Second Edition

MANAGEMENT

Ramon J. Aldag
Department of Management
University of Wisconsin - Madison

Timothy M. Stearns
Department of Management
Marquette University

COLLEGE DIVISION South-Western Publishing Co.

CINCINNATI   DALLAS   LIVERMORE

GC70BA

Publisher: Roger L. Ross
Developmental Editor: Edward A. Parker
Production Editor: Susan C. Williams
Production House: Carnes-Lachina Publication Services, Inc.
Cover and Interior Designer: Craig LaGesse Ramsdell
Marketing Manager: David L. Shaut
Photo Researcher: Kathryn A. Russell
Cover Photo: AXIOM INC. © 1990

Library of Congress Cataloging-in-Publication Data

Aldag, Ramon J.,
  Management / Ramon J. Aldag, Timothy M. Stearns. —2nd ed.
      p.   cm.
  Includes index.
  ISBN 0-538-80562-5   :
  1. Management. 2. Planning.   I. Stearns, Timothy M. (Timothy
Meeker).   II. Title.
  HD31.A357   1991
  658.4—dc20   90-40826
                                                   CIP

1 2 3 4 5 6 7 8 9 Ki 8 7 6 5 4 3 2 1 0

Printed in the United States of America

To Holly, Elizabeth, and Katherine

and

To Amy, Kira, and Cailin

RAMON J. ALDAG

Ramon J. Aldag is a respected researcher, author, and instructor in the field of management. At the University of Wisconsin–Madison, he is Professor of Management and Organization and Co-Director of the Center for the Study of Organizational Performance in the Graduate School of Business, and Participating Faculty Member in the Industrial Relations Research Institute. Professor Aldag is a past Chair of the Management Department and has served as Associate Director of the Industrial Relations Research Institute. He has served as Vice-President and Program Chair of the National Academy of Management for the 1990 annual meeting and is a Fellow of the Academy. He will assume the roles of President-Elect in 1990 and President of the Academy in 1991.

Professor Aldag holds a bachelor of science degree in Mechanical Engineering, a master's degree in Production Management, and a Ph.D. in Management—all from Michigan State University. He has 22 years of teaching experience and has served on more than 40 Ph.D. thesis committees. In addition, he is the co-author of five books and has published more than 50 journal articles on a vast array of research topics including job design, decision making, organizational environment, motivation, sex roles, social responsibility, and job search and choice. He has published in *Academy of Management Journal, Academy of Management Review, Administrative Science Quarterly, Decision Sciences, Journal of Applied Psychology, Journal of Management, Psychological Bulletin,* and elsewhere.

Professor Aldag has served in various previous roles in the Academy of Management, including Representative-at-Large on the Board of Governors; Public Sector Division Co-Founder, Program Chair, and Chair; Research Methods Interest Group Program Chair; Organizational Behavior Division Representative-at-Large, Program Chair, and Division Chair-Elect; and Midwest Academy of Management President. He also has held positions in the Decision Sciences Institute and the Industrial Relations Research Association and is a member of The Institute of Management Sciences.

A management consultant as well, Professor Aldag has served a wide variety of public and private sector organizations in such industries as information processing, health care, heavy machinery, insurance, law enforcement, and pharmaceuticals.

TIMOTHY M. STEARNS

Timothy M. Stearns, well known in the area of management as an instructor, researcher, and author, holds a bachelor of science degree in Sociology from San Jose State University and both a master's degree and a D.B.A. in Business Administration from Indiana University. He is currently Assistant Professor of Management in the College of Business Administration at Marquette University. He previously held teaching positions at the University of Wisconsin and Indiana University.

Professor Stearns has taught the subject of organization and management for more than 15 years. His research focuses on the way organizations interface with their environments. Professor Stearns has published in numerous academic journals, including *Academy of Management Journal, Administrative Science Quarterly, The Journal of Business Research, Social Science Quarterly,* and *Journal of Management.* He has lectured on the subject of organization performance at Shang-Hai Jiao Tong University, Beijing University, and Tsing Hua University in China. In addition, Professor Stearns has served as a consultant in U.S. Presidential campaigns and for numerous entrepreneurial firms throughout the Midwest.

We were very gratified by response to the first edition of MANAGEMENT, in terms of both adoptions and user and reviewer comments. We have attempted in MANAGEMENT, Second Edition, to continue to convey the excitement, richness, and importance of this fascinating field. To do so, we have built on the text's strengths while making several significant revisions. As with the first edition, we believe the resulting text is current, academically honest, relevant, interesting, and comprehensive.

In the preface to the first edition we wrote about the critical, challenging, and dynamic nature of modern management. Issues of productivity, quality of work life, organizational adaptability, product quality, innovation, corporate social responsibility, labor costs, and employee creativity all fall within the domain of management. Events of the last few years, reflected in changes in the second edition, underscore this view. If your students slept through the final years of the eighties, they can read here about Michael Milken, Tiananmen Square, the United States Football League, computer viruses, AIDS legislation, comparable worth, the 1989 San Francisco earthquake, genetic testing of workers, the Ben Johnson Olympic steroid scandal, whistle-blowers, and the Alaskan oil spill. Each of these examples is used in MANAGEMENT, Second Edition, to show the relevance of management to the modern world, and the impact of the modern world on management.

You will find many changes in this revision, as detailed below. In every case, the changes were made to enhance understanding, interest, and relevance. For instance, we have tried to minimize "academic" discussions of research in favor of a focus on material really necessary for the understanding and practice of management. The changes in this edition also are in keeping with our view of the "personality" of the text. We have drawn broadly from many fields and sources to provide a stimulating, involving, even entertaining book. Reviewers' enthusiastic comments about the first edition and the revisions for the second edition suggest that we have been successful in this effort. While many reviewers' comments focused on the writing style, comprehensiveness, and informativeness of the text, others picked up on its more engaging aspects. For instance, one reviewer wrote that "there were many points in reading the text where I found myself enjoying the experience (pretty rare in a principles book)"; another wrote that the book was "full of ideas that would be fun to introduce in class." Such comments reflect our efforts to give the book a personality which transcends a narrow view of management. We have drawn on a rich array of subject areas and sources to illustrate key management points. For instance, in MANAGEMENT, Second Edition, students can find answers to questions such as:

- What do the gift-giving rituals of the Siuai of the Solomon Islands tell us about leadership?
- How does the electronic grandmother in Ray Bradbury's "I Sing the Body Electric" provide clues about future developments in computers?
- What can we learn about management from Ben Franklin? From Albert Camus? From George Orwell? From Aristotle?
- What do the lobster gangs of Maine tell us about group processes?
- What does the Mitsubishi morning song reveal about group norms?
- How does the sad life cycle of a male mite teach us about creativity?
- What does the *Go Rin No Sho (A Book of Five Rings),* written in a cave in 1645, suggest about strategy?
- What does the advice to a young sailor, "If it moves, salute it; if it doesn't move, paint it," tell us about human decision processes?
- What is the relevance to strategic planning of "afterglow," "big-hat boys," "sharks," and "tombstones"?
- What do a hipo, a Wallenda, and an imagineer who order drinks at a bar tell us about communication?

Many personal events and activities of the last few years have helped shape the second edition of this text—far too many to detail here. Tim has traveled extensively to Asia, Australia, and elsewhere to meet with management practitioners and scholars and has gained new insights into international management. Most recently, he lectured to Chinese factory managers and scholars in Shanghai and Beijing on such topics as strategic planning and goal setting. Ray has served in various roles in the Academy of Management. As Vice-President and Program Chair, with responsibility for the 1990 San Francisco meeting, he again savored the breadth and depth of management. That program featured the participation of managers and scholars from dozens of firms and hundreds of universities, as well as from approximately 30 countries. Just as important, Tim's new twin daughters—now aged 3— and Ray's daughters—now aged 5 and 7—taught us lessons about motivation, social influences, individual differences, and (lack of) control. Our children, coupled with our dual-career situations, gave us each a renewed appreciation for career issues as well as for family-sensitive work practices. In addition, each of us has had reason to appreciate the roles of social support, group processes, and coping mechanisms.

TEXT ORGANIZATION

MANAGEMENT is divided into six parts, which are in turn divided into 24 chapters. Part 1 serves as an introduction to the study of management and an overview of the historical perspectives that have emerged to address specific managerial problems and issues in different eras. It also discusses key contextual dimensions of the organization as well as the social and ethical issues which confront managers.

Part 2 describes the procedures managers follow to perform the planning activity effectively. It does so by identifying the role that goals serve in the planning process, discussing the fundamental approaches necessary for effectively implementing plans, presenting techniques that can be used in the formulation of a strategy, and discussing a variety of quantitative tools for managing. Part 3 focuses on methods managers use in organizing and staffing activities. Issues concerning the appropriate design of the organization, staffing the organization, and careers in organizations are addressed in separate chapters.

Part 4 considers management issues and problems related to directing members of the organization. The topics of behavior in organizations, motivating others, designing jobs, effective communication, leadership, and the management of groups are individually addressed. Part 5 describes techniques that are used for controlling activities in organizations. Chapters in this part deal with the creation and implementation of control systems, information management, and operations management. Finally, Part 6 discusses additional topics in management that are critical to organizational vision and vitality. Specifically, we discuss issues related to problem solving and creativity, change and culture, small business management, entrepreneurship, and intrapreneurship, and management of the global organization.

CHAPTER ORGANIZATION

Each chapter contains the following learning devices:

- Learning objectives.

- Tables, graphs, and schematics presenting information and relationships in a visually appealing way.

- A profile of, and interview with, a noted management scholar or practitioner. Profiles of practitioners such as Rocky Aoki of Benihana of Tokyo, John Flicker of The Nature Conservancy, and Donald Newton of Hoosier Racing Tire Company let the student know how text material is relevant in the real world. Academic profiles permit noted scholars such as Kay Bartol, Keith Davis, Douglas T. (Tim) Hall, Henry Mintzberg, William Newman, Henry Tosi, and Victor Vroom to discuss the latest developments in their fields.

- "From the Field" features, based on questionnaires mailed to a total of 2,000 top managers. The comments of respondents are included as "From the Field" boxes throughout the text. They provide information on issues such as career tips, market trends, corporate goals, staffing practices, microcomputers in organizations, and encouraging creativity. These survey materials were developed specifically for this text and are presented nowhere else.

- An average of two "Management in Action" features, as well as other boxed examples. These are typically lengthier real-world examples than can be incorporated in the regular flow of the text material. Some of the "Management in Action" features are humorous or present a unique twist on topics of interest; all are real-world and interesting. Here is a sampling:

Downtime at Lotus	How to Draw a Plan
Profiting from the Past	The Death of Premier
A Body to Be Kicked	In Brazil, OK Is Not OK
One-Bean Motivation	Meeting Foreign Challenges with
Images of Organization	Operations Management
Decision Support for the	Productivity Spies
1992 Barcelona Olympics	Hell Camp, Malibu-Style
The Hollow Corporation	Bad Mickey
And Beta Makes 3	Stealth

- Implications for management. While management implications are stressed throughout the text, this concluding section in every chapter provides an opportunity to integrate material and to highlight implications for the practice of management which can be drawn from the body of knowledge presented in the chapter.

- Key terms and concepts presented in boldface type in the chapter and listed at the end of the chapter.

- Questions for review and discussion, testing recall and understanding and requiring students to integrate and apply text material.

- Two recent cases drawn from actual management situations give students the opportunity to apply chapter materials to real-world management problems. There are no "XYZ Corporations" in MANAGEMENT, Second Edition, and there is not a widget to be found. Cases are typically drawn from such sources as *The Wall Street Journal, Fortune,* and *Forbes.* Here is a sampling:

  Applying the Taylor System: The Watertown Arsenal
  100% Pure [on the Beech-Nut apple juice scandal]
  McVideo Attack [on Blockbuster Entertainment Corporation]
  Rough Play? [on competition in the toy industry]
  A Risky Stance [on Gerber Products Co.'s reaction to the finding of glass in its products]
  Designs for Avoiding the Blues [on the perils of copying IBM's decentralization]
  The Executive Addict
  A New Tide [on the decline of lifetime employment in Japan]
  Nobody Gets Fired in Portugal [on the strange labor situation in Portugal, where the law prevents companies from firing workers—but doesn't say workers have to be paid!]
  Benefits on the Bottom Line [on measuring the savings associated with

such new-wave benefits as day-care assistance, wellness plans, maternity leaves, and flexible work schedules]

Random Checks for Steroids [on the implications of learning theory for the Ben Johnson Olympic steroid scandal]

Riding the Product Through the South Bronx [on expanding roles for workers]

The Death of the Assembly Line?

Business Communication in the Fax Age

Teamwork—A Management Plot?

Controlling for the Crunch in Fresh Vegetables

Computerizing the Fast Track [on using computers for career management]

Project Saturn

How the Cookie Crumbled at Mrs. Fields

A Slice of Things to Come? [on how the Soviet Union is opening its doors to foreign business]

- Endnotes and references.

OTHER SPECIAL FEATURES

- MANAGEMENT provides the most comprehensive coverage of any management text. Detailed coverage of such topics as operations management, small business management and entrepreneurship, international management, and information management helps ensure compliance with AACSB guidelines. Further, the breadth of coverage, including topics such as management information systems, strategic management, career management, and problem solving and creativity, gives the instructor the flexibility to explore the full range of contemporary management or select chapters of particular interest. Suggested course outlines are provided in the supplementary materials to provide guidance for instructors wishing to adopt a general emphasis or to place relatively greater emphasis on organizational behavior, strategy, operations management, or decision making.

- The book features an attractive, full-color format and is written in a readable, conversational style.

- In every area the text presents the most recent coverage possible, with examples drawn primarily from the last few years. A sampling of contemporary topics covered includes decision support systems, career planning, computer crime, group decision tools, cafeteria-style benefit plans, the electronic cottage, and the factory of the future, to name just a few.

- Humor, including cartoons (typically Doonesbury, *New Yorker,* or The Far Side), is used where appropriate to reinforce points and add interest.

- The text emphasizes both public and private sector organizations as well as firms offering both products and services.

- Separate name, subject, and company indices are provided.

SUPPLEMENTARY MATERIALS

Instructor's Manual – includes sections on setting up your course, lecture outlines and resources (with, for each chapter, opening comments, chapter outlines, notes and expansions, chapter projects and activities, answers to questions for review and discussion, and answers to case questions), case analysis guidelines, self-assessment scales, and an operational guide along with 18 cases to be used with the *Decision Assistant* software (discussed below).

Resource Guide – contains three main types of resources: a comprehensive bibliography of print material relevant to setting up and teaching a course in management, a listing of visual aids in management with suggestions for their use, and a set of 100 transparency masters (50 original and 50 drawn from the text).

Study Guide – contains statement of chapter purpose, chapter outlines, self-test questions, "Focus on Managing" mini-cases using real companies and people in situations calling for management action, bibliographic excerpts, and an integrative bibliography with full publisher information.

Test Bank – contains 2,520 questions. There are 40 true-false, 60 multiple-choice, and 5 essay questions per chapter. The *Test Bank* has been designed to facilitate use by instructors with differing requirements regarding content and format. It is available in both printed or microcomputer (MICROSWAT III) versions. This software is provided free of charge to instructors at educational institutions that adopt this text.

Careers Supplement – contains material on obtaining a job in business, profiles of individuals in various careers, suggested careers readings, summaries of various careers and their salaries and projected growth rates, and sources of additional career information.

Transparencies – a set of 100 color transparencies. Half of these are reproductions of text illustrations, while the other half are new to the package. These are all different from the 100 transparency masters included in the *Resource Guide*.

The South-Western *Decision Assistant* – a computerized set of ten management tools and case applications developed for this text. Tools include decision process selection, strategic business analysis, threat-opportunity matrix, goal analysis, project planning chart, and others. This software is provided free of charge to instructors at educational institutions that adopt this text.

Video Supplements – Complimentary videotapes will be available to users of the text.

SIGNIFICANT CHANGES FROM THE PREVIOUS EDITION

- Visual appeal has been enhanced. Trim size has been enlarged to provide more white space and opportunities for photos and other features in the margins. The first edition of MANAGEMENT was the first full four-color management text; the second edition continues the tradition of providing a visually appealing text to increase student interest.

- A second *real-world* case has been added to each chapter. All cases are either new or have been fully revised as appropriate.

- All material is fully updated, including incorporation of recent developments regarding many companies and individuals as well as national and world events. There is coverage of many new topics including transformational leadership, scripts and schemas, self-management, transaction costs, intrapreneurship, the new careerism, clan control, and managing culture.

- A chapter has been added on "Quantitative Tools for Managing."

- The chapters on computers and on management information systems have been collapsed into one chapter, titled "Information Management," with a greater management emphasis.

- Profiles have been thoroughly updated, and many are new. For instance, some of the new Academic Profiles include George Huber, Henry Mintzberg, Greg Oldham, Barry Staw, and Ellie Weldon. New Practitioner Profiles include Rocky Aoki of Benihana of Tokyo, Claudio Gonzalez of Kimberly-Clark de Mexico, S.A., and Ben Cohen of Ben and Jerry's Homemade, Inc., among others.

- The chapter on small business and entrepreneurship, now called "Small Business, Entrepreneurship, and Intrapreneurship," has been completely updated and revised to include material on intrapreneurship and to provide expanded discussion of entrepreneurial strategies.

- A chapter titled "Change and Culture" presents substantially expanded material on managing organizational culture.

- Some chapters and related materials have been rearranged in response to user feedback. The chapter on ethics and social responsibility has been moved to Part 1 to reflect the importance of this material. The chapter on behavior in organizations has been placed later in the text to directly precede related materials on motivation, job design, communications, and groups. The job design chapter has been moved back to follow the chapter on motivation. The careers chapter has been moved up to follow the staffing chapter. The stress appendix has been integrated into text material. Material on self-management, formerly in a supplement, has also been integrated into text material. Each of these changes reflects more logical flow of materials and response to users' preferences.

- Along with subject and name indices, there is a new company index, providing quick reference to the hundreds of firms discussed in the text.

- "Review Questions" in the first edition have been replaced by "Questions for Review and Discussion." Rather than just asking for a restatement of text material, these questions demand integration and application of those materials.

- Readability has been tested throughout and improved where appropriate. The entire book was treated to a line-by-line readability analysis and material has been revised to provide an appropriate and uniform reading level.

- There are many improvements in supplements to the text. For instance, the *Instructor's Manual* and *Test Bank* have been fully revised and updated; the *Test Bank* has also been substantially expanded, and the *Instructor's Manual* indicates where each of the expanded set of transparencies should be included in lectures, with an accompanying description of each transparency. The *Careers Supplement* is new. Further, instructors now have a total of 200 transparencies and transparency masters from which to draw—an average of more than eight per chapter! Videotapes complete the teaching package.

- Footnotes have been changed to endnotes for better flow.

ACKNOWLEDGMENTS

Many people have contributed to the development of this text. For their helpful suggestions as reviewers of manuscript, we are especially grateful to the following individuals:

Billie Allen
University of Southern Mississippi

Chandler Wm. Atkins
Adirondack Community College

Larry G. Bailey
San Antonio College

Steve H. Barr
Oklahoma State University

Gerald L. Bassford
Arizona State University

Allen C. Bluedorn
University of Missouri – Columbia

Michael G. Bowen
University of Notre Dame

Elmer Burack
University of Illinois at Chicago

Gregory G. Dess
University of Texas at Arlington

Steven W. Floyd
University of Massachusetts
  at Amherst

Cynthia Fukami
University of Denver

Daniel C. Ganster
University of Arkansas – Fayetteville

Lindle Hatton
University of Wisconsin – Oshkosh

Neil J. Humphreys
Louisiana Tech University

Michael Koshuta
Purdue University – North
  Central Campus

David R. Lee
University of Dayton

Walt J. McCoy
University of Nebraska
  at Omaha

Susan Kay Smith
Central Michigan University

Charles B. Shrader
Iowa State University

Robert Vecchio
University of Notre Dame

Richard A. Wald
Eastern Washington University

Robert Woodhouse
College of St. Thomas

We are grateful to the team of individuals that helped to develop and produce this text. They include, at South-Western: Roger Ross, Publisher;

Ed Parker, Developmental Editor; Susan Williams, Production Editor; Dave Shaut, Marketing Manager; Craig Ramsdell, Designer; and Kathy Russell, Photo Researcher; and, at Carnes-Lachina: Nancy Tenney, Project Manager, and Laura Hush, Editorial Assistant.

Finally, we are indebted to Janet Christopher, Michael Maass, Andrea Macharek, Monica Tobin, and Jean Trager for their assistance with manuscript development and preparation.

Ramon J. Aldag
University of Wisconsin – Madison

Timothy M. Stearns
Marquette University

BRIEF CONTENTS

xiv

CONTENTS

MANAGEMENT

The Scope of Management

PART ONE

Introduction to Management

CHAPTER 1

After studying this chapter, you should be able to:
- *Identify the areas of the external context that influence organization activities.*
- *Describe the dimensions that characterize an organization.*
- *Describe the four functional areas of managerial activities.*
- *Define the concept of management and discuss why managers are needed.*
- *Identify three major categories of management.*
- *Discuss the skills that are necessary for effective management.*
- *Identify key roles of managers and discuss their differences.*

The events that shaped the fortunes of Lotus Corporation in the late 1980s, as described in Management in Action 1 on page 6, are not that dissimilar from those facing organizations in other industries. Consider these familiar corporations:

- Bell Laboratories
- Trammell Crow Company
- Delta Air Lines, Inc.
- Goldman, Sachs & Co.
- Hallmark Cards, Inc.
- Hewlett-Packard Company
- International Business Machines Corporation
- Pitney Bowes Inc.
- Northwestern Mutual Life Insurance Company
- Quad/Graphics Inc.

These corporations were identified in the 1980s as "the 10 best companies to work for in America."[1] Based on an extensive study, what did the authors conclude were the reasons behind selecting a "best company"? Profits? Growth? Satisfied stockholders? None of the above. It was the underlying philosophy of management and how that philosophy was translated to the activities of company employees.

Achieving excellence in an organization is no small matter. Indeed, few occupations are as challenging as managing a modern organization. Being a manager in today's world means being responsible to many different constituencies. Managers are responsible to their employees and for their welfare. They are accountable for attaining desired organization goals whether those goals are to increase profits, provide services to clients, or create a quality workplace for employees. And managers are answerable to society for upholding its values and ideals.

Managing an organization is not an easy task. This is true whether the organization is very large, such as Lotus Development Corporation, or very small, such as Paula's Auto Repair Shop. Most seasoned managers are wary of Murphy's Law: "If anything can go wrong, it will." Effectively managing an organization (or heading off Murphy's dire prediction) requires managers to make informed decisions about people and the production of products and services, to respond strategically to competition, to interpret correctly the laws that affect the organization, to plan for future activities, and to evaluate their own performance as well as the performance of others.

The situation described at Lotus Development Corporation underscores the many responsibilities and problems managers must contend with in today's business world. As evidenced by that case, managerial styles alone do not determine the degree of success an organization may achieve. Even years of prior experience as a manager cannot guarantee successful outcomes. Consumer demand, employee morale, the type of products produced, use of resources, and competitor tactics all play an important role in managing an organization successfully. Managers, by attaining an understanding of the total organization and how individual actions contribute to the performance of the organization, can act to reduce the chances that things will "go wrong."

To some extent, we are all managers, though not necessarily in an organizational sense. With varying degrees of skill, we have learned to manage our financial matters, our course work, our social activities, and our career de-

The use of computer software can help managers make effective decisions.

Four years ago, Jim P. Manzi joined skyrocketing Lotus Development Corp., and saw his own career take off as well. A newspaper reporter and manage-

ment consultant by experience, he had lucked into a company filled with inventive iconoclasts who couldn't do what he could: market and manage. Then in 1986, after just two years on the job, he watched the company's founder unexpectedly walk out the door, leaving Mr. Manzi at the top: chairman, chief executive, and president. To cap it all, Mr. Manzi last year earned nearly $1 million in salary and $25.4 million from stock options he exercised. That made him one of America's best-compensated chief executives.

But the good fortune of the 36-year-old executive may be running out, for there is trouble in Lotusland, and critics are pinning much of the blame on Mr. Manzi. The company has lost its premier spot in personal computer software to Microsoft Corp. of Redmond, Washington, and faces the prospect this quarter of an unaccustomed earnings decline. Market share has slipped, veteran managers are fleeing the executive suite, the company's stock price has plunged, and management has made a string of product announcements that industry techies ridicule as "vaporware"—software Lotus keeps promising, but hasn't delivered.

An updated version of Lotus's big-selling *1-2-3* financial calculation program, which Mr. Manzi calls "absolutely, the most important thing we're doing as a company," is months late, and competitors meantime are going after Lotus's customers. Lotus says it hopes to get the new product out by the end of the year. But if it misses that deadline by much, or if the product doesn't live up to its promise, Lotus may become just one more former highflier in the high-tech game.

Mr. Manzi is taking the heat both for Lotus's fumbling and for a personal style that some say has hurt the company's image. Mr. Manzi, who is vocally competitive, is sometimes sarcastic and smart-alecky, perplexing many industry analysts and reporters who influence customers and buyers of stock. One consultant recalls that one time, after Lotus introduced a new product, Mr. Manzi said to a gathering of analysts, "I've anticipated your questions and prepared answers. Here they are. Yes. No. No. I can't comment."

Much of Lotus's arrogant image has to do with Mr. Manzi's self-confident style. His corner office at Lotus has a view across the Charles River toward Boston, and a sign on a shelf reads: "IBM—You Mean the Lotus of Hardware." His attitude toward uninformed visitors: "I don't like to talk to people who aren't terribly well prepared." And toward the danger of losing business because of the delay in updating 1-2-3: "Our customers are hooked on our strategy."

In the past, criticism of Mr. Manzi was muted because Lotus's results were so spectacular. The history of the company is part of the mythology of the personal computer industry. Started by Mitchell D. Kapor, a former disk jockey and transcendental meditation instructor, Lotus succeeded beyond expectations. Its first product, 1-2-3, far surpassed the capabilities of its competition.

Mr. Kapor, an eloquent evangelist for his technol-

velopment. However, what many of us lack is a systematic and thorough understanding of the principles of effective management. This book will provide you with an understanding of how to manage in a variety of organizational situations. The topics and ideas will be useful not only to those who have been hired recently for their first management position but also to those who have a wealth of prior managerial experience. We will build from the foundation of management that you currently have, whether from your personal or career experiences, and introduce you to management techniques that are both practical and appropriate for solving organizational problems. You will learn from this book not only what managers actually do but what managers should do to make their organizations more effective.

ogy, wore Hawaiian print shirts and baggy chinos at the office. He quickly tired of management duties. As the company matured, he leaned increasingly on Mr. Manzi, a McKinsey & Co. consultant who joined Lotus to head sales and marketing. "That was the perfect balance, because you had a company with a lot of soul," says Katie Payne, one of the eight public-relations chiefs Lotus has had in its short history. Now, she adds, "it's all yuppie and no hippie."

Adding to the company's problems is the exodus of a number of management veterans, including six of 17 vice-presidents, in the past five months. While some retired or moved on to better opportunities, others were pushed out. By way of explanation, Mr. Manzi says: "Transitions are constant." Some executives, who thought they might be considered for the No. 2 job at Lotus, left after Mr. Manzi brought in Frank King, a widely respected 17-year veteran of IBM, as senior vice-president in charge of software products. Others simply say the graying of Lotus made it less fun.

Even before this exodus, disillusionment within the company was growing. Publicity about Mr. Manzi's big paycheck "didn't go over well at the company," says one former employee, particularly since Mr. Manzi had just recently sent out an "austerity" letter asking the staff to control spending.

Lotus, meanwhile, has stepped up marketing efforts. To assuage users impatient for the new spreadsheet, it is giving away a program that improves existing copies of 1-2-3, including removing a hated copy protection that blocked users from duplicating their software disks. It is expanding its list of authorized dealers to 5,500 from 3,500 to pursue small businesses and, for the first time, mass merchandisers, such as the Lechmere chain of discount stores. Most important, Lotus has worked to cement its ties with big customers, making sure they know what Lotus is doing and understand its strategy. "In the past [salespeople] spent all of their time offensively," says Steven Crummey, Lotus senior vice-president for sales. "This year, some of it is defensive."

But can Lotus hold the market with its strategy? Small companies and individuals aren't likely to respond to the pitch Lotus makes to big users about the compatibility 1-2-3 will allow among different computers. Also, Lotus expects to market its product primarily to company data-processing managers, even though computer use is still highly decentralized. In the past, software products often have caught on in companies first through individual use. Lotus says that pattern has changed and that data-processing managers are now the key decision makers.

Philippe Kahn, chairman of rival Borland, says Lotus is focusing too much on marketing, and has lost sight of the need for technical pizazz. "In terms of marketing acumen, Lotus is smarter than we are," he says. But, "when you have marketing groups designing a product and telling R&D guys to build it, you may have the wrong architects."

That notion, not surprisingly, raises Mr. Manzi's hackles: "Our bill for paper for 1-2-3," he boasts, "will be bigger than all of Borland."

The need for effective management has perhaps never been greater than it is today. In the last decade of the 20th century, we find ourselves rapidly becoming an international community. Events thousands of miles away can affect the management of an organization almost immediately. Managers can no longer presume that worldwide supplies will be plentiful, that the money markets will provide the organization with necessary capital, that governments will be stable, or that the products and services produced will not be subject to critical scrutiny by the consumer. It is a time for bold, innovative, and thoughtful management. It is a time for those who want to accept the opportunity to manage in an organization to prepare themselves for the challenges that await.

This chapter is designed to establish a working foundation for our discussion of effective management within the organization. We will explain the system in which managers act; identify what constitutes an organization; discuss the various activities of managers; and define critical concepts relevant to the nature of managerial actions.

THE CONTEXT OF MANAGEMENT

An understanding of the practice of management begins with the recognition that managers act within a system. A **system** is a set of coordinated activities that function as a whole.[2] Organizations, as systems, coordinate activities through subsystems in order to transform inputs (such as raw materials) into outputs (such as products or services). Coordinating these activities within an organization is central to the manager's task. For instance, managers at Lotus Development Corporation obtain resources (such as computer disks and program writers) from the environment (such as manufacturers of computer disks and universities) through such subsystems as purchasing departments and personnel departments; these resources are transformed (programs are written onto the computer disks), often in a production department; and the output becomes products and services (Lotus 1-2-3 and contacts with big customers) that fall under the responsibility of a sales department. The combination of characteristics that identify the organizational system and its relationship to the environment is referred to as the **context**.

Managers must be keenly aware of events outside their organization that may hamper the acquisition of resources. They must strive to transform raw materials in both an efficient and an effective manner. And they must distribute the products and services in a timely and competitive fashion. Coordinating these and other activities can make the difference between success and failure. Are the methods Mr. Manzi uses to coordinate the development of software with the sales of software adequate? Will they achieve success? Before we begin to address these critical issues, we need to understand the nature of activities external and internal to the boundaries of an organization.

External Context

We can identify six areas that make up the external context, or the environment, of an organization. Let's look at these in detail.

COMPETITORS

Organizations that provide the same or similar products or services to a market are known as competitors. Competitors may lower or raise the prices of their products, modify their products, or seek to capture a greater share of the market through increased advertising. It is important for managers to recognize and understand the activities of competitors in a market in order to make decisions about pricing, product modification, and advertising. How Borland, a competing software firm, responds to Lotus's new emphasis on marketing may determine the success of newer versions of 1-2-3.

TECHNOLOGICAL CHANGE

The development of new procedures for producing products or services or the development of an entirely new product involves technological change. Often, technological change can lead to a decrease in price due to the discovery of a cheaper method for manufacturing a product. Moreover, technological change can result in an organization's product becoming obsolete. For instance, if IBM were to replace its disk operating system (DOS) with a system based on a newer technology, could Lotus survive?

ECONOMIC CONDITIONS

Inflation rates, lending rates, gross national product, and money supply are among the economic conditions that influence the way managers operate in an organization. Indeed, failure of managers to understand economic conditions can result in substantial losses to an organization. For example, an increase in interest rates could cause companies to postpone the purchase of a computer installation and thus would decrease the sales of Lotus 1-2-3.

SOCIETAL VALUES AND ATTITUDES

Changing societal values and attitudes can affect how customers respond to a product; thus, they can influence sales. For instance, when the personal computer first came on the market, it was considered an expensive toy by many, useful solely for playing video games. By the mid-1980s, the personal computer was recognized as a valuable work tool in most businesses. This shift in attitude about the personal computer enabled Lotus to dramatically increase sales. Societal values can also shift within a firm. "It's all yuppie and no hippie" is a statement indicating that newer societal values have replaced older societal values of employees at Lotus Development Corporation.

POLITICAL PROCESSES

The actions of political parties, local school boards, and judicial systems are all part of a political process that influences managers in organizations. Lotus's copyright protection on its software is vital for sales of 1-2-3. If Congress or the courts were to rule against Lotus's right to enforce copyright protection, sales would diminish rapidly.

PHYSICAL CONDITIONS

Physical conditions involve natural events (e.g., sunny, rainy, or snowy weather) or acts of God (e.g., tornadoes, hurricanes, or earthquakes) that can influence or dictate how managers in an organization operate. The 1989 earthquake in the San Francisco area caused many firms in Silicon Valley to shut down for days or weeks. Shipments of computer disks and other supplies were halted until communication and transportation systems could be restored to service.

Each of these six areas of the external context influences the manner in which an organization acquires material resources. Political activities may regulate the quantity of resources available to an organization. Economic

*External events like the
earthquake that struck
the San Francisco area in
1989 require rapid
management response.*

conditions, such as high interest rates, may make it difficult to acquire capital resources through borrowing. Increased public awareness of business ethics may make it difficult for an organization that has been involved in unethical activities to attract or keep employees. Competitors may try to withhold important information in order to enhance their competitive advantage. Successful managers are those who understand how to prepare for and meet the demands of the external environment.

Internal Context

Transforming resources into products and services requires the coordinating of many activities. Many of these activities are coordinated through organizing subsystems, or departments. Purchasing acquires resources external to the organization, manufacturing makes a product or service, marketing delivers the product or service to the customer, personnel supplies the organization with needed labor, finance allocates capital to support productivity, maintenance keeps equipment in good working order, and data processing provides timely information to decision makers.

The job of a manager, whether coordinating activities within a department or across departments, is to recognize and understand the influence of both the internal and external context. For instance, Mr. Manzi of Lotus Development Corporation believes that R&D and marketing must develop closer coordination through greater input from the marketing group into the design of the product. But personnel in the marketing department may lack expertise in new technological trends in the environment. If so, they may resist any efforts to incorporate the new technology into their products. This is apparently a gamble that Mr. Manzi believes he can take in his effort to make Lotus more competitive.

As we will see, recognition of the relationships among and between these subsystems can have profound effects on the way managers design and staff the organization, direct and control task activities and behaviors of subordinates, and plan for the future. Figure 1–1 illustrates the context in which these major managerial activities are carried out.

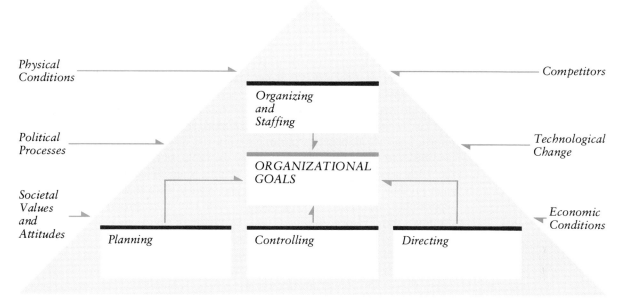

FIGURE 1–1
*The Context of
Management*

ORGANIZATION, MANAGEMENT, AND MANAGERS

Developing an understanding of how to manage begins with the definition and description of three key terms: organization, management, and managers. While these terms have been defined in different ways, we will establish one definition for each so that we can consider each from a common reference point.

What Is an Organization?

Most of our waking hours revolve around consuming products and creating activities. Awareness of our dependence on products such as food, transportation, and housing and on activities such as recreation and conversation can lead us to an understanding of the important role that organizations play in our daily lives. Indeed, it is difficult to think of a product or an activity that has not been influenced by some type of organization.

Food crops produced on farms or in gardens are made possible through the purchase of seeds, seedlings, tools, and equipment from nurseries and farm implement companies. Much of this food is distributed by trucking organizations to various supermarkets. These trucking organizations use streets and highways built and maintained by political organizations such as city hall, state governments, and federal agencies. Supermarkets are housed in structures built by contractors who utilize crews of masons, carpenters, electricians, plumbers, and other skilled laborers.

Activities that tend to produce intangible goods, such as conversation or recreation, are also heavily influenced by organizations. We get together with friends to consume food and beverages distributed by food processors and bottling plants, while engaging in discussions of topics we've read about in

The distribution of food crops involves many levels of organization.

newspapers and magazines issued by publishers. Likewise, we may go on vacations where organizations provide food, lodging, transportation, and entertainment. Organizations are so deeply intertwined in our daily lives that we often fail to recognize the extent of their influence.

An important question, then, is, "Why do organizations envelop our lives to the extent that they do? Is it because humans do not have the capacity to be independent and self-sufficient?" Hardly. One reason that organizations are so pronounced in our lives can be traced to Adam Smith's observation that two working together can produce more than two working alone. Smith referred to this as benefits obtained from the **division of labor** into specialized tasks to increase productivity. For example, in an English pin factory in the 18th century, Smith noted that 10 men specialized in their task could each produce about 4,800 pins a day. But if they were to have produced pins separately, one man working alone could not have produced more than 20 pins a day.[3] Hence, organizations, by virtue of dividing labor into specialized tasks, serve as vehicles for increasing individual productivity.

We define an **organization** throughout this text as a collectivity of people engaged in a systematic effort to produce a good or an activity. As we will learn, this definition of an organization is not complete. For now, however, let us use the definition to establish *when* a collectivity of people constitutes an organization.

Consider a chance meeting of three students in a student union. If we define a collectivity as two or more people, the group of friends in the student union will suffice. We can also note that an activity is being produced in the form of conversation which serves as an exchange of information about each other and perhaps other students. However, what is missing is a systematic effort to produce a good or an activity. By systematic we mean that the members of the collectivity have defined a set of coordinated roles in the "organization," are working toward a common goal (the desire to produce a good or an activity), and are doing so in a manner that enables some predictability of each other's activities. For instance, let us suppose that this same group of students decides to meet once a week in the student union for lunch to exchange information about each other's job search. One individual is assigned the responsibility for calling the other two to remind them of the meeting and to determine if they will make it that week. Another individual in the group is assigned the task of securing a table at the student union to guarantee that the group will not have to wait upon arrival. The third individual is assigned the duty of collecting money to pay for food. What has emerged from this process is a systematic effort to produce an activity; thus, the weekly meeting of three students that started as a chance encounter has evolved into a simple organization.

Certainly, this "organization" is not as formidable as General Motors, but it is an organization nonetheless. We may speculate that in time, new students join the group. Eventually the meeting is shifted to a hall at night in order to accommodate the number of people attending. We may also find the group engaging in multiple activities such as fund raising, organizing political events, and arranging social get-togethers. Officers may be elected and the organization may publish a brochure on job placement that is used to recruit more members to the organization. Ultimately, the members may even decide to produce a good or service, thereby leaving other jobs to take employment in this newly created company. Many organizations have gotten their start in this way.

For instance, Mitch Kapor, the founder of Lotus, was a student at the Massachusetts Institute of Technology Sloan School of Management when he developed a statistical program called "Tiny Troll." The program evolved from a statistical program at MIT called "Troll" and ran on the Apple® II computer. After showing the program to other students, he found an interest in its use. Through friends, Mitch Kapor was introduced to an executive of a software firm and signed an agreement to produce the program for his firm. Two years later, Kapor founded Lotus Development Corporation.

An organization can take on many shapes and forms. It is important for us not to be mentally locked into the idea that organizations are of one type, such as large profit-oriented firms. In fact, large profit-oriented firms constitute only a small percentage of all organizations that currently operate in the United States. Most organizations are small and may be profit oriented or not-for-profit oriented. It is also important to recognize that while each organization may have unique characteristics, such as the product produced, the personnel hired, or the rewards distributed to management, organizations can be classified into broad "types" based on contextual characteristics that are commonly shared.

For now, we need to recognize that organizations are multiple, influence much of our lives, and must contain two or more individuals engaged in a systematic effort to produce a good or an activity. In addition, we can note that organizations operate as a system influenced by both external and internal activities that managers must consider when engaged in planning, organizing and staffing, directing, and controlling.

What Is Management?

The term *management* is used in a variety of ways. It can refer to members of the organization who make key decisions regarding how and in what way products or services are produced. Or we may use the term to refer to a body of knowledge that has accumulated over the years through applications of scientific research and observation of managers in practice. Hence, management can also refer to the collective wisdom that has evolved from scientific study that can then be applied to specific managerial situations. Throughout this text, however, we will define **management** as a process of planning, organizing and staffing, directing, and controlling activities in an organization in a systematic way in order to achieve a common goal.

While uses of the term may be multiple, it is useful to think of management as a process, an ongoing and related set of activities and tasks. These activities, in turn, are systematic in that managers are required to introduce order into their activities and conduct their tasks in a manner that is recognizable and consistent with the expectations of other members in the organization. Finally, management is a systematic process in pursuit of a common goal. That is, the practice of management requires that tasks and activities be derived from the desire to achieve the goals set forth by the members of the organization.

We have defined management as a process whereby activities are systematized and directed toward a goal. As noted in the definition, management activities can be classified as planning, organizing and staffing, directing, and controlling. While managers may focus on one activity more than another depending on personal skills, aptitudes, and organizational requirements, all the activities are coordinated. We characterize these activities as follows:

- Planning. **Planning** is the selection and sequential ordering of tasks that are required to achieve an organizational goal. Plans may be short-term or long-term depending on the context of the organization and the importance of the goal to the success of the organization.
- Organizing and staffing. The assignment and coordination of tasks to be performed by members in the organization and the assignment and distribution of resources necessary to perform each task are known as **organizing and staffing**. This often requires activities directed toward the recruitment, placement, training, and development of organization members. Ideally, training and the assignment of tasks and resources evolve from the planning activity. Each member is thus required to contribute output in his or her activities which will ultimately contribute to the overall success of the organization.
- Directing. **Directing** is the process of motivating, leading, and influencing activities of subordinates. Managers are required to motivate employees to do their best in a task assigned, to lead them toward the appropriate goal, and to influence their approach in completing the task.
- Controlling. **Controlling** involves the collection, evaluation, and comparison of information in order to correct for tasks that are improperly performed as well as to identify where activities by members in the organization can be improved.

Managers continually coordinate the four activities in order to arrive at decisions that will lead to the attainment of organizational goals. Managers make plans to implement future activities. They organize and staff planned activities with members who will produce a good or service. Managers must then direct members by motivating and leading them in their task activities. Finally, task activities are controlled by managers who evaluate the task activities to determine if they are attaining the desired goal.

Again, we can think back to our example of the three students who decided to meet in the student union once a week for lunch. Management techniques were applied when efforts were made to systematize their meetings in order to achieve the common goal of enhancing their friendship. Plans were established to meet at a specific time and at a specific place. Tasks were organized by assigning individuals responsibility to perform certain activities with available resources. Efforts were directed to motivate attendance by offering a congenial atmosphere and an opportunity to revive friendships. And activities were controlled by establishing criteria directed toward attendance at the weekly meetings. If we assume this small organization grew in size and took on different goals, then we would find that its management might take on a different form. But the requirements to engage in management are still the same. Figure 1–2 depicts the four managerial activities and their interrelationships based on our example.

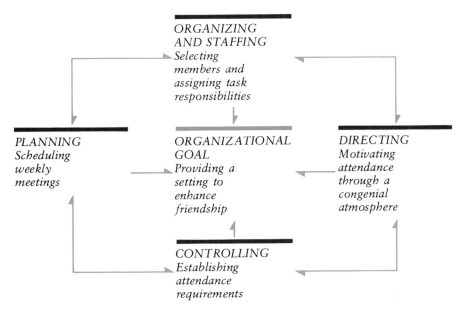

FIGURE 1–2
*Interrelationships of
Managerial Activities*

What Are Managers?

Managers are individuals who are responsible for completing tasks that require the supervision of other members or organizational resources. In many large organizations, managers can be sorted into levels of a hierarchy. This hierarchy, consisting of first-line managers at the lowest level, middle managers, and then top managers at the highest level, is a useful classification. It not only identifies a career path for many members of the organization but also provides a way to identify the types and varieties of skills and tasks that must be performed.

First-line managers are situated at the lowest level in the managerial hierarchy. They may be titled "foreman" or "supervisor" within a department or

*First-line managers
oversee the tasks of
employees.*

unit of the organization. As managers, their primary activity is to lead employees in the day-to-day tasks which contribute to the organization's goals. However, first-line managers must also be concerned with the control function in order to correct errors or solve problems directly related to the production of products or services. For many employees in the organization, first-line management offers the initial entrance into a management position.

Middle managers are more diverse in terms of titles and task responsibilities. However, a characteristic distinguishing them from other types of managers is that middle managers have supervisory responsibility for first-line managers and at times non-management personnel in the organization. More important, middle managers are responsible for implementing the plans and policies of the organization by focusing on the coordination of tasks performed to achieve organizational goals. Middle managers may be divisional heads, plant managers, or departmental directors.

The smallest grouping of managers in most organizations, top or **upper managers**, is responsible for the overall performance of the organization. Top managers engage extensively in the formulation of strategies. They must also provide leadership, evaluate and shape the method of organizing, and control the direction the organization is moving in an effort to accomplish goals. Top managers usually have such titles as "chief executive officer" (CEO), "chairperson," "senior vice-president," and "president." Figure 1–3 illustrates the hierarchy of management.

It is not necessary that organizations conform to any one specific configuration along the management hierarchy. Depending on the activities of the organization, top management may be quite large relative to middle and first-line management, or first-line management may be extremely small. For instance, many social service agencies have large numbers of top managers to maintain ongoing contact with the community. On the other hand, many high-technology firms have few first-line managers, relying instead on employees to fulfill the function of supervision by determining and evaluating their own individual activities. Figure 1–4 depicts how managers at different levels might distribute their time among the various managerial activities.

FIGURE 1–3
The Hierarchy of Management

FIRST-LINE MANAGEMENT	MIDDLE MANAGEMENT	TOP MANAGEMENT
Planning	*Planning*	*Planning*
Organizing and Staffing	*Organizing and Staffing*	
Directing	*Directing*	*Organizing and Staffing*
		Directing
Controlling	*Controlling*	*Controlling*

FIGURE 1–4
How Managers Distribute Their Time

Management Skills

In the previous section we identified four important managerial activities: planning, organizing and staffing, directing, and controlling. It was suggested that these activities need to be coordinated to achieve desired goals. In turn, the time an individual manager spends on each activity is dependent on the management hierarchy in the organization. One last element must be added to the managerial picture. Managers, upon joining the managerial ranks of an organization, must possess certain skills that will enable them to perform their tasks successfully. In many ways, the skills that managers possess in the organization are the most valued resources of the organization. Poor managerial skills can defeat the most successful activities and in many cases can lead to the demise of the organization, as related in the story of Sewell Avery in Management in Action 2.

Robert L. Katz suggests that three important managerial skills that must be cultivated and enhanced by the organization are technical, human, and conceptual.[4] The degree of development a manager has in each of these three skills will have a strong impact not only upon the success of the organization but also upon the career success of the manager.

Technical skills are those abilities that are necessary to carry out a specific task. Examples of technical skills are writing computer programs, completing accounting statements, analyzing marketing statistics, writing legal documents, or drafting a design for a new airfoil on an airplane. Technical skills are usually obtained through training programs that an organization may offer its managers or employees or may be obtained by way of a college degree. Indeed, many business schools throughout the country see their role as providing graduates with the technical skills necessary for them to be successful on the job.

Human skills involve the ability to work with, motivate, and direct individuals or groups in the organization whether they are subordinates, peers, or

Many managerial positions require technical skills.

Sewell Avery was born in Saginaw, Michigan, in 1874, the son of a wealthy Michigan lumberman. For many years of his life, his was an admirable success

story. He graduated from Michigan State University Law School in 1894 and started at the bottom in a small gypsum plant owned by his father. By the time he was 22 years old, he was manager of the plant. Then in 1901, the small firm was absorbed by the U.S. Gypsum Company. Four years later, Avery was president of U.S. Gypsum. *Time* magazine described him as a "suave and brilliant supersalesman," and he built U.S. Gypsum into one of the largest purveyors of building materials in the United States.

In the deep depression year of 1932, salesman Avery was called on by Montgomery Ward's directors and creditors to rescue the floundering company, which had suffered an $8.7 million deficit in 1931. Avery gathered around him sharp young executives. He added new luxury items to Ward's stock and reentered the fashion merchandise field. He said, "We no longer depend on hicks and yokels. We sell more than overalls and manure-proof shoes." The catalog was improved and seventy unprofitable stores were closed.

Avery was successful. In 12 years, he had changed a $5,700,000 loss (1932) into a $20,438,000 profit (1943). In 1932, the company lost 2.2 times as much money as Sears on a volume only 65 percent that of Sears; by 1939, Ward had 82 percent of Sears' business and 84 percent of Sears' profit.

Avery ruled Ward with an iron hand, with no regard for the feelings of employees or executives. He tolerated no dissension or deviations from his views. He ruled this billion-dollar firm as an old-fashioned tyrant and in the process lost dozens of capable high-level executives who found the management atmosphere he created to be intolerable. One such view

that Avery had was a no-growth strategy after World War II. He had an adamant belief that a depression was imminent after the cessation of hostilities. His basis for this was the depression that did occur after World War I. Avery foresaw that the nation would have difficulties trying to readjust to a peacetime economy as industries halted production of war materials and reverted to peacetime production and as millions of men and women returning from the service tried to find employment. He predicted that "economic conditions are terrorizing beyond what we have known before." And he noted, "We [Ward] are starting nothing of any size; we are being cautious."

However, after World War II most population growth was taking place in major metropolitan areas, particularly in their suburbs. Shopping centers were burgeoning and were inevitably taking business from downtown and from smaller business districts. But Ward, under Avery's direction, repudiated expansion during this period of major change in shopping patterns, deliberately leaving the field to Sears, Penney, and other competitors.

A manager can be outstandingly successful at one stage of his or her career. Sewell Avery certainly was in his years as president of U.S. Gypsum Company and in his early leadership of a badly floundering Ward in the 1930s. Yet in another age, the formerly successful leader may lead an organization to a debacle. The great leader who is rigid and unbending often becomes error-prone in later years and intolerant toward capable subordinates who do not accept all of his or her views.

Eventually, after Avery, Ward pulled itself around and tried to resurrect a growth pattern. However, the lost years could never be regained. Poor judgment, which permitted no deviating opinions, cast a sorry spell over the company. A man who for much of his life had evinced outstanding success led Ward down the wrong path and was too stubborn to admit it.

Source: Excerpted from *Management Mistakes* by Robert F. Hartley. Copyright © 1983, by John Wiley & Sons, Inc. Reprinted by permission of John Wiley & Sons, Inc.

superiors. Human skills, therefore, relate to the individual's expertise in interacting with others in a way that will enhance the successful completion of the task at hand. Some human skills that are often necessary for managers to display are effective communication (writing and speaking), creation of a

We asked executives in a variety of industries what tips they could provide for a student starting a career in business. Hundreds offered their advice. Here is a sampling:

"Be flexible, with a willingness to accept tasks and positions that meet the company's needs (versus adhering stringently to personal career goals). Continue to expand knowledge through every possible educational channel. Accept responsibility, then meet it with an urgency and with high-quality results." (The senior vice-president of a large pharmaceutical firm)

"Select courses requiring the development of problem-solving ability. Develop knowledge of the business and economic environment by outside reading such as *The Wall Street Journal* and *Business Week*. Develop competence in the analytical application of computer technology." (The vice-president for planning of a natural gas transmission firm)

"Prepare well in verbal skills, writing ability, and interpersonal skills. While good business practices are important to know and apply, the ultimate success of any manager is getting many people committed to a common set of priorities and goals." (The vice-president of a telecommunications firm)

"First, learn the technical skills. Second, prepare for management by observing and trying to understand how your superiors arrive at decisions." (The vice-president for finance of an air transportation firm)

"Get practical work experience. 'Street smarts' are critical to success. Work on people skills. Develop a winning attitude." (The president of a prepared-foods firm)

"Be flexible. Do not be afraid to try different career paths or different industries. All businesses need bright, energetic, hard-working, ambitious individuals and will pay to both obtain and keep them." (The vice-president and director of an industrial/commercial insulation firm)

"Learn to listen." (The vice-president for sales and marketing of a printing and publishing firm)

"Be inquisitive, open to new ideas. Be a student of both technology and human nature—neither can be effective without the other. There can be powerful synergy when the two are harmonized." (The senior vice-president for new product development of a computer software firm)

"Business is becoming increasingly global every year, especially the auto industry. Students should be prepared to handle the increased scope of worldwide business." (The director of international marketing for an automotive firm)

"The difference between a job and a career is about 20 hours per week. Most incoming people I see want a job with career benefits." (The vice-president for marketing of a soft-drink sales firm)

"Express your opinions but be a team player (unless that includes unethical practices)." (The executive vice-president of a transportation services firm)

A number of recurring themes appeared in the executives' suggestions: the importance of people management skills and of good communications; of enthusiasm and hard work and a willingness to accept responsibility; of problem-solving ability; of knowledge of the "real" business world; of presenting a favorable personal image; of flexibility; of being comfortable with the new technology; of being willing to get one's hands dirty. This book will deal with the key skills suggested in these tips. And, throughout, it will give you many glimpses of the "real world" of business.

positive attitude toward others and the work setting, development of cooperation among group members, and motivation of subordinates.

Conceptual skills require an ability to understand the degree of complexity in a given situation and to reduce that complexity to a level at which
specific courses of action can be derived. Examples of situations that require
conceptual skills include the passage of laws that affect hiring patterns in an
organization, a competitor's change in marketing strategy, or the reorganization of one department which ultimately affects the activities of other departments in the organization.

While successful managers must possess a high level of expertise in technical, human, and conceptual skills, it is also true that each skill will vary in
importance according to the level at which the manager is located in the organization. Generally, technical skills become least important at the top level
of the management hierarchy, replaced with a greater emphasis on conceptual skills. Technical skills are most pronounced at lower levels of management because first-line managers are closer to the production process, where
technical expertise is in greatest demand. Human skills are equally necessary
at each level of the management hierarchy. Conceptual skills are critical for
top managers because the plans, policies, and decisions developed at this level
require the ability to understand how a change in one activity will affect
changes in other activities. The skills needed for effective performance at
different levels of management are depicted in Figure 1–5.

Development of human and conceptual skills will be the main thrust of
the material in this book. This emphasis does not imply that technical skills
are believed to be less worthy, but simply that they are more easily developed
than human and conceptual skills. In many organizations, newly recruited
managers have obtained a foundation in technical skills through schooling.
In addition, many organizations provide in-house training programs to
develop the technical skills that are specific to the operations of the organiza-

FIGURE 1–5
*Managerial Skills
Necessary at Different
Levels of Management*

FIRST-LINE MANAGEMENT	MIDDLE MANAGEMENT	TOP MANAGEMENT
Conceptual	Conceptual	Conceptual
Human		
	Human	
		Human
Technical		
	Technical	
		Technical

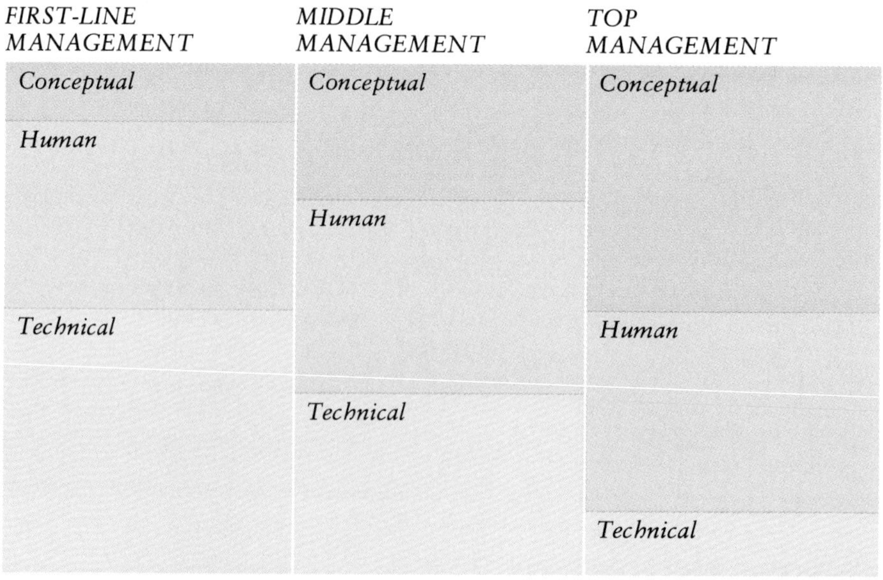

tion. These training programs can last from one day to several years depending on the complexity of the tasks.

Human skills can be developed through an understanding of human and group behavior. Conceptual skills can be developed through knowledge of the various factors that influence organizational activities. Both human and conceptual skills rest on information gathering, reflection, and critical analysis. Such skills are not developed through intuition. Rather, development of human and conceptual skills is enhanced by establishing a framework that will enable a manager to identify and respond to various factors that affect a given situation.

Managerial Roles

Managers must wear many different hats in formulating and implementing task activities related to their positions. In an attempt to understand the diversity of hats managers must wear, Henry Mintzberg examined managerial activities on a daily basis. His study enabled him to identify ten different but coordinated sets of behavior, or roles, that managers assume. These ten roles can be separated into three general groupings: interpersonal roles, informational roles, and decisional roles, as displayed in Figure 1–6.[5]

INTERPERSONAL ROLES

Three of the manager's roles come into play when the manager must engage in interpersonal relationships. The three roles of figurehead, leader, and liaison are each necessary under differing circumstances. Adopting one or another of the three interpersonal roles is made easier by the formal authority the manager obtains from the organization.

The **figurehead role** is enacted when activity of a ceremonial nature is required within the organization. A baseball manager attending a minor league all-star game, the head chef of a prominent restaurant greeting customers at the door, and the president of a bank congratulating a new group of trainees are all examples of the figurehead role. While the figurehead role is routine, with little serious communication and no important decision making, its importance should not be overlooked. At the interpersonal level, it provides

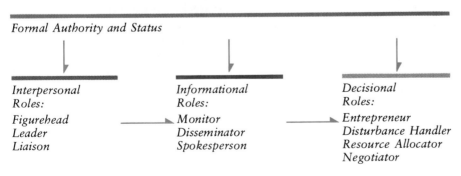

Formal Authority and Status

*Interpersonal
Roles:*

*Figurehead
Leader
Liaison*

*Informational
Roles:*

*Monitor
Disseminator
Spokesperson*

*Decisional
Roles:*

*Entrepreneur
Disturbance Handler
Resource Allocator
Negotiator*

FIGURE 1–6
*The Relationship of
Managerial Roles*

The manager gathers information, evaluates it, and transmits it as appropriate to members of the organization.

members and non-members alike with a sense of what the organization is about and the type of people the organization recruits.

The second interpersonal role, the **leader role**, involves the coordination and control of the work of the manager's subordinates. The leader role may be exercised in a direct or an indirect manner. Hiring, training, and motivating may all require direct contact with subordinates. However, establishing expectations regarding work quality, decision-making responsibility, or time commitments to the job are all outcomes of the leader role that are indirectly related to subordinates.

Quite often, managers are required to obtain information or resources outside their authority. The **liaison role** is enacted when managers make contact with other individuals, who may or may not reside in the organization, in order to complete the work performed by their departments or work units. An auto assembly plant supervisor may telephone a tire supplier to determine the amount of inventory available for next week; a prosecuting attorney may meet with the presiding judge and defense attorney to discuss the use of motions and evidence in a libel trial; or a college professor may meet with professors in a separate department on campus to obtain information on a prospective doctoral student. Ultimately, the liaison role enables a manager to develop a network for obtaining external information which can be useful for completing current and future work activities.

INFORMATIONAL ROLES

Monitor, disseminator, and spokesperson are the three informational roles that a manager may assume. These informational roles are created as a result of enacting the set of interpersonal roles already described. A network of interpersonal contacts with both subordinates and individuals outside the work unit serves to establish the manager as an informational nerve center of the unit, responsible for gathering, receiving, and transmitting information that concerns members of the work unit.

A manager assumes the **monitor role** by continually scanning the environment for information or activities and events that may identify opportunities or threats to the functioning of the work unit. Much of the manager's gathering of information is achieved through the network of contacts that has been established through the interpersonal roles. Hearing small talk at a banquet about a competitor's planned marketing program, learning through casual conversation at a ball game about the negative medical evaluation of an unsigned ball player, or daily reading of a business periodical are all examples of the kinds of information gathering involved in the monitor role.

The information a manager gathers as a monitor must be evaluated and transmitted as appropriate to members of the organization. The transmittal of information by a manager activates the **disseminator role**. Privileged information may be disseminated to subordinates, peers, or superiors in the organization. The manager may inform the marketing vice-president about the specific marketing strategy a competitor is planning to implement. A baseball manager may inform the team owner that an impending trade should be canceled because of the unfavorable medical report on one of the players. Or reading *The Wall Street Journal* may inform the manager that a shipping strike is looming and thus enable her to inform subordinates that temporary layoffs may occur next month.

Occasionally, a manager must assume the **spokesperson role** by speaking on behalf of the work unit to people inside or outside the organization. This might involve lobbying for critical resources or appealing to individuals who have influence on activities that affect the work unit. A top manager asking the board of directors to keep the work unit together during a reorganization period or a corporate president speaking to a college audience on the role the company plays in education would both constitute engaging in the spokesperson role.

DECISIONAL ROLES

Both interpersonal and informational roles are really preludes to what are often considered to be a manager's most important set of roles: the decisional roles of entrepreneur, disturbance handler, resource allocator, and negotiator.

The **entrepreneur role** comes into action when the manager seeks to improve the work unit. This can be accomplished by adapting new techniques to fit a particular situation or modifying old techniques to improve individual or group activity. Managers usually learn of new or innovative methods through information gathered in the monitor role. As a result, a supervisor purchases a new kiln which will shorten the drying process for ceramic tiles; a director of a youth club trains staff in the use of personal computers to increase file access; or a president establishes a new pension plan to improve employee morale.

Whereas the entrepreneur role establishes the manager as the initiator of change, the **disturbance handler role** establishes the manager as a responder to change. Organizations, unfortunately, do not run so smoothly that managers are never called upon to respond to unwelcome pressures. In these cases, the manager is required to act quickly to bring stability back to the organization. A law partner must settle a disagreement among associates in the

Kathryn M. Bartol (Ph.D., Michigan State University) is Professor of Organizational Behavior and Management of Human Resources in the College of Management, University of Maryland, College Park. She is a past president of the Academy of Management and a fellow of the Academy of Management and the American Psychological Association. Professor Bartol is the author of Male and Female Leaders in Small Work Groups and of numerous articles that have appeared in the Journal of Applied Psychology, Industrial and Labor Relations Review, Soviet Studies, Academy of Management Review, MIS Quarterly, and elsewhere. She is a specialist in performance appraisal and compensation sys-

ACADEMIC PROFILE
KATHRYN M. BARTOL

tems design. A former systems project leader in the computer field, she writes extensively on the management of human resources within high-technology environments. Professor Bartol is a consultant/trainer for a number of organizations and is an associate editor of the Academy of Management Executive.

Q: *Some writers of popular management books, and some managers, give the impression that management training in business schools may be irrelevant and misguided. What do you think causes such a view?*

A: Unfortunately, some managers and even writers of popular management books are not very aware of current trends in management training in business schools. As a result, their comments often are based on sources like hearsay, quick looks at a few management textbooks, or even their own management training, which may now be obsolete. Within the last twenty years, growth in the knowledge base about management has accelerated exponentially, and it is becoming more difficult than ever for managers and others to keep up with advances. At the same time, management professors share some of the responsibility for views that management training may be irrelevant or misguided. They frequently are so busy working on new research projects and exchanging information with each other that they neglect to communicate new research findings to managers, particularly through writing articles geared specifically to managerial needs. Management professors simply haven't worked hard enough to disseminate new knowledge to managers.

Q: *What do you think prospective managers gain from management training in business schools that they would not pick up on their own in the "real world"?*

A: I recently asked a group of 300 new MBA students at my university how many had worked for a manager whom they considered to be relatively ineffective in handling people. Every single hand went up, even though most of these students were under 30 and had only worked for a few years. Being a good manager is extremely difficult, and prospective managers will find that "trial and error" is a long and costly way to learn how to manage. Most of us wouldn't even consider trying to learn chemistry or engineering that way. Management training in business schools offers an opportunity to learn about many basic concepts in areas such as motivation, organizational design, strategy and planning, decision making, and communications—to name a few. Typically, there also is a great deal of emphasis on learning how to apply these concepts through cases, role plays, and other class exercises. These concepts help prospective managers learn how to evaluate conditions and decide what action to take in the variety of situations that they are likely to confront. Think of these concepts as important tools which aid managers. Without these tools, and the training that goes with them, a manager's job is much more difficult.

Q: *Do you have any other thoughts on this issue?*

A: One serious problem is that the management field is highly susceptible to fads. New approaches sometimes are embraced as if they are the key to unparalleled success. This is especially true if the new approaches are touted in the popular press, as was the case with Japanese management a couple of years ago. Then, when the new approach doesn't turn out to be the expected cure-all, it is summarily abandoned. Who is to blame for the fads? The popular writers, and sometimes the academics, who oversell the ideas? The managers who grab on to them? I suspect that the current generation of business school graduates will be more sophisticated as managers and will put an end to this faddism.

firm on who will present a case before a judge; a personnel director must negotiate with striking employees dissatisfied with the procedures for laying off employees; or a cannery first-line manager must respond to a sudden shortage of cans used to package perishable fruit because the supplier has reneged on a contract.

When a manager is placed in the position of having to decide to whom and in what quantity resources will be dispensed, the **resource allocator role** is assumed. Resources may include money, time, power, equipment, or people. During periods of resource abundance, this role can be easily performed by a manager. In most cases, however, organizations operate under conditions of resource scarcity; thus, decisions on the allocation of resources can be critical for the success of the work unit, division, or organization. As a decision maker, the manager must strive not only to appropriately match resources with subordinates but also to ensure that the distribution of resources is coordinated to effectively complete the task to be performed. An office manager must provide secretaries with appropriate equipment to generate and duplicate documents. A manager of a fast-food restaurant must coordinate work shifts to have the maximum number of employees working during the lunch hour. Corporate presidents may provide their administrative assistants with decision-making responsibility for day-to-day matters.

In addition to decisions concerning organizational changes, disturbances, and resources, the manager must enact a **negotiator role**. The process of negotiation is possible only when an individual has the authority to commit organizational resources. Hence, as managers move up the managerial hierarchy and obtain control over more resources, they become more involved in the negotiator role. For example, the president of a record company may be called in to discuss terms of a possible contract with a major rock group; a production manager must negotiate with the personnel department to obtain employees with specialized skills; or a college dean must negotiate with department heads over course offerings and the number of faculty to be hired.

The relative emphasis a manager places on these ten roles is highly dependent on the manager's authority and status in the organization. Length of time on the job, position in the management hierarchy, goals of the subunit to be achieved, and skills the manager possesses all play a part in determining which roles are more prominent than others at any given time. For instance, a marketing manager is more likely to emphasize the interpersonal roles because of the importance of personal contact in the marketing process. A financial manager, charged with responsibility for the economic efficiency of the organization, will probably focus on the decisional roles. A staff manager, or a manager who performs in an advisory capacity, is likely to be more heavily involved in the informational roles. Regardless of the differences that may occur, however, all managers enact interpersonal, informational, and decisional roles while performing their tasks.

IMPLICATIONS FOR MANAGEMENT

Effectively managing an organization is a demanding task. Managers not only must develop skills related to the functional areas of management but also must learn how to integrate these activities. What makes this process demanding is that events and activities external and internal to an organization can radically change the techniques and methods managers must use in order to arrive at successful outcomes. Managers cannot afford to be limited in their view of management, nor can they simply rely on how things were done in the past.

The situations at Lotus Development Corporation and Montgomery Ward underscore this point. Both companies enjoyed tremendous success at one point in time. However, the inability of management to plan effectively for the future, to organize and staff the companies with appropriately skilled employees, to direct activities that encouraged employees to make solid contributions, and to implement adequate controls resulted in serious difficulties for each organization. In addition, management in both companies failed to recognize how the context of their organizations had changed. Management at Lotus Development Corporation did not recognize that failure to update software in a timely manner would damage their position in the industry. Ward's Sewell Avery was convinced that the country was on the verge of a major economic depression after World War II and made the costly mistake of refusing to move stores to the suburbs.

Even the most seasoned and successful managers are prone to mistakes. However, a more complete knowledge of the managerial process can reduce the chances of mistakes that will have dire consequences for an organization. Such knowledge may help managers to better plan, organize and staff, direct, and control organization activities within the context of their organization.

KEY TERMS AND CONCEPTS

conceptual skills	liaison role
context	management
controlling	managers
decisional roles	middle managers
directing	monitor role
disseminator role	negotiator role
disturbance handler role	organization
division of labor	organizing and staffing
entrepreneur role	planning
figurehead role	resource allocator role
first-line managers	spokesperson role
human skills	system
informational roles	technical skills
interpersonal roles	upper managers
leader role	

QUESTIONS FOR REVIEW AND DISCUSSION

1. Discuss in which of the three managerial skills Jim Manzi appears to be most proficient. Least proficient.
2. What are the six areas of an organization's external context?
3. In what ways do you engage in managerial activities in your daily life? What methods do you use to interrelate these activities to accomplish goals?

4. Explain why division of labor should lead to increased productivity.
5. What are the key dimensions of an organization? How does an organization differ from a group of students who happen to meet in the student union?
6. List and discuss the four managerial activities. How does each activity contribute to the attainment of organizational goals?
7. How could Sewell Avery at Montgomery Ward have changed his approach to prevent the failures that occurred? What role did contextual factors play in producing poor firm performance?
8. In reference to the ten managerial roles, how would you describe Jim Manzi and Sewell Avery? In which roles did they seem to be effective? Which roles did they execute ineffectively?
9. Describe how your teacher uses the managerial activities of planning, organizing and staffing, directing, and controlling in this course. What are the goals the teacher is trying to accomplish? How are activities interrelated to attain these goals?
10. How were the various things you did today influenced by organizations?

CASES

1–1 THE CHAMPION OF THE MODERN CORNER STORE

It's 7:30 A.M., and the sun is beating down on the cars parked at the offices of Sunshine-Jr. Stores, Inc., in Panama City, Florida. The salient fact is not the sun (this is Florida) but the cars (so many, so early). Home base of a chain of four local supermarkets and 320 convenience stores in five southeastern states, the building is an essay in economy—corrugated steel painted an unprepossessing off-white. The only hints of hierarchy and privilege are four covered parking spaces close to the front door.

One of the spaces belongs to Lana Jane Lewis-Brent, president and chief executive officer, and it takes only a few minutes in her presence to realize that the setting meshes perfectly with her style. Matter-of-fact and open, Lewis-Brent inspires a trust that her executives consider inviolable. "Nobody wants to let her down," says Annette Trujillo, vice-president of marketing and a long-time friend. Adds Herman Daniels, director of data processing: "She puts a lot of confidence in you, and you don't want to betray it. It's easier to make things work than to go into her office and tell her you can't."

Lewis-Brent, 43, didn't win this trust overnight. She has been building it since she joined Sunshine-Jr. in 1967, after college. As the daughter of L. D. Lewis, the founder and only CEO the company had ever had, she clearly was on the fast track, although she was no shoo-in for his job. "He had great confidence in her, but it was hard for him to imagine women in top positions," says Lewis-Brent's mother, Leona Lewis, who is chairman of the board. "Lana Jane was ready so much sooner than he was ready to think she could succeed as head of the company."

An indefatigable businessman, L. D. died at the office in 1981, at the age of 73. Lana Jane, 35, had been with Sunshine-Jr. for 14 years, moving up by moving around, from accounting to shareholder relations.

She also was the mother of an 8-week-old son, Jensen, and the wife of a designer with an increasingly busy practice in architecture, painting, and graphics. "Because of my age and the new situation with Jensen, I think I could have waited five or ten years to step in and run the company," she says. "But within a very few days I decided that my next step should be to become president." (A full-time housekeeper and live-in nanny already were in place. Lana Jane and her husband, Paul Brent, had decided before the birth to give their careers as many domestic supports as possible.)

Backed by her mother, who owns over half of Sunshine-Jr.'s shares, Lewis-Brent immediately moved to assume control of the company, hoping to put a halt to troubles that had accumulated during the last few years of her father's life. The convenience-store chain had mushroomed to 354 stores, but it had grown without the discipline she thought necessary for a large-scale corporation in an extremely competitive industry. There was no human resources department, older stores had begun looking seedy, a worrisome number of outlets operated in the red, and top management was not exactly committed. "We had people who came to the office for only 30 or 40 minutes a day," says Lewis-Brent. The slack, it seems, was the result of L.D.'s soft heart. "He would fire people, then rehire them, three or four times," Leona Lewis says. "He also brought family members into the business, which is not always a good thing."

Facing the monumental task of restructuring the company, Lewis-Brent says she felt overwhelmed but not unprepared. "Over the years I had thought about what I would do differently. I had put some of my ideas on paper as a reference for the future, and these ideas became the basis of my plan." She wanted a more systematic approach to budgeting, a schedule for remodeling run-down stores, and formalized employee training. One of her first acts was to discuss these plans with the current president and offer him a chance to stay on. He declined.

His departure was the first of many. "I wanted people who were willing to make a big commitment in time and energy and effort and enthusiasm," Lewis-Brent says. "If they couldn't do that and couldn't be part of a team that was going forward fast, I had to either terminate or accept terminations." The task gave her no joy. "The hardest part was realizing that I was changing the direction of people's lives. For the benefit of the company, I'm concerned that managers be a cohesive group, all pulling in the same direction, but I'm also concerned about the impact of my decisions on the lives of individuals." When the broom finished sweeping, only one of her father's executives remained.

Even with new managers change came slowly, because the inertia at headquarters had spread through the entire organization. "There was paralysis in the stores," says Richard McAllister, chief operating officer. "People in the field knew what to do, but they had been trained not to do it without an OK from headquarters." That autocratic approach stifled initiative and slowed Sunshine-Jr.'s reactions to change—potentially fatal flaws in an industry with net-profit margins as thin as prosciutto. The typical convenience store—part gas station and part grocery store—also is a barometer of the world around it: sensitive to jumps in oil prices, the rise in drug-related crime, and changing consumer demands for everything from oat bran to round-the-clock service. The latest available industry figures, for 1988, show average pretax profits of 1.9 percent.

Also, competition has stiffened. In its first 15 years Sunshine-Jr. prospered simply by adding more stores. But in the mid-1970s, when oil companies and other convenience-store chains saw the money to be made in the booming Sunbelt, in they came. Real estate prices soared, driving up the cost of new stores and putting more pressure on profits.

While Lewis-Brent had a long list of problems to solve, she saw that her most critical task was to give employees a clear vision of her ambitions for the company. The vision had to be easy to communicate and broad enough to serve as a guide for making decisions. Sunshine-Jr., she decided, was going to be the best in the business. Its gas prices would be the lowest, its stores would gleam, it would move beyond the ordinary to prepared food and video rentals, and its service would be impeccable. (Clerks were renamed "sales associates" to upgrade their self-image and to underscore their role in selling.)

Sunshine-Jr. executives agree that the uniqueness of Lewis-Brent's drive to be the best lies in her intensity. "Lana Jane cares so much and works so hard, it's staggering," says Rich McAllister. "She is just not willing to give less than she can give." Employees are held to the same standard. "No matter what we achieve, she always challenges us to reach beyond that," Trujillo says. "She isn't driven by what the industry is doing but by how we can improve on what we're doing."

The words "demanding" and "perfectionist" surface repeatedly in assessments of Lewis-Brent's style, but so do "open-minded" and "a great listener." McAllister praises her reluctance to dismiss any idea, even one that failed in the past: "She will say, 'Well, we did that once before, but maybe we didn't do it right.'" When Lewis-Brent disagrees, she leaves the door open. "My mind can be changed," she likes to say.

When Lewis-Brent comes home, ideas picked up in her travels are immediately discussed with managers. So are news stories about competitors and industry issues. In a world where information is power (and where the first law of power is "Protect what you have"), Lewis-Brent's eagerness to tell all may seem naive. But she has enough self-confidence to believe that the rewards outweigh the risks. Only if the lines of communication are open in both directions, she feels, can she get the information—freely discussed and fully debated—she needs.

Source: Patricia O'Toole, "The Champion of the Modern Corner Store," *Working Woman* (September 1989): 114, 118. Reprinted with permission from *Working Woman* magazine. Copyright © 1989 by the WWT Partnership.

1. Compare the management styles of Lana Lewis-Brent, Jim Manzi, and Sewell Avery. Which management skills do they use effectively? Which skills are weak?
2. To which areas of the external context must Ms. Lewis-Brent be attentive in order to manage Sunshine-Jr. effectively? How does she learn about these areas of the external context?
3. How does Lana Lewis-Brent strive to achieve excellence in her company? What advice could you give her to help her achieve this excellence?
4. What managerial roles does Ms. Lewis-Brent emphasize as CEO of Sunshine-Jr? Are these roles appropriate? Should she emphasize other roles as well?

1–2 CARTER RACING

"What should we do?"

John Carter was not sure, but his brother and partner, Fred Carter, was on the phone and needed a decision. Should they run in the race or not? It had been a successful season so far, but the Pocono race was important because of the prize money and TV exposure it promised. This first year had been hard because the team was trying to make a name for itself. They had run a lot of small races to get this shot at the big time. A successful outing could mean more sponsors, a chance to start making some profits for a change, and the luxury of racing only the major events. But if they suffered another engine failure on national television . . .

Just thinking about the team's engine problems made John wince. There had been blown engines seven times in 24 outings this season with various degrees of damage to the engine and car. No one could figure out why. It took a lot of sponsor money to replace a $20,000 racing engine, and the wasted entry fees were no small matter either. John and Fred had everything they owned riding on Carter Racing. This season had to be a success.

Paul Edwards, the engine mechanic, was guessing the engine problem was related to ambient air temperature. He argued that when it was cold the different expansion rates for the head and block were damaging the head gasket and causing the engine failures. It was below freezing last night, which meant a cold morning for starting the race.

Tom Burns, the chief mechanic, did not agree with Paul's "gut feeling" and had data to support his position (see Exhibit 1). He pointed out that gasket failures had occurred at all temperatures, which meant temperature was not the issue. Tom has been racing for 20 years and believed that luck was an important element in success. He had argued this view when he and John discussed the problem last week: "In racing, you are pushing the limits of what is known. You cannot expect to have everything under control. If you want to win, you have to take risks. Everybody in racing knows it. The drivers have their lives on the line, I have a career that hangs on every

EXHIBIT 1
Note from Tom Burns

John,

I got the data on the gasket failures from Paul. We have run 24 races this season with temperatures at race time ranging from 53 to 82 degrees. Paul had a good idea in suggesting we look into this, but as you can see, this is not our problem. I tested the data for a correlation between temperature and gasket failures and found no relationship.

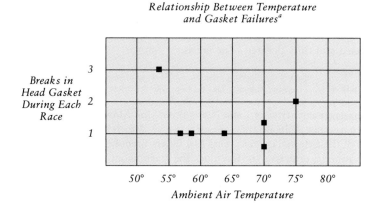

Relationship Between Temperature
and Gasket Failures[a]

Breaks in
Head Gasket
During Each
Race

Ambient Air Temperature

In comparison with some of the other teams, we have done extremely well this season. We have finished 62.5% of the races, and when we finished we were in the top five 80% of the time. I am not happy with the engine problems, but I will take the four first-place finishes and 50% rate of finishing in the money[b] over seven engines any day. If we continue to run like this, we will have our pick of sponsors.

Tom

[a]Each point is for a single race. A gasket can have multiple breaks, any of which may produce an engine failure.
[b]The top five finishers in a race are "in the money."

race, and you guys have got every dime tied up in the business. That's the thrill, beating the odds and winning." Last night over dinner he had added to this argument forcefully with what he called Burns's First Law of Racing: "Nobody ever won a race sitting in the pits."

John, Fred, and Tom had discussed Carter Racing's situation the previous evening. This first season was a success from a racing standpoint, with the team's car finishing in the top five in 12 of the 15 races it completed. As a result, the sponsorship offers critical to the team's business success were starting to come in. A big break had come two weeks ago after the Dunham race where the team scored its fourth first-place finish. Goodstone Tire had finally decided Carter Racing deserved its sponsorship at Pocono—worth a much-needed $40,000—and was considering a full-season contract for next year if the team's car finished in the top five in this race. The Goodstone sponsorship was for a million a year, plus incentives. John and Fred had gotten a favorable response from Goodstone's Racing Program Director last week when they presented their plans for next season, but it was clear that his support depended on the visibility they generated in this race.

"John, we only have another hour to decide," Fred said over the phone. "If we withdraw now, we can get back half the $15,000 entry and try to recoup some of our losses next season. We will lose Goodstone, they'll want $25,000 of their money back, and we end up the season $50,000 in the hole. If we run and finish in the top five, we have Goodstone in our pocket and can add another car next season. You know as well as I do, however, that if we run and lose another engine, we are back at square one next season. We will lose the tire sponsorship and a blown engine is going to lose us the oil contract. No oil company wants a national TV audience to see a smoker being dragged off the track with their name plastered all over it. The oil sponsorship is $500,000 that we cannot live without. Think about it—call Paul and Tom if you want—but I need a decision in an hour."

John hung up the phone and looked out the window at the crisp, fall sky. The temperature sign across the street flashed "40 DEGREES AT 9:23 AM."

Source: Jack W. Brittain and Sim B. Sitkin, "Carter Racing." Copyright © 1986. Reprinted by permission of Jack W. Brittain, School of Business, University of Texas at Dallas, and Sim B. Sitkin, Graduate School of Business, University of Texas at Austin.

1. Four decisional roles were identified in the text: entrepreneur, disturbance handler, resource allocator, and negotiator. Which of these four roles is John Carter being asked to fulfill?
2. Which of the following managerial activities appears to be most important to John Carter in the management of Carter Racing: planning, organizing and staffing, directing, or controlling?
3. Identify the internal and external contextual conditions that have the greatest impact on the decision to be made by John Carter.
4. If you were John Carter, would you enter the race or pass? Justify your answer.

ENDNOTES

1. R. Levering, M. Moskowitz, and M. Katz, *The 100 Best Companies to Work for in America* (Reading, MA: Addison-Wesley, 1984), 368. Also see R. Levering, *A Great Place to Work: What Makes Some Companies So Good (and Others So Bad)* (Reading, MA: Addison-Wesley, 1988).
2. L. von Bertalanffy, "The History and Status of General Systems Theory," *Academy of Management Journal* 15 (1972): 407-426.
3. A. Smith, *The Wealth of Nations* (London: J. M. Dent & Sons, 1910).
4. R. L. Katz, "Skills of an Effective Administrator," *Harvard Business Review* 52, no. 5 (September-October 1974): 90-102.
5. H. Mintzberg, "The Manager's Job: Folklore and Fact," *Harvard Business Review* 53, no. 4 (July-August 1975): 49-61.

History of Management

CHAPTER 2

After studying this chapter, you should be able to:
- *Understand the contributions that preindustrial organizations have made to the study of management.*
- *Discuss the significance of the Industrial Revolution in management thought and practices.*
- *Summarize the importance of classical management theory and behavioral management theory, and evaluate their limitations in application to management practices.*
- *Identify the contributions that quantitative management theory and systems theory have made to the practice of management.*
- *Discuss why contingency theory is useful for solving managerial problems.*
- *Describe emerging theories of management and their application to managerial practices.*

Many different perspectives on the practice of management have been advanced suggesting how managers should approach, diagnose, and solve organizational problems. Some perspectives attempted to solve problems of current interest to managers of that day. Other perspectives attempted to develop rules and guidelines for managers that could be useful in many different organizational settings. Regardless of the managerial issue or problem that was of central concern to these perspectives, it is fair to say that each differed in its assumptions and in the methods it recommended to managers for reaching a solution. A careful understanding of the events and issues that confronted managers in the past enables us to understand why different approaches have been recommended for solving managerial problems. As Management in Action 1 suggests, companies now frequently turn to historians to help them solve today's problems through knowledge of the past.

HISTORICAL FOUNDATIONS OF MANAGEMENT

The development of management theory and practice is best understood in the context of history. First, we will explore social and cultural developments that preceded the emergence of specific writings on management. Then we will examine the effects of the Industrial Revolution on management thought. Throughout the chapter we will discuss events that surrounded the introduction of new ideas in management to give you a clear picture of the problems and issues that theorists and managers have attempted to address.

Preindustrial Societies

While techniques of management have been around for a long time, the practice of management is relatively new. Prior to the beginning of the Industrial

Techniques of management were practiced long before a body of management theory was developed.

For years, Polaroid's W-3 plant in Waltham, Massachusetts, was a model of efficiency—the sort of small, collegial shop that the photography firm loved

to boast about. But relations with workers slowly soured, productivity slumped—and by the time 15 years had passed, no one could remember the reasons why. Enter Phelps Tracy, corporate historian. By interviewing employees and examining old records, the consultant, a trained social scientist, pieced together the puzzle: As the plant's employment and output had increased over the years, managers had imposed ever tighter controls that gradually sapped workers' morale. Employees and management pored over Tracy's findings. They soon discovered the source of the plant's problems and took the steps needed to solve them.

Company historians were once chiefly public-relations ploys, crafted to enshrine their subjects in a free-enterprise Hall of Fame. But along with Polaroid, firms like AT&T, Navistar, Consolidated Edison, and Wells Fargo Bank are now asking serious scholars like Tracy to research their past. Some firms have even hired their own in-house historian. As a result, companies may be acquiring the long-term perspective American management is often accused of lacking. Paul E. Johnson, a vice-president at Navistar, says, "It's beneficial to know your corporate roots."

Delving into corporate history still has its conventional marketing uses. Wells Fargo's history department manages an extensive collection of archives, some of which are used in the bank's advertising campaigns. But today's corporate historians stress that their research is primarily aimed at giving man-agers useful information for running their businesses. Sometimes the past proves valuable in simply keeping firms from repeating previous mistakes. One history graduate student working part-time at a California-based computer company discovered that the firm was unknowingly researching a potential product that it had researched a decade earlier. The company quickly offered him a full-time job.

Replenishing the corporate memory bank may help to solve "one of the facts of life—that people change jobs every year or two," says Harold Anderson, Wells Fargo archivist. The employees in line are often left with few clues as to why their predecessor reached a given conclusion. To remedy that problem, historian Philip Cantelon wrote a book for Consolidated Edison executives showing how former executives had grappled with corporate issues. At AT&T, consultants who conducted historical research for Bell in connection with the government's antitrust suit also compiled a history of the Western Electric acquisition that may assist in the system's breakup. When it comes to facing new competition, says consultant and lecturer George David Smith, managers will benefit from seeing just how Ma Bell evolved from a turn-of-the-century fledgling founded on a risky technological base.

Some historians wonder whether their objectivity is sufficiently protected. "'Historians for Hire' are constantly confronted with how they can do scholarly work while being paid for it," says Ted Karamanski, a history professor at Loyola University of Chicago. Guarding against mere vanity histories, Karamanski says, will require "a system of ethics." But it's the candid truth about their pasts that most firms now seem to be after—and today's corporate Toynbees seem determined to deliver the goods.

Source: Dentzer, "Profiting from the Past." From *Newsweek* (May 10, 1988). © 1988, by Newsweek, Inc. All rights reserved. Reprinted by permission.

Revolution in 17th-century England, several forms of organization had emerged requiring the use of "managers" to successfully achieve organizational objectives. Most prominent among these organizations were the state, the church, and the military. It is in these organizations that we can identify early notions about how management is to be practiced.

With the emergence of villages and cities in ancient civilizations, as represented by Greek, Roman, and Chinese societies, came the need to administer the building of roads; to establish judicial principles to oversee commerce and settle disputes; to provide means to distribute food supplies; to control the collection of taxes; and to supervise military activities both within the state and among conquered territories. We find in the writings of early Egyptians, Hebrews, Greeks, and Romans expressions of the need for effective managers with explications of the duties and responsibilities assigned to their position, the need for training, and the need for control over activities in the hands of a centralized authority such as the emperor.[1]

Religious institutions, most notably the Catholic church, also contributed to the body of knowledge concerning managerial principles. While the objectives of the church differed from those of the state, the church incorporated many of the same principles of management. In addition, the church developed methods and techniques directed toward commitment to values and attitudes, provided social support to the populace, and established conditions for membership.

Perhaps the most advanced form of organization was the military. Indeed, many of the more sophisticated principles created and developed by the military, from the Roman to the Prussian armies, are still applied by managers of modern businesses. Most notable of these principles are the following:

- **Chain of command.** The chain of command established clear, unbroken lines of authority and responsibility from the highest to the lowest level in the organization.
- **Delegation of authority.** Because of the length of the chain of command, it became essential that decision-making authority be granted to those in middle- and low-level positions. Without this provision, the individual occupying the senior position would be overwhelmed by the task of having to approve each activity necessary to the efficient functioning of the military units.
- **Staff.** As warfare became more sophisticated, those in command could not be fully aware of every tactic available in a given situation. Thus the need developed for a group of officers, called staff officers, who were recruited and trained to serve as advisers to managers faced with critical decisions. While staff officers accrued power because of their expertise, the final decision was the responsibility of the commanding officer.
- **Unity of command.** The principle that no individual has more than one supervisor is known as unity of command. Receiving orders or directives from two or more superiors can lead to confusion, contradictory requests, and instability in military operations.

The importance of these principles in military organizations cannot be overemphasized. As we will see later, organizations operating in threatening environments must reduce errors and plan their activities to a greater extent than organizations operating in nonthreatening environments.

Many other early examples of management principles and concepts could be cited. However, it was not until the emergence of the Industrial Revolution that a literature on management and organization began to be seriously developed.

The Industrial Revolution

The Industrial Revolution led to radical changes in the way people work, socialize, engage in politics, and carry on their daily lives. Prior to the Industrial Revolution in Europe and the United States, most human labor was performed in relation to the soil. Artisans comprised a small segment of labor which was primarily confined to the cities and concentrated in the production of goods such as cloth, shoes, tools, and weapons. However, it was the advancement of technology in several key spheres that culminated in the rapid emergence and growth of industrial manufacturing.[2]

Foremost among the technological advancements was the discovery of how to derive energy from steam. The steam engine, as perfected by James Watt, provided a mechanism for obtaining cheap and efficient energy. Moreover, steam power allowed for the development of machinery that could lower production costs, produce larger volumes of goods, and ultimately provide for swifter transportation of those goods to markets. However, this could not be achieved without a readily available labor force. As factories based on the use of this new technology were set up, the need for greater numbers of laborers generated political tension in many European societies. With most of the laborers dispersed on farmlands, often working under conditions of virtual servitude to large landowners, attempts to reform society began to occur. Indeed, much of the political unrest in Europe during the 19th century was due to political power struggles between the aristocratic classes and a new emerging class of factory owners struggling to define the role that labor would play in the Industrial Revolution.

Ultimately, many of the peasants moved to the city to obtain work in the developing factories. As a result, human labor and energy were augmented by machines, and industrial development spread throughout Western civilization. However, an additional technological advancement was necessary in order for factories and industries to grow. While goods could be produced in greater quantities, at lower costs, and in less time, customers had to be available. Again, steam power provided the solution. Where a single city may have constituted the total market for the goods produced in a factory, railroads and ships powered by steam could now efficiently transport the goods over a much wider area to be sold to new customers. Hence, it was both the invention of new forms of energy for the production and transportation of goods and radical social changes that promoted the Industrial Revolution.

The rapid growth of factories posed management problems different from those encountered in preindustrial organizations. The state could operate without competition or having to show a profit; the church could organize and manage its activities because of the devotion of the faithful; and the military could control large numbers of troops through a rigid hierarchy of discipline and authority. Managers of factories, however, had to find a different set of principles and techniques in order to be effective.[3]

As an individual factory grew in numbers of employees, it became more difficult for one person to oversee the operation. The obvious solution to this problem was to hire managers to oversee parts of the production process. Yet trained managers were in short supply. Most of those employed as managers had to learn their position based on ad hoc problem solving. To complicate the management task, many laborers had not had access to education; thus, literacy was low as was the ability to perform basic mathematical calculations. Great amounts of managerial time were spent in providing oral instructions and demonstrations of tasks to be performed. The focus of managers, therefore, was more on directing subordinates than on coordinating and motivating the work force. The effect of this situation was a loss of production efficiency.

During this time, several individuals began to address issues of management both in practice and in writings. Two of the best-known theorists of this period were Robert Owen and Charles Babbage.

ROBERT OWEN

Robert Owen (1771–1858) was the owner of a mill in New Lanark, Scotland. He came to recognize that human resources were as valuable to the production of goods as were financial and material resources. Owen believed that factory workers would be more productive if they were motivated through rewards rather than punishments. He experimented with several motivating techniques and became a strong advocate for improving working conditions through increasing the minimum working age of children to 10 years, providing regular meal breaks for workers, and reducing the workday to 10½ hours with no night work for children. While these ideas are widely accepted now, they were considered "too radical" by other manufacturers and politicians of that time. Frustrated by this opposition to his ideas, Owen left England for the United States and founded a communal township at New Harmony, Indiana, in 1824 which incorporated much of his philosophy. Many of Owen's ideas about the management of human resources were assimilated into a school of thought, referred to as behavioral theory, that emerged in the 1920s.

CHARLES BABBAGE

Charles Babbage (1792–1871) is considered a genius for his contribution to the development of the modern school of English mathematics, his application of mathematical principles to management, and his development of an "analytic engine" whose ideas are represented in the modern computer in the form of program control, microprogramming, multiprocessing, and array processing. Babbage's major contribution to management is his book *On the Economy of Machinery and Manufactures*, in which he described in great detail how mathematics could be applied to problems of inefficient use of materials and facilities.[4] Many of his ideas would be incorporated both in classical management theory and in quantitative management theory, which were espoused in the 1900s. Babbage also had a strong understanding of the importance of human resources as related to efficiency. He advocated profit-sharing plans and bonus systems as ways to achieve better relations between management and labor. Despite the significance of his contributions, Charles Babbage was considered by his contemporaries to be eccentric, if not on the verge of lunacy. Upset by the noise made by organ grinders on the street outside his house, he would counter by blowing a bugle in front of his house, much to the dismay of his neighbors. One friend noted that "he spoke as if he hated mankind in general, Englishmen in particular, and the English government and organ grinders most of all."[5]

Despite the work of Owen and Babbage, it was not until the late 1800s that owners and managers began to raise concerns about the problem of material and human inefficiency. By this time markets were becoming saturated and competition for greater profits had intensified. Emphasis on cutting costs and increasing efficiency led to the emergence of classical management theory.

CLASSICAL MANAGEMENT THEORY

It is important to recognize that while the Industrial Revolution was having similar impacts on Europe and America, some important distinctions can be made. Unlike Europe, America was undergoing rapid growth and expansion. Midwestern and western lands were sparsely inhabited and contained large quantities of untapped minerals, forest reserves, and fertile farmland. As the population moved westward, new markets were opened for enterprises, and the need for power, transportation, and communication became critical. With the development of rail systems and the establishment of telegraph lines, entrepreneurial activity was abundant and highly competitive. The need to develop management techniques that would integrate technology, materials, and worker activities in a productive and efficient manner was a central concern during this period. Because of these events in the United States and the impact of the Industrial Revolution in Europe, classical management theory evolved in an effort to develop techniques that would solve problems of organizational efficiency in the production of goods and services.

Classical management theory can be divided into two perspectives distinguished by the issues and problems that they address. One perspective, administrative theory, evolved from a concern by both European and American academicians and managers with the nature and management of the total organization. Issues and problems that they sought to address focused on the technical efficiency of the organization. A second perspective, scientific management, emerged primarily among American scholars and managers and focused on issues involved in the management of work and workers.

Administrative Theory

Administrative theory focuses on the total organization and attempts to develop principles that will direct managers to more efficient activities. Prominent writers in this perspective were Henri Fayol, Max Weber, and Chester Barnard.

HENRI FAYOL

Henri Fayol (1841–1925) was a French mining engineer who spent many of his later years as an executive for a French coal and iron combine. In 1916, as director of the company, Fayol penned the book *General and Industrial Management*. In this book, Fayol classified the study of management into several functional areas which are still commonly used in executive training and corporate development programs. The functional areas identified by Fayol are planning, organizing, directing, coordinating, and controlling.

Fayol set down specific principles for practicing managers to apply that he had found useful during his years as a manager. He felt these principles could be used not only in business organizations but also in government, the military, religious organizations, and financial institutions. Some of these principles, discussed in Chapter 1 and summarized in Figure 2–1, are still widely cited.

Fayol's principles were not meant to be exhaustive. Rather, his aim was to provide managers with the necessary building blocks to serve as guidelines

Division of Work	Like many writers before him, Fayol believed that dividing labor into specialized units would reduce inefficiency through less waste and increased output and would simplify the task of job training. Fayol advocated this specialization for both laborers and managers in the organization.
Authority	Fayol defined authority as the right to give orders and the power to exact obedience. Fayol believed that formal authority (granted to the position) and personal authority (derived from intelligence and experience) should be complementary. Further, authority carries responsibility, which is the obligation to carry out assigned duties satisfactorily.
Discipline	Poor discipline is the result of poor leadership. Good discipline exists when workers and managers respect the rules governing activities in the organization.
Unity of Command	The principle that no individual should have more than one supervisor was derived from military codes, and Fayol believed it was fundamental to effective management of an organization.
Unity of Direction	Tasks of a similar nature that are directed toward a single goal should be grouped under one manager.
Subordination of Interests	The goals of the organization should take precedence over individual goals. Fayol believed that when individual goals prevailed over organizational goals, the outcome would be conflict.
Remuneration	Rewards in the form of pay, bonuses, and benefits should be fair for all employees in the organization.
Centralization	The concentration of power and authority at the upper levels of the organization is centralization; when dispersed throughout levels, decentralization. Fayol believed that the optimum depended on special considerations, such as the size of the firm. Large firms generally required more decentralization than small firms.
Scalar Chain	The scalar chain, or chain of command, stipulates that authority and communication should be routed through positions from top to bottom in the organization.
Order	Human and material resources should be coordinated in such a way that there is a place for everything and everything has its place.
Equity	Justice and kindliness should be pursued by managers when dealing with subordinates.
Stability of Tenure	Staffing should be conducted through planning in order to avoid high employee turnover.
Initiative	Employees should be encouraged to act on their own volition when they have an opportunity to solve a problem.
Esprit de Corps	Managers should emphasize teamwork by building harmony and a sense of unity among employees.

Source: From *General and Industrial Management* by Henri Fayol (Revised by Irwin Gray). Copyright © 1987 by David S. Lake Publishers, 500 Harbor Boulevard, Belmont, CA 94002.

FIGURE 2–1
Fayol's Principles for Effective Management

for managerial activities. In sum, the principles emphasize efficiency, order, stability, and fairness. While they are now over 80 years old, they are very similar to principles still being applied by managers today. The problem with Fayol's principles of management is knowing when to apply them and how to adapt them to new situations.

MAX WEBER

Max Weber (1864–1920) was born to a wealthy family with strong political ties in Germany. As a sociologist, editor, consultant to government, and author, Weber experienced the social upheaval brought on by the Industrial Revolution and saw the emerging forms of organization as having broad implications for managers and society. Adhering to a perspective that viewed society as becoming increasingly rational in its activities, Weber believed that organizations would become instruments of efficiency if structured around certain guidelines. In order to study this movement towards "rationality" of organizations, Weber constructed an ideal type, termed a **bureaucracy**, that described an organization in its most rational form. The structural characteristics Weber identified are outlined in Figure 2–2.[6]

FIGURE 2–2
Weber's Structural Characteristics of a Bureaucracy

Hierarchical Structure	A well-defined hierarchy of authority is essential for rationally controlling the behavior of employees. Positions are established and linked by a chain of command in a continuous branching out so that multiple layers exist in the hierarchy. Power and authority increase as one moves up through the levels of positions in the organization. This is similar to a scalar chain.
Division of Labor	A bureaucratic organization will divide the tasks to be performed as narrowly as possible. The most rational division of labor would break down a complex task into several separate operations. This leads to greater efficiency because the individual performing the task develops a level of expertise and new employees can be trained in a narrower task more quickly.
Rules and Regulations	Critical to the bureaucratic form of organization are explicit rules and regulations governing decision making and interpersonal behaviors. Continuity in rules and regulations is necessary to maintain order and promote achievement of organizational goals. Where owners, managers, and workers may come and go, the rules and regulations provide organizational stability. Moreover, rules and regulations serve to restrict decision makers who may otherwise act in their own interests or beliefs rather than in the interests of the organization.
Technical Competence	Managers in a rational organization will assign personnel to positions based on adequate technical training, not on friendship, family ties, or other forms of favoritism. An organization that does not strive to match skills objectively to the position will ultimately end up being inefficient.
Separation from Ownership	Weber believed that owners were one cause of inefficiency in an organization because their decisions would be based more on the goal of achieving greater profits than on increasing production efficiency. By having organizational members separated from ownership, decisions would be less self-serving, based on what is best for achieving overall organizational goals.
Positional Power	Organizations achieve rationality when power and authority are vested in the position and not in the incumbent. If power and authority were individual attributes, individuals would use the power and authority for their personal goals rather than the goals of the organization. By vesting the position, not the incumbent, with power and authority, managers who did not perform adequately would lose all power and authority by simply being removed from their position.
Recordkeeping	Since the rational organization will outlive its members, it is necessary to develop a memory. Minutes of meetings, written documents, and financial statements are all essential information for future decisions. In order to maintain continuity and efficiency over time, managers should have access to an organization's records in order to avoid previous mistakes and identify those activities that were successful.

Because of the emphasis on efficiency that had developed around the turn of the 20th century, many management scholars and practitioners interpreted Weber's writings on bureaucracy as a prescription for organizing. Weber, however, was more interested in developing his bureaucratic type as a method for comparing organizational forms across societies. While he did not believe any organization would perfectly conform to the dimensions that compose his bureaucratic model, Weber felt that some organizations would come closer than others. The closer to the bureaucratic type, the more rational society was becoming, and it was Weber's interest in the rationality of social life that directed his attention to the study of organizations.[7]

CHESTER BARNARD

Chester Barnard (1886–1961) drew on his own experiences as a manager and his extensive reading of sociological theory in constructing a theory of the organization. Born on a farm in Massachusetts, Barnard received a scholarship to attend Harvard which he supplemented by tuning pianos and running a small dance band. He completed the requirements for an economics degree in three years but was denied a degree for failing to attend a science laboratory section. Even without a degree, however, he was hired by American Telephone and Telegraph in 1909 and became the president of New Jersey Bell in 1927. A tireless "organization man," Barnard was very active in volunteer work. Barnard's most famous work, *The Functions of the Executive*, viewed the organization as a "cooperative system" of individuals embodying three essential elements: (1) willingness to cooperate, (2) a common purpose, and (3) communication.[8] The absence of any one of these three elements would lead to the disintegration of the organization, according to Barnard.

Like Weber, Barnard viewed the distribution of authority as an important process within the organization. However, he felt that the source of authority did not reside in the person who gave the orders; rather, authority resided in the subordinates who could choose to either accept or reject directives from their superiors. Subordinates would assent to authority when four conditions were satisfied: (1) they could and did understand the communicated directive; (2) they believed that the directive was consistent with the purpose of the organization; (3) they believed that the directive was compatible with their own personal interests; and (4) they were mentally and physically able to comply with the directive.[9] This view of authority has become known as **acceptance theory.**

Scientific Management

Whereas administrative theory focuses on the methods by which managers could structure the overall organization to make it more effective, **scientific management** addresses issues concerning the management of work. Prominent contributors to scientific management were Frederick W. Taylor, Frank Gilbreth, Lillian Gilbreth, and Henry Gantt.

FREDERICK W. TAYLOR

Before the 1880s, there were almost no systematic efforts to find ways to properly manage workers. While the writings of Fayol, Weber, and Barnard later on were to provide a blueprint for structuring organizations and organizing managerial activities, the practice of management before 1880 was based primarily on experience, intuition, and common sense. Frederick W. Taylor (1856–1915), a self-taught engineer who worked his way up from clerk to chief engineer at the Midvale Steel Company by the age of 28, tried to change that approach, espousing the view that managers should study work scientifically in order to identify the important elements of a task. His engineering background provided a model for establishing principles of management that would guide scientific analysis of work so as to improve task efficiency. Taylor's principles can be summarized as follows:

- *Determine important elements of a task.* Taylor believed that managers should observe and analyze each task to uncover the most economical way to perform the job and then put that way into operation. To enable managers to study work scientifically, Taylor promoted the use of time studies. **Time studies** measure all task movements made by a worker and try to eliminate those that do not lead to increased productivity.
- *Scientific selection of personnel.* Taylor did not believe that any individual with proper training would necessarily be the most competent to perform a certain task. Taylor was a strong advocate of matching physical traits to the dimensions of the task to be performed. While recognizing that the application of scientific principles would increase efficiency in task production, Taylor felt that some individuals would be more suited to a task than others and that managers should seek out those with proper traits. For Taylor, the most important physical traits of a worker were production capability, muscle durability, and resistance to fatigue. Selection of workers based on personality was to be avoided.
- *Financial incentives.* While matching the correct worker with the task was essential to increasing worker efficiency, Taylor recognized that another element must be added to the equation. Workers had to be motivated. At the time, the most common basis of pay was the hourly rate. Taylor believed that motivation would be enhanced by a differential **piece-rate system** of financial incentives, where workers would be paid according to what they produced rather than the number of hours they worked.
- *Functional foremanship.* Responsibility should be divided between managers and workers. This principle specified that separate managers would plan, direct, and evaluate the work process; the individual worker was responsible for performing the actual task. Thus, a worker would take orders from the functional foreman depending on the stage of the work process.[10]

Under the Taylor system, the first three principles formed the core of the scientific management approach. The final principle was considered innovative in that it introduced the notion of relieving workers of the responsibility to plan, initiate, and evaluate their work. Instead they could focus more directly on the actual production process.[11]

The application of Taylor's ideas in the steel industry led to greatly increased production and higher wages. However, many of Taylor's methods were met with resistance as workers and unions feared that greater physical demands and increased layoffs would result from the implementation of the techniques. In addition, many owners and managers used the methods to increase their own profits and earnings, thus depriving workers of the benefits of increased production. Indeed, these were the outcomes when Taylor's methods were implemented in the Simonds Rolling Machine Company, a firm that manufactured ball bearings. By 1912, with strikes occurring at the Watertown Arsenal in Massachusetts and opposition from labor unions solidified, congressional hearings were held on Taylor's methods to assess their potential for exploitation of workers. Taylor argued before Congress that his methods would work only if labor and management shared equally in the rewards of increased productivity.[12]

Taylor's ideas for improving productivity and efficiency in the workplace had a long-lasting impact on American industry. Manufacturers turned increasingly to mass-production methods to which Taylor's methods were highly suited. Though strong evidence exists that Taylor may have falsified some of his findings to support the merits of his methods, the methods did lead to increased productivity and efficiency in many plants.[13]

While many of Taylor's techniques, such as time studies and piece-rate work, are commonly used in industry today, the philosophy of scientific management was not accepted in its entirety in the United States. Of interest is the fact that through the work of the International Management Institute (1926–1935) many European societies found Taylor's philosophy more suitable to their culture and incorporated many of Taylor's ideas in industry.[14] Even Lenin, at the time he was Premier of the Soviet Union, advocated the adoption of scientific management principles to Soviet industry.[15]

HENRY L. GANTT

Henry L. Gantt (1861–1919) had worked with Taylor in implementing his methods at Midvale, Simonds, and Bethlehem Steel. Believing that the piece-rate system developed by Taylor was not having the desired level of impact, Gantt focused his attention on techniques that would further motivate workers. One of his innovations, a modification of the piece-rate system, was a **task-and-bonus wage system** whereby production goals were established for the worker. If the worker achieved the goal, a bonus in addition to the day wage was provided. A worker who fell short of the goal would still receive the day wage. In addition, if the worker achieved the goal, the foreman or immediate supervisor would also receive a bonus. The assumption was that a foreman who stood to gain from a worker's efficiency would put more emphasis on training the worker to do the job.

Another of Gantt's contributions was his development of the **Gantt chart**, a technique to show on a graph the scheduling of work to be done and itemization of the work that has been completed. For example, a chart might show which machines will be used, or have been used, for various tasks over time. Although it is a simple idea, the Gantt chart was a major development in production control. The chart is used extensively today in many manufacturing firms.

Like Taylor, Gantt believed that production efficiency was the most important concern of a manager. However, Gantt had greater concern for the psychological well-being of the worker in relation to the production process. Gantt's development of the task-and-bonus system was spawned by his belief that a generous bonus system would lead to more-satisfied employees and therefore better output.

THE GILBRETHS

Lillian Gilbreth (1878–1972) and Frank Gilbreth (1868–1924), a wife and husband team, were early backers of Taylor's scientific management philosophy. With Lillian's knowledge of management and psychology, and Frank's understanding of the intricacies of work, a unique and effective team was formed. Whereas Taylor often tried to find ways to have a task done faster by speeding up the worker, the Gilbreths tried to increase speed by eliminating motions that were discovered to be unnecessary. For instance, Frank's early work experience as an apprentice bricklayer focused his attention on the process of laying brick. Using photo stills of bricklayers at work, the Gilbreths discovered that the number of motions a bricklayer made to lay a brick could be reduced from 18½ to 4, increasing the number of bricks laid during a workday from 1,000 to 2,700 without speeding up the worker.[16] Their success in this study led them to focus on tasks performed by workers in the manufacturing industries.

The Gilbreths did not limit their research to the discovery of the one best way of performing a task as Taylor did. Reducing the number of motions a worker made in performing a task was, of course, a way to increase output, but of equal interest to the Gilbreths was the reduction in worker fatigue that it would accomplish. Putting their focus on the psychology of management, which had been the topic of Lillian's doctoral thesis,[17] the Gilbreths devised methods for training and developing workers to rotate tasks under the assumption that variety in the workplace would boost morale.

The Gilbreths did not confine their ideas solely to the workplace. As documented in a book written by two of their 12 children titled *Cheaper by the Dozen* (later a popular movie), Frank and Lillian applied many of their ideas to ordinary daily activities. The children report that their father buttoned his vest from the bottom to the top, instead of top to bottom, because he could save four seconds. By shaving with two razors at the same time, he could reduce shaving time by 44 seconds, but he abandoned this technique because it took two minutes per bandage to treat the cuts. The children insist that it was the two minutes lost and not the cuts that bothered him the most.[18]

Evaluation of Classical Management Theories

Classical theories and the principles derived from them continue to be popular today with some modifications. Many criticisms have been directed at the classicists. Several major ones are discussed here.

RELIANCE ON EXPERIENCE

Many of the writers in the classical school of management developed their ideas on the basis of their experiences as managers or consultants with only certain types of organizations. For instance, Taylor's and Fayol's work came primarily from their experiences with large manufacturing firms that were experiencing stable environments. It may be unwise to generalize from those situations to others—especially to young, high-technology firms of today that are confronted daily with changes in their competitors' products.

UNTESTED ASSUMPTIONS

Many of the assumptions made by classical writers were based not on scientific tests but on value judgments that expressed what they believed to be proper life-styles, moral codes, and attitudes toward success. For instance, the classical approaches seem to view the life of a worker as beginning and ending at the plant door. Their basic assumption is that workers are primarily motivated by money and that they work only for more money. They also assume that productivity is the best measure of how well a firm is performing. These assumptions fail to recognize that employees may have wants and needs unrelated to the workplace or may view their jobs only as a necessary evil.

FAILURE TO CONSIDER THE INFORMAL ORGANIZATION

In their stress on formal relationships in the organization, classical approaches tend to ignore informal relations as characterized by social interchange among workers, the emergence of group leaders apart from those specified by the formal organization, and so forth. When such things are not considered, it is likely that many important factors affecting satisfaction and performance, such as letting employees participate in decision making and task planning, will never be explored or tried.

UNINTENDED CONSEQUENCES

Classical approaches aim at achieving high productivity, at making behaviors predictable, and at achieving fairness among workers and between managers and workers; yet they fail to recognize that several unintended consequences can occur in practice. For instance, a heavy emphasis on rules and regulations may cause people to obey rules blindly without remembering their original intent. Oftentimes, since rules establish a minimum level of performance expected of employees, a minimum level is all they achieve. Perhaps much more could be achieved if the rules were not so explicit.

HUMAN MACHINERY

Classical theories leave the impression that the organization is a machine and that workers are simply parts to be fitted into the machine to make it run efficiently. Thus, many of the principles are concerned first with making the organization efficient, with the assumption that workers will conform to the work setting if the financial incentives are agreeable.

STATIC CONDITIONS

As noted in Chapter 1, organizations are influenced by external conditions that often fluctuate over time, yet classical management theory presents an image of an organization that is not shaped by external influences. As we will see later in this chapter, systems theory attempts to correct this image.

Since many of these criticisms of the classical school are harsh, several points need to be made in defense of writers during this period. First, the work force was not highly educated or trained to perform many of the jobs that existed at the time. It was not common for workers to think in terms of what "career" they were going to pursue. Rather, for many, the opportunity to obtain a secure job and a level of wages to provide for their families was all they demanded from the work setting.

Second, much of the writing took place when technology was undergoing a rapid transformation, particularly in the area of manufacturing. Indeed, for many writers, technology was the driving force behind organizational and social change. Thus, their focus was on finding ways to increase efficiency. It was assumed that all humankind could do was to adapt to the rapidly changing conditions.

Finally, very little had been done previously in terms of generating a coherent and useful body of management theory. Many of the classical theorists were writing from scratch, obliged for the most part to rely on their own experience and observations. Thus their focus is understandably narrow. With this in mind, we now turn our attention to approaches that emerged later—approaches that benefited from the classicists' successes and were attempts to rectify their mistakes.

BEHAVIORAL MANAGEMENT THEORY

During the 1920s and 1930s, the United States was experiencing another force of upheaval not unlike that caused by the Industrial Revolution. Though more limited in scope, it had similar ramifications on the way people work and on the way managers manage those who work.

Culturally and socially the United States was undergoing change. People were moving to the cities in greater numbers. Rapid economic growth was giving people the opportunity to spend money on leisure and household items their parents could only dream about. Women were given the right to vote, unions were now organized and were playing an integral role in politics and the economy, and the first minimum-wage legislation had been passed. Prior to the stock market collapse of 1929, a genuine sense of optimism had swept the country, and values and attitudes toward government, people, families, and work were being transformed. As a result, many of the techniques applied by the classical theorists to the workplace no longer seemed to work effectively.

Several prominent theorists began to direct their attention to the human element in the workplace. Elton Mayo, Mary Parker Follett, Douglas McGregor, Chris Argyris, and Abraham Maslow were writers who addressed this issue by contending that increased worker satisfaction would lead to better performance. It was their belief that a greater concern by management for the work conditions of the employee would generate higher levels of satisfaction; thus evolved **behavioral management theory.**

Elton Mayo

One prominent pioneer of the behavioral school was Elton Mayo (1880–1949), an Australian psychologist who joined the Harvard Business School faculty in 1926. Convinced that economic incentives only partially explained individual motivation and satisfaction,[19] Mayo worked with Fritz Roethlisberger, William Dickson, and others to formulate theories concerning the factors that increased human motivation and satisfaction which were later to become the foundations of the human relations movement in management. Their ideas did not have wide circulation, however, until they were asked to assist in a research project that had apparently failed.

In 1924, a research team launched an experiment at the Hawthorne plant of the Western Electric Company in Cicero, Illinois. Their experiment was designed to identify factors other than fatigue that would diminish worker productivity. Initially, it was believed that physical surroundings (e.g., noise, light, humidity) would have an impact on productivity. Testing was conducted by selecting two groups of women who would perform an assembly operation, with each group in a separate room. One group was to be the control group, working in a room where no change in the physical surroundings would be made. The second group would perform their tasks under changing physical conditions. As various features of the physical surroundings were altered in the second room, the researchers would record the level of output and compare it with the output of the control group.

One such alteration of the physical surroundings was the level of lighting. Illumination was increased in stages, and the researchers recorded an increase in output as well. To further test their hypothesis, the light was dimmed. Much to their surprise, output by the women increased again. Even when the light level was reduced to the point where it resembled moonlight, output increased. What made this finding even more difficult to interpret was that the control group was also increasing its output without any alteration in the physical surroundings. Increased output was also obtained when the researchers expanded the length of the workday and eliminated rest periods. Indeed, many of the women reported that they were more satisfied with their jobs than before the experiments began.

In 1927, Mayo and his team were called in to assist in the interpretation of the results and to conduct further experiments as needed. One such experiment was to alter supervisory authority so that the women could determine on their own when they would take a rest break. Another was to increase the salary of the women in the experimental group while the women in the control group would keep the same pay. Again, productivity went up in both groups. After several years of intensive study, Mayo and his colleagues began to piece together what was happening. First, they concluded that financial incentives did not influence productivity since output went up in both groups though only the experimental group received more pay. Instead, they learned through interviews and observation that an "emotional chain reaction" was causing the increase in productivity.[20] Having been singled out to be participants in the experiment, the women developed a group pride that motivated them to increase their performance. No longer did they feel that they were isolated individuals in the plant; now they felt they were part of an important group. The support received from their supervisors and the opportunity to make decisions about their job contributed to this motivation.

Mayo and his colleagues realized that an important contribution to the study and practice of management had evolved from a seemingly failed experiment. First, the Hawthorne study suggested that workers were not so much driven by pay and working conditions as by psychological wants and desires which could be satisfied by belonging to a work group. Second, giving workers responsibility for decisions concerning the task, whether as individuals or in a group, was a stimulus to treat the task as more important. And finally, recognition by superiors made workers feel that they were making a unique and important contribution to the organization.

The Hawthorne experiment was a turning point in the study of management, suggesting that a worker is not simply an extension of the machinery. As the results of the study became known among theorists and practitioners alike, an outpouring of research was conducted based on many theories and discoveries made in psychology. Thus, the Hawthorne study opened the study of management to a whole new arena of ideas from the social sciences that had previously been ignored. And, as an unintended contribution to research methodology, the experiments led to a rethinking of field research practices. That is, the researcher can influence the outcome of the experiment by being too closely involved with the subjects who are participating in the experiment. This outcome, referred to as the **Hawthorne effect** in research methodology, is exemplified by subjects behaving differently because of the active participation of the Hawthorne researchers in the experiment.

Mary Parker Follett

Mary Parker Follett (1868–1933) was born near Boston and was educated at Radcliffe College and Cambridge University, studying politics, economics, philosophy, and law. Her successful work on committees set up to work out solutions to community problems led eventually to a concentration on the study of industrial management, with a particular interest in techniques for resolving conflicts in organizations.

Follett was a pragmatist who believed that conflict was neither good nor bad. She hypothesized that managers could resolve conflict in one of four ways: (1) one side giving in, (2) one side forcing the other to submit, (3) compromise, and (4) integration. Follett believed the first two alternatives were undesirable as they required the threat or actual use of power. Compromise was also unsatisfactory, merely postponing the conflict by not addressing the issues that led to the conflict. With integration, however, the efforts of both sides to identify the solution, according to Follett, would lead to discussion and resolution of the issues that caused the conflict.[21]

Douglas McGregor

A theorist who shared the views of Mayo and his colleagues was Douglas McGregor (1906–1964). McGregor felt that organizations were often designed based on faulty assumptions about human behavior. Those assumptions were that most workers disliked work, that workers preferred to be directed by supervisors rather than assume responsibility for their tasks, and that workers were more interested in monetary gains than in performing their jobs well. Because of these assumptions, McGregor felt that managers were prone to design organizations that were centralized in decision making, established numerous rules and regulations, and required close supervision of subordinates. For fear of technical and financial inefficiency, McGregor felt that organizations overemphasized control mechanisms.

Labeling these assumptions **Theory X**, McGregor developed an alternative set of assumptions which he labeled Theory Y. His **Theory Y** assumptions are that workers can enjoy their work under favorable conditions and can provide valued input to the decision-making process. Rather than develop needless mechanisms of control in the organization, McGregor felt that managers should emphasize coordination of activities by providing assistance to workers when problems are identified.[22]

Chris Argyris

Chris Argyris (1923–) also expanded on the work of the Hawthorne experiment by challenging the basic assumptions of the classical school concerning worker motivation and satisfaction. Argyris argued that an overemphasis on control by managers encouraged workers to become passive and dependent and to shirk responsibility. As a result, workers will become frustrated and dissatisfied with the workplace and will either quit their jobs or engage in behaviors that hamper the achievement of organizational goals. Many of his ideas were developed from the belief that as people mature, they develop new attitudes and behaviors that affect their life-styles. Some of these attitudes and behaviors are a movement toward independence, a broadening of interests, greater diversity in activities, and a desire to assume more control over their lives. Organizations that emphasize control are, in actuality, treating individuals as if they were immature.[23]

Abraham Maslow

Abraham Maslow (1908–1970) is most noted for suggesting a theory that humans are motivated by needs that exist in a hierarchy. At the bottom of the hierarchy are the physiological needs for food and shelter. Once these basic needs are satisfied, humans are then motivated to satisfy higher-level needs for safety, love, esteem, and self-actualization.[24] In Maslow's theory, a person moves up the ladder of needs as each level is satisfied. Maslow's theory of "hierarchical needs" will be described in more detail in Chapter 13.

Evaluation of the Behavioral School

Contributors to the behavioral school advanced our understanding of management by emphasizing the importance of the individual within the organization—an element essentially ignored by writers of the classical school. That is, social needs of individuals, group processes, and subordinate-superior relationships were all identified as integral components in the practice of management. No longer could managers confine their attention to technical skills. Rather, they had to use people skills as well and develop an understanding of the relationship between the technical and human sides of management.

However, the behavioral school did not completely resolve issues concerning the nature of human motivation. Later studies were to dispute the belief that worker satisfaction was the prime cause of productivity. Under certain conditions, satisfaction was found to play an inconsequential role. In addition, though money may not be the primary motivator, salaries do at times affect worker productivity, particularly in industries where salaries are low, causing high rates of absenteeism and turnover. Much like classical theory, behavioral theory also assumed that the external environment of the organization was static. Thus, the psychological and social dimensions of the indi-

Charles D. Wrege (Ph.D., New York University) is Professor of Management, School of Business, Rutgers University. Professor Wrege's teaching and research interests include both the history of management and the role of creativity and innovation in organizations. His publications include a historical analysis of the origins of the Hawthorne studies, Facts and Fallacies of Hawthorne, *and articles in the* Academy of Management Journal *and the* Academy of Management Review. *Professor Wrege has served as chairman of the Management History Division of the Academy of Management and is currently the historian and archivist of the Academy of Management and*

ACADEMIC PROFILE
CHARLES D. WREGE

vice-president of the Institute of American Historical Technology. Before joining academia, he was the owner of Yearound Displays, a New York City manufacturing company.

Q: Can you define history and indicate some of its important elements?

A: History is understood as knowledge of things said and done, presented in the form of a written description of past events based on careful research for the whole truth. In preparing any historical account, the historian considers four important elements: (1) research, the careful accumulation of all possible evidence; (2) critique, evaluating the evidence; (3) insight, the moment of understanding the true meaning of the evidence; and (4) presentation, a carefully written description presenting the results of steps 1 to 3.

Q: What is the importance of history to students of management?

A: Over the centuries, we have developed the written word to supplement the frail bonds of memory concerning events. The written record is the device that enables us to preserve the accomplishments, ideas, and activities of our predecessors. Unfortunately, the historian who attempts to uncover the facts concerning past events soon learns that knowledge of the past is limited by two factors: (1) false evidence deliberately planted in order to deceive, and (2) evidence which is misleading because it is incomplete. Research into management history reveals two examples of these two factors. In regard to the planting of false evidence, we can consider Frederick W. Taylor's famous pig-iron experiments in 1899. Taylor said he carefully selected, trained, and helped the workmen to increase their output. My discovery of the actual records of these experiments in 1963 revealed that Taylor fabricated this part of the story. In reality, the men had volunteered and worked without direction, and the increase in output was due to hard work and a desire for higher earnings. An example of how incomplete evidence can result in erroneous conclusions is illustrated by the uncritical acceptance by management scholars of Elton Mayo's 1939 conclusions that financial incentives did not cause the increase in output during the Hawthorne studies. I discovered the actual output figures, and a subsequent computer analysis of the wage incentive system revealed that Mayo's conclusions were incorrect. The wage incentive system caused inequities in pay among the workers which only could be overcome by higher output. This was the real cause of the increased output, not improved social conditions or morale.

Q: How can management scholars and managers of the future help to preserve historical evidence?

A: Management scholars and management students should be aware of the constant threats to the very existence of historical evidence. Every day records, research files, and the drafts of printed manuscripts are destroyed by neglect, accidents, or intent, by individuals and/or organizations. Sometimes the seeds of future destruction are sown when events are recorded on audiotape, videotape, or computer files or by color photographs. Such methods of recording are potentially dangerous because records obtained in this manner must be preserved under carefully controlled storage conditions. Typed copies of audiotapes, black-and-white film, and hard copies of computer files are superior methods for preserving historical evidence for future historians.

vidual only partially explain organizational outcomes and constitute only a part of the larger and more complex managerial picture.

QUANTITATIVE MANAGEMENT THEORY

The advent of World War II introduced a new set of problems related to the practice of management. Submarine warfare was introduced, as was the massive deployment of airplanes as a means of attack. These developments made the conduct of war more complex and reduced the margin of error that one could afford militarily. With Great Britain confronting the prospect of defeat, the British formed an operations research team consisting of mathematicians, physicists, and other experts to develop methods for countering the German offensive. The team was able to develop sophisticated mathematical models that could simplify scenarios of attack and counterattack and thus reduce tactical errors by military commanders. These models, based on mathematical equations, were credited with assisting the British military in effectively staving off the German attack.[25]

After World War II was over, interest in the application of operations research technology to industry began to emerge. This interest was accelerated by advances in computer technology that increased the speed with which many of the complicated mathematical models could be solved. In particular, operations research models were applied to solve production problems. Mathematical models were used to simulate a production problem, bringing to bear all the relevant factors affecting that problem. The values of these factors could be changed to develop different scenarios in the search for a solution. For example, a manager might be interested in the effect that delays in shipments of raw materials have on the cost of producing a good. By changing this variable in the equation, production costs under different scenarios can be estimated and managers can then make more-informed decisions on how to deal with this problem situation.

While operations research has provided management with a valuable tool in the planning and control of production activities, mathematical models have yet to account effectively for human behaviors. The difficulty, of course, is that the human factor is not as easily quantified as inanimate phenomena. The contributions of quantitative management theory will be discussed further in Chapters 8, 19, and 20.

SYSTEMS THEORY

In the 1950s, the expansion of the economy, the rapid growth of the middle class, the proliferation of larger and more complex corporations, and advances in communication and travel introduced new problems that had to be addressed by managers. At the same time, the Ford Foundation and Carnegie Corporation issued reports suggesting that business education in the United States was inadequate for developing managers because it focused more on vocational training than on organizational problem solving. As a result, management theorists and practitioners began to direct their attention to the question of how organizations as a whole could be made more efficient and effective.

The **systems theory** approach to management is based on the assumptions and ideas of a biologist named Ludwig von Bertalanffy. Von Bertalanffy approached the field of science from the perspective that each discipline studies forms of systems that are composed of interrelated subsystems. Basically, a **system** is an interrelated set of elements functioning as a whole. Examples of systems would be plant cells, a clock, a hospital, or the human body. In management theory, the system is the organization composed of subsystems such as departments or divisions. Von Bertalanffy emphasized that the survival or failure of the system was dependent on the interrelation of subsystems and their contribution to the overall purpose of the system. Hence, activities in a production department will be determined largely by the sales department, which in turn will be dependent on budget allocations from the accounting department, which in turn is dependent on the cost efficiency of the production department, and so forth. The implication is that no department is fully independent of another; it cannot act independently or make decisions without considering their effect on other departments.

Systems can be further classified as open or closed. A **closed system**, as depicted in Figure 2–3, is one that does not rely on resources from the environment to survive. In order to survive, a closed system must have internal resources to transform into goods and services which are then consumed by members of the organization. Very few organizations meet the criteria of a closed system. Monasteries situated in remote mountain ranges perhaps come

FIGURE 2–3

Closed System and Open System

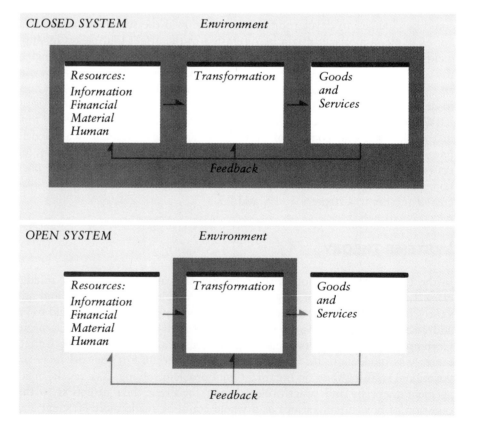

closest to being closed systems, but even monasteries must obtain inputs from the environment in the form of new members. Yet many earlier managerial theories treated the organization as if it were a closed system. The principles developed to solve problems were based on the assumption that the environment was static and thus focused on ways to make the organization more efficient through changes in internal design.

An **open system** is one that must continually seek resources from the environment in order to survive. Figure 2–3 indicates that an open system obtains information, financial, material, and human resources from the environment. The transformed resources must then be exported to the environment. Organizations characterize an open system in that resources must be purchased from outside suppliers, and customers must be willing to purchase the goods or services transformed by the production process of the organization in order for the organization to survive.

The introduction of von Bertalanffy's systems ideas to the subject of managerial theory spawned increased interest in their application to managerial problems. Efforts to enlarge on the subject of subsystems were conducted by Katz and Kahn, who distinguished the five types of formal organization subsystems shown in Figure 2–4:

- *Production.* A **production subsystem** produces a good or service to be exported to customers in the environment. The production subsystem focuses primarily on the transformation of inputs, such as raw materials, and includes employees who work on the production line as well as those in inventory control.
- *Maintenance.* The **maintenance subsystem** is concerned with the stable operation of activities in the organization. Here, the focus is on employee

FIGURE 2–4
*Subsystems of an
Organization*

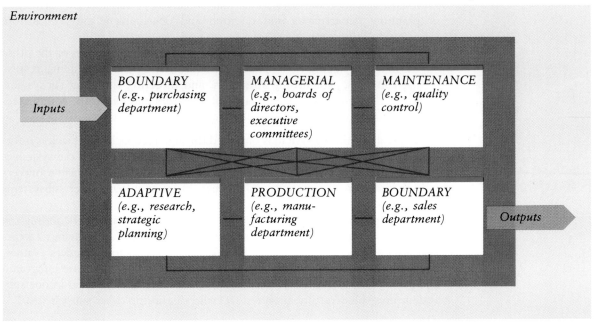

An assembly line is an example of a production subsystem.

selection procedures, cleaning and maintenance of buildings and machinery, and quality control.

- *Boundary.* **Boundary subsystems,** or **boundary-spanning subsystems,** handle transactions involving the procurement and disposal of necessary resources. These subsystems work in conjunction with the production subsystem but address issues concerning methods of obtaining resources from suppliers and distributing goods to customers. Thus, boundary subsystems work directly with individuals and organizations in the environment. Purchasing departments and marketing departments represent boundary subsystems.
- *Adaptive.* The responsibility to oversee organizational planning and change rests with **adaptive subsystems.** Members of adaptive subsystems scan the environment to obtain information about technological developments, competitor activities, and regulatory constraints. Strategic-planning departments and research and development units constitute adaptive subsystems.
- *Managerial.* The **managerial subsystem** oversees the activities of the other subsystems, placing its emphasis on coordinating the subsystems, resolving conflicts, establishing strategies, and directing the other subsystems toward system-level goals. Boards of directors and executive committees are examples of managerial subsystems.[26]

Control within the system is obtained through feedback. **Feedback** is information that is received about activities in the organization. As the system is functioning, information about activities is fed back to key decision makers who then can invoke measures to correct errors or inform other subsystems about the status of activities throughout the organization.

The implication of systems theory for managers is that understanding the nature of the organization begins with a knowledge of the various factors that impinge on organizational life. Workers, technology, leaders, values, goals, and motivations do not exist in a vacuum; all these factors are integrated and affect each other, and actions taken to correct a malfunction in one subsystem must be carefully analyzed to avoid disrupting other subsystems.

Systems theory has had a major influence on the study and practice of management. Viewing an organization as a system of interdependent subsystems enables managers to comprehend more fully the implications of their actions. Indeed, the power of the systems theory framework has not been solely confined to the study of management. The disciplines of physics, biology, sociology, and mathematics have all found the principles of systems theory useful.

The contributions of systems theory to the study of management, however, are somewhat limited. First, it is primarily descriptive rather than predictive. That is, the theory provides a useful way to describe an organization, but it has had less success in predicting outcomes based on changes that occur among subsystems. Second, advocates of systems theory often find themselves mired in the same problem for which classical theorists have been criticized. Like classical theory, systems theory views all organizations as similar and thus fails to account for the role that unique contextual, organizational, and human dimensions can play in organizational outcomes.

CONTINGENCY THEORY

The contingency, or situational, approach to management theory and practice emerged in the early 1960s from organizational research conducted in the United States and England. With the arrival of the sixties came the expansion of markets based not on the introduction of new products but rather on the differentiation of existing products. Consumers were demanding more variety in the products they purchased. The Henry Ford axiom from a previous generation, "You can buy a car of any color as long as it is black," was no longer acceptable. With consumer demand becoming more diversified, so did the types of organizations that were being founded. In addition, the work force was becoming less blue-collar and more white-collar. Many more workers were being employed in activities that did not directly involve the production of a good, but rather the production of a service. Indeed, some scholars began to write about the end of the Industrial Revolution with predictions about the dawning of a new age in American society.[27]

Contingency theory attempts to provide a perspective on organizations and management based on the integration of prior theories. **Contingency theory** starts with the theme of "it depends," arguing that the solution to any one managerial problem is contingent on the factors that are impinging on the situation. For instance, where little variation in materials exists in the production process, it is appropriate to break down the work into highly routine tasks. However, where variation is high, requiring many judgments concerning which material is appropriate and which is not, managers will want to avoid making tasks routine.

One of the first applications of contingency theory came from research conducted by two British scholars, Thomas Burns and G. M. Stalker. After studying several industrial firms in England, such as textile mills and electronics manufacturers, they concluded that the appropriate managerial techniques were highly dependent on the kind of task the organization was trying to accomplish.[28]

Burns and Stalker identified two organization types: **mechanistic**, for a task that is routine and unchanging, and **organic**, for a task that is nonroutine and changing. They discovered that the most successful firms were those that used whichever type was appropriate for a given task. When the task was routine and unchanging (mechanistic), the appropriate managerial approach was to emphasize efficiency, a high degree of specialization, and elaborate procedures for maintaining controls over behavior. On the other hand, when the task was nonroutine and changing (organic), the appropriate approach was to emphasize low job specialization, creativity rather than efficiency, and freedom for workers to control their own behaviors rather than relying on rules and procedures to keep them "in line." It is clear that this represents an integration of the classical and behavioral approaches.

Other theorists, namely Paul Lawrence and Jay Lorsch[29] and John Child,[30] have enlarged on this perspective and identified contingencies, such as environmental conditions, ownership patterns, strategies, and leadership, as important in assessing the appropriate approach to use in a given situation.

One attraction of the contingency approach among theorists and practitioners alike is its situational perspective. Those interested in research issues regarding organization and management can use the contingency perspective to explain why some factors influence situations in one setting but have virtually no influence in another setting. Indeed, one objective of research within the contingency framework is to specify those dimensions and conditions that do affect a situation and those that do not. For the manager, the requirement from the contingency perspective is to identify which technique will, in a particular situation, best contribute to the attainment of organizational goals. For instance, under some circumstances, an authoritarian leadership style may be more appropriate than a leadership style that tries to get workers internally motivated.

While the contingency approach is useful in recognizing that the complexity involved in understanding human and organizational systems makes it difficult to develop universal principles of management, there have been several criticisms of the approach. For one, it has been pointed out that the logical extension of the contingency approach is that *all* situations are unique. If this is true, then management can be practiced only by intuition and judgment, thereby negating the value of prior knowledge and wisdom.

On a research level, contingency theory has been criticized for being atheoretical.[31] One requirement of theory is the ability to test the validity of assumptions by showing that contradictory assumptions do not disprove the theory. In a contingency framework, if contradictory results are obtained, the contingency response would be that the situation is unique or that important dimensions affecting the situation were not tested. Thus, showing that contradictory assumptions disprove the theory would be difficult at best.

While these limitations are recognized, we will approach the study of management utilizing the assumptions of contingency theory. We believe that management is a highly complex discipline in both research and practice. We build the approach from previous research and practice and extend the findings to develop an understanding of how contextual, organizational, and human dimensions are integrated. Specifically, we draw ideas from classical management theory regarding the structuring of organizations to increase efficiency and productivity. Behavioral management theory provides knowledge about human needs and motivations that can lead not only to increased productivity but also to enhancement of the working environment. Systems theory serves to identify the context in which organizations operate, thus enabling managers to understand the environment and how the parts, or subsystems, of the organization are interrelated. In addition, we will draw from quantitative management theory for the application of specific tools and techniques that are useful for increasing managerial efficiency and effectiveness.

By applying contingency theory to the study of management, you will be able to identify and to solve problems under different situations. You will recognize that the successful application of a technique in one situation does not guarantee success in another. Rather, you will be able to examine each situation in terms of how it is affected by the contextual, organizational, and human dimensions. As a result, your overall ability to correct problems and to become more effective as a manager will increase. The contingency framework that we will be using is shown in Figure 2–5.

Consider the following situation. A shoe manufacturer is faced with decreasing profits. As a manager, this person may conduct a time study from the belief that the decline in profits is due to lower productivity on the part of the workers (classical management theory). The manager may attempt to involve workers more fully in decisions concerning the methods to use in producing the shoes based on the premise that this will motivate workers to produce more (behavioral management theory). Or the manager may establish a committee of sales and production personnel to coordinate the production and distribution of goods under the assumption that large inventories are responsible for the decline in profits (systems theory). Application of a contingency perspective will enable the manager to examine the situation and to determine the cause of decreased profits before a new procedure or program is implemented. Perhaps only one program needs to be implemented, or perhaps all three. However, only through an awareness of all possible solutions to the problem is the manager able to arrive at a correct solution. Contingency theory, as presented in this book, is designed to provide the manager with the capabilities to examine numerous possible solutions to a problem.

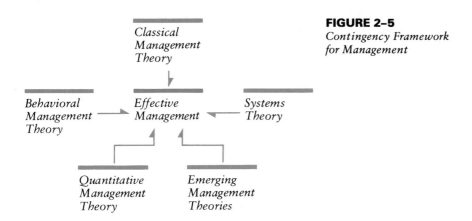

FIGURE 2–5
Contingency Framework for Management

In addition, we will extend the framework of the contingency approach by incorporating knowledge and ideas that have emerged from more recent perspectives on the study of organization and management. A discussion of these emerging perspectives follows.

EMERGING PERSPECTIVES IN MANAGEMENT

The 1970s and 1980s brought about a whole new set of problems for managers. Midway through the 1970s, the world experienced an economic downturn due to the sudden oil embargo imposed by the Organization of Petroleum Exporting Countries (OPEC). The reduction in supplies of oil to developed countries such as the United States, Japan, Great Britain, France, and Germany, accompanied by escalation in the price of oil, led to a dramatic adjustment in the way citizens in those countries engaged in leisure activities, consumed products, and conducted work. At about the same time, the United States was faced with a political crisis that threatened to undermine the faith of the American people in government institutions that had existed for almost 200 years. Referred to as Watergate, the crisis erupted in 1972 when several men close to the Republican President, Richard Nixon, were caught attempting to break into the national headquarters of the Democratic party in the Watergate building complex in Washington, D.C. As details of the scandal emerged, several high-ranking government officials, including President Nixon himself, were implicated. The situation culminated in Nixon's resignation in 1974. Of greater consequence for the nation was the cynical and suspicious attitude that the Watergate revelations spawned among the populace toward institutional power of any kind, including that held by large corporations and those who managed them.

Finally, the seventies witnessed the end of the Vietnam War. With the shift away from producing war goods came a downturn in the economy. Inflation, unemployment, and organizational failures became common experiences. By the 1980s, many foreign-based companies had made significant inroads into the United States economy by either supplying cheaper goods and services to American markets or by purchasing American corporations. The introduction of cheaper and sometimes better products placed pressure on American managers to become more competitive and efficient in their operations. During this time period, five perspectives on management began to emerge. One addressed institutional power; another addressed issues of organizational failure; the third was concerned with the relationship of values and attitudes in the workplace to productivity; the fourth considered competitive strategies for responding to industry forces; and the fifth attempted to explain how managers can make economic transactions more efficient.

Resource Dependence Perspective

The resource dependence perspective developed a framework to explain why organizations are often forced to establish linkages with other organizations in their environment. As resources become scarce, managers must expand the number of suppliers and receivers of goods in order to maintain stable operations and profits. However, these linkages place constraints on the decisions managers can make to guide the organization toward specific goals. That is, as the organization's activities become dependent on other organizations, there are fewer opportunities to guide the organization in different and novel directions. Thus, solving the problem of scarce resources can cause a loss of organizational power. The success or failure of the organization becomes more dependent on the decisions and behaviors of the other organizations in the linkage. For instance, a firm that relies heavily on borrowing funds from a bank may include the bank president on its board of directors to promote favorable access to funds. However, the bank president may vote against decisions of the firm that run counter to the interests of the bank (e.g., the firm's decision to issue bonds to raise capital).[32]

The resource dependence perspective is expanded to explain how dependence on organizational environments affects the fortunes of managers as they move up the career ladder. With changes in the environment, in terms of either resource distribution or organizational interdependence, the probability that managers will lose their jobs increases.[33] In line with the contingency approach, environmental changes produce new situations, and new situations may require managers who are better able to adapt.

Population Ecology

The second perspective to emerge in the late seventies is labeled population ecology. Borrowing principles from biology concerning the process of natural selection, theorists in this area have attempted to explain why some organizations survive and others fail based on conditions in the environment. In the population ecology framework, luck, chance, and randomness play an important role in explaining the survival or failure of an organization. This is the similar to the way biologists have accounted for the survival or failure of animal and plant species throughout time. New organizations are continually being formed by entrepreneurs with a new idea for a product or service. Theorists of the population ecology perspective argue that survival or success is more dependent on luck or chance than on the quality of the idea. Many new products and services are offered in the marketplace, but it may take a chance discovery by another person or organization to see their usefulness. The implication of this perspective is that managerial abilities and talents in the initial stages of organizational development have very little to do with organizational success. Rather, success is more dependent on the environment and the various changes that are going on in the environment.[34] As such, the perspective offers important insight into the relationships of organizations to a changing environment and how organizations either adapt to that change or experience failure. Hence, population ecologists would be in agreement with the old adage that success can be largely attributed to "being in the right place at the right time."

Theory Z

The third perspective addressing the problems facing organizations in the seventies was developed by William Ouchi and is labeled Theory Z.[35] **Theory Z** presents solutions to problems of human resource management. During the decade, many U.S. firms were losing their competitive advantage to foreign companies. For instance, with the oil embargo came a demand among consumers for more-fuel-efficient automobiles, resulting in an influx of Japanese and German car imports and a decline in market share among U.S. automobile manufacturers. To understand methods of increasing quality and efficiency in the production process to make U.S. goods more competitive with foreign products, Ouchi compared managerial practices in Japan, which he referred to as Theory J, with those in this country, Theory A. From these two theories, Ouchi formed Theory Z, which he believes combines the best of both Japanese and American management practices (see Figure 2–6).

Theory Z attempts to incorporate and integrate the best of American and Japanese styles of management. It advocates that workers should be guaranteed employment for longer periods of time, have a greater role in decision making by participating in group decision-making councils, and be personally responsible for their task activities. In addition, evaluation and promotion should proceed at a slower rate; there should be informal and implicit control mechanisms with formal and explicit measures; moderately specialized career paths; and more emphasis on integrating the workers' roles and responsibilities away from the workplace into the organization (such as family and civic roles). Ouchi contends that Theory Z retains the American cultural value of individualism by combining it with opportunities to become more a part of the organization's direction and activities through collective decision making. As a result, it is believed that employees will feel a greater sense of belonging to the organization; productivity and product quality will increase as employees take more pride in their work; and absenteeism and turnover, which are costly to most organizations, will decrease. Numerous corporations have studied the Theory Z approach and have integrated part or all of the theory into their managerial philosophy. Perhaps the most common example of the application of the Theory Z approach is the use of quality circles.

FIGURE 2–6
*Characteristics of
American, Japanese, and
Theory Z Organizations*

Theory A (American)	Theory J (Japanese)	Theory Z (combined American and Japanese)
Short-term employment	Lifetime employment	Long-term employment
Individual decision making	Consensual decision making	Consensual decision making
Individual responsibility	Collective responsibility	Individual responsibility
Rapid evaluation and promotion	Slow evaluation and promotion	Slow evaluation and promotion
Explicit, formalized control	Implicit, informal control	Implicit, informal control with explicit, formalized measures
Specialized career path	Nonspecialized career path	Moderately specialized career path
Segmented concern for employee as an employee	Holistic concern for employee as a person	Holistic concern for employee, including family

Source: William G. Ouchi and Alfred M. Jaeger, "Type Z Organization: Stability in the Midst of Mobility," *Academy of Management Review* 3 (April 1978): 308. Reprinted by permission of the publisher, William G. Ouchi, and Alfred M. Jaeger.

Competitive Strategy

One important theoretical development in the 1980s contributed to the study of industry competition and strategic activity. Michael Porter's theory and models of competitive strategies provide a framework for understanding how competition within an industry is shaped by the following forces:

- The threat of new entrants;
- The bargaining power of customers;
- The bargaining power of suppliers;
- The threat of substitute products or services; and
- Competition among existing firms.[36]

Porter's framework has been useful to managers in the formulation and implementation of competitive strategies by helping them to understand industry dynamics and anticipate future trends. Porter's framework for analyzing industries will receive further attention in Chapter 7, which discusses strategic planning.

Markets, Hierarchies, and Clans

Economist Oliver Williamson offers insight into how organizations can be inefficient in terms of costs.[37] Williamson notes that while a free market system serves to reward efficiency by weeding out those firms that are inefficient, many unnecessary costs still remain. These costs are related to transactions such as purchasing goods, employing labor, or providing a service. Because managers may lack knowledge about a situation, make mistakes in the securing or delivery of a good, or behave in ways that are not entirely rational, greater costs than necessary will result from the transaction. These are referred to as **transaction costs**. Since markets may not always be efficient, hierarchical organizations, or bureaucracies, evolve to reduce transaction costs by establishing rules to regulate exchanges and assigning coordination mechanisms to govern the allocation of goods and services. A third mechanism, other than markets and hierarchies, to regulate transactions is the clan, which governs transactions through commonly shared values and goals. In clan relationships, mutual trust is high, negating the need for rules and regulations. Clan systems of transaction are often found in Japanese firms.[38] Figure 2–7 summarizes effective methods for operating markets, hierarchies, and clans. Williamson was given an award for outstanding contribution to the field of management by the Academy of Management in 1988.

IMPLICATIONS FOR MANAGEMENT

The systematic study and practice of management has been in existence for over 100 years. During this time, our knowledge and understanding of managerial issues and problems have evolved from an approach concerned primarily with establishing principles to increase efficiency in the workplace to those approaches that attempt to understand the total organization by exam-

FIGURE 2–7
Requirements for Effective Operation of Markets, Hierarchies, and Clans

Method of Governing Transactions	Characteristics
Market	Regulates exchanges through competitive pressures that relate the value of a good or service to its price.
Bureaucracy (hierarchy)	Regulates exchanges with rules which determine who can interact with whom and coordinators who have formal authority to allocate goods and services among parties.
Clan	Regulates exchanges through a system of shared values and traditions.

Source: Daniel Robey, *Designing Organizations*, 2d ed. (Homewood, IL: Irwin, 1986), 54. Reprinted with permission.

ining the interrelationships among the contextual, organizational, and human dimensions of the workplace. The various theories each offer a different perspective for addressing managerial problems. Many of the differences between the theories are due to the types of problems that have historically emerged to confront managers.

As a manager, you should realize that no one method or technique is to be applied to all problems or situations. Rather, you should strive to develop a contingency perspective in your application of managerial techniques. This perspective will enable you to assess the different probable causes of a problem and to recognize which application is most appropriate. For instance, a contingency perspective would inform you that increasing work efficiency may speed up the flow of work, but may also lead to greater levels of worker dissatisfaction. As a result, you may incur greater turnover, absenteeism, and carelessness in the workplace.

A contingency perspective also enables you to weigh factors that exist in the environment of the organization and to understand how changes in one area of the organization may require changes in other areas as well. For instance, a decrease in sales may be the result of a devaluation in foreign currency, thus making goods or services produced by foreign competitors cheaper in price. An increase in production will, in many instances, require an increase in the sales force, an increase in budget, and perhaps the need to redefine organization goals.

Your understanding of the strengths and limitations of historical perspectives will provide you with the knowledge needed to perform your managerial tasks effectively. We have much to learn from the past in order to be successful in the future.

KEY TERMS AND CONCEPTS

acceptance theory
adaptive subsystems
administrative theory

behavioral management theory
boundary or boundary-spanning
  subsystems

bureaucracy	piece-rate system
chain of command	production subsystem
classical management theory	quantitative management theory
closed system	scientific management
contingency theory	staff
delegation of authority	system
feedback	systems theory
Gantt chart	task-and-bonus wage system
Hawthorne effect	Theory X
maintenance subsystem	Theory Y
managerial subsystem	Theory Z
mechanistic organization	time studies
open system	transaction costs
organic organization	unity of command

QUESTIONS FOR REVIEW AND DISCUSSION

1. Some managers have suggested that classical management theory is still the most appropriate approach for managing an organization. They contend that all managers should emphasize efficiency in their decisions. Do you agree? If not, how would you respond to this statement?
2. What are the key assumptions made by writers espousing classical management theory? What is the difference between administrative theory and scientific management?
3. Some contemporary writers have suggested that we are in the midst of an "information revolution" that will have the same impact on the practice of management as did the Industrial Revolution. Do you believe this to be the case?
4. Identify and discuss the major criticisms that have been directed at classical management theories.
5. Discuss the sequence of events involved in the Hawthorne experiment and identify its outcome.
6. Identify the strengths and weaknesses of the assumptions about human behavior advanced by behavioral management theory.
7. How did quantitative management theory originate? In what areas of management is it most applicable?
8. Discuss why a contingency approach to management is valuable, and identify the problems a manager might encounter using that approach.
9. What managerial issues does the resource dependence perspective address? Population ecology? Theory Z? Competitive strategy? Markets, hierarchies, and clans?
10. Identify and discuss current issues or problems in management that the theories discussed in this chapter seem unable to address or solve. Do you believe we may need an entirely new theory for effective management in the 21st century?

CASES

2–1 APPLYING THE TAYLOR SYSTEM: THE WATERTOWN ARSENAL

During the period when scientific management was being introduced, the Watertown Arsenal, situated eight miles west of Boston, became a focus of controversy. Frederick W. Taylor believed that the Watertown Arsenal, which manufactured weapons for the military, provided an opportunity to display the benefits of his system. We will describe the old management system at the Watertown Arsenal and then the system that Taylor implemented. To test your understanding of classical management theory, you may, after reading "The Old Management System" and before reading "The Taylor System," speculate on what Taylor would do to make the Watertown Arsenal more efficient.

The Old Management System

When an order for goods was received at the arsenal, the correspondence office, directly under the commanding officer, would prepare a shop order naming the product and the quantity to be manufactured. Copies of the order were then sent to the foreman, who was thereafter responsible for filling the order.

The foreman's duties included obtaining the drawings of what the workers had to make, compiling a list of parts to be manufactured, and making a list of the raw materials necessary. The foreman would then write out job cards for the workers and make requisitions for materials. In addition to these duties, the foreman was responsible for the supervision of the workers and the maintenance of shop discipline.

When workers finished a job, they would go to the foreman for another job assignment, find the necessary materials, and, either alone or with assistance, move them to their machines. They would track down the drawings and work specifications and go after the required tools. Meanwhile, the machines sat idle. The workers studied the drawings and planned the tasks required to complete the job. Machinists would grind their own tools, select their own speeds, and, if the machines were defective, repair them before starting the work. There was no attempt to coordinate jobs among machinists since the foreman had no idea when to expect the delivery of raw or semifinished materials. There was practically no stock on hand, and most of the material was bought only after an order was received. The dates of delivery were so uncertain that frequently there were inordinate delays. To keep the workers occupied during these periods, they were given busywork.

The Taylor System

Under the Taylor system, the order received was sent by the commanding officer to the engineering department, which then prepared a bill of materials, a list of parts, the suborders, and a set of drawings. The bill of materials was then sent to a property department, with notations on whether the materials required were in storage. If the materials were not in storage, a copy of the bill of materials was sent to the purchasing department, which would then purchase the materials. The original bill, along with the drawings and the suborders, went to the machine shop where the work was to be started.

When any of the suborders were completed, a report was submitted to the planning department and a shipment of the required pieces was made to the machine shop. In the meantime, the planning department would have already received from the engineering department copies of the order, the bill of materials, the list of parts, and the required drawings. From this information, the planning department determined the necessary operations for each part and the sequence in which these were to be carried out. These decisions were compiled on a master route and a schedule sheet from which the following smaller cards were prepared:

1. *Job cards.* One card for each operation giving the name and suborder, number of the part, the code number of the machine, and information on labor and overhead cost.
2. *Move cards.* One card for each part informing the workers how the part was to move through the manufacturing process.
3. *Move tags.* Small tags attached to each part with instructions to workers who were responsible for transferring the parts from one machine to another.
4. *Instruction cards.* One card for each operation explaining in detail how the operation was to be performed on the part.

A special department was set up to make periodic inspections and to complete necessary repairs. Most of the traditional duties of the foremen were performed by the planning and engineering departments. The foreman's new functions consisted of checking on the delivery of materials, obtaining special tools and fixtures, and making certain that workers understood the instructions from the planning department.

As a result of Taylor's system, production at the Watertown Arsenal doubled, saving the machine industry millions of dollars a year. The system was credited with contributing to the United States' victory in World War I in that production of munitions increased fivefold during this period.

Source: Adapted from Hugh G. J. Aitken, *Scientific Management in Action: Taylorism at Watertown Arsenal, 1908-1915.* Copyright © 1985 by Princeton University Press. Reprinted with permission of Princeton University Press.

1. Which of the four managerial activities—planning, organizing and staffing, directing, or controlling—did Taylor emphasize to increase efficiency in the Watertown Arsenal? Identify examples of each.
2. At the time the new methods were introduced, workers and managers at the arsenal protested the implementation of Taylor's methods, which later led to the creation of a Congressional committee to investigate the Taylor system. Why do you think workers and managers would be upset over this system?
3. How would Elton Mayo and other behavioral management theorists have approached this problem? Proponents of systems theory? Contingency theory? Theory Z?

2–2 WHO SAID WHAT?

Many of the people discussed in this chapter wrote extensively on the subject of management. You may want to test your understanding of their ideas by matching the writer with the following quotes. Your teacher can provide you with the correct match.

1. "The purely bureaucratic type of administrative organization . . . is superior to any other form in precision, in stability, in the stringency of its discipline, and its reliability."
2. "Our administrative methods . . . know how to organize for material efficiency. But problems of absenteeism, labor turnover, 'wildcat' strikes, show that we do not know how to ensure spontaneity of cooperation; that is, teamwork."
3. "I have never observed a group whose members wanted it to decay. I have never studied a group or an organization that was decaying where there were not some members who were aware that decay was occurring. Accordingly, one key to group and organizational effectiveness is to get this knowledge out into the open and to discuss it thoroughly."
4. "The problem of productivity in the United States will not be solved with monetary policy or through more investment in research and development. It will only be remedied when we learn how to manage people in such a way that they can work together more effectively."
5. "The executive functions serve to maintain a system of cooperative effort. They are impersonal. The functions are not, as so frequently stated, to manage a group of persons."
6. "It is in difficult moments above all that a plan is necessary. The best of plans cannot anticipate all unexpected occurrences which may arise, but it does include a place for these events and prepare the weapons which may be needed at the moment of being surprised."
7. "Whether or not individual organizations are consciously adapting, the environment selects out optimal combinations of organizations."

8. "One objective of my book is to 'try to convince the reader that the remedy for . . . inefficiency lies in systematic management, rather than in searching for some unusual or extraordinary man.' "

9. "We have all been wrong in scheduling on a basis of quantities; the essential element in the situation is time, and this should be the basis in laying out any program."

10. "People are not by nature passive or resistant to organizational needs. They have become so as a result of experience in organizations."

11. "The key to organizational survival is the ability to acquire and maintain resources."

ENDNOTES

1. For a more comprehensive discussion of early writings on management, see C. S. George, Jr., *The History of Management Thought*, 2d ed. (Englewood Cliffs, NJ: Prentice-Hall, 1972).

2. A. Tillett, T. Kempner, and G. Wills, *Management Thinkers* (Harmondsworth, Eng.: Penguin Books, 1970).

3. D. A. Wren, *The Evolution of Management Thought* (New York: Ronald Press, 1972).

4. C. Babbage, *On the Economy of Machinery and Manufactures* (London: Charles Knight, 1835); reprinted, 4th ed. (New York: Augustus M. Kelley, 1963).

5. "The Cranky Grandfather of the Computer," *Fortune* (March 1964): 112-113.

6. M. Weber, *The Theory of Social and Economic Organization*, trans. A. M. Henderson and T. Parsons, ed. T. Parsons (New York: Free Press, 1947), 329-333.

7. M. Weber, *Max Weber*, ed. S. M. Miller (New York: Thomas Y. Crowell, 1963), 10.

8. C. I. Barnard, *The Functions of the Executive* (Cambridge, MA: Harvard University Press, 1938).

9. Ibid., 163.

10. F. W. Taylor, *Principles of Scientific Management* (New York: Harper & Brothers, 1911).

11. Ibid.

12. Hearings before Special Committee of the House of Representatives to Investigate the Taylor and Other Systems of Shop Management Under Authority of House Resolution 90 (Washington, D.C.: U.S. Government Printing Office, 1912), 1451.

13. C. D. Wrege and A. G. Perroni, "Taylor's Pig-Tale: A Historical Analysis of Frederick W. Taylor's Pig-Iron Experiments," *Academy of Management Journal* (March 1974): 6-27.

14. Wren, *Evolution of Management Thought*, Chapter 8.

15. R. H. Miles, *Macro Organizational Behavior* (Glenview, IL: Scott, Foresman, 1980), 93.

16. Wren, *Evolution of Management Thought*, 162.

17. Like many women during this period, Lillian faced gender discrimination. In 1914, her thesis, "The Psychology of Management," gave her name as "L. M. Gilbreth" to avoid reference to her gender.

18. F. B. Gilbreth, Jr., and E. G. Carey, *Cheaper by the Dozen* (New York: Thomas Y. Crowell, 1948), 3.

19. E. Mayo, *The Social Problems of an Industrial Civilization* (Boston: Division of Research, Graduate School of Business Administration, Harvard University, 1945).

20. F. J. Roethlisberger and W. J. Dickson, *Management and the Worker: An Account of a Research Program Conducted by the Western Electric Company, Hawthorne Works, Chicago*; with the Assistance and Collaboration of Harold A. Wright (Cambridge, MA: Harvard University Press, 1939). Later research has indicated that Mayo did not understand the small-group incentive system. A subsequent analysis of the output data and the incentive system has shown that instead of the incentive system not contributing to the increase in output, it was the very cause of the increased output. For more details, see R. G. Greenwood and C. D. Wrege, "The Hawthorne Studies," paper presented at the annual Academy of Management meetings, Chicago, 1986.

21. For further discussion of the ideas of Mary Parker Follett see E. Fox, "Mary Parker Follett: The Enduring Contribution," *Public Administration Review* (November/December 1968): 520-529, and J. Stever, "Mary Parker Follett and the Quest for Pragmatic Administration," *Administration and Society* (August 1986): 159-177.

22. D. McGregor, *The Human Side of Enterprise* (New York: McGraw-Hill, 1960).

23. C. Argyris, *Personality and Organization: The Conflict Between the System and the Individual* (New York: Harper & Brothers, 1957).

24. A. H. Maslow, "A Theory of Human Motivation," in *Motivation and Personality*, 2d ed. (New York: Harper & Row, 1970), 35-58.

25. C. W. Churchman, R. L. Ackoff, and E. L. Arnoff, *Introduction to Operations Research* (New York: John Wiley & Sons, 1957).

26. D. Katz and R. L. Kahn, *The Social Psychology of Organizations* (New York: John Wiley & Sons, 1966), 86.

27. D. Bell, *The Coming of Post-Industrial Society: A Venture in Social Forecasting* (New York: Basic Books, 1973).

28. T. Burns and G. M. Stalker, *The Management of Innovation* (London: Tavistock Publications, 1961).

29. P. R. Lawrence and J. W. Lorsch, *Organization and Environment* (Cambridge, MA: Harvard University Press, 1967).

30. J. Child, "Organizational Structure, Environment, and Performance: The Role of Strategic Choice," *Sociology* 6 (January 1972): 1-22.

31. H. Koontz, "The Management Theory Jungle Revisited," *Academy of Management Review* 5 (April 1980): 175-187.

32. J. Pfeffer and G. R. Salancik, *The External Control of Organizations: A Resource Dependence Perspective* (New York: Harper & Row, 1978).

33. J. Pfeffer, "Size and Composition of Corporate Boards of Directors: The Organization and Its Environment," *Administrative Science Quarterly* 17 (1972): 218-228.

34. M. T. Hannan and J. H. Freeman, "The Population Ecology of Organizations," *American Journal of Sociology* 82 (March 1977): 929-964.

35. W. G. Ouchi, *Theory Z: How American Business Can Meet the Japanese Challenge* (Reading, MA: Addison-Wesley, 1981).

36. M. E. Porter, *Competitive Strategy: Techniques for Analyzing Industries and Competitors* (New York: Free Press, 1980).

37. O. E. Williamson, *Markets and Hierarchies: Analysis and Antitrust Implications* (New York: Free Press, 1975).

38. W. Ouchi, "Markets, Bureaucracies, and Clans," *Administrative Science Quarterly* 25 (1980): 129-141.

Managing the Context of Organizations

CHAPTER 3

After studying this chapter, you should be able to:

- Identify the important contextual conditions that influence organization and managerial activities.
- Describe six environmental domains used for classifying factors in an organization's environment.
- Identify six environmental dimensions that describe how organization factors are arranged in the environment.
- Discuss the role of environmental uncertainty in the development of managerial practices.
- Summarize and describe the techniques that managers can use for adapting and controlling factors in the environment.
- Discuss the concept of organization set and its impact on management.

68

In this chapter we will explore the impact of organization context on managerial performance. Managers must recognize that an organization's context affects and is affected by managerial decisions and activities. We will identify and discuss various contextual conditions that influence an organization. A **contextual condition** is a characteristic that is either external or internal to the boundaries of an organization. Knowledge of the context of an organization enables managers to understand more fully how events can affect their organization now and in the future. By the end of this chapter, you should have a basic understanding of how managers can formulate, analyze, and manipulate an organization's context to increase overall organization success. Figure 3–1 displays the contextual dimensions of an organization to be discussed in this chapter.

ORGANIZATION CONTEXT

Organization context can be thought of as "the ecology of the organization,"[1] comprising dimensions of activities and events that exist outside an organization's boundaries as well as dimensions that are unique to the organization. Contextual dimensions of an organization include the domains and dimensions of the external environment and the relationships organizations have with other organizations (i.e., the organization set) in the environment. Each of these contextual dimensions has important implications for the ways managers engage in planning, organizing and staffing, directing, and controlling the organization.

For most managers of organizations, the external context, or environment, is represented by the market for which they are trying to provide a good or service. Yet the external context can also include events and activities that do not exist in the market the organization is serving. For instance, a television station operates in a context in which viewers, advertisers, program producers, and news services all affect the broadcasting by the television station. Similarly, governmental regulations, technological changes in unrelated industries, national events, and other organizations that provide information and entertainment may also affect the operations of the television station. Contextual conditions are important because they influence the methods by which managers can effectively use resources to plan, organize and staff, direct, and control organization activities.

FIGURE 3–1
*Contextual Dimensions
of Organizations*

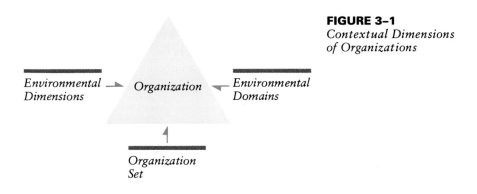

*Environmental
Dimensions* → *Organization* ← *Environmental
Domains*

*Organization
Set*

Contextual Conditions

We can think of an organization's context as an array of interrelated conditions, perceived or not perceived by organization managers, that influence activities and organization performance. By *interrelated*, we mean that the contextual conditions of an organization affect one another and, at times, managers must account for this interrelationship in their decision making. Contextual conditions that influence an organization or a manager may be fairly constant over time or they may change every hour. A change in a contextual condition—for example, entering a new market—requires an understanding of how the new environment will affect the organization and its activities. It also requires an understanding of how the environmental change will affect the role of other contextual conditions of the organization as well.

The task of the manager would be considerably less complicated if contextual conditions of the organization remained constant. Managers could then reduce the number of unique situations faced over the course of time and become quite skilled at handling recurring problems. In actuality, however, no organization exists that resides in a totally stable or unchanging context. Indeed, contextual change is occurring at a faster rather than a slower pace for most organizations today.

This observation raises an important question about our understanding of the contextual nature of an organization. What conditions would have to exist for an organization to operate in a context in which dimensions are stable over time? As discussed in Chapter 2, the answer to this question lies in viewing every organization as a system.[2]

ENVIRONMENTAL DOMAINS AND DIMENSIONS

We define **environment** as all factors outside an organization's boundaries that affect the activities of the organization. **Environmental factors** consist of information, capital, material, people, and other organizations. For example, consider a fast-food hamburger restaurant near a college campus. An environmental factor would be the supplier from whom the restaurant buys its ground beef. Statistics on college enrollment would be a factor. Information about patterns of hamburger consumption among college students would be another factor.

Often new factors are introduced into the environment that are important to managers. The campus bookstore may open a cafeteria serving hamburgers which is in direct competition with the fast-food restaurant. Dissatisfaction with the college food service may bring more students into the restaurant more often. The election of a new president in Argentina may result in a change in beef export policy that affects the price of ground beef in the United States. Managers need to know not only what factors affect their firm, but what effect these factors may have.

Environmental Domains

A manager's understanding of environmental factors is helped by learning to identify environmental domains which comprise groups of factors. We can conceptualize and analyze six environmental domains that influence the activities of an organization: economic, political, social, technological, competitive, and physical domains. Some organizations may have factors in each of these domains. Other organizations may have factors in only one domain. However, managers should be knowledgeable about each domain. Changes in the environment may transform domains once thought to be negligible into domains that heavily influence the firm. Management in Action 1 shows how environmental domains changed for AT&T after a federal court ordered its breakup.

THE ECONOMIC DOMAIN

Economic factors are the factors most readily identified by most organization managers. Interest rates, trade deficits, inflation rates, gross national product indicators, and the money supply are all economic factors that may influence an organization's activities. Factors in the economic domain are important because they have implications for the ability of organization managers to get the resources needed to produce goods and services and distribute those goods and services to a market.

One can identify economic factors for virtually all types of organizations. Suppliers, whether individuals or organizations, provide raw materials, labor, equipment, and financial inputs to an organization. The price a supplier charges for these inputs will often affect the profit and sales of the organization. Customers are also a factor in the economic domain through their willingness or unwillingness to buy a good or service at a particular price.

Managers spend considerable time forecasting economic changes because those changes influence the cost of borrowing money, the ability to engage in international trade, and the cost of materials from suppliers. Banks may raise their lending rates in anticipation of inflation. Computer manufacturers may delay building a new plant believing that interest rates will drop within the year. Steel manufacturers dependent on foreign imports are hurt when the value of the dollar declines in relation to foreign currencies. On the other hand, some organizations are insulated from economic conditions. Rolls-Royce, a manufacturer of expensive luxury cars, claims to be unaffected by economic factors because Rolls-Royce customers are not typically concerned about price. Health-food stores often find that the state of the economy has little effect on their sales.

AT&T has had to consider a wide array of economic factors throughout its history. Because the firm has operated in international markets, it has had to respond to changes in interest rates, trade deficits, and inflation in the United States and overseas. For instance, the value of a foreign country's currency will affect the cost of overseas long-distance calling. When foreign currency is increasing in value relative to the dollar, the cost of a long-distance call to the country will increase. When foreign currency is decreasing in value relative to the dollar, the cost of a long-distance call to the country will decrease. Since the value of a country's currency changes on a daily basis, AT&T management must be aware of the direction and rate of change in currency throughout the world.

The breakup of AT&T, as discussed in Management in Action 1, has transformed its economic domain. Pricing of goods and services to customers used to be determined by the cost of providing goods and services with respect to a regulated profit margin. With the introduction of competition and

On January 1, 1984, American Telephone and Telegraph Co. (AT&T) put into effect a federal court order which deregulated, in part, the company's op-

MANAGEMENT IN ACTION 1
THE CASE OF AT&T

erations. The court order signified the end of an era—the monopoly of the American domestic telephone service. This monopoly had provided, according to some, the best service in the world under the mission of "One System, One Policy, Universal Service." However, the American free-market mentality, antitrust climate, suspicion of monopolies, protests from would-be competitors, and AT&T's interest in diversifying to information systems were some of the forces driving that decree. As a result, seven regional telephone communications companies were dismembered from AT&T in an operation as painful to the employees as it was confusing to the public. A family of one million employees was torn apart and either sent to one of seven new regional companies or remained with the diminished parent. Employees not only suffered emotional shock but the aftermath of divorce proceedings. "Ma Bell doesn't live here anymore," proclaimed CEO Charles Brown prior to the decision heralding a change not only in structure, mission, and strategy but also in corporate culture.

The 107-year-old culture of AT&T was molded by a regulated monopolistic environment which protected the company from competition. At one point in time (1930s), the government was considering nationalizing the phone system as was being done in Europe, yet AT&T convinced the government to retain its independence. The watchful eye of the Federal Communications Commission would regulate interstate and international communications by virtue of the Communications Act of 1934. Nevertheless, AT&T would have a long history of legal battles with regulators and competitors, over patents at first and antitrust suits later. For example, the Justice Department of the United States sued AT&T, charging that telephone rates were kept artificially high because AT&T required equipment to be purchased from its manufacturing plant (Western Electric) by the local telephone companies. The government sought to have

AT&T divest itself of its manufacturing operations. The suit was finally settled without divestiture in 1956 when it was agreed that AT&T would limit its manufacturing operations, would not enter new markets, would restrict itself in common carrier communications, and would grant licenses to those who applied for technical information.

Prior to 1968, AT&T, as a monopoly carrier, held that no one could connect equipment to the AT&T network because of potential harm to the network. Therefore, AT&T provided the communications service and equipment. However, in 1968, the FCC decided in favor of Carter Electronics Corporation of Dallas in its petition to connect its equipment to the AT&T network. The 1968 "Carterphone" decision, though, required that "protective" equipment be installed between the network and the non-Bell device which by 1977 was no longer required. This enabled consumers to buy and use telephones from suppliers other than Bell.

The above actions began an erosion of the Bell monopoly that culminated in divestiture of the 22 operating telephone companies as settlement of yet another antitrust suit begun by the Justice Department in 1974 which ended January 8, 1982. The divestiture agreement which went into effect on January 1, 1984, left AT&T with long-distance, manufacturing (Western Electric), and research and development (Bell Labs) operations and grouped the 22 operating companies into seven regional telephone companies.

The new environment, however, is highly competitive, although some parts of AT&T remain regulated while the competition is not; telephone equipment is completely deregulated; long-distance AT&T remains regulated while all competitors are not; and computers and other products are deregulated. For example, the long-distance market is currently a mixed bag of monopoly and competitive players. AT&T is subject to old monopoly regulation while others operate without restrictions. Competitors claim this is fair by citing AT&T's huge market share and vast resources, which would crush fledgling competitors. According to reports, AT&T has lost market share in equipment and long distance while it has increased market share in international sales and automated office equipment.

entrance into new markets, AT&T is now required to price its goods and services based on competitive pricing and customer demand. In addition, resource suppliers were constrained in the price they charged AT&T. After the breakup, prices of supplies could be adjusted based on demand from the

Technology also pushed AT&T into the open. AT&T was prohibited from entering the data-processing market while functioning as a monopoly. It was determined that data processing and data communications were two distinct operations. However, ensuing technological innovation reduced this distinction, and as a result, AT&T was finally allowed to enter the market via a separate subsidiary, American Bell, on January 1, 1983. AT&T already had the new data-processing technology available for in-house use but could now commercialize it. Thus, before the major divestiture, part of AT&T had already entered into the competitive environment.

The breakup of the giant AT&T set the stage for a telecommunications upheaval. This also reestablished the earlier driving forces of AT&T to an emphasis on innovation. But prior to the breakup, innovation resulted from expanding new technology, whereas after the breakup, emphasis was placed on innovation to fulfill customer needs. For Bell Labs, whose employees had won several Nobel prizes for creating new technologies (e.g., the transistor and silicon chip), what was needed was a system to reduce the time between product development and production as well as to focus on customer needs rather than pure basic research.

Given competition, AT&T focused on changing from a service-oriented company to a market-driven company. For the customer, the AT&T breakup hit closer to home and to the wallet. In general, residential customers would pay more for phone service while business customers would pay less. Customers in some areas would face the danger of service deterioration because local service would no longer be subsidized by artificially high long-distance rates. Some customer groups have complained that cost-based pricing makes it impossible in high-cost, often rural areas to have a phone. As residential rates are tied closely to costs for the service, big variations in what people pay in different parts of the country have occurred.

Customers have found obtaining various services to be confusing. One company may provide long-distance service, another equipment, and yet another local service. Also, leased phones changed ownership. Local telephone companies originally owned them, but ownership was transferred to American Bell. As a result of these divisions, customers often receive at least three phone bills: local service, long distance, and equipment rental.

Finally, long-distance calling became more diverse. Many customers not only have to use long distance for interstate calls, but also for calls to areas within their metropolitan region. Customers can now choose from a variety of carriers, but those carriers vary in cost, methods of connection, services, and transmission quality.

For the investment community, divestiture was the largest corporate event in history. Once considered to be a safe and minimum-risk stock characterized by predictable earnings (even during the Great Depression AT&T continued to pay $9 dividends), AT&T stock was initially approached with caution and uncertainty. Wall Street was uncertain about AT&T's ability to adjust to the newly deregulated competitive environment. AT&T lost triple A ratings from Moody after 20 years because of the perceived risk of managing the split-up and entering new markets.

In response, AT&T applied pay freezes, employee layoffs, and plant closings all in an effort to make operations more efficient. Chairman Brown summarized the necessary steps taken in the 1984 annual report:

One of the principal adjustments we have had to make is to lower our cost structure and improve our margins. We had to come to grips with the fact that not all the work done when we were "the telephone company" has a place in this new business environment and that we could operate with a much smaller management force. As a result, jobs have been eliminated through attrition and voluntary and involuntary layoffs.

Source: Susan C. Schneider and Dr. Ellen Powley (now with NYNEX Service Company), "The Role of Images in Changing Corporate Culture: The Case of AT&T," paper presented at the Standing Conference on Organizational Symbolism, Antibes, France, 1985.

many organizations that are now providing telephone service to customers. This change in AT&T's economic domain has, of course, required management to set up new systems for determining the price and cost of its goods and services.

THE POLITICAL DOMAIN

The political domain of the organization environment rests on laws and regulations passed by governmental agencies and legislative bodies. Legislation has been directed toward the elimination of discrimination based on sex, race, and age. Other legislation has been designed to bring about an end to sexual harassment in the workplace, prevention of unfair pricing in markets, restrictions on pollution, consumer protection, and methods of corporate taxation. However, the enforcement of these laws and regulations often varies with the party or individual who occupies political office. For instance, enforcement of civil rights laws and pollution controls has varied because of differing beliefs by both political incumbents and the electorate about the need to enforce such legislation. Managers not only need to be aware of legislation, but must strive to understand how legislation will be interpreted in enforcement procedures.

Not all organizations are affected equally by such legislation. Some legislation is specific to industries—for example, requirements for the disposal of toxic wastes in the chemical industry, restrictions on licensing of banks in the financial industry, the mode of competition in the airline industry, and the choice of materials for the construction of products in the toy industry. Human service organizations may not have to be concerned with laws designed to control pollution, but would have to be concerned with laws that affect hiring practices. Steel companies may have to contend not only with pollution and hiring laws, but also with laws related to competition, occupational safety, consumer warranties, and methods of extracting and transporting iron ore. One industry that has been faced with multiple legislation and enforcement has been the tobacco industry. Laws have been passed restricting the advertising of cigarettes on television and requiring health warnings on the labels of packages and cartons of cigarettes.

The AT&T divestiture case clearly presents the impact that factors in the political domain have on an organization. After many years of legal maneuvering to determine whether AT&T was in violation of antitrust laws, an agreement was reached. AT&T would remove itself from local telephone service markets in exchange for the opportunity to compete in the data-processing market.

THE SOCIAL DOMAIN

The social domain of an organization's environment consists of societal values, attitudes, norms, customs, and demographics. Every society incorporates values and attitudes that may be uniform across a population or may vary by regional or ethnic groupings. Values are what people believe to be proper goals for members of the society to keep or achieve. Attitudes reflect what individuals think about issues and behaviors that occur within a society.

In the United States, most citizens value the freedom of speech as a necessary feature of their daily lives. They may, however, believe that this right is abused by other citizens. Citizens in other countries may feel that freedom of speech is unnecessary or is a value that only leads to disruption in their daily lives. Other values and attitudes that may differ by regions within a country or between countries concern the role of the family as a means to socialize the young, the importance of clean air to breathe, or the role of religion in political institutions. Values and attitudes are often expressed in the legal

The health care industry is strongly affected by changes in societal attitudes.

codes of countries. The First Amendment to the United States Constitution, for instance, guarantees the right of free speech to all citizens.

Values and attitudes, however, can change over time. Forty years ago in the United States, the role of motherhood was viewed by many as taking precedence over the mother's desire to work outside the home. This attitude has changed, despite some resistance, as over 50 percent of women with children under the age of six are now active in the work force. In 1950, the percentage of working mothers was only 12 percent.[3]

Attitudes toward the consumption of alcohol have undergone several changes over the years. In 1919, Prohibition was established with the passage of the Eighteenth Amendment, which forbade the manufacture, transportation, and sale of alcoholic beverages in the United States. Led by the Women's Christian Temperance Union, many had the attitude that alcohol consumption led to the decay of people's morals and the erosion of their sense of responsibility to their families. Enforcement of the law proved to be an insuperable problem, however, and public concern about the graft and violence surrounding illicit traffic in liquor led to the repeal of Prohibition in 1933. In the past decade, however, there has been a resurgence of concern about the effects of alcohol not only on those who consume it but also on those who do not. Concern about traffic deaths due to drunk driving, health hazards associated with alcohol abuse, and the increase in the number of alcoholics has led to efforts to restrict its use.

Naturally, these shifts in values and attitudes about alcohol consumption have had direct repercussions on the operations of organizations that manufacture alcoholic beverages. During Prohibition, many breweries and distilleries were either forced into bankruptcy or required to manufacture nonalcoholic beverages. With the end of Prohibition, legitimate producers of alcoholic beverages reappeared. Recently, in response to the growing concern about alcohol consumption, producers have issued public service messages cautioning consumers about the dangers of overconsumption. They have also added beverages lower in alcohol content to their product line.

Societal norms are common standards of behavior accepted by members of a society. Norms may be the product of values, attitudes, customs, religious teachings, or tradition. Forty years ago, for example, it was the norm for men attending sporting events to wear a suit and tie. In many ballparks today, this practice is more likely to draw stares from spectators in the stands. Norms also influence the way we speak or behave in the presence of friends, relatives, new acquaintances, or supervisors. Managers who fail to observe regional or societal norms in their dealings with people inside and outside the organization may become less effective.

Demographic factors are such characteristics of the population as age, sex, income, and buying patterns. The United States Bureau of the Census collects countless measures of population characteristics to identify shifts in the population and help organizations in their forecasts of future trends. The dramatic population growth of the postwar years of 1946 to 1962 has had a major impact on organizations as the baby-boom generation has matured. Manufacturers of baby food, clothing, and toys first enjoyed a large increase in sales only to suffer a decrease in sales as this portion of the population moved into their teens and became a significant market for the products of record companies, the automobile industry, and clothing manufacturers, which all experienced growth during the sixties. In the seventies, home-construction firms and companies catering to weddings grew rapidly. Businesses in the 1980s who benefited from the buying patterns of the maturing baby boomers were those associated with high technology, health, and travel. The 1990s will perhaps be prosperous for organizations that provide medical goods and services and products associated with status.

Demographics are important in other ways as well. They provide information about living patterns, the composition of the work force, migrations to new regions, levels of education, and wealth. Organizational managers who can interpret these trends successfully will be at an advantage in making decisions about entering new markets, producing or dropping products, and staffing the organization with essential human resources.

AT&T was forced to be responsive to factors in the social domain by assessing patterns of consumer behavior. This contributed to its decision to move not only into data processing for business but computers for home use as well. In addition, AT&T will have to identify the differences in demand for long-distance service in various regions of the country. Regions with greater numbers of corporate headquarters, such as the Northeast, will require more emphasis on business usage. Concern in the Southwest will be over growth in long-distance usage as the population expands in this region.

THE TECHNOLOGICAL DOMAIN

The technological domain, or technology, refers to the application of knowledge to the production and distribution of goods and services. It is often viewed as a major source of environmental change for an organization. Technology is greatly affected by innovation. **Innovation** is the creation or modification of a process, product, or service. Innovation can occur at different rates, as can its transfer throughout the environment. For instance, the use of silicon chips to replace transistors as the medium for storing computer information is an example of product innovation. Modifying a silicon chip to increase its storage capacity is an example of process innovation.

Technology transfer involves the application of innovation to processes, products, or services either within or between industries. Although innovation is often restricted to the process, product, or service for which the change was intended, innovations can also be applied to products or services for which the change was unintended. The National Aeronautics and Space Administration was instrumental in the innovation of a substance that would function under intense heat to protect spacecraft from burning upon reentry into the earth's atmosphere. An unintended application of this innovation was the use of the substance in cookware for both conventional and microwave ovens. The product, now known by its brand name "Pyrex," has undergone many changes in its application within this industry.

The rate of innovation varies by industry. Coal mining and the manufacture of farm machinery have low rates of innovation. On the other hand, innovations based on the application of bioengineering techniques have had impacts on medicine (serums), agricultural production (corn), and veterinary science (growth hormones) over a short period. While this suggests that some industries and organizations will have to deal with technological factors in their environment more than others will, technological factors should never be completely ignored. Regardless of the industry, there is always the risk that competitors will innovate a product which will make an organization's product obsolete—perhaps overnight. Examples include manufacturers who continued to produce electric typewriters without monitoring developments in the computer industry, razor manufacturers who failed to anticipate the introduction of electric razors to replace safety razors, and watch manufacturers hurt by the introduction of battery-operated watches that need no windup mechanism.

AT&T, through careful monitoring of technological trends, was able to identify the technological factors that would have the most impact on communication. As a result, AT&T management developed Bell Laboratories and hired researchers to develop and apply innovations in the communications field. It also led management to the realization that it had the skills and resources to compete in the computer industry. This helped the company to shift its activities after the breakup of the company in 1984.

THE COMPETITIVE DOMAIN

We often think of the competitive domain, or competition, as primarily an economic factor in an organization's environment. Indeed, competition is a strong influence on the economic activity of an organization and often requires managers to make economic decisions (e.g., the price to set for a product). However, competition needs to be considered beyond its economic implications.

Organizations can be faced with a wide variety of competitive conditions in their environment. Some large organizations compete only with small organizations, often giving them the advantage in the pricing of their products. Other competitive conditions arise from different mixes in the strategies that competitors pursue. For instance, a firm that produces 40 varieties of soup may have to compete with firms that also produce many varieties of soup as well as firms that produce only a few varieties. Competition for sales of soup may also differ in the areas of packaging (can versus frozen pouch), form of the product (wet versus dry soup), or varieties of cuisine (Oriental, European, Spanish).

Within a capitalist system, organizations can operate in one of four competitive market structures: monopoly, oligopoly, monopolistic competition, or perfect competition. A **monopoly** exists when an organization has sole access to the market for its goods and services. In a monopoly situation, competitors either have been restricted from access to customers or have voluntarily chosen not to compete in the market. Restrictions to markets may occur when regulatory agencies or governments grant a single organization the right to provide a good or service in the market. Utility companies are the most common form of organization operating under monopoly conditions. However, many governmental agencies, such as police departments, sanitation services, public schools, and transportation services, also operate under monopoly conditions that are purposely restricted by legal sanctions. Monopolies also can exist where competitors have chosen not to compete with a single firm operating in the market. Daily newspapers in many towns and cities are examples.

An **oligopoly** exists when only a few firms are in competition to provide goods and services to a market. In this situation the number of firms producing a good or service is so small that actions by any single firm in the industry concerning price, output, product style, and terms of sale have a perceptible impact on the sales of the other firms. The goods or services produced by oligopolists may be similar, as in the case of basic steel, aluminum, and cement. Or they may be different, as in the case of automobiles, cigarettes, home appliances, soaps, and detergents.

Monopolistic competition exists when many firms offer a similar good or service with only minor price differentials. Customers may recognize that the price of a sport coat is $5 lower at another store but may choose to spend the extra amount to avoid having to drive across town. Gasoline stations operate under conditions of monopolistic competition, as price differentials are often minor ($.01 to $.05 price variations for most retail sellers of gasoline). The extra amount is willingly spent by the customer. Indeed, most organizations that provide a specialized good or service operate under monopolistic competition. While small price differentials may have little effect on volume sales, managers must be sensitive to large discrepancies in price. Many customers may opt to absorb the inconvenience or extra expense to get a lower price. Often, managers try to respond to price discrepancies by marketing their products as unique (e.g., gel toothpaste) or by offering more pleasant surroundings (e.g., carpeting in a grocery store).

Perfect competition exists where many organizations offer essentially the same good or service. Price becomes the primary discriminator for the customer, who is presumed to have full knowledge of price disparities and wants to buy the good or service at the lowest available price. While perfect competition is rare in most industrial sectors, some sectors come close to meeting the conditions of perfect competition. The markets for many agricultural commodities, such as wheat, operate in a structure closely resembling perfect competition. One farmer's produce is essentially like any other farmer's produce. If a farmer chooses to demand a price for wheat higher than that of other farmers, buyers would probably not choose to buy the more expensive wheat.

AT&T represents a company that experienced a notable change in factors in the competitive domain as a result of its breakup. Earlier, it operated in a monopolistic market structure with noncompetitive conditions to provide phone service throughout the nation. With deregulation, the company was forced into a market of monopolistic competition, having to compete with

Airlines must respond to factors in the physical environment.

MCI, Sprint, Allnet, and many other companies providing long-distance communication services. Many economists correctly predicted that some competitors would fail or merge with other competitors, changing the market structure to an oligopoly. The challenge to AT&T management is whether it can effectively identify the changes in factors in its competitive domain and make the proper organizational adjustments.

THE PHYSICAL DOMAIN

All organizations must respond in some manner to factors in their physical domain. Weather conditions, for instance, may greatly influence the activities of a firm. Airlines must follow the location and movement of hurricanes in the southeastern United States when scheduling air traffic service on routes from, for example, Miami to New Orleans. Construction companies in the upper Midwest must schedule their activities to avoid construction of roads or homes during harsh winter months. Electric utilities must monitor both the heat and cold to make adjustments in the volume of electricity that must be generated to provide heat or air conditioning to customers. And orange growers must make quick decisions about harvesting when frost warnings are issued.

Many organizations, because of the type of good or service they provide, are relatively immune to factors in the physical domain. Financial securities companies that do most of their trading on Wall Street rarely find their activities disrupted by weather conditions. However, on September 27, 1985, Hurricane Gloria hit New York City, preventing members of the Wall Street exchanges from reaching their offices. This resulted in an uncommon closing of the stock and bonds market, and many financial securities companies were forced to close as well. Many brokerage houses experienced losses from the cessation of trading on that day.

AT&T is also sensitive to its physical domain. Earthquakes, tornadoes, freezing rain, and hurricanes each have the potential to destroy communication channels in different regions of the country. The curtailment of communication lines also prevents organizations, such as the Red Cross, from responding quickly to the needs of individuals who have suffered from such events. Hence, the management of AT&T must be prepared for such events by monitoring weather conditions and training employees to respond to damage to communication lines.

While AT&T represents an organization with factors in each of the environmental domains (see Figure 3–2), this is not the case for many organiza-

FIGURE 3–2
Environmental Domains of an Organization

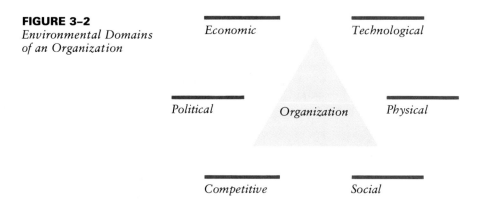

tions. Some organizations may be affected by factors in only one or two domains. A dry-cleaning business operating in a small town may be affected only by weather conditions (colder weather usually increases the demand for dry-cleaning services), but the political, economic, social, competitive, and technological domains may have virtually no impact on the operation of business. While this may be the case, a manager of a dry-cleaning business must still be aware of changes in these domains as new methods of cleaning, laws concerning liability, new competition, or changes in customer life-styles may occur at any time.

Managers need an understanding of the various domains to classify environmental factors that either have or do not have influence on the operation of their organization. Sometimes factors from different domains merge to produce unique or unusual products. Management in Action 2 gives an example of the merging of social and technological factors to produce a novel product. Further understanding of the relationships between an organization and its environment can be gained by examining environmental factors along several dimensions.

Environmental Dimensions

Six environmental dimensions characterize the arrangement of factors within the domains of the organization's environment. The six dimensions are munificence, dynamism, complexity, concentration, turbulence, and consensus.[4] Managers of organizations must not only be able to identify environmental factors but must also understand the arrangement of factors to make correct decisions.

MUNIFICENCE

The **munificence** of an organization's environment refers to the level of resources available to an organization. The degree of munificence may range from rich to lean. Rich environments usually exist where resources are plentiful. However, a rich resource environment attracts other organizations and, over time, environments will move from rich to lean. As such, rich resource environments usually exist in the early stages of industry development or under conditions of monopoly market structure.

You're a creature of your times. You want a baby. But you don't want diapers. You don't want midnight feedings.

Technology saves the day. For $19.95, and just 13 minutes out of your busy day, you can have "the full, rich experience of parenthood without the mess and inconvenience of the real thing." It's called Video Baby.

Let's slip it into the VCR and see. Why, it's a girl! A cuddly, blue-eyed little girl. Look at those fingers. Isn't she adorable?

The soothing voice of a narrator is heard, inviting you to name this little cherub. "You'll know immediately if you've chosen a name your baby likes," the narrator says. "Call your Video Baby by name now." There is a brief pause, while the proud parents say "Melissa" or "Penelope." Then the baby smiles glowingly.

"This is tailor-made for yuppies," says Peter Wild, the chairman of Creative Programming Inc., which has just brought the video infant into the world. "The enjoyment without the commitment."

He seems to know what he is talking about. The

MANAGEMENT IN ACTION 2
AND BETA MAKES 3

shelves of video shops are sprouting with tapes for people who will take their gratification electronically, just so long as it is instant.

Tired of lugging firewood and fiddling with dampers? One tape offers the yuletide warmth of a flickering fire, with Christmas carols in the background. And never any ashes to scoop.

For those who find even a fishbowl too taxing, one company offers Tropical Fish Tank. Turn it on and your television screen becomes an electronic aquarium full of exotic fish. Other products for the times are "Look Mom, I'm Fishing," Video Cat, and Video Dog which will, on command, "sit up," "get the ball," and "roll over."

When environments become lean, organizations are required to engage in several tactics to survive. Stockpiling through inventory, cutthroat competitive practices, and more efficiency in the use of resources are all tactics that will increase the chances of survival. Organizations unable to adapt to lean environments are faced with two prospects—failure, or movement to a richer resource environment by changing their product, their market, or both.

For instance, a lumber mill in the Pacific Northwest at the turn of the century would have found resources (trees) in plentiful supply. Over time, however, the number of trees would diminish, changing the resource environment of the lumber mill from rich to lean. In addition, the establishment of other lumber mills in the region would make the supply of trees even more scarce.

How did lumber mills respond to this situation? Many discovered ways to be more efficient in the location and cutting of timber. As more competitors moved into the region, competitive pricing of timber became more intense. Many lumber mills created large warehouses for the storage of lumber to ensure that they would have adequate supplies. Some lumber mills moved to other regions where timber supplies were richer. Others simply failed. And, of course, firms in the lumber industry recognize the importance of reseeding the forests to generate richer supplies for the future.

DYNAMISM

Dynamism refers to the degree of turnover in environmental factors. A low degree of turnover of factors creates a stable environment. A high degree in turnover of factors creates an unstable environment. A stable environment al-

FROM THE FIELD
ENVIRONMENTAL
DOMAINS

We surveyed corporate planners from a wide variety of industries to learn what environmental domains they felt were most important in forecasting trends. We asked each planner, "How would you rate each of the following environmental domains in overall importance to your organization?" Planners rated each domain on a scale of 1 to 5, with possible responses including 1 (very unimportant), 3 (neither important nor unimportant), and 5 (very important). Here are the results, ranked from most important to least important.

Rank	Environmental Domain	Average Rating
1	Competitive	4.91
2	Economic	4.45
3	Technological	3.79
4	Social	3.44
5	Political	3.23
6	Physical	3.18

These results show that planners responding to the survey see all six environmental domains as having some importance to their forecasting of trends. Not very surprising is that factors in the competitive and economic domains were ranked most important. This, of course, is probably attributable to the fact that all the planners are employed by for-profit firms. The results might be different if planners from the public sector or not-for-profit organizations had been included in the survey.

lows organizational members to follow routine procedures for getting resources and distributing goods or services to the market. It also rewards organizations which have been operating the longest amount of time. The longer an organization operates under stable environmental conditions, the more managers learn and the more able they are to reduce the number of mistakes. Under conditions of environmental instability, managers must constantly adjust their activities to adapt to new conditions. As a result, efficiency is problematic because the techniques learned and applied last year may no longer be appropriate.

Many manufacturers of children's toys find themselves in unstable environments. Each year, the type of toys children demand will change. One year, it may be Cabbage Patch dolls; the next year, it may be Masters of the Universe dolls. Because most toys are sold during the holiday season, manufacturers of toys must begin speculating in early spring on what toys will be in demand (to give adequate lead time for their design and production). Managers who fail to predict correctly in March what toys children want in December can make the difference between a profitable and an unprofitable year for the company.

While many firms operating in so-called fad industries (e.g., toys, fashion clothing, records) are considered to be operating in an unstable environment, firms in other industries must also deal with instability. Airlines (price of fuel, deregulation), banks (prime rates, inflation), and farming (weather conditions, government policies) are just a few examples. On the other hand, manufacturers of box containers who have a steady demand for their products as well as a steady supply of resources are an example of a stable industry.

COMPLEXITY

Complexity is the degree of similarity or diversity between the factors in an organization's environment. When factors are similar, the environment is referred to as homogeneous. When factors are diverse, the environment is referred to as heterogeneous. Organizations operating in homogeneous environments can specialize in producing one good or service to be distributed to the market. Homogeneous environments also allow an organization to simplify its operations as the knowledge and skills required of managers and workers are related to one product. Heterogeneous environments, on the other hand, require an organization to provide diverse products and services to the market. Managers operating in heterogeneous environments, therefore, must be knowledgeable in many areas and develop multiple skills to be effective. When organizations expand their market, they often move to a more heterogeneous environment.

Hospitals operate in a heterogeneous environment. Providing health care to patients requires the use of multiple skills and techniques depending on whether patients need diagnostic services, surgery, or treatment for diseases. In addition, many hospitals are now providing patients with "wellness" programs including exercise programs, health seminars, and rehabilitation. Hospitals are responding not only to complexity among patients but also to a wide range of regulations, economic conditions, and diverse technologies. In contrast, many chiropractic clinics operate in a relatively homogeneous environment by offering one service to their patients.

CONCENTRATION

Concentration, the degree to which factors are distributed in the environment, can have differing effects on an organization's activities. Whether factors are concentrated in one or several locations, managers must be able to identify their location and develop methods for using them. When factors are concentrated in one location, transportation costs can be reduced because members need not travel to multiple locations to get them. When factors are dispersed, or evenly distributed in the environment, the cost of learning about those factors increases, as does the cost of transportation to and from the factors. Thus, organizations in a concentrated environment will realize more efficiency in their operations than organizations in a dispersed environment.

Many firms have responded to customer dispersion by providing mail-order services. Sears, of course, developed this idea before the turn of the century through its catalogs. Some companies, such as Lands' End and many seed stores, use mail order almost exclusively to reach their customers. On the other hand, political lobbyists spend most of their time in Washington, D.C., because that is where most of the political factors are concentrated. Many brokerage firms locate in New York City because of the concentration of financial markets. And steel companies prefer to locate in the upper Midwest because ore and labor are concentrated in this region.

TURBULENCE

Turbulence is the extent to which environments are being disturbed by an increasing rate of exchanges between factors. Exchanges result from transfers

A business firm's environment can be affected by resource exchanges with nations far removed from its market.

of resources between organizations. As the rate of exchanges increases in the environment, so does the chance that organizations must change their internal operations. For instance, a hundred years ago business firms in the United States were rarely affected by events in the Middle East. As more resource exchanges were made by governments, energy firms, and defense contractors with nations in this region, events in the Middle East had more impact on firms in this country. Chain motels, such as Holiday Inns, for example, were greatly affected by rising oil prices. As the price of gas increased, the number of family vacations decreased. This led to a decline in the number of vacationers seeking lodging at motels. When turbulence increases in the environment, organizations increasingly must alter their operations to adapt to exchanges that are often far removed from their market. A low degree of turbulence reduces the need for managers to alter their operations.

CONSENSUS

Consensus refers to the degree to which an organization's claim to a specific activity is recognized or disputed by other organizations. Favorable recognition of an organization's activities by other organizations suggests that consensus exists. When the activity is disputed, however, the environment is in a state of dissensus. The very nature of private enterprise involves dissensus, as profit-oriented organizations in competition are engaged in contesting one another's right to participate. However, many business firms do seek to achieve consensus by encouraging protective legislation such as import quotas, tariffs, and licensing.

In the nonprofit sector, many social service agencies, such as Planned Parenthood, seek support for their activities by offering a unique service to the community. Consensus occurs when other organizations recognize the need for such service and are willing to provide support to aid the agency in achieving its goals. Indeed, in many communities, United Way serves as a major determinant of consensus simply by selecting an agency to receive funds and discouraging other agencies from providing duplicate services.

Each of the environmental dimensions addresses how factors can be organized and located in respect to the organization. Managers need to understand not only where an organization is located on each dimension, but the direction in which the organization is moving along the dimension. For instance, an organization in a rich environment benefits from plentiful supplies of resources. Managers, however, must recognize that if the environment shifts to a lean environment because of increased competition, adjustments in organization activities will have to be made. Figure 3–3 displays the six environmental dimensions and identifies organizations that are likely to be located at either extreme of the dimension.

ENVIRONMENTAL UNCERTAINTY

Factors in the external environment of an organization can be placed into six environmental domains and six environmental dimensions. Both methods of characterizing the environment are useful for managers when trying to un-

	RICH	LEAN
MUNIFICENCE	Salt producers Solar energy power plants in the Sun Belt Monopolies, such as public utilities	Manual typewriter manufacturers Plow manufacturers
	STABLE	UNSTABLE
DYNAMISM	Container manufacturers Limousine producers Flour producers	Greeting card manufacturers Preschools Political campaign organizations
	HOMOGENEOUS	HETEROGENEOUS
COMPLEXITY	Boys' military academies Corn seed producers Senior citizens clubs Salmon canneries	Automobile manufacturers Movie production companies Venture capital companies Large universities
	CONCENTRATED	DISPERSED
CONCENTRATION	City government agencies Prisons Newspapers Neighorhood organizations	Cable television networks Multinational companies College textbook publishers Political parties
	LOW INTERCONNECTION	HIGH INTERCONNECTION
TURBULENCE	Communes Rural churches Antique stores	National governments Oil companies Media organizations Post offices
	CONSENSUS	DISSENSUS
CONSENSUS	Public utilities Child welfare agencies Public transportation systems Sports franchises	Fast-food companies Airlines Soft drink manufacturers

FIGURE 3-3
*Organizations and Their
Environmental
Dimensions*

derstand how the environment influences their organization. However, some environmental conditions are easier to understand and predict than others. Until now, we have viewed the environment objectively—that is, any manager examining the same environment should arrive at the same conclusion on what domains the factors are located in and where the organization resides within the environmental dimensions. This will occur if all managers have full information about the environment. However, managers rarely have the opportunity to make judgments based on total information. Indeed, much information about the environment may be absent or erroneous. Hence, many environmental evaluations are subjective and lead to disagreements among managers about the true condition of the environment.

We surveyed marketing and sales executives from a wide variety of industries to learn what direction trends in their markets were taking. We asked each executive to identify the term that was most accurate for describing market trends in his or her industry. You will note that each question is designed to measure the environmental dimensions discussed in the chapter, except consensus and turbulence. See if you can identify which question is designed to measure which dimension. Numbers in parentheses are the percent of executives who identified the term that described market trends for their companies.

1. The number of competitors is decreasing (25%) or increasing (75%).
2. Consumers want more (81%) or fewer (19%) varieties of the products we produce.
3. Repeat customers are a small (13%) or large (87%) part of our business.
4. Most of our customers are located in a few (22%) or in many (78%) regions of the country.

If you associated measure 1 with munificence, measure 2 with complexity, measure 3 with dynamism, and measure 4 with concentration, you were correct. These results suggest that for most of the firms surveyed, the consumer environment is lean, complex, stable, and dispersed. However, these questions do not necessarily characterize the total environment of the organizations in which these executives work. Operations, finance, or personnel executives may respond differently to the questions, or they may want to consider factors other than customers and competitors.

When managers do not have information or have incorrect information about environmental factors, they have a difficult time predicting external changes.[5] When this occurs, managers must decide under conditions of uncertainty. As uncertainty increases, so also does the risk that managers will make decisions that harm rather than help the organization. Five types of managerial uncertainty can lead to poor decisions:[6]

- Uncertainty about information availability, accuracy, and clarity
- Uncertainty about cause-effect relationships
- Uncertainty about outcome preferences
- Uncertainty arising from the time span needed for definitive feedback
- Uncertainty arising from the inability to assign the probability of an outcome

Research suggests that uncertainty will increase for organizational managers when the environment becomes lean, heterogeneous, unstable, dispersed, turbulent, and is in a state of dissensus.[7] Each of these environmental conditions requires the gathering of more information. If the information is difficult to get or unobtainable, managerial uncertainty will increase even more.

The relationship between uncertainty and two of the environmental dimensions is displayed in Figure 3–4. Environmental dynamism and complexity can both create managerial uncertainty in different degrees. A manager in

Environmental Complexity

	Homogeneous	*Heterogeneous*
Stable	Cell 1 Low Uncertainty 1. Similar types of external elements 2. Elements remain the same or change slowly Example: Cardboard container manufacturer	Cell 2 Moderately Low Uncertainty 1. Diverse types of external elements 2. Elements remain the same or change slowly Example: Canned foods producer
Unstable	Cell 3 Moderately High Uncertainty 1. Similar types of external elements 2. Elements are in a continuous process of change Example: Country & Western record company	Cell 4 High Uncertainty 1. Diverse types of external elements 2. Elements are in a continuous process of change Example: Commercial airline

Environmental Dynamism

FIGURE 3–4
Environmental Dimensions and Uncertainty

an organization residing in cell 1, such as a manufacturer of cardboard containers, should experience low uncertainty because the environmental factors are basically similar and stable over time. Managers of organizations in cell 2 should have moderately low uncertainty in making decisions because the environment is stable, but information varies as a result of differences in environmental factors. Many companies producing canned foods are situated in this cell because they serve different types of customers, but the demands and needs for such products change little over time. Cell 3 environments pose more uncertainty for organizational managers. Though the environmental factors are basically similar, they are changing over time; thus, the uncertainty is moderately high. Companies that produce country music albums are in this cell. The artists are similar, as is the method of producing the albums, but the demand for the music varies as does the popularity of the performing artists. Managers in cell 4 face the greatest amount of uncertainty because the factors in the environment are both unstable and complex. AT&T is located in this cell as are many airlines and oil companies. Similar four-cell matrixes can be constructed using the four other environmental dimensions, with similar results for managerial uncertainty.

ORGANIZATIONAL ADAPTATION AND CONTROL

It is clear from our discussion that the environment of an organization has an enormous impact on organizational performance. Of paramount concern to all organizational managers is the attainment of necessary resources and

Gregory G. Dess (Ph.D., University of Washington) is Professor of Management at the University of Texas at Arlington. Professor Dess's teaching and research interests include the study of organization/environment relationships and executive decision-making processes, and the analysis of strategy variables contributing to organizational performance. His research has been published in Administrative Science Quarterly, Academy of Management Journal, Academy of Management Review, Strategic Management Journal, *and* Journal of Management. *He is a consultant to many organizations in the public and private sectors. Prior to his academic career, Professor Dess was a planning engineer for Western Electric Company, Inc., in Atlanta, Georgia.*

ACADEMIC PROFILE
GREGORY G. DESS

Q: Do you find some organizations or industries better equipped than others to handle change in their environments? If so, what would or would not account for this?

A: The ability to anticipate and to respond to unpredictable environmental change is not equally important in all industries. For example, based on interviews with executives and analysis of industry data, "paints and allied products" is a highly stable industry and "electronic computing equipment" is a highly unstable industry. Therefore, unpredictable change would be much higher in the latter industry and the ability to cope with uncertainty would be much more important. However, the importance of coping successfully with change varies significantly within industries. For example, in the paints and allied products industry, firms which manufactured "high-tech" products such as automobile finishes were required to closely monitor environmental change to keep up with important technological changes. Important means to this end included the review of technical publications and active participation in such trade associations as the National Paint and Coatings Association. On the other hand, firms which manufactured less sophisticated products such as house paint tended to be less active in trade associations as their executives felt it was less important to monitor environmental change.

Q: What are some of the major environmental challenges facing U.S. executives in the 1990s? How can they successfully meet them?

A: The 1990s pose many challenges for managers as they work to position their firms effectively in both domestic and foreign markets. Among these are the following:

- Potential new markets in Eastern Europe and other communist bloc countries
- Rapid technological change in many areas leading to the birth of new products such as high-definition television (HDTV) and increasingly sophisticated computers
- Federal and state governments' role in legislation on such key issues as trade, environmental protection, LBOs, and tax codes
- Possible recessionary pressures with macroeconomics factors such as a large federal deficit and trade deficit
- Changing demographic factors such as the growing influence of the baby-boom generation and two-wage-earner families
- Shortcomings of the U.S. educational systems for developing a trained work force for a complex information society.

Such highly complex and uncertain environmental conditions require executives to develop further their ability to scan the environment. The resulting knowledge must be integrated into a thorough understanding of what the organization should achieve. Clearly, executives must solve increasingly complex problems, become proactive in their perspective, and practice contingency planning—that is, the creation of strategic options. Furthermore, the increased competitive pressures in many mature industries such as automobiles and steel heighten the need for a variety of effective competitive strategies—tight cost control, technological and product market innovation, and quick reaction time to market changes.

I believe that future managers must recognize that the "law of requisite variety" applies to management education. An increasingly complex and sophisticated profession requires a more complex and sophisticated educational experience. Students of management should avoid focusing solely on their preferred area(s) of expertise in their course studies. Students must broaden their curriculum with advanced courses outside of business such as in the liberal arts and the physical sciences. Also, both managers and educational institutions need to work together to ensure that skill levels of managers are constantly improved and that the relevance of universities is enhanced.

customers from the environment in a timely and efficient manner. The distribution of organizational factors, namely those individuals, groups, or organizations in the environment who buy the organization's goods or services, provide raw materials, new technologies, capital, labor, information, and competition, will greatly affect how an organization operates. Managers have opportunities to respond to environmental factors in a variety of ways. Efforts to respond to environmental factors by changing organizational activities are referred to as adaptation. Managers may also choose to control environmental factors by setting up favorable linkages with them or by influencing their activities.

Depending on environmental and organizational circumstances, managers may choose to adapt the organization, control the environment, or both. The decision whether to adapt the organization or control the environment will depend on the domains in which the factors are located. For instance, a manufacturer of shoes may adapt to customer demands for style by collecting information about consumer tastes in footwear. At the same time, the firm may be active in lobbying Congress to restrict the import of shoes from manufacturers overseas. The next section describes approaches organizational managers can pursue as a response to their environment.

Organizational Adaptation

Organizational adaptation implies that part or all of the organization is transformed to make its activities more compatible with existing environmental conditions. The greater the amount of uncertainty arising from the environment, the greater the need for managers to seek a variety of ways to adapt the organization.

One way to identify the various techniques that managers can use to adapt the organization to the environment has been presented by James Thompson.[8] Thompson believed that for an organization to be successful when the environment is uncertain, managers must develop strategies and structures to protect the organization's technical core. The **technical core** is an organization's internal operations, which must be conducted in a predictable and orderly manner to be efficient. Thus, mechanisms must be set up that will "seal off" the technical core from environmental factors that might disrupt the internal operations of the organization. Thompson referred to these mechanisms as **coping strategies** because they are designed to cope with uncertainties produced by factors in the environment. The five coping strategies identified by Thompson are buffering, smoothing, forecasting, rationing, and boundary spanning. These and two other coping strategies related to Thompson's list—increasing structural complexity and providing for managerial succession—are discussed in the following sections.

BUFFERING

Organizations can absorb and cope with environmental uncertainty through **buffering**, or setting up buffers for both the input and output sides of organizational activities. **Buffers** may be programs or practices instituted to prevent environmental factors from upsetting the smooth functioning of the production process. On the input side, this may be achieved by stockpiling inventories so that supplies can be provided to the production unit at a steady

*Stockpiling ensures that
an organization can
provide customers with
goods at a steady rate.*

and predictable rate, regardless of changes in resource availability. Restaurants, for instance, may buffer the production of meals by purchasing and freezing large quantities of produce grown seasonally. Other buffering techniques may be stockpiling extra pitchers on a baseball team in case of injuries to the pitching staff during the season.

On the output side, organizations may choose to "dump" their goods or services in markets to prevent the stoppage of activities in production. (*Dumping* means selling a good or service at prices below production costs.) For instance, Japanese steel companies have been accused of dumping steel in the United States to avoid carrying inventory costs on finished goods. This move caused a drop in the price of steel in markets in their own country. The United States has been accused of dumping excess grain into foreign markets because distributing the grain in this country would drive the price of grain down and create unpredictable economic patterns in the commodities market. As a result, many farmers would face bankruptcy, thus affecting their technical core in the severest manner. Figure 3–5 shows how various departments of an organization can be viewed as buffers to safeguard the production process.

SMOOTHING

Organizations that face changes in the demand for their goods or services can cope by adjusting their operations to expected changes in demand. Where buffering absorbs environmental fluctuations, **smoothing** involves efforts to reduce changes in the environment.[9] For example, offering reduced rates for long-distance phone service after 11:00 P.M. serves to decrease demand during peak day hours and shift the demand to a period when demand is normally low. Discounting airline fares in October when vacation travel is low also represents an effort to smooth demand.

FORECASTING

When environmental fluctuations cannot be dealt with effectively by buffering or smoothing, organizations can become actively involved in forecasting

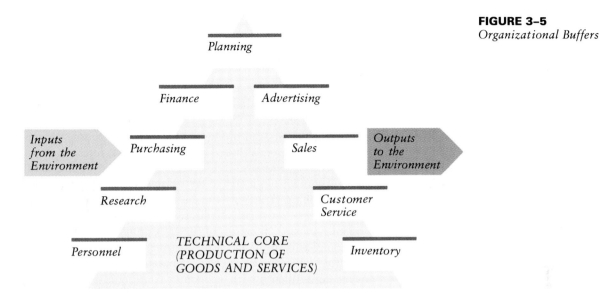

FIGURE 3–5
Organizational Buffers

to follow changes in the environment. **Forecasting** is the collection of past and current information to make predictions about the future. Financial institutions collect economic data to predict the future direction of financial markets. Heublein, Inc., the manufacturer of A-1 steak sauce, predicts future sales based on the price of grain in the commodities market. When the price of grain rises, more cattle are slaughtered for beef to avoid the high cost of feed. The increase in slaughtered cattle leads to a lower cost for beef and an increase in consumption. This, in turn, increases the sales of steak sauce. On the other hand, while the immediate effect is more beef consumption, increased slaughter of cattle also reduces the number of cows producing calves. This eventually leads to a shortage of beef and thus less consumption. Hence, Heublein must monitor the price of grain closely to determine how much steak sauce to manufacture based on this cyclical process.

RATIONING

Organizations can also implement coping strategies that are designed to preserve the most critical functions of the technical core. **Rationing** takes place when organizations ignore some operations and emphasize others. The United States Postal Service will at times ration its activities during high-volume periods, giving first-class mail more attention at the expense of second- and third-class mail. Thus, third-class mail will take a longer time than usual to reach its destination when rationing takes place.

BOUNDARY SPANNING

Boundary spanning is the process of creating roles to open exchanges and coordinate activities with factors in the environment. The creation of such roles serves to reduce uncertainty as boundary spanners gather and collect critical information which can be used for planning in the technical core. The information can be used further to develop activities for adapting the organization to predicted changes in the environment.

Personnel in strategic planning or market research departments serve as boundary spanners. They try to obtain and process information about changes in the external environment and channel that information to organization personnel. In addition, boundary spanners represent the organization to others in the environment.[10] As representatives, boundary spanners provide information about the organization and can develop more awareness of environmental factors. As a result, boundary-spanning activities can serve to reduce environmental uncertainty.

STRUCTURAL COMPLEXITY

A sixth mechanism that managers can use for coping with environmental uncertainty is structural complexity. While Thompson did not refer to **structural complexity** as a coping strategy, it is widely recognized as a critical mechanism by which organizations adapt to environmental uncertainty.[11] Indeed, Thompson's five coping strategies can be subsumed under structural complexity. As open systems, most organizations faced with environmental complexity must adapt to various domains of the environment. Managers can increase structural complexity by creating departments that focus on relationships with specific domains: marketing departments with consumer demands; accounting departments with economic considerations; and production departments with technological developments. Hence, the more complex the environment, the more the need for the organization to adapt by setting up departments (or subsystems) that will respond to specific groupings of factors. Changes in an organization's structure as a method of adaptation to the environment will receive further discussion in Chapters 9 and 22.

EXECUTIVE SUCCESSION

Organizations may try to adapt to environmental uncertainty through executive succession. **Executive succession**, or the replacement of a top manager by another manager, enables an organization to hire executives with new energy and vitality. In addition, the new executives can bring to the organization specific skills needed to analyze and respond to the environment. Increased financial uncertainty in an organization's environment, for instance, may lead to preference for a chief executive officer with financial training. Many large corporations purposely seek executives in their mid-fifties, knowing that tenure in the job will be limited to a decade.[12] New executives can then be hired to replace the retiring executives. In this way organizations can avoid the stagnation that may result when executive officers occupy key decision positions for lengthy periods.

The selection of an adaptive mechanism to cope with environmental uncertainty is critical to an organization's performance. An additional response to environmental uncertainty is to try to control environmental factors.

Environmental Control

Adaptation requires management to alter organizational activities to make them more compatible with existing environmental conditions. Environmental control, on the other hand, requires management to identify and seek to influence environmental factors to obtain more positive effects on organizational activities. Two categories of control methods are (1) creating favorable linkages with key organizations in the environment, and (2) manipulating the environmental domains that the organization wishes to control.[13]

CREATING FAVORABLE LINKAGES

Six methods for creating favorable linkages to reduce environmental uncertainty are available to organization managers.

Mergers

A **merger**, or the acquisition of another organization, can be a method for controlling the environment when the purchased firm is producing uncertainty in the environment. For instance, if a supplier of raw materials is erratic in its shipments to a retailer, managers may choose to buy the company to guarantee a stable flow of materials. Sears has used this technique extensively by purchasing not only raw material suppliers, such as Kenmore appliances, but also companies that provide direct service to customers, such as the Coldwell Banker Real Estate Group, Inc.

Joint Ventures

Joint ventures are used by many companies to reduce environmental uncertainty. Management of General Motors, experiencing uncertainty due to the inability to forecast Japanese auto sales in this country, decided to form a legal relationship with Toyota to produce a car jointly. This move enabled General Motors to become more involved in the sales of Japanese-style cars.

Interlocking Directorates

Managers can expand their boards of directors to include members who serve on the board of directors of other organizations. Such boards are known as **interlocking directorates**. Often the selection of these members is based on the individual's knowledge of a specific environmental domain that is causing uncertainty. Many firms appoint board directors of banks to their board of directors to get information about economic conditions and to receive favorable access to funds. Or individuals may be appointed to a board because they serve on the boards of the firm's competitors, suppliers, or distributors.

Executive Recruitment

Hiring executives with prior experience in other industries is another method that can be used to set up favorable linkages in the environment. Career executives from industries about which the organization needs extensive information can be important in the competition for contracts. Many firms that depend on government contracts hire former administrators of government agencies to learn about the decision process. This also provides the firms with access to the friends of the former administrators who may still work in the contracting agencies. Executive recruitment is different from executive succession in that recruitment is an effort to strengthen linkages with important factors in an organization's environment. Executive succession is an adaptive mechanism designed to hire executives who have skills and information about the organization's environment.

Advertising

Advertising can be used to attract customers and cast the organization in a favorable light. Hallmark Cards, for instance, not only produces advertisements to sell greeting cards but also funds and produces television programs to enhance its image in the minds of the public. Advertising serves to link the organization's goods or services to customers by promoting a favorable image.

Resource Flows

Managers of organizations can set up many types of resource exchanges with other organizations in the environment. They may choose to have exchanges that are frequent or infrequent. They may also choose to have exchanges that are many or few in number. For instance, a manager of a radio station may decide to set up relationships with many music companies to get albums or to rely on only one source. The manager may also want to use a source of albums on a regular basis or to use the source infrequently. How these resource exchanges are set up can be an important decision. For instance, when environments are lean, limiting the number of exchange relationships is better for the performance of the organization. Complex environments call for a more complex network of resource flows.[14]

MANIPULATING THE ENVIRONMENT

Three tactics can be pursued by organizations seeking to manipulate the environment in which they operate: changing domains, lobbying, and forming trade associations.

Changing Domains

Organizations may seek to manipulate their environment by changing one or more of the six domains in which they operate. Usually, this involves a change in markets or the addition of a product line. Many organization managers try to locate markets that have weak competition and are rich in resources. By entering a new domain, the organization can affect current activities in the market in ways that will make the external environment more favorable. For instance, Philip Morris's main line of business for many years was the production of cigarettes. With the realization that the cigarette industry was declining, the company began changing its competitive domain by expanding its line to include beer (Miller) and soft drinks (7-UP).

Lobbying

Lobbying tries to influence decisions made by governmental agencies or legislators. Lobbying usually involves paying an individual to represent the interests of the organization to governmental decision makers. Lobbyists may be employees of the organization or may be hired by the organization on a part-time or full-time basis. Television networks (ABC, CBS, NBC) not only hire lobbyists to influence decisions made by the industry's regulatory agency (the Federal Communications Commission) but also have one of their corporate vice-presidents located in Washington, D.C., to help in the lobbying effort. Lobbying involves persuading key decision makers to uphold existing laws or enact new laws that will be favorable to the organization.

Forming Trade Associations

Perhaps the most common method of manipulating the environment is through trade associations. **Trade associations** are associations of member organizations that share a common interest. Whereas lobbying is conducted by a single organization as an effort to manipulate the environment, trade associations represent a pooling of resources among organizations with similar concerns. The National Association of Realtors, the National Association of Car Dealers, and the National Educational Association are trade associations actively involved in lobbying agencies and legislators to get favorable decisions for their membership. However, since many different interests may be represented in a large trade association, trade associations are generally more concerned with influencing governmental policy than with promoting specific actions that affect the member organizations directly.

Organizations exist in environments that may be helpful or harmful to their survival. Environments take many forms, and it is critical that managers recognize their impact on the organization's activities. Managers can choose to adapt the organization to the environment or try to control environmental factors to make them more responsive to the needs of the organization, or both. In either situation, the goal of the manager is to reduce environmental uncertainty. As uncertainty decreases, the ability of the manager to carry out successful decisions should increase.

ORGANIZATION SET

Another method for understanding an organization's relationship to its environment is to examine the organization set. An **organization set** consists of all the organizations with which a firm has an exchange in order to get necessary resources and achieve goals. Identifying the organization set is useful to managers interested in understanding their organization's relationship with other organizations.

Organizations enter into exchange relationships with other organizations because they need resources to perform their activities. Auto manufacturers buy steel from steel companies. Cars are sold in volume to car-rental agen-

Auto manufacturers are engaged in an exchange relationship with the steel industry.

cies. Links are set up with the Environmental Protection Agency to determine acceptable levels of emitted pollutants. And contracts are made with the United Auto Workers to buy labor, with rubber and tire manufacturers to get specified wheel sizes, and with accounting firms to determine the best way to produce a quality car at the lowest price possible. Each exchange is made possible because the parties involved get a desired value from the exchange, usually in achieving their own organizational goals. Where a desired value is not achieved, exchanges will be ended or renegotiated. Thus, an organization set can be an ever-changing set of exchanges among organizations.

The value to managers of understanding their organization set is in the knowledge about who one must negotiate with as well as what is to be negotiated. Knowledge of the organization set also increases an understanding of the way the environment can force an organization either to adapt to or to control pressures that are external to its operations. The size of the organization set or number of organizations that an organization is linked to is largely determined by the nature of the organization's environment. Sets will usually grow in size as more uncertainty occurs. Expanding the organization set is one response aimed at guaranteeing the acquisition of necessary resources. The types of environmental conditions that are likely to increase the size of the organization set are leanness, instability, complexity, dispersion, turbulence, and dissensus.

Figure 3–6 shows the organization set of a commercial television station. Since the station does not have the capital necessary to produce all of its programming, it must set up exchanges with a major network or syndicated producers to get programs. Other critical exchanges are with advertisers, news services, trade associations, program-rating firms, viewer groups, the Federal Communications Commission, and program suppliers.

Identifying the organization set enables managers to understand the context of their organization with respect to other organizations in the environ-

FIGURE 3–6
*An Organization Set of
a Commercial Television
Station*

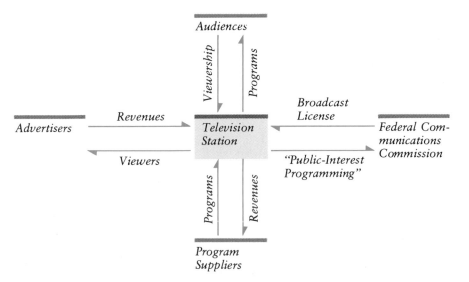

Source: Adapted from Timothy M. Stearns, "A Longitudinal Examination of Performance and Change in the Television Station Industry," unpublished dissertation (1983), 56.

ment. Much of an organization's success depends on understanding the needs of managers of firms within the organization set as well as deciding how to adapt to or influence exchanges with those firms.

IMPLICATIONS FOR MANAGEMENT

This chapter serves as an introduction to the major contextual dimensions of an organization. Early managers viewed the organization as a closed system, failing to consider how the context of the organization would influence activities within the organization. By analyzing the organization from an open-system perspective, we begin to understand the ecology of the organization in a way that will help managers become more effective decision makers.

The environment is an important contextual dimension. Much of what happens in an organization's environment cannot be controlled by its managers. Managers must learn to prepare the organization to respond to uncertainty in the environment. Several useful techniques can be employed to achieve this result. First, managers can distinguish which environmental factors are important and which are not. Factors that clearly affect the operations of the organization should be monitored closely.

Second, factors can be grouped into six environmental domains: economic, political, social, technological, competitive, and physical. Some organizations may have most or all factors located in one domain. Other organizations may have factors evenly distributed among all six environmental domains. Grouping environmental factors into separate domains serves to highlight those that require more attention and the collection of information. It also enables managers to develop mechanisms either to adapt to or to control those factors that influence the activities and performance of the organization.

Third, factors can be plotted along six environmental dimensions: munificence, dynamism, complexity, concentration, turbulence, and consensus. Each dimension has different implications for the organization and the way it relates to its environment. Thinking in terms of the six environmental dimensions enables the manager to understand the direction in which the environment is moving over time. Rich, stable, simple, concentrated, nonconnected, and consensual environments produce the most managerial certainty. Lean, unstable, complex, dispersed, turbulent, and dissensual environments produce the most managerial uncertainty.

While the six dimensions provide an objective view of the way environmental factors are arranged, it does not necessarily follow that managers will perceive the environment as such. When managers perceive a different arrangement of factors, erroneous decisions are likely to occur. This increases the chance of organizational problems or even failure. Hence, managers should be continually collecting information from the environment to understand its present condition and the direction in which the environment is moving over time.

Once an understanding of an organization's environment is achieved, managers can consider methods for either adapting to or controlling the environment. Buffering, smoothing, forecasting, rationing, boundary spanning, structural complexity, and managerial succession can be considered individually or in combination as methods for adapting to the environment. Control of environmental factors to achieve more desirable effects on the organization may be accomplished through linkage techniques such as mergers, joint ventures, interlocking directorates, executive recruitment, advertising, and resource flows. Or managers may manipulate the environment by changing domains, lobbying, or being involved in trade associations. The environment obviously places great demands on organization management in requiring not only an accurate understanding of its conditions but also a proper and timely response to those conditions.

The need for critical resources and markets to produce and distribute goods or services leads an organization to set up exchanges with other organizations in the environment. The number and nature of those exchanges have a significant impact on an organization's activities and performance. Managers should try to identify and understand the types of exchanges that exist not only for their own organization but also for organizations they interact with frequently. Understanding the organization set will enable managers to take into account the implications of their decisions on organizations with which they share resources.

An understanding of the contextual concepts in this chapter provides managers with a working knowledge of how conditions external to the organization shape internal activities. The difficulty of getting information about many contextual features further underscores the complexity of modern management. However, incorporating the ideas presented in this chapter in their decision making increases the chances that managers will produce results helpful to members of the organization and to society.

KEY TERMS AND CONCEPTS

boundary spanning	merger
buffering	monopolistic competition
buffers	monopoly
complexity	munificence
concentration	oligopoly
consensus	organizational adaptation
contextual condition	organization context
coping strategies	organization set
dynamism	perfect competition
environment	rationing
environmental factors	smoothing
executive succession	structural complexity
forecasting	technical core
innovation	trade associations
interlocking directorates	turbulence
joint venture	

QUESTIONS FOR REVIEW AND DISCUSSION

1. In what ways does an understanding of organization context help a manager to make better decisions?
2. In your opinion, which of the six environmental dimensions has the most impact on managerial activities? Which dimension do you believe is least important?

3. How does systems theory provide an understanding of how contextual conditions influence an organization?

4. What are the differences between the six environmental domains?

5. Can you design an organization that would have only factors located in the political domain? The social domain? The technological domain? The physical domain?

6. If a manager were provided with all the information available on the environment, would the environment be "certain"? Why or why not?

7. List the five types of managerial uncertainty that can lead to poor decisions.

8. What is the difference between organizational adaptation and environmental control?

9. What is an organization set? How can managers use knowledge of their organization set to increase their effectiveness?

10. Much public debate focuses on how much influence organizations should have on the political process. Should firms be restricted in using the mechanisms for controlling their environments?

CASES

3–1 MAKING SMALL GETS BIG

Oshkosh B'Gosh, the manufacturer famous for its children's overalls, has a problem that most companies wish they had; it has grown too big for its britches.

Oshkosh, a 91-year-old company long known for its drab overalls and other work clothes, experienced a phenomenal growth spurt in recent years after it discovered that parents adore putting their sons and daughters in pint-size overalls. As a result, Oshkosh's sales more than tripled to $162 million in 1985, from $47 million four years before.

"We had a few years of unbelievable growth," said Charles F. Hyde, Jr., the company's polished, white-haired president and chief executive officer. "All of that growth was a result of children's clothes."

But in selling so many children's overalls, dungarees, jumpers, knit shirts, and blouses, Oshkosh has suffered serious growing pains.

Despite contracting out work, its 11 factories often cannot keep up with demand. Deliveries sometimes arrive late. Stores have been put on an allocation, or quota, system.

"It's hard to sustain a growth rate of 40 percent to 50 percent a year," acknowledged Hyde, whose company is based in Oshkosh, a city of 55,000. "I don't know if we would want to grow that fast even if we could."

The 65-year-old chief executive expressed fears that if Oshkosh continued growing so fast, it might someday saturate the market and fall flat on its face, as Izod did when demand for its faddish alligator leveled off. So Hyde has throttled back the company's growth.

"They've decided to try to manage the growth rather than vice versa," said Jay E. Van Cleave, an analyst with Robert W. Baird & Co. in Milwaukee.

Instead of building factory after factory, Oshkosh has deliberately kept its capacity below demand. Last year it contracted out production of about one-third of the 21 million garments it sold. If demand trails off, Oshkosh will let its contracts lapse rather than get stuck with expensive idle capacity.

"There's more to running a profitable business than having it grow," said Hyde, whose father-in-law bought a controlling share of Oshkosh B'Gosh in 1934. "We're now looking at those things that have suffered in recent years. Our customers want a dependable resource that they can count on."

His goal is to limit sales growth to a still-ambitious 15 percent a year. At that rate, company sales would top $300 million in 1990. The firm's profit for 1985 was $14 million.

Hyde's decision to slow Oshkosh's growth comes after a generational skirmish at the company. "Some of us younger folks always say, 'Let's go for it. Let's run for the roses,'" said Michael D. Wachtel, Hyde's 32-year-old son-in-law and Oshkosh's director of operations. "But Mr. Hyde has some experience that teaches us. He often says, 'Fashion is fickle.'"

In its first 80 years, Oshkosh worried little about fashion. It sold sturdy, lackluster work clothes to farmers, railroad workers, and factory hands. In the last decade, its work clothes sales have slipped because economic changes caused a decline in factory, farm, and railroad employment.

But in the 1970s, Oshkosh happened upon an alternative market: children, the sons and daughters of the baby-boom generation. The discovery came soon after a mail-order house based in Oshkosh, Miles Kimball, included Oshkosh's children's denim overalls and hickory-striped overalls in its catalog. The overalls—the type one imagines Tom Sawyer used to wear—sold like hotcakes.

"Their success made us begin to see what we had," said Douglas W. Hyde, the chief executive's 35-year-old son and the vice-president for merchandising.

Because its sales force concentrated on work clothes, Oshkosh used direct mail to promote its children's wear to dozens of specialty shops and department stores.

Bloomingdale's placed a large order. Other department store buyers followed. Now, children's wear accounts for 80 percent of Oshkosh's sales, up from 15 percent in 1979.

"Oshkosh has become a status item dear to the contemporary mother," said Roger F. Farrington, manager of the youth apparel department for Marshall Field in Chicago. "It's basic everyday play wear that is well styled, has nice colors, and wears well."

As styles changed, Oshkosh moved from just plain denim and striped overalls to more fashionable ones. Indeed, it has done with children's overalls what George Washington Carver did with the peanut. Oshkosh has come up with baggy overalls, painter's overalls, overalls with crossover straps, overalls with short legs called shortalls, and overalls with bright prints that look like fingerpaint.

"It started out as a reverse snob appeal," said the elder Hyde of the denim and striped overalls. "It became popular when everyone was dressing down, wearing overalls and five-pocket jeans. They were dressing their children the same way as themselves.

"But today," he continued, "people are dressing with a more upbeat fashion look, so we have introduced a more upbeat product line."

In addition, Oshkosh—recognizing that parents buy two tops for each bottom that a child wears—started to sell knit blouses, shirts, sweaters, and jackets. The tops, which were introduced in 1981, now represent one-third of the company's children's wear sales.

Oshkosh officials say they are going after prosperous customers. The company's prices are lower than Ralph Lauren's Polo line for children, but generally more expensive than such competitors as Health-Tex, Carter's, and Buster Brown. Its children's shirts and blouses sell for $10 to $12 and its jeans, pants, and overalls sell for $12.50 to $25.

"More children are being born nowadays, and couples are having them later in life, when they're able to spend more on clothes," said Brenda Gall, an analyst with Merrill Lynch. "In addition, many families are having fewer children, so they have more money to spread around for clothes. And maybe they buy better things for their children because they feel guilty because both parents are working."

Charles Hyde said Oshkosh can thrive, even though production costs at its plants in Tennessee, Kentucky, and Wisconsin are higher than the cost of imported goods, because the company is known for high quality. Besides, he said, "We're perceived as an All-American product."

The company, which now focuses on girls and boys below the age of 6, plans to pay more attention to older children as the offspring of the baby boomers grow up.

"I'm less sanguine about the prospects for some of the newer areas," said Gall of Merrill Lynch. "I don't think mothers will necessarily spend premium prices on sleepwear. Since the neighbors don't see the sleepwear on the child, mothers might want to be more price conscious."

And she sees problems for Oshkosh in the market for ages 6 through 12. "As soon as children start picking out their own things, it becomes a different ball game," she said. "In the larger sizes, boys are going to want to wear what their big brother is wearing, not what their little brother is wearing."

But Oshkosh executives have heard critics say many times before that they were a fad.

"Our popularity has started to level off," Douglas Hyde acknowledged. "But I don't think that one day parents will wake up and say, " 'Ugh, we don't want Oshkosh anymore.' "

Source: Steven Greenhouse, "Growing Pains for Oshkosh," *The New York Times,* February 22, 1986. Copyright © 1986 by The New York Times Company. Reprinted by permission.

1. Identify the environmental domains that affect Oshkosh B'Gosh. Which environmental domain causes the most uncertainty for management? Why?
2. Locate Oshkosh B'Gosh on the six environmental dimensions. Which environmental dimension do you feel produces the greatest amount of uncertainty for the firm?
3. Identify and describe the firms that are part of Oshkosh B'Gosh's organization set. Which firm in the organization set is most responsible for generating rapid growth in sales? Why?
4. How might management of Oshkosh B'Gosh use the coping strategies identified in the text to adapt to their environment? How might management apply techniques of environmental control to handle their growth?

3–2 HOW MANY WAYS CAN YOU SLICE APPLE PIE?

From the offices of Claritas, Robin Page can see the Potomac River clearly. From the computer printout on his desk, he gets almost as vivid a picture of Thomaston, Georgia.

The printout shows that Thomaston is what Claritas calls a Norma Rae-ville.

That label suggests that people there read the *National Enquirer,* watch roller derby, buy plenty of curling irons, hairsetting lotions, and deviled ham, love Hardee's — and are just like people in Childersburg, Alabama, or Tarboro, North Carolina.

"Mill town south," says Mr. Page, a senior vice-president at the marketing firm. "Baptist church people, most of them, living small-town lives with small-town pleasures."

Huntington, New York, on the other hand, is no Norma Rae-ville. For the most part, it is classic Furs and Station Wagons. People there tend to belong to country clubs, Mr. Page says; they have new homes and new money and are big buyers of electric toothbrushes and depilatories.

By contrast, the Detroit suburb of Fraser is mostly Blue Chip Blues. "The top of the blue-collar world," says Mr. Page. Large families. Above-ground swimming pools. "These guys," he says, "have big powerboats in their driveways and lots of money in their jeans."

Claritas specializes in geo-demography. Through its computer system called Prizm, it has reduced the vast, diverse, and confusing U.S. market to its most basic common denominator, the neighborhood.

Sometimes, as in the case of Thomaston, Claritas can apply one label to an entire town. But most places aren't that homogeneous; so the firm has gone further. From such information as income, education, and occupations, it has pigeonholed the country's 240,000 neighborhoods into 40 different prototypes and can, often with amazing accuracy, describe life in each, from the type of aspirin in the medicine cabinet to the magazines on the coffee table. What's more, Prizm has fine-tuned its crunching of U.S. Census data, the guts of the system, and sliced its neighborhoods down in units of 340 households.

As rapid social change in America continues to unravel the mass market for most new products, the data sold by information packagers like Claritas are in increasing demand. The old labels aren't very useful anymore.

High-tech and service jobs have eroded the differences between white and blue collar; double incomes and divorce rates have blurred the differences between upper and lower class. Consumers are not only harder to understand but also harder reach, with their overstuffed mailboxes and their VCRs.

In this chaos, Prizm helps predict which consumers are likeliest to open an envelope, which will drive by a billboard, which will respond to a radio ad. "We try to help marketers get closer to their nirvana, which is to have the name, address, and 1001 facts about each of their customers," says Bruce Carroll, the managing general partner of Claritas. The concern's growing client list now ranges from Coca-Cola Company and General Motors Corporation to evangelist groups like the Oral Roberts organization.

Some marketers don't think the Prizm system works. "They try to be precise, but I'm not sure Prizm is anything more than sweeping generalizations," says Ronald Paul, a Chicago-based marketing consultant. "They try to make a case that people in Lake Forest, Illinois, are the same as the people in Buckhead [a section of Atlanta]," which may be true in the case of private schools, he says, but not when it comes to restaurants.

Prizm does seem extremely precise about the Honda Accord, though. You drive one? Prizm says you are likely also to own a VCR or a personal computer. You probably play racquetball at your health club, ski, and own a 35-mm camera. You are probably "somebody who at least fancies himself to be very discerning and discriminating—the kind who would read *Consumer Reports* to make an educated buy," says Daniel Wojcik, one Prizm marketer.

Such insights proved valuable to Matthew Peterson, a marketing manager for Mountain Bell Telephone Co. in Denver. Until recently, he was certain the best customers for his call-waiting and call-forwarding services were Young Suburbias and other parents. "Our internal analysis showed that kids were it," he says.

A Prizm breakdown of subscribers to those services showed that, on the contrary, his best customers were childless Young Influentials, who are ambitious and active and hate missing important phone calls. In fact, says Mr. Peterson, "we had missed our biggest market."

Through Prizm, General Motors' Buick division keeps an eagle eye on its markets, for it knows how quickly things change. By mid-1984, its once-prestigious Buick Electra had lost much of its cachet in ritzy neighborhoods and had become instead a status symbol in rural, downscale Norma Rae-villes and among Back-Country Folks and Sharecroppers. Those people "liked to buy cars for image and liked them to be big, prestigious, bulky," recalls Paula Travenia, a marketing research supervisor for Buick.

When Buick introduced a shorter, more svelte 1985 Electra, Ms. Travenia recalls holding her breath. "We really didn't know what to expect," she says. Within three months, however, Prizm showed Buick it had been right in its calculated risk. The new model had made steady gains in such neighborhoods as Furs and Station Wagons, Young Suburbias, and Pools and Patios—and, incidentally, lost some of its favor in the Sharecropper neighborhoods.

Many marketers are using Prizm-type data to trim or revamp their advertising budgets. Until last year, Days Inns Corporation spent $3 million on radio, TV, and newspaper ads designed to reach $25,000 to $45,000 households, on the hunch that such households contained penny-pinching travelers. "We would blast out and hope we'd hit," says Michael Leven, the president of the chain of low-price hotels. This year, Days Inns is spending instead about $2 million on a more targeted, Prizm-based mail campaign. "If we want to go to the Southeast, they'll tell us where," says Mr. Leven.

Source: Reprinted by permission of *The Wall Street Journal*. © Dow Jones & Company, Inc. (November 3, 1986). All Rights Reserved Worldwide.

1. In which environmental domain do you believe the services of Prizm are most helpful? Can you identify a company or industry that would not benefit from the services of Prizm?
2. What environmental dimension(s) does Prizm help managers to understand?
3. Does the information from Prizm increase or decrease uncertainty for managers? What type of uncertainty does it affect?
4. Does Prizm help managers to adapt to or control their environment? Explain.

1. J. Pfeffer and G. Salancik, *The External Control of Organizations: A Resource Dependence Perspective* (New York: Harper & Row, 1978), 1.
2. For a more extended discussion of the systems concept and its application to management theory, see L. von Bertalanffy, "The History and Status of General Systems Theory," *Academy of Management Journal* 15 (1972): 407-426.
3. *Capital Times*, Madison, WI (November 14, 1984), 2.
4. For an extended discussion of these dimensions and their application to organization theory, see Chapter 3 of H. E. Aldrich, *Organizations and Environments* (Englewood Cliffs, NJ: Prentice-Hall, 1979).
5. D. J. Hickson et al., "A Strategic Contingencies Theory of Intraorganizational Power," *Administrative Science Quarterly* 16 (June 1971): 216-229.
6. R. Miles, *Macro Organizational Behavior* (Glenview, IL: Scott, Foresman, 1980), 199.
7. See W. R. Scott, *Organizations: Rational, Natural and Open Systems* (Englewood Cliffs, NJ: Prentice-Hall, 1981), 168-169, for a partial summary of these conclusions.
8. J. D. Thompson, *Organizations in Action* (New York: McGraw-Hill, 1967), 20-21.
9. Ibid., 21.
10. H. Aldrich and D. Herker, "Boundary-Spanning Roles and Organization Structure," *Academy of Management Review* 2 (1977): 217-230.
11. See T. Burns and G. M. Stalker, *The Management of Innovation* (London: Tavistock, 1961), and P. R. Lawrence and J. W. Lorsch, *Organization and Environment* (Cambridge, MA: Harvard University Division of Research, 1967).
12. See O. Grusky, "Corporate Size, Bureaucratization, and Managerial Succession," *American Journal of Sociology* 67 (November 1961): 355-359.
13. J. P. Kotter, "Managing External Dependence," *Academy of Management Review* 4 (January 1979): 87-92.
14. T. Stearns, A. Hoffman, and J. Heide, "Performance of Commercial Television Stations as an Outcome of Interorganizational Linkages and Environmental Conditions," *Academy of Management Journal* 30 (March 1987): 71-90.

Ethics and Social Responsibility

CHAPTER 4

After studying this chapter, you should be able to:
- *Identify factors influencing ethical behavior and discuss how ethical behavior can be encouraged.*
- *Define social responsibility and present four viewpoints on the social responsibility of business.*
- *Identify parties to whom a business may have social responsibilities.*
- *Discuss costs and benefits of social responsibility.*
- *Identify guidelines for planning and organizing social actions.*
- *Discuss the social audit.*

In this chapter, we will examine the closely related topics of business ethics and the social responsibility of business. First, we will discuss business ethics. We will consider the demand for ethical behavior, examine the sorts of ethical dilemmas facing businesspersons, review factors known to influence ethical behavior, and highlight specific actions that firms can take to encourage their employees to behave ethically. We will then shift our focus from behavior of employees to social actions of the firm. We will examine differing views on the social responsibility of business, identify parties to whom business may have responsibilities, identify costs and benefits of social actions, outline steps in planning and organizing for social actions, and discuss the social audit.

BUSINESS ETHICS

Ethics are principles of morality or rules of conduct. **Business ethics** are rules about how businesses and their employees ought to behave. Ethical behavior conforms to these rules; unethical behavior violates them.

During the late 1980s, business ethics were regularly in the headlines. In October 1988, Stephen Sui-Kuan Wang, Jr., a former analyst for Morgan Stanley & Co., was sentenced to a three-year prison term, to be followed by three years of probation, for participating in a multimillion-dollar insider-trading scheme. That sentence followed prison sentences and stiff fines for Ivan Boesky and other Wall Street inside traders that sent shock waves through the investment community in 1987.[1] In December 1988, the Wall Street firm of Drexel Burnham Lambert agreed to plead guilty to six felony counts of mail, wire, and securities fraud and to pay $650 million in fines and restitution.[2] Michael Milken, head of Drexel's Beverly Hills, California, junk bond office, faced a 98-count federal government indictment charging him with racketeering and other offenses related to securities trading.[3] Also in 1988, several companies, including Rockwell International Corp., faced criminal indictments charging fraud on defense contracts, including double billing, making false statements to auditors, and mail fraud. Officials at Rockwell and other firms charged with fraud each faced fines of up to $500,000 and 30-year-maximum prison terms.[4] A 1987 book entitled *The Complete Book of Wall Street Business Ethics* featured 158 blank pages. Management in Action 1 presents the case of a major bank charged with laundering illegal drug money.

The Demand for Ethical Behavior

Businesses, governments, and the public are all paying more attention to business ethics. The Foreign Corrupt Practices Act of 1977 requires that companies operate ethically. When such conduct is not forthcoming, the government will use all legal means at its disposal to correct the problem.

Bribes and kickbacks have come under particularly close scrutiny lately. A kickback may be seen in the following example:

A retailer hires a market researcher to find a choice location for a new retail store. The retailer does not know that the researcher has previously agreed to recommend the property of a real estate developer in return for a secret percentage of the first year's rental payment on the property.

On October 11, 1988, in Tampa, Florida, the Federal Government charged that an international bank holding company had conspired with cocaine dealers

WE INVITE YOU TO BE WITH US

to launder millions of dollars in illegal drug money in a network that reached from the United States to Europe to the Medellin drug cartel in Colombia. The announcement capped a series of raids in the United States, France, and Britain that rounded up 44 suspects. In all, federal officials said 85 people in seven U.S. cities had been named in indictments in the case. Nine of them were executives of the bank, the Bank of Credit and Commerce International S.A., and its holding company, BCCI Holdings.

The officials said that BCCI, a Luxembourg-based concern owned by wealthy Persian Gulf investors, with assets of more than $20 billion and offices in more than 70 countries, was the first financial institution to be indicted for laundering money. The BCCI probe represents an acceleration of Washington's campaign to ferret out financial abuses involving foreign players, and was the first coordinated transatlantic effort against money laundering.

The indictments came after a two-year undercover investigation in which Customs Service agents posed as experts on money laundering, acting as intermediaries to transfer $14 million between drug dealers and the bank. Eleven of those indicted were arrested after coming to Tampa for what they thought would be the wedding of two friends. They had even received engraved invitations. "We invite you to be with us as we begin our new life together," the invitations had read. But the friends had, in fact, been among the undercover agents involved in the case for two years. The eleven were seized as they entered what they had expected to be a bachelor party before the wedding.

Although only BCCI was named in the case, Customs officials said they did not believe it was uncommon for banks to launder money for drug dealers — that is, to find ways to disguise the flow of cash to make it harder to link to criminal activities. The indictments state that the proceeds of drug sales in several major U.S. cities were received by BCCI from the undercover agents. BCCI next shifted the money by wire to branches in France, Panama, Luxembourg, and elsewhere. Then, through a series of financial maneuvers, the funds were shifted from country to country, making them difficult to trace.

The officials clearly hope the indictment will be a strong deterrent. Money laundering is punishable by a maximum term of 20 years in prison and a fine of $500,000 or twice the value of the property laundered, whichever is greater. BCCI, as an institution, would face a maximum fine of $28 million.

Source: Adapted from Jeffrey Schmalz, "Bank Is Charged by U.S. with Money-Laundering," *New York Times* (October 12, 1988): 1, 34, and "This Bank May Have Been a Laundry, Too," *Business Week* (October 24, 1988): 29-30.

Bribery is especially a problem in overseas dealings. The Justice Department conducted a three-year criminal investigation of the Lockheed Corporation's overseas payments. Lockheed subsequently pleaded guilty to charges of concealing payoffs to Japanese business and government officials and was fined $647,000. In another instance, Brunswick Corporation admitted to the Securities and Exchange Commission that it had paid bribes to two Latin American countries to win contracts. And the Joseph Schlitz Brewing Company faced a 747-count federal indictment for giving kickbacks and other inducements to beer retailers and distributors in exchange for their business. It later agreed to pay a $750,000 penalty in a settlement.

More recently, Rockwell International, General Dynamics, General Electric Company, and other large companies have been charged with defrauding the Pentagon, and insider-trading scandals have been rampant. E. F. Hutton was caught in an illegal check-kiting scheme. MiniScribe, an apparently successful manufacturer of computer disk drives, admitted that it had "cooked the books," giving the appearance of rising sales (and thus misleading investors and others) by shipping more disk drives than had been ordered and claiming to have shipped drives on a freighter that simply didn't exist; when the fraud was revealed, MiniScribe's stock price tumbled from $15 to less than $3.[5] The shocking case of Beech-Nut Nutrition Corporation's sale of phony apple juice for babies is discussed in Case 4–2.

Ethical Dilemmas

It is easy to say that individuals in organizations should behave ethically. Some behaviors, such as employee theft, are clearly unethical. In other situations, however, it is often very difficult to determine exactly what is or is not ethical. For instance, computer software is protected by copyright laws, and copying is punishable by fines of up to $50,000 and a year in jail. But illegal copying of software is a common practice. Many people who would quickly condemn theft apparently see no ethical problems with software copying. Further, in addition to making ethical decisions about our own acts, we must often face the issue of how to deal with the unethical behavior of others. For instance, how would you react if you learned that a colleague was making personal phone calls from work, or that your firm was secretly polluting a community lake, or if your boss suggested that you pad your expense account, or if you found that a colleague had lied on her job application?[6]

Whistleblowers

Consider now the case of an employee who learns that his or her company engages in bribery or some other illegal activity. The employee can keep quiet, report the incident to top management, or even tell the press about the incident. By going outside the company, the employee is "blowing the whistle." **Whistleblowers** may find their jobs and careers are in jeopardy.

For instance, Robert Wityczak was an employee of Rockwell International. He testified in 1985 before a Senate subcommittee that his supervisors

The copying of software is not always perceived as unethical behavior.

reacted angrily when he told them that he would no longer mischarge labor and other items to NASA's space shuttle project. Gradually, he reported, he was squeezed from his purchasing job at the company, stripped of his confidential clearance, and put to work making coffee and sweeping floors. A Vietnam veteran who had lost both legs and a hand in the war, Wityczak testified that such tasks aggravated a back problem and forced him to take a temporary medical leave. When he returned to work, he was fired. Rockwell recently settled a wrongful-discharge suit with Wityczak for an undisclosed sum.[7]

Factors Influencing Ethical Behavior

Unethical behavior does not occur in a vacuum. Like other behaviors in organizations, it is a function of the situation, reward systems, individual differences, and other factors.

For instance, one study found that such ethical violations by firms as price fixing and other illegal competitive relationships were more common when firms faced lean environments than when those environments were rich.[8] That is, difficult financial situations encouraged firms to engage in unethical activity.

Another series of studies assessed causes of unethical behavior.[9] They used simulations in which subjects played the role of regional sales manager for a large wholesaling firm. Subjects had to deal with decisions on whether to pay kickbacks to purchasing agents. The unethical behavior of offering kickbacks was related to personality characteristics, rewards and punishments, competition, and organizational policies and statements.

In particular, the researchers found that those with a Machiavellian orientation, those who felt they had little control over their own fates, and those with economic or political value orientations tended to engage more often in unethical behavior. When subjects felt unethical behaviors would increase their rewards, unethical behavior increased. When there was the possibility not only of increased rewards but also of public exposure and a fine, however, unethical behavior dropped to a level below even that when neither rewards nor punishment would result from the behavior. Unethical behavior increased when subjects were in competition. It decreased when a clear statement was issued in favor of ethical behavior by the organization's president or when an ethics objective was assigned by the organization.

Encouraging Ethical Behavior

The findings discussed in the previous section clearly suggest that organizations can encourage ethical behavior. If a firm is serious about the ethical behavior of its employees, it must take concrete actions such as those shown in Figure 4–1.

CODES OF ETHICS

Over 90 percent of U.S. companies have a **code of ethics** setting forth principles of appropriate behavior.[10] Such codes generally address such topics as conflict of interest, confidentiality of corporate information, misappropriation of corporate assets, bribes and kickbacks, and political contributions. Some also contain sections on the company's responsibilities to its various

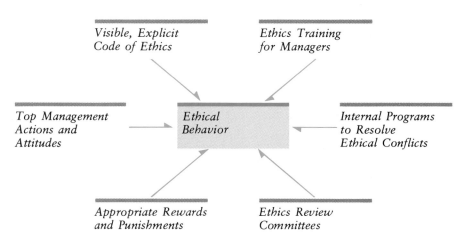

FIGURE 4–1
Ways to Encourage Ethical Behavior

Source: William H. Cunningham, Ramon J. Aldag, and Christopher M. Swift, *Introduction to Business,* 2d ed. (Cincinnati: South-Western Publishing Co., 1989), 589. Reproduced with permission.

constituencies. For example, the Bank of America's "Code of Corporate Conduct" includes 77 separate items that detail the responsibilities of the company and its employees. The code prohibits bribes and kickbacks and emphasizes the importance of full disclosure to prevent misconduct. McGraw-Hill, Inc., a publishing house, has a "Code of Business Ethics" guaranteeing the privacy of employee personnel and payroll records. Chevron Corp. produced a 31-page booklet titled "Our Business Conduct: Principles and Practices" which touches on accounting and internal standards, conflicts of interest and confidential information, government regulations, health and safety, antitrust, multinational operations, and other matters.

While companies have scrambled in recent years to adopt formal codes of ethics, such codes are not without their critics. Some employees feel pressured to accept the codes and resent having their values questioned. And many ethics specialists argue that codes of ethics are window dressing, intended to look good but not interfere with the realities of the business world.[11]

Clearly, if a code of ethics is to make a real difference, it must be carefully designed and implemented. A code is most likely to be accepted by employees if it is developed through a process that involves line managers and others who are affected by the code, rather than just by company lawyers.[12] Of course, employees must be made aware of the code—but in fact only about two-thirds of all companies with codes distribute them to all employees. In addition, a company should make sure that the code specifies procedures for handling violations and that these procedures are fairly enforced. Further, the code should be revised as the company's product line or competitive practices change. Also, the code must be internally consistent. Separate statements saying "Do not discriminate in hiring and promotion" and "Act affirmatively to hire and promote women and minorities" leave the manager torn.[13]

REWARDS AND PUNISHMENTS

The evidence we reviewed concerning factors influencing ethical behavior indicates that the ways in which employees are rewarded or punished for their ethical and unethical actions should influence the likelihood of future ethical violations. Some firms are making it clear that unethical behavior will be punished. For instance, a 1987 study revealed that 60 percent of 238 surveyed companies with ethics codes included specific penalties for code violations. Half of the companies included termination as a potential penalty, while 30 percent included suspension. Probation, demotion, and negative comments on performance appraisals were reported as potential penalties by 21, 19, and 14 percent, respectively, of the surveyed companies.[14] However, perhaps because ethical behavior is simply expected, examples of firms that specifically offer rewards for ethical behavior are notably lacking.

INTERNAL PROGRAMS

Besides developing an effective code of ethics, making it available and explicit, and providing appropriate rewards and punishments, a company can encourage ethical behavior through other positive actions. For instance, some firms have internal programs to resolve ethical conflicts. One example is IBM, which has had a "Speak Up!" program for more than 25 years. This program allows an employee to appeal any supervisory action and to get a mailed response to the appeal without having the employee's name communicated to the supervisor. A meeting between the employee and management is arranged if necessary. Unfortunately, few companies currently have such internal programs for resolving ethical conflicts.

ETHICS REVIEW COMMITTEES

Other corporations have review committees made up of people specially trained to deal with ethical issues. These committees are composed of people from both inside and outside the company. The committee's role is to advise directors on sensitive ethical matters. In a 1985 survey, about a third of 279 responding top U.S. corporations had created high-level ethics committees, and 17 had ombudsmen or hot lines to provide "escape routes" for employees reluctant to raise ethical problems through normal channels. A 1987 survey found that 18 percent of a group of the largest U.S. companies have an ethics committee, 8 percent have an ombudsman, and 1 percent have a formal judicial board.[15]

ETHICS TRAINING

Ethics training is a part of some management development programs. The training usually includes discussions among the program participants of real problems they have faced at work or of hypothetical situations such as were discussed earlier. Alternative ways of dealing with each problem are then explored, and probing questions are asked: "How would I feel if my family found out about my behavior? How would I feel if I saw it printed in the newspaper?"[16] In the mid-1980s, companies such as General Dynamics, McDonnell Douglas Corp., Chemical Bank, and American Can Company initiated such programs.

TOP-MANAGEMENT ACTIONS AND ATTITUDES

Whether employees behave ethically depends largely on the actions and attitudes of top management. For instance, if a code of ethics tells employees that bribing overseas clients is against company policy but management turns the other way when bribes are successful in winning large contracts, the code is unlikely to be taken seriously. Further, companies must not encourage unethical behavior by setting unrealistic goals that can be met only by cutting ethical corners, and they must not condone cheating to "help" the company. TRW Inc. in 1985 dismissed or disciplined 30 employees for "irregularities and unethical behavior." The employees had been overstating the time they spent on military projects in order to overcharge the government.[17]

THE SOCIAL RESPONSIBILITY OF BUSINESS

On December 3, 1984, a deadly cloud of methyl isocyanate gas leaked from the Union Carbide Corp. chemical plant in Bhopal, India, and covered a 25-square-mile area. By the time it cleared, 3,329 people were dead and the lives of hundreds of thousands were ruined. The company faced lawsuits totaling tens of billions of dollars, investigations into the company's safety procedures, and allegations about management's prior knowledge of the dangers. For four years, effigies of Warren Anderson, then chairman of Union Carbide, were destroyed on Bhopal's streets. The Union Carbide plant hasn't reopened; the graffiti on the plant gate—"Carbide Kills"—is fading. In February 1989 Union Carbide agreed to pay an Indian government-negotiated $470 million in compensation to resolve all civil and criminal claims. Many called the settlement appallingly low. A company spokesperson said, "This is the end of it."[18]

Union Carbide isn't the only company which has been the focus of vocal criticism in recent years. Nestlé Corp.'s sales of infant formula in developing countries sparked protests and boycotts charging that Nestlé was contributing to malnutrition by discouraging breastfeeding. General Motors is still feeling the effects of criticisms of the Corvair's safety record. And Burroughs Wellcome Co., the manufacturer of the acquired immune deficiency syndrome (AIDS) drug AZT, was stung by harsh criticisms that its $198 million profit in fiscal year 1988 was at the expense of AIDS victims; activists staged demonstrations in San Francisco, London, and New York calling Wellcome a corporate extortionist and pasted "AIDS profiteer" stickers on Wellcome products.[19]

But consider these facts: Celanese, a chemical company, gave the National Audubon Society $400,000 for research on the Atlantic puffin, the California condor, and other endangered bird species. Aetna Life and Casualty, an insurance firm, provided nearly $6 million in grants in a single year for such varied purposes as publishing a bilingual community newspaper, supporting a program of legal aid for female criminal offenders, and expanding a news service for American Indians. Shell Oil contributed $2 million for testing Interferon, an antiviral drug that may be effective against cancer. Lyphomed, Inc., a drug manufacturer, announced that it planned to distribute free to indigent patients an aerosol drug that can prevent a type of pneumonia that kills as many as 80 percent of all AIDS patients.[20]

Bhopal, baby formula, puffins, and papers are a strange assortment, reflecting the many sides of the topic of social responsibility. In this portion of the chapter we will explore viewpoints on social responsibility, identify interested parties, assess costs and benefits of social actions, consider planning and organizing for social issues, and discuss the social audit.

Corporations fulfill their social responsibility by sponsoring various community programs.

WHAT IS SOCIAL RESPONSIBILITY?

Most people would agree that the **social responsibility** of business reflects business's concern for the social as well as the economic effects of its decisions. That is, it relates to the need for business to fulfill social expectations, and perhaps needs, adequately. Beyond these general statements, there is less agreement. Some see economic and social effects as completely congruent, while others see them as potentially in conflict. To some, social responsibility might be evidenced by a company's willingness to incur costs that do not relate directly to the company's production of goods and services. To others, the acceptance of such costs would be seen as a violation of social responsibility. To some, such actions as voluntarily controlling smokestack emissions or building a Little League baseball diamond would fall under the mantle of social responsibility. Others would see those actions as clearly outside the legitimate social role of business. Some socially impacting actions by firms are presented in Figure 4–2.

VIEWS ON SOCIAL RESPONSIBILITY[21]

It is easy to say that firms should be socially responsible, but there is far less agreement on exactly what social responsibility means. Let's consider some viewpoints on this complex, important, and often emotion-laden issue.

The Classical View

The English economist Adam Smith in 1776 propounded what is now known as the **classical view** of market economics and social welfare. In essence, Smith argued against government involvement in a market economy to set price or determine output. Smith equated the self-interest of private enterprises, each acting individually, with the general interest of society. That is, when businesses attempt to maximize their profits by making appropriate decisions in a competitive market environment, they also unintentionally

FIGURE 4–2
*Some Notable Corporate
Social Actions*

- *Time, Inc.,* the nation's largest magazine publisher, donated 2,138 acres of land in Texas to the Nature Conservancy for use as a nature sanctuary. The land has great ecological significance, harboring 340 species of wildflowers.

- *The Fingerhut Corporation,* a Minnesota direct-mail marketing company, reimburses employees for cab fares when they take a taxi home rather than driving while intoxicated. The company also gave smoke detectors to its 2,600 employees for installation in their homes.

- *New England Mutual Life Insurance Company* pays all tuition costs to degree-granting institutions for its home-office employees. About 200, or 10 percent, of these employees are enrolled in such institutions.

- *Safeway Stores,* the nation's largest supermarket chain, has a specially designed shopping cart for customers in wheelchairs. The cart clamps firmly to the wheelchair for easy maneuverability. There is at least one cart in each of Safeway's 2,000 stores.

- *Portland General Electric Company,* at the urging of its senior citizens representative, implemented a seminar on the dangers of hypothermia. The seminar has been attended by about 2,000 people and is credited with saving at least four lives.

- *Aetna, Prudential,* and *Arco* are among 300 corporate sponsors of the Local Initiatives Support Corp. (LISC). LISC makes low-interest loans to neighborhood rehabilitation projects aimed at halting and reversing urban decay.

Source: William H. Cunningham, Ramon J. Aldag, and Christopher M. Swift, *Introduction to Business,* 2d ed. (Cincinnati: South-Western Publishing Co., 1989), 580. Reproduced with permission.

promote the public or social interest. They are guided, as if by an **"invisible hand,"** to use society's scarce resources for the greater good of all. According to this view, any action not in the best interest of the firm works against the invisible hand and reduces good to the community. As stated by economist Milton Friedman, "The business of business is business."

ARGUMENTS IN FAVOR OF THE CLASSICAL VIEW

Proponents of the classical view of business argue, first, that harm will result if a business tries to achieve any end except its own well-being. Classical thinkers believe that business has an implied contract with society to use resources effectively—or to use resources to promote the business, which in turn promotes society. If a business begins to spend time and money directly on some social issue, such as sponsoring a community drug rehabilitation program, then the business will be breaking the contract to use its resources for itself.

Second, classical thinkers believe that the voting public, not the people in business, should set social priorities. If the public wants certain social problems solved, then the public should work through legislative bodies for the passage of appropriate laws. Letting businesses set social priorities takes power away from the majority and gives it to the few.

Finally, proponents of the classical view may argue that social issues are better handled by expert social planners than by companies. Business managers should stick to what they know: running businesses.

ARGUMENTS AGAINST THE CLASSICAL VIEW

According to its many critics, the classical view of the role of business in society is based on narrow thinking and outdated assumptions. The classical view, the critics say, assumes that individual firms have no market power and no control over prices. Such perfect competition is more an ideal than a reality.

The classical view also assumes that businesses can stay healthy in a sick society. But in reality, say critics, the pace of industrial society places a great deal of stress on the environment and on the emotional and physical health of workers. In the long run, can a firm operate profitably if clean air and water are scarce, or if the work force deteriorates because of health problems?

Another argument against the classical view is that it does not acknowledge that society has certain expectations of how businesses should act. In fact, these expectations go beyond those set down in law. Society is made up of organizations—corporations, nonprofit groups, churches—as much as it is made up of people. Just as the actions of individuals affect society, so do the actions of organizations. Therefore, if we expect socially responsible behavior from individuals, why not expect the same from organizations?

In a sense, many of the attacks on the classical view reflect a variety of criticisms about business itself as it exists and operates in contemporary society. Neil Jacoby summarizes those criticisms as follows:[22]

- Big businesses exercise concentrated economic power contrary to the public interest.
- Big businesses are controlled by a self-perpetuating, irresponsible "power elite."
- Big businesses exploit and dehumanize workers and consumers.
- Big businesses degrade the environment and the quality of life.

Whether or not we agree with these criticisms, we must recognize that they are rather widely held. In response to arguments against the classical view, at least three alternative viewpoints have emerged.

The Constrainer View

Constrainers view business enterprises as essentially indifferent to the social consequences of their actions or feel that businesses tend to act irresponsibly unless constrained by legal and political means. This group calls for strict laws to govern product safety, advertising, pollution, and competitive practices. The excerpt "A Body to Be Kicked" reflects some concerns and reactions of constrainers.

The Foreboder View

Foreboders believe that businesses must contribute to social improvement; otherwise, social problems will worsen and government will be forced to step in. Promoting such social improvement was the goal of the 51-company partnership, including the Ford Motor Company and several life insurance firms, which backed the construction of the Detroit Renaissance Center. The Renaissance Center, built in a decaying section of the Detroit waterfront, contains the world's largest hotel and four massive office buildings. Whatever the im-

A BODY TO BE KICKED

A 19th-century English judge, Edward Baron Thurlow, lamented in a court decision, "Did you ever expect a corporation to have a conscience when it has no soul to be damned and no body to be kicked?" Then he whispered, "By God, it ought to have both."

A century later, Jay Magnuson went looking for a body to kick when an elderly Polish immigrant died of cyanide poisoning in the suburban Chicago plant of Film Recovery Systems, Inc. After an eight-month investigation, the Illinois assistant state's attorney general brought, in October 1983, what may be the first case in the United States charging corporate officials with murder in a work-related death.

Film Recovery's workers used cyanide to extract silver from film scraps. Prosecutors say that they may have evidence that the workers, mostly non-English-speaking immigrants, weren't warned about the dangers of cyanide and were provided minimal safety equipment.

In February 1983, Stephan Golab, a 61-year-old Polish immigrant, collapsed and died near an open vat of cyanide, his colleagues said. The Cook County medical examiner ruled that Mr. Golab died from cyanide poisoning and that his death was a homicide. The plant was closed and federal regulators fined the company $2,425 for safety violations. A Cook County grand jury indicted five company officials for murder.

Now the idea of applying criminal laws to corporate executives is getting increased attention worldwide. The impetus is the mass poisoning in Bhopal, India, where more than 2,000 people died after a Union Carbide Corp. plant accidentally released a cloud of deadly gas.

In the United States, the India tragedy is generating demands for tougher corporate-responsibility laws. Rep. John Conyers plans to introduce in Congress a bill that would subject a company manager who knowingly conceals a dangerous product or business practice to up to 10 years in prison, a maximum $250,000 fine, or both. "There's a growing consensus that the only way to deal with these problems is to impose very serious criminal penalties and actually put these people behind bars," an aide to the Michigan Democrat says.

mediate financial return for the investors, foreboders would see such urban renewal as a wise and forward-thinking move.

The Demander View

Demanders cite the **iron law of responsibility**, stating that responsibility must equal power. Since firms are not the powerless entities of perfect competition, they must be willing to exhibit a level of social involvement in proportion to their resources and power. Demanders argue that firms must actively address society's needs, diverting their excess resources to social ends. Demanders would see support of cancer research or protection of endangered species as appropriate uses of corporate funds.

These viewpoints on the social responsibility of business may systematically vary as a function of firm and individual characteristics. For example, research indicates that executives in larger firms hold relatively more classical, profit-maximizing orientations toward social responsibility and are less likely to favor allocation of excess corporate resources for social needs than are others. Young executives are more likely than older executives to adopt the demander orientation. Executives who feel they have little control over their fates tend to favor the classical view. Finally, executives with positive

The construction of the Detroit Renaissance Center was supported by corporations committed to social improvement.

faith in people are likely to be less skeptical about corporate claims of social responsibility than are others.[23]

INTERESTED GROUPS

In considering its responsibilities to society, business must weigh the interests of many groups. Some of these groups are shown in Figure 4–3 and are discussed in this section.

Shareholders

Since shareholders are the owners of the firm, we might expect that their interests would always be given highest priority. In fact, though, the managers of corporations often take actions that are not in the best interests of shareholders. Shareholders generally have little influence over the day-to-day management of their companies. Later in this chapter, the benefits and costs of social actions to shareholders will be examined separately.

Consumers

Consumers are an important societal group toward whom businesses must behave responsibly. One listing of consumer rights was expressed by President Kennedy in 1962:

- The right to choose from a range of brands of products and services.
- The right to be informed of important facts about a product or service, such as quality, health hazards, and durability.

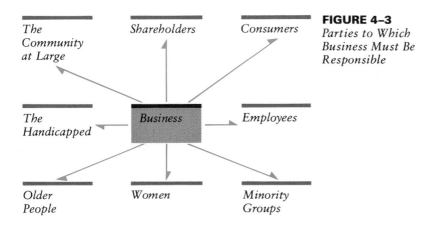

FIGURE 4–3
Parties to Which Business Must Be Responsible

Source: William H. Cunningham, Ramon J. Aldag, and Christopher M. Swift, *Introduction to Business*, 2d ed. (Cincinnati: South-Western Publishing Co., 1989), 577. Reproduced with permission.

- The right to be heard by business and government, to make complaints or suggestions, and to ask questions.
- The right to be safe when using products or services.

Johnson & Johnson showed its concern for consumer safety with its response to the Tylenol scares. In 1982, the company recalled all of its Extra-Strength Tylenol capsules from the market after capsules into which someone had introduced cyanide caused seven deaths. Although Johnson & Johnson was not responsible, it redesigned the Tylenol package to minimize the chances of future tampering. The total cost to the company of the recall and package redesign was $100 million. When capsules laced with cyanide were again found in 1986, the company decided to stop making the product in capsule form.

Many other companies have conducted massive recall campaigns because of safety or quality considerations. For instance, Procter & Gamble removed Rely tampons from the market one week after learning that the tampons had been linked with toxic-shock syndrome. It ran ads warning women not to use Rely, and it offered to buy back all Rely tampons, even those received as free samples.

Employees

Of course, firms should protect the health and safety of their employees. Occidental Petroleum closed the pesticide unit of one of its chemical plants when several male workers in the unit were found to be sterile. In a case against the Manville Corporation, a maker of asbestos products, a Los Angeles Superior Court jury awarded a former shipyard worker $1.2 million in compensation. The worker had contracted asbestosis, a lung ailment caused by inhaling the asbestos fibers. Manville, as well as other firms in the same industry, is facing hundreds of other damage suits across the country. And, in the case described in Management in Action 2, workers found themselves in the bizarre situation of being sworn to silence about the causes of their work-related illnesses.

Consumers must be able to make informed decisions.

John Flicker is executive director of the Florida State Program of The Nature Conservancy. He has been with The Nature Conservancy for 16 years and previously held a variety of positions, including director of U.S. operations, executive vice-president, and director of protection programs. A native of Minnesota, Mr. Flicker holds degrees from the University of Minnesota and William Mitchell College of Law.

Q: Could you briefly describe the general philosophy and goals of The Nature Conservancy?

A: The Conservancy's philosophy and goals are very closely related. We have only one goal—to protect the best remaining examples of ecologically significant natural areas and the diversity of life they support. Our philosophy in accomplishing this goal is to be pragmatic. We focus all of our resources on realizing that single goal, and we define our strategies in terms of what it will take to reach it. We are science-based, politically neutral, and nonconfrontational.

Q: Industry Week has called The Nature Conservancy "industry's favorite environmental group." The Nature Conservancy has chosen to work with the business community to further environmental concerns rather than to adopt a more traditional confrontational stance. Why has it taken this course?

A: Once again, we are pragmatic. We do it because it works better than any other approach. A confrontational or political approach might make better news headlines, but it would not be the best way to accomplish our goal. Good conservation is usually also good business. We can get much more done by working with business and industry than we can get by fighting them.

Q: Could you point out a few of the notable successes which have resulted from cooperation between The Nature Conservancy and the business community?

A: We protected much of the Great Dismal Swamp on the North Carolina–Virginia border through a 50,000-acre gift from Union Camp Corp. and an 11,000-acre donation from Weyerhaeuser Co. Similarly, International Paper has made land gifts to us over many years totaling more than 30,000 acres.

Corporate land donations have also been critical to the success of our trade lands program. Trade lands are nonecologically significant lands that we accept as donations and resell. We then use the proceeds to finance projects that further our objectives.

In addition to receiving outright donations of land, we've bought land from many corporations through "bargain sales." For example, Champion Inc. (formerly St. Regis) sold us critical habitat for Mississippi sandhill cranes at $1.2 million below its fair market value, taking the difference as a charitable write-off. Since we conducted the proceedings under friendly "threat of condemnation," the corporation also received a tax deferment on their long-term capital gains.

We've received more than $2 million in cash gifts from corporations during each of the past two years. We currently have 442 "corporate associates," a special membership category for corporations that make annual cash gifts of $1,000 to $10,000.

Q: Are there any specific environmental areas in which assistance of the business community is now especially important?

A: Assistance from the business community is probably most important in an area that's common to all efforts to protect the environment—money. For years, conservation organizations depended heavily on federal funds. This is especially true in the area of land conservation, where the government traditionally has spent tens of millions of dollars a year. Because of budget constraints, however, the government is now passing this expensive responsibility on to the private sector. The corporate community must take a leadership role if we are going to protect our remaining wildlife habitats.

Q: Is there a place for business school graduates within The Nature Conservancy?

A: Absolutely. In addition to scientists and attorneys, we hire many people with MBA degrees. We have the same organizational needs as any corporation, and it's vital to our success that we have people who understand areas such as tax structures, real estate negotiations, financial management, information systems, and strategic planning, to name a few. But most importantly, the Conservancy needs people who understand business concepts and perform well under the pressure associated with a corporate environment.

MANAGERIAL PROFILE
JOHN FLICKER

Clashes between basic values can present sensitive and difficult ethical questions. In a recent case involving Lockheed Corp., national security and workers' health may have come into fundamental conflict.

In late 1988, two federal agencies—the U.S. Occupational Safety and Health Administration and the Department of Defense—launched investigations into claims by workers at Lockheed's Burbank, California, plant that life-threatening chemicals or other materials are being used in the facility's secret projects. At least 160 workers at the Lockheed plant have become ill, including many who are believed to be working on the top-secret F-19, or Stealth, fighter plane. The Stealth fighter is thought to use materials similar to those believed to be used by the Stealth bomber being developed by Northrop Corp. Analysts say those materials don't reflect radar, making detection difficult.

About 75 workers are plaintiffs in a lawsuit filed in 1986 charging that the workers suffered from ailments induced by hazardous substances used in their top-secret jobs, and that Lockheed's facilities have not been adapted to the hazards. In addition to that lawsuit, about 150 workers have filed worker compensation claims, and union officials say they have received hundreds of grievances related to toxic sub-

stance concerns. The workers say they are suffering from a variety of health problems, including headaches, nausea, high blood pressure, disorientation,

MANAGEMENT IN ACTION 2
STEALTH

memory lapses, and cancer. Lockheed has denied the legal charges and has said that the plaintiffs knowingly assumed any risks that may have occurred at the plant.

The trouble is that, while many newspapers and technical publications have reported on the existence of the Stealth fighter, neither Lockheed nor the Defense Department has confirmed the existence of the Stealth fighter program. The program is so secret that workers cannot discuss their work, at the risk of dismissal and prosecution for violating laws against disclosing sensitive information. Scientists familiar with aerospace manufacturing argue that disclosing how the substances cited in the lawsuits are used could give other countries insights into the processes being used to build the secret aircraft.

In the meantime, workers are not allowed to fully explain what they believe to be causing their illnesses, even to their doctors. Five plaintiffs have died.

Source: Based on Kenneth B. Noble, "Illness Adds to Mystery of Stealth," *Wisconsin State Journal* (September 18, 1988): 3A, and Rhonda L. Rundle, "Lockheed Employees' Health Complaints Prompt Inquiries by 2 Federal Agencies, " *The Wall Street Journal* (October 3, 1988): B12.

More generally, it is believed that companies should offer salaries and other employee benefits that are appropriate to the work performed as well as to the skill, knowledge, and training of the worker. Many companies also share their good fortune with their employees. When Apple Computer had an especially good quarter in 1981, it gave each of its 2,500 employees an extra week's vacation.

Earlier in this chapter, we considered the right of employees to speak out. In coming chapters we will see examples of other rights of employees, including the right to privacy and the right to retain their jobs unless just cause for termination can be shown.

Minority Groups

Certain minority groups have been treated unfairly in the past. Some groups, blacks and Hispanics, for example, have been easily identifiable targets for discrimination in hiring and promotion. Several laws now help to prevent discrimination and, in some cases, to make up for past discrimination. Dean Witter Reynolds, a stock brokerage firm, agreed to make payments of $1.8 million to Hispanic, black, and female brokers who applied to or worked for the company from 1976 through 1981. These people had been discriminated against in hiring and promotion decisions. The company was also required to establish a $2.8 million affirmative action program to place minority persons in brokerage positions.

Women

Until fairly recently, most women working outside the home were employed as secretaries, nurses, teachers, receptionists, and retail sales clerks. Very few women were lawyers, doctors, or professional managers. Now, more and more women are pursuing careers in these areas. Federal law requires that businesses make a serious effort to recruit and retain female employees, as well as to treat them fairly. Otherwise, the businesses risk potentially serious legal consequences. For example, the Bechtel Corporation, a California engineering firm, settled a sex discrimination case by agreeing to pay $1.3 million in damages to former and current female employees. In another case, American Airlines agreed to rehire 300 flight attendants who had been fired because of pregnancy and to pay them a total of $2.7 million.

Older People

The average age of the U.S. work force is increasing. The reasons include longer life expectancy, a tapering off of the baby boom, the entry of increasing numbers of middle-aged women into the work force, and a relaxation of mandatory retirement rules.

The protection of the rights of older people in the workplace, therefore, is becoming more important. The Age Discrimination in Employment Act of 1978 specifically prohibits age discrimination in hiring and promotion. But apart from legislative protection, the attitude of employers toward older workers is important. Arbitrarily dismissing a skilled worker at age 60 or 65 hurts both the employee and the company.

The Handicapped

Business firms have begun to act more responsibly in hiring and promoting the handicapped. It is likewise the responsibility of businesses to see that curbs, stairways, and similar obstacles do not prevent handicapped people from doing their jobs properly.

Recent legal opinions have broadened the scope of the term "handicapped" to include workers with contagious diseases, including AIDS. For instance, an October 1988 Justice Department ruling held that fear of contagion by itself does not permit federal agencies or federally assisted employers to fire or discriminate against workers infected with the AIDS virus. Such rulings, coupled with other employees' fears of contamination, will present firms with sensitive and difficult decisions in coming years.[24]

The Community at Large

Many laws and watchdog groups now protect society from the potentially disruptive actions of business. One area of special concern is environmental protection. USX, formerly U.S. Steel, settled a lengthy dispute with the Environmental Protection Agency by agreeing to spend $400 million to clean up air and water pollution at its plants in Pittsburgh. Fines and negative publicity require that firms be especially careful about the effects of their actions on the environment and other aspects of community life.

Businesses operate in a highly diversified society; they affect many social and economic groups and are affected by these groups in turn. It is clear that a company manager must have a wide range of abilities and an open mind to be successful in such a setting.

BENEFITS AND COSTS OF SOCIAL ACTIONS

Is being socially responsible good for business? We'll approach this question from the perspective of the benefits and costs of socially responsible actions.

Benefits

A company may benefit directly and indirectly by taking socially responsible actions. One obvious benefit is improved employee satisfaction and motivation. Employees are likely to be more satisfied at work and more motivated to achieve the organization's goals if they believe the company actively contributes to society. For instance, many employees of Bristol-Myers—makers of Bufferin, Ban, Windex, and many other popular products—point with pride to the fact that their company spends more on cancer research than any other pharmaceutical company.

Other benefits may occur in the marketplace. By showing a genuine interest in social needs, a firm may become more aware of changing consumer tastes and preferences. The socially responsible firm may also find that its

American Express used donations based on its credit card usage to help finance restoration of the Statue of Liberty.

products and services are in greater demand because consumers recognize and appreciate such companies. These benefits relate directly to increased sales revenue and profitability. Some companies are trying to strengthen this link between marketing and social responsibility. As one example, American Express Company gave the Statue of Liberty–Ellis Island Foundation $1.7 million to help restore the Statue of Liberty. It generated the gift money by promising in a national ad campaign to donate a penny to the statue for each use of its charge card and a dollar for most new cards issued. Card usage during the quarter increased 28 percent over the same period in 1982. As another illustration, Carter Hawley Hale Stores Inc., parent of Neiman Marcus, is narrowing its giving to only the visual and performing arts and only in major cities. The reason: to make sure its efforts are evident to its socially upscale customers.[25]

Just as consumers may favor the products of responsible firms, so might investors prefer the stocks of such firms. A company with a highly visible social program may find that its stock sells at a higher market price. Several "social investing" mutual funds have sprung up recently. These funds seek out companies with "good" social records. Three companies included most often are Quaker Oats Co., which makes low-sugar cereals; Dayton Hudson Corp., which uses 5 percent of its federally taxable income for charitable purposes; and Magma Power Co., a leader in the development of geothermal energy. Performance of these funds has been mixed. Historically, returns on most "socially responsible" mutual funds have lagged those of averages such as the Standard & Poor's 500 stock index. In the first half of 1988, however, such funds did quite well, with most outperforming both the Standard & Poor's 500 and the average of general equity funds.[26]

In the long run, socially responsible actions by business may eliminate the need for legislative controls on business activity. Such controls often cost firms more in lost business opportunities than the socially responsible actions would have cost.

Control Data is one company that recognizes the benefits of socially responsible actions. It has invested millions of dollars in such projects as redeveloping rundown neighborhoods, assisting small farmers, and providing computer-based education systems. According to its statement of corporate mission, Control Data is "a worldwide corporation committed to a strategy of addressing society's major needs as profitable business opportunities."

Costs

Although social responsibility may be cheaper than government controls, it is not without costs. The most obvious cost is the money spent in direct support of social projects. A $50,000 grant to a community theater group is $50,000 that is no longer available for financing plant expansion. By diverting funds away from profitable investment opportunities, the company is not maximizing shareholder wealth. A firm's social goals are often less clearly defined than its profit goals; therefore, if hard financial goals are not pursued, it may be difficult to distinguish between good and bad management. In the long run, therefore, the market price of the stock of socially responsible companies may just as easily fall as rise.

A further cost relates to the issue of competitive parity. A company may stay on equal footing with its competitors if all the companies support social projects; but a company which alone supports such projects may lose business if its competitors use their surplus resources to strengthen their competitive positions.

Finally, it is possible that government may step in and regulate the private provision of social services and programs. Private companies have traditionally served society by providing goods, services, jobs, and a return on investment to shareholders. Venturing into this new area of social "product," well-intentioned companies may find that their actions bring forth more government regulation.

Comparing Benefits and Costs

Are the benefits of a proposed set of corporate social programs greater than the costs? How does the decision maker proceed? If we could clearly measure the benefits and costs in terms of dollars, the answer to this question would be easy: Implement the proposed program if total benefits exceed total costs; rethink the program if they do not. But this is an area lacking simple answers. Many factors affect the comparison of benefits and costs. Among them are the actions of competitors, possible government controls, the amount of cash on hand, and the "visibility" of the social programs themselves.

The USX case mentioned earlier in this chapter provides a good illustration of how difficult these decisions can be. Pollution controls at the company's mills produce the undeniable benefit of cleaner air to people living nearby. But the costs are undeniable too. Not only is there the cost of installing and operating the pollution control equipment, but there are also the costs involved in depressed output, lost jobs, and higher steel prices.

PLANNING AND ORGANIZING FOR SOCIAL ISSUES

Archie Carroll recommends that firms should systematically plan for social issues and organize for social response.[27] Here are some suggestions for carrying out social planning and organizing.

Planning for Social Issues

Planning for social issues involves social forecasting and social goal setting. These activities entail consideration of social trends and formulation of specific social goals.

SOCIAL FORECASTING

Kenneth Newgren defines **social forecasting** as follows:

Social forecasting . . . is a systematic process for identifying social trends and their underlying attitudes, analyzing these social trends for their relevance to the organization, and integrating these findings with other forecasts to cover a time period of at least five, and preferably more, years.[28]

Such social forecasting is carried out primarily in large firms. Some firms use one or more **futurists**, analysts who study the future in an attempt to identify social or political trends and determine their relevance to the firm. The alternative is to hire consultants and use the information they provide.

Executives in many firms, including Bristol-Myers, American Express, and Sears, Roebuck, participate in a program named "Strategic Trend Evaluation Process," or STEP, run by a New York consulting firm. The idea is to make the executives think like futurists. The consulting firm's staff reads periodicals ranging from *Technology Review* to *Mother Jones*. Staff members write abstracts of articles that suggest future trends. Executives consider these abstracts and meet every few months to discuss the issues and trends they have studied. One typical issue was the impact of government cutbacks in support of the arts and social services. Executives discussed how these cutbacks might lead to pressures on companies for support and how firms should respond.

Other firms are using **issues managers**, individuals much like futurists but concerned with the shorter term, say one to five years. Issues managers identify social issues and make specific recommendations for company response.

Atlantic Richfield formed an issues management group in the late 1970s, in part because it felt that its more traditional planners had failed to anticipate key energy and environmental developments. The group is very heterogeneous, comprising engineers, marketing managers, lawyers, a former English teacher, and others. The group monitors publications, opinion polls, and think-tank reports. It provides middle managers in the company with a daily publication called *Scan* which summarizes important developments. Carroll notes that issues management groups at various firms spurred such moves as removing fluorocarbons from aerosol sprays years before such action was federally mandated, lobbying to head off anticipated tax changes, and introducing nonflammable goods prior to their requirement by the government.

SOCIAL GOAL SETTING

Like all other goals, social goals should be specific and concrete. As one example, Carroll suggests that the general objective "To be a good community citizen by supporting community projects" can be replaced by such operational objectives as "To provide ten hours a week released time for each of two executives to serve on the community's Committee on Crime Prevention for two years at a cost of $18,000 to the company" or "To underwrite the costs of the annual Christmas concert put on by the Boys' Club of Athens at a cost of $5,000." Specific goals enhance credibility, make success more likely, and make appraisal of social performance more feasible.

Organizing for Social Response

Once firms have planned for social action, they must develop appropriate organizational patterns. The specific patterns will depend on industry and environmental characteristics, firm size and visibility, the importance of social issues to the firm, and other matters. Carroll identifies the following structural forms to deal with social issues:

- The corporate social/public responsibility officer, first appearing on organization charts in the late 1960s and early 1970s.

- The task force of executives, assigned on a temporary basis to deal with specific or general social issues. Since these are temporary committees, they lack continuity and may lead to hasty response.
- The permanent committee, giving the social function authority and prominence. This committee may be made up of members of the board of directors or a regular management group.
- The department, the most formal organizational method. Usually headed by an individual with high organizational status, such as a vice-president for public affairs, it also typically includes a full-time staff working on social issues. The departmental structure provides status, resources, continuity, planning, and professional management.

THE SOCIAL AUDIT

Our discussion so far has focused on the many issues involved in corporate responsibility and on the problems of evaluating the performance of these programs. We have also considered planning and organizing for social performance. One way to think constructively about social issues and problems, as well as to assess the effectiveness of social planning and organizing, is to conduct a social audit.

What Is a Social Audit?

A **social audit** is a step-by-step examination of all the activities comprising a firm's social programs. The firm may evaluate its own programs in terms of goals, and it may identify new programs that it ought to pursue. Goals are then formulated for these new programs. The general aim of the social audit is to make management more aware of the impact of corporate actions on society.

In some countries, social audits are mandatory. In Germany, about 20 of the largest firms now publish regular social reports. In France, all firms with more than 750 employees must publish a social report that includes information on 94 social indicators. Norway also requires a published social report, and many other European countries are considering such legal requirements. Figure 4–4 diagrams the social audit for a company evaluating past activities and considering new ones.

Conducting and Reporting on the Social Audit

Conducting a social audit is not easy. There are many difficult questions to be answered: What activities should be audited? How should each activity be evaluated? How should social performance be assessed? These questions generally have to be answered on a case-by-case basis.

REPORT TO SHAREHOLDERS

More and more companies are reporting on their social activities to shareholders and others. For example, Atlantic Richfield has published three corporate social reports, available to anyone who requests a copy. The most recent report, "Participation III," describes Atlantic Richfield's activities in consumer affairs, human resources management, occupational and environ-

FIGURE 4–4
The Social Audit

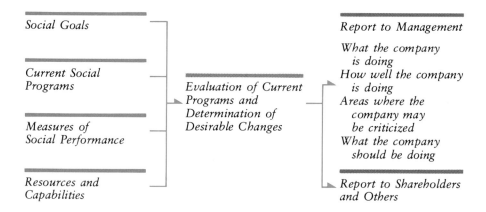

Source: William H. Cunningham, Ramon J. Aldag, and Christopher M. Swift, *Introduction to Business*, 2d ed. (Cincinnati: South-Western Publishing Co., 1989), 583. Reproduced with permission.

mental protection, energy conservation, philanthropy, and public-policy advocacy.[29] The report presents a comprehensive and generally positive picture of the company's social activities.

INDEPENDENT CRITIQUES

An impressive aspect of the Atlantic Richfield report is that it also includes independent critiques by outside experts. Although generally quite favorable in regard to most of Atlantic Richfield's social activities, some of the critiques are painfully candid. For example, one critique took the company to task for its all-white, all-male board of directors; its funding of memberships for company executives in private clubs discriminating against Jewish people, racial minorities, and women; and its lack of formal corporate social policies. Another critique pointed out the lack of a specific policy governing corporate donations. The company evaluated these criticisms and brought them to the attention of managers. Since publication of "Participation III," Atlantic Richfield has taken the initial step of adding a woman to its board of directors.

IMPLICATIONS FOR MANAGEMENT

As a manager, you will often be faced with difficult decisions concerning business ethics and social responsibility. These decisions will often require you to balance economic and social concerns.

While some ethical decisions seem clear-cut, others are in gray areas. Many people who consider themselves ethical routinely duplicate copyrighted computer software, take home office supplies, and make personal calls on company phones. Questions of ethics also loom large when unethical behavior is "standard business practice." A recent investigation of kickbacks in the oil industry found fraud to be flourishing at all levels, from the wellheads to the executive suite. Motorboats, barbecue pits, prostitutes, cocaine, and money were discovered to be routinely offered to get contracts. One operator said, "Any little oil service business who tells you he isn't paying kickbacks is lying. You got to buy your business to stay alive." How would you behave in such a situation?

Difficult questions also arise when you are aware that others are behaving unethically. Should you notify management, become a whistleblower, or simply keep quiet? Give some thought to these issues before you have to face them.

Certainly, if you are serious about encouraging ethical behavior among employees, you should try to create a climate conducive to such behavior. This would require publicizing the firm's commitment to ethics as well as the rewards and punishments associated with ethical and unethical behavior. It would demand that you avoid creating situations where unethical behavior is seen as the route to success. You may also want to encourage ethics training, ethics review committees, and company programs to resolve ethical dilemmas.

Along with ethical dilemmas at the individual level, you may also have to make decisions regarding the social actions of your firm. Give some careful thought to your views concerning social responsibility. Do you most agree with the classical, demander, constrainer, or foreboder views? What are the bases for your opinions?

When considering social actions, you will inevitably encounter tradeoffs. The socially "correct" decision may be costly and unpopular. Pursuing actions that you consider to be socially responsible may lead others to conclude that you don't care about "the bottom line." Take some time to think through your views concerning social responsibility. You may then be better able to deal with hard social tradeoffs in a consistent, reasoned way.

In making decisions about social issues, give some thought to possible costs and benefits of alternative actions. You may conclude that some actions could be better handled by others, or that the costs far outweigh the benefits. You may decide that the actions should definitely be undertaken, but that costs will somehow have to be passed along. The purpose of such a balancing should be not to seek ways to avoid social responsibilities but rather to best match social actions to the particular strengths of the firm.

Like other management activities, social issues management requires planning, organizing, and control. Forward-thinking managers carry out social forecasting and set specific social goals. They choose appropriate organizational patterns and conduct systematic social audits. These activities will almost certainly become more important in the future.

KEY TERMS AND CONCEPTS

business ethics

classical view

code of ethics

constrainers

demanders

foreboders

futurists

"invisible hand"

iron law of responsibility

issues managers

social audit

social forecasting

social responsibility

whistleblowers

QUESTIONS FOR REVIEW AND DISCUSSION

1. Define business ethics and cite four examples of potentially unethical behavior.

2. If it is impossible to do business in a country without using kickbacks and bribes, what should a company do?

3. What are some costs and benefits to the firm of employees who are whistleblowers?
4. What is meant by social responsibility? Give three examples of socially responsible actions by firms.
5. Define the classical, constrainer, foreboder, and demander viewpoints toward social responsibility. With which of these viewpoints do you most agree? Disagree? Why?
6. Identify five parties to whom business may have social responsibilities.
7. Cite some costs and benefits of social responsibility from the point of view of shareholders.
8. Present guidelines for planning social actions. In your answer, give four specific examples of social goals.
9. Identify different ways of organizing for social actions.
10. Describe the social audit.

CASES

4–1 GENETIC TESTING OF WORKERS

The expanding science of genetics is beginning to touch the American workplace. The prospect is full of promise and peril.

The promise is bright: Genetic screening of employees could identify those with special susceptibility to a disease and steer them away from work where dust or fumes might trigger it. Testing that found chromosomal damage among workers in a certain occupation would give an early warning of danger. Employers, and society, might save millions in medical costs.

That is one way it might work. Another is that employers, able to exclude the most vulnerable workers, might avoid cleaning up hazardous workplaces. Certain employees, labeled "susceptible," might find their careers and their health insurance lopped off. They might find their privacy invaded, or their race singled out. The employers might find themselves sued.

Employers have already done some genetic testing. A 1982 survey found 18 major U.S. companies that either were doing tests or had done them in the past. Another 59 thought then that they might begin genetic testing within five years. But now, owing partly to current scientific limitations and partly to the flak some companies drew, very little of such testing is being done. Many experts welcome the pause as a chance for people to think about the issues involved.

Genetic testing of workers comes in two varieties: screening and monitoring. They are distinct both in what they set out to do and in the attitudes toward them.

Screening is the one-time analysis of DNA taken from blood or other body fluids, aimed at finding genetic "markers" indicating that a person may be especially susceptible to harm from a particular substance. This is the procedure in which critics see the greatest social dangers. Another recent concern with genetic screening is that employers may use such procedures to screen out employees who are likely to develop debilitating or fatal genetic diseases such as Huntington's chorea or Alzheimer's.

Genetic monitoring, by contrast, involves periodically testing groups of employees to see whether they are showing any alarming chromosomal abnormalities, changes which might have arisen from their environment. Monitoring has the approval of many of the labor leaders and others who oppose screening. In fact, they would very much like to see more genetic monitoring of industrial employees to provide evidence of workplaces in need of sanitizing.

Source: Based on Alan L. Otten, "Probing the Cell: Genetic Examination of Workers Is an Issue of Growing Urgency," *The Wall Street Journal* (February 24, 1986): 1, 6; "Genetic Screening Raises Questions for Employers and Insurers," *Science* (April 1986): 317-319; Judy D. Olian, "Genetic Screening for Employment Purposes," *Personnel Psychology* (1984): 423-438; and Fern Schumer Chapman, "The Ruckus over Medical Testing," *Fortune* (August 19, 1985): 57-62.

1. Do you feel that genetic screening is ethical? Genetic monitoring? In each case, justify your position.
2. Do you see genetic testing as an invasion of privacy? If so, do you think concerns about privacy are overridden by legitimate need?
3. If genetic monitoring shows that an employee is especially susceptible to a workplace substance, who should decide whether the employee should be transferred, the employer or the employee? Why?
4. What sorts of policies or practices do you think companies should employ when deciding whether or not to employ genetic testing?

4–2 100% PURE

There is probably no product for which quality is seen as more important than baby food. As such, the revelation that Beech-Nut Nutrition Corp., a subsidiary of Swiss food giant Nestlé, had for years been selling a "100% Apple Juice" product for babies that contained little or no apple juice was startling. The juice, sold between 1978 and 1983, was in fact a "100% fraudulent chemical cocktail"—a cheap concoction of beet sugar, apple flavor, caramel color, and corn syrup.

The case emerged after a private investigator named Andrew Rosenzweig was hired in 1982 by a trade group to investigate possible adulteration in the apple juice industry. A year later, the Food and Drug Administration received an anonymous letter from a Beech-Nut employee, signed "Johnny Appleseed," alerting it to the problem.

In fact, Beech-Nut had known since at least 1981 that the "apple concentrate" supplied by Interjuice & Universal Juice Co.—at a price 20 percent below the standard market rate—was bogus. Beech-Nut's director of research and development, Jerome LiCari, alerted Beech-Nut's president, Neils Hoyvald, that a "tremendous amount of circumstantial evidence" constituted a "grave case" against the supplier, and recommended terminating Beech-Nut's contract with the company. Instead, Hoyvald criticized LiCari's loyalty and judgment, and threatened to fire him. In 1982, LiCari resigned.

Beech-Nut was under tremendous financial pressure, and the cheap, phony concentrate saved millions of dollars, helping to keep the company alive. Beech-Nut executives apparently rationalized their behavior on two grounds, both debatable. First, they reasoned that other companies were also selling fake juice, and thus Beech-Nut was just remaining competitive. Second, they were apparently convinced that the fake juice, even if adulterated, was perfectly safe. So, when the private investigator told Beech-Nut in 1982 that he had conclusive proof of adulteration and asked the company to join other juicemakers in a lawsuit against the supplier, Beech-Nut blatantly stalled in order to unload its $3.5 million inventory of tainted juice products. President Hoyvald ordered the inventories unloaded "fast, fast, fast" at deep discounts. Much of the product was sold in the Caribbean.

Beech-Nut's stonewalling angered government investigators, who brought indictments against Beech-Nut in 1986. In June of 1988, Beech-Nut's current president, Richard Theuer, admitted that the company "broke a sacred trust" but assured the public that Beech-Nut baby foods were now pure. But by then tremendous, and perhaps irreparable, damage had been done. Two former Beech-Nut executives—Hoyvald and former vice-president for manufacturing John Lavery—were each sentenced to a year and a day in prison and fined $100,000 for their roles in the scam, termed by federal judge Thomas Platt "the largest consumer fraud case ever." Beech-Nut pleaded guilty to 215 counts of introducing adulterated food into commerce and violating the Federal Food, Drug, and Cosmetic Act. The company paid a $250,000 fine to the state of New York. The Defense Logistics Agency suspended the company from all government contract work and is considering a permanent ban. The company also paid $7.5 million to settle a class-action suit brought by a supermarket chain over the issue, and it paid the government a $2.2 million fine. At least two civil suits are pending, and the company's market share has slipped from 20 percent to 17 percent, strengthening rival Gerber's competitive position. Various suppliers to the company are soon to be sentenced, and others are due to go on trial. And Beech-Nut's reputation, built since 1891 on purity, high quality, and natural ingredients, was forever tarnished.

Source: Based in part on J. Queenen, "Juice Men: Ethics and the Beech-Nut Sentences," *Barron's* (June 20, 1988): 37-38; A. Hagedorn, "Two Ex-Officials of Beech-Nut Get Prison Sentences," *The Wall Street Journal* (June 17, 1988): 39; "What Led Beech-Nut Down the Road to Disgrace," *Business Week* (February 22, 1988): 124-128; and S. Kindel, "Bad Apple for Baby," *Financial World* (June 27, 1989): 48.

1. What sorts of factors do you think might have led Beech-Nut executives to engage in these illegal, and risky, activities? What are your reactions to Beech-Nut's justifications for its actions?
2. In view of the widespread and apparently blatant nature of this fraudulent activity, are you surprised that it wasn't exposed earlier? What factors may have prevented potential "Johnny Appleseeds" from blowing the whistle sooner?
3. How would you characterize Jerome LiCari's actions? Should he have acted differently, either before or after his termination?
4. What sorts of penalties do you think are appropriate for Beech-Nut? For Neils Hoyvald?

ENDNOTES

1. A. Hagedorn and B. Wong, "Wang, Former Morgan Stanley Analyst, Sentenced to 3 Years for Insider Trading," *Wall Street Journal* (October 27, 1988): A3.
2. "Mixed Feelings About Drexel's Decision," *Wall Street Journal* (December 23, 1988): B1.
3. See "Drexel's Milken Finds Himself More Isolated As Indictment Nears," *Wall Street Journal* (December 23, 1988): A1, A5, and S. Swartz, "Why Mike Milken Stands to Qualify for Guinness Book," *Wall Street Journal* (March 31, 1989): A1.
4. E. W. Read, "Rockwell's Motion to Dismiss Charges of Fraud on Defense Contracts Is Denied," *Wall Street Journal* (September 20, 1988): 8.
5. A. Zipser, "How Pressure to Raise Sales Led MiniScribe to Falsify Numbers," *Wall Street Journal* (September 11, 1989): A1, A8.
6. For a presentation and discussion of various ethical dilemmas, along with the general public's and executives' reactions to such dilemmas, see R. Ricklefs, "Executives Apply Stiffer Standards Than Public to Ethical Dilemmas," *Wall Street Journal* (November 3, 1983): 27, 30.
7. *Wall Street Journal* (June 13, 1986): 16.
8. B. M. Staw and E. Szwajkowski, "The Scarcity-Munificence Component of Organizational Environments and the Commission of Illegal Acts," *Administrative Science Quarterly* 20 (1975): 345-354.
9. W. H. Hegarty and H. P. Sims, Jr., "Organizational Philosophy, Policies, and Objectives Related to Unethical Decision Behavior: A Laboratory Experiment," *Journal of Applied Psychology* 64 (1979): 331-338.
10. T. J. Murray, "Ethics Programs: Just a Pretty Face," *Business Month* (September 1987): 30.
11. See A. Bennett, "Ethics Codes Spread Despite Skepticism," *Wall Street Journal* (July 15, 1988): 13, and R. Wartzman, "Nature or Nurture? Study Blames Ethical Lapses on Corporate Goals," *Wall Street Journal* (October 9, 1987): 21.
12. *Human Resources* (October 1987): 1-2.
13. A. L. Otten, "Ethics on the Job: Companies Alert Employees to Potential Dilemmas," *Wall Street Journal* (July 14, 1986): 17.
14. *Human Resources* (October 1987): 1.
15. Otten, "Ethics on the Job," and Murray, "Ethics Programs."
16. Otten, "Ethics on the Job."
17. G. Stricharchuk, "Businesses Crack Down on Workers Who Cheat to Help the Company," *Wall Street Journal* (June 13, 1986): 16.
18. For instance, see "Union Carbide Agrees to Settle All Bhopal Litigation For $470 Million in Pact with India's Supreme Court" (February 15, 1989): A3; A. Spaeth, "Court Settlement Stuns Bhopal Survivors," *Wall Street Journal* (February 22, 1989): A10; and "The Ghosts of Bhopal," *The Economist* (February 18, 1989): 70.

19. M. Chase, "Burroughs Wellcome Reaps Profit, Outrage from Its AZT Drug," *Wall Street Journal* (September 15, 1989): A1.

20. A. Nomani, "Lyphomed to Give Indigent Patients Drug for AIDS," *Wall Street Journal* (October 19, 1988): A6.

21. For a detailed discussion of these viewpoints and references concerning their respective proponents, see R. J. Aldag and D. W. Jackson, Jr., "A Managerial Framework for Social Decision Making," *Business Topics* 23 (1975): 33-40.

22. N. H. Jacoby, *Corporate Power and Responsibility* (New York: Macmillan, 1973), 10-15.

23. See R. J. Aldag and K. M. Bartol, "Empirical Studies of Corporate Social Performance and Policy: A Survey of Problems and Results" in *Research in Corporate Social Performance and Policy,* vol. 1, ed. L. E. Preston (Greenwich, CT: JAI Press, 1978), 165-199, and R. J. Aldag and D. W. Jackson, Jr., "Measurement and Correlates of Social Attitudes," *Journal of Business Ethics* 3 (1984): 143-151.

24. A. Pastor and J. Davidson, "U.S. Agencies, in Reversal, Told to Bar Bias for Victims of AIDS," *Wall Street Journal* (October 7, 1988): B7.

25. Wendy W. Wall, "Helping Hands: Companies Change the Ways They Make Charitable Donations," *Wall Street Journal* (June 21, 1984): 1, 20.

26. E. D. Lee, "It's All Relative: Mutual Funds Discover 'Socially Responsible' Is in Eye of Beholder," *Wall Street Journal* (May 20, 1987): 35, and C. W. Stevens, "Socially Aware Investing Turns Profitable," *Wall Street Journal* (July 29, 1988): 23.

27. This section is based on A. B. Carroll, *Social Responsibility of Management* (Chicago: Science Research Associates, 1984).

28. K. E. Newgren, "Social Forecasting: An Overview of Current Business Practices" in *Managing Corporate Social Responsibility*, ed. A. B. Carroll (Boston: Little, Brown, 1977), 170-190.

29. *Participation III: Atlantic Richfield and Society*, ed. N. B. Whaley (Los Angeles: Atlantic Richfield and Company, 1980).

Planning

PART TWO

Organizational Goals

CHAPTER 5

After studying this chapter, you should be able to:
- *Explain why organizational goals are important to managerial activities.*
- *Discuss the three types of organizational goals and their application to the managerial hierarchy.*
- *Describe the factors that influence the goal-formulation process.*
- *Discuss the various techniques managers use for managing multiple goals.*
- *Recognize the distinction between organizational efficiency and effectiveness.*
- *Identify the various approaches managers use for assessing organizational effectiveness.*
- *Apply criteria for assessing organizational effectiveness.*

Managers of organizations set goals to help direct activities of members. An **organizational goal** is defined as a desired state of affairs which the organization tries to realize.[1] The activities directed toward goal achievement can differ widely from organization to organization. Also, goals often change as an organization grows or faces new situations in the environment. For example, if we examine organizations in a single industry, goals may differ depending on organization size and stage of growth. A new computer software firm may emphasize the goal of survival in its first years of operation. An older firm may have goals of growth and profit. Other computer firms may have goals of achieving dominance in the industry or recognition for quality software products. Managers of a hospital, on the other hand, may set goals of providing low-cost health care, avoiding labor strikes, and recruiting talented graduates from medical schools.

Managers must understand what goals are appropriate for their organization. Goals are important because they identify for members a direction in which the organization desires to move. Organizational goals also help managers in the selection of strategies and the identification of department goals. They inform the public about the organization's intentions. And they provide a basis for judging the effectiveness of the organization's activities.

This chapter will examine the role that organizational goals and effectiveness play in directing managers toward successful results. We will determine why goals are important and identify types of goals. We will also suggest techniques for managing multiple goals in an organization. Finally, we will introduce a framework for judging organizational effectiveness.

This chapter will also provide the base for our discussion of the planning function of management in Chapter 6 and strategic management in Chapter 7. We will learn that organizational plans evolve from goals and that plans lead to the selection of a strategy by managers for their organizations. Managers decide what organizational goals to pursue. These decisions are made in regard to the conditions in the organization's environment as described in Chapter 3.

THE IMPORTANCE OF ORGANIZATIONAL GOALS

After examining annual reports of organizations, many students conclude that the goals stated in these documents are simply "for show." Phrases such as "produce a quality product," "seek growth," "innovative leadership," "high profit," or "enhance humanity" seem to be more the work of a creative marketing director than the substance of what top organization managers are actually trying to accomplish. In some instances managers do ignore the stated goals of the organization. However, it would be wrong to assume that stated goals are of little or no importance to how an organization operates.

Organizational goals have two major functions. First, goals affect the way the organization relates to the environment, serving to clarify the connection between organizational activities and other organizations, groups, and individuals in the environment. The second major function of goals is to guide the internal activities of the organization, providing managers and members with knowledge of task scope, decision guidelines, methods of motivation, performance criteria, and a rationale for organizing. These attributes of

Making "Quality Job 1" is an organizational goal that Ford communicates to society through its advertising.

Ford, Mercury and Lincoln owners win again.

For the 7th year in a row, owners of Ford Motor Company cars and trucks have reported fewer problems than owners of any other vehicles designed and built in North America.* Not just when they're new, but thousands of miles down the road.

And all our new cars and light trucks are backed by a 6 year, 60,000 mile powertrain warranty.**

That's what happens when you make **Quality Job 1.**

*Based on an average of owner-reported problems in a series of surveys of '81-'87 models designed and built in North America.
Restrictions and deductible apply. Ask your dealer for a copy of this limited warranty. **Buckle up—Together we can save lives.

Courtesy of Ford Motor Company.

goals serve to generate member commitment and increase identification with the organization. Therefore, one responsibility of management is to define and communicate organizational goals to members and to society.

External Importance of Goals

Goals provide information about the purpose, mission, and legitimacy of organizational activities.

PURPOSE

The **purpose** of an organization is the reason for the organization's existence. We can view the purpose of an organization broadly as the desire to provide a good or service. Without some purpose, the organization need not exist. Goals serve to emphasize the purpose by announcing to society what the organization's intentions are. The purpose of the Art Institute of Chicago is to safeguard and display works of art. The purpose of the San Francisco Giants baseball team is to earn a profit for the team's owners. The purpose of the State of Florida is to provide citizens with social services and protection.

Organizations must also, however, be concerned with survival. For some organizations, particularly new ones, survival is the primary goal. On the other hand, some organizations are started with the express intent of dissolving when a particular goal is met. Many real estate partnerships schedule a self-liquidation program after so many years of operation with hopes of an adequate return on investment for the owners. Political campaigns designed to elect officials often cease operations the day after the election. The desire to cease operations, however, does not necessarily mean the organization can end its activities. The Committee to Re-elect the President was formed in 1970 to elect Richard M. Nixon to the Presidency but did not formally stop operating until 1985, 13 years after the election was over!

Who determines the purpose of an organization? Initially, the purpose of an organization is determined by the creators of the organization. Over time, managers may change the purpose if significant change in the environment or activities is expected. For example, during World War II, many manufacturing firms changed their purpose from generating owner profit to supporting the Allies through weapons production. When the war ended, the firms returned to their original purpose of profit generation. Hence, a temporary change in the organization's purpose was made by management.

MISSION

Identification of an organization's purpose leads to the creation of a mission. Organizational **mission** is defined as the path managers choose to achieve the purpose. Many organizations have the purpose of making a profit for the owners. But multiple paths can be pursued to achieve profit. In determining the mission of a business organization, founders or managers identify a product and a market in which to pursue customers. Specification of the product and market can be stated in broad or narrow terms. For example, a company that defines its mission as oil production will direct its marketing efforts toward consumers of oil. A company whose mission is more broadly viewed as energy production will identify the market not only for oil but also for water, sun, and wind as sources of power. Goals, as expressed in the organization's mission, direct managerial attention to the needs and wants of those customers it desires to reach.

Selecting an organizational mission is a critical decision. Stuckey's Inc., a restaurant chain, saw its mission as providing "convenient, moderately priced home cooking" to travelers along the interstates. The company enjoyed huge success until the late 1970s, when interstate travel decreased and consumer tastes shifted toward gourmet cuisine. By defining its mission as servicing interstate customers rather than dine-out customers in general, Stuckey's was forced to close most of its interstate facilities. Thus, the choice of mission can have a significant and long-lasting effect on an organization's ability to achieve its purpose. Goals should not only identify the customer the organization desires to reach, but also should be updated by management as conditions in the environment change.

LEGITIMACY

Legitimacy is the acceptance of the organization's activities by non-members of the organization. Organizational goals are important for legitimizing the activities of the organization to important elements in the external environment. In the United States, many organizations achieve initial legitimacy through governmental granting of a legal charter. Legal charters differ based on how government views the purpose and mission of the organization. Not-for-profit organizations are granted charters that allow managers to provide goods or services necessary for the welfare of society even when noncompetitive pricing is the result. For-profit organizations are granted rights to produce goods and services provided they do not engage in unfair trade practices. They also must file appropriate forms and agree to pay a percentage of their revenue to the government in the form of taxes.

Organizational legitimacy always comes from factors in the external environment. Consumers legitimize an organization through purchase of its products or services. Regulatory agencies determine whether the organization has faithfully fulfilled the criteria of its charter. Unions express approval or disapproval of organizational practices. Managers must continually relate the goals of the organization to external constituents to avoid the loss of legitimacy.

Many organizations have had to face a "crisis of legitimacy." Firms in the cigarette industry have had to contend with published medical research linking smoking with cancer. As a result, the government has decided that advertising of cigarettes on television is illegitimate. Amway, a distributor of home products, was challenged by the U.S. Internal Revenue Service on whether its goal was to produce and sell home products or to provide a tax shelter for those granted distributorships. Bookstores selling pornographic materials have been picketed by groups claiming the material is morally and legally without justification. And some political groups that advocate overthrow of governments or hatred toward minority groups find getting legitimacy in the broader society difficult.

Organization legitimacy is usually a product of the cultural and legal system in which the organization operates. Many organizations, recognizing that what is not legitimate in the United States may be legitimate in some foreign countries, will move their operations elsewhere. The formation of cartels, unlawful in the United States, is legal in many European countries. And some communist countries, such as Cuba, still will not allow the formation of organizations within their boundaries whose primary goal is to make a profit for the owners.

Managers of organizations must recognize that goals serve to generate and maintain support among non-members in the environment. Often, when managers recognize that their goal is losing legitimacy, they will seek a new purpose or mission for the organization. Recognizing that cigarette production was losing legitimacy, Philip Morris redefined its mission from that of a tobacco producer to that of a producer of consumable goods. The firm entered the beer industry through the acquisition of Miller Brewing, acquired Barbasol shaving cream, and has placed greater emphasis on the sale of cigarettes in overseas markets where smoking is viewed to be more acceptable.

Internal Importance of Goals

Goals also provide important information to members of the organization. Members are informed about task scope, decision guidelines, methods of motivation, standards of performance, and the rationale for organizing.

TASK SCOPE

Goals can affect how members of the organization view the scope of their tasks. Consider two stock investment firms. One has the stated goal of producing a safe, low-risk rate of return for its investors. The other has a stated goal of high growth but considerable risk in returns for investors. Managers in the low-risk investment firm will focus their tasks on the search for and purchase of financial instruments that guarantee a certain rate of return. One might expect the investment portfolio to be dominated by U.S. Treasury securities or AAA bonds. Managers in the high-risk investment firm will focus their tasks on the search for and purchase of financial instruments that have a promise of high growth but little guarantee of returns. Investment portfolios may consist of young firms in high-technology industries or firms that appear to be strong candidates for acquisition or merger. Hence, the stated goal of the organization serves to direct managers to task activities that will optimize their chances of achieving the goal.

While directing members of the organization toward desired results, goals also inform members which activities to avoid. One would not, for instance, expect a financial manager handling low-risk investments to be conducting research on the options or commodities market. Goals should provide all members of the organization with a clear understanding of what tasks are appropriate and what tasks are inappropriate.

DECISION GUIDELINES

Goals serve to set decision guidelines for organization managers. If the stated goal of an organization is to be responsive to customer needs, it would be appropriate for a sales manager to set up a payment and shipping schedule for purchased products that would conform to each major customer's cash flow position. But if the stated goal is to avoid delinquent accounts, the sales manager may have little opportunity to create a shipping and payment schedule other than one prescribed by upper management.

METHODS OF MOTIVATION

Goals provide the foundation to motivate organization members to perform at high levels. Goals serve as incentives for members, particularly when the achievement of the goal is linked directly to rewards such as promotions, salary increases, stock options, or recognition. Goals can further foster motivation through strong member identification with the purpose of the goal. Many Peace Corps volunteers were motivated to join not by the prospect of material rewards but by a firm belief in and commitment to the goal of helping people in countries with harsh living conditions.

STANDARDS OF PERFORMANCE

Goals provide a standard for assessing and rating performance. A goal of rapid growth requires upper management to set a specific performance criterion—for example, a 25 percent increase in sales over last year's record. Once the criterion has been set, individual standards can be assigned to members and their activities reflecting the contribution they are expected to make to the overall goal. At the end of the year, each member is rated to determine her or his degree of success in achieving the desired result.

RATIONALE FOR ORGANIZING

A continual concern of managers is the creation and maintenance of organization structures. Organizational goals provide the basis for selecting the correct form and fit of structure. In an uncertain environment like that facing a

Linking achievement of organizational goals to rewards serves as an incentive for employees.

computer software firm, managers need structures that are loose and flexible. Organizations facing environmental threats need structures that will enable decision makers to mobilize resources quickly and efficiently. The U.S. Air Force, for example, must be constantly on the alert for foreign intrusions of airspace. While a computer software firm may face threats from competitors, it is not a life-or-death situation for members of the firm. Rather, survival is usually dependent on the degree of member creativity. Thus, the U.S. Air Force adopts systems that emphasize rapid mobilization of combat units while a computer software firm adopts flexible systems that enhance member creativity.

TYPES OF GOALS

Organizations pursue multiple goals simultaneously. Organizational goals can be divided into three types, for which different parts of the organization assume responsibility. Top management is responsible for **official goals,** or those formally stated, of the organization. Middle management is responsible for **operative goals,** or those goals concerning operating policies of the organization. **Operational goals** are the responsibility of first-line supervisors and employees and include built-in standards of behavior, performance criteria, and completion time.[2]

Official goals are usually the most abstract and tend to be long-term. Long-term goals are those that lack specific measurement or time criteria for completion. Operational goals are the most concrete and are usually short-term. Short-term goals identify specific time and measurement criteria for the completion of the goal.[3] Operative goals are usually a mix of both long-term and short-term. They direct middle managers toward a desired outcome, but they do not specify an exact time for completing the activity or provide a specific measure of performance.

The three types of goals can be arranged on a managerial hierarchy in which operative goals are derived from official goals and operational goals are derived from operative goals. Figure 5–1 depicts the relationships among these three types of goals within the hierarchy of the organization.

FIGURE 5–1
Organizational Goals by Managerial Hierarchy

Abstract   *Long-Term*

Official Goals
Top Management

Operative Goals
Middle Management

Operational Goals
First-Line Management

Concrete   *Short-Term*

Official Goals

Official goals are the formally stated goals of the organization as described in a charter, annual report, or policy manual. As such, they express the purpose and mission of the organization. Usually abstract in content, official goals are not readily measurable. Official goals also lack closure—that is, there is nothing in the statement of a goal to indicate when the goal is to be accomplished. Merck & Company, a leader in the pharmaceutical industry, has set the following official goals:

- To enhance stockholders' wealth.
- To grow internally and externally.
- To strive for long-term improvement in the company's performance.
- To strengthen our position as a major drug company.
- To provide patients, physicians, and society with innovative products that represent high technology and high value.[4]

As stated, Merck's official goals identify to constituencies in the environment a purpose (e.g., to benefit stockholders); a mission (e.g., growth); and legitimacy (e.g., innovative products). The official goals also provide a basis for guiding members in task scope (e.g., providing innovative products); decision guidelines (e.g., providing products that represent high technology and high value); motivation (e.g., strengthening position as a major drug company); standards of performance (e.g., striving for long-term improvement in performance); and a rationale for organizing (e.g., providing patients, physicians, and society with innovative products). Thus, the five stated official goals of Merck & Company express the importance of creating links with the environment and encourage employee commitment to and identification with the firm.

The official goal statement of Merck & Company establishes links with both non-members and those who work for the firm. However, the wording itself does not provide specific direction or action to be taken. "Enhance stockholders' wealth," "strengthen our position," and "grow internally and externally" are statements open to debate among top managers. How is "stockholders' wealth" enhanced? What is a "strong position" versus a "weak position"? How is growth to be measured—and how much growth is desired? The official goal statements of Merck & Company are also long-term. The statements do not say when the goals will be accomplished. Rather, it is implied that the goals are to be ongoing concerns of top management.

Despite the level of abstraction and lack of closure, official goals can be helpful to the success of the organization over time. The abstract wording allows top management to adapt organizational activities to changes in the environment. On the other hand, the statements restrict top management from developing some activities. For instance, the official goals of Merck & Company make it clear that acquiring an automobile company would be inappropriate. By stating the official goals as long-term, top management and others in the organization are informed that the goals are not to be interpreted as temporary. Rather, they are to be accomplished on a continuing basis.

While top management has an opportunity to decide how goals will be accomplished, other responsibilities are important as well. Top management must set targets for middle and first-line managers in the organization.

If these targets are not met satisfactorily, it is often top managers who are removed from their positions. Thus, it is important for top management to establish clearly the targets to be reached in a given year and then communicate those targets to department heads.

Operative Goals

Operative goals are the ends sought through the actual operating policies of the organization. More concrete than official goals, operative goals consist of a mix between short-term and long-term dimensions. Operative goals are often redefined on a yearly basis. Adjustments to the operative goals are made with information from the prior year's performance, a forecast of environmental trends, and examination of competitors' performance. Peter Drucker has identified eight types of operative goals found within most organizations.[5]

MARKETING

Marketing goals are concerned with what the organization wants to accomplish within markets. Marketing goals are usually the responsibility of a marketing or sales department. Increases in customer satisfaction, changes in products, expansion of product lines, and growth in sales are examples of operative goals for a marketing department.

INNOVATION

Innovation goals are directed toward the development of new products, new services, or a new manufacturing process. Innovation goals are often the responsibility of research and development or engineering departments. Innovation goals may direct the research and development department to "develop two new products" or to "reduce production waste."

PROFITABILITY

Profitability in for-profit organizations is an overall organizational concern but also can be assigned to specific departments or profit centers. Profitabil-

To support innovation goals, a research and development team at TRW, Inc., works on the development of high-energy lasers for defense research.

ity goals can be expressed by return on investment, net income after taxes, or earnings per share. An increase in return on investment of a department store outlet in Fresno, California, or an annual increase in net income in the chemical division of Merck & Company would represent a profitability goal. Not-for-profit organizations often use financial ratios to set profitability goals such as decreasing average expenses per client served.

PHYSICAL RESOURCES

Physical resource goals address performance levels of the tangible assets of the organization. Plants and facilities, production capacity, inventory capacity, and the amount and quality of goods or services received from suppliers are examples of tangible assets. Physical resource goals, like profitability goals, can be assigned to many departments in the organization or to one department such as production. Additional classroom space may be a physical resource goal of a business school that is experiencing increased enrollment.

FINANCIAL RESOURCES

Financial resource goals are concerned with the acquisition of capital to maintain organizational operations. Short- and long-term debt, accounts receivable, and payments for raw materials and supplies are focuses of financial resource goals. Finance or purchasing departments would normally be assigned these goals. The repurchasing of outstanding common stock could be a financial resource goal of a firm seeking to prevent a takeover move by another firm.

HUMAN RESOURCES

Human resource goals relate to the recruitment and development of organization members. Human resource goals may address issues of staffing, absenteeism, turnover, training, and promotion of members. Though often the responsibility of a personnel department, human resource goals may also be assigned to all departments within the organization; for example, reduction of absenteeism may be a company-wide human resource goal.

PRODUCTIVITY

Productivity goals concern the levels of output per worker. The greater the level of output per worker, the more efficient the production process. Productivity goals are common in production departments, but also can be applied to other departments in the organization. Productivity of sales forces can be determined by dividing dollars of sales by total expenses required to make the sales. A productivity goal of Del Monte foods may be to decrease costs per unit of production in the pickle-packing plant.

SOCIAL RESPONSIBILITY

Social responsibility goals apply to the organization's relationship with the societies, states, or communities that are affected by its activities. Many organizations have set up consumer affairs and public relations departments or foundations to achieve social responsibility goals. Reduction in pollution emissions, increases in minority hirings, and contributions to public television are goals derived from social responsibility.

The attainment of operative goals is the responsibility of middle managers who receive directives from top management. Top management derives operative goals from the official goals and creates measures by forecasting environmental trends, evaluating past performance, and examining performance of competitors. Operative goals are then assigned to the department and manager that will be responsible for their completion. It is essential that top management communicate the intent and purpose of the operative goal to members of each department.

Operational Goals

Operational goals have built-in standards of behavior, performance criteria, and completion time. Operational goals are concrete and short-term. Operational goals inform first-line managers and members of the organization how and when the goal will be attained. An operational goal is derived from an operative goal. The linkage of official, operative, and operational goals, referred to as the **hierarchy of goals**, is shown in Figure 5–2. It is important to recognize that the achievement of operational goals leads to the achievement of operative goals. These achievements in turn enable the organization to fulfill official goals at the top level of the organization.

Operational goals give managers a concrete idea of what is expected from them. The operative goal of "increasing sales of product A" can be expanded into the operational goal of "increasing sales of product A in 1995 by 10 percent over last year through hiring five sales representatives to cover the New England states." Operational goals can be further specified, such as assigning one manager the task of locating 20 potential applicants for the sales representative job by October 1994. Additional managers can be assigned the responsibility of segmenting sales territory in New England into five units by November 1994. Figure 5–3 shows how Merck & Company might derive both operative and operational goals from its statement of official goals.

FORMULATING GOALS

Goal formulation is a critical task for top management. It must consider several questions. What goals does management want the organization to

FIGURE 5–2
The Hierarchy of Goals

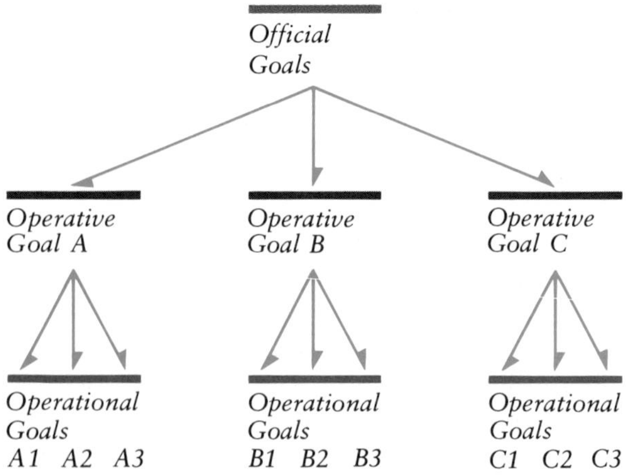

Official Goals	Operative Goals	Operational Goals
1. Enhance stockholders' wealth.	1. Increase quarterly dividend payments.	a. Reduce debt by 1 percent each quarter. b. Increase retained earnings for dividend payment at rate of 2 percent a quarter. c. Repurchase 0.05 percent of company stock each year.
2. Grow internally and externally.	2. Acquire a firm with a compatible product line.	a. Identify potential firms by May. b. Develop negotiation team by June. c. Submit offer by August.
3. Strive for long-term improvement in the company's performance.	3. Implement cost control programs.	a. Cut production costs by 15 percent on all product lines. b. Increase income-to-sales ratio by 5 percent. c. Reduce capital outlays by 12 percent of sales.
4. Strengthen our position as a major drug company.	4. Increase market share.	a. Increase sales force 10 percent by end of first quarter. b. Increase national advertising budget by 5 percent by end of first quarter. c. Open new facility in Asia by November.
5. Provide patients, physicians, and society with innovative products that represent high technology and high value.	5. Introduce five new products a year.	a. Double research and development staff by end of March. b. Survey patients and physicians on product needs by end of April. c. Acquire two patents from university faculty.

FIGURE 5–3

Possible Operative and Operational Goals Based on Merck & Company's Official Goals

achieve? What goals does it believe it can achieve? The type of competition the organization must face, the availability of resources to the organization, constraints imposed on organizational activities by laws, and skill levels among members of the organization must all be taken into account in the goal-formulation process. The desire to be profitable and provide quality products or services to consumers cannot be the only consideration when goals are formulated. Management also must have a clear understanding of the organizational context in which it operates to discriminate between unrealistic and realistic goals. Much of this understanding can be achieved by identifying external and internal factors associated with organizational goal formulation.

External Factors and Goal Formulation

James Thompson and William McEwen have provided a model for understanding the goal-formulation process based on the organization's relationship with its environment.[6] They stress that organizations can be placed on a continuum where at one end the organization has a strong influence over its environment and at the other end the environment has a strong influence over the organization. While most organizations reside somewhere in the middle, goals are formulated either through competitive factors or through cooperative factors such as bargaining, co-optation, or coalitions.

COMPETITION

Competition implies that an element of rivalry exists between two or more organizations. Competition can exist over customers, raw materials, personnel, or social legitimacy. With competition, managers are relatively free to formulate goals based solely on competitive considerations. However, even under conditions of competition, the organization can be constrained by noncompetitive factors. Suppliers may simply refuse to sell products or services to the organization because they dislike the management of the company. Governments may constrain goal formulation by dictating what are and are not acceptable goals of the company. Or, customers may choose to buy only products which are made in America.

Historically, large multinational corporations have come closest to organizations able to formulate goals based on competition. Recently, however, this type of goal formulation has been problematic. Opposition to apartheid in South Africa, for instance, has forced many multinational companies doing business in that country to reformulate goals based on ethical considerations. Revelations that officials of foreign governments have been bribed by managers of multinational companies have resulted in the expulsion of many firms from the host country. As a result, many companies doing business overseas have had to reformulate goals. Thus, even managers of organizations that have a large influence over their environment are not necessarily able to formulate goals based solely on competitive considerations.

COOPERATION

At the other end of the goal-formulation continuum is cooperation. **Cooperation** is pursued by managers when other organizations in the environment have a strong influence over their organization. There are three ways to formulate goals through cooperation: bargaining, co-optation, and coalition.

Agreements reached through labor/management bargaining play an important role in goal formulation.

Bargaining

Bargaining is the negotiation of an agreement for the exchange of goods or services between two or more organizations. Managers formulate goals directed toward maintaining agreements with suppliers or buyers. Goals that may lead to dissatisfaction among suppliers or buyers may be rejected by management if it believes it must continue to maintain the relationships.

The role of bargaining and its relationship to goal formulation are readily observed in negotiations between labor unions and management. Unions supply labor to an organization, usually under an agreement that is periodically renegotiated. Management must formulate its goals depending on the nature of the agreement that has been bargained with labor. For instance, the union representing baseball players has a strong impact on the formulation of goals by owners. The players' union can command strong influence largely because a substitute resource (i.e., baseball players) is not readily available.

Co-optation

Co-optation occurs when an organization must absorb new elements into the goal-formulation process to avert threats to the organization's stability or survival. Co-optation constrains the formulation of goals because the desired goal must be acceptable to the co-opted party.

For instance, when Chrysler Corporation faced the chance of failure in the late 1970s, it needed cooperation from labor to avoid costly strikes and to reduce labor costs. To get these guarantees, top management of Chrysler had to agree to accept Douglas Fraser, then the president of the United Auto Workers Union, as a member of the board of directors. While this move alarmed many corporate executives both within and outside the auto industry, the result was a more cooperative relationship between the union and the company. Indeed, many observers have credited this move as a major reason why Chrysler saved itself from bankruptcy. Co-optation is also common among young, entrepreneurial firms. Often, young firms must include bank executives or venture capitalists on their boards of directors to get the necessary cash to continue operations. The result is that some goals must be modified to satisfy the additional party in the decision process.

Coalition

A **coalition** is a combination of two or more organizations joined to achieve a common purpose. For some organizations, the failure to locate a partner to form a coalition results in an inability to achieve a desired goal. On the other hand, forming a coalition usually means that the desired goal becomes compromised as each organization in the coalition seeks to formulate the goal in a manner that is most advantageous for it. Coalitions also introduce veto power, which sets further constraints on the goal-formulation process.

For example, American Motors Corporation, prior to being bought out by Chrysler Corporation, teamed up with Renault of France because AMC lacked the ability to design and produce a small car on its own that would appeal to enough consumers. One condition of the venture was the emphasis on the Renault name over AMC, which provided Renault with direct access to the U.S. market.

Managers need to recognize that the environment introduces constraints on the goal-formulation process. While some goals may be highly desired by management, the pursuit of those goals may be infeasible without support from other organizations. Generally the larger and more dominant an organization is within its market, the more ability top management has to formulate goals based on its own desires.

Internal Factors and Goal Formulation

There are several internal factors that constrain management's formulation of goals. Richard Cyert and James March suggest that goal formulation is an outcome of competing claims for resources among groups within the organization.[7] Groups form when organization members have identified common interests they want to promote. The formation of groups with a common interest may be by department (e.g., research and development); by hierarchy (e.g., middle managers); or by distinct concerns or traits (e.g., women).

As groups within the organization compete for resources, three processes

Groups form when organization members have identified common interests they want to promote.

have an influence on goal formulation. These include side payments, prior commitments, and organizational slack.

SIDE PAYMENTS

Side payments are inducements that can be used by groups to encourage others to join them in pursuit of their desired goals. Side payments may include money, status, privileged treatment, authority, or promises. Side payments, therefore, are the price a group pays others to join it in support of a group goal. For example, stockholders are induced by dividends to support the goals of top management; production workers are induced through wage increases to avoid strikes; middle managers are offered promotions and more office space if they agree to support a goal; or a marketing department may be granted the opportunity to introduce a product line if it agrees to cut back on travel expenses. The result in each case is that goals are formulated based on the number and type of side payments available to groups in the organization.

PRIOR COMMITMENTS

Prior commitments are guarantees or promises made to others on actions to be taken in the future. Goal formulation can be influenced by prior commitments made to groups within the organization. Prior commitments influence the formulation of goals by limiting the amount of resources used for side payments within the organization. For example, let's suppose that research and development is guaranteed an annual increase of 20 percent in its budget by top management for the next five years if it will increase its work on high-technology products. With this commitment of funds to R&D, resources may not be available for side payments to other groups in the organization, such as marketing, which may favor expanding its sales force. Thus, prior commitments may serve to constrain the ability of a group to influence goals in the future by diminishing the resources available for side payments.

ORGANIZATIONAL SLACK

Basic to the processes of side payments and prior commitments is the notion of organizational slack. **Organizational slack** is the difference between the total resources available to the organization and the total side payments made to induce goal support among organizational groups. Organizational slack can be viewed as the balance of a bank account in which total resources are deposits and side payments are withdrawals. During times of excess resources (i.e., increased organizational slack), weaker groups often can participate in the goal-formulation process, as side payments tend to be generous. However, when organizational slack is low, hard bargaining between groups emerges and the weaker groups often must sacrifice the pursuit of their own goals.

The formulation of goals within organizations can be understood as the result of factors both external and internal to the organization. Managers must consider the constraints imposed on goal formulation by the organization's relationship with the environment and the degree of group bargaining resulting from levels of organizational slack. Figure 5–4 depicts both the external and internal factors of an organization that influence the goal-formulation process.

MANAGING MULTIPLE GOALS

It is clear from our discussion that organizations have multiple goals. Often, these goals are incompatible or are in conflict. Increasing a firm's contributions to charitable organizations may cause a decrease in profits. Expanding a firm's market share can also result in lower profit. Thus, managers must assess the tradeoffs when the achievement of two goals simultaneously is not possible. Four techniques that managers can use to decide which goals will be emphasized when conflicts exist are satisficing, sequential attention, preference ordering, and goal changes.

Satisficing

Managers of organizations can choose to satisfice their levels of performance across goals.[8] **Satisficing** a goal means identifying a satisfactory, or suboptimal, rather than optimal level of performance to be attained. This technique is most commonly used when management believes that the highest levels of performance cannot be achieved for all goals, but the organization cannot

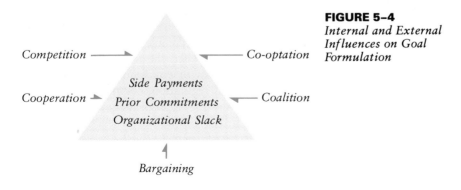

FIGURE 5–4
Internal and External Influences on Goal Formulation

Competition —→   ←— *Co-optation*

Side Payments
Cooperation ➤ *Prior Commitments*   ←— *Coalition*
Organizational Slack

Bargaining

afford to fail in its performance of any one goal. Thus, managers set acceptable levels of performance for each goal, recognizing that optimums may not be achievable.

Sequential Attention

Managers may choose to shift their attention sequentially from one goal to the next over time. **Sequential attention** is most commonly used when certain periods require greater attention to one goal than to others. Or it may be necessary when a crisis in the organization requires managers to redirect their attention until the problem is resolved.

Toy manufacturers, for instance, focus their attention on research and development goals during the spring and summer months, shift their attention to production in the fall months, and shift attention again to sales before the Christmas season in December. In 1984, IBM suffered a less-than-projected sales volume of its PCjr® home computer and was forced to redirect its attention to reviving sales. A concerted marketing campaign was started and the price of the computer was lowered. As a result, almost 200,000 PCjr home computers were sold in the fourth quarter of 1984 where only 75,000 units had been sold in the prior three quarters. This effort, however, did not correct the problem. After the marketing campaign ended and the price for the computer returned to its previous level, sales declined, forcing IBM to drop production of the PCjr computer in April 1985. Thus, management's attention to the crisis enabled the company to achieve its sales goals for the 1984 year, but the need to shift attention to other products led to the demise of the PCjr in the next year.

Preference Ordering

In some situations, managers may use **preference ordering**, ranking goals according to priorities. Management may decide that increasing profit goals is more important than increasing market share. Increasing market share may be considered more important than increasing product quality. During an economic recession, managers of companies often choose to sell product lines or company divisions to other firms to use the cash to bolster profits, even though it means a loss in total market share. Such decisions are often based on a previous management decision to rank profit increases over market share increases.

Changes in consumer tastes may require changes in organizational goals.

Goal Changes

Over time, some goals become outdated or are no longer appropriate in relation to current environmental conditions. Goal changes come about as managers reevaluate the importance of goals or when the measurement criteria become inappropriate as a result of changes in environmental conditions. Changes in consumer tastes, governmental regulation, competition, or technology may require managers to examine the appropriateness of the goal. The three major television networks in the United States (ABC, CBS, and NBC) have long had the goal of being first in market share among television audiences. With the growth of cable broadcasting in the 1970s and 1980s, this goal has become less important. Expanded cable broadcasting and VCR use has resulted in an overall decline in market share for the three major television networks. While being number one in market share is still a goal, it is much less of a priority than it used to be.

In some cases, goal change can be the result of success. One example is the Foundation for Infantile Paralysis, which pursued the goal of controlling polio in the 1940s. When an effective vaccine was developed, management selected the new goal of conquering birth defects and arthritis and changed the organization's name to the March of Dimes.[9]

ORGANIZATIONAL EFFECTIVENESS

An important concern of managers is the overall effectiveness of the organization. **Organizational effectiveness** can be defined as the extent to which an organization realizes its goals.[10] In this section, we will discuss various methods managers can use to assess the effectiveness of an organization.

Effectiveness Versus Efficiency

In the previous section, it was noted that organizations pursue multiple goals. One may assume that organizational effectiveness can be determined by comparing the actual performance with the intended performance for each goal and totaling the results. However, this would not provide a manager with an accurate picture of overall effectiveness. For instance, an organization that achieves its goals of increased market share, product innovation, product quality, consumer satisfaction, and social responsibility may still fail miserably at achieving the goal of profitability, forcing the organization into bankruptcy. Because the organization achieved five of six operative goals, would a manager be content with this measure of effectiveness? In all likelihood, probably not.

Managers should recognize that organizational goals are not necessarily equal in importance and that their importance can vary over time. In addi-

Does the use of robots help an organization improve its effectiveness, its efficiency, or both?

tion, a measure of organizational effectiveness must incorporate factors both inside and outside the organization. If the organization were to achieve the goal of high profits at the expense of consumer satisfaction, managers of other organizations might conclude that the organization is ineffective and decide to enter the industry. Thus, the diversity and inequality of organizational goals make measurement of effectiveness a highly complex problem.

Efficiency is less problematic for managers to assess in most organizations. **Organizational efficiency** is defined as the ratio of an organization's outputs to its inputs. Inputs consist of raw materials, labor, and capital. Outputs consist of products or services. When compared with similar organizations, an organization is considered more efficient when fewer inputs are used to achieve an equivalent number of outputs. Thus, efficiency is an internal measure of performance that focuses on *the degree to which* the organization achieves its goal rather than on *whether* the organization achieves its goal.

Managers sometimes confuse measures of efficiency with measures of effectiveness. Generally, measures of efficiency are related to organizational effectiveness, as reduced production costs can support the survival of the organization. However, efficiency and effectiveness can be entirely unrelated. The ability to produce a product at a relatively low cost does not promote organizational effectiveness if consumers have no interest in purchasing the product. On the other hand, an organization may be able to attract a market for its product, but inefficiencies in production may eliminate profits.

An example demonstrating that efficiency is not necessarily related to effectiveness is provided by a computer firm named Viatron, founded in 1968. Viatron set goals of (1) becoming a major force in the data-processing industry, (2) supplanting IBM as the industry leader, and (3) generating large capital gains for the founders and investors of the company. Achieving these goals would be supported by the application of a relatively new technology known as MOS/LSI. This new technology was to replace the current use of transistors and would allow data processing to be conducted through terminals rather than through one large unit. Application of the new technology enabled Viatron to achieve a ten-to-one cost efficiency over IBM in the production of its units. Because of a downturn in the economy in 1970, however, sales plummeted and Viatron was forced into bankruptcy in 1971. Despite the large cost efficiencies in production it achieved over its competition, the failure of the company to generate an adequate cash flow for corporate reinvestment led to its downfall.[11] Later, the same MOS/LSI technology led to the use of silicon chips by both Apple Computer and IBM to generate the home computer revolution in the mid-1970s.

Assessing Organizational Effectiveness

Assessing an organization's effectiveness is not a clear and easy task. While comparing intended goal performance with actual goal performance is perhaps the most common method, managers must also recognize that other factors have to be considered as well. Ways to rate overall organizational effectiveness include examining an organization's ability to get the resources it needs, to operate in a smooth and efficient manner, to optimize goals, and to satisfy external constituencies that have an interest in the organization. We will address each of these approaches separately.

SYSTEMS RESOURCE ASSESSMENT

The systems resource assessment of organizational effectiveness is an approach that examines the performance of the organization in getting the resources it needs.[12] Measures and evaluations of effectiveness in this approach come from assessing the organization's ability to get necessary inputs for transformation into a product or service. An inability to get necessary inputs will constrain or curtail organizational activities. New firms in high technology must be effective in getting start-up capital; bakeries must get flour, eggs, and other ingredients to continue operating; airlines must purchase gasoline to meet schedules; and social service agencies must receive federal, state, or municipal funding to continue offering services to the community.

Determining organizational effectiveness from a systems resource view includes two important assessments: (1) the amount of resources acquired from the external environment, and (2) the bargaining position the organization has with resource suppliers in the external environment. The first assessment directs managers to goals that will increase resource acquisition. Examples of such goals may be "to increase financial borrowing to expand product line," or "to increase coal reserves to avoid disruptions in production due to worker strikes." The second assessment directs managers' attention to goals that will optimize the company's bargaining position with suppliers—for example, "to improve contacts with suppliers to get faster delivery time," or "to expand the number of suppliers to get a more competitive price."

INTERNAL PROCESS ASSESSMENT

The internal process assessment of organizational effectiveness focuses on goals related to productivity and member development. The organization is judged in terms of production efficiency, integration of departmental activities, satisfaction of members, and level of conflict within the organization. Thus, the effective organization from the standpoint of internal process assessment is one that operates smoothly and efficiently without costly disruptions. Where systems resource assessment focuses on acquisition of organization inputs to determine effectiveness, internal process assessment focuses on how resources have been handled after they have been acquired. Lumber mills try to make use of the total tree to avoid waste; navy personnel are given shore leave to increase morale; and building construction firms schedule regular meetings between architects and engineers to coordinate plans.

Internal process assessment of organizational effectiveness is concerned with both production efficiency goals and member goals. Sometimes these goals compete with each other, creating a dilemma for managers. Emphasis on production efficiency, for instance, may lead to worker dissatisfaction as constraints are applied to activities. Efforts to increase worker satisfaction may reduce production efficiency as members spend more time on activities that do not directly contribute to the production of a good or service. Thus, managers must decide the tradeoffs between competing goals to increase effectiveness.

Examples of goals contributing to internal process effectiveness of the organization would be "to increase employee morale by encouraging participation in production decisions," "to reduce production waste by transferring unused materials to other departments," and "to establish coordinating committees across departments to engage in planning and resolving disputes."

Many organizations now provide exercise facilities at the work site to show their commitment to the health and well-being of employees and increase employee satisfaction.

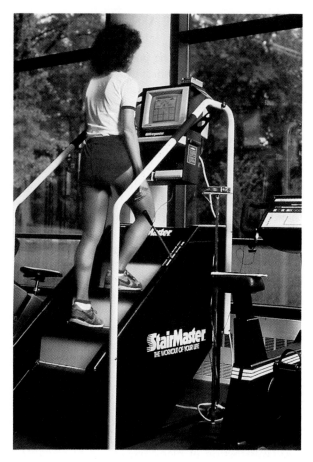

GOAL ASSESSMENT

Goal assessment focuses on the outputs of the organization. Outputs are the products or services that the organization produces to distribute to consumers. Output goals are usually described in terms of sales growth, market share, volume, revenues, or profits. Effectiveness is achieved when the organization has attained the desired level or target of the output goal. Business schools set goals for the successful placement of students in jobs; television networks strive to increase their market shares of audiences; and grocery stores try to increase sales volume of products on the shelves.

Many organizations rate their effectiveness of output by comparing current goal achievement with goal achievement from a prior period or by comparing goal achievement with that of competing organizations. "Increase our market share by 10 percent over last year" is a goal measure that compares last year's performance with this year's performance. "Increase market share to be largest in the industry" is a goal measure developed for comparison with competing organizations. It is usually inappropriate for organization managers to develop goals by setting targets based on organizations outside their industry. A 5 percent increase in revenue for a restaurant may be considered effective, but a 5 percent increase in revenue for a savings and loan may be considered ineffective.

STRATEGIC CONSTITUENCY ASSESSMENT

A strategic constituency assessment of organizational effectiveness places less emphasis on the inputs, the outputs, and the internal processes of the organization and more emphasis on groups that have a stake in the organization. A **strategic constituency** is any group internal or external to the organization that has more than a passing interest in how the organization performs. Stockholders, owners, creditors, suppliers, employees, communities, and customers can all be considered to be strategic constituencies of an organization. In this respect, effectiveness is determined by the degree to which the organization satisfies the expectations and demands of all these groups.

A strategic constituency assessment of organizational effectiveness is usually more difficult to make than assessments using the systems resource, internal process, and goal assessment approaches. Groups can vary widely in their expectations and demands. Stockholders rate the organization by financial returns on their investments; members judge the organization on the quality of the workplace; customers expect the organization to be responsive to their needs; suppliers check the organization on its promptness in payment; and communities assess the organization on how the organization improves the quality of life for the citizenry. The often contradictory demands and expectations of these groups hamper an organization's ability to be effective.

Goals that relate to a strategic constituency assessment would be "to increase support for our service in the community," "to increase dividend payments on stock," and "to be responsive to customer complaints." While such goals resemble those of the systems resource, internal process, and goal assessment approaches, strategic constituency assessment measures effectiveness by relative satisfaction across all groups with an interest in the organization. Hence, it is the combined satisfaction of these groups that is used to assess the effectiveness of the organization. Figure 5–5 shows the various constituencies that managers may have to consider.

The relationship among these four approaches for assessing organizational effectiveness is shown graphically in Figure 5–6. At times, managers may focus on one type of assessment, depending on circumstances. For instance, when the resource environment is lean and inputs are difficult to obtain,

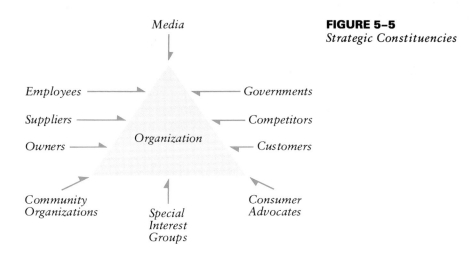

FIGURE 5–5
Strategic Constituencies

FIGURE 5–6
*Four Approaches for
Assessing Organizational
Effectiveness*

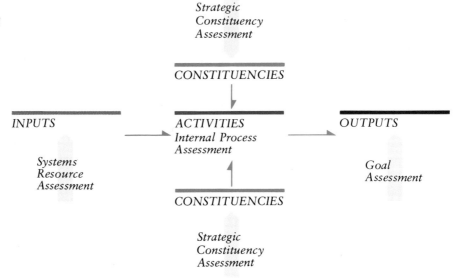

managers may emphasize systems resource assessment. A drop in production efficiencies may direct managers to an assessment of internal processes. Declining sales would require an assessment of output goals. A lessening of satisfaction among stockholders and communities would encourage an evaluation of strategic constituencies. Regardless of the emphasis chosen, managers must recognize that the four different assessments of organizational effectiveness are interrelated. Adjustments in goals to strengthen one area may require adjustments in goals affecting the other areas.

Criteria for Assessing Organizational Effectiveness

Managers can address several questions that will help them in making their organizations more effective. These questions enable managers to understand and reformulate, if necessary, the criteria they use for judging effectiveness. Important questions for managers to consider are the following:[13]

- To what extent are we applying our limited resources toward the attainment of our various goals? In many instances, resources are distributed throughout the organization without recognizing that the goals may be independent of the allocation. As a result, some goals may be unfunded, or activities may be funded that fail to support a goal. For example, funds may be allocated to hire quality-control inspectors to meet the goal of improved product quality, but the funds necessary to cover their travel to different plants may not have been allocated. Or, funds may be allocated to a research and development department to buy new equipment that is unrelated to the goal of developing new products.
- Is there a clear relationship between the amount of resources we spend on the various goals and the importance of each goal? If the organization is committed to increasing profits and generating community support and these two goals are considered to be equal, is the commitment reflected in the allocation of resources?

Q: What should corporate managers understand about the role of organizational goals?

A: Let's start with this premise: Organizational goals provide a point of focus for the members. When goals are stated and known to the different stakeholders, they tell an important story about what the organization is all about. I believe that too often managers forget the fundamental reason why an economic organization exists. A society needs economic goods and services and, in order to have them created, legitimizes a certain form of business organization. This legitimacy defines the priorities of the various stakeholders' claims on the firm, as well as the acceptable limits for those claims. For instance, in our society, firms must meet customer demands, achieve acceptable returns on investment, pay minimum wages, and be good citizens in many different ways. Other cultures define different structures of legitimacy, as can be observed in those which have more socialistic political systems.

Managers must develop a set of organizational goals which can accommodate the demands of these different constituencies. Further, managers must realize that, over time, these priorities will change. When they do, the firm has no choice but to accommodate, though it will incur costs. For instance, we are all aware of the growing concern with pollution and how many firms are now required, by law, to reduce toxic emissions. The management may not like the fact that it must increase costs, but it must do so or be forced out of business. The same thing happens with product preferences, though managers usually understand this market effect a little better. Over the years we have seen dramatic changes in what consumers want in cars, electronics, and clothing. When companies responded, they did well. When they did not, they lost market share.

Essentially what this means is that the overarching activity of top management is to continually negotiate and accommodate to these different constituencies. It is only in this way that the firm can survive.

Q: But is survival enough? Shouldn't managers be concerned with maximizing profits?

A: Of course to survive the firm must provide adequate returns to owners, set wages that will attract a managerial and skilled work force, and meet other social and legal requirements. These goals are usually articulated in mission statements which outline, in general terms, what the firm seeks to do.

But the real trick is to turn these mission statements into specific operative goals that mean something to those in the firm. This is a problem, because mission statements tend to be very general, which means that they may be translated into different operative goals and achieving them is the difference between success and failure. Some take a longer-term view of the market, place a different emphasis on product quality and price, and have a more enlightened view of their work force.

Q: Then doesn't the question become: "Why is it that some firms do better than others in developing and implementing goals?"

A: Yes, and there are at least three reasons for this. One is that some managers have more ability than others. This problem has to be addressed by careful selection and development of the managerial work force.

A second reason is that it is crucial to understand and create the proper relationship among the different operative goals. For example, market goals must define a product that consumers will purchase. If that is not done right, the other goals are not attainable. Sometimes we observe that managers define operative goals in a way that puts their own interests ahead of market goals.

The third reason is that, even when we get the goals right, it is difficult (1) to break them down into more specific objectives for those in different functions and levels of the firms and (2) to develop a system of incentives to reinforce organization members to achieve them. This is what management by objectives (MBO) is all about. It is the way to make organizational goals a meaningful concept for those who are working to achieve them.

Henry Tosi (Ph.D., Ohio State University) is the McGrift Professor of Management at the University of Florida. He has been on the faculty of the Graduate School of Business, Michigan State University. He previously taught at the University of Maryland, Cornell University, the University of California at Irvine, and Luigi Bocconi University in Milan, Italy. He is the co-author, with Stephen Carroll, of Management by Objectives: Research and Applications, *a book based on research at Black and Decker Inc. In addition, Professor Tosi is the author of four other books, including* Theories of Organization, *and the co-editor of two books,* Motivation and Compensation *and* Organization

ACADEMIC PROFILE
HENRY TOSI

Behavior: A Contingency Approach. *Professor Tosi has written several articles and papers on management that have appeared in the* Academy of Management Journal, Journal of Business, Administrative Science Quarterly, *and* Journal of Applied Psychology. *He is a fellow of the Academy of Management.*

- What kind of return on investment, per goal, are we getting on our resources? Some organizational goals considered to be more important may have a lower return on investment than lesser goals. For example, funding lobbying efforts in Congress to get favorable trade restriction laws may have a low return on investment, but the need to have contact with legislatures may outweigh the desire to get higher returns.

- Is the entire organization working together for goal attainment? It is often the case that departments or groups in the organization engage in activities that are more helpful to them than to the overall organization. For instance, marketing personnel may have a greater interest in conducting consumer research than in promoting sales if the former gives members more job autonomy and is more related to their skills. If this focus results in poor sales and revenue performance, however, management must make appropriate adjustments so that opportunities for goal attainment are not reduced.

- Is the "fit" between the organization and its environment changing? Environments are often unstable for organizations over time. As the environment shifts, so also should the goals of the organization. Managers need to raise questions continually about the nature of the environment and how the organization is situated in relation to its competition. Merck & Company must continually monitor new pharmaceutical products to judge their effectiveness. If physicians are changing their approach to certain illnesses, the firm must reevaluate its goals and adjust them accordingly.

IMPLICATIONS FOR MANAGEMENT

Organizational goals are important to members and non-members alike. As a manager, you should set and communicate the organization's goals clearly to external constituencies to get and maintain legitimacy for the organization's activities. Goals should be communicated clearly to members so they will understand how their tasks contribute to the organization and will recognize what are acceptable and unacceptable standards of performance. Many organizational activities fail or do not accomplish the goal they were designed to achieve because managers have not communicated clearly their purpose or informed members of their importance. This emphasis on goal communication should not be confined to your immediate subordinates. Rather, you should be attentive to the way in which official goals at the top of the organization are translated down to the operational level as well.

The formulation of goals is a critical activity in the organization. Many managers fail to recognize that many external and internal contextual conditions influence the way goals are formulated. Before formulating a goal, you should first determine the competitive strength of your organization. If your organization is a dominant force in the industry, goals should be formulated based on maintaining your competitive edge. If your organization is in an industry dominated by bigger competitors, you may want to formulate goals that will maintain cooperative agreements with suppliers and buyers.

As a manager you will want to identify which goals are of the greatest importance. It is useful, for instance, to rank goals based on what activities are most critical to the success of the organization. The ranked goals should be discussed with other managers to achieve consensus as well as to inform them of activities that should receive the greatest attention over the course of time. Be aware of when goals need to be changed, and be sure to inform other members of the organization why the change is being made.

Assess the effectiveness of the organization using different approaches. Use the systems resource approach for assessing input goals, the internal process approach for assessing activities in the production of goods or services, the goal approach for assessing output goals, and the strategic constituency approach for assessing goals related to groups in the broader environment. Be aware that the four approaches are interrelated; a high degree of success in three of the areas may not compensate for failure in the fourth.

KEY TERMS AND CONCEPTS

bargaining	organizational effectiveness
coalition	organizational efficiency
competition	organizational goal
cooperation	organizational slack
co-optation	preference ordering
hierarchy of goals	prior commitments
legitimacy	purpose
mission	satisficing
official goals	sequential attention
operational goals	side payments
operative goals	strategic constituency

QUESTIONS FOR REVIEW AND DISCUSSION

1. How do an organization's purpose and mission differ? How are they similar? How do goals lead to legitimacy of an organization? Who grants the legitimacy?
2. What five important types of information do goals provide members of the organization?
3. What types of organizations are most likely to have their legitimacy questioned? Is this questioning due to a change in the environment or to objections to the goals at the time the organization was created?
4. What problems might you encounter in formulating goals if resources are plentiful in the organization? If resources are scarce? What specific methods might you pursue under each situation?
5. Identify the eight types of operative goals that Peter Drucker found within most organizations. How would you assign each goal by department within an organization?
6. Under what conditions are organization managers likely to formulate goals based on competitive considerations? Based on cooperative considerations?
7. Define the terms side payments, prior commitments, and organizational slack. How do they influence goal formulation within the organization?
8. Identify four techniques that managers can use for deciding which of several conflicting goals will be emphasized.
9. The dean of the business school would like you to evaluate the effectiveness of the school. Where would you begin and how would you proceed? What assessment(s) would you apply in your evaluation?

10. Review the five important questions for managers to consider when developing criteria for assessing organizational effectiveness. Can you identify other questions that would be equally important to managers?

5–1 AMERICA'S MOST ADMIRED CORPORATIONS

The Greeks had a word for it: *eudoxia*—reputation. Shakespeare's Iago called it "the immortal part of myself." To his Richard II, it was "the purest treasure mortal times afford." Today's managers may put it more prosaically, but they know that in a fiercely competitive world where news spreads—and views can change—on a nanosecond's notice, a solid reputation has never been more important. Says David Glass, CEO of Wal-Mart stores: "It helps you with customers, suppliers, and employees. Your reputation is everything and should be protected at any cost."

No company has nurtured this invaluable asset better than Merck. For the fourth straight year, the New Jersey pharmaceuticals giant scored highest among the 305 major corporations in our annual poll of nearly 8,000 executives, directors, and financial analysts. But the competition is getting tougher. Rated on a scale of 0 to 10 in each of eight categories, Merck averaged 8.90 this year. It earned top honors by four measures, including quality of products and soundness of financial position. Two of the other categories were won by silver medalist Philip Morris, which scored 8.78 overall. Never during Merck's reign as champ has its lead been so narrow.

Several other corporations gained considerable ground in the view of executives and other experts, all of whom rated companies within their own industries. By pressing ahead with the most radical restructuring in its recent history, Procter & Gamble shed its image as the corporate Kremlin and leaped nine places to No. 4. Du Pont joined the first team for the first time, moving from No. 15 a year ago to No. 10. PepsiCo rose a notch to tie the retailing wizards at Wal-Mart for the No. 6 spot. Pepsi was joined in the top ten by Coca-Cola and Anheuser-Busch—an unprecedented trifecta for the three biggest U.S. beverage companies and a tribute to their ability to gain global market share without choking off profit growth.

Inevitably, some slipped. Boeing, which suffered a six-week strike, dipped to No. 11 from No. 8. Furniture maker Herman Miller, hammered by a slump in spending on office refurbishing, dropped 24 places to No. 33. Big Oil also looked smaller. Shell Oil slipped four places to No. 14. Exxon, wounded by the disastrous Alaskan oil spill, plummeted from the sixth spot to No. 110.

What does it take to win—and keep—a top reputation? For one thing, consistently spectacular profit growth. Merck's earnings per share have risen at least 25 percent for 14 consecutive quarters. On revenues over five times larger than Merck's, Philip Morris routinely logs 20 percent annual increases in earnings per share. Rubbermaid, which occupies the No. 3 spot and is a perennial star of this survey, has met or surpassed CEO Stanley Galt's goal of 15 percent annual sales and earnings growth for three years running. PepsiCo has spent some $8 billion on acquisitions since 1985 and increased earnings at a compound annual rate of over 20 percent while doing so. Says Chief Executive D. Wayne Calloway: "We are not letting building for the 1990s get in the way of everyday results."

Muscular profits, of course, lift share prices. In 1989, Philip Morris's stock rose 63 percent, Merck's 34 percent, Procter & Gamble's 61 percent. P&G's former chief, John Smale, and his successor, Edwin Artzt, successfully pushed management authority down and speeded up decision making. Better chemistry with shareholders also lifted Du Pont. By raising the quarterly dividend from $1.05 to $1.20 and announcing a $2 billion share repurchase program, new CEO Edgar Woolard improved his company's value as a long-term investment from 7.50 to 7.82 in the judges' rating.

The most admired are masters at rolling out new products and services. Merck holds one of the deepest hands among global players in the $100-billion-a-year prescription drug market. Last year 15 of its drugs had sales of over $100 million. Rubbermaid creates so many toys, trash cans, dish drains, and other plastic goodies that products less than five years old account for more than 30 percent of sales.

Laurel-resting and resistance to change are rarely found among those who top *Fortune's* honor roll. Consider 3M, which ranked fifth overall. Though awash in products—60,000 at last count—3M has spent $6 billion over the past five years redesigning its merchandise and reshaping manufacturing lines. Says security analyst Theresa Gusman of Salomon Brothers: "This is a company that develops a whole new process for making Scotch tape, even when it already dominates the market. They are amazing."

Merck, whose drugs have almost all been home-grown, is beginning to look beyond its own labs. To maintain strong earnings growth throughout this decade, the company is teaming with Johnson & Johnson to develop new over-the-counter drugs and with Du Pont on prescription pharmaceuticals that will help fight hypertension. PepsiCo—already the beverage industry leader in attracting, developing, and keeping talented people, according to our judges—gave each of its 100,000 employees stock options worth 10 percent of their salaries in 1989. Says CEO Calloway, who plans to continue the practice every year: "This just reinforces the theme that employees are the stewards of PepsiCo's assets."

Most Admired	Score*	Least Admired	Score*
Merck	8.90	Gibraltar Financial	2.24
Philip Morris	8.78	Wang Laboratories	3.08
Rubbermaid	8.42	Control Data	3.59
Procter & Gamble	8.37	Meritor Financial Group	3.61
3M	8.21	Texas Air	3.72
PepsiCo	8.16	LTV	3.86
Wal-Mart	8.16	National Steel	4.01
Coca-Cola	8.15	United Merchants and Mfrs.	4.03
Anheuser-Busch	7.96	K-H	4.05
Du Pont	7.93	Unisys	4.18

*Using a scale 0 (poor) to 10 (excellent), 8,000 executives, outside directors, and financial analysts were asked to rate companies in their own industries on eight attributes: (1) quality of management, (2) quality of products or services, (3) innovativeness, (4) long-term investment value, (5) financial soundness, (6) ability to attract, develop, and keep talented people, (7) community and environmental responsibility, and (8) use of corporate assets.

Source: Adapted from Sarah Smith, "America's Most Admired Corporations," *Fortune* (January 29, 1990): 58-63. © 1990 Time Inc. Reprinted by permission from *Fortune* Magazine. All rights reserved.

1. Identify the different approaches to effectiveness that each key attribute in the corporate reputation survey attempts to measure. Do the eight key attributes adequately measure an organization's effectiveness? Why or why not?
2. Which of the performance categories in the *Fortune* article does Merck & Company emphasize in its official goal statement (see page 141)? Why do you believe Merck has been more successful than other firms in the ratings?
3. Examine this year's *Fortune* ratings (published in January of each year). What changes have occurred? What circumstances may have led to those changes in corporate scores among the eight key attributes?

5–2 THE KING OF TIRES IS DISCONTENTED

After a ten-year battle to hold its position as the world's largest tire maker, Goodyear sits high atop the rubber heap these days. The Akron-based company has overwhelmed traditional U.S. competitors and faced down such formidable foreigners as France's Michelin and Japan's Bridgestone with production methods generally conceded to be the most efficient in the industry. Not content with a secure grip on one-third of the U.S. tire business and nearly one-fifth of the world market, Goodyear is diversifying into what it hopes will be less cyclical and more profitable industries. The company is looking for quick growth from an aerospace subsidiary and Celeron, a Louisiana-based oil and gas company that it recently bought. Can the reawakened giant of the tire industry make it in businesses where it is still a pygmy?

Back in the 1970s, the odds were against Goodyear in the battle for the tire business. Michelin had caught American tire makers by surprise when it invaded the U.S. market with steel-belted radials. Most American tire makers scurried to find safe havens in the rapidly changing marketplace.

Goodyear chose not to hide. Over the last ten years, the company spent $3.2 billion to upgrade plants and equipment around the world, $2 billion of it tied directly to radial production. Goodyear streamlined its production to offset the lower labor costs enjoyed by foreign competitors. "We could have sat here fat, dumb, and happy, being king of the buggywhip business," says Chairman Robert E. Mercer. "But we would have wound up in second place, and that's not our charter."

His current plans have the company striving for a target of $15 billion in sales within five years. That goal seems easily attainable unless car sales collapse again. Mercer says he wants to boost return on investment to 5 percent and return on stockholders' equity to 15 percent. He believes those goals, however, remain beyond reach while the company is so heavily tilted to the slow-growth, cyclical tire business. Car tires and related products account for three-quarters of the company's sales. Mercer grumbles that one cancellation from Detroit can force them to close a plant. Thus, the reason for moving the company into new markets such as aerospace and energy.

One way Goodyear has reduced its exposure to the foreign invasion is by concentrating on the quality end of the market, where most foreign tire makers lack the capital and technological prowess to compete. Nearly 15 percent of the company's tire sales last year were high-performance models. Mercer was so taken with an exotic new design Goodyear developed in conjunction with General Motors for the new Corvette that he traded in his Cadillac for one of the two-seaters, complete with a radar detector. He now tools around Akron at speeds unbecoming a chief executive.

Goodyear maintains a distinct advantage over both foreign and domestic challengers in the replacement market with the largest system of dealerships in the industry. The company owns about 1,100 retail outlets and also sells through more than 3,000 franchises and independent dealers. Goodyear's sales force is aggressive, offering special financing and training programs along with the company's broad product line, and is often able to nudge rival brands out.

None of this would matter much were it not for Goodyear's highly sophisticated production methods. It has also restructured the quality-control systems. The key was moving from what Goodyear calls "control model" management to "commitment model" management—meaning that individual workers, rather than supervisors, are now responsible for quality. Working with management consultants from Harvard and MIT, Goodyear tried to change the relationship between supervisor and worker from what it calls "parent-child" to "adult-adult."

Mercer is not without woes. Goodyear's overseas operations are faltering where high inflation and government price controls don't allow the company to pass on increases in the cost of raw materials. The problem, according to the joke around headquarters, is too many MBAs—Mexicos, Brazils, and Argentinas.

1. Write an official goal statement for Goodyear based on the information contained in the case. After writing the statement, go to the library and examine Goodyear's official goal statement in the annual report. How does your statement compare with the one in the annual report? Do you believe Robert Mercer's interpretation is accurate?
2. What operative goals has Robert Mercer identified as critical to the achievement of Goodyear's official goal?
3. Which goals discussed in the case appear to have highest priority and which are of lowest priority? Why has management made a decision to pursue some goals more vigorously over other goals?

ENDNOTES

1. A. Etzioni, *Modern Organizations* (Englewood Cliffs, NJ: Prentice-Hall, 1964), 6.
2. C. Perrow, "The Analysis of Goals in Complex Organizations," *American Sociological Review* 26 (1961): 854-866.
3. M. D. Richards, *Organizational Goal Structures* (St. Paul, MN: West Publishing Co., 1978).
4. See Merck & Company, Annual Report (1986).
5. P. F. Drucker, *Management: Tasks, Responsibilities, Practices* (New York: Harper & Row, 1974), 100.
6. J. D. Thompson and W. J. McEwen, "Organizational Goals and Environment: Goal-Setting as an Interaction Process," *American Sociological Review* 23 (1958): 23-31.
7. R. Cyert and J. March, *A Behavioral Theory of the Firm* (Englewood Cliffs, NJ: Prentice-Hall, 1963).
8. J. G. March and H. A. Simon, *Organizations* (New York: John Wiley & Sons, 1958).
9. D. L. Sills, *The Volunteers* (New York: Free Press, 1957).
10. Etzioni, *Modern Organizations*, 8.
11. L. T. Hosmer, *Strategic Management: Text and Cases on Business Policy* (Englewood Cliffs, NJ: Prentice-Hall, 1982), 14-34.
12. E. Yuchtman and S. E. Seashore, "A System Resource Approach to Organizational Effectiveness," *Administrative Science Quarterly* 12 (1967): 377-395.
13. R. M. Steers, "When Is an Organization Effective?" *Organizational Dynamics* (Autumn 1976): 50-63.

Fundamentals of Planning

CHAPTER 6

After studying this chapter, you should be able to:
- *Identify four levels of management that contribute to the planning process.*
- *Describe the role that a planning staff plays in an organization.*
- *Distinguish between single-use plans and standing plans.*
- *Describe the various planning horizons and tell how they are integrated by levels of management.*
- *Identify the conditions that lead to the need for contingency planning.*
- *Describe the steps in the planning process.*
- *Discuss the various barriers to planning and the techniques managers can use to overcome these barriers.*

164

A ban on the use of charcoal lighter fluid.

Electric trolleys replace diesel buses.

Elimination of aerosol in underarm deodorants.

The end of cars idling while in the drive-through lanes at fast-food outlets.

Mandated ride-sharing for employees of some firms.

Requirements that housing construction be closer to work sites.[1]

A vision of the future by some idealistic science fiction writer? No—just some of the proposals in a plan passed in 1989 by the South Coast Air Quality Management District for implementation by the year 2007. The goal? To achieve compliance with the federal clean air standards for the four-county Los Angeles basin. The plan is in three phases. The first phase would require conformity to a variety of emission-control standards for homes, work sites, and vehicles. The second phase involves further emission reductions through the use of existing technology. The third phase proposes the use of technologies that have yet to be developed. While the plan must be approved by other state and federal governing bodies, it represents a bold step in the direction of achieving the goal of a smog-free environment in the Los Angeles area.

The previous chapter discussed approaches to formulating organizational goals. However, formulating organizational goals is only part of the picture. Implementing a plan successfully is a critical activity of organization managers. Successful implementation requires managers at all levels of the organization to understand the specific tasks necessary to achieve the goals of the organization. The Los Angeles anti-smog plan can only be successful if managers at each level of the Air Quality Management District clearly understand how they will implement their tasks.

This chapter is concerned with the methods and techniques for implementing a plan in support of selected goals. We will discuss the importance and benefits of a well-developed plan. We will then identify the responsibilities that managers have at various levels of the organization for implementing the plan. Next, we will examine the techniques and time horizons for implementing plans. This examination is followed by a presentation of contingency planning, an important technique used by managers for planning organization activities in an uncertain and turbulent environment. The final section of the chapter is concerned with barriers to planning which managers must often face and how these barriers can be overcome. Certainly, the success of the Air Quality Management District plan will hinge on how well it is implemented over the next two decades.

INTEGRATING THE PLANNING PROCESS

A **plan** is a framework that details the methods and tasks involved in achieving a defined goal. Plans are developed once managers have selected goals they believe will direct the organization toward success. As defined in Chapter 1, planning is the process of identifying the methods to be used, tasks to be performed, and time horizons for sequencing the implementation of methods and tasks in the organization. Ultimately, a plan is designed to coordinate activities to enhance achievement of goals.

The Need to Coordinate Activities

The need to plan increases when managers must respond to uncertainty in the environment.[2] In an environment in which very little change has occurred or is expected to occur, minimal planning is necessary. Members of the organization need only learn the tasks that are required to achieve organizational goals and simply repeat those tasks in the future. However, certainty in the environment is a luxury that few if any organizations enjoy. Indeed, it is because environments of organizations have become more uncertain that planning has become a very critical activity for organization managers.

The need to coordinate organization activities through plans increases as an organization's environment becomes more uncertain. Coordination of organization activities requires that managers devise frameworks for integrating subunit activities (e.g., production with research and development) and linking organization activities with the environment (e.g., getting resources from suppliers and distributing products or services to buyers). Plans help specify the contribution of each subunit to the quantity, quality, cost, and timing of the production of outputs.

Planning to coordinate the activities of subunits and members within the organization and with the organization's environment is a function of management that must be attended to at all levels of the organization. Plans should help managers achieve the operational, operative, and official goals of the organization as defined in Chapter 5.

Levels of Planning

All managers participate in the planning process to some degree. Variations in the degree of participation in the planning process will depend on the size and the goal of the firm and the specific function of the manager. Some organizations, such as a manufacturer of goods for space exploration, may have plans that extend far into the future. The production manager of such a firm may have a detailed plan for producing a gyroscope two years from now. Other organizations, such as a company producing a weekly series for television, may have plans that extend for only three months. The casting director for a television series may make a major contribution to the development phase of the series (e.g., selecting the cast) but have little input once the cast has been selected.

NASA's plans for space exploration may extend far into the future; an organization producing a television series may have plans extending for only a few months.

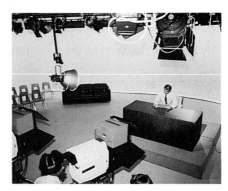

Four distinct levels of management can be identified that contribute to the planning process: boards of directors, executive officers, division heads, and first-line managers (we will be using the terms first-line managers and lower management interchangeably).[3] These levels are not present in all organizations. Small shops, such as local clothing stores, may not have division heads. However, identification of these four levels of management can be applied to most large organizations.

BOARDS OF DIRECTORS

Boards of directors are made up of individuals who are either appointed or elected to oversee the activities of the organization. Boards may be active in the planning process or may delegate planning to executive officers. When planning is delegated to executive officers, the board of directors will serve as a committee that reviews the plans once they have been formalized. Members of the board of directors may be elected by stockholders or, in the case of a social service organization, by other members of the board. Generally, the board evaluates formalized plans to determine if they will help to achieve the organization's official goal. If so, approval is granted and executive officers proceed to carry out the plans.

EXECUTIVE OFFICERS

As discussed in Chapter 1, executive officers are referred to as the top, or upper, management of the organization. In many organizations, executive officers are led by a chief executive officer (CEO) hired by the board of directors to manage the overall operations of the organization. Where the board of directors is an active participant in the planning process, the CEO will work closely with the board in the development of the plans. Where the board assumes the role of overseeing the formalized plan, the responsibility for planning rests with the CEO and other executive officers. Either way, executive officers play a critical role in the development and implementation of plans.

DIVISION HEADS

Division heads are individuals who manage a subunit or a division in an organization. In some organizations, they may be executive officers and participate in planning at that level. As a middle manager, a division head is responsible for developing plans that support the operating policies of the organization—its operative goals. For instance, at Chrysler Corporation, division heads run the Chrysler, Plymouth, and Dodge divisions. Division heads consult with executive officers during the planning process to share information about the operations of their divisions. Division heads also contribute to the formulation of any plan that will directly affect how their division operates.

FIRST-LINE MANAGERS

First-line managers oversee specific tasks within the organization. A first-line manager in General Motors may be the head of production or the head of marketing for the Saturn division. First-line managers work with division heads in the planning process by providing information about what they need to operate effectively under the plan. First-line managers play a critical role in the execution of activities that support the plan.

These four levels of an organization's management serve as a mechanism for developing and implementing effective plans that will direct the organization toward the accomplishment of goals. The integration of these four levels, from top to bottom, is often referred to as the **hierarchy of plans**. Figure 6–1 illustrates these relationships. Not all organizations use this approach to planning. Some organizations, such as General Electric, 3M, and Johnson & Johnson, place a greater burden of responsibility for planning at middle and lower levels of management. This is done in the belief that because middle and lower-level managers have a better understanding of the direction their divisions and departments need to pursue, they should have more say in the implementation of plans. In these companies top management reviews and authorizes the plans submitted by middle and lower-level managers.

The Planning Staff

In some instances, top management of an organization may create and develop a planning staff.[4] A **planning staff** is a group of individuals whose sole responsibility is the formulation of plans. The creation of a planning staff to advise managers in the organization is useful when managers need to devote more time to other activities, lack the expertise to solve particular problems, or are dispersed across the country or around the world, thereby reducing contact with headquarters. Under these conditions, as is the case with many large multinational corporations, planning is best conducted by a staff of individuals who can work exclusively on the formulation of plans.

A planning staff is usually composed of individuals who have attained expertise in areas that are critical to the planning process. Members may be chosen for their expertise in statistical modeling of environmental trends or

FIGURE 6–1
The Hierarchy of Plans

Level in the Organization	*Responsibilities*
Board of Directors	Reviews and evaluates plans when formulating is delegated to executive officers. May assume direct responsibility for formulating plans.
Executive Officers	Assume major responsibility for formulating plans and overseeing the implementation of plans directed toward the accomplishment of official goals.
Division Heads	Contribute to the formulation of plans and assume responsibility for the implementation of plans directed toward the accomplishment of operative goals within their divisions.
First-Line Management	Contributes to the formulation of plans by providing specific information about task activities. Responsible for the implementation of plans that will lead to the accomplishment of operational goals.

production applications, analysis and forecasting of consumer behavior, sophisticated financial analysis, or industry analysis. In most instances, the planning staff is composed of individuals who have had professional training and experience in a specialized field.

When setting up a planning staff, upper management must decide how much responsibility for planning the staff will assume. In some organizations, all planning is done by the planning staff. Upper management reviews and checks the plans that have been formulated. In other organizations, the planning staff is assigned responsibility for collecting information that is needed for planning. The information is assimilated and upper management, such as the executive officers, uses that information to formulate plans. Still another approach is to assign smaller units of staff to specific divisions and have them report to middle managers, or division heads, rather than to upper management.

Regardless of how a planning staff is used in an organization, it should be recognized that the formation of the unit has several important purposes. First, the planning staff can help management in developing goals and strategies for the organization by scanning the environment for important trends that may affect the organization. Second, the planning staff can coordinate the plans of various subunits in the organization. If production is planning to increase the output of a product by 500 units in the month of May, then sales should have plans to increase the promotion of the product. Finally, the planning staff can serve as a valuable source of information to managers at all levels of the organization in matters concerning the formulation or implementation of plans.

ACTION PLANS

In this section, we will examine **action plans**, plans that identify day-to-day activities in support of the goals of the organization. Action plans provide the details on how the overall plan will lead the organization to the accomplishment of its goals.

Action plans can be classified into two types. **Single-use plans** are used to direct activities in the achievement of a specific goal and will not be repeated in the future. **Standing plans** are developed to guide activities toward achievement of goals of a recurring nature. Both types of action plans help members coordinate and direct their activities toward goal accomplishment. For this reason, the development and implementation of action plans can prove to be the difference between success and failure in the implementation process.

Mickey Mouse's 50th-birthday celebration at Disneyland was orchestrated through a single-use plan.

Single-Use Plans

Single-use plans are developed when the likelihood of repeating activities is low. Construction of new plant facilities would exemplify a single-use plan. Managers may also develop single-use plans when a one-time promotion for a product needs to be carried out. The three types of single-use plans are programs, projects, and budgets.

FROM THE FIELD
CORPORATE GOALS

We surveyed corporate planners from a wide variety of industries to learn what corporate goals they felt were important to the planning process. We asked each planner, "How would you rate each of the following corporate goals in terms of their overall importance to the development of plans for your organization?" Planners rated each goal on a scale of 1 to 5, with possible responses including 1 (very unimportant), 3 (neither important nor unimportant), and 5 (very important). Here are the results, ranked from most important to least important.

Rank	Corporate Goal	Average Rating
1	Increase market share	4.60
2	Improve return on investment	4.55
3	Reduce production inefficiencies	4.18
4	Improve cash flow	4.05
5	Improve relations with buyers and suppliers	3.79

Improvements in market share and return on investment emerged as the most important corporate goals to consider in the development of plans. Of interest is the importance that the planners placed on reducing production inefficiencies, slightly ahead of the goal of improving cash flows. This may reflect a new emphasis on productivity in the face of increased domestic and foreign competition.

PROGRAMS

A **program** is designed to coordinate a large set of activities. As a single-use plan, a program contains a set of guidelines that identify (1) the goal to be achieved, (2) the major steps needed to attain the goal, (3) the members or subunits that will be responsible for implementing each step, (4) a schedule that orders and times the implementation of each step, and (5) an estimate of the cost associated with the implementation of each step.

Programs may be developed that involve the entire membership of an organization or only a few members. For instance, the Statue of Liberty–Ellis Island Centennial Commission was set up to raise funds for the refurbishing of perhaps the most famous monument in the United States. The commission coordinated its activities through a program that required soliciting and collecting funds, locating and employing skilled workers, and developing public relations events. The success of this program was dependent on explicit goals, identification and sequencing of major steps to be performed, assignment of responsibility, and detailed estimates of costs. Programs that may be limited to a few members but are large in scope would be represented by a company's effort to engage in a corporate merger. Activities involved in setting up the merger are extensive, but the program designed to carry out the activities may include only a small handful of senior managers. The program is ended once the merger has been completed.

PROJECTS

A **project** is a single-use plan that is usually more limited in scope than a program. A project may be developed in support of a program when a specific set of activities to be conducted at one time is required to complete a step in the program. A project linked to the program developed to refurbish the

All managers must plan and manage projects. You may be in production, trying to determine a better way to cut costs in the plant. You may be in marketing, charged with laying out a marketing plan for a new product. You may have to audit the books in one office of your company, in hopes of improving efficiency. All of these projects, and numerous others in your organization, involve deadlines, particular results, budgets, and ambiguity. They require coordination among numerous people, and they require innovation to solve problems. Indeed, projects are the lifeblood of innovation, and today's managers must create innovation in order to compete in a changing world. All managers can do a better job of getting innovation projects done on time, within budget, and according to desired quality standards.

All too often, ineffective managers try to complete a project without a well-designed plan. They use a fix-it mentality. But effective project managers realize that good planning leads to smaller problems during implementation. The idea is to go slower early, so you can go faster later. . . . Projects involve a merging of technical and people issues, and effective managers know how to follow ten principles for planning and managing projects:

1. Set a clear project goal. To get a job done effectively, you must mentally start at the finish and work backward.
2. Determine the project objectives. Once you have gone through the goal-setting process, you can begin to add more detail to the plan. Objectives help to break the goal down into specific responsibilities for each team member, and they help the team members understand how their contributions relate to the overall goal.

MANAGEMENT IN ACTION 1
WHAT EVERY MANAGER NEEDS TO KNOW ABOUT PROJECT MANAGEMENT

3. Establish checkpoints, activities, relationships, and time estimates.
4. Draw a picture of the project schedule.
5. Direct people individually and as a project team. The most fundamental but overlooked principle of managing a project is this: You cannot do it alone.
6. Reinforce the commitment and excitement of the project team.
7. Keep everyone connected with the project team informed.
8. Build agreements that vitalize team members.
9. Empower yourself and others on the project team. Project managers often do not have enough power. How often have you heard a project manager lament, "If I only had the authority to get those people on track." Project managers have to realize that influencing others arises at least as much from personal competence as it does from formal authority.
10. Encourage risk taking and creativity. Thomas Edison is quoted as saying, "I failed my way to success." Would he have survived in your organization?

Statue of Liberty was the organization of a gala event to celebrate the completion of work on the statue.

A project can also be self-contained, without any link to a broader program. A personnel manager may be required to review the salaries and benefits of all employees in the firm to determine whether allegations of discrimination based on age or sex of employees are true. Interest in techniques used to manage projects has grown rapidly. Management in Action 1 identifies ten principles for every manager involved in project management.

BUDGETS

A **budget** is a single-use plan that specifies allocations of financial resources required to support specific activities within a given period. Budgets also prescribe methods by which financial resources are to be distributed in a project or program. By setting limits on the amount that can be spent, budgets are important devices for controlling activities.

Depending on the level of financial resources committed to a program or project, budgets can have a powerful impact on how tasks are carried out in the organization. If budgets are inadequate for support of a program or project, managers are forced to simplify steps and may in the process jeopardize the successful accomplishment of the goal. If budgets are too generous, managers may include many unnecessary steps in the implementation process of a program or project to use up the funds.

Standing Plans

In many instances, managers must plan for activities in the organization that recur continually. In these situations, standing plans are developed that can be recycled for as long as they are believed to be appropriate for coordinating member activities. Standing plans are useful to managers because they allow managers to conserve time and energy by focusing attention on activities or events that do not recur. The three types of standing plans are policies, standard operating procedures, and rules and regulations.

POLICIES

A **policy** is a standing plan that provides managers with a general guideline for decision making. As such, a policy defines boundaries or limits that are to be observed by managers when decisions are required. A policy is carried out within an organization to increase the chances that managers will respond uniformly to problems or situations that require their attention. A policy also provides guidelines about the methods managers are to employ to attain the goals they are working toward.

In some organizations, policies are developed to provide managers with guidelines for hiring employees. Policies such as "All employees of the organization must have a college degree" provide managers with a guideline in making decisions about hiring. However, note that the policy as stated does not provide the manager with a guideline for discriminating among applicants who do have a college degree. If further limits or boundaries are believed important, additional policies can be carried out, such as "All employees must have three years of prior work experience."

Generally, policies are set by the top management of the organization. Policies reduce the need for close supervision of subordinates and further express the intentions of organizational strategies and goals. In the implementation of a policy, top management can direct behaviors and decisions toward the attainment of organizational goals, express values and ideas that are believed to be important, and serve to reduce confusion or conflict about issues or concerns that subordinates may have in carrying out their tasks.

Top management should make every effort to ensure that policies are internally consistent and direct activities toward desired goals. As the environment of organizations changes, accompanied by changes in goals, the change or removal of older policies is sometimes necessary. This is particularly important with policies about hiring and promotion of employees. Many older policies in organizations have been found to be discriminatory toward women, racial and ethnic minorities, and the handicapped, and thus can expose the organization to lengthy and costly litigation.

STANDARD OPERATING PROCEDURES

A **standard operating procedure (SOP)** is another form of standing plan. An SOP governs specific actions that members of the organization are required to perform under certain circumstances. Normally, an SOP is more explicit and detailed than a policy, specifying step-by-step the procedure to be followed. Thus, an SOP is useful for employees who meet a particular situation or circumstance on a regular basis. Once the SOP has been set, new employees can be trained easily in the procedures.

The procedure for handling goods returned to a retail store is spelled out for salespeople in an SOP.

An example of a standard operating procedure would be one set up to guide a floor salesperson in a retail store when a customer returns a product and asks for a cash refund. For instance, the SOP may direct the employee to (1) request a receipt from the customer; (2) fill out a form stating the date of purchase and reason for exchange; (3) attach the receipt to the form; (4) contact the immediate supervisor for approval of a refund; (5) take the approved form and receipt to the refund department; (6) obtain a refund and have the customer sign the form noting receipt of cash; (7) provide the customer with the yellow copy of the form, submit the blue copy of the form to the refund department, and keep the white copy of the form in the employee's assigned cash register; and (8) submit all refund forms to the supervisor at the end of the day. The detail included in this example of an SOP ensures that employees will perform the task consistently and correctly over time.

RULES AND REGULATIONS

Rules and regulations are statements that either require or forbid a certain action. Rules and regulations are the most explicit form of standing plan. While SOPs are also explicit, they differ from rules and regulations in that they identify the specific steps to follow in a particular situation. A typical rule or regulation is "No smoking except in designated areas" or "All employees must be at their desks by 8:00 A.M." Note that a rule or regulation may be accompanied by an SOP detailing the procedures supervisors are to follow if a rule or regulation is violated.

While rules and regulations serve to eliminate the need for decision making under certain circumstances, they can also be suspended. A manager may, for instance, suspend the rule of having to be at one's desk at 8:00 A.M. if the employee must attend a funeral because of a death in the family. Members of an organization may feel stifled in their efforts to attain goals if rules become excessive or are either enforced too rigidly or violated without penalty.

Action plans such as single-use or standing plans are important tools for coordinating and directing activities toward the implementation of organizational strategies and the attainment of organizational goals. Figure 6–2 depicts the relationship that action plans have with the goals of the organization. It is crucial for managers who formulate and implement action plans to make sure that the plans will focus member activities on tasks that are critical for overall success.

FIGURE 6–2
The Relationship of Action Plans with Organizational Goals and Strategy

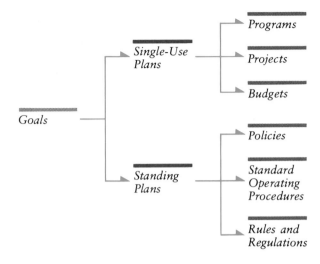

Goals

- *Single-Use Plans*
  - Programs
  - Projects
  - Budgets
- *Standing Plans*
  - Policies
  - Standard Operating Procedures
  - Rules and Regulations

PLANNING HORIZONS

An important part of any plan is the **planning horizon,** the length of time the plan specifies for activities to be carried out. Three planning horizons can be identified: long-range, intermediate, and short-range.

Long-Range Planning

Long-range planning involves identifying those activities to be performed over an extended period of time. In some cases, long-range plans may extend for several decades. For instance, a firm in the forestry industry may have long-range plans that extend over a century to reforest cut timberland. Plans of this type help guarantee a continual supply of resources long after present managers of the company have retired. Large corporations such as Dow Chemical and General Motors engage in long-range planning that covers several decades. As a general rule, we identify any plan that extends beyond five years as a long-range plan.

Long-range planning is different from strategic planning, which will be discussed in Chapter 7. Strategic planning is primarily concerned with how the organization will position itself among competing firms in a market. Long-range planning identifies the activities to be performed that will lead to the accomplishment of official goals.

In one important feature, a long-range plan is necessarily different from plans with shorter planning horizons. In a plan covering 20 years, for example, attempts to be specific in year 1 about activities to be carried out in year 20 would be essentially wasted effort. It is more useful simply to develop general guidelines. As the planning horizon gets closer and more is known with certainty about the internal and external environment facing the organization, managers can add specifics to suit current conditions.

Intermediate Planning

Intermediate planning identifies activities to be carried out over a period of one to five years at the middle or divisional levels of the organization. Inter-

Development of superconductivity as an alternate energy source at IBM is an example of long-range planning.

mediate planning is critical in most cases to the success of long-range planning. For instance, a long-range plan may identify several points in time when the organization is to consider the introduction of new products. In three years, a new product is to reach the market. Six years hence, or three years after its introduction, the new product is to be changed based on consumer feedback gathered from surveys, and so on. In this situation, an intermediate plan would focus on the introduction of the new product, specifying the necessary financial and material resources, and time horizons for completing necessary tasks in support of the new product. Whereas long-range planning must cope with highly uncertain conditions in the future, intermediate planning is focused more on the activities that have to be carried out within a planning horizon that contains fewer uncertainties.

Short-Range Planning

Developing plans for implementation within a planning horizon of less than one year is referred to as **short-range planning**. Short-range plans are those that are pertinent primarily to first-line managers and general employees of the organization. Short-range plans may specify activities to be carried out that will achieve certain production levels each week. The aggregation of these weekly production levels will then serve to meet the goals of production for the year. While short-range plans are necessary for most organizations, they can have drawbacks. Often managers become so focused on short-range plans because of the immediate attention they require that they lose sight of the intermediate and long-range plans. Ultimately, this can lead to failure in the accomplishment of organizational goals.

Integrating Planning Horizons

A critical concern of managers engaged in the planning process is the integration and balancing of organizational goals and strategies with long-range, intermediate, and short-range plans. Short-range plans, for instance, should be supportive of intermediate plans and intermediate plans supportive of long-range plans. Long-range plans support the official goals of the organization. Recall from Chapter 5 our discussion of the hierarchy of goals. We can use that framework for depicting the relationship between goals, managers, and planning horizons. Figure 6–3 portrays these relationships.

Managers at various levels of the organization assume responsibility for the implementation of plans. First-line managers oversee the activities in the short-range plans which seek the attainment of operational goals. Divisional managers guide activities identified in the intermediate plans which serve to accomplish operative goals. Executive management focuses on activities in long-range plans that are directed toward official goals of the organization and are derived from the selected strategy.

Suppose top management believes that continuous growth is necessary. This matches the official goal of the organization to seek long-term growth and greater profits. The long-range plan would identify at specified intervals of time the construction of new plants located close to markets that the organization seeks to enter. Intermediate plans would focus on the construction of the plants, which requires managing capital flows, contracting with construction companies, and purchasing machinery. Short-range plans would

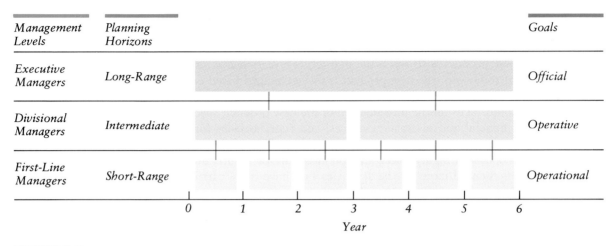

Management Levels	Planning Horizons		Goals
Executive Managers	Long-Range		Official
Divisional Managers	Intermediate		Operative
First-Line Managers	Short-Range		Operational

0 1 2 3 4 5 6

Year

FIGURE 6–3

Integrating Planning Horizons with Organizational Goals

then be developed to train workers, stock inventories, set targets for production levels, and designate budgets necessary to achieve the operational goal of increased production.

Once the plans have been developed for the three planning horizons, managers must balance the plans depending on the degree of success achieved in each time frame. It would not be useful, for instance, to train workers if for some reason the construction of a plant is delayed for several years. Thus, integration of the three planning horizons is an important task of management.

Where many adjustments are necessary in the overall plans, many managers choose to develop a planning staff that will not only make a major contribution to the development of plans but also monitor the implementation process and make adjustments to plans when necessary.

CONTINGENCY PLANNING

In Chapter 3 we pointed out that organization managers must contend with environmental uncertainty. Environmental uncertainty makes it difficult for managers to project critical conditions in the future. Under these conditions, managers will try to develop contingency plans.

Contingency planning involves identifying alternative courses of action in advance of implementation to meet possible conditions in the future. For instance, an organization that seeks to expand its production levels to enter new markets can set up a contingency plan to respond in the event of a sudden downturn in the economy that increases the cost of borrowing money and lowers the demand for the product. If management believes this is possible, the contingency plan may be to put plans for new plant construction on hold and instead reduce production levels and curtail the hiring of new employees.

On the other hand, management may also believe there is a chance for accelerated demand for the product which would require expanded production levels beyond those established in the original plan. In this case management may set up another contingency plan that calls for subcontracting with other firms to produce the product. Hence, through contingency planning, management is prepared to carry out the original plan, to respond to a decline in demand, or to meet an acceleration in demand.

Contingency planning provides several benefits to managers in the organization. First, contingency planning can reduce the need for **crisis management**, which is the scramble for answers to problems within a very short time frame. In many instances, crisis management produces decisions that are ineffective or actually damage the chances that the organization will achieve its desired goals. Second, contingency planning further develops managerial skills by requiring managers to understand the dynamics of their environment. And third, it enables managers to develop more effective decisions by using a variety of decision-making techniques.

The process of contingency planning is best understood through the identification of action points. **Action points** are points in a plan at which conditions may be moving in a direction that requires the modification or abandonment of the original plan. Action points are incorporated into the original plan at stages considered critical for committing resources. Action points are set up and checked in a plan by the following methods:

- In the development of the plan, managers examine each step in the implementation process and pose a "what if" question affecting each step to be completed—for example: What if there is a sudden downturn in the economy? Managers assign probabilities to the occurrence of the event and then identify alternative plans to be carried out should the event actually occur. Not all possible events can be included, as this could be an infinite number. Assigning probabilities enables managers to narrow the number of contingency plans required. For example, management may decide that a set of contingency plans will not be developed for any event that has less than a 25 percent chance of occurring.

- During the implementation process, information is gathered to identify trends that may lead to one of the possible events identified in the contingency plans. For instance, management may believe that a decline in the gross national product (GNP) of more than 2 percent will lead to a severe decline in demand for the organization's product. Thus, if the GNP has been declining over several quarters, managers may have good reason to believe that an event covered by one of the contingency plans may occur in that year.

- If a decision is made that an event is likely to occur, implementation of the appropriate contingency plan takes place. In the case of a downturn in the economy that would affect demand for the company's product, the plan may be to halt construction of new plants and discontinue programs designed to train new employees.

- Action points are continually checked to assess the chances that further contingency events will take place.

THE PLANNING PROCESS

While we have discussed various aspects of planning in previous sections, it is useful to identify the procedures managers use in planning and the conditions that promote planning effectiveness. Though the sequencing and implementation of steps in planning may vary among organizations, identification of a general process helps in understanding the planning function.

Steps in Planning

Steps in the planning process can be illustrated through the formal process used by large, diversified corporations:[5]

1. *Statement of official goals.* The chief executive of the firm sets the official goals, usually presenting them to division heads or middle management. A formal statement of the official goals provides a common focus for planning and identifies those goals that top management seeks to emphasize.
2. *Forecast of economic conditions.* Forecasts are usually prepared by top management for three time frames (short, intermediate, long) and often include contingency forecasts (best case, worst case, most likely case). The purpose of forecasting is to provide divisional managers with a common set of assumptions for preparing their divisional plans. As the news article in Management in Action 2 illustrates, the lack of a common set of assumptions can play havoc with planning.
3. *Development of the divisional plans.* Divisional managers receive copies of the official goals and forecasts and begin to develop divisional plans. Operative goals are identified that support the official goals. Managers develop operative goals by reviewing the past performance of their division in terms of sales, market share, revenues, manufacturing costs, gross margins, and so forth.
4. *Consolidation of the divisional and departmental plans.* Each division submits its plans to top management, which then consolidates the divisional objectives into a consistent "package" across divisions. In this step top management may either reject plans, accept plans, or request revisions in the plans submitted by the divisions.
5. *Preparation of the detailed divisional and departmental plans.* After approval of the overall divisional plan has been granted by top management, divisional managers prepare detailed plans for allocating resources such as capital, labor, and materials. Divisional plans often include predicted cash flows, identification of work activities, and plans for capital expenditures.
6. *Coordination of the divisional plans.* After preparation of the divisional plans has been completed, the plans are returned to top management. Top management aggregates the divisional plans, checks computations, and evaluates the plans based on financial criteria.
7. *Preparation of the divisional and departmental budgets.* After approval for funding of the divisional budget has been granted, division managers prepare budgets for departments within the division. Lower managers are assigned budgets for their departments, performance standards, revenues by product lines, staff support, and so forth. This process is often done in monthly or quarterly segments completed in consultation with managers of departments in the division.
8. *Integration of divisional budgets.* The completion of divisional budgets leads to the final step where the budgets are submitted to top management. Top management reviews the budgets but rarely rejects them. Why? It is often felt that top management does not have the detailed knowledge of operations at the lower levels of the corporation to make a critical examination of these plans.

Figure 6–4 depicts this eight-step planning process in a corporate setting.

How big is Brookfield, Wisconsin, a suburb of Milwaukee? What will the city's population be 20 years from now? The answer depends on who's providing the response.

Discrepancies in population figures arose last week when consultants, architects, and city officials discussed the civic center site plan and possible future buildings there. Library officials had used a 51,000 estimated population for the year 2010; other officials insisted a 39,000 figure was more accurate.

And Police Chief Jerome Wolff said neither figure was meaningful when applied to the population police and fire departments serve, because the daytime population, with its influx of office workers, rises to 100,000 now. Wolff contended the figure most accurate is that referring to the number of people served rather than actual city population.

But Mayor Kathryn Bloomberg pleaded for uniformity. "We have to have the same population assumption and then go from there," she said. "When we give population statistics to the public, we'd better not have a 50 percent variance."

The 39,000 number came from the Southeastern Wisconsin Regional Planning Commission, according to architects for the civic center site plan. The 51,000 figure came from commercial sources, the school district, and the public works department, according to library officials.

MANAGEMENT IN ACTION 2
WHAT'S THE POPULATION? DEPENDS ON WHO'S COUNTING

"Our population is so volatile," said William Muth, public works director. He reminded officials of the problems the school district has had projecting enrollments for the district in the face of changing economic and age patterns in the community. The city used to have an average of 4.5 people per family, he said; now that figure is about 2.5.

Mayor Bloomberg still asked for one population projection to be used by all groups. The library, she said, can logically cite that number and perhaps a statistic showing that more than the average number of Brookfield residents use that facility. And police and fire officials can say the number of people they serve has gone up because of increased commercial developments. "But we've got to get some basic assumptions about population—and everybody's should be the same," she said.

Source: Reprinted by permission of *The Brookfield News* (August 25, 1988): 4.

FIGURE 6–4
Steps in Planning

Management Level Responsible	Time →				
Top Management	1. State official goals	2. Forecast economic conditions	4. Consolidate divisional plans	6. Coordinate divisional plans	8. Integrate divisional budgets
Middle Management			3. Develop divisional plans	5. Prepare detailed divisional plans	7. Prepare divisional budgets
Lower Management				Prepare departmental plans	Prepare departmental budgets

Making Planning Effective

To make planning effective, managers should attend to several considerations in the planning process:

- To the greatest degree possible, use techniques and systems already established in the organization to carry out the plans. While some changes may be necessary, introducing changes increases the chance that mistakes will be made. Having to spend time to learn new techniques and adapt to a new system may get in the way of achieving goals.
- Planning should be participative. The greater the number of organization members involved in the planning process, the deeper the level of commitment to the final plan and the greater the number of perspectives, information, and viewpoints that can be brought into consideration. This often requires the involvement of lower-level managers, as well as top and middle management, in the planning process.
- Communicate to subordinates the reasons why specific activities are being carried out. Understanding how the activities relate to goals and strategies of the organization enables subordinates to make a greater contribution.
- Plans should be simple. While planning can be a complicated process and deals with complex issues, the plan itself should strive to simplify the operations to be performed and the goals to be attained.
- Plans should be flexible. Though managers should not change plans without communicating their intent to top management, adjustments may be needed to adapt to unforeseen circumstances.
- Monitor implemented activities. Managers have to go beyond directing subordinates as to what has to be done. They must also check the implementation of those activities to make sure they are being done correctly and to help in solving problems that may occur.

When many organization members are involved in the planning process, a variety of different perspectives are considered and commitment to the final plan is strengthened.

MANAGING THE PLANNING PROCESS

Creating a comprehensive plan for guiding organizational activities toward the achievement of desired goals does not guarantee that the implementation of the plan will be without problems. In most cases, managers discover that several barriers to planning must be overcome in order for their plans to be effective. This section discusses the major barriers to planning, techniques for overcoming planning barriers, and reasons why planning has failed in some organizations.

Barriers to Planning

Barriers to planning include the environment, reluctance to establish goals, an inadequate reward system, resistance to change, and time and expense.

ENVIRONMENT

The environment of an organization can take many forms. Where the environment is very unstable and complex, planning becomes highly difficult. When the environment changes rapidly, plans soon become obsolete and useless. For example, managers in firms that are engaged in advancing bioengineering techniques, such as the cloning of plant and animal cells to produce hybrids, find that new knowledge and techniques evolve daily. As a result, it is difficult to predict how the new knowledge and techniques will affect current research activities. In many cases, plans have to be radically changed, and managers may be reluctant to expend the effort to develop a comprehensive plan for the organization.

RELUCTANCE TO ESTABLISH GOALS

Setting goals is the essential first step in the planning process. In some instances, managers are reluctant to set goals for themselves and their subunits. Several reasons for this reluctance can be identified:[6]

- *Unwillingness to give up alternative goals.* In developing a plan, managers consider multiple goal alternatives. Some managers may prefer one goal to others, feeling that it is more important or better suited to their skills. If their preferred goal is not chosen to direct activities in the organization, their commitment to the goal selected may be half-hearted and their performance inadequate to achieve the goal.
- *Fear of failure.* Goals identify desired outcomes. With the designation of a goal come expected levels of performance. Some managers may be reluctant to set a goal because of the risk of failure. Failure can be a threat to one's job security, leading to a loss of support from other workers and a loss of self-esteem for the manager. Thus, the fear of failure may influence managers to set only those goals that do not involve risk.
- *Lack of organizational knowledge.* Successful planning requires the integration of activities within and across subunits of the organization. Some

managers, particularly those who are new or have failed to develop information networks within the organization, may lack sufficient knowledge about the organization to understand how their goals integrate with other goals in the organization. When this occurs, managers may avoid setting goals because they are unsure the activities necessary to complete the goals will be supported by the organization.

- *Lack of confidence.* Managers may believe the organization does not have the resources or commitment to successfully complete a goal.

INADEQUATE REWARD SYSTEM

Managers of an organization engage in varied activities with varied reward systems. Depending on where top management places its emphasis, some activities may reap higher rewards than others. In an organization whose focus is on activities that increase efficiency or increase profits, planning may be one activity that managers are not rewarded for adequately.

RESISTANCE TO CHANGE

Resistance to change is a fourth barrier to the planning process. Planning is much more than timing activities to be performed; planning implies that some change is to occur in the organization. Insecurity about the effect of the change on their role or prestige in the organization causes some managers to avoid any planning that might promote change. Further discussion of organizational change and various forms of resistance to it will be found in Chapter 22.

TIME AND EXPENSE

Some managers may avoid planning because it involves too much time and expense. Effective planning often requires working in committees to coordinate the plans throughout the organization as well as to assess various options. For many managers, committee work is viewed as too time-consuming. They would prefer to engage in tasks that have more immediate results. Managers may also avoid the planning process because they feel there is a lack of funds available to get the necessary resources. The development and implementation of an effective plan may require additional expense for hiring experts, expanding data bases, or purchasing new equipment. If managers believe the funds are not available, they may elect not to engage in the planning process.

Overcoming Barriers to Planning

Having identified barriers to the planning process, we can turn our attention to several techniques that can be used for overcoming planning barriers.

SUPPORT FROM UPPER MANAGEMENT

For planning to be effective throughout the organization, support from upper management must exist. Upper management can express and display this support by taking the initiative in clarifying the mission and official goals of the organization and by selecting a strategy that will guide activities toward their attainment. In addition, upper management can encourage middle and lower-level managers to engage in the planning process by setting up rewards for planning and assigning adequate time and resources to planning.

COMMUNICATION

Throughout the planning process, the intent of the strategy to be carried out and the methods for integrating and coordinating plans should be communicated to all participants. Communication enables managers and workers of the organization to maintain an accurate understanding of the direction they are to pursue. Managers should continually try to specify goals to be attained and encourage others to direct their activities toward those goals.

PARTICIPATION

Planning should not be exclusive. That is, planning should not be confined to any one subunit or level of management in the organization. Rather, it should encompass all those members, managers and workers alike, who will have an effect on the activities to be carried out through the plan.

REVIEW AND UPDATES

Reviewing and updating plans are important activities in the implementation process. Determining whether sudden changes in the environment call for a change in the plan should be an ongoing task. If reviews and updates are not performed and important environmental shifts have taken place, managers may abandon planning altogether. As we discussed earlier, contingency plans should be developed if managers suspect that a change in the environment is possible within the time horizons of the plan.

INFORMATION

Managers at all levels of the organization should receive information about the successes and failures of activities in other subunits of the organization. This information enables managers to identify problems in other areas of the organization that might be solved by adjusting activities in their own area. Exchanges of information can also help reduce resistance to change as managers are informed that change is occurring not only in their subunits, but throughout the organization. Management in Action 3 describes an unusual technique that is used to help executives make effective plans for the organization as a whole.

Reasons for Planning Failure

A survey of managers in 350 American and European corporations suggests that planning failures are the result of one or more of the following factors:[7]

- Strategic plans are not integrated into the total management system.
- Planning is done haphazardly; there is a lack of systematic procedures for the formulation and implementation of plans.
- Planning does not encompass all of the members of the organization who will be affected by the plans.
- Departments of planning are created with the sole responsibility of formulating plans rather than sharing responsibility with managers.
- Management assumes that a formulated plan is a substitute for an implemented plan.
- Plans try to do everything at once.
- Management "plans its work but fails to work its plan."

Donald B. Newton is Vice-President of Manufacturing for Hoosier Racing Tire Company. He joined the company in 1974, and prior to that he taught in the public school systems in California. Hoosier Racing Tire Company, located in South Bend, Indiana, manufactures and distributes specialty tires for automobile racing. In 1990, its gross sales were approximately $16 million through a worldwide distribution network that includes sales in Australia and throughout Europe. Since 1979, the growth in sales has increased nearly 25 percent a year. The company is vertically integrated from manufacturing its own rubber to retail selling. It has two manufactur-

MANAGERIAL PROFILE
DONALD B. NEWTON

ing plants and corporate offices in Indiana employing 175 people, with regional warehouses nationwide. Production is cyclical because of the seasonality of the sport and the constant obsolescence of the product. The product mix consists of over 250 models of racing tires produced on a short-run basis. Models are modified in response to the competitive pressures exacted by auto racing and by other racing tire manufacturers. Mr. Newton received an M.B.A. in administration from Indiana University.

Q: How would you describe the approach to planning that takes place at Hoosier Racing Tire?

A: Planning takes several forms at Hoosier. The organization is small enough that the president has daily communication with all department heads. Usually the president spends mornings with the sales and administrative people, often on a one-to-one basis. He has a structured sales meeting weekly. Afternoons are spent talking with manufacturing personnel including the designer, plant manager, and compounder. It is through daily contact that short-range plans emerge, are altered, and are implemented. Often, one department is informed only about that portion of the plan it is involved in, thus at times leaving a fragmented view of the whole picture. Problems arise when the president thinks he has informed all vital personnel but has left a key person out. On the other hand, this unstructured daily contact allows for fast response to product and schedule changes, thus avoiding the time-consuming nature of structured meetings.

Q: Is the short-term focus for planning purposive or simply necessary because of the nature of your market?

A: Our inability to engage in long-range planning stems primarily from a lack of information about our market. We have yet to define our market concretely. We know there are other areas like drag racing and off-road racing that we don't even provide a product for. However, we're running at capacity, in spite of the aggressive expansion of production by competitors, just to meet the demand for oval car racing. We feel our market is like digging in a coal mine; we do not know the extent or size of the coal vein or in which direction it will take us. Ideally, I would like to know the total sales of all my competitors, which would give us an understanding of market size and definition. Because of the undetermined nature of the market, we practice what we call incremental planning—adding foreseeable information to our short-range plans. Another feature of the market that disrupts the planning process is the constant obsolescence of racing tires. Most people not in the business have a hard time understanding this. Competitors are constantly changing the design and composition of the product, which can occur as often as weekly. Because of this, we're unable to create large inventories for fear of having an outdated product.

Q: For someone seeking a job in your industry, what managerial skills do you believe are important in order to be effective?

A: I would suggest to anyone who wants to enter this industry that communication skills are necessary. I have a policy of no verbal orders. By this I mean that any instructions or orders should always be in written form—not in any formal sense—but rather, a few words scratched on a pad and handed to a subordinate along with verbal instructions. This will always produce better results than verbal instruction alone. Personal organization is an important skill. I always carry a pocket spiral notebook in which I constantly write notes to myself and for others. I begin my day by reading my notebook and moving ideas to a sheet on my desk which is divided into today's projects (items such as phone calls that can be handled quickly) and long-term projects (items such as sales forecasts, machinery modifications, and so forth). At the end of the day, I review daily production, scrap and maintenance reports, quality control, and personnel reports, in an attempt to identify problem areas.

Take a metaphorical leap. Imagine your company as a vehicle. Any kind of vehicle. Now draw it on a piece of paper and describe it in a few words. The result might make you a better manager.

Since 1979, the Wharton Applied Research Center at the University of Pennsylvania has given seminars on strategic management and leadership to more than 1,000 senior executives. The seminars are designed to help executives set long-term goals and deploy resources to achieve those goals. Drawing a picture is one part of the executives' training. The seminar's director, Peter Davis, says the exercise forces the participants to think of their company as a whole, which is essential to productive corporate planning. "Corporations go through transitions, and you need to reexamine the nature of the company periodically," Mr. Davis says. The drawings, he says, "express a holistic sense of where the company is and where it is going."

Or not going. One executive pictured his company as a bicycle with two sets of handlebars. The ones on the front wheel faced backward, and the ones on the back wheel faced forward—an outfit that didn't know if it was coming or going. Such depictions are typical of fast-growing firms, Mr. Davis notes. When an organization expands rapidly, he says, "directional issues are important," and managers often feel that the company isn't on a steady course.

People often reveal more in a drawing than in words, Mr. Davis says. Expressions of anger, helplessness, and frustration are common. For example,

one executive who drew a fierce aircraft doesn't think kindly of his employer, a large baking company. His description of the concern: "Fast, mean,

MANAGEMENT IN ACTION 3
HOW TO DRAW A PLAN

sleek, aggressive, doesn't turn back, ruthless." The company apparently is not one to be trifled with or one that is prone to failure.

Executives draw automobiles more than any other kind of vehicle. But some of the renderings look like a car designer's nightmare. Imagine trying to get to work in a car that has the front end of a race car joined to the front end of a Model T. Travel might be difficult, but the art is revealing. The vehicle was drawn by an executive at a company "struggling to get into another field," Mr. Davis says. Obviously, the old phase of the business is a drag on the new one.

Psychologists don't agree on the usefulness of such pictures in making executives more effective managers. Chris Argyris, a professor of organizational behavior at Harvard University, says pictures will disclose someone's feelings of helplessness, anger, and frustration, but not show the situation that creates those feelings. One of Mr. Davis's favorite pictures was done by a son in the family's business. He drew an armored vehicle without doors or windows, explaining that there was no way for outsiders to get inside the company and no way for an insider like himself to get out.

- There is an overemphasis on forecasting trends and an underemphasis on developing plans to respond to trends.
- There is a lack of adequate information.
- Too much emphasis is placed on one area of the plan.

IMPLICATIONS FOR MANAGEMENT

Planning is a process in which all managers are involved. As a manager, you will need to determine what task activities are necessary for the implementation of a plan. These task activities are to be formulated so as to support the selected goals of upper management. You must remember that all planning is related to the mission and goals of the organization. Task activities that do not lead to the attainment of the organization's mission and goals should be avoided.

Several types of plans should be considered by managers. Single-use plans are useful when a manager believes the task activity will not be repeated in the future. When implementing a single-use plan, managers should make sure that the program or project has identified all of the necessary tasks to be performed. Special consideration should be given to the budget that has been assigned to the program or project. Sometimes the budget may not be adequate to complete every task. When this occurs, managers must reevaluate their single-use plan, identifying those tasks that can be cut or changed to meet the budget constraints. Standing plans should be continually changed to meet the requirements of the organization. Sometimes managers must change procedures or rules, because external change has made them obsolete. Standing plans should be understood as mechanisms for guiding tasks and directing them toward desirable goals.

Plans can be classified into three planning horizons. It is important that short-range plans support intermediate plans and that intermediate plans support long-range plans. If working with a short-range plan, managers should report to upper management any problems they are having in carrying out the plan. Managers responsible for the next stage of the planning horizon will need to know about delays or inadequate levels of performance that may necessitate adjustments in their own plans.

Increasingly, organizations are using contingency planning. As external conditions become more volatile, one must ask "what if" at each step of the planning process. When participating in the planning process, you should consider events that may require a change in the plan. Those that seem to have a high chance of occurrence should be identified and a contingency plan developed.

You may find yourself in an organization where planning is not done in a consistent manner. Try to determine the reason why managers are not engaged in planning. Do they feel that the environment is too uncertain? Are they reluctant to set clear goals? Are some managers fearful of change? Are rewards absent for managers who plan? Do they lack the time to plan? If the answer is "yes" to any of these questions, the organization is not taking full advantage of the planning process. These barriers to planning can be overcome. This may be accomplished by having upper management express its support for planning, increasing communication about the goals to be achieved, involving more members of the organization in the planning process, having managers review and update their plans, and setting up a system of information sharing which will lead to greater integration of plans within the organization.

KEY TERMS AND CONCEPTS

action plans	planning staff
action points	policy
budget	program
contingency planning	project
crisis management	rules and regulations
hierarchy of plans	short-range planning
intermediate planning	single-use plans
long-range planning	standard operating procedure (SOP)
plan	standing plans
planning horizon	

1. Describe the difference between a plan and planning.
2. When does the need to coordinate activities increase? How do plans help in the coordination of activities?
3. Is a planning staff useful for all types of organizations? If not, which organizations would not benefit from having a planning staff and which organizations would benefit?
4. What is an appropriate planning horizon for a business school or department at your university or college? What factors did you consider in making that judgment?
5. Describe the differences between a single-use plan and a standing plan. What type of departments in a company would be most likely to develop single-use plans? Standing plans?
6. Identify the three planning horizons and describe how they are integrated.
7. What is contingency planning? What benefits can it provide for managers?
8. Is it possible for an organization to "overplan"?
9. A manager once said she was "too busy to plan." Can this be the case in some organizations? What advice might you give her?
10. Describe the major barriers to planning. Discuss how these barriers can be overcome.

6–1 GENERAL MOTORS BETS BILLIONS

Pssst. Wanna gamble? Forget Las Vegas and Atlantic City. The real action is on W. Grand Boulevard in Detroit.

That's where the top economists and executives from General Motors Corporation play their multibillion-dollar numbers games, placing bets that could flush the face and scramble the nerves of the most ardent risk taker.

The automaker's biggest lottery involves choosing the correct number of new vehicles that will be sold in the United States in a calendar year. Guessing right helps automakers set the appropriate schedules for deciding how many vehicles to produce and what kinds to make. Guessing wrong can devastate profits, wipe out thousands of jobs, or upset the United States economy.

Variations of this fiscal roulette game take place at thousands of companies, whether the task is to project the number of washing machines to be sold, shirts to be made, or crops to be planted.

But with annual sales of $102 billion, General Motors' performance is of particular importance. Its success, or lack thereof, in a given quarter could add or subtract one point from the gross national product—the dollar amount of goods made by and services provided to the nation in a specific period.

With those stakes, General Motors invests millions of dollars a year—it won't say exactly how much—in gathering and analyzing information to make market predictions.

Every car, truck, or bus produced by an automaker is eventually sold. But if production matches market demand, those vehicles can be sold at higher prices.

General Motors' economic handicapping is done by two groups: its macroeconomics staff, headed by George C. Eads, the company's chief economist; and the market product-planning group directed by Jay I. Stark.

The macroeconomics group looks at the big picture, plotting data like disposable income, interest rates, consumer confidence, gasoline prices—factors that it thinks affect United States car sales.

The market-planning group examines changing consumer demographics such as the aging population or the growing affluence of the baby-boomer set, which might give the company a chance to increase its Cadillac sales and market more pricey cars, such as the swanky Buick Reatta two-seater.

Both Eads and Stark describe their groups' work as friendly competition, a way of helping the company cover the odds by getting information from two sources.

"These are deliberately overlapping and competing forecasts," said Eads, who served on President Carter's economic council. "In effect, the company wants to make sure that not any one way of looking at things goes unchallenged."

Both economic-research staffs provide monthly reports to four committees: one that decides how many vehicles should be made in a given period, another that sets prices, one that reviews marketing campaigns, and another that determines the kinds of products that should be pushed in a selling period.

Each committee has at least one top General Motors executive, and can operate with a certain degree of autonomy. The scheduling committee, for example, can approve production cuts or overtime work at any of General Motors' 30 United States assembly plants.

But on the really tough decisions—matters such as plant closings and product introductions—only General Motors Chairman Roger B. Smith or one of his top four officers can call the shots.

Good information helps. But sometimes those executive decisions require a healthy dose of guts and intuition gained from years of experience in the business.

Take General Motors' decision last year to scrap production of its sporty Pontiac Fiero two-seater. The car was beginning to win consumer nods after several years of derision and disappointing sales, which led many in the company to think the Fiero could stage a comeback.

But Eads' economics staff couldn't ignore the fact that rising insurance costs could dampen sales of sports cars like the Fiero. Stark's staff couldn't downplay the growth of intense competition from "affordable sports cars" like the Toyota MR2. Neither Stark nor Eads could put aside the tea leaves indicating the natural constituency for entry-level sports cars—young singles—was shrinking.

So Roger Smith, in the face of strong outside criticism from Fiero supporters, killed the car.

For 1989, General Motors is betting the economy will grow slowly, that short-term interest rates will rise and then fall this year, that long-term interest rates will remain stable in the first half of the year before moving downward, but that all the back-and-forth movement of interest rates will result in some weakening of consumer confidence.

The upshot, according to General Motors' prognosticators, will be 15 million vehicle sales in the United States in 1989.

For the record, Ford is betting consumers will snap up 15.4 million cars and trucks, and Chrysler is laying odds that General Motors is right in putting its chips down on 15 million.

Source: Reprinted by permission from the *Washington Post*. Warren Brown, "General Motors Bets Billions Its Economic Forecasts Are Right" (January 23, 1989).

1. How much responsibility for planning do the macroeconomics and market-product groups have at General Motors? Is this level of responsibility appropriate?
2. Is the information gathered by the macroeconomics and market-product groups appropriate for action plans, contingency plans, or both? Explain.
3. Sales at the end of 1989 fell far short of 15 million cars. None of the three automakers was prepared. What might they have done in the planning process to prepare for a large shortfall in sales?

6–2 McVIDEO ATTACK

Wayne Huizenga is a 50-year-old in a hurry. At 33 he co-founded Waste Management Inc., now the nation's largest waste disposal company. He was its president and chief operating officer until 1983, when he tired of commuting between Waste Management's Chicago headquarters and his home in Fort Lauderdale. He left the company in 1984. Now Huizenga wants to repeat the Waste Management trick in a different industry: videotape rental. His vehicle: Blockbuster Entertainment Corporation.

Videotape rental is one of the country's fastest-growing and most fragmented industries; more than half of United States television households now have at least one VCR. The rental market for tapes is around $5 billion a year. So far, no single company has claimed much of that revenue.

There are now over 25,000 video rental stores, mostly small storefront entrepreneurs. Throw in the rental departments of grocery, record, and convenience stores and mass merchants, and there are over 57,000 rental outlets. Many of these stock only a few hundred tapes. Few stock as many as 3,000.

A shakeout seems inevitable, and Huizenga intends to speed it up by creating the first nationwide chain, offering huge selections. Blockbuster now has over 200 stores (129 of them company-owned) in 30 states. Each store stocks a minimum of 6,500 different titles—with multiple copies, some 10,000 tapes in all. All stay open from 10 A.M. to midnight, seven days a week. In the 12 months since Huizenga took control of Blockbuster, the company has become the country's fifth largest in 1987 revenues, according to Video Store magazine.

Blockbuster began life as Cook Data Services, a Dallas-based public company that supplied computer software to the oil and gas business. When the oil business went bad, Cook's founder, David Cook, cast around for something else to do. At the urging of his ex-wife—a movie buff—he began looking at the video rental business.

Almost immediately, Cook was struck by the number of complaints he heard about lack of selection. To have a large tape selection required a heavy investment (distributors typically charge $70 per tape for a box office hit) and a good computer system to manage the inventory and run the store. Cook figured he could play a role in rationalizing the fragmented business. After months of research, primarily by former wife Sandy Cook, David Cook sold the oil and gas software business to its managers. In October 1985 he opened the first Blockbuster superstore, in Dallas. Cook's store started out with 8,000 tapes and 6,500 titles, thousands more than his largest competitor.

But depth and control of inventory weren't Cook's only innovations. Other stores keep their tapes behind the counter, to avoid theft. That means a customer must order his tape at the counter and wait until an employee finds it, if it is available. Then the transaction has to be written up. A time-consuming process. From the start, Blockbuster's tapes were stacked face forward on shelves in the display area—more like a bookstore than a library—so customers could browse and then bring their selections to the counter themselves. A magnetic stripe on each tape discouraged theft, and laser guns scanned bar codes on tape boxes and members' cards and printed up a transaction in seconds. Just like a supermarket checkout counter.

The Dallas store, says Cook, was wildly successful. "People weren't just renting the top 50 hits," he says. "They were renting everything. There seemed to be a latent demand that no one knew about. No one had put 8,000 tapes out there before."

By the summer of 1986 Cook's Blockbuster had three stores. But then, just days before an equity offering in September 1986 to raise money for expansion, a financial columnist sneered at Blockbuster's oil industry antecedents and questioned Cook's business acumen. Cook blames the columnist for killing the stock offering. In any case, Blockbuster began to run out of cash.

This is where Huizenga came in. In February 1987 Huizenga, John Melk, and Donald Flynn invested $18.6 million in newly issued Blockbuster stock. This gave the Huizenga group almost 35 percent of Cook's company, with warrants to buy more stock in the future, and set the stage for Cook's departure. Whereas Cook had envisaged a company that would primarily franchise its name and computer system, much like McDonald's, Huizenga wanted most of the growth to come from company-owned stores.

"I don't believe that just franchising gives you quality of earnings," Huizenga explains. "If you want to build a quality company, you have to have company-owned operations." He ruled that franchises would be granted only for towns too small to justify several stores. Where possible, Huizenga decreed, franchised territories would be bought back. Ultimately, Blockbuster plans to own 60 percent of its stores.

Huizenga and Cook also disagreed over Huizenga's plan to acquire chains that dominated local markets, convert them to the Blockbuster format, and achieve instant dominance. He'd used the technique at Waste Management, once buying up 100 local waste-haulers in a nine-month period. In April 1987 Cook left, and Huizenga, Melk, and Flynn took over. They haven't tampered with Cook's fundamental format: the Blockbuster superstore, with its huge selection and a rental policy that allows customers to have tapes for three evenings for slightly more than other stores charge for a 24-hour rental. That encourages customers to rent more than one tape at a time.

Blockbuster's emphasis on selection goes counter to prevailing wisdom in the industry. "The video rental industry says that this is a hit-driven business, so why carry all the newer stuff?" says Huizenga. "That's good. I like them saying that." Huizenga says the rental of hits accounts for under 30 percent of Blockbuster's rental revenues. Because the nonhit tapes cost far less to buy (around $30), their return on investment sometimes exceeds that of hits.

Blockbuster also differs from its competitors by not stocking X-rated films. "When we started, we thought people would stop in on the way home from work and pick up a tape or two," says Huizenga. "But generally, they go home, pick up the kids, and come back to shop around. That's the atmosphere that we like." To foster it, Blockbuster edits the trailers that it shows in stores to eliminate violence, bad language, and sex.

To manage the rapid growth, Huizenga has built a strong organization in six regional offices. The distribution center in Dallas repacks tapes into bar-coded boxes and stocks enough inventory for the next 20 new superstores. As with Toys "R" Us, another company that dominates a fragmented industry, Blockbuster has developed the most sophisticated computer system in its business. The system permits parents to block the rental of R-rated films by their children by coding membership cards to prohibit such rentals. Information from the system allows Blockbuster to cull tapes that aren't doing well. It is mainly this information system that franchisees are buying when they give Blockbuster a franchise fee of $35,000 and a royalty of up to 7 percent of gross revenues.

"We have the best concept by far in the industry," Huizenga says. "One little problem: It's not proprietary, so people can copy it. That's why we need to move rapidly." Thanks to David Cook and Wayne Huizenga, copying Blockbuster won't be easy.

Source: Subrata N. Chakravarty, "Give 'em Variety," *Forbes* (May 2, 1988): 54–56.

1. David Cook's plan to provide a system where customers could access tapes directly from the shelf and check out the tape by way of computer scan represents what type of action plan discussed in the text?
2. Is Wayne Huizenga's plan for rapid growth a reasonable planning horizon? Should he lengthen or shorten his planning horizon when it comes to growth of Blockbuster? Explain.
3. How might Blockbuster benefit from a contingency plan? What specific contingencies might it prepare for?

ENDNOTES

1. See *Los Angeles Times*, "Vote on Wide-Ranging Pollution Controls Set" (March 17, 1989): 1, and "Key Southland Panels OK Stringent Air-Control Plan" (March 19, 1989): 1; *Wall*

Street Journal, "Los Angeles Area Gets Anti-Smog Plan That Calls for Big Changes in Society" (March 20, 1989): B2.
2. P. F. Drucker, *Managing in Turbulent Times* (New York: Harper & Row, 1980).
3. R. F. Vancil and P. Lorange, "Strategic Planning in Diversified Companies," *Harvard Business Review* (January-February 1975): 81-90.
4. W. H. Newman, *Administrative Action: The Techniques of Organization and Management* (Englewood Cliffs, NJ: Prentice-Hall, 1963).
5. Vancil and Lorange, "Strategic Planning."
6. D. A. Kolb, I. M. Rubin, and J. M. McIntyre, *Organizational Psychology: An Experiential Approach to Organizational Behavior* (Englewood Cliffs, NJ: Prentice-Hall, 1984).
7. K. A. Ringbakk, "Why Planning Fails," *European Business* (Spring 1971): 15-26.

Strategic Planning

CHAPTER 7

After studying this chapter, you should be able to:
- *Understand the role that an organization's purpose, mission, and goals play in formulating a strategic plan.*
- *Identify specific conditions in the environment that have increased the need for strategic planning.*
- *Describe the methods managers use for conducting a SWOT analysis.*
- *Identify the role of strategy selection at three levels of the organization.*
- *Identify various grand strategies that managers can select during the process of formulating the strategic plan.*
- *Describe the role that departments play in implementing the strategic plan.*

In February 1989, Sears, Roebuck & Co. announced that it was closing all 824 of its U.S. stores for 42 hours the next week. This was the first such closing in the firm's 99-year history. The closing was to give employees time to permanently cut prices on 50,000 items in line with a new policy of "everyday low pricing." In addition to closing its stores, Sears bombarded television viewers, radio listeners, and newspaper readers with advertising about the change. Thomas E. Morris, vice-president of marketing for the Sears merchandise group, said: "Our goal is to reach everyone in America several times" with information about the new strategy.

Why the new strategy? Sears had been suffering from sagging retail sales, losing market share to trendy merchants and discount chains. With this new approach Sears wants to be identified as a store that has a "sale that never ends."[1]

In addition to price cutting, Sears also is expanding its product line to give customers a wider selection. Now the products that Sears manufactures exclusively for its own stores (such as the Kenmore and Craftsman brands) will have to compete directly with products manufactured by other firms. The decision to revamp Sears' merchandising effort follows its attempts to sell the Sears Tower in Chicago and deliberations over selling off several business units such as Coldwell Banker (real estate) and Dean Witter Reynolds (investments).

Why did managers at Sears choose to alter the firm's strategy? How did they arrive at their decision? What led them to implement the new strategy? These questions and others will be addressed in this chapter. We define **strategy** as a method of competition. **Strategic management** is that set of managerial decisions and actions that determines the long-run competitive performance of the organization. It includes the formulation, implementation, and evaluation of a strategic plan. The **strategic plan** of an organization is a systematic blueprint of management's answers to three basic questions: (1) What will we do and for whom will we do it? (2) What goals do we want to achieve? (3) How are we going to manage the organization's activities so as to achieve the chosen goals?[2]

Managers at Sears, Roebuck & Co. established a systematic blueprint based on these three basic questions. The critical goal was maintaining dominance in the retail industry. Advertising was found to be an inadequate method of competition for achieving this goal, and management chose to change the price and variety of products in hopes of expanding its market share. In addition, restructuring the firm through changes in business holdings was part of the overall strategic plan.

This chapter will begin with a discussion of the importance of strategic planning. Next we will examine key parts of the strategic plan. The formulation of the strategic plan will be discussed with an emphasis on developing effective strategic plans. Identification of a full range of strategic alternatives available for consideration by managers will follow. Finally, several models for conceptualizing organizational strategies will be discussed.

THE IMPORTANCE OF STRATEGIC PLANNING

The subject of strategic planning is relatively new to organization managers. Twenty years ago, few managers participated in strategic planning. Those

Part of Nissan's strategy for wooing consumers away from other makes of luxury automobile in a volatile market was a series of ads for its Infiniti that piqued interest by not revealing what the new model looked like.

Infiniti, A Division of Nissan Motor Corp. in U.S.A.

who did lacked sophisticated techniques for the formulation and implementation of plans. Today, such planning is widespread. Many organizations have set up departments whose personnel do nothing but perform this function. Indeed, more and more business schools have added courses in strategic planning. Some schools now even offer degrees in this area.

Why the recent interest in setting up and staffing strategic planning departments within organizations? One reason is that the relative increase in the size of many organizations has led to a need for greater coordination among organizational activities. A strategic plan helps managers understand how various departments, such as accounting, manufacturing, marketing, engineering, and research, are linked together. A second major reason for the interest in strategic planning is an increase in environmental uncertainty. Events within an organization's context are no longer as predictable as they once were. In addition, many contextual events have a greater impact on organizational activities than was true in the past.

Recall our discussion in Chapter 3 of the six environmental dimensions that influence an organization's operations. They include munificence, dynamism, complexity, concentration, turbulence, and consensus. You may wish to review these concepts. Increases in environmental uncertainty have placed greater pressure on organizational managers to engage in strategic planning. Strategic planning helps managers to identify and understand important environmental trends and to develop responses to those trends, leading to greater organizational effectiveness.

Strategic planning is important to managers because it links the goals of the organization with the organization's environment. If the environment of the organization remained constant, strategic planning would be less important to the organization. However, few if any organizations operate in a certain environment.

LEVELS OF STRATEGIC PLANNING

While greater environmental uncertainty has increased the need for strategic planning, we still need to learn what specific activities managers perform to create and manage a strategy. We can address these questions by examining first the levels of strategic planning.[3]

Strategic Planning at the Corporate Level

Strategic planning at the corporate level must consider the entire organization. Corporate-level managers must decide which businesses to expand and which to contract. They must consider the amount and manner in which resources are to be allocated to many different business units and product lines. Plans concerning acquisitions, mergers, joint ventures, and divestitures are usually made at this level. At Sears, Roebuck & Co., corporate-level planners decided to pursue a strategy of price leadership and made decisions to divest Coldwell Banker Realty Group. A guiding question for managers at this level is "What business are we in?"

Strategic Planning at the Business-Unit Level

Strategic planning at the business-unit level is focused on a closely related group of products or services for a recognized class of customers. For instance, the Saturn Division of General Motors is a business unit of General Motors. Sears has such business units as Allstate Insurance and Dean Witter Reynolds. A guiding question for managers at this level is "How do we compete in our industry?"

Strategic Planning at the Department Level

Within each business unit are departments or operating subdivisions of the business unit—marketing, production, finance, personnel, R&D, and so forth. Managers at this level are responsible for implementing the strategic plan. At Sears, it was the responsibility of store managers to oversee the price markdowns during the 42-hour closing. The marketing department was responsible for developing advertisements and securing time and space for the distribution of those advertisements. A guiding question for managers at this level is "How do we support the strategic plan of the business unit?"

Managers at all levels of the organization are critical to the success of the strategic plan. A book currently popular with managers who are involved in strategic planning is *A Book of Five Rings* by Miyamoto Musashi, which describes the "Way" to learn the "art" of strategy (see Management in Action 1).

THE PROCESS OF STRATEGIC PLANNING

Strategic planning consists of several key components. Figure 7–1 lists these components and shows the way in which they are linked together into the process of strategic planning.

Born in 1584, Miyamoto Musashi was one of Japan's most renowned warriors. He was a samurai and, by the age of 30, had fought and won more than 60 con-

tests by killing all of his opponents. Satisfied that he was invincible, Musashi then turned to formulating his philosophy of "the Way of the sword." He wrote *A Book of Five Rings* [Go rin no sho] while living in a cave in the mountains of Kyusu a few weeks before his death in 1645. Musashi believed that timing was the key to everything and that timing could not be mastered without a great deal of practice. This is how he describes timing and the "Way of strategy":

"There is timing in the whole life of the warrior, in his thriving and declining, in his harmony and discord. Similarly, there is timing in the Way of the merchant, in the rise and fall of capital. All things entail rising and falling timing. You must be able to discern this. In strategy there are various timing considerations. From the outset you must know the applicable timing and the inapplicable timing, and from among the large and small things and the fast and slow timings find the relevant timing, first see-

ing the distance timing and the background timing. This is the main thing in strategy. It is especially important to know the background timing, otherwise your strategy will become uncertain.

"You win in battles with the timing . . . born of the timing of cunning by knowing the enemies' timing, and thus using a timing which the enemy does not expect.

"If you practice day and night . . . your spirit will naturally broaden. Thus is large-scale strategy and the strategy of hand-to-hand combat propagated in the world. This is recorded for the first time in the five books of Ground, Water, Fire, Tradition (Wind), and Void. This is the Way for men who want to learn my strategy:

1. Do not think dishonestly.
2. The Way is in training.
3. Become acquainted with every art.
4. Know the Ways of all professions.
5. Distinguish between gain and loss in worldly matters.
6. Develop intuitive judgment and understanding for everything.
7. Perceive those things which cannot be seen.
8. Pay attention even to trifles.
9. Do nothing which is of no use."

Source: Miyamoto Musashi, *A Book of Five Rings: The Classic Guide to Strategy* (Woodstock, NY: Overlook Press, 1974), 48-49.

Defining Organizational Purpose and Mission

The stated purpose and mission of an organization, as discussed in Chapter 5, are the starting point in formulating a strategic plan. The purpose and mission serve to define for management the markets, products, and environmental domains in which the organization seeks to be successful. The purpose and mission further serve to guide managers in setting official, operative, and operational goals.

Setting Organizational Goals

Organizational goals specify desired long-run results, as in the case of official goals, and desired short-run results, as in the case of operative and operational goals. Goal setting is an essential part of strategic planning in that it specifies performance targets for managers at all levels of the organization. The setting of goals is directly derived from the purpose and mission of the organization.

Usually, existing goals are the result of prior strategic plans and are reset when they have been achieved, have gone unmet, or the context of the organization has changed substantially. For instance, events such as governmental deregulation of the industry, the emergence of new competitors, unionization

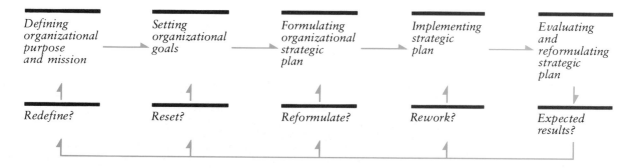

| Defining organizational purpose and mission | → | Setting organizational goals | → | Formulating organizational strategic plan | → | Implementing strategic plan | → | Evaluating and reformulating strategic plan |

| Redefine? | Reset? | Reformulate? | Rework? | Expected results? |

Source: Adapted from A. A. Thompson, Jr., and A. J. Strickland, *Strategic Management: Concepts and Cases* (Plano, TX: Business Publications, Inc., 1990), 5. Reproduced with permission.

FIGURE 7–1
Components of Strategic Planning

of workers, lowered demand for products or services, or the retirement of top executives can each necessitate a reevaluation of the current strategic plan. When this occurs, managers examine the organization's purpose and mission and determine whether goals need to be reset or the existing goals are desirable and achievable.

Setting organizational goals provides managers with a base for formulating strategies. Goals further provide managers with criteria for selecting and rejecting alternative strategies based on an evaluation of each strategy's potential for achieving goals at all levels of the organization.

Formulating the Strategic Plan

Suppose you are the manager of a division in a large company with the operative goal of increasing profit by the end of the year. Would you propose to lower the price of the product and increase production? Raise the price of the product and decrease production? Expand the advertising budget? Increase the commissions that the sales force receives? Cut back on budget allocations to the departments in the division? Hire or fire employees? A combination of these proposals? Every goal in an organization can, on paper, be reached by one or more strategic paths. Much like a coach of a football team who enters the stadium each Sunday with a "game plan" that was developed during the week, organization managers must also develop a game plan that will enable the organization to achieve its desired results over the course of several years.

In formulating a strategic plan, managers must assess the organization's prior performance, current position, and desired outcomes. Four strategic questions should be addressed:[4]

- How do we respond to new opportunities in the environment, lessen the impact of environmental threats, and strengthen the mix of the organization's activities by doing more of some things and less of others?
- How do we assign resources among the various subunits, divisions, and activities of the organization?
- How do we compete with other organizations for customer groups and customer needs through allocation of existing or new products and services?
- How do we effectively manage organizational activities at the departmental, divisional, and corporate level of the organization?

Like football coaches, organization managers must develop a game plan that will achieve desired outcomes.

In summary, the formulation of a strategic plan is a process in which management assesses the opportunities and threats that exist in the environment and rates the organization's internal strengths and weaknesses. When management has conducted this assessment of the organization, it is ready to select a strategy that will be compatible with the organization's purpose and mission.

Implementing the Strategic Plan

Vince Lombardi, the famous coach of the Green Bay Packers football team, was once quoted as saying, "The best game plan in the world never blocked or tackled anybody." Like a football coach, organization managers are faced with the difficult task of converting the strategic plan from paper into action. In general, to carry out a strategic plan successfully, managers must effectively communicate the plan; assign proper authority and responsibility for activities within the plan; develop methods for measuring the results of activities; and, when necessary, develop procedures for taking corrective action should the results not be supportive of the plan. Similarly, on the day of the game, a football player must understand the overall intent of the plan, his responsibilities in executing the plan, the criteria that will be used for judging his performance, and the methods that will be used should he fail to carry out his assigned tasks successfully.

On a broader level, we can think of the implementation of a strategic plan as a process where management has to fit the plan to several different aspects of the organization's operations. "Fits" needed are between:

- Strategy and organizational structure;
- Strategy and organizational skills and capabilities;
- Strategy and the allocation of resources;
- Strategy and the organization's system of rewards and incentives;
- Strategy and internal policies and procedures;
- Strategy and the values shared by organizational members;
- Strategy and budgets and programs; and
- Strategy and the organizational culture.[5]

The difficulty in implementing a strategic plan comes from the need not only to satisfy each of these fits, but also to satisfy all the fits simultaneously. That is, an implemented strategic plan can achieve success only when all the various fits are coordinated by management.

Evaluating the Strategic Plan

Equally critical to the success of a formulated and implemented strategy is the evaluation of results. Managers must continually watch the results of the implemented strategy and make adjustments if necessary. No strategic plan can predict with total accuracy such environmental variables as customer response to products, economic indicators, legislation, or actions of competitors. Throughout the implementation process, managers must get information both on the environment and on activities within the organization. For example, early signs of low consumer purchases of a new product may require managers to alter their advertising campaign or to consider whether product quality is low because workers are not yet experienced at producing the new product. If results of the implemented strategy are less than predicted, management may have to reevaluate the strategic plan. This, of course, can result in high financial and human costs within the organization.

Managers should always keep in mind that the ultimate test of a strategic plan rests with how well the organization can achieve its appointed goals. The remainder of this chapter will focus on steps involved in formulating the strategic plan.

TECHNIQUES IN STRATEGIC PLANNING

Formulation of a successful strategic plan requires managers to have an accurate and complete understanding of the external environment and internal capabilities of the organization. This understanding must precede the selection of a strategy by managers. One technique for understanding an organization's environment and internal capabilities is the SWOT analysis.

SWOT Analysis

SWOT is an acronym for Strengths and Weaknesses of an organization's internal capabilities and Opportunities and Threats in the organization's external environment. SWOT analysis enables managers to develop a strategic profile of the organization based on information they have collected. SWOT analysis assumes that an organization will achieve strategic success by increasing strengths and opportunities and lessening weaknesses and threats. Figure 7–2 lists key questions to guide managers in a SWOT analysis.

STRENGTHS

A strength is a distinctive competence, resource, or skill that provides the organization with a competitive advantage in the marketplace. Access to higher-quality materials, good financial relations, a strong image, exclusive ownership of patents, extensive distribution channels, or highly talented managers are all strengths that an organization may hold over its competitors.

WEAKNESSES

A weakness is a negative internal condition that can lead to a lowering of organizational performance. A weakness can be the result of an absence of necessary resources or skills, or a deficiency in the development of necessary resources and skills. Divisions with inadequate strategy skills, overextended credit accounts, poor product image, outdated machinery, or poor plant locations can be weaknesses for an organization.

OPPORTUNITIES

An opportunity is a current or future condition in the environment that is favorable to an organization's current or potential output. Favorable conditions may consist of changes in laws that give the organization a competitive edge, a growing number of customers, introduction of new technologies that the organization can easily exploit, or improved relationships with suppliers.

FIGURE 7–2
*Questions for
Conducting a SWOT
Analysis*

Internal

Strengths

A distinctive competence?
Adequate financial resources?
Good competitive skills?
Well thought of by buyers?
An acknowledged market leader?
Well-conceived functional area
    strategies?
Access to economies of scale?
Insulated from strong competitive
    pressures?
Technology leader?
Cost advantages?
Competitive advantages?
Product innovation abilities?
Proven management?
Other?

Weaknesses

No clear strategic direction?
A deteriorating competitive position?
Obsolete facilities?
Sub-par profitability?
Lack of managerial depth and talent?
Missing any key skills or competencies?
Poor track record in implementing
    strategy?
Plagued with internal operating
    problems?
Vulnerable to competitive pressures?
Falling behind in research?
Too narrow a product line?
Weak market image?
Competitive disadvantages?
Below-average marketing skills?
Unable to finance needed changes in
    strategy?
Other?

External

Opportunities

Serve additional customer groups?
Enter new markets or segments?
Expand product line to meet broader
    range of customer needs?
Diversify into related products?
Vertical integration?
Ability to move to better strategic group?
Complacency among rival firms?
Faster market growth?
Other?

Threats

Likely entry of new competitors?
Rising sales of substitute products?
Slower market growth?
Adverse government policies?
Growing competitive pressures?
Vulnerability to recession and business
    cycle?
Growing power of customers or
    suppliers?
Changing buyer needs and tastes?
Adverse demographic changes?
Other?

Source: Adapted from A. A. Thompson, Jr., and A. J. Strickland, *Strategic Management: Concepts and Cases* (Plano, TX: Business Publications, Inc., 1990), 91. Reproduced with permission.

Opportunities should not be examined solely in light of current conditions, but rather for their long-range effects on organization activities.

THREATS

A threat is a current or future condition in the environment that is unfavorable to an organization's current or potential output. Unfavorable conditions may consist of entry of a powerful competitor into the organization's market, a decline in the number of customers, introduction of new technologies that would make existing products obsolete, passage of regulations that would constrain an organization's ability to compete, or difficulty locating reliable suppliers.

One of the strengths of Hewlett-Packard is its corps of highly talented managers.

Upon completion of a SWOT analysis, managers are ready to check their organization's existing position and make adjustments that will better prepare the organization for the future. SWOT analysis is useful for strategic planners in a variety of ways. First, it provides managers with a logical framework for assessing their organization's current and future position. Second, from this assessment managers can identify a set of alternative strategies. And finally, the SWOT analysis can be conducted periodically to keep managers informed about what external or internal factors have either increased or decreased in importance to the organization's activities. Ultimately, of course, SWOT analysis should lead to improved organizational performance. Not until Chrysler Corporation conducted a SWOT analysis after near-bankruptcy did managers fully understand what environmental threats and internal weaknesses faced them. The SWOT analysis enabled Chrysler's management to reassess its situation clearly and turn the company around successfully.

Formulating Strategic Goals

Recall the hierarchy of goals introduced in Chapter 5. Strategic planning can provide the basis for transforming official goals into operative and operational goals.

A SWOT analysis helps managers identify what organizational activities can be realistically achieved over the course of time. Increasing a firm's market share from 20 percent to 50 percent may be desirable but unrealistic if the firm is externally threatened by the entry of several large corporations into the market. Increasing production capacity by 30 percent may not be realistic if a current internal weakness is a high debt-to-asset ratio. In cases where strategic planners discover many external threats and internal weaknesses, a total reassessment of the organization's purpose and mission may be required.

SELECTING A STRATEGY

Once managers have assessed the organization's environment, checked its internal operations, and set goals to be achieved, the process of selecting a strategy begins. A variety of **strategic alternatives,** or different methods of competition for attaining organizational goals, may be considered by managers at all levels of the organization. We will first examine corporate-level strategies, then business-level strategies, and finally departmental-level strategies.

Corporate-Level Strategies

Corporate-level strategies serve to identify a unified direction for the total organization. Managers at the corporate level define a strategic direction that includes business units and departments within those business units. Managers often select either grand strategies or portfolio strategies for guiding their company.

GRAND STRATEGIES

A **grand strategy** is a broad plan to guide an organization toward completion of its official goals. Depending on the size of the organization and the nature of the goals to be achieved, managers may choose to implement one of three grand strategies: growth, stability, or retrenchment.[6]

Growth
Companies can grow through internal development or external acquisition of additional business units. A **growth strategy** is common in new, emerging industries or industries that are themselves undergoing rapid growth and thus gaining many new external opportunities. There are several methods for achieving growth. One method is for the firm to expand operations to reach new customers. Franchise operations like McDonald's have used this strategy successfully throughout the world. A second method is to change an existing product or create a new product that is very similar to the existing one. Changing the product or service or producing related products or services enables the organization to keep existing customers who are satisfied with the product while at the same time attracting new customers with similar tastes. Procter & Gamble has been highly successful with this strategy. The leading product of Procter & Gamble has been Tide detergent. The original Tide is still manufactured, but consumers may also purchase Lemon Tide and Unscented Tide. Creation of a new product similar to an existing one is common in the recording industry. Firms in the industry have followed a path of continual innovation in the transmission of recorded music, from Thomas Edison's invention of recorded sound on a wax cylinder at the turn of the century to compact discs based on laser technology in the 1980s. A third method of growth is through acquisition of another firm. The acquired firm may be

The grand strategy of the Walgreen Company is to achieve growth by opening new stores.

a competitor, as when Bristol-Myers acquired Squibb in 1989 to become the second largest company in the pharmaceutical industry. Or the acquired firm may be a supplier or customer of the firm. Sony's acquisition of Columbia Pictures gives it a large supply of movies and music recordings that can be used with Sony electronic equipment.

Stability

Managers select a **stability strategy** when they want to protect the existing market share of the firm from environmental threats or have just completed a phase of rapid growth or divestment. A stability strategy allows corporate managers to concentrate on increasing the internal strengths of the firm. After many years of growth, Holiday Inn chose to stabilize its operations by curtailing growth and focusing on upgrading its hotels to compete more effectively.

Retrenchment

When managers of an organization are faced with declining performance due to internal weaknesses and external threats, a **retrenchment strategy** is often selected. Managers who select this strategy believe they can correct existing problems by invoking techniques for improving operational efficiency. Often this requires cutbacks in labor and management and divestiture of existing business units. It may also require curtailment of research expenditures, a reduced marketing budget, and a decrease in organizational benefits such as pay, travel, and supplies. General Motors, faced with declining profits and market share, was forced in the late 1980s to cut back on hiring, lay off workers, reduce salaries, and sell many automobile manufacturing plants to streamline the operations of the organization. Stiff competition due to foreign imports as well as inefficiency in overall operations forced GM managers to pursue this alternative to avoid further losses. Retrenchment can be a painful choice for managers because it implies that management has failed. However, it can provide management with an opportunity to engage in creative tactics for making the organization viable once again.

Figure 7–3 provides a useful matrix for understanding how SWOT analysis can serve as a guide to the selection of a grand strategy. After conducting a SWOT analysis, managers can locate the quadrant that best describes their present position and forecast their possible position in the future. An empirical study of 247 top managers in 88 organizations suggested that SWOT analysis helped managers make an effective choice among strategic alternatives.[7]

PORTFOLIO STRATEGIES

A **portfolio strategy** considers the business mix of the corporation—that is, the types of business units and product lines the company controls. The BCG matrix and the GE matrix are two models used by many corporations in selecting a portfolio strategy.

BCG Matrix

Developed by the Boston Consulting Group, the **BCG matrix** model of strategy emphasizes the nature of the internal mix, or the diversification, of business units that are under the control of management. The BCG matrix views the overall investment an organization has made in various lines of business. The objective of the BCG matrix is to help managers decide about the deployment of resources to each business unit or product line owned and operated by an organization.

Business units or product lines of an organization are classified according to two dimensions: overall market growth rate and market share held by the business unit. Market growth rate and market share can be classified as high or low, enabling managers to situate a business unit within a 2 × 2 matrix. The classification of business units within the matrix leads to identification of the four strategic types shown in Figure 7–4: stars, cash cows, question marks, and dogs. Each strategic type describes a business in a different stage of development which has unique implications for overall organization cash flow and profit.

FIGURE 7–3
Grand-Strategy Selection Matrix

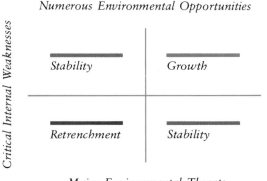

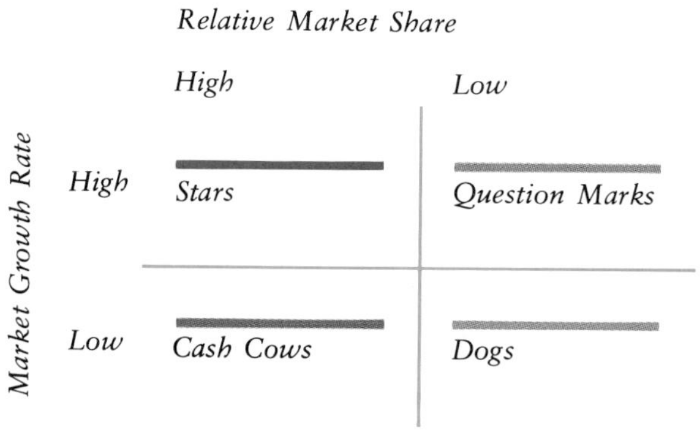

Relative Market Share

FIGURE 7–4
*The BCG Portfolio
Matrix*

	High	Low
High	Stars	Question Marks
Low	Cash Cows	Dogs

Market Growth Rate

Source: *Perspectives,* no. 66, "The Product Portfolio." Reprinted by permission from The Boston Consulting Group, Inc., Boston, Massachusetts/ © 1970.

STARS. A **star** is a business unit that has both high market growth rate and a relatively large share of the market. Typically, this is a product line or business unit that has high potential for growth and needs large amounts of short-run cash to support rapid growth. Stars are attractive to organizations because they have the potential to increase sales and therefore to generate large amounts of profits in the future. An example of a star would be a producer of high-definition television sets.

CASH COWS. A **cash cow** is a business unit or product line in a mature industry. The business has a large share of the market, but there is little growth. Many cash cows were formerly successful stars. Cash for investment in expanded facilities or advertising is no longer required. Rather, large amounts of surplus cash can be "milked" from a cash cow and can then be channeled into new business units or products that have high potential for growth, but are short on cash (e.g., stars). An example of a cash cow business unit would be Mars, the producer of candy bars.

QUESTION MARKS. A **question mark** is the most problematic for managers formulating a strategic plan. Question marks exist in a rapidly growing market but have a small market share. Managers must decide whether to invest more capital into the business unit or product to take advantage of the high growth opportunity (i.e., transform it into a star), or divest to emphasize other business units or products in the portfolio. Either way, managers are faced with some risk—either in making a large investment that may result in failure or in passing up an opportunity that may later turn out to be highly profitable. In the early 1970s, the management of W. R. Grace decided to sell Miller Brewing to Philip Morris in the belief that the unit could not be transformed into a star. The management of Philip Morris saw Miller Brewing differently. With the introduction of Lite beer after the purchase, Miller became a major source of revenue for Philip Morris.

DOGS. A **dog** is a poor performer because of little growth in the market and its small market share. Usually, dogs are a cash drain on the organization because they are unable to support themselves with what little revenue they can generate. Management must either try to sell the business unit to another company or liquidate its assets. An example of a dog would be a producer of transistor radios.

The BCG matrix is designed to provide managers of diversified organizations with an understanding of the contributions business units or product lines can make to the overall profit of the company. As depicted in Figure 7–5, managers should develop a portfolio in which cash cows are available to provide cash for new ventures in the form of stars or question marks. Question marks are needed to become the stars of the future. Stars are needed to become the cash cows of the future. Current cash cows are most likely to become dogs over time and are therefore divested. Managers who formulate and implement a balanced portfolio among cash cows, stars, and question marks should achieve successful outcomes for the organization.

GE Matrix

The **GE matrix**, sometimes called the **GE nine-cell matrix**, provides upper managers with a means of evaluating existing business units and those they might like to acquire. Developed by General Electric with the help of the consulting firm McKinsey and Company, the GE matrix is considered to have advantages over the BCG matrix by introducing multiple factors for evaluating business units.[8] As shown in Figure 7–6, business units are plotted in the matrix on two dimensions: industry attractiveness and business strength. Industry attractiveness includes such factors as market size, market growth rates, seasonality, types of competitors, and technical complexity of products. Business strength is determined by such factors as profit margins, market share, quality of management, and manufacturing technology.

Based on where the business unit is located on the two dimensions, one of three basic strategies is recommended: investment/growth, selective investment, or divestment. Business units falling in the blue cells of Figure 7–6 are candidates for investment and growth because they rank high in both industry attractiveness and business strength. Business units falling in the gray cells should only be invested in selectively. Investments should be cautious until a change in the unit's strength or degree of industry attractiveness occurs. Business units in the red cells are candidates for divestment because they rank low in both industry attractiveness and business strength.

Grand strategies and portfolio strategies are useful for corporate strategists whether they seek to build their organization through internal growth or through acquisitions. The 1980s saw extensive use of portfolio strategies

FIGURE 7–5
Strategies of Portfolio Types

	Portfolio Types			
	Stars	*Cash Cows*	*Question Marks*	*Dogs*
Strategy	Invest for rapid growth, convert to cash cow	Channel revenues to stars and question marks	Evaluate for future potential as star, divest remainder	Divest or liquidate

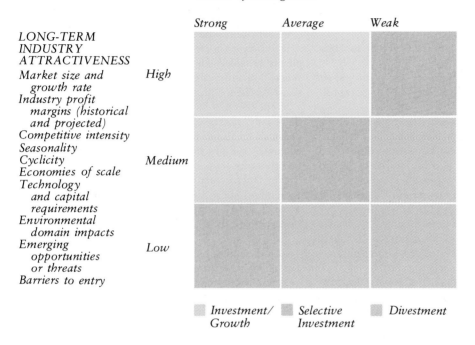

FIGURE 7–6
The GE Matrix

BUSINESS STRENGTH/
COMPETITIVE POSITION
Relative market share
Profit margin relative to competitors
Ability to compete on price and quality
Knowledge of customer and market
Competitive strengths and weaknesses
Technological capability
Caliber of management

LONG-TERM
INDUSTRY
ATTRACTIVENESS
Market size and
    growth rate
Industry profit
    margins (historical
    and projected)
Competitive intensity
Seasonality
Cyclicity
Economies of scale
Technology
    and capital
    requirements
Environmental
    domain impacts
Emerging
    opportunities
    or threats
Barriers to entry

as a means of evaluating business units as candidates for acquisition. Some of the colorful language used by corporate strategists during this period is displayed in Management in Action 2.

Business-Unit-Level Strategies

Several models have been developed for describing and explaining different types of business-unit-level strategies. Two such models that are useful to managers in understanding how the strategy of their business unit relates to their industry are the adaptation model and the competitive model. Each model makes different assumptions about the relationships between strategy, organization, and the environment. The following discussion of each strategic model will focus on its assumptions, alternative strategies that managers can consider, and the way the strategy can be implemented for success.

ADAPTATION MODEL

Raymond Miles and Charles Snow developed the adaptation model of organizational strategy.[9] The **adaptation model** contends that a major thrust of afterglow   postmerger euphoria of acquirer and/or acquiree, usually soon lost.

Age of Acquireus   post-1967 to date.

MANAGEMENT IN ACTION 2
THE LANGUAGE OF CORPORATE TAKEOVERS

ambush   swift and premeditated takeover attempt.

big-game hunting   plotting and executing takeovers of large companies.

big-hat boys   Texas moneymen interested in "big-game hunting."

black knights   unfriendly acquirers drawn to a target by news that the company is already being propositioned by others.

courtship   merger discussions, relatively friendly, between top executives of two firms.

cyanide pill   anti-takeover finance strategy in which the potential target arranges for long-term debt to fall due immediately and in full if it is acquired.

double Pac-Man strategy   target firm makes tender offer for the stock of its would-be acquirer.

friendly offer   merger proposal cleared in advance with the target company's board and top management; usually leads to the firm's recommending it favorably to shareholders for approval.

golden parachutes   provision in the employment contracts of top executives that assures them a lucrative financial landing if the firm is acquired in a takeover.

greenmail   a firm's purchase of its own stock, at a premium, from an investor who it fears will otherwise seek to acquire it or else initiate a proxy fight to oust its present management.

hired guns   merger and acquisition specialists, other investment bankers, and lawyers employed by either side in any takeover.

junk bonds   high-risk, high-yield debt certificates traded publicly, so called because they are rated below investment grade, either by Moody's or by Standard & Poor's; junk bonds are often used to help finance hostile takeovers.

marrying   accomplishing a merger.

matchmaking   searching for possible deals to join two companies; a major activity of investment banking houses.

mushroom treatment   postmerger problems from an acquired executive's standpoint: "First they buried us in manure; then they left us in the dark awhile; then they let us stew; and finally they canned us."

pirates or raiders   hostile acquirers.

sharks   takeover artists.

shark repellent   protective strategies for preventing or combating a hostile tender offer.

shoot-out   climax of a takeover battle, usually conducted by "hired guns."

takeover   the purchase of majority ownership in a corporation; usually resisted by the target company but accomplished nonetheless by paying a premium above the current market price for the firm's shares.

tender offer   proposal to purchase a firm's stock from its shareholders for an amount higher than its current market price.

tombstones   advertisements in the financial press containing announcements of interest to investors and the business community (e.g., tender offers, stock underwritings, mergers, and divestments).

unfriendly offer   proposal to transfer a firm's ownership to parties viewed as hostile or unworthy by its current board and executives; usually resisted and seldom endorsed by the target company.

white knight   acceptable acquirer sought by a potential acquiree to forestall an unfriendly takeover; the preferred suitor.

wounded list   executives of an acquired firm who develop health or career problems from the deal.

Source: Adapted from Paul M. Hirsch, "From Ambushes to Golden Parachutes: Corporate Takeovers as an Instance of Cultural Framing and Institutional Integration," *American Journal of Sociology* 91, no. 4 (January 1986): 830-835. Published by The University of Chicago Press. Reprinted with permission.

strategic management should be the alignment of organization activities with key dimensions of the organization's environment. To accomplish this end, managers must set up a strategy that will adapt to environmental conditions and also manage internal activities of the organization to support the selected strategy. Adaptation of the organization to the environment is accomplished by simultaneously solving three critical strategic problems: the entrepreneurial problem, the engineering problem, and the administrative problem.

The **entrepreneurial problem** considers what managers believe to be their market. It is solved by determining what goods or services the organization will produce for a defined product-market domain. In a real sense, the entrepreneurial problem is solved by the organization's mission as well as by management's decisions on commitment of resources to achieve goals related to the mission.

The **engineering problem** is one of deciding which methods are appropriate for the production and distribution of goods and services. The solution to the engineering problem is determined by the solution of the entrepreneurial problem, or management's decisions on what products or services will be provided to a market. The solution usually involves implementing a system for producing, controlling, and distributing the goods or services that support the organization's mission. Using robots on the production line, providing employees with authority to decide the pace of work, and distributing goods or services to specific markets can be solutions to the engineering problem.

The **administrative problem** addresses the need to develop an appropriate administrative system within the organization. It is solved by designing an organizational system that will enhance the coordination of activities to achieve the solutions to the entrepreneurial and engineering problems. Decisions about the degree of bureaucracy in the organization, spans of control for management, and methods of hiring employees may be questions that must be answered to solve the administrative problem.

The adaptation model of organization strategy contends that managers must interrelate the three solutions to the entrepreneurial, engineering, and administrative problems. Organizations that are most successful, according to this strategic model, will be those that have correctly matched the solutions to the conditions in the organization's environment. Four types of organizations, classified by the different ways they solve these problems, are identified by Miles and Snow: defenders, prospectors, analyzers, and reactors.

Defenders

The **defender strategy** is carried out when management seeks or creates an environment that is stable. Managers will emphasize protecting the market share they have gained. A defender solves the entrepreneurial problem by defining a narrow market segment and producing only a few products or services to provide to the market. The engineering problem is solved by emphasizing efficiency in the production of goods or services to lower costs and thus be able to set a price that competitors cannot match. Rigid bureaucratic controls offer a solution to the administrative problem by reducing errors and increasing efficiency in member activities. The defender strategy is similar to the stability strategy previously discussed. McDonald's exemplifies a defender organization by focusing on a narrow market segment (fast-food consumers), maximizing efficiency in production (cooking methods that lead to product uniformity), and strict employee controls (dress and behavior codes for employees).

Prospectors

The **prospector strategy** is the opposite of the defender strategy. The prospector seeks or creates an unstable environment in the form of rapid change and high growth in the market. Management emphasizes organizational activities that will locate and exploit new product opportunities. The entrepreneurial problem is solved by defining the environment in broad and general terms to encourage innovation and diversity in activities. Since internal activities must be diverse and adaptable to new opportunities, managers solve the engineering problem by avoiding long-term commitments to any single method of production. Instead, multiple methods of production that can be changed when necessary are used. Large capital investments in plants and machinery are avoided so that activities can be shifted to new or different products readily without having to scrap old equipment or invest in new methods of production. Administratively, managers encourage flexibility in member activities through loose controls to maximize growth and change. Johnson & Johnson represents a prospector organization by broadly defining its market (home and personal products), employing multiple methods of production (over 150 product divisions that are continually changing), and setting loose administrative controls (each division manager selects the administrative structure believed to be appropriate for his or her employees).

Analyzers

An analyzer is an organization that exists between the two extremes of defender and prospector. The **analyzer strategy** involves adapting solutions from both the defender and prospector strategies to the three problems. Consistency is maintained by identifying two areas of activity for the organization. One area of focus is a stable market, where a defender strategy is pursued. The other area of focus is an unstable market, where a prospector strategy is pursued. The major concern of managers is to maintain a balance between organization subunits that are defender-oriented and subunits that are prospector-oriented. The entrepreneurial problem is solved by identifying two market segments—one stable and the other changing. The engineering problem is solved by managers who emphasize methods of efficiency in production for the stable subunits and methods of flexibility for those subunits oriented to a changing market. The administrative problem is solved by structuring the organization around tight controls over stable subunit activities and loose controls for subunits engaged in developing new products. Organizations such as RJR Nabisco represent the analyzer strategy. RJR Nabisco's original base of business is tobacco products, where profits are high but growth is slow. The management of RJR Nabisco chose to expand into more unstable markets by entering into food products (e.g., Chun King, Del Monte, and Patio Foods), which have high competition and rapid growth. Thus, original technologies and bureaucratic controls remain for the tobacco business while multiple technologies and loose controls have been set for the food-product lines of business.

Reactors

A reactor organization is basically one that has suffered strategic failure. Strategic failure can be due to inappropriate managerial decisions about the formulation and implementation of the strategic plan. As Miles and Snow note, factors that can force the use of the **reactor strategy** include the following:

- Top management may not have clearly articulated the organization's strategy.

- Management has not fully shaped the organization's structure and processes to fit a chosen strategy.
- Management has had a tendency to maintain the organization's current strategy/structure relationship despite overwhelming changes in environmental conditions.[10]

In order for the organization to end the reactor mode of strategy, management must develop new solutions for the entrepreneurial, engineering, or administrative problem, or solutions for all three, depending on what has caused the failure. Reactor strategies are similar to the retrenchment strategy discussed earlier. An example of a reactor organization was International Harvester Company in the early 1980s. A producer of farm machinery and trucks, International Harvester had expanded into construction equipment and gas turbine engines. Beset by a worldwide recession, lower demand for farm equipment due to high interest rates, and a lengthy labor strike, management of International Harvester was faced with a short-term debt of over $1 billion and a loss of $397 million for the year ended in 1980.[11] Although management's decision to expand into other product lines was initially correct as a method of diversifying, costs and conflicts within its core businesses of farm machinery and trucks were not adequately controlled. As a result, a shift in the environment severely damaged the firm's financial and market position. The president of John Deere, a competitor in the farm machinery market, stated, "For years, Deere has outperformed its arch-rival, International Harvester. Harvester's allegiance was divided between its truck business and farm machinery. Deere, by contrast, knew what its business was, who its customers were, and what they wanted."[12] Ultimately, International Harvester was forced to divest major holdings outside its truck and farm machinery businesses to raise capital. The company filed for Chapter 11 bankruptcy to restructure its debts. In 1986, International Harvester officially changed its name to Navistar. Figure 7–7 summarizes the solutions to the three problems that each strategic type attempts to implement.

COMPETITIVE MODEL

The competitive model of organizational strategy was developed by Michael Porter.[13] The **competitive model** contends that the nature and degree of competition in an industry determine the strategy that is appropriate for managers to formulate and implement.

Industry Structure

Porter identified five industry forces that determine the degree of competition within an industry:

- The threat of new entrants to compete in the industry.
- The bargaining power of suppliers in the industry.
- The bargaining power of customers in the industry.
- The threat of substitute products or services from potential competitors.
- Competitive rivalry among existing firms.[14]

THREAT OF ENTRY. New competitors entering an industry often bring with them large resources with the goal of gaining market share and profits. This may be achieved through the creation of a new company, as was the case with

Problems	*Solutions by Strategic Types*			
	Defender	*Prospector*	*Analyzer*	*Reactor*
Entrepreneurial	Aggressive maintenance of narrow and stable domain	Rapid growth through monitoring broad and continuously developing domain	Steady growth through surveillance of hybrid domain	Reformulate organization mission
Engineering	Routine and efficient methods of production	Flexible and innovative methods of production	Combined routine, efficient and flexible, innovative methods of production	Reformulate method of production
Administrative	Tight control of activities and decisions	Loose control of activities and decisions	Tight control of older product lines, loose control of new product lines	Reformulate organization structure

Source: Adapted from Raymond E. Miles and Charles C. Snow, *Organizational Strategy, Structure, and Process* (New York: McGraw-Hill Book Company, 1978). Copyright © McGraw-Hill Book Company. Reproduced with permission.

FIGURE 7–7
Problems and Solutions for Adaptive Strategies

K mart in the retail industry, or by diversification of a firm in one industry into another industry through acquisition, as Philip Morris did with the purchase of Miller Brewing. How serious the threat of entry is depends on barriers to entry that exist in the industry and on the reaction from existing competitors that the new entrant can expect.

BARGAINING POWER OF SUPPLIERS. In some industries, suppliers of materials to competing organizations can gain power by either raising prices for their materials or lowering quality. Thus, powerful suppliers can squeeze profitability out of an industry by dictating the price and quality of the materials that are bought by the competing firms.

Suppliers should not be thought of solely as firms that manufacture a product to provide to an industry. Labor unions can also be a supplier group. For instance, in the sports industry, players' unions can exert a strong influence over the profit of team owners since the unions are more concentrated, there are few substitutes, the product is important to the buyer's business, products are differentiated (e.g., fan loyalties), and players could conceivably start their own league (i.e., forward integration).

BARGAINING POWER OF CUSTOMERS. The conditions that make customers powerful are similar to those that make suppliers powerful. Customers can force down prices, demand higher-quality goods and services, and play competitors against each other—all of which serve to lower overall profitability in the industry.

Customers, of course, include individual consumers as well as organizations. Returning to the example of the sports industry, one can identify two types of customers for sports entertainment: fans who attend games and television networks that provide games to viewers in their homes. It is easy to understand why television networks have more bargaining power over team owners than do fans attending the games.

SUBSTITUTE PRODUCTS. Substitute products limit the potential prices of goods or services in an industry. If the price of a product is too high, buyers will seek substitutes. Producers of sugar have been faced with many substitutes that have greatly eroded profits and have kept the price of sugar low. Saccharin, corn syrup, and aspartame have been introduced as substitutes for sugar and have been marketed at lower prices. As a result, sugar producers have been forced to accept a smaller share of the sweetener market.

INTENSITY OF RIVALRY AMONG EXISTING COMPETITORS. Rivalry among existing competitors takes the form of such tactics as price competition, advertising battles, new product introductions, and increased customer service or warranties. Rivalry occurs because managers of competing organizations believe that they can improve their position in the industry by implementing one or more of these tactics.

Figure 7–8 shows the relationship of these five forces to the industry of which the organization is a part. The goal of a competitive strategy is to find a position in the industry where the organization can best defend itself

Attracting new customers by offering superior service or warranties is a tactic used to beat the competition.

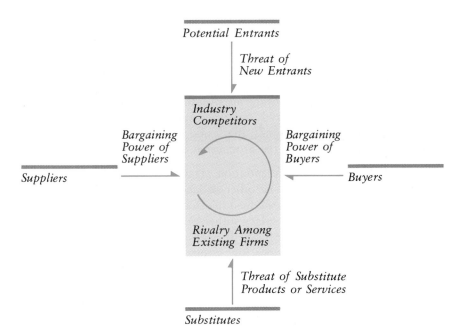

FIGURE 7–8
Forces Affecting Industry Competition

Source: Redrawn and adapted with permission of The Free Press, a Division of Macmillan, Inc., from *Competitive Strategy* by Michael E. Porter. Copyright 1980 by The Free Press.

against these forces or can influence them in its favor. Managers of organizations who best understand these forces, according to Porter, will have greater success at selecting a strategy that will be suited to conditions in the industry.

The competitive model provides a mapping of industry conditions that managers can examine to develop a strategy that will improve organizational performance. Once management has assessed the factors that influence competition within the industry, competitive opportunities and threats can be determined. Identification of organization strengths and weaknesses will then enable management to identify a strategy that will help the organization compete effectively.

Competitive Strategies

Porter identifies three strategies that managers can implement to compete against other organizations in the industry: (1) overall cost leadership, (2) differentiation, and (3) focus. The degree of success of each competitive strategy depends on the amount of commitment members have to the strategy and the effectiveness of managers in implementing the strategy.

OVERALL COST LEADERSHIP. The **overall cost leadership strategy** requires management to formulate and implement a strategic plan that will lead to construction of efficient facilities; attainment of cost reductions; tight cost and overhead control; avoidance of marginal customer accounts; and minimal costs in areas such as research and development, service, sales, and advertising. By maintaining an efficient and low-cost organization, management can attain above-average returns in the industry and make it difficult for less efficient competitors to match the price of the product. If less efficient competitors are successful at matching the product price of the overall cost leader, their returns will be much lower because of their higher costs.

The ability to achieve a position of overall cost leadership often requires a high market share, favorable access to raw materials, design of products for ease in manufacturing, maintenance of a wide line of related products, and service to all major customer groups to build volume. Organizations known for their success in implementing an overall cost leadership strategy are Briggs and Stratton, which holds a 50 percent worldwide market share in small-horsepower gasoline engines; Black and Decker, in the manufacture of power tools; and Du Pont, in the production of chemicals.

DIFFERENTIATION. The **differentiation strategy** recognizes that a firm's product is unique in relation to other products produced in the industry. Management cannot ignore costs in implementing the differentiation strategy; however, costs are a secondary rather than a primary consideration. A differentiation strategy is successful through emphasis on strong marketing abilities, creative product engineering, strong commitment to research and development, a reputation for quality or technological leadership, and a long tradition in the industry for having highly skilled employees.

Often the adoption of a differentiation strategy means that a high market share must be sacrificed. When the product is perceived to be superior, margins can be raised. However, customers may recognize the superiority of the product but be unwilling to pay the high price. Organizations that have successfully implemented a differentiation strategy are Mercedes, in the automobile industry; MacIntosh, in stereo components; Coleman, in camping equipment; Hyster, in lift trucks; Fieldcrest, in towels and linens; and Bloomingdale's, in retail stores.

FOCUS. The **focus strategy** pursues either an overall cost leadership strategy or a differentiation strategy by focusing on a narrow customer group, product line, or geographic market. The focus strategy provides products or services to a narrow segment, or niche, in the industry. Examples of successful focus strategies are Illinois Tool Works, which designs fasteners; Fort Howard Paper, which provides industrial-grade paper, thus avoiding broad consumer paper markets; and Cray Computers, which manufactures highly sophisticated computers for the government.

The competitive model identifies five industry forces that managers must consider in formulating and implementing strategies that will lead to organizational effectiveness. Analysis of these five forces by management should enable it to devise a strategic plan that will lead to efficiency in operations (overall cost leadership), uniqueness of product (differentiation), or targeting a narrow market segment and developing efficiency or uniqueness (focus). Those organizations that develop the best methods for achieving these goals will be the most successful in the industry. Management in Action 3 describes the prominent role the competitive model played in the National Football League's attempts to ward off the newly formed United States Football League in the mid-'80s. As some have noted, however, the model can be applied in a manner that may violate antitrust and other laws.[15]

Department-Level Strategies

Management of strategy at the department level is vital to the success of the organization. It is at the department level that strategies are often directly implemented. Departments implement strategies through plans, programs, and projects. As discussed in Chapter 6, plans, programs, and projects provide a set of action assignments that support the strategy of the business unit. Business units can have numerous and varied departments. We will briefly discuss the role of four traditional departments in relation to the implementation of strategy: marketing, production, personnel, and finance.

MARKETING

A marketing department serves as the direct contact with the organization's customers. It must find customers, identify their needs, convince them to buy the product, and provide service after the product has been purchased. These activities can be performed by developing programs, plans, or projects to address the following departmental issues:[16]

1. Lines of products and services offered to customers.
2. Types and locations of customers preferred by the company.
3. Prices to be charged.
4. Marketing mix of sales appeals to be stressed and sales promotion efforts.

These four issues correspond to the popular "four P's" that are taught in marketing: product, place, price, and promotion. Marketing management must evaluate each issue and determine how best to support the strategy.

The Goodyear blimp is a highly visible marketing effort to keep the company name before the buying public.

Almost every day in the trial of the United States Football League's antitrust suit against the National Football League, someone refers to an exhibit that is

MANAGEMENT IN ACTION 3
PORTER PRESENTATION IS TRIAL'S
EXHIBIT A

now known as the Porter Presentation. Entitled simply "U.S.F.L. vs. N.F.L.," the exhibit was introduced into evidence by the U.S.F.L. and has become a focal point of the case.

The exhibit is a 46-page outline of a presentation made in 1984 by a Harvard Business School professor, Michael E. Porter, at a seminar arranged by the N.F.L. Management Council and attended by 65 league executives. Its celebrity, after just six days of testimony in a trial expected to last more than two months, has grown as a result of two major points of contention between the leagues:

1. Some of the ideas put forth by the professor are considered by the U.S.F.L. to be proof of "intent" by the N.F.L. to drive the U.S.F.L. out of business. The N.F.L. has denied that it implemented any of the ideas. It offered for evidence another document, a letter in which Jay Moyer, the N.F.L. executive vice-president, told the Management Council that many of the professor's ideas are "largely impractical or legally impermissible."
2. Commissioner Pete Rozelle has testified that he did not know of Porter's presentation until a week after it was given and that when he learned of it, he said he grew "physically ill." The U.S.F.L. seems to think Rozelle had known about it and, perhaps, condoned it.

Only the jury can ultimately decide which side is right and how the evidence fits into the overall picture. That aside, however, the exhibit serves to show several fascinating elements about the case. Not the

least of them is how Porter . . . portrayed the nature of the competition between the two leagues at the time.

In keeping with the "war" metaphor that easily attaches itself to football—throwing the bomb, winning the game in the trenches, blitzing linebackers—Porter carried the metaphor into his presentation. Here are some examples:

- "The conflict is primarily one of guerrilla warfare."
- A two-paragraph explanation of different forms of "generalship" is preceded by "The Art of War—China 500 B.C."
- Those forms of "generalship" are broken down into practical applications under the headings "Conquer by alliance," "Conquer by battles" and "Besieging walled cities."

Later in the exhibit, which is filled with charts and graphs, are two pages of ideas that the U.S.F.L. attorney, Harvey Myerson, cited as ways in which the N.F.L. executives were shown they could "conquer" the U.S.F.L.

Ideas that appear under the heading "Defensive strategies" include "Sign current 'star' players to contract extensions" so as to "deter the U.S.F.L. from attempting to gain control of players later when they have more funds" and "Establish very strong relations with college coaches and/or agents to reduce U.S.F.L. credibility." Another idea was to "'dissuade' ABC from continuing U.S.F.L. contract."

"Offensive strategies" include moving the N.F.L. draft to one week after the U.S.F.L. draft and "do it secretly if possible," actively encourage sending undesirable players to the U.S.F.L., help encourage strong unionization of the U.S.F.L. so as to "drive up player costs with fringe benefits," and "attempt to co-opt the most powerful and influential U.S.F.L. owners with promises of N.F.L. franchises."

Source: Michael Janofsky, "Porter Presentation Is Trial's Exhibit A," *New York Times*, May 25, 1986. Copyright © 1986 by The New York Times Company. Reprinted with permission.

Should the product be unique or standard? Should we try to sell to everyone or just to a particular segment of consumers? What price is appropriate? How will we reach the customer through promotion? Answers to each of these questions can be approached through a plan, program, or project.

PRODUCTION

All organizations engage in the production of a good or service. For most manufacturing firms, the production department employs the most people and oversees control of the most assets. Successful implementation of the business-unit strategy is therefore of highest priority for managers of the production department. Like marketing, production activities can be organized around plans, programs, and projects. Four issues are of concern to production managers:[17]

1. The creation of a differential advantage.
2. The make or buy decision.
3. Selection of the technology for the manufacture of the good or service.
4. The level of production capacity required for producing the good or service.

Differential advantage is accomplished through a variety of techniques. Production managers may want to pursue a low-cost, high-volume method of production which encourages economies of scale and takes advantage of learning-curve effects. Or they may elect to introduce variety into the products in response to variations in consumer demand. The decision whether to make or buy the good or service can have important consequences. Although buying a component of the product from a supplier eliminates expenditures for additional labor and plant facilities, the organization may lose control over quality if the component is purchased. Making the component may reduce costs, but will require additional expertise; should the component fail, added responsibility falls on production managers. The choice of technology will center on whether the organization wants to mass-produce by way of assembly line, introduce robots into the production process, establish workstations for customized production of goods, and so forth. Finally, a decision on production capacity must be made. If we expand our facilities, will they be useful in the future? Do we need to modernize our facilities to manufacture a new or existing product? Where should we locate new facilities?

Each answer to these issues can be addressed through the development of a program, plan, or project. Chapter 20 will give additional insight on issues related to the management of a production department.

PERSONNEL

The personnel, or human resource, department plays an important role in the implementation of strategy. A mismatch between tasks and the people who perform them can doom a strategy. Selecting, training, and motivating employees of the organization often requires well-developed plans, programs, or projects. Key issues for personnel managers as related to business-unit strategy are:

1. Selecting and developing personnel.
2. Matching skills to required tasks.
3. Pay and benefit packages for personnel.
4. Industrial relations.

Personnel managers must examine the selected strategy and determine methods for addressing each issue. Chapter 10 will treat each of these issues in greater detail.

FINANCE

The finance department provides an essential resource in support of a business-unit strategy. Common to strategic planning are expenses for equipment

Richard J. Jordan retired as Director and Executive Vice-President of Brunswick Corporation in 1989. He also served as President and General Manager of Mercury Marine, a division of the Brunswick Corporation, from 1982 until the time of his retirement. Before joining the Mercury Marine Division he was General Manager of the Monoject Division of Brunswick's Medical Group, Director of the Medical Group's international operations, and Vice-President of Marketing for Brunswick's International Division. Mr. Jordan attended the University of Dayton and graduated from the Advanced Management Program at the Harvard Graduate School of Business Administration. In 1989 he received the

honorary degree of Doctor of Laws from Marian College, Fond du Lac, Wisconsin. He is a member of the advisory board of Marquette University's College of Business Administration, Milwaukee, Wisconsin, and is a director of Todd Corporation, St. Louis, Missouri.

Q: At the time you implemented a change in the strategy at Mercury Marine, what strengths and weaknesses of your firm did you identify and what strategy did you select based on this assessment?

A: In my opinion any strategy must address the existing strengths and weaknesses of the company. At that time Mercury's strengths were a reputation for product quality with an emphasis on speed and performance; a position of leadership in product innovation and technology in outboard horsepower; recognition under its founder, E. C. Kielhaefer, as a "leader with integrity" within the industry; and a worldwide dealer organization with a core of dedicated and loyal dealers. Mercury's weaknesses included the following: (1) In the low horsepower range, the outboard product line was perceived as less than competitive; (2) The outboard product line had "aged" and needed selective modernization; (3) The company's dealer and distributor organization was overpopulated and its overall quality was poor; (4) Mercury's profitability was marginal because of high manufacturing costs and excess overhead; and (5) The company lacked a coordinated effort. We weren't all "marching to the same drumbeat."

The following strategies were put in place to capitalize on our strengths and minimize our weaknesses:

New product development. R&D was expanded more than twofold.

Cost reduction. We put together a task force of a dozen key managers to analyze our situation and develop a plan to achieve cost parity with our major competitor, Japan. The plan implemented the following programs: (*a*) daily production of every model (versus batches every few months); (*b*) just-in-time inventory management; (*c*) teamwork versus individual work; (*d*) enhanced operator skill flexibility; (*e*) reduced levels of managerial supervision; (*f*) involvement of engineering and manufacturing with product development from the start; and (*g*) an attitude of "continuous improvement." We called this program QUEST (Quality by United Effort Secures Tomorrow).

Increased dealer professionalism. This program called for a commitment to quality dealers.

"Beat the drum." This was an effort to achieve cohesiveness and coordination in the firm through better communication between the various functions of the company.

Q: Many manufacturers are concerned about the "Japanese threat." Is there such a threat in the outboard motor industry and can you compete effectively?

A: The Japanese have been marketing in this country for 15 years and internationally even longer. They are good competitors through products, pricing, and service. During the early and mid-1980s when the Japanese yen was weak, they tried low pricing and were somewhat successful outside the United States. Now that the yen is strong, their prices are essentially equal and their market strength has been reduced. Why? For the following reasons: (1) U.S. manufacturers produce a full line of product from 2 horsepower to 300 horsepower. Hence the Japanese do not have a product advantage; (2) The quality of U.S. products is equal to and in some cases superior to that of Japanese products. Again no advantage; (3) U.S. manufacturers have dealers that are profitable and successful and hence loyal. The Japanese have trouble getting dealers to handle their product. If you think about the above in the context of Mercury's strategy, you will see that our strategy meets the Japanese threat head-on.

Q: The United States appears to be losing its leadership in world markets. What can managers of U.S. firms do to reassert that leadership?

A: One of my associates who shaped my career said, "In order to create shareholder wealth we must design things, manufacture things, and sell things." To reassert our leadership we must commit ourselves to technology leadership; we must commit ourselves to manufacture quality products at competitive world cost; and we must aggressively market the products we design and produce.

and materials, promotion, employees' salaries, and administration. Financial managers will be primarily concerned with methods of distributing and acquiring capital in the most cost-efficient manner. Again, cost efficiency can be obtained through careful development of plans, programs, or projects. Three general issues are relevant to managers of finance regarding the implementation of a strategy:

1. Methods for allocating capital.
2. Instruments used for obtaining capital.
3. Cash flow management.

A wide variety of methods and instruments have been developed by financial experts for evaluating the allocation of capital. Break-even analysis, net present value analysis, liquidity ratios, and profitability ratios are some of the more common. Instruments used in the obtaining of capital are bond and stock issues and short-term credit. Cash flow considers the timing of payments and the receipt of cash to the organization.

Departments play a crucial role in the successful implementation of a strategy. Marketing, production, personnel, and finance departments are common to most organizations. Other departments that may play a key role in the implementation of a strategy are research and development, information systems, purchasing, and customer service. Coordination of the departmental activities in support of the strategic plan is a critical activity of department and business-unit level management.

IMPLICATIONS FOR MANAGEMENT

The subject of strategic planning has increasingly dominated discussions in corporate boardrooms. The past decade has seen large-scale changes in the structure of many industries. These changes have meant that many company managers who once made decisions in a benign environment must now adjust to making decisions in an environment that may be uncertain and perhaps hostile.

Strategic planning assists managers by reducing the chances of making erroneous decisions and increasing awareness of opportunities that may be helpful to the organization in the future. As a manager, you should be attentive to changes in your organization's environment or industry. This is true whether you are a first-line manager or a top executive. First-line managers, though not responsible for strategic decisions, can usually identify important changes in the environment or industry before top management can. This is particularly true for those first-line managers who are in a department that spans the boundaries of the organization. By reporting changes to upper management, managers at all levels of the organization can make an important contribution to the formulation and implementation of a strategy.

Managers who fail to understand the goals of the organization risk implementing strategies that will not lead to successful results. Managers at all levels of the organization should have a clear understanding of the goals and how those goals are to be pursued. Misreading of the goals can lead to misreading of the strategy that is being implemented. Often an incorrect interpretation of an organization's goals leads to the selection of a strategy that may emphasize internal weaknesses rather than strengths. As a manager, you should be constantly aware of the company's strengths and try to formulate and implement strategies that will exploit those strengths. Awareness of an organization's strengths and weaknesses, as well as external opportunities and threats, can be obtained from a SWOT analysis.

As a strategic planner, do not be afraid to adjust or reformulate a new strategy. Managers often feel "married" to a strategy because they have committed resources or their careers to the success of the strategy. Staying with a strategy that is not achieving desired results may not only be costly for the organization, but may also jeopardize the fortunes of many employees, including the manager. An excellent manager is one who knows when to change the organization's strategic direction.

Finally, you should understand your organization's strategy by asking broad questions about positioning within the industry or market. Is the industry highly competitive? If so, develop an understanding of the industry forces and identify whether your company is more capable of pursuing with success an overall cost leadership, differentiation, or focus strategy. Are the fortunes of your organization dependent on how well you adapt technology and administrative structures to the environment? If so, consider whether a defender, prospector, or analyzer strategy best exploits your organization's strengths. Does your company pursue a diversification strategy? If so, you may want to examine the portfolio of business units or product lines your organization controls in order to assess which units have potential for growth; which units can generate large amounts of resources; which units may need further support or should be divested; and which units are poor performers with few opportunities.

KEY TERMS AND CONCEPTS

adaptation model	growth strategy
administrative problem	overall cost leadership strategy
analyzer strategy	portfolio strategy
BCG matrix	prospector strategy
cash cow	question mark
competitive model	reactor strategy
defender strategy	retrenchment strategy
differentiation strategy	stability strategy
dog	star
engineering problem	strategic alternatives
entrepreneurial problem	strategic management
focus strategy	strategic plan
GE matrix	strategy
grand strategy	SWOT

QUESTIONS FOR REVIEW AND DISCUSSION

1. Define and explain the differences between the terms strategy, strategic management, and strategic plan.

2. How do an organization's purpose, mission, and goals contribute to the formulation of a strategic plan?

3. Identify the environmental conditions that would have to exist for managers of a company to be unconcerned about strategic planning. Do these conditions resemble those of any organization with which you are familiar?

4. A strategic planner for a major corporation once claimed that the environment had become so uncertain that strategic planning was a waste of time. Do you agree or disagree with this conclusion?

5. What is a SWOT analysis? How often do you believe an organization should conduct a SWOT analysis? Monthly? Semiannually? Yearly? Every five years? Identify the factors you considered in making this decision.

6. What are the major grand strategies? Can corporations try to implement several grand strategies at the same time, or must only one be selected? Explain.

7. Identify the three problems that managers must solve according to the adaptation model. How does each strategic type solve these problems?

8. What are the five industry forces that managers must consider according to the competitive model? How does each strategic type respond to the five forces?

9. Describe the two dimensions used in the portfolio model. Under what conditions would managers want to use a BCG matrix? In what ways is the GE matrix more or less useful to corporate strategic planners?

10. Review the key issues of strategy implementation at the departmental level for all four departments discussed in the chapter. How would responses differ between a cost leader and a differentiator strategy? A defender versus a prospector?

CASES

7–1 TOYS "R" US, BIG KID ON THE BLOCK, WON'T STOP GROWING

Last Christmas, a Florida newspaper ran a cartoon of a couple, laden with gifts, emerging from a Toys "R" Us store. "Broke 'R' Us," the caption read. Company executives liked the cartoon so much that copies now hang in their offices.

The toy industry may be in a slump, but not Toys "R" Us Inc. Overall, toy sales have grown an average of just 2 percent the past couple of years, but sales at Toys "R" Us have increased a robust 27 percent annually. Last year, its cash registers rang up 20 percent of the $12.5 billion in toys sold in the U.S., up from just 13 percent in 1984.

"Every time a Toys 'R' Us moves in, our sales go down 20 percent the first year," laments Michael Vastola, chairman and chief executive officer of Lionel Corp., a competing toy-store chain.

But Charles Lazarus, who earned $60 million last year as the company's chairman and chief executive officer, mostly by exercising stock options, isn't satisfied. His goal: to sell half of all toys sold in the U.S.

Securities analysts predict that by 1995 the retailing giant will be close to Mr. Lazarus's goal, selling 40 percent of the toys in this nation. Sean McGowan, vice-president of research at Balis Zorn Gerard Inc., sums up Toys "R" Us approach: "Its strength isn't its product, but the way it sells it."

The giant retailer's strategy has remained essentially the same since it emerged from bankruptcy proceedings in 1978. It sells toys as if Christmas were always around the corner: Each store, stuffed to the rafters, offers 18,000 toys in convenient locations at low prices. The company's buying clout, and its use of computers to spot emerging hits, mean that it usually is stocked with hot items even when other retailers aren't. It also tries to win over new customers by selling baby products, such as disposable diapers, at or below cost.

In the past couple of years, Toys "R" Us has fine-tuned the success formula. Last Christmas, for example, it installed scanners at the cash registers to speed up check-outs. And the company now also uses a computer to schedule work shifts to increase efficiency.

Perhaps as much as anything, growing customer loyalty explains its continued growth. "Look at these baseball cards," says a smiling Mary Lou Kuegler as she leaves a Toys "R" Us store in Dedham, Mass. "I got them for $4.50 apiece. Everywhere else they're six bucks." Ms. Kuegler, a Newton, Mass., housewife, says she drives seven miles past other discounters and department stores to do most of her toy shopping at Toys "R" Us.

Although some of Toys "R" Us sales growth of late has come from an increase in the number of stores, much has come from existing stores at the expense of retailers that don't specialize in toys. K mart Corp. and Service Merchandise Co. have slowly shrunk the size of their toy departments, at least in part because Toys "R" Us has taken away business.

Discount and department stores simply can't compete very well by offering only 3,000 toys and occasional sales. "Seasonal sellers competing against Toys 'R' Us is like amateurs going up against professionals," says Richard Nager, an analyst at Ladenburg Thalmann & Co.

Toys "R" Us also has managed, at least so far, to fend off imitators. Two chains—Child World Inc. and Lionel—have designed almost identical stores. "But neither imitator has been able to carry out the concept better than the master," says Dorothy Lakner, an analyst for Deutsche Bank Capital Corp. One reason for Lionel's 56 percent profit decline in 1987 was competition from Toys "R" Us, says Jane Gilday, an analyst for McKinley Allsopp Securities.

While Toys "R" Us sells $330.80 of goods per square foot a year, Child World manages $221.70 and Lionel $193.10, Ms. Lakner says. Put another way, Toys "R" Us averages $8.4 million in sales a year per store, compared with $4.9 million for Child World and $4.4 million for Lionel—though their stores are about the same in size.

Toys "R" Us offers low prices, but it still could be vulnerable in a price war, analysts say. Late last year, Child World deliberately undersold Toys "R" Us in an effort to gain market share, and it worked. Child World's Christmas-season same-store sales rose 21.2 percent, compared with 12 percent for Toys "R" Us. But Child World dismissed the architect of the strategy, President Gilbert Wachsman, last February, apparently because the low prices reduced profits too much. "Both Toys and Lionel are resting easier now that Wachsman is gone," says Ms. Gilday of McKinley Allsopp.

Toys "R" Us also enjoys clout with toy makers and is able to get larger quantities of scarce toys, some say. Toys "R" Us officials deny the company enjoys special favor with toy makers. Instead, they say, smart planning through computer surveys and the financial ability to buy toys earlier in the year, when supplies are more plentiful, enable the company's stores to be well stocked.

The way it's growing, Toys "R" Us is becoming even more formidable. The 314-store chain plans to open 45 stores this year in the U.S. And, with 52 stores abroad, it is continuing its expansion overseas. Foreign countries, where mom and pop shops and department stores dominate the toy market, are ripe for a Toys "R" Us style of selling, analysts say. For example, 70 percent of the toys in Europe are sold at Christmas, which means Toys "R" Us can exploit the off-season market, Ms. Lakner of Deutsche Bank Capital says.

After five years, the company's move into children's clothes with its Kids "R" Us stores is finally showing a profit, analysts add. Kids "R" Us—112 stores and growing—sells brand-name clothes at a discount.

Succeeding in the $15 billion children's clothing business is tougher than toys, both because there is more competition and because retailers have only about 10 weeks to sell merchandise before the change of season. But Kids "R" Us says it is more than holding its own. It sells 85 percent of its clothing at a profitable price, marking down just 15 percent—compared with an industry average of 22 percent—to clear inventory, says Michael Searles, president of Kids "R" Us.

Toys "R" Us has relatively little turnover among its middle and upper management ranks, analysts note. Through its employee stock option plan, more than 40 employees have become millionaires in the past 10 years. But, says Norman Ricken, Toys "R" Us president and chief talent scout, the company demands hard work in return. "I like to recruit people who like to work, not people who like to get rich," he says. "Toys 'R' Us is not a 9-to-5 but an 8-to-faint job," Mr. Ricken jokes.

"At Toys 'R' Us, we have a theory," he says. "If you're really dominant, no one can compete with you. Our goal is to be that dominant in the business."

Source: Reprinted by permission of *The Wall Street Journal,* © Dow Jones & Company, Inc. (August 11, 1988). All Rights Reserved Worldwide.

1. Review the grand strategies discussed in the chapter. Which grand strategy does Toys "R" Us pursue? Justify your conclusion. How might the use of portfolio models be applied to the business units of Toys "R" Us?
2. What are the internal strengths and weaknesses of Toys "R" Us? What are the external opportunities and threats in the toy and children's clothing industries? Based on this analysis, is Toys "R" Us pursuing the appropriate grand strategy? Why or why not?
3. Describe the strategic type of each business unit of Toys "R" Us according to Porter's competitive model. Based on the information provided in the case, how would you describe each business unit's relationship to its suppliers? Its buyers? How intense is rivalry in the industry?
4. How do the various departments (marketing, production, personnel, and finance) of Toys "R" Us assist in the implementation of the strategy? Which has a bigger role in the implementation of the strategy?

7–2 ROUGH PLAY?

As children across America revel in their Christmas gifts, toy manufacturers are tallying up the final rush of sales. For one grand old name of the playroom, Christmas proved to be anything but merry.

Fisher-Price, whose Pull-A-Tune xylophone and Little People farm have been favorites among toddlers for decades, recently said it expected to post a loss of $5 million to $15 million in the quarter ending December 31.

The reason, analysts say, is brutal competition from Hasbro, Mattel, and Rubbermaid's Little Tikes division in Fisher-Price's core infant and preschool businesses along with production foul-ups and disappointments on Fisher-Price's end. Fisher-Price's loss will depress the results of the toy maker's parent, Quaker Oats of Chicago.

And it has once again stoked speculation that Quaker might try to shed Fisher-Price. Neither Quaker nor Fisher-Price would comment on the rumors. What is clear is that Fisher-Price's time as undisputed king of the infant and preschool playroom toy categories is over.

Recently, Hasbro's Playskool division has assaulted Fisher-Price with an array of lower-priced rattles, shape sorters, musical mobiles, and stacking toys. Mattel has eaten into Fisher-Price's market share with its successful Disney line of characters. And Little Tikes, which had focused on outdoor toys like seesaws and sandboxes, has pushed successfully into Fisher-Price's arena with make-believe kitchens and toy vehicles.

The incursions have begun to hurt Fisher-Price's results. Sales in the three months ended September 30 fell 13 percent, to $227.5 million from $257.2 million a year earlier. Operating earnings slumped to $28.9 million from $42.7 million. The drop in earnings, with the projected loss for this quarter, suggest to analysts that Fisher-Price could be a less profitable company in the future.

During 1989, the company has developed new products. But many have fizzled or were so plagued by production delays that they arrived late on retailers' shelves for this year's Christmas season. Given Fisher-Price's impressive performance until recently, it is no surprise that competitors decided to move in on the company's market. More than anything, competitors covet Fisher-Price's market because it is so stable. Unlike faddish toys tied to movies or cartoon shows, Fisher-Price's product line emphasizes more established toys like stacking rings, colorful crib playthings, and plastic vehicles and play houses.

Competitors see "the inherent stability we have had from this business," said Bruce Sampsell, Fisher-Price's president. "The purchaser is an adult so you don't get the fast-driven, in-and-out purchasing." Big toy retailers got burned by promotional toys like dolls based on the movies *Annie* and *Batman*.

The Teddy Ruxpin experience also was quite sobering to the industry. Teddy Ruxpin was a battery-operated talking teddy bear with eyes and a mouth that moved in tandem. At $60, the bear was a hit a few years ago. But after an initial flirtation with toy stardom, Worlds of Wonder, the manufacturer, saw sales plummet.

Fisher-Price has had flops when it ventured too far from its strong suit of making imaginative yet simple toys. The most visible disappointment has been the company's Sport Car. A miniature convertible jeep, the Sport Car was a success among buyers for toy and department stores who placed hefty orders after the industry's annual trade show in February. Buyers were dazzled by the car's electronic dashboard, intricate plastic engine complete with spark plugs, and five-piece tool kit.

But technical flaws showed up when Fisher-Price was testing the product in homes—too late to fix the cars in time to roll them out for the start of the Christmas selling season. The car's $300 price also gave sticker shock to many consumers, who already were paying well above $100 for a far more popular toy, the Nintendo video game set. The result: Many retailers are being forced to take steep markdowns on Fisher-Price's car to move slow-selling inventory.

While such markdowns are technically the merchants' problem, analysts say Fisher-Price must somehow make it up to them, presumably in the form of retroactive discounts, if it wants to maintain positive relationships with them. Analysts say Fisher-Price must focus customers' attention even more than in the past on the qualities that made the company a success. Market research consistently places Fisher-Price at or near the top in terms of the durability, safety, and appeal of its toys.

Fisher-Price's next step will be to resume growth. To do that, analysts say, the company must come up with new products and market them aggressively, competing with the large promotion budgets of Mattel, Hasbro, and Little Tikes. But the company's current competitive battle makes analysts more certain that Fisher-Price will not enjoy the returns it has earned in the past.

Sampsell admits as much. Asked whether his company would cut prices and suffer an erosion in profits to protect its business, he said: "We are prepared to go toe-to-toe with anyone who wants to take a run at our position."

Source: Eric N. Berg, "King of the Playroom Hath Fallen," *New York Times,* December 25, 1989. Copyright © 1989 by The New York Times Company. Reprinted by permission.

1. Conduct a SWOT analysis for Fisher-Price. Based on this analysis, is it appropriate for Fisher-Price to pursue a growth strategy? Why or why not?
2. Analyze the toy industry based on the five industry forces in the competitive model. Which of the five industry forces are having the greatest impact on Fisher-Price and which are having the least impact?
3. Which departments of Fisher-Price appear to be most problematic for implementing its current strategy? Explain. What can management do to correct this situation?

ENDNOTES

1. Francine Schwadel, "Sears Will Close Stores 42 Hours To Cut Prices," *Wall Street Journal* (February 24, 1989): B1, B4.
2. A. A. Thompson, Jr., and A. J. Strickland, *Strategic Management: Concepts and Cases* (Plano, TX: Business Publications, 1987), Chapter 1.
3. W. H. Newman, J. P. Logan, and W. H. Hegarty, *Strategy: A Multi-Level, Integrative Approach* (Cincinnati, OH: South-Western Publishing Co., 1989).
4. Thompson and Strickland, *Strategic Management*, 8.
5. Ibid., 11.
6. J. A. Pearce, "Selecting Among Alternative Grand Strategies," *California Management Review* (Spring 1982): 23-31.
7. L. Hrebiniak and C. C. Snow, "Top-Management Agreement and Organizational Performance," *Human Relations* 35, no. 12 (1982): 1139-1158.
8. For an insightful critique of the Boston Consulting Group matrix, see J. A. Seeger, "Reversing the Images of the BCG's Growth/Share Matrix," *Strategic Management Journal 5* (1984): 93-97.
9. R. E. Miles and C. C. Snow, *Organizational Strategy, Structure, and Process* (New York: McGraw-Hill, 1978).
10. Ibid.
11. "End of a Troubled Reign," *Fortune* (May 31, 1982): 7.
12. T. J. Peters and R. H. Waterman, Jr., *In Search of Excellence: Lessons from America's Best-Run Companies* (New York: Harper & Row, 1982), 300.
13. M. E. Porter, *Competitive Strategy: Techniques for Analyzing Industries and Competitors* (New York: Free Press, 1980).
14. Ibid.
15. V. H. Fried and B. M. Oviatt, "Michael Porter's Missing Chapter: The Risk of Antitrust Violations," *Academy of Management Executive* 3, no. 1 (1989): 49-56.
16. Newman, Logan, and Hegarty, *Strategy*.
17. Ibid.

Quantitative Tools for Managing

CHAPTER 8

After studying this chapter, you should be able to:

- *Discuss four ways that models may be classified, and identify five specific types of models that may be useful to management.*
- *Identify and use tools and criteria for making choices under certainty, risk, and uncertainty.*
- *Describe game theory and specify business situations in which it might be useful.*
- *Identify characteristics of ill-structured decision situations and discuss how heuristics may be helpful in such situations.*
- *Describe linear programming and indicate the sorts of problems for which it might be useful.*
- *Explain three forecasting techniques and discuss their relative strengths and weaknesses.*
- *Discuss simulation and specify when computer models may be appropriate.*
- *Explain how queuing models are used.*

The AIL Division of Cutler-Hammer, Inc. (now a division of Eaton Corporation), had the opportunity to acquire the defense market rights to a new flight-safety system patent. The inventor claimed he had a strong patent position as well as technical superiority. However, the market for the product was very uncertain, mostly because of pending legislative action. Since the inventor wished to make an offer to other companies if AIL was not interested, he asked AIL to decide whether or not to purchase an option on the patent in a few weeks, a period clearly inadequate to resolve any uncertainties AIL might be aware of. AIL turned to formal decision analysis, using a variety of techniques including a decision tree. The decision tree analysis suggested that the best course of action for AIL was not to purchase an option on the patent.

AIL's resorting to formal, systematic decision tools is not unique. Ford, Honeywell, Pillsbury, ITT, and many other firms routinely use such tools when making major decisions. As the environments facing organizations become more complex and dynamic, and as organizational resources become scarcer, systematic decision tools become increasingly necessary.[1]

The use of systematic decision tools has many advantages. First, their application highlights the sorts of information that the decision maker must think about and gather. Second, the tools serve as external memory devices and displays, permitting the decision maker to deal with much more information than would otherwise be possible. Third, the availability of quantitative techniques which are appropriate to the task at hand makes decision making a more comfortable process. In view of the great cognitive strain caused by decision making, this is no small benefit. Fourth, if quantitative tools are consistently applied, they typically result in decisions which are much more reliable than those made by the unaided decision maker. Making decisions more reliable should improve their quality.[2] Finally, systematic aids make it possible for the decision maker to explain to others precisely how a decision was made. This ability to justify a decision is likely to improve its acceptability. It also makes life a little easier for the decision maker.

Several quantitative tools for managing, including PERT, inventory-control models, break-even analysis, and control charts, are considered at appropriate points in later chapters. In this chapter, we will examine a variety of additional quantitative models which have proved to be valuable aids for the management decision maker.

MODELS

Models are simplifications of reality. Once developed, they can be manipulated more easily and inexpensively than the real situation they depict.

Classification of Models

Models can be classified in many ways—by their purpose, by their mode of representation, by their degree of objectivity, and by the role that chance is assigned.

PURPOSE

Models may be descriptive or prescriptive. A descriptive model describes the way things actually are. A prescriptive (or normative) model is used to determine the way things *should* be. In this chapter, we will be concerned primarily with prescriptive models.

MODE OF REPRESENTATION

Models may be iconic, analog, or symbolic. An iconic model retains a physical relationship to the thing it represents. A scale, blueprint, or picture is an iconic model. An analog model establishes a relationship between a variable in a system and an analogous variable in the model. For instance, an analog computer uses electrical circuits to simulate the behavior of other types of physical systems. The "old-fashioned" watch with hands rather than numbers directly presenting the time is now sometimes called an analog watch. A symbolic model substitutes symbols for variables in the real world. Those symbols are typically represented mathematically. An equation such as $E = mc^2$ is a symbolic model. The models we will consider are primarily symbolic.

DEGREE OF OBJECTIVITY

Models may be objective or subjective. An objective model is based only on concrete facts. A subjective model incorporates the feelings and beliefs of the decision maker.[3] In some cases, we will want to make decisions which are unaffected by personal opinions. In others, it will be appropriate to incorporate the decision maker's feelings and beliefs about the satisfactoriness of alternatives, the probabilities of events, and so on.

ROLE OF CHANCE

Models may be deterministic or probabilistic. A deterministic model precisely specifies what will occur. There is no chance involved. A probabilistic (or stochastic) model considers probabilities of occurrence. That is, chance plays a role. We will consider both deterministic and probabilistic models.

Types of Models

Models may help to solve a variety of types of problems. Here is a sampling of model types, based on the sorts of problems they address:

- **Choice-making models** are used when a decision maker is faced with an array of alternatives and can choose only a subset of those alternatives. A selection committee required to choose a single candidate for a job opening or an operations manager who is asked to select the three best plant sites from among many options might make use of such models.
- **Allocation models** permit the decision maker to make optimal use of scarce resources by allocating them where they will do the most good. For instance, a firm may be manufacturing several products, each of which requires processing time on three different machines. Since the available time on the machines is limited, allocation models can be used to determine the most profitable product mix.
- **Forecasting models** allow the decision maker to obtain estimates of future levels of variables, such as sales or employment levels or prices. These models typically make use of past information to predict future levels.

This scale model of an office building is an iconic model.

- **Simulation models** are used to develop simplified versions of reality. Manipulations of the models can then be performed to give clues about the probable impact of similar changes in the real world. While in a sense all models are simulations of reality, simulation models deal specifically with problems of such complexity that analysis by other techniques is not feasible.
- **Queuing models** are useful in determining the sorts of waiting lines which are likely to develop at machines, service stations, or other facilities. The models can be used to examine how the lines and associated costs are likely to change as the number of facilities, service times, or other variables are altered.

CHOICE-MAKING MODELS

Decision makers must somehow weigh a variety of information to arrive at good choices. Models are available to help with that task, but different models are needed for different situations. In particular, the appropriate model depends on whether the decision is made in a situation characterized by certainty, risk, uncertainty, conflict, or ill structure. A **decision matrix**, shown in Figure 8–1, helps to clarify the differences among these situations. A decision matrix is one way to display the sorts of information a decision maker needs to make an optimal choice.

The information in the decision matrix includes the following:

- The alternatives available to the decision maker;
- The events (sometimes called states of nature) which might occur to affect the quality of the choice;
- The probabilities of the various events;
- The outcomes which would result from various combinations of alternatives and events; and
- The utilities (that is, levels of satisfactoriness) of each outcome.

The various decision situations are defined by the amount of information available to the decision maker, as follows:

- **Certainty.** The problem solver has all the information needed to construct the decision matrix and knows which event will occur.

FIGURE 8–1
Decision Matrix

Alternatives	Events				
	1 p_1	*2* p_2	*3* p_3	...	*m* p_m
1	O_{11} (U_{11})	O_{12} (U_{12})	O_{13} (U_{13})	...	O_{1m} (U_{1m})
2	O_{21} (U_{21})	O_{22} (U_{22})	O_{23} (U_{23})	...	O_{2m} (U_{2m})
3	O_{31} (U_{31})	O_{32} (U_{32})	O_{33} (U_{33})	...	O_{3m} (U_{3m})
...	...	...	...	...	...
n	O_{n1} (U_{n1})	O_{n2} (U_{n2})	O_{n3} (U_{n3})	...	O_{nm} (U_{nm})

- **Risk**. The problem solver has all information needed to construct the decision matrix. While the event which will occur is not known, the probabilities of events are known.
- **Uncertainty**. The problem solver has all information needed to construct the decision matrix. The event which will occur is not known, and the probabilities of events are not known.
- **Conflict**. The problem solver has all the information needed to construct the decision matrix. The events are actions of a competitor, and their probabilities are unknown.
- **Ill Structure**. The problem solver does not have enough information to construct the decision matrix.

DECISION MAKING UNDER CERTAINTY

In the case of decision making under certainty, the event which will occur is known. It is only necessary to decide which alternative is best when that event occurs. Sometimes the alternatives under consideration differ on only a single attribute, such as cost. Sometimes they differ on many attributes. These situations call for somewhat different approaches.

Dealing with Single-Attributed Alternatives

Sometimes alternatives have only one relevant attribute, such as return or quality or size. If so, it is only necessary to find the degrees of satisfactoriness corresponding to the various levels of that attribute. Then the alternative with the most satisfactory level of the attribute can be selected.

Utility is the relative satisfactoriness of something to an individual. The unit of measurement of utility is called a utile. If one alternative has higher utility to the decision maker than another, it is more satisfactory than the other. The definition highlights important points about utility. First, utility has only relative, not absolute, meaning. The statement "This plant location has a utility of 20" has no meaning unless the utility can be compared with something else, such as the utilities of other locations. Second, since utility is a measure of satisfactoriness to an individual, it is inherently subjective. There is no "real," or objective, utility waiting to be discovered.

A **utility curve** is a plot of the utiles corresponding to the various levels of an attribute. The simplest way to get utility curves is called the direct estimation method. The decision maker assigns 100 utiles to the best level of an attribute. Then other levels of the attribute are assigned utilities based on the answer to the question, "Relative to the best level, how satisfied would you be with this level?"

To illustrate this process, consider Figure 8–2. It shows a decision maker's utility curve for size of a decision-making group. Since the decision maker feels that a group size of five is most satisfactory, that size receives a utility of 100. Relative to a size of five, a size of seven receives a utility of 80, a size of three receives a utility of 50, and so on.

The shape of a utility curve provides information about an individual's risk preferences. Figure 8–3 shows utility curves for money reflecting risk neutrality, risk aversion, and risk seeking, respectively. Faced with identical

The utility of a plant location is a relative measure, meaningful only in relation to the utilities of other locations.

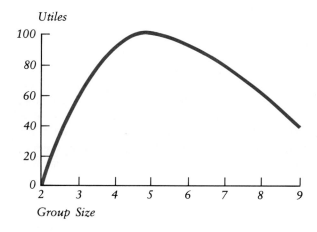

FIGURE 8–2
A Utility Curve for Size of a Decision-Making Group

sets of alternatives, individuals with different utility curve shapes—and thus different risk preferences—may make different choices.

Ralph Swalm examined utility curves of managers in a variety of organizations.[4] He found that decision makers have a wide range of curve shapes, reflecting different orientations toward risk. Sometimes decision makers in the same position in the same organization had markedly different curve shapes. In general, Swalm found that the predominant shape of utility curves among the managers he studied reflected risk aversion. Swalm reasoned that corporate reward systems—which penalize losses more than they reward gains—may foster such risk aversion.

Dealing with Multi-Attributed Alternatives

Managers often face problems in which they must choose from among alternatives that differ on several dimensions. For instance, they may have to decide which of five employees to promote. One is superior in years of experience, another in previous performance appraisal ratings, another in letters of reference, and so on. There are two ways to address such problems. They are called screening approaches and scoring approaches.

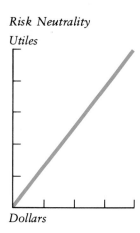

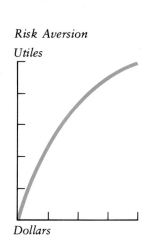

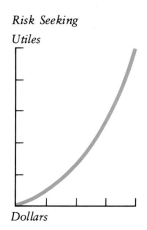

FIGURE 8–3
Utility Curves for Money

SCREENING APPROACHES

A **screening approach** identifies each alternative as satisfactory or unsatisfactory. The unsatisfactory alternatives are then screened out. This is done by use of a **decision structure table**. Figure 8–4 presents a simple example of a decision structure table. It arrays the information for a job choice decision. The table simply presents the alternatives (listed on the vertical axis), their relevant attributes (listed along the top horizontal axis), attribute levels (shown in the cells), and constraint levels (listed along the bottom horizontal axis). For convenience, the attributes are arrayed in Figure 8–4 from the most important to the problem solver (pay, at the left) to the least important (location, at the right).

FIGURE 8–4
Decision Structure Table for the Job Choice Decision

		Attributes			
		Pay	*Job Challenge*	*Promotion Potential*	*Location*
Alternatives	Comrent	26000	High	Low	Midwest
	Enmart	21000	Moderate	Moderate	Northeast
	Sencorp	33000	High	High	Southwest
	Alamar	19500	Low	Moderate	Southwest
Constraints		≥20000	≥Moderate	≥Moderate	Northeast or Southwest

Two rules are most commonly used to screen out unacceptable alternatives. The **satisficing rule** considers alternatives sequentially. The first alternative which satisfies all constraints is chosen. In Figure 8–4, the first alternative, Comrent, fails to satisfy the promotion potential constraint and the location constraint, so it is eliminated. The second, Enmart, does satisfy all constraints, and it is chosen. The other rule, called the **elimination-by-aspects rule**, screens out unacceptable alternatives on an attribute-by-attribute basis, generally working from the most important to the least important. Here, both Enmart and Sencorp satisfy all constraints and thus would survive application of the elimination-by-aspects rule. In such a case, the constraints could be tightened until only one alternative remained, additional attributes could be considered, or the surviving alternatives could be examined to see the degree by which they exceed the constraints. Since Sencorp is better than Enmart for each of the three most important attributes and is as good on the fourth, it would probably be chosen. Note that if the satisficing rule were used, Sencorp would never even be considered.

While a screening approach is easy to use, it provides only a satisfactory alternative, not one that is optimal (that is, the best possible). Further, it doesn't allow good levels of one attribute to compensate for poor levels of another. So, even though an alternative may be far superior on all dimensions but one, it will be dropped from consideration if it fails to meet the remaining constraint by even one unit. Nevertheless, screening approaches provide systematic ways to make choices. In many situations, such as when all we need is a satisfactory alternative, they are fine.

SCORING APPROACHES

When an optimal alternative is needed, a **scoring approach** called a multi-attribute utility can be used. A **multi-attribute utility (MAU) model** is a tool to determine the overall satisfactoriness of something that has a number of relevant characteristics.[5] It considers the utility of each alternative on each attribute and weights the relative importance of the attributes. Then, by comparing the levels of overall satisfactoriness, or utility, of various alternatives, the best can be chosen.

Here are the steps in development and use of a MAU model:

1. Determine the n relevant attributes and their feasible ranges.
2. For each attribute, i, develop the single-attribute utility curve or figure by use of the direct estimation method, as discussed previously.
3. Determine the relative importance weights, w_i, of the attributes.
4. Combine this information by a linear additive model of the sort:

$$\text{Multi-Attribute Utility}_j = \sum_{n}^{i=1} (w_i U_{ij})$$

where U_{ij} is the utility of alternative j on attribute i

To illustrate, let's again use the job choice example detailed in Figure 8–4 and find the multi-attribute utilities for Comrent, Enmart, Sencorp, and Alamar. Suppose the decision maker's single-attribute utilities for various levels of each of the four relevant attributes were found by direct estimation. These are shown in Figure 8–5.

Suppose the decision maker felt that pay was the most important of the attributes and assigned it a weight of 10. Feeling that job challenge was almost as important as pay, the decision maker assigned it a weight of 9. Promotion potential and location were felt to be relatively much less important and were given weights of 5 and 3, respectively. The multi-attribute utility model is thus:

$$\text{MAU}_j = \sum_{4}^{i=1} (w_i U_{ij}) = 10U_{1j} + 9U_{2j} + 5U_{3j} + 3U_{4j}$$

The single-attribute utilities can be drawn from Figure 8–5. For the first alternative, Comrent, the utility of pay is $U(26000) = 75$; the utility of job challenge is $U(\text{High}) = 100$; the utility of promotion potential is $U(\text{Low}) = 0$; and the utility of location is $U(\text{Midwest}) = 0$. So:

$$\text{MAU}_{\text{Comrent}} = 10 \times 75 + 9 \times 100 + 5 \times 0 + 3 \times 0 = 1650$$

Similarly:

$$\text{MAU}_{\text{Enmart}} = 10 \times 25 + 9 \times 50 + 5 \times 60 + 3 \times 80 = 1240$$
$$\text{MAU}_{\text{Sencorp}} = 10 \times 100 + 9 \times 100 + 5 \times 100 + 3 \times 100 = 2700$$
$$\text{MAU}_{\text{Alamar}} = 10 \times 20 + 9 \times 0 + 5 \times 60 + 3 \times 45 = 635$$

The best alternative is clearly Sencorp. The alternative selected by the satisficing rule, Enmart, is a distant third.

While MAU models are used primarily for choice making, they can also be valuable communication tools. That is, since the models set down the weights

FIGURE 8–5
*Single-Attribute Utility
Curve and Figures for
Job Choice Example*

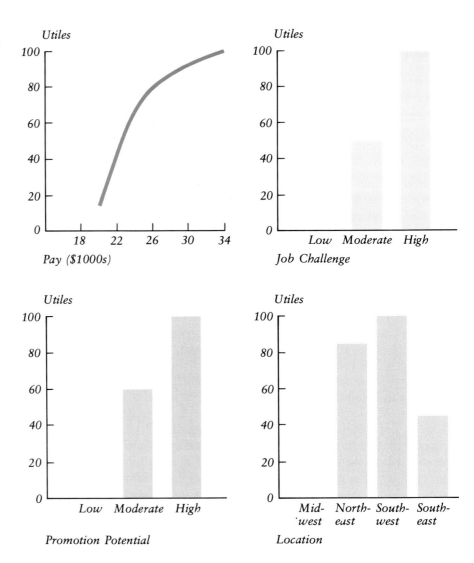

individuals attach to attributes and the values they attach to various levels of those attributes, once an individual's model is developed it can be shown to others. Points of agreement or disagreement about weights and values may then become clear. Or, by aggregating the MAU models of a group of individuals, a "consensus" model can be developed and discussed. Such a "consensus corporate utility function" was developed for the members of the geotechnical engineering and environmental consulting firm Woodward-Clyde Associates. The model incorporated ten attributes—such as retained earnings, growth in retirement plan, base compensation, incentive compensation, geographical scope of services offered, and professional development—which were identified by the firm's long-range planning committee. The consensus model was used to facilitate communication among officers of Woodward-Clyde and to serve as an input to their decision making.[6]

PRO-CON COMPARISON

Another useful and simple tool for decision making under certainty is called pro-con comparison. As the name suggests, **pro-con comparison** simply involves the comparison of pros and cons of alternatives. For each alternative, a listing is made of favorable and unfavorable aspects. Then the two columns can be compared. While pro-con comparison lacks the precision and sophistication of a MAU model, it is quick and easy to use and may be acceptable for many purposes.

In 1722, Joseph Priestley was invited to become librarian for the Earl of Shelburne. He asked the advice of Benjamin Franklin, whose reply is an excellent example of pro-con comparison:

Dear Sir:

In the affair of so much importance to you, wherein you ask my advise, I cannot, for want of sufficient premises, advise you what to determine, but if you please I will tell you how. When these difficult cases occur, they are difficult chiefly because while we have them under consideration, all the reasons pro and con are not present to the mind at the same time; but sometimes one set present themselves, and at other times another, the first being out of sight. Hence the various purposes or inclinations that alternately prevail, and the uncertainty that perplexes us.

To get over this, my way is to divide half a sheet of paper by a line into two columns; writing over the one Pro, and over the other Con. Then during three or four days' consideration I put down under the different heads short hints of the different motives that at different times occur to me, for or against the measure. When I have got them all together in one view, I endeavour to estimate their respective weights; and where I find two (one on each side) that seem equal, I strike them both out. If I find a reason pro equal to some two reasons con, I strike out the three. If I judge some two reasons con equal to some three reasons pro, I strike out the five; and thus proceeding I find at length where the balance lies; and if after a day or two of further consideration, nothing new that is of importance occurs on either side, I come to a determination accordingly. And though the weight of reasons cannot be taken with the precision of algebraic quantities, yet when each is thus considered separately and comparatively, and the whole lies before me, I think I can judge better, and am less likely to make a rash step; and in fact I have found great advantage from this kind of equation, in what may be called moral or prudential algebra.

Wishing sincerely that you may determine for the best, I am ever, my dear friend, yours most affectionately.

B. Franklin[7]

DECISION MAKING UNDER RISK

In the case of decision making under risk, the problem solver does not know which event will occur. Therefore it is not possible simply to apply the criterion of utility maximization. Instead, the various events which may occur must be taken into consideration. A different choice criterion is thus needed.

Expected Utility Maximization

Since the probabilities of events are known in this situation, the decision maker can weight the utilities of outcomes by their probabilities of occurrence to get **expected utilities**. The alternative with the highest expected utility can then be chosen since it is expected to yield the highest degree of satisfaction.[8] Where there are n events which may occur, the expected utility of an alternative can be calculated as:

$$\text{Expected Utility of Alternative } j = \sum_{n}^{i=1} (p_i U_{ij})$$

For instance, suppose there were three possible events, with probabilities of 0.2, 0.5, and 0.3, respectively. Then suppose an alternative would yield a utility of 20 if the first event occurred, of 30 if the second event occurred, and of 0 if the third event occurred. The expected utility of the alternative would be:

$$\text{Expected Utility} = 0.2 \times 20 + 0.5 \times 30 + 0.3 \times 0 = 19$$

Subjective Probabilities

Often, good estimates of the probabilities of events are not available to decision makers. In such cases, they can either try to make decisions without the use of probabilities—an option we would argue against—or they can come up with their own best estimates of those probabilities. These estimates are referred to as **subjective probabilities** because they reside in the mind of the subject (the decision maker) who is considering the object (the event). Techniques are available to help decision makers quantify their subjective probabilities, and the evidence concerning the validity of subjective probabilities is generally quite favorable.[9] Decision makers should not take the absence of good "objective" probabilities as a reason (or excuse) to abandon tools for decision making under risk.

Decision Matrices

A decision matrix is a compact means of arraying the information needed in the case of decision making under risk. For instance, consider the decision matrix shown in Figure 8–6, where the numbers in the matrix are the utilities corresponding to the various combinations of alternatives and events.

The expected utilities corresponding to each of the four alternatives can be calculated by multiplying each utility by the probability of the corresponding event and summing across the events.

Thus, alternative 3 has the highest expected utility and should be chosen. It can be expected to yield greater satisfaction to the decision maker than any of the other alternatives.

Using a decision matrix is an easy way to display information, but it is not appropriate for all problems. Basically, it is most applicable for a one-time decision in which all the alternatives are influenced by the same events.

Decision Trees

Use of a **decision tree** is another way to display the information needed to make a decision under risk. A decision tree is composed of act forks and

FIGURE 8–6
Using the Decision Matrix for Decision Making Under Risk

	Event		
	1 $p_1 = 0.4$	2 $p_2 = 0.5$	3 $p_3 = 0.1$
1	12	1	6
2	8	0	14
3	16	4	0
4	9	6	3

Alternative

So: Expected Utility$_1$ = 12 × .4 + 1 × .5 + 6 × .1 = 5.9
Expected Utility$_2$ = 8 × .4 + 0 × .5 + 14 × .1 = 4.6
Expected Utility$_3$ = 16 × .4 + 4 × .5 + 0 × .1 = 8.4
Expected Utility$_4$ = 9 × .4 + 6 × .5 + 3 × .1 = 6.9

event forks. Act forks, emanating from square nodes, display alternatives. Event forks, emanating from round nodes, display events. Associated with each event fork is a corresponding probability. As we discussed earlier, this may be either an objective or a subjective probability. At the end of each terminal branch in the tree is an outcome value or utility.

Once the tree is constructed, the best alternative can be found by the rollback method. This involves moving from right to left in the tree and finding the expected value or expected utility at each successive node. Any time an act fork is encountered in the tree, it is treated as a separate decision.

To illustrate, consider the decision tree shown in Figure 8–7. The decision maker is considering two alternatives, A and B. If alternative A is chosen, either of two events may occur, C or D. The probability of C is 0.6 and the probability of D is 0.4. Note that, since one or the other of these events must occur, their probabilities sum to 1. If C occurs, the utility will be 80; if D occurs, the utility will be 50. If the decision maker chooses alternative B, things are a bit more complicated. Either of two events, E or F, may occur, each with a probability of 0.5. If event E occurs, the utility will be 90. However, if event F occurs, the decision maker faces another choice (as seen by the square node)—taking G, with a sure utility of 60, or taking H. If H is chosen, either of two events—I or J—may occur, with probabilities of 0.8 and 0.2, respectively, and utilities of 100 and 20, respectively.

To determine the expected utility of each alternative, it is only necessary to roll back from right to left. The expected utility of alternative A is simply 0.6 × 80 + 0.4 × 50 = 68. To find the expected utility of alternative B, it is first necessary to determine whether G or H should be chosen. The expected utility of H is 0.8 × 100 + .2 × 20 = 84. Since this is greater than the utility of 60 offered by G, H should be chosen. So, the expected utility of 84 can be rolled back to the square node. Then the expected utility of alternative B is 0.5 × 90 + 0.5 × 84 = 87. Since 87 > 68, the decision maker should choose alternative B. Then if event F occurs, the decision maker should choose alternative H.

While less compact than the decision matrix, the decision tree has some relative advantages. For example, it can display alternatives for which differ-

FIGURE 8–7
Decision Tree Example

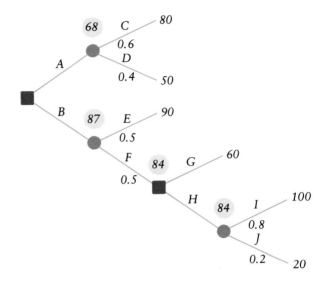

ent events are relevant. Also, it can handle complex situations involving a series of decisions.[10]

As an example of the use of decision trees, consider the case of Tomco Oil, Inc. Independent oil and gas producers typically operate in the sort of complex decision environment where decision trees are most useful. When Tomco was planning to drill for oil in Butler County, Kansas, it used decision trees to choose between two sites. The trees considered geological and engineering factors as well as the decision maker's attitudes toward risk and money. The president of Tomco stated, "Decision tree analysis provided us with a systematic way of planning these decisions and a clearer insight into the numerous and varied financial outcomes that are possible given the choice of any one alternative."[11]

DECISION MAKING UNDER UNCERTAINTY

In the case of decision making under uncertainty, we do not know the probabilities of various events—not even whether one is a bit more or less likely than another. This is a very uncomfortable situation because there is really no right answer available to the decision maker. Instead, all that can be done is to apply one or more of a variety of criteria. Some of these criteria are well known and widely used. However, we should stress that each of them is somewhat flawed in the sense that it violates at least one principle of rational behavior.

To see how these criteria might be applied, consider the decision matrix presented in Figure 8–8. Note that there are no probabilities for the events since, by definition, the probabilities are unknown.

Criterion of Optimism

The **criterion of optimism** says, "Assume things will work out as well as they possibly could." When this criterion is adopted, the decision maker picks the

Having to make a decision under uncertainty is uncomfortable.

alternative that will give the best possible outcome. For a matrix of returns, this is called the *maximax* criterion, since it says to maximize the maximum return. In Figure 8–8, the maximum returns for alternatives 1, 2, and 3 are 10, 8, and 20, respectively. The maximum maximum is 20, corresponding to alternative 3.

Criterion of Pessimism

The **criterion of pessimism** sees nature as out to get the decision maker. It assumes that, for any alternative the decision maker chooses, the worst possible event will take place. So, the reasonable thing to do is to choose the alternative that has the best outcome if the worst happens. For a matrix of returns, this is called the *maximin* criterion, since the alternative with the maximum minimum return would be chosen. In Figure 8–8, the minimum returns for the alternatives are, respectively, 0, 8, and −2. The maximum minimum is 8, corresponding to alternative 2.[12]

Laplace Criterion

The **Laplace criterion**, also called the **criterion of insufficient reason**, argues, "If you really don't know anything about the probabilities of events, it seems reasonable to assume that the probabilities are equal." So this criterion calls for setting the probabilities equal and treating the problem as a decision under risk. Since there are three events in Figure 8–8, the probabilities of each

	Event 1	Event 2	Event 3
Alternative 1	10	6	0
Alternative 2	8	8	8
Alternative 3	−2	20	20

FIGURE 8–8
Decision Making Under Uncertainty

event would be set at ⅓. The resulting expected values of the three alternatives are 5⅓, 8, and 12⅔, respectively. The best return is 12⅔, corresponding to alternative 3.

Savage Criterion

The **Savage criterion**, also known as the **criterion of minimax regret**, says that people should act in ways to minimize their maximum possible regret; that is, so they won't be sorry. Regret is determined by considering how sorry the decision maker would be if a particular alternative were chosen and a particular event occurred. For instance, if alternative 1 in Figure 8–8 were chosen and event 1 took place, the decision maker would experience no regret since that was the best outcome for the event. On the other hand, if alternative 2 had been chosen, there would be 2, that is, $(10 - 8)$, units of regret, and choosing alternative 3 would result in 12, that is, $[10 - (-2)]$, units of regret. A regret matrix is thus developed by subtracting each number in a column from the best number in the column. The regret matrix resulting from Figure 8–8 is presented in Figure 8–9. The maximum levels of regret corresponding to the three alternatives are, respectively, 20, 12, and 12. The minimax (minimum maximum) level of regret is thus 12, corresponding to alternatives 2 and 3.

Choosing Among the Criteria

Given all these criteria and their often conflicting recommendations, which should the decision maker apply? Unfortunately, as we suggested earlier, there is no right answer to this question. Each of the criteria, however apparently reasonable, is somehow flawed. If all the criteria happen to yield the same alternative, that alternative can perhaps be chosen with some confidence. And there may be cases in which one of the criteria seems especially appropriate. A decision maker facing a severe cash shortage may, for instance, want to play it safe and apply the criterion of pessimism. The process of setting up the decision matrix can be helpful in itself, and some alternatives (such as alternative 1 in this case) may be eliminated from consideration if they do best on none of the criteria. However, the bottom line is that decision makers should do all they possibly can to avoid decision making under uncertainty. They should try somehow to come up with probability estimates, either objective or subjective, even if these estimates are crude.

DECISION MAKING UNDER CONFLICT

In the case of decision making under conflict, the decision maker no longer faces an uncaring "nature." Instead, the decision maker is dealing with a

FIGURE 8–9
Regret Matrix

	Event 1	Event 2	Event 3
Alternative 1	0	14	20
Alternative 2	2	12	12
Alternative 3	12	0	0

competitor. These conflict situations are sometimes referred to as games. Games can have several relevant dimensions. One dimension is the number of players of the game—that is, the number of different sides. A bridge game, for instance, is a two-person game because there are two sides. A football game is also a two-person game, whereas a poker game with six players is, barring collusion, a six-person game. Another dimension of a game is the number of strategies per player. For instance, one player may have three feasible strategies and the other player may have five. Still another dimension is whether the game is zero sum or non–zero sum. A zero-sum game is a game in which one player's gain is the other player's loss (thus, gains and losses sum to zero). Here, the "pie" is fixed in size, so hungry competitors must fight fiercely to get their shares. In a non–zero-sum game, the pie can grow or shrink in size depending on the behaviors of the players. A win-win situation in which players can increase their total returns through cooperation would be non–zero sum. A situation such as all-out war, in which both sides may lose, would also be non–zero sum.

The game of chess is an example of decision making under conflict.

Many business situations either are zero sum or can be usefully treated as zero sum. For instance, firms competing for shares of a fixed market, departments fighting for shares of a fixed budget, or individuals striving for the same promotion are essentially in zero-sum situations.

In two-player, zero-sum situations, game theory is useful. **Game theory** is used to find the optimal strategy or mix of strategies of each competitor, or player, in a zero-sum conflict situation.[13] According to game theory, each player should behave in such a way as to do as well as possible in the face of an adversary that is trying to minimize the player's welfare. That is, each competitor should adopt a maximin strategy (if gains are being considered) or a minimax strategy (if costs are being considered).

Consider the game matrix shown in Figure 8–10. That matrix shows that the player on the vertical axis (generally called blue) has four strategies, while the player on the horizontal axis (generally called red) has three strategies.

The numbers in the matrix are returns to the player on the vertical axis (blue). For instance, if blue plays blue strategy 1 and red plays red strategy 3, the return to blue is 8. The maximin value for blue is 4, while the minimax value for red is also 4. When blue's maximin value is equal to red's minimax value, as in this case, the intersection of the strategies is called a **saddle point**. When a saddle point exists, each player should always play the strategy corresponding to the saddle, and the expected return to blue (called the **value of**

FIGURE 8–10
Game Matrix

	Red			
	1	2	3	Minimum
1	6	3	8	3
2	9	④	5	④ ← Maximin
3	−2	3	6	−2
4	10	2	−1	−1
Maximum	10	④	8	

Saddle Point

Minimax

the game) is the value of the saddle. Notice that if blue plays any strategy other than blue 2 while red correctly plays red 2, the return to blue will be less than 4. If red plays any strategy other than red 2 while blue correctly plays blue 2, the cost to red will be greater than 4.

Saddle points are common in very small matrices, but increasingly rare as the matrix gets larger. When there is no saddle point, further calculations are needed to find the optimal mix of strategies for each player. It may be found, for example, that one player should play one strategy half the time and another half the time. The other player may find it best to play one strategy one-quarter of the time and another strategy three-quarters of the time.[14]

When the game is non–zero sum, things get considerably more complicated. A classic example of the perplexing nature of the non–zero-sum game is illustrated by the **Prisoner's Dilemma,** shown in Figure 8–11. In the Prisoner's Dilemma, each of two accused criminals is independently given the one-time choice of confessing or not confessing. While each is much better off if neither confesses than if both confess, one will be badly hurt if the other is the only one to confess.

The Prisoner's Dilemma is a one-time game. Sometimes game players face a situation of continuing interaction. For instance, representatives of union and management may go through a sequence of steps in negotiating a labor contract rather than making just one offer.

In an interesting test of alternative decision rules in such a case, Robert Axelrod invited experts on the Prisoner's Dilemma to compete in a computer tournament.[15] Contestants in the tournament were asked to create a computer program that would generate either a C, for cooperate, or a D, for defect. If both programs produced a C, each received three points. If one offered a C while the other generated a D, the defecting program received five points and the cooperating program received none. If both programs produced a D, each received one point. Instead of the game being played only once, it was repeated about 200 times.

Each program was pitted against each other program in a series of one-to-one competitions. The winner, called TIT-FOR-TAT, was the simplest of all of the programs. Its first move was to cooperate. After that, it matched the previous move of the competitor. By its nature, TIT-FOR-TAT could never perform better than its competitor. However, because it encouraged cooperation on the part of competitors, it tallied the highest total score by the end of the competition.

Game theory has been applied to many business situations. These include pricing, labor-management negotiations, conflict management, plant location, and merger agreements.

FIGURE 8–11
The Prisoner's Dilemma

		Prisoner 2	
		Not Confess	*Confess*
Prisoner 1	Not Confess	1 year each	10 years for 1; 3 months for 2
	Confess	3 months for 1; 10 years for 2	8 years each

DECISION MAKING IN ILL-STRUCTURED SITUATIONS

The common element of the situations we have considered to this point is the ability of the decision maker to develop a decision matrix. Unfortunately, there are many situations in which information is so lacking or ambiguous that construction of a decision matrix is not feasible. In such situations, the formal tools we have considered cannot be directly used. These ill-structured decision situations will be discussed in Chapter 19.[16]

Ill-structured decision situations may be quite important. In fact, strategic decisions at upper levels of the organization are often ill structured. As we will discuss in Chapter 21, it may be dangerous to use heuristics, or rules of thumb, when we are not aware that we are using them. However, many scholars, including Nobel Prize winner Herbert Simon, have argued that such heuristics may provide needed guidance in difficult ill-structured situations.[17] A taxonomy of heuristics is presented in Figure 8–12.

As shown in that figure, there are four types of heuristics. A simple generalized heuristic can apply to any of a wide range of problems.[18] Here is a sampling:

- Draw a figure.
- Work backwards from the desired solution to the current situation.
- Change your assumptions.
- Break the problem down into parts.
- Restate the problem from another perspective.

A simple specialized heuristic is devised for a specific purpose. "Reorder whenever inventory level reaches five units" is an example.

A specialized heuristic program is a series of heuristics which are contingently linked, much like a flowchart, and are meant to be applied to a specific problem. An example would be a flowchart detailing appropriate steps for a firm to take in response to various pricing moves by competitors.

Finally, a generalized heuristic program is a contingently linked set of heuristics which is meant to be applicable to any of a wide range of problems. Because of their complexity, these programs are generally available as software for microcomputers. The user of such a program interacts with the computer and is guided through the problem-solving process. Heuristics included in the program may give tips on problem definition, generation of al-

	Single Rule	Multiple, Contingently Linked Rules
General Purpose	Simple Generalized Heuristics	Generalized Heuristic Programs
Specific Purpose	Simple Specialized Heuristics	Specialized Heuristic Programs

FIGURE 8–12
A Taxonomy of Heuristics

Source: From D. J. Power, "A Criteria-Based Review of 14 Generalized Heuristic Programs," *Proceedings of the Midwest Academy of Management,* April 1979, 278-285.

ternatives, evaluation and choice of alternatives, and other phases of the problem-solving process. By providing structure, these programs permit the use of MAU models and other techniques we consider in this chapter. In Chapter 19 we will discuss one form of generalized heuristic program called a decision insight system.

SUMMARY OF CHOICE MODELS

We have seen that the nature of decision situations must be taken into account when deciding which choice-making model is appropriate. Figure 8–13 summarizes the various decision situations we have considered, their characteristics, appropriate criteria to be applied, and suitable tools.

ALLOCATION MODELS

As we indicated earlier, allocation models are used when a decision maker wishes to use scarce resources where they will do the most good. One well-known allocation technique is linear programming. **Linear programming** seeks to optimize something subject to various constraints. For instance, a firm may want to maximize sales revenues subject to material and staffing constraints, or to maximize advertising exposure subject to an advertising budget. Linear programming is appropriate when it can be safely assumed that all relationships in the problem are linear.[19]

Simple linear programming problems can be solved graphically. Here is a manufacturing example. Suppose that we can make two products, X and Y, and each product requires time on two machines, A and B. The situation is as follows:

	Minutes per Unit		Time Available
Machine	Product X	Product Y	on Machine (Minutes)
A	3	3	120
B	1	4	100

FIGURE 8–13
Summary of Choice Models

Decision Situation	Characteristics	Appropriate Criterion/a	Suitable Tools
Certainty	Event which will occur is known	Maximize utility	Utility model MAU model Decision structure table
Risk	Probabilities of events are known	Maximize expected utility	Decision tree Decision matrix
Uncertainty	Probabilities of events are unknown	Various	Decision matrix
Conflict	Events are the strategies of a competitor	Maximize minimum gain or minimize maximum loss	Game matrix
Ill-Structured	Inability to develop a matrix	Uncertain	Heuristics

What we are trying to maximize or to minimize is called the **objective function**. In this case, each unit of product X will add $5 to profit, while each unit of product Y will contribute $8, so the objective function is:

Profit = $5 (Units of Product X) + $8 (Units of Product Y)

The various constraints are represented by inequalities. In this case, the inequalities are:

[1] $3X + 3Y \leq 120$
[2] $X + 4Y \leq 100$

There are also nonnegativity constraints. These simply say that we can't produce less than none of a product. In this case, they are:

[3] $X \geq 0$
[4] $Y \geq 0$

We can depict the inequalities graphically as shown in Figure 8–14.

The **feasible region** is the area that satisfies all of the constraints. In this case, it is the region bounded by ABCD. The optimal point in the feasible region can be found by constructing isoprofit (equal profit) lines. For instance, 8 units of X yield the same profit ($40) as 5 units of Y. So an isoprofit line can be drawn from X = 8, Y = 0 to X = 0, Y = 5. Similarly, a $160 isoprofit line can be drawn from X = 32, Y = 0 to X = 0, Y = 20. In fact, an infinite number of parallel isoprofit lines can be drawn, expanding outward. Some of these isoprofit lines are also shown in Figure 8–14.

The best mix of X and Y can be found by locating the outermost isoprofit line which touches the feasible set. In this case, it is the $260 isoprofit line, touching the feasible set at X = 20, Y = 20. Thus, the best possible combination of X and Y is 20 units of X and 20 units of Y, yielding a profit of $260.

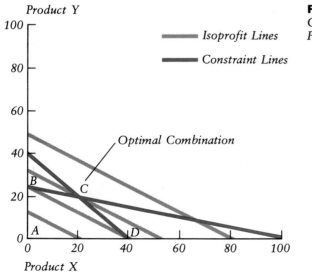

FIGURE 8–14
Graphical Linear Programming Solution

Two other important linear programming terms are slack and shadow price. **Slack** is the amount left over on each constraint when the objective function is optimized. Plugging the optimal combination of 20 units of X and 20 units of Y into inequalities [1] and [2] above, we see there is no slack in either case: each is "at the limit." The **shadow price** associated with a constraint tells us how much the objective function would improve if we loosened that constraint by one unit. If there is slack associated with a constraint, the shadow price is zero since the constraint is not really limiting the objective function. If there is no slack, the shadow price is positive. An examination of shadow prices can suggest where we might best add resources to loosen constraints profitably.

Many companies have made use of linear programming. For instance, during early 1985, the Financial Services Group, a division of Canada Systems Group, Incorporated, anticipated a surge in transaction processing needs because of the popularity of its registered retirement savings program. To plan for resulting manpower needs, a linear-programming model (containing 202 constraints and 226 variables!) was developed and implemented. The model resulted in savings of over $320,000 over a six-week period relative to the previous year, despite higher wages and a 25 percent increase in volume.[20]

As another example, United Airlines has developed and implemented a computerized manpower-planning system for scheduling shift work at its reservations offices and airports. The system uses linear programming and related techniques. It encompasses the entire scheduling process from forecasting of personnel requirements to printing employee schedule choices. Since its implementation in 1983, it has been used to develop work schedules for 4,000 employees, and will eventually schedule 10,000 employees. The system has produced direct labor savings of $6 million annually. It has been favorably received by United's upper management, operating managers, and affected employees. One manager described the model as "magical . . . just as the [customer] lines begin to build, someone shows up for work; and just as you begin to think you're overstaffed, people start going home."[21]

FORECASTING MODELS

In early 1984, Compaq Computer Corporation, a manufacturer of IBM-compatible microcomputers, faced a critical decision. Compaq knew that

Computerized manpower-planning systems are widely used in the airline industry.

IBM was about to introduce its own version of the portable microcomputer and threaten Compaq's dominance in that profitable market. Compaq had two options. It could specialize in this product line and market its portables aggressively, or it could expand its offerings to include desktop microcomputers. The latter option would pit Compaq head-to-head with IBM on its home ground. The company would also have to make major investments in product development and working capital and expand its organization and manufacturing capacity.

Compaq's management faced many unknowns, including the potential market's size, structure, and competitive intensity. Several new developments in the markets, including the introduction of laptop portables by Hewlett-Packard and Data General and the introduction of desktop computers by Sperry, NCR, ITT, and AT&T, were creating further uncertainties. Management felt that Compaq's vitality might erode if the company did not expand. Further, successful expansion would lead to economies of scale that would help Compaq survive in the dynamic and competitive industry. If the market assumptions were wrong, however, Compaq's future might be bleak.

The two Compaq executives most directly involved in the decision—the vice-president of marketing and the CEO—used a series of consumer and dealer surveys coupled with periodic evaluations of technology to assess the future market and to guide the development of products and programs. Based on their forecasts, Compaq entered the desktop segment of the market. While other competitors restricted their programs or even went into receivership, Compaq prospered. Despite the complexities and uncertainties of the situation, Compaq was able to show that forecasting techniques *can* be used to help reach important decisions.[22]

As this example suggests, forecasting is crucial to planning and many other management activities. We will discuss one qualitative forecasting technique, the Delphi process, in Chapter 21. In this section, we will consider three quantitative techniques for forecasting.[23] Each of these techniques uses information from past periods to forecast for future periods.[24]

Moving Average

One simple way to take past data into account when making a forecast is to use a moving average. A **moving average** forecasts the next period on the basis of actual levels over a particular number of past periods. Thus, a three-period moving average forecasts the next period's level as the average of levels for the last three periods, a four-period moving average as the average of levels for the last four periods, and so on. For instance, consider the following sales data:

Period	Sales
1	30
2	35
3	38
4	44
5	47

A three-period moving average forecast for period 6 would be based on sales for the last three periods; that is, $(38 + 44 + 47)/3 = 43$. A four-period moving average forecast would be $(35 + 38 + 44 + 47)/4 = 41$.

Exponential Smoothing

A moving average provides an easy way to forecast on the basis of past information, but it has some undesirable characteristics. For one, it considers information for only a specified number of periods and ignores other information. Also, it gives equal weight to all of the information considered. It would be preferable to consider all past data, but to give heavier weight to more recent data. **Exponential smoothing** is a forecasting technique that provides an estimate which weights all previous observations, but the weights diminish with the age of the observation.

The new forecast is called the smoothed exponential mean, or SEM. The smoothed exponential mean for a given period (SEM_{new}) is equal to the forecast for the previous period (SEM_{old}) plus an adjustment for the error in the old forecast:

$$SEM_{new} = SEM_{old} + \alpha(Actual_{old} - SEM_{old})$$

Because of the way the smoothed exponential mean is determined, SEM_{old} actually contains information about all past levels of the variable. As the formula shows, the error in the old forecast (that is, ($Actual_{old} - SEM_{old}$)) is weighted by α, called the smoothing constant. The higher α is set, the more weight is given to the error in the forecast for the last period, and thus to recent data. A low α gives relatively heavier weight to the old forecast, and thus less to recent data.

Suppose for the data presented above that the smoothing constant, α, was set at 0.3. Let's forecast for period 6 using exponential smoothing. Since we need an initial value of SEM_{old}, we will set it at the actual level for period 1 (that is, 30). Using the formula:

$SEM_2 = SEM_1 + 0.3 (Actual_1 - SEM_1) = 30 + 0.3 (30 - 30) = 30$

$SEM_3 = SEM_2 + 0.3 (Actual_2 - SEM_2) = 30 + 0.3 (35 - 30) = 31.5$

$SEM_4 = SEM_3 + 0.3 (Actual_3 - SEM_3) = 31.5 + 0.3 (38 - 31.5) = 33.45$

$SEM_5 = SEM_4 + 0.3 (Actual_4 - SEM_4) = 33.45 + 0.3 (44 - 33.45) = 36.615$

$SEM_6 = SEM_5 + 0.3 (Actual_5 - SEM_5) = 36.615 + 0.3 (47 - 36.615) = 39.7305$

Since exponential smoothing is based entirely on weighting of past data, it will lag a trend. With a low value of α, as in this example, that lag may be considerable. If α had been set higher, the forecast would have better reflected the trend. For instance, with an α of 0.8, the forecast for period 6 would be 46.128.[25]

Linear Regression

Linear regression predicts future levels of a variable by identifying the line that best fits through past levels of the variable. The line can then be extended to future years to estimate the variable level at those times. In general, the equation for a line is:

$$Y = a + bX$$

where:

Y is the dependent variable for which we would like to make forecasts;

X is the independent variable, such as the period or year;

a is the intercept of the line with the Y axis;

b is the slope of the line.

Similarly, we can substitute the mean levels of X and Y in the equation, as follows:

$$\overline{Y} = a + b\overline{X}$$

The formula to determine the slope of the best-fitting line is:

$$b = \frac{\sum\limits_{i=1}^{n} XY - \overline{X}\sum\limits_{i=1}^{n} Y}{\sum\limits_{i=1}^{n} X^2 - \overline{X}\sum\limits_{i=1}^{n} X}$$

For our example:

$$b = \frac{(1 \times 30 + 2 \times 35 + 3 \times 38 + 4 \times 44 + 5 \times 47) - 3 \times 194}{(1 + 4 + 9 + 16 + 25) - 3 \times 15}$$

$$= \frac{625 - 582}{55 - 45} = \frac{43}{10} = 4.3$$

Then, since $Y = a + bX$:

$$38.8 = a + 4.3 \times 3 = a + 12.9$$

So: $a = 38.8 - 12.9 = 25.9$

The equation of the best-fitting line is thus:

$$Y = 25.9 + 4.3X$$

This is shown in Figure 8–15.

To forecast for any future period, it is then necessary only to plug in the appropriate value for X. The forecast for the next period (period 6) would be:

$$Y_6 = 25.9 + 4.3 \times 6 = 25.9 + 25.8 = 51.7$$

Similarly, the forecast for period 7 would be:

$$Y_7 = 25.9 + 4.3 \times 7 = 25.9 + 30.1 = 56.0$$

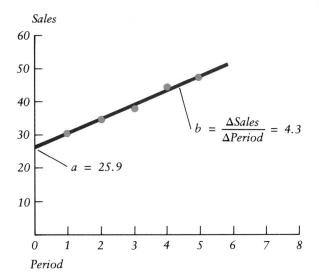

FIGURE 8–15
The Regression Line

George P. Huber (Ph.D., Purdue University) is the Fondren Foundation Chaired Professor of Business at the University of Texas–Austin. His research focuses on decision making, information systems, and organizational design, and he has written three books and over seventy other publications on these topics. Professor Huber has held positions in the Emerson Electric Company, Procter & Gamble, the U.S. Department of Labor, Execucom Systems, and the Universities of California and Wisconsin and has served as a consultant to many corporations and public agencies. He recently completed a two-year study of information use in research and development organizations for

ACADEMIC PROFILE
GEORGE P. HUBER

the National Science Foundation and is now directing a five-year research program on organization design for the U.S. Army Research Institute for Behavioral and Social Sciences. Professor Huber is a fellow of the Decision Sciences Institute.

Q: Why should managers bother to improve their decision-making abilities?

A: The careers and lives of good decision makers are more professionally rewarding and personally satisfying than the careers and lives of poor decision makers. Managers who are good decision makers tend to spend their time capitalizing on the results of their wise choices. Managers who are poor decision makers expend their energy dashing around remedying mistakes and "fighting fires"; they always seem to have had a frustrating day. Theirs are difficult lives; so also are the lives of their subordinates, superiors, and co-workers. In contrast, the quality of life and professional success of managers who make good decisions are significantly greater.

Q: Which decision-making techniques do you think offer the greatest benefits for practicing managers?

A: Managerial problems are always more complex than our minds can encompass, so we tend to oversimplify them and fail to consider and process information that could make the difference between a good choice and a bad one. Decision-making techniques that help us deal with problem complexity, and yet are easy to use, offer the greatest benefits. The best of them help managers do three things: organize their thoughts, determine what information is relevant, and use information effectively. Good examples of such techniques are decision matrices, decision trees, and multi-attribute utility models.

Q: Why do you think some managers resist use of formal decision-making techniques?

A: Some managers aren't able to sort decision situations; they tend to see all situations as if they were one type. If their bias is to see all decision situations as social or political, they will tend to resist the view that facts and analysis are relevant and so resist the use of formal decision-making techniques. We are increasingly becoming aware that the formal decision-making techniques can be very useful in collective choice and political decision situations. They are, for example, extremely effective as communication aids for the participants in a collective choice situation, and are frequently helpful in identifying alternatives that all parties in a political situation can live with.

Q: Do you expect use of formal decision-making techniques in organizations to grow?

A: There is no doubt that the use of formal decision-making techniques will continue to grow. One reason is that improvements in communication and transportation technologies will make the world more complex, and the techniques allow us to deal with complexity effectively. The second reason is that these same technologies are making the world more competitive, thus making differences in the quality of decisions even more important than they have been in the past.

250

SIMULATION MODELS

As we stated earlier, simulation models are used to develop simplified versions of reality. These models can be manipulated to gain insights into the more complex real-world situation. We consider simulation techniques throughout this text. For instance, role playing and in-baskets, which we will consider in Chapter 10, simulate the real world of managers. In a sense, many of the quantitative models we have considered in this chapter, and will examine in future chapters, are simulations. That is, they are simplifications of reality used to provide insights that may then be extrapolated to the real-world situation.

Computer Simulation

Simulation relies heavily on experimentation. That is, once the simulation is developed, variables can be experimentally manipulated and the consequences of those manipulations noted. Through such systematic manipulation of key variables, near-optimal solutions can often be found. Because simulations are generally complex, and because many experimental manipulations may be desired, simulations are often computerized.

For example, General Motors of Canada has committed more than $20 billion (Canadian) to meet the productivity and quality challenges posed by overseas manufacturing. As one response, it modernized its Oshawa, Ontario, assembly plant. Automatic guided vehicles (AGVs) and robotics and other automation will be used in the body-framing area. A computer simulation model was developed linking output to AGV needs. The simulation found that the framing system could produce 20 percent more cars per shift, but this increase beyond the targeted output would require 70 percent more AGVs.[26]

In an unusual application, General Motors Corp. recently settled a class-action lawsuit alleging discrimination against salaried black employees in pay and promotion. As part of the agreement, GM agreed to set up a computer simulation model to monitor future personnel practices. The computer model will generate an expected percentage of black promotions, taking into account six major factors that determine the qualifications of covered black GM employees. These factors are the length of time spent at the company, time spent in the current job, years of education, degrees obtained, area of study, and when the degrees were obtained. If, taking into account these factors, the percentage of promotions among blacks differs substantially from that among whites, GM will have to make up the difference.[27]

QUEUING MODELS

We are all familiar with waiting lines, or queues. They are common occurrences in supermarkets and during registration for classes. There may also be waiting lines for products to be processed on a particular machine, waiting lines of letters to be typed by a secretary, and waiting lines at truck depots. Waiting lines are not necessarily bad. To eliminate them completely might be very costly. Instead, it is important to study how they form and to evaluate the costs of congestion against the costs of reducing the queues. As noted earlier, queuing models can be used for these purposes.[28]

As shown in Figure 8–16, there are some common elements to queuing systems. They are arrivals at the service facility, the queue, the various stations of the service facility, and departures.

By using a queuing model, it is possible to examine the consequences of adding more or fewer lines, of changing service time, and so on. Then, by considering the costs associated with the lines (perhaps in delayed production or in customer ill will) and the costs associated with altering their length, decisions can be made about how to minimize total costs.[29]

USING THE TOOLS TOGETHER

In our discussion of quantitative tools for managing, we have tended to treat the tools separately. In complex real-world applications, the tools are often used together. For instance, when Baltimore Gas and Electric Company was considering alternatives for adding 600 megawatts of electrical generating capacity, it examined several technology choices, some of which were not commercially available at the time of the analysis. Because several criteria were important to BGE, such as customer cost, shareholder return, corporate image, health and safety, and feasibility, multi-attribute utility analysis was used. Because many events, such as success or failure of new technologies, were probabilistic, decision trees were employed. Because of the great complexity of the overall problem, a computer simulation was developed and implemented. These and other quantitative tools were used together to provide insights into the complex problem of technology choice.[30]

Also, the quantitative tools we have considered may be used as complements to other, often more qualitative, approaches. As an example, during 1984 and 1985 Citgo Petroleum Corporation invested in a wide range of tools and approaches including mathematical programming, expert systems, artificial intelligence, organization theory, and cognitive psychology. These and related applications resulted in an estimated annual profit improvement of $70 million.[31]

IMPLICATIONS FOR MANAGEMENT

We stress throughout this text that managers are facing increasingly complex and dynamic situations. Together, complexity and dynamism create uncer-

FIGURE 8–16
A Queuing System

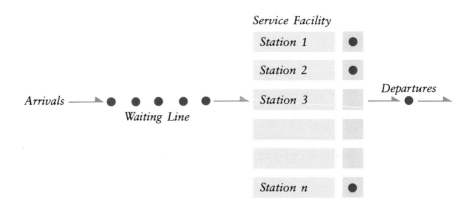

tainties. As a result, decision making is typically both difficult and important. Further, in current times of resource scarcity, both the importance of decisions and the need to justify them are especially great. Managers are stressed in such situations and are likely to put off making decisions, to avoid information that disagrees with their preferred alternatives, and to engage in other unproductive decision behaviors. They need all the help they can get. The techniques discussed in this chapter provide some of that help. You should find them a useful, though partial, tool kit for managerial decision making.

In conditions of change, complexity, and constraint, certainty is generally the stuff of managerial fantasies. Instead, you as a manager will often have to venture into risky, uncertain, conflictive, and even ill-structured situations. You will have to recognize these situations and to master the appropriate techniques to deal with them. Utility models, decision trees and matrices, game matrices, and heuristic programs all have their place and may make decision making more manageable. Further, forecasting becomes both more difficult and more crucial in times of rapid change.

With increasing foreign competition and other constraints, growth in many industries has stagnated. In fact, many managers find themselves burdened with the unpleasant task of managing decline. These developments have important consequences for decision making. First, it may become harder to find win-win solutions, though they should certainly be sought. In these cases, gaming approaches may become more applicable. Second, difficult tradeoffs will have to be made, often involving many variables. Decision structure tables and multi-attribute utility models can be used to address these tradeoffs. Third, effective use of resources will be crucial, calling for heavier reliance on allocation models. Finally, managers will have fewer opportunities to do costly experimentation in the real world, or to try hit-or-miss strategies. Instead, computer simulation will become increasingly appropriate. By mastering the techniques we have discussed, you will have a substantial competitive advantage in trying circumstances.

KEY TERMS AND CONCEPTS

allocation models	ill structure
certainty	Laplace criterion (criterion of
choice-making models	insufficient reason)
conflict	linear programming
criterion of optimism	linear regression
criterion of pessimism	models
decision matrix	moving average
decision structure table	multi-attribute utility (MAU) model
decision tree	objective function
elimination-by-aspects rule	Prisoner's Dilemma
expected utilities	pro-con comparison
exponential smoothing	queuing models
feasible region	risk
forecasting models	saddle point
game theory	satisficing rule

Savage criterion (criterion of minimax   slack
   regret)   subjective probabilities
scoring approach   uncertainty
screening approach   utility
shadow price   utility curve
simulation models   value of the game

QUESTIONS FOR REVIEW AND DISCUSSION

1. What is a model? Which of the models considered in this chapter are primarily objective? Subjective? Which are primarily deterministic? Probabilistic?
2. Identify and define five decision situations and indicate the appropriate choice criterion for each situation.
3. Describe a situation in which a screening approach would probably be more appropriate than a scoring approach. Then, describe a situation in which a scoring approach would probably be more appropriate than a screening approach. Finally, discuss the key differences between the two situations.
4. Describe a situation in which a decision maker is faced with a choice among three specific alternatives. Identify the events that might be expected to influence the outcome of each alternative, and specify the probabilities of those events. Then, indicate the utility you would attach to each outcome. Finally, use a decision tree to array the information and to choose the best alternative.
5. Identify four criteria for decision making under uncertainty. Of these criteria, which seems most reasonable to you? Least reasonable? Why?
6. What is the TIT-FOR-TAT strategy? In view of the success of that strategy in the computerized competition described in this chapter, why do you think it is not more often used in real-world bargaining situations?
7. Suppose that a manufacturing firm purchases three component parts from three suppliers. Each supplier has limited capacity and thus can't meet all of the manufacturing firm's needs. Further, the suppliers differ in the amount they charge for each component. Discuss how linear programming could be applied to this problem to determine how many units of each component should be purchased from each supplier.
8. Describe three forecasting techniques and identify the strengths and weaknesses of each. In your answer, be sure to discuss the degree to which each technique:
   a. is easy to use;
   b. is responsive to changing conditions; and
   c. can forecast for periods far into the future.
9. Identify at least two costs that might be associated with long waiting lines at a lathe in a manufacturing facility. Then, identify at least two costs of making the line shorter.

CASES

8–1 A RISKY STANCE

Gerber Products Co. keeps a stash of teddy bears and cookies in the lobby of its headquarters in Fremont, Michigan, to welcome its chief customers—children. But, battered by a wave of complaints about glass in its baby food, the company is shedding its paternal, cuddly image.

In March of 1986, Gerber started talking tough. Noting that the Food and Drug Administration had yet to substantiate any of the complaints, the company contended that a recall was pointless and blamed the media for helping to fuel the panic. "We feel this is a lynch mob," said James Lovejoy, Gerber's director of corporate communications. "Nobody wants to wait for due process. We're guilty until proven innocent."

The company's problems were getting plenty of scrutiny because they involved the emotionally charged issue of safe baby food. The scare also followed close on the heels of what has been termed a "textbook" response to public concerns about product safety: Johnson & Johnson's answers to the Tylenol scares. In 1982, and again in 1986, Johnson & Johnson quickly recalled capsules of the pain reliever after some were found to be laced with cyanide. In the name of public safety, the company launched big advertising campaigns announcing the recalls and, in 1986, decided to stop making the product in capsule form.

Gerber, however, took a very different course. Believing that the complaints would eventually be proved false, the company made no recalls and no changes in packaging or product offerings. If Gerber, the largest U.S. baby-food producer, is right, it can ride out the crisis with minimal damage. But if the company is wrong, the results could be devastating.

"If there isn't a problem, then it's probably advisable to be quiet, let the misperception die a natural death," says James Gaudino, who teaches public relations at Michigan State University. But, he adds, consumers will wonder what company officials have done "to safeguard me today. Should they find out next week that babies have been eating glass for a month, then that's going to make people real mad. The risk is realized."

The objective now is "not to get panicked," says the company's Mr. Lovejoy. "We have felt all along that this is not a product-quality story—it's [public] perceptions." Gerber's quality-control people have been gathering suspect food samples from around the country, looking for a common denominator in the more than 225 complaints the FDA has received to date. Top executives from sales, quality control, consumer relations, and other departments have formed a crisis-management team and meet each day to coordinate investigations.

"Gerber has to lose either way, whether they do something or do nothing, because people will perceive a risk," says Charles Goodman, professor of marketing at the Wharton Business School at the University of Pennsylvania. "If people believe there is a danger, it doesn't matter if there really is no danger."

Source: Reprinted by permission of *The Wall Street Journal*, © Dow Jones & Company, Inc. (March 6, 1986). All Rights Reserved Worldwide.

1. Set up a decision matrix which describes this situation. Include at least three alternatives that Gerber could pursue in responding to this situation and three events that might influence the outcomes. Remember that events must be mutually exclusive and exhaustive. Also include an estimate of the probabilities of each of the events.
2. Consider each possible outcome in the matrix. Attach a utility to the outcome reflecting your perception of its desirability.
3. Treat this as a decision under risk and select an optimal course of action. Then treat this as a decision under uncertainty and apply each of the criteria discussed in this section. Based on these analyses, which course of action would you recommend?

8–2 SITE SELECTION FOR A UNITED TECHNOLOGIES CORP. MANUFACTURING PLANT IN EUROPE

United Technologies Corp. (UTC) has experienced major growth and diversification since the 1970s, moving from an aerospace firm with $2 billion in sales to a $17 billion, broadly based corporation with over 300 plants in 26 countries. Its divisions include Pratt & Whitney, Carrier Air Conditioning, Otis Elevator, Hamilton Standard, Norden Systems, and Sikorsky. These divisions are a major global presence, maintaining the number one or two market-share position in their markets (in terms of revenues) worldwide.

In the late 1980s, United Technologies' Automotive Products Division (APD) began site search and selection for a new European facility to provide additional capacity for the 1989 model year and beyond as APD continues to grow in Europe. Several countries were initially considered for the site, but Portugal was quickly chosen because of its very low labor costs, stable economic and political environment, availability of manufacturing and engineering talent, and other factors.

Once Portugal was selected, it was necessary to determine the specific location of the facility. APD decided, based largely on transportation considerations, to locate near Porto, Portugal's second largest city. Porto offered excellent access to APD's Spanish operations and the rest of Europe. Further, some managerial and professional employees may wish to live in Porto and commute to the facility.

APD was seeking a site with these primary characteristics:

- Adequate labor supply. APD would need to hire 1,000 people within three years.
- Minimal distance from Porto.
- Adequate facility available immediately or with reasonable renovation costs.
- Adequate access to transportation.
- High quality of life.

Three cities—Serem, Ilhavo, and Valongo—were considered as possible sites for the APD plant. Serem is in a rural area 40 miles south of Porto. Approximately 1,100 people are employed within a five-mile radius of Serem. Serem is on the main highway between Porto and another large city, Coimbra. An appropriate facility would have to be constructed to APD's specifications.

Ilhavo is located 50 miles south of Porto in an industrialized area with an ample labor supply, but it is not on a main highway. The only acceptable building would require considerable renovation. Both Serem and Ilhavo are in the Aveiro district, noted for its fishing, dairy farming, and porcelain works.

Valongo is five miles from Porto and nearest to the airport of the three cities under consideration. Valongo has a population of 91,000 and also has access to the Porto labor supply. An available building under construction in Valongo consisted only of a shell without floors and utilities and could be finished to APD's specifications. With its proximity to Porto, Valonga is close to many museums, educational facilities, recreation, and entertainment.

Source: Information in this case is drawn in part from T. L. Rees, "Site Selection in Europe—A Case Study," *Site Selection and Industrial Development* (October 1988): 13-15.

1. Set up a decision structure table for the three potential sites. In developing the table, set constraints regarding minimum or maximum acceptable levels of each attribute. Given those constraints, which alternative(s) would be chosen by the elimination-by-aspects rule? By the satisficing rule? (When applying the elimination-by-aspects rule, proceed from the most important attribute to the least important attribute.)
2. For each attribute listed above, draw your utility curve using the direct estimation method. Then, determine the utility of each alternative site on each attribute.
3. Assign weights to each of the attributes using the procedure discussed in this chapter. Using these weights and the utilities developed above, calculate the multiattribute utility for each city.
4. Compare the results of the screening and scoring approaches. Are they the same or different? If different, how do you explain any discrepancies?

ENDNOTES

1. These examples are drawn from J. W. Ulvila and R. V. Brown, "Decision Analysis Comes of Age," *Harvard Business Review* (September-October 1982): 130-141.

2. Reliability refers to consistency. For instance, a bathroom scale which gives a very different weight each time we step on it is inconsistent or unreliable. Validity refers to accuracy. For instance, if the bathroom scale gives an accurate weight it is valid. Unreliability reduces validity; if we see that the scale is giving us inconsistent weights, we know that we can't trust its accuracy. So, improving consistency will increase accuracy.

3. This distinction is not as clear as it may seem. For instance, information which seems quite objective may actually have been influenced by subjective elements in its gathering and recording.

4. R. O. Swalm, "Utility Theory—Insights into Risk Taking," *Harvard Business Review* 44 (1966): 123-136. For a recent discussion of this issue, see J. G. March and Z. Shapira, "Managerial Perspectives on Risk and Risk Taking," *Management Science* 33 (1987): 1404-1418.

5. G. P. Huber, "Methods for Quantifying Subjective Probabilities and Multi-Attribute Utilities," *Decision Sciences* 5 (1974): 430-458, and *Managerial Decision Making* (Glenview, IL: Scott, Foresman, 1980); and R. L. Keeney and H. Raiffa, *Decisions with Multiple Objectives: Preferences and Value Trade-Offs* (New York: John Wiley & Sons, 1976), provide discussions of derivation and use of multi-attribute utility models.

6. R. L. Keeney, "Examining Corporate Policy Using Multiattribute Utility Analysis," *Sloan Management Review* (Fall 1975): 63-76. For another application of multi-attribute utility analysis, see F. E. Wenstop and A. J. Carlsen, "Ranking Hydroelectric Power Projects with Multicriteria Decision Analysis," *Interfaces* (July-August 1988): 36-48. This article discusses application of MAU approaches to the ranking of 542 hydropower projects for the Norwegian master plan for water resources.

7. B. Franklin, Letter to Joseph Priestley, in *Ben Franklin's Autobiographical Writings*, ed. C. Van Doren (New York: Viking Press, 1945).

8. For an interesting application of expected utility maximization to the decision of whether to kick an extra point after a touchdown or to try for a two-point conversion, see C. T. L. Janssen and T. E. Daniel, "A Decision Theory Example in Football," *Decision Sciences* 15 (1984): 253-259.

9. See Huber, "Methods for Quantifying," 430-458, and T. S. Wallsten and D. V. Budescu, "Encoding Subjective Probabilities: A Psychological and Psychometric Review," *Management Science* 29 (1983): 151-173, for reviews.

10. S. E. Bodily, "When Should You Go to Court?" *Harvard Business Review* (May-June 1981): 103-113; J. E. Magee, "Decision Trees for Decision Making," *Harvard Business Review* (July-August 1964): 126-138; Ulvila and Brown, "Decision Analysis"; T. J. Madden, M. S. Hyrnick, and J. A. Hodde, "Decision Analysis Used to Evaluate Air Quality Control Equipment for Ohio Edison Company," *Interfaces* (February 1983): 66-75; and R. E. Luna and R. A. Reid, "Mortgage Selection Using a Decision Tree Approach," *Interfaces* (May-June 1986): 73-81, give examples of business applications of decision trees.

11. J. Hosseini, "Decision Analysis and Its Application in the Choice Between Two Wildcat Oil Ventures," *Interfaces* (March-April 1986): 75-85. The quote is from page 85.

12. Another criterion, called the Hurwicz criterion, combines the criterion of pessimism and the criterion of optimism. It weights the worst outcome by α, the coefficient of pessimism, and the best outcome by $(1 - \alpha)$. α may vary from 0 (if the individual is completely optimistic) to 1 (if the individual is completely pessimistic). If α is set at 0.5, the best and worst outcomes are equally weighted.

13. R. D. Luce and H. Raiffa, *Games and Decisions* (New York: John Wiley & Sons, 1957), and J. Von Neumann and O. Morganstern, *Theory of Games and Economic Behavior* (Princeton, NJ: Princeton University Press, 1944), provide technical discussions of game theory. For an excellent and very readable presentation, see J. D. Williams, *The Compleat Strategyst*, rev. ed. (New York: McGraw-Hill, 1966).

14. We don't have space to demonstrate how these mixed strategies are determined, but they assume that each player chooses a mix of strategies such that the actions of the competitor do not matter. The value of the game will be the same regardless of the competitor's actions.

15. W. F. Allman, "Nice Guys Finish First," *Science* 84 (October 1984): 25-32.

16. C. Churchman, "Wicked Problems," *Management Science* 14 (1967): B141-B142, provides a discussion of ill-structured problems.

17. H. A. Simon, *The New Science of Management Decision*, rev. ed. (Englewood Cliffs, NJ: Prentice-Hall, 1977).

18. G. Polya, *How to Solve It: A New Aspect of Mathematical Method*, 2d ed. (Princeton, NJ: Princeton University Press, 1957), nicely shows how simple, generalized heuristics may be used to solve ill-structured problems such as riddles.

19. D. R. Anderson, D. J. Sweeney, and T. A. Williams, *An Introduction to Management Science: Quantitative Approaches to Decision Making*, 4th ed. (St. Paul, MN: West Publishing Company, 1985), show how linear programming can be applied to a wide range of business problems.

20. C. Haehling von Lanzenauer, E. Harbauer, B. Johnston, and D. H. Shuttleworth, "RRSP Flood: LP to the Rescue," *Interfaces* (July-August 1985): 27-33.

21. T. J. Holloran and J. E. Byrn, "United Airlines Station Manpower Planning System," *Interfaces* (January-February 1986): 39-50. The quote is from page 49.

22. D. M. Georgoff and R. G. Murdick, "Manager's Guide to Forecasting," *Harvard Business Review* (January-February 1986): 112-114, 119-120. For a review of forecasting research and a set of suggestions for making better forecasts, see J. S. Armstrong, "The Ombudsman: Research on Forecasting: A Quarter-Century Review, 1960-1984," *Interfaces* (January-February 1986): 89-109.

23. Quantitative forecasting techniques may be used along with "eyeball" extrapolation and judgmental adjustment. For one study on this point, see R. Carbone and W. L. Gorr, "Accuracy of Judgmental Forecasting of Time Series," *Decision Sciences* 16 (1985): 153-160. In that study, the authors concluded that objective methods proved more accurate than eyeball extrapolation. However, judgmental adjustment improved the accuracy of some objective forecasts.

24. As another example of use of forecasting, the Export Credits Guarantee Department (ECDG) is a British government department which insures United Kingdom exporters against the risk of nonpayment of goods sold to overseas buyers. Because of the many uncertainties involved in such insurance, the ECDG uses a computer-based model that forecasts premium income, buyer claims, administrative costs, and other variables on the basis of past levels of those variables. For a discussion, see H. Pullinger and A. P. G. Hare, "Corporate Financial Planning in Insurance—A Case Study," *Journal of the Operational Research Society* (October 1987): 957-964.

25. For an application of exponential smoothing to the forecasting of total daily demand for teller services in a bank, see W. L. Berry, V. A. Mabert, and M. Marcus, "Forecasting Teller Window Demand with Exponential Smoothing," *Academy of Management Journal* 22 (1979): 129-137.

26. J. H. Bookbinder and T. R. Kotwa, "Modeling an AGV Automobile Body-Framing System," *Interfaces* (November-December 1987): 41-50.

27. J. M. Schlesinger, "GM Settles Class Lawsuit Accusing It of Racial Bias," *Wall Street Journal* (February 1, 1989): B1.

28. Real-world queuing systems can be very complex and ill defined, and they may resist application of exact mathematical approaches. For a discussion of simple, flexible approaches to cover a variety of queuing problems, see W. K. Grassman, "Finding the Right Number of Servers in Real-World Systems," *Interfaces* (March-April 1988): 94-104.

29. For case studies of applications of queuing theory to airport runway design, the London bus problem, traffic delays at toll booths, and the arrival of ships at wharfs, see A. M. Lee, "Four Selected Case Histories," in *Applied Queuing Theory* (New York: St. Martin's Press, 1966), 142-151. For some other applications and discussions of queuing theory, see J. S. Annino and E. C. Russell, "The Seven Most Frequent Causes of Simulation Analysis Failure—and How to Avoid Them," *Interfaces* (June 1981): 59-63; G. P. Cosmetatos, "The Value of Queuing Theory—A Case Study," *Interfaces* (May 1979); and H. Deutsch and V. A. Mabert, "Queuing Theory and Teller Staffing: A Successful Application," *Interfaces* (October 1980): 63-67.

30. R. L. Keeney, J. F. Lathrop, and A. Sicherman, "An Analysis of Baltimore Gas and Electric Company's Technology Choice," *Operations Research* (January-February 1986): 18-39.

31. D. Klingman, N. Philips, D. Steiger, and W. Young, "The Successful Deployment of Management Science Throughout Citgo Petroleum Corporation," *Interfaces* (January-February 1987): 4-25.

Organizing
and Staffing

PART THREE

Organizational Design

After studying this chapter, you should be able to:
- Identify the basic elements of organizational structure.
- Discuss the criteria managers can use to group jobs and activities.
- Describe the factors that influence managerial span of control.
- Identify ways activities can be coordinated in an organization.
- Identify and discuss the strengths and weaknesses of the functional, divisional, hybrid, and matrix designs.
- Describe and discuss how environment, strategy, size, and technology influence an organization's design.

What do General Motors, International Business Machines, Textron, Inc., Digital Equipment Corporation, American Can Corporation, and Texas Instruments have in common? Like many other major U.S. corporations, these companies underwent an extensive restructuring during the 1980s. Restructuring is the "current buzzword, which has swept U.S. industry, [and] involves taking companies apart and putting them together again in different forms."[1]

Managers may choose to restructure their organization for a variety of reasons. Current structures may be seen as contributing to inefficiency and related problems. Or management may see the current structures as incompatible with projections of future growth and goals. Faced with the prospects of more aggressive competition in the future, managers may seek to change the organization's structure now.

ORGANIZATIONAL STRUCTURE

All organizations arrange their activities around structures. We will first define organizational structure and then identify its basic elements.

Defining Organizational Structure

The concept of structure is simple and has application to many scientific and applied disciplines. Physiologists, for example, consider the skeletal framework as a basic structure of the human body. Similarly, **organizational structure** can be defined broadly as mechanisms that serve to coordinate and control activities of organizational members. Coordination is the process by which tasks and departments are interrelated to achieve organizational goals. Control is the regulation of activities in a manner that will enable members to predict and stabilize relationships within the organization. Both coordinating and control mechanisms, or structures, must be matched to the organization's context in order for the organization to be effective.

What are the mechanisms that managers use to structure their organization to coordinate and control activities? There are five general mechanisms that serve these functions. We refer to them as the basic elements of organizational structure.

Basic Elements of Organizational Structure

Managers make decisions about the structure of their organization when they consider ways in which activities will be coordinated and controlled in the organization. Structural decisions addressing issues of coordination and control focus on the degree of work specialization, the manner of departmentation, the pattern of authority, the span of control, and mechanisms of activity coordination.

WORK SPECIALIZATION

Work specialization is the degree to which tasks are divided in the organization. From Chapter 1, we can recall Adam Smith's observation that greater specialization often leads to greater productivity. Smith observed that one individual working alone could produce only 20 pins a day. If the work was divided into 10 specialized tasks, however, each of 10 individuals trained in one of the tasks could produce the equivalent of 4,800 pins a day.

Managers may decide on a high degree or a low degree of specialization in their organization. When there is a high degree of work specialization, we find individuals focusing on one or a few tasks. When work specialization is low, we find individuals performing many different tasks in the organization. The degree of work specialization in an organization can vary both within and across industries. For instance, managers of an automobile company may choose to have a high degree of work specialization on the production line. In this instance, we may find workers whose sole task is to rivet the bolts that hold the left passenger door to the frame of the car. Other workers may then attach the window handles to the door, while others install the door lock mechanism. Indeed, in a highly specialized automobile assembly line, one will find thousands of workers assigned to specific tasks that lead to the production of an automobile. On the other hand, managers of an automobile company may choose instead to specialize work to a low degree. Here, workers may operate as a team of eight who "walk" the car down the assembly line, each performing a wide variety of tasks until the automobile is completed.

Work specialization is not, however, confined only to tasks directly related to the production of a good or service. Managerial activities may also be divided into high or low work specialization. A manager who hires and fires personnel, keeps financial records, contacts suppliers to purchase raw materials, and travels to sell the organization's products is operating in a situation of low work specialization. Assigning a manager to perform each of these tasks separately would lead the organization to higher degrees of work specialization at the managerial level.

Work specialization is an important structural mechanism that managers can use to coordinate and control member activities. Increasing work specialization enables managers to achieve greater levels of control over tasks. In highly specialized work, an individual can learn the necessary methods

Testing radios with a computer is the specialized task of this employee.

quickly, and managers can observe the activity to make sure the task is being performed correctly. At the same time, however, increased work specialization can make coordination of activities more difficult. An individual performing five separate tasks can coordinate the various activities, as that person has a better understanding of what tasks have been accomplished and what tasks have to be completed in the future. If five individuals are performing each task separately, the activities must be coordinated to make sure each person completes the task at the right time. Hence, managers must recognize that work specialization can solve problems of control but increase problems of coordination. The issues surrounding work specialization will be discussed further in Chapter 14.

DEPARTMENTATION

Another basic element of organizational structure is departmentation. **Departmentation** is the grouping of jobs based on criteria that managers believe help in the coordination and control of activities. The six criteria for grouping jobs include the following:

- *Knowledge and skills.* Positions are grouped according to the specialized knowledge and skills that members bring to the job. For example, universities assign professors to departments such as chemistry, business, and engineering that have been created based on the grouping of knowledge and skills.
- *Work process and function.* Positions are grouped according to the process or activities to be performed. With this kind of grouping, separate departments are set up to handle such activities as production, marketing, research and development, engineering, and finance.
- *Time.* Grouping of positions is based on when the work is to be done. For example, when the organization performs the same work 24 hours a day, as may occur in food processing, members are grouped into daytime, evening, and night shifts. Time may also serve as a basis of grouping when work varies within a 24-hour period. For example, telephone operations vary according to whether they are performed on weekdays, weekends, evenings, or late at night; thus, different work skills may be required for the groups assigned to these time slots.
- *Product.* Positions in the organization are grouped on the basis of the good or service that is being produced. A computer manufacturer may have separate departments handling office computers, home computers, and scientific computers.
- *Customer.* Groups may be formed based on the need to deal with different types of customers. A television production company may have groups formed to handle programming for children, for teenagers, and for adults.
- *Location.* Positions may be grouped by location. Thus, one may find the midwestern division, the western division, and the international division, which have been formed based on a geographically defined area of operation.[2]

The choice of criteria by which managers choose to group positions in an organization is critical. Implications of grouping will be discussed later in the chapter when we examine organizational designs. For now, we need to recognize that the decision on grouping based on one of the six criteria is important. Grouping defines both the tasks to be combined into one department and the members who belong to that group.

A hospital administrator, for instance, may make a decision about departmentation that can have a wide range of implications. The decision can affect the way hospital management assigns authority, distributes resources, rewards performance, and sets up communication. In addition, it has implications for the quality of the goods and services it provides to patients. Figure 9–1 provides six hypothetical groupings that could be applied to a hospital.

Grouping has four basic implications for employees and how organizational activities are carried out:

- Grouping sets up a system of common supervision. Once jobs have been assigned to a department, a manager can be named to coordinate and control the activities within the department.
- Grouping typically requires a sharing of resources. Budgets, facilities, and equipment that are necessary to complete activities can be assigned to the department.
- Grouping typically creates common measures of performance. Joint sharing of resource inputs and joint responsibility for outputs enable members of the department to be measured on common performance criteria. Recognition of joint performance measures encourages members to coordinate their activities.
- Grouping encourages communication. Departmentation and sharing of common facilities usually bring employees into close proximity. This closeness encourages frequent communication among employees, enabling them to coordinate their tasks more effectively.[3]

FIGURE 9–1
*Six Hypothetical
Groupings of a Hospital*

KNOWLEDGE AND SKILLS:

Physicians — Nurses — Lab Technicians

WORK PROCESS AND FUNCTION:

Admittance — Diagnosis — Treatment

TIME:

8:00A.M.-4:00P.M. — 4:00P.M.-12:00P.M. — 12:00P.M.-8:00A.M.

PRODUCT:

Cardiology — Ear, Nose, & Throat — Internal Medicine

CUSTOMER:

Pediatrics — Women's Health — Geriatrics

LOCATION:

Downtown — Suburbs — County

PATTERN OF AUTHORITY

Decision-making authority is the right of a member to make decisions without having to get approval from another member of the organization. We will discuss authority in greater detail in Chapter 16. A pattern of authority becomes set in an organization when authority is distributed to all positions in the organization. The distribution of authority through positions can be patterned into a centralized or decentralized structure.

Centralized authority exists when decision-making authority is concentrated in the hands of higher-level managers. **Decentralized authority** exists when decision-making authority has been granted to middle and lower-level positions in an organization. In this respect, organizations can distribute their authority along a continuum with centralization at one end and decentralization at the other end.

With a centralized structure, decision-making authority is concentrated in the hands of higher-level managers.

Let us consider how managers of an organization may choose to have a centralized or decentralized structure. Suppose you have just bought a small store that sells premium wines from around the world. Six positions exist in the store: store manager, purchaser, stockperson, cashier, custodian, and accountant. You may decide to pattern authority in the store using a centralized structure. To do so, you announce that the purchaser, stockperson, cashier, custodian, and accountant must receive approval from the store manager for any decisions made. This may mean that the purchaser cannot close a deal to buy cases of vintage wine without first receiving approval from the manager. The stockperson would not be allowed to open cases of wine and shelve bottles until the manager decides to let her do so. The cashier is restricted from cashing checks without the manager's signature; the custodian must schedule repairs and cleaning at the request of the manager; and the accountant is unable to make payments without the manager's signature on the checks. Obviously, in this situation the store manager will be highly involved in the day-to-day operations of the store!

On the other hand, you may choose to decentralize the pattern of authority in the store. In this case, the store manager would grant greater decision-making authority to the other positions. The purchaser may be granted authority to close a deal on a wine buy without prior approval from the manager; the stockperson would have the authority to decide when wine is to be shelved; and so on. By decentralizing, the store manager is removed from the day-to-day decisions of each position and is allowed more time to check the environment and plan activities for the future. The choice of whether to centralize or decentralize decision making is discussed further in Chapter 16.

No organization is ever completely centralized or completely decentralized. Rather, organizations lean toward one end of the authority continuum more than the other. For instance, the manager of the wine store would probably apply conditions to the decision-making authority of the subordinate positions. Requiring the purchaser to get the prior approval of the store manager for purchases over $10,000 or requiring the cashier to get the manager's approval to cash a customer's check for over $25 are examples of techniques used to avoid relinquishing total control.

When should an organization centralize and when should it decentralize? This structural decision is based on several factors: the nature of the environment, the decision style of top managers, the type of strategy that the firm pursues, the skills and experience of lower managers, and the number of boundary-spanning personnel in the organization. For instance, in 1986 the management of Eastman Kodak Company announced that it planned to decentralize its research and development operations to achieve compatibility with technology and strategy. Under the reorganization, Kodak said it would divide operations of its research laboratories in Rochester and San Diego into six research centers. The research centers would be attached to separate business groups within the photographic and information management divisions. A seventh laboratory would be used for long-term research in new technologies, mainly unrelated to current products.[4] Later in this chapter, we will discuss specific contingencies and how they influence the authority structure in an organization.

SPAN OF CONTROL

Span of control is the number of subordinates reporting to a single supervisor. Narrow spans, or few subordinates reporting to a supervisor, allow for greater control over subordinates' activities. Wide spans, or many subordinates reporting to a supervisor, make close supervision difficult. However, wide spans have the advantage of reducing costs by reducing the number of supervisory positions in the organization.

Figure 9–2 illustrates two approaches for structuring positions in the previously discussed wine store using wide and narrow spans of control. An organization that has narrow spans of control is referred to as a **tall organization,** since it requires increased levels of management. In our example, the store manager at the top level directly supervises the accountant and

FIGURE 9–2

Two Approaches for Structuring Span of Control in a Wine Shop

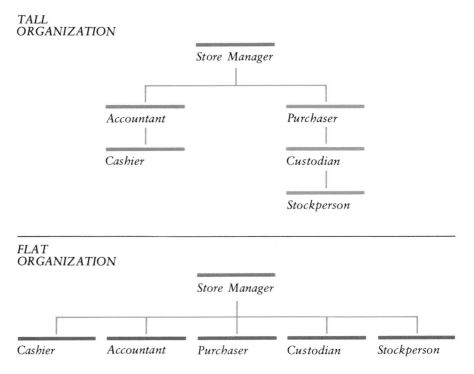

TALL ORGANIZATION

Store Manager

Accountant   Purchaser

Cashier   Custodian

Stockperson

FLAT ORGANIZATION

Store Manager

Cashier   Accountant   Purchaser   Custodian   Stockperson

the purchaser. The accountant directly supervises the cashier, the purchaser supervises the custodian, and the custodian supervises the stockperson. Hence, three levels of management have been set up in a store with a total of six positions. A **flat organization** has wider spans of control and thus fewer levels of management. Using the wine shop example again, the cashier, accountant, purchaser, custodian, and stockperson report directly to the store manager. Thus, only one level of management has been set up: the store manager.

The wine store provides an example of how the span of control can be adjusted and readily understood in a small firm. Imagine structuring an organization that has 1,000 or 10,000 or over 100,000 employees, as many multinational corporations do! A decision to reduce or expand by one the span of control in a large company can have an enormous impact on organizational costs (as well as on the control of activities). Management in Action 1 shows a growing trend among many U.S. corporations to reduce costs through the elimination of middle-management levels. This "flattening" of the organization will certainly reduce costs by saving on salaries and fringe benefits, but it may increase uncontrolled activities.

Is there an optimum span of control? This question has been of major concern to many managers and researchers. Classical theorists recommended a narrow span of control, contending that managers cannot effectively watch the activities of more than six or seven subordinates at one time. V. A. Graicunas (1933) noted that managers must not only control activities of a subordinate in a direct one-to-one relationship, but must also control the relationships that exist among the subordinates themselves. As each subordinate is added to the group, the number of relationships to control grows geometrically and can easily exceed the manager's ability to control activities among subordinates effectively. This view has received additional support from George A. Miller (1956), who suggested that humans are unable to process information beyond the "magic number of seven, plus or minus two."

Other writers were to qualify a strict adherence to an optimum number of subordinates within a supervisor's span of control. Ralph C. Davis (1951), for instance, noted that the level of management will determine the number of subordinates a supervisor can handle effectively. Wide spans of control are possible among lower levels of management and narrow spans of control effective among upper management.

The argument that an optimal or effective span of control exists has been questioned by other management scholars. James Worthy (1950) found that Sears, Roebuck and Co. used a span of control of 40 or more that worked very effectively. Subordinates were found to have greater job satisfaction and to be more productive because of the greater job responsibility they gained with looser controls. And J. M. Pfiffner and F. Sherwood (1960) noted that in California, the Bank of America had over 600 branch managers reporting directly to corporate headquarters!

Eight factors should be considered when determining a manager's span of control:[5]

- *Professionalism.* The more professional the subordinates are, the less supervision they will need.
- *Task uncertainty.* If tasks performed by subordinates contain frequent and hard-to-solve problems, closer supervision may be required to help the subordinate come up with solutions.

- American Telephone & Telegraph is laying off 24,000 employees at its Information Systems group; nearly one-third of them are in manage-

MANAGEMENT IN ACTION 1
MIDDLE MANAGER A FAVORITE TARGET OF THE JOB-CUTTER

ment.
- Ford is committed to trimming its management by 9,000 over the next five years.
- Since 1983, Eastman Kodak has reduced its worldwide work force from 136,500 to 124,000 and is not adding to its management ranks.

These events, multiplied many times throughout American industry, demonstrate the new plight of middle managers. Middle managers, the staff people long thought essential to a smooth-running corporate operation, are becoming increasingly expendable because of the rapid increase in office automation and a new corporate emphasis on pushing decision making far down into the operations.

Nowadays, companies want managers who contribute directly to the value of the enterprise through research, product development, manufacturing, and sales. That shift spells trouble for managers whose expertise lies in administration or staff support. Quinn Mills, a Harvard Business School professor who consults for International Business Machines, General Motors, and Bethlehem Steel, says: "Companies simply can't afford to carry people who don't directly contribute to the bottom line. If they reorganize, they can push middle-management functions lower down into the work force and save a good deal of money."

The reason? "Many times, middle management and clerical groups are involved in work that doesn't add value to the product. In international competition, jobs that don't add value to the product are not needed," says Peter C. Van Hull of Arthur Andersen Co.

The idea is to renew a focus on the core elements of the enterprise—design, manufacture, and sales—and to eliminate the managerial redundancy that was once key in assuring that top management edicts were followed. Gone are the days of "checkers checking checkers checking checkers."

Source: Michael Schrage and Warren Brown, "Middle Manager a Favorite Target of the Job-Cutter," *Milwaukee Journal* (December 1, 1985). © The Washington Post. Reprinted with permission.

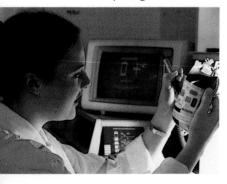

Subordinates with a high degree of professional training can perform their work without the need for tight controls.

- *Training.* The more training subordinates have, the more they will be able to perform their work without close supervision.
- *Physical dispersion.* Supervisors may have subordinates located in one plant facility, or subordinates may be scattered throughout the country. The more dispersed subordinates are, the narrower the span of control should be.
- *Required interaction.* The more interaction required between a superior and subordinate, the narrower the span of control should be.
- *Similarity of tasks.* When tasks among subordinates are similar, a wider span of control for the supervisor is possible.
- *Standardized procedures.* If uniform and specific procedures have been applied to the tasks performed by subordinates, the span of control can be wide.
- *Task integration.* When the tasks of subordinates require integration, a narrower span of control may be necessary.

These factors suggest the complex nature of deciding on a proper span of control for managers in an organization. Some factors may be contradictory when taken together, as in the case of the supervision of professionals (wide span) who may be performing dissimilar tasks (narrow span). Under these circumstances, managers must assess the relative importance of each factor and decide on a span of control that will fit the situation.

COORDINATION OF ACTIVITIES

The final structure that serves as a building block of organizations is the coordination of activities. **Coordination** is the linking of activities in the organization that serve to achieve a common goal or objective. As task activities are divided in the organization, managers must try to develop mechanisms that will link the tasks together in order for the desired goal to be accomplished. The result of such a linkage of activities is the creation of various forms of activity interdependence. The degree to which activities are interdependent can vary from low to high. The four configurations of activity interdependence are pooled, sequential, reciprocal, and team.[6] The type of interdependence among activities performed in an organization will largely determine the appropriate coordination mechanisms. Figure 9–3 diagrams each type of interdependence and the kinds of coordination mechanisms that are associated with each.

Pooled Interdependence

Pooled interdependence exists where there is minimal direct contact between individuals or groups performing an activity. Work does not flow between activities; rather, the results of activities are "pooled" at a higher level in the organization. For example, individual members of a planning staff may be assigned the task of preparing a forecast on a specific domain of the organization's environment. After each member has performed the task, the forecasts are submitted to the executive vice-president of strategic planning, who has the task of integrating the material from each report into a broader, long-range plan. Other examples of pooled interdependence exist for franchisees, such as McDonald's outlets. Each outlet performs its tasks independently of other outlets but gives or pools some revenues to corporate headquarters to pay for national advertising.

With this configuration, coordination is most readily achieved through rules and regulations, standardized procedures, direct supervision, and training programs. Rules and regulations serve as guidelines for the same activity performed separately. Thus, the vice-president of strategic planning can create the rule that each report is due on the 15th of the month, that a 10-year time frame is to be used in the analysis, and that forecasts will assume a prime rate of 10 percent. McDonald's is noted for having extensive rules and regulations governing the operations of each franchise. This enables the parent organization to coordinate national advertising for products and services that applies to all locations.

Sequential Interdependence

Sequential interdependence exists when the output of one activity becomes the input of another activity. This form of interdependence characterizes a typical assembly line where one worker installs the axle on an automobile and the next worker places the wheel rim on the axle. Sequential interdependence can also operate at the plant level, with one plant manufacturing the axle and wheel rim and shipping them to another plant for assembly. In either case, the activity of one worker or plant cannot be conducted until another worker or plant has completed its activity.

Coordination in sequential interdependence is attained through standardization, with emphasis on the use of plans and schedules. Setting deadlines, establishing performance targets, and identifying linkages between activities are

FIGURE 9–3

Interdependence and Its Relationship to Coordination Mechanisms

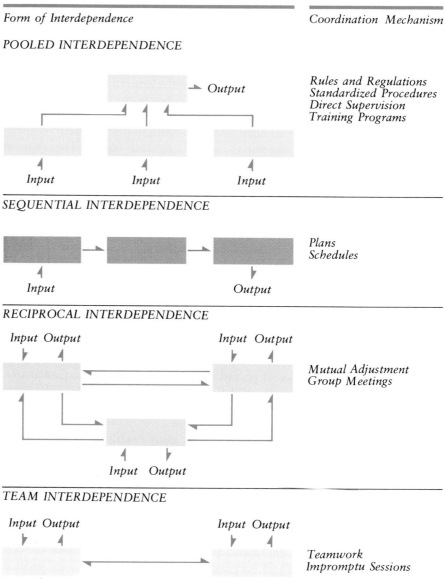

Form of Interdependence

POOLED INTERDEPENDENCE

Rules and Regulations
Standardized Procedures
Direct Supervision
Training Programs

SEQUENTIAL INTERDEPENDENCE

Plans
Schedules

RECIPROCAL INTERDEPENDENCE

Mutual Adjustment
Group Meetings

TEAM INTERDEPENDENCE

Teamwork
Impromptu Sessions

Coordination Mechanism

all critical managerial decisions which must be made before members or units engage in the work process. Sequential interdependence, therefore, requires managers to spend time planning for an effective level of coordination.

Reciprocal Interdependence

When units provide each other with activity inputs, **reciprocal interdependence** exists. For example, a legal department in a savings and loan may review applications from borrowers that have been submitted to the loan department. After an application has been reviewed, it is sent back to the loan department so that the request or denial of the loan can be processed. The output of the loan department becomes the input for the legal department and the output of the legal department becomes the input of the loan department. There is a two-way flow between departments.

To coordinate the activities of units engaged in reciprocal interdependence, mutual adjustment is required in addition to standardization of plans and schedules. Mutual adjustment is the process of direct communication and joint decision making among the members or units involved in the task activities. While rules and regulations, direct supervision, training, planning, and scheduling help to smooth the coordination among units, not all the problems that result from high levels of interaction between units can be anticipated. Hence, it is important that the linkages between activities are continually adjusted through direct communication to facilitate effective task completion.

Team Interdependence

The most intense form of interdependence results when the completion of activities requires teamwork. **Team interdependence** exists when work is interactive, or acted on jointly by members of different groups or units rather than simply being transferred back and forth. Team interdependence is most commonly used when an activity cannot be broken down easily into distinct tasks because there is uncertainty about what tasks have to be performed to accomplish the goal. Basic research in space exploration, cancer research, and new product development often require the use of team interdependence.

Teamwork is the most important method of coordination in team interdependence. Direct contact among activity participants can be accomplished through regularly scheduled meetings, impromptu sessions, and informal get-togethers. Therefore physical separation of participants makes coordination through teamwork difficult to achieve.

DESIGNS OF ORGANIZATIONS

Organizational structures provide the basic building blocks for the overall design of an organization. Managers can combine various structures to create the design they believe will enhance the accomplishment of goals. First, we will identify the four designs most frequently used by managers to structure their organizations. We must recognize that each design is only a blueprint. In much the same way that building construction crews change blueprints to conform with land and weather conditions, managers will be required to make changes in design to accommodate specific or unusual needs. In the last section of this chapter, we will identify several important contextual factors that influence a manager's choice of an organizational design. But first, let's examine the four basic organizational designs: functional, divisional, hybrid, and matrix.

Functional Design

The most basic organizational form is **functional design,** in which employees are grouped together in separate departments on the basis of common tasks, skills, or activities, as shown in Figure 9–4. All sales personnel are located in

FIGURE 9–4
Functional Design

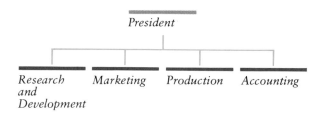

the marketing department; all engineers are located in the research and development department; all members performing accounting activities are located in the accounting department, and so on. The grouping of tasks or skills in one department enables the assignment of one senior manager to whom all members of the department report. In many organizations, this position is labeled vice-president.

Functional designs are most common in small to medium-size organizations, because they work best when there are few products and there is a need for a high level of work specialization. The functional design tends to centralize decision making at the top of the organization. Decisions about the coordination of activities across departments must be made at the top of the organization. Top management also serves as an arbitrator for problems resulting from interaction between departments. Spans of control within departments are usually wide, as supervisors are chosen for their extensive knowledge of the tasks subordinates have to perform.

Functional designs have a variety of strengths and weaknesses.[7] Several important strengths of the functional design are as follows:

- *Efficient use of resources.* By grouping common tasks together, economies of scale are possible. Each department can serve other departments efficiently by mobilizing problem-solving expertise quickly. Physical resources are also used efficiently because members who share facilities or machinery are in the same location.
- *In-depth skill development.* More intensive training of members is possible within departments because of the similarity of knowledge and prior skill development. Members have opportunities to specialize their skills to a greater extent by sharing information with colleagues in the department.
- *Clear career paths.* Employees have a clear understanding of job requirements and the path that will lead to promotion. By watching colleagues with similar backgrounds and expertise, an employee will learn quickly which activities are desired by the organization and which are not.
- *Unity of direction.* A centralized decision structure helps in achieving unity of direction, as top management provides coordination and control to the organization. Departments can be provided with goals and objectives that will support the overall strategy of the organization.
- *Enhanced coordination within functions.* Common backgrounds of members within a department facilitate communication and enhance collegiality. This in turn helps the coordination process, as members of the department are more likely to work as a team to accomplish the department's goals.

Weaknesses of the functional design include the following:

- *Slow decision making.* With decision making located at the top, senior managers may have an overload of decisions if multiple problems emerge in departments. As a result, decisions may be slowed or of lower quality, causing delays and additional problems in the organization.

- *Less innovation.* Members of a department may become focused only on departmental goals rather than on the overall goals of the organization. Ideas for new products, implementation of new technology, or suggestions for new methods of solving problems often get lost because of the need to communicate or to generate support across departments.
- *Unclear performance responsibility.* The successes and failures of an organization are an outcome of activities by all departments. However, the individual contribution of each department to the success or failure of a goal is not easy to pinpoint.
- *Limited management training.* While functional departments excel at training members to solve problems related to specific skills, they do poorly at training members to solve problems affecting the organization as a whole. Top management must have an understanding of how departments can be linked together effectively. Extensive training and experience in one department reduce the opportunity for developing broader management skills.
- *Poor coordination across functions.* Members of an individual department may feel isolated from members of other departments or even hostile toward them. As a result, they may be unwilling to support or compromise with other departments to achieve organizational goals.

Divisional Design

As organizations grow in size, the weaknesses of a functional design can begin to offset the strengths. This is particularly true when the growth of the organization is accompanied by an expanded product line, more customers, or geographic expansion. When this occurs, top management can create self-contained units, or divisions, that will design, produce, and market their own products. In a **divisional design**, all activities needed to produce a good or service are grouped together into an independent unit.

A divisional design sets up self-contained units responsible for designing, producing, and marketing a product.

Divisional designs can be distinguished from functional designs by their emphasis on grouping by organizational output. Functional designs are based on grouping by input, such as the tasks, skills, and knowledge required to perform an activity. The divisional design considers the output, such as the product, the customer, or the geographic location, and sets up for each output a self-contained unit composed of research and development, marketing, production, and accounting. The divisional design serves to increase coordination around a specific output. With this design, a firm that manufactures both farm equipment and recreation vehicles, for example, has a separate production department for each product. Figure 9–5 shows how a functional design can be changed into a divisional design.

A divisional design uses one of three patterns:

- **Product division.** In product division, each unit is responsible for a single product or a group of related products. Division by product is usually created when a product or group of products has a production process and marketing method that are different from those for other types of products in the organization (see Figure 9–6).
- **Customer division.** When the organization sells products to a diverse group of customers, customer division may be the proper design. A single customers who may differ from region to region in tastes and needs. By product may have diverse customers, or managers may believe there are groups of customers with special needs that have to be met. By instituting a customer division, a close relationship can be set up between a division and its customers. For instance, some computer firms have divisions for business, research, and home customers (see Figure 9–7).
- **Geographic division.** Large organizations that distribute their output nationally or internationally often develop divisions based on geography. Geographic division is helpful when one must locate facilities close to customers who may differ from region to region in tastes and needs. By

FIGURE 9–5
Changing a Functional Design into a Divisional Design

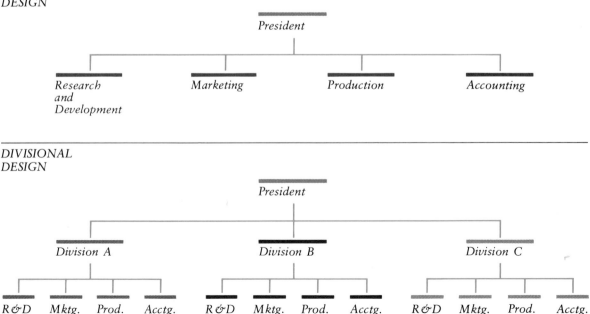

FUNCTIONAL DESIGN

DIVISIONAL DESIGN

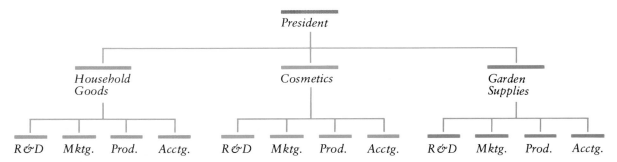

FIGURE 9–6
Divisional Design Based on Product Divisions

creating geographic divisions, the organization can improve coordination of activities within each region. Large retail grocery stores, for example, often create divisions by region. A manager in charge of the region can then coordinate the purchasing, warehousing, stocking, and advertising of food products that are commonly bought in each region (see Figure 9–8).

Divisional designs have several implications for organizational structures. They often make decision making more decentralized by pushing authority and responsibility down to the level of division or unit manager. Since divisions are based on unique output traits, managers at this level are more prepared to respond to problems than top management would be. Work can be specialized by output, and the span of control is reduced for department heads. Finally, coordination for the overall organization is achieved through pooling, as each division operates independently of other divisions. Coordination is achieved through each division's contribution to the corporation.

A divisional design has the following strengths:[8]

- *Adaptation to unstable environment.* Since each division is relatively small, it can adapt more readily to changes in product developments, customers, or regions. The decision to change a rule, for instance, does not have to be applied across all divisions, but can be made by the divisional manager and applied to a single division. Since divisional managers are closer to the action, they can respond more quickly to changes in the environment.
- *High customer satisfaction.* Customers receive more attention under a divisional design because there is more tailoring of the product to customers' needs and wants. Customers can more easily relay their ideas as well as their complaints about the product to someone empowered to respond.
- *High task coordination.* Employees feel a stronger identification with the product than with the specific department to which they are assigned

FIGURE 9–7
Divisional Design Based on Customer Divisions

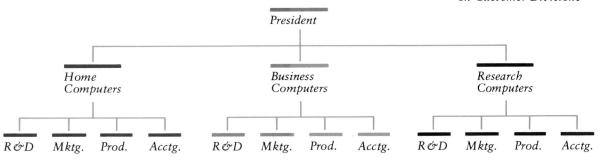

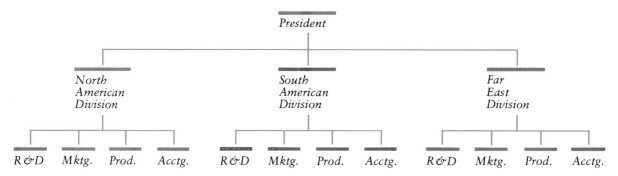

FIGURE 9–8
*Divisional Design Based
on Geographic Divisions*

within the division. As a result, there is more communication and team-work across departments in the division.

- *Clear performance responsibility.* Each division can be made a profit center, thus permitting specific objectives to be assigned. Top management can assess the performance of each division separately to determine where success and failure have occurred.
- *General management training.* Divisional managers learn how to coordinate and control activities among several departments within a division. In addition, managers can be shifted to different divisions to become familiar with other product lines as well as other operating methods. This provides strong experience for top management training.

The weaknesses associated with a divisional design include the following:

- *Inefficient use of resources.* One major problem of a divisional design is the dispersion of resources across divisions. In a functional design, for example, a sales force of 20 employees may be sufficient for selling five products. Sales personnel can shift readily from one product to another as supply and demand require. In a divisional design, four salespeople would have to be assigned to each of the five product divisions. However, some products may have cyclical demand, requiring eight sales personnel during the summer and two during the winter. The division would then be faced with either hiring eight full-time salespeople or requesting transfers from other divisions. Either way, the costs associated with hiring or moving personnel or providing additional training would be incurred.
- *Low in-depth training.* A decrease in the number of personnel reduces the opportunity for members of the division to specialize. Rather, they must focus on the basic tasks required to produce and deliver a product.
- *Focus on division objectives.* Coordination across divisions is often difficult. Members of a division become focused on the unit's objectives rather than on the broader goals of the organization. Often this results in direct competition between divisions. For example, a company with a detergent division and a paper towel division may have the detergent salesperson vying with the paper towel salesperson for shelf space in a supermarket.
- *Loss of control.* Divisions may become so different that top management may be unable to impose rules and regulations or establish plans and schedules across all divisions. Hence, the overall goals of the organization may be difficult to achieve.

Hybrid Design

In some instances, managers may find that a purely functional or purely divisional design is inappropriate for their organization. In practice, many corporations incorporate elements of both functional and divisional designs to reduce weaknesses and capitalize on strengths. A **hybrid design** includes divisional units as well as functional departments centralized and located at corporate headquarters.[9] For example, a company may choose to have the personnel department located at headquarters. The personnel department services the various divisions of the company by providing applicant screening, employee training, and maintenance of employee files for all divisions of the company, thus eliminating the considerable cost of maintaining separate personnel staffs in each division.

Banks are examples of organizations that frequently use hybrid designs, as depicted in Figure 9–9. Each branch operates as a geographic division under the centralized functional departments of personnel, legal, accounting and auditing, operations, marketing, and loan servicing. Personnel provides hiring and training services for each branch. Legal problems are channeled to the corporate office, which reduces the number of lawyers that have to be hired. Accounting and auditing helps each branch in the compilation of its financial performance records. Operations provides a central location for storing customer information and accounts. Advertising, such as informing consumers about interest rates, can be coordinated through one centralized marketing department. This means large savings of time and money since each branch will have the same interest rates, and managers of the branch do not have to contract independently with advertising sources. Finally, loan servicing located at company headquarters prevents wide differences in lending requirements across branches.

FIGURE 9–9
A Commercial Bank as a Hybrid Design

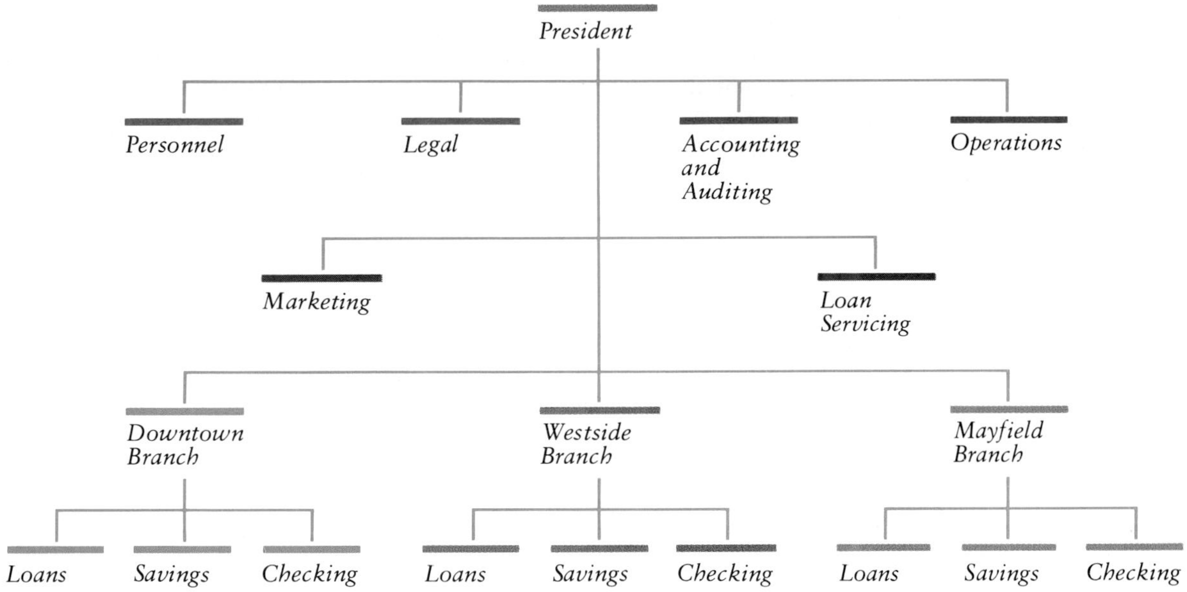

The strengths of the hybrid design include the following:

- *Simultaneous coordination.* Coordination across and within divisions can be achieved with a hybrid structure. Centralized functions enable coordination across divisions by setting up activities that direct each division toward a common purpose. Coordination is achieved within each division by locating functions together.
- *Integration of goals with objectives.* The hybrid structure provides autonomy for divisions to change their objectives based on unique situations or circumstances. However, the centralized functions serve to generate awareness of the overall corporate goals among divisions.
- *Adaptability and efficiency.* The divisional units can adapt to the opportunities and constraints of their environment. The functional units can focus on efficiency of operations. Thus, the hybrid structure can attain both adaptability and efficiency within one structural design.

The weaknesses of the hybrid design include the following:

- *Slow response to exceptional situations.* When a division faces a unique problem, resolution must be obtained from headquarters. This can result in delays and may also lead to inefficiencies, since the division itself may be better equipped than headquarters to handle the case.
- *Conflict between headquarters and divisions.* Though functional departments at headquarters do not typically have supervisory authority over divisions, they often try to influence divisional activities. Contradictory suggestions from different functional departments may hamstring decision making at the divisional level.
- *Administrative overhead.* Functional departments at headquarters have a tendency to grow as staff are added to help in the control of divisions. This can lead to excessive cost and duplication and result in bottlenecks in decision making.

Matrix Design

Most organizations use functional, divisional, or hybrid structural designs. However, not all managers believe that these designs satisfy the needs of their organization. A functional design promotes technical expertise, but it sacrifices efficient coordination across departments in the production of goods. A divisional design allows for the development of multiple products, but technical expertise may be underdeveloped. The hybrid design enables managers to set up some departments as functional to encourage technical expertise, while creating divisional departments to achieve coordination in the production of goods. Managers may, however, feel the need for an organizational design that generates technical expertise and product coordination simultaneously.

The matrix design may be the solution for managers who believe the other designs are inadequate. As shown in Figure 9–10, the **matrix design** implements functional and divisional structures simultaneously in each department. The result is a system in which employees in each department are supervised by two bosses having equal authority within the organization— the functional manager and the divisional manager. The functional manager is responsible for the work performed by specialists from the functional de-

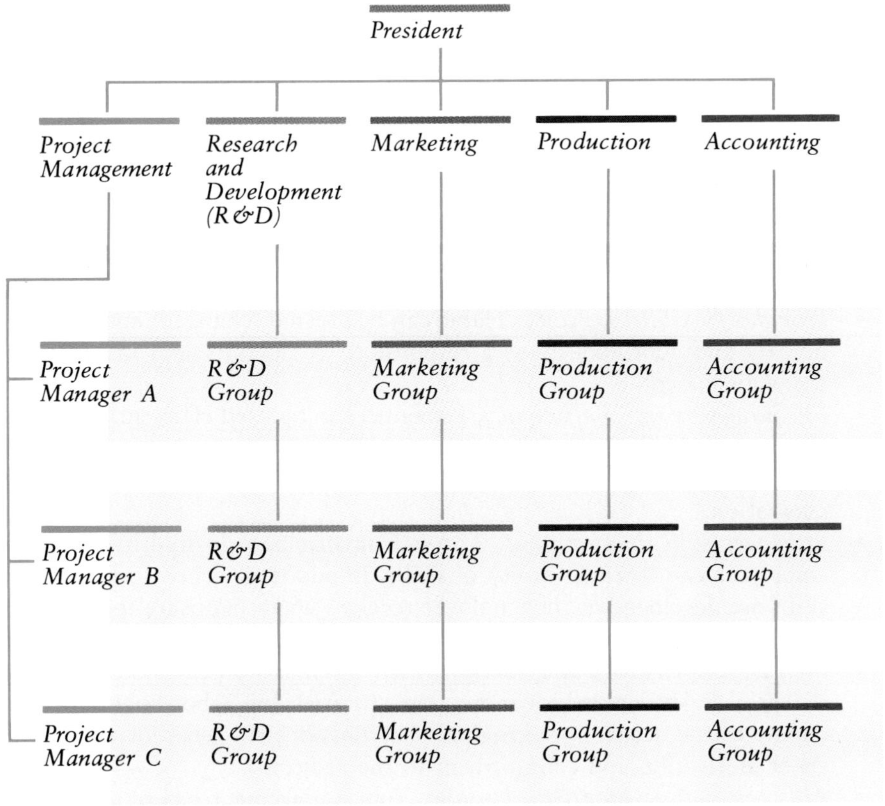

FIGURE 9–10
Matrix Design

partment. The divisional manager, or project manager, is responsible for integrating the activities of the specialists across functional departments.

The matrix design is a more complicated structural arrangement than the functional, divisional, or hybrid designs. For this reason, managers should consider instituting the matrix design only when the following conditions exist:[10]

- *Environmental pressures exist for a dual focus.* Competition, regulatory requirements, or consumer demand may require the organization to provide not only multiple and innovative products, but also products of high technical quality. This dual pressure requires that both product and technical quality be given equal attention through a dual authority structure.
- *Large amounts of information must be processed.* An unstable and complex environment often requires processing information that is extensive and rapidly changing. Separation of task responsibilities by product and technical expertise allows information to be sent more quickly throughout the organization.
- *Efficiency is needed in the use of resources.* The organization does not have the capabilities to assign separate facilities and personnel to each product. Matrix design allows for shifting personnel and sharing facilities across product lines as needed.

Matrix designs were first developed and implemented in the aerospace industry and by the National Aeronautics and Space Administration. Now the matrix design is commonly used in organizations such as CPA firms, hospitals, consulting firms, advertising agencies, insurance companies, banks, and law firms.

As noted, the matrix design is not for all organizations. It is a complicated design and should be used only when certain conditions exist. Even then, managers should be aware of the strengths and weaknesses of the matrix design. The strengths include the following:[11]

- *Allows demands from the environment to be met simultaneously.* Pressures for technical quality as well as multiple products and innovation can be addressed more efficiently and promptly.
- *Provides flexibility.* Project teams can be created, changed, and dissolved quickly and continuously as a response to complexity and instability in the environment.
- *Encourages resource efficiency.* Personnel can be used efficiently by rotating them through projects based on need or by assigning one individual to several projects. This reduces the need to hire multiple experts in the organization.
- *Enhances skill development.* Through involvement in multiple projects, employees can learn a variety of skills. In addition, general management skills are developed as the employee receives wider exposure to the multiple operations of the organization.
- *Increases motivation and commitment.* Emphasis on decision making at the project level provides more opportunities for subordinates to contribute to the decision-making process. This in turn generates higher levels of motivation and commitment to the project.
- *Aids top management in planning.* Top management has more time for long-range planning as the matrix design allows for day-to-day operational decisions to be delegated to the functional and project managers.

The weaknesses of the matrix design include the following:

- *Creates dual-authority confusion.* The assignment of two superiors to one subordinate leads to confusion and conflict. Recall that this structure violates the unity-of-command principle which stipulates that no subordinate should report to more than one superior. As a result, subordinates may receive contradictory directives or instructions. On the other hand, some subordinates may infer that the matrix is a form of anarchy and thus that they are free to do what they want.

The matrix design has been adopted successfully at Dow Corning Corporation.

- *Spawns power struggles.* The equal sharing of authority by the functional and project managers can lead to unproductive power struggles. The functional manager may emphasize technical quality at the cost of production delays. The project manager may emphasize meeting a schedule at the cost of lower technical quality. Efforts to resolve this situation can lead to intense conflict between managers.
- *Is time-consuming.* The matrix design requires large amounts of time because frequent meetings are necessary to integrate activities. This can result in long delays if meetings get bogged down in discussions not directly related to the project.
- *Requires interpersonal skill training.* Matrix designs require high levels of interpersonal interaction. Chances for success are greatly diminished if employees are combative, distrustful, or poor communicators. Thus, large investments in interpersonal training may be required.
- *Generates high implementation cost.* Achieving a permanent balance of power between the functional and project managers may take many years. Additional project managers and staff have to be hired and trained in order for the design to be successful.

The matrix design is just one of four organizational designs that managers can consider in the structuring of their organization. Pittsburgh Steel Company, Chase Manhattan Bank, Prudential Insurance, Monsanto, and Dow Corning are some notable corporations which have adopted the matrix design successfully. However, other firms—Citibank, Philips, and Texas Instruments—have adopted the matrix design only to abandon it after disenchantment with its results.

While functional, divisional, hybrid, and matrix designs are believed to be the most common options available to managers, perhaps a new design is on the horizon. Management in Action 2 describes what this new futuristic design may look like.

CONTEXT AND ORGANIZATIONAL DESIGN

How do managers know what structural design is best for their organization? While no single indicator is available that will answer this question, there are several important contextual dimensions that can help managers make their decision. These contextual dimensions are the environment, strategy, size, and technology.

No one contextual dimension need dictate the organizational design. Managers must weigh and consider how each contextual dimension fits with an appropriate organizational design. The remainder of this chapter will examine each contextual dimension and discuss how it influences the choice of a structural design.

Environment and Design

Tom Burns and G. M. Stalker (1961) provided the first extensive formulation of the relationship between an organization's structural design and the environment. After studying 20 industrial firms in England, Burns and Stalker

A new type of organizational design is appearing—the hollow corporation. As we look back through the evolution of corporate organization design, we first

MANAGEMENT IN ACTION 2
THE HOLLOW CORPORATION

had the simple owner-managed structure, then the functional, divisional, hybrid, and matrix designs. Now the network design, the so-called hollow corporation, is developing. Why this name? Akio Morita, chairman and co-founder of Sony Corporation of Japan, has this comment: "American companies have either shifted output to low-wage countries or come to buy parts and assembled products from countries like Japan that can make quality products at low prices. The result is a hollowing of American industry.

The United States is abandoning its status as an industrial power."

Can the network design succeed? Maybe, but it will require state-of-the-art technology in communication systems. In the traditional corporation, particularly those with functional, divisional, hybrid, and matrix designs, there is a vast infrastructure with several reporting levels and internal structures. The network design is very different, because it relies on a small central organization to coordinate the principal functions of distribution, marketing, research and development, manufacturing, and other essential functions performed in other organizations. You can visualize this by thinking of a small central core linked by telecommunications to other businesses, both foreign and domestic.

Source: "The Hollow Corporation." Adapted from March 3, 1986, issue of *Business Week*.

---

identified two forms of organizational design: mechanistic and organic. In a **mechanistic design**, which resembles a bureaucratic organization, the structures emphasized rules, specialized jobs, and centralized authority.

In an **organic design,** rules and regulations were minimal, tasks were more often done in groups than individually, and authority was decentralized. Members often had to gather information on their own and figure out what to do rather than rely on directives from superiors. Figure 9–11 summarizes the differences between mechanistic and organic organization forms.

Burns and Stalker also studied the environments of organizations with mechanistic and organic designs. They concluded that a mechanistic design was best suited to a stable environment. In a stable environment, tasks can be specialized and rigidly defined, as they are likely to be performed in the same manner. With a lack of environmental and thus task change, rules can be de-

FIGURE 9–11
*Mechanistic and Organic
Organization Forms*

Mechanistic	Organic
1. Tasks are broken down into specialized, separate tasks.	1. Employees contribute to common task of department.
2. Tasks are rigidly defined.	2. Tasks are adjusted and redefined through employee interactions.
3. Strict hierarchy of authority and control and many rules.	3. Less hierarchy of authority and control and few rules.
4. Knowledge and control of tasks are centralized at top of organization.	4. Knowledge and control of tasks are located anywhere in organization.
5. Communication is vertical.	5. Communication is horizontal.

Source: Adapted from *Innovations and Organizations* by Gerald Zaltman, Robert Duncan, and John Holbek. Copyright © 1973 by John Wiley & Sons, Inc. Reprinted by permission of John Wiley & Sons, Inc.

veloped and applied over time to maintain control over activities. With a reduced need for decisions at the task level, decision making can be centralized
with communication flowing from top to bottom in the organization.

Organic designs were discovered to be more appropriate in an unstable
environment. Tasks are completed through group efforts and are adjusted
and redefined to cope with demands made by the changing environment. Decision making is carried out by those close to the task, since they have a more
immediate understanding of problems. Communication is primarily horizontal as members exchange information about adjustments in tasks and changes
that have occurred in the environment.

The relationship between environment and organizational design discovered by Burns and Stalker received additional support from Paul R. Lawrence
and Jay W. Lorsch (1967). In a study of ten companies in the United States,
they found that the match between an organization's design and conditions
in the environment influences organizational performance. In addition, they
examined the designs of three departments—manufacturing, research, and
sales—of each company and concluded that the environment has different effects on the subsystems or units of the organization. That is, they discovered
that each unit of the organization developed its structural design based on its
own unique environment. Thus, a research department working on a high-
technology project may need an organic design because of the high degree of
change in the environment. The manufacturing department, on the other
hand, may need a mechanistic design, assuming that little change is required
in the way goods are produced.

Lawrence and Lorsch suggested that environmental factors will cause organizations to vary along two dimensions: differentiation and integration.
Differentiation is the extent to which the organization is broken down into
departments that differ by managers' orientations and structures. An organization that has many departments which operate differently has a high level
of differentiation. An organization that has few departments, each operating
similarly, has a low level of differentiation. **Integration** is the degree of collaboration that exists among departments. High integration occurs when
managers must coordinate their activities with other departments. Low integration occurs when departments can operate independently and coordination between departments is not required.

A complex and rapidly changing environment increases the need for differentiation and integration in an organization. In a complex environment
managers must create highly specialized departments to develop expertise
and handle environmental uncertainty. Increased integration is necessary because frequent change requires more information processing and adjustments
within and across departments.

Strategy and Design

After analyzing the histories of about 100 of America's largest organizations,
such as General Motors, Sears, and Du Pont, Alfred Chandler (1962) advanced the notion that "structure follows strategy." Chandler concluded that
an organization's strategy was closely related to its environment and that this
relationship influenced the structure of the organization. For example, a firm
that saw an opportunity to grow by expanding geographically would be re-

quired to alter its structure. This could mean a change to the production of a wider range of goods and a shift from a functional to a divisional structure.

In Chapter 7, three adaptive strategies were presented: defender, prospector, and analyzer. These three strategic types parallel and expand on the ideas of Chandler and others by suggesting which organizational designs are most appropriate for each strategic type. Each strategy has an administrative "problem" to be solved. The solution to the administrative problem for each strategy is presented in Figure 9–12.

Further efforts to understand the link between an organization's strategy and an appropriate structural design have been advanced by Henry Mintzberg. Mintzberg identifies five design configurations, each of which gives greater or lesser prominence to the following key parts of the organization:

- *Strategic apex.* Top management and its staff.
- *Middle line.* Middle and first-line management.
- *Operating core.* Members who perform tasks and activities that directly produce a good or service.
- *Technostructure.* Analysts such as engineers, researchers, planners, and accountants.
- *Support staff.* Members engaged in such tasks as maintenance, clerical, and mailroom services.

As shown in Figure 9–13 and discussed in the following sections, Mintzberg's formulation rests on variations in an organization's environment, strategy, age and size, and technology. His five design configurations

FIGURE 9–12

Design Solutions to Administrative Problem: Defender, Prospector, and Analyzer Strategies

Defender	Prospector	Analyzer
Strategy: To protect the organization's market.	Strategy: To seek high growth in the organization's market.	Strategy: To protect some markets while seeking growth in other markets.
Problem: How to maintain strict control of the organization to ensure efficiency.	Problem: How to help and coordinate numerous and diverse operations.	Problem: How to differentiate the organization's structure and processes to accommodate both stable and dynamic areas of operation.
Solutions: 1. Functional design with extensive division of labor and high degree of formalization. 2. Centralized control. 3. Simple coordination mechanisms and conflict resolved through hierarchy.	Solutions: 1. Divisional design with low division of labor and low degree of formalization. 2. Decentralized control. 3. Complex coordination mechanisms and conflict resolved through mutual adjustment.	Solutions: 1. Matrix design combining both functional departments and product divisions. 2. Moderately centralized control. 3. Extremely complex and expensive coordination mechanisms; some conflict resolution through project managers, some through hierarchy.

Source: Adapted from Raymond E. Miles, Charles C. Snow, Alan D. Meyer, and Henry J. Coleman, "Organizational Strategy, Structure, and Process," *Academy of Management Review* (July 1978): 546-562. Reprinted with permission.

	Simple Structure	*Machine Bureaucracy*	*Professional Bureaucracy*	*Divisionalized Form*	*Adhocracy*
Environment	Simple and dynamic, sometimes hostile	Simple and stable	Complex and stable	Simple and stable within diversified markets	Complex and dynamic
Strategy	Survival and growth	Efficiency	Effectiveness and quality	Efficiency and profits	Innovation and adaptation
Key Part of Organization	Strategic apex	Technostructure	Operating core	Middle line	Technostructure and operating core
Age and Size	Young and small	Old and large	Varies	Old and very large	Young
Technology	Simple	Machines, but not automated	Service	Divisible, like machine bureaucracy	Very sophisticated, often automated

Source: Henry Mintzberg, *The Structuring of Organizations*, © 1979, pp. 466-471. Adapted by permission of Prentice-Hall, Inc., Englewood Cliffs, New Jersey.

FIGURE 9-13
Dimensions of Context and Structure of Organization Designs

are labeled simple structure, machine bureaucracy, professional bureaucracy, divisionalized form, and adhocracy.

SIMPLE STRUCTURE

The simple structure is most common among small and young organizations run by an aggressive entrepreneur. Coordination of activities is maintained by a top manager who directly supervises employees in the operating core. The technostructure, support staff, and middle line are underdeveloped or absent. Decision-making authority is retained by the CEO, who is often the owner. Tasks tend not to be specialized. The overall strategy and goals of the organization are directed toward survival and growth. The organization is suited to a simple and dynamic environment with an emphasis on adaptability. Because of its small size, the organization can change quickly with the environment and thus outmaneuver powerful competitors. Examples of organizations with simple structures are new government departments, small automobile dealerships, and medium-size retail stores.

MACHINE BUREAUCRACY

The machine bureaucracy closely resembles Burns and Stalker's mechanistic design. The organization is large and old, and it divides tasks according to an assembly-line technology. Coordination is achieved through standardization of work processes. The technostructure and support staff are large in number because of the great need for engineers, market researchers, financial analysts, and systems analysts. Key decisions are made in the strategic apex with rigid patterns of authority. Spans of control are narrow. The machine bureaucracy is best suited to a stable and simple environment with goals directed toward increased efficiency. Steel companies, the U.S. Postal Service, prisons, and automobile manufacturers are examples of the machine bureaucracy.

PROFESSIONAL BUREAUCRACY

The professional bureaucracy is characterized by an operating core that is primarily composed of professionals, as is common in universities, hospitals, public accounting firms, social work agencies, and craft production firms. Coordination is achieved through standardization of skills. Usually services rather than tangible products are produced in a professional bureaucracy. The technostructure and middle line are often absent, though a large support staff is necessary to handle the organization's administrative affairs. Decision making is decentralized, as professionals in the operating core are powerful. Age and size can vary, while the environment is most often complex and stable. Goals are designed to achieve overall organizational effectiveness with an emphasis on quality of service.

DIVISIONALIZED FORM

The divisionalized form of organizational design achieves coordination through standardization of output. It operates in an environment that is relatively stable and simple, but diversified by product, customer, or geography. Middle managers, who are responsible for division activities, are large in number and make many decisions about their divisions. The organization itself tends to be old and very large. Goals direct activities toward efficiency and profit. Divisions tend to structure tasks and activities as in a machine bureaucracy. Examples come largely from Fortune 500 organizations. Procter & Gamble, Ford, Westinghouse, and IBM are divisionalized organizations.

ADHOCRACY

The final design based on Mintzberg's framework is the adhocracy, typically found in dynamic and complex environments. As in Burns and Stalker's organic design, coordination is achieved through mutual adjustment, avoiding specialization, formality, and centralized authority. Often, adhocracy takes the form of a matrix design with emphasis on activities in the operating core and technostructure. Task activities are highly sophisticated and technical as can be found in aerospace, computer software, and avant-garde film companies. Goals emphasize innovation and adaptation.

Mintzberg's five organizational designs provide unique insight into how various contextual and structural dimensions can be molded into compatible relationships based on a selected strategy. Managers can identify important contextual features, such as the environment, to guide them in the development of an appropriate organizational design. While Mintzberg's framework is a departure from the more traditional approaches to design discussed earlier, it does have elements in common with them. Adhocracy is similar to matrix design, divisionalized form is similar to divisional design, and machine bureaucracy is similar to functional design. Managers can also consider a simple structure in the early growth stage of their organization and a professional bureaucracy when efficiency and quality of services offered are the official goals of the organization.

Size and Design

Another contextual dimension that is important in understanding how to design an organization is size. The size of an organization can be measured in a variety of ways. Examples include market share, total revenues, number of employees, and scope of operations. Often we use the total number of employees in the organization as the basis for defining an organization's size. However, we should recognize that some organizations, such as an FM radio station, may garner millions of dollars in revenues with very few employees. A company that manufactures shoes may get less than a million dollars in revenue but have many employees. As a general rule, an organization's size should be measured against that of other organizations in the same industry. Thus, an FM radio station may be small or large only in respect to the size of other FM radio stations.

From many studies conducted on the relationship of organizational size and structural design, one conclusion seems to be consistent: Large organizations are more bureaucratic than small organizations.[12] As organizations grow in size, there are more pressures on managers to control and coordinate activities. The result is an increase in specialization, departmentation, and decentralization:[13]

- *Specialization.* As size increases, more specialized work practices are likely to result. An increase in the division of labor requires more supervision and coordination to make the parts of the organization work together.
- *Departmentation.* Growth in organizational size is usually accompanied by expanded departmentation. Large organizations often require additional specialties. These specialties become grouped into departments which also grow in size with the organization. Often departments become so large and unmanageable that they are broken down into several smaller departments, thus increasing departmentation in the organization.
- *Decentralization.* In large organizations, decision making is pushed downward and thus becomes decentralized. Top management is unable to make every decision in a large organization because of the long chain of command and the many decisions that have to be made regularly. Thus, routine decisions are made at lower levels in the organization. However, these decisions must often be made in conformity with explicit rules and procedures that set up boundaries in the decision-making process.

While organizational size is not a perfect determinant of organizational design, managers should be knowledgeable about the effects that size has on structure. This will enable them to understand the types of changes that may be necessary as the organization grows.

Technology and Design

Technology is a conversion process that transforms organizational inputs into outputs. Technology is not merely machinery, but also includes knowledge, tools, techniques, and actions that are necessary to complete the transformation process.[14] Thus, the concept of technology can be applied not only to manufacturing firms, but also to organizations that engage in information processing (e.g., universities) and service clubs (e.g., Rotarians).

Current management understanding of the relationship between technology and organizational design begins with the pioneering research of Joan Woodward (1965). Her research showed the way in which technology in manufacturing firms affected the overall design of the organization. Woodward and her colleagues studied 100 firms in South Essex, England, with the original intent of finding what universal principles of management were being applied. Through interviews, observation, and examination of company records, the team of researchers measured such characteristics as management practices and styles, manufacturing processes, size, economic performance, and structural dimensions.

At first, analysis of the data showed that no management principles were being applied consistently and that differences in their application had no relationship to economic performance. These results directly refuted classical management contentions that there is "one best way" to manage an organization. However, Woodward was not satisfied with merely discrediting classical management theory. Rather, she searched for an alternative explanation that would account for the variations. She discovered that technical complexity, or the firms' technology, accounted for the differences among organizations.

Three classes of technology were identified:

- **Unit, or small-batch, technology.** Organizations using unit, or small-batch, technology resemble job-shop operations that manufacture custom-made products. The production process is primarily in the hands of individuals who must provide knowledge and skill to the transformation process. Organizations using this kind of technology tend to be low in mechanization, and the transformation outcome cannot be predicted with certainty. Examples include makers of custom-built cars, custom-jewelry designers, and hairdressers.
- **Large-batch, or mass-production, technology.** With large-batch, or mass-production, technology, the transformation process is performed in an assembly-line fashion characterized by long production runs with standardized parts. Output can be inventoried because products are not designed to satisfy custom needs of the purchaser. Examples of companies that use large-batch technology are automobile manufacturers, large food canners, and soft-drink bottlers.
- **Continuous-process technology.** Continuous-process technology represents the most mechanized and automated transformation process. Machines handle the production process almost entirely; thus, output is highly predictable. Often, there is no starting and stopping of the production process, and quantity of output is geared toward storage for later sales. Examples would include petroleum and chemical refineries, large breweries, and electrical and nuclear power plants.

Woodward identified unit, or small-batch, as the least complex class of technology and continuous process as the most complex class. By studying the types of technology employed by the firms in her sample, Woodward found that structural dimensions were fairly consistent with each technology. Figure 9–14 presents some of the findings from her study.

Note that large-batch technology is best suited to a mechanistic design. Unit and process technologies are best suited to organic designs. Large-batch

Q: *This text discusses the five design configurations you identified in* The Structuring of Organizations. *You have suggested in later writings that a sixth design may be also appropriate for managers to consider: the "missionary." Under what conditions would you recommend that members of a firm adopt this design?*

A: In my writings on power in and around organizations, I added a sixth and also a seventh form. The "missionary" form coordinates by standardizing norms, in effect building a strong culture as many Japanese corporations do. The seventh, called the "political arena," describes the situation where organizational processes break down into political infighting, as when a group of Young Turks challenges the Old Guard. But I do not believe these to be very common in pure form, and so I prefer to see them as *forces* that act on organizations. One is the force for cooperation—pulling together—and the other is the force for competition—pulling apart. All organizations experience both; indeed, politics can be a positive force, bringing about change that may be blocked in other ways, while strong culture can be a negative force, turning people inward so that the organization cannot adapt to changes in its environment.

Q: *How powerful an effect do you see telecommunications having on the design of organizations?*

A: I see it as having little effect on the senior management levels. In fact, one recent study showed that despite personal computers, fax machines, and all the rest, the executives of the most successful international firms climbed aboard an airplane when they had to communicate seriously. At the operating levels, the effect can obviously be profound in certain kinds of organizations; in my opinion, companies that can automate much of their operating work tend to shift toward the adhocracy form, for reasons I spell out in my book on structure.

Q: *How will designs of a firm in the 21st century be different from designs of a firm in the 20th century?*

A: I prefer not to predict anything—there are too many discontinuities that no one can foresee. I believe, in fact, that most predictions are merely extrapolations of preferred trends. So let me do only that. If things continue the way they are going now, I believe we shall see more adhocracies and fewer bureaucracies, especially of the machine type. People are less tolerant of the latter, although they may get a surprise from the former—an adhocracy is not exactly the place for the good life, calm and relaxed.

Q: *Where should a manager start the process of selecting a new design if it is felt that the current design is inappropriate?*

A: "Selecting" suggests choosing one of the five configurations, or something similar. More and more, I believe managers have to *design* for the special needs of their own organizations, rather that slotting into a given structure. That means playing with all the forms—finding combinations that work for their organizations. To do this, managers should start with the fundamental needs of their own organizations, whether that be the central vision of a simple structure, the efficiency of a machine bureaucracy, the proficiency of a professional bureaucracy, the market concentration of a diversified form, or the innovative capacity of an adhocracy. Sometimes one of these needs will dominate and the organization will find a structure close to one of the configurations; at other times various needs will have to be attended to in rough balance, and then the organizations will have to design some kind of hybrid structure. The latter organizations may still be able to achieve harmony among the elements of their structures, but in their own particular ways. A student of mine once characterized this as playing "organizational LEGO" instead of jigsaw puzzle!

Henry Mintzberg (Ph.D., Sloan School of Management, Massachusetts Institute of Technology) is a Bronfman Chair at the McGill University Faculty of Management in Montreal, Canada. In his research and writing on management and organizations Professor Mintzberg's current focus is the process of strategy formation, the design of organizations as well as the impact of design on organizations, and the roles of intuition, insight, and inspiration in a world of "thin" management. Dr. Mintzberg is the author of The Nature of Managerial Work, The Structuring of Organizations, Power In and Around Organizations, *and* Mintzberg on Management: Inside Our Strange World of Organizations. *His articles number about seventy, including two* Harvard Business Review *McKinsey prizewinners, "The Manager's Job: Folklore and Fact" (first place, 1975) and "Crafting Strategy" (second place, 1988). In addition, Dr. Mintzberg became president of the Strategic Management Society in 1988 and is a fellow of the Royal Society of Canada. He now does all of his management training with experienced managers either in public seminars or within their own organizations throughout Europe and North America.*

FIGURE 9-14
Technology and Structural Dimensions in Woodward's Study

Structural Dimensions	Technology		
	Unit	Large Batch	Continuous Process
Number of management levels	3	4	6
Supervisor span of control	23	48	15
Manager/total employee ratio	Low	Medium	High
Number of "skilled" workers	High	Low	High
Formalized procedures	Low	High	Low
Centralization	Low	High	Low
Amount of verbal communication	High	Low	High
Amount of written communication	Low	High	Low
Structural design	Organic	Mechanistic	Organic

Source: Adapted from Joan Woodward, *Industrial Organization: Theory and Practice* (London: Oxford University Press, 1965).

technology requires more division of labor and workers with fewer skills than do unit or process technologies. As a result, more bureaucratic structures are necessary to coordinate and control activities. Structural dimensions, such as span of control, centralization, rules and procedures, and written communication, are also high in large-batch technology because of the standardized nature of the work. The use of more highly skilled workers, decentralization, verbal communication, and few rules and procedures allows unit and process technologies to be more adaptable to changing conditions.

The most important of Woodward's findings was the evidence that organizations applying designs complementing the technology were better economic performers than organizations that strayed from the associated structural design. This led Woodward to conclude there was a technological "imperative" in the design of organizations. That is, technology dictates the design of the organization.

Later research was to discount the technological imperative by noting that the firms in Woodward's sample were, on the whole, small and oriented toward manufacturing. Questions were raised concerning whether the technological imperative was applicable to large organizations and organizations that operated in service industries. Later research largely concluded that, while technology should be considered in the design of an organization, other factors, such as size, strategy, and environment, must be considered as well.[15]

IMPLICATIONS FOR MANAGEMENT

Organizational design has important influences on activities and achievement of goals. Managers must understand how the five basic elements of organizational structure influence the performance of the organization. Work specialization can be increased or decreased; departments can be created based on a variety of criteria; authority can be retained by top management or distributed to middle and first-level management; varying numbers of subordinates can be assigned to supervisors; and activities can be coordinated by several different methods. Managers must consider not only which structures are most effective for their organization but also how those structures interact with each other.

Organizational designs provide a general framework for structuring organizations and understanding how the structures relate to each other. The most basic design is functional, where departments are based on grouping employees by task similarity. As organizations grow in size, managers should consider changing their design to a divisional arrangement. Hybrid designs are useful when support staff is required in the organization but it is not necessary to have staff distributed across divisions. Matrix design offers managers a proper structure when environmental pressures exist for a dual focus, when large amounts of information must be processed, and when there is a need for efficient use of resources.

When thinking about a new design for your organization, consider the importance of such contextual dimensions as the environment, strategy, size, and technology. Remember that organic designs are most appropriate when the organization is in a complex and dynamic environment; when the strategy emphasizes adaptation and innovation; when the organization is small; and when the technology is of low or high complexity. Mechanistic designs, on the other hand, should be considered when the environment is simple and stable; when the strategy requires an emphasis on efficiency in production; when the organization is large; and when technology is large-batch.

KEY TERMS AND CONCEPTS

adhocracy
centralized authority
continuous-process technology
coordination
customer division
decentralized authority
departmentation
differentiation
divisional design
divisionalized form
flat organization
functional design
geographic division
hybrid design
integration
large-batch or mass-production
    technology

machine bureaucracy
matrix design
mechanistic design
organic design
organizational structure
pooled interdependence
product division
professional bureaucracy
reciprocal interdependence
sequential interdependence
simple structure
span of control
tall organization
team interdependence
technology
unit or small-batch technology
work specialization

QUESTIONS FOR REVIEW AND DISCUSSION

1. Discuss how each of the five basic elements of organizational structure serves to coordinate activities in an organization. How does each serve to control activities in an organization?

2. Under what conditions should managers consider restructuring their organization? Why do you believe "restructuring" became a buzzword for U.S. industry during the 1980s?

3. Identify and discuss the six criteria managers can use for grouping jobs and activities in an organization.

4. Is it possible for an organization to have a division that is simultaneously a by-product of product, customer, and location grouping? Explain.

5. When is functional design preferable to divisional design?

6. How do flat and tall organizations differ?

7. After you graduate and secure your first job, which type of organizational design do you believe would be best for you? Would you prefer to work within the same design throughout your career, or do you think another design would be more beneficial later on?

8. What are the key differences between the four methods of coordination through interdependence of tasks?

9. How does organizational context influence the choice of structure? Are some contextual variables more important than others? Discuss.

10. Based on the discussion of mechanistic and organic designs, how would you classify functional, divisional, hybrid, and matrix designs in terms of their similarity to these designs? How would you classify Mintzberg's designs using the same criteria?

CASES

9–1 DESIGNS FOR AVOIDING THE BLUES

Since International Business Machines Corporation's announcement that it would decentralize its management structure, management consultants have been predicting that other companies will follow. For many companies, it could be an expensive imitation.

In recent years an increasing number of companies have learned that pushing decision making down the ranks is a management luxury they can't always afford, especially in a competitive environment. The benefits can be undermined by staff duplication, marketing confusion, and out-of-control local units. That's been especially true as companies shed units and return to a single, core business.

As a result, many companies, including Hewlett-Packard Company and Minnesota Mining & Manufacturing Company, are in fact moving slightly in the other direction—either consolidating functions or reining in their divisional managers. "The worst thing is companies will decide IBM has done it, and that makes it right for them," says Robert M. Tomasko, a consultant with Temple, Barker & Sloan, of Lexington, Massachusetts. "But there's no right or wrong reason for everyone."

IBM, hoping to become more responsive to customers and spur innovation, shifted broad responsibility from corporate headquarters to six product and marketing groups that will have wide latitude in decision making. In addition, the company says that over the next couple of years "many thousands" of corporate staff members will be moved into positions that put them closer to customers.

Students of corporate history have plenty to look at in gauging the effectiveness of such a move. For the past 50 years, decentralization has come and gone several times as a management trend. And so its pitfalls are well known. The first is that it can lead to costly duplication. Hewlett-Packard, for instance, has since 1959 allowed its units to operate as minicompanies, each with its own manufacturing, marketing, finance, and personnel staffs. But about three years ago, the company decided that sometimes such duplication was too expensive.

For example, each of Hewlett-Packard's units manufactured circuit boards for its particular product—even though the boards are often interchangeable. This setup allowed unit managers flexibility and control over volume and quality. But the company says that that system was "redundant" and a cost it no longer could afford in the face of strong competition. To eliminate the overlap, the company has consolidated the circuit-board manufacturing at fewer sites, says Lewis E. Platt, executive vice-president of Hewlett-Packard's technical systems sector.

Stiffer global competition has forced companies like Johnson & Johnson, cited by management experts as a model of a well-run decentralized company, to make adjustments to trim duplication. Last year, it consolidated about 75 percent of the manufacturing of sanitary-protection products in Europe into a single plant in Germany. The products had been made at plants run by previously autonomous units. But as more and different types of sanitary-protection products were developed, a spokesman says, the company could no longer afford installing in each plant the necessary sophisticated machinery. "To compete with the products consumers want, we can't afford to manufacture locally," a company spokesman says.

Companies have also found that small, decentralized sales forces can be inefficient when dealing with large customers. 3M used to sell products like stethoscopes, elastic bandages, scrub brushes, and plastic hospital drapes out of two different medical-products divisions. That worked well when individual doctors made buying decisions, because 3M's slew of sales agents could contact each one and tout the products' features. But when buying decisions began to be made by hospital groups, 3M's decentralized sales strategy became inefficient. Hospitals were more interested in price and bulk purchases, and they preferred buying from one sales representative rather than dealing with sales agents from two divisions. So the company merged the two divisions in 1984. "We can now offer bundles of products to large hospital groups and have fewer people in the field," says Jerry E. Robertson, executive vice-president, life sciences sector.

Another problem with decentralization has arisen when companies find that their units are competing with each other. While that may spur innovation and aggressiveness at some companies, sometimes it leads to confused customers. Hewlett-Packard, for instance, had at least three autonomous divisions making different—and incompatible—computers aimed at the professional and office markets. "The fact is, those products were being sold competitively against one another by the various divisions," a spokesman says. "Customers were telling us we didn't have a coherent strategy." So last year the company stripped the divisions of their autonomy, placing them under one group, reporting to one manager. Among the first changes: Products were made technologically compatible.

Companies that have decentralized also have found that managers tend to make decisions in the best interests of their units, but that doesn't always coincide with what's best for the corporation. John Hoffman of Cresap, the consulting arm of Towers Perrin Company, says it's common to find "an operating unit taking care of its short-term needs at the expense of the corporation's long-term needs." For example, he says, a chemical division looking to pump up immediate profits sells its product to an outside customer at a price higher than it could have gotten from a sister division. But the corporation ultimately loses because the sister division would have made even higher profits by adding greater value to that product.

Wall Street firms in particular have been plagued by maverick units, with headquarters exercising little oversight, says Robert B. Lamb, a New York University management professor. "There were a number of prima donnas who were able to create their own departments, expand their staffs on their own, decide their own capital-risk exposure and, because they were so successful, the corporate parent was reluctant to monitor," he says.

Some companies have the opposite problem with decentralization: It fails because managers prefer the security of corporate control. They are therefore reluctant to embrace the newfound freedom. As part of a decentralization plan begun in 1984, for example, many managers at TRW Inc. are required to submit financial forecasting and reporting plans only once a year instead of monthly. But some managers are resisting, continuing to require their subordinates to submit the plans more frequently, says Howard Knicely, TRW's vice-president for human relations. "To get them to get rid of that detailed financial reporting is a tough sell," he says. As a result, employees are tied up with providing unnecessary information.

Despite all the problems, however, nobody thinks decentralization will go away— if only because of the image it presents. "Nobody wants to admit to being centralized," says Jay Lorsch, a Harvard Business School professor. "The American feeling is it's good to let people make decisions and be autonomous."

Source: Reprinted by permission of *The Wall Street Journal*, © Dow Jones & Company, Inc. (February 19, 1988). All Rights Reserved Worldwide.

1. What are the pros and cons that managers give for decentralization? How do these compare with the advantages and disadvantages of the divisional design discussed in the chapter?
2. In view of the problems of decentralization identified in the case, is there an alternative design these companies should consider? Explain.
3. Which do you consider to be the most important factor that encourages managers to consider the restructuring of their company: the environment, strategy, size, or technology?

9–2 A NEW WAY TO INSURE SUCCESS

Thanks to a sweeping change in the way it organizes its offices and employees, an unassuming, nonprofit insurance company has suddenly discovered celebrity. Over the past two years, Aid Association for Lutherans (AAL) has been moving a sizable portion of its work force into "self-managing work teams"—doing more, by some estimates, than any other service-sector employer in the nation to give its lowest-level employees more responsibility on the job.

"They're the best example we know of in the country of this kind of a change taking place," said Joan Sickler, a vice-president at the Work in America Institute, a workplace think tank in Scarsdale, N.Y. "They have done a superb job at changing their organization."

Employees at AAL, once assigned specific functions, now share a broader range of duties as part of work teams. The change resembles the change occurring on some U.S. factory floors as more blue-collar workers form teams whose individuals can perform a variety of assembly tasks instead of continually attaching the same part to the same product as it goes by on the line.

Where life-insurance underwriters at Aid Association for Lutherans worked separately from the employees who entered a policy on the association's books, for example, the two now may work together. They also may be cross-trained in each other's jobs, and in the jobs of other team members. Each team serves a geographic area within one of four national regions.

Under the old arrangement, one of the company's 1,900 field representatives around the country would get bounced from department to department for help with questions, new policy applications, and changes in existing policies. Now a single team, working regularly with the agent, can handle life-insurance underwriting, issue a life policy, oversee quality control and premium calculation, and handle health-insurance matters and a variety of other tasks.

The changes have helped the association boost productivity while trimming the size of its work force. Comments from employees suggest that the changes have made their jobs more interesting, if sometimes more stressful. "I'm an independent person," said Diane Hesse, a life-insurance processor, during a panel discussion last month as part of a daylong seminar AAL held for managers from other firms. "I wouldn't want to go back to my manager standing over me." But "it hasn't been easy for people who weren't trained as managers," said Mary Harp-Jirschele, director of public information for the association. "And now everyone's a manager."

Trouble often gives rise to this sort of sea change. But David Sielaff, second vice-president of insurance product services at AAL, said the organization wasn't in trouble when it decided to reshape itself—at least not in the conventional sense.

As AAL moved through the 1980s, however, top executives realized the company faced growing competition, a changing market, massive changes brought on by advances in computer technology, and evolving government regulations. It also faced the happy challenge of absorbing an unexpected surge in sales of an immensely popular new line of life insurance, called Horizon, begun in 1982.

The company retained a management consultant and interviewed 200 employees at all levels. Their comments were blunt: "We have become over-managed and under-led," said one. "We're just another big company," said another. "Nothing but stress."

AAL set a goal of trimming 250 jobs from its work force of 1,500 over five years through attrition and early retirements; there have been no layoffs. The cuts focused on layers of middle management. To make that possible, while also improving productivity and the work environment, AAL pushed more of the day-to-day decisions to the lowest possible level. In the insurance services division alone, with 425 employees, the number of supervisory positions was cut to 22 from 62, said Jerome Laubenstein, vice-president for insurance product services.

Giving employees more authority has already cut the time for processing insurance applications, claims, and other paperwork from a high of 21 days to a low of 5. Teams manage their own work flow, schedule their own hours, and set goals and objectives. Individual members also take responsibility for learning new jobs. And AAL aims to have team members review each other's performance, decide how to distribute bonus pay, and play a role in hiring new team members as openings occur.

"We've learned that you can trust people," said Tim Schwan, an AAL regional manager.

Source: Reprinted by permission of *Milwaukee Journal* (April 16, 1989): Business Section, 1D, 4D.

1. Why does top management at Aid Association for Lutherans see a need to change the way decisions are made?
2. What is the old method for achieving task interdependence? How does this method differ from the new approach?
3. Do you believe management at Aid Association for Lutherans should consider a matrix organization? What strengths and weaknesses might the company acquire by becoming a matrix organization?

ENDNOTES

1. G. Slutsker, "Some Call It Restructuring," *Forbes* (September 16, 1985): 40.
2. H. Mintzberg, *The Structuring of Organizations* (Englewood Cliffs, NJ: Prentice-Hall, 1979), 108-111.
3. Ibid., 108.
4. *Wall Street Journal* (February 28, 1986).
5. C. W. Barkdull, "Span of Control—A Method of Evaluation," *Michigan Business Review* 15, no. 3 (May 1963): 27-29, and H. Steiglitz, *Organizational Planning* (New York: National Industrial Conference Board, 1966), 15.

6. J. D. Thompson, *Organizations in Action* (New York: McGraw-Hill, 1967), 51-65, and A. H. Van de Ven, A. L. Delbecq, and R. Koenig, Jr., "Determinants of Coordination Modes Within Organizations," *American Sociological Review* 41 (1976): 322-338.

7. R. Duncan, "What Is the Right Organization Structure? Decision Tree Analysis Provides the Answer," *Organizational Dynamics* (Winter 1979): 59-80.

8. Ibid.

9. S. A. Allen, "Organizational Choices and General Management Influence Networks in Divisionalized Companies," *Academy of Management Journal* 21 (1978): 341-365.

10. S. M. Davis and P. R. Lawrence, *Matrix* (Reading, MA: Addison-Wesley, 1977), 11-24.

11. K. Knight, "Matrix Organization: A Review," *Journal of Management Studies* (May 1976): 111-130, and Duncan, "What Is the Right Organization Structure?"

12. J. R. Kimberly, "Organizational Size and the Structuralist Perspective: A Review, Critique, and Proposal," *Administrative Science Quarterly* 21, no. 4 (1976): 571-597.

13. P. M. Blau and R. A. Schoenherr, *The Structure of Organizations* (New York: Basic Books, 1971), and D. S. Pugh and D. J. Hickson, *Organization Structure in Its Context: The Aston Programme I* (Lexington, MA: D. C. Heath, 1976).

14. C. Perrow, "A Framework for the Comparative Analysis of Organizations," *American Sociological Review* 32 (1967): 194-208.

15. D. Gerwin, "Relationships Between Structure and Technology," in *Handbook of Organizational Design 2*, ed. P. C. Nystrom and W. H. Starbuck (London: Oxford University Press, 1981), 3-38.

REFERENCES

Burns, T., and Stalker, G. M. 1961. *The Management of Innovation.* London: Tavistock.

Chandler, A. D., Jr. 1962. *Strategy and Structure: Chapters in the History of the American Industrial Enterprise.* Cambridge, MA: MIT Press.

Davis, R. C. 1951. *Fundamentals of Top Management.* New York: Harper & Row.

Graicunas, V. A. 1933. "Relationships in Organizations." *Bulletin of the International Management Institute* 7: 39-42.

Lawrence, P. R., and Lorsch, J. W. 1967. *Organization and Environment.* Homewood, IL: Richard D. Irwin.

Miller, G. A. 1956. "The Magical Number Seven, Plus or Minus Two: Some Limits on Our Capacity for Processing Information." *Psychological Review* 63: 81-97.

Pfiffner, J. M., and Sherwood, F. 1960. *Administrative Organization.* Englewood Cliffs, NJ: Prentice-Hall.

Woodward, J. 1965. *Industrial Organization: Theory and Practice.* London: Oxford University Press.

Worthy, J. C. 1950. "Organizational Structure and Company Morale." *American Sociological Review* 15: 169-179.

Staffing the Organization

CHAPTER 10

After studying this chapter, you should be able to:
- Discuss the elements of staffing.
- Explain the steps in human resource planning.
- Identify key laws influencing staffing.
- Identify approaches to selection and hiring and explain their relative benefits and problems.
- Describe the elements of placement.
- Explain why training is needed and identify training methods.
- Discuss why performance appraisal is important to the firm and how employee performance can be measured.
- Describe how job worth, labor market conditions, pay systems, and employee performance determine levels of employee compensation.

Staffing involves bringing new people into the organization and making sure they serve as valuable additions to the work force. It is a vital part of personnel management. The aim of staffing is to match, or align, the abilities of the job candidate with the needs of the firm.

In staffing, management is faced with a balancing act. As one option, it can work especially hard to recruit, select, and place individuals who are very well qualified to meet the firm's needs. The alternative is to put less emphasis on these processes and focus instead on training and development. Figure 10–1 illustrates this balancing act.

Careful selection and placement certainly have their advantages. The new employees can be productive immediately, showing results today rather than in six months at the conclusion of a training program. SEDCO and other offshore drilling companies like to hire undersea welders who are already competent and can do their jobs safely. Individuals are hired because they already have proven skills acquired through years of experience; the firm does not have to gamble that they will learn them properly. Brokerage companies, such as Prudential-Bache, offer high bonuses to brokers who come from other companies. These brokers already have the needed skills and are of proven ability; Prudential-Bache doesn't have to worry about hiring a dozen brokers and having only three or four work out.

On the other hand, a focus on training and development also has advantages. For one thing, people can be hired at lower rates of pay if they come to the firm untrained. Also, the training and development can be tailored exactly to the company's needs. Westinghouse, for example, hires students with degrees in advertising, but the company completely retrains them in a training institute. Ford, Bell Telephone, and even McDonald's have similar training programs for employees who need special skills that cannot be obtained anywhere else. In addition, people trained by a firm often develop strong loyalties to it.

The choices made in resolving this balancing act depend upon careful consideration of human resource objectives, legal constraints, the nature of internal and external labor supplies, and other factors. Even after such choices are made, the firm is faced with the continuing need to evaluate employee performance and to determine equitable levels of employee compensation.

In this chapter we will first consider human resource planning and will then address laws influencing staffing. Next, we will discuss the four basic stages of staffing: recruiting, selection and hiring, placement, and issues of performance appraisal and employee compensation.

HUMAN RESOURCE PLANNING

It would be unthinkable for a company to fail to plan for its future needs for materials, plant capacity, or financing. Similarly, firms must plan for their human resource needs. **Human resource planning** is the process of analyzing an organization's human resource needs under changing conditions and developing the activities necessary to satisfy those needs.[1] Human resource planning requires consideration of where the firm is in terms of staffing and

Recruitment, Selection, and Placement	Training and Development	**FIGURE 10–1** *Balancing the Staffing Options*

Fitting the New Employee and Job Together

Making Sure That Employees Grow with Their Jobs

where it wants to be. Then, strategies can be developed to move from the current to the desired situation. This process requires the following steps:

1. *Specification of human resource objectives.* These objectives flow from the larger organizational goals discussed in Chapter 5.
2. *Inventory of current internal personnel.*[2] Current employees not only accomplish today's tasks but also serve as the human resource base of the future. For this reason, a clear picture of the current personnel status is a necessary step in human resource planning. An inventory of current personnel might include such information as numbers of people in various positions, their skills, time in the organization, performance records, and wage levels. Other useful internal supply information would include turnover and absenteeism rates by position and movement rates between positions.
3. *Estimation of external labor supplies.* Such developments as terminations, retirement, organizational growth, and changes in the organization's focus, as well as the simple wish to bring in "new blood," may require that organizations look beyond current internal labor supplies. This requires identification of labor markets and of labor supply and wage rates within those markets.
4. *Consideration of current and projected organizational and job design.* For instance, how will the size of the organization and its units change over time? How will the required skill mix be altered? Answers to these questions, in turn, may depend upon forecasts of economic conditions, consumer tastes, and other factors.
5. *Development of a forecast of labor demand.* This forecast, based on information gathered in steps 1–4, is developed in terms of the number of people required, the qualifications required, and the time at which they will be needed. For instance, it might be determined that an additional 35 salespersons with particular expertise will be needed in five years. There are many sophisticated models available to provide guidance at this step.
6. *Development of human resource strategies.* Once future supply and demand are estimated, alternative strategies can be devised to equate the two. These may involve, for instance, the manipulation of such variables as hiring rates and policies, promotion and transfer rates and policies, and termination policies. Again, use of mathematical models may ease the development and testing of alternative strategies.

LAWS INFLUENCING STAFFING

The legal environment has a major impact on staffing. Laws specifying required, acceptable, or prohibited activities place many constraints on recruiting, selection, placement, and other staffing practices. We will review key legislation dealing with employee health, safety, and security; with employment discrimination; and with labor unions.

Health, Safety, and Security

A substantial amount of legislation deals with various forms of employee protection. In this section, we will review statutes relating to working hours, working conditions, and benefits.

WAGES AND HOURS

The Fair Labor Standards Act of 1938 introduced both the minimum wage and the 40-hour workweek. At the time of passage, the minimum wage was set at 40 cents per hour. The law also said that workers must receive time-and-a-half pay for time spent on the job in excess of the 40-hour standard.

Not all employees are covered by the Fair Labor Standards Act. People in managerial, professional, or sales positions, for example, are not protected by the act.

CHILD LABOR

The Fair Labor Standards Act also regulates child labor. The minimum age for most jobs is now 16. The employment of 14- and 15-year-olds is restricted to a few types of jobs such as filing and sales. The range of jobs for children under 14 years of age is even more restricted: they are permitted only to deliver newspapers, work as actors or actresses, or hold selected farm jobs.

SOCIAL SECURITY

The Social Security Act, passed in 1935, established our social security system. The aim of the system is to provide a minimum guaranteed income to retired and disabled persons. Today, about one out of every seven people in the United States receives a social security check each month.

The social security system is funded by a tax on employees and employers. In 1989, employees were required to pay into the system an amount equal to 7.51 percent of their first $48,000 earned; employers were required to match that amount. The rate for self-employed persons was 15.02 percent on the first $48,000 earned, though a 2.0 percent credit reduced the effective rate to 13.02 percent. Currently, more than 90 percent of working people in this country pay into the social security system regularly. The average worker pays about the same amount in social security tax as in federal income tax.

UNEMPLOYMENT BENEFITS

Each state has a program for protecting people who lose their jobs through no fault of their own. These programs differ in cost and coverage, but they must all meet certain federal guidelines. Under these programs, employers pay a tax to the state—usually equal to 1 percent or less of the wage of each employee earning $1,500 or more during any single quarter of the year. Recently unemployed workers may then draw upon these funds for the duration of their unemployment, subject to certain restrictions.

In order to be eligible for unemployment benefits, people must have worked at least 12 weeks before losing their jobs. Those fired for poor performance, leaving the job voluntarily, or refusing to accept work for which they are qualified are not entitled to the benefits.

SAFETY AND HEALTH HAZARDS

The goal of the Occupational Safety and Health Act, passed in 1970, is to reduce the number of safety and health hazards in the workplace. The law established the **Occupational Safety and Health Administration (OSHA)** and gave the Secretary of Labor the authority to set health and safety standards for individual industries. Recently, OSHA has been considering the merits of expanding its monitoring of workers' exposure to toxic substances and of broadening testing for the medical consequences of such exposure.[3]

Employment Discrimination

It has been necessary for Congress to pass several laws that directly address the problem of employment discrimination. The Civil Rights Act of 1964, the Equal Employment Act of 1972, and the Civil Rights Restoration Act of 1988 are three of these laws. They make it illegal to discriminate on the basis of race, color, religion, national origin, or sex in hiring or promotional decisions. In 1988, the Justice Department ruled that an antidiscrimination law protecting the handicapped extends to employees with the acquired immune deficiency syndrome (AIDS) virus if they are in the federal work force or have jobs in programs receiving federal aid.[4]

Federal law prohibits discrimination against the handicapped in hiring and promotion decisions.

ENFORCEMENT PROCEDURES

The Civil Rights Act established the **Equal Employment Opportunity Commission (EEOC)**, which is responsible for enforcing federal law relating to job discrimination. The EEOC can take a firm to court if it violates the law. The more usual practice is to persuade the offending firm to change its policies and pay damages to any person discriminated against. When AT&T was charged by the EEOC with keeping women and minorities in low-paying jobs, the phone company agreed to change its policies and to pay 15,000 of its employees a total of $15,000,000 in damages.[5]

MAJOR PROVISIONS OF THE LAW

The Civil Rights Act and the Equal Employment Act have been strengthened by other federal legislation. Let's look at the most important parts of current federal law relating to discrimination:

- *Race, color, or national origin.* The law clearly states that it is illegal to discriminate on the basis of race, color, or national origin. There are no exceptions.
- *Sex.* In only a few cases is it legal to discriminate on the basis of sex. In such cases, it is the responsibility of the firm to prove that a woman would not be able to perform the job in question.
- *Appearance.* Many firms want their employees, especially those who deal with the public, such as salespeople and receptionists, to meet certain standards of appearance and grooming. Although there have been cases of "appearance" discrimination, business firms generally have the right to require their employees to meet appearance standards.
- *Age.* It is now illegal in most cases to force employees to retire before age 70. One exception is top executives with a planned retirement income of $27,000 a year or more. Some states now have laws prohibiting forced retirement because of age, period. Former President Reagan, the nation's oldest chief executive in the history of the United States, worked hard to see that such a law was passed on a national basis. The age law also specifically protects persons between the ages of 40 and 70 from age discrimination.
- *Handicap.* Every employer who has a contract with the federal government worth $2,500 or more must actively seek to hire and promote handicapped people. A handicapped person is defined as any individual with a physical or mental problem that limits the person's normal activities. However, the law does state that the handicapped person must be qualified to perform the particular job for which he or she is being considered.

EQUAL PAY AND COMPARABLE WORTH

The 1963 Equal Pay Act requires that men and women receive equal pay for equal work. What is important is not whether the job titles are the same, but that the content of the jobs is substantially similar. If a company pays men and women differently, it must prove that their jobs differ in terms of skill or effort required, responsibility, or working conditions.

Some people go further, arguing that there should be equal pay not only for equal work, but also for **comparable worth**; that is, if the work of a secretary is of equal worth to that of a carpenter, the pay should be the same. The concept of comparable worth is now being hotly contested in the courts. Ontario, Canada, passed a law in 1987, with a January 1990 compliance deadline, that requires public-sector organizations and private companies with 10 or more employees to restructure pay rates so that women and men are compensated equally for comparable work. It is predicted that the law will cause massive changes in salaries. As one example, a distribution firm is now paying its men who pick warehouse stock from bins $30,000 annually, while female typists are paid $18,000. Under the new law, the typists are expected to have salaries of at least $30,000. Firms are watching such developments closely.[6]

AFFIRMATIVE ACTION

Affirmative action is a legal requirement that employers must actively recruit, hire, and promote members of minority groups if such groups are underrepresented in the firm. That is, if the labor pool in a community is 15 percent black and 10 percent Mexican-American, then 15 percent and 10 percent of the labor force of a firm operating in that community should be black and Mexican-American, respectively.

Labor Unions

As discussed in Chapter 3, and as examples throughout this book make evident, labor unions are major forces influencing many firms. They give workers a source of collective power and may act as intermediaries between labor and management. They may influence wages and benefits and may constrain many management actions. As a result of social, economic, and legal changes, the roles of unions have evolved over the last 50 years and will doubtless continue to change. Although unions have experienced a decline in membership in recent decades, they remain powerful in many sectors and are taking steps to regain lost ground.

Early in this century, labor-management relations were generally unregulated. With the coming of the Great Depression, however, Congress passed laws that encouraged collective bargaining and tried to bring a better balance between management and labor. The major provisions of some of these laws are presented in the box on the following page.

RECRUITING

The first step in staffing is to put together a group of job applicants from which to choose. This step is called **recruiting**. No matter how employees are later selected, trained, and motivated, it is important to start out with a good group of applicants. The greater the number of applicants and the better their qualifications, the more likely the firm is to build a solid personnel base.

Sources of Applicants

Job applicants can be found in many ways. Six sources of applicants are presented in the box on page 307. These sources differ in terms of ease of use, cost, and the quality of applicants obtained.[7]

MAJOR LABOR LAWS

Norris-LaGuardia Act (1932). Until the early 1930s, employers could go to court to prevent organizing, bargaining, and striking activities. They could also force workers to sign "yellow-dog contracts"—a promise that they would not join a union if hired by the company. The Norris-LaGuardia Act outlawed these contracts and prohibited the courts from standing in the way of lawful union activities. The act strengthened the position of unions but did not deal with the rights of individual workers.

Wagner Act (1935). The Wagner Act, formally known as the National Labor Relations Act, recognized the right of employees to engage in union activities, to organize, and to bargain collectively without interference from employers. The act stipulates that when a majority of employees in a given work unit wants union representation, the employer must bargain collectively regarding wages, hours, and terms of employment. The act also established the National Labor Relations Board, which is responsible for conducting representation elections and for investigating charges of unfair labor practices.

Taft-Hartley Act (1947). The Taft-Hartley Act, also known as the Labor-Management Relations Act, restricted the power of unions, which some people felt had been given an unfair advantage in the bargaining relationship by the Wagner Act. Passed over President Truman's veto, the Taft-Hartley Act attempted to restore a balance between labor and management. Specifically, it said that employees were free to refrain from, as well as engage in, union activities; it recognized that both unions and employers are capable of unfair labor practices; it established the Federal Conciliation Service to provide help in negotiations when both parties request it; it outlawed the closed shop; and it gave the President the authority to halt a strike for 80 days if the strike posed a threat to national security. The act also allowed states to pass "right-to-work" laws. These laws prevent unions from negotiating labor contracts which make union membership mandatory.

Landrum-Griffin Act (1959). The Landrum-Griffin Act, also called the Labor-Management Reporting and Disclosure Act, was passed to combat corruption. Under the terms of the act, unions and management must provide the government with a variety of information concerning their activities. Unions must report their constitution and bylaws, administrative policies, and financial dealings. Employers must report any expenditures designed to prevent employees from organizing. The act also provided a Bill of Rights of Union Members, under which every union member has the right to nominate candidates for union office, vote in union elections, attend union meetings, examine union accounts and records, and seek relief in court if deprived of these rights.

Civil Service Reform Act, Title VII (1978). Executive Order 10988, issued by President Kennedy in 1961, established the right of government employees to be represented by labor organizations and to enter into agreements concerning working conditions. However, these employees were not given the right to strike, to demand that unsettled grievances go to arbitration, or to make demands concerning job security or economic matters.

The Civil Service Reform Act of 1978 replaced Executive Order 10988 and clarified the relationship between federal employee unions and the government. It set up a Federal Labor Relations Authority as an independent body to monitor labor-management relations in this area and required binding arbitration of unresolved grievances. However, government workers still did not have the right to strike.

The Realistic Job Preview

Most companies present overly favorable pictures of themselves and their job openings in order to attract job applicants. Partly as a result, many new employees are dissatisfied when they learn the "truth" about the company. Some may even quit after a short time there. To avoid this, some companies now use realistic job previews. The aim of the **realistic job preview (RJP)** is to give the recruit an accurate picture of what the company and job are like. For example, films of people on the job and uncensored comments of current employees may be used to acquaint new employees with the day-to-day reality of the job.

SOURCES OF APPLICANTS

Newspaper Advertisements. Newspaper and magazine advertisements are easy to use and bring in many applicants, but few of the applicants may be qualified.

Referrals from Current and Past Employees. Employees understand the firm's personnel needs and may know suitable job candidates. However, referrals by employees tend to reaffirm the demographic status quo, perhaps conflicting with affirmative-action considerations.

Private Employment Agencies. These firms charge fees for their services, sometimes to the job seeker and sometimes to the hiring firm. In effect, when a company contracts with an employment agency, it is turning over the task of recruiting and screening applicants to someone else.

Public Employment Agencies. Most cities have an office of the state employment agency whose role is to find jobs for unemployed people and to keep track of people receiving unemployment compensation.

Educational Institutions. Educational institutions may be good sources of job applicants. For jobs in great supply, companies may send recruiters to campuses for the purpose of finding and interviewing job applicants.

Labor Unions. Labor unions are often a good source of applicants. Some unions have hiring halls where employers and job seekers are brought together.

The RJP is one example of what is more generally called emotional inoculation. People who are given a dose of the reality they are to face—whether it is the truth about the probable outcomes of a surgical procedure, about the possible aftermath of a flood, or about undesirable aspects of a job—are emotionally inoculated against that reality and better able to deal with it.[8] In the case of the realistic job preview, studies suggest that such inoculation results in increased job satisfaction, commitment to the organization, and performance, and in decreased turnover after hiring. And, perhaps surprisingly, the RJP does not seem to "turn off" qualified employees.[9]

The opening pages of a new General Motors Corp. recruiting brochure give the impression of a realistic job preview gone wild. It describes legal practice at GM as "incredibly dull and boring," says the attorneys are "just a bunch of lazy, inefficient corporate types who have and want no challenges, work short hours, do low-level routine work, take endless vacations, and work for meager pay," and claims that people doing such work are "not real lawyers." However, the brochure goes on to say that these statements are only myths associated with working in a corporate legal department, and then sets about countering those myths.[10]

Preparing employees in advance for the pressures they can expect on the job is an aim of the realistic job preview.

SELECTION AND HIRING

The role of recruiting is to locate job candidates; the role of **selection and hiring** is to evaluate each candidate and to pick the best one for the position available. Some business firms use informal selection procedures such as reviewing completed application blanks and résumés. Others ask their job candidates to take a battery of personality and ability tests. Still others have assessment centers where procedures for selecting and hiring new employees are all very systematic.

Careful selection procedures can be time-consuming and costly. However, if the costs of a wrong decision are high, if there are a large number of appli-

cants relative to the number of openings, and if selection tools have high degrees of accuracy, careful procedures are probably worth the cost. Some companies are now using expensive selection procedures even for positions which would historically have been filled without much screening. For instance, when Toyota Motor Corp. wanted to fill positions at its new auto-assembly plant in Kentucky, it received 90,000 applications from 120 countries for its 2,700 production jobs, and thousands more for the 300 office jobs. To select workers who would conform to the Japanese emphasis on teamwork, loyalty, and versatility, Toyota required applicants to spend about 25 hours completing written tests, workplace simulations, and interviews, in addition to undergoing a physical examination and a drug test. The tests examined not only literacy and technical knowledge, but also such things as interpersonal skills and attitudes toward work.[11] Let's look at some of the ways in which firms determine whether the qualifications of a job candidate are in line with the requirements of the job.

Application Blanks

The first source of information about a potential employee is the application blank. An **application blank** provides the hiring firm with information about educational background, work experience, and outside interests. Much of this information is especially useful for applicant screening purposes. For example, an applicant for a position as a computer analyst should have had courses in data processing. The application blank would tell the employer right away whether the applicant had the necessary training.

However, there are at least three problems with application blanks as sources of information about potential employees. First, the information provided by the applicant may not be relevant to performance on the job. Second, applicants may give incorrect or misleading information on application blanks or in résumés. Finally, there are legal restrictions on what can and cannot be asked on an application blank. Figure 10–2 is a partial listing of questions considered to be unfair by the Washington State Human Rights Commission. Clearly, many of the questions routinely asked on application blanks are violations of state or federal law.

References

References are another popular selection tool. **References** are written by previous employers, co-workers, teachers, or other acquaintances. The evidence suggests, however, that references are generally of little value in the employee-selection process. The people asked to provide references sometimes do not really know much about the person requesting a reference. At other times, they are not frank because they do not want to say anything uncomplimentary about a person, especially in writing. As a result, references are generally biased in the applicant's favor.

Interviews

Interviews involve asking the job candidate a series of questions. In what is called a structured interview, the questions are precise and are asked in a

- Any inquiry that implies a preference for persons under 40 years of age.
- Whether applicant is a citizen. Any inquiry into citizenship which would tend to divulge applicant's lineage, ancestry, national origin, descent, or birthplace.
- All inquiries relating to arrests.
- Inquiries which would divulge convictions which do not reasonably relate to fitness to perform the particular job or relate to convictions for which the date of conviction or prison release was more than seven years before the date of application.
- Specific inquiries concerning spouse, spouse's employment or salary, children, child-care arrangements, or dependents.
- Any inquiries concerning handicaps, height, or weight which do not relate to job requirements.
- Whether the applicant is married, single, divorced, engaged, or widowed.
- Type or condition of military discharge.
- Request that applicant submit a photograph.
- Whether the applicant is male or female.
- Any inquiry concerning race or color of skin, hair, eyes, etc.
- All questions as to pregnancy, medical history concerning pregnancy, and related matters.
- Any inquiry concerning religious denomination, affiliations, holidays observed, etc.
- Requirements that applicant list all organizations, clubs, societies, and lodges to which applicant belongs.
- Inquiry into original name where it has been changed by court order or marriage.

FIGURE 10–2
Unfair Preemployment Inquiries

fixed order. In unstructured interviews, there is a looser interchange between the interviewer and the job candidate.

Interviews are widely used. More than 90 percent of all people hired for industrial positions are interviewed at least once. Despite the popularity of interviews, however, it has been shown that a successful interview does not always mean that the recruit will perform well on the job. Interviewers sometimes show many biases, disagree with one another over which recruits are likely to do best, and ignore information available about recruits. And interviewers may make their decisions on the basis of things they aren't aware of while slighting factors they consider to be important.[12]

One view of interviews is that they are essentially games or rituals:

In one sense the interview is a battle of wits. The applicant, who wants to put his best foot forward, engages in "impression management," seeking both to cover up his deficiencies and to provide answers that will please the interviewer. The latter tries to penetrate these defenses and catch a glimpse of the "real person" underneath.[13]

Unfortunately, it seems that these gaming aspects and other problems largely undermine much of the potential value of interviews as a selection tool. Nevertheless, there are many reasons why firms continue to use them. For one thing, it is easier to ask someone a series of questions than to construct a rigorous test such as an ability test. Also, companies may use interviews to give the applicant information about the job duties of the position being filled and about the organization in general. Interviews may be used to "sell" the company to the applicant. They may also be used to get missing or incomplete

Job interviews are a widely used selection procedure.

data from interviewees. Finally, good candidates might be unwilling to seriously consider a job without being given the chance to ask questions and gather information.

If interviews are used, steps should be taken to minimize their drawbacks. It is typically best to use a structured interview format, with a specific list of topics to be covered, the order in which the topics should be covered, and/or a list of specific questions to be asked. Interviewers should be trained in asking questions, probing for details, and listening carefully, and they should be careful to avoid discriminatory questions. Written records of the interview should be carefully kept. Whenever feasible, multiple interviewers should be used. Interviews should never be the sole basis for selection of a candidate. Instead, they should be used along with other selection devices to provide additional information on candidates' strengths and weaknesses.[14]

Testing

Testing is a relatively objective means of determining how well a person may do on the job. Unlike interviews, which rely on the clinical judgment of the interviewer to put information together and come up with a decision, testing is an actuarial approach. That is, information is collected which is known to be related to some criterion of interest such as performance. Then a relatively objective score is calculated and used to make staffing decisions. Many human resource experts and personnel managers believe that testing is the single best selection tool. Tests yield more information about a person than does a completed application blank, and they have less bias than do interviews.

TYPES OF TESTS

Let's examine four different types of tests: ability, personality, interest, and work sample tests.

Ability Tests

An **ability test** measures whether the applicant is able to perform the tasks required on the job. Mental ability tests assess memory, problem-solving speed, verbal comprehension, ability to deal with numbers, and so on. Mechanical ability tests measure an applicant's grasp of spatial relations—seeing how parts fit together into a whole. Candidates for dental school are often given a block of soap and a knife and asked to carve a tooth or other readily identifiable shape. The idea is that a candidate who can create a tooth in the correct proportions will be able to perform well when working in a patient's mouth. Psychomotor ability tests assess reaction time and finger dexterity. They are given to people applying for jobs involving physical, rather than mental, tasks. Psychomotor tests are routinely given to draftees for professional football teams.

Personality Tests

A **personality test** measures personality characteristics that might be important on the job. Job applicants are asked to describe themselves in terms of traits or behavior. The Ghiselli Self-Description Inventory, for example, lists 64 pairs of adjectives such as the following:

capable	defensive	weak
discreet	touchy	selfish

Applicants are asked to pick the trait in each pair that best (or, in some cases, least) describes themselves. On the basis of responses to such pairs, scores on personality dimensions—initiative, decisiveness, self-assurance, and so on—are obtained.[15]

One controversial form of personality assessment is handwriting assessment, or graphology. With graphology, an attempt is made to determine a person's personality profile by analyzing a handwriting sample. There appears to be little evidence that these tests are accurate, and there are legal questions about their use, but the use of graphology appears to be on the rise.[16]

Interest Tests

An **interest test** measures a person's likes or dislikes. One popular interest test is the Kuder Vocational Preference Record, in which the person is given sets of three activities (e.g., play baseball, work a puzzle, watch a movie) and asked to pick his or her favorite. The responses result in scores on ten interest categories including literary, outdoor, and mechanical.

Work Sample Tests

A **work sample test** measures how well applicants perform selected job tasks. An applicant for a job that requires typing skill is typically given a typing test; a police officer candidate might be given judgment tasks. Work sample tests generally predict subsequent job performance quite well.

VALIDITY AND RELIABILITY

It is important that tests (and, in fact, any selection tools) be valid and reliable. Validity is the degree to which the test measures what it is supposed to be measuring. Reliability is the degree to which the test provides consistent results. Since a measure cannot be valid unless it is reliable, examination of a test's reliability can provide insights into its validity. Several measures of validity may be relevant. Some deal with the content of the test or other scale, others with whether the scale looks valid on the surface, and still others with the relationship of the scale to other scales. Ideally, test scores of job applicants should be related to their performance months or years later. This is a difficult, time-consuming, and costly process, but it is necessary if the test is to legally be used for purposes of selection or placement. This same restriction holds for all selection tools—interviews, application blanks, or whatever. If a claim is made that any of these tools works in a discriminatory fashion, such evidence of validity must be presented.

In general, it seems that work sample tests and ability tests do a good job of predicting who will do well on the job. Research indicates that the validities of ability tests may be generalizable from job to job. As a result, there is likely to be increasing use of such tests for selection in the future.[17] However, research on the validity of interest and personality tests has been less encouraging, suggesting that while some such tests may prove useful for certain occupations, they are less helpful in predicting success across a variety of occupations.

As a result of concerns about both validity and invasion of privacy, a 1988 federal law outlawed most private uses of pre-employment polygraph tests, aimed at assessing employee honesty. However, a reaction to the federal law has been a proliferation of written "honesty" tests, many of which may be even less valid than the polygraph tests they are supplanting.[18]

© King Features Syndicate, Inc.

FAIRNESS IN TESTING

Everyone would agree that tests should be fair. What may bring disagreement is the definition of a fair test. To some, it means a test that doesn't contain items that would be unfamiliar to some people because of their race or ethnic origin. Others might focus on whether the test measures abilities and traits really needed on the job or just acts as a hurdle to block entry.

In the eyes of the law, a fair test is one that does not systematically underpredict or overpredict performance of one subgroup of employees relative to another. For instance, if a test predicts that white males will do better than black males on the job when in fact both groups do equally well, the test is unfair.

FAKING TESTS

There is a danger that tests may be faked. That is, people may guess what they feel to be the "correct" or desired answers and then give those answers rather than their true beliefs. If tests are "transparent"—that is, easy to "see through" or figure out—the possibility of faking increases.

Assessment Centers

Instead of just using an interview or a test, many large companies approach the employee-selection process more systematically. They use a variety of procedures combined in the form of an **assessment center**. These centers have psychologists and other experts on human behavior as well as providing tests, interviews, group discussions, and other approaches. Often, managers from within the firm serve as assessors.[19]

One approach used in assessment centers is role playing, in which job recruits pretend they are, for instance, marketing managers or first-line supervisors in a real decision situation. In another approach to discovering how recruits hold up under fire, the recruit is given an in-basket piled high with memos, phone messages, letters, and other matters requiring attention. Each person's performance is evaluated in terms of how the tasks are sequenced, how promptly they are completed, whether the most important ones in the pile are finished, and how good the proposed problem solutions are.

Assessment centers have many uses beyond selection. They may help with early spotting of management potential. They may pinpoint weaknesses that employees should focus on to improve their career prospects. And, when assessors are managers within the firm, the training they receive on how to run assessment centers is also valuable in helping them to understand the firm, to observe and rate behavior, and to develop skill at making judgments.

On the average, assessment centers cost about $100,000 to maintain each year. But they may be worth the cost to the large firms which use them, such as AT&T, IBM, and General Electric. Virtually every study of assessment centers has shown them to make better predictions of employee performance than other approaches to selection, and employees typically report that assessment centers have given them a fair chance to show their abilities.

PLACEMENT

Placement means fitting people and jobs together. It includes everything from helping new employees feel at home in the firm to promoting them to positions of greater pay and responsibility or demoting them to less desirable positions when necessary.

Orientation

Orientation involves introducing new employees to their jobs and to the company. It is their first inside look at the company, and it can make an important impression. If properly done, job orientation reduces employee uncertainties, makes company policies and expectations clear, and provides a good idea of what the firm, plant, and co-workers are like. Often, both the personnel department and the new employee's supervisor are involved in the orientation efforts.

We will discuss orientation further in Chapter 11. We will see that the orientation process may have an impact that will extend throughout the employee's career.

Lateral Moves

Firms may sometimes move employees laterally. For instance, as discussed in the previous chapter, systematic job rotation may build worker skills. At Union Carbide, three executive vice-presidents traded jobs to get a better feel for the total organization and to prepare for the presidency. Such lateral moves can provide valuable learning experiences, building a more solid base for subsequent promotions.

Sometimes lateral moves are dictated by organizational changes. For instance, when International Business Machines Corp. announced in 1988 that it would undertake a major staff redeployment in an attempt to lower costs, the plan required several thousand people to change jobs, often from staff positions to the sales force.[20]

Promotion

The most pleasant job move is the promotion. A **promotion** is a move up, generally to a new title, more responsibility, and greater financial rewards.

Promotions are handled carefully because they usually mean moving a person into a position having greater potential impact on the firm. Legal restrictions also complicate the promotion process. In addition, the fact that the promoted individual did well at the old job is no guarantee that that person will do well at the new, higher-level job. Jobs at different levels in the firm may require vastly different skills and interests. All too often, a good salesperson or engineer becomes a poor manager.

This tendency is called the Peter Principle. The **Peter Principle**, proposed by Laurence Peter, asserts that good workers are continually promoted to positions of greater authority. Eventually, they reach their "level of incompetence" and will not be promoted again. Carried to its extreme, the Peter Principle says that employees are ultimately promoted to positions for which they are not qualified. Most practicing managers can point to examples of the Peter Principle at work in their firms.

Promotions can also cause problems for the people promoted. Some employees may be happier in their current jobs than they would be in positions requiring greater responsibility, new skills, and geographic moves. Such changes can cause stress. To make the move a bit less scary, some firms have instituted fallback positions. Employees accepting promotions are guaranteed that if they are unhappy, they can "fall back" to the old positions or positions of equal stature.

These caveats notwithstanding, it is certainly the case that most people welcome promotions. Further, there is no guarantee that promoted employees will be subject to the Peter Principle. Indeed, many employees may experience an "inverse Peter Principle," performing better as they have the opportunity for increased responsibility and challenge.[21]

Demotion

A movement downward in title, responsibility, or benefits—called **demotion**—is rare in organizations. Demotions are especially stressful for employees, of course, and they are likely to be resisted by unions. Still, especially during economic recessions, employees may have to make the choice between demotion and unemployment. Some companies have experimented with demoting employees temporarily so that they can relate better to their subordinates. Also, as noted above, some employees ask for their old, lower-level jobs back if they are unhappy with their promotions.[22]

Termination

Another painful reality, especially in hard times, is the need to terminate employees. As a result of technological changes, mergers, altered strategies, for-

eign competition, and other factors, firms may have to downsize. In such cases, they often engage in firings—sometimes of major proportions—even at the executive level. For instance, in the wake of deregulation of the telephone industry, AT&T quickly made plans to cut 11,000 jobs at a savings of $400 million to $500 million a year. It also moved to shrink its first five layers of management to four, both to cut costs and to streamline decision making.[23]

Such firings are extremely stressful to individuals and firms. While the terminated employees may subsequently find jobs for which they are better suited, the short-run pressures are nevertheless great. In some cases, outplacement firms are hired by the terminating organization to assist affected individuals. These firms help the employer with the dismissal—offering advice and sometimes getting involved in the termination interview—and then counsel the individual on how to carry out a job search and cope with the period of transition between jobs. They may also actually help the individual find a job.[24]

Sometimes employers hire consulting firms to act as "hatchet men" when many jobs must be cut. One such consulting firm, Alexander Proudfoot, has worked with companies such as Citicorp, Amoco Corp., and New York Life Insurance Company to streamline their work forces. For a typical fee of about $1 million, Alexander Proudfoot uses various efficiency management techniques to find jobs that can be eliminated and other cost savings.[25]

It is no longer the case that companies can easily terminate employees at will. The idea of **termination at will** was that management had the right to fire employees for any reason, much as Mr. Dithers regularly fires Dagwood Bumstead, even on a whim. While courts generally recognize management's right to terminate employees who are incompetent, lazy, or uncooperative, they are increasingly attacking firings for some other reasons. For instance, firings for reasons of convenience, to make the employee a scapegoat, or to avoid pension costs have been challenged. Nevertheless, many critics of the current situation argue that workers in the United States are still much more vulnerable to unjust discharge than are workers in other democratic, industrialized nations, and they call for national laws providing general protection against such treatment.[26]

TRAINING AND DEVELOPMENT

The training of employees and the development of their skills and careers have many advantages for the firm, not the least of which is helping the firm meet its immediate human resource needs. Over the long run, however, it ensures that the firm's employees are ready to meet future challenges. A wide range of approaches to **training and development** have been devised, some with notable success.[27]

Determining Training and Development Needs

Training needs may arise for many reasons. In some situations, specific skills may be required which are not readily available, such as computer programming, accounting, and mechanical skills. Other training efforts are undertaken in anticipation of future personnel needs or are designed to promote career development among employees. Sometimes training takes the form of counseling employees on how to handle stress, overcome dependence on alcohol or other drugs, or manage their time. It may also be necessary for firms to set up special training programs for women, minorities, and the handicapped in order to meet affirmative-action goals.

By the mid-1980s, more than 57 percent of the Fortune 500 companies had such **employee assistance programs (EAPs)**. Illinois Bell Telephone Co., Navistar, the U.S. Postal Service, Du Pont Co., and Control Data Corp. have reported favorable results from such programs, including fewer absences due to illness, reduced grievances and disciplinary actions, and increased performance. Control Data estimates that its program saves the company $3.5 million annually.[28]

Technological change has made many jobs obsolete, creating tremendous demand for retraining. However, a *Business Week*/Harris poll showed that 64 percent of companies surveyed offered no formal retraining programs for the displaced.[29]

Approaches to Training and Development[30]

The two general aims of training and development are to teach specific skills, such as how to operate fiberglass-molding equipment, and to improve organizational processes such as communications among widely scattered plants and warehouses of the same company. There are many ways to conduct training programs. These can be classified as on-the-job and off-the-job training.

ON-THE-JOB TRAINING

As the term implies, **on-the-job training** is conducted while employees perform job-related tasks; they are not taken out of the office or plant and put in a classroom. On-the-job training is the most direct approach to training and development, offering the employer the quickest return in terms of improved performance. Such training is also conducted in anticipation of future job requirements. For example, many large companies rotate their managers through a variety of positions in order to broaden their knowledge of the company. Other sorts of on-the-job training for managers might include regular coaching by a superior, committee assignments to involve individuals in decision-making activities, and staff meetings to help managers become acquainted with the thinking of other managers and with activities outside their immediate areas.

OFF-THE-JOB TRAINING

It is often necessary to train employees away from the workplace. Role playing and in-baskets, which we discussed in conjunction with assessment centers, are often used for training purposes. Other popular off-the-job training techniques are described in the following sections.

Classroom Method

Classroom training allows many trainees to be taught by relatively few instructors. It may employ lectures, films, videotapes, and other audiovisual media. With **vestibule training**, trainees are given instruction in the operation of equipment like that found in their departments. For managers, classroom training might also include case studies. Case studies involve the presentation of a large amount of information about a business problem such as how to finance expansion of a new plant. Trainees are asked to analyze the material

Vestibule training gives trainees instruction in how to operate equipment.

and present recommendations. This may both enhance their knowledge of specific matters and improve their decision-making skills.

Programmed Instruction Method

With **programmed instruction**, subject matter is broken down into organized, logical sequences. The trainee is presented with a segment of the information and must respond by writing an answer or by pushing a button on a machine. When a correct response is given, the trainee is presented with the next segment of material. An incorrect response is met with an explanation and a "try again" response. Computer-assisted instruction (CAI) is a more sophisticated version of programmed instruction in which use of computer memory and computational ability permits teaching of more complex topics.

Management Game Method

With **management games,** trainees are faced with a simulated situation, such as a hypothetical business, and are required to make an ongoing series of decisions such as quantity of a product to manufacture and price to charge. Generally, trainees are members of teams competing with other teams. Feedback is given to trainees about the impacts of their decisions, often by a computer. If carefully developed, the games give a feeling of "real" decision making and generate considerable enthusiasm.

Sensitivity Training Method

Sensitivity training is used with small groups, called T (for training) groups. Through extended sessions in which group members attempt to share their feelings and be open to the views of others, sensitivity training attempts to develop participants' sensitivity, self-insight, and awareness of group processes. Increasingly, sensitivity training is focusing on job- and organization-related issues rather than solely on personal feelings. A recent development, the "New Age" training program, combines elements of sensitivity training with techniques drawn from other sources, from Eastern mysticism to positive thinking. Some programs include meditation and hypnosis. These programs are now being challenged as infringements on employees' religious beliefs.[31]

Behavior Modeling Method

Behavior modeling gives supervisory trainees an opportunity to deal with actual employee problems and provides immediate feedback on their performance. Behavior modeling tries to bring about behavioral change through four steps:[32]

1. Trainees view films or videotapes in which a model supervisor is portrayed dealing with an employee in an effort to improve or maintain the employee's performance. The model shows specifically how to deal with the situation.
2. Trainees participate in extensive practice and rehearsal of the behaviors demonstrated by the models. The greatest percentage of training time is spent on these skill-practice sessions.
3. As the trainee's behavior increasingly resembles that of the model, the trainer and other trainees provide such social reinforcers as praise, approval, encouragement, and attention. Videotaping such behavior rehearsals adds feedback and reinforcement.
4. The principles of transferring the training to the job are emphasized throughout the training period.

PERFORMANCE APPRAISAL

Performance appraisal is the measurement of employee performance. Before we look at techniques for performance appraisal, let's consider why performance should be appraised in the first place.[33]

Why Appraise Performance?

There are many reasons for measuring how well employees are performing. First, many administrative decisions, such as those dealing with promotions, salary increases, and layoffs, depend on performance appraisals. Second, if employees are to do their jobs better in the future, they need to know how well they have done them in the past so that they can make adjustments in their work patterns as necessary. Finally, performance appraisal is necessary as a check on new policies and programs. For example, if a new pay system has been implemented, it would be useful to see whether it has had a positive effect on employee performance.

Pitfalls in Performance Appraisal

Performance appraisal is a difficult process. Problems may occur because of the nature of the job, the rater, or the situation. For instance, accurate appraisal is particularly difficult when work is nonroutine, when the rater and ratees have differing perspectives, and when the appraisal system is incompatible with organization structure or technology. Further, many of the perceptual problems to be discussed in Chapter 12 plague the performance-appraisal process. Clearly, great care needs to be exercised in selection, use, and refinement of performance-appraisal systems.

Types of Performance Measures

There are three major ways by which performance may be appraised. Appraisal can focus on traits, behaviors, or accomplishments.

TRAIT APPROACHES

Under trait approaches, a manager or performance appraiser rates an employee on such traits as friendliness, efficiency, and reliability. Presumably, these traits are related to performance. One such approach asks the appraiser to check the word or phrase (such as "outstanding," "average," or "poor") that best describes how an employee rates on each trait.

These trait approaches are very popular, but they suffer from a number of problems. For instance, words such as "superior" and "average" may mean different things to different people. The people appraising performance may feel uncomfortable giving someone a low score on such traits as efficiency, decisiveness, or supervisory ability, especially if their ratings will be shown to the person being rated. Appraisers may also be prone to various biases and rating errors.

BEHAVIORAL APPROACHES

Behavioral approaches involve the recording of specific employee actions. With the **critical incidents method**, for example, the performance appraiser keeps a list of all the things the employee did that were especially good or bad. Sometimes, such incidents are gathered from job incumbents and/or supervisors, and a list of incidents discriminating between high and low performers is developed. Such a list, illustrated in Figure 10–3, can then be used by others.

A newer and somewhat related approach, the **behaviorally anchored rating scale (BARS)**, presents a list of possible employee actions, ranging from very desirable to very undesirable.[34] An example of good performance for a grocery checker might be "By knowing the price of items, this checker would be expected to look for mismarked and unmarked items." An example of poor performance might be "In order to take a break, this checker can be expected to block off the checkstand with people in line." The rater checks the action on the scale that the employee would be most likely to engage in.

Traits such as friendliness are the focus of trait approaches to performance measurement.

FIGURE 10–3
Critical Incidents

Position: PERSONNEL OFFICER

In classifying a position, fails to take into account other functions in the unit or in the larger organization which impact the position being classified.

In discussions related to filling a difficult position, will explore all possible mechanisms for filling the position and talk to program officials to ascertain cause of difficulty in locating applicants before making a recommendation.

Does not ask employees for additional information which might help in becoming qualified for a position.

Agrees with supervisor's request that an overgraded employee be overlooked during the review period.

Identifies potential interpersonal conflicts due to differences in personality, age, race, etc., between parties to a grievance before making a decision.

Source: From *Performance Appraisal and Review Systems* by S. J. Carroll and C. E. Schneier. Copyright © 1982 by Scott, Foresman and Company. Reprinted by permission.

By focusing on specific actions, behavioral approaches are an improvement on the earlier trait approaches because they consider things under the control of the employee rather than things which might be heavily influenced by other factors. They specify exactly what the employee needs to do to get a good rating, and they provide the basis for concrete feedback. Sometimes, however, they give employees the uncomfortable feeling that there is always a rater looking over their shoulders.

OUTCOME APPROACHES

Rather than consider traits or actions, some appraisal techniques rate what the employee is supposed to accomplish on the job. One of these approaches, management by objectives, will be discussed in Chapter 13. Such approaches may be time-consuming, and they may also cause appraisers to focus only on objectives that can be easily expressed in numbers. They do, however, get directly at the things that the company cares most about, and they let the employee know specifically which outcomes are most important.

Who Appraises Performance?

Our discussion of performance appraisal has focused on the evaluation of employees' performance by their superiors. However, employees may also be rated by peers or subordinates. Peer assessment has been widely used, and it is generally considered to be highly valid and reliable. There is also growing use of ratings by subordinates. General Electric, Libby-Owens-Ford Co., and Southern California Edison are among the companies in which workers rate their bosses. It is argued that subordinates may be in ideal positions to evaluate their bosses for leadership, organization, and crisis-management skills. Subordinates tend to be tougher raters of their supervisor than is the supervisor's boss. Unfortunately, many managers find it hard to deal with criticisms from their subordinates, and they may ignore the appraisals.[35]

COMPENSATING EMPLOYEES

The salary or wages paid to employees, as well as other job benefits, depend in part on how well employees perform on the job. Other factors influencing employee compensation are the relative worth of each job within the firm, labor market conditions and prevailing wage rates, and the type of pay system used. Let's take a look at these determinants of employee compensation.

Job Analysis

The systematic study of a job to determine its characteristics is called **job analysis**. How is the information gathered for a job analysis? One common method is to observe workers on the job, noting which tasks they perform, the order in which the tasks are performed, and the time it takes to perform each task. Another method is to interview employees about the nature of their work. Sometimes employees are asked to supply the needed information by filling out written questionnaires. The value of this information, however gathered, is that it allows the job description to be written.

Job Description

A **job description** is a short summary of the basic tasks making up a job. A job description usually includes the title of the job, work activities and procedures, work conditions, and hours and wages.

Job descriptions serve a number of important functions. First, they clarify organizational structure by specifying who is to perform each task; they also minimize job overlap, wherein two people are assigned the same task. Second, job descriptions can be used to introduce new employees to their jobs, giving them a good idea of what to expect on the job before they actually start work.

Other uses of job descriptions are also worth noting. For example, they are important in developing job specifications, performance standards, and the criteria for job evaluations. A **job specification** is a summary of the qualifications needed for a specific job. A job specification is especially useful in recruiting job applicants and making hiring decisions. **Performance standards** define the goals to be achieved by a worker over a specified period of time. The purpose of a **job evaluation** is to determine the relative worth of a job in the firm. The job analysis and the job description provide the information needed for the job evaluation. The result of the job-evaluation process is a rank ordering or rating of job importance which, of course, is useful in setting wage and salary scales. Figure 10–4 shows the overall process of setting wage and salary rates on the basis of the factors discussed.

Demand for nurses is high in the labor market.

Labor Market Conditions

Supply and demand cause the wages for some jobs to be higher than for others, even though the jobs may be of similar difficulty, responsibility, and so on. The level of wages is also influenced by the competitive wage in the local area. For example, machine shops in the same town will all tend to pay the same wage, especially if a union contract is in effect. Because of this tendency, some companies conduct surveys of local wages to make sure that their own are in line. As shown in Figure 10–5, there is quite a bit of vari-

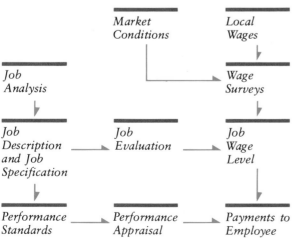

FIGURE 10–4
The Wage Determination Process

Job	Jackson, Mississippi	Minneapolis, Minnesota	San Francisco, California	St. Louis, Missouri	Washington, D.C.	Houston, Texas
Secretary	$ 9.38	$10.01	$12.40	$10.52	$11.25	$11.48
Truck driver	10.92	13.09	13.42	12.52	11.29	8.88
Computer operator	9.12	10.53	11.66	9.84	10.84	10.76
Drafter	9.85	12.37	15.47	11.51	9.88	14.50
Forklift operator	8.34	12.07	13.14	11.87	10.50	9.40
Accounting clerk	7.30	6.52	11.10	8.12	8.45	9.02
Shipper and receiver	8.33	9.58	11.51	9.73	10.35	8.72
Key entry operator	7.83	7.28	9.92	6.84	7.45	8.13

Wage quotation for Jackson, MS, is for January 1989; for Minneapolis, MN, is for February 1989; and for Houston, TX, is for April 1989. All other quotations are for March 1989.

Source: U.S. Department of Statistics, Area Wage Surveys (1989).

FIGURE 10–5
Average Hourly Wage Rates

ability in average hourly wage rates for the same job in different parts of the country.

Pay Systems

Even after the value of a job is determined (and the local and regional wage differences are taken into consideration), one person may be paid more for the same job than another person. We can identify at least five other factors that may account for wage differentials. They include seniority, individual performance, group performance, plant-wide productivity, and profit sharing.

SENIORITY

Seniority refers to the number of years spent with the company. In some companies, the more years of seniority, the greater the level of pay. Wage and salary increases are automatic rewards for duration of service. The idea is that seniority reflects loyalty to the company as well as experience.

INDIVIDUAL PERFORMANCE

How much individual employees are paid may also be based on how well they do on the job. Under a piece-rate system (see Chapter 2) of compensation, total wages are tied directly to output. For example, a worker in a toy factory may get one dollar for every puppet produced. Obviously, the more efficient the worker, the bigger the paycheck. As we'll see in Chapter 13, piece-rate pay systems increase employee motivation. One survey showed that about 70 percent of employees felt their productivity would go up if their pay were tied to performance. There has been a distinct recent trend toward pay-for-performance plans. For instance, General Motors in 1986 established a pay-for-performance system for salaried employees. GM now ranks employees against each other. Supervisors have to pick the top 10 percent, the next 25 percent, the next 55 percent, and the bottom 10 percent of their group, and must enforce pay differences between the tiers.[36] Sometimes, employees are rewarded with stock options rather than cash. These options give holders the right to purchase stock at some specified price, typically well be-

Q: *Some of the personnel policies of your company are quite innovative. For instance, you have a five-to-one salary ratio which limits salaries of top executives to five times those of the lowest-paid employee. What do you see as the benefits of this five-to-one ratio?*

A: The benefit of the five-to-one pay ratio is that it makes the clear statement that everyone who works at Ben & Jerry's is a major contributor to the success of the company. That builds a worker dignity and ownership that, hopefully, builds a better work environment. The bottom line is that the quality of work is maintained.

Q: *Ben & Jerry's has a "Joy Committee," charged with putting more fun into the workday. The company stresses teamwork and trust, and tries to put considerable power in the hands of lower management. It hires the handicapped, provides free therapy sessions to any employee who needs them, and even has changing tables for babies in the men's room as well as the women's room. All of this suggests that you care about the well-being of your employees and your community. Do you feel that such practices and attitudes also influence the company's "bottom line"?*

A: We have a saying around here at Ben & Jerry's that if it ain't fun why do it? There's no question that if you can make things fun there's a greater willingness to do things and do them well. We really emphasize the quality of our ice cream. It takes a quality work force to make quality ice cream. If you have a happy, motivated work force producing that ice cream it's easier to maintain quality. Quality affects the bottom line. If people buy a bad pint, they're probably not going to come back for more. We don't want that to happen. Keeping the work force happy and motivated is a way to prevent this from happening.

Q: *Ben & Jerry's has been noted for its social activism. For instance, it has supported the notion that a law should be passed committing 1 percent of the U.S. defense budget to citizen and cultural exchanges and cooperative international ventures in science, business, the arts, education, and other fields, and it has donated funds toward the preservation of Brazilian rain forests. You have also proposed an "Ice Cream for Peace" joint venture with the Soviet Union which would put American ice cream parlors in Russian cities and would channel any profits into student exchange between the two countries. What does all this say about your view of the proper social role of Ben & Jerry's?*

A: I believe very strongly that business is the most powerful force in society. I see business as organized human energy and money that equal power. Add to that equation the communication resources that business has and uses and you have a superpower. So, business has a lot of potential and a lot of responsibilities. Business is the organization within society that is best suited to transform society into one that meets the needs of society a lot better than what we're doing right now.

Ben & Jerry's is incorporating that social responsibility into every business decision we make. We're looking for suppliers that share these values, such as Community Products Incorporated, which makes a product whose sales benefit Rainforest and other environmental preservation efforts. Our brownies for our Chocolate Fudge Brownie are baked at the Greyston Bakery in Yonkers, N.Y. Greyston trains, employs, and counsels the homeless, the underskilled, and others in difficult situations and helps them improve the quality of their lives. These are the kinds of things business can do that are incorporated right into profitability and responsibility to the business and society.

MANAGERIAL PROFILE
BEN COHEN

Ben Cohen is co-founder, chairman, and chief executive officer of Ben & Jerry's Homemade Inc. Before founding Ben & Jerry's with his childhood friend Jerry Greenfield, Cohen held such jobs as Pinkerton guard, pottery-wheel deliveryperson, pediatric emergency-room clerk, and crafts teacher. Ben & Jerry's began as an ice cream parlor in a renovated Burlington, Vermont, gas station in 1978. It has since grown dramatically, with 1989 sales of over $58 million and approximately 300 employees. Cohen sees the company as an experiment and a force for social change. The company's culture emphasizes fun, charity, and goodwill toward fellow workers. Cohen and Greenfield have received the Corporate Giving Award from the Council of Economic Priorities for the firm's many charitable contributions, were named U.S. Small Business Persons of the Year in 1988, and have garnered many other honors. Cohen is active in social causes and has taught courses on social responsibility.

FROM THE FIELD
STAFFING PRACTICES

We surveyed human resources executives in a variety of industries to learn more about current organizational staffing practices. We first asked the executives the degree to which various selection tools were used in their firms. Possible responses were 1 (no use), 2 (very little use), 3 (moderate use), and 4 (substantial use). Here are the average responses for the tools, ranked from most used to least used:

Rank	Tool	Average Rating
1	Interviews	4.0
2	Application blanks	3.5
3	References	3.4
4	Ability tests	2.1
5	Work sample tests	1.9
6	Assessment centers	1.6
7	Personality tests	1.3
8	Interest tests	1.2

These results are not too surprising. Recall, though, that the techniques most widely used here are each prone to misrepresentation, biases, or other sources of error.

Using the same scale, here are the results for a question concerning the degree to which compensation in the executives' firms is based on various factors. The bases of compensation are ranked from most used to least used:

Rank	Basis of Compensation	Average Rating
1	Individual performance	3.9
2	Company profits	2.7
3	Seniority	2.0

low the market price. Once reserved for executives at the top of the corporate ladder, these stock options are increasingly being made available to middle and lower managers, and even to non-management employees.[37]

GROUP PERFORMANCE

Workers performing similar or related tasks are sometimes organized into work groups. In such situations, pay scales are often tied to group performance. How much each person takes home, therefore, is based on how well the group as a whole does. Because wages for one worker are determined by the efforts of others, group members have an incentive to push slow workers to do better. Again, we see that compensation systems and employee motivation are related.

PLANT-WIDE PRODUCTIVITY

Rates of pay for employees can be based on how well the entire organization does. If the company has a good year, each worker receives a bonus. One popular plan of this type is the Scanlon Plan, under which groups of employees suggest to management how productivity might be improved. Then, at regular intervals, such as once a year, the productivity of the organization is evaluated.

| 4 | Group performance | 2.0 |
| 5 | Plant-wide productivity | 1.9 |

Since reward systems based on individual performance have powerful motivating consequences, the heavy reliance on such a basis for compensation is encouraging. What we cannot see from these data, of course, are the extent to which the organizations actually carry through on using these bases or the extent to which employees perceive this to be the case.

Finally, we presented the executives with a series of statements concerning some important recent staffing issues. Scores ranged from 1 to 5, with possible responses including 1 (completely disagree), 3 (neither agree nor disagree), and 5 (completely agree). Here are the average responses:

Statement	Average Rating
It is generally a good idea to give potential employees as realistic a picture of the company and job as possible, rather than to paint an overly rosy picture.	4.8
Comparable worth is an issue whose time has come.	2.2
In general, unions do more harm to American businesses than good.	3.3
The laws which apply to personnel management are becoming increasingly strict.	3.8

It is apparent that executives believe in the realistic job preview. Staffing executives—to whom comparable worth is presenting serious challenges and difficulties—are apparently not yet embracing that issue. Further, these staffing executives have mixed feelings about the benefits of unions, and they see legal constraints on staffing as tightening.

If productivity is up, each worker is rewarded with a bonus. Some Japanese companies have adopted an interesting variation of this plan: they have annual picnics at which new ideas, inventions, and improvements devised by their employees are exhibited and demonstrated by the company president.

PROFIT SHARING

Many companies today feature **profit-sharing plans**. The idea is simple: If company profits are high, employees are given a bonus in the form of either a cash payment or company stock. For instance, in 1988 General Motors paid out a total of $90 million in bonuses to 450,000 blue-collar and salaried workers based on a profit-sharing formula. Ford Motor Company's hourly and salaried workers received an average of about $3,700 each from profit sharing in 1987, and about $2,800 in 1988.[38] Unlike a plant-wide productivity plan in which payments are tied to productivity standards, here they are tied to profit. Such plans have the nice feature that firms make payments only when they can best afford them.

One problem with profit-sharing plans, as well as with tying bonuses to plant productivity, is that employees are not rewarded on the basis of individual performance. As we'll discuss in Chapter 13, research evidence clearly shows that the more closely rewards are tied to individual performance, the more strongly the employee will be motivated. Also, employees do not like to be penalized for things outside their control such as low company productivity or profit. When Du Pont Co.'s fiber division instituted a profit-sharing program in 1989, there was considerable support, but many employees complained that they felt powerless to influence profits, and that they had no control over costly management mistakes.[39] For this reason, although plant-wide productivity plans may result in more positive employee attitudes toward the company, they probably do not have much impact on individual performance.

IMPLICATIONS FOR MANAGEMENT

Throughout your career as a manager, you will be called on to make or to be involved in staffing decisions. Give them the attention they deserve. Like other resources, the people recruited, selected, placed, and trained by the organization are crucial inputs. Unlike many of the firm's resource inputs, however, they may play important roles for many years. To complicate matters, they may change in both nature and purpose over time. Decisions concerning such important, long-lasting, changeable inputs will certainly be difficult.

Whether you are involved in a final staffing decision or are asked to make inputs, a knowledge of relevant laws is crucial. For instance, many questions you might be tempted to ask a recruit may violate state or federal laws. Some things you might want to try during a union recruiting drive may also be illegal. Similarly, you should try to be well versed in laws concerning employee benefits, health and safety, and selection and placement.

As a manager, you should keep in mind the need for valid and reliable selection tools. Invalid or unreliable tools lead to poor selection decisions—often at tremendous cost to the firm—and invite legal redress. Since application blanks, references, and interviews are easy to use and seem to be informative, you may find it tempting to rely on them heavily for selection decisions. Keep in mind their flaws. If you do rely on interviews, be very careful to plan the interview in advance, to build some structure into the process, and to focus on job-relevant information. Don't rely on interviews in an attempt to skirt legal requirements for tests; all selection tools are treated similarly by such laws. When possible, employ properly validated tests and, especially for decisions concerning managerial positions, consider setting up assessment centers. These approaches are sometimes difficult and expensive to use. However, there is little doubt that, when properly implemented, they can improve the selection process.

Regardless of your managerial position, you will to some degree be involved in placement. Sometimes you will be asked to help with orientation of a new employee. At other times, you may be asked to make or assist in decisions about who should be promoted or transferred or terminated. These decisions will have tremendous impacts on the lives of the people involved and on the firm. Treat them accordingly. Carefully weigh the personal, financial, and other costs and benefits of alternative moves.

Good managers recognize that firms must be concerned both with immediate human resource needs and with meeting future challenges. Proper training and development methods can help meet these dual concerns. As a manager, you will regularly be involved in on-the-job training of subordinates and perhaps in other training programs. In all likelihood, you will also be a participant in a variety of developmental activities. Take advantage of developmental opportunities; seek them out if necessary and make sure they are provided for your subordinates. Managers are judged by how well they train and develop subordinates, and many managers have been passed over for promotions because they have not developed a replacement.

Like many managers, you may find performance appraisal difficult. It is often hard to decide on proper performance criteria, to give subordinates "bad" ratings, or to provide negative feedback on their performance. Nevertheless, these are all key managerial activities. A carefully developed appraisal system that focuses on behaviors or outcomes rather than on employee traits may ease your appraisal task. Conscious attention to possible rating biases may also help.

Finally, you may be involved in decisions about compensation. In making your inputs, keep in mind that successful compensation programs are both equitable and motivating. A system must pay careful attention to employee inputs if it is to be regarded as fair. It must somehow tie compensation to performance criteria if it is to be motivating.

KEY TERMS AND CONCEPTS

ability test
affirmative action
application blank
assessment center
behavior modeling
behaviorally anchored rating scale
    (BARS)
comparable worth
critical incidents method
demotion
employee assistance programs
Equal Employment Opportunity
    Commission (EEOC)
human resource planning
interest test
interviews
job analysis
job description
job evaluation
job specification
management games
Occupational Safety and Health
    Administration (OSHA)

on-the-job training
orientation
performance appraisal
performance standards
personality test
Peter Principle
placement
profit-sharing plans
programmed instruction
promotion
realistic job preview (RJP)
recruiting
references
selection and hiring
seniority
sensitivity training
staffing
termination at will
testing
training and development
vestibule training
work sample test

QUESTIONS FOR REVIEW AND DISCUSSION

1. What is the basic goal of staffing?
2. What is human resource planning? In what ways are human resources like other resources of the firm? In what ways are they different?

3. Identify five key laws influencing staffing. In your opinion, are such laws too strict or too lenient? How do you think they should be changed, if at all?

4. In what sense do recruiting, selection, and placement differ from training and development? Discuss factors that would influence the relative desirability of selection and placement on the one hand and training and development on the other.

5. What is a realistic job preview? What do you see as potential dangers of using realistic job previews?

6. Name the six primary sources of job applicants. Which of these do you believe is generally most useful? Generally least useful? Why?

7. In the selection and hiring process, how does a personality test differ from an interest test?

8. In the eyes of the law, what is a fair test? Do you agree with that definition? Why or why not?

9. Explain how the Peter Principle works. Give an example. What are some things that might prevent the Peter Principle from occurring?

10. What are the two basic aims of training?

11. What are some situations in which demotion in rank or responsibility would be preferable to firing an employee?

12. Which of the approaches to performance appraisal do you prefer? Why?

13. What is a job description? What is it used for? Write a job description for a business student.

14. Which of the pay systems discussed in this chapter do you think you would prefer as an employee? As an employer? Why?

10–1 PERSONALITY TESTING FOR BLUE-COLLAR JOBS

For many years, companies have used sophisticated role playing or psychological tests to decide what manager gets what job. Now, more companies are using similar techniques when hiring people for such entry-level jobs as customer-sales representatives and clerks, as well as for blue-collar positions.

The trend is most prevalent at companies that are espousing so-called participatory management, giving workers more responsibility in running operations. And companies like financial service and insurance firms, forced to improve service in the face of increased competition, say they are searching harder for employees with greater "people" skills—empathy, ability to communicate, and an overall motivation to please others.

"Ten years ago, we didn't expect as much from people," says Robert Goehring, manager of human resources development for Kimberly-Clark Corp., the paper-products concern. "Now we have participative organizations that foster a high degree of responsibility, even at the operator level."

At Kimberly-Clark's newest plants, for example, applicants for nonunion machine-operator jobs are put through "leadership-simulation" exercises. In one session, the job candidate is asked to play the role of a supervisor directing a seasoned subordinate to switch to a more demanding job.

Mr. Goehring and many other personnel experts contend that such tests accurately predict future job performance. But critics have long maintained that personality tests or simulation exercises sometimes depict wrong or irrelevant traits needed for a particular job. Personality tests, in which applicants answer a long series of questions, may accurately describe such traits as aggressiveness, but they won't necessarily "measure how well that person will do on the job," says D. Quinn Mills, a Harvard Business School professor.

Simulations also are considered only as accurate and fair as the person judging them. Further, applicants with experience in a job—even if they have performed poorly—may fare better in role playing than potentially outstanding, but inexperienced, candidates.

Another concern: A spokesperson for the AFL-CIO says the union believes that some companies use personality tests to weed out prospects with union inclinations. "They can make sure every new hire has the traits of an independent or a nonjoiner, someone who won't take part in group action," the spokesperson says.

Still, a growing number of companies, while acknowledging the tests' flaws, feel that the changing workplace and demand for better service require them to hone their hiring process through testing.

Source: Reprinted by permission of *The Wall Street Journal*, © Dow Jones & Company, Inc. (January 16, 1986). All Rights Reserved Worldwide.

1. Do you think it is appropriate to use personality tests for entry-level positions and blue-collar jobs? Why or why not?
2. A professor in the case says that personality tests may accurately describe traits but won't necessarily "measure how well that person will do on the job." What procedures
   could be used to assess whether the tests do in fact relate to job performance?
3. Would it be better for firms to use interviews rather than tests to determine whether people have "people" skills such as empathy and ability to communicate? Why or why not?

10–2 THE EXECUTIVE ADDICT

Unarmed and uncomfortable about it, Ed Loyd, chief of security for a West Coast company, parked in a deserted area near Stevens Creek Reservoir in Cupertino, California, and headed up a forest trail shrouded from the noon sunlight by a thick canopy of leaves. Loyd was there to confront a blackmailer, an employee of the company, who had sold drugs, threatened co-workers, and lately had sent death threats to senior executives. Both the security chief and his company's executives judged the man perfectly capable of making good on the threats. An ex-Marine, he was clearly on drugs himself and seemed haunted by flashbacks to his experiences in Vietnam.

Nothing in Loyd's 18 years as a narcotics detective and corporate security chief had prepared him for what was waiting in the forest. He found the employee, an American Indian, sitting before a camp stove, decked out with Indian armbands and feathered headdress, his face smeared with war paint. The man carried an ax and had a bow and arrows within easy reach. The security chief was weaponless on orders from the company. Squinting at this vision through the shimmering heat from the fire, Loyd realized that the man could kill him, probably even without weapons. Instead, the two men struck a deal: In return for being kept on the payroll as a disability case, the employee would stay away from the company and leave its executives alone.

The order to buy off the blackmailer had come from the top, Ed Loyd says. The employee had threatened to tell the press that executives at the company were using and dealing in cocaine and marijuana.

The abuse of drugs by executives has become a serious problem nationwide. While there are no solid statistics on this illegal activity, those in the best position to gauge its extent—doctors who treat executives, people who run rehabilitation centers for them, and executive addicts themselves—are virtually unanimous in saying that executive drug abuse is widespread and increasing rapidly. . . . Dr. Joseph A. Pursch, medical director of Comprehensive Care Corp., which operates 160 hospitals devoted to treating alcoholism and drug addiction, says, "We've seen a 100 percent increase in the number of high-level executives coming to us for treatment compared with five years ago. I'm sure that a year or two from now it'll be another 100 percent or more. Drugs have taken the business world by storm."

Source: Abridged from Steven Flax, "The Executive Addict," *Fortune* (June 24, 1985): 24-31. © 1985 Time Inc. All rights reserved.

1. From a human resource management perspective, identify costs associated with this increasing drug use among executives.

2. What are the implications of this growing drug use for the issues discussed in this chapter, including selection, placement, training and development, and performance appraisal?

3. Do you agree with the company's decision to instruct Ed Loyd to strike a deal with the employee rather than to take other action? In general, what actions do you think are appropriate when companies become aware of illegal drug use by their employees? What actions are inappropriate?

ENDNOTES

1. This definition is drawn from J. W. Walker, *Human Resource Planning* (New York: McGraw-Hill, 1980). This section is based on M. J. Wallace, Jr., N. F. Crandall, and C. H. Fay, *Administering Human Resources: An Introduction to the Profession* (New York: Random House, 1982), 142-152.

2. For a discussion of procedures to carry out a human resource audit, see E. Flamholtz, *Human Resource Accounting* (Encino, CA: Dickenson, 1974).

3. A. R. Karr, "OSHA Mulls Rules That May Expand Worker Monitoring," *Wall Street Journal* (September 29, 1988): 4.

4. "AIDS Workers Get Protection," *Wisconsin State Journal* (October 7, 1988): 6A.

5. R. N. Corley, R. L. Black, and O. L. Reed, *The Legal Environment of Business* (New York: McGraw-Hill, 1981), 352.

6. J. Solomon, "Pay Equity Gets a Tryout in Canada—and U.S. Firms Are Watching Closely," *Wall Street Journal* (December 28, 1988): B1.

7. See P. G. Swaroff, L. A. Barclay, and A. R. Bass, "Recruiting Sources: Another Look," *Journal of Applied Psychology* 70 (1985): 720-728, for a discussion of evidence regarding the impact of alternative recruiting sources on tenure and productivity of employees provided by the source.

8. For a thorough discussion of emotional inoculation, see I. L. Janis and L. Mann, *Decision Making: A Psychological Analysis of Conflict, Choice, and Commitment* (New York: Free Press, 1977).

9. For a recent review of this literature, see S. L. Premack and J. P. Wanous, "A Meta-Analysis of Realistic Job Preview Experiments," *Journal of Applied Psychology* 70 (1985): 706-719.

10. C. Harlan, "Why Were the Lawyers Nodding When They Started Reading This?" *Wall Street Journal* (October 17, 1988): B1.

11. R. Koenig, "Toyota Takes Pains, and Time, Filling Jobs at Its Kentucky Plant," *Wall Street Journal* (December 1, 1987): 1.

12. On this point, see E. Valenzi and I. R. Andrews, "Individual Differences in the Decision Processes of Employment Interviewers," *Journal of Applied Psychology* 58 (1973): 49-53.

13. G. Strauss and L. R. Sayles, *Personnel: The Human Problems of Management* 4th ed., © 1980, pp. 372-373. Reprinted by permission of Prentice-Hall, Inc., Englewood Cliffs, NJ.

14. This discussion of the benefits of interviewing and suggestions for improvement of the interviewing process are drawn from D. C. Feldman, *Managing Careers in Organizations* (Glenview, IL: Scott, Foresman, 1988), 53-55.

15. For a discussion of the development of this inventory, including the inventory and norm data, see E. E. Ghiselli, *Explorations in Managerial Talent* (Pacific Palisades, CA: Goodyear Publishing Co., 1971).

16. M. J. McCarthy, "Handwriting Analysis as Personnel Tool," *Wall Street Journal* (August 25, 1988): 17.

17. F. L. Schmidt and J. E. Hunter, "The Future of Criterion-Related Validity," *Personnel Psychology* 33 (1980): 41-60.

18. C. Harlan, "Written 'Honesty' Tests Draw Interest As Law Bars Polygraphs as Hiring Tool," *Wall Street Journal* (January 3, 1989): B4.

19. For an excellent discussion of assessment centers, see G. C. Thornton III and W. C. Byham, *Assessment Centers and Managerial Performance* (New York: Academic Press, 1982).

20. P. B. Carroll, "IBM Is Planning Another Staff Redeployment," *Wall Street Journal* (June 27, 1988): 3.

21. We are indebted to Gregory Dess for making this point.

22. For a discussion of steps that companies can take to manage downward moves, see D. T. Hall and L. A. Isabella, "Downward Movement and Career Development," *Organizational Dynamics* 14 (1985): 5-23.

23. For discussions of downsizing, see G. E. L. Barbee, "Downsizing with Dignity: Easing the Pain of Employee Layoffs," *Business And Society Review* (Spring 1987): 31-34; A. B. Fisher, "The Downside of Downsizing," *Fortune* (May 23, 1988): 42-52; and E. R. Greenberg, "Downsizing: Results of a Survey by the American Management Association," *Personnel* (October 1987): 35-37.

24. For a discussion of the adverse effects of involuntary job loss and of possible interventions by government, unions, and business organizations to help employees deal with such loss, see C. R. Leana and J. M. Ivancevich, "Involuntary Job Loss: Institutional Interventions and a Research Agenda," *Academy of Management Review* 12 (1987): 301-312. For a discussion of the possible positive impact of involuntary job loss on career growth, see J. C. Latack and J. B. Dozier, "After the Ax Falls: Job Loss as a Career Transition," *Academy of Management Review* 11 (1986): 375-392. For a discussion of the growth of outplacement, see J. Main, "Look Who Needs Outplacement," *Fortune* (October 9, 1989): 85, 88, 92.

25. J. Bailey, "A Consulting Firm Thrives by Handling Clients' Dirty Work," *Wall Street Journal* (September 27, 1988): 1, 14.

26. R. C. Rodgers and J. Stieber, "Employee Discharge in the 20th Century: A Review of the Literature," *Monthly Labor Review* (September 1985): 35-41.

27. For a thorough discussion of training and development, see K. N. Wexley and G. P. Latham, *Developing and Training Human Resources in Organizations* (Glenview, IL: Scott, Foresman, 1981).

28. For more on EAPs, see R. T. Hellan, "An EAP Update: A Perspective for the '80s," *Personnel Journal* (June 1986); R. I. Lehr and D. J. Middlebrooks, "Legal Implications of Employee Assistance Programs," *Employee Relations Law Journal* 12 (August 1986): 262-274; and M. Rothman, "Mental Health and the Workplace: A Case for Employee Assistance Programs," *Compensation and Benefits Review* 18 (1988): 33-43.

29. *Business Week* (April 25, 1983): 64.

30. This section is based on H. J. Chruden and A. W. Sherman, Jr., *Managing Human Resources*, 7th ed. (Cincinnati, OH: South-Western Publishing Co., 1984), 192-199.

31. M. Brannigan, "Employers' 'New Age' Training Programs Lead to Lawsuits over Workers' Rights," *Wall Street Journal* (January 9, 1989): B1.

32. From B. L. Rosenbaum, "A New Approach to Changing Supervisory Behavior," *Personnel* 52, no. 2 (1975): 40-42.

33. For good discussions of performance appraisal, see S. J. Carroll and C. E. Schneier, *Performance Appraisal and Review Systems* (Glenview, IL: Scott, Foresman, 1982), and D. R. Ilgen and J. L. Barnes-Farrell, *Performance Planning and Evaluation* (Chicago: Science Research Associates, 1984).

34. The following examples are drawn from L. Fogli, C. L. Hulin, and M. R. Blood, "Development of First-Level Behavioral Job Criteria," *Journal of Applied Psychology* 55 (1971): 3-8. For a review of BARS, see D. P. Schwab, H. G. Heneman III, and T. A. DeCotiis, "Behaviorally Anchored Rating Scales: A Review of the Literature," *Personnel Psychology* 28 (1975): 549-562. Behaviorally anchored rating scales are also known as behavioral expectation scales (BES).

35. L. Reibstein, "Firms Ask Workers to Rate Their Bosses," *Wall Street Journal* (June 13, 1988): 15.

36. J. M. Schlesinger, "GM's New Compensation Plan Reflects General Trend Tying Pay to Performance," *Wall Street Journal* (January 26, 1988): 33.

37. J. Bettner, "Firms Give Stock Options to Wider Range of Workers in Effort to Instill Loyalty," *Wall Street Journal* (October 3, 1988): B1.

38. J. B. White, "GM to Pay Out Profit Bonuses, First Since 1985," *Wall Street Journal* (December 13, 1988): B11.

39. L. Hays, "All Eyes on Du Pont's Incentive-Pay Plan," *Wall Street Journal* (December 5, 1988): B1.

Managing Careers

After studying this chapter, you should be able to:
- Explain why careers are important.
- Identify the stages of career choice.
- Discuss how careers and the life cycle are related.
- Describe career stages in the organization and identify key career issues at each stage.
- Explain three models that recognize individual differences in careers.
- Discuss mobility in organizations, including the rules for success chess.
- Identify guidelines for self-management of careers.
- Describe steps that companies can take to enhance careers of women and minorities.

At Fairchild Control Systems Company, each of ten experienced managers is assigned as a mentor to one high-potential protégé. The mentor and protégé meet on a monthly basis. A two-year development plan is put together. It focuses on ways to enhance the protégé's education, exposure, responsibility, and skills training. The mentor develops goals for the protégé which are reviewed biannually, and the mentor has the responsibility for goal completion.[1]

Syntex runs assessment centers that provide management candidates with inputs about capabilities and give them the opportunity to participate in career planning. Syntex has also developed a career-planning workbook, *How to Work for a Living and Like It*, which sets down the basic steps and processes necessary to develop a career plan. Regular seminars, open to all employees, deal with career issues, including views of the various functional areas and the experience, education, and skills required for each area. The information has been especially helpful to women entering the work force.[2]

AT&T uses several selection and development procedures for career management. An important element of the AT&T approach is provision of challenging initial jobs. Competent, demanding superiors are identified who hold high expectations for the new employee.[3]

These are just a few examples of systematic attempts by organizations to manage their employees' careers effectively. Others are presented in the box on page 334. We will see in this chapter that several forces are demanding that careers no longer be left to chance. Both individuals and organizations have a stake in careers, and both can take steps to make careers more rewarding and productive.

We will first discuss alternative views of careers and consider why careers are important. Next, we will examine career choice and see how careers change over the life cycle. We will then address key issues that occur during career stages in organizations. After a review of models of individual differences in careers, we will examine ways to predict and enhance career mobility. Then we will provide guidelines for self-management of careers. Next, we will consider ways of enhancing careers of women and minorities. Finally, we will consider the management of career stress and examine the new careerism.

WHAT IS A CAREER?

Certainly a career has something to do with getting jobs, and perhaps with moving between jobs, places, and levels of responsibility and challenge. However, a career means more than that.[4]

The Protean Career

Proteus was a character in Greek mythology who could change shape in any way he wanted—from fire to lion to dragon to tree. Douglas T. Hall has drawn on this mythological figure to coin the term **protean career**. The essence of this idea is that there is much more to a career than just moving up the hierarchies of organizations:

The protean career is a process which the person, not the organization, is managing. It consists of all of the person's varied experiences in education, training, work in several organizations, changes in occupational field, etc.

SOME INNOVATIVE APPROACHES TO CAREER MANAGEMENT

Here are some examples of companies that have taken leadership roles in adopting innovative career management practices, and of the key ingredients of their programs:

Minnesota Mining and Manufacturing. 3M has a two-day management assessment program that helps employees identify career goals, training needs, and placement opportunities. Each program consists of about 15 participants chosen from young non-management employees who have volunteered or been nominated by management. 3M also has a career information center, a staff of career counselors, and a regular series of career development workshops. Particularly noteworthy are 3M's "transition workshops," which provide intensive help on self-assessment and active job-search techniques for those identified as available for transfer and promotion.

Exxon. To ensure a disciplined approach to the development of managerial talent, Exxon has implemented a Compensation and Executive Development (COED) system. The system is run by the CEO and a committee made up of members of Exxon's board. Meeting nearly every Monday, the committee regularly reviews the development and placement of the top 250 Exxon executives. It examines the perfor-

mance of these executives, plans for their developmental needs, and provides training and appropriate job assignments for potential backup candidates. In addition, each major subsidiary of Exxon has its own COED as well, so that the overall system reaches the top 2,000 managers at Exxon.

RCA. RCA asks its managers to suggest five to seven individuals who have had substantial work relationships with them to comprehensively assess their performance. Then each employee is anonymously evaluated by these individuals on 40 concrete performance practices, dealing with everything from creativity to analytical abilities. RCA uses the data to plan training programs and to provide in-depth career counseling.

Hewlett-Packard. Hewlett-Packard uses six devices to help employees assess their career goals and personal needs: autobiographical sketches, vocational interest tests, personality tests, diaries completed by employees themselves, tape-recorded interviews, and symbolic depictions of their lives (through pictures, photos, and so forth). After these self-assessment exercises, employees meet with department managers to discuss career objectives and to chart sequences of job changes and training courses.

Source: From *Managing Careers in Organizations* by Daniel C. Feldman. Copyright © 1988 by Scott, Foresman and Company. Reprinted by permission.

> *The protean career is not what happens to the person in any one organization. The protean person's own personal career choices and search for self-fulfillment are the unifying or integrative elements in his or her life. The criterion of success is internal (psychological success), not external.*[5]

Viewed in this light, a career is an ongoing sequence of events, some of which may have little or nothing to do with money or prestige. Also, according to this view, a career extends over the entire work life. What happens in one year or in one corporation is just a small piece of the rich career mosaic. Finally, determining whether or not a career is successful is up to the individual. If people are happy with the way their careers turn out, how can anyone say that their careers are failures? Figure 11–1 summarizes key differences between the traditional career and the protean career.

Why Are Careers Important?

Most people probably agree that careers are important. Unfortunately, most management students leave college knowing more about how to manage a

The protean career is a self-managed process of choices in a search for personal satisfaction and self-fulfillment.

company than about how to manage their own careers. Douglas T. Hall has suggested reasons why managers should care about careers. They include the following:[6]

- The career represents a person's entire life in the work setting, and work is a key factor in influencing the quality of a person's life. Work has the potential to satisfy, directly or indirectly, most human needs.
- Work is a way to get social equality and social freedom. For example, the entry of more and more women into the work force has changed the way society views women, the amount of power they have, and the rhythms of family life. Similarly, as more blacks and members of other minority

FIGURE 11–1

The Protean Versus the Traditional Career

Issue	Protean Career	Traditional Career
Who's in charge?	Person	Organization
Core values	Freedom; growth	Advancement; power
Degree of mobility	High	Lower
Important performance dimensions	Psychological success	Position level; salary
Important attitude dimensions	Work satisfaction; professional commitment	Work satisfaction; organizational commitment
Important identity dimensions	Do I respect myself? (self-esteem); What do I want to do? (self-awareness)	Am I respected in this organization? (esteem from others); What should I do? (organizational awareness)
Important adaptability dimensions	Work-related flexibility; current competence (measure: marketability)	Organization-related flexibility (measure: organizational survival)

groups get high-prestige jobs, their roles in society will change, too. Nothing speaks louder than success. A successful career brings recognition, respect, and freedom from economic want.

- People are increasingly willing to change organizations and even occupations. And, with growing emphasis on personal freedom, people are less likely to move passively at the company's whim or to make other personal sacrifices. As a result, the employee represents a greater unknown than in the past. Managers must now pay more attention to employees' career desires.

- Successful managers understand the needs and wants of their subordinates. As career management becomes a major concern of subordinates, managers must understand career interests and career dynamics to manage effectively.

- Finally, managers have their own careers to think about. They need to understand careers to manage their own careers effectively. Unfortunately, studies show that people often do not consider such vital career issues as how to make well-informed career choices, how to cope with conflicts between work and personal life, and how to arrive at career goals. Instead, they often let others make their career choices for them.

Stages of Career Choice

People develop career choices over a period that spans much of their lives. These choices often involve three stages. The **fantasy stage** generally occurs between the ages of 6 and 11. Typically unrealistic, it may reflect desires to be a cowboy or cowgirl, a sorcerer, or an astronaut. The **tentative stage** usually occurs between the ages of 11 and 16. In this stage, people first realize they have an important decision to make about their future. They begin to consider how various careers might fit their abilities, interests, and values. Finally, in the **realistic stage**, people seriously explore career options, firm up their preferences, and make an occupational choice. This is often a stage of compromise between what they want and what is available. The realistic stage may last for years—perhaps even a decade or more.[7]

Self-Analysis

Honest self-analysis is crucial to realistic job choice. Ideally, a job (and career) will be chosen that offers a good fit with an individual's abilities, values, and interests. A job that isn't right may seem attractive in the short run but will almost certainly lead to problems.[8] When considering your abilities, try to recognize both what you can do well and what you can't do well. It might be useful to make listings both of your strengths and weaknesses and of abilities you possess that may be particularly useful in certain jobs. These latter abilities might include knowledge of electronics, real estate, payroll procedures, or foreign languages. As we will discuss in the next chapter, values are broad, general beliefs we hold about how we should behave (such as behaving honestly or frugally) or what life goals we would like to achieve (such as a comfortable life or freedom). When thinking about jobs, determine whether they might clash with your values. Finally, interests are the things you like or dislike. Interests often develop from more general values. Think about your interests and how various jobs might satisfy them.

CAREERS AND THE LIFE CYCLE

Understanding how careers may evolve over time can help individuals and organizations to plan for career change and to manage it properly. Since the early 1970s, several life-cycle theories of careers have been developed, partly as a result of psychological examination of adult development. These theories find their roots primarily in the work of Carl Jung and Erik Erikson.[9]

Jung wrote of a "noon of life" transition from youth to middle life, occurring between the ages of 35 and 40. This noon of life is the "last summons to attain all of one's capabilities." Psychosomatic symptoms at this age and such ailments as depression and ulcers were seen as resulting from the failure to attain goals set during youth.

Erikson suggested that there are eight stages of life, each characterized by the individual's facing and attempting to resolve a crisis. He identified the following four adult stages:

1. *Adolescence*. This is the identity crisis stage. Childhood adaptations are reexamined. The adolescent searches for a new, creative, and independent role through which to contribute to society and derive a sense of meaning and faith.
2. *Young adulthood*. At this stage there is an intimacy crisis. The individual tries to develop intimacy and sharing with others.
3. *Adulthood*. Here, the individual faces a generativity crisis. There is concern with others beyond the immediate family. He or she tries to act as a mentor for the next generation.
4. *Maturity*. At the maturity stage the individual experiences a second identity crisis. There is a sense of nearing completion. This is a stage of reflection. The individual tries to accept the rightness of his or her life, and of all reality.

Graduation traditionally marks an individual's entry into the adult world.

Among the most interesting and influential attempts to relate careers to life stages is a model developed by Daniel Levinson.[10] He and his colleagues interviewed men ranging in age from 35 to 45 at the beginning of their study. Based on their research, they see adult life as punctuated by a rather predictable sequence of personal and career crises. Here are some of the important stages they identified during the work life up to the age of 50, at which age their research ended:

1. *Pulling up roots (ages 17–22).* The individual is breaking away from family ties and trying to become independent. There is still some reliance on family for financial support, and the separation may be difficult.
2. *Entering the adult world (ages 22–28).* Here, the individual has completed his or her education and made future commitments. He or she chooses a career and life-style.
3. *Age 30 transition (ages 28–33).* At the transition stage the individual reviews career and personal progress to date. If progress has not been satisfactory, there may be radical changes, such as divorce, career or job change, or a geographic move.
4. *Settling down (ages 33–39).* At this stage the individual devotes time heavily to the job and career, subordinating social contacts to advancement. He or she tries to find a "sponsor" who will ease upward movement.
5. *Mid-life transition (ages 40–45).* At the mid-life transition the individual may again review career progress. If progress has been satisfactory, a sense of pride and accomplishment may develop. If not, there may be a frustrating "mid-life crisis." This is a time of tumultuous struggles within the self and with the external world. The mid-life crisis may be reflected in a major change in life-style, often with drastic effects on the career.
6. *Entering middle adulthood (ages 45–50).* At this stage, it is time to get past the mid-life transition and begin forming a new life structure. The life structure that emerges varies in its satisfactoriness. Some individuals, because of defeats in prior stages, lack the resources to create a minimally adequate structure. They face a middle adulthood of constraints and decline. Others will find middle adulthood to be a time of special satisfactions and fulfillments. They have achieved many of their ambitions and can now enjoy a full and creative period.

CAREER STAGES IN ORGANIZATIONS

In the previous section we considered how careers and the life cycle might be related. Several writers have proposed career stages which are related more specifically to the sequence of roles an individual may adopt while in an organization. Figure 11–2 shows four such roles.[11]

At the apprentice stage, the individual is directed by others and is concerned with helping, learning, and following directions. Next is the colleague stage, when the individual becomes an independent contributor to the organization. At the mentor stage, the individual assumes responsibility for others, spending time on such activities as training and guidance. Finally, at the sponsor stage, the individual is concerned with directing the organization as a whole and shaping its direction. As people pass through these stages in their early, middle, and late careers, their task needs and socioemotional needs

	Stage 1	Stage 2	Stage 3	Stage 4
Central Activity	Helping Learning Following directions	Independent contributor	Training Interfacing	Shaping the direction of the organization
Primary Relationship	Apprentice	Colleague	Mentor	Sponsor
Major Psychological Issues	Dependence	Independence	Assuming responsibility for others	Exercising power

FIGURE 11–2
Four Career Stages

change. Figure 11–3 presents Douglas Hall's summary of these evolving needs. Let's consider some important aspects of each of these stages.

Early Career Issues

Early in their careers, people often experience great uncertainty about their competence and performance potential.[12] They are likely to need guidance and support to get their careers moving. This stressful time can have a major influence on the remainder of the career.

FIGURE 11–3
Developmental Needs in Careers

Stage	Task Needs	Socioemotional Needs
Early Career	1. Develop action skills 2. Develop a specialty 3. Develop creativity, innovation 4. Rotate into new area after 3–5 years	1. Support 2. Autonomy 3. Deal with feelings of rivalry, competition
Middle Career	1. Develop skills in training and coaching others (younger employees) 2. Training for updating and integrating skills 3. Develop broader view of work and organization 4. Job rotation into new job requiring new skills	1. Opportunity to express feelings about mid-life (anguish, defeat, limited time, restlessness) 2. Reorganize thinking about self (mortality, values, family, work) 3. Reduce self-indulgence and competitiveness 4. Support and mutual problem solving for coping with mid-career stress
Late Career	1. Shift from power role to one of consultation, guidance, wisdom 2. Begin to establish self in activities outside the organization (start on part-time basis)	1. Support and counseling to help see integrated life experiences as a platform for others 2. Acceptance of one's one and only life cycle 3. Gradual detachment from organization

Young managers may experience frustration when the job that seemed to offer high-level responsibility and excitement involves instead many late nights at the office just to complete routine tasks.

CAREER PROBLEMS OF YOUNG MANAGERS

Based primarily on his interviews and discussions with hundreds of young managers, Ross Webber identified some of the problems that young managers most commonly face.[13]

Early Frustration and Dissatisfaction

Young managers' job expectations often exceed reality. Since their academic training may have focused on cases in which they took the roles of top-level executives, they may now expect to get a lot of responsibility quickly. Instead, they are often placed in routine, boring jobs until they have proven themselves. As a result, young managers may experience severe reality shock, become frustrated, and perhaps leave the firm. If the company has painted an overly bright picture when recruiting, this reality shock may be especially great.[14]

Insensitivity and Passivity

Organizations are political. Often young managers are either insensitive to the political aspects of organizations or may resent them. Or they may simply be passive, hoping that things will turn out for the best. As a result, they may not actively explore the organizational environment to understand relationships and attitudes and clarify their own positions. Further, they may be unaware of the real criteria by which performance is rated. In some cases hard criteria such as performance are difficult to assess, and superiors may focus instead on whether the young manager fits their prejudices. Appearance, speech habits, managerial style, and other subjective measures may be used for evaluation.

Loyalty Dilemmas

Most people in authority value subordinates' loyalty, variously defined. However, there are many versions of loyalty. Some see loyalty as obedience—subordinates are loyal if they do what they are told. Others interpret loyalty as putting in effort and long hours to prove concern for the company. To still others, loyalty is successful completion of tasks, or protection of the superior from ridicule and adverse evaluation by others, or giving the superior honest information about mistakes and potential failures. Unfortunately, young managers often do not know which version of loyalty the organization or superior expects. Sometimes multiple versions are demanded simultaneously. For instance, the superior may expect strict obedience but be angry if obedience leads to poor performance. These uncertainties and conflicts may cause the young manager to conform to power and authority, to try to change the superior's expectations, or to leave.

Personal Anxiety

Young managers may experience anxiety. They often find that, just at the time they are beginning to reap the rewards of their jobs, they question the value of what they are doing. They may say, "I am making $30,000 a year, but I don't think what the company produces has much value to society." As a result, young managers may fear that they are "selling out." These concerns can lead to difficult choices. Young managers can change their personal values, appear to be troublemakers, or leave their jobs. Young managers may also feel anxiety about commitment to the organization. Though they may feel they would benefit from conforming to the norms of the organization and having a sense of certainty about their careers, they don't want to close doors and shatter illusions about possibilities. Finally, young managers may feel anxious about being dependent on others in the organization. Just at the point in their lives when they are declaring psychological independence from home and parental authority, they are becoming dependent on superiors and others in the firm. They may also feel anxiety because others in the organization—subordinates, peers, and even superiors—are dependent on them.

Ethical Dilemmas

Most young managers face unexpected career dilemmas that force them to think about what is ethical and unethical. In making ethical choices, young managers may find themselves torn between economic self-interest, obedience to the law, observance of religious principles, obedience to a superior, and doing the greatest good for the greatest number. Business ethics were discussed in detail in Chapter 4.

THE IMPORTANCE OF EARLY CAREER CHALLENGE AND SUCCESS

Douglas Hall and Fran Hall have presented a model of the career-growth cycle.[15] The model, shown in Figure 11–4, suggests the importance of early career challenge. According to Hall and Hall, a job that provides challenging, stretching goals triggers the process of career growth. The clearer and more challenging the goals and the more support the job provides, the more effort will be exerted and the greater will be the chance of good performance. A person who does a good job and receives positive feedback will feel successful. These feelings of psychological success will enhance self-esteem and increase job involvement, leading, in turn, to the setting of future stretching goals and continued career growth.[16]

These arguments make it sound as though early career success is crucial to later development. James Rosenbaum has presented evidence that supports this view.[17] He interprets this evidence as favoring a **tournament model of mobility**. In the tournament model, careers are seen as a series of competi-

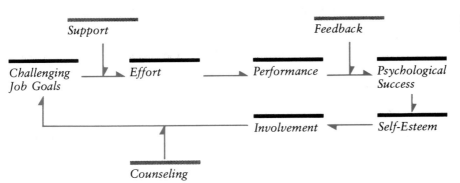

FIGURE 11–4
The Career-Growth Cycle

tions, each of which has implications for an individual's chances of mobility. Winners at a given level can compete at a higher level. Losers are out of the tournament or can compete in only lower-level contests.

Rosenbaum found that very early job moves are related to mobility even a decade later, after employees have moved on to second and third jobs. In fact, he concluded that mobility in the earliest stage of one's career bears an unequivocal relationship with one's later career, predicting chances of promotion and demotion in subsequent periods as well as the final career ceiling to which the individual would rise. The disadvantages of not being promoted early were so great, Rosenbaum concluded, that it is reasonable to conclude that employees who were not promoted in the first period are no longer competing in the same system with employees who were. They are in a different tournament, somewhere in the minor leagues.

These findings have important implications, some of them disturbing. First, of course, they bolster Hall and Hall's claim that early career experiences are crucial. False steps at a tender career age can be permanently crippling. Second, Rosenbaum feels that tournament mobility may represent a self-fulfilling prophecy.[18] Early winners will be seen as "high-potential" people and will be given challenging socialization processes to foster further development. Early losers will be socialized into undemanding, alienating roles. Third, it is possible that awareness of tournament mobility could inhibit risk taking. Conscious that a slip at any rung of the tournament ladder may be fatal to the career, managers may elect safe, conformist strategies.

Middle Career Issues

By mid-career, individuals are becoming fully independent contributors. They have learned the ropes of organizational life and put their focus on exposure and advancement. There can be many new stresses at this stage, and some individuals may find their movement thwarted.

COPING WITH MID-CAREER STRESS[19]

At mid-career—as suggested by the Levinson model—the employee experiences many physiological, attitudinal, occupational, and family changes. There is an awareness of aging and a recognition that many ambitious career goals will never be attained. New life goals may be sought. A disturbing sense of obsolescence may develop, coupled with a feeling that one is becoming less mobile and less attractive in the job market.

At mid-career, employees may choose to undergo some retraining in preparation for new career opportunities.

Having realistic expectations about mid-career crises and transitions seems to ease the stress and pain of this period. In addition, mid-career employees can receive training to provide exposure to new skills and ideas. They may also be trained to help younger employees, thereby keeping fresh and up-to-date. Mid-career employees can be encouraged to face their feelings of restlessness and insecurity, to re-examine their values and life goals, and to set new goals or recommit themselves to old ones. Life planning and career planning exercises may be especially valuable. The company can take steps to deal with obsolescence through seminars, workshops, degree programs, and other forms of "retreading." It can also try to prevent obsolescence in the first place by providing challenging job assignments which force the individual to build new skills and learn about new developments in the professional field. A later section in this chapter discusses stress in organizations and suggests steps that individuals and organizations can take to manage stress.

THE CAREER PLATEAU

The **career plateau** is the point in a career where the likelihood of additional hierarchical promotion is very low.[20] Employees often experience this plateau at mid-career. Some people may plateau because they have no desire for future promotion. They may enjoy their current jobs and do them well but be reluctant to take on additional responsibilities. Others may have plateaued because of poor performance. Still others find there is simply no place to go: There are no openings at higher levels. The fact that an employee has plateaued may say nothing about desires or performance.

Workers who have plateaued because of slack demand for labor or because of poor performance often have little to do. Japanese white-collar excess workers are called *madogiwazoku*, or "window watchers," because they have little to do but stare out the window. They may be assigned to lawn or maintenance work. In the United States, Eugene Jennings has written of "shelf sitters," executives whose careers have stagnated and who have been "put on the shelf" in make-work, dead-end positions.[21]

Figure 11–5 presents a model of managerial career states. The model classifies four principal career states on the basis of current performance and likelihood of future promotion.

Learners have high potential for advancement, but are now performing below standards. Trainees or employees recently promoted into new positions which they have not yet mastered would be examples. Stars, performing well and having high potential for continued advancement, are on a "fast track." Solid citizens have good current performance but little promotion potential. Finally, deadwood are poor performers with little potential for advancement. The solid citizens and deadwood have plateaued, though for different reasons. Deadwood are "ineffective plateauees." Solid citizens are "effective plateauees." Some are organizationally plateaued because of lack of openings. Because organizations are typically pyramid-shaped, such organizational plateauing is common. Others are personally plateaued either be-

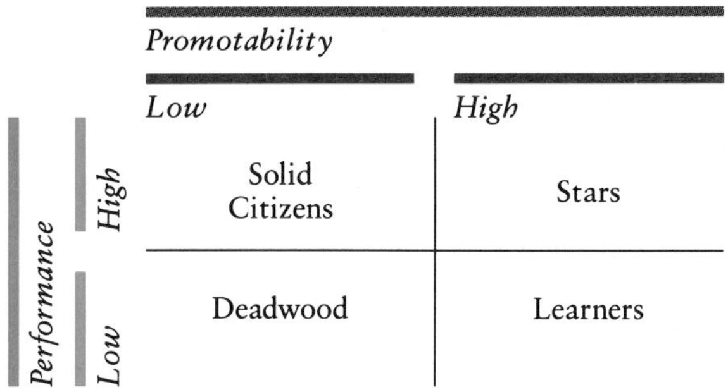

FIGURE 11–5
Performance and Promotability

	Promotability	
	Low	**High**
High (Performance)	Solid Citizens	Stars
Low (Performance)	Deadwood	Learners

Source: Adapted, by permission of the publisher, from "Managing the Career Plateau," by T. P. Ference, J. A. F. Stoner, and E. K. Warren, *Academy of Management Review* 2 (1977): 603. Reproduced with permission.

cause they do not desire higher-level jobs or because they are not seen as having the abilities needed for such jobs.

One study of managers who describe themselves as plateaued found them to show surprisingly little dissatisfaction with the promotion policies of their firms.[22] Further, they were only slightly less satisfied with their jobs and lives than were their non-plateaued counterparts. Apparently, many plateaued managers can cope with and adapt to the career plateau. As we have said, some genuinely may not want promotions. Others who did not receive desired promotions may rationalize, emphasizing the longer hours and increased pressure that promotions would bring. Still others may divert their energies to activities outside the job. Finally, some plateaued managers may move to new jobs within the firm to hide their embarrassment from their peers.

Whatever the satisfaction level of plateaued managers, plateauing may cause problems for more than just the plateaued employee. One survey found that younger employees were often demoralized by the stalled careers of older, plateaued employees, thinking this might be a vision of what the future holds for them. Plateaued employees were also seen as clogging promotion channels, lowering morale of co-workers and subordinates, and harming relationships with customers and clients.[23]

This model of managerial career states raises some interesting issues. For instance, firms may want to take steps to ensure that their solid citizens are not neglected. They can appraise, counsel, and develop career paths for solid citizens and provide them with training, skill upgrading, and development. They can try to identify deadwood early and act to restore performance through a variety of means. For instance, they might employ education programs to upgrade technical skill, development programs focusing on emotional and intellectual recharging, and job rotation through new duties, skill demands, or location.

Late Career Issues

By late career, many individuals have already experienced considerable advancement and may turn their attention to aiding and developing others. If their careers have been fulfilling, this can be a satisfying and rewarding time. If their careers have been frustrating, this can be a difficult period of trying to cope with disappointments. In late career individuals also begin to turn their thoughts toward separation from the organization.

MENTORING

Mentor relationships are relationships between younger and older adults that contribute to career development.[24] D. J. Levinson et al., in their study of adult males, note that the mentor plays an important role in the young adult's development:

He may act as a teacher to enhance the young man's skills and intellectual development. Serving as sponsor, he may use his influence to facilitate the young man's entry and advancement. He may be a host and guide, welcoming the initiate into a new occupational and social world and acquainting him with its values, customs, resources, and cast of characters. Through his own virtues, achievements, and way of living, the mentor may be an exemplar that the protégé can admire and seek to emulate. He may provide counsel and moral support in times of stress.[25]

Increasingly, of course, the mentor and/or the protégé may be female. Indeed, if mentors are really as important as many suggest, it may be crucial for women to find mentors. However, since most mentors are still likely to be male, many women will find themselves in cross-gender relationships. These may be stressful because of fears of intimacy and because of public scrutiny. Females may also find male mentors to be unsatisfactory role models because males have not experienced similar personal and professional dilemmas.[26]

While most mentoring is informal, some firms do have formal mentoring programs. In some cases, companies assign mentors only to minorities and females. In others, experienced executives volunteer to work with high-potential employees to set goals, review progress, and give feedback outside the formal chain of command.[27]

The mentor relationship can be helpful to both parties. In addition to the help it provides the protégé, it gives the mentor a feeling of technical and psychological support from loyal subordinates. Also, peers may recognize mentors for effectively developing talent, and mentors may receive satisfaction from passing on wisdom and developing the next generation of managers.

For many couples, freedom from work pressures and time to enjoy each other's company are a retirement bonus.

ADJUSTMENT INTO RETIREMENT

Retirement gives some individuals a sense of loss and finality. Many workers fantasize that they will die soon after retirement. For other people, retirement is a chance to escape a frustrating or high-pressure job and to enjoy free time and pursue hobbies. In any case, this is a major transition. As discussed later in this chapter, life change—whether desirable or undesirable—is stressful. Retirement combines changes in work patterns with personal, financial, and perhaps health changes. Those happiest in retirement have prepared for it over time and have made plans for their retirement years.

One large midwestern utility has developed a series of retirement seminars.[28] A year before planned retirement, employees attend these seminars to prepare for the transition. The seminars cover topics such as pension and benefits. In addition, experts in other areas meet with the employees to discuss such issues as use of leisure time, psychological adjustments, relocations, and second careers.

A THREE-DIMENSIONAL MODEL OF CAREERS

The view of stages we have just considered focused primarily on upward movement in the organization. However, movement may be more complex. As shown in Figure 11–6, Edgar Schein sees movement through the organization as taking place in three dimensions:[29]

- *Vertical*—up and down, such as a promotion or demotion. This is the traditional way to view movement in organizations.
- *Radial*—toward or away from the inner circle or the core of the system. Radial movement takes the individual closer to or further from central tasks, people, or power. Generally radial movement will be related to vertical movement. However, as illustrated by people who are "kicked upstairs," some individuals may experience vertical movement while remaining on the periphery. Others may stay on a level but move closer to the core as they gain experience and trust.

FIGURE 11–6
Schein's Conical Model

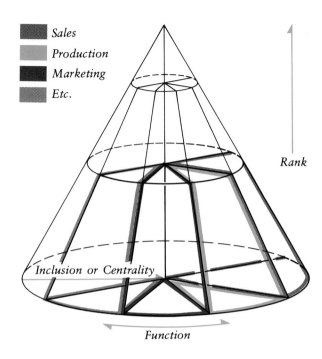

Sales
Production
Marketing
Etc.

Rank

Inclusion or Centrality

Function

Source: Reprinted with permission from NTL Institute, "The Individual, the Organization, and the Career: A Conceptual Scheme" by Edgar H. Schein, *Journal of Applied Behavioral Science* 7 (4): 404, copyright 1971.

- *Circumferential*—to a different function, program, or product in the organization, such as to production from sales. Such moves may be a useful broadening experience, providing the base for future vertical moves.

Different organizations have different structures and boundaries relating to these dimensions and, thus, have different types of mobility. Corresponding to the types of movement are the following boundaries:

- Hierarchical boundaries, separating the hierarchical levels from one another;
- Inclusion boundaries, separating individuals or groups who differ in their degree of centrality;
- Functional or departmental boundaries, separating departments or different functional groupings from each other.

These boundaries may differ in the number of each that exist in the organization, in their permeability, and in their criteria for movement. During career progress, individuals and organizations influence each other. When the individual moves vertically or radially, there are attempts at socialization to instill in the manager the values and attitudes needed for the new position.[30] When a circumferential move is made, training is used to give the individual the new skills and knowledge required. In turn, managers influence the organization through innovation, bringing their own views with them and introducing change. Such innovation generally occurs later in the manager's career, after experience, status, and power have been acquired.

FITTING INDIVIDUALS TO CAREERS

Several theories try to fit individuals to careers. Such theories might help organizations select appropriate individuals and tailor programs to their particular needs. They might also help individuals find suitable positions. In this section, we will examine three models that point out individual differences in the way people view occupations or jobs.

Holland's Occupational Personality Types

John Holland reasoned that people gravitate toward environments that match their personal orientations. He proposed six personality types and six matching occupational environments:[31]

- *Realistic.* Involves aggressive behavior and physical activities requiring skill, strength, and coordination. (Examples: forestry, trucking, farming.)
- *Investigative.* Involves cognitive activities (thinking, organizing, understanding) rather than affective activities (feeling, acting, or interpersonal and emotional). (Examples: biology, mathematics, oceanography.)
- *Social.* Involves interpersonal rather than intellectual or physical activities. (Examples: clinical psychology, foreign service, social work.)
- *Conventional.* Involves structural, rule-regulated activities and subordination of personal needs to an organization or person of power and status. (Examples: accounting, finance.)
- *Enterprising.* Involves verbal activities to influence others and to attain power and status. (Examples: management, law, public relations.)
- *Artistic.* Involves self-expression, artistic creation, expression of emotions, and individualistic activities. (Examples: art, music education.)

The Vocational Preference Inventory (VPI) can be used to measure these orientations. The VPI is a list of 160 occupational titles toward which individuals indicate their likes and dislikes.[32] Holland proposed that if one of the orientations dominates the others, the individual will gravitate toward an occupation consistent with that orientation. If two or more are equally strong, the individual will vacillate in choosing an occupation.

Holland has developed a hexagonal model of the relationships between personal orientations, presented in Figure 11–7. According to Holland's research, the closer two orientations are in the figure, the more compatible they are. People with high scores on opposite categories in the hexagon (such as on Artistic and Conventional) are likely to have internal conflicts about their occupational choices.

Research on Holland's model shows that people do gravitate to a small subset of jobs. Further, when people choose a career consistent with their personality, they are more likely to be satisfied with their career choice and not change professions. They are also more likely to remain excited by the nature of the work they do and to be satisfied with their colleagues at work.[33]

Schein's Career Anchors

Based in part on his decade-long study of a panel of alumni of the Sloan School of Management, Schein has presented the idea of **career anchors**.[34] These anchors are "a syndrome of motives, values, and self-perceived compe-

People who choose a career consistent with their personality are more likely to find satisfaction.

FIGURE 11–7
*Occupational
Personality Types*

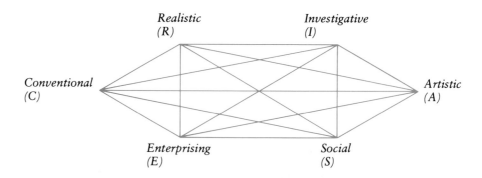

Source: John L. Holland, *Making Vocational Choices: A Theory of Vocational Personalities & Work Environments*, © 1985, p. 29. Reprinted by permission of Prentice-Hall, Englewood Cliffs, New Jersey.

tencies which function to guide and constrain an individual's entire career."[35] An anchor can be thought of as a "master motive," or the thing the person will not give up under any circumstances. Schein's study led him to conclude there are at least five career anchors:

- *Anchor 1: Managerial Competence.* The career is organized around the competencies and values inherent in the managerial process. The most important components of this concept are the ability to influence and supervise, the ability to analyze and solve complex problems, and emotional stability.
- *Anchor 2: Technical-Functional Competence.* The career is organized around the challenge of the actual work being done, whether it is related to marketing, financial analysis, corporate planning, or some other area of business or management. The anchor is the technical field or functional area rather than the managerial process itself. Individuals with this anchor don't want to be promoted out of the kind of work they are now doing.
- *Anchor 3: Security.* The individual has an underlying need for security and tries to stabilize the career by tying it to a given organization. More than others, individuals with this anchor are likely to accept an organizational definition of their careers. They rely on the organization to recognize their needs and competencies and to do what is best for them.
- *Anchor 4: Creativity.* Individuals with this anchor have a strong need to create something. This anchor is most evident among entrepreneurs, but corporate employees may also hold it.
- *Anchor 5: Autonomy and Independence.* The concern here is with freedom and autonomy. Individuals with this anchor often find organizational life too restrictive or intrusive into their personal lives and seek careers that offer more autonomy.

These five anchors reflect predominant concerns. An employee may still care about other things, but the anchor is overriding. Schein argues that, to the extent that these anchors are stable, it is crucial for employing organizations to identify them early and to create appropriate career opportunities. For instance, a person with a technical-functional anchor may not welcome a promotion to a management position. Instead, organizations will have to learn to think about the kinds of contributions people with various anchors can make. They will also have to develop multiple reward systems and career paths to permit the full development of diverse kinds of individuals.

Driver's Career Concept Types

Michael Driver sees four basic **career concept types**. They include the following:[36]

- *Transitory.* There is no clear pattern of career movement. Some transitory individuals may drift in a relatively passive way from job to job. Others may be entrepreneurial types who launch new activities but move on as soon as stabilization sets in.
- *Steady-state.* The individual chooses a lifetime occupation. Steady-state types settle into an organization and prefer stability to change.
- *Linear.* A career choice is made early and there is emphasis on steady upward movement on a career ladder.
- *Spiral.* There is a planned search for increasing self-development and creative growth. The career choice may change periodically.

Driver has linked his career concept types to Schein's career anchors. For instance, individuals having security as the career anchor might fit the steady-state career concept. Those with autonomy as the career anchor might adhere to the transitory or spiral career concepts.

Driver reasons that organizations might be categorized in terms of the four career concept types. A transitory organization is loose, temporary, and entrepreneurial, with few formal procedures. Linear and steady-state organizations both have classical pyramidal structures with tight controls. However, linear organizations put stress on vertical movement and steady-state organizations have units of great stability. Some high-technology or artistic organizations may show spiral patterns. Some departments in linear or steady-state organizations may also operate in a spiral mode.

An employee would generally best fit into an organization of a corresponding type—a transitory individual in a transitory organization, and so on. A linear individual, for instance, would be uncomfortable in a transitory organization. However, Driver also takes a dynamic view of the career concept types. He reasons that as a result of work or other social learning, or the inner dynamic of human development, career concepts may evolve during a lifetime. Therefore, organizations must do more than simply be concerned with fit to an unchanging employee; they must also cultivate human resource planning systems, employee development programs, and even strategies and structures that recognize transitions between career concept types.

CAREER MOBILITY

We have argued that mobility is not the only gauge of career success. However, many people, especially the linears in Driver's classification, certainly do value it.[37] Mobility often leads to greater responsibility and status, as well as to increased pay and benefits. Further, some people may value mobility in

Douglas T. (Tim) Hall (Ph.D., Massachusetts Institute of Technology) is Professor of Organizational Behavior at Boston University. He is the author of Careers in Organizations *and co-author of* Organizational Climates and Careers, The Two-Career Couple, Experiences in Management and Organizational Behavior, *and* Human Resource Management: Strategy, Design, and Implementation. *He is editor of* Career Development in Organizations. *Professor Hall is the recipient of the American Psychological Association's James McKeen Cattell Award for research design. He is a fellow of the American Psychological Association and of the Academy of Management, where he served on*

the board of governors. His research and consulting activities have dealt with career development, women's careers, career burnout, and two-career couples. He has served as a consultant to organizations such as Sears, AT&T, American Hospital Supply, General Electric, Borg-Warner, Price Waterhouse, Ford Motor Company, Eli Lilly, and the World Bank.

Q: You wrote a decade ago about the protean career, discussed in this chapter. Have your views concerning the protean career changed at all since then? Do you now see other people as adopting this view?

A: The protean career seems to have been a model for many people for a long time. The differences now are that there are more people who want this sort of flexible, self-directed career pattern (e.g., two-career couples, baby boomers, working parents, late-career people phasing into retirement); and the protean career is now more acceptable to management in that it is more "OK" for an employee to admit that he or she wants a protean career. As organizations are downsizing, restructuring, merging, divesting, de-layering, growing, and making all kinds of other changes, they need employees who are more flexible and adaptive (to make the organization more flexible and adaptive). Further, more higher-level managers and executives are becoming concerned about flexibility in their *own* careers.

Q: Do you think organizations are generally taking a greater interest in managing their employees' careers?

A: There is not more interest in managing employees' careers directly, but in helping employees manage their own careers (i.e., career planning, to get a better fit between the employee and the organization). There is also more interest in career management, which entails formal systems for the utilization, development, and movement of employees to meet organizational human resource management objectives. A cutting edge development here is in linking career planning and career management through self-paced, computerized career information systems. Organizations such as IBM, Xerox, and Monsanto have been leaders in this area.

Q: You and others have argued that individual differences should be considered when managing careers. Do you feel that organizations are in fact recognizing such differences? If so, how are they dealing with them?

A: Career stage, which is loosely related to age, is being recognized as a critical individual difference. Special career programs are often found for newly hired employees (entry stage), fast-track, high-potential employees (establishment), mid-career employees, and pre-retirement employees. Also, special interest is now being shown in the varied needs of a very diverse work force. Companies that value these differences will have a competitive edge in the future.

Q: Your writings suggest that early career experiences are crucial. What recommendations would you make for individuals who are about to begin their careers?

A: First, realize that you are choosing an organization as well as a job. Be sure that the first job will be challenging, but also look ahead to future job assignments and future bosses, to see if later jobs will also be challenging. Talk to people who have been in the organization for four or five years, as the five-year point is where many people realize that future career growth in that organization may be limited.

Find out who your boss would be in the first job. Your boss will have a major impact on how challenging the job is. Be sure the boss has confidence in you and will set high expectations for you.

Finally, make sure the job and organization provide an environment where you would enjoy working. Make sure it is a good fit for you personally. Do not choose the job just because it is in a high-status or high-paying organization. To be successful, you will have to perform at your best on every assignment. And to perform at your best, you will have to enjoy the work environment.

itself. Eugene Jennings has identified what he calls the **mobicentric man,** someone who values mobility as an end rather than as a means:

The mobicentric man values motion and action not so much because they lead to change, but because they are change and change is his ultimate value. . . . Freedom to him is a form of movement. He frequently changes positions, sometimes just within one company (though never just within one department) and sometimes between companies. . . . For him, success is represented less by position, title, salary, or performance than by moving and movement.[38]

Jennings has outlined nine rules of what he calls **success chess** to increase mobility:

- *Rule No. 1: Maintain the widest possible set of options.* Don't get stereotyped. Don't stay in technical work too long. And, while it may be necessary to get staff experience, a good line reputation is also necessary.
- *Rule No. 2: Don't get trapped in a dead-end position.* Try not to work under a superior who hasn't moved in more than three years. Check to see that there are upward job routes open. If there are not, try to get out of the situation.
- *Rule No. 3: Become a crucial subordinate to a mobile superior.* A **crucial subordinate** is one that the boss needs as much as that person needs the boss. A crucial subordinate will move when the boss moves.
- *Rule No. 4: Always try for increased exposure and visibility.* **Exposure** refers to how often you are seen by those above you in the organization. **Visibility** is how often you can see those above you. Decades ago, people were told that the way to get to the top was to have a desk near the boss's door. This advice—that you don't get promoted if you aren't noticed—is still valid.
- *Rule No. 5: Be willing to practice self-nomination.* That is, let people in power know when you want a job. Generally at least two moves in a career span are due to self-nomination. Don't just wait for your boss or someone else to determine your options.
- *Rule No. 6: If you decide to leave a company, do it at your convenience.* Leave on the best of terms. Don't wait for the situation to get really bad or for a nasty face-off to occur. Quit while you're ahead.
- *Rule No. 7: Rehearse before quitting a job.* Don't leave in a state of high emotion. Write out your resignation and wait a week. Think the decision through. Tell your family, take a week-long vacation, and bring your biographical data sheet up to date. After a week, decide whether or not to quit. But don't keep on rehearsing; one way or another, make up your mind.
- *Rule No. 8: Think of the corporation as a market place for skills.* Learn which skills are in demand in a particular company or industry at a particular time. Read business publications such as *The Wall Street Journal* or *Fortune* to find out which companies need your skills.
- *Rule No. 9: Don't let success cut off your options.* Successful people in one area often can be successful in other areas. Consider new careers. Don't spend your life in a rut.

SELF-MANAGEMENT OF CAREERS

Many forces affect career development. Organizational practices clearly play a role, and even luck may be important.[39] Certainly, though, individuals should be proactive, acting to manage their own careers. Jennings' rules for success chess may help in that regard. Also, Douglas T. Hall has presented the following guidelines for self-management of careers:[40]

1. *Develop basic career competencies.* John Crites has identified five such competencies: self-appraisal, occupational information, goal selection, planning, and problem solving.[41] Each of these competencies can be developed.

   a. *Self-appraisal.* Mature career development requires self-awareness. The counseling, guidance, career planning, or personnel offices on most campuses can help at this stage. Counseling interviews, aptitude and interest tests, and career-planning exercises may all be helpful. Also, just asking others, such as an instructor or boss, to give you feedback about your performance can be enlightening.

   b. *Occupational information.* Career development requires a fit between you and your job, so it's important to learn about potential jobs. Some sources that provide information about types of work, skill requirements, occupational developments, worker trait requirements, and other relevant factors include the *Dictionary of Occupational Titles*, the U.S. Department of Labor's *Occupational Outlook Handbook*, and the *Occupational Outlook Quarterly*. Also, some interactive computer methods for providing career information are now available.

   c. *Goal selection.* Career success, according to the approach taken in this chapter, means achieving one's goals, so the process of properly setting goals is crucial. Chris Argyris argues that goals leading to growth are challenging, relevant to the person's self-image, set by the person (alone or in collaboration with another), and implemented by the person's independent effort.[42] Proper goal setting depends upon awareness of oneself and of occupations. That is, goals must be consistent with career capabilities. Counselors, supervisors, or one's own work experiences may be useful in defining proper goals. Also, some useful career-planning exercises are now available.

   d. *Planning.* Once a goal is set, it is necessary to specify the steps to meet that goal and to determine the order of those steps. Both counseling and career-planning exercises may help at the planning stage.

   e. *Problem solving.* Because problems constantly arise during careers, competence in problem solving can be crucial to successful movement through a career. Many of the techniques we will discuss in Chapter 21, Problem Solving and Creativity, can readily be applied to career problems.

2. *Choose an organization carefully.* Your choice of an organization to work for is extremely important. The organization will control many important rewards, may determine where you live, and may even influence the sorts of competencies you develop and the kinds of skills you exercise. Also, your initial choice of an employer may have lasting consequences in terms of the chances of future moves to other organizations. For example, in a

university setting it is unlikely that those seeking to fill a faculty position at a high-status institution such as Stanford or Yale would seriously consider the application of someone now teaching at what they consider to be a lower-status institution, despite that individual's impressive credentials.

3. *Get a challenging initial job.* In choosing a first job, you should generally give such short-run considerations as salary and location less weight than challenge and potential for career growth. If you do take a job that offers little challenge, you should probably either try to make a later job change or try to redefine your job to assume more responsibility.

4. *Be an outstanding performer.* Good performance enhances your esteem both in the eyes of others, such as your boss, and in your own eyes. Ask your boss to help you set challenging goals, to give feedback, and to coach you.

5. *Develop professional mobility.* More options are better than fewer. Mobility and potential mobility are crucial to career success.

6. *Plan your own and your spouse's careers collaboratively.* If both spouses are working, or may work, severe strains can result unless careful career planning takes place. It is unrealistic and unfair to assume that one partner will go along passively when the other takes a job transfer.

7. *Get help in career management.* Seek advice from experts in your school or organization. Consider using professional job counselors or placement specialists.

8. *Anticipate chance events.* No matter how precisely you plan, chance will play a role. Develop contingency plans that specify what you will do if various things—good or bad—happen.

9. *Continually reassess your career.* Mid-course corrections may be needed. You will have to make career choices all through life, not just when you leave school. Continually ask where you are, where you want to be, and how you are going to get there.

ENHANCING CAREERS OF WOMEN AND MINORITIES

The nature of the workplace in general, and of managerial ranks in particular, is changing. Many of these changes are the result of laws and social trends which are encouraging females and minorities to cast off traditional roles. Nevertheless, women and minorities may still face an invisible but real "glass ceiling" that acts as a subtle barrier to promotions into high-level executive jobs.[43] In this section we will consider three issues in career management for women and minorities.

Women's Career Development

A phenomenal recent social trend has been the rapid increase in the number of married women in the work force. This trend is in part a result of economic necessity and in part a reflection of changing values: jobs are a liberating influence, a key to new life choices. Over half of all mothers with children under six years of age are in the work force. Between 1986 and 2000, there will be an estimated net increase of 13 million female workers, compared with 7.7 million male workers.[44]

This trend presents opportunities and challenges to organizations. If women's potential is to be fully utilized, companies must take steps to foster their career development. As shown in Figure 11–8, companies have chosen several routes to such development.

Some of these routes take the form of such traditional means as visible posting of job opportunities, career counseling, and training programs. Others are more innovative, such as opportunities for part-time jobs at advanced hierarchical levels and a variety of family-sensitive work practices.

Also, mentoring—discussed earlier in this chapter—can be critical to women's career development. Unfortunately, many women and minority workers complain that it is difficult to find mentors, especially at upper-management levels. At such levels, many executives have had little experience working closely with women and minorities. Also, many mentoring relationships are based on friendship and nurturing developed outside a 9-to-5 schedule. If whites and blacks do not interact socially, the relationships upon which much mentoring is based are never forged. It is partly for these reasons that, as noted previously, some firms are formally assigning mentors to females and minorities.[45]

One recent, and very controversial, suggestion to accommodate women in the work force is the so-called Mommy Track. The idea of the Mommy Track is that firms should permit women who are more committed to family than career to have greater flexibility—but that they should be eased off the fast track. Although presented as a way for some women to have careers while raising a family, it was met with anger and frustration by many women and women's groups. They protested that the Mommy Track reinforces the view of some executives that women can be active parents only at the expense of their careers.[46]

Dual-Career Couples

Another result of the influx of women into the work force is the growth in the number of dual-career couples. By late 1988, that number had reached

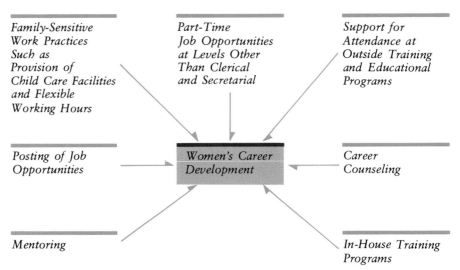

FIGURE 11–8
Company Practices to Enhance Women's Career Development

Family-Sensitive Work Practices Such as Provision of Child Care Facilities and Flexible Working Hours

Part-Time Job Opportunities at Levels Other Than Clerical and Secretarial

Support for Attendance at Outside Training and Educational Programs

Posting of Job Opportunities

Women's Career Development

Career Counseling

Mentoring

In-House Training Programs

24.8 million.[47] Such couples enjoy the benefits of two careers, including increased income, but face many constraints and problems. For starters, it is often difficult to find two suitable jobs in the same geographical location. When one member of the couple is offered a transfer, often a promotion, the decision of whether or not to accept becomes much more complicated. Also, about one-fourth of the nation's working wives earn more than their husbands. That can create strains in marriages where men have always held the breadwinner role, and the chance of divorce increases.[48] Add to these pressures the fact that the couple also has to juggle home and family roles, and the picture of the dual-career couple becomes less than bright.

There seem to be four critical factors in successful dual-career relationships, as identified by Rhona Rapoport and Robert Rapoport: mutual commitment to both careers, flexibility, coping mechanisms, and energy and time management.[49]

MUTUAL COMMITMENT TO BOTH CAREERS

Successful dual-career couples share a commitment to work and to each other's need and right to pursue a career. Often, the couple's self-concept is built around themselves as a working team.

FLEXIBILITY

Two types of flexibility are important: personal flexibility and flexibility in the job. Personal flexibility is the willingness and ability to adapt and improvise to find ways to deal with problems affecting both members. Flexibility in the job exists when at least one member of the couple has enough autonomy to schedule time to cope with conflicts and enough geographic mobility to allow the spouse to accept transfers.

COPING MECHANISMS

Dual-career couples must develop a variety of coping mechanisms. They may cope by restructuring roles, with the members negotiating to make their roles more compatible with their responsibilities. A husband and wife may, for instance, agree to take turns with cooking, or may trade some responsibilities for others. Coping may also take the form of setting priorities or working harder on the planning and scheduling of activities.

ENERGY AND TIME MANAGEMENT

Effective dual-career couples are willing to devote energy to making the relationship work and to allocating time. They recognize the importance of maintaining the relationship and give it a high priority.

Companies are developing a variety of strategies for dealing with the dual-career couple.[50] Effective programs should have the following characteristics:

- Flexible career-development tracks and experiences.
- Skill development in coping with conflict and life/career management.
- Spouse involvement in career planning and problem solving.
- Support services for career couples.

FROM THE FIELD
CAREER
MANAGEMENT
PRACTICES

We surveyed human resources executives in a wide variety of industries to learn more about current organizational career management practices. Of the respondents, 67 percent indicated that their firms took steps to plan and manage their employees' careers. Only 9 percent indicated "Employees are entirely responsible for planning and managing their own careers."

Here is a summary of responses to the question, "Which of the following career-planning and management techniques are used in your firm?" The techniques are ranked from most frequently used to least frequently used:

Rank	Technique	Percent Using
1	In-house training programs	95
2	Tuition reimbursement programs	91
3	Outside management seminars	86
4	Regular reviews of management personnel's strengths and weaknesses	67
5	Posting of job openings	67
6	Pre-retirement counseling	67
7	Counseling for terminated employees	52
8	Career pathing to help managers acquire the necessary experience for future jobs	48
9	Succession planning or replacement charts	48
10	Planned job progression for new employees	43
11	Career management seminars and workshops	38
12	Computerized skills inventories to assist with career planning	38
13	Career counseling	33
14	Five-year or other long-term career plans for management personnel	29
15	Counseling for downward transfers	24
16	Systematic job rotation of supervisors to prepare them for higher-level positions	19

Since the surveyed executives were employed primarily in large organizations, these figures probably overstate the average degree of use of these techniques across organizations. It is clear, though, that organizations use an elaborate array of tools for the planning and management of employee careers.

Some companies now offer parental leave for fathers as well as mothers of newborns.

Some companies' attempts to help dual-career couples, as well as single working parents, are noteworthy.[51] For example, Merck & Co. uses extensive employee surveys and focus groups to help determine how best to mesh work and family life. It offers both men and women unpaid parental leave of up to 18 months for preparation for childbirth and for care after the birth or adoption of a child. Merck invested $100,000 to set up a child-care center near its headquarters. It is planning to provide child-care resource and referral information to its employees nationwide. Du Pont Co. has a new Corporate Work and Family Committee whose 19 members meet monthly. The company formed the committee after conducting a survey of 20,000 employees at four corporate sites. The survey found that 70 percent of all employees with children under the age of 13 used some form of child care outside the home. International Business Machines Corp. offers flexible work schedules, up to $1,750 for adoption expenses, and up to $500 to help relocating spouses find new jobs. It offers both men and women up to a year of unpaid leave for child care or special projects, provides a huge child-care consultation and referral program, and has just set up a similar program to help employees care for elderly parents. Campbell Soup Co. grants up to three months of unpaid leave to mothers and fathers for taking care of newborn, adopted, or seriously ill children or other family members. The company has an on-site child-care facility at its headquarters and subsidizes 60 percent of the costs. It also has flexible scheduling and job sharing available to most employees.[52]

Moving Females and Minorities into Managerial Ranks

Many companies are concerned that not enough women and minorities have achieved managerial ranks. As a result, some firms are considering novel ways to identify, train, and develop promising female and minority candidates. Identification may take place through job sampling and other ways of simulating management jobs, including assessment centers, discussed in the previous chapter. Douglas Hall and Fran Hall have discussed three steps, summarized in the following sections, that companies are taking to foster training and development of women and minorities.[53]

ASSESSMENT CENTERS FOR DEVELOPMENT

In recent years, companies have used assessment centers for employee development. Trained staff members give the employee feedback about strong and weak points, illustrated with examples of specific behaviors. Once the employee understands and accepts the feedback, the discussion turns to counseling and planning for future training experiences and developmental assignments that would lead to a particular target job in management.

JOB PATHING

Job pathing involves a carefully planned sequence of job assignments aimed at developing certain job-related skills. The paths are designed to ensure that important skill-building experiences are provided in increments small enough not to overwhelm the individual but large enough to require stretching. The goal is to minimize the career time needed to reach a target job. Through the use of job pathing, one large retail organization feels it can reduce the time to develop a store manager from 15 years to 5. Plotting career paths not only speeds employee growth but also forces the organization to think about the career paths it is now using. It may find that some potential paths are not being used, and perhaps that paths can be plotted through different functional areas to develop managers with broader views.

TALENT DEVELOPMENT AMONG HOURLY EMPLOYEES

Companies are trying to find ways to attract more female and minority hourly workers into pre-supervisory programs. One problem is perceptual: Females and minorities sometimes feel that opportunities for upward mobility are lacking, or that barriers exist to their upward mobility. Some also do not perceive themselves as fitting into supervisory roles. Firms must act to alter these perceptions. Some firms are also relying on training programs conducted by professional or trade organizations to develop female and minority employees. Many of these employees see training provided by such associations as being less competitive and more supportive than company-sponsored programs.

MANAGING CAREER STRESS

Earlier in this chapter we discussed the kinds of stress that may arise at various career stages. In this section we will consider the nature, causes, and consequences of stress in organizations. Then we will examine individual and organizational approaches to stress management.[54]

People at work are faced with a wide variety of stressors. As shown in Figure 11–9, **stressors** are environmental factors such as deadlines, noise, rules, and demanding bosses that influence stress levels. **Stress** is a physiological state resulting from stressors. It is caused by a complex set of reactions which result in the coursing of adrenaline into the bloodstream and then to muscles and organs. **Stress reactions** are mental and physical responses to stress. They might include psychological health reactions such as depression and anxiety, physical reactions such as backaches and high blood pressure, affective reactions such as job dissatisfaction, and behavioral reactions such as absenteeism and high turnover.[55]

Stress is not without its benefits. At low levels, it is an activating force, called *eustress* from the Greek *eu*, meaning good. However, as shown in Figure 11–10, excessive levels of stress—called *distress*—have negative consequences. It is probably the case that most workers already face at least moderate levels of stress: More than 30 million prescriptions are written in the United States each year for Valium alone, and over 150 million for all tranquilizers.[56] So, almost any increases in organizational stressors are likely to cause distress.

Costs of Stress

Stress results in a variety of costs for firms. First, as suggested by the preceding discussion of stress reactions, it is a threat to employee health. Stress has been associated with coronary heart disease, ulcers, diarrhea, high blood pressure, backaches, gastrointestinal distress, headaches, depression, and the related use of alcohol and other drugs. Workers are also more likely to incur accidents on the job when under stress. The cost to business of stress-related problems and mental illness is estimated at $150 billion annually in health insurance and disability claims.[57] Second, stress is likely to have an impact on long-term organizational effectiveness. Stress is associated with dissatisfac-

FIGURE 11–9
Stress Model

Stressors ⟶ Stress ⟶ Stress Reactions

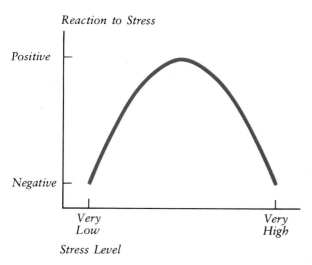

FIGURE 11–10
*The Relationship
Between Stress Level
and Reactions*

tion, absenteeism, and high turnover. It may also result in a climate that stifles creativity. Such factors may more than offset any short-term gains associated with stress.[58] Third, organizational stressors can lead to legal liability on the part of firms. Courts are increasingly ruling that firms are responsible for worker depression, anxiety, or other mental problems resulting from on-the-job stressors. The California labor code now allows compensation for injuries caused by "repetitive mentally or physically traumatic activities extending over a period of time, the combined effect of which causes any disability or need of medical treatment."[59]

Causes of Stress

Almost anything can be a source of stress—job insecurity, noise, too much responsibility, job loss, office politics, family concerns, and so on.[60] Three very important factors seem to be whether the individual exhibits a Type A or Type B behavior pattern, the amount of change the individual is facing in life, and conflicts and uncertainties faced at work.

- *Type A Behavior Pattern.* The **Type A behavior pattern** is characterized by feelings of great time pressure and impatience. Type A's work aggressively, speak explosively, and find themselves constantly struggling. The opposite pattern—relaxed, steady-paced, and easygoing—is called the **Type B behavior pattern.** Individuals with Type A behavior patterns are much more likely than others to experience high stress levels and to show a variety of symptoms of stress. There is considerable, though somewhat conflicting, evidence linking Type A behavior to coronary heart disease.[61]
- *Life Change.* Individuals experiencing high rates of life change—whether or not the changes are desirable—experience elevated stress levels and many health problems. Many organizational actions, such as geographical reassignments, promotions, early retirements, reprimands, and firings, can have a tremendous cumulative life change impact.[62]
- *Conflicts and Uncertainties at Work.* Jobs in which there are conflicting or unclear expectations concerning what an employee is supposed to do

lead to high stress levels. Such role conflict and role ambiguity, to be discussed in Chapter 17, translate into low satisfaction with work, high absenteeism and turnover, and somatic tension.[63]

Individual Strategies for Stress Management

Individuals experiencing stress in their careers may want to consider several approaches to stress management:

- *Social Support.* Seek out social support. Individuals who have the support of friends and loved ones experience many fewer symptoms of stress than do those without social support. If you feel you are lacking social support, seek it out. Social groups, churches, and local support organizations are possibilities.[64]
- *Priorities.* Try to reduce Type A tendencies. Attempt to reestablish priorities. Allow more time for activities. Ask which activities can be curtailed. Learn to say no.
- *Coping.* Develop effective coping strategies.[65] In general, those who cope with a stressful situation by treating it as an opportunity to show skills and abilities tend to do best. Those who simply try to run away from stressful situations usually find they can't. Those who deal with stress by treating its symptoms—especially by use of alcohol or drugs—often find themselves in a downward spiral.
- *Fitness.* Get fit and stay fit. Exercise reduces tension and strengthens the cardiovascular system. Physically fit individuals are better able to master stressful situations.[66]
- *Relaxation.* Learn to relax. A variety of relaxation techniques have been developed. Some of them seem a bit mystical, but most do seem to be useful.[67] The relaxation response is an anti-stress response in which muscle tension decreases, heart rate and blood pressure decrease, and breathing slows. It is brought about by a quiet environment, closed eyes, a comfortable position, and a repetitive mental device. Another approach, transcendental meditation, or TM, is a popular form of meditation which involves sitting comfortably with eyes closed and engaging in the repetition of a special sound for 20 minutes twice a day. Studies show TM to be related to reduced heart rate, lowered oxygen consumption, and decreased blood pressure. Finally, with biofeedback, small changes in the body and brain are detected, amplified, and displayed to the person. For instance, heart rate, blood pressure, temperature, and brain-wave patterns can be displayed. The ability to understand and perhaps control one's bodily processes may be helpful.
- *Managing Change.* Avoid unnecessary change. Think through the cumulative impact of planned changes.
- *Counseling.* Especially if stress is severe, seek out professional guidance. Most campuses and many firms have people whose key role is to provide assistance in times of stress. Take advantage of them.

Organizational Strategies for Stress Management

With the recognition that stress has important consequences for organizations and their members, firms have begun to adopt a wide range of approaches to the management of employee stress:

- *Emphasis on Wellness.* Some organizations are now placing great emphasis on the physical and mental wellness of their employees. For example, the Sentry Insurance Company has extensive physical fitness facilities at its corporate headquarters that its employees can use at any time. There is also a pleasant "quiet room" where employees can go to meditate, think, cool down, or simply be alone.

  Control Data Corporation has an elaborate program called StayWell. Employees in the program have a screening session in which a team of professionals collects data on health and life-style and then develops a health risk profile. This computer-generated profile analyzes the employee's health condition and provides a report that includes the chronological age, the risk age (how old the employee is in terms of risk), and the achievable age (how old the employee could expect to become if appropriate changes in health-related behavior were made). Employees then choose from a variety of activities related to their individual needs, including wellness education and life-style change courses. CDC has almost total participation of its employees and their spouses in the program.[68]

- *Family-Sensitive Work Practices.* A variety of work practices, some of which will be discussed in Chapter 14, can substantially reduce stresses for many employees, especially those with conflicting family responsibilities. These include flexible work schedules, job-sharing opportunities, and provision of child care facilities.

- *Programs to Develop Stress-Management Skills.* Many organizations are providing relaxation training, training in coping and social skills, and other programs to enhance employee stress-management skills. For instance, with the merger of Gulf Corporation with Standard Oil Company of California, now called Chevron, it became clear that many Gulf employees at the Pittsburgh headquarters would have to be terminated involuntarily. Needless to say, the threat of such termination is highly stress inducing. To help employees cope with that stress, Gulf hired a psychiatrist, a special psychologist, and a nurse to teach stress-management techniques to employees on company time. A third of the 700-person staff signed up for the stress-management classes.[69]

- *Selection and Placement.* Firms can recognize individual differences in family situations, degree of Type A behavior, and other dimensions and consider them when making selection and placement decisions.

- *Career Management.* Career-management programs can be designed with stress in mind. The probable impacts of job changes and other career elements can be taken into consideration in career planning.

- *Job Redesign.* Enriched jobs, characterized by use of a variety of skills, feedback about performance, and the completion of a large part of the task, tend to have lower stress levels and to permit use of more effective coping strategies than do specialized jobs.[70]

THE NEW CAREERISM

Throughout this chapter we have seen many signs that our views of careers and career success have changed dramatically in recent decades. While career success was historically defined in terms of salary and occupational status, it now takes on a personal dimension. Career success may now be defined in terms of having a comfortable job, of being able to maintain a satisfying personal life off the job, or of personal growth. Further, there is a growing expectation that the employee's entire work life will not be spent in a single company, or even in a single industry or profession. With this changed perspective has come the parallel recognition that organizations do not have unilateral control over employees' careers, nor are they likely to take care of employees in a paternalistic fashion. Even the cast of actors has expanded, with people at all levels of the organization paying more attention to their careers, and with a growing influx of women into the work force.

Daniel Feldman has labeled this set of changes the **new careerism.**[71] According to Feldman, there are some positive consequences of the new careerism. For one, employees are getting better feedback, since they seek more frequent appraisals from their employers and they engage in more critical self-analysis. Also, employees are showing more self-assertiveness about career progression. They make sure their organizations know what their career goals and expectations are, and they are more likely to refuse promotions and transfers that interfere with those goals. Finally, the new careerists are more conscious of buffering their personal lives from their work lives. They may show less concern than past employees about living in the "right" place or marrying the "right type" of spouse, and they are less likely to ignore the needs and demands of their families.

However, Feldman also sees a variety of unintended consequences of the new careerism.[72] For instance, turnover is high for the new careerists, both because they leave a job when they are dissatisfied and because they believe that "switching jobs looks good on the résumé." Also, because employees expect to be moving on to another job and another organization, they may lack involvement in the job and commitment to the organization (topics we will discuss in more depth in the next chapter). They may not invest time to develop interpersonal relationships with colleagues, except to the degree that those relationships are useful in attaining career goals. This short-term orientation may also cause employees to ignore long-term strategy on major business decisions, trying instead for a "home-run" strategy—make the big play, and move on. In the long run, this may lower standards of excellence and the sense of integrity of organizations. And, even if the current job seems great on conventional dimensions, employees may be dissatisfied because they don't see it as a good launching pad for the next career move.

There is room for argument about both the pervasiveness of the new careerism and its consequences. However, it is clear that major changes have taken place in how individuals and organizations are thinking about and dealing with careers. Those changes will have important and far-reaching results, and they demand serious attention.

IMPLICATIONS FOR MANAGEMENT

The issues we have discussed in this chapter present a variety of new challenges for organizations. At the same time, they suggest that enlightened organizations may have a growing array of tools for dealing with those challenges.

Changing employee values are creating difficulties for the firm. Many employees will no longer passively accept transfers or even promotions calling for a geographic move that would disrupt their life-styles. Some, especially those with security or technical-functional competence as career anchors and those with steady-state orientations, may actually show little desire for promotions, preferring stability. The growing number of dual-career couples is further complicating the picture, decreasing the firm's flexibility in dictating transfers, schedules, and rewards. As a manager, you are likely to face a complex scenario in which employee desires will have increasing weight in organizational decisions.

Further, changing social norms, laws, and other pressures for affirmative action are demanding that firms improve the career situations of women and minorities. Career progress is seen as a way to achieve social equality, and firms and their managers are being asked to play an active role in promoting that progress. You may be called on to foster the development of women and minorities.

In times of high company growth and profitability, career progress is often rapid, and firms can absorb the costs of errors in career management. As growth slows and profitability declines, the situation becomes more difficult. Mobility channels may be blocked as the firm stagnates and managers remain longer in their positions. The impact of errors magnifies as the firm lacks the resources needed to buffer mistakes. Unfortunately, you may find yourself in the situation of managing stagnation or decline. In such a situation, you will need creativity and flexibility in your career-management practices. You will need a thorough knowledge of a full arsenal of career tools.

Together, these forces—changing values, social pressures, and environmental scarcity—strip firms of the luxury of deciding whether to practice career management. Instead, firms must manage careers, and they must manage them well if they are to be successful. As a manager, you will probably find that you are increasingly devoting your time to career management.

The perspective we have considered suggests that career success means different things to different people. Effective career management allows the realization of potential, whether the potential is for mobility, competence, or creativity. You may find yourself counseling one subordinate on how to gain a desired promotion, another on ways to develop valued skills, and still another on how to achieve a satisfying balance of work and family life. To do all that, you will need an understanding of the different career needs and desires of your subordinates.

Your knowledge of the problems your subordinates are likely to face during the stages of their careers should prepare you to deal with them. Early career shock and pressures for accomplishment; mid-career crises and plateauing; and late career frustrations, reflection, and preparation for retirement all create special demands. An understanding of the models of individual differences in careers should help you anticipate and deal with those demands. Further, the material in this chapter may help you deal with your career stress and that of your subordinates.

Finally, of course, all this knowledge should help you manage your own career. Many firms do not pay much attention to their employees' careers. Regardless of the firm's practices, though, self-management of careers is important. You should prepare yourself to play an active role in achieving your own career success, however you define it. The various perspectives, models, and guidelines presented in this chapter should give you some direction in that quest.

KEY TERMS AND CONCEPTS

career anchors
career concept types
career plateau
crucial subordinate
exposure
fantasy stage
job pathing
mentor
mobicentric man
new careerism
protean career

realistic stage
stress
stressors
stress reactions
success chess
tentative stage
tournament model of mobility
Type A behavior pattern
Type B behavior pattern
visibility

QUESTIONS FOR REVIEW AND DISCUSSION

1. What is the protean career? How does it differ from the traditional view of careers? What is your definition of career success?
2. Give three reasons why careers are important.
3. Describe the stages of career choice. Do you think all people go through these stages? Do you think some people go through some of the stages more than once?
4. Identify three of Levinson's stages of adult work life.
5. What are some steps that firms might take to ease the stress faced by managers in their first jobs?
6. Describe the tournament model of mobility. Do you find such a model to be encouraging or disturbing? Why?
7. What is a learner? A star? A solid citizen? Deadwood?
8. Can you foresee any problems that a mentor might cause for a protégé?
9. Identify the three sorts of movement through the organization in the Schein model. Which boundary is associated with each type of movement?
10. Which of Schein's career anchors do you think best characterizes your motives, values, and competencies? Why? What does this say about the sort of career and position that would be most appropriate for you?
11. What sorts of problems do you think a spiral individual would face in a steady-state organization? A linear individual in a spiral organization?
12. Discuss ethical questions that may arise as companies more actively manage employees' careers.
13. Give five rules for self-management of careers. Are there any of these rules that you disagree with? Why?
14. Should companies adopt the Mommy Track? Defend your position.
15. Do you think companies should take special steps to help dual-career couples? Why or why not?

11–1 FEMALE EXECUTIVES

Women executives have mixed feelings about the men they work with. Most of them have been helped by men, and many would rather work for a man than for a woman. "I have always worked for a man and liked it," says a senior vice-president in manufacturing. "The men have that network," says a vice-president in a retail firm. "They are in higher positions. It's lonely out there."

Yet, at the same time, executive women are likely to feel thwarted and obstructed by male prejudices. "I have been stepped on because I am frank and have opinions," says a bank vice-president. "And every few days, I have an instance where I'd like to punch someone out."

The Wall Street Journal and the Gallup Organization surveyed 722 female executives with the title of vice-president or higher to find out how it feels to be a woman in the male corporate world. Their answers (see below) show that it often feels very difficult.

Executive women readily acknowledge that some men have played major roles in their careers. Eighty-two percent say that the one person who has been most helpful in their advancement has been a man. Even among younger women, who are more likely to have been preceded by other women in management positions, nearly four out of five say a man has filled the role of professional mentor.

In general, the women say it makes little difference to them whether their boss is a man or a woman. But 29 percent say they'd rather work for a man; only 4 percent prefer a female boss. While two-thirds of the women cited one or more advantages to being female, four out of five can think of an equal number of disadvantages.

How Being Female Affects Personal/Social Behavior

Have you ever:	
Been mistaken for a secretary at a business meeting?	61%
Felt cut off from social conversations or activities among your male colleagues?	60%
Felt you were being patronized by older executives?	44%
Felt the presence of female executives made male executives more appearance conscious?	33%
Felt uncomfortable about socializing with a male colleague because it would not look right?	24%

How Being Female Affects Job Performance/Evaluation

Have you ever:	
Felt you were being paid less than a man of equal ability?	70%
Had the impression that your views were not respected as much as a man's in certain areas?	60%
Felt that a male subordinate resisted taking orders from you because he felt threatened by a female boss?	41%
Felt that you were being judged more on the basis of dress and appearance than a man in your position would be?	37%
Felt that your personal life was being scrutinized more than those of your male colleagues?	29%

Felt that your professional advancement was accelerated
  because of pressure to promote women?   20%
Felt that you were pitted against other women in
  competition for a token top job?   7%

1. Which of the survey's findings do you find to be the most encouraging for the future progress of women in managerial ranks? The most disturbing? Why?
2. What might be some causes of the finding that some women prefer a man as a boss? Of the finding that most—even among the younger women—have had men as their mentors? What are some implications of these findings?
3. If this survey were repeated in the year 2000, which of its findings do you think would have changed the most? The least? Why?

11–2 A NEW TIDE

Not long ago, colleagues would have branded Kensuke Yukimura a traitor for what he did. Even now, the 31-year-old engineer confesses to being "in pain for a year" because of it.

His transgression? Mr. Yukimura changed jobs. While that may not sound like a big thing to Americans or Europeans, changing companies in mid-career is nothing less than revolutionary in Japan. And it's a revolution that more and more Japanese are joining. In 1987 about 2.7 million people, or 4.4 percent of the work force, jumped for greener pastures. That's up 80 percent from five years earlier.

"It's a new tide," says Kimihasa Sato, a director of Mitsubishi Research Institute who follows management trends. It's also a new boon for foreign companies trying to compete in Japan. They now find it much easier to hire experienced Japanese employees, given that Japan's job market is acting more like a free market. Recently, for example, Lotus Development landed a Sony marketing whiz, LSI Logic nabbed a top NEC manager, and Daimler Benz and BMW each recruited an executive from Toyota. "It's become very easy to meet foreign companies' needs," says Hiroo Takahashi, a director of Nippon Manpower Co., a recruiting firm. "It's a complete change from 5 to 10 years ago."

For Japanese companies, though, the new labor mobility is a double-edged sword. They stand to gain more flexibility in recruiting, but they also will probably pay more in personnel costs and lose some of the group harmony that is so cherished here.

For years, management experts have trumpeted Japan's "lifetime employment" system—no layoffs, but no quitting either—as one of the secrets of the country's success. Simply put, managers and workers see themselves in the same boat, dependent on each other for survival. Japanese workers so thoroughly identify their fates with their companies' that they give up their vacations, accept unwanted transfers, and work overtime (sometimes without pay), all the while peppering their bosses with suggestions on how to run the business better. In many cases, this job performance is what gives Japanese an edge over foreign competition. No one expects this system or its spirit to disappear, but job hopping will tend to undermine it.

The new trend is as much home-grown as inspired from abroad. Japan is plagued with labor shortages; thus, many companies, desperate for trained professionals, are hiring people from the competition.

Some Japanese companies also seem intent on diluting the monolithic corporate cultures that have ruled in postwar Japan. The old, group-oriented approach worked well when the objective was perfecting mass-production techniques, but many top managers think the future now puts a premium on creative corporate strategies. They figure that by bringing in mid-career managers from the outside, they can acquire fresh perspectives and, in turn, a sharper corporate image.

Source: Reprinted by permission of *The Wall Street Journal,* © Dow Jones & Company, Inc. (November 11, 1988). All Rights Reserved Worldwide.

1. What do you see as some costs and benefits of this new labor mobility from the point of view of the organization? Of the individual?
2. Discuss how workers with different career anchors would be likely to react to these changes.
3. Discuss how workers with different career concept types would be likely to react to these changes.

ENDNOTES

1. H. A. Levine, "Career Planning," *Personnel* 62, no. 3 (March 1985): 67-72.
2. D. B. Miller, "Career Planning and Management in Organizations," *S.A.M. Advanced Management Journal* (Spring 1978): 36.
3. For instance, see D. T. Hall, *Careers in Organizations* (Glenview, IL: Scott, Foresman, 1976), 154, 166-167.
4. For good discussions of career management, see Hall, *Careers in Organizations*, and M. L. London and S. A. Stumpf, *Managing Careers* (Reading, MA: Addison-Wesley, 1982).
5. From *Careers in Organizations* by D. T. Hall. Copyright © 1976 by Scott, Foresman and Company. Reprinted by permission.
6. These are drawn from Hall, *Careers in Organizations*.
7. These stages are drawn from E. Ginzberg et al., *Occupational Choice* (New York: Columbia University Press, 1951), 60-72.
8. There are some useful books to guide your self-analysis. For instance, see R. Bolles, *What Color Is Your Parachute?* (Berkeley, CA: Ten Speed Press, 1982), and J. G. Clawson et al., *Self-Assessment and Career Development*, 2d ed. (Englewood Cliffs, NJ: Prentice-Hall, 1985).
9. C. Jung, *Modern Man in Search of a Soul* (New York: Harcourt & Brace, 1933), and E. Erikson, *Childhood and Society*, 2d ed. (New York: Norton, 1963).
10. D. J. Levinson, *The Seasons of a Man's Life* (New York: Alfred A. Knopf, 1978).
11. For other models of career stages, see D. T. Hall and K. Nougaim, "An Examination of Maslow's Need Hierarchy in an Organizational Setting," *Organizational Behavior and Human Performance* 3 (1968): 12-35; D. C. Miller and W. H. Form, *Industrial Sociology*, 2d ed. (New York: Harper & Row, 1964); and D. E. Super and M. J. Bohn, Jr., *Occupational Psychology* (Belmont, CA: Wadsworth, 1970).
12. See M. R. Louis, "Managing Career Transition: A Missing Link in Career Development," *Organizational Dynamics* (Spring 1982): 68-74, for a discussion of the stresses faced during career transitions and of steps that firms might take to ease those transitions.
13. R. A. Webber, "Career Problems of Young Managers," *California Management Review* 18 (1976): 11-33.
14. Recall from Chapter 10 that the realistic job preview from J. P. Wanous, *Organizational Entry: Recruitment, Selection, and Socialization of Newcomers* (Reading, MA: Addison-Wesley, 1980), may help alleviate reality shock.
15. D. T. Hall and F. S. Hall, "What's New in Career Management?" *Organizational Dynamics* (Summer 1976): 17-33.
16. J. S. Livingston, "Pygmalion in Management," *Harvard Business Review* 47, no. 4 (1969): 81-89, presents an interesting discussion of the powerful role that early career challenge and superiors' high expectations play in career growth.
17. J. Rosenbaum, "Tournament Mobility: Career Patterns in a Corporation," *Administrative Science Quarterly* 24 (1979): 220-241.
18. For an excellent discussion of self-fulfilling prophecy, see L. Jussim, "Self-Fulfilling Prophecies: A Theoretical and Integrative Review," *Psychological Review* 93 (1986): 429-445.

For more on the Pygmalion effect, see D. Eden, "Self-Fulfilling Prophecy as a Management Tool: Harnessing Pygmalion," *Academy of Management Review* 9 (1984): 64-73, and "Pygmalion, Goal Setting, and Expectancy: Compatible Ways to Boost Productivity," *Academy of Management Review* 13 (1988): 639-652; and D. Eden and A. B. Shani, "Pygmalion Goes to Boot Camp: Expectancy, Leadership, and Trainee Performance," *Journal of Applied Psychology* 67 (1982): 194-199.

19. This discussion is based primarily on Hall, *Careers in Organizations*.

20. T. P. Ference et al., "Managing the Career Plateau," *Academy of Management Review* 2 (1977): 602. For additional perspectives on career plateaus, see J. W. Slocum, Jr., W. L. Cron, and L. C. Yows, "Whose Career Is Likely to Plateau?" *Business Horizons* (March-April 1987): 31-38; W. Kiechel III, "High Up and Nowhere to Go," *Fortune* (August 1, 1988): 229-231; and F. Rice, "Lessons from Late Bloomers," *Fortune* (August 31, 1987): 87-91.

21. *Business Week* (September 5, 1983): 96, and E. E. Jennings, *The Mobile Manager: Study of the New Generation of Top Executives* (Ann Arbor: Bureau of Industrial Relations, Graduate School of Business Administration, The University of Michigan, 1967).

22. J. Near, "Reactions to the Career Plateau," *Business Horizons* (July-August 1984): 75-79.

23. M. J. McCarthy, "Plateaued Workers Cause Big Damage," *Wall Street Journal* (August 17, 1988): 21.

24. For further discussions of mentoring, see L. Baird and K. Kram, "Career Dynamics: Managing the Superior-Subordinate Relationship," *Organizational Dynamics* (Summer 1983): 46-64; E. Collins and P. Scott, "Everyone Who Makes It Has a Mentor," *Harvard Business Review* (July-August 1978): 89-101; K. E. Kram, *Mentoring at Work: Developmental Relationships in Organizational Life* (Glenview, IL: Scott, Foresman, 1985); G. R. Roche, "Much Ado About Mentors," *Harvard Business Review* 57, no. 1 (1979): 14-17, and M. H. Reich, "The Mentor Connection," *Personnel* (February 1986): 50-56.

25. D. J. Levinson et al., *The Seasons of a Man's Life* (New York: Alfred A. Knopf, 1978), 98. Reprinted with permission.

26. Roche, "Much Ado," 14-17.

27. M. H. Reich, "Executive Views from Both Sides of Mentoring," *Personnel* 82, no. 3 (March 1985): 42-46.

28. M. A. Morgan, D. T. Hall, and A. Martier, "Career Development Strategies in Industry: Where Are We and Where Should We Be?" *Personnel* (March-April 1979): 17-18.

29. E. H. Schein, *Career Dynamics: Matching Individual and Organizational Needs* (Reading, MA: Addison-Wesley, 1978).

30. For a thorough discussion of organizational socialization, see J. Van Maanen and E. H. Schein, "Toward a Theory of Organizational Socialization," in *Research in Organizational Behavior,* vol. 1, ed. B. M. Staw (Greenwich, CT: JAI Press, 1979), 209-264.

31. J. Holland, *The Psychology of Vocational Choice* (Waltham, MA: Blaisdell, 1966).

32. See S. H. Osipow, *Theories of Career Development*, 2d ed. (New York: Appleton-Century-Crofts, 1973), 65-66, for an intensive and supportive review of the literature and theory relating to the VPI. For an extension of Holland's model to conflict between the individual and the demands of the organizational role (called person/role conflict), see J. C. Latack, "Person/Role Conflict: Holland's Model Extended to Role-Stress Research, Stress Management, and Career Development," *Academy of Management Review* 6 (1981): 89-103.

33. D. C. Feldman and H. J. Arnold, "Personality Types and Career Patterns: Some Empirical Evidence on Holland's Model," *Canadian Journal of Administrative Sciences* 2 (1985): 192-210.

34. For more on Schein's anchors, see E. H. Schein, "The Individual, the Organization, and the Career: A Conceptual Scheme," *Journal of Applied Behavioral Science* 7 (1971): 401-426, and *Career Dynamics*; and D. C. Feldman, *Managing Careers in Organizations* (Glenview, IL: Scott, Foresman, 1988), 101-106.

35. E. H. Schein, "Career Anchors and Career Paths: A Panel Study of Management School Graduates," in *Organizational Careers: Some New Perspectives*, ed. J. Van Maanen (London: Wiley-Interscience, 1977), 63.

36. The following discussion is based largely on M. J. Driver, "Career Concepts and Career Management in Organizations," in *Behavioral Problems in Organizations*, ed. C. L. Cooper (Englewood Cliffs, NJ: Prentice-Hall, 1979).

37. For a discussion of mobility influences during career stages, see J. F. Veiga, "Mobility Influences During Managerial Career Stages," *Academy of Management Review* 8 (1983): 64-85.

38. Eugene E. Jennings, "Mobicentric Man," *Psychology Today* (July 1970): 35. Reprinted with permission from *Psychology Today*. Copyright © July 1970, American Psychological Association.

39. D. Seligman, "Luck and Careers," *Fortune* (November 16, 1981): 60-66, 70, 72, presents an interesting discussion of the role of luck in careers.

40. Hall, *Careers in Organizations*.

41. J. O. Crites, *Theory and Research Handbook, Career Maturity Inventory* (Monterey, CA: McGraw-Hill, 1973).

42. C. Argyris, *Integrating the Individual and the Organization* (New York: John Wiley & Sons, 1964).

43. For a discussion of the "glass ceiling" and companies' attempts to break it, see L. E. Wynter and J. Solomon, "A New Push to Break the 'Glass Ceiling,'" *Wall Street Journal* (November 15, 1989): B1, B10.

44. *Capital Times*, Madison, WI (November 14, 1984): 2, and *Wall Street Journal* (March 7, 1989): B1.

45. S. Feinstein, "Women and Minority Workers in Business Find a Mentor Can Be a Rare Commodity," *Wall Street Journal* (November 10, 1987): 33.

46. The idea of the Mommy Track (but not the name) was proposed by Felice N. Schwartz in her article, "Management Women and the New Facts of Life," *Harvard Business Review* (January-February 1989): 65-76. The Mommy Track was subsequently *Business Week*'s March 20, 1989, cover story and the subject of the subsequent article, "Is the Mommy Track a Blessing—or a Betrayal?" *Business Week* (May 15, 1989): 98-99. See also J. Solomon, "Schwartz of 'Mommy Track' Notoriety Prods Firms to Address Women's Needs," *Wall Street Journal* (September 11, 1989): B7A.

47. U.S. Department of Labor, Bureau of Labor Statistics, *Employment Statistics and Earnings Characteristics of Families* (Washington, DC: U.S. Government Printing Office). This section is based in part on Hall and Hall, "What's New in Career Management?" and "Dual Careers—How Do Couples and Companies Cope with the Problems?" *Organizational Dynamics* (Spring 1978): 57-77.

48. L. Hays, "Pay Problems: How Couples React When Wives Out-Earn Husbands," *Wall Street Journal* (June 19, 1987): 19.

49. R. Rapoport and R. Rapoport, *Dual-Career Families* (Baltimore: Penguin, 1971).

50. These are drawn from Hall and Hall, "What's New in Career Management?" 17-33.

51. C. Trost, "Best Employers for Women and Parents," *Wall Street Journal* (November 30, 1987): 21.

52. While these benefits are often available to both men and women, it appears that men typically do not take advantage of them. See Cathy Trost, "But Do Dads Do It?" Labor Letter column, *Wall Street Journal* (July 19, 1988): 1.

53. Hall and Hall, "What's New in Career Management?"

54. For some discussions of stress at work, see "Stress: The Test Americans Are Failing," *Business Week* (April 18, 1988): 74-76; "Stress on the Job," *Newsweek* (April 25, 1988): 40-45; and "Cool Cures for Burnout," *Fortune* (June 20, 1988): 78-84.

55. A pioneer in the area of stress research is H. Selye, *The Stress of Life* (New York: McGraw-Hill, 1956). For other overviews of stress, see J. C. Quick and J. D. Quick, *Organizational Stress and Preventive Management* (New York: McGraw-Hill, 1984); R. S. Lazarus and S. Folkman, *Stress, Appraisal and Coping* (New York: Springer, 1984); and T. A. Beehr and R. S. Bhagat, *Human Stress and Cognitions in Organizations: An Integrated Perspective* (New York: John Wiley & Sons, 1985).

56. H. Peyser, "Stress and Alcohol," in *Handbook of Stress*, ed. L. Goldberger and S. Breznitz (New York: Free Press, 1982). The idea of a curvilinear relationship between stress and outcomes was first proposed by R. M. Yerkes and J. D. Dodson, "The Relation of Strength of Stimulus to Rapidity of Habit Formation," *Journal of Comparative and Neurological Psychology* 18 (1908): 459-482.

57. "The Crippling Ills That Stress Can Trigger," *Business Week* (April 18, 1988): 77-78. See also B. D. Steffy and J. W. Jones, "Workplace Stress and Indicators of Coronary-Disease

Risk," *Academy of Management Journal* 31 (1988): 11-19; S. Dentzer, J. McCormick, and D. Tsuruoka, "A Cure for Job Stress," *Newsweek* (June 2, 1986): 46-47; and R. Winslow, "Workplace Turmoil Is Reflected in Depression Among Employees," *Wall Street Journal* (December 13, 1989): B1.

58. For an examination of the consequences of job stress, see P. E. Spector, D. J. Dwyer, and S. M. Jex, "Relation of Job Stressors to Affective, Health, and Performance Outcomes: A Comparison of Multiple Data Sources," *Journal of Applied Psychology* 73 (1988): 11-19.

59. J. M. Ivancevich, M. T. Matteson, and E. P. Richards III, "Who's Liable for Stress on the Job?" *Harvard Business Review* (March-April 1985): 60. See also W. C. Nugent, "When Employees Seek Workers' Compensation for Stress," *Employee Relations Law Journal* 14 (1988): 239-252.

60. For instance, see J. L. Latack, "After the Ax Falls: Job Loss as a Career Transition," *Academy of Management Review* 11 (1986): 375-392, and S. J. Motowidlo, J. S. Packard, and M. R. Manning, "Occupational Stress: Its Causes and Consequences for Job Performance," *Journal of Applied Psychology* 71 (1986): 618-629.

61. See M. Friedman and R. Rosenman, *Type A Behavior and Your Heart* (New York: Alfred A. Knopf, 1974); K. A. Matthews, "Psychological Perspectives on the Type A Behavior Pattern," *Psychological Bulletin* (1982): 293-323; V. A. Price, *Type A Behavior Pattern* (New York: Academic Press, 1982); J. Fischman, "Type A on Trial," *Psychology Today* (February 1987): 42-50; and J. E. Bishop, "Hostility, Distrust May Put Type A's at Coronary Risk," *Wall Street Journal* (January 17, 1989): B1.

62. See B. S. Dohrenwend and B. P. Dohrenwend, "Some Issues in Research on Stressful Life Events," *Journal of Nervous and Mental Disease* 166 (1978): 7-15; T. H. Holmes and M. Masuda, "Life Change and Illness Susceptibility," in *Stressful Life Events: Their Nature and Causes*, ed. B. S. Dohrenwend and B. P. Dohrenwend (New York: John Wiley & Sons, 1974), 45-72; T. H. Holmes and R. H. Rahe, "The Social Readjustment Rating Scale," *Journal of Psychosomatic Research* 11 (1967): 213-218; and S. M. Monroe, "Major and Minor Life Events as Predictors of Psychological Distress: Further Issues and Findings," *Journal of Behavioral Medicine* (June 1983): 189-205.

63. For instance, see J. Schaubroeck, J. L. Cotton, and K. R. Jennings, "Antecedents and Consequences of Role Stress: A Covariance Structure Analysis," *Journal of Organizational Behavior* (January 1989): 35-58.

64. For discussions of social support, see S. Cobb, "Social Support as a Moderator of Life Stress," *Psychosomatic Medicine* 38 (1976): 300-314; B. H. Gottlieb, *Social Support Strategies* (Beverly Hills, CA: Sage Publications, 1983); and D. C. Ganster, M. R. Fusilier, and B. T. Mayes, "Role of Social Support in the Experience of Stress at Work," *Journal of Applied Psychology* 71 (1986): 102-110.

65. For discussions of coping strategies, see S. Folkman and R. S. Lazarus, "An Analysis of Coping in a Middle-Aged Community Sample," *Journal of Health and Social Behavior* 21 (1980): 219-239; J. C. Latack, "Coping with Job Stress: Measures and Future Directions for Scale Development," *Journal of Applied Psychology* 71 (1986): 377-385; *Journal of Health and Social Behavior* 19 (1978): 2-21; and J. C. Latack and R. J. Aldag, "The Dynamic Constellation of Coping: An Examination of Measures Across Samples and Job Situations," *Proceedings of the 1986 Annual Meeting of the Decision Sciences Institute* (1986): 974-976.

66. See "Effects of CEO Fitness: The Performance Plus," *Psychology Today* (May 1989): 50-53, and P. D. Tomporowski and N. R. Ellis, "Effects of Exercise on Cognitive Processes: A Review," *Psychological Bulletin* 99 (1986): 338-346.

67. For more on the relaxation response, see H. Benson, *The Relaxation Response* (New York: Avon Books, 1975), and H. Benson and R. Allen, "How Much Stress Is Too Much?" *Harvard Business Review* (September-October 1980): 86-92. On meditation, see P. Carrington, *Freedom in Meditation* (New York: Anchor Press/Doubleday, 1978). For discussions of biofeedback, see G. D. Fuller, "Current Status of Biofeedback in Clinical Practice," *American Psychologist* 33 (1978): 39-48; and L. Tarler-Benlolo, "The Role of Relaxation in Biofeedback Training: A Critical Review of the Literature," *Psychological Bulletin* 85 (1978): 727-755.

68. M. P. Naditch, "They 'StayWell' at Control Data," *Sales and Marketing Management* (May 18, 1981): 60-62. See also M. Roberts and T. G. Harris, "Wellness at Work," *Psychology Today* (May 1989): 54-58.

69. *Wall Street Journal* (August 17, 1985): 15.

70. For instance, see A. P. Brief and R. J. Aldag, "Correlates of Role Indices," *Journal of Applied Psychology* 61 (1976): 468-472, and R. J. Aldag, H. J. Joseph, and J. C. Latack, "An Examination of Determinants and Consequences of Coping Behaviors," paper presented at the 16th Annual Meeting of the American Institute for Decision Sciences (Toronto, November 1984).

71. Feldman, *Managing Careers in Organizations.*

72. For a more detailed listing of these unintended consequences, see Feldman, *Managing Careers in Organizations*, 206-209.

Directing

PART FOUR

Behavior in
Organizations

CHAPTER 12

After studying this chapter, you should be able to:
- *Discuss three sets of important employee behaviors.*
- *Identify three major categories of ability.*
- *Describe the perceptual process and understand major influences at each stage in the process.*
- *Differentiate between three types of learning.*
- *Describe four theories of personality and identify eight key personality characteristics.*
- *Identify key work attitudes and analyze their links to employee behaviors.*
- *Describe values and the roles they play.*

Since managers are responsible for getting work done through others, they must be concerned with employee behaviors and with factors that influence those behaviors. In this chapter we will consider some important employee behaviors, including participation, effort, and performance. Then we will look at several factors which may be related to those behaviors. These factors include ability, perceptions, learning, personality, attitudes, and values.

Knowledge of these factors should help the manager in understanding, predicting, and influencing employee behaviors. We will touch on all these topics again in later chapters, and some will be examined in much more depth. Other determinants of behavior, such as job characteristics, leadership, and group influences, are not directly considered here. However, we'll need to refer to many of the issues discussed in this chapter when we do address those topics.

SOME IMPORTANT WORK BEHAVIORS

While it is tempting to focus just on performance as the "bottom line" work behavior, many employee behaviors are important. In this section we'll consider measures of participation, effort, and performance.

Participation

Participation is simply being at work to do the job. Three key measures of participation are attendance, timeliness, and retention. We often see these behaviors discussed in terms of their negative "flip sides": absenteeism, tardiness, and turnover.

ATTENDANCE

Attendance relates to whether or not an employee reports for work on a given day. Failure to attend—absenteeism—can be quite costly for companies. Typically, companies continue to pay absent employees. Furthermore, absenteeism causes costly disruptions, such as the need to reschedule work and reassign employees. One estimate is that such disruptions cause productivity to drop by as much as 2.5 percent for every 1 percent increase in absenteeism.[1] Those disruptions may also result in products of decreased quality, since regular employees are replaced by "swing" employees who move from one job to another. The defect-plagued "Monday car" is one example. An estimated 400 million person-days are lost in the United States annually through absenteeism—about four times the amount lost in strikes. Total annual costs of absenteeism have been put as high as $26.4 billion.[2]

In recent years, absenteeism in the United States has averaged about 2 to 3 percent of total workdays annually. It is hard to sort out how much of this absenteeism is avoidable (that is, due primarily to the employee's desire simply not to go to work that day) or unavoidable (due to factors such as illness or transportation problems). Even if companies tried to keep track of that distinction, it is unlikely that employees would cooperate by "calling in bored." It is probably the case, though, that avoidable absenteeism makes up a large share of the total.

TIMELINESS

Timeliness is a measure of the degree to which employees come to work on time. Few data are available on timeliness. The costs of the lack of timeliness—tardiness—will depend on the situation. If many jobs are tightly linked and if the employee is hard to replace, such costs could be high.

RETENTION

Retention is the term used to mean remaining with the organization. Its opposite—turnover—has many costs, including disruption of the work process, recruitment and training of new employees, and low productivity of new employees during the training period. In some industries, turnover rates may actually exceed 100 percent annually. Overall, rates in the United States are about 15 percent annually.[3]

Some companies may actually be more concerned with retention than with performance levels. This is because in some instances there may be relatively little the firm can do about improving performance, but turnover, as we'll see later, may be more amenable to organizational influence.

Turnover may be voluntary (initiated by the employee) or involuntary (initiated by the firm because of poor performance, disciplinary problems, or the like). Voluntary turnover may be avoidable, due to factors such as dissatisfaction with the firm, or unavoidable, due to factors such as transfer of a spouse. Clearly, firms should closely examine voluntary, avoidable turnover.

Unlike absenteeism, which has few redeeming features (to organizations, if not to employees), turnover is not a complete evil. That is, turnover by low-performing employees may be a blessing to the firm, and perhaps to mismatched employees. This is especially true when the firm is constrained from firing such employees.[4] Also, "fast-trackers" in some industries may make many moves between firms. While this may be upsetting in the short run to the firms they leave, the overall effect of such turnover may be positive. It may enhance development of employees and expose them to a variety of perspectives, thereby improving their skills and increasing their value to the organizations they join. And, from the perspective of the employees, such turnover may also result in increased rewards.

Effort

Effort is behavior directed toward some goal. Whether or not the goal is achieved may depend upon many things beyond effort. These include ability, situational constraints, and whether there is a clear understanding of what is to be accomplished. However, since goals are unlikely to be achieved unless an effort is made to reach them, management places much of its emphasis on increasing employee effort.

Performance

Performance is the accomplishment of some organizational goal. The goal may be quantity or quality of output, creativity, flexibility, dependability, or anything else desired by the organization. The emphasis may be on the short term or the long term. It may be at the level of the individual, group, unit, or

Output per worker-hour may be the productivity measure for assembly of computer components.

organization. Furthermore, performance may refer to the completion of a task such as decision making or teaching a class or analyzing a stock. The key point to recognize here is that performance should be thought of broadly. Focusing just on quantity of output, for instance, would probably have unfortunate results.

One performance measure which has been in the spotlight in recent years is productivity. **Productivity** is a measure of the output of goods or services per unit of input such as human resources, land, and capital. Often, the productivity measure of interest is output per worker-hour. Output per worker-hour in the United States remains greater than in any other nation; Japan's output, for instance, is about two-thirds as great. However, the rate of growth of U.S. productivity is declining, causing the productivity gap between the United States and other countries to narrow. As we'll discuss elsewhere, this trend has disturbing implications for U.S. business. It is the catalyst for a variety of proposals for productivity improvement.

ABILITY

Ability is the capacity to perform. Along with effort, it is a key determinant of performance. Abilities may be classed as mental, mechanical, and psychomotor.[5] Each may be important to employee behavior.

Mental or intellectual abilities are important for problem solving. We possess a great variety of mental abilities—one popular model puts the number as high as 120! We will explore these abilities in Chapter 21. For now, suffice it to say that mental ability is more than just being able to come up with the solution to a problem. It may involve the capacity to transform information, generate alternatives, memorize, seek implications, or many other capacities.

Mechanical abilities relate to the person's capacity to comprehend relationships between objects and to perceive how parts fit together.

Psychomotor abilities include such things as manual dexterity, eye-hand coordination, and motor and manipulative ability. Such abilities involve skilled muscular performance and typically some degree of visual control.

There are many other ways to classify abilities. The key points here are that abilities may differ in importance from one task to another and that employees may vary substantially in their levels of those abilities. Such recognition is crucial to understanding and predicting work behaviors. In Chapter 10 we considered ways to measure abilities and discussed ways management can make use of differences in abilities.

PERCEPTIONS

Each of us lives in our own world. It is a world created by our attempts to sift through, to organize, and to interpret the tremendous number of things we see, hear, feel, and otherwise constantly sense. It is different from all other worlds—the unique product of a complex process.

Ms. Johnson, a fast-rising executive, exists in the world of one of her colleagues as hard-working and competent. In the world of another, she is driven and ruthless. The job which in Sam's world is boring and routine exists in Carol's world as a source of challenge and opportunity. Mr. Björnson's subtle messages to Mr. Peterson, carefully crafted and potentially powerful in Mr. Björnson's world, are nowhere to be found in the world of Mr. Peterson.

The "truth" in our unique world depends on whether something is consistent with the rest of that world. Moreover, the nature of our unique world helps determine how we behave. How are these private worlds created? What makes each unique? How are we to deal with people living in other worlds?

In this section we will consider the nature of the perceptual process, noting key influences and associated problems at each step. We will then review the related process of causal attribution. Finally, we will discuss ways to reduce perceptual error.

The Perceptual Process

Knowledge of the world is sent to our brains through our sensory systems—seeing, hearing, tasting, touching, and smelling. **Perception** is the complex process by which we select, organize, and interpret sensory stimuli into a meaningful and coherent picture of the world.[6] As shown in Figure 12–1, perception involves several steps. In the first step, sensation, many stimuli impact on our sensory filters, but only some are sensed. Others are filtered out, perhaps because they are at very low levels or are not within a particular range. In subsequent steps, stimuli which are sensed are selected, organized, and translated. Let's consider some things that occur at each of these steps.

SELECTING STIMULI

In this step, selection, some stimuli are selected for further processing. If our perceptions were not selective, we would be overwhelmed. Though ideally we

"Here's to the truth as perceived by you."

Drawing by Victor, *The New Yorker Magazine*, Inc., 1980.

should select only the most important stimuli, many other factors affect selection, some of which are potentially troublesome. For instance, we have all heard the saying "I'll believe it when I see it." Turning the statement around to "I'll see it when I believe it" is a good way to characterize another factor involved in perception. That is, we are more likely to see things we are expecting to see. This is called **perceptual readiness.**

In a classic study, Dewitt Dearborn and Herbert Simon asked executives in various departments of a manufacturing firm to read a detailed case study from a business policy course. All the executives were told to analyze the case from a company-wide perspective. In spite of this instruction, what they did instead was focus on their own areas—the areas where they were ready to see problems. Sales executives, for instance, saw marketing problems as needing attention; production executives identified organization and production problems as the most pressing.[7] Thus, perceptual readiness may cause managers to fail to "see the big picture." Perceptual readiness, as we'll discuss shortly, also influences the way we interpret stimuli.

Needs and Personality

Different people will select different stimuli based on their needs and personalities. A hungry person is likely to focus on the food pictured in an adver-

FIGURE 12–1
The Perceptual Process

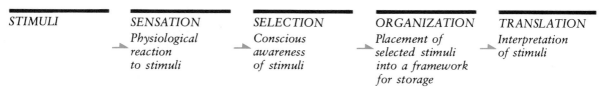

STIMULI	SENSATION	SELECTION	ORGANIZATION	TRANSLATION
	Physiological reaction to stimuli	*Conscious awareness of stimuli*	*Placement of selected stimuli into a framework for storage*	*Interpretation of stimuli*

tisement for china, whereas a person who is not hungry may focus on the color and pattern of the china.

Contrast

Stimuli that contrast with the surrounding environment are more likely than others to be selected. That contrast could be in color, size, flavor, or some other factor. The only person talking in a theater or the only blue shirt in a sea of Wisconsin red on a football weekend almost demands attention.

Frequency

Repetition of a stimulus has an additive effect, making it more likely to be selected for attention. Advertisers, of course, make use of this fact, regularly repeating a message. And you have probably had an experience similar to the following: You say "Hello" to a friend, Bob. Bob doesn't respond. You say "Hello" again. Bob replies, "Oh, hi. Sorry, I didn't hear you the first time." In fact, of course, Bob *had* to hear you the first time to make that statement.

Other Factors Influencing Selection

Other things being equal, more intense stimuli—a bold flavor or a shout—are more likely to be selected. A changing stimulus, or one which is novel, is also more likely to be selected. A stimulus presented along with many others, such as a request for more money that arrives at the same time as twenty similar requests, may not receive attention.

ORGANIZING STIMULI

Once stimuli have been selected, they must be organized into a useful framework. The way we organize stimuli is important. Things we group together

In a forest of green, a tiny figure in red catches the eye.

THE FAR SIDE   By GARY LARSON

"Wait! Wait! . . . Cancel that, I guess it says 'helf.' "

THE FAR SIDE COPYRIGHT 1982 CHRONICLE FEATURES. Dist. by Universal Press Syndicate. All rights reserved.

tend to be recalled together, and their meanings tend to influence one another. In general, we are likely to group things together that are somehow similar (for instance, in shape, size, or color) or which are close together in time or space (two accidents on the same day or two people seated together). Also, we tend to organize things so that closure occurs. **Closure** is "closing up" or "filling in" missing parts to create a meaningful whole.

INTERPRETING STIMULI

Finally, we interpret stimuli at the translation step in the perceptual process. The way we translate the stimuli we have selected and organized depends on the situation (for instance, whether it is friendly or hostile, relaxed or frantic), our characteristics, and the characteristics of the thing being perceived. The many distortions of objective reality that are possible at the translation stage have important implications for management.

Stereotyping

Walter Lippmann coined the term **stereotyping** in 1922, writing of "pictures in people's heads" that distorted their perceptions of others.[8] The term is now often used to mean forming an opinion of a person based not on individual characteristics but on the group to which the person belongs. Stereotyping, if it is accurate, may be useful, since it efficiently places information into categories. When we face new situations, stereotypes provide guidelines to help classify people.

Unfortunately, stereotyping based on false premises may lead to a distorted view of reality. For instance, one study asked respondents to give their impressions of a person in a photograph. One group was told that the person was a management representative; the other group, that he was a union leader.[9] Entirely different impressions emerged from the same picture. In another study, hiring decisions were made on the basis of matched pairs of dossiers.[10] The dossiers differed only in one way: one in each set had a male name and the other had a female name. The dossier with the male name was more likely to be picked. Research suggests that stereotyping in work organizations may be harmful to minority-group members, older workers, and females.

Perceptual Readiness

We noted earlier that perceptual readiness influences the stimuli we select. It also influences how we interpret those stimuli. A prime example is the self-fulfilling prophecy, or **Pygmalion effect**.[11] In one study, teachers who were told at the beginning of the school term that certain of their new students were especially intelligent (when, in fact, they were not) later perceived those students to show signs of greater intelligence and higher performance. As a result, they treated them differently. These "intelligent" students then showed gains in intellectual capacity, while others in the class did not.[12] Similar findings have occurred when leaders were told (again, incorrectly) that certain of their subordinates were high performers. Apparently perceiving these "high-performing" subordinates differently, the leaders gave them considerable decision-making authority but closely supervised "low performers."[13] Our expectations may color our perceptions.

Halo Effect

The **halo effect** refers to a process in which a person judges specific traits on the basis of a general impression. Sometimes one trait, such as a subordinate's honesty or enthusiasm, forms the halo. Given this favorable impression, the subordinate may also be seen as loyal, efficient, courteous, and so on. That is, people have a tendency to perceive links between traits. If they make evaluations on the basis of a halo when the traits really aren't linked, halo error is the result. Of course, many traits are in fact related, so not all judgments based on the halo effect are really halo error.

Projection

An unconscious tendency to project one's own characteristics onto others is called **projection**. For example, people may relieve their own guilt by projecting blame on others. Fearful people tend to see others as fearful. People with certain undesirable personality characteristics, such as stinginess or obstinacy, tend to see others as having the same traits.

Primacy/Recency Effects

The time at which we receive a stimulus influences the weight we give it. Quite often, the first information we receive has a very strong influence on our final impressions. This is called a **primacy effect**. It has important consequences when several alternatives are being considered, as in the case of a sequence of job choice decisions. Sometimes the information received most recently has the strongest influence—a **recency effect**.

Perceptual Defense

When we face information we find to be threatening or unacceptable, our perceptions try to defend us. We may fail to perceive the troublesome stimuli, or we may distort our perceptions of the stimuli to make them less troublesome. Perceptual defense is especially evident when long-held beliefs or attitudes are challenged.

To illustrate, in one study college students were given descriptions of factory workers.[14] These descriptions included the word *intelligent*. Since ascribing intelligence to factory workers was contrary to the students' beliefs, their perceptual defenses came to the rescue. Some students simply denied that the workers were intelligent. Most frequently, they modified or distorted the description. For instance, they might accept the term *intelligent* but would couple it with another characteristic, such as lack of initiative, to maintain their overall perception of the workers. Clearly, perceptual defense can result in a very distorted and potentially biased view.

Implicit Theories

Implicit theories are preconceptions in people's minds. For instance, we may believe that jobs offering more challenge also provide more authority. Or we may believe that leaders who let their subordinates participate in decision making also care more about their subordinates. Whether correct or incorrect, these implicit theories may influence perceptions at the selection, organization, and translation stages. For instance, if we see evidence concerning one element of the theory, we will be likely to perceive other elements also. So, if our boss lets us participate in decision making, we may also be more likely to see caring behaviors, to organize caring behaviors with opportunities for participation, and to translate particular behaviors as more caring. We will explore the roles of implicit theories in later chapters.[15]

Causal Attribution

A crucial task for managers is to form accurate perceptions of the causes underlying others' behaviors. This process is called **causal attribution**. As an example, a district sales manager may want to determine what caused a salesperson's poor performance in the fall quarter. It may be especially important to determine whether the behavior was the result of internal factors such as the person's motives or traits or of external factors such as luck or the situation. If the sales manager feels that her subordinate's poor performance was due to lack of effort (an internal factor), she may want to consider disciplinary actions. If she feels the poor performance was due to an economic downturn, such actions would seem unfair.

According to Harold Kelley, we try to sort out the causes of an individual's behavior by considering three factors.[16] For instance, in the case of the poorly performing salesperson noted above, the boss might ask three questions. First, did other salespersons act the same way in this situation? That is, did others also have a poor period in the downturn? Second, does this salesperson always act this way in this situation? That is, does he always do poorly in economic downturns? Third, does this salesperson act differently in other situations? That is, does he do better in the absence of an economic downturn? If the boss answered yes to each of these questions, she would probably not blame her subordinate. On the other hand, if other people had done well in the downturn and this subordinate always does poorly, it would be hard to blame the situation.

Unfortunately, causal attribution is a process which is prone to error. For instance, people tend to attribute the behavior of others to internal factors, even when this is not appropriate. That is, we often blame or commend people for things that are really outside their control. Furthermore, there is a tendency to attribute the causes of our own behaviors to external factors and of others' behaviors to internal factors. Finally, the **self-serving bias**—the tendency to take credit for successes and deny personal responsibility for failures—is often seen.[17] In Chapter 10, we saw some ways these errors may result in biased performance appraisals.[18]

Reducing Perceptual Errors

Since perception is such an important process and plays a major role in determining our behavior, we must try to do it right. For instance, people who are aware of their own traits make fewer errors in perceiving others and are less likely to see the world in black-and-white terms.[19] Also, people who are able to accept themselves as they are can see a wider range of characteristics in others. They may also be less prone to projection. Further, simple knowledge of such tendencies as halo error, stereotyping, and self-serving bias may help to avoid them. Finally, it is important to make a conscious effort to attend to relevant information and to test reality. Actively seek evidence of whether or not your perceptions are accurate. Compare your perceptions with those of others and try to account for any differences. Look for objective measures relating to the perceptions. If you think Mr. Tanaka is a poor performer, check his output levels.

LEARNING

Learning is any relatively permanent change in behavior produced by experience. Changes in behavior due to physical variations, such as growth, deterioration, fatigue, or sleep, are not learning. Similarly, temporary changes are not true learning. Also, the changes may not be desirable; we have probably all learned some behaviors which have caused us to be less effective or adaptive than before. Here, we will briefly review three types of learning: classical conditioning, operant conditioning, and social learning. Together, these learning theories help explain how our behaviors are determined through our own experiences as well as the experiences of others.

Classical Conditioning

To many people, mention of learning theory brings to mind thoughts of Pavlov's dog. In Pavlov's experiments, a dog was taught to salivate in response to a variety of stimuli, such as a touch on the paw or the sound of a bell.[20] This was done by continually pairing the bell or other stimulus, which originally produced no increase in saliva, with food. Salivation was a normal physiological response to food in the mouth. The repeated pairing of the bell with the food caused the dog to salivate simply upon hearing the bell. Figure 12–2 shows this process.

The learning that took place in these experiments is called **classical,** or **Pavlovian, conditioning.** It occurs when, through pairing of stimuli, a new stimulus is responded to in the same way as the original stimulus. The thought of dangling rewards in front of salivating employees is a bit unseemly. Happily, this is not the sort of learning that is of most relevance in organizational settings.

People who are rewarded for desired behavior will tend to continue that behavior.

Operant Conditioning

Most learning in organizations relies on the law of effect. The **law of effect** states that behavior which is rewarded will tend to be repeated; behavior which is not rewarded will tend not to be repeated. So, if we want people to continue acting in a certain way, we should see that they are somehow rewarded for acting in that way. If we want them to stop particular undesirable behaviors, we should make sure we are not rewarding them for those behaviors. The sort of conditioning which relies on the law of effect is called **operant conditioning** or, after its best-known researcher and theorist, **Skinnerian conditioning.**[21] Figure 12–3 illustrates operant conditioning.

We will discuss specific operant-conditioning techniques in the next chapter. For now, we will simply point out that individuals enter organizations, and particular situations within organizations, with very different histories of reinforcement. That is, they have learned different things. Some have learned that working hard is the way to get ahead. Others have learned to be stubborn in the face of challenge. Still others have learned to avoid troublesome situations. Many differences in behaviors among employees may be due to the different ways their behaviors have been rewarded or punished in the past.

Social Learning

Both classical conditioning and operant conditioning focus on learning as something that develops out of our own experiences. However, much of what we have learned comes from the experience of others. Because others have been burned by a hot stove or have failed in their attempts to start a new

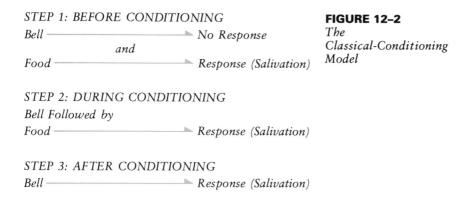

STEP 1: BEFORE CONDITIONING

Bell ─────────────────────→ No Response
             and
Food ─────────────────────→ Response (Salivation)

STEP 2: DURING CONDITIONING

Bell Followed by
Food ─────────────────────→ Response (Salivation)

STEP 3: AFTER CONDITIONING

Bell ─────────────────────→ Response (Salivation)

FIGURE 12–2
The Classical-Conditioning Model

FIGURE 12–3
The Operant-Conditioning Model

STIMULUS ──────▶ RESPONSE ──────▶ CONSEQUENCE

company or have found that certain leader behaviors are ineffective, we don't have to get burned ourselves to learn those things. Instead, we can benefit from social learning. **Social learning** is learning that occurs through any of a variety of social channels—newspapers, books, television, conversations with family members, friends, co-workers, and so on. As we will discuss in the next chapter, social learning accounts for much of our knowledge. In Chapter 14, we will consider the role of social learning in determining how employees view their jobs.

PERSONALITY

Personality is the organized and distinctive pattern of behavior that characterizes an individual's adaptation to a situation and endures over time.[22] The distinctive character of personality allows us to tell people apart. The enduring character of personality permits us to recognize people and to anticipate their behaviors. Try to imagine a situation in which people had no enduring qualities. For instance, suppose your boss acted "like a different person" from day to day. This might be interesting in the short run but would soon lead to chaos.

Personality Theories

Several theories of personality have been proposed. Some early personality theories saw behavior as being related to innate traits, such as independence, sociability, and humility. These traits were felt to be stable, enduring, and interrelated. The unique combination of these traits was seen as the clue to personality.[23]

According to another early approach, Sigmund Freud's **psychoanalytic theory**, we are motivated by drives or instincts.[24] We may be unaware of these drives, and they are largely out of our control. In this theory, the unconscious mind plays an overwhelming role, sometimes revealed to us by "Freudian slips." These are inadvertent mistakes in speech or writing that suggest what is happening in a person's unconscious mind. The psychoanalytic model sees personality as a conflict between basic pleasure-seeking drives and a restrictive society. Unhappiness, neuroses, and psychoses are seen as the result of that conflict.

Humanistic-existential theories focus on the total personality of the individual instead of on the separate behaviors that make up the personality. They downplay the roles of the environment and biology, stressing instead individual choice and personal responsibility. Instead of focusing on conflict, as in the Freudian model, the emphasis is on striving for awareness and fulfillment of the human potential. These strivings are seen as the basic force motivating human behavior. The work of Abraham Maslow, a key practitioner of this relatively optimistic approach, will be discussed in the next chapter.

Finally, learning theories see personality as a set of patterns of learned behaviors. That is, personalities differ because people have different experiences in childhood and throughout life. So, while personalities may be extremely complex, they are based upon simple learning principles.

Q: *One of your major contributions deals with escalation of commitment. You have characterized this tendency to commit increasing levels of resources to losing courses of action as throwing good money after bad. What are the causes of escalation of commitment?*

A: First, and most obviously, there are projects that logically demand further investment. That is, the economics of the situation may lead decision makers to "rationally" decide that putting in more resources will pay off. Second, there are psychological forces that seem to lock people into courses of action. For instance, individuals may try to justify their own prior decision making by continuing to invest in a losing course of action. Third, attempts to salvage a poor decision may also be based on social forces. Here, the individual may privately admit the failure of the course of action, but still need to defend it to salvage his or her job and credibility within the organization. Finally, losing projects or endeavors can sometimes become so ingrained in the organization that they are supported by more structural forces. The decision of British Columbia to stage the world's fair, Expo 86, despite large expected losses was a prime example of such larger, more institutional forces preventing withdrawal from a losing course of action.

Q: *You have also advocated a dispositional approach to work attitudes. Could you briefly discuss this approach and its practical implications?*

A: Most current approaches to work attitudes have taken a situational perspective, positing either that objective job conditions account for the way people feel about their work or that job attitudes are a function of social influences. These approaches are not wrong; they are just incomplete. They fail to take into account the degree to which job attitudes are determined by a person's disposition or personality. Using this dispositional approach, our research has shown substantial consistency in job attitudes over time. We have also shown that knowledge of the person's affective disposition (i.e., tendency to be happy or not) at an early age can predict job satisfaction through later adult life.

There are two general interpretations of the dispositional approach to job attitudes. The most pessimistic argues that because it is difficult to make people happy through job conditions, one might more profitably select "happy people" for the organization. The more optimistic view, and the one we advocate, is to admit that people have some tendency toward consistency in their job attitudes, but to argue that this is precisely the reason why we need strong improvements in the work situation. Without major changes in the way jobs are organized or structured we cannot expect long-lasting changes in work attitudes.

Q: *Could you summarize your research on the use of self-serving attributions by organizations when reporting performance information to shareholders?*

A: Our research showed that organizations, like individuals, tend to make self-serving attributions for their performance. They are quick to take credit for positive events and to blame negative performance on outside, extenuating circumstances. This biased reporting of results is widespread and does not seem to be disapproved of by stockholders. In fact, they may either be deluded into believing some of these rationalizations or come to expect them as a standard element in stockholder relations. I would expect some long-term fallout from self-serving biases. If companies using such biased reporting continue to perform poorly, they may later pay the price in diminished investor confidence. And, if companies start to believe their own rhetoric (e.g., that poor U.S. auto sales are mainly due to unfair competition), then future adaptiveness of the firm will likely be compromised.

Barry M. Staw (Ph.D., Northwestern University) holds the Lorraine T. Mitchell Chair in leadership and communication at the Business School of the University of California–Berkeley. His research has focused on the tendency of individuals and organizations to become locked into courses of action. He has also conducted many studies in the areas of job attitudes, work motivation, and creativity. Professor Staw founded and has served as co-editor of the annual series Research in Organizational Behavior *for the last 13 years. He has served on the editorial boards of such journals as* Administrative Science Quarterly, Academy of Management Journal, Journal of Applied Psychology, Motivation and Emotion, Journal of Occupational Psychology, *and* Organizational Behavior and Human Decision Processes. *He is a fellow of the Academy of Management and the American Psychological Association.*

ACADEMIC PROFILE
BARRY M. STAW

387

People differ markedly in their propensity to take risks.

Each of these theories of personality makes different assumptions about things such as the role of the environment and biology, the degree to which people are active or passive, and motivating forces. Together, the approaches provide a variety of potentially useful perspectives for examining and predicting human behavior.

Important Personality Dimensions

It is especially important for managers to understand how people with particular personalities may behave. In this section we review some personality characteristics which are related to behavior or performance.

RISK-TAKING PROPENSITY

People—even those in the same position in the same organization—differ markedly in their risk-taking propensity.[25] Some are risk averse. They like to "play it safe," choosing alternatives that are likely to give a relatively low but certain return. Others, called risk seekers, like to gamble. They prefer alternatives which may turn out very well or very poorly to those with little variance in outcomes. Risk takers tend to make fast decisions based on relatively little information.[26] Managers with different levels of risk-taking propensity will make very different decisions in the same situation.

AUTHORITARIANISM

Authoritarian individuals believe that power and status should be clearly defined and that there should be a hierarchy of authority.[27] They feel that authority should be concentrated in the hands of a few leaders and that this authority should be obeyed. As leaders, authoritarians expect unquestioning obedience to commands; as subordinates, they willingly give it. If a leader is authoritarian and his or her subordinate is not, frustration or conflict may result.

DOGMATISM

Dogmatic individuals are closed-minded. They have rigid belief systems and doggedly stick to their opinions, refusing to revise them even in the face of conflicting evidence. Dogmatics make decisions quickly based on relatively little information and are confident in those decisions. Dogmatics like to follow the rules and are unlikely to consider novel alternatives. They may perform acceptably in well-defined, routine situations, especially if there are time constraints. In other situations, especially those demanding creativity, they do poorly.[28]

LOCUS OF CONTROL

Locus of control refers to the degree to which individuals feel that the things which happen to them are the result of their own actions.[29] Those who feel that such things are within their own control have an internal locus of control. Those who see their lives as being controlled by fate, circumstance, or chance have an external locus of control. Externals are unlikely to believe that they can do better if they try harder or that the rewards and punishments they receive depend upon how well they do. For each of these reasons, internals may be more highly motivated than externals.

TOLERANCE FOR AMBIGUITY

Individuals with high **tolerance for ambiguity** welcome uncertainty and change. Those with low tolerance for ambiguity find such situations threatening and uncomfortable. Since managers are increasingly facing dynamic, unstructured situations, tolerance for ambiguity is clearly an important characteristic.

MACHIAVELLIANISM

Individuals with **Machiavellian** personalities feel that any behavior is acceptable if it achieves their goals. Machiavellians try to manipulate others. They are unemotional and detached. They "look out for Number One" and aren't likely to be good team players.

SELF-MONITORING

Self-monitoring is the extent to which people emulate the behavior of others.[30] High self-monitors pay close attention to the behaviors of others and try to model their behaviors after those of the individuals observed. For instance, a subordinate may watch how a co-worker behaves when dealing with the boss and then try to emulate that behavior when next interacting with the boss. Low self-monitors react to situations without looking to others for behavioral cues.

This discussion of personality should not be taken to suggest that people have no control over their actions. Instead, personality characteristics suggest tendencies to behave in certain ways. People's conscious decisions may help them overcome troublesome behavior patterns. For instance, people may be able to make a conscious effort to take the needs of others into account, to consider more information before making a decision, and to modify their risk preferences.

ATTITUDES

Attitudes are the beliefs, feelings, and behavioral tendencies held by a person about an object, event, or person (called the *attitude object*). In this section we will consider the nature of attitudes and examine some specific work attitudes. We will discuss how attitudes are formed and examine the relationships of work attitudes to work behaviors.

The Components of Attitudes

The definition of attitudes indicates that they have three components: cognitive, affective, and behavioral tendency. The cognitive component of attitudes is our cognitions or beliefs about the facts pertaining to the attitude object. We may, for example, believe that salespersons in our firm receive high pay or that our firm is the oldest in the industry. These beliefs may be correct or incorrect. The second component, the affective component, is made up of our feelings toward the attitude object. It involves evaluation and emotion. For instance, we may think favorably or unfavorably about another

Our attitudes affect our ability to get along well with others.

employee or think a particular rule is good or bad. The third component, the behavioral tendency component, is the way we intend to behave toward the attitude object. We may, for example, intend to tell off the boss or ask for a raise or outperform a co-worker.

Sometimes, our cognitions may influence our feelings, which may, in turn, influence our behavioral tendencies. However, it is important to recognize that different people with the same beliefs may develop different feelings, and that different people with the same feelings may develop different behavioral intentions. Also, we'll see there may even be cases in which our beliefs will be influenced by our feelings, or even by our actual behaviors.

Why Care About Attitudes?

It might seem that managers should be concerned about the behaviors, not the attitudes, of their employees. In fact, however, there are a number of reasons why employee attitudes should be of concern to managers. First, as we suggested earlier, attitudes may influence behaviors. If so, managers may try to improve behaviors by bringing about changes in attitudes. Widely repeated statements such as "A satisfied employee is a productive employee" show that many people do believe that attitudes (in this case, satisfaction) are related to work behaviors (here, productivity). For this reason, it is important to determine what links, if any, really do exist between employee attitudes and employee behaviors.

Second, work attitudes may influence things of direct concern to the employee such as stress levels, ability to sleep, and attitudes toward other aspects of life. Furthermore, attitudes are important for their own sake, independent of their consequences. Employees spend half their waking lives at work. Caring managers may want to learn how to make the working hours of employees more pleasant.

Some Important Work Attitudes

The most commonly studied work attitude is job satisfaction. Two other important work attitudes are job involvement and organizational commitment.

JOB SATISFACTION

Job satisfaction is the affective component of work-related attitudes. Managers are often concerned about employees' satisfaction with specific facets of the job, as well as about overall job satisfaction.

The best-known scale to assess facets of job satisfaction, the Job Descriptive Index (JDI), measures satisfaction with the work itself, pay, co-workers, supervision, and promotions.[31] Figure 12–4 presents sample items from the supervision subscale of the JDI. By tapping satisfaction with particular job facets, a scale such as the JDI helps managers to pinpoint sources of dissatisfaction and to take appropriate actions.

Overall job satisfaction, or general job satisfaction, is concerned with the overall affective reactions of an employee to the job. While examination of facet satisfaction is very useful, it may fail to see the forest for the trees. That is, measures of facet satisfaction can't give us the complete picture because employees may give differing weights to various job facets and may combine information about facets in different ways. Thus, overall satisfaction measures provide useful additional information. Many such measures are short and easy to use.

Figure 12–5 and Figure 12–6 present two measures of overall satisfaction. The first measure, called the Faces Scale, can easily be completed by employees regardless of their language skills. It is sometimes criticized for seeming a bit *too* simple, but it has good validity and reliability. If instructions on the Faces Scale are reworded to focus on a particular job facet, the scale can also be used to measure satisfaction with that facet. The second scale, developed by Arthur Brayfield and Harold Rothe, is also easy to use. Employees simply indicate their degree of agreement with each of 18 statements about the job.[32]

Many studies have focused on job satisfaction levels. To a great extent, the results of those studies seem to depend on the wording of questions and

---

FIGURE 12–4
*Job Descriptive Index:
Supervision Subscale
Sample Items*

The following adjectives and phrases describe five aspects of a job: the work itself, supervision, pay, promotions, and co-workers. Carefully consider each adjective or phrase and indicate whether or not it is true of your job by circling:

   Y   for YES, this is true of my job.
   ?   for I cannot decide if this is true of my job.
   N   for NO, this is not true of my job.

The Supervision on My Job

- Asks my advice............   Y   ?   N
- Hard to please ....   Y   ?   N
- Impolite...................   Y   ?   N
- Influential................   Y   ?   N
- Stubborn ....   Y   ?   N
- Knows job well............   Y   ?   N

Source: P. C. Smith, L. M. Kendall, and C. L. Hulin, Job Descriptive Index (Revised), Bowling Green State University (Department of Psychology), Bowling Green, OH. Copyright 1985, Bowling Green State University. Reprinted with permission.

FIGURE 12–5
*Measures of General
Satisfaction: The Faces
Scale*

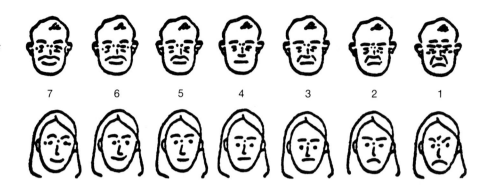

Source: The male faces scale was developed by T. Kunin, "The Construction of a New Type of Attitude Measure," *Personnel Psychology* 8 (1955): 65-78, and the female scale by Randall B. Dunham and J. B. Herman, "Development of a Female Faces Scale for Measuring Job Satisfaction," *Journal of Applied Psychology* 60: 629-631. Copyright 1975 by the American Psychological Association. Reprinted by permission.

the interpretation of findings. Major surveys conducted over periods of twenty years or more show that 80 percent to 90 percent of the work force report they are at least reasonably satisfied with their jobs.[33] Yet everything we hear about "blue-collar blues" and high levels of absenteeism and turnover in many jobs, as well as complaints we regularly hear about jobs, suggests that this is too bright a picture.

Perhaps as revealing are studies that show that most workers—over three-quarters of blue-collar workers and almost 60 percent of white-collar workers—say they would not choose the same line of work again.[34] A survey looking at average levels of general satisfaction may give an incomplete pic-

FIGURE 12–6
*The Brayfield-Rothe
Scale (Selected Items)*

Some jobs are more interesting and satisfying than others. We want to know how people feel about different jobs. Cross out the phrase below each statement which best describes how you feel about your present job. There are no right or wrong answers.

1. My job is like a hobby to me.

STRONGLY AGREE   AGREE   UNDECIDED   DISAGREE   STRONGLY DISAGREE

2. My job is usually interesting enough to keep me from getting bored.

STRONGLY AGREE   AGREE   UNDECIDED   DISAGREE   STRONGLY DISAGREE

5. I enjoy my work more than my leisure time.

STRONGLY AGREE   AGREE   UNDECIDED   DISAGREE   STRONGLY DISAGREE

7. I feel fairly well satisfied with my current job.

STRONGLY AGREE   AGREE   UNDECIDED   DISAGREE   STRONGLY DISAGREE

17. I find real enjoyment in my work.

STRONGLY AGREE   AGREE   UNDECIDED   DISAGREE   STRONGLY DISAGREE

Source: These items are from A. H. Brayfield and H. F. Rothe, "An Index of Job Satisfaction," *Journal of Applied Psychology* 35 (1951): 307-311.

ture. For instance, it may fail to isolate specific facets of the job that cause much dissatisfaction or particular sorts of jobs that are particularly distasteful.[35] Some jobs, and some parts of many jobs, may be "the pits."

JOB INVOLVEMENT

As the term suggests, **job involvement** is the degree to which employees really are involved with—that is, "get into"—their jobs. Job involvement may be reflected in the job's importance to the employee's life or to the employee's self-concept. A person with a high degree of job involvement would agree with statements such as:[36]

- The most important things that happen to me involve my job.
- The major satisfaction of my life comes from my job.
- I live, eat, and breathe my job.

While companies want their workers to be involved in their jobs, overly high levels of job involvement may be undesirable. At the extreme, employees who are "workaholics" may neglect their families and outside activities and may even suffer health problems.[37]

A related attitude, **work involvement**, is the degree to which an employee is involved with work in general, rather than with a specific job. "Priorities of Life" suggests that Japanese employees are highly involved with their jobs and work.

ORGANIZATIONAL COMMITMENT

Organizational commitment reflects the degree to which the employee is committed to the organization's values and goals. An employee with strong organizational commitment agrees with statements such as the following:[38]

- I find that my values and the organization's values are very similar.
- I am proud to tell others that I am part of this organization.
- I really care about the fate of this organization.
- I am willing to put in a great deal of effort beyond that normally expected in order to help this organization be successful.

PRIORITIES OF LIFE

In 1986, the average Japanese worked 2,150 hours a year while Americans worked 1,924 hours and West Germans, 1,655 hours. Relatively few Japanese work only a 40-hour week or even take the vacation time they are entitled to. In the Japanese scale of values, the worker rates the economic welfare of his company higher than he does his own good. He also sees to it that his children attend school five and a half days per week, including 8:30 A.M. to 1 P.M. on Saturdays.

Several years ago the Japanese Department of Statistics and Information of the Ministry of Health and Welfare asked workers a question of priorities, which went something like this: "If you were heading to your job and an earthquake broke out, and you were limited to a single phone call, who would you phone—your wife, your physician, your children, your employer, or your parents?" The overwhelming majority selected "employer."

Source: Excerpted from "Priorities of Life," *Parade Magazine* (September 4, 1988): 21.

Organizational commitment is much like loyalty. It would seem that a company would like to see high levels of organizational commitment among its work force. In fact, while that is generally true, there may be exceptions. For one thing, if low-performing employees are very committed to the organization, they may be reluctant to leave. If management is constrained from terminating low-performing employees, such commitment could be costly to the firm. Also, we have all heard of cases in which employees have been so committed to an organization or to a cause that they have been afraid to "rock the boat" or to criticize others in the firm. In extreme cases, commitment has led to commission of illegal or unethical acts. More commitment, like more of most things in life, is not necessarily better.

Attitude Formation

The earlier section on learning suggests ways in which we may form attitudes. For one, we may have direct personal experience with the attitude object. We may, for instance, have met a candidate for public office. Second, we may form attitudes through association. That is, we may transfer an attitude about a particular attitude object to a new attitude object which is somehow similar. For example, if we like all of our current acquaintances who are runners, we may like a new acquaintance upon learning that she runs. Finally, we may form attitudes indirectly through social learning. Here, attitudes are influenced by information provided by others. We may read about an object, for instance, or may hear it discussed on TV or listen to co-workers weighing its pros and cons.

Attitudes formed in any of these ways may be intensely held. However, attitudes formed through personal experience are more clearly defined, held with greater certainty, more stable over time, and more resistant to counterinfluence than attitudes that are formed indirectly.[39]

The Relationships of Attitudes to Behaviors

Knowledge of the relationships of work attitudes to work behaviors can be valuable to managers. Here we explore two possible ways they may be related—attitudes may cause behaviors, or behaviors may cause attitudes.

DO ATTITUDES CAUSE BEHAVIORS?

We said earlier that one reason managers care about employee attitudes is that those attitudes may influence behaviors. This seems to make sense. If we don't like our jobs, for instance, we may not put our full effort into them. In fact, though, many researchers have found that sometimes the link between attitudes and behaviors is weak.

In the first such study, R. T. LaPiere reported on his travels through the United States with an Oriental couple in the early 1930s.[40] During those travels, the couple was almost always treated hospitably at hotels and restaurants. However, a survey of owners of the establishments found their attitudes toward Orientals to be very negative. In fact, 90 percent said that as a matter of policy Orientals would not be served. Clearly, attitudes were not being translated into behaviors.

More recent attempts to sort out this puzzle have suggested reasons why the attitude-behavior linkage may be weak. For instance, even though people have certain attitudes, they may have no choice but to behave in certain ways. Also, a person's behavioral tendency is the result of many things beyond attitude, including pressures exerted by others, the nature of the job market, and personality characteristics. Let's briefly consider evidence concerning the relationships between satisfaction and work behaviors.

Satisfaction and Turnover

Research shows a negative relationship between satisfaction and turnover. That is, more-satisfied workers are less likely to leave the firm. One review of the literature found this negative relationship to be evident in 35 of 39 studies.[41] The average correlation was about -0.40, indicating that about 16 percent of the variance in turnover was related to satisfaction.[42]

Many things besides satisfaction also seem to influence turnover, including economic conditions, family pressures, skill levels, and personality. It is probably the case that satisfaction is a better predictor of turnover in good economic times than in bad.[43] In good times, a dissatisfied employee may feel confident that other jobs will be available and therefore quit. In bad times, an employee may simply put up with dissatisfaction rather than take a chance of being out of work.

Satisfaction and Absenteeism

While satisfaction and absenteeism are also negatively related, the association revealed by studies is not as strong as we might expect—most correlations do not exceed -0.35. However, satisfaction may play a larger role in determining absenteeism than such figures might indicate. This is because, as we noted earlier, much absenteeism is unavoidable, caused by such things as illness or family emergencies. If the relationship of satisfaction to avoidable absenteeism could be adequately assessed, it would probably be considerable.

There are many times when workers and managers need to be away from their desks. However, chronic absenteeism may be a sign that an employee finds the job unsatisfying.

Satisfaction and Performance

Findings concerning the relationship of satisfaction to performance show us why research is often needed to augment common sense. While it seems reasonable to expect that satisfied workers would be more productive, many studies suggest that this is really not the case, at least to any appreciable degree. Major reviews of the satisfaction-performance relationship have concluded that the correlations are so low as to be negligible, and that satisfaction does not imply motivation for strong performance.[44] Across 20 major studies, the median correlation was only 0.14.[45] With a correlation of that magnitude, only about 2 percent of variance in performance is associated with variance in satisfaction. We will try to make more sense of these surprising findings in the next chapter.

Before we leave this topic, however, we should point out that the question of the relationship of satisfaction to performance is still not settled. For instance, Dennis Organ has noted that most studies of the satisfaction-performance relationship have used narrow definitions of performance, such as quantity of output or quality of craftsmanship. He argues that broader performance behaviors—such as helping co-workers with a job-related problem, following orders without a fuss, making timely and constructive comments about the work unit or its head to outsiders, and protecting and conserving organizational resources—may in fact result from satisfaction.[46] A subsequent study by Thomas Bateman and Organ found that relationships between job satisfaction and these **citizenship behaviors** were much stronger than is typical of studies of the satisfaction-performance relationship. The authors argue that the stronger relationships may be because citizenship behaviors generally represent actions more under the control of workers than conventional performance measures.[47] These citizenship behaviors have received little attention, but in many cases they may be just as important as narrower performance measures.

The Financial Impact of Attitudes

The failure to find that satisfaction causes better performance, at least narrowly defined, should not lead us to conclude that attitudes don't influence financial performance. Instead, as we've tried to show, absenteeism, turnover, and other employee behaviors also have costs. The area of **behavioral accounting** is now trying to assess the financial impact of attitudes. It does this by examining the costs of such behaviors as turnover and absenteeism and the strength of their links to attitudes. While this is a new field, and fraught with measurement problems, some of its conclusions are remarkable.

For instance, Philip Mirvis and Edward Lawler used behavioral accounting to estimate the costs of absenteeism, turnover, and balancing shortages of 160 bank tellers.[48] They concluded that moderate improvements in attitudes averaging perhaps 0.7 on a seven-point scale would yield the bank total savings of $781,892, or $4,886.83 per employee. One study has estimated that, on a national basis, a very modest improvement in employee attitudes of perhaps 0.15 on a seven-point scale would result in a total financial benefit of over one billion dollars.[49]

DO BEHAVIORS CAUSE ATTITUDES?

Leon Festinger has proposed a theory of cognitive dissonance, which suggests that behaviors may actually cause attitudes.[50] Cognitions are thoughts and dissonance is lack of harmony. So, **cognitive dissonance** is a situation in which we have conflicting thoughts. For example, if we don't like a co-worker, Janet, but must treat her nicely because of job demands, we may experience such conflict.

As detailed by Festinger, cognitive dissonance is such a tense, uncomfortable state that people will do something to reduce that tension. One way to reduce the tension is to change one or both of the cognitions to make them consistent.

Furthermore, Festinger proposed that some cognitions are more resistant to change than others. For instance, cognitions based on physical reality, such as the fact that we just treated Janet nicely, are more resistant to change than are cognitions based on opinions and attitudes, such as our negative feelings toward Janet. The bottom line, then, is that we may change our attitudes to make them consistent with our behaviors. We may actually begin to like Janet.

We said earlier that the high levels of job satisfaction reported may be artificially high. Dissonance theory suggests another reason why that may be the case. A pair of conflicting thoughts, such as "I continue to work on this job, yet it does not give me satisfaction," reflects dissonance. To reduce that dissonance, employees may convince themselves that they are in fact satisfied with their jobs.

There is an important second route by which behaviors may influence attitudes. That is, behaviors may lead to consequences which may impact on attitudes. For instance, a high-performing employee may get a big raise, which may in turn increase satisfaction with pay. We'll explore this avenue more fully in the next chapter.

VALUES

Values have an enduring quality and are less specific than attitudes. **Values** are broad, general beliefs about some way of behaving or some desired end state. Ways of behaving, for instance, might include behaving honestly, frugally, or cautiously. Desired end states might be financial security, happiness, freedom, or a sense of accomplishment. Values may influence whether an individual accepts or resists organizational goals or pressures, what limits the individual sets to determine what is and is not ethical behavior, how the individual perceives other individuals and groups, how the individual defines individual and organizational success, and many other factors.[51]

Types of Values

Values can be classified in many ways. George England has described two distinct types of value systems—the pragmatic and the ethical-moral.[52] A person with a pragmatic value system determines whether or not to engage in a particular act principally by asking the question, "Will engaging in the act help me become more successful?" A person with an ethical-moral value system instead asks the question, "Is the act ethically right or wrong?"

Another useful way to classify values has been presented by Gordon Allport, Philip Vernon, and Gardner Lindzey:[53]

- *Theoretical values.* Individuals with strong theoretical value orientations are primarily interested in the discovery of truth and the systematic ordering of knowledge.
- *Economic values.* Adherents to economic values are oriented toward practical and useful aspects of work. They are interested in the production and consumption of goods and the uses and creation of wealth.
- *Aesthetic values.* Those with dominant aesthetic values are interested in the artistic features of an object, with an emphasis on form, symmetry, grace, and harmony.
- *Social values.* Individuals with strong social values place primary emphasis on the love of people and the warmth of human relations. They value people as ends, rather than means, and tend to be kind, sympathetic, and unselfish.
- *Political values.* Those with primary political value orientations are concerned with power, influence, and recognition. Competition plays an important role in their lives, and power is the key motive.
- *Religious values.* People with strong religious values have an orientation toward unity and creation of satisfying relations with the environment.

Such value differences can cause people to make different decisions, and probably to choose different sorts of occupations. Using the two classification schemes identified, how would you describe your values? The values of the "typical" college student? The values of the "typical" businessperson?

Work Values

In recent years there has been a concern that work values have been changing. Instead of valuing "an honest day's labor" and a quality product, younger workers are seen as valuing "the easy way" and as caring little about whether they can be proud of their work. The work values whose decline is lamented are encompassed in the Protestant work ethic. The **Protestant work ethic** is the belief that work is valuable, important, and a central life interest. Individuals adhering to the Protestant work ethic agree with statements such as the following:[54]

- Hard work makes one a better person.
- Wasting time is as bad as wasting money.
- If all other things are equal, it is better to have a job with a lot of responsibility than one with little responsibility.
- A good indication of one's worth is how well that person does a job.

If there has been a marked change in work values, it could have a substantial impact on organizations. We will explore this issue further in Chapter 14.

IMPLICATIONS FOR MANAGEMENT

As a manager, you should be concerned with a variety of work behaviors, including absenteeism, turnover, tardiness, effort, and quantity and quality of performance. Focusing just on a single behavior is inappropriate. In particular, you will find that greater gains can often be achieved by emphasizing work quality and employee turnover levels than by concentrating solely on quantity of output.

You will often need to formally or informally evaluate the work behaviors of subordinates and others. This chapter shows that there are many causes of behaviors, some learned and others innate. Some behaviors are caused by internal factors, such as ability, and others by external factors, such as illness in the family or business fluctuations. If you make faulty assumptions about the causes of behaviors, your actions will probably be misguided.

Much of this chapter dealt with perceptions, and with good reason. Perceptions guide behavior. The ways employees respond to leader behaviors, rewards and punishments, and job characteristics all depend on perceptions. If you as a manager fall prey to perceptual errors, you will make mistakes in the ways you behave and respond to the behaviors of others. If you are unable to influence the perceptions of others, you will be powerless.

Learning continues throughout our lives. You will certainly learn during your years as a manager, and you will be responsible for much of the learning of your subordinates. In teaching subordinates, you will rely primarily on operant conditioning and social learning. You will not have a choice of whether or not to use those tools; learning will take place whether you like it or not. Your task will be to see that it is done right.

In your work life, you will find yourself responding daily to superiors, peers, and subordinates who may differ in terms of such personality characteristics as risk-taking propensity, locus of control, dogmatism, and Machiavellianism. It will often be tempting to simply curse what seem to be maddeningly irrational, unreasonable, or manipulative acts on the part of others. A better course of action will be to try to understand the personalities of those you must deal with and to assess how they are likely to cause them to behave. Such an understanding will make behavior in organizations more predictable and thus more manageable.

As a manager, you may be criticized if you seem to place emphasis on the attitudes of your subordinates. Some may argue, for instance, that you are forgetting the bottom line. The material in this chapter suggests some responses. For one, you can point out that attitudes are important in themselves. When workers are satisfied with their work, involved in their jobs, and committed to the organization, they are likely (within limits) to have richer, more meaningful lives. Also, you can respond that there are many roads to the bottom line. Attitudes directly influence such contributors to organizational success as levels of employee turnover, absenteeism, and health. We will see later that they may, in some situations, also influence work quality and quantity.

Finally, throughout your career you will deal with people who have a variety of values, some probably very different from your own. Because values are enduring and general in nature, you will find it much more difficult to influence your subordinates' values than, say, their attitudes. Similarly, you will probably find it fruitless to argue with others on the basis of their values. Those with aesthetic values, for instance, are not going to be convinced that political values are correct, and vice versa. Instead, you will have to recognize those value differences and behave accordingly.

In sum, successful managers recognize that they must understand, predict, and influence the behavior of others in organizations. The concepts presented in this chapter—many of which we will address later in more depth—are essential for the accomplishment of these important aims.

KEY TERMS AND CONCEPTS

ability
attendance
attitudes
authoritarian
behavioral accounting
causal attribution
citizenship behaviors
classical or Pavlovian conditioning
closure
cognitive dissonance
dogmatic
effort
halo effect
humanistic-existential theories
implicit theories
job involvement
job satisfaction
law of effect
learning
locus of control
Machiavellian
operant or Skinnerian conditioning

organizational commitment
participation
perception
perceptual readiness
performance
personality
primacy effect
productivity
projection
Protestant work ethic
psychoanalytic theory
Pygmalion effect
recency effect
retention
self-monitoring
self-serving bias
social learning
stereotyping
timeliness
tolerance for ambiguity
values
work involvement

QUESTIONS FOR REVIEW AND DISCUSSION

1. Which of the work behaviors discussed in this chapter do you think would be most important in a fast-food restaurant? In a firm manufacturing top-of-the-line stereo equipment? In a child-care center? Justify each of your choices.
2. Identify three categories of abilities. Describe jobs for which each of these abilities would be especially important.
3. Of the things influencing the perceptual process, which three do you think pose the greatest problems from the point of view of management? Why?
4. Describe a situation in which you tried to figure out the cause of someone's behavior. To what extent did you consider the factors suggested by Kelley? Did you come to the same conclusion that his approach would suggest?
5. What is the difference between classical conditioning and operant conditioning? How are they each different from social learning?

6. Can you imagine a situation in which classical conditioning might be used in business? Does any advertising make use of classical conditioning?

7. Pick three people—friends, co-workers, television personalities, or corporate executives—and describe them in terms of each of the personality characteristics considered in this chapter.

8. Do you think management should place more emphasis on increasing worker job satisfaction? On increasing job involvement? On increasing organizational commitment? In each case, defend your answer.

9. Describe the relationships of satisfaction to turnover, absenteeism, and performance. Why should management be concerned about assessing those relationships?

10. Do you feel that belief in the Protestant work ethic is declining? Why or why not? If it is declining, what are three implications for management?

CASES

12–1 NOBODY GETS FIRED IN PORTUGAL

Nobody gets fired in Portugal unless the boss has a very good reason. That is the law as set down more than a decade ago after the radical left took over the government.

The government has since softened, and the economy has hit bottom. But the law stands and performs miracles for employment. Over in Spain, the jobless rate tops 18 percent. Here, it tickles 11 percent. Anybody who goes to work in Portugal today can almost certainly go to work tomorrow.

Bosses hate this. They want to consolidate, modernize. They are aching to fire people. Luckily for them, the radicals who wrote the law to protect jobs forgot to write a law to protect salaries. So Portugal's bosses have devised a new way to increase cash flow. They don't fire workers; they just don't pay them. "It can't really increase efficiency," a labor expert says, "but it does cut costs."

Among Portugal's workers, enthusiasm for this innovation has been limited. "It isn't a normal basis for civilized society," says José Luis Judas of the communist labor federation. "You work, you get paid. This is not the case in Portugal at the moment."

The absence of pay, however, hasn't led workers to do anything rash—like stay home. Portuguese pay averages $165 a month. Some workers haven't gotten an escudo in over a year. Others get paid in dribs and drabs, and months behind. By various guesses, 500 companies owe 150,000 employees $70 million. Yet almost everybody keeps on working.

How come? Well, according to the law, if somebody doesn't show up for work just because that person isn't being paid, he or she could get fired.

In some countries, a worker might quit and apply for unemployment benefits. For a quitter to qualify for benefits in Portugal, the company would have to certify that it has stopped paying the individual. But no company wants to do that. Some officials might decide that nonpayment of wages is tantamount to dismissal. Dismissals, remember, are generally illegal.

Source: Reprinted by permission of *The Wall Street Journal*, © Dow Jones & Company, Inc. (December 12, 1984). All Rights Reserved Worldwide.

1. Discuss what impact a situation like this would be likely to have on the cognitive, affective, and behavioral tendency components of employees' attitudes toward work. What links, if any, are likely among those components in this case?

2. Which of the personality characteristics discussed in this chapter do you think would be positively related to continued participation in work in this situation? Which of the characteristics might be positively associated with turnover?

3. How would you predict that this situation would influence employee performance levels? Why?

12-2 BENEFITS ON THE BOTTOM LINE

In January 1987, Union Bank opened a new profit center in Los Angeles. This one, however, doesn't lend money. It doesn't manage money. It takes care of children.

The profit center is a day-care facility at the bank's Monterey Park operations center. Union Bank, 77 percent owned by Bank of Tokyo, provided the facility with a $105,000 subsidy last year. In return, it saved the bank as much as $232,000.

There is, of course, nothing extraordinary about a day-care center. What is extraordinary is the $232,000.

The number is part of a growing body of research that tries to tell companies what they are getting—on the bottom line—for the dollars they invest in such new-wave benefits as day-care assistance, wellness plans, maternity leaves, and flexible work schedules.

The research poses the problems typical of any social science subject: almost endless variables, subjective evaluations, and the kinds of benefits—such as corporate loyalty—that seem impossible to quantify.

But however difficult, the measurements are crucial: Squeezed corporate budgets mean pressure to justify any expense. Union Bank, for instance, approved spending $430,000 to build its day-care center only after seeing savings projections.

For some researchers, the answer is to measure problems they believe could be alleviated by such benefits. In other words, the cost of *not* providing them: turnover, absenteeism, tardiness, or time at work spent phoning babysitters.

Some of these calculations can be made fairly simply. In 1986, for instance, Corning Glass Works decided to measure out-of-pocket expenses associated with turnover—such as interview costs and hiring bonuses. The number—$16 million to $18 million annually—led to investigations into the causes of turnover, and in turn to new policies on flexible scheduling and career development. American Telephone & Telegraph Co. and Merck & Co. are among other firms that have assessed the savings associated with benefits programs.

The Union Bank study, designed to cover many questions left out of other evaluations, offers one of the more revealing glimpses at the savings from corporate day-care centers. For one thing, the study was begun a year *before* the center opened, giving researchers more control over the comparison statistics.

Using data provided by the bank's human resource department, Sandra Burud, a child-care consultant in Pasadena, Calif., compared absenteeism, turnover, and maternity leave time the first year of operation and the year before. She looked at the results for 87 users of the center, a control group of 105 employees with children of similar ages who used other day-care operations, and employees as a whole.

Her conclusion: The day-care center saves the bank $138,000 to $232,000 a year—numbers she calls "very conservative."

Ms. Burud says savings on turnover total $63,000 to $157,000, based mostly on the fact that turnover among center users was 2.2 percent, compared with 9.5 percent in the control group and 18 percent throughout the bank.

She also counts $35,000 in savings on lost days' work; users of the center were absent an average of 1.7 days less than the control group, and their maternity leaves were 1.2 weeks shorter than for other employees. Ms. Burud also added a bonus of $40,000 in free publicity, based on estimates of media coverage of the center.

Despite the complexities of measuring, she says, the study succeeds in contradicting the "simplistic view of child care. This isn't a touchy-feely kind of program. It's as much a management tool as it is an employee benefit."

Source: Excerpted and adapted from Jolie Solomon, "Companies Try Measuring Cost Savings from New Types of Corporate Benefits," *The Wall Street Journal* (December 29, 1988): B1.

1. Do you believe the costs and savings of benefits such as day-care facilities, flexible work schedules, and wellness plans can be measured with enough accuracy to permit meaningful management decisions? Why or why not?

2. Do you feel attempts to assess the savings and costs of benefits as described in this case will be more widely adopted by firms in the future? Why or why not?

3. What do you see as some benefits to firms of use of this approach? Some potential dangers or costs?

ENDNOTES

1. Bureau of National Affairs, "Absenteeism Policy Guide," *BNA Policy and Practices Manual no. 518* (1981): 23.

2. See S. F. Yolles, P. A. Carone, and L. W. Krinsky, *Absenteeism in Industry* (Springfield, IL: Charles C Thomas, 1975), and R. M. Steers and S. R. Rhodes, "Major Influences on Employee Attendance: A Process Model," *Journal of Applied Psychology* 63 (August 1978): 391-407.

3. Some writers consider all job changes, including movements within the organization, as turnover. We are maintaining the more traditional use of the term.

4. For discussions of this issue, see D. R. Dalton, W. D. Todor, and D. M. Krackhardt, "Turnover Overstated: The Functional Taxonomy," *Academy of Management Review* 7 (1982): 117-123, and J. R. Hollenbeck and C. R. Williams, "Turnover Functionality Versus Frequency: A Note on Work Attitudes and Organizational Effectiveness," *Journal of Applied Psychology* 71 (1986): 606-611.

5. E. McCormick and J. Tiffin, *Industrial Psychology*, 6th ed. (Englewood Cliffs, NJ: Prentice-Hall, 1974).

6. B. Berelson and G. A. Steiner, *Human Behavior: An Inventory of Scientific Findings* (New York: Harcourt, Brace & World, 1964).

7. D. C. Dearborn and H. A. Simon, "Selective Perception: A Note on the Departmental Identifications of Executives," *Sociometry* 21 (1958): 140-144.

8. S. S. Zalkind and T. W. Costello, "Perception: Some Recent Research and Implications for Administration," *Administrative Science Quarterly* 7 (1962): 218-235.

9. M. Haire, "Role Perceptions in Labor-Management Relations: An Experimental Approach," *Industrial and Labor Relations Review* 8 (1955): 204-216.

10. J. R. Terborg and D. R. Ilgen, "A Theoretical Approach to Sex Discrimination in Traditionally Masculine Occupations," *Organizational Behavior and Human Performance* 13 (1975): 352-376.

11. The term "Pygmalion effect" comes from mythology. As told by Ovid, a sculptor named Pygmalion created a sculpture of a young woman so beautiful that he fell hopelessly in love with it. Venus, the goddess of love and beauty, was fascinated by this new kind of lover and brought the sculpture to life. Pygmalion named the maiden Galatea and they had a son, Paphos. The Pygmalion effect, then, refers to creating something in the image you had of it. For a discussion of Pygmalion applied to management, see D. Eden, "Self-Fulfilling Prophecy as a Management Tool: Harnessing Pygmalion," *Academy of Management Review* 9 (1984): 64-73. For a more general discussion of self-fulfilling prophecies, see L. Jussim, "Self-Fulfilling Prophecies: A Theoretical and Integrative Review," *Psychological Review* 93 (1986): 429-445.

12. R. Rosenthal and L. Jacobson, *Pygmalion in the Classroom: Teacher Expectation and Pupils' Intellectual Development* (New York: Holt, Rinehart & Winston, 1968).

13. A. Lowin and J. R. Craig, "The Influence of Level of Performance on Managerial Style: An Experimental Object Lesson in the Ambiguity of Correlational Data," *Organization Behavior and Human Performance* 3 (1968): 440-458.

14. M. Haire and W. F. Grunes, "Perceptual Defenses: Processes Protecting an Organized Perception of Another Personality," *Human Relations* 3 (1950): 403-412.

15. For a thorough discussion of implicit theories, see R. J. Sternberg, "Implicit Theories of Intelligence, Creativity, and Wisdom," *Journal of Personality and Social Psychology* 49 (1985): 607-627.

16. H. H. Kelley, "The Processes of Causal Attribution," *American Psychologist* 28 (1973): 107-128.

17. For more on these sources of error, see F. Heider, "Social Perception and Phenomenal Causality," *Psychological Review* 51 (1944): 358-374; R. E. Nisbett et al., "Behavior As Seen by the Actor and As Seen by the Observer," *Journal of Personality and Social Psychology* 27 (August 1973): 154-164; and C. S. Carver, E. DeGregorio, and R. Gillis, "Field-Study Evidence of an Attribution Among Two Categories of Observers," *Personality and Social Psychology Bulletin* 6 (March 1980): 44-50.

18. Of course, managers must make causal attributions about many things, not just behaviors. For instance, for a model to explain how managers' attributions of the causes of organizational performance downturns influence their subsequent strategies, see J. D. Ford, "The Effects of Causal Attributions on Decision Makers' Responses to Performance Downturns," *Academy of Management Review* 10 (1985): 770-786.

19. R. D. Norman, "The Interrelationships Among Acceptance-Rejection, Self-Other Identity, Insight into Self, and Realistic Perception of Others," *Journal of Social Psychology* 37 (1953): 205-235, and D. T. Benedetti and J. G. Hill, "A Determiner of the Centrality of a Trait in Impression Formation," *Journal of Abnormal and Social Psychology* 60 (1960): 278-279.

20. I. P. Pavlov, *The Work of the Digestive Glands*, trans. W. H. Thompson (London: Charles Griffin, 1902).

21. B. F. Skinner, *Contingencies of Reinforcement: A Theoretical Analysis* (East Norwalk, CT: Appleton-Century-Crofts, 1969).

22. J. M. Darley, S. Glucksberg, L. J. Kamin, and R. A. Kinchla, *Psychology*, 2d ed. (Englewood Cliffs, NJ: Prentice-Hall, 1984).

23. R. B. Cattell, *Personality: A Systematic, Theoretical, and Factual Study* (New York: McGraw-Hill, 1950), and G. W. Allport, *Pattern and Growth in Personality* (New York: Holt, Rinehart & Winston, 1961).

24. S. Freud, "Civilization and Its Discontents," ed. and trans. J. Strachey, in *The Standard Edition of the Complete Psychological Works 2* (New York: Macmillan, 1962).

25. R. O. Swalm, "Utility Theory—Insights into Risk Taking," *Harvard Business Review* 44 (1966): 123-136.

26. R. N. Taylor and M. D. Dunnette, "Relative Contribution of Decision-Maker Attributes to Decision Processes," *Organizational Behavior and Human Performance* 12 (October 1974): 286-298.

27. T. W. Adorno, E. Frenkel-Brunswik, D. J. Levinson, and R. N. Sanford, *The Authoritarian Personality* (New York: Harper, 1950).

28. B. H. Long and R. C. Ziller, "Dogmatism and Predecisional Information Search," *Journal of Applied Psychology* 49 (1965): 376-378.

29. J. B. Rotter, "Generalized Expectancies for Internal Versus External Control of Reinforcement," *Psychological Monographs* 80 (1966): 1-28.

30. For applications of self-monitoring, see M. Snyder, S. Gangestad, and J. A. Simpson, "Choosing Friends as Activity Partners: The Role of Self-Monitoring," *Journal of Personality and Social Psychology* 48 (1983): 1061-1071, and A. W. Siegman and M. A. Reynolds, "Self-Monitoring and Speech in Feigned and Unfeigned Lying," *Journal of Personality and Social Psychology* 48 (1983): 1325-1333.

31. P. C. Smith, L. M. Kendall, and C. L. Hulin, *The Measurement of Satisfaction in Work and Retirement* (Chicago: Rand McNally, 1969).

32. A. H. Brayfield and H. F. Rothe, "An Index of Job Satisfaction," *Journal of Applied Psychology* 35 (1951): 307-311. To score the scale items, give a 5 for "Strongly Agree," a 4 for "Agree," and so on down to 1 for "Strongly Disagree." Then, sum the scores for the five items to get an overall score for these items.

33. G. H. Gallup, *The Gallup Poll* (New York: Random House, 1972), and R. P. Quinn and G. L. Staines, *The 1977 Quality of Employment Survey* (Ann Arbor, MI: Institute for Social Research, 1979).

34. R. L. Kahn, "The Meaning of Work: Interpretations and Proposals for Measurement," in *The Human Meaning of Social Change*, ed. A. A. Campbell and P. E. Converse (New York: Basic Books, 1972).

35. C. N. Weaver, "Job Satisfaction in the United States in the 1970s," *Journal of Applied Psychology* 65 (June 1980): 364-367.

36. These items are drawn from T. M. Lodahl and M. Kejner, "The Definition and Measurement of Job Involvement," *Journal of Applied Psychology* 49 (1965): 24-33.

37. For a discussion of this issue, see A. W. Schaef and D. Fassel, *The Addictive Organization* (New York: Harper & Row, 1988).

38. These items are drawn from L. W. Porter et al., "Organizational Commitment, Job Satisfaction, and Turnover Among Psychiatric Technicians," *Journal of Applied Psychology* 59 (October 1974): 603-609.

39. Darley et al., *Psychology*.

40. R. T. LaPiere, "Attitudes and Actions," *Social Forces* 13 (1934): 230-237.

41. P. M. Muchinsky and M. L. Tuttle, "Employee Turnover: An Empirical and Methodological Assessment," *Journal of Vocational Behavior* 14 (February 1979): 43-77, and L. W. Porter and R. M. Steers, "Organizational, Work, and Personal Factors in Employee Turnover and Absenteeism," *Psychological Bulletin* 80 (1973): 151-176.

42. The percent of variance in one variable that is associated with another is determined by simply squaring the correlation coefficient and multiplying by 100. In this case, $(-.40)^2 \times 100 = 16\%$.

43. P. M. Muchinsky and P. C. Morrow, "A Multidisciplinary Model of Voluntary Employee Turnover," *Journal of Vocational Behavior* 17 (December 1980): 263-290.

44. R. Likert, *New Patterns of Management* (New York: McGraw-Hill, 1961); F. Herzberg et al., *Job Attitudes: Review of Research and Opinion* (Pittsburgh: Psychological Service of Pittsburgh, 1957); and A. H. Brayfield and W. H. Crockett, "Employee Attitudes and Employee Performance," *Psychological Bulletin* 52 (1955): 396-424. On the issue of attitude-behavior relationships, see also M. Fishbein and I. Ajzen, *Belief Attitude, Intention, and Behavior* (Reading, MA: Addison-Wesley, 1975).

45. V. H. Vroom, *Work and Motivation* (New York: John Wiley & Sons, 1964).

46. D. W. Organ, "A Reappraisal and Reinterpretation of the Satisfaction-Causes-Performance Hypothesis," *Academy of Management Review* 2 (1977): 46-53.

47. T. S. Bateman and D. W. Organ, "Job Satisfaction and the Good Soldier: The Relationship Between Affect and Employee 'Citizenship,'" *Academy of Management Journal* 26 (1983): 587-595.

48. P. H. Mirvis and E. E. Lawler III, "Measuring the Financial Impact of Employee Attitudes," *Journal of Applied Psychology* 62 (1977): 1-8.

49. R. B. Dunham, *Organizational Behavior: People and Processes in Management* (Homewood, IL: Richard D. Irwin, 1984).

50. L. Festinger, *A Theory of Cognitive Dissonance* (Evanston, IL: Row, Peterson & Company, 1957).

51. M. Rokeach, *Beliefs, Attitudes, and Values: A Theory of Organization and Change* (San Francisco: Jossey-Bass, 1968), and *The Nature of Human Values* (New York: Free Press, 1973); and G. W. England, O. P. Dhingra, and N. C. Agarwal, *The Manager and the Man: A Cross-Cultural Study of Personal Values* (Kent, OH: Kent State University Press, 1974), 2.

52. G. W. England, "Personal Values of American Managers," *Academy of Management Journal* 10 (1967): 53-68.

53. G. Allport, P. Vernon, and G. Lindzey, *Study of Values*, 3d ed. (Boston: Houghton Mifflin, 1960).

54. These items are based on M. R. Blood, "Work Values and Job Satisfaction," *Journal of Applied Psychology* 53 (1969): 456-459.

Motivating

CHAPTER 13

After studying this chapter, you should be able to:
- *Describe motivation and explain why it is important in organizations.*
- *Identify four content theories of motivation and discuss their similarities, differences, and relative validities.*
- *Discuss three process theories of motivation and how they can be used to explain employee effort and performance.*
- *Describe management by objectives, including its potential costs and benefits.*
- *Explain how learning theory may be used in organizations, including rules for application of organizational behavior modification.*
- *Describe self-management and give guidelines for self-management.*
- *Explain how schemas and scripts may influence behavior.*

Managers have always tried to find ways to motivate their employees to work harder, more efficiently, and more intelligently. For instance, consider the way workers are motivated at Lincoln Electric, described in Management in Action 1. Notice the many factors, such as pay, strikes, turnover, pressure, interpersonal relationships, and quality, which attempts at motivation may affect.

Recently, motivation has gained increased attention. This is partly out of feelings of despair over what many people call "the sorry state of worker motivation" today and partly out of hope. One reason for concern about motivation grows out of the awareness that the annual productivity growth rate for the United States is declining. It is now far lower than that of Japan and West Germany (though absolute levels of productivity remain relatively high). While much of the U.S. decline is due to relatively low investments in new technology, there is also a concern that worker motivation to produce has eroded. Such concerns are bolstered by regular reports of the high job involvement and company loyalty of some foreign workers, particularly the Japanese.

WHAT IS MOTIVATION?

Motivation is a set of forces, originating both within and outside the individual, that initiate behavior and determine its form, direction, intensity, and duration.[1] This definition indicates that motivation drives people to behave in certain ways. It recognizes that many forces, internal and external to the individual, may simultaneously play roles. And it sees motivation as not only initiating behavior but also guiding it, influencing its strength, and determining whether or not it is sustained.

As shown in Figure 13–1, one view of motivation suggests that it flows from a state of need deficiency—people want something. It continues as people search for a way to satisfy that need and then as they perceive a potential need-satisfying goal. Next, people try to attain the goal. If they are successful, the state of need deficiency will become less strong and thus less motivating.[2]

THEORIES OF MOTIVATION

Theories of motivation may be classified as content theories, process theories, or reinforcement theories. **Content theories** focus on the underlying needs

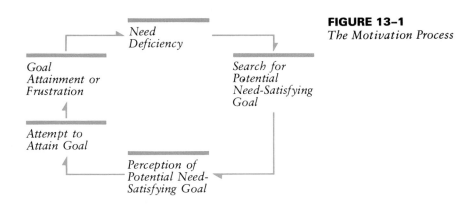

FIGURE 13–1
The Motivation Process

Lincoln Electric Company decided in 1907 on the way it wanted to motivate workers. It has liked the results ever since. The company pays most of its

MOTIVATING AT LINCOLN ELECTRIC

2,500 employees on a piecework basis. In 1933, it added an annual bonus system. Bonuses, based on performances, can exceed regular pay. Employees have averaged as much as $45,000 a year in good times.

Lincoln Electric has no unions, and it avoids strikes. Turnover is only 0.3 percent a month. Sales volume and profits have risen over the years to record levels. Customers praise product quality, and Lincoln is now one of the leading makers of arc-welding equipment.

Employees can buy stock in the company at book value. About 70 percent own stock, holding a total of nearly half the shares outstanding.

Employees are each responsible for the quality of their own work. They inspect their own parts and correct any imperfect work on their own time. If customers or Lincoln's quality-control people discover defects that have slipped by, the worker's pay is lowered.

Workers complain of the pressure, saying they sometimes want to slow down. They may have to work 50 hours or more a week in boom times, and they must accept any position in any department, even at a cut in pay. A certain number of merit points are given to each department, so a high rating for one person usually means a lower rating for another. One worker with nearly 20 years service says, "There's a saying around here that you don't have a friend at Lincoln Electric."

Source: Reprinted by permission of *The Wall Street Journal*, © Dow Jones & Company, Inc. (August 12, 1983). All Rights Reserved Worldwide.

which motivate a person. We will consider four examples—Maslow's need hierarchy theory, Alderfer's ERG theory, McClelland's achievement motivation theory, and Herzberg's motivation-hygiene theory. **Process theories** consider the processes which lead a person to behave in a certain way. Three theories examined in this chapter, expectancy theory, equity theory, and goal theory, are process theories. Finally, **reinforcement theories** focus on the environmental events which influence behavior. We will see in this chapter that current applications of learning theory have characteristics of reinforcement theories as well as (in their cognitive forms) of process theories. We will see some differences among the approaches, and will review evidence suggesting that some of the theories are flawed. However, the various perspectives when viewed together provide a solid and generally consistent set of tools for employee motivation.[3]

MASLOW'S NEED HIERARCHY

Figure 13–1 suggests that motivation is the attempt to satisfy needs. One very well-known theory of needs was presented by Abraham Maslow, a humanistic psychologist.[4] Maslow believed that human needs could be placed in five groups:

- *Physiological*. These are basic bodily needs such as needs for food, water, sex, and air.
- *Security*. These include needs for safety, freedom from illness and pain, and stability.

- *Social or affiliation.* This category covers needs for belonging, interaction with others, friendship, and love.
- *Esteem.* Needs both for respect and recognition from others and for personal feelings of accomplishment fit here.
- *Self-actualization.* These are needs to become all that one is capable of becoming—to realize one's potential. Self-actualization needs are desires for growth, creativity, and constructive accomplishment.

Maslow felt these needs were arranged in a hierarchy from "lowest" to "highest." Maslow said that as needs at the "lowest" level—physiological— were satisfied, those at the next "higher" level—security—would become most important, and so on. This movement up the hierarchy is called **satisfaction progression.** Maslow's hierarchy and the idea of satisfaction progression are shown in Figure 13–2. Furthermore, Maslow argued that a satisfied need is not a motivator; as a need becomes more fully satisfied, it becomes less important.

Abraham Maslow began his career as a Freudian psychologist studying primate behavior.[5] At that time, people's basic drives, such as hunger and sex, were viewed as the key to understanding human behavior; as discussed in the previous chapter, conflict between these drives and society's expectations was believed to result in neuroses and psychoses. Maslow's work with primates, as well as his subsequent research with college students, led him to conclude that states of psychological health may transcend lower drives. Maslow's greatest contribution in his later work was to focus attention on positive psychological health rather than solely on neuroses and psychoses. His hierarchy, with its recognition that higher-order needs such as self-actualization are as real as deficiency needs such as hunger and sex, fostered a basic reorientation of thinking about motivation.

Maslow's need hierarchy has great intuitive appeal. We can all think of acquaintances or public figures who seem to focus on one or another of the various needs in the hierarchy. And we recognize in ourselves that if we're very hungry or thirsty, we temporarily set aside thoughts of esteem or self-actualization. The theory can also be used to explain historical developments. For instance, workers first focused on economic rewards to satisfy physiological and security needs. Once these needs were satisfied, they then shifted more of their attention to social needs and job challenge.

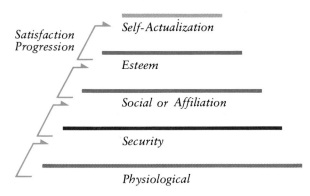

Satisfaction
Progression

Self-Actualization

Esteem

Social or Affiliation

Security

Physiological

FIGURE 13–2
Maslow's Need Hierarchy

However, Maslow intended his theory to provide a basis for further testing, not as the final word on human needs. In fact, he wrote with refreshing candor about his concern that the need hierarchy was "being swallowed whole by all sorts of enthusiastic people, who really should be a little more tentative in the way that I am."[6] Research on the Maslow need hierarchy yields mixed results. People do seem to have a variety of needs and to be motivated to fulfill them. And the importance of needs does change over time. However, other findings contradict some of the specifics of Maslow's theory. For instance:[7]

- People's needs don't seem to fall into five distinct sets. Instead, research suggests that there are no more than two or three meaningful sets of needs.
- While need satisfaction and need importance are negatively related for needs near the base of the hierarchy, they are positively related for those needs near the top. As we eat, the importance of eating temporarily declines. But, as we realize that we're capable of achievement and acceptance of responsibility, we may emphasize them even more.
- While people typically place great importance on physiological needs which aren't satisfied, they don't proceed up the hierarchy in any orderly fashion once these basic needs are satisfied. No clear pattern is evident concerning which needs will become most important when physiological needs are satisfied.

Despite these negative findings, the value of Maslow's work should not be underestimated. Maslow provided a testable framework which could be used to build refined theories of human needs. Perhaps more important, he forced us to divert our gaze to the higher reaches of the human mind.

ALDERFER'S ERG THEORY

Maslow's need hierarchy provided a starting point for an improved theory of human needs. Clayton Alderfer developed the **existence-relatedness-growth (ERG) theory,** which revised Maslow's theory to make it consistent with research findings concerning human needs.

There are three key differences between Alderfer's ERG theory and Maslow's need hierarchy theory. First, since studies have shown that people have two or three sets of needs rather than the five Maslow hypothesized, Alderfer collapsed his needs into three sets:

- **Existence needs.** These include all forms of material and physical desires.
- **Relatedness needs.** These include all needs that involve relationships with other people. Relatedness needs include anger and hostility as well as friendship. For instance, we may feel the need to yell at one person and befriend another. Isolation from others would cause deprivation of relatedness needs in either case.
- **Growth needs.** These include all needs involving creative efforts that people make on themselves and their environment.

Alderfer revised Maslow's theory in other ways as well. First, he argued that the three need sets form a hierarchy only in the sense of increasing abstractness, or decreasing concreteness. As we move from existence to related-ness to growth needs, the ways to satisfy the needs become less and less concrete.

Second, Alderfer recognized that, while satisfying our existence and relat-edness needs may make them less important to us, such is not the case for growth needs. Instead, our growth needs become increasingly important as we satisfy them. As we are able to become creative and productive, we raise our growth goals and are again dissatisfied until we satisfy these new goals.

Finally, Alderfer reasoned that we are likely to focus first on needs which can be satisfied in concrete ways. We then attend to those with more abstract means of satisfaction. This is similar to Maslow's idea of satisfaction progres-sion. However, Alderfer added the idea of frustration regression. **Frustration regression** occurs when our inability to satisfy needs at a particular level in the hierarchy causes us to regress and focus on more concrete needs. If we are unable to satisfy growth needs, we will "drop back" and focus on relatedness needs. If we are unable to satisfy relatedness needs, we will focus on exis-tence needs. Alderfer's needs, as well as satisfaction progression and frustra-tion regression, are illustrated in Figure 13–3. The combination of satisfaction progression and frustration regression can result in cycling as we focus on one need, then another, then back again.

Since Alderfer's ERG theory was in part a response to research findings which contradicted Maslow's theory, it was designed to be consistent with those findings. The relatively little research undertaken to test the theory has generally been supportive. For instance, it supports the contentions that there are three independent sets of needs and that growth needs (and perhaps relat-edness needs) become more important as we satisfy them. Further, some re-search suggests that people do move through the three needs in the ways Alderfer proposed.[8]

McCLELLAND'S ACHIEVEMENT MOTIVATION THEORY

Maslow felt that people were born with a particular set of needs. Those needs might be viewed as buckets of rather fixed sizes. We would first focus on one bucket. Then, when it was filled to a certain level, we would shift our attention to another, unfilled bucket. Henry Murray believed that people ac-quire needs through their interaction with the environment.[9] That is, he viewed needs as being like seeds. Some are nurtured by the environment and grow. Others remain dormant, or grow only a little, because they are not en-

FIGURE 13–3
Alderfer's ERG Theory

couraged by the environment. This idea of acquired needs is important. It suggests that needs may actually be developed or diminished.

Murray developed a very lengthy list of acquired needs. While his work had little direct impact on organizations, it did draw the interest of David McClelland and others. McClelland was particularly interested in one of Murray's needs—need for achievement. Murray defined **need for achievement** as the need

to accomplish something difficult. To master, manipulate, or organize physical objects, human beings, or ideas. To do this as rapidly and as independently as possible. To overcome obstacles and attain a high standard. To excel oneself. To rival and surpass others. To increase self-regard by the successful exercise of talent.[10]

Like Murray, McClelland felt that need for achievement was an acquired need, developed in childhood as the result of encouragement and reinforcement of autonomy and self-reliance by parents. He also felt, though, that adults could be taught need for achievement.

Measuring Need for Achievement

McClelland used a variety of interesting techniques to assess the strength of need for achievement, as well as of need for power and need for affiliation.[11] For instance, he measured the achievement needs for various nations by looking at the number of achievement ideas per 100 lines in children's stories in public school textbooks. He reasoned that the spirit prevailing in the country would be reflected in the orientations of the stories. McClelland also felt that national achievement levels were tied to achievement motivation as expressed in that literature:

Normally, we found, a high level of concern for achievement is followed some 50 years or so later by a rapid rate of economic growth and prosperity. Such was certainly the case in ancient Greece and in Spain in the late Middle Ages. Furthermore, in both cases, a decline in achievement concern was followed very soon after by a decline in economic welfare.[12]

McClelland also studied needs by use of projective tests. With projective tests, individuals view a series of pictures and write stories based on each picture. An achievement motivation score is calculated based on the number of achievement-oriented ideas in the story. These ideas might include thinking of ways to solve problems or anticipating the consequences of success or failure. McClelland felt this technique was useful in measuring differences between groups of people. For instance, he found that business managers in several countries generally scored much higher on achievement motivation than did professionals. He also found major differences across countries. As an example, the average score for professionals in the United States was twice that of Italian professionals.

Characteristics of Individuals with Strong Needs for Achievement

McClelland argued that people with high needs for achievement shared the following characteristics:[13]

A strong need for achievement motivates Olympic stars like Carl Lewis.

- A strong desire for personal responsibility.
- A desire for quick, concrete feedback about the results of their actions.
- The derivation of intrinsic satisfaction from doing a job well. For people with strong achievement needs, the monetary and other material rewards associated with accomplishment are more a kind of feedback concerning performance than ends in themselves.
- A tendency to set moderate achievement goals.

This last characteristic may seem surprising. That is, we might expect that people with strong need for achievement would set very high goals. Instead, they set goals which are easy enough to be within their abilities but difficult enough to be meaningful.

Developing Need for Achievement

Again, McClelland believed that adults could develop need for achievement. He felt this required a four-stage process in which the individual would be encouraged to:[14]

1. Speak the "language of achievement." The individual is encouraged to think, talk, act, and perceive others as would a person with a high achievement motive. He or she learns how to take moderate risks to maximize expected payoff and how to code thoughts and fantasies to measure achievement needs.
2. Feel that he or she can and should change and focus on specific personal goals for change in the near future.
3. Develop an honest picture of himself or herself, and his or her desires and possibilities.
4. Feel emotionally supported by instructors and other group members in attempts at self-change.

McClelland used these techniques with some success. For instance, he found that American executives he trained were promoted faster than similar executives he had not trained. He also trained businessmen in India and found their degree of unusual achievement activity (such as starting a business, sharply increasing profits, or diversifying) almost to double. That of businessmen who couldn't get in the program because of space constraints remained about the same.

Need for Achievement and Job Success

McClelland didn't feel that achievement motivation would be necessary or even particularly useful in all occupations. He reasoned that individuals with strong need for achievement would choose certain occupations—such as sales, entrepreneurship, or promotion—which offered quick feedback and personal responsibility for results. Jobs such as accountant, research scientist, or personnel manager would probably not be suitable for such individuals. McClelland found that even Nobel Prize–winning research scientists—who must often wait years to learn whether their ideas are successful—had only moderate levels of need for achievement.

Need for Affiliation and Need for Power

McClelland also considered two other needs—need for affiliation and need for power. **Need for affiliation** is the desire to establish and maintain friendly and warm relations with other persons. It is much like Maslow's social needs. Persons high on need for affiliation welcome tasks requiring considerable interaction, while those low on the need may prefer to work alone.

Need for power is the desire to control other persons, to influence their behavior, and to be responsible for other people. While McClelland felt that need for achievement was most important for entrepreneurs, he saw need for power as quite important in large organizations. Those high on need for power can try to satisfy the need in either of two ways.[15] **Personalized power seekers** try to dominate others for the sake of dominating, deriving satisfaction from conquering others. Use of personalized power appears to be undesirable for the organization. Personalized power seekers often divert their attention from organizational goals to their own ends. They have also been found to engage in heavy use of alcohol and to fantasize about power. **Socialized power seekers**, on the other hand, satisfy their power needs through means that help the organization. They may show concern for group goals, find goals to motivate others, or work with a group to develop and achieve goals. McClelland felt that need for power, when exhibited in the form of socialized power acquisition, was the most important determinant of managerial success. Persons high in need for achievement, he felt, might be too concerned with personal achievement. Those with high need for affiliation might be reluctant to take necessary actions which could offend the group.

HERZBERG'S TWO-FACTOR THEORY

Frederick Herzberg tried a different approach to the study of employee motivation. He reasoned that if we could understand what satisfies or dissatisfies employees, we could get a handle on ways to motivate them.

Motivators and Hygiene Factors

Herzberg began by interviewing 200 engineers and accountants in nine companies. He used the critical incidents method, asking these individuals to describe past work experiences that were critical in the sense of being "exceptionally good" or "exceptionally bad."

Herzberg analyzed these interviews and concluded there are two relatively distinct sets of factors in organizations. One set, which he called **satisfiers** or **motivators**, resulted in satisfaction when adequate. The other set, labeled **dissatisfiers** or **hygiene factors**, caused dissatisfaction when deficient. Herzberg's theory is thus known as the **two-factor theory** or the **motivation-hygiene theory.**

Figure 13–4 lists some motivators and hygiene factors. The motivators are typically **intrinsic factors**, largely part of the job itself or administered by the employee. The hygiene factors are **extrinsic factors**, under the control of the supervisor or someone else other than the employee.[16]

The important point here was that Herzberg did not see satisfaction and dissatisfaction as being at opposite ends of the same continuum. Instead, as Figure 13–5 shows, he saw them as two separate continua. According to Herzberg, the opposite of satisfaction is not dissatisfaction but no satisfaction. The opposite of dissatisfaction is not satisfaction but no dissatisfaction.

Organizational Implications of the Two-Factor Theory

If valid, Herzberg's theory has profound implications for organizations. It says that things such as pay, fringe benefits, and working conditions don't cause worker satisfaction and motivation. Below a certain level, they may cause dissatisfaction, but once improved to that level, they will have little positive impact. As a result, it would make sense to direct attention away from dissatisfiers and toward such satisfiers as opportunities for achievement, challenge, growth, and recognition. For many firms, this would demand a major reorientation of reward systems.

Evaluation of the Two-Factor Theory

There have been many criticisms of the two-factor theory.[17] For instance, Herzberg implies that satisfaction and motivation are essentially the same. We know, though, that motivation is often the result of dissatisfaction. Therefore it is dangerous to draw conclusions about what motivates employees on the basis of what satisfies them.

Also, if research results are valid, we would expect them to hold up when other methodologies are used to test them. Herzberg's findings are tied to his critical-incidents methodology. That is, the two factors revealed by Herzberg show up only when employees recall satisfying and dissatisfying events. Using any other methodology, this distinction breaks down. Is Herzberg's methodol-

A delighted Jessica Tandy, honored as Best Actress for her performance in Driving Miss Daisy, *acknowledges the recognition of her peers at the 1990 Oscar awards ceremony.*

Motivators (Satisfiers)	Hygiene Factors (Dissatisfiers)
Achievement	Pay
Challenging job	Technical supervision
Responsibility	Working conditions
Growth	Work rules and company policy
Advancement	Fringe benefits
Recognition	Seniority rights
Work itself	

FIGURE 13–4
Herzberg's Motivators and Hygiene Factors

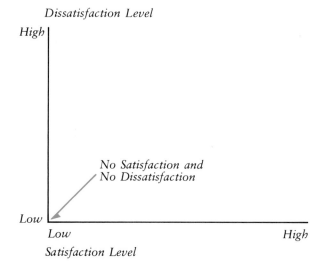

FIGURE 13–5
The Two-Factor Theory

ogy the only one which is correct, or does it erroneously "cause" the findings? The latter explanation is more likely. Recall from Chapter 12 the self-serving bias in causal attribution—that is, our tendency to attribute good things to internal factors and bad things to external factors. Herzberg's results may just be a reflection of this self-serving bias. When asked to recall a satisfying event, individuals make an internal attribution. When asked to recall an event that caused dissatisfaction, they find an external source. So, rather than revealing something new about employee motivation, Herzberg's findings may simply be a reflection of bias in attribution.

Further, Herzberg classified items as satisfiers or dissatisfiers on the basis of the *relative* number of times employees mentioned them as causing satisfaction or dissatisfaction. For instance, as shown in Figure 13–6, achievement was called a satisfier because it was associated with satisfying events about four times as often as with dissatisfying events. Conversely, relations with superiors was called a dissatisfier since it was associated with dissatisfying events about four times as often as with satisfying events. However, we can interpret the data in Figure 13–6 differently. If we consider the *absolute* number of times items are mentioned as satisfying or dissatisfying, achievement and recognition are actually more often associated with dissatisfaction than are the so-called dissatisfiers of working conditions, relations with superiors, and relations with peers.

These criticisms notwithstanding, Herzberg's work has had a major impact on organizations. It has caused managers to pay increasing attention to

FIGURE 13–6
"Satisfiers" and "Dissatisfiers" in Six Studies Reported by Herzberg

Item	Times Mentioned as Satisfying	Times Mentioned as Dissatisfying
Achievement	440	122
Recognition	309	110
Working conditions	20	108
Relations with superiors	15	59
Relations with peers	9	57

intrinsic factors, rather than just to pay and other extrinsic rewards. This altered focus is appropriate since research shows that intrinsic rewards are very important, both for satisfaction and for dissatisfaction. Herzberg's work was certainly a major impetus for the job enrichment movement, to be discussed in the next chapter, with its heavy emphasis on intrinsic rewards.

EXPECTANCY THEORY

Expectancy theory is an approach to the understanding of motivation which examines the links in the process from effort to ultimate rewards. Thus, unlike the theories we have just considered, it is a process theory of motivation rather than a content theory. Developed by Victor Vroom, it says that three conditions must be present if an employee is to be motivated to behave in a certain way.[18] First, the employee must believe that more effort will in fact make the desired behavior more likely. Second, the desired behavior must lead to various outcomes. Third, the employee must value those outcomes.

Expectancy Theory Concepts

Figure 13–7 presents the key elements of expectancy theory. They are as follows:

FIRST-ORDER OUTCOME

A **first-order outcome** is the direct result of effort. The first-order outcome may be performance, creativity, low absenteeism, low turnover, or any other desired behavior. There may be more than one first-order outcome.

FIGURE 13–7
The Components of Expectancy Theory

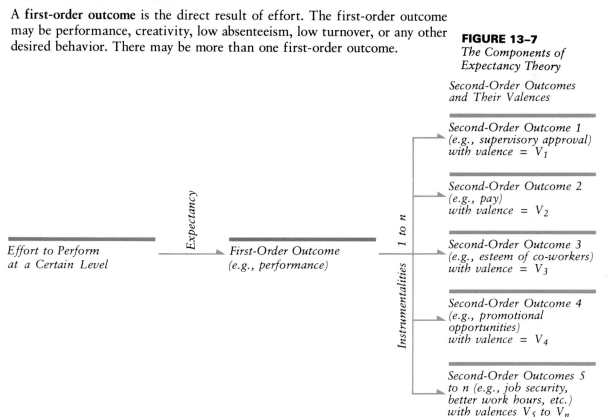

Second-Order Outcomes and Their Valences

Second-Order Outcome 1 (e.g., supervisory approval) with valence = V_1

Second-Order Outcome 2 (e.g., pay) with valence = V_2

Second-Order Outcome 3 (e.g., esteem of co-workers) with valence = V_3

Second-Order Outcome 4 (e.g., promotional opportunities) with valence = V_4

Second-Order Outcomes 5 to n (e.g., job security, better work hours, etc.) with valences V_5 to V_n

Effort to Perform at a Certain Level

Expectancy

First-Order Outcome (e.g., performance)

Instrumentalities 1 to n

SECOND-ORDER OUTCOME

A **second-order outcome** is anything, good or bad, which may result from attainment of the first-order outcome. Typically, there are many second-order outcomes, such as pay, esteem of co-workers, approval of the supervisor, and so on.

EXPECTANCY

Expectancy is the perceived linkage between effort and the first-order outcome. There is an expectancy for each first-order outcome. If a worker feels that trying harder won't improve his or her performance, the expectancy of effort for the attainment of performance would be low. If a worker feels that more effort will translate directly into higher performance, expectancy would be high. Expectancies are often expressed as probabilities.

Figure 13–8 shows some of the things that may affect the actual linkage between effort and the first-order outcome of performance. One of these, of course, is ability. If ability is completely lacking, effort won't help much. Another is the situation. In some situations, such as an assembly line, the employee is constrained. Greater effort simply won't speed up the line. A final factor is role perceptions. If employees don't know what their roles are (that is, what management expects of them), they will probably misdirect their efforts. Each of these factors is likely to influence expectancies.

INSTRUMENTALITY

Instrumentality is the perceived linkage between a first-order outcome and a second-order outcome. There is an instrumentality for each combination of first- and second-order outcomes. Like expectancies, instrumentalities are often expressed as probabilities.[19] If an employee feels that higher performance will lead to pay increases, the instrumentality of performance for the attainment of pay increases would be high. If an employee feels that performance and pay are unrelated, that instrumentality would be zero.

VALENCE

Valence is simply the value an individual attaches to an outcome. The valences of second-order outcomes are the values of such things as pay increases, supervisory approval, security, and esteem of co-workers. The valence of a first-order outcome, such as performance, depends upon the valences of second-order outcomes and on the instrumentalities of the first-order outcome for the attainment of those second-order outcomes. In particular, it is the sum of

FIGURE 13–8
The Linkage of Effort to a First-Order Outcome

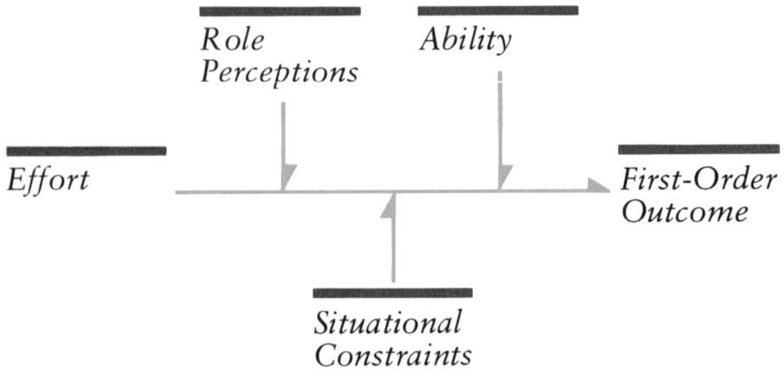

the products of the valences of the second-order outcomes and the instrumentalities of the first-order outcome for the attainment of the second-order outcomes. That is:

$$\text{Valence of First-Order Outcome} = \sum_{i=1}^{n} \begin{array}{c}\text{Valence of} \\ \text{Second-Order} \\ \text{Outcome } i\end{array} \times \begin{array}{c}\text{Instrumentality of First-Order} \\ \text{Outcome for the Attainment of} \\ \text{Second-Order Outcome } i\end{array}$$

FORCE TO PERFORM, OR EFFORT

As Figure 13–9 shows, the degree to which an employee exerts **force to perform**, or **effort**, to attain a first-order outcome depends on both the expectancy that effort will lead to an increase in that first-order outcome and the valence of the first-order outcome. For instance, expectancy theory would predict that an employee would exert no effort to perform at a higher level if he or she either saw no possibility that effort would lead to higher performance or did not value higher performance. Formally:

$$\begin{array}{c}\text{Effort to Attain} \\ \text{First-Order Outcome}\end{array} = \text{Expectancy} \times \begin{array}{c}\text{Valence of the} \\ \text{First-Order Outcome}\end{array}$$

Expectancy theory is at base, then, a theory which focuses on values and perceived (or subjective) probabilities. People may place different values on outcomes, and they may have very different perceptions about probabilities. Expectancy theory suggests that managers should not assume they know what employees want or think. Instead, valences, expectancy perceptions, and instrumentality perceptions should be directly assessed. Questionnaires can be used to make these assessments. In those questionnaires, valence is usually rated on a scale of -10 to $+10$. Expectancies and instrumentalities are usually rated on scales of 0 (no chance the outcome will occur) to 1 (it will definitely occur). The box on the following page provides an example of how expectancy theory can be used.

Evaluation of Expectancy Theory

Expectancy theory treats individuals as rational, maximizing their expected values. Evidence concerning related theories making similar assumptions in the decision theory literature suggests that they do a reasonably good job of predicting behavior. Of course, people are not entirely rational, and the instruments used to assess valences, expectancies, and instrumentalities are not perfect. Further, there is some question whether people combine information in the ways that expectancy theory assumes.

Reviews of expectancy theory typically show that it can explain about 25 percent of the variance in workers' satisfaction (though that is not its primary goal) and about 10 percent of the variance in their performance when

Valence of First-Order Outcome

Expectancy

→ *Effort*

FIGURE 13–9
The Determinants of Effort to Perform at a Particular Level

AN EXPECTANCY THEORY EXAMPLE

Suppose a survey reveals that a particular employee has the following valences for second-order outcomes (note that some of the outcomes may be seen as undesirable):

Second-Order Outcome	Valence
Higher pay	10
Supervisory approval	5
Supervisory reprimand	−5
Peer group approval	8
Peer group reprimand	−8
Intrinsic rewards	10
All others	0

These valences show that intrinsic rewards and higher pay are very important to this employee. Approval and reprimand by peers are a bit less important than these, but more important than supervisory approval and reprimand.

Suppose the survey also indicates that the employee perceives that increased performance (a first-order outcome) will have the following instrumentalities for the attainment of the second-order outcomes just discussed:

Second-Order Outcome	Instrumentality
Higher pay	0.2
Supervisory approval	0.1
Supervisory reprimand	0.0
Peer group approval	0.0
Peer group reprimand	0.9
Intrinsic rewards	0.5

The instrumentalities show the employee feels that higher performance is rather weakly related to higher pay and supervisory approval, though it does have a moderately strong link to intrinsic rewards. On the other hand, there is a very high probability that peers would react negatively to higher performance.

Finally, suppose that expectancy = 0.6. That is, the employee feels there is a moderately high probability that higher effort would lead to higher performance. According to expectancy theory:

$$\text{Valence of Performance} = \sum_{i=1}^{6} \begin{array}{c} \text{Valence of} \\ \text{Second-Order} \\ \text{Outcome } i \end{array} \times \begin{array}{c} \text{Instrumentality of Performance} \\ \text{for the Attainment of} \\ \text{Second-Order Outcome } i \end{array}$$

$$= (10 \times 0.2) + (5 \times 0.1) + (-5 \times 0.0) + (8 \times 0.0) + (-8 \times 0.9) + (10 \times 0.5)$$
$$= 0.3$$

And:

$$\begin{aligned} \text{Force to Perform (Effort)} &= \text{Valence of Performance} \times \text{Expectancy} \\ &= 0.3 \times 0.6 \\ &= 0.18 \end{aligned}$$

What does a score of 0.18 mean? First, the sign is positive, indicating that on balance there is a positive force to perform. However, the magnitude is clearly quite low. To interpret it fully, we would need some basis for comparison. For instance, what was the score last month? How does it compare with the scores of other employees in the department? How does it compare with the average score for employees in the firm? Whatever those comparisons reveal, it does seem that force to perform is very low in an absolute sense.

To make sense of the score, we can examine its components. Expectancy seems reasonable, but valence of performance is low. Since valence of performance is a function of valences of second-order outcomes and instrumentalities, we can examine these components to gain insight into why valence of performance is low. In this case, the instrumentalities are quite revealing. They show that the employee sees both pay and supervisory approval as only loosely linked to performance. Quite simply, the employee doesn't feel higher performance will be extrinsically rewarded. Further, there is a very strong perceived link between performance and peer group reprimand. This is apparently a situation where there is agreement among employees to restrict production. Employees working faster are apparently seen as "rate busters," endangering the pay of others and making them look bad. Each of these components—expectancy, instrumentalities, and valences—provides valuable information for managers and suggests where action could be taken to improve employee effort.

predictions are made across people; that is, when it is used to predict relative levels of motivation across a variety of individuals. When expectancy theory is used to predict the various levels of effort an individual will exert on different tasks (as it was originally intended to do), it does quite a bit better, explaining 25 percent to 35 percent of the variance in effort.[20] Any theory that can explain such a large proportion of employees' behaviors is a valuable management tool.

An Expanded Model

We can now present an expanded model of employee behavior. To do so, we first need to discuss one other relationship. In the previous chapter we noted that it does not appear that satisfaction leads to performance. In fact, the evidence suggests that performance leads to satisfaction. Performance leads to rewards which, after comparison with perceived equitable rewards, influence satisfaction. We will explore the issue of perceived equitable rewards shortly.

Figure 13–10 presents a more complete model of employee behavior which incorporates this reasoning as well as Figures 13–8 and 13–9. It also includes two feedback loops—from satisfaction to valence of performance and from performance to expectancy. That is, as our needs are satisfied, their importance changes. And, as we are able to perform successfully at a certain level our expectancy perceptions are likely to increase, and vice versa.

EQUITY THEORY

Equity theory is one of a family of theories which argues that people want to maintain balance. By focusing on the balance of the inputs, or contributions, that people make to the outcomes they receive, equity theory helps us understand how employees determine whether they are being treated fairly.

Why Be Fair?

According to equity theorists, people want to maintain distributive fairness. **Distributive fairness** is the perception that people are getting what they de-

FIGURE 13–10
A Model of Employee Behavior

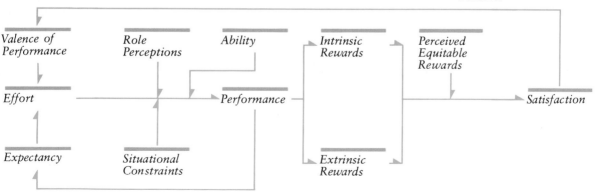

Source: L. W. Porter and E. E. Lawler, *Managerial Attitudes and Performance* (Homewood, IL: Dorsey-Irwin, 1968). Reproduced with permission.

serve—not less, certainly, but not more either. Research evidence supports this contention.[21] There are several reasons why people want distributive fairness.[22] For instance, when people experience a situation they feel is not fair, they experience an unpleasant state of tension. Restoration of distributive fairness reduces that tension. Also, some people try to be fair because they think others will reward them for being fair. Further, behaving fairly may bolster a person's self-esteem. Finally, most people find it comforting to believe that life is fair. By giving others what we think they deserve, we strengthen that belief.

Employers may have other, more specific reasons for wanting to treat their employees fairly.[23] They may, for instance, want to conform to business norms. For example, people in business generally agree that employees who do better work should get more rewards. They may want to attract superior workers to their company and to weed out inferior workers. If rewards are fairly tied to performance, a positive relationship between satisfaction and performance should result. Thus, high performers should be satisfied and disposed to stay with the firm, while low performers should be dissatisfied and leave the firm. Finally, employers may want to motivate employees to produce. As expectancy theory indicates, tying rewards to performance should enhance instrumentality perceptions and thus increase motivation to perform well.

Determining Equity

How do people determine whether outcomes are equitable? J. Stacey Adams proposed the following equation for an equitable relationship.[24] It is based on the writings of an earlier student of behavior, Aristotle:[25]

$$\frac{O_p}{I_p} = \frac{O_o}{I_o}$$

Where:

O_p is the person's perception of the outcomes he or she is receiving.
I_p is the person's perception of his or her inputs.
O_o is the person's perception of the outcomes some comparison person (or comparison other) is receiving.
I_o is the person's perception of the inputs of the comparison other.

This equation says that equity exists when a person feels the ratio of his or her outcomes to his or her inputs is equal to that ratio for some comparison other. Neither is seen as getting less or more than their inputs justify. Note that each of the elements in the equation is a perception. While actual conditions may (or may not) influence those perceptions, they do not directly enter the equity calculations.

The comparison other may be another individual (such as a co-worker or friend), a group of other people (such as workers on another job), or some abstract combination of people. It may even be the perceiving person at an earlier point in time.

Inputs and Outcomes

At base, inputs are anything employees believe they are contributing to the job. Outcomes are anything they believe they are getting from the job. So, inputs might include such things as seniority, time, performance, appearance, dedication to the organization, effort, intelligence, or provision of needed tools. Outcomes might include pay, promotional opportunities, job status, job interest, esteem of co-workers, monotony, praise, fatigue, and dangerous working conditions. Note that employees may view some outcomes of the job, such as fatigue and dangerous working conditions, negatively. Obviously, different people care about different inputs and outcomes. An input for one person may even be an outcome for another. For instance, one worker may value increased responsibility, viewing it as an outcome. Another may see that same increased responsibility as a burdensome input.

Restoring Equity

If an individual perceives a situation to be inequitable, there are many ways to restore equity. For instance, suppose that Frank feels underpaid relative to his co-worker, Karen. He could try to restore equity by:

- *Raising his actual outcomes.* For instance, Frank might demand and get a raise.
- *Lowering his inputs.* Frank might slow down on the job, withhold important information, or stop doing unpaid overtime work.
- *Perceptually distorting his inputs and/or outcomes.* Frank could reason that he was actually getting things out of the job he hadn't been considering, or he could downgrade the values of his inputs.
- *Perceptually distorting Karen's inputs and/or outcomes.* Frank could devalue the nonpay outcomes Karen is receiving, or he could increase his estimates of Karen's inputs.
- *Leaving the situation.* With a big enough feeling of inequity, Frank might psychologically withdraw from the situation or might actually apply for a transfer or quit.
- *Acting to change Karen's inputs and/or outcomes.* Frank could try to convince Karen to raise her inputs, could talk to the boss about lowering Karen's pay, or could take steps to try to make Karen leave her job.
- *Changing the comparison other.* Frank could begin to compare his situation to that of Paul, rather than that of Karen.

People do use these mechanisms to restore equity. For instance, field studies and laboratory experiments have shown that individuals withdraw from tasks when they are inequitably treated—even, in some cases, when they are overpaid.[26] There is also considerable evidence that people change their perceptions to restore equity.[27] Underpaid workers often perceive that they have made relatively low inputs and begin to see themselves as less qualified than others.[28] Some also exaggerate their outcomes, rating their jobs as far more interesting than others do.

The most intriguing findings concerning equity theory relate to changes in actual inputs as a result of perceived inequity. J. Stacey Adams and William Rosenbaum reasoned that employees' reactions would depend upon whether they were underpaid or overpaid and on whether they were paid on an hourly basis or for each unit of output.[29] Figure 13–11 shows the input changes that would restore equity in each case.

This figure suggests that underpaid workers will sometimes reduce their output, and will sometimes raise it. Overpaid workers will sometimes in-

Robert P. Vecchio (Ph.D., University of Illinois) is Franklin D. Schurz Professor of Management at the University of Notre Dame. Professor Vecchio's research has focused on issues in the areas of motivation, social influence, and leadership. His work has been published in a variety of major management and psychology journals. He is a member of the editorial review board of Academy of Management Review, Journal of Management, *and* Employee Responsibilities and Rights Journal.

Q: Your work on equity theory has been widely cited. In your opinion, what does a manager gain from an equity theory perspective?

A: Equity theory offers an important perspective for the understanding of attitudes and behavior in that feelings of inequity can underlie a great range of dysfunctional acts (e.g., employee sabotage, restricted production, grievances, etc.). Managers need to be sensitive to issues of equity and to display a commitment to maintaining equity in the work setting. More specifically, managers must explore employee perceptions of personal inputs and outcomes and question employees on their beliefs regarding the inputs and outcomes of comparison others. Further, equity theory suggests that managers must be aware of, and help to manage, the norms that relate to what rewards an employee may expect as a return for his or her efforts.

Q: What problems do you think managers face when trying to apply equity theory? How can those problems be alleviated?

A: Application of equity theory principles can present some unique problems. For example, one would not want to deliberately create a sense of underreward inequity within an hourly-based compensation scheme in order to increase the quantity of output, as the likely negative consequences for morale would offset any hoped-for gain in productivity. However, creating a sense of guilt by making others feel overrewarded is used with some frequency by employees to influence their co-workers. Similarly, an employee may try to create the belief in the mind of a supervisor that underreward inequity exists (in the hope of getting the supervisor to increase compensation or otherwise improve conditions). Also, some managers deliberately seek to induce a sense of inequitable treatment in the minds of poor performers in order to encourage them to quit. The effectiveness of this tactic is, of course, open to question. Perhaps the biggest problem managers face in applying notions which are derivable from equity theory is the creation of systems of performance appraisal and reward distribution which will be seen as being equitable.

Q: Equity theory predicts that individuals who feel overrewarded will feel guilty and dissatisfied and take steps to restore equity. How would you respond to a student or manager who says that this "just doesn't happen in the real world"?

A: In fact, guilt motivates many people to engage or not engage in certain activities. Of course, not all people feel such moral imperatives or constraints, or at least not to the same degree. It appears that an individual's degree of conscience may play a critical role in determining a person's reaction to overreward inequity. To be sure, the type of guilt that occurs in overreward inequity is probably quite transitory in that it can be quickly reduced by employee rationalizations. Most people find persistent guilt uncomfortable and, therefore, are motivated to find self-satisfying explanations and justifications for being overrewarded. Employees are rarely told that they are overpaid or made to feel incompetent regarding their ability to perform their jobs. Also, employees are typically in an exchange relationship with an organization rather than with another person. Employees who view themselves as overcompensated usually have a difficult time seeing the organization as being treated unfairly, as no specific individual is clearly injured by their being overrewarded.

Basis of Pay	Basis of Inequity	
	Underpayment	Overpayment
Hourly	Produce Less and/or Lower-Quality Work	Produce More and/or Higher-Quality Work
Piece-Rate	Produce More and/or Lower-Quality Work	Produce Less and/or Higher-Quality Work

FIGURE 13–11
Changes in Inputs to Reduce Perceived Inequity

crease their output and, surprisingly, they will sometimes reduce it. There is a great deal of controversy over the question of how workers change actual inputs in response to inequity. This is partly because it is hard to change equity perceptions in an experiment without also influencing other things such as self-esteem and feelings of job security. Also, relatively few long-term studies have assessed the overreward condition. However, of 22 studies involving hourly workers, almost 70 percent at least partially supported Adams's predictions. More than 85 percent of studies involving piece-rate workers gave partial or full support to those predictions.[30] A study by Robert Vecchio of piece-rate workers at four different geographic locations over a 13-month period was similarly positive. It supported equity theory performance predictions in 11 of 12 comparisons. In overpayment conditions, quantity of performance decreased an average of 17 percent relative to equitable situations, while quality increased 26 percent. In underpayment conditions, quantity increased 34 percent while quality decreased 12 percent.[31]

While equity theory would permit any of a wide range of adjustments to restore equity, it would be useful to know specifically which change is most likely to occur. Adams has provided the following set of propositions concerning how people choose from among the alternatives available to reduce inequity:[32]

- They will first try to maximize valued outcomes.
- They will be reluctant to increase inputs that are difficult or costly to change.
- They will resist actual or perceived changes in inputs or outcomes that are central to their self-concept and self-esteem.
- They will be more resistant to changing perceptions about their own inputs and outcomes than about their comparison other's inputs and outcomes.
- They will leave the situation only when inequity is great and other means of reducing it are not available. Partial withdrawal, such as absenteeism, will occur more frequently and under lower conditions of inequity.
- They will be reluctant to change their comparison others.

Other Rules for Determining Distributive Fairness

Equity theory is based on the contributions rule. The **contributions rule** says that distributive fairness is determined by equating contributions (inputs) with outcomes. However, people may use other rules when determining distributive fairness. They may, for example, employ the **needs rule**, feeling it is

An employee who deserves—and gets—a promotion probably favors the contributions rule of equity theory.

fair to give people what they need rather than what they contribute. Or, they may employ the **equality rule**, arguing that it is fair for everyone to get the same amount.

A variety of factors determine the weights we give to these various rules. They include the following:

- *Self-interest.* People tend to assign higher weights to rules that favor them. A high performer will be likely to favor the contributions rule, while a needy person will favor the needs rule.
- *Conformity.* People tend to conform to the beliefs and behaviors of others with whom they regularly interact. So, if all of a manager's co-workers favor the equality rule, the manager may also apply that rule.
- *Availability of relevant information.* People are reluctant to use a rule for which they don't have sufficient information. For instance, if a manager doesn't know what subordinates need, the needs rule probably won't be applied.

In addition, some things affect the weights given to specific rules. For instance, if it is important that high performers maintain their output levels, the contributions rule will be weighted heavily. When someone feels responsible for the receivers' welfare, the needs rule is likely to be applied. And, since the equality rule is easy to apply, people may also turn to the equality rule when needs and contributions are hard to assess.[33]

Procedural Fairness

Distributive fairness depends on whether receivers get what they deserve. People may also be concerned with procedural fairness. **Procedural fairness** is the perception that the process used to allocate outcomes is fair. If procedures seem unfair, people may also question the distribution of rewards. On the other hand, even if people don't get what they want, they may be satisfied as long as they believe the allocation process was fair.

Not surprisingly, people tend to think procedures that favor their interests are fair. They also believe procedures to be more fair when they have some control over the allocation process. Further, they are likely to consider a procedure unfair when it uses questionable means to get information about the receivers' behavior (such as the use of hidden cameras) or if the evaluations of receivers seem to be based on unreliable or irrelevant information (such as faulty performance appraisals).

GOAL SETTING

A **goal** is simply a desired end state. Edwin Locke has written that:

A cardinal attribute of the behavior of living organisms is goal directedness. It may be observed at all levels of life: in the assimilation of food by an amoeba, in the root growth of a tree or a plant, in the stalking of prey by a wild animal, and in the activities of a scientist in a laboratory.[34]

Certainly, goal directedness can be seen in employee behavior. Employees may strive to reach quotas, to win a contest, to make it through the workday, or to outperform their co-workers. Sometimes their goals are difficult, sometimes easy. Sometimes they are very specific, and sometimes vague. We will see that the nature of employee goals, and how they are set, can be very important.

Figure 13–12 summarizes results of a review of studies that reported the effects on performance of individual monetary incentives, group monetary incentives, goal setting, job enrichment, and participation. Figure 13–12 clearly shows that monetary incentives help. And, as we discussed in Chapter 10 as well as elsewhere in this chapter, individual incentives often work better than group incentives. Job enrichment, to be discussed in the next chapter, also typically leads to increased performance[35] (we will see that many of its other benefits relate to employee satisfaction and well-being). Participation doesn't seem to do very well, with only a median 0.5 percent performance increase. We'll see later that this may be a bit misleading. In some cases, participation may be very important and in others it may be unnecessary or even harmful. The figure also shows that goal setting can be very beneficial. Since, relative to monetary incentives and job enrichment, it is simple and inexpensive, goal setting certainly deserves a closer look.

Functions of Goals

The reasons goals are so important become clear when we review their many functions. For instance:[36]

- Goals can clarify expectations. They make it clear to employees what they are expected to do.
- Goals can relieve boredom. Consider how boring most games would be if you didn't keep score and try to reach goals.
- When people attain goals and get feedback indicating that the goals have been reached, they have increased liking for the task and satisfaction with their performance on the job.
- Feedback on goal accomplishment gives a person recognition by peers, supervisors, and others.
- People who are able to attain goals report feelings of increased self-confidence, pride in achievement, and willingness to accept future challenges.

Goal Characteristics

Figure 13–13 shows a variety of goal attributes which may make a difference. Let's review evidence concerning their roles.[37]

Motivational Technique	Median Improvement in Performance
Money (individual incentives)	30%
Money (group incentives)	20%
Goal setting	16%
Job enrichment	9%
Participation	0.5%

FIGURE 13–12
Motivation and Performance

Source: From "The Relative Effectiveness of Four Methods of Motivating Employee Performance," by E. A. Locke, D. B. Feren, V. M. McCaleb, K. N. Shaw, and A. T. Denny, in *Changes in Working Life*, ed. K. Duncan, M. Gruneberg, and D. Wallis. Copyright © 1980 John Wiley & Sons, Ltd. Reprinted by permission of John Wiley & Sons, Ltd.

FIGURE 13–13
*Goal Characteristics and
Performance*

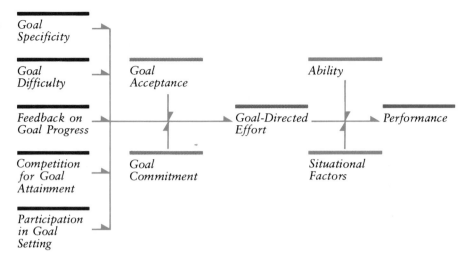

GOAL SPECIFICITY

Quite simply, specific goals lead to higher performance than just "do your best" goals. One review found this result to hold up in a remarkable 51 of 53 studies.[38] In fact, "do your best" goals have about the same effect as no goal at all. Imagine a runner circling a track, shouting to her coach, "How much farther do I have to go?" A reply from the coach of "Just do your best" won't help much.

Specific goals are so powerful as to overwhelm other things. In one study, subjects were assigned to either a "low-motivation" or a "high-motivation" group based on performance, ability, and attitude ratings.[39] The low-motivation group received specific task goals, while the high-motivation group was told to "do your best." Performance of the low-motivation group quickly caught up to that of the high-motivation group.

Of course, goals must be appropriate. If some goals are specific and others are not, the nonspecific goals will not receive much emphasis. Also, there is a danger that a manager may really care about X but, because Y is easier to quantify, will set goals for Y instead.

GOAL DIFFICULTY

There is a positive, linear relationship between goal difficulty and task performance. This relationship holds for various kinds of tasks, time horizons, and ages of subjects. However, employees must believe the goal is attainable. If not, they will not accept it. Also, people pursue many goals at the same time. If they believe one is too difficult, they will focus on other, more attainable goals. Interestingly, when people face difficult goals, they engage in more problem analysis and creative behavior than when faced with simple goals. So, they work both harder and smarter.

FEEDBACK ON GOAL PROGRESS

Feedback keeps behavior on track. Feedback may also stimulate greater effort (we will see in the next chapter that feedback from the job itself is a major determinant of the motivating potential of a job). A video game without a score would soon be abandoned. And, when people get feedback concerning their performance, they tend to set personal improvement goals. The nature of the feedback makes a difference. As we will discuss in the next chapter, feedback from the job itself is generally better than that provided by others. Finally, feedback is clearly more important to some people than to others. We've seen elsewhere, for instance, that people with high need for achievement have especially strong desires for feedback.

PEER COMPETITION FOR GOAL ATTAINMENT

If employees are working toward individual goals, such as salespersons pursuing independent sales goals, competition for goal attainment may be useful. Its impact is especially great in zero-sum situations; that is, where there is a fixed pie to divide. However, competition can hurt if tasks are interdependent. In such a case, an employee's attempts to excel may harm the performance of another. Also, if competition focuses on the quantity of output, quality may suffer.

GOAL ACCEPTANCE

Goal acceptance is the degree to which individuals accept particular goals as their own. If a goal is not accepted, the other goal attributes don't matter. Goal acceptance is likely to be lacking if the individual sees goals as unreachable or sees no benefit from reaching the goal.

GOAL COMMITMENT

Goal commitment is the degree to which individuals are dedicated to trying to reach the goals they have adopted. Like goal acceptance, it is a necessary condition for goal-directed effort. Goal commitment is affected by the same factors as goal acceptance. Those factors influence goal acceptance before the goal is set and goal commitment once the individual is pursuing the goal.

PARTICIPATION IN GOAL SETTING

Participation is not a panacea. Some people simply don't like to participate, and in some situations (such as under severe time constraints) participation may be inappropriate. In general, though, participation increases understanding and acceptance of the goal. Participation often leads to setting of more difficult goals, which may in turn lead to higher performance.[40]

Of course, most goal setting involves changes in a number of goal attributes. As one example, Gary Latham and James Baldes conducted a field experiment in the logging industry. Trucks carrying logs from the woods to the mill varied in the number of trees they hauled from one time to the next since the trees varied in size. As a result, considerable judgment entered into the decision of what was a full load. However, analyses showed that trucks were carrying an average of only about 60 percent of their legal net weight. Eventually the researchers, management, and the union decided that a goal of 94 percent of legal net weight was difficult but reachable. The drivers, who were responsible for loading the trucks, were assigned this 94 percent goal. After about a month, performance increased from the initial 60 percent to about 80 percent of capacity. It then dipped to 70 percent for another month before rising to 90 percent, where it remained for the next six months. Company accountants estimated the results translated into a savings to the company of a quarter of a million dollars' worth of new trucks alone. Several goal attributes had been changed—goals were difficult, were more specific than in the past, and had apparently been accepted.[41]

Management by Objectives (MBO)

Management by objectives (MBO) was introduced by Peter Drucker and Douglas McGregor in the 1950s and has been widely adopted in organizations.[42] While it has many variants, there are four basic steps:

1. The employee and his or her superior jointly set goals.
2. The employee tries to meet the goals.
3. Performance is evaluated against the goals.
4. The employee and superior jointly set new goals for the next time period.

This seems like a simple enough process, and it combines a variety of desirable characteristics. For example:

- MBO forces planning.
- Concrete feedback is a basic part of the MBO process.
- Goals are specific.
- The process guarantees that the superior and subordinate agree on the goals.
- The employee participates in the goal-setting process and is therefore more likely to understand and accept the goals.
- MBO allows for individual differences in the goal-setting process and permits tailoring of goals to the employee.
- MBO serves as a control mechanism, regularly checking to see if performance is on track.

Unfortunately, MBO hasn't been evaluated as rigorously as its popularity would suggest. It does seem that MBO is generally successful—one review estimated that successes were at least five times as common as failures.[43] However, that review defined success only as a statistically significant increase in performance, not as full realization of the potential of goal setting.

In fact, there have been several criticisms of MBO. For instance, in some cases it may be very difficult to set goals. Also, MBO requires as much as three to five years for proper implementation, requires visible top-management commitment, is time-consuming, and may involve a lot of paperwork. MBO may also build rigidity into the system; employees may continue to pursue fixed goals even though conditions have changed. Further, since MBO focuses on concrete, quantifiable goals, less tangible criteria may suffer. For example, MBO may reward productivity while downplaying creativity. Finally, the favorable impact of MBO may deteriorate over time. Thus, MBO is not a cure-all. As with any major program, its probable costs and benefits should be weighed. If undertaken, it should be carefully planned and implemented and steps should be taken to monitor its effectiveness over time.

LEARNING THEORY

In Chapter 12 we discussed three sorts of learning—classical conditioning, operant conditioning, and social learning. We will see now how managers can use learning theory to increase employee motivation. We will first see how rewards and undesirable consequences can be used to influence behavior. Next, we will examine partial reinforcement schedules. Finally, we will briefly consider organizational behavior modification.

Arranging the Contingencies of Reinforcement

Recall from the previous chapter that operant conditioning uses rewards or unpleasant consequences to strengthen desired behaviors or to weaken undesired behaviors.[44] Positive reinforcement and avoidance learning are two basic ways to strengthen desired behaviors. Nonreinforcement and punishment are ways to weaken and ultimately eliminate undesired behaviors. (Elimination of an undesired behavior—or failure to continue a desired behavior—is called **extinction**).

POSITIVE REINFORCEMENT

Positive reinforcement involves giving a reward when desired behavior occurs in order to increase the likelihood that the behavior will be repeated. A bonus for a job well done or a pat on the back for a good effort would be examples. In many jobs, bonuses and other forms of merit-based compensation are very important, sometimes exceeding base salaries. As an extreme example (perhaps the most extreme example in history), Michael Milken, the former head of Drexel Burnham Lambert Inc.'s junk bond department, received $550 million in bonuses in 1987, and his estimated income was twice that: $1.1 billion! The $550 million was more than Guyana's gross national product, would pay for about two B1 bombers, and approached the estimated value of Pablo Picasso's lifetime work. Unfortunately for Milken, the figures were disclosed as part of the U.S. government's 98-count indictment filed against him. The indictment charged Milken with racketeering and other offenses related to securities trading.[45] In a plea-bargaining agreement, Milken pleaded guilty in April 1990 to six felonies and agreed to pay $600 million in restitution.

ESCAPE CONDITIONING

Another way to increase the likelihood of desired behavior is to remove some unpleasant consequence when that behavior occurs. For example, suppose a rat is subjected to a loud, irritating noise until it presses a lever. Once it presses the lever, the noise stops. The rat would soon learn to press the lever to escape the grating noise. This is called **escape conditioning**. If pressing the lever would actually prevent the onset of the noise, this would be called **avoidance conditioning**. In some companies, there are certain jobs that employees feel are very good, and others that are clearly "the pits." If employees feel that they will be transferred from the bad jobs to the good jobs if they perform well, we have an example of escape conditioning. Clearly, though, escape conditioning is not easy to use in organizations.

NONREINFORCEMENT

Nonreinforcement causes extinction of an undesired behavior by removing the reinforcing consequence that previously followed the behavior. Consider the case of Sam. We have (unintentionally) been teaching Sam to make constant unwarranted demands by regularly giving in to those demands. How can we get him to stop? One answer is simply to stop rewarding him for that undesired behavior. That is, don't give in to the demands. He will learn that unwarranted demands aren't rewarded, and he will eventually stop making them.

PUNISHMENT

Another way to try to stop Sam's unwarranted demands would be to punish him whenever he makes those demands. **Punishment** is defined as presenting an unpleasant consequence, or removing a desired consequence, whenever an undesired behavior occurs. So, when Sam makes such demands, we could put a letter of reprimand in his file (an unpleasant consequence), or we could stop interacting with him socially (removal of a desired consequence). Note that both nonreinforcement and punishment can involve removal of a desired consequence. With nonreinforcement, the reward we would withhold (agreeing to demands) was the one previously tied to the behavior. With punishment, the reward withheld (social interaction) was not previously a reinforcer for that behavior. As a novel example of punishment, consider the story of the "40 Worst."

Most managers don't like to punish others. And punishment is likely to embitter the employee, leading to dissatisfaction and perhaps to turnover. Further, managers who use punishment frequently may find that their subordinates obey their orders only when they are present. When they are absent, the employees may secretly rebel. Finally, since punishment only stops undesirable behavior, the task of increasing desired behavior remains.

Partial Versus Continuous Reinforcement

There are many ways to reinforce behavior. One basic distinction is whether or not behavior is reinforced every time it occurs (such as for every widget produced). **Continuous reinforcement** occurs if every behavior is reinforced. Continuous reinforcement leads to rapid learning. However, if for some reason it is necessary to stop reinforcing (for instance, if the supervisor must leave the room), rapid extinction occurs. Most of the time, it is simply impractical to reinforce on a continuous basis, so a **partial reinforcement schedule** is used.

Partial reinforcement schedules can be time-based or behavior-based. Also, they can be administered on a fixed, unchanging basis, or can be varied around some mean. There are four basic partial reinforcement schedules.

FIXED INTERVAL

With a **fixed-interval schedule**, a reinforcer is given at fixed time intervals, such as once a week. Weekly paychecks and monthly inspections are common examples. Fixed-interval schedules, while easy to use, result in slow learning and moderately fast extinction rate. They also have a low response rate (that is, frequency of response per reinforcement) and very low response stability (people speed up just before the time of reinforcement and then slow down).

VARIABLE INTERVAL

A **variable-interval schedule** also is time-based. However, a reinforcer is administered randomly around some average interval. For instance, an instruc-

40 WORST

In China, a land of guaranteed employment, there is plenty of recognition for a job well done. You might be named a "model worker" and awarded a television set as a special bonus. Or, like proud employees at the Xian Instruments Factory near Xian, China, you might be handed a gold plaque declaring your firm a "civilized enterprise."

But, in a country that abhors the sordid capitalist practice of firing, what do you do when the workers of the world won't work? The Chinese are choosing a traditional medicine: When all else fails, try humiliation.

Amid much fanfare recently, the Xian Department Store, which has about 800 employees, publicly named its "40 Worst Shop Assistants," a move meant to spur better performance from the tardy and the rude. The large retail operation in this medieval walled city even went a step further: It made the transgressor's workplace his pillory, hanging a plaque overhead, complete with picture, that proclaimed him a member of the "40 Worst."

"It's the only system we've found to pressure workers to do better," says Bai Shouzheng, the store's burly Communist Party secretary. He flashes a broad smile, showing off a solid row of silver teeth. "Those designated the 'worst' feel embarrassed," he reasons. "Otherwise, our efforts would have no effect."

Is it working? Listen to Chen Jie, a dimpled, 19-year-old salesclerk sanctioned for snapping at a customer. "I accept my punishment, since my error hurt the store's reputation," says Ms. Chen, who sells synthetic-fur coats. "Today, I view my little three-foot shop counter as a window on socialist civilization."

Source: Reprinted by permission of *The Wall Street Journal*, © Dow Jones & Company, Inc. (January 24, 1989). All Rights Reserved Worldwide.

tor might announce there will be four pop quizzes during the semester, but will not say when they will occur. Learning rate, extinction rate, response rate, and response stability are all better for the variable-interval than for the fixed-interval schedule. However, they are generally not as good as for ratio-based schedules.

FIXED RATIO

A **fixed-ratio schedule** provides a reinforcer after a given number of acceptable behaviors. Commissions given on the basis of sales and bonuses given for periods of perfect attendance are examples. Fixed-ratio schedules have very high response rates—pigeons have been trained to peck at rates faster than machine-gun fire—and response stability. They have high learning rates but, unfortunately, rapid extinction rates as well.

VARIABLE RATIO

While a fixed-ratio schedule reinforces every n responses, a **variable-ratio schedule** reinforces on average every n responses. For instance, a one-armed bandit might have a payoff an average of once in every ten pulls of the handle. However, precisely when the payoff will occur is unknown. Response rates and response stability are similar to those for fixed-ratio schedules, but learning is slower. However, extinction is very slow. Companies have made some creative attempts to use variable-ratio schedules. For instance, in one firm, names of employees who didn't use their sick leave were placed in a lottery for a large prize. Sick-leave costs fell by 62 percent.[46]

Figure 13–14 summarizes how these schedules differ in terms of learning rate, response rate, response stability, and extinction rate.

FIGURE 13–14
Comparison of Schedules of Reinforcement

Measure	Schedule of Reinforcement				
	Continuous	Fixed Ratio	Variable Ratio	Fixed Interval	Variable Interval
Learning Rate	Very Fast	Fast	Slow	Very Slow	Moderate
Response Rate	Very Low	Very High	Very High	Low	Moderate
Response Stability	Very High	High	High	Very Low	Low to Moderate
Extinction Rate	Very Fast	Fast	Very Slow	Moderately Fast	Slow

Organizational Behavior Modification

Organizational behavior modification (OB Mod) is the use of the principles of learning theory to manage behavior in organizations. OB Mod practitioners and theorists typically use a combination of operant conditioning techniques and social learning to achieve their goals. That is, they use both cognitive and noncognitive approaches.

RULES FOR USING LEARNING TECHNIQUES IN ORGANIZATIONS

Clay and Ellen Hamner have presented the following set of rules for effectively using learning techniques in organizations:[47]

1. *Don't give the same reward to all.* Reward those who exhibit desired behaviors (such as high performance) more than those who don't.
2. *Failure to respond to behavior has reinforcing consequences.* Managers must remember that inaction, as well as action, has reinforcing consequences. They should ask, "What behavior will I reinforce if I do nothing?"
3. *Tell a person what behavior gets reinforced.* Make the contingencies of reinforcement clear to workers. Don't make them guess which behaviors will be rewarded.
4. *Tell a person what he or she is doing wrong.* If the manager does not make clear to the employee why a reward is being withheld, the employee may attribute the action to a past desired behavior rather than the behavior the manager wants to extinguish.
5. *Don't punish in front of others.* When workers are punished in front of others, they "lose face" and are doubly punished. This can cause a variety of problems.
6. *Make the consequences equal to the behavior.* Overrewarding desired behavior makes a worker feel guilty. Underrewarding desired behavior causes anger.

Notice that most of these rules rely heavily on cognitions, recognizing that employees can learn through observation and receipt of advice as well as from their own experiences.

BEHAVIORAL SHAPING

OB Mod often uses behavioral shaping. **Behavioral shaping** is the learning of a complex behavior through successive approximations of the desired behavior. Initially, the employee gets a reward for any behavior which is in any way related to the desired behavior. Subsequently, responses are not reinforced unless they are more and more similar to the desired behavior. Responses are "shaped" until the desired complex behavior is achieved.

Evaluation of Learning Theory

Properly applied, learning theory works. Many firms, including Emery Air Freight, General Electric, and Weyerhaeuser, have implemented very successful programs. In fact, some critics worry that learning theory works *too* well, possibly pushing the employee to exhaustion or to other undesirable behaviors. They see this as especially troublesome since this behavior—especially when noncognitive, operant conditioning is used—is to some extent outside the control of the employee, overriding free will. Learning theory has also been criticized for ignoring the fact that people value rewards differently and for focusing on quantity rather than quality.

We feel that, intelligently applied, learning theory can be very useful. After all, managers are reinforcing behavior all the time; the trick is to do it right. Cognitive approaches, in which employees know why they are being rewarded or punished and are aware of the contingencies of reinforcement, overcome some of the concerns that employees are being ruthlessly manipulated.

COMMON THEMES OF THE THEORIES

Now that we have reviewed several motivation theories, it may be useful to ask how they agree. In fact, while there are some differences among these theories, they share some important themes. They are unanimous, for example, in stressing the need to determine what employees want. Managers who treat all employees the same, or who assume they know what is important to their subordinates and others, are likely to do a poor job of motivating.

Managers can deal with individual differences in needs in a variety of ways. One possibility is to try to learn what each employee wants—perhaps through surveys—and tailor programs, behaviors, and rewards to the individual. Another possibility is to use cafeteria-style benefit plans. With **cafeteria-style benefit plans**, employees can choose from a wide range of alternative benefits. In that way, employees of differing ages, marital status, and needs can tailor benefits to their particular situations. One employee may choose all salary with no other benefits, another may use part of the total allowance for pension and insurance contributions, and so on.[48] Still another way to help ensure that rewards are satisfying is to invite employees to participate in the reward-setting process.[49]

Another point on which the content theories agree (and on which the process theories and reinforcement theory are silent) is that managers should pay attention to their subordinates' higher-order or growth needs. We will see in the next chapter that these growth needs are important determinants of how employees respond to enriched task characteristics. While it is unwise automatically to assume that employees have particular need structures, it is probably safe to say that growth needs have often been neglected in the past.[50] Thus, managers should consider their full arsenal of potential rewards, intrinsic as well as extrinsic, when developing motivational strategies.

While the various approaches have much in common, some may be more useful than others for explaining or influencing particular behaviors or attitudes. For instance, expectancy theory seems especially useful for dealing with choice-making. Equity theory and need theories may best explain worker satisfaction. Reinforcement theories, equity theory, and goal theory all seem useful for application to performance. That is, rather than trying to find the "best" theory for all purposes, it may be better to consider the particular strengths of each approach for the particular variables of interest.[51]

Of course, while choice of a technique is important, it is also critical that the technique be used properly. Some managers apply new tools without really considering whether they are appropriate. Others simply apply them incorrectly. For example, how would you feel if you were a sales manager in Management in Action 2?

SELF-MANAGEMENT

To this point, we have discussed ways that managers can motivate others. Often, though, people must motivate themselves. Consider the case of G. Neil Anderson. Anderson, a salesman for Apple Computer, travels a wide route through Idaho in his aging Falcon. He is basically on his own, striving to meet his monthly sales quota of eight computer systems. There is no boss around to tell Mr. Anderson what to do, no time clock to order his day. He says, "A salesman's got to have goals—and rewards." He keeps a fishing pole in his car. "If I sell a computer in the morning, I go fishing in the afternoon." Mr. Anderson is practicing self-management. His reward is immediate and valent.[52]

Advocates of self-management argue that, instead of relying on others to reward and punish, to direct, to set goals, to provide feedback, and so on, individuals should learn to manage themselves. Such self-management may be necessary in cases in which the individual is relatively isolated, such as an employee working at home. It may also be beneficial when there are low levels of supervision or when employees are supposed to be self-directing (we will consider two such cases—job enrichment and self-managing work groups—in coming chapters). However, self-management may serve as a useful supplement or complement to hierarchical leadership in almost any situation.

Being able to work on one's own without supervision is a valuable skill.

Benefits of Self-Management

Self-management has several potential benefits. It is a continually available skill, ready to be drawn upon for any task. It can be relatively inexpensive, especially when compared to formal organizational reward systems. It puts the individual in control of his or her own destiny. It serves as a substitute for leadership in many cases, such as that of Mr. Anderson.

Nevertheless, self-management has until recently received relatively little attention in the management literature. In fact, it has been called the missing

La Costa's sales department and special events coordinators sometimes get some rather unusual and bizarre requests, but Electrolux, the national vacuum manufacturing company, has to be near the top of the list in originality for its recent national sales managers' meeting at the resort.

At the meeting's dinner banquet, the room was divided with chicken wire and the company's top grossing sales managers sat separately from the others during the evening. Caterers decorated one side of the room with tables covered with white cloths, china, silver, and fresh flower centerpieces for those bringing the best number of sales to the company.

The top sales managers dined on filet mignon,

MANAGEMENT IN ACTION 2
ONE-BEAN MOTIVATION

potatoes, asparagus, and chocolate mousse, while their counterparts on the opposite side of the banquet hall ate baked beans and jello, washing it down with a cup of hot water laced with a single coffee bean.

Source: From *The Reporter*, newsletter of the La Costa Hotel and Spa Conference Center, Carlsbad, CA (January 1984), as reported in the *New Yorker* (January 2, 1984).

link in managerial effectiveness.[53] Recently, self-management has been successfully used to reduce employee absenteeism.[54] Research in other settings, such as programs for weight loss, smoking cessation, and improving study habits, has been quite positive.[55]

Guidelines for Self-Management

Frank Andrasik and Judy Heimberg have provided a number of useful guidelines for self-management.[56] These guidelines include self-analysis, modifying antecedents, modifying consequences, contracting, monitoring program effectiveness, and maintaining the desired change.

SELF-ANALYSIS

There are two steps in self-analysis, pinpointing and self-monitoring. The first step is to pinpoint the behavior you would like to change. You may want to keep track of how you spend your time in order to pinpoint specific behaviors to be altered. For instance, some of the time you may be working on jobs that should be delegated to others or you may be daydreaming instead of working. Decide exactly what you would like to change about the behavior (for instance, quantity, timing, duration, or frequency). Once behaviors have been pinpointed, the self-monitoring step involves keeping track of their frequency, duration, and any other dimensions of interest (such as the quality of the behavior or the time and place it occurs). Diaries, graphs, and timing devices may help with self-monitoring.[57] Figure 13–15 is a sample graph. In some cases, the mere act of self-monitoring will be enough to lead to changes in the behavior.

MODIFYING ANTECEDENTS

Sometimes the behavior we're interested in changing is prompted by other events. We may find, for example, that we are failing to get work done because of constant phone interruptions. A solution might be to have the secretary hold calls. Or we may increase desired behaviors by so simple a prompt as a list of things to be done.

FIGURE 13–15
Self-Management
Progress

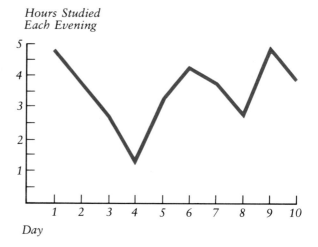

MODIFYING CONSEQUENCES

Here we want to reward or punish ourselves to alter our behavior. In the opening vignette, Mr. Anderson rewarded himself for selling a computer system by going fishing. The reward for a student working on a term paper might be as simple as a cup of coffee after five pages are written. Punishment for undesirable behavior might include not watching a favorite TV show or skipping a concert. Sometimes it is also helpful to reorder behavior. That is, we often do some rather enjoyable tasks in order to put off others that we don't care for. To prevent this, we can make the pleasant task contingent upon completion of the unpleasant task. For instance, if we enjoy opening and reading the mail, but find writing project reports unpleasant, we can put off opening the mail until we have finished the project reports.

CONTRACTING

Contracting is simply the act of writing a contract with ourselves. It may specify that we are to self-monitor, that we should not delay in rewarding desirable behaviors or in punishing undesirable acts, and so on. The contract should be clearly written and conspicuously posted.

MONITORING PROGRAM EFFECTIVENESS

It is important to check your progress on a regular basis. As you fill in your diary or graph, check to see whether the pinpointed behavior is changing in the way you wished. If you are making good progress, fine. If not, some corrective action may be necessary. For instance, a change in the prompts or rewards you are using may help. It may be that you are not rewarding yourself promptly, or that you are rewarding yourself even when the pinpointed behavior does not occur. Carefully assess the elements of your self-management program.

MAINTAINING THE DESIRED CHANGE

It is useful to plan strategies to maintain behavior which is successfully changed. That is, there is a tendency to fall back into prior habits if you do not take care to support the gains you have made. On the other hand, you may not want to continue indefinitely to use the same stringent system of rewards and punishments that were needed to bring about the change. So you may decide to reduce the frequency or intensity of pleasant consequences following desired behavior or to change the consequence to one that occurs more naturally.

You may want to apply these self-management guidelines to behaviors you would like to influence. For instance, you might start by pinpointing two behaviors you would like to change. One of those behaviors could be very short-term, such as your dating behavior over the next week. Another could be intermediate in length, such as your study habits over the rest of the year. For each, go through the steps we have outlined, including the writing of contracts. It may help to find friends or colleagues to provide support with the process. They may, for instance, check on a regular basis to see that you are maintaining the desired behaviors. In this way, they can help you enforce the contracts. Your progress may initially seem slow, but there is evidence that those who persevere and use a variety of self-management procedures are most likely to be successful.

SCRIPTS AND SCHEMAS

In the preceding sections of this chapter we have considered a variety of ways that people can motivate others and themselves. In this section we consider an approach based on the idea that people have pictures or stories in their minds that lead them to behave in certain ways. **Schemas** are cognitive frameworks that an individual uses to give structure and meaning to social information. These are essentially pictures in our minds about the way things fit together. We may, for instance, have a schema for the way that personality traits occur together.[58]

More directly relevant to motivation, **scripts** are schemas for behavior. They are schemas held in memory that describe events or behaviors appropriate for a given context. A script might indicate how we should behave during a formal meeting, a conversation with our supervisor, or the annual company picnic. So, when we are in an employment interview, the employment interview script is triggered. This allows us to enact the appropriate behaviors for the interview. We may learn scripts either by directly experiencing the events that take place in a situation or by indirect means. These indirect means might include viewing training films, watching role models, or conversing with co-workers.

This idea of scripts is interesting since it suggests that much of our behavior may be relatively automatic. Also, we may recall previously experienced events by fitting them into the script for the situation. Unfortunately, this may lead to "false remembering," in which we may recall events which are typical of a situation even though they did not occur in a particular case. For instance, an interviewing script may cause an interviewer to incorrectly be "sure" that she asked a job prospect about geographic preferences because she typically asks such a question. Scripts may have other dangers. For instance, they may cause us to respond automatically without fully considering the subtleties of a situation. They may also dampen creativity.

Scripts are probably more useful in explaining routine than novel behaviors. Further, there is still very little research about script-based models of behavior. Nevertheless, the idea of scripts provides a fascinating perspective and may offer new insight into behavior in organizations.[59]

IMPLICATIONS FOR MANAGEMENT

Motivation of employees is an ongoing and crucial task of the manager. As a manager, you will need to energize your employees to initiate, direct, intensify, and sustain their desired behaviors. By properly motivating your employees, you can enhance both performance and the quality of work life. The theories presented in this chapter should serve as useful tools.

As a manager, be willing to employ creativity in applying motivational techniques. Unusual benefits, a variety of arrangements of contingencies of reinforcement, and even lotteries may all have their place.

Expectancy theory provides some very useful managerial guidelines. For instance, it suggests that managers should try to examine carefully the expectancies and instrumentalities perceived by their employees. If expectancies are low, the manager should see whether the cause is perceived inability, situational constraints, or ambiguity concerning expected behaviors. If instrumentalities are low, the manager should ask why. Is there actually a weak link between the first-order and second-order outcome, or is the employee misperceiving the situation? If the former, actions to strengthen the linkage may help. If the latter, the manager may need to communicate the true nature of the link.

Good managers recognize that they must treat employees and others fairly. Keep in mind when trying to be fair to employees that perceptions are critical. Try to learn what your subordinates see as inputs to the job, and what they view as outcomes. Recognize, too, that some employees will base their equity perceptions on the contributions they make, others on their needs, and still others on the desire for equal outcomes. Finally, remember that fairness in procedures, as well as in distribution of outcomes, is important.

Few areas provide clearer, easier-to-apply guidelines to the manager than goal theory. As a manager, try to set specific and difficult goals and make sure that employees receive feedback, preferably from the task itself. Keep in mind that goal acceptance and commitment are necessary. Take steps, perhaps including the participation of subordinates in the goal-setting process, to secure such acceptance and commitment.

As a manager, you may use self-management techniques to change your own behaviors in desired ways. You may also want to provide self-management training for your subordinates so that they can effectively motivate themselves in your absence. The need for self-management will almost certainly increase in the future.

Finally, remember that you can apply these motivational tools to any behaviors, not just productivity. You may want to use them, for instance, to increase attendance, retention, creativity, or flexibility. The range of behaviors you may want to change, and the variety of ways in which you can use motivational techniques to attempt those changes, are limited only by your imagination.

KEY TERMS AND CONCEPTS

avoidance conditioning
behavioral shaping
cafeteria-style benefit plans
content theories
continuous reinforcement
contributions rule
dissatisfiers or hygiene factors
distributive fairness
equality rule
equity theory
escape conditioning
existence needs
existence-relatedness-growth (ERG)
   theory
expectancy
expectancy theory
extinction
extrinsic factors
first-order outcome
fixed-interval schedule
fixed-ratio schedule
force to perform or effort
frustration regression
goal
growth needs
instrumentality
intrinsic factors
management by objectives (MBO)

motivation
need for achievement
need for affiliation
need for power
needs rule
nonreinforcement
organizational behavior modification
   (OB Mod)
partial reinforcement schedule
personalized power seekers
positive reinforcement
procedural fairness
process theories
punishment
reinforcement theories
relatedness needs
satisfaction progression
satisfiers or motivators
schemas
scripts
second-order outcome
socialized power seekers
two-factor theory or
   motivation-hygiene theory
valence
variable-interval schedule
variable-ratio schedule

QUESTIONS FOR REVIEW AND DISCUSSION

1. What is motivation? Which of the motivation theories discussed in this chapter do you agree with the most? The least? Why?
2. How valid is Maslow's need hierarchy theory?
3. In what ways does Alderfer's ERG theory differ from Maslow's need hierarchy theory? How is it similar?
4. What is need for achievement? What are characteristics of individuals with strong need for achievement?
5. In what ways are expectancy theory and learning theory similar? How do they differ?
6. What are the three rules for distributive fairness? Indicate situations with which you are familiar in which each rule was used.

7. Think of three goals you set for yourself in the past. Describe each goal. Indicate how specific, difficult, and competitive the goal was and the degree to which you accepted the goal and were committed to it. What sort of feedback did you have concerning the degree to which you were attaining each goal? Finally, were you successful in attaining each of the goals? Indicate how each of the goal characteristics might have been relevant.

8. What is MBO? In what sorts of situations do you think MBO would be most useful? Least useful?

9. Compare and contrast need for self-actualization and need for achievement.

10. Do you think it is ethical to try to change the strength of employees' needs? Why or why not?

11. Describe a way—other than those described in the chapter—in which a firm might use fixed-interval, variable-interval, fixed-ratio, and variable-ratio reinforcement schedules.

12. If you were an employee, do you think you would want your boss to use organizational behavior modification techniques? Why or why not?

13. Select a behavior you would like to change. Explain how self-management techniques might be useful in changing that behavior.

14. What is a script? Think of some situation in which you routinely engage, and provide your script for that situation.

CASES

13–1 TYING MANAGERS' PAY TO PERFORMANCE

David Margolis works for a generous company—a very generous company. Last year, Mr. Margolis, the president, chairman, and chief executive officer of Colt Industries Inc., received a bonus of $555,000, more than double the bonus for chief executives of similar-size companies. And, that bonus was $115,680 more than his base salary. Total compensation: close to $1 million.

Colt says its largess is well founded. In 1984, the year on which the bonus was based, the company had a record return on equity and several other benchmarks. "We have no shame or trepidation about the fact that our people are highly paid," says Karyl Lynn, Colt's personnel director. "They've earned it."

A similar attitude can be found in increasing numbers of board rooms across the country. After years of regularly receiving hefty increases in salaries and bonuses—regardless of their company's success or failure—more top executives are now finding their compensation linked directly to corporate performance. The trend is even extending to division managers.

"There's been so much scrutiny that boards have been taking a closer look at compensation," says Pete Smith, national director of Wyatt Co.'s compensation consulting business. As a result, companies are relying less on salary and more on bonuses and other performance-linked compensation to reward executives. They are also tightening the criteria for earning those rewards.

Bonuses and other long-term compensation are becoming more important. In 1975, salary made up 60 percent of the pay of a chief executive officer of a company with $1 billion to $2 billion in sales. By 1985, the proportion fell to 50 percent.

During the last recession, ailing companies were still obliged to pay salaries that had risen at double-digit rates in the preceding years. Now, directors reason, they can trim compensation costs swiftly, if necessary, by putting more money into bonuses and less into salaries. "Salaries are a fixed cost; bonuses are a variable cost," says Charles Peck, a compensation specialist at the Conference Board.

Executive bonuses were always supposedly tied to targets such as growth in earnings per share, but the bonuses came to be looked on simply as additional salary. "The past standards were so loose that bonus plans were designed to pay off no matter what," says a corporate compensation manager. Such plans also gave executives an incentive to maximize short-term profits at the expense of long-term goals. Now, however, more compensation is being pegged to three-year or five-year gains in such performance measures as return on equity, return on assets, and earnings per share.

Source: Reprinted by permission of *The Wall Street Journal*, © Dow Jones & Company, Inc. (February 28, 1986). All Rights Reserved Worldwide.

1. According to expectancy theory, what impact would the changes noted in this case have on motivation? According to learning theory?
2. Does goal theory suggest any benefits of this approach? Any dangers?
3. In view of the potential benefits of performance-contingent bonuses, why do you think they are not universally applied?

13–2 RANDOM CHECKS FOR STEROIDS

In the 100-meter dash of the 1988 Olympics in Seoul, Korea, Carl Lewis glanced to his right in surprise at Ben Johnson of Canada. Johnson had exploded from the starting block and muscled his way to a clear victory, the Olympic gold, and the title of World's Fastest Human. Within days, though, Johnson was unceremoniously stripped of his medal and sent home. The reason: He had tested positive for the use of the anabolic steroid stanozolol, a substance that is supposed to help build lean muscle mass.

There had long been rumors about steroid use among track-and-field stars, and athletes had been disqualified from the 1983 Pan-American Games and the 1984 Olympics for drug use. Nevertheless, the Johnson case was startling. By the end of the 1988 Olympics there were a total of ten drug-related disqualifications. Almost immediately there were calls for stricter penalties for illegal drug use as well as for more stringent enforcement procedures. The next month, officials from 29 countries met in Borlange, Sweden, to draw up tough drug-testing proposals aimed at stamping out the use of anabolic steroids by athletes. The group recommended that random checks for steroids be carried out during training as well as actual competition. Refusal to submit to such checks would carry the same penalty as discovery of use, including disqualification and long-term bans from competition.

1. According to learning theory, what might have caused this apparently widespread drug use among track-and-field athletes?
2. What sort of partial reinforcement schedule does this random check for steroids represent? What are some probable consequences of use of such a schedule?
3. Which of the rules for use of learning theory in organizations discussed in this chapter does the proposed action incorporate?

ENDNOTES

1. This definition is based on C. C. Pinder, *Work Motivation: Theory, Issues, and Applications* (Glenview, IL: Scott, Foresman, 1984), 8.
2. While this is a useful framework, we will see that not all approaches to motivation are need based.
3. For recent reviews of the motivation literature, see M. G. Evans, "Organizational Behavior: The Central Role of Motivation," *Journal of Management* 12 (1986): 203-227; D. R. Ilgen and H. J. Klein, "Individual Motivation and Performance: Cognitive Influences on Effort and Choice," in *Productivity in Organizations*, ed. J. P. Campbell and R. J. Campbell (San Francisco: Jossey-Bass, 1988): 143-176; F. J. Landy and W. S. Becker, "Motivation Theory Reconsidered," in *Research in Organizational Behavior*, vol. 9, ed. L. L. Cummings and B. Staw (Greenwich, CT: JAI Press, 1987): 1-38; E. A. Locke and D. Henne, "Work Motivation Theories," ed. C. L. Cooper and I. Robertson, *International Review of Industrial and*

Organizational Psychology (New York: John Wiley & Sons, 1986), 1-18; and T. R. Mitchell, "New Directions for Theory, Research, and Practice," *Academy of Management Review* 7 (1982): 80-88.

4. A. H. Maslow, "A Theory of Human Motivation," *Psychological Review* 50 (1943): 370-396.

5. For an interesting discussion of Maslow's life and professional development, see G. Leonard, "Abraham Maslow and the New Self," *Esquire* (December 1983): 326-336.

6. A. H. Maslow, *Eupsychian Management* (Homewood, IL: Dorsey-Irwin, 1965), 56.

7. For discussions of Maslow's theory and its validity, see D. T. Hall and K. E. Nougaim, "An Examination of Maslow's Need Hierarchy in an Organizational Setting," *Organizational Behavior and Human Performance* 3 (1967): 12-35; E. E. Lawler III and J. L. Suttle, "A Causal Correlational Test of the Need Hierarchy Concept," *Organizational Behavior and Human Performance* 7 (1972): 265-287; A. H. Maslow, "A Theory of Human Motivation," *Psychological Review* 50 (1943): 370-396; and M. A. Wahba and L. G. Bridwell, "Maslow Reconsidered: A Review of Research on the Need Hierarchy Theory," *Organizational Behavior and Human Performance* 15 (1976): 212-240.

8. For discussions of Alderfer's theory and related research, see C. P. Alderfer, "An Empirical Test of a New Theory of Human Needs," *Organizational Behavior and Human Performance* 5 (1969): 142-175, and *Existence, Relatedness, and Growth: Human Needs in Organizational Settings* (New York: Free Press, 1972); R. E. Kaplan and K. A. Smith, "The Effect of Variations in Relatedness Need Satisfaction on Relatedness Desire," *Administrative Science Quarterly* 19 (1974): 507-532; J. P. Wanous and A. A. Zwany, "A Cross-Sectional Test of Need Hierarchy Theory," *Organizational Behavior and Human Performance* 18 (1977): 78-97; and V. Florian, "The Meaning of Work for Physically Disabled Clients Undergoing Vocational Rehabilitation," *International Journal of Rehabilitation Research* 5 (1982): 375-378.

9. H. A. Murray, *Explorations in Personality* (New York: Oxford University Press, 1938).

10. Henry A. Murray et al., *Explorations in Personality* (New York: Oxford University Press, 1938), 164. Reprinted with permission.

11. For instance, see D. C. McClelland, "Business Drive and National Achievement," *Harvard Business Review* 40 (1962): 99-112; and D. C. McClelland and D. H. Burnham, "Power Is the Great Motivator," *Harvard Business Review* (March-April 1976): 100-110. Measurement of manifest needs is troublesome. Both projective tests such as the TAT and more standard paper-and-pencil tests have psychometric problems. For one attempt to develop an improved measure of manifest needs, see M. J. Stahl and A. M. Harrell, "Evolution and Validation of a Behavioral Decision Theory Measurement Approach to Achievement, Power, and Affiliation," *Journal of Applied Psychology* 67 (1982): 744-751.

12. Reprinted by permission of *Harvard Business Review*. An exhibit from "Business Drive and National Achievement" by David C. McClelland (July/August 1962). Copyright © 1962 by the President and Fellows of Harvard College; all rights reserved.

13. For a model of factors influencing achievement motivation, see H. S. Farmer, "Model of Career and Achievement Motivation for Women and Men," *Journal of Counseling Psychology* 32 (1985): 363-390.

14. For a successful application of this process in an educational setting, see P. Ashton, "Motivation Training and Personal Control: A Comparison of Three Intervention Strategies," *Education* 106 (1987): 454-461.

15. D. C. McClelland et al., *The Drinking Man: Alcohol and Human Motivation* (New York: Free Press, 1972). See also D. G. Winter, "The Power Motive in Women—and Men," *Journal of Personality and Social Psychology* 54 (1988): 510-519.

16. For a more thorough discussion of intrinsic and extrinsic rewards, see A. P. Brief and R. J. Aldag, "The Intrinsic-Extrinsic Dichotomy: Toward Conceptual Clarity," *Academy of Management Review* 2 (1977): 496-500.

17. The two-factor theory remains quite controversial, with both critics and supporters. For instance, see F. Herzberg, *Work and the Nature of Man* (Cleveland: World Publishing, 1966), and "One More Time: How Do You Motivate Employees?" *Harvard Business Review* (January-February 1968): 53-62; R. J. House and L. A. Wigdor, "Herzberg's Dual-Factor Theory of Job Satisfaction and Motivation: A Review of the Evidence and a Criticism," *Personnel Psychology* 20 (1967): 369-389; and D. A. Whitsett and E. K. Winslow, "An Analysis of Studies Critical of the Motivator-Hygiene Theory," *Personnel Psychology* 20 (1967): 391-415.

18. V. H. Vroom, *Work and Motivation* (New York: John Wiley & Sons, 1964).

19. Both expectancies and instrumentalities are also sometimes expressed as correlations. Unlike probabilities, correlations can take on negative values. Outcomes would be restated accordingly.

20. For evaluations of expectancy theory, see H. G. Heneman III and D. P. Schwab, "Evaluation of Research on Expectancy Theory Prediction of Employee Performance," *Psychological Bulletin* 79 (1972): 1-9; R. J. House, H. J. Shapiro, and M. A. Wahba, "Expectancy Theory as a Predictor of Work Behavior and Attitude: A Re-Evaluation of Empirical Evidence," *Decision Sciences* 5 (1974): 481-506; D. P. Schwab, J. D. Olian-Gottlieb, and H. G. Heneman III, "Between-Subjects Expectancy Theory Research: A Statistical Review of Studies Predicting Effort and Performance," *Psychological Bulletin* 86 (1979): 139-147; and D. D. Baker, R. Ravichandran, and D. M. Randall, "Exploring Contrasting Formulations of Expectancy Theory," *Decision Sciences* 20 (1989): 1-13.

21. See E. Walster, G. W. Walster, and E. Berscheid, *Equity: Theory and Research* (Boston: Allyn & Bacon, 1978), for a review of studies on this issue.

22. G. S. Leventhal, "Fairness in Social Relationships," in *Contemporary Topics in Social Psychology*, ed. J. Thibaut, J. T. Spence, and R. Carson (Morristown, NJ: General Learning Press, 1976).

23. This listing is based on G. S. Leventhal, "The Distribution of Rewards and Resources in Groups and Organizations," in *Advances in Experimental Social Psychology*, vol. 9, ed. L. Berkowitz and E. Walster (New York: Academic Press, 1976).

24. J. S. Adams, "Inequity in Social Exchange," in *Advances in Experimental Social Psychology*, vol. 2, ed. L. Berkowitz (New York: Academic Press, 1965).

25. While there are some more sophisticated equity formulations (for instance, see Walster, Walster, and Berscheid, *Equity*), this formulation is adequate in most cases.

26. For instance, see E. Jaques, *Equitable Payment* (New York: John Wiley & Sons, 1961), and R. D. Pritchard, M. D. Dunnette, and D. O. Jorgenson, "Effects of Perceptions of Equity and Inequity on Worker Performance and Satisfaction," *Journal of Applied Psychology Monograph* 56 (1972): 75-94.

27. See Walster, Walster, and Berscheid, *Equity*, for a review of related studies.

28. Ibid.

29. J. S. Adams and W. B. Rosenbaum, "The Relationship of Worker Productivity to Cognitive Dissonance About Wage Inequities," *Journal of Applied Psychology* 46 (1962): 161-164.

30. Ibid.

31. R. P. Vecchio, "Predicting Worker Performance in Inequitable Settings," *Academy of Management Review* 7 (1982): 103-110. For recent successful applications of equity theory to wage structures and layoffs, see J. E. Martin and M. M. Peterson, "Two-Tier Wage Structures: Implications for Equity Theory," *Academy of Management Journal* 30 (1987): 297-315, and J. Brockner, J. Greenberg, A. Brockner, J. Bortz, J. Davy, and C. Carter, "Layoffs, Equity Theory, and Work Performance: Further Evidence of the Impact of Survivor Guilt," *Academy of Management Journal* 29 (1986): 373-384.

32. Adams, "Inequity."

33. Also, some people may be more concerned with fairness than others. For instance, individuals with higher levels of moral development may behave more in accordance with equity theory than others. And some people may be more sensitive to equity considerations than others. See R. C. Huseman, J. D. Hatfield, and E. W. Miles, "A New Perspective on Equity Theory: The Equity Sensitivity Construct," *Academy of Management Review* 12 (1987): 222-234, and R. P. Vecchio, "An Individual-Differences Interpretation of the Conflicting Predictions Generated by Equity Theory and Expectancy Theory," *Journal of Applied Psychology* 66 (1981): 103-110.

34. Reprinted with permission of the author and the publisher from E. A. Locke, "Purpose Without Consciousness: A Contradiction," *Psychological Reports* 25 (1969): 991-1009.

35. We will see that these performance improvements are generally in terms of quality rather than quantity.

36. This listing is drawn from E. A. Locke and G. P. Latham, *Goal Setting for Individuals, Groups, and Organizations* (Chicago: Science Research Associates, 1984).

37. This section is based primarily on reviews by R. M. Steers and L. W. Porter, "The Role of Task-Goal Attributes in Employee Performance," *Psychological Bulletin* 81 (1974): 434-452, and E. A. Locke et al., "Goal Setting and Task Performance: 1969-1980," *Psychological Bulletin* 90 (1981): 125-152. See also M. E. Tubbs, "Goal-Setting: A Meta-Analytic

Examination of the Empirical Evidence," *Journal of Applied Psychology* 71 (1986): 474-483; J. R. Hollenbeck and H. J. Klein, "Goal Commitment and the Goal-Setting Process: Problems, Prospects, and Proposals for Future Research," *Journal of Applied Psychology* 72 (1987): 212-220; and T. Matsui, T. Kakayama, and M. L. U. Onglatco, "Effects of Goals and Feedback on Performance in Groups," *Journal of Applied Psychology* 72 (1987): 407-415.

38. E. A. Locke, K. N. Shaw, L. M. Saari, and G. P. Latham, "Goal Setting and Task Performance: 1969-1980," *Psychological Bulletin* 90 (1981): 125-152.

39. J. F. Bryan and E. A. Locke, "Goal Setting as a Means of Increasing Motivation," *Journal of Applied Psychology* 51 (1967): 274-277.

40. For a series of studies relating to the role of participation in goal setting, see G. P. Latham, M. Erez, and E. A. Locke, "Resolving Scientific Disputes by the Joint Design of Crucial Experiments by the Antagonists: Application to the Erez-Latham Dispute Regarding Participation in Goal Setting," *Journal of Applied Psychology* 73 (1988): 753-772. These studies are particularly interesting since they were carried out by two researchers (Latham and Erez) who had previously reported conflicting findings on this issue, and a neutral mediator (Locke) who facilitated the design of crucial experiments to help resolve those conflicts.

41. G. P. Latham and J. J. Baldes, "The 'Practical Significance' of Locke's Theory of Goal Setting," *Journal of Applied Psychology* 60 (1975): 122-124.

42. See P. Drucker, *The Practice of Management* (New York: John Wiley & Sons, 1954); D. McGregor, *The Human Side of Enterprise* (New York: McGraw-Hill, 1960); and G. S. Odiorne, *MBO II: A System of Managerial Leadership for the 80s* (Belmont, CA: Fearon Pitman, 1979).

43. J. N. Kondrasuk, "Studies in MBO Effectiveness," *Academy of Management Review* 6 (1981): 419-430.

44. B. F. Skinner, *Contingencies of Reinforcement* (East Norwalk, CT: Appleton-Century-Crofts, 1969).

45. S. Swartz, "Why Mike Milken Stands to Qualify for Guinness Book," *Wall Street Journal* (March 31, 1989): A1.

46. W. Nord, "Beyond the Teaching Machine: The Neglected Area of Operant Conditioning in the Theory and Practice of Management," *Organizational Behavior and Human Performance* 4 (1969): 375-401.

47. W. C. Hamner and E. P. Hamner, "Behavior Modification on the Bottom Line," *Organizational Dynamics* 4 (1976): 3-21.

48. For more on cafeteria-style benefit plans and other innovative approaches, see D. C. Feldman and H. J. Arnold, *Managing Individual and Group Behavior in Organizations* (New York: McGraw-Hill, 1983).

49. For more on this issue, see G. D. Jenkins, Jr., and E. E. Lawler III, "Impact of Employee Participation in Pay Plan Development," *Organizational Behavior and Human Performance* 28 (1981): 111-128, and E. E. Lawler III, "New Approaches to Pay: Innovations That Work," *Personnel* 53, no. 5 (1976): 11-23.

50. This does not mean that money and other extrinsic rewards are not important. For a discussion of this issue, see A. P. Brief and R. J. Aldag, "The Economic Functions of Work," in *Research in Personnel and Human Resources Management*, vol. 7, ed. K. M. Rowland and G. R. Ferris (Greenwich, CT: JAI Press, 1989), 1-23.

51. This idea of matching of motivation theories to behaviors or attitudes of interest is drawn from Landy and Becker, "Motivation Theory Reconsidered."

52. This example is from "Door-to-Door Salesman Creates Needs in Pocatello, Idaho," *Wall Street Journal* (June 14, 1984): 1,19. Self-management is based largely on the work of Albert Bandura. For discussions of applications of Bandura's ideas to management, see A. P. Brief and R. J. Aldag, "The 'Self' in Work Organizations: A Conceptual Review," *Academy of Management Review* 6 (1981): 75-88, and M. E. Gist, "Self-Efficacy: Implications for Organizational Behavior and Human Resource Management," *Academy of Management Review* 12 (1987): 472-485.

53. F. Luthans and T. R. V. Davis, "Behavioral Self-Management: The Missing Link in Managerial Effectiveness," *Organizational Dynamics* 8, no. 1 (1979): 42-60.

54. C. A. Frayne and G. P. Latham, "The Application of Social Learning Theory to Employee Self-Management of Attendance," *Journal of Applied Psychology* 72 (1987): 387-392, and C. A. Frayne and G. P. Latham, "Self-Management Training for Increasing Job Attendance:

A Follow-Up and a Replication," *Academy of Management Best Paper Proceedings* (1988): 206-210.

55. For instance, see M. J. Mahoney, N. G. Moura, and T. C. Wade, "The Relative Efficacy of Self-Reward, Self-Punishment, and Self-Monitoring Techniques for Weight Loss," *Journal of Consulting and Clinical Psychology* 40 (1973): 404-407; F. H. Kanfer and J. S. Phillips, *Learning Foundations of Behavior Therapy* (New York: John Wiley & Sons, 1970); and C. S. Richards, "When Self-Control Fails: Selective Bibliography of Research on the Maintenance Problems in Self-Control Treatment Programs," *JSAS: Catalog of Selected Documents in Psychology* 8 (1976): 67-68.

56. These guidelines are drawn from F. Andrasik and J. Heimberg, "Self-Management Procedures," in *Handbook of Organizational Behavior Management*, ed. L. W. Frederiksen (New York: Wiley-Interscience, 1982). Andrasik and Heimberg go into considerably more detail on these points and provide a useful troubleshooting guide.

57. Self-monitoring is used here in the sense of checking one's own behavior, rather than as a personality variable as in Chapter 12.

58. Schemas are similar to implicit theories, discussed in Chapter 12.

59. For discussions of scripts and schemas, see D. A. Gioia and P. P. Poole, "Scripts in Organizational Behavior," *Academy of Management Review* 9, no. 3: 449-459, and R. G. Lord and M. C. Kernan, "Scripts as Determinants of Purposeful Behavior in Organizations," *Academy of Management Review* 12 (1987): 265-277.

Job Design

CHAPTER 14

After studying this chapter, you should be able to:
- Describe quality of work life, and define some of its categories.
- Discuss the benefits and problems associated with job simplification.
- Differentiate between job enlargement and job enrichment, and explain the benefits and costs of each.
- Explain the job characteristics model, and identify the core task dimensions.
- Discuss steps in implementation of job redesign.
- Identify the sorts of jobs and people for which job enrichment is likely to be successful or unsuccessful.
- Explain the social information-processing approach to job design.
- Describe flextime, job sharing, and the compressed workweek.

Jobs are central to the lives of most people. They consume a large part of our days, and often our nights. To a large extent, many of us rate our success in life on the basis of the status, pay, and other characteristics of our jobs. And others often size us up by our response to, "Tell me, what do you do?" Indeed, it is hard to imagine not working. Consider the case of $40-million-lottery winner Michael Wittkowski, described in Management in Action 1.

Albert Camus has written, "Without work, all life goes rotten. But when work is soulless, life stifles and dies." What is it about jobs that makes them important to people? What makes them exciting? Why are some soulless? What makes jobs "good" or "bad"? Does everyone want the same things from jobs? What can management do to improve jobs and increase their motivating potential?

In this chapter we will examine job design, the design of employees' tasks (recall that the issue of the design of organizations was addressed in Chapter 9). We will first look at the issue of quality of work life, in which job design figures prominently. We will then explore the merits and demerits of job specialization and consider calls for "bigger" jobs. Then, we will discuss job enrichment. Next, we will consider an approach to job design that emphasizes social cues. Finally, we will examine additional approaches to job redesign, focusing on work schedules.

THE QUALITY OF WORK LIFE

The recent calls for job redesign reflect the growing emphasis on the **quality of work life**. Quality of work life is an elusive term, used in many ways. To some, it means a "humane" work environment or increased worker participation in decision making or the full use and development of human capacities. To others, it means making working conditions more conducive to good health and even distributing the firm's income and other resources more fairly. Richard Walton provided the following list of categories for quality of work life:[1]

- Adequate and fair compensation
- Safe and healthy environment
- Development of human capacities
- Growth and security—the opportunity to maintain and expand capabilities, to use those capabilities in future work assignments, and to advance in organizational or career terms
- Social integration—the opportunity to achieve personal identity and self-esteem
- Constitutionalism—the degree to which a worker has rights and can protect those rights
- The total life space—the extent to which a person's work has a balanced role in his or her life, not demanding so much time, effort, or other inputs as to severely disrupt leisure and family time
- Social relevance—the degree to which the worker views what the organization does as socially responsible and, therefore, sees his or her work as being of social value

What these categories have in common is the intent to make organizations better places to work, more comfortable and satisfying. Because the na-

A 28-year-old Chicago man became North America's biggest lottery winner when he stepped up to claim a fat $40-million prize in the Illinois State Lottery.

MANAGEMENT IN ACTION 1
CHICAGO MAN WINS $40-MILLION LOTTERY

Michael E. Wittkowski, a printer for Deluxe Check Printers, Inc., his father, and seven other family members appeared at a jammed news conference yes-

terday, ending speculation over who would claim the huge prize.

The lottery will invest $15,093,125 in an annuity to pay Mr. Wittkowski $2 million a year, before taxes, for the next 20 years.

The winner, smiling broadly, said he hadn't any special plans for the money except to pay some bills and hasn't any intention of quitting his job. "If I quit," he said, "all I have to do is sit around and count my money."

Source: Reprinted by permission of *The Wall Street Journal*, © Dow Jones & Company, Inc. (September 4, 1984). All Rights Reserved Worldwide.

ture of jobs is so central to work life, calls for job redesign are common among those concerned with the quality of work life.

THE CASE FOR SPECIALIZATION

As discussed in Chapter 2, Frederick Taylor introduced scientific management. According to scientific management, the "one best way" to perform a job should be found.[2] That "one best way" usually results in job simplification, with each worker performing the same few activities over and over. Advantages cited for specialization include the following:

- The worker should be better able to perform the task and should find it to be easier.
- Time is not lost moving from one piece of machinery to another.
- The use of specialized machinery is encouraged.
- Replacement of employees who are absent or who leave the organization is easier since the job is simpler and easier to learn.
- Especially where assembly lines are used, the worker will adjust to the required pace and be drawn along by "traction."

Scientific management was credited with some notable successes. For instance, application of its principles in one case increased the number of bricks laid per worker-hour from 120 to 350. Further, scientific management permitted the worker to maximize performance by focusing on a narrow range of activities. If the worker was paid on a piece-rate basis, this would result in higher pay. As a result, scientific management was widely adopted in the United States and elsewhere.

Today, however, Taylor is often criticized for his emphasis on efficiency at the possible expense of employee satisfaction. He did consider the human element, but many of his views now seem inhumane. He wrote, for instance, that the kind of person who made a good pig-iron handler was "of the type of the ox." Whether or not criticisms of Taylor are valid, it does seem that reducing jobs to a simplified routine may have some unforeseen results. For instance, it may lead to boredom, dissatisfaction, and other negative outcomes.

There is little doubt that many jobs are quite boring. Figure 14–1 presents boredom ratings for a variety of jobs.

Criticisms of specialization have led to demands for larger, more challenging jobs. A Saab advertisement which appeared in the 1970s, shown in Figure 14–2, is one reflection of those demands. Case 4–2 illustrates a more recent automaker's response to concerns about specialization.

In many companies, the role of the worker is now much broader than in the past. For example, consider the changes presented in Management in Action 2.

JOB SIZE

If we believe "small" jobs are demeaning and unsatisfying to workers, a logical question is how we can make jobs larger. There are at least two major dimensions to job size. They are job depth and job scope, or range.

Job depth refers to the degree to which employees can influence their work environments and carry out planning and control functions. **Job scope** is the number of different activities the worker performs, regardless of their content. Increases in job depth are usually called **job enrichment**; increases in job scope are referred to as **job enlargement**. Though most job changes are likely to influence both depth and scope, they are separate dimensions and can be independently changed. Figure 14–3 shows jobs differing in their levels of job depth and scope.

Benefits of Increased Scope

Among the suggested advantages of increases in scope are the following:[3]

- There should be less fatigue of particular muscles since a greater variety of muscles may be used.
- Since the employee will complete a larger part of the task, there may be more of a feeling of accomplishment.
- The employee may exercise a greater variety of skills.

Jobs differ dramatically in their boredom levels. Here is a listing of some of the more and less boring jobs, according to a study conducted by researchers at the University of Michigan. An average boredom rating is 100.

FIGURE 14–1
Job Boredom Ratings

Job	Boredom Rating
Assembler (work paced by machine)	207
Forklift truck driver	170
Monitor of continuous-flow goods	122
Accountant	107
Electronic technician	87
Blue-collar supervisor	85
Administrator	66
Air-traffic controller (small airport)	51

Source: Institute for Social Research, University of Michigan.

FIGURE 14–2
*A 1970s Advertisement
Reflecting Concerns
About Specialization*

Bored people build bad cars. That's why we're doing away with the assembly line.

Working on an assembly line is monotonous. And boring. And after a while, some people begin not to care about their jobs anymore. So the quality of the product often suffers.

That's why, at Saab, we're replacing the assembly line with assembly teams. Groups

of just three or four people who are responsible for a particular assembly process from start to finish.

Each team makes its own decisions about who does what and when. And each team member can even do the entire assembly singlehandedly. The result: people are more involved. They care more. So there's less absenteeism, less turnover. And we have more experienced people on the job.

We're building our new 2-liter engines this way. And the doors to our Saab 99. And we're planning to use this same system to build other parts of our car as well.

It's a slower, more costly system, but we realize that the best machines and materials in the world don't mean a thing, if the person building the car doesn't care.

Saab. It's what a car should be.

Photo courtesy of Saab-Scania of America, Inc.

• Large increases in scope may enhance managerial flexibility. For instance, if (as in the Saab ad) a company uses assembly teams rather than assembly lines, it can shut down a small number of the benches used by assembly teams rather than the entire line.

We should note that some of the presumed advantages of scope confound scope with depth. For instance, the assembly teams described in Figure 14–2 usually provide employees with more things to do and also with increased opportunities for planning and control.

The old picture of bosses giving orders and employees simply following them is changing at many companies. Employees at A&P's Super Fresh Food

Markets in Philadelphia have had a hand in advertising, inventory, and operating decisions. Workers at a Bethlehem Steel Corporation plant in Johnstown, Pa., recommended improvements in the steel wire they produce and helped the firm keep a customer. At a Midwest Steel plant in Portage, Ind., a labor-management participation team started a publicity campaign to persuade local soft-drink companies to switch from aluminum cans to tin cans, which the company produces.

Partly in return for wage and other concessions, workers in ailing industries are winning greater roles in corporate decision making. For badly needed wage concessions, Chrysler Corporation in 1980 granted Douglas A. Fraser, then head of the United Auto

Workers, a seat on its board of directors and gave him access to sensitive financial information. More and more unions are demanding what were traditionally management rights. Many people now consider this to be a basic realignment of labor-management relations.

To some, this change is seen as a scary thing, handcuffing management. For instance, Ford Motor Company in 1982 had to agree to a 24-month prohibition against plant closings caused by work being contracted out to either foreign or nonunion domestic plants. Several airlines have gained needed concessions only by accepting agreements barring them from creating nonunion subsidiaries.

Others argue that these changes are simply part of a healthy trend toward greater worker participation. That participation may improve workers' attitudes toward their companies and their jobs. By feeling they have more of a hand in the destiny of the company, employees may take greater pride in their work and improve the competitive strength of their firms.

Benefits of Increased Depth

The presumed benefits of increased depth are primarily psychological. For instance, Chris Argyris has suggested that since small, routine jobs are frustrating to the drives of "mature" individuals, they may result in use of a variety

FIGURE 14–3
Jobs Varying in Depth and/or Scope

Source: From *Managerial Process and Organizational Behavior* by A. C. Filley, R. J. House, and S. Kerr. Copyright © 1976 by Scott, Foresman and Company. Reprinted by permission.

Job depth is increased when employees are given a problem to work out on their own.

of defense mechanisms.[4] These **defense mechanisms** are ways in which the employee may try to reduce the tensions caused by frustration. They might involve physically leaving the source of frustration (such as through absenteeism or turnover), mentally leaving (through apathy or daydreaming), or striking back (perhaps by slowing down on the job or by making negative comments about the company). As shown in Figure 14–4, Argyris has argued that the typical firm's response to such defense mechanisms is to make jobs even more specialized, to tighten up on rules, and to emphasize authority relationships. These actions further frustrate maturity drives, and a self-reinforcing cycle occurs. Argyris reasons that to break out of that cycle, it is necessary to treat employees as mature individuals. Giving them more opportunity for planning and control is one step in that direction.

M. Scott Myers has made similar arguments.[5] Myers said the assumption underlying work simplification is that there are two groups of workers. One group, responsible and highly motivated, is known as managers. The other, irresponsible and in need of close supervision, is called workers. Because of these assumed differences, companies call on managers to plan, direct, and control. They expect workers simply to carry out orders. Myers argues that companies must break down this artificial dichotomy and "make every employee a manager." This would involve turning many planning and control functions over to workers. That is, it would require enriching their jobs.

THE JOB CHARACTERISTICS MODEL

If we want to redesign jobs, we must know which job dimensions are important to employees. In particular, before we can undertake job enrichment, we must determine the characteristics of an enriched job.

Arthur Turner and Paul Lawrence tried to identify a set of job attributes that would influence employees' responses.[6] Building on that work, J. Richard Hackman and Edward Lawler and later Hackman and Greg Oldham refined

FIGURE 14–4
The Argyris Maturity Drive Frustration Cycle

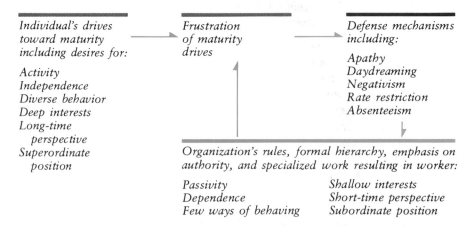

Source: Based on *Integrating the Individual and the Organization* by Chris Argyris. Copyright © 1964 by John Wiley & Sons, Inc. Reprinted by permission of John Wiley & Sons, Inc.

what is known as the **job characteristics model** of job design.[7] As presented by Hackman and Oldham, the job characteristics model describes jobs as having five core task dimensions and two interpersonal dimensions.[8]

Core Task Dimensions

The five **core task dimensions** are characteristics of the job itself that are believed to be key influences on employee motivation. They include the following:

- *Skill variety*. The degree to which the job requires employees to perform a wide range of operations in their work and/or the degree to which employees must use a variety of equipment and procedures in their work.
- *Autonomy*. The extent to which employees have a major say in scheduling their work, selecting the equipment they will use, and deciding on procedures they will follow.
- *Task identity*. The extent to which employees do an entire piece of work and can clearly identify the result of their efforts.
- *Task significance*. The extent to which the job has a strong impact on the lives and work of other people.
- *Feedback*. The degree to which employees receive information while they are working that reveals how well they are performing on the job.

Interpersonal Dimensions

The two **interpersonal dimensions** are job characteristics that influence the degree to which employees engage in relationships with others on the job. They include the following:

- *Dealing with others*. The degree to which a job requires employees to deal with other people (customers, other company employees, or both) to complete their work.
- *Friendship opportunities*. The degree to which a job allows employees to talk with one another on the job and to establish informal relationships with other employees at work.

Giving employees opportunities to deal with other people to complete their work is a means of job enrichment.

Figure 14–5 presents sample items from each of the core task dimensions. Can you match each item to the appropriate dimension?

Hackman and Oldham see the core task dimensions as impacting on three **critical psychological states**: experienced meaningfulness of work, experienced responsibility for work outcomes, and knowledge of the actual results of work activities. Further, they have argued that perceptions of the core task dimensions fit together, as shown in Figure 14–6, to yield the **motivating potential score** of the job. This model implies that if any of the three components is very low, overall motivating potential of the task will be low. Further, as long as any of the three remains at very low levels, increases in the others will do little to improve overall motivating potential.

Research on the Job Characteristics Model

The job characteristics approach has dominated recent research into job design. Questions have been raised concerning whether all employees actually view their jobs on these specific dimensions.[9] It does seem, however, that the dimensions may serve as useful guides for understanding reactions to jobs and for planning redesign strategies.

Studies show that perceptions of the core task dimensions are related to job satisfaction, job involvement, organizational commitment, and other favorable attitudes. However, these perceptions are usually not related in any consistent way to performance.[10] Since employees on enriched jobs typically get the benefits of enrichment simply by carrying out the task, regardless of their performance levels, we would expect the core task dimension percep-

FIGURE 14–5

Selected Items to Measure Task Dimensions

Listed below are several statements that may (or may not) describe your job. You are to indicate the degree to which each statement is an accurate description of the job on which you work. Do this by writing the appropriate number in the left-hand margin, based on the scale below.

Please make your descriptions as objectively and factually accurate as possible, without regard for whether you like or dislike your job.

1	2	3	4	5	6	7
Very untrue of the job	Mostly untrue of the job	Slightly untrue of the job	Uncertain	Slightly true of the job	Moderately true of the job	Very true of the job

1. The job requires me to use a variety of complex or high-level skills.
2. The job gives me considerable opportunity for independence and freedom in how I do the work.
3. The job provides me with the chance to finish completely the pieces of work I begin.
4. Just doing the work required by the job provides many chances for me to figure out how well I'm doing.
5. The job is one where a lot of other people can be affected by how well the work gets done.

Source: J. Richard Hackman and Greg Oldham, *Work Redesign*, © 1980, Addison-Wesley Publishing Co., Inc., Reading, MA. Reprinted with permission of the publisher.

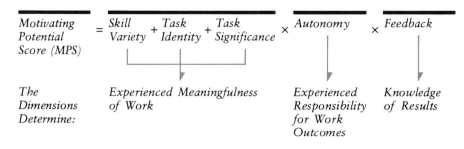

Source: Adapted from J. Richard Hackman and Greg Oldham, *Work Redesign*, © 1980, Addison-Wesley Publishing Co., Inc., Reading, MA. Reprinted with permission of the publisher.

FIGURE 14–6
Determining a Job's Motivating Potential Score

tions to translate into increased performance only when persistence on the task is important.[11]

Research shows that the combinatory model proposed by Hackman and Oldham (in which a very low level on one dimension would neutralize the impact of changes in other dimensions) is probably not valid. That is, task dimension perceptions seem to combine in an additive (rather than multiplicative) fashion to influence reactions.[12] This is a welcome finding since it suggests that improvements on any of the dimensions may influence outcomes.[13]

The Focus on Perceptions

We must keep in mind that the job characteristics approach focuses on employee perceptions of task characteristics. This is appropriate since people behave on the basis of their perceptions. However, many things may affect perceptions. For instance, Eugene Stone asked students to perform a simple assembly task.[14] The task was the same for all students, but the way they perceived the task depended on their ages and personalities. Older students felt the task offered more skill variety and feedback but less task identity than did younger students. In general, we might expect that an employee with considerable experience and training on a task would see it very differently than a rookie would.[15]

This makes job design more difficult. It is not enough to make objective changes in feedback, skill variety, or the other task dimensions. We must also discover how those objective changes translate into perceptions. Alternatively, as we'll see a bit later, it may even be possible to change perceptions without altering objective task characteristics.

IMPLEMENTING JOB ENRICHMENT

Hackman and Oldham have proposed a set of job changes that might influence the core task dimensions.[16] Referred to as implementing principles, these changes—and their possible effects on core job characteristics—are shown and explained in Figure 14–7.

These principles may be useful as suggestions for how companies can change jobs to increase levels of the core task dimensions. However, their use must take place as part of a systematic assessment of the particular situation.

FIGURE 14–7
Implementing Principles

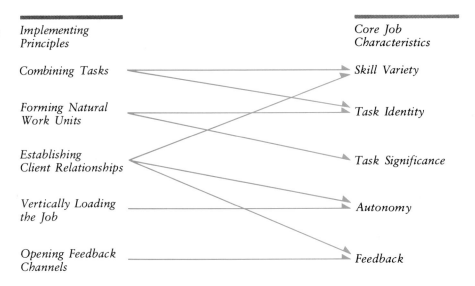

Where:

Combining tasks involves "putting together" simplified jobs to make a larger job.

Forming natural work units means arranging the items of work done by employees into meaningful, logical groups. For instance, tasks might be grouped by customers, geography, or type of business.

Establishing client relationships involves putting employees in direct contact with the "clients" or recipients of the work and giving them responsibility for dealing with those clients.

Vertically loading the job means pushing down to the employee responsibility and authority that were formerly held at higher levels.

Opening feedback channels involves creating conditions for employees to directly learn how they are doing, from the job itself.

Source: © 1975 by the Regents of the University of California. Adapted by permission from the *California Management Review*, Vol. 17, no. 4, p. 62. By permission of The Regents.

For instance, if job enrichment is to be successful, it must fit with the organization's employees, practices, structure, and technology.

The Conditions for Successful Redesign

A family of jobs should be considered for redesign if:[17]

- The employees perceive their jobs to be deficient in the core task dimensions. It is important to stress here that worker perceptions, not just the assumptions of management or consultants, are crucial.
- Employees are fairly well satisfied with pay, fringe benefits, and working conditions. If workers are unhappy with these factors, they are likely to resent and resist job redesign.
- The current structure and technology of the unit where the jobs are housed are hospitable to enriched jobs. If the overall organization has a

mechanistic structure or long-linked technology, redesign attempts may be expensive and hard to implement. They are also likely to ultimately fail.

- Employees want the sorts of things—variety, autonomy, feedback, and so on—that enriched jobs provide.

Steps in Implementation

If conditions seem appropriate for redesign, a job-redesign task force made up of management and labor representatives should proceed through the following steps:

1. Identification of the actual activities which now make up the family of jobs.
2. Identification of the specific relationships between those activities and the job incumbents' perceptions of salient task attributes (such as variety, autonomy, task identity, feedback, and task significance).
3. Specification of a detailed job-redesign intervention derived from study of the job activities–task attribute linkages detected in Step 2.
4. Evaluation of the proposed intervention through experiments in selected parts of the organization.
5. If evaluation is favorable, diffusion of the intervention throughout the family of jobs.

Figure 14–8 summarizes these conditions and steps.

WHO WANTS ENRICHED JOBS?

You probably know some people who would like their jobs to offer more challenge, variety, and responsibility and others who might not care. Still others might say, "If you're going to give me all the decision-making responsibility of my boss, give me my boss's pay. And if you want me to do more things, you'd better be ready to pay me even more." Consider the following:

Anyone who has read Studs Terkel's series of interviews, Working *(1974), has to be struck by the different ways in which people view their work in terms of the aspects of the work they consider important and of their reactions to job characteristics. A former quiz kid who has gone through a succession of jobs likes his current work in a greenhouse because his mind is at ease all day long. Conversely, a garbage collector keeps his mind occupied by analyzing how families live on the basis of what they throw out. Some workers are willing to put up with monotonous jobs in order to make money to do other things. A cab driver says his work is just a way to get enough money to buy a car wash and, ultimately, buy a schooner he'll charter in the West Indies. Other workers stress job ease. A fashion model feels guilty because she is spending her life doing something she doesn't like. "It's not very fulfilling," she says, ". . . but I'm lazy, I admit it. It's an easier thing to do" (p. 54). Still others find a variety of ways to make their jobs more meaningful. An elevator starter has assumed security functions and acts as an information source, giving room numbers. A steelworker sometimes deliberately dents his work as a way of making an imprint that he can recognize as his own.*[18]*

FIGURE 14–8
Stages in Job Redesign

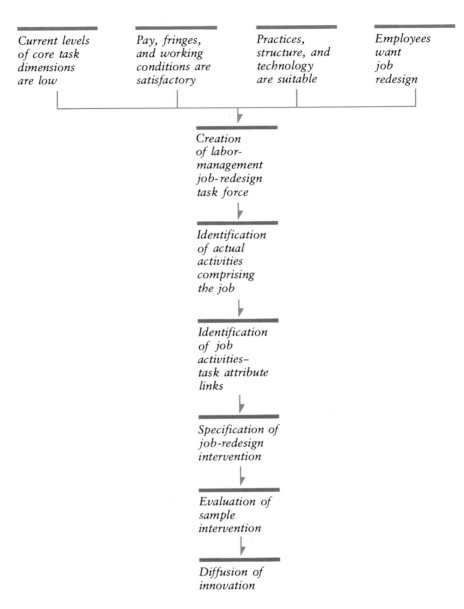

Terkel's examples highlight the need to determine what particular workers or sets of workers may want from their jobs. Who wants enriched jobs and who doesn't? In seeking answers to this question, researchers have struck out in several directions. They have examined whether the employees grew up in urban or rural areas, their degree of adherence to the Protestant work ethic, and their age, sex, and race.[19] Each of these attempts has come up short, failing to identify with any degree of consistency who would be likely to respond positively or negatively to job enrichment.[20]

A more promising measure is what has been labeled **higher order need strength (HONS)**. This is basically the degree to which an individual wants such things as challenge and responsibility, a topic we explored in Chapter 13. While most employees respond positively to high levels of the core task dimensions, those with strong HONS react most favorably.

*People differ widely in
what they want from
their jobs.*

THE CASE AGAINST JOB ENRICHMENT

Job enrichment is not a panacea. If workers don't want enriched jobs, if pay
and working conditions are poor, or if the firm's technology or structure is
inappropriate, job enrichment may be infeasible or unsuccessful. Several
other criticisms of job enrichment have been raised.[21] For instance, it has
been argued that work speedups, rather than "the blue-collar blues," may be
the real cause of much worker dissatisfaction. Also, some have argued that
there is only so much to be done; if a company gives some workers more challenge and responsibility, it must make the jobs of others more trivial. Further,
employees whose jobs are enriched may demand more pay because of the
greater skill requirements of the altered jobs. In fact, the job redesign may automatically lead to pay increases if the firm's reward system ties pay to such
skill requirements.[22]

These criticisms may each contain a grain of truth. At the very least, they
raise some issues companies should keep in mind when contemplating a job
enrichment program. Even when properly done, job enrichment may be time-
consuming and expensive. It should not be taken lightly.

DOONESBURY   **by Garry Trudeau**

Greg R. Oldham (Ph.D., Yale University) is IBE Distinguished Professor of Business Administration and Professor of Labor and Industrial Relations at the University of Illinois at Urbana-Champaign. He is author of numerous articles concerned with the design of work and employee motivation and is co-author (with J. Richard Hackman) of Work Redesign. Professor Oldham is a fellow of the American Psychological Association and a member of the Academy of Management. He is past chair of the Organizational Behavior Division of the Academy of Management and has served as a consultant to numerous organizations.

Q: You were one of the developers of the now-dominant Job Characteristics Approach to job design. Would you now recommend any extensions or revisions of the approach?

A: I still believe that the core job characteristics we identified are those that prompt the internal work motivation of employees. However, one potential modification of the Job Characteristics Model itself involves the Motivating Potential Score (MPS) that we proposed for combining the job characteristics into an index that reflects a job's overall potential to foster internal motivation. Recent studies show that it is better to simply add up the scores of the five job characteristics, rather than to use the more complex MPS formula. Also, in the 1980 version of the Job Characteristics Theory we argued that employees should be satisfied with the context of their work if they are to respond positively to jobs high on the five core characteristics. Perhaps we overemphasized the importance of context satisfactions. Recent studies have shown that employees who are dissatisfied with their work context respond as positively to well-designed jobs as employees who are satisfied with the context. Finally, we argued that employees with high Growth Need Strength (GNS) are most likely to respond positively to well-designed jobs and that GNS is a relatively stable characteristic of people. While most research indicates that high-GNS employees are more responsive to jobs high on the five core characteristics, there is now research which suggests that employees' needs may *change* or adjust to meet the demands of the situation. Thus, individuals may actually become more "growth oriented" when they are confronted with the demands of a complex, challenging job.

Q: How do you evaluate the social information-processing approach?

A: I think the idea that employees' job perceptions and attitudes might be influenced by "informational cues" about the job provided by supervisors and co-workers probably has some merit. However, I am not yet convinced that informational cues have long-lasting or permanent effects on employees' job perceptions. My best guess is that the effects of these cues are relatively short term—especially when compared to the effects of the structural changes produced by work redesign. I would also like to see a more thorough examination of the conditions under which informational cues have their most (and least) substantial effects. Individuals who have relatively little experience with a job may be more responsive to cues than employees with substantial job experience. And it may be that informational cues from certain sources (such as supervisors or managers) will have stronger effects than those from co-workers, colleagues, or subordinates.

Q: What new developments do you see in job design?

A: One promising new research development examines the influences of jobs on people, and of people on their jobs. This line of research may help us better understand the conditions under which individuals' personal characteristics are shaped by jobs, as well as the conditions that permit individuals to modify their jobs. Also of interest is research on the effects of jobs on the health and well-being of employees. Important work is now being conducted that examines the contribution of job design to employee reactions such as stress and burnout. A third interesting area of research tries to identify features of the organizational context (such as the physical layout and technology) that are appropriate for various job designs. This research could help us to design jobs that "fit" the contexts of organizations. Finally, in the area of team job design, research focusing on the role of group processes, the organizational context, and leadership on team effectiveness has real promise.

THE SOCIAL INFORMATION-PROCESSING APPROACH

A recently popular view of job design relies on the **social information-processing approach**. This approach says that socially provided information, such as comments from peers or supervisors, plays a major role in determining how people perceive jobs and respond to them. That is, workers may experience a "socially constructed reality."[23] For instance, if new employees hear their co-workers saying the job provides a lot of freedom, they are likely to perceive it as offering autonomy. In fact, some lab experiments have shown that socially provided information, such as written job descriptions and verbal cues, may have as much influence on worker perceptions of the job and their affective responses as do the objective characteristics of the job.[24]

In one field experiment, Ricky Griffin changed objective job characteristics in ways that were intended to increase variety, autonomy, feedback, and task identity.[25] At the same time social information was also manipulated by having supervisors make comments concerning these task dimensions. Each supervisor's goal was to give five such cues each day. Both objective changes and social information were found to influence employee perceptions of the job and affective reactions. However, while objective changes had a significant impact on productivity, social cues did not.

This social information-processing approach is appealing, and some research—especially that using laboratory experiments—is supportive. However, there are some serious questions about generalizing from laboratory results to the work setting. First, the studies have generally used students or other individuals who knew nothing about the jobs to which they were assigned. In the absence of other information, it is not surprising that subjects paid attention to social cues. Second, in order to sort out the roles of objective task characteristics and social cues, experiments have typically manipulated social cues so that they were different from the objective characteristics. In an actual job setting, social cues probably reflect whether a job really is boring or challenging, easy or difficult. That is, social cues may largely be determined in a work setting by objective characteristics, so the objective characteristics are still important. Third, while naive individuals may be "fooled" by social cues for the duration of an experiment, they are unlikely to continue to be fooled for a month, let alone 20 years.[26]

The bottom line here is that in real-world situations, workers may use social cues to quickly learn aspects of the job, but over time the objective characteristics of the job probably become more important. For this reason, the job characteristics and social information-processing approaches can be viewed as complements rather than competitors.[27] That is, both social cues and objective task characteristics may play important roles, though perhaps at different times. Thus, the social information-processing approach gives managers one more way to influence employee task perceptions and subsequent responses, especially for employees who are new on a task.

OTHER JOB CHANGES

There are several other approaches to changing jobs. Three which seem to have promise are flextime, job sharing, and the compressed workweek. Each represents a departure from traditional work schedules.

One of the advantages of flextime is avoiding rush-hour traffic.

Flextime

The **flextime** approach requires employees to work a certain number of hours during a core work period in the middle of the day ("coretime"). However, the employees are free to decide when they want to come to work and when they want to leave ("flexband"). Figure 14–9 shows a typical flextime schedule. Under flextime, one employee may decide to arrive at work at 6:00 in the morning and leave at 3:00 in the afternoon. Another might arrive at 10:00 in the morning and leave at 7:00 in the evening. In 1989, over 9 million full-time wage employees (13 percent) had flexible schedules, and flextime was offered by about one-third of all U.S. firms.[28] This percentage varies widely, ranging as high as 30 percent in some occupations, such as computer scientist. Further, the percentage is higher for part-time workers.[29]

Flextime reduces the stress of getting to work during busy rush hours, gives a sense of freedom, and lets employees work during their "best" hours. It may be especially welcome for young families trying to juggle child-rearing responsibilities with work schedules.

Not surprisingly, most employees seem to like flextime. For instance, one recent experiment carried out in a Midwestern utility found that satisfaction levels of an experimental flextime group, initially similar to those of members of a comparison group, became much higher after implementation of flextime. Further, this difference in satisfaction was still seen six months after the change.[30] One summary of flextime studies showed that worker support for adoption or continuation of flextime across nine samples of workers ranged from 80 percent to 100 percent.[31]

The few studies dealing with the impact of flextime on performance have concluded that flextime sometimes helps and in any case doesn't seem to hurt.[32] However, flextime productivity gains may be due to the Hawthorne effect.[33] That is, workers have been singled out to participate in the flextime experiments and may behave differently as a result.

Not all jobs are suitable for flextime. For instance, if teamwork is important, flextime may cause coordination problems. Flextime may also result in increased costs for administration and overhead, such as for heating and air conditioning, because of the expanded length of the workday.

Job Sharing

Job sharing, or **worksharing**, is a simple idea, but it can cause a major re-thinking of work roles. With job sharing, two or more people share a single job. For instance, Anita may work at a job in the morning and Carlos may take over the same job in the afternoon. Job sharing is popular with couples, enabling a husband and wife to each work half a day while taking turns with housekeeping and child-rearing responsibilities at home.

Job sharing may provide considerable flexibility for both workers and organizations. In the 1982 recession, Motorola wanted to cut production at its

FIGURE 14–9
A Typical Flextime Schedule

6:30 A.M.	10:30 A.M.	3:00 P.M.	6:00 P.M.
Flexible	*Core*		*Flexible*

9,000-employee Phoenix plant without laying off workers. Layoffs would have created hardships for many employees. They also would have meant high costs for training and recall when it was time to resume full production. Motorola chose job sharing as its approach for cutting production. In so doing, it cut costs by $1.5 million and saved more than a thousand jobs.[34] A 1987 survey by the Bureau of Labor Statistics found that 15.5 percent of firms with 10 or more employees provide opportunities for job sharing.[35]

Compressed Workweek

In the United States, most workers get up Monday mornings facing five working days. However, an increasing number of employees now work ten hours a day for four days, or what is called **4/40**. In some cases, companies stagger work schedules so that they can operate for a full five days. In others, the firm is open only four days a week, saving on overhead costs. From 1973 to 1985 employment in compressed workweeks grew almost five times as fast as total employment.[36]

The 4/40 workweek gives workers a three-day weekend, with the opportunity for longer vacations or even a second job. Having a larger block of free time could serve to increase worker satisfaction and reduce absenteeism and tardiness. However, workers are more likely to be fatigued by the end of a ten-hour day, and both accidents and poor performance could result. The company may also find it difficult to coordinate with firms that are working traditional five-day schedules.

Studies on the 4/40 workweek are sparse. Worker reactions to 4/40 are usually positive, but acceptance is not uniform among workers.[37] Support is greatest from younger workers with low-level jobs and those who feel the change has upgraded their status and responsibility.[38] One study which examined the impact of 4/40 on productivity showed short-run gains which disappeared about two years later.[39] As with flextime, the Hawthorne effect may be playing a role.[40]

IMPLICATIONS FOR MANAGEMENT

As a manager, you will be concerned with such goals as ensuring that products and services are of acceptable quality, that costs of absenteeism and turnover are low, and that levels of employee satisfaction and motivation are high. Your job-design efforts may help to achieve each of those goals.

Your actions as a manager will, to a large extent, define the jobs of your subordinates and others. By the way you supervise and assign tasks, you will be able to influence directly such key task elements as feedback, autonomy, and task significance. In addition, you may be in a position to carry out or push for major changes such as job enrichment, flextime, job sharing, and the compressed workweek.

Based on the information in this chapter, you know that such job changes offer various benefits, but they may prove difficult, expensive, or ill advised. You will have to decide whether subordinates want the changes, whether the situation is appropriate for redesign, and whether benefits are likely to outweigh costs. In making these decisions, you may have to consider current levels of the core task dimensions, adequacy of pay and working conditions, the structure and technology of the firm, and employee desires.

If you decide that job enrichment is a desirable approach, you will face the challenging task of actually changing your subordinates' perceptions of their jobs. A key lesson of this chapter is "Don't assume." Perceptions of the job are complex and sometimes surprising. To redesign jobs properly to change perceptions in desirable ways, it will be necessary to get employee inputs and to carry out a systematic redesign effort involving study, experimentation, and diffusion. You may also be able to use social cues, such as comments or literature about the job, to further influence worker perceptions.

Implementation of flextime, job sharing, or the compressed workweek is usually more straightforward than job enrichment, though problems can certainly occur. Employees have usually responded favorably to each of these innovative approaches, and the approaches seem well suited to reducing levels of employee stress. Nevertheless, you should use them cautiously. In each case, evidence concerning hard organizational outcomes is sparse, and some jobs are clearly not suited to the approaches. Your job as a manager will be to decide whether the very real benefits to employees and the potential benefits to the firm justify the increased administrative costs and coordination problems that will probably ensue.

There are few panaceas in management, and job design is no exception. It does offer the promise of enhancing the quality of work life while influencing organizational outcomes, but it demands care and restraint. As in any new or volatile area of management, it will be important that you update your knowledge on a regular basis. There will certainly be exciting new developments in job design in the coming decades.

KEY TERMS AND CONCEPTS

core task dimensions	job depth
critical psychological states	job enlargement
defense mechanisms	job enrichment
flextime	job scope
4/40	job sharing or worksharing
higher order need strength (HONS)	motivating potential score
interpersonal dimensions	quality of work life
job characteristics model	social information-processing approach

QUESTIONS FOR REVIEW AND DISCUSSION

1. Albert Camus was quoted in this chapter as stating, "Without work, all life goes rotten. But when work is soulless, life stifles and dies." Do you share this view? Why or why not?

2. What are four quality-of-work-life categories? Which of the categories do you feel is most important? Least important? Which do you feel the firm has a responsibility to improve?

3. Give four benefits of specialization. Give three problems associated with simplified, routine jobs.

4. The world is still full of boring jobs. In view of the problems associated with such jobs, why do you think they continue to exist? Try to think of some reasons that go beyond simple economics.

5. Chris Argyris argues that the typical firm responds to employees' frustrations with small, routine jobs by increasing specialization, tightening up on rules, and emphasizing authority relationships. Do you feel this is a fair view of how firms treat employees? Why or why not?

6. Write a one- or two-paragraph description of your ideal job. Which of the core task dimensions and interpersonal dimensions do you want in that description?

7. What are the underlying assumptions of the job characteristics model? Of the social information-processing approach? Which of those views do you believe is most valid? Why?

8. Some people feel that all jobs should be enriched, and that people could then "grow into" their enriched jobs. Others argue that if people say they don't want additional challenge and responsibility, it is unfair and paternalistic to enrich their jobs. Which view do you accept? Why?

9. Describe flextime, job sharing, and the compressed workweek. In view of the potential benefits of these approaches, why do you think many firms have not adopted them? Try to specify conditions under which each would not be suitable.

CASES

14–1 RIDING THE PRODUCT THROUGH THE SOUTH BRONX

When Robert Felts's supervisor at Bethlehem Steel Corp. asked him to visit a customer, the veteran line operator jumped at the chance. But there was one problem: The client was in East Texas, and Mr. Felts had to fly for the first time in his life. "I didn't like that. And they put me on four planes to get me there," he recalls with a shudder.

Mr. Felts's adjustment is only a small part of a general upheaval in traditional management-labor roles in the country's basic industries. Increasingly, management is turning to hourly workers for help with problems formerly handled only by field engineers and select executives. Employees like Mr. Felts are calling on customers and, in some instances, even visiting foreign competitors to determine firsthand how their own products stack up.

Whether the concept is called "employee involvement" or "worker education," the goals are the same: to improve quality, heighten competitive verve, and open a new channel for client relations. An Aluminum Co. of America senior executive says, "It's useless to ask employees to do a better job if they aren't empowered to take steps toward that goal."

Jobs are becoming so specialized that decisions about products often have to be made closer to the work area. Thus, more companies are ensuring that certain hourly employees understand how their products or services are viewed by customers or compare with those of competitors.

Workers are sometimes sent as far afield as Japan. Such a trip made by Clay Adams, a machine operator at a Westinghouse Electric Corp. turbine plant, left him with the impression that "the Japanese aren't going to slack up."

Westinghouse recently sent 30 hourly workers who produced subway generating equipment to New York to appraise their workmanship on the city's transit system and to underscore the need for reliability. "There's a difference between putting wires into a black box and riding the product through the South Bronx," contends Jack Geikler, general manager of Westinghouse's transportation business unit near Pittsburgh.

The changes are difficult for both management and labor. While management delayed bringing wage earners into the bigger picture, workers and their unions were initially suspicious of dropping an adversarial role. A mill supervisor at Bethlehem Steel explains that many workers who agreed to visit major customers were hounded during their shifts by co-workers who claimed they were "turncoats" to labor's cause.

At Bethlehem Steel's facility at Sparrows Point, Maryland, general manager John G. Roberts is largely credited with starting the employee visitation program. "Management still has to make the tough economic decisions. But they are easier to make when employees understand the issue and also trust management," he says.

Source: Reprinted by permission of *The Wall Street Journal* © Dow Jones & Company, Inc. (December 12, 1984). All Rights Reserved Worldwide.

1. Which of the core task dimensions are likely to be altered by "employee involvement" of the sorts discussed in this case?
2. What are probable positive consequences of such employee involvement? Possible negative consequences?
3. As an employee of Bethlehem Steel Co. who is participating in the visitation program, how would you respond if accused by co-workers of being a "turncoat" to labor's cause?

14–2 THE DEATH OF THE ASSEMBLY LINE?

Volvo's new, worker-designed assembly plant in Uddevalla, Sweden, looks like a great postmodernist tin barn. At full capacity, it can produce 80,000 of the company's top-end 700 Series cars a year. If Uddevalla seems quiet for an auto plant, it is because there are almost no machines; the plant looks like the service area of a huge car dealership.

In full production since early 1989, the plant employs teams of 7 to 10 hourly workers. Each team works in one area and assembles a complete car in about two hours. Team members are trained to handle all assembly jobs and work an average of three hours before repeating the same task. This avoids the short work cycle times of conventional assembly lines and the resulting boredom, inattention, poor quality, and high absenteeism.

By most measures, Volvo is a notable success. Its sales totaled $16.1 billion in 1988, a 50 percent increase since 1983, and operating profits totaled $1.2 billion. Volvo has no net debt and has a healthy return on equity of over 15 percent. But the company knows it must streamline and internationalize to meet continuing challenges. And it has a problem that haunts all Swedish manufacturers: The country's highly educated, well-trained labor force doesn't like to work in factories.

Volvo's Swedish plants suffer absenteeism of 20 percent, and almost one-third of its workers quit yearly. More pay does not motivate Swedes; taxes take up to 70 percent of any overtime pay. With unemployment at 1.6 percent, there is no lack of jobs. The problem of Swedish firms is to keep a work force.

Uddevalla is divided into six assembly plants, each of which has eight teams. The teams largely manage themselves, handling scheduling, quality control, hiring, and other duties normally performed by supervisors. Indeed, there are no first-line foremen and only two tiers of managers. Each team has a spokesperson/ombudsman, who reports to one of six plant managers, who in turn report to Leif Karlberg, president of the entire complex.

Morale seems high at Uddevalla. Absenteeism is only 8 percent. Workers have a spectacular view of a fjord. The plant is well lighted, and noise is subdued. Volvo gives its workers 16 weeks' training before they are allowed near a car, and on-the-job orientation lasts 16 months more. Pay averages $10 per hour.

Volvo's volume is relatively small compared with that of most auto plants. Other Volvo plants produce all of the 740's components and perform the major operations of stamping, welding, and painting car bodies that are shipped to Uddevalla.

After entering the plant, the car bodies glide noiselessly on magnetic tracks to the assembly points, where Volvo-designed machines lift and tilt the body to any angle. More than 80 percent of the assembly can be done from a comfortable working position with no bending or stretching. Tools have been redesigned with narrower grips and more internal torque and power to better accommodate the 40 percent of the work force which is female. Teams determine how long they'll work on a car and take responsibility for fixing defects. Volvo's Karlberg claims that, "This isn't just new production technology. It is the death of the assembly line. We've brought back craftsmanship to auto making."

But skeptics question whether Volvo's approach will spread. They argue that, while Uddevalla can achieve a high level of quality, it cannot match the productivity of efficient, mass-production systems, Japanese or American. Indeed, Volvo could have achieved at least 15 percent to 20 percent lower costs with a traditional plant design.

Source: Based on S. Kindel, "Check Your Brakes," *Financial World* (October 31, 1989): 32–34, and J. Kapstein, "Volvo's Radical New Plant: 'The Death of the Assembly Line'?" *Business Week* (August 28, 1989): 92–93.

1. Do you think the job design at Uddevalla will help Volvo achieve its stated goals? Why or why not?
2. What are some likely costs or difficulties associated with Uddevalla's design?
3. Do you think this approach would be successful in U.S. auto plants? In your answer, be sure to consider relevant similarities and differences between the situations in the United States and in Sweden.
4. Is Uddevalla likely to herald "the death of the assembly line"? Justify your position.

ENDNOTES

1. R. E. Walton, "Quality of Work Life: What Is It?" *Sloan Management Review* 15 (1973): 11-21.
2. F. W. Taylor, *The Principles of Scientific Management* (New York: Harper & Brothers, 1911).
3. R. J. Aldag and A. P. Brief, *Managing Organizational Behavior* (St. Paul, MN: West Publishing Co., 1981), 200.
4. C. Argyris, *Integrating the Individual and the Organization* (New York: John Wiley & Sons, 1964).
5. M. S. Myers, *Every Employee a Manager: More Meaningful Work Through Job Enrichment* (New York: McGraw-Hill, 1970).
6. A. N. Turner and P. R. Lawrence, *Industrial Jobs and the Worker: An Investigation of Response to Task Attributes* (Boston: Harvard University Division of Research, 1965).
7. J. R. Hackman and E. E. Lawler III, "Employee Reactions to Job Characteristics," *Journal of Applied Psychology Monograph* 55 (1971): 259-286, and J. R. Hackman and G. R. Oldham, "The Job Diagnostic Survey: An Instrument for the Diagnosis of Jobs and the Evaluation of Job Redesign Projects," *Technical Report No. 4* (New Haven, CT: Department of Administrative Sciences, Yale University, 1974).
8. For other discussions of this model, see the following: R. J. Aldag, S. H. Barr, and A. P. Brief, "Measurement of Perceived Task Characteristics," *Psychological Bulletin* 90 (1981): 415-431; Aldag and Brief, *Task Design and Employee Motivation* (Glenview, IL: Scott, Foresman, 1979); R. W. Griffin, *Task Design: An Integrative Approach* (Glenview, IL: Scott, Foresman, 1982); and K. H. Roberts and W. Glick, "The Job Characteristics Approach to Task Design: A Critical Review," *Journal of Applied Psychology* 66 (April 1981): 193-217. For a review comparing this model to other approaches to employee motivation, see E. A. Locke and D. Henne, "Work Motivation Theories," in *International Review of Industrial and Organizational Psychology*, ed. C. L. Cooper and I. Robertson (New York: John Wiley & Sons, 1986), 1-35.
9. R. B. Dunham, R. J. Aldag, and A. P. Brief, "Dimensionality of Task Design As Measured by the Job Diagnostic Survey," *Academy of Management Journal* 20 (1977): 209-223. See also Y. Fried and G. R. Ferris, "The Dimensionality of Job Characteristics: Some Neglected Issues," *Journal of Applied Psychology* 71 (1986): 419-426.
10. Aldag, Barr, and Brief, "Task Characteristics," 415-431.

11. Ibid.
12. Ibid. The first term is actually divided by three in the original formula. However, the multiplicative form of the model makes this irrelevant since scores of all jobs are divided by the same constant.
13. For instance, consider a simple two-characteristic case where characteristic A has a score of 0 on a scale of 0 to 5 and characteristic B has a score of 3. If an employee combines the scores with an additive model, the job would have a score of 0 + 3 = 3. With a multiplicative model, the job would have a score of 0 × 3 = 0. That is, it would not motivate at all. Suppose then that job changes were made to improve the score on characteristic B to 5. If an employee combines those scores with an additive model, the score becomes 0 + 5 = 5, an improvement of 2. With a multiplicative model, the score remains at 0 × 5 = 0.
14. E. F. Stone, "Some Personality Correlates of Perceptions of and Reactions to Task Characteristics" (Working paper, Purdue University, 1977).
15. See Aldag and Brief, *Employee Motivation*, 93-95, for more on this issue.
16. J. R. Hackman and G. R. Oldham, *Work Redesign* (Reading, MA: Addison-Wesley, 1980).
17. Aldag and Brief, *Employee Motivation*, 62-70.
18. From *Task Design and Employee Motivation* by R. J. Aldag and A. P. Brief. Copyright © 1979 by Scott, Foresman and Company. Reprinted by permission.
19. See ibid., 81-92, for a review of these studies.
20. A variable such as higher order need strength which influences, or moderates, the relationship between two other variables is typically called a moderator variable. Thus, the search for variables influencing the relationship between task characteristics and outcomes is often called a search for moderators.
21. Aldag and Brief, *Organizational Behavior*, 210-211.
22. R. B. Dunham, "Relationships of Perceived Job Design Characteristics to Job Ability Requirements and Job Value," *Journal of Applied Psychology* 62 (December 1977): 760-763.
23. For an interesting discussion of this idea, see K. E. Weick, "Enactment Processes in Organizations," in *New Directions in Organizational Behavior*, ed. B. M. Staw and G. R. Salancik (Chicago: St. Clair Press, 1977), 267-300.
24. For a discussion of this approach, see G. Salancik and J. A. Pfeffer, "A Social Information Processing Approach to Job Attitudes and Task Design," *Administrative Science Quarterly* 23 (June 1978): 224-253.
25. R. W. Griffin, "Objective and Social Sources of Information in Task Redesign: A Field Experiment," *Administrative Science Quarterly* 28 (1983): 184-200.
26. For a recent study supporting these arguments, see R. J. Vance and T. F. Biddle, "Task Experience and Social Cues: Interactive Effects on Attitudinal Reactions," *Organizational Behavior and Human Decision Processes* 35 (1985): 252-265. In that study, the impact of social cues on task-related attitudes and behavioral intentions declined with task experience. For a review of research on the social information-processing approach to task design and a study using actual workers, see M. E. Schnake and M. P. Dummler, "The Social Information Processing Model of Task Design," *Group and Organization Studies* (June 1987): 221-240. In this study social cues had little impact on task characteristics but did influence other variables such as role clarity and role overload.
27. For a perspective on task design which integrates the job characteristics approach with the social information-processing view, see R. W. Griffin, "Toward an Integrated Theory of Task Design," in *Research in Organizational Behavior*, vol. 9, ed. L. L. Cummings and B. M. Staw (Greenwich, CT: JAI Press, 1987), 79-120. For a laboratory experiment testing that integrated perspective, see R. W. Griffin, T. S. Bateman, S. J. Wayne, and T. C. Head, "Objective and Social Factors as Determinants of Task Perceptions and Responses: An Integrated Perspective and Empirical Investigation," *Academy of Management Journal* 30 (1987): 501-523.
28. S. Newman, "Working Alternatives," *Supervision* (July 1989): 13.
29. E. F. Mellor, "Shift Work and Flexitime: How Prevalent Are They?" *Monthly Labor Review* (November 1986): 14-21. For a discussion of the success of flextime at Steelcase, Inc., see B. Cohn, "A Glimpse of the 'Flex' Future," *Newsweek* (August 1, 1988): 38-39.
30. R. B. Dunham, *Organizational Behavior: People and Processes in Management* (Homewood, IL: Richard D. Irwin, 1984), 528-530.
31. R. T. Golembiewski and C. W. Proehl, "A Survey of the Empirical Literature on Flexible Workhours: Character and Consequences of a Major Innovation," *Academy of Manage-*

ment Review 3 (October 1978): 837-853. For a discussion of recent experience with flex-time see J. Solomon, "The Future Look of Employee Benefits," *Wall Street Journal* (September 7, 1988): 23.

32. For instance, see J. S. Kim and A. F. Campagna, "Effects of Flexitime on Employee Attendance and Performance: A Field Experiment," *Academy of Management Journal* 24 (1981): 729-741; V. E. Schein, E. H. Maurer, and J. F. Novak, "Impact of Flexible Working Hours on Productivity," *Journal of Applied Psychology* 62 (August 1977): 463-465; and S. Ronen, *Flexible Working Hours: An Innovation in the Quality of Work Life* (New York: McGraw-Hill, 1981). For a review of the evidence concerning flextime, see R. E. Kopelman, "Alternative Work Schedules and Productivity: A Review of the Evidence," *National Productivity Review* (Spring 1986): 150-165.

33. P. M. Muchinsky, *Psychology Applied to Work*, 2d ed. (Homewood, IL: Dorsey Press, 1987): 703.

34. For a discussion of job sharing and flextime at Steelcase Inc., see Cohn, "A Glimpse of the 'Flex' Future." For more on job sharing as a tool to prevent layoffs, see K. Watford, "Shorter Workweeks: An Alternative to Layoffs," *Business Week* (April 14, 1986): 77-78.

35. H. V. Hayghe, "Employers and Child Care: What Roles Do They Play?" *Monthly Labor Review* (September 1988): 38-44.

36. S. J. Smith, "The Growing Diversity of Work Schedules," *Monthly Labor Review* (November 1986): 7-13.

37. On these points, see J. G. Goodale and A. K. Aagaard, "Factors Relating to Varying Reactions to the 4-Day Workweek," *Journal of Applied Psychology* 60 (February 1975): 33-38; W. R. Nord and R. Costigan, "Worker Adjustment to the Four-Day Week: A Longitudinal Study," *Journal of Applied Psychology* 58 (August 1973): 60-66; A. R. Cohen and H. Gadon, *Alternative Work Schedules: Integrating Individual and Organizational Needs* (Reading, MA: Addison-Wesley, 1978); and R. B. Dunham and D. L. Hawk, "The Four-Day/Forty-Hour Week: Who Wants It?" *Academy of Management Journal* 20 (December 1977): 644-655.

38. M. D. Fottler, "Employee Acceptance of a Four-Day Workweek," *Academy of Management Journal* 20 (December 1977): 656-668.

39. J. M. Ivancevich and H. L. Lyon, "The Shortened Workweek: A Field Experiment," *Journal of Applied Psychology* 62 (February 1977): 34-37.

40. For a review of research on the compressed workweek, see R. E. Kopelman, "Alternative Work Schedules and Productivity: A Review of the Evidence," *National Productivity Review* (Spring 1986): 150-165. For a discussion of human resource managers' feelings about alternative work schedules, including the compressed workweek, flextime, and job sharing, see H. Z. Levine, "Alternative Work Schedules: Do They Meet Workforce Needs? Part 1," *Personnel* (February 1987): 57-62.

REFERENCE

Terkel, S. 1974. *Working.* New York: Pantheon Books.

Communicating

CHAPTER 15

After reading this chapter, you should be able to:

- *Explain the communication process and indicate reasons for communication failures.*
- *Discuss ways managers can help ensure that they receive accurate communications.*
- *Identify techniques for upward, downward, and horizontal communication in organizations.*
- *Recognize important characteristics of communication channels, including the roles of nonverbal channels.*
- *Describe the characteristics and consequences of various communication networks.*
- *Explain how the grapevine works and why it is important.*
- *Discuss how new information technologies are affecting communication in organizations.*

472

Thomas Peters and Robert Waterman sought in their book, *In Search of Excellence: Lessons from America's Best-Run Companies*, to discover the secrets of America's truly excellent companies.[1] Their findings led them to the conclusion that "the nature and uses of communication in the excellent companies are remarkably different from those of their nonexcellent peers" (p. 121). They further concluded, "The intensity of communications is unmistakable in the excellent companies" (p. 122). Peters and Waterman found their sample of excellent companies to use a variety of philosophies, practices, and structures to encourage communication. At IBM and Delta Air Lines, open-door policies were pervasive. At Hewlett-Packard and United Airlines, versions of "Management by Wandering About" were practiced, in which managers were encouraged to get out of their offices and communicate informally. Corning Glass installed escalators rather than elevators in its new engineering building to increase the chance of face-to-face contact. At Citibank, the desks of operations officers and lending officers were moved to the same floor and intermingled to encourage communication. Intel's new buildings in Silicon Valley were designed with numerous small conference rooms equipped with blackboards to facilitate communication, where people can eat lunch or meet for problem solving. What these examples have in common, according to Peters and Waterman, is "lots of communication" (p. 122).

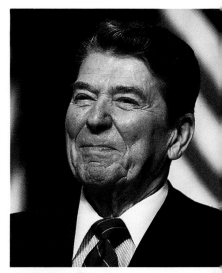

Former President Ronald Reagan came to be known as The Great Communicator because of his skill as a speaker.

This emphasis on communication is not surprising. Communication affects virtually every area of work. Communication to employees about plant closings, performance appraisals, organizational goals, probable salary increases and job changes, and the date of the company picnic is essential to the proper functioning of the firm. If communication is inaccurate or inadequate, the likely results are uncertainty, apprehension, errors, and dissatisfaction.

Organizations also must communicate effectively with parties outside their boundaries. Lee Iacocca's televised messages concerning Chrysler's resurgence and Sanford Sigoloff's television commercials declaring the Wickes Cos. to have come back strong were credited with a significant part of the success of those firms. And companies regularly find themselves communicating with the public to quell rumors—McDonald's, to combat reports that it was putting red worms in its hamburgers; Squibb, to deny that its Bubble Yum contained spiders' eggs; Procter & Gamble, to fight persistent reports that its corporate logo had hidden satanic meanings; and Barton Brands, importer of Corona Extra beer, to counter a whispering campaign that the beer was contaminated with urine.[2]

Further, much of managers' time is spent communicating. Henry Mintzberg's observations of chief executive officers showed them to spend 78 percent of their time on communication-related activities involving direct contact with others, including scheduled and unscheduled meetings, telephone calls, and tours of facilities. Even the 22 percent of time spent on what Mintzberg called "desk work" included answering mail and was thus related to communication. Mintzberg also found that managers considered activities involving direct communication with others to be more interesting and valuable than more routine activities. Figure 15–1 shows that Mintzberg's chief executives regularly communicated with peers, clients, suppliers, associates, subordinates, members of the board of directors, and others. Face-to-face communication appears to demand large amounts of time at all managerial levels. Mintzberg estimates that such communication takes 59 percent of the time of supervisors and 89 percent of the time of middle managers.[3]

FIGURE 15–1
The Chief Executive's Contacts

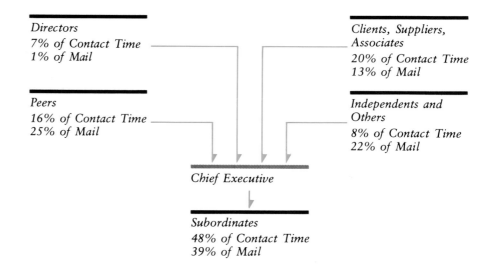

Directors
7% of Contact Time
1% of Mail

Clients, Suppliers, Associates
20% of Contact Time
13% of Mail

Peers
16% of Contact Time
25% of Mail

Independents and Others
8% of Contact Time
22% of Mail

Chief Executive

Subordinates
48% of Contact Time
39% of Mail

In this chapter we will examine the functions of communication. We will then discuss the nature of the communication process as well as barriers to effective communication and ways to overcome them. We will consider various techniques for communicating in organizations and examine communication channels and networks. After a discussion of informal communication, we will conclude with a look at how new information technology is affecting communication.

FUNCTIONS OF COMMUNICATION

Communication is the transfer of information from one person to another. Our discussion to this point suggests that communication may serve several important purposes. William Scott and Terence Mitchell have identified the following four major functions of communication:[4]

- *Information function.* Communication provides information to be used for decision making. Managers require information concerning alternatives, future events, and potential outcomes of their decisions to make reasoned choices.
- *Motivational function.* Communication encourages commitment to organizational objectives, thus enhancing motivation. Lee Iacocca's visible role as the spokesperson for the Chrysler Corporation was credited as being motivational both for Chrysler employees and for Americans in general.[5]
- *Control function.* Communication clarifies duties, authority, and responsibilities, thereby permitting control. If there is ambiguity concerning such matters, it is impossible to isolate sources of problems and to take corrective actions.

- *Emotive function.* Communication permits the expression of feelings and the satisfaction of social needs. It may also help vent frustrations. After the breakup of AT&T, there was a marked increase in the number of customers who yelled at operators, a convenient target for anger.

Communication is also central to many of the managerial roles discussed in Chapter 1. For instance, the roles of leader, liaison, disseminator, spokesperson, disturbance handler, and negotiator, among others, rely heavily on communication.

THE COMMUNICATION PROCESS

Communication is a process involving several steps. Figure 15–2 presents a model of the communication process.

The process begins when a message sender wants to communicate some fact, problem, idea, or opinion. The message has meaning to the sender, but that meaning cannot be directly transmitted. Instead, an **encoder** is first needed to put the meaning in an appropriate form such as words or symbols or body gestures. Next, a **transmitter** places the message into the **message channel**, the actual medium of information exchange. For instance, the transmitter may be the mouthpiece of a telephone and the channel may be the phone lines. Then, the **receiver** picks up the message and the **decoder** translates the message so it has meaning to the recipient. Finally, the recipient of the message may or may not provide feedback to the sender. As the figure shows, **noise**—anything that distorts the intended message—can occur at any step of the process.

SOME CAUSES OF COMMUNICATION FAILURE

Unfortunately, many things can interfere with effective communication. Here are some of the more common.

Code Noise

Code noise occurs when the meaning of a message to the sender differs from its meaning to the recipient. Too often, this may be because the sender has used "jargon," pretentious terminology or language specific to a particular profession or group. As an example of pretentious terminology, *The Wall*

FIGURE 15–2
The Communication Process

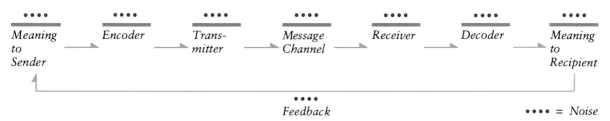

Street Journal reported on a federal tax case in which a fire alarm was described as a "combustion enunciator," a door as a "removable partition," a manhole as "equipment access," and windows as "decorative fixtures."[6] Management in Action 1 provides a fascinating glimpse of the ways that some companies consciously use jargon.

Distraction

Distraction, or **psychological noise**, occurs when a recipient does not understand the sender's message because he or she is simply thinking about something else. For instance, the recipient may be distracted by financial worries or upcoming deadlines. Often, of course, recipients don't understand senders' messages because they are thinking about their own replies rather than concentrating on the message to which they are going to reply. Thus, effective listening is an important communication skill.

Misrepresentation

Misrepresentation may also cause the failure of communication and may take various forms. Deliberate lies are an extreme example. Quite frankly, people do at times lie on their résumés (sometimes called padding), in their advertising messages (sometimes called puffery), and in their campaign promises (sometimes called politics). More often, information may be subtly distorted to the sender's benefit. A memo that focuses on sales increases but downplays drops in profit, an annual report that tries to hide changes in accounting format, and a brochure from a drug manufacturer that ignores hazardous side effects would be examples of this kind of misrepresentation.

Indeed, some forms of misrepresentation are so common that examples to the contrary are newsworthy. For instance, it is almost "common practice" for company annual reports to present the year's events in a favorable light. The "Dear Stockholder" letter in the 1988 annual report of poultry producer Holly Farms Corp. broke that mold. It began, "You already know the Bad News about our past fiscal year. We were wrong about chickens. The chicken market did not recover from salmonella publicity and we entered a sharp chicken depression. We lost money in chickens—our worst year in history. And the poor performance was mostly our fault."[7]

Information Retention

As we will discuss in more detail in Chapter 19, information is a valuable resource. Those who control it are in positions of power. Some employees may retain specific sorts of information, such as a formula or a filing system, and thereby make themselves more necessary. Others are in positions that give them the ability to channel—or not channel—information to various individuals inside and outside the organization. Still others are in positions in which they process information, sending only some of it along. Each of these sorts of individuals has the potential to create barriers to proper communication.

A hipo, a Wallenda, and an imagineer order drinks at a bar. They do a little work—edit a violin, non-concur with a wild duck, take care of some bad mickey—and then ask for the bill. "This is on the mouse," says one of the three. Who picks up the tab?

It's not uncommon to hear chatter like this from the mouths of corporate employees. Sometimes, translating it requires knowing the jargon not of MBAs, industries, or regions—but of particular companies.

For instance, an employee at International Business Machines Corp. who is fluent in IBM-speak knows that a "hipo" is an employee on the fast track to success—someone with "high potential." (According to one IBMer, an employee with low potential is known as an "alpo.") IBM-speakers don't disagree with their bosses—they non-concur. And anyone who non-concurs often and abrasively, but constructively, is a "wild duck" in IBM-speak. Former Chairman Thomas Watson Jr. borrowed that tag from Kierkegaard.

Like other tribal entities, corporations develop their own dialects as a way of linking members of the tribe and delineating their ranks. "It has the double purpose of bonding the user to the group and separating the user from general society," says Robert Chapman, editor of the *New Dictionary of American Slang*. "It makes us feel warm and wanted. This works in any society—a company, a school, a family, a saloon."

Slang often occurs in offices where words are the company's business, such as newspapers and magazines. *Newsweek*'s top editors are known as

Wallendas, after the famous family of aerialists—a reference to the precarious nature of their jobs. *Newsweek* writers also call each week's top story

MANAGEMENT IN ACTION 1
BAD MICKEY

the "violin." A spokesman says that's because the story is supposed to "reflect the tone" of the news.

Most of all, slang flourishes at corporations with rich histories and cultures. At McDonald's Corp., where employees take corporate training classes at Hamburger University, loyal workers "have ketchup in their veins." Patriotic citizens of Eastman Kodak Co. say they work for "the great yellow father."

Walt Disney Co., one of the world's shrewdest manufacturers of cultural imagery, is a rare example of a company that has consciously invented its own jargon. It calls the division that plans its theme parks "Walt Disney Imagineering." At orientation sessions (at Disney University), new theme-park employees are carefully told to say they are "on stage" while at work and "backstage" while taking a break. They are also told to consider each other not as employees but as "cast members."

Jack Herrman, a former Disney World publicist, recalls that his colleagues would brand anything positive "good Mickey" and anything negative—like a cigarette butt on the sidewalk—"bad Mickey." He also remembers putting lunch on the Disney World expense account and calling it "on the mouse." "You're immersed in the jargon they impose upon you as a way of life," he says.

Source: Reprinted by permission of *The Wall Street Journal*, © Dow Jones & Company, Inc. (December 29, 1987). All Rights Reserved Worldwide.

Perceptual Factors

Most perceptual errors are directly relevant to communication. Stereotyping, for example, may cause us to ignore or distort the messages of people we have classified in certain ways. A manager may, for instance, feel that union representatives are not trustworthy. As a result, the manager may misinterpret conciliatory gestures from the union. Selective perception may cause us to ignore communication that conflicts with our beliefs and expectations. Halo error may lead us to bias our evaluation of a message because of some unrelated characteristic of the message sender such as physical appearance. Projection may lead us to infer information in a message we receive based upon our own feelings. If we are angry, for instance, we may see anger in the message. Primacy and recency effects may cause us to give differing weights to

Is she really listening to the sender's message?

various communications depending on when we receive them. At this point, you may want to review the discussion of these and other perceptual errors in Chapter 12.

Other Factors

Several other things can contribute to communication failure. Time pressures and communication overload can each cause us to ignore messages. They may also cause us to focus on information that helps us make a choice quickly. For instance, a harried employment interviewer may look for reasons to reject many of the job candidates she is considering. Noise in the channel, such as static, can distort messages, especially when channels are long or not well shielded from outside influences. Short circuiting, in which a message fails to reach an intended recipient because of an error, can cause confusion, resentment, and mistakes.

Overcoming Communication Problems

There are many ways to eliminate the causes of communication failures. For instance, problems due to code noise, selective perception, and distraction may be reduced by use of feedback, repetitions of the messages, use of multiple channels, and simplified language. Figure 15–3 provides some guides for improved readability of written communications.

Communication overload may be reduced by careful review of the material needed by the recipient and by use of the exception principle. The **exception principle** states that only exceptions should be reported—there is no need for messages stating that the production line didn't break down or that absenteeism or competitive conditions are unchanged. Short circuiting may be reduced through careful consideration of who has a "need to know" the material. Electronic data-processing techniques that automatically route messages to certain people may also help.

FIGURE 15–3
Guides to Readable Writing

- Use simple words and phrases, such as "improve" instead of "ameliorate" and "like" instead of "in a manner similar to that of."
- Use short and familiar words, such as "darken" instead of "obfuscate."
- Use personal pronouns, such as "you" and "them," if the style permits.
- Use illustrations, examples, and charts. These techniques are even better when they are tied to the reader's experiences.
- Use short sentences and paragraphs. Big words and thick reports may look impressive to people, but the communicator's job is to inform people, not impress them.
- Use active verbs, such as "The manager said . . ." rather than "It was said by the manager that . . . ."
- Use only necessary words. For example, in the sentence "Bad weather conditions prevented my trip," the word "conditions" is unnecessary. Say, "Bad weather prevented my trip."

Source: From *Human Behavior at Work: Organizational Behavior*, 7th ed., by K. Davis and J. W. Newstrom. Copyright © 1985 by McGraw-Hill Book Company. Reproduced with permission.

Information retention and misrepresentation are more difficult problems and have led to some very different prescriptions. Some call for tightened formal controls and even organizational audit groups. An **organizational audit group** is designed to ferret out the points at which omissions or distortions are taking place. Others have argued just the opposite, saying that fewer formal controls and a more open, trusting organizational climate are needed.

These suggestions make it clear that there is no free lunch when dealing with communication. Things that lessen one problem are likely to worsen another. For instance, feedback, redundancy, and multiple channels may make communication overload worse. The exception principle makes misrepresentation and information retention easier. This does not mean that the situation is hopeless, only that we must pay serious attention to these problems and carefully weigh the resultant tradeoffs.

RECEIVING ACCURATE COMMUNICATION[8]

Along with communicating accurately and effectively to others, managers also want to make sure that the communication they receive is appropriate and undistorted. In this section, we will consider factors known to influence the quality of communication to you as a manager. Along the way, we will make suggestions to help ensure that quality is high.

Good News Versus Bad News

Quite simply, people are more likely to distort or suppress bad news than good news. This may be because people don't like to disappoint others. Or it may be because they feel they will be associated with the bad news. In ancient Persia, marathon runners charged with delivering messages were often associated with the messages they carried. One unfortunate messenger who arrived to inform the king that his side was losing a battle was slain. This practice almost certainly served to delay or distort some messages—if not to spur unionization attempts! In an organization, failure to receive bad news can lead to inaccurate assessment of performance, misallocation of resources, and a climate of secrecy and distrust.

Number of Information Sources

If the information source recognizes that you can check the information, he or she is more likely to provide accurate information in the first place. Multiple sources for the same information are useful both to decrease the likelihood of distortion from each source and to serve as checks on validity.

Your Influence over the Sender's Career

The more influence you have over a sender's career, the greater the danger that the sender will introduce bias into the message. If your reactions are unimportant to the message source, there will be relatively little pressure to distort. As those reactions gain importance, pressure to distort increases. For instance, a manager may openly discuss a mistake she made at work when

When the receiver is in a position to influence the sender's career, the sender may introduce bias into the message.

talking to a co-worker, but may try to cover up the mistake when reporting to her boss.

Your Trustworthiness

If you are not perceived by the message sender to be trustworthy, there is more motivation to distort the message. Further, when you have high influence over the sender's career and you are not trusted, distortion is high.[9]

Discretion Permitted

The more discretion allowed in reporting, the more biasing may occur. This is why courts sometimes force witnesses to answer questions with a simple "yes" or "no." This suggests that to reduce biasing you should take care to:

- Ask specific questions.
- Indicate that specific answers will be required.
- Use a specific reporting format. Indicate, for instance, whether you want the answer in written form and whether you require supporting documentation.

Difficulty in Communicating to You

As people find it more difficult to communicate with you, distortion will increase. Such difficulty may be due to physical barriers (such as geographic distance, walls, or computer mediation) or social barriers (such as differences in status or level of education). Some of these we cannot change, but others we can. For instance, we can reduce social distance by avoiding unnecessary authority trappings and by remaining accessible.

Workloads

As the workload of the sender increases, he or she will tend to simplify messages. Such simplification may include the omission of valuable information. The perceived workload of the receiver is also important. People generally want to avoid disturbing others, especially the boss, when they seem busy. If your subordinates think you are overloaded already, they will screen out more and more information before sending you a message.

Number of Links in the Communication Chain

As the number of links in the communication chain increases, the degree to which a message is compressed and distorted as it is relayed through the chain increases. In the case of rumors, as Figure 15–4 shows, the fraction of details correctly retained falls below 40 percent after as few as three reproductions.

The lesson here is simple: Keep message chains short. If possible, go directly to the original source of the message.

TECHNIQUES FOR COMMUNICATING IN ORGANIZATIONS

One useful way to classify communication is on the basis of whether messages flow downward, upward, or horizontally through the organization structure. Each direction of flow has its own purposes and associated techniques.

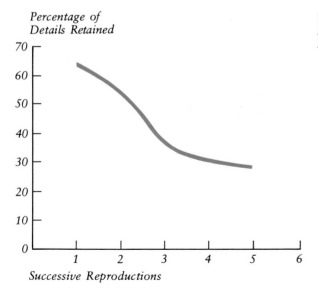

FIGURE 15–4
Retention of Rumor Details

Source: Figure 9 from *The Psychology of Rumor* by Gordon W. Allport and Leo Postman, copyright 1947 and renewed 1975 by Holt, Rinehart and Winston, Inc., reprinted by permission of the publisher.

Drawing by Ziegler; © 1982 *The New Yorker Magazine.*

Downward Communication[10]

Downward communication involves messages from senders relatively high in the organizational structure to receivers in lower-level positions, such as messages from a supervisor to a subordinate. It is used for such purposes as giving instructions, providing information about policies and procedures, giving feedback about performance, and indoctrinating or motivating.[11] A survey of CEOs found that 97 percent believe that communicating with employees has a positive impact on job satisfaction and 79 percent think it affects the bottom line, but only 22 percent actually do it weekly or more often.[12]

LETTERS, MEETINGS, AND THE TELEPHONE

Three common channels for communicating downward in organizations are written letters or memos, group meetings, and the telephone. Oral media, including meetings and the telephone, provide personal interchange, are highly adaptable to a wide variety of situations, and are useful when time is crucial. Written communication is required when the action called for is complex and must be done in a precise way. Further, written communication provides a permanent form of record keeping and can reach a large number of people easily. However, each of these techniques can be overused.[13]

MANUALS

A company manual is an integrated system of long-term instructions, brought together between covers, classified, coded, indexed, and otherwise prepared to maximize its reference value.[14] Manuals have a high degree of authority.

They deal primarily with policy, procedure, or organization. Since manuals are technical and complex, employees should be trained to use them.

HANDBOOKS

Handbooks are usually less authoritative, formal, and lengthy than manuals and generally apply at lower organizational levels. The employee handbook, for example, outlines the duties and privileges of the individual worker. Handbooks generally have a low-key, friendly, personal approach.

NEWSLETTERS

Company newsletters are usually issued biweekly or monthly. Informal in tone, they are used to disseminate information to many employees. Newsletters might announce company social functions, contain stories about employees cited for superior performance or attendance, or provide answers about employment issues. Unlike a manual, a newsletter has a mix of personal, social, and work-related information.[15]

Upward Communication

Upward communication involves communication from senders in lower-level positions to receivers in relatively higher positions. It is often used to give information on achievement or progress, to point out problems which are being encountered, to pass on ideas for improvement of activities, and to provide information about feelings on work and non-work activities. Three techniques which are especially useful in upward communication are suggestion systems, grievances, and attitude surveys.

SUGGESTION SYSTEMS

A suggestion system permits employees to submit ideas or suggestions for improving company effectiveness. The suggestions are then evaluated, generally by a panel of managers, and the valuable ones are acted on. The initiator of the idea may get a cash award, letter of commendation, or insignia. The idea behind a suggestion system is that employees are in the best position to contribute ideas to make their jobs more effective.

GRIEVANCES

Grievances are formal written complaints submitted by employees regarding alleged unfair treatment on the job. They may cover such topics as working conditions, promotions, pay, disciplinary action, supervision, and work assignments. Grievance procedures often involve several steps. In the first step, the employee's immediate supervisor reviews the grievance. Failure to resolve the grievance at that step may lead to appeals at higher levels, perhaps including the company's industrial relations office or an outside mediator. Grievances allow employees to channel their frustrations and feelings of injustice in productive ways.

ATTITUDE SURVEYS

Attitude surveys are often conducted annually or biannually. The organization uses the survey to learn about employees' feelings and attitudes on many

Drawing by Chas. Addams; © 1976 *The New Yorker Magazine*.

employment issues. The surveys are often administered by an outside consultant, and responses are usually anonymous so that employees can feel free to speak their minds. Results of the surveys are tabulated and a report is prepared. The company then acts on the information provided.[16] About 45 percent of large firms currently use surveys, often for a wide range of purposes.[17] For instance, at Wells Fargo & Co. in San Francisco, employees have been asked about such things as the effectiveness of the bank's advertising, the quality and innovation of its products, and its responsibility to the community.[18]

Horizontal Communication

Horizontal communication takes place among individuals or groups at the same organizational level. While organizations tend to ignore horizontal communication, it is quite important and common. Horizontal communication is used to coordinate activities, to persuade others at the same level of the organization, and to pass on information about activities or feelings. As organizations become more diversified and individual tasks become more specialized, the need for horizontal communication increases.[19] Some of the channels mentioned above, such as memos, meetings, and the telephone, are appropriate for horizontal communication. Committee meetings, for instance, may be useful for both vertical and horizontal communication. In addition, conferences or retreats may be arranged in which individuals can meet for one or more days away from the pressures and distractions of the workplace. Picnics, dinners, and other social affairs can also encourage horizontal communication.

COMMUNICATION CHANNELS

As we said earlier, a communication channel is the medium through which a message is sent. This would include both human channels, such as speech and body movements, and mechanical channels, such as computer networks, the mail, and the telephone. In choosing appropriate channels, managers may want to consider several channel dimensions.[20]

Channel Dimensions

Here are eight important channel dimensions:

CAPACITY

Channel capacity is the amount of information that can be sent through a channel over a given period of time without significant distortion. A telephone, for instance, has greater capacity than a memo since the memo is constrained by reading speed.

MODIFIABILITY

Modifiability is the degree to which the rate of transmission can be varied. Modifiability of a memo or other written message is high; the manager can read at a chosen speed and even set the memo aside for a while. A televised message is typically less modifiable (though VCRs are changing this).

DUPLICATION

It is sometimes useful to use subchannels to reiterate or elaborate on a message, especially when it is complex or novel. A television commercial, for instance, may use both visual and auditory subchannels to sell a product.

IMMEDIACY

Immediacy is the speed at which a message can be transmitted. Sophisticated computer networks now transmit reports and other information almost instantly. The U.S. Postal Service may take a few days, or more, to deliver the same message.

ONE-WAY VERSUS TWO-WAY

Some channels, such as a memo or a videotaped lecture, are essentially one-way. **One-way communication** gives a message without opportunity for immediate feedback. In contrast, **two-way communication**, such as a telephone or a face-to-face conversation, allows the message recipient to ask questions and provide feedback. Harold Leavitt has conducted some interesting research on this issue.[21] His, and other, research shows that:

- One-way communication is considerably faster than two-way.
- Two-way communication is more accurate than one-way.
- Receivers are more sure of themselves and make more correct judgments of how right or wrong they are with two-way communication.
- The sender may feel less secure in two-way communication. The message recipients can point out errors, interrupt a stream of thought, disagree, and otherwise challenge the sender.

- Two-way communication is relatively noisy and disorderly. One-way communication appears neat and efficient to an outside observer, but the communication is often less accurate.

NUMBER OF LINKAGES

As we said earlier, longer channels invite omission and distortion. Whenever possible, managers should use as few linkages as possible.

APPROPRIATENESS

Some channels are "made for" certain types of messages and may be completely inappropriate for others. A billboard may be fine for an advertising message, but it is probably not the place to reprimand an employee.

RICHNESS

Richness is defined as the potential information-carrying capacity of data. If something so simple as a wink conveys substantial new information, the communication is considered rich. If it provides little new understanding, it is low in richness. Face-to-face communication is the richest form of communication since it permits immediate feedback; with that feedback, understanding can be checked and interpretations corrected. Face-to-face communications also permit the observation of multiple cues, including body language, facial expression, and tone of voice. Face-to-face communications are followed by the telephone, written personal communications, written formal communications, and computer output in declining order of information richness.[22]

Selecting Channels

When sending messages, managers should consider the characteristics we have just presented. How much information must be transmitted? How fast? Does the message require elaboration? Is speed of the essence? Is feedback necessary? Are certain channels unsuited to the nature of the message? The manager may decide after weighing these factors that available channels must be somehow modified, or that multiple channels are needed. Whatever the result, the choice of channels should be carefully weighed.

Nonverbal Communication

We shouldn't leave this discussion of communication channels without mentioning nonverbal communication channels. **Nonverbal communication** includes all communication that either does not use words at all or uses words in a way that conveys meaning beyond their strict definition.[23] It may take place through such channels as the body, the face, the tone of voice, and interpersonal distance. A wink, a touch, or a change of body position can all convey worlds of meaning. Further, that meaning can vary markedly depending on the situation, the sex of the parties, the culture, and other factors. Interestingly, our definition indicates that nonverbal communication may even involve using words to carry meaning beyond that inherent in the words themselves. For instance, the words "They'll have to drag me out of my position kicking and screaming" conveys a different overall message than "I won't leave voluntarily."

Studies often conclude that over 50 percent of the impact of communication comes through facial expressions, another 30 percent from inflection and tone of voice, and less than 10 percent from the content of the message.[24] Whatever the validity of these specific figures, it does seem clear that nonverbal communication is quite important. And, since it is typically harder to disguise the meaning of nonverbal communication than of verbal communication, listeners are likely to pay close attention to it to search for confirmation or contradiction. Figure 15–5 provides a summary of nonverbal communication techniques.

Facial expression and body position can convey worlds of meaning.

COMMUNICATION NETWORKS

Communication channels may be linked in a variety of ways to form **communication networks**.[25] These networks are used to structure the information flows among network members. Communication networks influence decision quality, member satisfaction, message quality, and other variables. Figure 15–6 shows six commonly used networks.

The chain network links members sequentially. The Y network modifies the chain to have one member communicating to three others. With the wheel network, all communication must flow through a central individual. The circle network permits each member to communicate directly with two

FIGURE 15–5
Nonverbal Communication

Subsystem	Description
Hand Movements	There are three types of hand movements: 1. Emblems are hand movements that are understood in a specific culture or occupation. An example is a thumbs-up gesture. 2. Illustrators are gestures that relate to what is being said, such as pointing or accentuating. 3. Adaptors are touching of oneself or other objects. Self-adaptors are often associated with anxiety, guilt, hostility, and suspicion.
Facial Expressions	When used, these are generally understood. Examples are smiling and frowning. Even when people suppress facial expressions, they may make very short expressions lasting only a fraction of a second that reflect their true feelings.
Eye Contact	Eye contact is a major regulator of conversation. Although there are individual differences, eye contact suggests understanding and interest.
Posture	Posture is the way people position their bodies with regard to other people. This can be a closed position with arms folded to reflect exclusion or the opposite to show inclusion. Having congruent positioning reflects agreement or acceptance.
Proxemics	How people use interpersonal space can express intimacy, social distance, and public distance. For example, standing close indicates intimacy, and sitting at the head of a table indicates status. Sitting alongside a desk indicates openness; sitting behind the desk while the other person is in front indicates a superior-subordinate relationship.
Body Rhythms	How people move in relation to others, frequency of speaking, and speaking turns provide clues to meaning being conveyed.
Speech	Choice of words can reflect involvement or distance, or enthusiasm or lack of it.

Source: From *Management Information Systems: Conceptual Foundations, Structure, and Development*, 2d ed., by G. B. Davis and M. H. Olson. Copyright © 1985 by McGraw-Hill Book Company. Reproduced with permission.

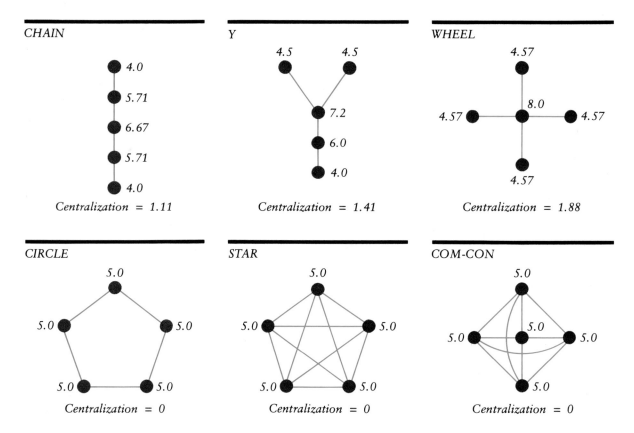

CHAIN

4.0
5.71
6.67
5.71
4.0

Centralization = 1.11

Y

4.5   4.5
7.2
6.0
4.0

Centralization = 1.41

WHEEL

4.57
4.57   8.0   4.57
4.57

Centralization = 1.88

CIRCLE

5.0
5.0   5.0
5.0   5.0

Centralization = 0

STAR

5.0
5.0   5.0
5.0   5.0

Centralization = 0

COM-CON

5.0
5.0   5.0   5.0
5.0

Centralization = 0

Note: Member relative centralities are shown next to each member. Centralization was calculated as the variance of relative centralities.

FIGURE 15–6
Communication Networks

others. With the star network, any member can communicate directly with any other. A variant of the star, called the com-con network, permits all members to communicate directly but also has a central member who is considered to be the leader.

These networks clearly differ on a number of dimensions. For instance, with networks such as the chain and the circle, it may be necessary for a message to pass through multiple links to reach its destination. With the star and com-con networks, one link is sufficient. The networks also vary in degree of centralization. The circle and star networks are decentralized—everyone is as central as everyone else. On the other hand, the wheel network clearly has a central member.

Relative centrality is the degree of centrality of an individual in a network. It can be calculated by summing the total number of links between the member and each other member in the network and dividing the sum for all members by that sum.[26] Figure 15–6 presents relative centrality scores of each member for each network. In the wheel network, there is clearly a central member. Since information more often flows through central members, they are likely to be perceived as leaders and to have high status. They are also likely to be more satisfied than their less central counterparts. In the circle and star networks, all members are equally central.

Along with the degree of relative centrality of members within a network, the overall centralization of the network is also of interest. **Centralization** is a measure of the variability in member relative centralities. The wheel, with one relatively central member and all others much less central, is highly centralized. The star, with equal member relative centralities, is completely decentralized. Figure 15–6 also presents network centralization scores.

Centralized networks tend to permit rapid decision making, but average member satisfaction is low. Centralized networks may be efficient for simple problems, but as complexity increases, more decentralization (and thus more participation in decision making) is needed. The wheel network might be appropriate for routine, well-structured tasks, especially if there are time constraints. For tasks requiring creativity and a wide range of member inputs, however, a network such as the circle or star would probably be better. We will look more at the issue of appropriate degree of participation in the next chapter.

THE GRAPEVINE[27]

Our discussion to this point has dealt primarily with formal communication channels in organizations. We all know that much information in organizations flows in other, officially unrecognized ways. The **grapevine** consists of information which is communicated informally among employees. The term comes from the Civil War practice of hanging telegraph lines loosely from tree to tree like a grapevine. Since messages sent over these lines were often garbled, incorrect information was attributed to the grapevine.

While much grapevine information is transmitted orally, handwritten, typewritten, and even electronic messages may be used. Studies show that over three-fourths of the information sent over the grapevine is accurate.[28] However, since even one error can change the overall meaning of a message, such a figure may be misleading. Further, grapevine information is often incomplete, giving a partial picture. As a result, many people view the grapevine negatively. In one study, 53 percent of managers and white-collar employees viewed the grapevine as a negative factor, and only 20 percent saw it as a positive factor.[29] In another study, the grapevine was ranked second as a source of information, but only fifteenth as a preferred source.[30]

Despite their problems, grapevines do fill some needs. For instance, they often carry messages that formal systems will not. They are fast and flexible, and they provide messages that are understandable to employees. Further, the tendrils of the grapevine wind their ways around often formidable barriers, seeking out needed information from people in the know. Whatever the actual validity of information carried over the grapevine, employees do tend to view it as accurate. As such, grapevine information carries considerable weight.

As Figure 15–7 shows, the grapevine may take many forms. In its most typical form, the cluster, one person passes the message on to a number of others. Some of them—perhaps only 10 or 20 percent—repeat the message and others do not. As the message gets old and a large percentage of people know it, those who receive it are less likely to repeat it, and it dies out.

As we all know, some people simply like to talk more than others. However, there are other reasons why people become active on the grapevine. For

Information transmitted informally through the grapevine can carry considerable weight.

FIGURE 15–7
Types of Grapevine Chains

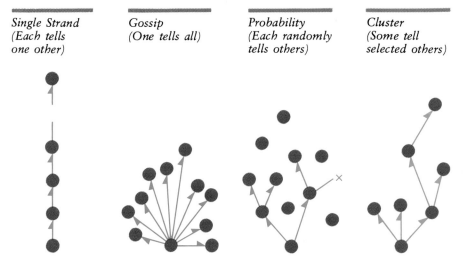

Single Strand (Each tells one other)   *Gossip (One tells all)*   *Probability (Each randomly tells others)*   *Cluster (Some tell selected others)*

Source: From *Human Behavior at Work: Organizational Behavior*, 7th ed., by K. Davis and J. W. Newstrom. Copyright © 1985 by McGraw-Hill Book Company. Reproduced with permission.

instance, if people have interesting news, they are likely to pass it on. If there is a great deal of excitement and uncertainty, such as when a new boss takes over, the grapevine thrives. Finally, some jobs that allow opportunity for contact and conversation have high levels of grapevine activity. One study, for instance, found that secretaries to managers were four times more likely to be key communicators on the grapevine than were other employees.[31]

Whatever managers think of the grapevine, they must accept it as a fact. Smart managers try to learn who is in the grapevine and how it works. They act to reduce misunderstandings and other negative effects of the grapevine. They may, for instance, carefully provide accurate information to squelch unfounded rumors. They also may try to harvest the grapevine, using it to get feedback about employee attitudes, feelings, and ideas.[32] Managers may also use the grapevine as a message channel to carry information which is somehow inappropriate for formal channels.

THE IMPACT OF NEW TECHNOLOGIES ON COMMUNICATION

New information technologies are rapidly changing organizational communications.[33] Telephone-answering devices and services, closed-circuit television systems, and videotaping, for instance, all provide new communication flexibility. The emerging technology of **electronic mail** or **E-mail**, the long-distance electronic transmission of written information, provides a very fast, inexpensive, and efficient means of communicating. It has been estimated that 16 billion E-mail messages will be sent annually by 1992, and 60 billion by the year 2000.[34] Management in Action 2 describes the benefits of electronic mail at Metropolitan Life Insurance Company.

Further, **teleconferencing**—two-way communication by both video and audio equipment between persons at different locations—offers tremendous

Q: *Your work shows that people in organizations rely very heavily on the grapevine as a source of information. What is the allure of the grapevine?*

A: People cannot resist the grapevine. It offers the latest news, and usually that news is reasonably accurate. Much of the news is about people, such as their friendships, conflicts, and experiences. Since formal communication carries very little of this type of information, we must listen to the grapevine in order to be fully informed. In addition, much of the grapevine occurs by person-to-person contact, which helps us become a part of social groups and receive social satisfactions.

Q: *Many managers view the grapevine as a negative factor. Should managers try to prevent employees from using the grapevine? Should they ignore the grapevine?*

A: Managers should not try to prevent their employees from using the grapevine. They cannot stop the grapevine, and those who occasionally try tend to find that their efforts stir up a larger, often more negative, grapevine. Even if we assume that managers could stop the grapevine, they would not want to do so, because then their employees would become less informed and less interested in their jobs. As an alternative, managers could ignore the grapevine, but that is poor management because they are ignoring an important part of their jobs. A better alternative is to join the grapevine and develop a reputation as a reliable sender and a trusted receiver of information.

Q: *Do you see any ethical problems with managers "harvesting" the grapevine to learn what subordinates and others are saying?*

A: No ethical problems arise with normal grapevine listening known to employees. They usually expect and want a manager to be in on some of their grapevines so that they can communicate upward some of the news they want their manager to receive. Of course, secret spies and listening devices are an unethical invasion of privacy and are universally condemned.

Q: *If managers are concerned that information passed through the grapevine is inaccurate, what can they do about it?*

A: First, they need to build an environment of trust so that employees will believe what managers say. Then, stop inaccurate rumors with the true facts. Nothing defeats rumors better than the truth. In rare instances when true facts are so confidential that they cannot be told, then explain why they are confidential. Face-to-face communication is quicker and allows response to individual employee questions. Furthermore, managers need to walk out of their offices and visit with their employees to establish a climate of trustworthy two-way communication. When managers bring accurate news to their employees, a social transaction is started that obligates employees in return to keep managers informed. This two-way trustworthy communication will substantially reduce inaccurate information.

Q: *How will new information technologies affect the role of the grapevine?*

A: New information technologies mean that the grapevine can travel much faster and reach many more people at once. In addition, more units of information can be transmitted within a short time. The patterns also are changing more to those who are on various electronic networks. Even the eavesdroppers are changing to those who are able to tap secretly into a network. The electronic grapevine is becoming more important and is here to stay.

Keith Davis (Ph.D., Ohio State University) is Professor Emeritus of Management at Arizona State University and formerly was a faculty member at Indiana University and the University of Texas. He is a past president of the Academy of Management and a fellow of both the Academy of Management and the International Academy of Management. He has been a consultant for a number of public and private organizations. Professor Davis is known internationally for his research on the organizational grapevine, and his other research interests are organizational behavior, human resources management, and social issues in business. He has published six books (four of which have been translated into other languages) and over 150 professional articles.

ACADEMIC PROFILE
KEITH DAVIS

Metropolitan Life Insurance Company describes its electronic mail system as a "general management tool for supplying information." Using this system helped

MANAGEMENT IN ACTION 2
ELECTRONIC MAIL SAVES METROPOLITAN
LIFE MORE THAN $100,000 EACH YEAR

to streamline message and reporting capabilities. It eliminated the need for duplicate hardware and helped save the company over $100,000 each year.

According to Vice-President Bruce J. Goodman, Metropolitan Life had to ensure rapid communication within its firm after decentralizing its New York home office functions in 1970. By establishing nine head offices across the country, the $52 billion company gained an opportunity to enhance customer service and to tap diversified labor markets. Because of cost considerations, these head offices serviced old policies whose historical paper records remained in the New York headquarters.

"It became the responsibility of head offices to administer several million policies issued some 30 to 40 years ago," said Goodman. "Thus, rapid communication between the head offices and New York became crucial in providing a high level of service to our policyholders."

Before instituting its electronic mail service, the head offices requested policy information from New York via a Telex system. Even though the system met the company's basic business needs, it required addi-

tional staffing and was prone to mechanical failure and human error. For instance, a correspondent received a request and filled in a form, and someone else cut the Telex paper tape, which was clumsy and occasionally ripped. Others would keypunch and batch multiple messages, which could only be transmitted to the home office at specific times. A total of 39 separate paper-handling steps were required in the overall work flow for one inquiry under the old system.

Using an electronic mail system, Metropolitan's head office customer service representatives send requests directly from their terminals. As a result, each head office saved from one-half to one full-time clerk. At the home office, the previous 39 separate paper-handling steps decreased to 22 steps, and the service time lapse improved by one to two days. Twelve clerical positions were no longer needed for processing message requests.

The system was first used to deliver daily operation status reports to head office end users and corporate management from the computer centers located in four cities. Computer center employees previously called in such reports by telephone. Not only did it take time to contact all necessary offices, but it usually took more than one phone call to reach the right person. One operator can now key a message, send it simultaneously to several offices, and not be restricted by multiple time zones.

Source: From *Management Information Systems: Conceptual Foundations, Structure, and Development*, 2d ed., by G. B. Davis and M. H. Olson. Copyright © 1985 by McGraw-Hill Book Company. Reproduced with permission.

savings of time, energy, and money. Many firms are now using teleconferencing for such purposes as sales meetings, editorial conferences, and job interviews. When the CEO of Atlantic Richfield Company (ARCO) complained that he had traveled 600 to 700 miles every day of his life for 35 years, ARCO began a two-year project to build a $20 million telecommunication network. The network links regional centers, permitting executives to meet with their counterparts elsewhere via widescreen color television. The executives can use another screen to exchange graphics, statistics, and photographs.[35]

Finally, **faxing**, the use of facsimile machines to send and reproduce copies of a document over telephone lines, has exploded in use in recent years. While hardly a new technology (it is about 150 years old!), faxing is a technology which is now rapidly changing the way many firms are doing business.[36] Faxing is discussed in Case 15–2.

We will more thoroughly explore the roles of the new information technologies in Chapter 19.

Faxing is rapidly changing the way many firms are doing business.

IMPLICATIONS FOR MANAGEMENT

It is hard to imagine someone becoming a truly successful manager without having a good grasp of communication skills. Communication is central to virtually all managerial roles and serves a variety of necessary functions.

Think about communication as a crucial skill you need to cultivate, much as you would try to master computer programming or finance. Learning to communicate, to ensure accurate communication from others, and to listen will probably reap greater returns than almost any other skill and will also make life a bit more pleasant.

Develop the ability to analyze organizational communication. Use the tools we have discussed to consider the nature of communication as well as communication channels, sources and recipients, timing, and difficulty. Once you assess each of these factors, steps toward improvement are possible.

Take into consideration the various causes of communication failure and try to avoid them. Keep language as simple as possible. Recognize that people will retain and distort information. Reward those who provide you with complete and accurate messages, and try to get objective confirmation of information. Beware of perceptual problems. Remember that selective perception, projection, and other perceptual difficulties can interfere with accurate communication. Use redundancy, feedback, and multiple channels as necessary to make sure your message has been correctly perceived. And take the time to listen.

When expecting communications from others, take steps to reduce the likelihood of problems. If possible, use multiple sources. Be clear about precisely what information you want and how and when you want it. Break down unnecessary communication barriers. Keep communication chains short. Create a climate of trust.

Master the array of techniques for communicating in organizations. Try not to overuse a single technique. Instead, fit the method to the needs of the message. Don't forget the importance of upward communication, and remember that horizontal communication is often useful.

Fit communication channels to your messages. Consider required immediacy, modifiability, capacity, and other channel dimensions, and ask whether feedback is needed. You may decide that multiple channels, such as both a telephone call and a written confirmation, would help, or that you must tailor channels specifically to the purpose. Attend to nonverbal as well as verbal aspects of your communication and keep them consistent. If you develop networks, design them with their required tasks in mind. Centralized networks may be fine for some purposes, but complex tasks demand the free flow of information that decentralized networks permit.

Don't assume that communication will, or should, neatly follow the branches of the organization chart. Instead, it may flow in unexpected ways—the grapevine winds everywhere. Pay attention to informal communication. If it seems inaccurate, try to provide corrective information, but don't treat the grapevine as an enemy. Use it as a supplement to formal channels.

Finally, follow developments concerning new communication technologies. Electronic mail, teleconferencing, faxing, and other innovations provide new flexibility and power to organizational communication. They promise to significantly change the way much of business is done.

KEY TERMS AND CONCEPTS

centralization	message channel
code noise	noise
communication	nonverbal communication
communication networks	one-way communication
decoder	organizational audit group
downward communication	psychological noise
electronic mail or E-mail	receiver
encoder	relative centrality
exception principle	teleconferencing
faxing	transmitter
grapevine	two-way communication
horizontal communication	upward communication

QUESTIONS FOR REVIEW AND DISCUSSION

1. What are four key functions of communication? Provide examples relating to each of these functions.
2. Which of the causes of communication failure discussed in this chapter do you think would be especially troubling in a firm in a stable, simple environment? In a dynamic, complex environment? Why?
3. Choose three of the perceptual problems discussed in Chapter 12 and show how each is relevant to communication in organizations.
4. Describe a situation of which you are aware in which bad news was suppressed. What were the consequences of that suppression?
5. Describe a situation in which one-way communication would be preferable to two-way communication.

6. Define nonverbal communication and give four examples. What are some of the things organizations might do to improve the effectiveness of the nonverbal communication of their managers?

7. Draw a star network and a wheel network. When would the wheel network be preferable to the star network? Why?

8. What is the grapevine? Do you feel grapevines should be stamped out in organizations? Why or why not?

9. What might be some problems associated with electronic mail? With teleconferencing?

CASES

15–1 TO APOLOGIZE OR NOT

Continental Airlines' chairman publicly begged the pardon of disgruntled airline passengers. "We grew so fast that we made mistakes," Frank Lorenzo confessed in a full-page advertisement in *Newsweek* in October 1987. "Misplaced baggage. Delays. Reservation errors. You were frustrated and angry. And a lot of hard-working people at Continental were pretty embarrassed."

Delta Air Lines took a different tack. Although hit by a string of mishaps, including a pilot landing a plane in the wrong city, the airline's ads ignored the problems. "Delta gets you there," its slogan maintained.

Until recently, companies seldom even considered confessing a mistake or shortcoming. "The standard was, 'Don't admit anything, bulldoze your way through a situation,'" says Thomas Garbett, a Watertown, Conn., corporate advertising consultant. Now it's not that easy. Consumers are smarter, and media coverage of business more scrupulous, he says, so the old strategy is no longer an automatic choice.

A virtual prerequisite to an apology, consultants say, is a chief executive with a strong interest in communications. Consider Chrysler Corp.'s response in the summer of 1987 when two executives were indicted in connection with disengaged odometers. After a storm of negative publicity, Chairman Lee Iacocca apologized for the practice at a news conference. "I'm damn sorry it happened and you can bet that it won't ever happen again, and that's a promise," he said. Ads in 23 newspapers carried the same message.

Consultants say Mr. Iacocca is more likely than many executives to offer an apology—both because of his interest in communications and because his name is so closely aligned with Chrysler that a black mark against the company tarnishes him personally. Likewise, an apology can boost or preserve credibility. Says Linda Golodner, executive director of the National Consumer League, "A lot of companies are starting to realize it's good PR to look vulnerable and concerned about customer service."

In 1986, for example, when Coca-Cola Co. reintroduced original Coke as Coke Classic, it confessed that it had misread consumer tastes in pulling the brand in the first place. The president called it "a humbling experience." The result: "Coke almost achieved a warmth and humanity out of having made a mistake," says Mr. Garbett.

Communications consultants say companies decide not to apologize chiefly because their lawyers advise against it. Indeed, a Chrysler spokesman says company lawyers didn't want Mr. Iacocca to apologize in the odometer episode, especially because the case hadn't gone to trial. Legal issues were so thorny in the case that the company had to clear the ads with the lawyer prosecuting the case, so that the company wouldn't be accused of trying to influence potential jurors by generating goodwill.

Others say an apology isn't appropriate in case of a serious problem. After 2,000 people died in the Bhopal, India, poison-gas leak, Union Carbide Corp. never considered an advertised public apology, says spokesman Earl Slack. "It's one thing to apologize for poor service," he says. "When you have something the magnitude of Bhopal, you address it with concerns and actions."

Continental Airlines spent months researching how best to convince the public that service was improving, but even so, many employees had misgivings about its ads. "Down deep, those people felt that if we ever admitted weakness, that would be it and the world would write us off," says James O'Donnell, vice-president of marketing services.

Apologizing publicly and vowing to make amends involves one other risk, says Leo J. Shapiro of the consumer research firm of Leo J. Shapiro & Associates. What happens, he asks, when the company makes another mistake? "Are you going to believe Frank Lorenzo if your luggage gets lost again?"

Source: Reprinted by permission of *The Wall Street Journal*, © Dow Jones & Company, Inc. (November 24, 1987). All Rights Reserved Worldwide.

1. Which of the four major functions of communication discussed in this chapter do you think are fulfilled by a company's apology for a shortcoming?
2. What do you see as the costs of a policy of publicly admitting mistakes? The benefits?
3. Consider a magazine ad and a news conference as two alternative channels a CEO might use to make a public apology. Weigh the relative merits of those alternatives by contrasting them on the channel dimensions discussed in this chapter.

15–2 BUSINESS COMMUNICATION IN THE FAX AGE

The facsimile machine, which can send and reproduce copies of a document over telephone lines, is suddenly everywhere. In broadest terms, it has divided the business world into the faxers and fax-nots. And as it blends into the corporate landscape, it is subtly changing how people communicate. It has, for instance, squeezed the breathing room that mailing allows. It has also helped to fuel the impatience that comes with automation.

The facsimile machine, invented in the 1840s but grown vastly more sophisticated in recent years, began its latest boom in Japan, where modern times demanded quick visual reproduction of a language with thousands of characters. Steve Joerg, vice-president of sales for fax machines at Ricoh Co. of Japan's U.S. subsidiary, says the Japanese also like to fax because their business culture encourages last-minute decision making and relies on consensus.

With a projected 1.5 million fax machines in use in the United States by the end of 1988, the technology's brief life as a competitive advantage is nearly over. "Like a lot of modern technology, if everyone gets it, it just becomes a condition of doing business," says JoAnne Yates, a senior lecturer at Massachusetts Institute of Technology's School of Management.

One of the great virtues of faxing is that it combines speed with useful "visual cues," says Ms. Yates. She explains that like a letter—and unlike electronic "mail" sent by computers—fax lets the sender signal "different levels of formality" by choosing between typing and handwriting, and among corporate letterhead, personal stationery, or sheets from a memo pad.

Faxing is especially appealing for international communications. Besides offering the comfort of "having it spelled out in a document," and the freedom to communicate despite time differences, faxing promotes a "much more direct" exchange, says Craig Murphy, a professor of political science at Wellesley College. While mailed materials from abroad often include a lot of verbal bowing and scraping, he notes, faxing encourages a straightforward memorandum style.

Despite the machine's charms, however, there are those who aren't going gently into the age of fax. Mark White, a Birmingham, Ala., lawyer, complains that faxing has destroyed a precious period of communications float. When sending something by mail or even overnight express, he says, "you'd get it off your desk and wouldn't have to deal with it for 48 hours. Now it's back to you in 10 minutes."

Because fax machines are often installed in the mail room or some central location, they can raise security problems. Experienced users say they are amazed at the material some people send, apparently without regard for who will see it at the other end. The more advanced machines now store communications, which recipients retrieve by punching in a code or using a passkey. Some machines can also load the material into a personal computer, where it will wait until the user calls it up.

And no one has yet solved the problem of fax junk mail. Mr. Joerg of Ricoh says fax operators in mail rooms around the country are reaping bounties of videocassette recorders, fur coats, and other merchandise for turning over to marketers or fax-directory publishers the logs of numbers called by their machines.

Source: Reprinted by permission of *The Wall Street Journal*, © Dow Jones & Company, Inc. (October 27, 1988). All Rights Reserved Worldwide.

1. Which of the communication problems discussed in this chapter do you think would probably be made worse by fax machines? Which would probably be alleviated?
2. Discuss faxing in terms of each of the communication channel dimensions discussed in this chapter.
3. In view of your answers to questions 1 and 2, for what sorts of messages do you think faxing would be most appropriate? Least appropriate? Why?

ENDNOTES

1. T. J. Peters and R. H. Waterman, *In Search of Excellence: Lessons from America's Best-Run Companies* (New York: Harper & Row, 1982).
2. See, for instance, R. Rowan, "Where Did That Rumor Come From?" *Fortune* (August 13, 1979): 130-137. The Corona Extra example is from *The Wall Street Journal* (August 17, 1988): 23.
3. H. Mintzberg, *The Nature of Managerial Work* (Englewood Cliffs, NJ: Prentice-Hall, 1973).
4. W. G. Scott and T. R. Mitchell, *Organization Theory: A Structural and Behavioral Analysis* (Homewood, IL: Richard D. Irwin, 1976).
5. For a discussion of the motivating roles of language, see J. J. Sullivan, "Three Roles of Language in Motivation Theory," *Academy of Management Review* 13 (1988): 104-115.
6. *Wall Street Journal* (November 12, 1982): 1.
7. *Wall Street Journal* (September 30, 1988): 23.
8. The structure of this section is based largely on talks by George Huber, Graduate School of Business, University of Wisconsin–Madison (1981).
9. W. H. Read, "Upward Communication in Industrial Hierarchies," *Human Relations* 15 (1962): 3-15.
10. The techniques for downward and upward communication are drawn from P. M. Muchinsky, *Psychology Applied to Work: An Introduction to Industrial and Organizational Psychology*, 2d ed. (Chicago: Dorsey Press, 1987), 547-554.
11. L. W. Rue and L. Byars, *Communication in Organizations* (Homewood, IL: Richard D. Irwin, 1980).
12. A. Farnham, "Trust Gap," *Fortune* (December 4, 1989): 70.
13. K. H. Roberts, *Communicating in Organizations* (Chicago: Science Research Associates, 1984).

14. C. E. Redfield, *Communication in Management* (Chicago: University of Chicago Press, 1953).

15. Japanese firms sometimes send out newsletters in the form of comic books. Comic books, or *mangas*, are widely read in Japan, and dozens of Japanese companies now use this form to convey information to employees. See S. Solo, "Japanese Comics Are All Business," *Fortune* (October 9, 1989): 143-149.

16. See R. B. Dunham and F. J. Smith, *Organizational Surveys: An Internal Assessment of Organizational Health* (Glenview, IL: Scott, Foresman, 1979), for a good discussion of organizational surveys.

17. Farnham, "Trust Gap," 57. This article provides a good discussion of the importance of upward communication.

18. *Wall Street Journal* (October 27, 1986): 23.

19. J. Hage, M. Aiken, and C. B. Marrett, "Organization Structure and Communications," *American Sociological Review* 36 (1971): 860-871.

20. This listing of channel characteristics is drawn from R. B. Dunham, *Organizational Behavior: People and Processes in Management* (Homewood, IL: Richard D. Irwin, 1984).

21. H. J. Leavitt, *Managerial Psychology*, rev. ed. (Chicago: University of Chicago Press, 1964), 138-152.

22. R. L. Daft and R. H. Lengel, "Information Richness: A New Approach to Managerial Behavior and Organization Design," in *Research in Organizational Behavior*, ed. B. Staw and L. L. Cummings (Greenwich, CT: JAI Press, 1984), 191-233.

23. For interesting discussions of nonverbal communication, see M. B. McCaskey, "The Hidden Messages Managers Send," *Harvard Business Review* (November-December 1979): 135-148, and Roberts, *Communicating in Organizations*.

24. See, for instance, R. Harrison, "Nonverbal Communication," in *Dimensions in Communication*, ed. J. H. Campbell and P. W. Harper (Belmont, CA: Wadsworth, 1970), and A. Mehrabian, *Non-Verbal Communication* (Chicago: Aldine, 1972).

25. Two key papers relating to communication networks are H. Guetzkow and H. Simon, "The Impact of Certain Communication Nets upon Organization and Performance in Task-Oriented Groups," *Management Science* 1 (1955): 233-250, and M. E. Shaw, "Communication Networks," in *Advances in Experimental Social Psychology*, ed. L. Berkowitz (New York: Academic Press, 1964), 111-147.

26. A. Bavelas, "Communication Patterns in Task-Oriented Groups," *Journal of the Acoustical Society of America* 22 (1950): 725-730. For instance, the central member in the wheel network in Figure 15-6 has a total of four links to the other four members (that is, one to each). Each of the other four members has one link to the central member and two links to each of the other three members (that is, a link to the central member and then another to the target member)—a total of seven links. So, the total number of links in the network is $4 + 7 + 7 + 7 + 7 = 32$. The relative centrality of the central member is $32/4 = 8.0$. For each other member, the relative centrality is $32/7 = 4.57$. Centralization is computed as the variance of the relative centrality scores.

27. This section is based primarily on K. Davis and J. W. Newstrom, *Human Behavior at Work*, 8th ed. (New York: McGraw-Hill, 1989), 370-378. See that source for a fuller discussion.

28. J. W. Newstrom, R. E. Monczka, and W. E. Reif, "Perceptions of the Grapevine: Its Value and Influence," *Journal of Business Communication* (Spring 1974): 12-20.

29. International Association of Business Communications survey reported in *Arizona Republic* (November 14, 1982): C-1.

30. Davis and Newstrom, *Human Behavior at Work*, 315.

31. K. Davis, "Grapevine Communication Among Lower and Middle Managers," *Personnel Journal* (April 1969): 269-272.

32. On this point, see H. B. Vickery III, "Tapping into the Employee Grapevine," *Association Management* (January 1984): 59-63.

33. For a good overview of electronic communications, see R. V. Ruch, *Corporate Communications: A Comparison of Japanese and American Practices* (Westport, CT: Quorum Books, 1984).

34. *Business Week* (May 8, 1989): 135, 138-139. See this article for a good update on the problems and prospects of E-mail.

35. *Business Week* (July 7, 1980): 81.

36. See J. Solomon, "Business Communication in the Fax Age," *Wall Street Journal* (October 27, 1988): B1.

Leading

CHAPTER 16

After studying this chapter, you should be able to:
- *Discuss how leaders can gain power in organizations.*
- *Identify traits that are sometimes associated with successful leadership and point out problems associated with the trait approach.*
- *Explain how democratic and autocratic leadership styles affect the way subordinates respond.*
- *Discuss the roles of leader consideration and initiating structure.*
- *Describe three models of leadership which take situational factors into account and explain their similarities and differences.*
- *Discuss substitutes for leadership.*
- *Explain the difference between transactional leadership and transformational leadership.*

Harry V. Quadracci is the founder and president of a commercial printing company, Quad/Graphics. In 1971, he bought a small, abandoned factory for $150,000 and paid for it with a rubber check for $10,000 as the deposit, a second mortgage on his home, and the hope that he could arrange more financing by the time the deal closed. Almost two decades later, Quad/Graphics has over $400 million in sales and more than 3,500 employees. Over the last decade, it has had an average annual growth rate of over 40 percent in an industry where 10 percent growth is considered exceptional. Quadracci practices what his employees call Theory Q—a blend of "hunchmanship" and active risk-taking. There are no budgets at Quad/Graphics—things change too quickly—and Quadracci shuns planning. "We're guerrillas," says Quadracci, describing his management strategy. "We're street fighters. We're not planners. We are doers." Quadracci sometimes describes the company as a circus, a continuous performance of highly creative and individualistic troupes. And he compares the company's management to clowns—they are not wedded to conventional wisdom, and they retain their childlike ability to be surprised and the flexibility to thrive on change. Quadracci's leadership style has clearly had an enormous, positive effect on the fortunes of Quad/Graphics. Just as clearly, his style might be disastrous in other situations.[1]

The potential impact of successful leadership is reflected in the tremendous compensation of some top executives. In 1988, Michael Eisner, chairman of Walt Disney Company, was the highest-paid U.S. chief executive, with a total of $40.1 million in salary, bonuses, and stock options. Frank Wells, Walt Disney Company's president, was runner-up at a mere $32.1 million.[2] The belief that leadership can make a difference is also evidenced by the turnover at the top of major organizations. A survey of the Fortune 500 companies found that almost 60 percent had changed their CEOs at least once over the 1976–85 period. On average, CEOs remained in their positions for only six years. Such turnover appears to be rapidly increasing.[3]

Of course, there are leaders throughout the organization, not just at the top. All of them must be concerned with the performance and satisfaction of their subordinates. But what is leadership?

Leadership can be viewed in terms of the ways that leaders behave or in terms of their characteristics. Arthur Jago provides the following definition:

Leadership *is both a process and a property. The process of leadership is the use of noncoercive influence to direct and coordinate the activities of the members of an organized group toward the accomplishment of group objectives. As a property, leadership is the set of qualities or characteristics attributed to those who are perceived to successfully employ such influence.*[4]

Note that in Jago's definition, leadership is not only some quality or characteristic of the person but also what that person does. Further, leadership is not limited to managers, supervisors, or superiors. Anyone in a group may take on leadership roles.

In this chapter we will first examine bases of leader power. Then we will consider a variety of approaches to the study of leadership. Those approaches focus on traits, styles, and behaviors, as well as on situational factors that influence successful leadership. Together, they may help you become a better leader.

POWER

Most people would agree that "leaders influence followers." There might be less agreement, though, on just what "influence" means. Further, how are leaders able to influence? In this section, we will consider authority, power, influence, and control. We will then discuss ways by which managers may acquire power.

What Is Power?

To help understand the nature of power, we must first define some terms. We should note that the one term found in each of the following definitions, *force,* does not necessarily imply coercion. Rather, it is used more generally to mean pressure for movement in a given direction, or pressure to resist movement. This broader meaning might be captured by a phrase such as "the force of one's arguments."

Chrysler Corporation's comeback from near financial collapse in 1979 was effected through the powerful leadership of Lee Iacocca.

- **Authority** is the right to exert force on another.
- **Power** is the ability to exert force on another.
- **Influence** is the actual exertion of force on another.
- **Control** is the exertion of enough force on another to alter behavior.

Bases of Power

John French and Bertram Raven have developed the best-known scheme for classifying bases of power.[5] They have identified five power bases:

- **Legitimate power** results when one individual feels it is legitimate, or right, for another to give orders or otherwise exercise force. A worker who says, "I ought to do as my boss says" is reflecting a belief in legitimate power. Legitimate power may:

  a. Be culturally specified. In some cultures, it is considered right that older people or people of certain castes or with certain characteristics should be given respect and obedience.
  b. Come from acceptance of the social structure. If individuals accept the social structure as legitimate—whether it is the hierarchy of an organization, the status ranking in a street gang, or a country's governance system—they are likely to see demands of those perceived to be higher in the structure as legitimate.
  c. Be designated by a legitimizing agent. Those with legitimate power may choose to share it with others. A firm's CEO may appoint an assistant. In democratic societies, the holders of legitimate power—the people—may pass on that power through elections.

  Legitimate power sounds much like authority. The difference is that authority is the right to exert force while legitimate power is the individual's belief that another has that right. Unless subordinates accept authority, there is no legitimate power.

- **Reward power** is power whose basis is the ability to reward. It depends on one person's ability to administer desired outcomes to another and to decrease or remove outcomes that are not desired. If Rosa feels that Carol controls things Rosa wants, and that getting those rewards depends upon whether or not she does what Carol wants, Carol has reward power over Rosa.

- **Coercive power** is based on one person's ability to affect punishment that another receives. The strength of Heidi's coercive power over Tom depends on the degree to which the threatened punishment has a negative valence for Tom and the degree to which Tom perceives that the probability of punishment will decrease if he conforms. Our previous discussions of punishment suggest that we should use coercive power sparingly, if at all. Recall that the definition of leadership given at the beginning of this chapter excludes coercive power. The gist of that definition is that use of coercion is not true leadership.
- **Referent power** comes from the feeling of identity, or oneness, that one person has with another or the desire for such identity. Diana's statement, "I want to be like Maria, so I will behave as she does or says," reflects Maria's referent power over Diana.
- **Expert power** is based on one person's perception that another has needed relevant knowledge in a given area. Doctors, lawyers, and computer specialists all may have expert power.

These bases of power, coupled with the definitions given above, suggest some characteristics of power. First, it is perceptual. If a subordinate perceives that the boss can reward or punish or has expertise or controls information, that person will behave accordingly, regardless of the objective situation. Second, power is relative. It is not, for instance, the absolute level of expertise one has that determines power over another but the expertise relative to the other. A superior may have considerable expert power relative to one subordinate and virtually none relative to another. Third, power is latent. It is the ability to use rewards, punishments, or other power bases. Even though those bases may never actually be used, power still exists. Finally, power is dynamic. Power relationships evolve over time as individuals gain or lose power bases relative to others or as perceptions change.

Power can vary in range and domain. The **range of power** is the number of different areas in which one person can influence another. The **domain of power** is the number of individuals over whom someone can exert influence with respect to a specified range. The bases of power defined above differ in range. Typically, referent power has the broadest range, while the range of expert power is limited.[6]

Some Specific Sources of Power

The French and Raven bases described earlier help us to get a feel for the many ways people can acquire power. However, there are other specific sources of power which may not fit neatly into those classes.[7] While we will focus on ways that individuals gain power, organizations may also use the following sources to acquire power:

- *Provision of resources.* Those who provide resources—whether financial, material, or human—have power since they can cut off the supply. Workers gain power by threatening to strike. A bank has power through its control of loan funds. Steel suppliers have power due to their ability to cut off supplies to auto plants.

- *Ability to cope with uncertainty.* Organizations, and parts of organizations, regularly face change, complexity, and other sources of uncertainty. Those who can handle this uncertainty gain power. These are often people at the "skin" of the organization, dealing directly with elements of the environment. Personnel managers and market researchers would be examples.
- *Irreplaceability.* Members of organizations who carry out necessary functions and are irreplaceable may have considerable power. Often, people take actions to ensure their irreplaceability. For instance, a computer programmer may fail to document programs so others can't use them without his or her input. Other ways to make replaceability more difficult include limiting access to the profession or using jargon that few others can understand.
- *Control over the problem-solving process.* Problem solving is a central, crucial process in organizations, and those who control it gain power. The ability to set the criteria used to make strategic choices or to dictate which alternatives will be considered carries power.
- *Control of information.*[8] People often gain power through access to or control of information. For instance, some people gradually acquire power over time through their growing knowledge of how things work and where things are. Some secretaries may know all the ins and outs of the organization and gain power as a result. Also, recall from Chapter 15 that people who are central in communication networks gain power through their access to information and their ability to decide who does—and does not—receive it.
- *Political skills.* Some people get power through their possession and use of political skills. Some simply have greater negotiation skills than others. Some are especially Machiavellian and therefore more inclined to rely on political skills. Some are capable of creating an "illusion of power," giving the false impression that they are capable of great influence. Since power is inherently perceptual, these political tactics may be powerful.[9]

Now that we have considered some ways that leaders may gain the ability to influence others, let's examine views on what makes leaders effective. We will take a historical perspective.

TRAIT APPROACHES TO LEADERSHIP

The earliest approach to the study of leadership was to try to identify characteristics, or traits, of successful leaders. For instance, one early study found links between leadership success and intelligence, education, high preference for risk, desire for independence, and other variables.[10] Literally thousands of studies have now explored leadership traits. Some of these traits relate to physical factors, some to ability, many to personality, and still others to social characteristics. Of the traits, activity, intelligence, knowledge, dominance, and self-confidence are most often found to be linked to successful leadership.[11]

Unfortunately, most reviews of studies relating to leadership traits have concluded that the trait approach has not been fruitful.[12] One early survey of

this literature noted that of all traits that showed up in one study or another as related to leadership effectiveness, only 5 percent were common to four or more studies.[13] In another early study, some high school students emerged as leaders on one type of task, and others on other tasks.[14] These findings suggest that the traits needed by leaders may depend on the situation. To illustrate how traits of successful leaders may vary, consider the profiles of current business leaders in Figure 16–1. How are they similar? How do they differ?

A further concern with the trait approach relates to the question of how the findings can be used. Since traits are relatively stable, it is unlikely that leaders can develop them through training. So, while information concerning traits of successful leaders might be useful for selection and placement, it is otherwise of limited value. In part, this is because the trait approach considers only the characteristics of the leader while ignoring the characteristics of followers and situations.

This doesn't mean that we should abandon the trait approach. For instance, it may be useful to determine which traits are associated with success in particular situations. However, it is safe at this point to say that more is likely to be gained by looking directly at what successful leaders *do* than at what they *are*.

DEMOCRATIC AND AUTOCRATIC STYLES

An early approach to the study of leadership considered the degree to which leaders are autocratic or democratic. **Autocratic leaders** make decisions themselves, without inputs from subordinates. **Democratic leaders** let subordinates participate in decision making. Autocratic and democratic styles are at opposite ends of a single continuum, differing in degree of delegation of decision-making authority. They differ only on this dimension, not necessarily on other variables such as sensitivity or caring. There are benevolent autocrats and there are uncaring democrats, as well as their opposites.

Research shows that democratic style is consistently linked to higher levels of subordinate satisfaction. However, the relationship of style to performance is more complex. Democratic style is usually positively, but weakly,

FIGURE 16–1
Leader Profiles

Here are some sketches of chief executives of U.S. firms. While only glimpses, they give some feel for the different styles of big business leaders.

Lee Iacocca, Chairman, Chrysler

Iacocca is an action-oriented, decisive, master communicator. He says, "There comes a time when you've got to say, 'Let's get off our asses and go,' whether you're running a war or whatever. . . . I have always found that if I move with 75 percent or more of the facts, I usually never regret it" (Iacocca and Novak, 1984, 71). "What the last fifty years have taught us was the difference between right and wrong, that only hard work succeeds, that there are no free lunches, that you've got to be productive" (p. 51). Iacocca "is a consummate salesman with an eye for product and styling . . . has credibility and visibility . . . directness, humor, and salty language that appeal to the public" ("Executive Pay," 90).

John F. Welch, Jr., Chairman, General Electric

Welch wants to make each GE business Number 1 or 2 in every market it serves. He tries to inspire discipline and respect and to promote risk-taking behavior. According to former employees, Welch "conducts meetings so aggressively that people tremble. He attacks almost physically with his intellect, criticizing, demeaning, ridiculing, humiliating" (Flax, 1984, 19). "Since taking over, Welch has announced the closing of 25 plants. This has earned him the nickname 'Neutron Jack.' Employees joke that, like the aftermath of a neutron bomb, after Welch visits a facility, the building is left standing, but a lot of people are dead" (p. 19). Welch wants "leaders" in GE, not just "managers." Managers, he says, start managing things and getting in the way. Leaders must be tough and decisive. Welch says, "It takes courage and tough-mindedness to pick the bets, put the resources behind them, articulate the vision to employees, and explain why you said yes to this one and no to that one" (Sherman, 1989, 50).

Carl Reichardt, Chairman and President, Wells Fargo Bank

Reichardt is a performance-oriented leader who likes to motivate people by offering rewards for good work. He believes in teamwork and shares decision making with subordinates. Reichardt considers time cards an insult to people. "If we don't trust them, they shouldn't be here, so we're eliminating time cards" (Garcia, 1983, 85). He encourages staff to "walk in here and talk to me and not feel they're going around someone's back" (p. 85). Reichardt says, "I communicate clearly, I delegate, but I like to understand the detail of things also. . . . When I have confidence in people, there's complete freedom to act around here. We're a decentralized organization" (p. 83). But Reichardt's performance emphasis has also led to his reputation as a Scrooge; he is notorious for such things as cutting a Christmas tree from the bank's budget and for refusing to replace worn carpets. He has closed dozens of operations that failed to meet profit goals and laid off thousands of employees in the process. He admits, "We do have a fetish about this expense control thing" (Bennett, 1989, 18).

related to productivity. There are many factors that determine whether a democratic style is appropriate, including the nature of the task and the personalities of subordinates. When tasks are simple and repetitive, participation has little effect because "there is little to participate about."[15] When subordinates are intelligent and desire independence, participation is especially important. Later in this chapter, we will examine a model that more thoroughly addresses this issue.

Also, we noted in Chapter 12 that people vary their behaviors depending on their perceptions of others; recall that this is a cause of the Pygmalion effect. So we might expect that managers who see their subordinates as high performers may treat them differently, giving them more responsibility. As a result, the correlation between democratic style and performance could be due to the impact of performance on style rather than vice versa. We'll see that this issue is also relevant to other areas of leadership research.

KEY DIMENSIONS OF LEADER BEHAVIOR

We've said that democratic and autocratic leadership styles differ on only a single dimension—the degree of delegation of decision-making authority. This is an important but rather narrow focus, ignoring many potentially important leader behaviors. A more promising approach might begin by taking a broader view, generating a lengthy list of leader behaviors. Then, it would be possible to see which behaviors group together and to examine how the groupings relate to subordinates' responses. This is the approach taken in a major research program carried out at Ohio State University.

The Ohio State researchers developed a scale called the Leader Behavior Description Questionnaire (LBDQ). The LBDQ asked subordinates to indicate the extent to which they agreed with a wide variety of statements about behaviors of their leaders. Statistical analyses revealed that two independent underlying factors were most important in explaining subordinates' responses:[16]

- **Consideration**. This is behavior "indicative of friendship, mutual trust, respect, and warmth." Sample LBDQ items are "Does personal favors for group members" and "Finds time to listen to group members."
- **Initiating structure**. This is behavior which indicates that "the [leader] organizes and defines the relationship between himself and members of the crew." Sample LBDQ items are "Rules with an iron hand" and "Schedules the work to be done."[17]

Consideration and initiating structure have emerged as key dimensions of perceived leader behavior in many later studies in a wide variety of settings. These are independent dimensions. A manager may be both considerate and structuring, considerate but not structuring, and so on. That is, a high score on one dimension does not imply a low score on the other.

A manager who takes the time to talk things over with a subordinate is exhibiting leader consideration.

Evidence Concerning Consideration and Initiating Structure

Evidence concerning the roles of consideration and initiating structure is mixed. Consideration is often, but not always, positively related to subordinate satisfaction and unrelated to performance. Initiating structure is often positively related to group performance and negatively related to satisfaction, though exceptions again crop up.

To try to make some sense of this literature, it would be useful to explore three issues: First, is leader behavior a cause or consequence of subordinates' responses? Second, do consideration and initiating structure act separately, or do they somehow interact? Third, what role does the situation play in subordinates' responses to leader behavior?

What Causes What?

One reason it is hard to isolate the roles of consideration and initiating structure is that research in this area has relied heavily on survey methodology and on correlations as the measure of association. Correlations show only how two variables are related, not whether one causes the other.

In fact, as we suggested earlier, it could be that leader behavior is as much a response to the behavior of subordinates as the reverse. It makes sense, for instance, that if we think our subordinates are working hard and doing a good job, we will treat them differently than if we see them as loafers.

For example, subjects in one early experiment were told they had been hired to supervise a "Job Corps trainee" who was typing letters. The "Job Corps trainee" was really a confederate of the experimenters, and the quality of the letters he typed was experimentally varied. When subjects thought their "trainee" was not competent, they supervised him more closely, exhibiting more initiating structure and less consideration than when they saw him as competent.[18]

Leader behaviors and outcomes also may be spuriously related. That is, the influence of some third variable may cause them to move in similar ways even though they are not themselves causally related. For instance, the nature of some jobs might cause employees to be satisfied and might encourage their leaders to allow high levels of participation. Other jobs might cause dissatisfaction and encourage autocratic behavior. A comparison across jobs might suggest that satisfaction and leader behavior are causally related when in fact job characteristics influence them both.

The Interaction of Leader Behaviors

While most studies have considered the separate roles of consideration and initiating structure, they may in fact interact to influence subordinates' reactions. For instance, consider Management in Action 1. How do you think you would react to such "Walk Around Management"? Chances are, if you thought the boss was considerate, such personal visits would be pleasant. If not, you might view them as spying or as an unwelcome intrusion.

In fact, some research shows that subordinates are often most satisfied when leaders exhibit high levels of both consideration and initiating structure.[19] Apparently, the way employees react to initiating structure depends on how considerate they feel their superiors are. If employees feel their superiors are considerate, initiating structure is apparently viewed as helpful. If employees see their superiors as inconsiderate, they interpret such structuring as evidence of lack of trust and as "breathing down the neck" of the employees.

Reflecting this focus on the possible beneficial effects of concern for both people and tasks is the popular **managerial Grid®** developed by Robert Blake and Jane Srygley Mouton, shown in Figure 16–2.[20] The axes of the Grid are concern for people and concern for production. These are similar to consideration and initiating structure, respectively, except that they deal with attitudes (that is, concern) rather than actual behavior. A manager can fall into any of the cells of the Grid. Blake and Mouton argue that a 9,9 approach, integrating high concern for both people and production, is preferable. Through well-developed training programs, Blake and Mouton help managers achieve that approach.

However, research suggests that it is not *always* best for the leader to exhibit high levels of both consideration and initiating structure. For instance, as we will see, sometimes the task is so well structured that further structuring behaviors would be unnecessary or even harmful. This does not necessar-

At Apple Computer's headquarters, many of the company's employees wear large badges labeled WAM. The initials stand for "Walk Around Manage-

MANAGEMENT IN ACTION 1
WALK AROUND MANAGEMENT

ment" and reflect an attempt to preserve the entrepreneurial atmosphere that contributed to Apple's success. At Hewlett-Packard, this approach is called "Management by Wandering Around." Motorola Chairman Robert Galvin often sets aside a day or more outside of headquarters to devote primarily to chatting with employees. These examples—and more could be cited—show that many managers feel it is important to break through the layers of bureaucracy and see what is going on among the workers. Such an approach may aid worker morale, help prevent executive insulation, and point out important problems or opportunities. If carried too far, however, it may cause executives to be bogged down in details and may undermine lower-level managers by breaking the chain of command.

Source: Adapted from "Where's the Boss? Taking a Walk," *Forbes* (August 29, 1983): 62

FIGURE 16–2
The Managerial Grid

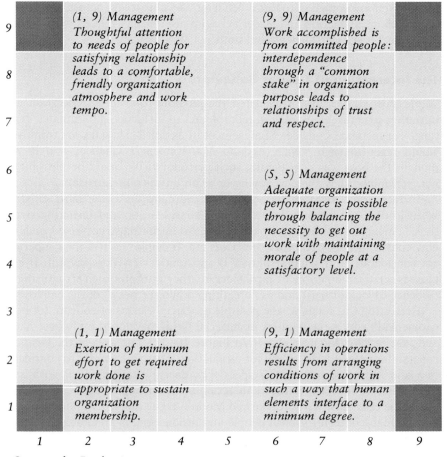

Concern for People

(1, 9) Management
Thoughtful attention to needs of people for satisfying relationship leads to a comfortable, friendly organization atmosphere and work tempo.

(9, 9) Management
Work accomplished is from committed people: interdependence through a "common stake" in organization purpose leads to relationships of trust and respect.

(5, 5) Management
Adequate organization performance is possible through balancing the necessity to get out work with maintaining morale of people at a satisfactory level.

(1, 1) Management
Exertion of minimum effort to get required work done is appropriate to sustain organization membership.

(9, 1) Management
Efficiency in operations results from arranging conditions of work in such a way that human elements interface to a minimum degree.

Concern for Production

Source: The Managerial Grid figure from *The Managerial Grid III: The Key to Leadership Excellence*, by Robert R. Blake and Jane Srygley Mouton. Houston: Gulf Publishing Company, Copyright © 1985, page 12. Reproduced by permission.

ily contradict the Blake and Mouton arguments—they reason that the leader should show *concern* for people and production. In some situations, the concern would not have to translate into behavior. Instead, behaviors are appropriate in some situations but not in others.

The Role of the Situation

Steve Kerr and his colleagues have identified a variety of factors that influence the way leader behaviors affect subordinates' responses.[21] Some of those factors are the following:

- *Pressure.* When the situation involves stress, time pressures, task demands, and physical danger, subordinates view leader initiating structure more favorably than in calm, secure situations. Historically, subordinates have accepted autocratic, structuring leaders in times of war or other national emergency.
- *Task-related satisfaction.* When jobs are not intrinsically satisfying, leader initiating structure may increase performance, but it leads to resentment and dissatisfaction. If subordinates don't like the job, they see little to gain from being told how to do it. Also, when the task is not intrinsically satisfying, leader consideration becomes more important. A friendly, supportive boss may not be very important if you really enjoy your work, but a bit of warmth and comforting helps ease the pain of an unsatisfying job.
- *Subordinates' need for information.* When subordinates lack knowledge about the task, perhaps because they are new on the job or because the job is very ambiguous, they like initiating structure.
- *Subordinates' expectations.* Subordinates react more positively to levels of consideration and initiating structure which they expect than to unexpected levels of those behaviors.

Together, these findings suggest some straightforward and logical guidelines for leaders. If the situation calls for structure, provide it. If it doesn't, subordinates will see structuring behaviors as redundant and bothersome. If the situation is one in which subordinates clearly could use some support, consideration would be especially helpful. If not, consideration may be less important (though it rarely hurts). And, subordinates (and others) value some predictability in behavior. If leaders behave erratically, subordinates are likely to react with suspicion and caution.

This recognition of the importance of the situation is reflected in three major theories of leadership which we will examine in the following sections. Each of these theories examines the fit between the leader and the situation, and each gives managers ways to achieve an effective fit. The first of these theories shows how the leader can assess and change the situation to bring about that fit. The others indicate how leaders can tailor their behaviors to the situation.

ENGINEERING THE JOB TO FIT THE MANAGER

Fred Fiedler developed the **contingency model of leadership**.[22] We have seen the term contingency before. It simply means that something is contingent upon (that is, depends upon) something else. In Fiedler's theory, leadership effectiveness depends upon whether situational characteristics fit the manager.

Nature of the Theory

Fiedler reasoned that if a fit could be found between some leader trait or behavior and the situation, that information could be used in one or more of four ways. It would be possible to try to:

- Change the leader's traits or behaviors.
- Select leaders who have traits or behaviors fitting the situation.
- Move managers around in the organization until they are in positions that fit them.
- Change the situation.

Fiedler felt that the first three options—training, selection, and placement—simply don't work well enough to make meaningful improvements. Instead, he reasoned, we should "engineer the job to fit the manager." The logic of his approach is as follows:

- Find a stable characteristic of the leader.
- Find some aspects of the situation which the leader can manipulate.
- Find the fit between the characteristics of the leader and of the situation.
- For a particular leader, see if fit is correct or incorrect.
- If fit is incorrect, change the situation to achieve correct fit.

Fiedler's measure of the leader—called the **LPC** (for least-preferred co-worker) **scale**—is unique and controversial. It requires the manager to describe on several dimensions the individual he or she least liked to work with in the past.[23] A manager with a high LPC score sees the least-preferred co-worker in relatively favorable terms, and vice versa. Fiedler sees a high-LPC leader as relationship-oriented and a low-LPC leader as task-oriented and directing.[24] LPC scores are generally quite stable.[25]

Fiedler identified three characteristics which leaders could alter as needed to make the situation more favorable:

- *Leader-member relations.* This involves the degree to which group members trust and like the leader and are willing to follow his or her guidance.
- *Task structure.* This involves the degree to which the task is spelled out step by step for the group and the degree to which the task can be performed according to a detailed set of standard operating procedures.
- *Leader position power.* This is the power of the leadership position, as opposed to personal power. This might include reward power, coercive power, and legitimate power.

According to Fiedler, the most favorable situation from the point of view of the manager is one in which leader-member relations are positive, the task is highly structured, and the leader has considerable position power. If the three dimensions of the situation are classified as high or low, there are a total of eight ($2 \times 2 \times 2$) octants differing in the level of what Fiedler calls situational favorability.

On the basis of research on over 800 groups in settings ranging from heavy-machinery plants to research labs, from bombers to bowling alleys, Fiedler concluded that the best LPC depended on the situation. Figure 16–3 summarizes his findings. The vertical axis of that figure shows the median correlation between the leader's LPC score and the performance of his or her group. The figure shows that high-LPC leaders do well (relative to low-LPC

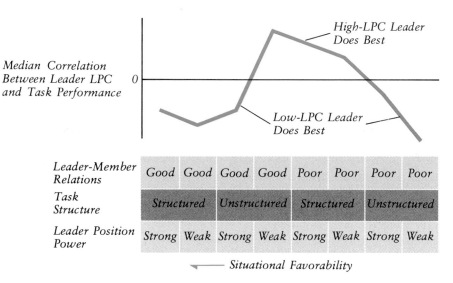

FIGURE 16–3
*How Effective
Leadership Varies with
the Situation*

Source: Reprinted by permission of *Harvard Business Review*. An exhibit from "Engineering the Job to Fit the Manager" by Fred E. Fiedler (September/October 1965). Copyright © 1965 by the President and Fellows of Harvard College; all rights reserved.

leaders) in moderately favorable situations. On the other hand, low-LPC leaders do relatively well in situations that are either very favorable or very unfavorable. Fiedler made sense of these findings as follows:

In very favorable conditions, where the leader has power, formal backing, and a relatively well-structured task, the group is ready to be directed about how to go about its task. Under a very unfavorable condition, however, the group will fall apart unless the leader's active intervention and control can keep the members on the job. In moderately unfavorable conditions, the accepted leader faces an ambiguous task, or his relations with group members are tenuous. Under these circumstances, a relationship-oriented, nondirective, permissive attitude may reduce member anxiety or intragroup conflict, and this enables the group to operate more effectively (i.e., the members would not feel threatened by the leader, and considerate, diplomatic leader behavior under these conditions may induce group members to cooperate).[26]

Fiedler developed a program called LEADER MATCH to train managers to apply his theory. LEADER MATCH uses a self-paced programmed manual which trainees can complete on their own time in about five hours. Lectures, group discussions, or films may also be used. The manual explains the model and shows trainees how to compute scores for LPC and situational factors. It then suggests ways to alter the situation to match the trainee's LPC.

Implications of the Theory

If Fiedler's theory is valid, it would have important implications for management. Clearly, managers should attempt to analyze their situations, assess their LPC scores, and make any necessary changes in the situation.

The theory also suggests that some types of leader training may actually be harmful if they move the leader to an inappropriate octant. As an example, human relations training may improve leader-member relations and thereby improve situational favorability. According to the theory, such training might be harmful for a high-LPC leader now in a moderately favorable situation.

Finally, the theory suggests that, because the firm can change the situation, it can focus selection processes on finding talented individuals rather than on trying to find managers who fit the current situation.

Evaluation of the Theory

Some people have criticized Fiedler's contingency theory, arguing that it is not clear what the LPC is really measuring, that the theory doesn't explain *how* the LPC causes high or low group performance, and that different leaders may assess the same situation differently.[27] These criticisms notwithstanding, studies tend to support the theory. For instance, each of 12 studies of the effectiveness of the LEADER MATCH program found that leaders who were trainees later received better performance ratings than leaders in control groups.[28] Another investigation examined 145 hypothesis tests of the theory, as well as the 33 results used to develop the theory. It concluded that there was strong statistical support for the theory's predictions of group performance.[29]

In sum, this is an interesting approach with considerable potential. Perhaps its greatest strength lies in the fact that it encourages managers to carefully and systematically assess their position power, leader-member relations, and task structure, and teaches them how to alter those situational characteristics in desired ways.

ADAPTING LEADER BEHAVIORS TO THE SITUATION: THE PATH-GOAL THEORY OF LEADERSHIP

Robert House developed the **path-goal theory of leader effectiveness,** an extension and revision of the work of Martin Evans.[30] House based this approach on expectancy theory (discussed in Chapter 13). House and Terence Mitchell explain the theory as follows:

According to this theory, leaders are effective because of their impact on subordinates' motivation, ability to perform effectively, and satisfaction. The theory is called path-goal because its major concern is how the leader influences the subordinates' perceptions of their work goals, personal goals, and paths to goal attainment. The theory suggests that a leader's behavior is motivating or satisfying to the degree that the behavior increases subordinate goal attainment and clarifies the paths to these goals.[31]

To couch these statements more explicitly in expectancy theory terms, the path-goal theory sees the leader as having three motivational functions. The leader can increase valences associated with work-goal attainment, instrumentalities of work-goal attainment for the acquisition of personal outcomes, and the expectancy that effort will result in work-goal attainment.

Nature of the Theory

Path-goal theory examines how the effectiveness of four sets of leader behaviors is influenced by two sets of contingency factors.

According to path-goal theory, a leader's behavior has an important influence on the goal attainment of subordinates.

BEHAVIORS CONSIDERED IN THE THEORY

The theory considers four kinds of leader behaviors:

- **Directive leadership** is characterized by a leader who lets subordinates know what is expected of them and tells them how to do it. This is similar to initiating structure.
- **Supportive leadership** is characterized by a friendly and approachable leader who shows concern for the status, well-being, and needs of subordinates. This is much like consideration.
- **Participative leadership** is characterized by a leader who consults with subordinates and asks for their suggestions, which he or she seriously considers before making a decision.
- **Achievement-oriented leadership** is characterized by a leader who sets challenging goals, expects subordinates to perform at their highest level, and shows confidence that subordinates will meet such expectations.

The theory tries to explain how each of these types of leadership affects (1) satisfaction of subordinates; (2) subordinates' acceptance of the leader; (3) the degree to which subordinates feel their effort will result in performance (expectancy); and (4) the degree to which subordinates feel their performance will result in rewards (instrumentalities). The theory essentially argues that subordinates will see each style of leadership as acceptable, satisfying, and motivating if they believe it is either an immediate source of desired outcomes or is useful in leading to such outcomes in the future.

CONTINGENCY FACTORS

The model considers two contingency factors—personal characteristics of the subordinates and the nature of the task to be performed. As an example, subordinates who don't feel they have the ability to master their tasks will probably react positively to directive leadership. And, if the job is highly structured, subordinates will see directive leadership as unnecessary and will resent it.

Evaluation of the Theory

Research on the path-goal theory has focused primarily on two hypotheses:

- Directive leadership will contribute to the satisfaction of followers engaged in ambiguous (that is, unstructured) tasks and will contribute to the dissatisfaction of followers engaged in clear (that is, structured) tasks.
- Supportive leadership will have its most positive effect on the satisfaction of members engaged in clear (that is, structured) tasks.

These hypotheses are intuitively reasonable, but findings concerning their validity are mixed. About an equal number of studies appear to support and refute each hypothesis.[32] Nevertheless, the theory does give concrete guidelines concerning potentially important leader behaviors and situational variables and provides a logical framework to examine how they might interact to influence follower satisfaction and performance. Also, it emphasizes the need for leaders to be sensitive and flexible. That is, it encourages managers to be sensitive to the characteristics of their subordinates and the task, and to recognize that they may need to tailor their behaviors accordingly.

ADAPTING DEGREE OF DELEGATION TO THE SITUATION: THE VROOM AND YETTON MODEL

We've seen that participative leadership styles are not always best. In fact, their value depends upon the situation. Participative approaches are more useful when (1) it is important that subordinates accept the chosen alternative (especially if subordinates would not accept an autocratic decision); (2) managers don't have the information necessary to make an autocratic decision; or (3) the problem is unstructured. Autocratic styles may be best if (1) acceptance is unimportant; (2) subordinates don't share the goals of the organization; or (3) time is short and an autocratic decision would be accepted. Victor Vroom and his colleagues used such information to build a normative model, usually called the **Vroom and Yetton normative model of leadership.** The model prescribes the proper leadership style(s) for various situations.

Nature of the Model

Figure 16–4 details the logic of the Vroom and Yetton model. The model begins with a set of feasible styles, ranging from completely autocratic to completely participative. The manager then answers a series of questions, each with a yes or no. The answers to these questions eliminate some styles which violate one or more rules. The styles which violate none of the rules are all appropriate. That is, they meet all quality and acceptability requirements.

| Various Alternative Processes (AI–GII) | Screening According to Questions Relating to Quality and Acceptability Criteria | Remaining Acceptable Processes | Scoring on the Basis of Another Criterion, Such as Time Taken | Selected Process |

The manager can use some other criterion to choose from among the acceptable styles. If time is short, the most autocratic of the styles can be chosen. If development of subordinates' decision-making skills is important, the most participative style can be chosen.

Figure 16–5 shows the specific styles considered in the Vroom and Yetton model. The styles range from the completely autocratic AI style, in which subordinates play no role, through consultative styles, to a pure group style.[33]

While the model is couched in terms of superiors and subordinates, it is really more general than this would suggest. It can be applied in any situation where an individual is asking whether others should be involved in the decision process. Based on past research which examined when participation is

FIGURE 16–5
Alternative Leadership Styles in the Vroom and Yetton Model

AI You solve the problem yourself using information available to you at that time.

AII You get the necessary information from your subordinate(s), then decide on the solution to the problem yourself. You may or may not tell your subordinates what the problem is when getting the information from them. The role played by your subordinates in making the decision is clearly one of providing the necessary information to you, rather than generating or evaluating alternative solutions.

CI You share the problem with relevant subordinates individually, getting their ideas and suggestions without bringing them together as a group. Then you make the decision that may or may not reflect your subordinates' influence.

CII You share the problem with your subordinates as a group, collectively obtaining their ideas and suggestions. Then you make the decision that may or may not reflect your subordinates' influence.

GII You share the problem with your subordinates as a group. Together, you generate and evaluate alternatives and attempt to reach agreement (consensus) on a solution. Your role is much like that of a chairperson. You do not try to influence the group to adopt "your" solution, and you are willing to accept and implement any solution that has the support of the entire group.

and isn't helpful, Vroom and Yetton developed a series of diagnostic questions which guide the manager through a tree diagram. The questions and tree are presented in Figure 16–6.[34]

At the end of each branch in the tree is the number of a problem type as well as a specific style. Figure 16–7 shows the acceptable styles for each problem type. The specific style at the end of each branch in Figure 16–6 is the fastest (that is, most autocratic) of the acceptable styles.

Using the Model

The tree seems rather complex, but its use is straightforward. Here is a case to show how it is used:

> You are on the division manager's staff and work on a wide variety of problems of both an administrative and a technical nature. You have been given the assignment of developing a standard method to be used in each of the five plants in the division for manually reading equipment registers, recording the readings, and transmitting the scorings to a centralized information system.
>
> Until now, there has been a high error rate in the reading and/or transmittal of the data. Some locations have considerably higher error rates than others, and the methods used to record and transmit the data vary among plants. It is probable, therefore, that part of the error variance is a function of specific local conditions rather than anything else, and this will complicate the establishment of any system common to all plants. You have the information on error rates but no information on the local practices that generate these errors or on the local conditions that necessitate the different practices.
>
> Everyone would benefit from an improvement in the quality of the data; it is used in a number of important decisions. Your contacts with the plants are through the quality-control supervisors who are responsible for collecting the data. They are a conscientious group, committed to doing their jobs well, but are highly sensitive to interference on the part of higher management in their own operations. Any solution that does not receive the active support of the various plant supervisors is unlikely to reduce the error rate significantly.[35]

To choose a proper style for the situation described in this case, the manager must answer the seven diagnostic questions in Figure 16–8. First, there is a quality requirement—the data are used for a number of important decisions. Second, you do not have sufficient information to make a high-quality decision—you lack information on local practices and local conditions. Third, the problem is not well structured—there are many variables to consider and no obvious way to use them all to arrive at a right answer. Fourth, acceptance is vital—without the active support of plant supervisors, the effort is unlikely to succeed. Fifth, it is unlikely that subordinates would accept an autocratic decision. The plant supervisors are sensitive to interference on the part of higher management. Sixth, the plant managers do seem to share the organization's goals—everyone would benefit from improved data quality. Finally, there is likely to be conflict among plant managers—variations in local practices and local conditions complicate establishing a common system.

The answers to the seven diagnostic questions are thus yes, no, no, yes, no, yes, and no, respectively. Moving along the corresponding branches in Figure 16–6, we see that the number at the end of the branch is 12, showing the problem type is 12. As Figure 16–7 indicates, only the GII style is appropriate in that case.

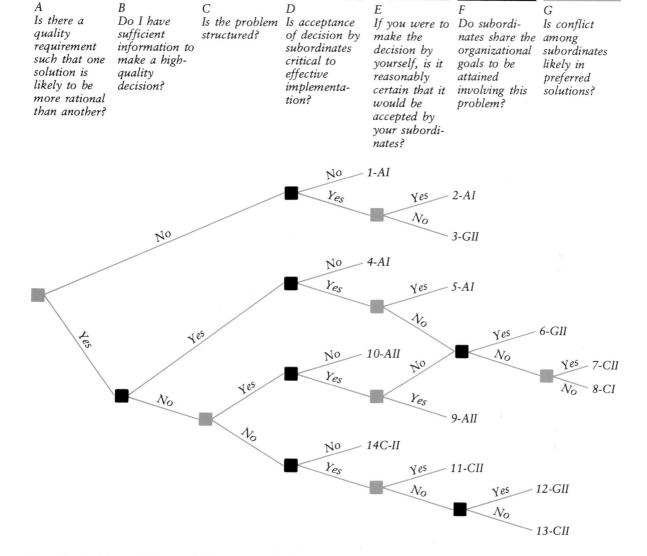

A	B	C	D	E	F	G
Is there a quality requirement such that one solution is likely to be more rational than another?	*Do I have sufficient information to make a high-quality decision?*	*Is the problem structured?*	*Is acceptance of decision by subordinates critical to effective implementation?*	*If you were to make the decision by yourself, is it reasonably certain that it would be accepted by your subordinates?*	*Do subordinates share the organizational goals to be attained involving this problem?*	*Is conflict among subordinates likely in preferred solutions?*

Source: Reprinted, by permission of the publisher, from "A New Look at Managerial Decision Making," by Victor H. Vroom, *Organizational Dynamics* (Spring 1973): 70. Copyright © 1973. American Management Association, New York. All rights reserved.

FIGURE 16–6
The Vroom and Yetton Model

Evaluation of the Model

Two sorts of questions have been examined regarding the Vroom and Yetton model. The first asks the degree to which unaided managers already behave in ways the model says they should. The second asks whether managers make better decisions when they apply the model than when they don't.

Four sets of findings regarding the first question are worth noting. First, research shows that unaided managers behave as the model says they should for two-thirds of their decisions. For one-third of their decisions, then, they use decision styles which the model says are inappropriate. Second, managers are less flexible in their choice of styles than the model says they should be. That is, they don't vary their styles as much from one situation to another as

FIGURE 16–7
Appropriate Decision Styles*

Problem Type	Acceptable Styles
1	AI, AII, CI, CII, GII
2	AI, AII, CI, CII, GII
3	GII
4	AI, AII, CI, CII, GII*
5	AI, AII, CI, CII, GII*
6	GII
7	CII
8	CI, CII
9	AII, CI, CII, GII*
10	AII, CI, CII, GII*
11	CII, GII*
12	GII
13	CII
14	CII, GII

*Acceptable only when the answer to question F is yes.

FIGURE 16–8
Problem Attributes and Questions in the Vroom and Yetton Model

Problem Attributes	Diagnostic Questions
A. The importance of the quality of the decision.	Is there a quality requirement such that one solution is likely to be more rational than another?
B. The extent to which the leader possesses sufficient information/expertise to make a high-quality decision by himself [or herself].	Do I have sufficient information to make a high-quality decision?
C. The extent to which the problem is structured.	Is the problem structured?
D. The extent to which acceptance or commitment on the part of subordinates is critical to the effective implementation of the decision.	Is acceptance of the decision by subordinates critical to effective implementation?
E. The prior probability that the leader's autocratic decision will receive acceptance by subordinates.	If you were to make the decision by yourself, is it reasonably certain that it would be accepted by your subordinates?
F. The extent to which subordinates are motivated to attain the organizational goals as represented in the objectives explicit in the statement of the problem.	Do subordinates share the organizational goals to be obtained in solving this problem?
G. The extent to which subordinates are likely to be in conflict over preferred solutions.	Is conflict among subordinates likely over preferred solutions?

the model dictates. Third, managers tend to behave a bit more autocratically than the model says they should. Finally, the ways managers behave depends much more on the situation they are in than on individual differences. That is, managers' choices of behaviors are more a function of whether the situation calls for autocratic or democratic behavior than of whether the managers are generally "autocrats" or "democrats."

The second of these findings highlights a potentially crucial leadership skill—flexibility. That is, the model suggests that, rather than asking whether they should be autocratic or democratic in general, managers should adapt to the situation. Curiously, there has been almost no attention in the leadership literature to flexibility itself.

To the second question, whether it helps to obey the model, research indicates the answer is yes. For instance, one study asked managers to recall a successful decision they had made, as well as the characteristics of the decision situation and the style they had used.[36] The managers then did the same for an unsuccessful decision. For each decision, the Vroom and Yetton model was applied to the information about the situation to determine which styles were appropriate. For 85 percent of the successful decisions, managers used styles agreeing with the model. Managers used styles agreeing with the model for only 43 percent of unsuccessful decisions.

As a further test of the Vroom and Yetton model, business students were placed in teams.[37] Each team was told to solve five decision-making problems, differing in their situational attributes. Further, each team was told to use different styles for each problem. Results supported the model. Decisions made with styles which the model said were appropriate were significantly more effective than inappropriate styles. An interesting footnote to this study was that the researcher had to discard data for over 40 percent of decisions because the (simulated) leaders did not behave in the ways they were supposed to. They were unable or unwilling to adopt the proper style, especially when told to use the AI or AII style. This suggests again that it is not enough simply to know the "right" way to behave. Some individuals may lack the ability to handle certain styles or the flexibility to vary styles appropriately.

A variety of concerns have been raised about the model. For instance, some have argued that answering questions with a yes or no is simplistic and that many variables not considered by the model may be important. Also, managers may err in defining the situation and thereby misuse the model. Further, use of the model may cause managers to treat the situation as fixed and to choose a style accordingly rather than try to change the situation. For instance, some critics say that if conflict is likely among subordinates over a preferred solution, managers should try to reduce the conflict potential rather than treat it as a given.

Finally, the CII style usually falls in the set of acceptable styles. Of 14 problem types in Figure 16–7, the CII style is acceptable in 11. The only exceptions occur when the model calls for the GII style. So it might be easier to ask if this is a situation requiring a group style and, if not, to employ the CII style.

In response to such criticisms, Vroom stated, "The criterion for social utility is not perfection but improvement over present practice."[38] If a manager is aware that the model has not considered important factors, it may be appropriate to override its suggestions. And there is nothing to stop a manager from improving the situation before applying the model. Further, while

Victor H. Vroom (Ph.D., Psychology, University of Michigan) is the John G. Searle Professor of Organization and Management at Yale University. Professor Vroom is an internationally recognized expert on leadership and decision making. As a teacher and researcher, he has focused on the psychological analysis of behavior in organizations. He is author of several books, including Work and Motivation, *and* Leadership and Decision Making, *and co-author of* The New Leadership: Managing Participation in Organizations, *with Art Jago. Professor Vroom has been elected president of the Society of Industrial and Organizational Psychology and a fellow of the American Psychological Association*

ACADEMIC PROFILE
VICTOR H. VROOM

and the Academy of Management. He has been active as a consultant to many organizations.

Q: For many years, you have been developing models which purport to give managers a concrete way to choose an appropriate leadership style. Can you summarize the status of this work?

A: In the early 1970s, Philip Yetton and I developed the Vroom-Yetton model. This model does not deal with all aspects of leadership style but rather attempted to advise managers on the forms and degrees of participation in decision making likely to be effective on problems they were facing. The model had a significant impact on both scholars and practitioners in management. It was, however, a rather primitive model. I think of it as somewhat like the Ten Commandments in the sense that it told managers what not to do rather than what to do. As is true in the biblical analog, there were an unduly large number of instances in which all the alternatives were acceptable (inside the feasible set), and therefore it provided no guidance.

Fifteen years ago, Art Jago and I capitalized on the accumulated experience and research with its predecessor, and developed a new model. While it shares the goal of advising managers about participation in decision making, this model is positive rather than negative. It is based on verifiable assumptions about the consequences of participation for the quality of decisions, subordinates' commitment to decisions, the time consumed by the decision process, and the likely development of subordinates that might result from their involvement in decision making. This model is also more complex. It utilizes a set of 12 situational variables (as opposed to 7 in the original) and permits up to five levels of attributes rather than the dichotomous judgments to which the Vroom-Yetton model was restricted. It can be represented as a decision tree but is more appropriately thought of as an expert system which can be run on a personal computer.

Q: How would you summarize evidence concerning the degree to which use of the models can improve decision-making effectiveness?

A: In the Vroom and Jago book we summarize the evidence concerning the Vroom-Yetton model. Six of the studies, carried out in three different countries, utilized comparable methodology. Across all six studies, if a manager's behavior conformed to that of the model, the rate of successful decisions was 62 percent; on the other hand, if a manager's behavior failed to conform to the model, the rate of success was only 37 percent.

There is much less information available concerning the validity of the new model. Since data concerning the validity of its predecessor were part of the empirical evidence that informed its construction, we believe strongly that it is a far better forecast of actual decision outcomes. The research that has been done to date supports this view.

Q: How widespread is use of these models in management training?

A: The Vroom-Yetton model has a long history of use in managerial education and training. The number of textbooks containing the model now number in the hundreds. Over a hundred thousand managers have taken courses dealing exclusively with the model.

The new model is rapidly replacing its predecessor both in textbooks and in formal management training programs. While the Vroom-Jago book gives the information necessary for managers to write their own computer program for the model, a company called Leadership Software markets a floppy disk which contains the model. To date thousands of the disks have been sold, largely to graduates of formal training programs.

Some of the applications of the model are much more subtle than we had originally imagined. The terms AI, GII, etc., are becoming standard vocabulary in many organizations for managers to label their own behavior as well as that of others. One large corporation is systematically training all managers and their subordinates in these terms, to provide some universal language for use in "expectation setting."

use of the CII style is usually acceptable, there will often be other acceptable styles, most of them requiring less time from the manager and subordinates.

This model may serve as a useful guide for the manager. It may also be helpful as a training device. That is, managers can compare their past or anticipated decisions with prescriptions of the model. They can then see what important factors they may have failed to consider and can gain self-insight concerning their styles. The model is, of course, meant to be a tool rather than a substitute for judgment.

As discussed in the Academic Profile for this chapter, a newer version of the model has been developed. The model uses equations rather than the tree form and has not yet received much formal testing.

TRANSFORMATIONAL LEADERSHIP

We have considered many leader behaviors and styles to this point. For instance, we have looked at such things as whether the leader is considerate, delegates authority, and structures tasks. Conspicuously lacking in our discussion—yet central to many people's views of successful leadership—has been any mention of inspiration, vision, or stimulation. Until quite recently, there has been virtually no attention paid to such aspects of leadership. However, some writers are now making an important distinction between transactional and transformational leadership.[39]

According to Bernard Bass, **transactional leaders** (1) recognize what actions subordinates must take to achieve outcomes; (2) clarify these roles and task requirements; and (3) recognize subordinates' needs and clarify how they will be satisfied if necessary efforts are made. This type of leadership is an exchange process. It involves a transaction in which followers' needs are met if their performance measures up to their contracts with their leader. **Transformational leaders** motivate followers to do more than they expected to do. They accomplish this by (1) raising levels of consciousness about the importance and value of designated outcomes and ways of reaching those outcomes; (2) encouraging followers to transcend self-interests for the sake of the team or organization; and (3) causing employees to focus on higher-order needs, such as the need for self-actualization.[40] Such leaders transform both their followers and the organizations they lead. Bass argues that transactional leadership may result in marginal performance improvements, but that transformational leadership is needed for major gains.

Bass's research, using a sample of senior U.S. Army officers, found three factors underlying transformational leadership. They were: (1) **charismatic leadership** (leaders aroused enthusiasm, faith, loyalty, and pride and trust in themselves and their aims); (2) individualized consideration (leaders maintained a developmental and individualistic orientation toward subordinates); and (3) intellectual stimulation (leaders enhanced the problem-solving abilities of their associates). These three transformational factors were more closely associated with perceived unit effectiveness and subordinates' satisfaction with the leader than were two transactional factors.[41]

One of these elements—charismatic leadership—dates back to the ancient Greeks (*charisma* is a Greek word meaning "divinely inspired gift") and was discussed by Max Weber over 60 years ago. Weber described a charismatic

Examples of charismatic leadership in the business world include Coca-Cola's Roberto Goizueta.

leader who was perceived by subordinates as possessing exceptional qualities which set him apart from ordinary men. He said that such leaders "reveal a transcendent mission or course of action which may be itself appealing to the potential followers, but which is acted upon because the followers believe their leader is extraordinarily gifted."[42] There are many conspicuous cases in which individuals have had a major impact on the founding or redirection of organizations. Examples include Gandhi's leading of India toward self-government, Jesus' founding of Christianity, and Hitler's responsibility for the Nazi war movement.[43] Examples of this kind of leadership in the business world might include Lee Iacocca of Chrysler, John F. Welch, Jr., of General Electric, Gordon McGovern of Campbell Soup, and Roberto Goizueta of Coca-Cola.[44]

The modern development of charismatic leadership theory is generally associated with the work of Robert House (who, you will recall, was also the developer of the path-goal theory of leadership). House wrote that the literature on charismatic leadership attributes three personal characteristics to charismatic leaders: extremely high levels of self-confidence, dominance, and a strong conviction in the moral righteousness of his or her beliefs. He drew on the sociological and political science literature to isolate these behaviors of charismatic leaders: (1) role modeling—charismatic leaders express by their actions a set of values and beliefs to which they want their followers to subscribe; (2) image building—charismatic leaders take actions consciously designed to be viewed favorably by followers; (3) goal articulation—charismatic leaders articulate a "transcendent" goal which becomes the basis of a movement or cause; and (4) exhibiting high expectations for subordinates and showing confidence in their ability to meet those expectations.[45]

Noel Tichy and David Ulrich see three programs of activity associated with transformational leadership: creation of a vision of a desired future state, mobilization of commitment to the new mission and vision, and institutionalization of change.[46] Richard Byrd proposes that transformational leadership will require new skill categories, including: (1) anticipatory skills—the ability to intuitively and systematically scan the changing environment; (2) visioning skills—the process of persuasion and example by which an individual or leadership team induces a group to take action that is in accord with the leader's purposes or, most likely, the shared purposes of all; (3) value-congruence skills—the ability to be in touch with employees' needs in order to engage employees on the basis of shared motives, values, and goals; (4) empowerment skills—the ability to effectively share power with employees so that they can also share the satisfaction derived from accomplishment; and (5) self-understanding skills—introspective skills as well as frameworks with which leaders understand both themselves and their employees.[47]

Despite the appeal of the idea of transformational leadership, and the ease with which examples of transformational leaders can be cited, there has been very little research on either transformational leadership itself or on the related concept of charismatic leadership. There may be several reasons for this.[48] For instance, the topic is elusive and has mystical connotations, rendering it a "suspect" subject for research. Also, a systematic framework for study of transformational or charismatic leadership has been lacking, making it difficult to identify, define, and operationalize key variables. Finally, researchers have found it difficult to gain access to transformational leaders. Whatever the reasons for this dearth of research, it seems clear that this is an important topic which deserves more attention.

On the other hand, we should not let the intuitive appeal of transformational leadership blind us to other aspects of leadership. First, as we have just said, solid evidence concerning the nature, distribution, and roles of transformational leaders is still lacking. Second, transformational leadership may be most important at times of organizational birth and rebirth. This still leaves a lot of organizational living in which leadership functions must be maintained. In fact, Weber argued that charismatic leadership is inherently transitory: "Indeed, in its pure form charismatic authority may be said to exist only in the process of originating. It cannot remain stable, but becomes either traditionalized or rationalized, or a combination of both."[49] In this regard, Alan Filley and his colleagues have argued, and demonstrated through their research, that charismatic leader characteristics may be appropriate during times of rapid organizational growth, but that reliance on formal procedures then becomes necessary.[50] A final caution is that it is still not clear whether transformational leadership can be taught. To the degree that transformational leader characteristics reflect inherent traits, making desired changes may prove difficult.

THE IMPACT OF LEADERSHIP

Anyone who has ever served as a leader (or as a subordinate) would probably agree that the way the leader behaves makes a difference. *Some* leader behaviors must have *some* impact on subordinates' satisfaction or performance. Perhaps surprisingly, then, we should point out that many writers are now arguing that leadership really doesn't matter much.[51] They reason that rules, laws, and societal forces effectively handcuff the leader. Also, various characteristics of situations or of subordinates may act as **substitutes for leadership**. Figure 16–9 lists some of these substitutes. The figure indicates, for instance, that structuring leadership will be neutralized when subordinates have high levels of ability, when tasks are well structured, and when there is a considerable distance between the superior and subordinate. That is, it will be redundant or ineffective. Similarly, relationship-oriented, supportive, considerate leadership will be neutralized when subordinates have high needs for independence, when the task is intrinsically satisfying, and when work groups are cohesive.

We don't share the pessimistic view that leadership has no impact. One study which examined the impact of substitutes for leadership found that hierarchical leadership was still important, even in the presence of potential substitutes for leadership.[52] Further, the evidence we have reviewed in this chapter does provide some consistent findings concerning leadership. Also, most studies of leadership have been carried out in large organizations. Leadership probably makes more of a difference in small and developing firms.[53] Finally, there has as yet been almost no examination of the potential impact of transformational leadership. As we expand our perspectives, the importance of effective leadership should become increasingly clear.

IMPLICATIONS FOR MANAGEMENT

As a manager, you will often find yourself in positions of leadership or of potential leadership. Your leadership role will sometimes be formally prescribed,

	Substitutes for Leadership Will Tend to Neutralize	
Characteristic	Relationship-Oriented Supportive, Considerate Leadership	Task-Oriented Directive, Structuring Leadership
Of the Subordinate		
1. Ability, experience, training, knowledge		x
2. Need for independence	x	x
3. "Professional" orientation	x	x
4. Indifference toward organizational rewards	x	x
Of the Task		
5. Unambiguous and routine		x
6. Standardized methods		x
7. Provides its own feedback concerning accomplishment		x
8. Intrinsically satisfying	x	
Of the Organization		
9. Formalization (explicit plans, goals, and areas of responsibility)		x
10. Inflexibility (rigid, unbending rules and procedures)		x
11. Closely knit, cohesive work groups	x	x
12. Highly specified and active advisory and staff functions		x
13. Organizational rewards not within the leader's contract	x	x
14. Considerable distance between superior and subordinate	x	x

Source: S. Kerr and J. M. Jermier, "Substitutes for Leadership: Their Meaning and Measurement," *Organizational Behavior and Human Performance* 22 (1978): 375-403. Reproduced with permission.

FIGURE 16–9

Substitutes for Leadership

and at other times may develop informally. In either case, your actions may have an impact on the performance and satisfaction of your subordinates and others. Give your leadership behaviors the attention they deserve.

To carry out your leadership duties, you will often need to draw on bases of power. Successful leaders draw on a variety of power bases. They recognize that referent power has a broad range and that heavy reliance on coercive power can be dangerous. As a leader, remember that control over resources, information, and the problem-solving process all serve to increase power.

When selecting people for leadership positions or assigning them to leadership tasks, it may be useful to consider such traits as intelligence, self-confidence, decisiveness, and need for occupational achievement. However, be sure to ask whether the position really calls for such traits. Recall from Chapter 10 that it is illegal to use selection criteria that are unrelated to task performance.

Remember that a leader must show concern for both task accomplishment and fulfillment of subordinate needs. This does not mean that as a leader you will always need to emphasize each of these factors. Often, the nature of tasks or of subordinates will take care of some concerns or make them less important. However, you must be ready to step in to see that these dual needs are somehow satisfied.

Remember, too, that the same style or behavior may not work in every situation. In deciding how to behave, consider the maturity and needs of your subordinates, the structure and other characteristics of the task, and the nature of the organization. The models discussed in this chapter should be useful in highlighting factors to keep in mind. Treat them as guides rather than as absolute rules. If you are using styles or behaviors that violate the suggestions of the models, ask yourself why. Do you disagree with the model? Is it ignoring variables that you feel are important, or are you somehow failing to assess the situation properly?

In general, behaviors reflecting consideration on the part of the leader are satisfying to subordinates and don't harm productivity. Further, consideration makes initiating structure more palatable. So, if the situation is one that calls for leader initiating structure, consideration will be important.

Leadership can be frustrating. Structured tasks, separation of superiors and subordinates, bureaucratic constraints, and other factors can sometimes handcuff the leader. Try to be aware of such substitutes for leadership. If they seem helpful in enhancing the satisfaction and performance of your subordinates, it may be best to accept them. If you feel they are constraining performance or satisfaction, you may want to try to circumvent them. For instance, if your subordinates are indifferent toward organizational rewards, you may try to determine what other kinds of rewards are important to them. You may also need to rely on alternatives to constrained power bases.

Also, as a leader you should not accept the situation as fixed. You may be able to change task structure, your power, relations with subordinates, and other dimensions. Before accepting the constraints, try to loosen them. Before fitting your behaviors to the situation, tailor the situation to your liking.

Perhaps more than anything else, the models reviewed in this chapter show that leader sensitivity, critical thinking, and flexibility are crucial. Leaders must be sensitive to the characteristics of tasks, workers, and other dimensions of the situation. They must choose suitable behaviors, avoiding those that are inappropriate or redundant. Finally, they must then have the flexibility to adopt those behaviors. These are difficult attributes to develop, but they will become increasingly important. You would be wise to try to cultivate them.

Finally, remember that vision and inspiration are important. Don't let a narrow focus on structuring of tasks and dealing with subordinates' needs on a day-to-day basis cause you to ignore broader, more transformational aspects of the leadership role.

KEY TERMS AND CONCEPTS

achievement-oriented leadership
authority
autocratic leaders
charismatic leadership
coercive power

consideration
contingency model of leadership
control
democratic leaders
directive leadership

domain of power   power
expert power   range of power
influence   referent power
initiating structure   reward power
leadership   substitutes for leadership
legitimate power   supportive leadership
LPC scale   transactional leaders
managerial Grid®   transformational leaders
participative leadership   Vroom and Yetton normative model of
path-goal theory of leader effectiveness   leadership

QUESTIONS FOR REVIEW AND DISCUSSION

1. Name four approaches to the study of leadership. Which of these approaches do you most agree with? Least agree with? Why?
2. Of the French and Raven power bases, which do you think is easiest to use? The hardest to use? The most ethical? The least ethical? The most widely applicable? The least widely applicable? The most characteristic of good leaders? The least characteristic of good leaders?
3. Do you think it is right to acquire power through use of political skills? Defend your viewpoint.
4. Identify three traits which the chapter identified as sometimes being related to leadership success. Then select three successful leaders and compare them on the basis of these traits, as well as on their abilities. Do the same for unsuccessful leaders. Are there more similarities or differences within the sets? Among the sets?
5. Describe a situation in which a leader displays a democratic style but is low on consideration. Then describe a situation in which a leader is autocratic but considerate. In general, do you think democratic style and consideration are linked?
6. What is the managerial Grid®? What are its underlying assumptions?
7. Name three situational factors that influence the way that leader behaviors affect subordinate responses. Which of those do you believe would be easiest for a manager to change? Hardest?
8. Give two ways managers might influence subordinates' expectancy perceptions, instrumentality perceptions, and valences of work-related outcomes.
9. What are four of the questions asked in the Vroom and Yetton normative model of leadership? Would you feel comfortable using this model to choose an appropriate leadership style? What factors might cause you to reject the style(s) it suggests?
10. Do you feel that all leaders have the ability to be flexible? If not, what are the implications for each of the theories discussed in this chapter?
11. Do you think modern leaders make much of a difference in organizations? Cite three examples in support of your position.
12. If you were to give a lecture concerning successful leadership, what three points would you stress most?

CASES

16–1 THE "BIG MEN"

Anthropologists have long been interested in the rise of "pristine states." These are states, such as Mesopotamia about 3300 B.C., Peru about the time of Christ, and Mesoamerica about A.D. 100, that developed without stimulation from preexisting states. Many anthropologists believe that such states developed when village societies intensified their food production to support growing populations.

Anthropologists refer to the intensifiers of agricultural production as "big men." In their purest, most egalitarian phase, known best from studies of many groups in Melanesia and New Guinea, "big men" play the role of hard-working, ambitious, public-spirited individuals who entice their relatives and neighbors to work for them by promising to hold a huge feast with the extra food they produce. When the feast takes place, the "big man," surrounded by his proud helpers, ostentatiously parcels out piles of food and other gifts but keeps nothing for himself. Under certain ecological conditions, and in the presence of warfare, these food managers could have gradually set themselves above their followers and become the original nucleus of the ruling classes of the first states.

Among the Siuai on Bougainville in the Solomon Islands, a "big man" is called a mumi. To achieve mumi status is every youth's highest ambition. A young man proves himself capable of becoming a mumi by working harder than everyone else and by carefully restricting his own consumption of meat and coconuts. Eventually, he impresses his wife, children, and near relatives with the seriousness of his intentions, and they vow to help him prepare for his first feast. If the feast is a success, his circle of supporters widens and he sets to work readying an even greater display of generosity. He aims next at the construction of a men's clubhouse in which his male followers can lounge about and in which guests can be entertained and fed. Another feast is held at the consecration of the clubhouse. If this is also a success, his circle of supporters — people willing to work for the feast in order to come — grows still larger, and he will begin to be spoken of as a mumi. What do supporters get from all this? Even though larger and larger feasts mean that the mumi's demands on his supporters become more irksome, the overall volume of production goes up. So if they occasionally grumble about how hard they have to work, the followers nevertheless remain loyal as long as their mumi continues to maintain or increase his renown as a "great provider."

Finally the time comes for the new mumi to challenge the others who have risen before him. This is done at a muminai feast, where a tally is kept of all the pigs, coconut pies, and sago-almond puddings given away by the host mumi and his followers to the guest mumi and his followers. If the guest mumi cannot reciprocate in a year or so with a feast at least as lavish as that of his challengers, he suffers great humiliation, and his fall from "mumihood" is immediate. In deciding on whom to challenge, a mumi must be very careful. He tries to choose a guest whose downfall will increase his own reputation, but he must avoid one whose capacity to retaliate exceeds his own.

Source: Adapted by permission of Random House, Inc. from *Cannibals and Kings: The Origins of Cultures*, by Marvin Harris. Copyright © 1977 by Marvin Harris.

1. What bases of power do the "big men" employ?
2. How would you characterize the leader behaviors of the "big men"?
3. In what ways is the role of the "big man" similar to that of modern leaders in organizations? What are some key differences?

16–2 LEADERS AND MANAGERS

Abraham Zaleznik knows how to start an argument. The Harvard Business School professor just delivers his favorite speech, dividing the executive ranks into "leaders" and "managers."

Leaders, he recently told 150 Philadelphia business people, are often dramatic and unpredictable in style. They tend to create an atmosphere of change, ferment, even chaos. They "are often obsessed by their ideas, which appear visionary and consequently excite, stimulate, and drive other people to work hard and create reality out of fantasy." He considers Lee Iacocca of Chrysler Corp. a classic leader.

Managers, Mr. Zaleznik told the Philadelphia group, are typically hard-working, analytical, tolerant, and fair-minded. They have a strong sense of belonging to the organization and take great pride in perpetuating and improving upon the status quo. But managerial executives focus "predominantly on process, whereas leaders focus on substance." The late Alfred Sloan, the architect of General Motors, was a classic manager, he said.

By the time the speech ended, it had touched some raw nerves. Five Philadelphia top executives took to the microphones, and several argued that they were combination "leader-managers." But by the time they finished, at least a few audience members felt they had heard five managers, no leaders.

The incident suggests that the issue of management style is a lively one in business circles these days. The Philadelphia crowd of 150 paid $75 apiece to have lunch with Mr. Zaleznik and hear him talk. Other executives, from Edward Telling of Sears, Roebuck & Co. to John Sculley of Apple Computer Inc., have been thinking and talking about organizational style of late. Some chief executives have even commissioned studies of their personal styles.

Theodore F. Brophy, the chairman and chief executive of GTE Corp., has asked his ten direct subordinates to comment anonymously on his management style. The purpose, he says, is to find out, among other things, "the impact that my style may be having upon them and their operations."

Source: Reprinted by permission of *The Wall Street Journal*, © Dow Jones & Company, Inc. (September 11, 1984). All Rights Reserved Worldwide.

1. To what factors do you attribute this recent burst of interest in leadership among business people?
2. Would you characterize the approach taken by Professor Zaleznik as primarily a trait, a style, or a behavioral approach? Why?
3. Do you think a manager can be both a "leader" and a "manager" as the terms are used in this case? Why or why not?
4. In what sort of situation do you think a "leader" would be most effective? A "manager"?

ENDNOTES

1. Based on D. M. Kehrer, "The Miracle of Theory Q," *Business Month* (September 1989): 45-49.
2. "Executive Pay," *Business Week* (May 1, 1989): 46.
3. J. Y. Lee and R. A. Milne, "Does High Executive Turnover Promote a Short-Term View?" *Business Forum* (Summer 1988): 25-28.
4. From Arthur Jago, "Leadership: Perspectives in Theory and Research," *Management Science* 28, no. 3 (March 1982). Copyright 1982 by The Institute of Management Sciences. Reprinted by permission of the publisher.
5. J. R. P. French and B. Raven, "The Bases of Social Power," in *Group Dynamics*, 2d ed., ed. D. Cartwright and A. F. Zander (Evanston, IL: Row Peterson, 1960), 259-269.
6. While this is a useful typology of power bases, well-done empirical studies of the typology are lacking. For instance, see P. M. Podsakoff and C. A. Schriesheim, "Field Studies of French and Raven's Bases of Power: Critique, Reanalysis, and Suggestions for Future Research," *Psychological Bulletin* 97 (1985): 387-411.
7. J. Pfeffer, *Power in Organizations* (Marshfield, MA: Pitman Publishing Co., 1981), 101-135.
8. Later formulations of the French and Raven power bases included information power as a sixth base. See B. H. Raven and A. W. Kruglanski, "Conflict and Power," in *The Structure of Conflict*, ed. P. Swingle (New York: Academic Press, 1970).
9. See J. P. Kotter, "Power, Dependence, and Effective Management," *Harvard Business Review* (July-August 1977), for more on these tactics.
10. T. A. Mahoney, T. H. Jerdee, and A. N. Nash, *The Identification of Management Potential: A Research Approach to Management Development* (Dubuque, IA: William C. Brown, 1961).

11. For one systematic approach to examination of leadership traits, see E. E. Ghiselli, *Explorations in Managerial Talent* (Pacific Palisades, CA: Goodyear Publishing Co., 1971).

12. See W. O. Jenkins, "A Review of Leadership Studies with Particular Reference to Military Problems," *Psychological Bulletin* 44 (1947): 54-79; R. M. Stogdill, "Personal Factors Associated with Leadership: A Survey of the Literature," *Journal of Psychology* 25 (1948): 35-71; and C. A. Gibb, "Leadership," in *Handbook of Social Psychology*, ed. G. Lindzey (Reading, MA: Addison-Wesley, 1954).

13. C. Bird, *Social Psychology* (New York: Appleton-Century, 1940).

14. L. F. Carter and M. Nixon, "An Investigation of the Relationship Between Four Criteria of Leadership Ability for Three Different Tasks," *Journal of Psychology* 23 (1949): 245-261.

15. A. C. Filley, R. J. House, and S. Kerr, *Managerial Process and Organizational Behavior*, 2d ed. (Glenview, IL: Scott, Foresman, 1976), 226.

16. The statistical technique used is called factor analysis. Factor analysis seeks to isolate the underlying factors that explain a set of responses. While a very large number of factors may be extracted, the factors extracted first are the most powerful in explaining the responses. In this case, factors other than consideration and initiating structure emerged but were much less powerful.

17. These definitions are from A. W. Halpin and J. J. Winer, "A Factorial Study of the Leader Behavior Descriptions," in *Leader Behavior: Its Description and Measurement*, Monograph No. 88, ed. R. M. Stogdill and A. E. Coons (Columbus, OH: Ohio State University, Bureau of Business Research, 1951), 42.

18. A. Lowin and J. R. Craig, "The Influence of Level of Performance on Managerial Style: An Experimental Object Lesson in the Ambiguity of Correlational Data," *Organizational Behavior and Human Performance* 3 (1968): 440-458. Also, see G. F. Farris and F. G. Lim, "Effects of Performance on Leadership Cohesiveness, Influence, Satisfaction, and Subsequent Performance," *Journal of Applied Psychology* 53 (1969): 490-499, and N. Rosen, *Leadership Change and Group Dynamics: An Experiment* (Ithaca, NY: Cornell University Press, 1969).

19. A. P. Brief and R. J. Aldag, "The Impact of Leader Behavior and Task Characteristics on Subordinate Job Satisfaction," Proceedings of the Southeast American Institute for Decision Sciences Conference, Columbia, SC, 1976.

20. R. R. Blake and J. S. Mouton, *The Managerial Grid* (Houston: Grid Publishing Co., 1961).

21. S. Kerr, C. Schriesheim, C. J. Murphy, and R. M. Stogdill, "Toward a Contingency Theory of Leadership Based upon the Consideration and Initiating Structure Literature," *Organizational Behavior and Human Performance* 12 (1974): 62-82.

22. F. E. Fiedler, "Engineering the Job to Fit the Manager," *Harvard Business Review* 43 (1965): 115-122.

23. Fiedler initially used an ASO (for assumed similarity of opposites) score, based on the difference between the MPC (most-preferred co-worker) and LPC scores. Since there was little variance in MPC scores, the LPC became the focus of attention.

24. It has been suggested that the LPC may also be a measure of the leader's ability to deal with complex information (called cognitive complexity). A high-LPC leader is able to differentiate between different traits of the least-preferred co-worker, rating some high and some low. A low-LPC leader, on the other hand, sees things as all good or all bad, rating the least-preferred co-worker low on all dimensions. So, a low LPC score may reflect halo error, discussed in Chapter 12.

25. The one apparent contradiction to this statement is that LPC scores sometimes fall when people enter the military. See P. M. Bons, A. R. Bass, and S. S. Komorita, "Changes in Leadership Style as a Function of Military Experience and Type of Command," *Personnel Psychology* 23 (1970): 551-568.

26. From *A Theory of Leadership Effectiveness* by Fred E. Fiedler. Copyright © 1967 by McGraw-Hill Book Company. Reprinted with permission.

27. C. Schriesheim and S. Kerr, "Theories and Measures of Leadership: A Critical Appraisal of Current and Future Directions," in *Leadership: The Cutting Edge*, ed. J. G. Hunt and L. Larson (Carbondale, IL: Southern Illinois University Press, 1977), 9-45, 51-56, and G. A. Yukl, *Leadership in Organizations* (Englewood Cliffs, NJ: Prentice-Hall, 1981).

28. F. E. Fiedler and L. Mahar, "The Effectiveness of Contingency Model Training: A Review of the Validation of LEADER MATCH," *Personnel Psychology* 32 (1979): 45-62.

29. See M. J. Strube and J. E. Garcia, "A Meta-Analytic Investigation of Fiedler's Contingency Model of Leadership Effectiveness," *Psychological Bulletin* 90 (1981): 307-321. The authors

used meta-analysis in this investigation. Meta-analysis basically involves applying statistical tests to a thorough literature review.

30. R. J. House, "A Path-Goal Theory of Leader Effectiveness," *Administrative Science Quarterly* 16 (1971): 321-338, and M. G. Evans, "The Effects of Supervisory Behavior on the Path-Goal Relationship," *Organizational Behavior and Human Performance* 5 (1970): 277-298.

31. R. J. House and T. R. Mitchell, "Path-Goal Theory of Leadership," *Journal of Contemporary Business* (Autumn 1974): 81-98; a publication of the Graduate School of Business, University of Washington, Seattle. Reprinted with permission.

32. C. A. Schriesheim and M. A. Von Glinow, "The Path-Goal Theory of Leadership: A Theoretical and Empirical Analysis," *Academy of Management Journal* 20 (1977): 398-405.

33. You may be wondering what happened to the GI style. The model presented here is called the group model. There is also an individual model which can be used when consultation with only one subordinate is being considered. The DI (for delegate to a subordinate) style in the individual model corresponds to the missing GI style in the group model.

34. The last of these questions may need explanation. The logic of the model is that if subordinates are likely to be in conflict over a preferred solution, a group process may be needed to resolve the conflict. Any other process would leave some subordinates unhappy and may cause them to reject the solution. Research suggests that this is the single question in the model which managers typically do not obey. Perhaps they feel that in a situation of potential conflict, they need to maintain control.

35. Reprinted, by permission of the publisher, from "A New Look at Managerial Decision Making," by Victor H. Vroom, *Organizational Dynamics* (Spring 1973): 73-74. Copyright © 1973. American Management Association, New York. All rights reserved.

36. V. H. Vroom and A. G. Jago, "On the Validity of the Vroom-Yetton Model," *Journal of Applied Psychology* 63 (1978): 151-162.

37. R. H. G. Field, "A Test of the Vroom-Yetton Normative Model of Leadership," *Journal of Applied Psychology* 67 (1982): 523-532.

38. V. H. Vroom and P. W. Yetton, *Leadership and Decision Making* (Pittsburgh: University of Pittsburgh Press, 1973), 80.

39. The terms "transactional leadership" and "transformational leadership" were first used in J. M. Burns, *Leadership* (New York: Harper & Row, 1978).

40. B. M. Bass, "Leadership: Good, Better, Best," *Organizational Dynamics* (Winter 1985): 26-40.

41. Ibid., p. 33.

42. M. Weber, *The Theory of Social and Economic Organization*, trans. and ed. A. M. Henderson and T. Parsons (London: Oxford University Press, 1947), 358.

43. These examples are drawn from A. C. Filley and R. J. Aldag, "Organizational Growth and Types: Lessons from Small Institutions," in *Research in Organizational Behavior, vol. 2*, ed. B. M. Staw and L. L. Cummings (Greenwich, CT: JAI Press, 1979).

44. These examples are drawn from N. M. Tichy and D. O. Ulrich, "The Leadership Challenge—A Call for the Transformational Leader," *Sloan Management Review* (Fall 1984): 59-68.

45. R. J. House, "A 1976 Theory of Charismatic Leadership," in *Leadership: The Cutting Edge*, ed. J. G. Hunt and L. L. Larson (Carbondale: Southern Illinois University Press, 1977). For a more recent discussion of House's work on charismatic leadership, see B. Shamir, R. J. House, and M. B. Arthur, "The Transformational Effects of Charismatic Leadership—A Motivational Theory," Working Paper, Suffolk University, 1989.

46. Tichy and Ulrich, "The Leadership Challenge," 63-64.

47. R. E. Byrd, "Corporate Leadership Skills: A New Synthesis," *Organizational Dynamics* (1987): 34-43.

48. These reasons are drawn from J. A. Conger and R. N. Kanungo, "Toward a Behavioral Theory of Charismatic Leadership in Organizational Settings," *Academy of Management Review* 12 (1987): 637-647.

49. Weber, *Social and Economic Organization*.

50. For instance, see A. C. Filley and R. J. Aldag, "Characteristics and Measurement of an Organizational Typology," *Academy of Management Journal* 21 (1978): 578-591.

51. M. W. McCall, Jr., and M. M. Lombardo, eds., *Leadership: Where Else Can We Go?* (Durham, NC: Duke University Press, 1978).

52. J. P. Howell and P. W. Dorfman, "Substitutes for Leadership: Test of a Construct," *Academy of Management Journal* 24 (1981): 714-728.
53. On this point, see Filley and Aldag, "Organizational Growth and Types."

REFERENCES

Bennett, R. A. "The Banker Who Would Be Scrooge." *The New York Times Magazine*, Part 2 (December 3, 1989): 16-18, 36, 40.

"Executive Pay: The Top Earners." *Business Week* (May 7, 1984): 90.

Flax, S. "The Toughest Bosses in America." *Fortune* (August 6, 1984): 18-23.

Garcia, A. "The New Stage at Wells Fargo." *Euromoney* (July 1983): 85.

Iacocca, L., and Novak, W. *Iacocca: An Autobiography.* New York: Bantam Books, 1984.

Sherman, S. P. "Inside the Mind of Jack Welch." *Fortune* (March 27, 1989): 39-44, 46, 50.

Managing
Groups

CHAPTER 17

After studying this chapter, you should be able to:
- *Explain why groups are important in organizations.*
- *Discuss the characteristics of various types of formal and informal groups.*
- *Identify reasons why people join groups.*
- *Discuss such group processes and characteristics as cohesiveness, roles, status, norms, and coalition formation.*
- *Describe the impacts of group size and spatial arrangements.*
- *Discuss the stages through which groups progress as they move toward maturity.*
- *Discuss guidelines for the effective management of group meetings.*
- *Identify techniques for managing conflict.*

In his popular book *Theory Z*, William Ouchi contrasts the model Japanese organization with the model American organization.[1] A key difference is the greater Japanese emphasis on collective decision making and collective responsibility. Teamwork, group (rather than individual) bonuses, concern for consensus, and attention to interpersonal relationships are conspicuous in the Japanese model. As discussed in previous chapters, Ouchi's Type Z organization incorporates many of these characteristics. What the characteristics have in common is attention to groups.

A **group** is a collection of individuals who have a common goal, are interdependent, and perceive themselves as a unit.[2] Harold Leavitt has suggested several reasons why groups are important and should be taken seriously by managers:[3]

- Small groups seem to be good for people. They may satisfy membership needs and provide a useful range of activities for members. They provide support in times of stress. They provide settings in which people learn about trust and cooperation.
- Groups seem to be good problem-finding tools. As we will explore in Chapter 21, groups may be useful in promoting creativity and innovation.
- In a wide variety of situations, groups make better decisions than individuals. In the previous chapter we saw that groups outperform individuals in many problem-solving contexts.
- Groups are great tools for implementation. They gain commitment from their members so that group decisions are more willingly carried out.
- Groups can control and discipline their members in ways that are often very difficult through more impersonal disciplinary systems.
- As organizations grow larger, small groups appear to be useful mechanisms for fending off many of the negative effects of large size. They help prevent communication lines from growing too long, the hierarchy from getting too steep, and the individual from getting lost in the crowd.
- Groups are natural phenomena and facts of organizational life. They can be created, but their development cannot be prevented. The question is not whether groups should exist, but whether they should be planned.

In this chapter we will consider the effective management of groups in organizations. Figure 17–1 provides a rough outline of the issues to be considered. We will first discuss types of groups. Then, we will identify reasons why people join groups. Third, we will examine a variety of important group processes and characteristics. Fourth, we will consider issues in group development, including an examination of group movement toward maturity. Finally, we will consider issues in the effective management of groups, including the management of conflict. The factors we will discuss influence such outcomes as group performance and member satisfaction. Those group outcomes, in turn, cycle back to affect the future condition, behavior, development, and management of the group.

FIGURE 17–1

Issues to Be Considered in Managing Groups

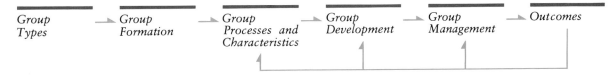

| Group Types | Group Formation | Group Processes and Characteristics | Group Development | Group Management | Outcomes |

TYPES OF GROUPS

Groups may be formal or informal. **Formal groups** are created by the organization to help accomplish some organizational objective. Their members work together to get a job done. **Informal groups** are created by the members themselves. Both types of groups are important in organizations.

Types of Formal Groups

Formal groups may be classified as command groups or task groups. These group types differ in their membership and duties.

COMMAND GROUPS

Command groups, or **functional groups,** consist of managers and their subordinates and show up on the organization chart. The group made up of a director of marketing and her immediate subordinates would be an example. As shown in Figure 17–2, these command groups "fit together" to make up the hierarchy. The leader of each group is typically also a member of a higher-level group and thus serves as a **linking pin,** coordinating activities and communications between levels.[4] Command groups generally are relatively permanent.

TASK GROUPS

Task groups, or **committees,** are formed for a specific purpose, such as exchange of information, coordination of activities, generation of recommenda-

FIGURE 17–2
How Linking Pins Connect Command Groups

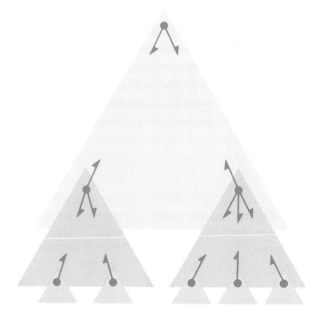

Source: Adapted from *New Patterns of Management* by Rensis Likert. Copyright © 1961 by McGraw-Hill Book Company. Reproduced with permission.

tions, development of new procedures, or solution of specific problems. Their members may be drawn from various parts of the organization as needed. **Ad hoc committees** are typically created for a short-term purpose and have a limited life. A search-and-screen committee organized to nominate candidates for a key managerial position would be an example. **Standing committees** are relatively permanent task groups that deal with issues on an ongoing basis. An example would be an ethics review committee set up to advise top management on the ethical implications of decisions.

The fact that groups are formed by the organization does not necessarily imply that they are simply puppets of management. For instance, J. Richard Hackman has discussed **self-managing work groups**.[5] These are "intact (if small) social systems whose members have the authority to handle internal processes as they see fit in order to generate a specific group product, service, or decision."[6] The self-managing work group is in essence job enrichment at the level of the group.

Types of Informal Groups

Informal groups may be classified as interest groups or friendship groups. Together, they make up the informal organization.

Interest groups arise when individuals unite to achieve some common purpose. As an example, a group might be formed to petition for a recall of a judge, to file a grievance, or to pitch in to do a job. **Friendship groups** are formed because of some attraction, due perhaps to similar values, backgrounds, or ages. Friendship groups may engage in a wide variety of activities both on and off the job.

Informal groups give members a forum to communicate, to gain some control over their environments, and to provide status and recognition. While they are formed by members themselves rather than by the organization, informal groups may help achieve organizational purposes. For instance, a group that forms so that members can help one another accomplish a task may help both the members and the organization. Informal groups are a reality that management cannot wish or coerce away. Because of this, management should recognize them and try to work with them for mutual benefit. We will take a closer look at the informal organization later.

GROUP FORMATION

Individuals join groups for a variety of reasons. We suggested earlier that formal groups are formed to promote organizational purposes and that individuals may join informal groups because of friendship or common interests. Some other, though perhaps related, reasons for group formation include proximity, need satisfaction, collective power, and group goals.

Proximity

Physical proximity and contact provide the opportunity for group formation. If people are not able to somehow get together, they will have little chance to interact and to form a group. George Homans sees proximity as one factor

A softball team is a group of people united by a common interest.

Elizabeth Weldon (Ph.D., Industrial/Organizational Psychology, Ohio State University) is Associate Professor of Organizational Behavior at the Kellogg Graduate School of Management, Northwestern University. Prior to taking her position at the Kellogg School, Professor Weldon taught in the Department of Business Administration at the University of Illinois in Urbana-Champaign. Professor Weldon's research in the area of group dynamics and effective team performance has appeared in journals such as Organizational Behavior and Human Decision Processes, Human Performance, *and* Journal of Applied Social Psychology.

Q: Much of your work has dealt with groups in organizations. What prompted you to focus on groups?

A: My interest in group dynamics was stimulated by a course in social psychology. That course showed that social dynamics have a strong impact on the attitudes and behavior of group members and that the quality of their interaction is an important determinant of outcomes achieved by the group. When I began my study of organizations, I applied the principles of social psychology to the study of work groups.

Q: Do you believe that managers are now "taking groups seriously"? Do you see any concrete evidence of growing use of groups?

A: Managers are beginning to recognize that groups can be more effective than individuals when groups are designed and managed properly. The use of quality circles and task forces to solve organizational problems and the increased use of self-managing work teams demonstrate this new appreciation for groups.

This new appreciation for groups is driven in part by the demands of today's economy. Rapid changes in the technical, legal, and regulatory environments and rapidly changing customer demands require rapid organizational response. Because effective coordination and cooperation determine in part the organization's ability to respond, effective group management is crucial to the organization's success.

Q: Your current research focuses on the impact of specific performance goals on group dynamics and group performance. What are the interesting developments in that area?

A: Many studies show that specific performance goals can improve group performance. My own research tests factors that account for that result. Specifically, I tested the relative importance of working smarter (group planning) versus working harder on the task (increased effort).

These studies show that the introduction of a specific performance goal impacts both these processes—group members work harder at their task and work together to improve the group's performance plan. This result is important because improvements in performance produced by planning and effort together should be easier to maintain than those produced by effort alone. Improvements produced by effort alone would be temporary because group members soon tire of working hard at the task. However, improvements produced by planning should be maintained as improved strategies become standard operating procedure. In practical terms, this finding suggests that group members should be encouraged to plan when faced with a difficult performance goal.

Q: What do you see as some unanswered questions relating to the management of groups in organizations?

A: Human resource management now focuses primarily on the management of individual performance. This focus must expand to include the group. Systems to select and train effective group members must be designed, and reward systems to promote effective group performance must be created. To meet this end, characteristics of effective group members and the skills required to work effectively in groups must be identified, and techniques for assessing these characteristics and training these skills must be developed. In addition, research testing the impact of different combinations of individual and group rewards on individual motivation and group performance must be conducted.

influencing a complex interplay of activity, interaction, and sentiment. Proximity gives people the chance to share ideas, opinions, and feelings. Such sharing may lead to feelings of liking. Those feelings, in turn, may lead to desires to carry out more activities together, and thus to interact.[7]

Need Satisfaction

Most people join groups because they feel that membership may help satisfy their needs. One function of groups is to provide safety and security in numbers. Unions, investment clubs, and street gangs are examples of groups that help satisfy such needs in various ways. Group membership clearly may directly satisfy needs for affiliation and social support. Groups may also help fulfill esteem needs—for instance, membership in a particular law firm or sorority may be seen as prestigious. Even growth needs may be met by group membership. As examples, memberships in literary groups, art clubs, or chess societies may all provide opportunities for growth.

Collective Power

People may form groups because of the collective power afforded by the group. Quite simply, the fact that a number of individuals have pooled their efforts affords power, and thus the ability to accomplish objectives, which would not otherwise be possible. Members of the Nature Conservancy or of the National Rifle Association, for instance, believe that group membership provides leverage. Collective power is also another reason for union membership. Later in this chapter we will consider the related topic of coalition formation.

Group Goals

Finally, individuals may join groups because they agree with the goals of the group. The authors, for instance, both serve on the boards of community organizations because they agree with the goals of those organizations, family enhancement and matching children with adult role models. Similarly, many people join fund-raising or advocacy groups to help the groups attain their goals.

GROUP DIMENSIONS INFLUENCING EFFECTIVENESS

Groups are complex, dynamic entities. Their effectiveness depends upon the rich and sometimes subtle interplay of many variables. In this section we will consider some of the most important of the processes and characteristics influencing group effectiveness.

Cohesiveness

Group cohesiveness is the degree to which members are attracted to one another, reflected in their desires to retain membership and to resist leaving. More-cohesive groups are generally more effective in achieving their goals. There is usually greater communication among members, higher member satisfaction, decreased member tension and anxiety, and heightened pressure toward conformity.

The sources of cohesiveness are much like those of group formation. For instance, they may reside in the personal attractiveness of group members, the attractiveness of the group task, or the prestige of group membership. As the group achieves its goals, cohesiveness increases. Large groups are less cohesive than small groups. High status of the group and outside pressures on the group both increase cohesiveness.

Roles

Group members play a variety of roles, both inside and outside the organization. A **role** is a set of shared expectations concerning appropriate behavior. There might be an expectation, for instance, that a nurse should behave, and should not behave, in certain ways. The group of people who have these expectations concerning appropriate behavior is called the role set, and the set of expectations they convey to the individual is called the sent role. The received role is the individual's perception of that sent role. The enacted role is the way the individual behaves in response to received roles.

Unfortunately, role expectations may be unclear or may cause conflict. **Role ambiguity** occurs in an organization when:

- Employees lack clear information about what people expect them to accomplish.
- Employees know what outcomes people expect but don't know how to achieve those outcomes.
- Employees don't know what personal costs or benefits are associated with meeting particular expectations.

Role conflict occurs when employees are expected to engage in activities that clash with their own expectations or are somehow inconsistent. There are five types of role conflict:

- *Intersender role conflict* results from conflicting expectations of different role senders. For example, supervisors sometimes find that their subordinates expect them to identify with labor while their superiors expect them to see themselves as part of management.
- *Intrasender role conflict* occurs when a single role sender transmits incompatible expectations. This sort of conflict might occur if a boss says to place more emphasis on quality but at the same time is demanding greater quantity.
- *Person-role conflict* results from clashes between role demands and personal values and expectations. A police officer who is called on to evict an aging tenant, or a manager who must fire loyal employees because of budget cuts, may experience such conflict.
- *Inter-role conflict* comes about through the incompatible demands of different roles. A person's role as operations manager of a company that needs wetlands to expand production capacity may conflict with her role as officer of a local conservation group.
- *Role overload* occurs because various role expectations, while not inherently inconsistent, simply cannot all be satisfied in the time available. The

increasing number of women entering the work force, often already heavily burdened by the demands of the roles of spouse and mother, may face such role overload.

Both role conflict and role ambiguity contribute to role stress, discussed in Chapter 11. Role stress has been associated with an array of negative consequences, including dissatisfaction, anxiety, turnover, and low performance.[8]

Status

Status, or social ranking within a group, is of two kinds—achieved status and ascribed status. Achieved status depends on a person's achievements. Ascribed status depends not on achievements but on such factors as age, lineage, or sex. While ascribed status is generally relatively fixed, achieved status may be altered.

Several things affect achieved status.[9] The answer to the icebreaking question, "What do you do?" gives one quick gauge of relative status. Figure 17–3 shows that there are substantial differences in the levels of status associated with different occupations.[10] In addition, achieved status is related to rank in the formal hierarchy, pay, skill or knowledge required to do the job, seniority, the status of one's associates, and the type of materials one works on.

Typically, one's rank in the social system is marked by **status symbols**. These are concrete signs of status. Titles, offices, clothing, and access to special facilities (such as the executive dining room or exercise room) may all serve as status symbols.

Status is important to organization members, many of whom would rather have a change in title than a pay hike. When individuals are forced to take actions which are inconsistent with their perceived status, tension is likely to occur. For instance, an employee with 20 years of seniority and consider-

Job	Score
Physician	95.8
Stockbroker	81.7
Advertising executive	80.8
Accountant	71.2
Office manager	68.3
Stenographer	52.6
Inspector in manufacturing plant	51.3
Bookkeeper	50.0
Cashier	35.6
Assembly-line worker	28.3
Delivery truck driver	26.9
Warehouse clerk	22.4
Janitor	12.5
Ragpicker	4.6

FIGURE 17–3
Prestige Scores of Selected Jobs

Source: C. E. Bose and P. H. Rossi, "Gender and Jobs: Prestige Standings of Occupations As Affected by Gender," *American Sociological Review* (June 1983): 327-328. Reprinted with permission.

SOME STATUS SYMBOLS

A survey of 143 chief executive officers by the American Society of Interior Design revealed the following:

- 75% have offices with a view
- 73% have corner offices
- 61% have offices on the top floor
- 62% have private washrooms
- 51% have a separate office for a secretary
- 45% have private adjoining waiting rooms
- 67% have original artwork in their offices
- 12% have wet bars
- 4% have exercise areas

Source: Adapted from *Forbes* (July 4, 1983): 10. Reprinted with permission.

able job skills may see taking orders from a young MBA with no experience as demeaning.

Norms and Conformity

Norms are expectations about how group members ought to behave. There may be a norm, for instance, that suits should be worn when making important sales presentations. Other norms might relate to performance, honesty, teamwork, loyalty, or anything else the group feels is important. The norms of loyalty and harmony are reflected in the song sung each morning by employees of Matsushita Electric, presented in Figure 17–4.

According to J. Richard Hackman, norms:[11]

- Are structured characteristics of groups that simplify the group influence process;
- Apply only to behavior and not to private thoughts and feelings of group members;
- Generally develop only in relation to those matters that most group members consider important;
- Usually develop slowly over time; and
- Sometimes apply only to certain group members.

FIGURE 17–4
The Matsushita Worker's Song

For the building of a new Japan,
Let's put our strength and minds together,
Doing our best to promote production,
Sending our goods to the people of the world,
Endlessly and continuously,
Like water gushing from a fountain.
Grow, industry, grow, grow, grow!
Harmony and sincerity!
Matsushita Electric!

Source: From *The Emerging Japanese Superstate* by Herman Kahn. © 1970 Hudson Institute. Reprinted by permission of the publisher, Prentice-Hall, Inc., Englewood Cliffs, New Jersey.

If individuals behave in ways that violate group norms, group members exert pressure for conformity to those norms. Pressure might take the form of "friendly" comments, threats, ridicule, ostracism, or even physical abuse. Conformity pressures are especially strong when the norm is very central to the group, when the situation is ambiguous, and when a large percentage of members accept the norm. Conformity pressures are also strong in cohesive groups, where members are attracted to the group and want to retain membership. Cohesive groups with strong norms have the potential to contribute to or undermine organizational performance.

Whether group pressure for conformity to norms is desirable from the point of view of the firm depends on the norm. Conformity to norms of high performance, an honest day's work, and creativity will generally be beneficial. Conformity to norms of rate restriction, leaving work early, and pilferage is clearly unwelcome. Donald Roy, a sociologist, took a job in a machine shop in order to observe work culture. Read his classic description of group norms in Management in Action 1.

As Roy's experience suggests, new group members are gradually integrated into the group through **socialization**. This is a process of "learning the ropes"—gaining an understanding of norms, values, and behavior patterns.

Conformity pressures are powerful, and they may lead to incorrect decisions. For instance, Muzafir Sherif conducted a classic study in which subjects were placed in a dark room where all they could see was a small point of light in the distance. The light was stationary, but a stationary light appears to move because of muscle twitches in the eye (this is a physiological process called the autokinesis—self-movement—effect). With no other visual cues present, those watching the light can't assess actual movement. Sherif first tested subjects individually to measure their movement estimates without social influence. He then tested them in groups over a series of trials. Subjects' estimates of movement were greatly influenced by estimates of other group members. After a series of trials the estimates began to converge; those reporting large movements reduced their estimates while those reporting small movements increased theirs.

In another experiment Sherif used confederates to create a group norm regarding the amount of movement. Then the confederates were replaced one by one with naive subjects over a series of trials. The group norm survived after all the confederates had been removed from the group membership and persisted even after several more subjects had been rotated through the group membership.[12] In another classic experiment, Solomon Asch showed that, if group pressures are great enough, people will often conform to a majority opinion that is clearly false. In that experiment, subjects were asked to indicate which of three lines on a card was the same length as a comparison line. Even though the answer was obvious, in about one-third of the cases subjects tended to agree with others who first, as confederates of the experimenter, unanimously picked the incorrect line.[13]

Sometimes, conformity can take on ominous hues. Stanley Milgram carried out a series of experiments on obedience to authority. He found that many subjects would conform to the demands of authority figures even when they thought they were administering dangerous, and potentially fatal, electric shocks to other subjects.[14] When conformity leads to acceptance of wrong choices, to unethical behavior, or to the stifling prospect of the "Organization Man," it is dangerous.[15]

Group norms may include expectations about what kind of clothing is appropriate for the business setting.

From [my first] to my last day at the plant, I was subject to warnings and predictions concerning price cuts. Pressure was the heaviest from Joe Mucha, day

MANAGEMENT IN ACTION 1
QUOTA RESTRICTION AND GOLDBRICKING
IN A MACHINE SHOP

man on my machine, who shared my job repertoire and kept a close eye on my production. On November 14, the day after my first attained quota, Mucha advised:

"Don't let it go over $1.25 per hour, or the time-study man will be right down here! And they don't waste time, either! They watch the records like a hawk! I got ahead, so I took it easy for a couple of hours."

Joe told me that I had made $10.01 yesterday and warned me not to go over $1.25 an hour. He told me to figure the set-ups and the time on each operation very carefully so that I would not total over $10.25 in any one day.

Jack Sharkey defined the quota carefully but forcefully when I turned in $10.50 one day, or $1.31 an hour.

Jack Sharkey spoke to me after Joe left. "What's the matter? Are you trying to upset the apple cart?"

Jack explained in a friendly manner that $10.50 was too much to turn in, even on an old job.

"The turret-lathe men can turn in $1.35," said Jack, "but their rate is 90 cents, and ours 85 cents."

Jack warned me that the Methods Department could lower their prices on any job, old or new, by changing the fixture slightly, or changing the size of drill. According to Jack, a couple of operators (first and second shift on the same drill) got to competing with each other to see how much they could turn in. They got up to $1.65 an hour, and the price was cut in half. And from then on they had to run that job themselves, as none of the other operators would accept the job.

According to Jack, it would be all right for us to turn in $1.28 or $1.29 an hour, when it figured out that way, but it was not all right to turn in $1.30 an hour.

Well, now I know where the maximum is—$1.29 an hour.

Source: D. Roy, "Quota Restriction and Goldbricking in a Machine Shop," *American Journal of Sociology* 57 (1952): 430-437. Copyright © 1952 by The University of Chicago Press. Reprinted with permission.

Coalition Formation

Coalitions are alliances of organizational members combining their individual powers, resources, and persuasive efforts to achieve greater influence on decision processes than the members could accomplish alone.[16] Coalitions may be used to gain the upper hand in elections, resource allocation decisions, promotion decisions, and the like. Richard Cyert and James March saw coalition formation as a basic element in organizational functioning.[17] Individuals work for the firm but have their own specific interests. To advance their interests, they join coalitions. Negotiations occur between conflicting coalitions to resolve differences. That resolution may come about through the dominance of one coalition or through compromise.

Various hypotheses have been advanced concerning how coalitions form. Experiments tend to support the **minimum resource theory**, which argues that members would like to form a coalition that controls the minimum amount of resources necessary to gain the upper hand.[18] If a majority is needed, for instance, members controlling 51 percent of resources might form a coalition. In that way, they have substantial leverage, being able to share the full 49 percent "spoils." If more resources were included in the coalition, there would be fewer spoils to share and perhaps more members with which to share them.

EFFECTS OF GROUP SIZE AND SPATIAL ARRANGEMENTS

Many of the group dimensions we have considered are influenced by group size and spatial arrangements. For instance, we will see in this section that size and spatial arrangements may influence status perceptions, interaction patterns, leadership, and coalition formation. Ultimately, they can affect member satisfaction, decision quality, and other group outcomes.

Group Size

Groups of various sizes have their own special characteristics. As we will see, some of those characteristics interfere with effective group functioning. Many of the dynamics we will discuss are relevant for groups of all types. However, the following discussion is primarily directed at interacting groups which will be used for problem-solving purposes.[19]

SMALL GROUPS

In a two-person group, or dyad, each member knows that if the other leaves, the group task will not be accomplished. Also, the dyad has none of the mechanisms that are available in larger groups to resolve disputes—members can't appeal to group norms, to majority opinion, or to another group member to help settle disagreements. As a result, dyads are characterized by tension and anxiety. Each member is reluctant to give opinions and continually asks for opinions. There are either high levels of antagonism or conscious attempts to hide latent antagonism. Not surprisingly, dyads are unstable.

Three-person groups, triads, have a tendency for coalition formation, with two members uniting against the other. The minority member in a triad is necessarily an isolate and is likely to be resentful. Triads also tend to be unstable, with considerable shifting of coalitions.

With four-person groups, there is a good chance of a tie vote, and thus of a stalemate. While ties are possible with any even-sized group, the chances decrease as the group gets larger. Further, interactions in groups of four or fewer members tend to be highly personalized. Members feel that they are personally tied to their statements. As a result, it is hard for them to change their opinions without losing face.

LARGE GROUPS

When groups are larger than six or seven members, a variety of difficulties arise. For example:

- As size increases, the potential number of interactions increases geometrically. As a result, coordination becomes very difficult.
- Because of difficulties in coordination, there are tendencies to centralize communication flows.
- As size increases, each person has less chance to make inputs.
- In large groups, dominant members become increasingly aggressive.
- When group size exceeds six or seven members, it is difficult to think of members as individuals.
- In large groups, some members become passive, sitting back and remaining quiet.

Large groups do have some advantages. They permit a wide range of member inputs, so they may be helpful if a very large number of alternatives must be generated, or if much information must be brought to bear on a problem.

FIVE-PERSON GROUPS

Five-member groups seem to have a number of benefits. For instance:

- If all members vote, there cannot be a tie.
- In the event of a disagreement, the group tends to split into a majority of three and a minority of two. So, there does not tend to be a single isolated individual.
- The group is small enough to let everyone make inputs but big enough to allow members to change their opinions and roles.

CHOOSING AN APPROPRIATE GROUP SIZE

The characteristics of groups of various sizes suggest that for most purposes a five-person group is best. If creativity is needed, a larger group may be helpful. These suggestions are supported by empirical evidence, summarized in Figure 17–5.

We should note, however, that if larger groups are needed, it may be best to use a group technique that avoids some of the problems of large interacting groups. We will consider two such techniques—the nominal group technique and the Delphi process—in Chapter 21. Sometimes, of course, it may simply be best not to use a group. Finally, common sense should be used. It may be too costly to bring more than a few individuals together. On the other hand, there may be reasons why more than five people must be involved.

Group Spatial Arrangements[20]

Spatial arrangements of group members may have an impact on such things as anxiety, perceptions of leadership and status, communication flows, and the propensity to behave in various ways.

TERRITORIALITY

Individual territory and **group territory** refer to fixed areas over which an individual or a group takes a proprietary interest. An example of individual territory would be a favorite chair, or a work space that is considered to be private. A gang's turf, a section of the corner eatery that is used only by locals, or a conference room reserved for meetings by executives would be examples of group territory. "The Harbor Gangs" discusses an example of group territoriality and also provides insights into other aspects of informal

---

FIGURE 17–5
How Group Size Influences Outcomes

Maximized at Small Size (<5)	*Maximized at Size 5 or 6*	*Maximized at Larger Size (>6)*
Member participation Member consensus	Emergence of effective leadership Decision quality Member satisfaction	Range of member inputs

THE HARBOR GANGS

James Acheson, in *The Lobster Gangs of Maine*, provides a fascinating discussion of group territoriality among harbor gangs in the lobster industry. Harbor gangs are informal groups. Lobstermen pay no dues and have no membership cards, but the groups are real. The gangs meet regularly and share information, problems, and skills. Further, they restrict entry into the group and claim and defend fishing areas. Gang members share a set of values, view outsiders with distrust, and have a clear hierarchy distinguishing the most successful fishermen ("highliners") from "moderates" and "dubs." Gang territories are unofficial and illegal. Nevertheless, every fisherman knows that if he sets his pots outside certain limits, his buoys will be cut. Territorial rights conserve resources and result in higher incomes.

Source: J. M. Acheson, *The Lobster Gangs of Maine* (Hanover, NH: University Press of New England, 1988).

group processes. Whether individual or group, territoriality is jealously guarded. When entering another's territory, one is a bit uncomfortable.

PERSONAL SPACE

Personal space is the self-established area of privacy and control which surrounds a person. Like territoriality, it implies a sort of ownership. However, personal space moves with the individual. Edward Hall has characterized personal space in terms of four zones as follows:[21]

- The **intimate zone** is a bubble extending, for Americans, to about 18 inches from the skin. As the name implies, we allow others to enter this space for only the very best of reasons, such as lovemaking, protecting, and comforting. When other circumstances—such as a crowded elevator—force us to allow people into our intimate space, we tend to treat them as objects rather than persons.
- The **personal zone** ranges from about one and a half to four feet from the person. It is used for comfortable interaction with others and connotes closeness and friendship.

When we are forced to allow people into our intimate zone, we tend to treat them as objects rather than persons.

- The **social zone**, from 4 to 12 feet, is used for most impersonal business. People working together use the inner part of this zone. The outer part is used for more formal interactions.
- The **public zone**, more than 12 feet, is beyond the range of comfortable interaction.

These distances vary by culture. Businesspersons entering other cultures must be especially careful to learn appropriate zones for various interactions. Typically, people experience discomfort when their personal space is improperly entered. They will generally protest or leave the situation rather than accept it.

SEATING ARRANGEMENTS

Seating arrangements are important. High-status individuals choose positions of high potential eye contact with others, such as the front of a room or the head of a table. Interestingly, a person randomly placed in a position of high eye contact is more likely to be perceived as a leader, or is more likely to be selected as a leader, than a person in a position of low eye contact. Also, communication flows are likely to be directed to this visible person, and he or she is likely to be perceived as having high status.

Further, if individuals are allowed to seat themselves around a table, they tend to choose arrangements deemed appropriate for the task. When people expect to be cooperating, they sit side by side. When they expect to compete, they tend to sit face to face. It may be that these positions are most comfortable for the particular tasks, or that they are simply the "expected" positions.

People seated in formal arrangements experience greater anxiety than those allowed to choose positions.[22] And, when people are seated in ways suggesting a particular interaction style, their potential for cooperation or competition changes accordingly.

STAGES OF GROUP DEVELOPMENT

In this section, we will examine how groups grow (or do not grow) toward maturity. Groups rarely function effectively when they are first formed. Members need to get to know one another, to understand the group's goals, to see how they fit into the group, and so on. Some groups never leave this disoriented, groping state. Others achieve a sort of maturity. Mature groups are characterized by members functioning as a unit, participating effectively in the group effort, and being oriented toward a single goal. Members in a mature group have the equipment, tools, and skills necessary to attain the group's goals, and they ask and receive suggestions, opinions, and information from each other.[23]

Groups generally go through five stages in reaching maturity, but they do not necessarily move neatly from one stage to another.[24] They may be in different stages simultaneously, and they may even move backward in the stages. Although proper development requires that groups deal with each stage, few groups fully realize their potential by reaching the final stage.

Stage 1: Membership

In this first stage people are deciding the degree to which they want to become committed to the group. They ask whether the benefits of membership outweigh the costs of time, effort, and personal vulnerability which may be required. People are "feeling their way" at this stage, testing how they fit in the group. They are generally unwilling to take strong stands. Group goals at this stage are often unclear, and it is hard for the group to be productive. Members size one another up, begin to make linkages with others, and see how their personal goals fit with group goals.

Stage 2: Subgrouping

In this stage, members form subgroups with others who are similar in terms of interests, values, needs, perceptions, or other characteristics. This gives them a sense of support and encourages them to take risks and voice disagreements. There is a sense that subgroups, rather than individuals, are interacting. At this stage group goals become more clear, most members have made a commitment to those goals, cohesiveness and norms develop, and group output increases. However, subgroup loyalties may lead to harmful rivalries between subgroups and reluctance to disagree with other subgroup members. Leaders may encourage development beyond this stage by highlighting disagreements within subgroups and similarities across subgroups.

Stage 3: Confrontation

Once individuals feel that they can take an unpopular position without being isolated, they are willing to express disagreements and engage in conflict. Such conflict typically first occurs across subgroups. While initially unsettling, conflict brings out diverse viewpoints and ensures that issues will be dealt with rather than avoided. When the group can handle confrontation and deal with disagreements constructively, real progress is possible. Such resolution tends to unify the group and to make subgroups more fluid in composition. However, there is a danger that, having successfully resolved some conflict and desiring to remain a congenial group, members will become afraid to "rock the boat." Good leadership is needed here to see that disagreements continue to be aired and that conflict remains depersonalized.

Stage 4: Individual Differentiation

In Stage 4, groups begin to approach their potential. Since it is now recognized that members are pursuing commonly agreed upon goals, members feel free to be themselves. Members are given considerable autonomy to pursue their own areas of responsibility. Groups at this stage are hard-working and effective. Meetings are intense. Because there is an emphasis on self-reliance, however, members may be unwilling to seek support from others. Relatively few groups reach this stage.

Stage 5: Collaboration

This stage differs from the fourth in that members are now mutually supportive in reaching the group's goals. Support may be either with assignments or in interpersonal areas. While conflicts continue to occur, they are task oriented. If members don't successfully carry out their duties, there is initial confrontation followed by assistance to prevent future failure.

GUIDELINES FOR MANAGING GROUP MEETINGS

Many managers regularly face the task of conducting group meetings. While these meetings can be structured in many ways, a common form is the committee meeting. In such a meeting members are typically free to interact as they explore issues, generate alternatives, make choices, and so on. Committee meetings are often among the most frustrating of humanity's inventions. In far too many cases, dominant members control the process, the discussion wanders off on wondrous tangents, and some members are reluctant to make inputs.

In the next chapter we will consider a variety of alternatives to the committee. In this section, we present George Huber's useful set of guidelines for managing committees.[25] Basically, Huber calls for definition of the committee's assignment and application of the traditional management functions of planning, organizing and staffing, directing, and controlling to committee management. Following is a summary of Huber's guidelines.

Defining the Committee's Assignment

Defining the committee's assignment involves specification—in written form, if possible—of the committee's purpose, responsibility, and needs. Answers to the following questions will guide this step:

- What is the issue with which the group must deal? What is its scope?
- What is the group's responsibility? To make the final decision? To give advice? To exchange information?
- What are the requirements the group must meet? For instance, what are the deadlines? What should be the format of the group output?

Planning the Overall Group Effort

Once the group's assignment is defined, it is necessary to plan the group effort systematically to accomplish that assignment:

- Divide the group's overall assignment into parts. This helps overcome psychological hurdles and makes it easier to develop estimates of time and resource needs.

- Estimate the time and other resources needed to complete each part of the assignment and the overall assignment.
- Determine the time and other resources available, and take appropriate actions to reduce any gaps between what is needed and what is available. This may involve changing the assignment, getting the deadline extended, or making other adjustments.

Organizing and Staffing the Committee

The group's composition has a major effect not only on how well it achieves its purpose but also on how satisfied its members feel. The following suggestions may prove helpful:

- Make sure that key information is available. It is important to specify information needs early and to staff accordingly.
- To reduce later resistance to the group's decision, make sure that those who will be affected get to participate. Participation may take many forms, such as group membership, interviews, or hearings.
- Do not allow past practices to dictate group membership. New members provide a fresh perspective and different kinds of expertise. In addition, participation is in itself a developmental experience.
- Appoint a leader who is group oriented yet willing and able to exert control. The leader should try to facilitate the group's efforts rather than enforce his or her will. Still, groups with leaders who are unwilling to control when needed tend to be ineffective and to have dissatisfied members.
- Consider having different members participate in different parts of the overall assignment. For instance, it may be useful to have one set of members explore the problem, another (such as a search committee) generate alternatives, and so on.

Directing and Controlling the Committee

At this point, it is time to actually have the committee carry out its assignment:

- Help the group members get acquainted. For instance, distribute biographical sketches, hold coffee hours for members to chat, or have members introduce themselves at the first meeting.

Visual displays are an effective tool in presentations to groups.

- Help the group follow the plan. To do this:
  a. At the beginning of each meeting, review the progress made to date and establish the task of the individual meeting.
  b. As early as possible in the meeting, get a report from each member with a preassigned task.
  c. At the end of the meeting, summarize what was accomplished, where this puts the group on its schedule, and what will be the group task at the next meeting.
  d. At the end of the meeting, make public and clear which members have which assignments to complete by the next meeting.
- Use information displays such as chalkboards, flipcharts, and handouts.
- Help the group achieve equitable participation by managing the discussion. This may involve use of guiding comments such as, "We've heard the case for this proposal. Now let's hear the arguments against it." Or members can be asked to take turns when giving their views.
- Focus on agreement about the soundness of the reasoning rather than on agreement about the choice itself.
  a. Early in the choice-making step, have the group agree on how it will ultimately make its choice.
  b. Have the group agree to be satisfied with the situation when members understand the reasoning that leads to the group choice.
  c. Obtain an explicit indication that the prevailing reasoning is understood by each group member.

ORGANIZATIONAL CONFLICT

Conflict is pervasive in organizations, and it can have disruptive effects on organizational and member activities. Opposing groups often put their own goals above those of the organization, lessening the organization's effectiveness. Organization members find that time which could have been used productively has to be diverted to a conflict situation. Finally, many of us have experienced the situation in which conflict becomes so intense that, win or lose, we are emotionally and physically drained and cannot be effective.[26]

Despite these adverse effects, many theorists and practitioners today see conflict as a useful force in organizations which, if managed correctly, may promote innovation and change. Controlled conflict may prevent an organization from stagnating and producing myopic decisions.[27] In a survey of top and middle managers, managers rated "conflict management" as at least equal in importance to planning, communicating, motivating, and decision making. Though the managers spent about 20 percent of their time on conflicts, they did not consider the conflict level in their organizations to be excessive. Instead, they rated it as about right.[28]

Sources of Conflict

There are many sources or causes of conflict in an organization. While conflict may take place between members, between individuals and groups, or between groups, we can usually trace the source of these conflicts to task interdependence, goal incompatibility, the need to share limited resources, differentiation between units or departments, environmental uncertainty, or the reward system of the organization.

TASK INTERDEPENDENCE

Task interdependence refers to the nature of the dependence among organizational units for information, financial, material, or human resources. Chapter 9 presented four forms of task interdependence: pooled, sequential, reciprocal, and team.

Generally the greater the interdependence between units of an organization, the greater the potential for conflict.[29] With pooled interdependence, interaction is low and thus conflict potential is low. Interaction in sequential interdependence is limited to units that provide input and the units to which the output is being provided. Thus, conflict potential is greater among these interacting units. Reciprocal and team interdependence are likely to produce the most conflict. The need to coordinate and share resources, often in an unpredictable manner, is likely to generate conflict if one unit does not receive expected resources from other units.

GOAL INCOMPATIBILITY

Different departments or units may have different, and perhaps incompatible, goals. Such differences may lead to conflict even though both units of the organization agree on the overall goal of the organization. In the aftermath of a hijacking or bombing, for example, personnel responsible for airport security may institute more stringent and time-consuming procedures at security checkpoints. At the same time, personnel in the control tower are committed to the goal of maintaining take-off and landing schedules. The delays caused by increased security may lead to conflict between the two groups.

SHARED RESOURCES

The limited resources of most organizations increase the potential for conflict. Units want to obtain the necessary money, facilities, people, and information to attain their goals successfully. If it appears that resources are scarce, efforts will be made to secure resources, often to the detriment of the goals of other groups. Inflating budgets, challenging the legitimacy of activi-

Delays caused by increased security after a hijacking or bombing may lead to conflict between airport personnel.

ties by other units, and covert efforts to prevent budget cuts are all forms of conflict over resources in an organization.

DIFFERENTIATION

Differentiation is a frequent source of unit conflict.[30] As each unit or department in an organization tries to cope with the unique demands of its own environment, it necessarily develops its own types of procedures, cherished values, and point of view. For example, a research department in a chemical firm might be run very democratically, and its personnel might develop a long-term time perspective since most of the things they are working on will not reach fruition for years. On the other hand, the production department might be run more autocratically, and its managers might be expected to put a much greater emphasis on immediate results. Because of these differences, communication and agreements about the sharing of resources will be difficult.

UNCERTAINTY

Uncertainty is often the result of an unstable environment. As the environment shifts, so must the activities of the unit. This often results in the shifting of the task scope and responsibilities of the unit. As units increase or decrease their tasks and responsibilities, they disrupt the activities of other units. This disruption may result from learning that a unit no longer is providing a resource that is critical to your unit's goal attainment or from finding out that another unit is performing essentially the same activity as your unit. For instance, a public relations unit in an organization may, because of increased encounters with potential customers, begin soliciting sales. Conflict may result when the sales department learns that it is losing commissions by not recruiting the customers itself.

REWARD SYSTEM

The reward system of an organization often governs the degree to which units will cooperate or engage in conflict. If units are given incentives that will reward the attainment of the organizational goal, cooperation is likely to result. However, if the incentives are designed to reward units for the attainment of their assigned goals, then the potential for emergence of conflict over cooperation is greater. For instance, if annual salary increases for managers are based on overall organization profits, then managers across departments are more likely to cooperate and seek compromise. However, if salary increases are distributed based on the performance of each department, little incentive exists for managers to cooperate, and conflict is likely.

Outcomes of Conflict

As noted earlier, many people regard conflict as undesirable in an organization. Indeed, early writers on management, from both the classical and behaviorist perspectives, felt that conflict was a sign that something was wrong within the organization.[31] A manager's primary responsibility was, at the very least, to reduce conflict and at best to eliminate it entirely from the organization. In other words, the most effective organization was one that was built entirely upon cooperation.

More recently, a "pluralistic" view of conflict has been prevalent. This perspective argues that conflict is inevitable in organizations and has beneficial qualities to its members.[32] Indeed, it is argued that the absence of conflict may actually reflect unhealthy complacency and stagnation. Figure 17–6 summarizes the differences between the traditional and pluralistic views of conflict.

Figure 17–7 suggests that a moderate level of conflict will lead to higher levels of performance for the organization. When conflict is too low, complacency and stagnation will result, causing the organization's performance to decline. When conflict is too high, performance is low because members divert their energies from efforts to achieve goals. Perceptions become less accurate. Units that lose in the conflict develop "loser effects" and seek scapegoats, and coordination among units is reduced.

There are several benefits of moderate conflict levels. Moderate conflict encourages members to focus more on their tasks and less on superfluous issues or disputes. It generates cohesion by building a "we" feeling. A balancing of power can be achieved through moderate conflict, and greater energy is directed toward the attainment of goals. It is important that managers understand the intensity level of conflict in their organization in order to facilitate a movement toward higher levels of performance.

MANAGING CONFLICT

According to the pluralistic view of organizational conflict, managers will want to maintain a moderate level of conflict in the organization. This means that conflict may have to be reduced, stimulated, or maintained. The traditional view suggests that conflict should be reduced and, if possible, prevented. Whichever view a particular manager espouses, techniques are available to prevent conflict, reduce conflict, or increase conflict in the organization.

FIGURE 17–6
Views of Organizational Conflict

Traditional View	Pluralistic View
1. Conflict, by and large, is bad and should be eliminated or reduced.	1. Conflict is good and should be encouraged; conflict must be regulated, however, so that it does not get out of hand.
2. Conflict need not occur.	2. Conflict is inevitable.
3. Conflict results from breakdowns in communication and lack of understanding, trust, and openness between groups.	3. Conflict results from a struggle for limited rewards, competition, and potential frustration of goals—conditions that are natural in organizations.
4. People are essentially good; trust, cooperation, and goodness are givens in human nature.	4. People are not essentially bad, but are nevertheless driven by achievement, self-seeking, and competitive interests.

Source: Adapted from Donald Nightingale, "Conflict and Conflict Resolution," in *Organizational Behavior: Research and Issues*, ed. George Strauss, Raymond Miles, Charles Snow, and Arnold Tannenbaum (Belmont, CA: Wadsworth Publishing Company, 1976). © by Kent Publishing Company. Reprinted by permission of PWS-KENT Publishing Company, a division of Wadsworth, Inc.

FIGURE 17-7
*The Relationship
Between Conflict and
Performance*

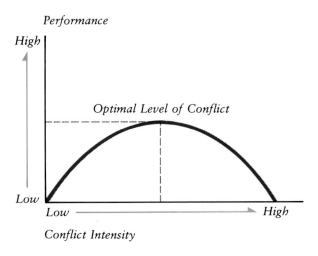

Preventing Conflict

In this section we consider a number of techniques that managers can use for preventing conflict:

- *Emphasize organizational goals over unit goals.* If members focus their attention on the goals of the organization, they are less likely to promote the differences between unit goals. This technique requires continual communication of organizational goals in order to make sure members are constantly focusing on the "big picture."
- *Structure tasks so that they are predictable and stable.* Well-structured tasks help members understand their activities and the activities of other members. This reduces ambiguity and uncertainty, thereby reducing the potential for conflict.
- *Develop and promote communication between members in different units of the organization.* The more misperceptions members have concerning the activities of another department or division, the greater the potential for conflict. Managers should facilitate communication either by encouraging contact between the groups or providing information about their activities.
- *Avoid win-lose situations.* A win-lose situation is one in which a member or group attains advantage through the deprivation of another. Where resources are scarce, managers should devise mechanisms for distributing resources equitably. For instance, if budget cuts are necessary, managers should avoid drastic cuts in one department with few cuts in other departments.

Reducing Conflict

The techniques discussed in this section can be applied by managers to reduce conflict which already exists in an organization:[33]

- *Physically separate conflicting groups.* The physical separation of conflicting groups is a quick and direct way to reduce conflict. Though it does not necessarily reduce the hostility felt between groups or members, it prevents the conflict from flaring up. Obviously, physical separation is not an option when groups are working on a joint task.

- *Apply bureaucratic rules and regulations.* Invoking or developing bureaucratic rules and regulations enforces a code of behavior that can lead to the suppression of conflict. For example, a rule stating that only top management can approve employee travel to training sessions may reduce a conflict between production and personnel departments arising from the latter's previously having authority for such approval.

- *Limit group interaction.* Often conflict arises because groups focus on where their goals differ rather than on where they agree. Such conflict can be reduced by confining group interaction to issues and tasks having compatible goals.

- *Establish integrator roles.* An integrator role is one that bridges two groups or departments in an organization. Managers can establish an integrator role by assigning authority to an individual who then maneuvers between the conflicting groups in order to achieve a solution. The integrator role is usually filled by an individual who is trusted by both groups.

- *Encourage confrontation and negotiation.* A face-to-face meeting between the conflicting members or groups is appropriate when managers believe a direct and open discussion of the problems causing the conflict may be fruitful. However, confrontation and negotiation will be successful only if the groups seek a win-win solution as opposed to a win-lose solution.

- *Bring in third-party consultants.* An outside or third-party consultant with expertise in human behavior can often facilitate the reduction of conflict. The third-party consultant can meet with representatives of both groups and work out an agreement that is acceptable to both. Third-party consultants should be used when suspicion between groups has resulted in a deadlock. Because third-party consultants have no vested interest in the dispute or organization, groups are often willing to trust and abide by their recommendations.

- *Rotate members between groups.* The temporary transfer of members from one group to another can have long-term consequences on the reduction of conflict. Members of one group learn the problems and constraints of another group. Rotation also encourages the establishment of personal bonds due to interaction with members in the other group. Such bonds should reduce the likelihood that conflict will result from misunderstandings or lack of recognition of the problems confronted by the other group.

- *Develop superordinate goals.* Superordinate goals can turn the focus of members or groups from conflict to cooperation. Threats of bankruptcy, loss of jobs, or deterioration of product quality can often encourage conflicting groups to cooperate to achieve a mutually beneficial goal. The need to "save the company" encourages conflicting groups to set aside their hostilities and unite for the purpose of keeping the organization going.

- *Use intergroup training.* With intergroup training, members of two or more groups in the organization are brought together in order to undergo similar training experiences. The objective of intergroup training is to develop permanent mechanisms that encourage groups to work together. This often requires the use of outside workshops and training programs

To energize organization members, a company may offer a vacation trip as an award for increased productivity.

where participants are removed from the day-to-day problems of their jobs.

Stimulating Conflict

Conflict may be stimulated by simply avoiding or reversing the application of the techniques mentioned above. However, managers seeking to increase conflict between groups may also want to consider the following techniques:

- *Increase competition and opportunities for conflict.* When competition intensifies, groups usually seek opportunities to engage in conflict. Creating awards for competitive activities, such as a trophy for the division that sells the most products, can energize members and groups in an organization. Conflict can result when one group suffers from loser effects. That group may demand that the rules of the competition be changed to make the contest fairer. Through modification of the rules, competition continues and the organization may benefit from this new-found energy by an increase in sales.

- *Increase uncertainty among groups.* Stagnation in organizations often results when activities are unchanged over long periods of time. Members and groups know exactly what tasks are to be performed each day and can predict the results of those tasks. Introducing uncertainty by assigning new tasks, hiring new personnel, and withholding information are techniques that foster a new interest in activities and increase the potential for conflict.

- *Change the reward system.* A change in reward systems can increase both competition and uncertainty. For instance, a group that receives rewards based on this quarter's performance compared with last quarter's performance is in competition with itself. Changing the system to one that distributes rewards based on how well the group performs in this quarter relative to other groups can encourage competition. In addition, introducing a new reward system creates uncertainty as members or groups try to determine how they will be affected by the new system. Often this leads to increased conflict due to misinterpretations or miscalculations of how the reward system operates.

Ineffective Techniques for Managing Conflict

A number of techniques for managing conflict have proved to be generally ineffective. We refer to them as nonaction, administrative orbiting, due-process nonaction, secrecy, and law and order.[34]

- *Nonaction.* A popular but ineffective strategy for managing conflict is simply to do nothing, hoping that the conflict will go away. When managers use this approach, they are simply encouraging the conflict to escalate. Ignoring problems usually only increases frustration and anger among the participants.

- *Administrative orbiting.* With this technique, appeals for change or attention are placed "under study" until "more information is received." Coming to realize after a while that the administrative orbit is not going to provide solutions, the conflicting parties increase their hostilities and undertake destructive action aimed at the organization or manager. Strikes, work stoppages, or sabotage may result.

- *Due-process nonaction.* A third ineffective technique for handling conflict is termed due-process nonaction. Here, recognized procedures are established for members or groups to redress grievances. However, the procedures turn out to be costly, time-consuming, and complicated, with no guarantee of a successful outcome. Because tangling with the bureaucratic machinery takes so much time and energy, due-process nonaction hopes to wear down the hostile groups or members. It may succeed in that goal, but the hostility remains.

- *Secrecy.* Some managers believe that secrecy regarding the way they operate and make decisions will avoid questions and challenges from those who are affected. Managers using this technique disclose only those activities that they feel shed a positive light on their activities. This "none of your business" attitude generates distrust and frustration among members of the organization. Thus, any effort to formulate and implement a solution to a conflict situation is met with suspicion.

- *Law and order.* This technique requires the suppression of conflict through force. In the name of the overall good and welfare of the organization, stringent rules often unrelated to the conflict situation are invoked. Those who persist in the conflict are labeled as troublemakers and their motives are questioned. Managers use this technique with the idea that suppressing conflict is the way to eliminate it. However, conflicting groups forced to curtail their hostilities will often forge a coalition directed at management out of resentment toward the technique.

IMPLICATIONS FOR MANAGEMENT

As a manager, you will regularly be called on to work with groups as a leader, member, observer, or even adversary. It is crucial that you have an understanding of group characteristics and processes, as well as of how groups form and mature.

You will deal with both formal and informal groups. People join these groups for many reasons and, for generally similar reasons, want to remain in them. The groups will not easily dissolve. They can certainly not be wished away. Be especially careful to recognize the importance of informal groups and to work with them to achieve organizational goals. Remember that, because of the workings of the informal organization, actions required by management may meet with resistance and other unintended consequences. Try to anticipate such reactions and consequences.

When specifying desired behaviors for group members, try to make your expectations clear in order to avoid role ambiguity. Ask, too, whether you are contributing to role conflict. See if there are things you can do to help your subordinates deal with role overload.

Most managers expect their subordinates to show some degree of conformity to norms. After all, norms reflect important group sentiments. However, conformity may be good or bad for the organization, depending on the norm. Further, very high levels of conformity, whatever the norm, may be undesirable. At the extreme, they may lead to unethical behavior, unquestioning obedience to authority, and lack of creativity.

When forming and organizing a group, give some consideration to the issues of size and spatial arrangements. For instance, a group size of five is optimal for many purposes. And, if cooperation is desired, face-to-face seating of potential adversaries should be avoided.

When managing groups, be aware of the stages of development through which they must pass on the rocky road to maturity. Don't expect harmony and consensus at each of those stages; in fact, disagreement and differentiation can be positive signs that the group is not experiencing stagnation. Anticipate conflicts and view them as necessary steps to group progress.

If you run group meetings, provide enough structure to head off the tangents, passivity, and other problems for which such meetings are noted. Plan, organize and staff, direct, and control the group process. Group members will usually welcome such structure.

As a manager, you should begin to realize that conflict can be both beneficial and destructive to an organization. Learn techniques for preventing, reducing, and stimulating conflict. Try to identify what you believe are the optimal ranges of conflict between groups or members that you are supervising. Then determine where conflict in your organization resides. Finally, apply techniques that will move the conflict situation into this optimal range in order to increase performance. Avoid the use of ineffective techniques for handling conflict. Though tempting and often used, such techniques may alleviate short-run symptoms, but they will most likely compound problems in the long run.

KEY TERMS AND CONCEPTS

ad hoc committees	norms
coalitions	personal space
command groups or functional groups	personal zone
formal groups	public zone
friendship groups	role
group	role ambiguity
group cohesiveness	role conflict
group territory	self-managing work groups
individual territory	social zone
informal groups	socialization
interest groups	standing committees
intimate zone	status
linking pin	status symbols
minimum resource theory	task groups or committees

QUESTIONS FOR REVIEW AND DISCUSSION

1. Identify three groups of which you are a member. Then, for each group, (a) indicate whether it is a formal or an informal group; (b) specify why you joined the

group; (c) describe, to the best of your knowledge, how the group developed over time; and (d) specify a central norm and the probable consequences for members who violate the norm.

2. What is cohesiveness? Describe a situation in which high levels of informal group cohesiveness would be harmful to the organization.

3. Describe four of your current roles. For each, identify the members of your role set. How clearly defined is each role? Are you experiencing any role conflict? If so, what sort?

4. Do you believe that American workers would be willing to conform to the norms of loyalty and harmony to the same degree as the employees of Matsushita Electric, as reflected in the Matsushita morning song? Why or why not?

5. What is conformity? Do you think the extreme sorts of conformity evidenced in the Asch and Milgram experiments are common in organizations today? Why or why not?

6. Think of three situations in which you recently interacted with someone else. For each situation, describe the purpose of the interaction, the interaction distance, and other relevant aspects of spatial arrangements.

7. Many managers try to prevent the formation of informal groups, or to break them up if they do form. Why do you think this happens? What might be some unintended consequences of such actions?

8. Define the stages of group development. Discuss a group of which you were a member as it developed over time. Did it seem to proceed through these stages?

9. Think of a recent conflict situation that you experienced. What were the sources of the conflict? The outcomes? How might you have managed the conflict differently?

10. Knowing that such techniques as "nonaction" and "administrative orbiting" are ineffective, why do you suppose managers continue to use them for resolving conflict? How might you encourage managers to avoid such techniques?

CASES

17-1 NURSE-MANAGED NURSING

For a long time, nursing has been the quintessential number two position: It combines a lot of responsibility with little autonomy or glory. The idea of being stuck in perpetual second place has driven some educated, ambitious nurses right out of the profession.

But some of the ambitious ones who stayed have begun to shape a new role for themselves: number one. And as these nurses change their jobs, they also forge new relationships with doctors and patients.

In their new roles, nurses—not doctors or hospital administrators—manage their own businesses. Some nurses have set up independent practices, hanging out shingles and seeing patients without doctors present. Other nurses have set up nurse-managed clinics or centers.

The idea that nurses can have a practice separate from doctors may be hard for some to digest. Nursing has evolved in the public consciousness as a kind of assistant doctor position, the job of carrying out orders, cleaning up, and holding hands after the real work is done.

Actually, nurses say, their work can be different from, and can complement, doctors' work. Doctors tend to see patients who are ill or injured and in need of immediate attention. Nurses can keep watch over people's health from month to month; they can monitor long-term problems like emphysema, diabetes, heart disease, arthritis, or Parkinson's disease. And they can do routine physical exams to spot minor ailments before they become major ones. Certain groups of the population—especially children, the elderly, and women, all of whom need regular exams—are the nurses' natural constituency.

Many doctors are uneasy about nurse-controlled nursing. The doctor glut in this country means no welcome to potential competitors. More than that, doctors say they worry that nurses will overstep their bounds, assuming a medical role without the training. "If a nurse wants to practice medicine, a nurse should go to medical school," says William R. DeLay of the American Academy of Family Physicians. "And if more physicians' services are needed in a community, another physician should be brought there."

Source: Reprinted by permission of *The Wall Street Journal*, © Dow Jones & Company, Inc. (January 7, 1986). All Rights Reserved Worldwide.

1. What needs of nurses do you think are fulfilled by the establishment of nurse-managed clinics or centers?
2. How is nurse-managed nursing likely to impact on nurses' roles? On their status? On their power?
3. This case indicates that some doctors oppose nurse-managed nursing because of potential competition and concerns about competence. Can you suggest other possible reasons for their opposition?

17–2 TEAMWORK—A MANAGEMENT PLOT?

Teamwork has become a popular management buzzword, and teams are becoming common in many organizations. Problem-solving teams such as quality circles typically meet for an hour or two a week to discuss ways to improve quality, efficiency, and the work environment. Special-purpose teams introduce work reforms and new technology, meet with suppliers and customers, and link separate functions; they may collaborate with management on decisions at all levels. Self-managing work teams, a recent development, produce an entire product; members learn all tasks and rotate from job to job. Self-managing work teams actually take over managerial duties such as work and vacation scheduling, hiring new members, and ordering materials.

A General Electric Company plant in Salisbury, North Carolina, typically changes product models dozens of times a day by using a team system, along with "flexible automation" and other computerized systems, to produce lighting panelboards. Productivity at the plant rose 250 percent over GE plants that made the same products four years earlier. In the early 1980s, workers on assembly lines at the A. O. Smith Corp. automotive works repeated the same tasks every 20 seconds. Union stewards constantly argued with foremen over work rules, and 20 percent of the frames produced on a Ford Ranger line had to be repaired before they were shipped. In 1987, Smith began reorganizing workers into production teams that essentially manage themselves; the ratio of foremen to workers was cut from 1 to 10 in 1987 to the current 1 to 34. In 1988, the productivity growth rate doubled and defects on the Ranger line plummeted to 3 percent. Because of such results, many other U.S. companies, including Procter & Gamble, General Motors, Ford, LTV Steel, General Foods, Boeing, and Champion International, have adopted the team idea. At General Electric itself, the goal was to have 35 percent of the work force in teams by the end of 1989.

Teamwork offers potential benefits to both management and workers. For management, work teams provide flexibility and, often, productivity improvements. Robert Erskine, manager of production services at GE, says, "When you combine automation with new systems and work teams, you get a 40 percent to 50 percent improvement in productivity." Further, the spirit of cooperation fostered by teamwork may serve to reduce labor strife. In turn, workers are given more say in decision making and they have more enriched jobs—they exercise greater autonomy on the job and can use more of their valued skills.

But not everyone is pleased with teamwork. A militant minority of workers is actively attacking the concept. They reason that work teams are used by management as union-busting devices, that work teams serve to coopt workers, and that the greater flexibility of work teams allows management to shift workers more easily and treat them as interchangeable. Further, they argue that the greater responsibility and variety of tasks given to workers on work teams produce "management by stress." John Brodie, President of Local 448 of the United Paperworkers, says, "What the company wants is for us to work like the Japanese. Everybody go out and do jumping jacks in the morning and kiss each other when they go home at night. You work as a team, rat on each other, and lose control of your destiny. That's not going to work in this country."

A United Auto Workers local election in May of 1989 reflected the division caused by the team concept at General Motors Corp.'s Los Angeles Camaro factory. Candidates critical of the system won five of seven positions as delegates to the UAW's annual national convention. These opponents of teamwork are part of a nationwide movement within the UAW that calls itself New Directions and favors a more confrontational approach with GM management. However, at the annual convention in June of 1989, a large majority of UAW delegates endorsed the cause of labor-management "jointness" and defeated the dissidents. That's good news for General Motors, Ford Motor, and Chrysler. They contend that cooperation is necessary to match the quality and productivity of Japanese producers. But New Directions leaders promise to continue the fight against teamwork, and a recent union commission discovered that anxieties about teamwork are widespread among UAW members.

Sources: Based on "The Payoff from Teamwork," *Business Week* (July 10, 1989): 56-62; "The Cultural Revolution at A. O. Smith," *Business Week* (May 29, 1989): 66, 68; "Is Teamwork a Management Plot? Mostly Not," *Business Week* (February 20, 1989): 70; "Teamwork at General Foods," *Personnel Journal* (May 1988): 62-70; and "GM's 'Team Concept' Splits UAW Local," *Capital Times*, Madison, WI (May 18, 1989).

1. Discuss how work teams might influence worker: (a) job satisfaction; (b) motivation; (c) power; and (d) role ambiguity.
2. How might work teams influence the nature and impact of group norms?
3. Do you agree with the dissidents' view that work teams of the sort discussed in this case are a subtle means of exploiting workers? Why or why not?

ENDNOTES

1. W. G. Ouchi, *Theory Z* (Reading, MA: Addison-Wesley, 1981).
2. This definition is based on D. L. Bradford, *Group Dynamics* (Chicago, IL: Science Research Associates, 1984). For a discussion of definitions of groups, see D. Cartwright and A. Zander, *Group Dynamics: Research and Theory*, 3d ed. (New York: Harper & Row, 1968), 46-48.
3. H. Leavitt, "Suppose We Took Groups Seriously," in *Man and Work in Society*, ed. E. L. Cass and F. G. Zimmer (New York: Van Nostrand Reinhold, 1975), 67-77.
4. The idea of the linking pin originates with R. Likert, *New Patterns of Management* (New York: McGraw-Hill, 1961).
5. J. R. Hackman, "The Design of Self-Managing Work Groups," in *Managerial Control and Organizational Democracy*, ed. B. King, S. Streufert, and F. E. Fiedler (Washington, DC: Winston & Sons, 1978).
6. J. R. Hackman and G. R. Oldham, *Work Redesign* (Reading, MA: Addison-Wesley, 1980), 164.
7. G. Homans, *The Human Group* (New York: Harcourt, Brace, 1950).
8. See, for instance, A. P. Brief, R. S. Schuler, and M. Van Sell, *Managing Job Stress* (Boston: Little, Brown, 1981), and R. S. Schuler, R. J. Aldag, and A. P. Brief, "Role Conflict and Ambiguity: A Scale Analysis," *Organizational Behavior and Human Performance* 20 (1977): 111-128.
9. J. A. Litterer, *The Analysis of Organizations* (New York: John Wiley & Sons, 1965).

10. This study was specifically interested in the role of gender in prestige ratings of occupations. In general, males and females tended to rate the status of various occupations quite similarly; only 8 of 110 occupations were rated more than 10 points differently by males and females on a 100-point scale. However, "female" jobs (those with a very high percentage of female job holders) were rated an average of 12 points lower than "male" jobs (those with a very low percentage of female job holders).

11. J. R. Hackman, "Group Influences on Individuals in Organizations," in *Handbook of Industrial and Organizational Psychology*, ed. M. D. Dunnette (Chicago: Rand McNally, 1976).

12. M. Sherif, "A Study of Some Social Factors in Perception," *Archives of Psychology* 27, no. 187 (1935).

13. S. E. Asch, "Effects of Group Pressure upon the Modification and Distortion of Judgment," in *Groups, Leadership, and Men*, ed. H. Guetzkow (Pittsburgh: Carnegie Press, 1951): 177-190.

14. S. Milgram, *Obedience to Authority: An Experimental View* (New York: Harper & Row, 1974).

15. For recent examples of the dangers of conformity, see S. K. Yoder, "Japan's Scientists Find Pure Research Suffers Under Rigid Life Style," *Wall Street Journal* (October 31, 1988): A1, and P. Ingrassia and K. Graven, "Nissan Shakes Free of Hidebound Ways to Mount a Comeback," *Wall Street Journal* (November 1, 1989): A1.

16. B. Bass, *Organizational Psychology* (Boston: Allyn & Bacon, 1965), 105.

17. R. M. Cyert and J. G. March, *A Behavioral Theory of the Firm* (Englewood Cliffs, NJ: Prentice-Hall, 1963).

18. W. A. Gamson, "A Theory of Coalition Formation," *American Sociological Review* 26 (1961): 373-382.

19. Much of this discussion is based on F. A. Shull, A. L. Delbecq, and L. L. Cummings, *Organizational Decision Making* (New York: McGraw-Hill, 1970), 144-154. For examinations of the role of group size, see L. L. Cummings, G. P. Huber, and E. Arendt, "Effects of Size and Spatial Arrangements on Group Decision Making," *Academy of Management Journal* 17 (1974): 460-475, and C. E. Manners, Jr., "Another Look at Group Size, Group Problem Solving, and Member Consensus," *Academy of Management Journal* 18 (1975): 715-724.

20. This section relies heavily on A. C. Filley, *Interpersonal Conflict Resolution* (Glenview, IL: Scott, Foresman, 1975).

21. E. T. Hall, *The Hidden Dimension* (Doubleday, 1968).

22. R. K. Myers, "Some Effects of Seating Arrangements in Counseling," unpublished doctoral dissertation (University of Florida, 1969).

23. Bass, *Organizational Psychology*.

24. These stages are based on S. L. Obert, "The Development of Organizational Task Groups," unpublished doctoral dissertation (Case Western Reserve University, 1979). For a fuller discussion, see Bradford, *Group Dynamics*, 33-36. For other views of stages of group development, see L. N. Jewell and H. J. Reitz, *Group Effectiveness in Organizations* (Glenview, IL: Scott, Foresman, 1981), and B. W. Tuckman and M. A. C. Jensen, "Stages of Small Group Development Revisited," *Group and Organizational Studies* 2 (1977): 419-427.

25. G. P. Huber, *Managerial Decision Making* (Glenview, IL: Scott, Foresman, 1980).

26. While the terms conflict and competition are used interchangeably, they are different. Conflict is a disagreement between two or more units resulting from perceived or real efforts by another party to interfere with the achievement of a goal. Competition, on the other hand, exists when goals are incompatible, but no opportunity exists for interference in the other party's efforts to achieve the goal.

27. S. P. Robbins, "Managing Organizational Conflict," in *The Progress of Management*, ed. J. Schnee, E. Kirby Warren, and H. Lazarus (Englewood Cliffs, NJ: Prentice-Hall, 1977), 163-176.

28. K. Thomas and W. Schmidt, "A Survey of Managerial Interests with Respect to Conflict," *Academy of Management Journal* 19 (1976): 315-318.

29. R. Walton and J. Dutton, "The Management of Interdepartmental Conflict: A Model and Review," *Administrative Science Quarterly* 14 (1969): 73-84.

30. P. R. Lawrence and J. W. Lorsch, *Organization and Environment* (Homewood, IL: Richard D. Irwin, 1969).

31. S. P. Robbins, *Managing Organizational Conflict: A Nontraditional Approach* (Englewood Cliffs, NJ: Prentice-Hall, 1974).

32. D. Nightingale, "Conflict and Conflict Resolution," in *Organizational Behavior: Research and Issues*, ed. G. Strauss, R. Miles, C. Snow, and A. Tannenbaum (Belmont, CA: Wadsworth Publishing Co., 1976), 141-164.

33. E. H. Neilsen, "Understanding and Managing Conflict," in *Managing Group and Intergroup Relations*, ed. J. Lorsch and P. Lawrence (Homewood, IL: Irwin, 1972), 329-343.

34. R. H. Miles, *Macro Organizational Behavior* (Santa Monica, CA: Goodyear, 1980), 125-126.

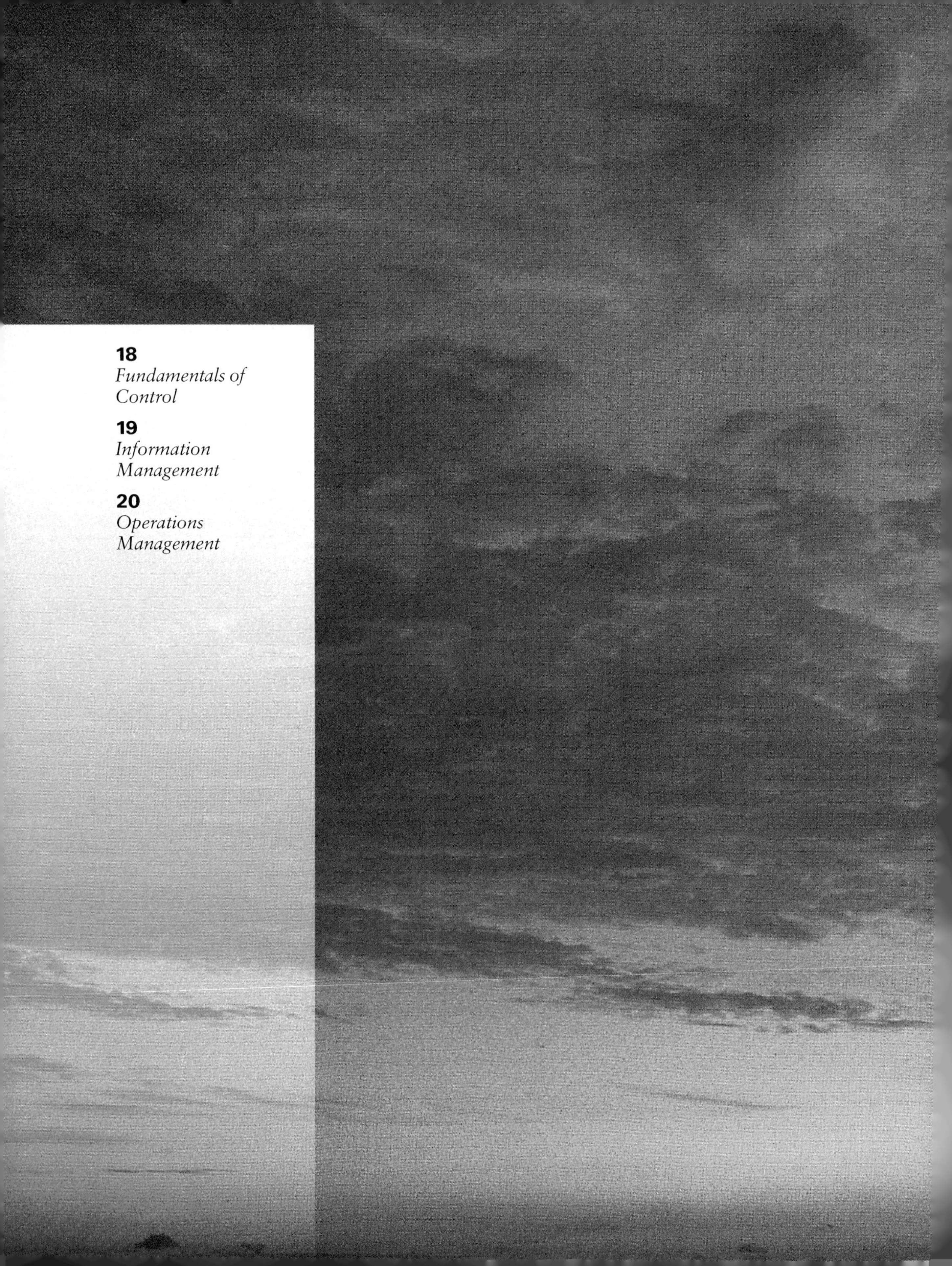

Controlling

PART FIVE

Fundamentals of Control

CHAPTER 18

After studying this chapter, you should be able to:
- *Discuss the importance of control systems to a firm.*
- *List the elements of control systems and explain the four functions of control.*
- *Explain the different levels of control systems.*
- *Explain how control systems may be categorized by managerial discretion, timing, and information.*
- *Describe the four main activities involved in a control process and their importance.*
- *Identify three control strategies and explain the differences between them.*
- *Discuss control techniques appropriate for the financial, material, human resources, and information dimensions of the internal context of the firm.*
- *Examine five dysfunctional side effects of control and explain why they occur.*
- *Discuss five guidelines for the design of effective control systems.*

Consider these examples of control in organizations:

In 1985, Wang Laboratories, a producer of word-processing and data-processing equipment, was having financial problems. Wang elected to examine its control systems for managing costs and for delivering products. The company's rapid growth had led to difficulties in meeting its performance goals. An Wang, the founder, came out of retirement to help develop cost-cutting controls in a company that previously had not paid much attention to items such as travel budgets and discretionary expenses. After Wang's death in the spring of 1990, the company was thrown into uncertainty.

Incidents involving the cyanide contamination of Extra Strength Tylenol led to an industry-wide evaluation of the packaging and quality controls of medications. Johnson & Johnson, the maker of Tylenol, decided to remove all capsule products from the shelves of stores and to stop manufacturing or selling capsules. Spokespersons for the company said that the safety of the capsules could not be guaranteed using the safety standards set by Johnson & Johnson.

Merrill Lynch & Company was surprised to learn that one of its top brokers had tampered with data and changed information in the firm's computer files. The result was that the computers produced falsified reports. These reports led a client to believe that he had a balance of about $36 million while the balance was actually roughly $8 million. Merrill Lynch was put into the compromising position of explaining how its control systems could have missed the discrepancies and tampering.

An Exxon Corporation tanker, the *Exxon Valdez*, rammed an underwater reef in Alaskan waters, causing the largest oil spill in U.S. history and an outpouring of anger from the American public. Evidence suggested that the captain of the tanker was intoxicated at the time of the accident and was not on the bridge. The captain had a history of alcohol-related problems, but Exxon's control system did not prevent him from again taking command of a huge tanker.

General Motors has hired undercover detectives to help control drug and alcohol abuse in its plants. Some employees have been found to be high on drugs or alcohol while operating dangerous equipment. This behavior affects worker productivity, plant safety, and product quality. GM is not alone in this problem: About 25 percent of the Fortune 500 companies use tactics for controlling the use of drugs in the workplace.

These are just a few examples of attempts by firms to control their operations, budgets, product quality, plant safety, and worker behavior. This chapter helps to identify the importance of the control function for firms and its role in keeping the firm competitive. As the examples illustrate, effective control can improve the firm's overall performance and reputation. Ineffective control can be disastrous.

Control is a process that tries to ensure that the actual activities performed match the desired activities, or goals, that have been set. Control ensures that deviations from the goals are corrected. It provides feedback that

This chapter is based in part on material prepared by Dr. Marjorie A. Lyles for the first edition of this text.

can aid in setting future goals and standards. The **control process** involves setting standards, measuring actual performance, comparing actual performance to the standards, and taking corrective action when necessary. Control is effective when the desired activities or objectives are achieved.[1]

We are all familiar with various kinds of control techniques: budgets, college entrance requirements, waiting lines at ticket stands, performance evaluations, product quality controls, and so on. A **control technique** is a mechanism designed to help achieve the desired performance. It can be specifically designed for the activity being controlled. Since there are many different organizational activities, control techniques are numerous and varied. For example, on assembly lines, workers usually have a minimum work rate to meet; restaurants are inspected to see if they meet health codes; and most organizations issue parking stickers to control who parks in their lots.

Sometimes firms use too many control techniques and too much control, causing dysfunctional side effects such as bureaucratic red tape. At other times, the control systems are not tight enough, allowing undesirable actions to occur.

The purpose of this chapter is to describe the nature of the control process and to examine its importance to management. We will explore the types of control methods, analyze control strategies, and describe resistance to control and how to overcome it.

IMPORTANT OF CONTROL

Every year, *Fortune* magazine lists America's most-admired corporations. IBM, 3M, Merck, and Coca-Cola frequently receive high ratings. Why?

The Coca-Cola Company is admired for a control system that coordinates the activities of all the members of the organization, from managers at the home office to drivers all around the country.

Besides having excellent records, the firms are admired for their ability to control ongoing activities, to meet their performance goals, and to attract quality management.

Companies that are considered excellent, such as IBM, have well-thought-out and thoroughly designed control systems. Various management systems, such as the budgeting process, the planning process, the reward system, and the organizational structure, are evaluated to see that the planned activities are actually being carried out. Control systems are designed to ensure that this occurs.

Control systems direct behavior toward important goals. For example, the Massachusetts Eye and Ear Infirmary designed a productivity-oriented method of control that related labor costs to a patient's needs, thus creating a billing system that truly reflects the resources used. Performance evaluation systems, such as MBO systems, develop evaluations based on projected objectives. Control systems are important because they monitor, reward, and reinforce the behavior and activities that management desires.

All organizations must control their activities, and the management of every kind of organization must be aware of how to design effective control systems. Not-for-profit organizations, such as social service agencies or hospitals, must keep track of their resources. Religious organizations maintain budgets to keep track of how and where they spend money. Publicly held organizations must report financial and other business-related information to the government.

Control systems coordinate the activities of all members of the organization. They provide methods of integration and measurement. Control ensures that the efforts of all members of the firm are coordinated through stan-

ZIGGY COPYRIGHT 1985. Ziggy & Friends/Distributed by Universal Press Syndicate. All rights reserved.

William H. Newman (Ph.D., University of Chicago) is Bronfman Professor Emeritus and Chairman of the Strategy Research Center at the Graduate School of Business, Columbia University, New York. Professor Newman has authored or co-authored such books as Strategy, Policy, and Central Management, Managerial Control, Managers for the Year 2000, *and* Constructive Control: Design and Use of Control Systems. *Because of his recognition as a scholar around the world, many of his works have been translated into foreign languages, Japanese in particular. Professor Newman is an international consultant and has served as a director or consultant for many prominent corpo-*

ACADEMIC PROFILE
WILLIAM H. NEWMAN

rations in the United States. In addition, he is a past president of the Academy of Management and has served as dean of fellows. Previously, Professor Newman was employed by McKinsey & Company, Marshall Field & Company, and was a consultant to the War Production Board from 1942 to 1943.

Q: Management has many facets. What prompted you to focus one of your recent books on control?

A: In most companies, and in organizations in general, controls have been neglected. There are all sorts of opportunities to improve results by giving closer attention to control. Because of past neglect, a manager or a young assistant can often make a greater impact by working on control than on a more glamorous topic like strategy. The pay dirt is richer.

Q: Do the many executives that you deal with recognize this need for more attention on control?

A: Only partially. There is a sharp increase in their concern with actually getting results—in contrast to fancier planning models. But control is only one of the tools executives grasp to "make things happen." I think such bypassing of controls is due to a mistaken view that some executives have of controlling. These executives think of controls as number-crunching and negative, whereas people with positive motivation seem to be the key to the good execution of plans.

Q: Don't you stress the behavior of people in your approach to controlling?

A: Yes, indeed. The design of standards that are meaningful to persons doing the work, the emphasis on steering controls rather than post-action controls, the operator's acceptance—even internalization—of control targets, all contribute to positive behavioral responses. This is crucial. Anybody who thinks of controlling only as a numbers game, comparing actual expenses versus budget, is lost in procedures. In a ballgame, we do need a scorekeeper, but it's the behavior on the field that really matters. When control is seen from this behavioral perspective, it becomes a vital tool for achieving results.

Q: In this regard, what future role do you see for computers in controlling actions in the workplace?

A: For effective controls, computers are both good news and bad news. The good news is that computers coupled with electronic communication can feed some useful information back (and forward) very rapidly. If a good control loop has already been established, corrective action can take place rapidly. The bad news is that computers will further emphasize quantitative features. Accounting data already dominate many control systems, and there is real danger that computers will overwhelm operating people with even more bewildering numbers—moving the game from something like checkers to chess. I recognize that chess is a sophisticated sport, but it is not the motivator needed in the vast majority of control situations. So, the danger of misusing computers is a further reason for designing controls with care and human empathy.

dards, rules, norms, budgets, and reporting systems. In a sense, control offers the mechanism for providing order to the diverse activities of a firm.

The need to manage uncertainty is another reason for the importance of control. Control systems limit options in decision making by setting rules to handle repetitive situations. This limits idiosyncratic behavior and provides standards for future events. For example, banks have credit standards that loan officers use in issuing loans. If these standards did not exist, each officer would use different standards for issuing loans.

The importance of control systems lies in their purpose of evaluating, monitoring, and correcting the performance of the firm. They provide a co-ordinating, integrating, and motivating force for every type of organization. They reduce the uncertainty of dealing with repetitive decisions and situations. Well-managed firms have effective control systems that enhance their ability to execute their strategies.

THE NATURE OF CONTROL

Elements of Control

Although each firm has its own unique control systems, there are certain elements that are common to all control systems.[2] Figure 18–1 lists these elements.

The way these elements are defined will determine the character of the control system. The monitoring systems measure and assess ongoing activities to determine the actual performance. The evaluation systems compare the actual performance with the desired performance. This information is fed back to management, who determines whether corrective actions are necessary. Standards, rules, and regulations are part of every control system and serve to set guidelines for activities and decisions. Goals are an integral element of a control system, because they communicate what performance is expected. Management uses influence techniques to control behavior. Reward systems help the effectiveness of the control systems by rewarding the desired behaviors.

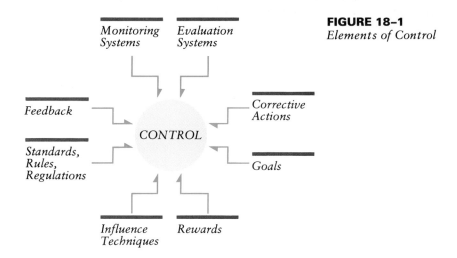

FIGURE 18–1
Elements of Control

Every control process includes these elements that serve to carry out the functions of control. A discussion of the four functions of control follows.

Functions of Control

Control systems serve four interrelated functions in organizations. Each function should be present for the control system to be effective. The functions, shown in Figure 18–2, are overseeing, comparing, correcting deviations, and influencing future decisions.

OVERSEEING

Control systems oversee ongoing activities to achieve the desired performance level. They ensure that the appropriate action is taking place while the activity is in progress. The immediate supervisor oversees through observing or conferring, usually at the place of the activity. Overseeing is particularly useful when the process is well understood, such as the preparation of food at a fast-food restaurant.

COMPARING

Comparing the degree of agreement between actual performance and performance standards can take place at or away from the point of operation. It is possible to use actual budgets to compare with projected budgets. However, the manager does not have to be physically in the department when the comparison is taking place. Comparing involves measuring, collecting data, evaluating, disseminating information, and reporting to the decision makers.

An important aspect of comparing is assessing the significance of any deviation from the plan. The aim is to compare the difference between actual performance and desired performance and then to decide whether that difference is acceptable. Some deviation is expected for most activities, and a certain amount of deviation is acceptable. Management must determine what level of deviation is unacceptable. To some extent, this level will depend on the activity. In some activities, even a small deviation may not be tolerated. For example, before the shuttle disaster of 1986, NASA's control system allowed some deviation from standard in the design of the booster rockets. After the disaster, the extensive control systems were tightened to tolerate very little deviation.

FIGURE 18–2
Functions of Control

Function	Purpose	Methods
Overseeing	To ensure that appropriate action is taking place	Observing Conferring
Comparing	To determine the degree of agreement between actual performance and desired performance and assess the significance of any deviation	Measuring Collecting data Evaluating Disseminating information Reporting
Correcting Deviations	To correct unacceptable deviations from desired performance	Immediate Basic
Influencing Future Decisions	To provide feedback to management to assess future goals	Reporting Goal setting

CORRECTING DEVIATIONS

Control involves correcting the deviations that may occur or altering the plan to allow for any obstacles that cannot be removed. There are two types of corrective action: immediate and basic. **Immediate corrective action** is taken to influence present performance. For example, putting employees on over-time to meet a deadline is an immediate corrective action. **Basic corrective action** influences performance in the future. It involves an analysis of the causes of the deviations to prevent their occurrence in the future. Disciplinary actions or new hiring practices are basic controls that affect future performance.

The recall of the Lexus only a few months after its highly publicized introduction is an example of immediate corrective action.

INFLUENCING FUTURE DECISIONS

Providing feedback to management for future decision making is another function of control. It maintains the momentum of the organization by influencing and rewarding employees. Learning from past performance and from current problems provides information to help control future activities.

Control Cycle

Figure 18–3 shows a simplified version of the control process. It includes all of the control elements and represents a control cycle. First, goals and standards are set. Behavior and ongoing activities are then monitored to determine actual performance. This output is measured and compared with the desired performance. If corrective action is needed, steps are taken to redirect the activities toward the desired standards. Finally, rewards are given to reinforce the desired behaviors and activities, and the cycle continues.

Management uses the measurement of results to evaluate current goals and standards. Apple Computer was not able to sell as many Macintosh™ computers as it expected to sell. This information was fed back through the established control system to managers, who used it to develop new goals and standards. Past performance gives information to management that is useful for setting new projections of performance.

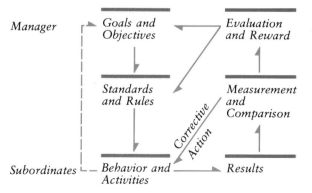

FIGURE 18–3
Process of Management Control

Source: Figure from *Organization: A Guide to Problems and Practice* by John Child. Copyright © 1984 by John Child. Reprinted by permission of Harper & Row, Publishers, Inc.

A difficult aspect of control is determining when a situation is controllable. The more certain, predictable, and simple an activity or a situation is, the easier it is to develop a mechanism for controlling it through formalized rules and procedures. For example, a car dealership has a much easier time keeping track of the number of cars on the lot than it has controlling when and what kind of car it will receive from the automobile manufacturer. The more an activity must be individually designed or evolves as the activity progresses, the more difficult it will be to establish standardized methods and controls.

Control systems should be adaptive and responsive to changes because of environmental uncertainty and changing conditions. New corporate goals or new governmental standards may require new control methods to achieve the desired performance level. Sometimes a control technique may grow stale over time and lose its effectiveness. Leeway should be built in to allow individual managers some discretion in handling situations or exceptions that develop.

Control in large organizations differs from control in small organizations. A small firm may rely more on informal, personal control techniques; a larger firm may have more formal methods. Larger firms will spend more time integrating their subunits, developing reports, and processing information. A small firm may rely simply on the president's walking around and talking with employees.

Top-Down Versus Bottom-Up Approaches

The control cycle shown in Figure 18–3 is a circular process involving decisions made at the top which influence the types of controls that are implemented. Input from those at lower levels in the organization indicates what is possible to implement and control. The three levels of management in a firm are concerned with different control questions. We will discuss these in the next section. In this section we describe the differences between a top-down approach and a bottom-up approach. The control cycle usually involves the interaction of these two approaches.

TOP-DOWN APPROACH

The left side of Figure 18–3 shows management setting the goals and objectives that subordinates then implement. This is a **top-down approach** in which management sets the direction and gives directives to subordinates. A typical set of management control concerns might be the budget, implementation of the strategic plan, the allocation of resources such as personnel or computers, or the timing of specific activities. The top-down approach addresses the control process from the perspective of upper management and from the vantage point of seeing how all the control techniques fit together.

BOTTOM-UP APPROACH

The dotted line in Figure 18–3 represents the **bottom-up approach**. Through means such as the budgetary process or planning for capital investments, subordinates influence the goals and standards. The budgetary process and the planning process allow ideas to filter up to top management and to be incorporated in new goals.

Levels of Control

Within every firm, the nature of control changes with the level of management. Upper-level management is concerned with issues relating to strategic control, while lower-level management is concerned with operational issues. The three levels of control—strategic, managerial, and operational—are shown in Figure 18–4. These correspond to the levels of management discussed in Chapter 1.

STRATEGIC CONTROL

Strategic control concerns the direction of the firm, the evaluation of strategy, the interrelationships of the business units, external reporting, and the maintenance of cash flows across business units. Strategic control involves a long time frame in which information about the future is frequently sketchy. If the environment is constantly changing, feedback from current performance may not be a good indicator of future opportunities or new goals.

Frequently, control at this level is that of overseeing and monitoring the implementation of strategy and making changes as events change. Decisions are made to determine the priorities of the firm and its various activities. Control is also concerned with corporate-wide capital expenditures, dividends paid, the performance of business units, environmental surveillance, and external reporting.

MANAGERIAL CONTROL

Managerial control allocates resources so that businesses, units, and departments have what they need to accomplish their goals, to schedule activities, and to monitor progress. It pertains to a business unit, a department, or a division as a whole and has a periodic time frame. The collection of data and its assembly into meaningful reports help the evaluation process. Managerial control is also concerned with scheduling, taking corrective actions, and rewarding the functional areas.

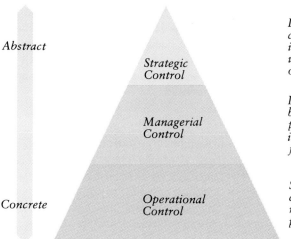

FIGURE 18–4
Levels of Control

Abstract

Strategic Control

Managerial Control

Concrete

Operational Control

Long time frame; corporate-wide; remote; interrelationships among units; corporate cash flow; overseeing strategy

Periodic time frame; business level or department performance; interrelationships among functional areas

Short time frame; compliance with schedules, rules, and budgets; personal surveillance

OPERATIONAL CONTROL

Operational control oversees individual tasks and performance and is concerned with the integration of work groups. Usually, we think of operational controls as those that deal directly with getting the job done, monitoring absenteeism, and keeping to a schedule. This type of control ensures compliance with rules and regulations and ensures that work will be completed within the constraints given. The time frame is short, and most of the information is concrete and quantitative. Case 18–1 provides an example of the use of computers for operational control.

TYPES OF CONTROL SYSTEMS

Let's consider three main ways to categorize control systems: by managerial discretion, by timing, and by information. The first classification relates to the amount of discretion that an individual manager has in completing the task. By discretion, we mean the freedom or authority to make decisions about a particular situation. Some control systems allow management little or no discretion, while other systems allow a great deal of discretion.

The second approach to classification of control systems depends upon when the control technique is used.[3] It can be used before the activity begins, during its execution, or after it is completed.

The third classification scheme identifies the type of information the control system handles.[4] For example, the control system and the techniques used may be designed to handle financial data or human resource data.

Managerial Discretion

The first classification of control systems is based on managerial discretion. Such systems may be either cybernetic or noncybernetic in nature.

CYBERNETIC CONTROLS

Cybernetic control systems are self-operating, self-regulating systems with built-in devices to correct automatically any deviations that occur. In such systems, there is little need for managerial discretion or, ideally, for human intervention of any kind. Robotics and automatic factories are incorporating cybernetic controls that try to eliminate the need for people to oversee the tasks. This type of system is useful for tasks and processes in which all the steps and standards are very clear-cut. If a deviation occurs, it can be automatically corrected without human intervention.

NONCYBERNETIC CONTROLS

Many organizational activities are not completely routine or standard, and thus do not lend themselves to cybernetic controls. These activities benefit from a system using noncybernetic controls. With **noncybernetic controls**, managers use their own discretion in deciding how best to complete an activity and meet performance goals. The more creative and unusual the task, the more managerial discretion is needed. Quality circles allow the discretion of work groups in determining how best to complete the job and eliminate problems. At the strategic level, there is more reliance on self-control and managerial discretion than there is at the operational level.

Timing

The second approach to classifying control systems is based on timing. Controls may be steering, yes-no, or post-action in nature.

STEERING CONTROLS

A **steering control** tries to control an activity before it occurs. This is also called a **preliminary**, or **feedforward, control**. Such controls anticipate results and guide activities before the operation begins. New product development frequently involves the use of steering controls to predict market demand, set production schedules, and define expected delivery dates in advance. As the activity progresses, corrective actions are taken based on the predicted results.

A quality circle at Ford Motor Company meets to decide on its own how to solve a problem.

Steering controls face several problems. Predictions based on estimates using current conditions may be wrong, or current conditions may change, leading to an error in the predicted results. Steering controls build in a lead time between the start and the completion of the project. Sometimes the estimates of these lead times may be incorrect or other factors may interfere.

YES-NO CONTROLS

A **yes-no control** assesses an activity while it is in progress. At specified checkpoints progress is okayed, corrective action is taken, or progress is halted. **Behavioral controls** monitor, measure, and evaluate behavior as it occurs. The more that is known about the tasks to be accomplished, the greater will be the tendency to use yes-no or behavioral controls.[5] Yes-no controls are used in the scheduling and timing of steps or procedures, such as the critical path method (CPM) or the program evaluation and review technique (PERT).

POST-ACTION CONTROLS

A **post-action control** or **output control** measures and evaluates the results of an activity after it is completed. Changes in performance levels or goals are based on these evaluations, and rewards are determined by these controls. Post-action controls are used to control activities in which the processes are not well known.

Information

Finally, control systems may be categorized based on the type of information being handled. Control systems are designed to monitor and evaluate certain activities; therefore, they are designed to accumulate and evaluate certain types of information—financial, production (physical), and human or administrative being the most common. Figure 18–5 identifies several control mechanisms and the types of information they are designed to handle.

Information about financial resources is usually in the form of figures that show the dollar amounts allocated and spent. Budgets, capital expendi-

Resource to Be Controlled	Typical Mechanism for Control	Focus of the Control System
Financial	Budgets Capital expenditures Cash-flow analysis	Expenditure projections Capital investments Cash management
Operations	Production scheduling Quality control Resource control	Volume produced Quality of product Amount and cost of supplies and resources
Human Resources	Absenteeism records Performance records Socialization	Days worked Evaluation of personnel Conformity of personnel

Source: J. A. Pearce and R. B. Robinson, Jr., *Strategic Management* (Homewood, IL: Richard D. Irwin, © 1982), 305. Reprinted with permission.

FIGURE 18–5
*Control Systems by
Information Type*

tures, and cash-flow analysis require a set of targets or standards against which current expenditures are compared.

To control the production operations of a firm, information about scheduling, inventories, quality control, and material resources has to be collected, stored, and retrieved. This information reports such things as the volume produced, product quality, inventory levels, and the amount and cost of supplies.

Human resource or administrative information is collected showing the employment and performance record of each employee. Information about absenteeism, pay raises, involvement in training seminars, and performance evaluations may be kept. Benefits information may include background information about such things as health care benefits, retirement or pension information, and stock options.

These are just three examples of the kinds of information control that are necessary in a firm. They do not represent all the types of information needed. For example, firms must control their marketing information, including sales and customer data. In the next chapter we address the topic of how to manage and design a system for control of information.

ACTIVITIES IN THE CONTROL PROCESS

Previously we pointed out that all control systems include several common elements that are important to managers at all levels, whether they are controlling the strategy of the firm or the costs of new product development. The four main activities in the control process that incorporate these elements are shown in Figure 18–6.

Monitoring the Environment

Many factors, including changes that occur outside the organization, affect the control process. Resources are affected by environmental changes that may lead to internal changes in goals and in resource allocations. To keep information up-to-date, management must keep track of events as they occur. These might include governmental regulations, IRS reporting requirements,

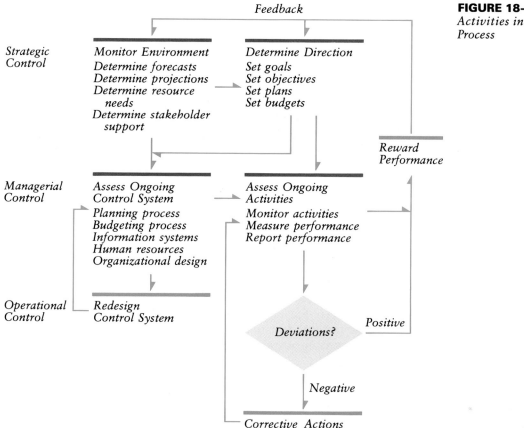

FIGURE 18–6
Activities in the Control Process

safety regulations, consumer attitudes, and social responsibility concerns. Every organization has contracts with other organizations. The firm must be aware of the availability of resources and the attitudes of its suppliers and distributors. Joint ventures are becoming more and more common, and sales are often determined by environmental demands.

Determining Direction

The control process depends upon the goals, objectives, plans, and resource allocations that are determined in the planning, goal-setting, and budgetary processes. They determine which subunits should grow or retrench, which new projects can be funded, and how much money will be available for raises. They provide the targets against which ongoing activities are compared, and they reflect the strategy of the firm.

Assessing Ongoing Operations

Measuring, comparing, and evaluating ongoing operations involve a continual monitoring of activities. Comparing actual results with standards or goals requires gathering and interpreting information about performance.

WIZARD OF ID   BY BRANT PARKER & JOHNNY HART

By permission of Johnny Hart and News America Syndicate.

Acceptable levels of deviation from standards or goals must be established. Management usually sets upper and lower performance limits that indicate how much deviation from the standard is acceptable.

If actual performance deviates beyond these limits, management must decide whether corrective actions are needed. Taking corrective actions only when there is an unusual deviation is called **management by exception**. Sometimes the feedback from assessing ongoing operations indicates that the goals or standards should be changed because the original goals were set too high or too low.

Assessing the Control System

Part of the control process involves a continual assessment of the control system itself to determine if it is remaining effective. The information provided must be timely, accurate, and relevant to the decisions being made. Resistance to controls, boredom with rules, and poorly developed standards have an effect on actual performance. The objective of the control process is to get the desired behavior and performance from the people within the firm; consequently, control systems need to be continually evaluated, updated, and improved.

CONTROL STRATEGIES

There are several strategies for managers to consider when deciding to design a control system. We will examine three strategies developed by William Ouchi that represent different approaches to control.[6] All three strategies may be used within the same organization. In fact, some form of all three strategies is used in most organizations, since each serves a different purpose.

These control strategies rest on the theory that cooperation between the subunits of a firm depends upon exchanges taking place. People exchange their time and efforts for money, security, and excitement. Firms exchange money, products, and services to achieve a goal or purpose. As discussed in Chapter 2, transaction costs may be accrued to ensure that the value assigned to any good or service is considered fair.[7]

The three control strategies identified by Ouchi are market control, bureaucratic control, and clan control. Figure 18–7 shows their components. It

Type	Components	Focus
Market Control	Self-contained units Prices Exchange relationships Clear responsibilities Specified outputs Semi-autonomy	Coordination
Bureaucratic Control	Rules Identifiable task elements Routine decision-making Hierarchy Rewards enforcing conformity	Compliance
Clan Control	Culture Personal commitment Social norms	Commitment

FIGURE 18–7
Control Strategies

also shows that the strategies differ in their focus: market control emphasizes the importance of coordination of activities, bureaucratic control stresses compliance to standards and rules, and clan control relies on worker commitment to the organization.

Market Control

A **market control strategy** assumes that the price of certain exchanges or transactions can be set most efficiently through market mechanisms such as competition. For example, many organizations have their subunits charge other internal subunits for products or services used. Thus, the marketing department might be charged for the computer or human resource services that it uses. Market control relies on the assumption that a competitive price can be determined for these services.

Implementing a market control strategy requires clearly defined outputs for which a price can be set. It puts a cost on all activities and develops a quantitative measurement of the contribution of the business unit, department, subunit, or person. Frequently, divisions within the firm become profit centers, and their performance is measured by their contribution to profits.[8] This strategy requires clear responsibilities for activities, specified outputs, and some sense of the market value of an activity. The value of individuals is frequently assessed by market-like measures such as salaries or merit raises.

Generally, the firm should be engaged in competition with other firms in order to establish a market value for the output. Because this strategy relies solely on the measurement of outputs, semi-autonomy develops and there is little need for reporting on the internal activities, such as the cost of personnel within the subunit.

Bureaucratic Control

Since market mechanisms do not always operate efficiently, especially when there is no competition or when a subunit has a great deal of power, it may be necessary to rely on legitimate authority, such as upper management, to set standards and rules. Upper management is assumed to be wise and fair; thus, it is considered to be qualified to set fair methods for handling exchanges. Legitimate authority is the key element in a **bureaucratic control strategy**.

The bureaucratic control strategy depends upon tight controls based on rules that ensure standardization and upon data management that reports the current level of activity to management. If this strategy is used, clearly defined tasks, authority relationships, and hierarchy must exist.

This approach depersonalizes decision making and reduces the potential for conflict. When rules and procedures are clearly spelled out, employees can resist pressures to do things a different way. Also, employees can blame rules for bad outcomes, thus avoiding personal responsibility. In order for this approach to be effective, rewards must reinforce conformity to rules.

Paul Lawrence and Davis Dyer have found that organizations that use bureaucratic controls rely on rules and on leaders.[9] They are usually large organizations concerned with order and well-defined communication and decision channels. Most American organizations use a combination of market and bureaucratic controls.

Clan Control

A **clan control strategy** capitalizes on people's need to belong to a group and develops control through rituals and myths. The market strategy may not work when there is an absence of competition or when costs get too high. The bureaucratic strategy may not work when the unique characteristics of a situation make it impossible to set concrete standards and rules. In these cases, the clan strategy helps control the organization by achieving a commitment to higher-level organizational goals, such as the usefulness of a firm or its ability to contribute to society, and by allowing differences in individual performance. William Ouchi suggests that goal congruity and a strong sense of community are important for clan control, and it occurs "where team-work is common, technologies change often, and therefore individual performance is highly ambiguous."[10]

The clan strategy is becoming more popular in America as firms pay more attention to developing their organizational cultures. One recent example is Ford Motor Company, which is trying to move away from its reputation for competitive personalities and autocratic management to that of a firm known for its team orientation.

The clan strategy relies on the individual to use self-control and to perform as desired. It manages through informal mechanisms for control. Establishing trust, making informal contacts, and developing a company culture comprise part of this strategy.[11] Thomas Peters and Robert Waterman describe it this way:

Without exception, the dominance and coherence of culture proved to be an essential quality of the excellent companies. Moreover, the stronger the culture and the more it was directed toward the marketplace, the less need was there for policy manuals, organization charts, or detailed procedures and rules. In these companies, people way down the line know what they are supposed to do in most situations because the handful of guiding values is crystal-clear.[12]

Japanese management approaches incorporate clan strategies for keeping employees committed and working hard.[13] Lincoln Electric Company has been cited as an American firm that uses a control system similar to that of the Japanese. It uses no formal budgeting system; the managers are trusted to keep expenses to a minimum, and they do.

The clan strategy uses few formal controls. It emphasizes selection, training, and socialization of employees. It is particularly appropriate in smaller firms, at higher levels of management in larger firms, and in firms needing to encourage innovation.

Walt Disney Company has been extremely successful, with 1988 revenues of $3.5 billion and sharply rising returns to shareholders. Central to that success are the "cast members" in its theme parks, which contribute over half of Disney's revenue. These members are primarily high school and college students, and they must be trained and motivated to perform repetitive, sometimes routine work at low pay while conveying the Disney fantasy and creating happiness. The challenge of this situation is increased by the fact that the work force is heavily unionized; Disneyland alone has 24 unions. As a result, Disney has made a concerted effort to develop a sense of community and shared values. It does this largely through selection, training, and socialization, and it has developed Disney University to help in the process. Management in Action 1 provides a glimpse of just a few of the elements of clan control utilized at Disney.

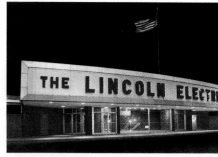

Lincoln Electric uses a control system similar to that used by the Japanese.

CONTROL TARGETS

In this section we will address techniques for the control of financial, material, human, and information resources.

Budgets and Financial Controls

Firms can be viewed as pools of funds that provide monies for the implementation of the firms' various activities. These funds are limited, however, and careful attention must be given to their allocation to ensure that all major activities are funded. Financial controls aim to control and predict the use of funds to help meet organizational goals. Financial control methods include budgets, financial analysis, and financial audits. These techniques help ensure the survival of the firm by managing profitability, cash flow, and capital investments.

BUDGETS

A **budget** is a formal statement of the expenditures needed for future activities for a specific time period. Monetary terms serve as a common denominator for comparing all the diverse activities of the firm, including earnings and expenses. Each project, unit, department, or division has an operating budget that shows expenses for items such as salaries, rent, and travel. Budgets clarify responsibilities by identifying which managers are responsible for which activities. Comparisons are frequently made on a monthly basis to determine how actual expenditures compare with the amount budgeted.

Managers are expected to meet their budgets, and a performance appraisal criterion evaluates how well they succeed. Consequently, the amount set in a budget becomes very important to the manager. If costs are budgeted too low, managers will feel unfairly constrained. If they are budgeted too

Disney's philosophy is a comprehensive approach to employee relations. It's reinforced with activities, management style, and language. For example, em-

MANAGEMENT IN ACTION
HOW DOES DISNEY DO IT?

ployees are called "cast members," and they don't work at a job, they're cast in a role. Furthermore, cast members work either onstage or backstage, and they wear costumes, not uniforms.

Because the company's clean-cut image and conservative reputation help potential workers self-select, it usually attracts the type of applicants it wants. To narrow the field even more and make sure everyone knows what's expected before the interviews proceed, would-be employees may be shown a film that details some of the discipline, grooming, and dress codes. People with extreme styles know in advance that they must adapt if they want a role in the show.

Virtually all of the 39,000-plus cast members begin their Disney career with an orientation. Rather than a single program, this entertainment giant's orientation is an ongoing process that continually reinforces the values, philosophies, and guest service standards.

Orientation is the core of the company's training. Designed to be sensitive to new cast members, university teachers reflect the group they're instructing.

For example, rather than have a corporate-type lead a group of new college-age cast members through the Park, Disney uses outstanding cast members, dressed in full costume, to teach the classes.

When orientation is completed, cast members begin a series of learning experiences at on-site practice and classes at the university. The next step—paired training—allows exceptional cast members to act as role models. The benefits of such a training are twofold: The new cast member rehearses with a respected member of the troupe, and the veteran is recognized by management, as well as his or her peers, and held in esteem.

To encourage enthusiasm and commitment, a variety of recognition, communications, and social-relations programs are especially important. For instance, Disney offers service recognition awards, peer recognition programs, attendance awards, and milestones banquets for 10, 15, and 20 years of service. In addition, informal recognition parties, during which root beer floats are served in employee cafeterias, help boost morale. The company also has the requisite softball and volleyball teams. During the Christmas holiday, the parks reopen one night just for cast members and their families. Management says "Happy Holidays" by dressing in costume and operating the parks. All events are designed to build a sense of camaraderie and identification with the organization.

Source: Abridged and adapted from C. M. Solomon, "How Does Disney Do It?" *Personnel Journal* (December 1989): 50-57.

high, unnecessary spending may result. If changes in the budget are made, managers should be involved and informed.

The budget represents the yearly plan of the firm in financial terms. It indicates the expenditures, revenues, or profits planned. The amount has usually been approved at several levels of the firm, and the manager is expected to operate within the amount that has been set. Actual expenditures will be compared to the budget to identify when corrective actions are needed.

Budgeting is the process by which the firm divides up its resources and allocates them to the various business units. The process involves the development of budgets, comparisons between organizational units, adjustments to the initial budgets, and approval. The figures used in the budgets may be based on past performance, projections of future activities, or the personal experience of the manager.

Two key types of budgets are operating and financial budgets. An **operating budget** summarizes the raw materials, goods, and services the unit expects to consume during the time period. A **responsibility center** is a unit which has responsibility for achieving certain goals.[14] A responsibility center uses resources measured in inputs or costs to produce a set of products or services measured in outputs or revenues. The operating budget corresponds to the business unit's activities and to the type of responsibility center; some are responsible for revenues, others for expenses, and still others for profits.

The **financial budget** estimates the amount of cash needed to support the expected level of activities during the specified time period. It documents the sources of cash and how it will be spent. The purpose of these budgets is to help the firm achieve its financial goals through the efficient use of capital.[15]

Because the budgeting process is so important, there is always a desire to improve the process. Two recent attempts are zero-based budgeting and the planning, programming, budgeting system. **Zero-based budgeting (ZBB)** was developed in the 1970s at Texas Instruments as an alternative to the incremental budgeting process. In the incremental budgeting process, the focus is on changes from current levels of funding, and those levels are not necessarily reevaluated. Incremental budgeting builds in inequities and unnecessary costs that may go unquestioned from year to year.[16]

Zero-based budgeting tries to avoid this problem by beginning from scratch each budgeting period and justifying the entire budget. Questions are asked about whether an activity is necessary and at what level it should be funded based on its importance to desired objectives. Many firms, including Xerox, Westinghouse, and Ford, have adopted ZBB. These firms think the advantages of ZBB are that it forces managers to evaluate carefully all elements of the budget before it is submitted for review and that it eliminates unnecessary costs. The disadvantages of ZBB are that it is time-consuming and is often resented by managers because of the amount of justification deemed necessary.

The **planning, programming, budgeting system (PPBS)** is used for analyzing and deciding among program or activity proposals. The Defense Department tried to implement this approach during the Kennedy administration to eliminate duplications and to integrate activities. It serves as a starting point for the annual budget process and is meant to tie together strategic and long-range planning with conventional budgeting.

PPBS includes the following steps: (1) determining the desired direction through goals, (2) analyzing the goals of a program or an activity to see the fit with overall goals, (3) determining the program costs for a specified time period (1 year, 2 years, and so on), and (4) reviewing and approving program plans. It uses a budgeting and planning process that is output oriented. Resources are allocated over the planning period. The disadvantages of this system are that it is time-consuming to prepare the plans; the reports become bulky and extensive; and it involves considerable management time at all levels of the organization.

FINANCIAL ANALYSIS

In order to control the firm, the budgeting process helps to assess the revenues and expenditures of the divisions. It is also helpful to do a financial analysis. A **financial analysis** assists in identifying the major financial strengths and weaknesses of a firm by determining whether funds are used efficiently and the firm is financially viable. It indicates whether a firm has enough cash to meet obligations; a reasonable accounts receivable collection period; an efficient inventory management policy; sufficient plant, property, and equipment; and an adequate capital structure. A financial analysis helps to determine the financial condition of the firm, its liquidity position, and its profitability. The financial analysis assesses how well the firm is doing in comparison with past years and with other firms in the industry.[17]

Completing a financial analysis sometimes involves analyzing components drawn from the balance sheet and the income statement and combining these components in financial ratios. At other times, it involves comparing a series of statements that represent different accounting periods to identify trends. For example, a balance sheet showing the figures for 1986 through 1990 makes it possible to see the differences in amounts across the years.

The **income statement** shows revenues, expenses, taxes, and profits. It shows the profitability of the firm over time and the net increase or decrease (revenues minus expenses) over the same period. The **retained earnings statement** provides a summary of the changes in the earnings retained in a business for a specific period of time.

Ratio Analysis

A **financial ratio** is a relationship that indicates something about a firm's activities, such as the ratio between the firm's assets and liabilities. No single financial ratio can answer all questions, but ratio analysis can provide a good indication of how the firm is performing, especially in comparison with other firms in the industry.

There are two approaches to ratio analysis: (1) to evaluate performance over several years, and (2) to compare performance with that of similar firms in the same industry. The first approach usually compares current performance with past performance. For example, it is possible to see how well the firm is doing this year compared with last year. The second approach can be used for one point in time or over a period of time. The performance of the firm is compared with that of others in the same industry to see if it is performing up to industry averages. Dun & Bradstreet, Inc., compiles industry average ratios for over 100 industries.

Break-Even Analysis

Another form of financial analysis is **break-even analysis**. This is a method for analyzing at what point a project will cover its costs. The **break-even point** is the point at which there is neither a profit nor a loss. Figure 18–8 demonstrates a break-even analysis by showing the level of activity or production that would be necessary in order to break even. Such analysis looks at the relationship among fixed costs, variable costs, and profits. Because it has fixed costs, a firm must produce at a certain level in order to avoid a loss.

A break-even analysis considers the amount of fixed costs and the amount of variable costs per unit that must be covered. This determines the total cost line. The income line is based on the selling price per unit for the volume produced. Beyond the break-even point, the firm begins to earn a profit. All new projects, products, and businesses should be analyzed with break-even analysis to show the expected profits and losses at different expected sales volumes.

The formula for the break-even point is:

$$\text{Break-Even Point in Units} = \frac{\text{Total Fixed Costs}}{\text{Unit Selling Price} - \text{Unit Variable Cost}}$$

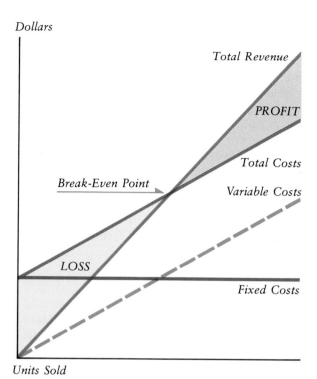

Dollars

FIGURE 18–8
Break-Even Analysis

Total Revenue

PROFIT

Total Costs

Variable Costs

Break-Even Point

LOSS

Fixed Costs

Units Sold

As an example, suppose the total fixed costs for producing a product are $200,000, the unit selling price is $5, and the unit variable cost is $4. Then, the break-even point would be $200,000/($5 − $4) = 200,000 units. The break-even point in sales dollars would be 200,000 × $5 = $1,000,000. Alternatively, if the unit selling price is $6, the break-even point would be $200,000/($6 − $4) = 100,000 units. The corresponding break-even point in sales dollars would be 100,000 × $6 = $600,000.

FINANCIAL AUDIT

Control systems are designed to specify how departments and organizational units should budget their activities and what procedures these units must follow for reporting and correcting their actions. The role of an **audit** is to provide an independent and unbiased evaluation of the data reported and the procedures used.[18] There are two primary types of audit: external and internal. With an external audit, individuals external to the firm—usually certified public accountants—report on the firm's activities and provide an expert opinion that the statements fairly represent the firm's condition. Most large firms also have some of their own staff serve as auditors who verify the amounts and methods reported but who also examine the efficiency and effectiveness of the accounting procedures. An internal audit periodically appraises the overall system to evaluate whether or not goals are being achieved. While the external auditor verifies the overall financial statements reported externally, the internal auditor evaluates the operations and makes recommendations for their improvement.

In some cases, such as when it appears that a company has engaged in a major fraud, additional auditors, called forensic accountants, may be brought in. Such was the case when ZZZZ Best, a carpet-cleaning company, went bankrupt, leaving creditors with $70 million in losses. A forensic accounting firm, John Murphy & Associates Inc., was brought in and conducted an exhaustive audit which revealed evidence of fraud, money laundering, and racketeering.[19]

Operations Control

Operations control concerns the management of the transformation of inputs into outputs. Chapter 20 covers operations management, including operations control, in detail.

Roger Schroeder suggests that there are five key decision categories in operations control.[20] We will briefly discuss four of these: process, capacity, inventory, and quality controls. The fifth, work force, will be covered under behavioral controls.

PROCESS CONTROLS

Process controls address the method of transformation and facility planning. They are long-term in nature and frequently involve capital investment decisions, such as purchase of plants or equipment, that cannot be readily changed. Developing a product or service takes a series of interrelated steps. Process control attempts to analyze the series of steps involved in an activity. For example, in material flows analysis each product is divided into its parts and each part is followed through the assembly process.

CAPACITY CONTROLS

Capacity controls link long-range forecasts to the amount of product or service being produced, generating alternative capacity plans, scheduling operations, and deciding on a plan for implementation. Primary among capacity controls are those concerning facilities or plant decisions. These controls are concerned with predicting how much capacity is needed, and when and where it is needed.

INVENTORY CONTROL

Most firms keep raw materials and finished products on hand to meet demand. These are inventories, and they allow the firm to have some slack in the ordering time for materials and the production schedule. Inventory management must balance the need to keep inventories low to minimize storage costs and the need to keep inventories high to meet customer demands. **Inventory control** manages the costs of ordering, storing, and handling inventory. It involves deciding when to order and how much.

QUALITY CONTROL

In order to make a product that meets certain specifications, **quality control** measures must be taken to monitor the transformation process and to correct deviations. Product quality control ensures the maintenance of standards for the product. Process quality control ensures that the processes of transformation and delivery meet certain standards.

Behavioral Controls

Behavioral controls influence the behavior of the work force—the firm's human resources. These controls are of two primary types: (1) formal behavioral controls such as job analysis, performance appraisals, selection and training, and staffing levels; and (2) informal behavioral controls such as culture, socialization, and executive power. **Formal behavioral controls** are tied to the rules and regulations of the firm. They serve to formalize hiring practices, the assignment of work, and evaluation procedures. These controls were discussed in Chapter 10. **Informal behavioral controls** try to influence the employees of the firm through unobtrusive methods. Here, we consider three forms of informal behavioral control.

CULTURE

As will be discussed in Chapter 22, the culture of the organization consists of the shared beliefs, ideologies, and norms that influence organizational decision making. Many firms are attempting to develop an organization culture that is helpful in motivating their employees and keeping them committed to the firm. At General Motors, "culture cards" are carried around by executives to remind them of their new missions. Japanese firms use the culture of the firm for controlling behavior by having songs, uniforms, and team-building exercises. This helps to build identification with and commitment to the firm and thus increases the likelihood that individuals will act in the best interest of the firm.

SOCIALIZATION

Socialization (discussed in Chapter 17) refers to the process by which an individual attains the attitudes, values, and beliefs of the organizational culture.

Herb Kelleher, CEO of Southwest Airlines, has developed an organization culture based on warmth and informality in employee and customer relationships.

Organizational programs, rewards, and rituals are means used by organizations to socialize their members.[21] Other employees also serve as an important means for socializing new members by showing them the ropes or telling them the way things are done. The objective of the socialization process is to get the individual to conform to the accepted norms and behave in a way that is considered desirable by management.

EXECUTIVE POWER

Power can be an important technique for influencing people and for getting them to do what is desired. In fact, powerful people may influence the attitudes and values of others.[22] The power of people in leadership positions works to control behavior, because others believe these people can influence the future of the firm and can back up promises and threats. Rosabeth Moss Kanter found that employees try to be in the network of powerful people because it helps their careers.[23] At the same time, John Kotter suggests that the networks developed by powerful people help them to gain information and ideas, to communicate their planned agendas, to implement their agendas, and to achieve their objectives.[24]

There is a growing trend which suggests that the sharing of power is one of the most effective ways for executives to control behavior in the workplace; however, delegation is not a substitute for having powerful people making key decisions. Frequently, sharing power involves delegating the task of directing how things are done, but not what things need to be done. Thus, even delegation becomes an informal control technique of executive power.[25] For example, Roger Smith's campaign at General Motors to change the GM culture has included the decentralization of decision making and of power. Some managers have called it "do-it-yourself management," because they are given the jobs to be done and are expected to make the decisions necessary to get them done.

Information Control

One of the central problems for today's firm is the control of information. Part of the reason is that as firms have become larger and more complex, it is no longer physically possible for management to oversee all activities directly. Consequently, it must rely on information and reports to monitor activities. Management must have accurate information for making decisions.

The rapid growth of computer technology means that it is easier to process more pieces of information at a faster pace. With the development of distributed networks, it is now possible to get information from geographically dispersed offices and foreign subsidiaries.[26] Management must control the large capital expenditures associated with computer systems and allocate computer time and space as scarce resources within the firm. Management defines the objectives for information control and systems development, determines estimates of the values and costs, and evaluates the information quality and system performance. The next chapter will address many of the issues relating to information control.

DESIGNING EFFECTIVE CONTROL SYSTEMS

To design effective control systems, management must assess the impact of the control systems on the organization. In this section, we will first consider some general objectives for the design of effective control systems. Then, we will examine some dysfunctional side effects of control systems and their causes. We will conclude with guidelines for designing control systems to maximize effectiveness while avoiding such dysfunctional side effects.

Goals of Effective Control Systems

Here are some general goals of effective control systems. Note that these goals relate to more than simply keeping things on track. They deal with such things as maintaining order, ensuring adequate information, and encouraging compliance:

- To establish order and consistency in the methods used to handle recurring problems.
- To provide information about what should get done, how it should get done, and when.
- To meet corporate objectives and to correct deviations in performance.
- To provide information to management that is accurate and useful for evaluating current goals and operating procedures.
- To encourage compliance with regulations, but also to encourage innovation and commitment.

Dysfunctional Side Effects of Control

An inherent contradiction built into control systems may hamper the attainment of these goals. Control systems are meant to standardize activities, establish order, and enhance compliance, but they are not meant to dampen commitment, motivation, or innovativeness. In many cases, however, control systems limit self-initiative and freedom, and this may cause dysfunctional side effects that range from game playing to actual sabotage to generation of inaccurate information. These side effects are often amplified because people tend to view control negatively, and control techniques may create resistance.

GAME PLAYING

One of the behavioral consequences of control systems is that people look at controls as something to be beaten.[27] For example, many people view filling out their income tax forms as a game to beat the IRS. Similarly, people may look at rules and regulations simply as things to circumvent. Another problem, since a rule establishes minimum standards, is that people may try to do "just enough" to satisfy the rule.[28]

One common form of game playing in organizations is the budget game.[29] It is frequently a version of "Pad the Budget" or "Pad the Expense Account." The objective of this game is to get more money for expenses. University departments frequently play a version of "Beat the Clock" in which every penny of money allocated to them is used before the next budgeting period begins.

The need for more resources can thus be justified. People play games within the limits set by the control system; they don't often try to change the rules of the game.

Another type of game playing is impression management. With **impression management** workers attempt to beat controls by appearing to be busy or to otherwise be meeting job requirements.[30] Clark Molstad took a job as a brewery worker and studied how his co-workers reacted to the repetition and boredom of their jobs, as well as to the lack of freedom associated with being closely controlled by supervisors.[31] He writes of the impression management that the brewery workers engaged in:

The most effective of these worker tactics combine the acts of looking busy and disappearing into one process. When a worker is on foot and being observed, this procedure requires appearing busy and active, even preoccupied and harassed, and then managing to drop out of the supervisor's sight, either by going into the distance or by disappearing behind obstacles such as machinery. The idea is to look intense and involved to the point that one can't be bothered with more work or with silly questions and conversation. . . . These ploys will not necessarily fool all experienced supervisors, but by disappearing the worker can hope that something else will distract the supervisor's attention (p. 357).

SABOTAGE

In sabotage, employees attempt to create such damage to the control system that it will not work in the future and will be abandoned by management. Computerized time clocks are frequently broken or manipulated by workers. Another form of sabotage is to create confusion. Experts can make projects seem so complex that management cannot understand them or understand the resources necessary to support the project. To ignore the rules and to do whatever pleases you is a subtle form of sabotage.

INACCURATE INFORMATION

Control systems rely on the accuracy and timeliness of the information provided about the actual performance and its comparison with projected goals. Managers may supply inaccurate information to make themselves appear better. It is well documented that subordinates will report what they perceive management wants to hear.[32] Realistic progress reports and expenses may not be reported if they contradict what management expects. Sometimes management will ask for information that has not been collected, and subordinates will make up the numbers or give their best guess.

ILLUSION OF CONTROL

Appearing to be in control is particularly important at the upper levels of the firm. If the firm reports good financial results, the president takes full credit. If the firm has had poor performance, the results are blamed on unforeseen environmental changes that the president could not control.[33] Managers try to appear in control and to assure their superiors that everything is in order and flowing smoothly. Even in performance evaluation sessions, subordinates will try to appear in control and to deny the existence of any negative deviations from performance standards.

BUREAUPATHOLOGY

For some people, control becomes almost a sickness. For instance, supervisors may rely very heavily on control mechanisms to overcome the anxieties arising from their positions—anxieties that are reinforced by the knowledge that they may be blamed for the sins of their subordinates. They may demand constant reports, supervise closely, fail to delegate responsibility, remain aloof from subordinates, and make and enforce many regulations for subordinates' behavior. This pattern of supervisory behaviors aimed at maintaining tight control has been called **bureaupathology**.[34]

Causes of Dysfunctional Effects

The occurrence of dysfunctional effects in control systems is the result of a myriad of complex administrative, technical, and behavioral processes. However, these effects are not inevitable. We will first discuss some of the causes of these effects and then consider design tactics to deal with them.

PERSONAL DIFFERENCES

As we discussed in previous chapters, people are motivated by different things at different times, and they will uniquely perceive the same situation or instructions based on their own backgrounds. For example, one manager in a department might report that the department is doing well and meeting its goals. Another manager in the same department might be more aware of poor morale and report that the department is not doing well. Sometimes managers simply are not aware that they are reporting inaccurate information or that they are game playing. They may sincerely believe that they are doing the best job that they possibly can.

Differences in mental capabilities can produce cognitive strain for some individuals who are afraid of making mistakes and who need to follow rules and procedures very carefully.[35] Some subordinates resent having their superiors oversee their activities and intervene to make adjustments. Individuals best understand standards which they have been involved in setting. Individual differences cause differences in perceptions and reactions to the control system.

OVERCONTROL

Too much control can be as much of a problem as too little control. People need to feel some responsibility for themselves and for their work. Frequent evaluations, too many rules, and repeated interventions by superiors can be distracting and disturbing. Overcontrol can cause people to do only what is necessary and no more. As long as the rule is followed, behavior is defensible. A draftsperson may refuse to work overtime because it is not part of his or her job description. A salesperson may decide to rigidly follow the rules rather than treat customers with flexibility.[36]

CONFLICTING GOALS

Often, one aspect of the control system conflicts with another. For example, many firms require their managers to put together a long-range plan, but the performance evaluations are based on short-term activities. In such a situation managers filling out reports to meet management's expectations face conflicting standards and may generate inaccurate information.

As organizations grow and specialized subunits develop, those subunits may generate their own subgoals. So, marketers and production people may each pursue their own subgoals while losing track of larger organizational goals. This can result in a product which meets market needs but can't be produced economically, or one that is easy to manufacture but not what customers want.[37]

Standardized procedures are usually based on what happened in the past and are an attempt to avoid conflict in the future. Over time, these procedures may become outdated but still be in effect, even though the reasons for maintaining them are no longer valid. These procedures may conflict with getting the work done efficiently and effectively now. The firm may also view the questioning of authority and rules as an act of insubordination.

The linkages between the rules, regulations, standards, and schedules have a combined effect. The combined effects of the technological control processes, performance evaluations, allocations of resources, and work procedures may be different from that produced by each one separately.

IMPACT ON POWER AND STATUS

The ability to control the making of rules, to disseminate information, and to set rewards gives a person power over other people. People may feel threatened by a change in the control system because it will also change their power and status.

Control systems can create new experts and eliminate old ones. People familiar with new aspects of the control system become experts and gain power to obtain resources and to withhold information from others. Changing the organizational structure of AT&T created new work groups with new leaders, new rules, and new power relationships.

Guidelines for Effective Design

The nature of appropriate control varies according to the environmental conditions, nature of the work, type of firm, and people involved.[38] It depends upon the amount of managerial discretion necessary, interdependencies among subunits, time span, and type of information required for evaluations. An effective control system must be designed for each organization, but there are certain guidelines that are appropriate for all firms. These guidelines are aimed at developing control systems that overcome the dysfunctional side effects we have considered.

CREATE VALUABLE INFORMATION

Valuable information is information that is timely, accurate, and relevant to the decision makers. If information is to have value, it must be gathered, processed, and disseminated in time to influence decisions. Further, managers must have information that truly reflects actual performance, and it should be objective, comprehensible, and appropriate to the task. Valuable information contributes to designing well-conceived standards and goals. The next chapter goes into more depth on how to design a management information system effectively.

BE PRACTICAL

Control systems should be economically and organizationally practical. The benefits of effective control systems must outweigh costs. To help ensure a proper benefits/cost balance, the control system should be focused on points at which deviations are most likely to occur or are likely to be especially costly. It should also focus on points at which effective corrective action is most feasible. Also, efforts should be made to see that the system is appropriate to the task. For instance, if a manager needs only weekly information about production figures for certain control purposes, a system providing hourly information would incur costs without corresponding benefits. Further, the control system should be consistent with organizational realities. If performance standards are unrealistic, if the system ignores political realities, or if no link is seen between performance standards and rewards, the system may fail.

CREATE A CONTROL CULTURE

A culture consists of shared values and norms. For control systems to be effective, a culture must be developed in which the purpose and limits of the controls are recognized and fully understood. This is a particularly important contribution of upper management. Organizations that have been successful at implementing control systems spend a great amount of energy developing trust, flexibility, and shared understandings of the purpose of controls and rules. Controlling is not an exact science, and employees should understand that the control systems are solely a means to reach desired goals. Reaching those goals depends upon everyone in the firm. Participation leads to shared understandings, a sense of ownership, and a more effective system.

PRACTICE CONTINUOUS REDESIGN

Rules, procedures, and standards should be fixed only in the short term. The control system should be flexible and responsive to changing events that influence the firm. There should be a continual assessment of current levels of controls, standards used, and control methods. Evaluation should center as much on the information presented as on how that information was collected and how it will be used.

MAINTAIN GRIEVANCE PROCEDURES

IBM has a procedure by which anyone can present to upper management something that is perceived to be a major deviation from the plan. If necessary, individuals can bypass the normal hierarchical communication lines. This illustrates a nonthreatening method for alerting management to problems within the existing control system. Lawrence Hrebiniak suggests that to create more effective control systems, organizations must embrace error rather than feel threatened by deviations.[39] Sometimes errors, mistakes, deviations, and bad luck are punished. Yet these provide important learning experiences and may represent the acceptance of risk taking and creative approaches to a problem. Control systems should provide for deviations that may occur and for a discussion of the causes without the threat of punishment.

IMPLICATIONS FOR MANAGEMENT

The control function will be part of your job as a manager. The control systems you use will help you to monitor your own performance and to look better to your superiors. However, control can have dysfunctional effects. You must carefully analyze the impact of each control technique to determine if it is functioning effectively.

There are many types of control that you can use in all aspects of your work. All levels of management are involved in and responsible for developing and assessing financial, operations, behavioral, and information control. As a manager, you will have to assess what is needed and its impact on the activities for which you have responsibility.

It is also important for you to recognize that the techniques used within the firm have an impact on how the firm is viewed by those outside it. For example, different accounting controls and procedures create different types of accounting statements. These influence how the firm is seen by the financial community and can determine whether the firm gets investors or loans. Similarly, the type of behavioral controls implemented frequently affects the firm's reputation as a good place to work. Inventory and quality controls influence customer satisfaction with the product or service.

It would be helpful to involve your subordinates in determining appropriate controls rather than imposing these controls on them. Participation in designing controls does mean that the process may take longer and that you may have to negotiate on some of the controls used. However, it does produce a better understanding of and commitment to the controls.

Remember that control systems must have some flexibility in order to handle the exceptions that may occur. Customer relations are very important, and customers like to feel that their problems are being individually addressed. They do not like receiving routine answers. Even when proper procedures are being followed, it is helpful to make it seem that a solution was designed especially for the situation. Control systems provide guidelines that should incorporate some flexibility.

As a manager, you need to recognize that control techniques have a life cycle; at some point, they are no longer as effective as they once were. About the time that the control technique is most effective, other things begin to change. For example, new technology may be introduced, better-educated employees may start work, or government regulations may change. All of these factors may influence the effectiveness of the technique. Change and redesign can keep the control system more viable.

The most important implication is to understand your own individual strengths and weaknesses in managing other people. Some people may be very uncomfortable with informal controls; others may be uncomfortable with formal controls. You need to find what works best for you to get the job done and keep your subordinates motivated and committed.

KEY TERMS AND CONCEPTS

audit	informal behavioral controls
basic corrective action	inventory control
behavioral controls	management by exception
bottom-up approach	managerial control
break-even analysis	market control strategy
break-even point	noncybernetic controls
budget	operating budget
budgeting	operational control
bureaucratic control strategy	operations control
bureaupathology	planning, programming, budgeting
capacity controls	system (PPBS)
clan control strategy	post-action or output control
control	preliminary or feedforward control
control process	process controls
control technique	quality control
cybernetic control	responsibility center
financial analysis	retained earnings statement
financial budget	steering control
financial ratio	strategic control
formal behavioral controls	top-down approach
immediate corrective action	yes-no control
impression management	zero-based budgeting (ZBB)
income statement	

QUESTIONS FOR REVIEW AND DISCUSSION

1. Give an example of a control system that made you angry and tell why.
2. Do you think it is better to have too little control or too much control? Why?
3. Identify some control systems used in your university. Characterize them as cybernetic, noncybernetic, steering, yes-no, or post-action controls.
4. How do assumptions about people differ in the market control strategy, the bureaucratic control strategy, and the clan control strategy? Which of these approaches do you think is most effective? Why?
5. If you were a manager, how could you determine that your control system was no longer effective? What signals would you watch for?
6. From the point of view of the organization, what are the advantages of informal behavioral controls over formal behavioral controls? The disadvantages?
7. What is the relationship between planning and control?
8. Is control inherently manipulative? Justify your position.
9. Describe four dysfunctional side effects of control systems.
10. If you were a manager, what sorts of controls would you feel comfortable implementing in your department? What sorts would make you uncomfortable?

CASES

18–1 PRODUCTIVITY SPIES

Vaughn Foster has U.S. 85 all to himself as he swings his truck onto the highway for his last trip of the day. To his right, the sun is disappearing behind the Rockies; ahead, the road stretches straight and empty for miles. With one eye on the speedometer, he eases into the right lane and starts creeping ahead at 50 miles an hour.

"I've been out all week," he says. "My wife's home, my kids are home, and I'd just as soon be there with them. There's no doubt about it: If that computer wasn't there, I'd be running 60 easy."

Mr. Foster is talking about a black box the size of a dictionary that sits in a compartment above his right front tire. At the end of his trip, his boss at Leprino Foods Co. in Denver will pull a cartridge out of the box and pop it into a personal computer. In seconds the computer will print out a report showing all the times the truck was speeding.

Computers are transforming thousands of jobs at companies like Leprino in a significant new way: They are watching over employees and monitoring their productivity.

Typists in word-processing pools generate reports that show how many pages they produce in a day and how many keystrokes they produce in a minute. Supervisors of telephone operators scan summaries of how many calls each operator answers and how long each call takes. In production plants making everything from spark plugs to Tupperware, supervisors glance at terminals and see instantly which machine operators are ahead of schedule and which are behind.

To many managers, computer monitoring has brought wondrous results. They say it motivates employees to meet company standards and makes them more productive workers. Some managers also find that a printout provides an objective way to rate a worker's performance and determine raises and promotions without giving scapegoats or pets special treatment. And at least one employer has used monitoring technology to ferret out an episode of apparent office sabotage and build a case against a suspect.

But as electronic watchdogs move into the workplace, they are stirring alarm among a growing number of unions, government officials, and labor experts. These people worry that the practice breeds stress and dehumanizes employees. In 1985, seven states considered legislation to restrict the practice. Twenty unions have adopted official positions against monitoring, and one, representing claims processors at Equitable Assurance Society, has succeeded in fashioning a contract that it credits with establishing limits.

Source: Reprinted by permission of *The Wall Street Journal*, © Dow Jones & Company, Inc. (June 3, 1985). All Rights Reserved Worldwide.

1. Do you agree that computer monitoring motivates employees to meet company standards and makes them more productive? Do you agree that computer monitoring breeds stress and dehumanizes employees?
2. Which of the dysfunctional side effects of control discussed in this chapter do you think might result from these "electronic watchdogs"?
3. For what sorts of jobs might monitoring of this sort be most appropriate? Least appropriate?

18–2 CONTROLLING FOR THE CRUNCH IN FRESH VEGETABLES

Amid the growing emphasis on fitness and good nutrition, it's become trendy to seek out fresh and exotic fruits and vegetables in the supermarket. Per capita consumption of fresh produce has risen 12 percent in the United States over the past 10 years. As a result, the fresh-produce section in a typical supermarket has expanded to 15 percent of the store's total area, twice the size of a decade ago. And most produce aisles now stock about 200 items, a fourfold increase in the same period.

But the vogue for unprocessed produce has a few soft spots. The increased demand has caused inventory and quality-control problems for both suppliers and retailers, and shoppers have become warier about the products they buy—particularly with regard to the additives that distributors and retailers sometimes use to extend shelf life. Moreover, many young consumers—children of parents who preferred the convenience of canned and frozen foods—are unversed in the selection and preparation of fresh produce. "They're like a species that's lost the use of its tail," says Faith Popcorn, owner of BrainReserve, a New York marketing concern that specializes in the food industry. "They see the beautiful vegetables. They know they're supposed to do something with them, but what?"

From the start, so-called fresh produce isn't always as fresh as consumers might think. Many items are still in transit, or in ripening rooms losing nutrients and taste, long after their canned and frozen counterparts have had those qualities sealed in at the processing plant. Though packing and refrigeration techniques have improved, the harvest-to-consumer cycle in some parts of the country can stretch to ten days or more. And if the cooling in a warehouse or truck is inadequate, "you can lose all the good you're doing in about 30 minutes," says Larry Wheeler, director of marketing, fresh vegetables, at Minneapolis-based Pillsbury Company.

In many cases, quality and freshness go unchecked, as Department of Agriculture inspectors have been hard-pressed to keep up with the burgeoning shipments of fresh goods. According to department officials, an estimated 76 billion pounds of fruits and vegetables will be inspected in 1986, a 17 percent increase over five years. But during this time, the number of federal inspectors, about 200, has remained virtually unchanged. At present, more than 50 percent of the food in supermarket produce aisles gets from farm to store without government inspection, the officials say.

Given the rise in volume and variety, retailers too have less opportunity to weed out inferior produce, and rising labor costs have meant less expertise in produce departments. "You just don't get the guy who's been in the produce department for years and knows how to handle the product. You get a guy going to college who's just there to make a little extra money," says Duane Eaton, staff vice-president of the Produce Marketing Association, a trade group. "What it comes down to," adds marketing consultant Mona Doyle, "is that consumers are the inspectors."

Increased volume and variety are also making it harder for produce managers to estimate what they'll need for stock. Retailers say they're throwing away up to 15 percent of their produce—nearly twice the amount of five years ago—because it gets old before they can sell it. Such problems along the supply line are affecting shoppers. "The consumer is suspicious," says Ms. Doyle. "He's got the notion there's something rotten in the bottom of every bag." But what arouses suspicion isn't always the food itself. In a recent survey of 484 shoppers by Ms. Doyle, 94 percent of the respondents said they would be willing to switch supermarkets if they could find fresh food that wasn't "waxed"—that is, coated with a preservative commonly used to enhance cosmetically such items as apples and cucumbers. Indeed, the use of preservatives on fresh produce is causing growing concern among shoppers. Consumer complaints to the Food and Drug Administration about illnesses caused by sulfite preservatives—which, depending on the amount used, may leave a residue after washing—more than tripled to 1,000 between 1984 and 1985. In 1986, the FDA banned their use.

To correct the situation, produce sellers must take steps to inform consumers and allay their fears, says BrainReserve's Ms. Popcorn. "There's going to have to be more labeling with information about how produce has been grown and handled. Consumers want a white-glove imagery," she explains.

Source: Reprinted by permission of *The Wall Street Journal*, © Dow Jones & Company, Inc. (January 27, 1986). All Rights Reserved Worldwide.

1. Review the section on "Designing Effective Control Systems." How might supermarket managers successfully meet the five objectives for designing an effective control system?
2. What causes of dysfunctional side effects of control systems established by growers, shippers, and sellers of fresh produce have forced customers to become "inspectors"?
3. Would a top-down or bottom-up approach be most effective for creating and establishing controls over fresh produce? Why?

ENDNOTES

1. R. N. Anthony, J. Dearden, and N. M. Bedford, *Management Control Systems*, 6th ed. (Homewood, IL: Irwin, 1989).
2. For a discussion of these elements and of their determinants and consequences, see W. H. Newman, *Constructive Control: Design and Use of Control Systems* (Englewood Cliffs, NJ: Prentice-Hall, 1975), and W. G. Ouchi, "The Relationship Between Organizational Structure and Organizational Control," *Administrative Science Quarterly* 22 (March 1977): 95-113.
3. Newman, *Constructive Control*.
4. E. E. Lawler and J. G. Rhode, *Information and Control in Organizations* (Santa Monica, CA: Goodyear, 1976).
5. Ouchi, "Organizational Structure and Organizational Control," and W. G. Ouchi and M. A. Maguire, "Organizational Control: Two Functions," *Administrative Science Quarterly* 20 (December 1975): 559-569.
6. W. G. Ouchi, "A Conceptual Framework for the Design of Organizational Control Mechanisms," *Management Science* 25 (1979): 833-848.
7. W. G. Ouchi, "Markets, Bureaucracies, and Clans," *Administrative Science Quarterly* 25 (March 1980): 130.
8. R. L. Daft, *Organization Theory and Design*, 2d ed. (St. Paul: West Publishing Co., 1986).
9. P. R. Lawrence and D. Dyer, *Renewing American Industry* (New York: Free Press, 1983).
10. Ouchi, "Markets, Bureaucracies, and Clans," 136.
11. R. L. Dunbar, "Designs for Organizational Control," in *Handbook of Organizational Design* vol. 2, ed. P. C. Nystrom and W. H. Starbuck (Oxford: Oxford University Press, 1981).
12. T. J. Peters and R. H. Waterman, Jr., *In Search of Excellence* (New York: Harper & Row, 1982), 75-76.
13. A. M. Jaeger and B. R. Baliga, "Control Systems and Strategic Adaptation: Lessons from the Japanese Experience," *Strategic Management Journal* 6 (1985): 115-134.
14. R. N. Anthony, J. Dearden, and N. M. Bedford, *Management Control Systems: Text and Cases* (Homewood, IL: Irwin, 1989).
15. R. P. Neveu, *Fundamentals of Managerial Finance*, 3d ed. (Cincinnati, OH: South-Western Publishing Company, 1989).
16. P. A. Pyhrr, "Zero-Based Budgeting," *Harvard Business Review* (November-December 1971): 111.
17. Neveu, *Fundamentals of Managerial Finance*.
18. D. N. Ricchiute, *Auditing Concepts and Standards*, 2d ed. rev. (Cincinnati, OH: South-Western Publishing Company, 1989).
19. D. Akst and L. Berton, "Accountants Who Specialize in Detecting Fraud Find Themselves in Great Demand," *Wall Street Journal* (February 26, 1988): 17.
20. R. G. Schroeder, *Operations Management: Decision Making in the Operations Function*, 3d ed. (New York: McGraw-Hill, 1989).
21. H. J. Reitz, *Behavior in Organizations*, 3d ed. (Homewood, IL: Richard D. Irwin, 1987).
22. H. Mintzberg, *Power in and Around Organizations* (Englewood Cliffs, NJ: Prentice-Hall, 1983), and J. Pfeffer, *Power in Organizations* (Marshfield, MA: Pitman Publishing Co., 1981).
23. R. M. Kanter, *Men and Women of the Corporation* (New York: Basic Books, 1977).
24. J. Kotter, *General Managers* (New York: Free Press, 1982).

25. S. Srivastva and Associates, *Executive Power: How Executives Influence People and Organizations* (San Francisco: Jossey-Bass, 1986).

26. R. McLeod, Jr., *Management Information Systems*, 2d ed. (Chicago: Science Research Associates, 1983).

27. Dunbar, "Designs for Organizational Control."

28. A. W. Gouldner, *Patterns of Industrial Bureaucracy* (Glencoe, IL: Free Press, 1954).

29. R. J. Swieringa and R. H. Moncur, "The Relationship Between Managers' Budget Oriented Behavior and Selected Attitude, Position, Size, and Performance Measures," *Empirical Research in Accounting: Selected Studies*, Supplement to *Journal of Accounting Research* 10 (1972): 194-209.

30. For instance, see J. T. Tedeschi and V. Melburg, "Impression Management and Influence in the Organization," *Research in the Sociology of Organizations* 3 (1984): 31-58.

31. C. Molstad, "Control Strategies Used by Brewery Workers: Work Avoidance, Impression Management and Solidarity," *Human Organization* 4 (1988): 354-360. As the title suggests, this article provides an interesting discussion of how workers may try to exert control in frustrating jobs.

32. E. Carter, "Behavioral Theory of the Firm and Top-Level Corporate Decisions," *Administrative Science Quarterly* 16 (December 1971): 413-439.

33. G. R. Salancik and J. R. Meindl, "Corporate Attributions as Strategic Illusions of Management Control," *Administrative Science Quarterly* 29 (June 1984): 238-254.

34. V. A. Thompson, *Modern Organization* (New York: Knopf, 1961).

35. R. T. Lenz and M. A. Lyles, "Managing the Planning Process: A Field Study of the Human Side of Planning," *Strategic Management Journal* 3, no. 2 (April-June 1982): 105-118.

36. R. K. Merton, "Bureaucratic Structure and Personality," *Social Forces* 18 (1940): 560-568.

37. P. Selznick, *TVA and the Grass Roots* (Berkeley: University of California Press, 1949).

38. R. F. Vancil, "What Kind of Management Control Do You Need?" *Harvard Business Review* (March-April 1973): 75-86.

39. L. G. Hrebiniak, *Complex Organizations* (St. Paul, MN: West Publishing Co., 1978).

Information Management

CHAPTER 19

After studying this chapter, you should be able to:
- *Identify important characteristics of information.*
- *Describe the characteristics and design of a management information system.*
- *Identify keys to the success of management information system implementation and use.*
- *Discuss the impact of management information systems and related management decision aids on organizations and society.*
- *Describe computer applications in job design, staffing, communications, control, and operations management.*
- *Discuss uses of computers to improve decision making, including decision support systems, decision insight systems, and expert systems.*
- *Identify problems with computers.*

602

The following vignettes suggest some of the ways managers are acquiring and using information to increase their efficiency and effectiveness:

- Xerox Corp. is reaping the rewards of faster information—savings of almost 20 percent of the manufacturing costs in its copier division. It now exchanges quality-control information with its suppliers via computer terminals to eliminate the expensive inspection of incoming parts. In turn, the copier maker gives suppliers its master manufacturing schedule so they can ship parts at precisely the time Xerox needs them in its production line, thus keeping inventories lean.[1]
- Many managers through their microcomputers can currently access up to 2,400 on-line databases. The full texts of stories and articles from hundreds of journals, newspapers, and trade publications can be called up instantly. Information on credit markets and currency quotes, industry developments, pending legislation, skiing conditions, and Japanese baseball scores are a few keystrokes away.[2]
- When AMP Inc. ran a sales contest in 1980, executives of the $1.2 billion maker of electrical connectors were chagrined to discover they could not declare a winner. The reason: They didn't have the necessary information. Although the Harrisburg (Pa.) headquarters regularly received sales reports, it did not have the breakdown by product line it needed to find the best salesperson. Now, AMP has an information center. Among other things, the center allows managers to determine how fast each of AMP's product lines is moving and how fast the divisions are writing off inventories that are not selling. As a result of such analyses, AMP restructured its inventory and was able to increase domestic sales by 25 percent while shrinking inventories by 2.5 percent.[3]

The daily output of U.S. offices includes an estimated 600 million pages of computer printout, 234 million photocopies, and 76 million letters.[4] And these figures don't include information that managers receive through phone calls, meetings, or day-to-day observations. Having to handle such tremendous amounts of paperwork and other data is a burden to many managers and may hurt their productivity.

In this chapter, we will see what can be done to better manage and use information. We will first consider information and information management. Next, we will examine the nature, design, implementation, and impact of management information systems. Then, we will discuss computer applications for job design, staffing, communications, control, operations management, and management decision making. Finally, several potential problems associated with the use of computers in organizations will be addressed.

INFORMATION AND MANAGEMENT

Information is the lifeblood of organizations. Flows of information allow the organization to function, to coordinate its parts, and to respond to new challenges. Clearly, managing information is an important and difficult task.[5]

Information Defined

The dictionary defines **information** as knowledge communicated or received concerning a particular fact or circumstance. Information, therefore, is not

Information is any knowledge that is passed along to enlighten or to inform.

just facts and figures and charts and maps. Rather, it is any knowledge that is passed along to enlighten or to inform.

Many, if not most, of the data that managers receive are not really information. Rather than informing, they overwhelm. Still, the problem is not just one of cutting down on paperwork, phone calls, and the like. Much of the information managers need simply does not reach them, or it is in the wrong form, or it comes too early or too late.

How Managers Get Information

Henry Mintzberg studied managers as they went about their day-to-day work.[6] What he saw was a bit surprising. Rather than finding long-range planners who would block out days to analyze important issues, Mintzberg saw managers performing a wide variety of brief, often unrelated tasks. Instead of getting all information from a single all-knowing computer terminal, the managers used five different media—documents, telephone calls, scheduled meetings, unscheduled meetings, and observational tours. Of these, managers strongly favored telephone calls and meetings. The manager's job emerged as hectic, overloaded, and fragmented. And, Mintzberg concluded, things will only get worse.

Information Resource Management

Information resource management is the name given to a new field that has developed in recognition of the fact that information is a valuable resource in need of systematic management. Our society has seen tremendous growth in the area of information services in this century. Whereas in 1890, 46 percent of the population was involved in agriculture and 4 percent in information services, that figure had reversed by 1979. Only 4 percent of the population was in agriculture and 46 percent was in the information business.[7] Despite this growth in the personnel devoted to information services, only in very recent years has much attention been given to the need to recognize information as a valuable resource.

In fact, information has all the characteristics of a resource. Information is clearly a valuable asset to the firm. And it costs money to collect, store, send, and display information. Like other resources, information has qualities: it may vary in timeliness, accuracy, and form. Furthermore—and this is of prime importance for management purposes—the amount or degree of these qualities can be altered. Information-handling systems can be designed to deliver information sooner or later, of higher or lower quality, in the form of text, numbers, or images. Many firms are now using their information as a valuable strategic weapon. For instance, financial service companies are spending millions of dollars to create information management systems that are faster and more flexible than those of their competitors. Fidelity Brokerage Services Inc. spent $8 million for a proprietary system that has vaulted it to the No. 2 slot in the discount brokerage business. Its system allows a broker using a desktop terminal to execute stock trades more quickly and less expensively than most competitors who buy their services from outside computing companies.[8]

Information Value

Several things determine the value of information to a manager. For instance, Roman Andrus has suggested four sorts of information utility:[9]

- *Form utility*. As the form of information more closely matches the requirements of the decision maker, its value increases. Information that uses an unfamiliar format or jargon will probably be ignored.
- *Time utility*. Information has greater value to the decision maker if it is available when needed. For this reason, some data-processing equipment has been designed to provide instantaneous (real-time) delivery and display. While real-time information is generally not needed, missing or tardy information can cause costly errors or delays.
- *Place utility (physical accessibility)*. Information has greater value if it can be accessed or delivered easily. On-line systems, with which managers immediately access needed information, maximize both time and place utility.
- *Possession utility (organizational location)*. Internal structure and external effectiveness are functions of the location of information within the firm. The possessor of information strongly affects its value by controlling its dissemination to others.

This discussion suggests that information appropriateness, availability, accessibility, and possession all affect the value of information to a manager. In addition, information value depends upon the degree of information accuracy and whether the amount of information is consistent with the manager's needs (that is, neither too little nor too much).[10]

Of course, information is generally not free. Acquisition, processing, storage, and use of information all incur costs for the firm. As with any other resource, management must make tradeoffs, balancing costs with expected benefits.

Like many other U.S. Presidents, George Bush depends on uncertainty absorbers to sift through masses of information and identify the key material needed for decision making.

Information Managers

To some extent, everyone in organizations manages information. However, some people have more control over the way information is acquired, manipulated, distributed, or used than others. For instance, **gatekeepers** decide who should receive information—they open and close the gates of information.

Individuals who summarize information or change its form in other ways to make it more understandable or concise are called **uncertainty absorbers.** They try to make the information more "certain" by taking out unnecessary parts, clarifying issues, bringing together key points, and so on. For instance, some U.S. Presidents have had uncertainty absorbers who read a wide range of newspapers and then put together a collection of key editorials, articles, and other information for the President to read.

As discussed in Chapter 3, **boundary spanners** are employees at the "skin" of the organization, the boundary between the organization and its environment. Recruiters and salespeople are boundary spanners. Boundary spanners are often able to gather valuable information about changes in the environment of the organization. Especially when those environments are complex and rapidly changing, boundary spanners are valuable.

Gatekeepers, uncertainty absorbers, and boundary spanners are all information managers. However, their control of information often comes about less because of organizational needs than through personal circumstance. In an attempt to manage the information resource more systematically, many firms are now developing management information systems.

WHAT IS A MANAGEMENT INFORMATION SYSTEM?[11]

To organize and use information more effectively, many firms are developing management information systems. As Figure 19–1 shows, a **management information system (MIS)** is an integrated system of information flows designed to enhance decision-making effectiveness. Good management information is accurate, timely, complete, relevant in form and content, and available when needed.

FIGURE 19–1
The Basic Meaning of an MIS

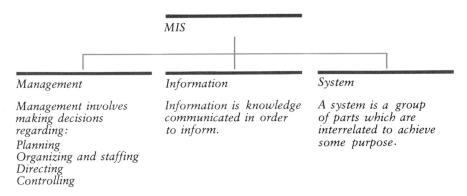

MIS		
Management	*Information*	*System*
Management involves making decisions regarding:	*Information is knowledge communicated in order to inform.*	*A system is a group of parts which are interrelated to achieve some purpose.*
Planning		
Organizing and staffing		
Directing		
Controlling		

Source: Robert G. Murdick and Joel E. Ross, *Introduction to Management Information Systems,* © 1977, p. 8. Adapted by permission of Prentice-Hall, Inc., Englewood Cliffs, NJ.

DESIGN OF THE MANAGEMENT INFORMATION SYSTEM[12]

To design an MIS, it is necessary to set objectives, identify constraints, determine information needs and sources, and put the system together.

Setting Objectives for the MIS

Ultimately, the MIS aims to make managers more effective decision makers. They will be more effective to the extent that:

- They get early warning signals of trouble ahead.
- They get information to assist in decision making.
- The system automatically makes certain decisions that don't require managerial input.
- Routine clerical operations are automated.

Specific objectives should be set to help managers accomplish these purposes. Figure 19–2 shows how these purposes tie in with MIS objectives and related company objectives. Figure 19–3 presents MIS objectives for some specific functions of the organization, such as purchasing and project control.

Identifying System Constraints

Constraints on MIS design may be externally or internally imposed. External constraints may include government regulations, customer demands, and supplier needs.

One internal constraint is cost. Costs must be compared to anticipated benefits. Too often, information managers simply try to get the fanciest, most complete MIS possible, regardless of cost. Policy considerations are another internally imposed constraint. They may determine how centralized the system should be, or they may require that certain information be available for internal auditing purposes. Also, the degree of top management support sets limits on the kind of MIS that can be set up. Computer capacity, availability of personnel, and possible reactions of employees affected by the system are other internal constraints.

FIGURE 19–2
Examples of MIS Objectives

Type	Typical MIS Objective	Related Company Objective
Early warning signals	Prevent surprises due to technological breakthroughs affecting the firm's products.	Avoid crash development programs or loss of market share.
Decision-assisting information	Supply financial trends and ratios to management.	Make good cash and capital investment decisions.
Programmed decision making	Allocate advertising expenditures among selected magazines.	Provide economical and broad support for salespersons.
Automation of routine clerical operations	Automate payroll computations.	Provide timely and accurate pay of employees at minimum cost.

Source: Robert G. Murdick and Joel E. Ross, *Introduction to Management Information Systems,* © 1977, p. 147. Adapted by permission of Prentice-Hall, Inc., Englewood Cliffs, NJ.

Subsystem	Objective
Inventory	Optimize inventory costs through the design of decision rules containing optimum reorder points, safety stock levels, and reorder quantities, each capable of continuous and automatic reassessment.
Accounts Payable	Pay 100 percent of invoices before due date.
Purchasing	Provide performance information on buyer's price negotiations with suppliers in order that purchase variance can be controlled within set limits.
Production Control	Identify cost and quantity variances within one day in order to institute closer control over these variables.
Project Control	Identify performance against plan so that events, costs, and specifications of the project can be met.

Source: Robert G. Murdick and Joel E. Ross, *Introduction to Management Information Systems*, © 1977, p. 149. Adapted by permission of Prentice-Hall, Inc., Englewood Cliffs, NJ.

FIGURE 19–3
Objectives for MIS Subsystems

Determining Information Needs

Once MIS goals and constraints have been identified, the next step is to write a clear statement of information needs. One way to determine these needs is to ask managers what goes on in their decision-making process. Then, questions that must be answered in the process can be determined. Another approach is to ask managers to list their major responsibilities and four or five specific items required to carry out those responsibilities. Typically, various groups of MIS users will have different uses for the systems, as shown in Figure 19–4.

Information needs will also depend on the individual manager. Some managers want great detail; others want less. Some desire a sophisticated, computerized system; others want to "keep things simple." Some say, "Get me all the facts"; others say, "Get me only what I need to know."[13]

The nature of the organization and its environment is also important in determining information needs. In general, the larger and more complex the firm is and the more complex and rapidly changing its environment, the more sophisticated its information needs will be. And, in "looser," more organic sorts of organizations, it may be harder to determine information needs than in a very structured, mechanistic firm.

FIGURE 19–4
Major Users of an MIS

User	Uses
Clerical personnel	Handle transactions, process input data, and answer inquiries.
First-line managers	Obtain operations data. Assistance with planning, scheduling, identifying out-of-control situations, and making decisions.
Staff specialists	Information for analysis. Assistance with analysis, planning, and reporting.
Management	Regular reports. Ad hoc retrieval requests, analyses, and reports. Assistance in identifying problems and opportunities. Assistance in decision-making analysis.

Source: From *Management Information Systems: Conceptual Foundations, Structure, and Development*, 2d ed., by G. B. Davis and M. H. Olson. Copyright © 1985 by McGraw-Hill Book Company. Reproduced with permission.

Determining Information Sources

Once information needs are determined, sources can be identified. Some of these are **primary data sources**. Data from these sources are gathered specifically for the current purpose. Others are **secondary data sources**. Data from these sources were initially collected for other purposes, but fit the current needs. Two secondary data sources are internal records and published sources of business information.

There is often a surprising wealth of information available in the firm's own internal records. For instance, purchase orders may give clues about which market segments are growing or declining. Personnel files can be used to see whether there is especially high turnover in certain areas of the firm, or whether some groups of employees are being promoted faster than others. Memos, letters, and various records of inputs and outputs of the firm may all prove useful.

Much of the information that businesses need may be found in the library. Newspapers, magazines, annual volumes of data, and many other sources provide information concerning just about every imaginable topic of interest to management.

Putting the System Together

As a final step, the system must be put together. This usually involves charting the needed flows of information, such as marketing and sales information and reports, and determining which information should be stored in data banks. Then decisions are needed concerning how inputs to the MIS, such as personnel information, will be coded and what form system outputs will take. Finally, computer hardware and software needs must be assessed.

Other Issues in MIS Design

Several authors have presented additional guidelines for successful MIS design and implementation. Here are some of those guidelines:[14]

INVOLVE THE USER

The technicians who develop an MIS often have perspectives and attitudes that differ from those of users. When this is the case, the system they develop may not adequately meet the users' needs.[15] An additional reason to involve users in MIS design is that they feel greater ownership of the resulting system.[16]

CONSIDER ORGANIZATIONAL TECHNOLOGY

Richard Daft and Norman MacIntosh have argued that organizational technology must be considered when designing and implementing information systems.[17] In particular, they reason that two technological dimensions—task variety and task knowledge—are crucial. **Task variety** is the frequency of unexpected and novel events that occur as inputs are transformed into outputs. **Task knowledge** is the degree to which the transformation process is well understood. If the technology is well understood and there is little task variety, as in programmable technology, a concise information system is appropriate. In such a system, small to moderate amounts of precise and unambiguous information are available to users and the information is used in a quick and decisive way. At the other extreme, if the technology is not well understood and task variety is high, a diffuse information system fits best. A diffuse MIS is characterized by moderate to large amounts of information covering a wide range of material. The information is frequently ill defined and imprecise, and it is typically used in a slow, deliberate manner.

CONSIDER DIFFERENCES AMONG USERS

There are at least two reasons for considering differences among individual users in MIS design. First, as noted earlier, various users may have different information preferences and needs. Second, some users may want to contribute to MIS design and subsequent refinement while others may not.[18]

TAILOR INFORMATION TO THE MANAGEMENT LEVEL

Figure 19–5 shows how management information needs vary by level in the organizational hierarchy. At upper levels, information is needed for strategic and policy planning and decision making. At middle levels, information needs focus on tactical and operational planning and decision making. At lower levels, those needs relate to more routine activities, such as transaction processing.

There are other differences in information requirements across levels. For instance, at upper levels information often is drawn from external sources, has a future orientation, is qualitative, and lacks detail. By its nature, it often suffers from low degrees of accuracy. By contrast, information at lower levels is generally drawn from internal sources, oriented toward the present, quantitative, detailed, and accurate.[19]

OTHER GUIDELINES

As with any attempt at major change, it is important to anticipate and plan for sources of resistance to the MIS. Further, to the greatest extent possible,

FIGURE 19–5
*Management
Information by
Organizational Level*

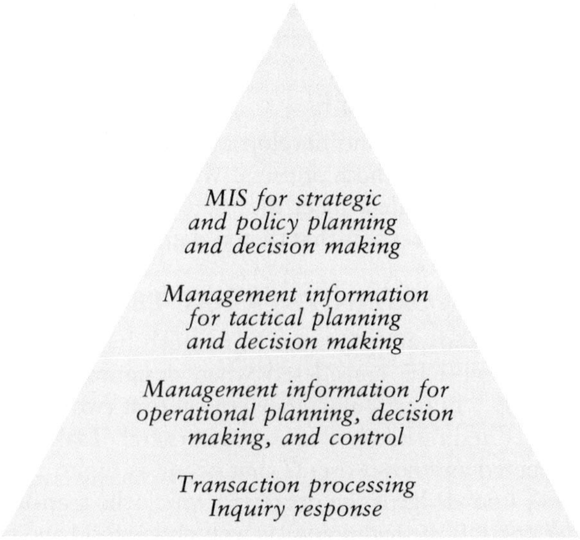

*MIS for strategic
and policy planning
and decision making*

*Management information
for tactical planning
and decision making*

*Management information for
operational planning, decision
making, and control*

*Transaction processing
Inquiry response*

Source: Reprinted with permission of *Datamation*, © Copyright by Technical Publishing Company (May 1967).

the information system should be kept as simple as possible and designed in a compatible way throughout the organization. And it is important to test and evaluate the information system before implementation. Any bugs that remain after implementation may lead to errors, frustration, and—perhaps—calls to scrap the system. Finally, careful thought must be given to implementation. The implementation schedule should be realistic, users should be given adequate training, and time should be provided for system evolution; it is unreasonable to expect a "final" system to be put in place immediately.

THE IMPACT OF MIS

The use of management information systems may have an impact at many levels—societal, industry-wide, organizational, and individual. At the societal level, for instance, Alvin Toffler has argued that MIS developments may cause demassification, in which mass production gives way to such things as the growth of home industries. At the industry level, the use of management information systems is influencing the nature of competitive strategies. For instance, airlines are working together with one another and with hotels, customers, and others in large airline reservation systems.[20]

At the level of the organization, the use of management information systems may influence organizational structure and flexibility as well as, one would hope, performance. As an example of impact on structure, management information systems will displace some people, changing the nature and shape of the organization. The ease with which executives will be able to access and process information will permit them to manage with fewer middle managers.[21] It is interesting that information technology provides the opportunity for both centralization and decentralization. Centralization is possible because top managers have the information to exert control more easily. Decentralization is facilitated because decision making can be more easily delegated when information is readily available at lower levels.

The probable impact of the use of management information systems on individuals has been hotly debated. For instance, Chris Argyris has argued that the rationalization and systematization of management information systems threatens the individual and also inhibits the openness and adaptiveness essential for a healthy organizational climate.[22] He has argued further that the use of management information systems reinforces the status quo and generates forces that favor efficiency over effectiveness. Others have taken a more positive view of the consequences of information technology. Especially when user needs are taken into consideration in information system design and changes are humanely introduced, individual reaction to information technology can be quite positive.[23]

COMPUTERS IN MANAGEMENT

Time magazine's Man of the Year for 1982 was not a man, woman, or child. The contributions of any individual, *Time* concluded, were small in comparison to the contributions of the computer—*Time*'s choice for 1982's "greatest influence for good or evil."

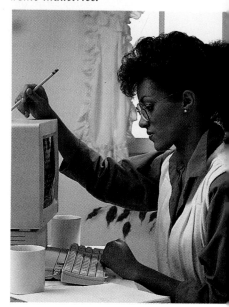

Some analysts believe that MIS developments will spark the growth of home industries.

Daniel Robey (D.B.A., Kent State University) is Professor and Chairman of the Department of Decision Sciences and Information Systems at Florida International University. He is the author of Designing Organizations *and* Managing Computer Impact: An International Study of Management and Organizations. *He has published widely in the administrative science and information systems fields, including articles in such journals as* Management Science, MIS Quarterly, Communications of the ACM, Human Relations, Academy of Management Review, Academy of Management Journal, *and* Decision Sciences. *Dr. Robey currently serves on the editorial review boards of* Information Systems Re-

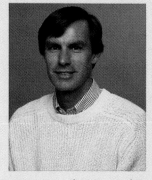

ACADEMIC PROFILE
DANIEL ROBEY

search, Organization Science, *and the de Gruyter and John Wiley series on information systems. He has also served on the editorial boards of the* Academy of Management Review *and the* Journal of Management *and as an associate editor for* MIS Quarterly. *His current research deals with the consequences of information systems in organizations and the process of system development. Dr. Robey has served on the faculties of the University of Pittsburgh, Marquette University, and the Copenhagen School of Economics and Business Administration.*

Q: Why should firms be concerned with MIS?

A: I like the term "information systems" (IS) better than MIS because many applications of the technology do not directly affect management decisions. For example, office automation and communication systems help to make organizations more effective, but they are indirectly concerned with management. Firms should be concerned with IS because IS supports a number of important organizational functions. Strategic planning, operations, decision making, communication, and control are all affected by computers and IS. One problem is that many managers consider computers to be too technical and don't bother learning anything about them. This is unfortunate because managers are best equipped with the vision to understand the most productive uses of IS. Managers who resist IS because of the technical barrier cannot make good decisions about their use, and are less effective as a result.

Q: Are information systems primarily useful only for large organizations?

A: No. Historically, larger organizations have been the ones that could easily make the capital investment required. However, the past ten years have seen the so-called micro revolution in computers. Now, very small organizations and independent professionals are using small computers for many of the functions mentioned above.

Q: There is some controversy concerning whether or not individual differences should be considered when designing an IS. How would you summarize your views on this issue?

A: Individual differences in preferences may be related to user satisfaction in working with an IS. For instance, people who prefer "the big picture" may dislike detailed tabular displays and feel more comfortable with graphs that portray overall patterns. Individual differences in ability may be related to performance differences. For example, color graphic displays help some people with perceptual limitations to perform better than they do with monochrome displays.

One problem with these generalizations is that they treat individual differences too rigidly. The human nervous system is a very flexible information processor in its own right, and very capable of adjusting to the different demands placed upon it. I don't think that individual differences should be used to deny some people the opportunity to work with computers or to hold certain jobs where computing is necessary. That would be unfair discrimination. Perhaps the best way of dealing with individual differences is to make systems flexible in the options they offer to the user.

Q: How would you characterize the current state of decision support systems? Do you think they will take on a larger role in the future?

A: Most DSS continue to support rather structured decision processes despite claims that DSS fit unstructured problems. DSS depend on mathematical models and sufficient databases to make the models run. In many cases managers have neither models nor data, and I look for DSS in the future to be expanded to include even less structured situations where real creativity is needed.

In this capacity, DSS could be used to probe the human mind with questions rather than giving answers to inquiries. A DSS could help managers move away from conventional thinking by introducing surprise questions at just the right moment. DSS can also be applied to group problem solving by assisting in the combination of judgments of group members. I see DSS as having an exciting future, as long as DSS designers understand the potential of information technology to support the creative aspects of human problem solving.

In the years since that selection, the computer's potential for good and evil has begun to be realized. Computers are providing the opportunity for personal growth and autonomy at work, but they are also increasing tedium and resulting in tighter, sometimes stifling, control. They are creating jobs for people who would otherwise be homebound, but they are making many other workers unnecessary. They are easing access to needed information, but they are threatening privacy. They are valuable tools for decision making and handy aids for sabotage and larceny. They are everywhere, and they are not going away.

In this section, we will examine computer applications for job design, staffing, communications, control, and operations management. Then we will examine ways computers are being used as decision aids. Finally, we will address a variety of potential problems associated with the use of computers in organizations.

COMPUTER APPLICATIONS

We have touched on computer applications in management throughout this text, and we will continue to do so. For instance, we have seen examples of how computers are transforming communications, how they are used in training and career planning, and how they permit automated decision conferencing. In Chapter 20 we will discuss their roles in robotics and in a wide variety of other operations management applications. Further, of course, computers are widely used for routine data processing and, increasingly, for word processing. Here are some additional uses.

Job Design Applications

Computers are permitting some fundamental changes in the design of jobs and organizations. For instance, a supervisor who once would have walked around the plant to check on employees' performance can now stand over a computer screen. In general, people are talking more with machines and less with other people, and work becomes more abstract. Further, jobs that were once quite different are now becoming more similar, with bank auditors and pulp-mill operators alike sitting in front of computer screens and monitoring on-line information.[24]

In addition, with the advent of small home computers that can communicate with remote office locations, the electronic cottage has become a reality. The **electronic cottage** is the name given to stay-at-home computer work. Employees can carry out their tasks on their home computers and then transfer the results to the office without ever leaving their homes. The electronic cottage provides employment opportunities for the disabled, homebound parents, and others who previously would have been unable to get to work on a regular basis.

Staffing Applications

Computers have many applications in staffing, including interviewing, training, keeping track of information on job applicants, developing selection tests, and storing a wide variety of information on personnel.[25]

Computer interviews are being used to screen job applicants. These computer interviews may be used to question applicants about work attitudes, theft, or substance abuse—subjects that some interviewers are reluctant to discuss face-to-face. Further, the computers never forget to ask a question, and they can put the same question to each applicant in exactly the same way (though flexibility is also possible). When Bloomingdale's was staffing its new Miami store, it turned to computer screening of applicants. The screening helped the Miami outlet achieve the lowest turnover rate of any new store in the company.[26]

Computers can now train employees more rapidly, more economically, and even more enjoyably than through conventional means. Unlike early computer training, in which the computer was basically a book on a TV screen, new systems are more fully interactive and able to react to the student. Computers are now used to train mechanics at Ford dealerships, to teach inventory control techniques at J. C. Penney, and to train IBM repairpersons.[27]

Application of computers to the management of employee careers, particularly to decisions concerning promotions, is described in Case 19–1. Such applications are especially important in dynamic situations and in those in which pressures for affirmative action are great.

Management in Action 1 discusses some of the computer software that managers may use to deal with staffing and other concerns.

Communications Applications

In Chapter 15 we discussed the impact of new technologies on communication, including electronic mail. Computers facilitate communications through modems and networking.

MODEMS

A **modem** (short for modulator-demodulator) is a device that permits computers to communicate over telephone lines. With a modem, one microcomputer user can phone another and transfer letters, financial data, or other information. A user can also call a mainframe computer, carry out computations on the mainframe via a keyboard, and output the information through the microcomputer. Further, modems let microcomputer users access **electronic bulletin boards**, thereby providing those users with a wide array of information. After the modem is used to call the board, messages can be read from the bulletin board or added to it. Electronic bulletin boards are now available containing financial information, job opportunities, newspapers and magazines, airline schedules and prices, the status of pending legislation, weather data, and almost anything else imaginable.[28]

NETWORKING

New developments in technology which link previously incompatible computers are making large-scale networking of computers more feasible. Such **networking** ties computers together, permitting them to communicate without modems and to access tremendous amounts of information. For instance, local-area networks are turning Travelers Corp. into "one big switch." They are moving around financial data and linking 3,000 databases and thousands of computers in several hundred offices. The company has spent $10 million lay-

With the use of a modem, a microcomputer user can communicate with other computers.

New software has surfaced that takes a shot at overcoming managerial reluctance to step personally into the computer age. Many of these programs are "knowledge-based"—so-called because they permit an executive to tap into compendiums of rules and suggestions for how to handle specific situations, much in the way that some of the popular "how-to" books might do. They deal with negotiating skills, training, strategic planning, and other areas that managers cannot delegate. And they have been written for desktop computers.

"These programs get at the essence of what a manager does," says Jack B. Levine, president of Thoughtware Inc., a new company in Coconut Grove, Florida, that offers 14 managerial programs. "The benefits are not ephemeral. They are real, and they should give people the motivation to use them." Mr. Levine maintains that many of the programs can eliminate the need for off-site management training programs or outside consultants, and that once business people discover this, the market for all types of managerial software will explode to $1 billion annually.

Human Edge Software has five programs that sell for between $50 and $295 each and draw extensively from published literature in psychology dealing with the relationships of managers and their staffs, sales representatives and customers, and people engaged in negotiations.

For example, someone using Human Edge's Ne-

MANAGEMENT IN ACTION 1
MANAGEMENT SOFTWARE TO GET THE BOSS INVOLVED

gotiating Edge program would be asked to agree or disagree with more than 50 statements. A few samples: "Fair play is a losing strategy," "I would rather travel than have a desk job," and "Others on the job count on me to stir up some action."

Next, the user describes the person with whom he or she is about to negotiate. To do this, the user agrees or disagrees with each of more than 40 adjectives such as manipulative, empathetic, precise, and double-dealing.

Lastly, there are a few questions about the circumstances of the meeting, such as whether others will be present, how much time will be available, and whether the two main players will ever bargain with each other again.

After the data are entered, the program generates a 2,500-word character analysis of the person with whom the manager will negotiate and suggests ways in which the user can get the best of the meeting.

Source: Abridged and adapted from Thomas C. Hayes, "Management Software to Get the Boss Involved," *New York Times* (December 2, 1984): 8F. Copyright © 1984 by The New York Times Company. Reprinted by permission.

ing two million feet of cable in its new Manhattan headquarters building so it can ultimately link computers for 8,000 employees. Joseph Brophy, a senior vice-president at Travelers, envisions the day in the 1990s when 400,000 machines, including 30,000 home computers, will be linked to 60 data and claims centers and 300 field offices. This will allow one-stop shopping at the computer screen for auto, health, and life insurance.[29]

Control Applications

While some computer applications, such as the electronic cottage, offer workers additional autonomy and responsibility, computers may also increase management control. Worker performance can be constantly monitored and related to goals and norms. For example, at Fleming Companies, a food wholesaler, workers insert cards in computer terminals when they begin work. The computer tells them how long management thinks a job should take. When they complete their jobs, workers again insert their cards. If they beat the clock, the screen flashes, "Good job." If not, the computer indicates how far below capacity performance is.[30]

Operations Management Applications

Computers now design products, run production lines, check product quality, control machine loads, and guide machines automatically. As we will discuss in the next chapter, computers are essential to material requirements planning. Two additional manufacturing applications are computer-assisted design and computer-controlled production.

COMPUTER-ASSISTED DESIGN

To avenge the loss of the America's Cup to Australia, U.S. designers turned to the computer. They used a program that enabled them to view in three-dimensional diagram form each boat model or model part from any angle and test it against hypothetical competition and sailing conditions.[31] Figure 19–6 shows an example of this procedure, called **computer-assisted design (CAD)**. CAD is a popular tool used by auto makers and architectural firms for speeding up design projects and reducing the number of drafters needed. It has been used in the volatile sportswear industry—in which product lines may change five times a year—to help deal with fashion obsolescence.[32]

COMPUTER-CONTROLLED PRODUCTION

Many businesses use computers to run and control manufacturing processes. For example, **numerical control** is a system that relies on punched tape or some other automatic control mechanism to direct machine operations. Lathes, looms, and riveting machines are often run by numerical control. Computers have been used extensively in chemical production, oil refining, and other industries that involve large-volume processing. Computers also put a layer of dye only a few ten-thousandths of an inch thick on Polaroid film.

COMPUTERS AS DECISION AIDS

Computers are valuable aids to management decision making. Each of the applications discussed in the previous section illustrates use of computers to assist with decision making in particular functional areas. Here, we consider three applications of computers to improvement of decision making per se.

FIGURE 19–6
Computers have become instrumental in rapid completion of design projects.

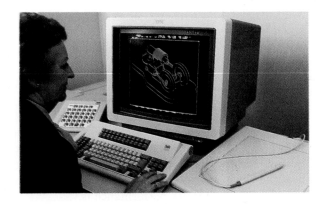

FROM THE FIELD
MICROCOMPUTERS IN
ORGANIZATIONS

We surveyed executives in a variety of industries to learn more about the use of microcomputers in organizations. We asked, "How would you characterize the degree of use of microcomputers in your firm?" On a scale of 1 to 5, with possible responses including 1 (declining rapidly), 3 (neither growing nor declining), and 5 (growing rapidly), the average response was 4.1. The controller of a food-processing firm commented, "Education in the function and use of microcomputers will be an absolute necessity to succeed in the future business world."

The most common applications of the microcomputer were reported to be financial analysis (100%), word processing (85%), statistical analyses (85%), budgeting (85%), and accessing the mainframe computer (80%).

We asked, "What do you see as the major benefits to your firm of the use of microcomputers?" Ranked in decreasing order, the responses were improved efficiency (86%), enhanced flexibility (79%), time savings (71%), improved information access (64%), and cost savings (50%).

To the question, "What do you feel are the chief barriers to the use of microcomputers in your firm?", the five most commonly reported were as follows:

Rank	Barrier	Percent Reporting
1	Cost considerations	50
2	Concerns about confidentiality of information	43
3	Lack of availability of necessary software	28
4	Resistance on the part of management	14
5	Lack of applicability to specific needs of the firm	14

Interestingly, employee resistance, possible malfunctions, and concerns about technological obsolescence were rarely cited as barriers. The vice-president for computers and information systems of an aerospace manufacturing firm added, "Micros have proven to be of great value. However, they do raise questions of management control with respect to software configural control, data accuracy, data integrity, data security, and data element definition."

It is evident that executives see microcomputers as useful and that applications are growing. Executives do feel, though, that microcomputers present new challenges for management.

They are termed decision support systems, decision insight systems, and expert systems.[33]

Decision Support Systems

The term **decision support system (DSS)** refers to a class of systems which support the process of making decisions. They are a type of MIS application that allows managers to ask a series of "what if" questions about the problems they face.

DSS ASSUMPTIONS

The idea of a DSS is based on certain assumptions about the proper role of the computer in decision making.[34] First, a DSS supports, but does not replace, the manager. This takes advantage of computer strengths that are appropriate

Decision support systems include spreadsheet software that enables the user to get quick answers to "what if" questions.

for the problem and leaves the rest to the manager. Second, a DSS is likely to be most helpful for semistructured problems. In such problems, parts of the analysis can be systematized for the computer, but the decision maker's insight and judgment are needed to control the process. Many problems in organizations fall into this category. Third, the word *system* in decision support system suggests that effective problem solving is interactive, employing a dialogue between managers and machines. Finally, since the problem can be only partially structured, and since managers grow in their understanding and needs over time, a DSS must grow and evolve as the user adapts and learns.

DSS SUBSYSTEMS

Decision support systems provide tools to managers which they can use to help them to analyze problem situations systematically. They have four subsystems:[35]

- Interactive capability which enables the user to communicate directly with the system.
- A data manager that makes it possible to extract necessary information from both internal and external databases.
- A modeling subsystem that permits the user to interact with management science models by inputting parameters and tailoring situations to specific decision-making needs.
- An output generator with graphics capability which provides the user with the capability to ask "what if" questions and get output in easily interpretable form.

An example of how such a system will be used for the 1992 Barcelona Olympics is provided in Management in Action 2.

DSS GOALS

Decision support systems aim at increasing managerial effectiveness through an interactive, supportive, evolving process. Steven Alter has suggested that DSSs may enhance effectiveness in at least five ways:[36]

- *Improving personal efficiency.* At a minimum, a manager with a DSS may be able either to perform the same task in less time or to perform the same task more thoroughly in the same amount of time. More optimistically, increased efficiency may mean that a person is performing a more appropriate task in a different way and using less time and effort.
- *Expediting problem solving.* A DSS may ease problem solving by permitting fast access to required data, by improving consistency and accuracy, and by providing better ways of viewing problems.
- *Facilitating interpersonal communication.* DSSs may standardize mechanics and vocabulary. In large, complex organizations, terms may have different meanings across divisions. A DSS defines terms and procedures in standard ways. Also, a DSS provides a conceptual basis for decision making. That is, it can combine separate potential decisions by various people by filtering those decisions through a single model that would estimate the total result. For instance, production, marketing, and finance managers could use the model to show the "objective" effects of one group's proposals on other groups' actions and on the total outcome.

In order to prepare for the 1992 Olympic Games, the city of Barcelona needs to prepare a schedule of the games. This is not a trivial task. At the outset, a huge number of schedules are possible, as more than 2,000 events have to be scheduled in a 15-day period. Although several well-defined constraints help to bring that number down (some obvious, like semifinals having to be played before the finals, or not having two events scheduled at the same time and place, and some less obvious, like tradition saying that the marathon is run the last day of the games, and that swimming and track and field don't go on at the same time), it is still very large.

In such an environment, selecting "the best" possible schedule is not a well-defined problem at all, mainly because it is not clear what is meant by "best" in this context. The problem is one of multiple criteria; for example, a good schedule should try to ensure the maximum audience for each Olympic event, while avoiding inconveniences for the athletes. Or, a schedule in which the number and quality of finals goes in crescendo will probably be perceived as better than a less rhythmic one. At the same time, constraints on available equipment (for example, TV cameras) or personnel (for example, security personnel) have to be met. And one would also like to avoid traffic jams caused by two or more events scheduled in facilities located near each other at approximately the same time. Further, because TV is broadcast live, the time at the Olympic site really is equivalent to

MANAGEMENT IN ACTION 2
DECISION SUPPORT FOR THE 1992 BARCELONA OLYMPICS

different times in different countries, where interest in different sports can vary widely.

In order to help the person preparing the schedule, a DSS was built to allow him or her to develop alternative schedules and to evaluate them in light of various criteria. The DSS, now called SUCCCES92, is very complex internally, containing information about the nature and duration of events, facilities and equipment, traffic flows, TV and live audience characteristics, effectiveness criteria, and many other variables. Despite its internal complexity, SUCCCES-92 is easy to use; it is interactive and contains graphical aids to help compare certain characteristics of a given schedule with those set at the outset as ideal. With the DSS, the person preparing the schedule can develop alternative schedules and evaluate them in light of various criteria. Early reactions to SUCCCES92 have been very positive. The real test will be the 1992 Olympics.

Source: Adapted by permission of R. Andreu and A. Corominas, "SUCCCES92: A DSS for Scheduling the Olympic Games," *Interfaces* 19, no. 5 (September-October 1989): 1-12. Copyright 1989 The Institute of Management Sciences, 290 Westminster Street, Providence, Rhode Island 02903 USA.

- *Promoting learning or training.* Users of a DSS gradually learn the concepts incorporated in the models. In fact, some companies are now explicitly using DSSs as training tools.
- *Increasing organizational control.* Some DSSs have been extended to provide data for purposes of overall organizational control. For instance, the systems may be used to automatically develop reports comparing managers' decisions to those of standard formulas. Of course, in many situations where judgment is required, standard formulas are not available.

There have been many impressive examples of savings and other benefits derived from decision support systems. For instance, the Delco Electronics Division of General Motors has plants in Wisconsin and Mexico which ship finished goods such as radios and speakers to an Indiana facility for product consolidation before order filling and shipping by truck directly to 30 GM assembly plants across the country. While Delco could ship directly from the Delco plants to the GM assembly facilities, saving some inventory costs, this would increase shipping costs since loads would be less than full and schedules would be irregular. Delco developed a decision support system called TRANSPART to examine the tradeoff between its inventory costs and shipping costs. Shipment sizes, shipment frequencies, shipping routes, and other variables were included in the model. TRANSPART was used to examine the total costs of various shipping strategies, resulting in annual savings of $2.9 million. It has now been applied at over 40 GM facilities, with documented savings of $35,000 to $500,000 per year for each application.[37]

Decision Insight Systems

One interesting recent MIS-related development has been dubbed the decision insight system.[38] Unlike a decision support system, which is typically developed for a specific application, the **decision insight system** is aimed at improving decision making in general. That is, its purpose is to lead the manager through the problem-solving process. Such systems are especially useful in ill-structured decision situations.

An **ill-structured, or wicked, decision situation** may be described as non-routine and unprogrammed, with delayed feedback and incomplete information.[39] This difficult situation is typical of many management decisions, especially those at higher, strategic levels. In ill-structured situations, the speed, reliability, lack of emotion, and memory of the computer may serve as valuable complements to the abilities of the human decision maker.

Several decision insight systems have been developed. For instance, STRATANAL (for STRATegic ANALysis) "leads the analyst through a decision process of choosing the right mix of factors for an efficient organizational strategy." CONCORD (for CONference COoRDinator) is a program designed to tutor groups in general strategies for problem solving. DECAID (for Decision Aid) is a collection of heuristic programs to assist in management education and actual strategic management decisions.[40]

One common element of such programs is their general focus; that is, they are each applicable to a broad range of problems. As such, they do not contain databases. Another common element is their complex, tree-like structure. They contain a series of branching instructions to lead the manager through the problem-solving process. For instance, DECAID can be used to address any problem situation (though it is especially helpful when the situation lacks structure). It has stages that help the manager define the problem, generate alternatives, evaluate alternatives, make a choice, question the desirability of the choice, and so on.

Expert Systems

At the National Aeronautics and Space Administration (NASA), turnover in top and middle-level managers, engineers, and scientists threatened to cripple operations within five years. NASA's solution: It turned to intelligent computers to replace its skilled humans.[41] An **expert system** is a computer application that guides the performance of ill-structured tasks, which usually require experience and specialized knowledge (that is, expertise). Using an expert system, a non-expert can achieve performance comparable to that of an expert in that particular problem domain. Expert systems are a sort of decision support system. Their distinguishing characteristic is the knowledge base, the data and decision rules which represent the expertise.[42]

Expert systems often rely on **artificial intelligence (AI)**. With artificial intelligence, a computer can reason as people do, as well as learn from experience and communicate in human language. Complete artificial intelligence has not yet been achieved, but developments are promising. For instance, an expert system named PROSPECTOR was used to find a rich deposit of molybdenum ore buried deep under Mount Tolman in eastern Washington. While geologists had long believed that the ore existed, over 60 years of mining and drilling had failed to yield pay dirt. Written into PROSPECTOR's software was the accumulated knowledge of nine geologists who were intensively interviewed about how they locate minerals from what they observe in the field. This information was reduced to a series of rules and combined with a huge storehouse of geological information. When PROSPECTOR was told to locate the ore, it asked a series of factual questions about the Mount Tolman area. After considering all the answers, it pinpointed the ore in a small, unexplored area ringed by earlier borings and mines.[43]

Many applications of expert systems are now being reported.[44] For instance, expert systems may one day be more common than people on factory floors. They will be the brains that make robots intelligent and flexible. And they will assist engineers and managers in such diverse tasks as designing products, supervising orders and inventories, and coordinating production. An expert system at Hewlett-Packard Co. advises how to manufacture integrated circuits; at Digital Equipment Corp., an expert system manages scheduling on the shop floor.

American Telephone & Telegraph Co.'s expert system called ACE quickly locates faults in telephone cables. It does in an hour a job that previously took a team of technicians a week to accomplish. Digital Equipment spent two years building an expert system that its salespeople use to configure computer systems for their customers. The system has cut error rates from 25 percent to 5 percent, at an estimated annual savings of more than $10 million. Expert systems are also ideally suited to a variety of insurance underwriting and banking tasks, to medical diagnosis, and to almost any other area where expert judgment plays a role.

There are problems associated with expert systems. For one, they are difficult to develop, sometimes requiring several person-years of effort and millions of dollars. Further, it is generally not easy to capture an expert's knowledge to include in such programs. Experts may use complicated problem-solving techniques of which even they are not consciously aware. Further, they may be reluctant to share their valuable knowledge.[45] These problems notwithstanding, expert systems are a promising and exciting new development.

PROBLEMS WITH COMPUTERS

We noted earlier *Time* magazine's choice of the computer as the "greatest influence for good or evil." We have considered many of the potential benefits of computers. Now let's take a look at problems sometimes associated with computers.

Malfunctions

All of us have heard about computer malfunctions. A computer error caused false alarms on the Air Force's NORAD missile detection system, moving us

DOONESBURY   by Garry Trudeau

DOONESBURY. Copyright 1982 by G. B. Trudeau. Reprinted with permission of Universal Press Syndicate. All rights reserved.

to the brink of war. On a smaller scale, computer malfunctions can be devastating for businesses. The increasingly heavy reliance of firms on computers creates a situation of dependence. For instance, business organizations were surveyed to learn how long they would be able to operate without the information-processing capabilities of computers. Many firms reported that they would quickly be immobilized by a major computer failure. After five and a half days without a computer, only 28 percent of operational activities would be functioning. Among finance firms that responded, it was estimated that only 13 percent of operations would be functioning after five and a half days without computing.[46]

Because of the dangers of such malfunctions, some firms are spending millions of dollars to develop backup operations, work out contingency plans, and otherwise prepare for electronic disasters. Nevertheless, specialists say that most firms are ill prepared to cope with failures of critical computer facilities.[47]

Often, of course, computers are blamed for human mistakes. By simply saying, "We had some computer problems," it is easy to shift responsibility to a guileless computer. Such a statement is typically greeted with a resigned nod and the unspoken understanding that "these machines aren't as smart as they think they are."

Errors in Use

Unfortunately, many people operate computers without proper training. Further, users may fail to do routine checks for errors. As one example, there is concern that users of the very popular electronic spreadsheet programs, such as *VisiCalc* and Lotus 1-2-3, may fail to carry out simple checks on the accuracy of their results. One California executive used an electronic spreadsheet on his personal computer to predict that a computer his company planned to introduce would reap $55 million in sales in its first two years. Based on that projection, other managers began making aggressive plans to add staff and inventory. Unfortunately, the executive had failed to include in the program a price discount planned for one key component, thus inflating the sales estimate by $8 million. Had the mistake not been caught, it would have cost the new company profits, momentum, and investor confidence.[48] Managers who routinely check and recheck their own manual computations and logic may fail to do so when using a computer.

Invasion of Privacy

In his novel *Nineteen Eighty-Four*, George Orwell portrayed computers as all-seeing intruders into people's private lives. Our government now has billions of records on individuals, stored on thousands of data systems. Personal finances, health, travels abroad, and traffic violations are among the data that are available from government computers. Because of fears that such systems could be misused, plans to develop even larger networks of computers, such as a massive network called FEDNET tying together all government computers, have been scrapped.

Businesses also have vast quantities of sensitive information. Medical records, past arrest records, or military discharge information could prove harmful to employees if made public. In response to such concerns, firms are spending huge sums on complex access systems and other forms of security. For instance, Metropolitan Life Insurance Company spends from 2 to 3 percent of its annual data processing budget on security precautions and has a staff of six full-time employees guarding its data.[49] Some firms, such as Cummins Engine Company, have refused to computerize their personnel records. Others, including IBM, have removed much information from their files to guard employee privacy. General Electric, Eastman Kodak, and Caterpillar Tractor allow employees access to their files.

Hackers

Hackers—computer buffs who illegally gain access to, and sometimes tamper with, computer files—are becoming a growing threat to businesses. Some see hackers as fun-loving pranksters, others as angry rebels, and still others as wanton criminals. While some hackers' actions, such as interrupting another computer user's work and flashing "Gimme Cookie!" on the screen, may seem harmless, others are very costly to organizations.

The potential danger of hackers was vividly illustrated by a series of incidents in November 1988. Between 9 and 10 P.M. on a Wednesday evening, computers in Berkeley, California, and Cambridge, Massachusetts, slowed to a crawl, the victims of a surprise attack. Shortly thereafter, Princeton University was struck. Before midnight, the National Aeronautics and Space Administration Ames Research Center in California's Silicon Valley, as well as the Los Alamos National Laboratory in New Mexico, were targeted. Then Johns Hopkins University in Baltimore and the University of Michigan in Ann Arbor were hit. In each case, computers mysteriously slowed and ran strange programs. At 2:28 A.M., a Berkeley scientist sent a bulletin around the nation: "We are currently under attack." A "worm," a self-contained program that entered computers via a communications network, had been developed by a Cornell University hacker. When the worm—a form of computer virus—entered a computer, it used information in the computer to establish links with other computers in the network, and it spread rapidly.

Computer buffs who illegally gain access to computer files are becoming a growing threat to businesses.

Fortunately, this virus was relatively benign; it merely used empty storage space. However, it could just as easily have wiped out files, or it could have been programmed to wreak havoc on systems days or months later. Ultimately, a "vaccine" was developed to counter the attack, but only after computer operations were widely disrupted and hundreds of person-years of work went into purging the virus.[50]

Computer Crime

A 25-year-old computer terminal operator used computer trickery to receive pension checks under 30 different names. An accountant working for a fruit wholesaler used a computer to inflate prices on invoices and to send the extra money to dummy vendors. He amassed $1 million over six years. In the infamous Equity Funding fraud, computers were used to build a confusing pyramid of fake assets. By the time the fraud was uncovered, $185 million in fake assets had been created.

Computers have spawned a whole new class of criminals. Often computer experts, these criminals take advantage of flaws in systems or of access to files to steal an estimated $300 million a year. The FBI figures that, while the average armed bank robbery nets about $10,000, computer crimes often bring in more than $1 million.

Robert H. Courtney, a security consultant and former director of data security and privacy for International Business Machine Corp., says the likelihood of prosecution is inversely proportional to the amount of money involved. "The bigger the theft, the greater the embarrassment to the company," he says. One of his clients, an insurance company, lost $38.1 million to a crooked senior officer and didn't report the crime to police.[51]

Terminal Tedium

Some people see computers as the new assembly lines. People who once interacted with one another and carried out at least some physical activities now may sit and stare at video displays for eight or more hours a day. There is concern that such "terminal tedium" may be stressful, and even that there may be health hazards associated with constant exposure to the displays. While most claims of health hazards are now speculative, fears about the consequences of stress and social isolation are harder to dismiss.

Negative Human Reactions

People's reactions to computers run to extremes. Some view them as all-knowing. They treat anything coming out of a computer as "truth," beyond challenge. In fact, of course, what the computer produces is no better than what is put into it and how the computer is instructed to process it. This "garbage in–garbage out" principle is too often forgotten.

Other people fear the computer, believing it will threaten their jobs either by replacing them or by requiring skills they don't have. Others are concerned that they will become too dependent on computers. For still others, the computer represents change and the unknown. Each of these sources of fear may lead to resistance, and all should be seriously considered.

To some extent, computers are becoming more "user friendly." In his science-fantasy story "I Sing the Body Electric," Ray Bradbury wrote of an "electric grandmother," a computerized robot designed to look, talk, and act like a warm, supportive grandmother. Computers are rapidly becoming more grandmotherly.

IMPLICATIONS FOR MANAGEMENT

It would be inconceivable for a firm to ignore such resources as personnel, materials, and finances. Until recently, though, information was the neglected sibling of the resource family. This situation is rapidly changing. The impact of information and information systems on organizations and their members can hardly be overestimated, and all signs suggest that such impact will continue to grow.

Like other resources, information must be used intelligently and managed carefully. Just as an inventory-control system or a human resource development system is designed to fit a particular organization with its own specific characteristics, an information system must be tailored to the particular situation. Organizational structure, technology, and context should all be evaluated in designing and implementing an MIS.

Further, information systems represent not only a remarkable technological development but also a major social change. As with any social change, the human factor must be considered. Since changes in information technology have a direct impact on members of organizations, and since the acceptance of that change is crucial to its success, the needs of MIS users must be considered if the MIS is to be successful. In many cases, user involvement in the design and implementation process may be necessary.

Computers are becoming pervasive in organizations, and there seems to be no end to their potential applications. They are involved in all stages of the management process, and as a manager you will have to be prepared to use and deal with them.

An increasing number of jobs in organizations will be intimately tied to computer use. If you find yourself in such a position, it will obviously be critical that you master computer skills. Since your future career moves are to some degree uncertain, anticipate such needs.

Further, with the growth in use of microcomputers, you are likely to find yourself using computers on a regular basis. They will be an integral part of almost any job, much like a typewriter or file cabinet. You may turn to a computer to write a memo, check the latest quote on oil prices, design an object, sort customer lists, or make a decision. Basic computer literacy will become a selection criterion for many positions, even those seemingly far removed from information management. Actively seek opportunities to become acquainted and comfortable with microcomputers.

Whether or not you personally use computers, you and your job will be influenced by them. You may be selected by a computer, trained by a computer, and monitored by a computer. Your boss may turn to a computer to decide how to supervise and reward you, and may use a computer to plot your career moves. Computers may influence the amount of authority you receive and may dictate with whom—if anyone—you directly interact. Computers will permeate the fabric of organizations.

The presence of computers will cause managers to face some difficult questions. Should computers be used as control devices? Who should have access to their information? What steps should be taken to prevent abuse and unauthorized access? What can or should be done to counteract the depersonalizing influences of computers? Should decisions be turned over to computers? You will find yourself facing these and other questions on a regular basis. Give serious thought to the issues raised in this chapter so that you will be prepared to respond to these emerging issues.

Remember that computers are tools, not crutches. They will not transform bad inputs into good outputs. They will not make a dull idea creative. They will not accept ultimate responsibility for bad decisions. Try to take advantage of the benefits of computers, but don't be lulled into complacency.

The impact of information technology is really just beginning to be felt. It is already clear that basic changes at the levels of society, industries, organizations, and individuals will result. The organizations you will manage will be fundamentally different from those of 20 years ago and, quite likely, those of today. Welcome to interesting times.

KEY TERMS AND CONCEPTS

artificial intelligence (AI)
boundary spanners
computer-assisted design (CAD)
decision insight system
decision support system (DSS)
electronic bulletin boards
electronic cottage
expert system
gatekeepers
hackers
ill-structured, or wicked, decision
    situation

information
information resource management
management information system (MIS)
modem
networking
numerical control
primary data sources
secondary data sources
task knowledge
task variety
uncertainty absorbers

QUESTIONS FOR REVIEW AND DISCUSSION

1. In what ways is information a resource? How does information *differ* from other resources? What might be some implications of those differences for the design of an MIS?
2. What sorts of impacts do you think MIS and DSS might have on leadership? On job design?
3. Describe a management situation in which you think a formal MIS would *not* be helpful.
4. Do you think that formal information systems pose dangers to organizations? To society? Why or why not?
5. Is it right for managers to use computers to monitor employee performance? Is such monitoring different from other forms of control?
6. What are the key benefits of the interactive capability of decision support systems?
7. What sorts of people do you think would be most enthusiastic about the use of expert systems? Who might be most likely to oppose them?

8. Do you think the benefits of giving computers access to tremendous amounts of information about individuals and businesses outweigh the costs? Justify your conclusion.

9. Should hackers be dealt with more severely? Why or why not?

10. In your opinion, are current microcomputers really user friendly? What would be the characteristics of a *totally* user friendly computer?

CASES

19–1 COMPUTERIZING THE FAST TRACK

The career paths of a growing number of corporate managers are now being charted on computers. With the advent of software designed to monitor executive talent, personnel specialists are using computers to plan successions, regulate affirmative-action programs, and watch out for junior managers on their way up. Human resources consultants say that, just as electronic spreadsheets improved financial planning by making complex projections easy to do, computerized executive-tracking systems are improving personnel planning.

Computers increase objectivity and allow for a wider scope when considering candidates for promotion, personnel managers claim, thus loosening the ties of the old-boy networks that govern movement within many companies. And, by uncovering inside talent, they lessen dependence on headhunters and can reduce the cost and disruption of outside hiring.

For example, Southland Corp., the Dallas-based parent of the 7-Eleven convenience store chain, has computerized its search for fast-trackers. Twice yearly, Southland managers file reports about the promotability of their subordinates. By consolidating the reports on a computer, "We find out whether there will be a deficit of people coming up through the ranks," says Blake Frank, Southland's manager of personnel research. A separate program helps produce career development plans, pinpointing weaknesses and suggesting solutions—university courses, in-house training, a different job, or a special assignment.

Many personnel departments, for these applications and others, are writing their own executive-management programs or snapping up the half-dozen sold by independent companies. Frank Gains, a Greenwich, Connecticut, consultant who ran Exxon Corp.'s executive development program for 15 years, says, "It's like playing chess; you're trying to optimize every vacancy. With the computer, you can play the game and consider more alternatives."

Fast-growing companies often need computerized tracking systems to find scarce talent. But mature companies need them to discover good people who might be stalled. Similarly, affirmative-action software makes it easy to locate areas in which there are few women and minorities and then find qualified people who might be overlooked in informal brainstorming sessions.

Source: Reprinted by permission of *The Wall Street Journal*, © Dow Jones & Company, Inc. (September 18, 1985). All Rights Reserved Worldwide.

1. Which of the strengths of computers do programs such as these incorporate?
2. What are the benefits of computer programs for career-planning purposes? The costs and dangers?
3. Would you like your career to be charted by a computer? Why or why not?

19–2 INFORMATION AND TIMING

Of the thousands of phone lines at Merrill Lynch & Co.'s trading desks, seven are confidential. Only the chief of block trading uses them when he wants information fast, without alerting anyone else in the trading room. Several of them go straight to New York's biggest banks. Another line reaches Merrill Lynch's chairman, William Schreyer. And one line goes to the firm's most powerful customer: Michael Steinhardt.

When Merrill Lynch phones Mr. Steinhardt, it reaches a pudgy 45-year-old in a polo shirt who can sometimes be found eating Japanese takeout food at his desk. But appearances deceive; Mr. Steinhardt has built up one of the nation's most feared and respected private investment firms. Last year, Steinhardt Partners earned as much as 56 percent on its portfolios, nearly double the market's gain. Assets have surged to more than $600 million including at least $50 million of Mr. Steinhardt's own money.

Much of Mr. Steinhardt's clout comes from his rapid-fire—and sometimes controversial—trading. He will buy a stock in the morning, then sell it two hours later at a profit. He spends $22 million a year in brokerage commissions, putting him in the same league as the biggest institutions.

Brokers salivate for these commission dollars. As a result, Wall Street's top firms gladly swap market insights with Mr. Steinhardt several times a day. "Sometimes his market intelligence is better than ours," says a Merrill Lynch executive.

A look at Mr. Steinhardt's recent trading shows how he combines intensity, charm, and a far-reaching information network to make profits. From his 33rd-floor office in midtown Manhattan, he storms into dozens of different stocks. And in one case, an informant passes on what Mr. Steinhardt calls "fancy information"—a tip that helps him make $90,000 in an afternoon's trading.

All through the day, phone calls bring Mr. Steinhardt the news he needs. Other investors study annual reports, read trade journals, or visit companies to get investment ideas. Not Mr. Steinhardt. He thinks the last time he visited a company was in 1973. Instead, he munches on bran muffins and hears daily from Wall Street personalities.

Mr. Steinhardt's office layout reveals his fondness for split-second decisions. Instead of a normal desk, Mr. Steinhardt sits at the helm of an L-shaped trading juggernaut. Six video screens surround him. They churn out a running tape of stock trades, the latest headlines, and prices of more than 100 securities he owns. No matter what Mr. Steinhardt discusses, one eye is always on the screens.

Above all, Mr. Steinhardt wants profits. With an ear to the rumor mill last summer, he bought at least 250,000 shares of General Foods Corp. just before Philip Morris agreed to acquire the company. "We're nimble enough that we can quickly buy 200,000 shares if something seems to be happening," an aide says.

Source: Reprinted by permission of *The Wall Street Journal*, © Dow Jones & Company, Inc. (March 3, 1986). All Rights Reserved Worldwide.

1. In what ways is information a resource to Mr. Steinhardt?
2. Analyze the information acquired by Mr. Steinhardt in terms of the dimensions discussed in this chapter. Are the characteristics appropriate to the task?
3. Does Mr. Steinhardt have a management information system? Why or why not?

ENDNOTES

1. *Business Week* (August 22, 1983): 98.
2. D. Seligman, "Life Will Be Different When We're All On-Line," *Fortune* (February 4, 1985): 68-72.
3. *Business Week* (September 13, 1982): 118, 123.
4. *Data Management* (November 1981): 43.
5. For detailed discussions of information and information management, see J. G. Burch, Jr., and G. Grudnitski, *Information Systems: Theory and Practice*, 5th ed. (New York: John

Wiley & Sons, 1989); B. R. Ricks and K. F. Gow, *Information Resource Management*, 2d ed. (Cincinnati: South-Western Publishing Co., 1988); and J. F. Magee, "What Information Technology Has in Store for Managers," *Sloan Management Review* (Winter 1985): 45-49.

6. H. Mintzberg, "The Manager's Job: Folklore and Fact," *Harvard Business Review* 53 (1975): 49-61.

7. M. U. Porat, "The Information Economy" Unpublished thesis, Stanford University. As reported in *Wall Street Journal* (February 23, 1981): 1.

8. *Business Week* (August 22, 1983): 98.

9. R. A. Andrus, "Approaches to Information Evaluation," *MSU Business Topics* (Summer 1971): 42-43.

10. R. H. Gregory and R. L. Van Horn, "Value and Cost of Information," in *Systems Analysis Techniques*, ed. J. D. Couger and R. W. Knapp (New York: John Wiley & Sons, 1974), 473-489.

11. For further discussions of management information systems, see G. B. Davis and M. H. Olson, *Management Information Systems: Conceptual Foundations, Structure, and Development*, 2d ed. (New York: McGraw-Hill, 1985); J. C. Weatherbe, *Executive Guide to Computer-Based Information Systems* (Englewood Cliffs, NJ: Prentice-Hall, 1983); and J. I. Cash, Jr., F. W. McFarlan, J. L. McKenney, and M. R. Vitale, *Corporate Information Systems Management*, 2d ed. (Homewood, IL: Irwin, 1988).

12. This section is based in part on R. G. Murdick and J. E. Ross, *Management Information Systems* (Englewood Cliffs, NJ: Prentice-Hall, 1977), 8, 147, 149.

13. People preferring details are called sensing types while those preferring the "big picture" are called intuitives.

14. These are drawn in part from J. O. McClain and L. J. Thomas, *Operations Management: Production of Goods and Services* (Englewood Cliffs, NJ: Prentice-Hall, 1985), 215, and Weatherbe, *Computer-Based Information Systems*, 151. The first point is empirically demonstrated by P. H. Cheney and G. W. Dickson, "Organizational Characteristics and Information Systems: An Exploratory Investigation," *Academy of Management Journal* 25 (1982): 170-184.

15. K. Kaiser and A. Srinivasan, "User-Analyst Differences: An Empirical Investigation of Attitudes Related to Systems Development," *Academy of Management Journal* 25 (1982): 630-631.

16. For instance, see J. J. Baroudi, M. H. Olson, and B. Ives, "An Empirical Study of the Impact of User Involvement on System Usage and Information Satisfaction," *Communications of the ACM* 29 (1986): 232-238, and W. J. Doll and G. Torkzadeh, "A Discrepancy Model of End-User Computing Involvement," *Management Science*, 10 (1989): 1151-1171.

17. R. L. Daft and N. B. MacIntosh, "A New Approach to Design and Use of Management Information," *California Management Review* 21 (1978): 82-92.

18. See R. W. Zmud, "Individual Differences and MIS Success: A Review of the Empirical Literature," *Management Science* 25 (1979):975. This issue is far from resolved. George Huber in "Cognitive Style as a Basis for MIS and DSS Designs," for instance, has argued that considering cognitive style in MIS design—a favorite target of study—is "much ado about nothing" (p. 567). For more on this issue, see I. Benbasat and R. N. Taylor, "The Impact of Cognitive Styles on Information System Design," *MIS Quarterly* (June 1978): 43-54; Davis and Olson, *Management Information Systems*; Kaiser and Srinivasan, "User-Analyst Differences"; D. Robey, "User Attitudes and Management Information System Use," *Academy of Management Journal* 22 (1979): 527-538; and D. Robey and W. Taggart, "Measuring Managers' Minds: The Assessment of Style in Human Information Processing," *Academy of Management Review* 6 (1981): 375-383.

19. G. Anthony Gorry and M. S. Scott Morton, "A Framework for Management Information Systems," *Sloan Management Review* (Fall 1971): 55-70.

20. For more on the impact of information technology on competitive strategies, see F. W. McFarlan, "Information Technology Changes the Way You Compete," *Harvard Business Review* (May-June 1984): 98-103, and G. L. Parsons, "Information Technology: A New Competitive Weapon," *Sloan Management Review* (Fall 1983): 3-13.

21. For an interesting discussion of alternative scenarios about organizational impacts of information systems, see D. J. Power, "The Impact of Information Management on the Organization: Two Scenarios," *MIS Quarterly* 7, no. 3 (1983): 13-20.

22. C. Argyris, "Management Information Systems: The Challenge to Rationality and Emotionality," *Management Science* 17 (1971): B275-B292.

23. For more on this point, see P. G. Keen and M. S. Scott Morton, *Decision Support Systems* (Reading, MA: Addison-Wesley, 1978).

24. These examples are drawn from J. Main, "Work Won't Be the Same Again," *Fortune* (June 28, 1982): 58-65.

25. See, for instance, T. S. Darany, "Computer Applications to Personnel (Releasing the Genie — Harnessing the Dragon)," *Public Personnel Management Journal* (Winter 1984): 451-473, and M. A. McDaniel and F. L. Schmidt, "Computer-Assisted Staffing Systems: The Use of Computers in Implementing Meta-Analysis and Utility Research in Personnel Selection," *Public Personnel Management* (Spring 1989): 75-86.

26. S. Feinstein, "Computers Replacing Interviewers for Personnel and Marketing Tasks," *Wall Street Journal* (October 9, 1986): 35.

27. J. Main, "New Ways to Teach Workers What's New," *Fortune* (October 1, 1984): 85, 86, 90, 92, 94. See also H. L. Schuette, "Educating Executives: Computers Bring the Factory into the Classroom," *Management Review* (March 1984): 15-21; S. Schwade, "Is It Time to Consider Computer-Based Training?" *Personnel Administrator* (February 1985): 25-35; and W. A. Kleinschrod, "The Trend to Electronic Training," *Administrative Management* (April 1988): 29-33.

28. Seligman, "Life Will Be Different."

29. D. Kneale, "Computer Caution: Linking of Office PCs Is Coming, but Plenty of Obstacles Remain," *Wall Street Journal* (January 28, 1986): 1, 20.

30. "Fleming's Fast Rise in Wholesale Foods," *Fortune* (January 21, 1985): 54.

31. G. Bronson, "Shiver Me Bits and Bytes," *Forbes* (June 2, 1986): 214-216.

32. K. H. Shaffir, "Information Technology for the Manufacturer," *Management Review* (November 1985): 61-62.

33. A fourth approach involves designing a computer model of the specific decision maker, called a model of man, and using that model to replace the decision maker. Such models may free the decision maker's time, provide insight concerning how he or she uses information, and serve as training tools for novices. Also, since they don't get fatigued or have mood swings or mental lapses, the models are perfectly reliable, and thus potentially more valid than the decision maker who was modeled. For instance, see L. R. Goldberg, "Man Versus Models of Man: A Rationale, Plus Some Evidence, for a Method of Improving on Clinical Inferences," *Psychological Bulletin* 73 (1970): 422-432, and I. Zimmer, "A Comparison of the Prediction Accuracy of Loan Officers and Their Linear-Additive Models," *Organizational Behavior and Human Performance* 27 (1981): 69-74.

34. Davis and Olson, *Management Information Systems*, 368-369. For more on decision support systems, see G. P. Huber, "Decision Support Systems: Their Present Nature and Future Applications," in *Decision Making: An Interdisciplinary Inquiry*, ed. G. R. Ungson and D. N. Braunstein (Boston: Kent Publishing Co., 1982); R. J. Sprague, Jr., and E. D. Carlson, *Building Effective Decision Support Systems* (Englewood Cliffs, NJ: Prentice-Hall, 1982); M. S. Silver, "Descriptive Analysis for Computer-Based Decision Support," *Operations Research* 36 (1988): 904-916; R. Sharda, S. H. Barr, and J. C. McDonnell, "Decision Support System Effectiveness: A Review and an Empirical Test," *Management Science* 34 (1988): 139-159; and R. Sabherwal and V. Grover, "Computer Support for Strategic Decision-Making Processes: Review and Analysis," *Decision Sciences* 20 (1989): 54-76.

35. R. D. Anderson, D. J. Sweeney, and T. A. Williams, *An Introduction to Management Science*, 4th ed. (St. Paul, MN: West Publishing Co., 1985), 722.

36. This listing is condensed from S. L. Alter, *Decision Support Systems: Current Practice and Continuing Challenges* (Reading, MA: Addison-Wesley, 1980), 95-104.

37. D. E. Blumenfeld, L. D. Burns, C. F. Daganzo, M. C. Frick, and R. W. Hall, "Reducing Logistics Costs at General Motors," *Interfaces* (January-February 1987): 26-47. For a discussion of how a DSS for planning and scheduling of blender operations saves Texaco $30 million annually, see C. W. DeWitt, L. S. Lasdon, A. D. Warren, D. A. Brenner, and S. A. Melhem, "OMEGA: An Improved Gasoline Blending System for Texaco," *Interfaces* (January-February 1989): 85-101.

38. There is considerable confusion over terminology in the MIS area. The term decision insight system is suggested by B. Golden, A. Hevner, and D. J. Power, "Decision Insight Systems: A Critical Evaluation," *Computers and Operations Research* 13, nos. 2-3 (1986): 287-300. It is used here to differentiate these systems from decision support systems which rely on data bases, are task specific, and are less applicable to ill-structured situations.

39. C. Churchman, "Wicked Problems," *Management Science* 14 (1967): B141-B142.

40. For more information on these and other decision insight systems, and for an evaluation of DECAID, see R. J. Aldag and D. J. Power, "An Empirical Assessment of Computer-Assisted Decision Analysis," *Decision Sciences* 17 (1986): 572-588.

41. W. J. Broad, "'Smart' Machines Ready to Assume Many NASA Duties," *New York Times* (March 6, 1989): 1, 11.

42. Davis and Olson, *Management Information Systems*, 375. For more on expert systems, see C. W. Holsapple and A. B. Whinston, *Business Expert Systems* (Homewood, IL: Irwin, 1987); W. E. Leigh and M. E. Doherty, *Decision Support and Expert Systems* (Cincinnati, OH: South-Western Publishing Company, 1986); and T. Liang, "Development of a Knowledge-Based Model Management System," *Operations Research* 36 (1988): 849-863.

43. *Business Week* (July 9, 1984): 54-55.

44. Ibid., 54-62.

45. For an interesting example, see F. Rose, "An 'Electronic Clone' of a Skilled Engineer Is Very Hard to Create," *Wall Street Journal* (August 12, 1988): 1, 14.

46. D. O. Aasgaard et al., "An Evaluation of Data Processing 'Machine Room' Loss and Selected Recovery Strategies," University of Minnesota, Management Information Systems Research Center WP-79-04, p. 70.

47. On this point, see W. L. Wall, "Few Firms Plan Well for Mishaps That Disable Computer Facilities," *Wall Street Journal* (May 31, 1988): 25.

48. "How Personal Computers Can Trip Up Executives," *Business Week* (September 24, 1984): 94.

49. "Computer Security: What Can Be Done?" *Business Week* (September 26, 1983): 126.

50. "How Computer Science Was Caught Off Guard by One Young Hacker," *Wall Street Journal* (November 7, 1988): A1, A4. See also A. Q. Nomani, "'Bug Busters' Devise Electronic Vaccines for Computer Viruses," *Wall Street Journal* (June 17, 1988): 1, 8, and D. Stipp and B. Davis, "New Computer Break-Ins Suggest 'Virus' May Have Spurred Hackers," *Wall Street Journal* (December 2, 1988): B4.

51. E. Larson, "Crook's Tool: Computers Turn Out to Be Valuable Aid in Employee Crime," *Wall Street Journal* (January 14, 1985): 1, 10.

Operations Management

CHAPTER 20

After studying this chapter, you should be able to:
- *Discuss the strategic role of operations management.*
- *Describe five types of transformation processes.*
- *List the steps in capacity planning.*
- *Identify key cost and noncost considerations in facility location.*
- *Describe four types of facility layout.*
- *Explain the purchasing cycle.*
- *Identify the basic elements of inventory control and discuss just-in-time systems and material requirements planning.*
- *Identify the steps in the production planning and control process.*
- *Define quality control and discuss how statistical quality control and quality circles work.*
- *Describe three basic forms of maintenance.*
- *Discuss the factory of the future, including the role of robotics.*

Hewlett-Packard executive George Henry got a startling bit of advice on a 1982 trip to Japan. "You Americans are so good at agriculture," said a Japanese business executive. "Why don't you go back to agriculture and leave manufacturing to us?"[1] Events of recent years suggest that, however reluctantly, American firms have in fact increasingly been leaving manufacturing to foreign competitors. For the last two decades, the "Made in America" label has been vanishing as overseas manufacturers dominate entire industries. In 1969 U.S. manufacturers produced 82 percent of the nation's television sets, 88 percent of its cars, and 90 percent of its machine tools. Today, they produce almost no TVs and have given up half the domestic machine-tool market and 30 percent of the auto market. Even in the new area of semiconductors, the United States' world market share plunged from 85 percent in 1980 to 15 percent in 1989.[2]

Maintaining satisfactory productivity and quality are among the most pressing challenges facing American business today. Though the absolute level of productivity in the United States is still quite high relative to other nations, in recent decades the growth rate of productivity has not compared so favorably. While output per worker grew at a rate of more than 2 percent per year in the 1960s, the annual growth rate since 1973 has averaged less than 1 percent. Over that period, productivity growth rates in countries such as West Germany, Japan, France, and the United Kingdom were substantially greater.[3] A "productivity paradox" exists: American manufacturers have been putting almost $20 billion a year into automation and there are productivity czars, committees, and campaigns across the country, but there has been relatively little to show for it. While there has been a productivity upturn since 1982, it has been less impressive than other postwar upturns, and many doubt that it will be sustained.[4] Quality differentials between U.S. products and those of other developed countries have also generally narrowed in recent years, if not reversed. Meeting these productivity and quality challenges will depend largely on operations management.

Many U.S. firms are taking active steps to use operations management to counter foreign threats. For instance, Management in Action 1 shows how three U.S. companies are responding. Note that the changes in technology and structure represented in these examples are not carried out in isolation from the other sorts of steps we have discussed in previous chapters. Instead, operations changes are often coupled with altered authority relationships, job design, and reward systems. Note also that American firms are sometimes taking on foreign partners to tackle global challenges.

In this chapter we will explore the nature of operations and operations management. We will examine capacity planning, facility location, and facility design and layout. We will discuss materials purchasing, inventory control, and the production planning process. Then, we will consider quality control and maintenance policies. Finally, we will take a look at the factory of the future, including the role of robotics. Throughout the chapter, we will see that operations management plays a central role in firms' strategic arsenals.

THE NATURE OF OPERATIONS AND OPERATIONS MANAGEMENT

Let's first examine the nature of operations and operations management and the tasks of the operations manager.

Stiffer competition from foreign firms forced General Electric Co. managers to restructure the company's circuit breaker business from top to bottom.

MANAGEMENT IN ACTION 1
MEETING FOREIGN CHALLENGES WITH OPERATIONS MANAGEMENT

In short order, they decided to consolidate the circuit breaker's unit at one automated assembly plant in Salisbury, N.C., and shut five others in diverse U.S. locations. They also simplified the box's design, reducing its total parts to 1,275 from some 28,000. Furthermore, they installed a computerized system so that with each order, the factory machines were automatically programmed to make the boxes. In addition, GE eliminated all line supervisors and quality inspectors and gave those middle-management responsibilities to production workers. These people and process changes have sparked impressive results. Productivity jumped 20 percent while manufacturing costs declined 30 percent in a year. Most telling: it now takes just three days—not three weeks—to fill an order, and the plant's backlog has dropped to two days from three weeks.

Corning Glass Works undertook a similar approach to GE with two new factories that manufacture pollution-control devices. The Corning, N.Y., company examined each of the 235 manufacturing steps involved, eliminating 115 unnecessary operations to cut production time to three days from four weeks. At the same time, Corning insisted on just two job classifications at the plant: operations associate and maintenance engineer. Plants now have just a single layer between workers and plant managers. While the plants are unionized, all workers will next year begin receiving bonuses for achieving goals.

Some manufacturers are edging toward so-called small-batch manufacturing, using advanced computer technology to make a broader array of products quicker. Surprisingly, one is a casket manufacturer. With automated equipment, Batesville, Ind.-based Hillenbrand has slashed the time in which it can turn out a casket model from an array of designs. On a larger scale, a Charlottesville, Va., plant operated jointly by General Electric and Japan's Fanuc Ltd. has automated the production of sophisticated programmable logic controllers used in factory automation equipment. The plant is capable of custom making each controller in batch sizes of one—at a competitive price—to fit customers' needs.

Operations

Operations include any process that accepts inputs and uses resources to change those inputs in useful ways.[5] A basic operations system is shown in Figure 20–1. Inputs to the system include labor, capital, and materials. The **transformation process** alters the inputs in some useful way. The outputs are goods or services. The nature of the outputs may provide feedback to those responsible for both the inputs and the facility concerning needed changes in quality, strategy, or other factors.

Inputs may be transformed in a variety of ways. An assembly line, in which a radio or other product moves from one workstation to the next, is an example of a process involving a transformation in form. Whenever raw and semifinished materials are processed and converted into finished products, a form transformation occurs. In a synthetic transformation process, basic parts, components, or chemicals are combined to form a finished product. The production of appliances from steel, plastic, and other inputs is an example of a synthetic transformation in form. In an analytic transformation process, a basic material is broken down into one or more final products. Examples include the refining of iron ore or crude oil and the milling of logs into lumber, plywood, composite board, and other building materials.

Inputs can also be transformed in time or space—temporal transformation and spatial transformation, respectively. Storage is an example of a temporal

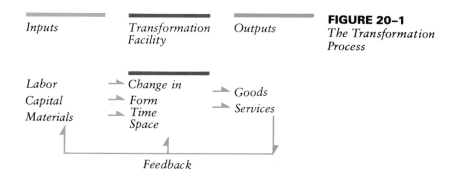

FIGURE 20–1
The Transformation Process

transformation. Rental warehouse space is the output, and it is purchased for a period of time. A transportation service, such as commercial air travel or package shipment via Federal Express, is an example of a spatial transformation. Here, the transformation process involves the movement of people or packages from one place to another.

As these examples show, operations may include both production operations and service operations. Production operations, aimed at producing goods, include such organizations as computer manufacturers, building contractors, and coal mines. The goal of service operations, such as a hospital, university, or bank, is to provide personal services. Figure 20–2 shows examples of production and service operations, based on the degree of process repetitiveness and the purpose of the operation. While there are some basic differences between production and service operations, many operations management techniques can be applied to either.

Operations Management

Operations management is the process of planning, organizing, and controlling operations to reach objectives efficiently and effectively.[6] As we will see, this may include such activities as capacity planning, purchasing, quality control, and maintenance. Again, while operations management is often associated with production operations (owing in part to common use of the term production management to describe the area), it is equally relevant for service operations.

The refining of crude oil is an analytic transformation process.

Degree of Process Repetitiveness	TYPE OF OPERATION—PRODUCTION		
	Manufacturing	Converting	Repairing
Continuous flow	Paper mill	Electrical power plant	Water-treatment plant
Mass	Automobile assembly plant	Open-pit coal mine	Large auto paint shop
Large batch	Winery	Scrap-metal reduction plant	Road-repair contractor
Job lot	Furniture maker	Custom slaughterhouse	Auto-body shop
Unique item	Office-building construction firm	Ship salvage company	Major ship-repair yard

Degree of Process Repetitiveness	TYPE OF OPERATION—SERVICE		
	Protection	Logistics	Well-Being
Continuous flow	Prison	Gas pipeline	Hospital intensive-care ward
Mass	U.S. Secret Service	Airline	Public school
Large batch	Traffic court	Grain elevator	Military basic-training camp
Job lot	Fire department	Trucking firm	Travel tour guide
Unique item	Lloyd's of London insurance	House mover	Management consulting firm

Source: Stephen E. Barndt and Davis W. Carvey, *Essentials of Operations Management*, © 1982, p. 9. Reprinted by permission of Prentice-Hall, Inc., Englewood Cliffs, NJ.

FIGURE 20–2
Examples of Operations

The Tasks of the Operations Manager

Economists make a basic distinction between the short run and the long run. In the short run, the basic plant and equipment cannot be changed in size or design; in the long run, they can. That is to say, production capacity of the plant is fixed in the short run but variable in the long run.

The operations manager's task in the short run is to use existing facilities in the best ways possible through such actions as proper maintenance, inventory control, and production scheduling. In particular, the operations manager can:

- Vary the amount or type of inputs such as by purchasing fewer materials.
- Use the facility more effectively through multishift operations, overtime, or improved work methods.
- Temporarily add capacity by hiring another company to do part of the work (this is called subcontracting).

Over the long run, the operations manager's job is to search for ways to improve existing facilities and to modify or expand them as needed. Inland Steel Company, the nation's seventh-largest steel producer, recently completed a $1 billion plant expansion and modernization program to lower production costs, improve product quality, and increase its share of the steel market.

CAPACITY PLANNING[7]

The capacity planning of a firm is a primary reflection of its long-range operations strategy. In capacity planning, the firm must consider many issues, such as market size and trends, probable technological changes in products or services, the possible addition of new products or services, the likelihood that new production methods will be developed in the future, and the desirability of a single or multiple facilities.

The process of capacity planning includes several steps. First, future demand must be predicted. Then, these predictions are translated into physical capacity requirements. Next, alternative capacity plans related to these requirements are generated; these might involve decisions concerning adding capacity, using overtime or multiple shifts, employing outside capacity sources, or absorbing lost sales. The economic effects, risks, and strategic effects of these alternative plans are then analyzed. Plans may have an impact on economies of scale, competition, flexibility of operations, market locations, labor policies, market share, and so on. Finally, a plan for implementation is needed.

Capacity planning involves the operations manager in decisions with key strategic implications. These decisions interface with such functional areas as marketing, finance, and engineering and have an impact on most other operations management activities.

FACILITY LOCATION

For most companies, the decision of where to locate a new facility or to relocate an old facility is critical. The location of a manufacturing plant with respect to raw materials, a skilled work force, or customer markets can mean the difference between success and failure. Firms compete with one another by keeping transportation, labor, and distribution costs low. A bioengineering firm without a nearby supply of college graduates or a sod farm located far from its customers would be at a severe competitive disadvantage.

Figure 20–3 suggests some important factors in facility location decisions. As the figure shows, the decisions involve both cost and noncost factors. When General Motors was deciding on the location of its new Saturn plant, it used computers to weigh the many relevant variables. States competed aggressively for the facility.

In times of economic slump, states and localities work especially hard to attract desirable industries. Many states have recently been granting tax breaks to attract firms. In addition, Ireland, Puerto Rico, and Canada are actively vying for new facilities. Federal minimum wage laws and other nationwide standards may make locating outside the United States more attractive in years to come.

FACILITY DESIGN AND LAYOUT

The goal of facility design and layout is to develop a plan that, when executed, will result in a businesslike environment that allows and promotes ef-

Factors	Industry Where This Might Be Especially Important	Recent Developments
Cost Factors		
Labor Costs	Apparel	Labor costs tripled from 1970 to 1986, but minimum wage laws and nationwide competition for skilled labor have acted to even costs out across the country. Labor costs tend to be higher in unionized areas.
Transportation Costs	Cement	These have gone up very rapidly in the last fifteen years. Trucking rates more than doubled and rail rates went up more than fourfold.
Construction Costs	Warehousing	These have more than doubled since 1975. They tend to be lower in areas where unions are less dominant, such as the South and West.
Utility Costs	Steel	Energy resources are quickly being used up. Costs are skyrocketing and will continue to be a major consideration.
Taxes	Oil	Many states and territories (particularly Puerto Rico) are now giving industries substantial tax breaks.
Noncost Factors		
Environmental Conditions	Paper	New laws and social pressure have had great impact on many companies. Industry has spent tremendous amounts on air pollution and waste disposal equipment.
Living Conditions	High Technology	Many employees are no longer willing to just go where the company tells them. Quality of life in the community is becoming more important.
Availability of Resources	Canning	Industry use of water will increase substantially by the year 2000. Supplies are low in Los Angeles, Denver, and Chicago. The Gulf Coast from Texas to Alabama suffers from a shortage of groundwater.
Availability of Skilled Labor	Genetic Engineering	The labor force will decline in numbers in coming years, creating new labor shortages.

Source: William H. Cunningham, Ramon J. Aldag, and Christopher M. Swift, *Introduction to Business*, 2d ed. (Cincinnati: South-Western Publishing Co., 1989), p. 268. Reproduced with permission.

FIGURE 20–3
Factors in Facility Location Decisions

ficiency. Specifically, facility design and layout efforts try to reduce the machine and employee idle time otherwise resulting from unnecessary movement, bottlenecks, and uneven utilization; minimize in-process inventories; minimize materials-handling costs; minimize facilities operation and maintenance costs; and provide a safe and pleasant place to work and do business.[8]

Depending on the function of the facility, facility layouts may be classified as process layouts, product layouts, group technology layouts, and fixed-position layouts. A **process layout** groups work of a similar function in a single department or work center. In a clinic, for instance, radiology may be in one location, occupational therapy in another, and internal medicine in yet another.

In a **product layout,** the organization of the work is dictated by the sequence of production or service steps common to all jobs. Parts move from one operation to the next with a minimum of movement required. The auto assembly line is a well-known form.

A **group technology layout** groups dissimilar machines into work centers (or cells) to work on products having similar shapes and processing requirements. A group technology layout is similar to a process layout in that cells are designed to perform a specific set of processes, and it is similar to a product layout in that the cells are dedicated to a limited range of products. This layout may foster employee motivation since cells consist of a few workers who form a work team and turn out complete units of work. There should also be less in-process inventory and material handling; a cell combines several production stages, so fewer parts travel through the shop. Further, production setup should be faster since fewer jobs mean reduced tooling and thus faster tooling changes.[9]

Finally, in a **fixed-position layout** the workers, rather than the material or part, move from one work center or machine to another. Such a layout is used when the product is very large, such as an aircraft carrier, or could be damaged by movement. The fixed-position layout is costly since tools and skills are duplicated across projects, so it is generally used only when there is no good alternative. One advantage is that many workers prefer to move about rather than being tied to one spot.

While the choice of a proper layout depends on many things, primary considerations are the nature of the technology (discussed in Chapter 9), repetitiveness, and volume. A product layout is appropriate for mass and continuous production technology, where repetitiveness is continuous and volume is high. A process layout is appropriate for job lot and large batch technology, with intermittent repetitiveness and intermediate volume. A fixed-position layout is suitable when a unique item is produced; repetitiveness is one-time and volume is low. Group technology may offer some flexibility in application. Generally, though, it is treated as an alternative to process technology and as applicable in similar situations.

The choice of facility design and layout depends on the kind of product being manufactured.

MATERIALS PURCHASING

Purchasing is the link between the firm and its suppliers. It involves decisions about which supplies to buy, when, from whom, and for how much. Purchasing and materials handling have a major impact on company profits. For instance, moving materials from one place to another, such as from a pipe company to a plumbing supply house, accounts for an estimated 20 to 50 percent of all production costs. The total amount of money spent on supplies and raw materials in any given year exceeds the gross national product, and 50 percent of the sales dollar of most large firms is spent on purchasing.[10] Clearly, even a small savings in the purchasing budget can be very important. There are six steps in the purchasing cycle:

1. *Requisitions.* Personnel from various production units turn in purchase requisitions to the purchasing agent or buyer. These requisitions indicate the type and number of items needed.
2. *Value analysis.* The purchasing agent conducts a systematic appraisal of the purchase requisition to find the lowest-cost way to satisfy the request. Questions asked by management at this stage are: Do the requested items include too many unnecessary features? Can packaging or shipping requirements be reduced? How available are these items in the form needed?

3. *Supplier selection.* A list of approved suppliers is developed. The list rates suppliers on the basis of price, quality, reliability, and services. The purchasing agent then gets quotes on prices and delivery times.
4. *Order placement.* A formal purchase order is completed. The purchase order describes the goods requested, unit prices, quantities desired, shipping instructions, and so on. The purchasing agent can obtain quantity discounts by ordering large amounts of requested materials at one time.
5. *Order monitoring.* The purchasing agent regularly checks important orders to make sure they are on schedule. Communicating with the supplier is crucial at this stage.
6. *Order delivery.* A receiving clerk checks the delivered goods against a copy of the purchase order. If the shipment is correct, the purchase is recorded and payment is made.

INVENTORY CONTROL

Inventories held by firms in the United States exceed $700 billion in value.[11] By maintaining inventories, firms protect themselves from such threats to their supply as a strike by the employees of a supplier. Ample inventories of finished goods also enable firms to meet a sudden surge of customer demand. So, we say that inventories cushion against supply-side and demand-side shocks. Holding inventories is expensive, however, and this forces the operations manager to balance the benefits of large inventories against the costs. Figure 20–4 pictures this and other typical operations management tradeoffs.

Inventory Costs

Three types of costs must be considered for proper inventory control: holding costs, ordering costs, and stockout costs. **Holding** or **carrying costs** are the expense of storing the inventory in the firm's warehouse or on its stock shelves. Examples of such costs are warehouse rental and utility bills. Holding costs may total over $125 billion annually, or about 4 percent of the gross national product.[12] **Ordering costs** are the expenses involved in placing an order. These result largely from paperwork and management time. **Stockout costs** result when the firm runs out of inventory. The dollar value of lost production time or the value of a lost sale and the possible decline in customer goodwill are examples of stockout costs.

As an example, holding costs for a Toyota retail dealership include the interest on loans required to purchase an order of cars from the factory, the cost of showroom space, and the costs of accessories (such as radios and tape decks) which are mounted in the cars and cannot be sold separately. Ordering costs include the cost of paperwork, customs fees, arranging shipping to the dealer's lot, taxes and title fees, and so on. If the dealership is out of a model, stockout costs include the profits lost when customers give up on a Toyota and buy a Honda instead. The long-term costs of stockout include the failure of those customers to return to the Toyota dealer when they buy another car. Also, repeated reports of stockouts may spread to other potential customers.

Inventory costs often dictate major corporate decisions. For instance, when inventories of Oldsmobile's Cutlass Supreme averaged a 95-day supply

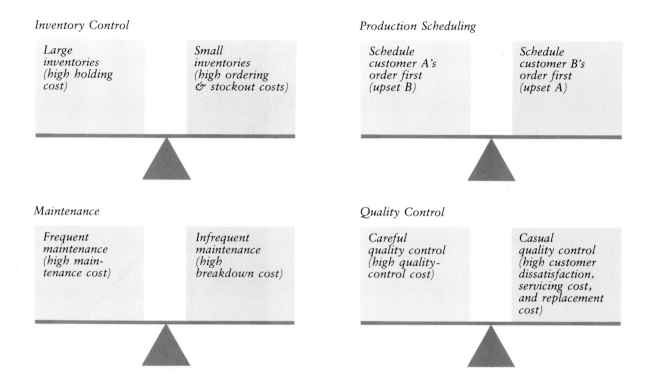

Inventory Control

| Large inventories (high holding cost) | Small inventories (high ordering & stockout costs) |

Production Scheduling

| Schedule customer A's order first (upset B) | Schedule customer B's order first (upset A) |

Maintenance

| Frequent maintenance (high maintenance cost) | Infrequent maintenance (high breakdown cost) |

Quality Control

| Careful quality control (high quality-control cost) | Casual quality control (high customer dissatisfaction, servicing cost, and replacement cost) |

Source: William H. Cunningham, Ramon J. Aldag, and Christopher M. Swift, *Introduction to Business*, 2d ed. (Cincinnati: South-Western Publishing Co., 1989), p. 265. Reproduced with permission.

FIGURE 20–4
Operations Management Tradeoffs

in early 1989, General Motors closed its Doraville, Ga., plant for a month. It also offered low-interest financing and substantial rebates to purchasers of Oldsmobiles.[13]

Reorder Point and Reorder Quantity

The total of the three inventory costs depends on the size of inventories at the **reorder point** (when an order is placed) and the **reorder quantity** (size of the order). Figure 20–5 shows possible variation of inventory levels over time, the reorder point, and reorder quantity. If demand is known and steady from one day to the next, the reorder point is chosen so that new supplies arrive as the last product moves off the shelf. In the figure, average daily demand is 20 units, and the time from order placement to delivery, called **lead time**, is 5 days. The firm reorders when the level of inventory drops to $20 \times 5 = 100$ units, and the reorder quantity is 240 units.

It is usually best to build some slack into an inventory-control system. For example, it might be safer to reorder when inventory levels drop to 120 units rather than 100.

Economic Order Quantity

The choice of the best reorder quantity requires a balancing of the various inventory costs. If the reorder quantity is large, average inventories will be

FIGURE 20–5
Inventory Levels

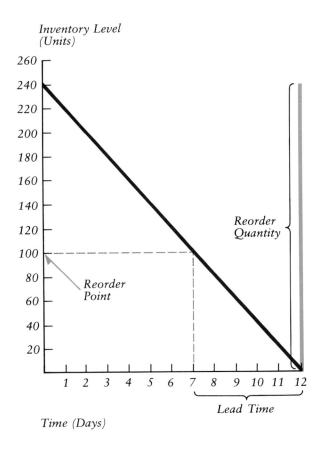

high, so holding costs will be high. If the reorder quantity is small, the number of separate orders will be high, so total ordering costs will also be high. If demand is uncertain, which is almost always the case, small inventories may result in disappointed customers. In this case, a small reorder quantity may lead to high stockout costs. Holding costs, on the one hand, versus ordering and stockout costs, on the other, determine the least-cost reorder quantity, or the **economic order quantity (EOQ)**.

A Safeway store, which holds inventories of perishable goods, must determine an accurate EOQ for each of its products. Accuracy is especially important since profit margins are extremely small in the grocery trade and quickly vanish if inventories are too large and produce spoils, or if inventories are too small and customers are lost to other stores. The EOQ will be different for fresh lettuce than for canned soups or dried beans.

For the simple case where demand and lead time are known and constant (and where stockouts, therefore, need not occur):

$$EOQ = \sqrt{\frac{2DO}{H}}$$

Where:

D = annual demand for the product
O = fixed cost of placing and receiving an order
H = annual holding cost per unit

For instance, if:

D = 8,000 units per year
O = \$20 per order
H = \$2 per unit per year

Then:

$$EOQ = \sqrt{\frac{2DO}{H}} = \sqrt{\frac{2 \times 8000 \times 20}{2}} = \sqrt{160000} = 400 \text{ units}$$

Keeping Track of Inventories

Many companies today keep a running count of their inventory levels—a **perpetual inventory**. Under such an inventory system, the firm knows exactly how much inventory it has at any moment. Items either added to inventory or taken from it are immediately noted on the inventory records. This continuous method of accounting for inventory is maintained on a transaction-by-transaction basis, often using computers.

Under a **periodic inventory** system the firm does not keep a continuous count of inventory. Rather, at the end of each accounting period—six months or a year—the firm takes a physical count of the inventory. These periodic counts often serve as a check on the accuracy of a perpetual inventory system.

New Developments in Inventory Control

Two recent developments are changing the nature of inventory control. These are known as just-in-time and material requirements planning.

JUST-IN-TIME

Just-in-time (JIT) or **kanban** (a Japanese term for the cards used in the process) is a method of inventory control in which the firm maintains very small inventories.[14] When an order arrives for a finished product, a kanban is issued instructing workers to finish the product. The finishing department chooses components and assembles the product. The kanban is then passed back to predecessor stations to replenish the components. This process continues all the way back to the material suppliers. At each stage, parts and other materials arrive "just in time" for use.

One consequence of just-in-time is that all inventories remain extremely low. Thus, firms markedly reduce their holding costs. However, beyond this, JIT represents a fundamental rethinking of the relationship between producer and supplier. For JIT to work, a stable, symbiotic relationship must be developed. Long-term contracts reduce ordering costs and increase predictability. Since supplies arrive only as they are needed, lot sizes are small and deliveries are made frequently—perhaps more than once a day. This may require suppliers to devote themselves exclusively to one purchaser and locate nearby.

John McClain and L. Joseph Thomas suggest that there are three basic JIT philosophies:[15]

- *Setup time and cost must be reduced.* The goal is to make them so low that small batch sizes are economical—preferably batches of size 1!

With just-in-time inventory control, parts and other materials are moved to the appropriate workstation "just in time" for use.

- *Safety stock is a bad thing.* It costs money and hides problems such as inefficient production methods. Just-in-time should replace just-in-case.
- *Productivity and quality are inseparable.* JIT is not possible if poor-quality components are produced. The firm will not be able to test, rework, and deliver products in a timely fashion. Thus, JIT requires not only small batches, low inventories, and quick production, but also a very high level of quality. The goal is 100 percent good items at each step.

JIT offers many benefits to producers.[16] They include the following:

- Reduced part costs—low scrap costs, low inventory holding costs.
- Improved quality—fast detection and correction of unsatisfactory quality and, ultimately, higher-quality purchased parts.
- Responsive design—fast response to engineering change requirements.
- Increased administrative efficiency—fewer suppliers, minimal expediting and order release work, simplified communications and receiving activities.
- Higher productivity—reduced rework, reduced inspection, and reduced parts-related delays.
- Reduced capital requirements—reduced inventories of purchased parts, raw materials, work in process, and finished goods.

For suppliers, JIT provides the benefit of a long-term, stable relationship. A supplier often becomes the sole supplier to a purchaser, thus reducing the long-run risk of doing business. Communication with the buyer is frequent, reducing communication problems. Capacity needs can be better predicted. And, if the supplier adopts JIT with its own suppliers, its own purchased inventories are reduced.

The cost savings of reduced storage under a precision JIT approach can be substantial. Fireplace Manufacturers Inc., a maker of prefabricated metal fireplaces, was having cash-flow problems because it needed to carry $1.1 million in inventory to support annual sales of $8 million. Using JIT principles, the company has now cut inventories to $750,000 even though sales have doubled. The vice-president of manufacturing said, "I don't think we'd be here today if it wasn't for JIT."[17] Ford and Chrysler have recognized savings of hundreds of millions of dollars by applying JIT techniques. General Motors spends an estimated $3 billion annually to maintain inventories valued at $9 billion. With JIT, analysts believe General Motors could cut this cost to about $1 billion. The Buick Motor Division of GM is rejuvenating a complex in Flint, Michigan, dubbed "Buick City," which will rely heavily on JIT. Auto production will take place in about half the space of conventional facilities. Within Buick City, major vendors will be located in eight adjacent industrial parks.

In the United States, JIT is currently well developed at Kawasaki Motors, a manufacturer of motorcycles and jet skis in Lincoln, Nebraska. Kawasaki began JIT work-in-process parts delivery on the factory floor and in the purchasing department in 1980. One of its suppliers, TRICON, has been supplying motorcycle seats on a just-in-time basis since 1977, typically making two deliveries a day. It followed the standard Japanese supplier practice of moving close to the parent firm, and it uses JIT with its own suppliers. Kawasaki is now expanding the JIT concept to other suppliers.

JIT doesn't work everywhere. It is most difficult to implement when a product line is very diverse, when there is very high variation in demand throughout the year, when setup times and costs are high and cannot be reduced, or when scrap rates are high. Further, JIT may limit flexibility in the range of products produced, and vendors must be willing to locate nearby.[18] While these situations limit the applicability of JIT, each should be carefully evaluated before JIT is rejected.

MATERIAL REQUIREMENTS PLANNING

Material requirements planning (MRP) is a method of planning and controlling inventories in which projected inventory levels are computed from present inventories and from planned transactions affecting inventory levels.[19] When component parts are assembled into products such as automobiles, they are not used independently of one another; instead, they are needed at exact times in the production cycle. They must be ordered to fit that cycle. This is a job of material requirements planning.

As shown in Figure 20–6, there are three major inputs to material requirements planning.[20] First, the **master production schedule** is the overall production plan for the end items. It is expressed in terms of timing and quantity requirements. Second, the **inventory record file** contains information about the status of each item held in inventory. Finally, the **bill of material** is a listing of the components of an end item. Working down from the final product, it shows the subassemblies used in the final product, the components going into each subassembly, and the raw materials needed for the components. MRP relies on computer programs to coordinate this information and provide outputs which help to ensure that materials are available when needed.

Figure 20–6 also presents some of the regular outputs of the MRP system. They include planned order releases, open-order due dates altered as a result of rescheduling, notices of cancellation or suspension of open orders, and inventory status data. In addition, there are a variety of optional MRP outputs. These include exception reports, which note errors or inconsistencies, and performance reports, which supply information needed by management to control the major elements in the functioning of the overall system.

Typical reductions of inventory levels with MRP are 30 percent or less, though figures as high as 50 percent are sometimes cited. Direct labor costs for some companies using MRP have fallen as much as 10 percent, and indirect labor costs as much as 25 percent. There have been up to 35 percent re-

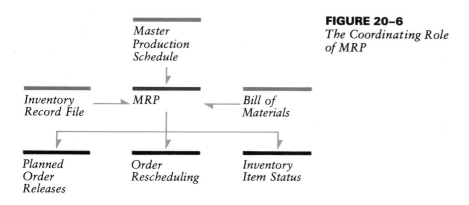

FIGURE 20–6
The Coordinating Role of MRP

ductions in late orders and total service improvements of up to 20 percent. However, these figures are from selected experiences and may overstate the average impact of material requirements planning.[21]

PRODUCTION PLANNING AND CONTROL

Production planning and control is concerned with the ordering and monitoring of work in process. It includes control of the flow of materials, people, and machines. The aim is to use these resources in the most efficient way possible.

The Planning and Control Process

Effective planning and control involves seven basic steps or actions. Let's examine each of these steps.

ROUTING

The movement of a mechanical part or other piece of work from one operation to the next traces out a route. **Routing** is the process of determining these work flows. In the case of an assembly line, the routing of work is built into the design of the plant itself. Volvo, for example, is famous for the efficiency of its automobile assembly lines. Even the Japanese auto makers have inspected Volvo plants closely before building their own factories.

LOADING

Loading is the process of determining how long it takes to perform a particular operation at a machine or workstation and then adding that amount of time to the time needed for work already scheduled there. The result is a "load chart" showing how much each machine or workstation will be used. Because of setup time, maintenance, and other factors, most machine tools cannot be used for more than seven hours of an eight-hour shift.

General Electric faces heavy production schedules for its Hotpoint air-conditioner assembly plants just before the summer starts. The company prefers to schedule its maintenance around this busy period so that it can load its plant as fully as possible. When the assembly line has to be set up for a new product, maintenance work is often done at night so it does not interfere with normal shift operations.

SCHEDULING

The planning and control function of **scheduling** is the process of determining when an operation is to be performed at a machine or workstation. At McLouth Steel, foundries sometimes must be booked weeks or months in advance for an operation that may take only a few hours. If the facilities are not available on time, an expensive batch of iron can be lost.

DISPATCHING

After the routing, loading, and scheduling functions are performed, the start of each operation on the shop floor is authorized through **dispatching**, or the preparing and issuing of work orders. For example, if four machine operations are required, work orders for each operation are prepared and issued at this point.

FOLLOW-UP

Another function of production planning and control is keeping track of work completed and any time lags or delays that may have occurred. This is called **follow-up**. Some jobs will run behind schedule and others will run ahead. With effective follow-up procedures, the time savings from jobs running ahead of schedule can be used to bring lagging jobs back on schedule.

CORRECTIVE ACTION

We might think that a well-managed plant would have everything running on schedule. In fact, though, a plant that does not sometimes encounter production delays probably is not being used efficiently. Because delays have to be expected in a well-run plant, management should be ready to deal with them. It may take such corrective action as scheduling overtime or shifting work to other machines.

The United States Postal Service usually operates at maximum capacity. When delays occur, post office managers schedule overtime or send part of their volume to post offices with additional automation, where sorting and delivery can be completed more efficiently.

REPLANNING

In response to changing market conditions, manufacturing methods, or labor force availability, new plans may sometimes be needed. The development of new routing, loading, and scheduling is called **replanning**. In the semiconductor industry, operations managers have to develop new production schedules for new products weekly or monthly.

Planning and Control Procedures

Operations managers have several analytical tools available to help them with production planning and control. We'll consider two such tools.

SCHEDULE CHARTS

One simple way to keep track of work in process is with the schedule chart. The **schedule chart** shows when each of a series of job orders is to be performed at each machine, workstation, or department. Figure 20–7 shows one such schedule chart, known as a Gantt chart.

According to this figure, the operations manager has scheduled several job orders on each of three lathes over a six-week period. Notice that lathe No. 1 is frequently idle and that the operations manager has anticipated maintenance time and delays on lathes No. 2 and No. 3. Also, job order No. 16 is ahead of schedule. With scheduling charts, operations managers can monitor the flow of materials through a production process or the flow of work through a job shop. And the operations manager always knows the status of work performed in relation to work scheduled.

FIGURE 20–7
A Gantt Chart

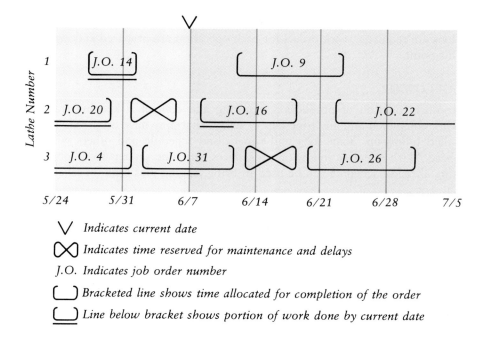

V   Indicates current date

⋈   Indicates time reserved for maintenance and delays

J.O. Indicates job order number

⟮ ⟯ Bracketed line shows time allocated for completion of the order

⟮⟯ Line below bracket shows portion of work done by current date

Source: William H. Cunningham, Ramon J. Aldag, and Christopher M. Swift, *Introduction to Business*, 2d ed. (Cincinnati: South-Western Publishing Co., 1989), p. 270. Reproduced with permission.

PERT AND THE CRITICAL PATH

An operations manager frequently has a major project to finish by a contract deadline. The project is made up of many separate activities or steps, each of which requires a certain amount of time for completion. Usually, one activity cannot be started until another is completed. This activity, in turn, is followed by still others. The goal is to coordinate all these activities. Most projects, from the company picnic to the construction of an offshore oil-drilling platform, fit this description. Some projects can involve many thousands of separate activities.

The operations manager facing such a project often develops a **program evaluation and review technique (PERT) chart**. Figure 20–8 is an example of a PERT chart. It depicts each activity involved in the completion of a project, the sequencing of these activities, and the time allotted for each activity.

Whenever possible, it is desirable to carry out several activities at the same time ("in parallel") rather than one after another ("in series"). In Figure 20–8, activities B and C can be performed at the same time because the start of one does not depend on the completion of the other. However, activity A and activities B and C must be performed in series. In an employee attitude survey, for instance, the choice of specific research goals necessarily precedes the writing of the survey questionnaire and the selection of data analysis methods.

The aim of a PERT network is to minimize project delays through effective scheduling of project activities. Such scheduling depends on the identification of the critical path. The **critical path** is the sequence of in-series activities requiring the longest time for completion. In Figure 20–8, the sequence of activities along the critical path is such that the project cannot be completed in fewer than ten weeks. Activities B and C are in parallel, but activity B is along the critical path because that path (ABDFG) takes the most time to complete. Since activity C is on a path (ACEG) which takes only seven weeks to complete, it could be delayed as much as three (10 − 7) weeks without slowing project completion. Because activity C can be delayed without slowing down the project, it is not on the critical path. Instead, it is said to have three weeks of **slack time**.

It should be clear by now that the completion of a project on time depends on the careful management of activities along the critical path. When necessary, the operations manager can divert resources from noncritical activities to critical activities to get them done sooner. Also, the operations manager can look for opportunities to schedule activities in parallel which are now in series.

QUALITY CONTROL

At one time, the label "Made in Japan" was synonymous with cheap products and inferior construction. It usually appeared on the bottom of products found in discount bins. Now, however, consumers speak with pride about their Japanese autos, cameras, television sets, stereo systems, watches, and porcelain dinnerware. More often than not, it is American products that are now thought to be of inferior quality. For instance, one researcher visited every Japanese manufacturer of room air conditioners and all but one American manufacturer.[22] He found tremendous variations in failure rates across companies—sometimes by a factor of 500 or 1000. The average Japanese plant had assembly-line defect rates 70 times lower than those of American plants. First-year service call rates were almost 17 times better for the Japanese plants. The poorest Japanese company typically had a failure rate less than half that of the best American manufacturer.[23]

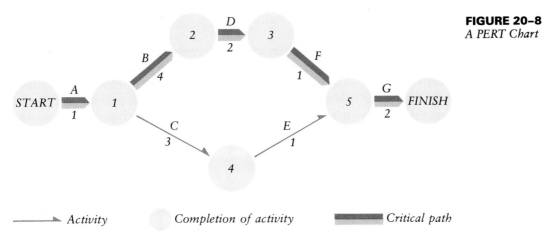

FIGURE 20–8
A PERT Chart

———▶ *Activity*   *Completion of activity*   ▰▰▰ *Critical path*

Activity time shown below activity

Source: William H. Cunningham, Ramon J. Aldag, and Christopher M. Swift, *Introduction to Business*, 2d ed. (Cincinnati: South-Western Publishing Co., 1989), p. 271. Reproduced with permission.

Many companies in this country have responded to the problem of declining quality by setting up quality-improvement programs for employees. For instance, "zero defects" programs use a combination of posters, slogans, pep talks, and praise to encourage employees to work more carefully. In general, firms are placing greatly increased emphasis on quality control.

Inspection

We can define **quality control** as the process of setting manufacturing standards and measuring products against these standards.[24] The second part of the definition refers to inspection. **Inspection** involves comparing products with the standards, approving those that meet them, and rejecting those that do not. Inspection serves as a check on the quality of incoming material and finished goods.

Many advanced techniques, including ultrasonic and magnetic tests, x-rays, computerized scanners, and television cameras, are used for inspection. But some judgments, such as whether a wine tastes "bad" or a flaw is "serious enough" to cause rejection, cannot be made so objectively.

Statistical Quality Control

The assumption behind **statistical quality control** is that most quality problems, perhaps as many as 85 percent, are the result of flaws in manufacturing systems, not of errors by production workers. Statistical quality control was first applied in the Bell Telephone Laboratories in the early 1920s. W. Edwards Deming introduced statistical quality-control concepts to Japan in 1950 and is widely credited with turning around product quality there in just a few years. Figure 20–9 presents Deming's "14 Points."

Deming's work has received considerable attention in recent years, and it seems clear that his statistical quality control principles may lead to substantial improvements in product quality.[25] However, Deming's "14 Points" have not received systematic testing. Some of these points, such as the calls for supervision, for training and education, and for teamwork, would lead to little argument. Others, such as the need to "drive out fear" and "to improve constantly and forever every activity in the company," are goals rather than specific operational suggestions. Still others, such as the calls to eliminate merit rating, management by objectives, quality and productivity targets, and numerical quotas, have not been convincingly supported. In fact, we have seen in previous chapters that each of these approaches may be valuable,

Testing an automobile in a wind tunnel is one of many techniques used to ensure the quality of the finished product.

FIGURE 20-9
Deming's 14 Points

1. Create constancy of purpose toward improvement of product and service, with the aim of becoming competitive to stay in business and to provide jobs.
2. Adopt the new philosophy: We are in a new economic age, created by Japan. Transformation of Western style of management is necessary to halt the continued decline of industry.
3. Cease dependence on mass inspection to achieve quality. Eliminate the need for inspection on a mass basis by building quality into the product in the first place.
4. End the practice of awarding business on the basis of price tag. Purchasing must be combined with design of product, manufacturing with sales, to work with the chosen supplier. The aim is to minimize total cost, not merely initial cost.
5. Improve constantly and forever every activity in the company, to improve quality and productivity and thus constantly decrease costs.
6. Institute training and education on the job, including management.
7. Institute supervision. The aim of supervision should be to help people and machines and gadgets do a better job.
8. Drive out fear, so that everyone may work effectively for the company.
9. Break down barriers between departments. People in research, design, sales, and production must work as a team, to foresee problems of production and in use that may be encountered with the product or service.
10. Eliminate slogans, exhortations, and targets for the work force asking for zero defects and new levels of productivity. Such exhortations only create adversarial relationships, since the bulk of the causes of low productivity lie beyond the power of the work force.
11. Eliminate work standards that prescribe numerical quotas for the day. Substitute aids and helpful supervision.
12a. Remove the barriers that rob the hourly worker of his pride of workmanship. The responsibility of supervisors must be changed from sheer numbers to quality.
12b. Remove the barriers that rob people in management and in engineering of their right to pride of workmanship. This means abolishment of the annual or merit rating and of management by objectives.
13. Institute a vigorous program of education and retraining. New skills are required for changes in techniques, materials, and service.
14. Put everybody in the company to work in teams to accomplish the transformation.

Source: Reprinted from *Out of the Crisis* by W. Edwards Deming by permission of MIT and W. Edwards Deming. Published by MIT, Center for Advanced Engineering Study, Cambridge, MA 02139. Copyright 1986 by W. Edwards Deming.

at least in some instances. While Deming's statistical quality-control principles deserve attention, the "14 Points" should be viewed more cautiously.

RANDOM VARIATION OR OUT OF CONTROL

The goal of statistical quality control is to determine whether something has gone wrong with the manufacturing system. It relies on the laws of probability to do this. By checking a sample of the output of a process and applying the right statistics, it is possible to tell whether the system is "out of control."

To illustrate, suppose that our plant produces a machine part for oil well pumps. The part is designed to be 6 inches in diameter, but we know from experience that an individual part is sometimes slightly more or less than

6 inches. Now suppose we pull one of the finished parts off the assembly line and find its diameter to be 6.01 inches. Is this deviation of 0.01 inch simply a random, unimportant variation, or is the deviation a sign that the production process is out of control, therefore requiring adjustment?

THE CONTROL CHART

To answer this question, we need to look at the past outputs of our production process and determine their average characteristics (such as the average diameter of 6 inches) and the typical variation around these averages. We also need to know the probability that various deviations may have occurred by chance alone. These probabilities are provided by statistical analyses.

For example, it might be known that a part with a 6.01-inch diameter occurs ten times in a hundred by chance alone. Thus, our sampled part with the 6.01-inch diameter does not concern us very much because the deviation is very likely due to chance. But suppose the diameter of the sampled part was 6.03 inches and the probability of this occurring by chance was known to be only one in ten thousand. What then? In this case, we can be fairly sure that the production process is out of control and that it will produce more defective parts.

A **control chart** is used in conjunction with statistical control. Figure 20–10 shows a control chart for our example. The chart shows the average diameter as well as an upper control limit and a lower control limit. If a part has a diameter greater than the upper control limit or smaller than the lower control limit—in this case, 6.02 inches and 5.98 inches, respectively—the production system is somehow flawed. If the diameter is within that range, then the system is operating satisfactorily. These control limits might be measurements (such as the diameter in our example), frequencies (such as the number of bad light bulbs in a sample), or number of defects per unit (such as the number of flaws on a piece of glass).

FIGURE 20–10
A Control Chart

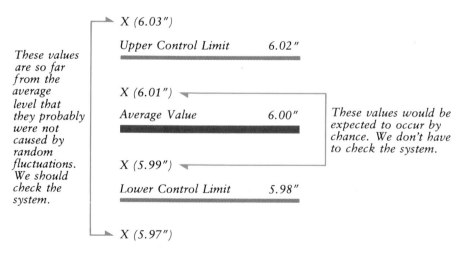

Source: William H. Cunningham, Ramon J. Aldag, and Christopher M. Swift, *Introduction to Business*, 2d ed. (Cincinnati: South-Western Publishing Co., 1989), p. 274. Reproduced with permission.

Quality Circles

Another outgrowth of Deming's statistical quality control concepts was the quality circle. **Quality circles (QC)** use a committee of workers that analyze and solve quality problems. They provide a form of participative management by letting workers make important inputs to key decisions. Typically, the committee consists of 6 to 12 volunteers from the same work area.[26] They receive training in problem solving, statistical quality control, and group processes. A facilitator, usually a specially trained member of management, helps with training of circle members and sees that things run smoothly. The circles typically meet for about four hours a month on company time. QC objectives include quality improvement, productivity enhancement, and employee involvement.

Widely adopted in Japan since the 1950s, quality circles first appeared in the United States at Lockheed Missile and Space Company in 1974. Lockheed estimated that the circles saved the company about $3 million, and that savings from the circles exceeded costs by a ratio of six to one. Over 200,000 U.S. employees have participated in quality circles,[27] and over 90 percent of the Fortune 500 companies have QC programs.[28] In fact, the acceptance of quality circles in the United States has been so rapid and widespread that they took on the appearance of "the managerial fad of the 80s."[29]

Quality circles have some appealing characteristics—they encourage worker participation, provide an enriched job experience, develop problem-solving skills, and encourage goals of workers and the firm to be congruent—and their success in Japan is hard to deny. Further, since the circles only make recommendations, management does not give up control. Many successes of quality circles have been reported, and involvement in quality circles has been shown to be related to positive employee attitudes.[30]

Nevertheless, a variety of concerns about QCs have been expressed. For instance, many people question whether the culture of the United States is right for quality circles. American management and workers differ in many ways from those in Japan, and a transplant may not take. Further, despite the initial appeal of QCs and the many anecdotes about their success, research shows that as many as 75 percent of initially successful QC programs were no longer in operation within a few years.[31]

Until the last few years, rigorous empirical evidence on the effectiveness of quality circles has been scarce. Recent research suggests that quality circles are more successful when there is top management involvement and support and when the circles have been together for some time.[32] However, the bottom line seems to be that quality circles often work and they often fail. Managers who consider using QCs must have realistic expectations and must consider their costs—often $20,000 or more for a modest effort—as well as their potential benefits.[33] Quality circles cannot be forced onto organizations, nor do they seem to work well in situations of high stress. Finally, managers should make sure that the issues to be addressed by quality circles can realistically be expected to be improved by quality circle involvement. Quality circles will not remedy problems caused by poor management planning or an inappropriate product mix.[34]

Monitoring the Quality of Supplies

Quality-control problems in production are often the result of poor-quality inputs. Some companies have strong programs for ensuring the quality of incoming production materials and supplies. Xerox has a four-point program to assist suppliers. From the beginning of its new product development process, Xerox involves its suppliers in writing specifications for production materials and components. Xerox makes sure that its suppliers understand these specifications before supply orders are placed. It also operates a hotline for suppliers who have any last-minute questions. Finally, Xerox uses statistical quality control on its suppliers' manufacturing systems, and it uses a team approach for a check on the packing and handling of materials. Xerox's program has been credited with marked quality improvements.

MAINTENANCE POLICIES

A breakdown in a large piece of production machinery can be extremely expensive in terms of lost production time and repair costs. Keeping production equipment in good repair is a big job: companies in the United States spend more than $14 billion a year on maintenance.[35] Maintenance can take one of three forms:

- **Corrective maintenance.** Fixing a machine that is not working properly.
- **Preventive maintenance.** Designing, inspecting, and servicing machinery so that breakdowns are less likely to occur.
- **Predictive maintenance.** Employing monitoring instruments to estimate when machine failure is most likely to occur.

Preventive maintenance is preferred by most operations managers because it is usually less costly than corrective maintenance. Predictive maintenance is especially appropriate for complex, highly automated production processes.

Management should answer several questions concerning maintenance. For instance, how much maintenance is needed? Can computers and statistical methods be of help? Should an in-house maintenance staff be used or should outside people be brought in? Would preventive or predictive maintenance be less expensive?

Most maintenance policies are just good common sense. For instance, it is usually best to try to schedule maintenance for periods when things are slow. If much maintenance is needed during peak periods, thought should be given to contracting out some work. And, there is usually a "best" time to replace or service equipment. If it is done too early, money is wasted; if it is done too late, repair may be costly or impossible.

THE FACTORY OF THE FUTURE

The increasing competition American manufacturers are facing in world markets has made them keenly aware of the need to improve their efficiency and effectiveness. To do so, some U.S. firms are now making major technological investments in what has been called the factory of the future. The **fac-**

tory of the future represents the computer-based integration of design, process, and control functions in the manufacturing environment. Such integration is made possible by the proliferation of inexpensive, yet powerful computers; advances in data communication technology and data base concepts; and the emergence of a computer software industry that can supply a growing selection of computer application software packages.[36] Management in Action 2 provides a glimpse of a factory of the future at General Motors.

Manufacturing has historically been based on economies of scale, in which large numbers of identical components were manufactured on automated equipment to achieve low unit production costs. In contrast, the factory of the future tries to capture **economies of scope**, in which computerized controls allow the same automated machinery to produce a variety of products cheaply.[37] In this section we will describe the factory of the future and then look at one of its key elements, robotics.

Characteristics of the Factory of the Future

Mariann Jelinek and Joel Goldhar have presented the following characteristics of the factory of the future:[38]

- *Flexibility.* With the flexible automation of the factory of the future, custom products can be produced at close to mass-production costs. Firms will find it easier to respond to needed change, quickly updating products and increasing their complexity and technological content as required.
- *Information richness.* As computers and inexpensive electronic circuitry proliferate, firms will enjoy information richness at low cost. It will be easy to monitor, analyze, and ultimately optimize almost any operation process.
- *Control.* Through the use of computer controls, memory, and the sensors that generate improved knowledge of production processes, factory operations can be optimized far more efficiently than in the past. Quality will increase while costs for waste are reduced. More reliable operations will permit maintenance to be scheduled more predictably to ensure fewer stoppages and less downtime.
- *Integration.* Computer integration offers benefits beyond those of automation of individual processes. **Computer-integrated manufacturing (CIM)** will link computer-aided engineering (CAE), computer-assisted design (CAD), and computer-aided manufacturing (CAM), each of which was discussed in Chapter 19, multiplying their individual benefits.
- *Closely coupled systems.* In the factory of the future, the various functions of the firm will be tightly linked. For instance, close relations must be fostered among manufacturing, design, and marketing to ensure timely response to new features or product designs and to make sure that promises to customers are based on sufficient knowledge of manufacturing capabilities and schedules.

Robotics

One of the authors attended a week-long conference on new developments in operations management. Of the many topics covered and facts presented,

Saginaw Vanguard has been called the world's most futuristic factory. Created by General Motors Corp. as a laboratory for tomorrow's technology, the

$52 million plant in Saginaw, Michigan, began fully automated production of complicated front-wheel-drive axles in 1988.

The plant is a futuristic wonderland where lasers inspect parts and check for wear on machine tools, experimental robots assemble components shaped by automated equipment, and driverless, automatically guided vehicles whiz about, picking up and delivering parts. The technological overkill is intentional; if failures are going to occur, the company wants to see them here before diffusing them elsewhere.

Only 42 hourly workers are spread over two shifts, and eventually the plant will add an overnight shift with no human presence of any kind. All employees are volunteers. They were carefully screened and given well over 1,000 hours of training in tech-

nical and socio-technical systems. There is careful integration, not just of technology but also of people with technological systems.

The factory is run by a handful of engineers and technicians. Seated at a bank of computer terminals in an overhead, glass-walled command room, they dispatch production orders to the shop floor and monitor the results. Computer integration of machines permits the plant to switch from one product line to another in less than 10 minutes, compared to as much as 10 days in conventional factories.

Saginaw Vanguard reflects the GM viewpoint that manufacturing technology is the ultimate key to competitiveness. Vanguard was launched after GM executives traveled to Japan in 1982 and were impressed by a highly automated Fanuc Ltd. servomotor plant. Vanguard now serves a dual role, as a production facility and as a showcase industrial laboratory for testing ways to apply technology to manufacturing. Technologies nurtured at Vanguard will be transplanted throughout General Motors.

Source: Based on "GM Bets an Arm and a Leg on a People-Free Plant," *Business Week* (September 12, 1988), and R. N. Stauffer, "Saginaw Steers Toward Tomorrow's Factory," *Manufacturing Engineering* (July 1988): 37–38.

perhaps the most thought-provoking was a simple photograph. It was solid black, with only a pinpoint of white in the lower right-hand corner. The photograph showed the third shift at a Japanese auto plant. No lights were needed by the sightless robots that completely ran the plant. The pinpoint of white was from the flashlight of the lone guard.

The word *robot*, introduced by Czech playwright Karel Čapek over 65 years ago, comes from the Czech *robota*, meaning drudgery, servitude, or forced labor. His satirical play *R. U. R. (Rossum's Universal Robots)* raised questions about the dehumanizing impact of technological progress on humankind.[39] Today, a **robot** is defined as a machine that can be programmed to do a variety of tasks automatically.

The variety of robots is remarkable. There is now a bureaucratic robot that stamps signatures on letters, a nurse robot to assist handicapped persons in wheelchairs, a robot "janitor and dog" for the home, and talking robots to give training to illiterates and to advertise products. Some industrial robots are mobile and have many arms, but most are nothing more than a mechanical arm attached to a stationary base. A programmable computing device controls the operations of the arm. Robots in U.S. factories are now performing such manufacturing tasks as spray painting, arc welding, die casting, assembling, and materials handling. In 1980, there were an estimated 3,500 robots in use in this country. The 1990 robot population in this country was estimated at between 75,000 and 150,000 units.[40]

The science-fiction-like qualities of robots have captured the public's imagination. Further, robots can handle dangerous or unpleasant jobs, lift

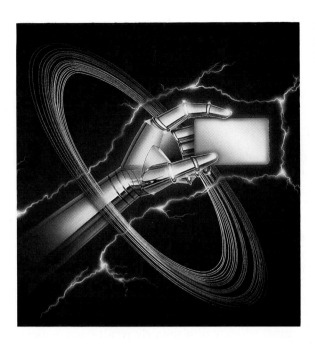

*One of the key elements
in the factory of the
future is robotics.*

heavy loads, work odd hours, and provide flexibility. However, the great growth in use of robots is largely the result of simple economics. About 25 years ago, an assembly line robot cost $4.20 an hour to operate, a figure that was slightly higher than the hourly rate paid to an average factory worker. By 1988, auto manufacturers were able to operate robots for $5 to $6 per hour (including maintenance and depreciation) versus $23 to $24 for skilled labor. Further, each robot may do the work of as many as five or six humans, and robots have an uptime of 95 percent versus 75 percent for the average blue-collar worker.[41] Roger Smith, chairman of the board of General Motors, stated, "Every time the cost of labor goes up $1 an hour, 1,000 more robots become economical."[42] A Swedish household appliances company compared a conventional line and a robot line for parts manufacture. The results are presented in Figure 20–11. Because of its superiority, the robot line was chosen. Further savings of $900,000 provided by shorter lead times with the robot plant paid back its higher initial investment in a year and a half.[43]

	Conventional Line	Robot Line
Number of operators	28	6
Floor space	1,700 m²	300 m²
Lead time for part design change	3–4 weeks	4 minutes
Investment costs	$450,000	$850,000

FIGURE 20–11
*A Conventional Versus a
Robot Production Line*

Source: Reprinted from "The Strategic Implications of the Factory of the Future," by Mariann Jelinek and Joel D. Goldhar, *Sloan Management Review*, 25, no. 4 (Summer 1984), p. 30, by permission of the publisher. Copyright © 1984 by the Sloan Management Review Association. All rights reserved.

The number of robots in use in the United States is growing rapidly. At its Lordstown, Ohio, plant, GM has 26 advanced Unimate robots that apply 450 welds to every car that comes off the line. The Unimates have "super seniority"—they stay in the plant during layoffs and shutdowns and are back at work as soon as they are needed. A Unimate costs $45,000 and pays for itself in less than 15 months by replacing two $28,000-a-year welders. Robots are a key part of GM's revolutionary new Saturn plant, discussed in Case 20–2.

Since robots replace human labor, many workers see robots as a threat. While the belief that someone would have to build the robots made some workers feel more secure, there are now instances of reproductive robotics, in which robots build robots. Unemployment is a possibility that cannot be ignored. For instance, a Carnegie-Mellon study concluded that the current generation of robots has the technical capability to perform nearly seven million existing factory jobs—one-third of all manufacturing employment. Sometime after 1990 it will be technically possible to replace all manufacturing operatives in the automotive, electrical equipment, and fabricated-metals industries. At the Fujitsu Fanuc Company, robots are allowed to join the union. The company pays their dues.[44]

The amount of unemployment which will ultimately result from automation is hotly debated. One estimate is that the effect of automation would be the loss of 1 percent per year of U.S. manufacturing jobs, and one-fourth percent per year of all U.S. jobs.[45] Others argue that negative effects will be short-term and are overstated. According to this view, automation will result in higher productivity and, with it, new jobs.[46] While many people agree that long-run effects may well be beneficial, someone has accurately pointed out that in the long run, we're all dead. There will almost certainly be major short-term displacements as a result of automation. Companies, unions, and government will have to seek creative ways to deal with them.[47]

Bud Grace © 1984 Science '84

Q: What is world class manufacturing?

A: World class manufacturing (WCM) is a set of processes designed to achieve a sustained global competitive advantage through the continuous improvement of manufacturing capability. This movement has grown out of increasing awareness of global competition in the last decade and the notion that management approaches transcend national boundaries. WCM bases the competitive strength of the business on its ability to design and produce superior products, rather than on its financial or marketing abilities. It combines the best of German, Japanese, American, and other manufacturing management practices. Thus, WCM is based on the idea that the success of Japanese manufacturing, and manufacturing in other parts of the world, derives not from cultural characteristics but from using good management practices to continuously improve manufacturing capability.

Q: What sorts of management practices will lead to WCM?

A: While different practices may be appropriate for different organizations, the common focus will be on the continuous improvement of every aspect of manufacturing, across functional lines. The manufacturing process management practices of WCM include just-in-time (JIT), improved process technology, an interactive research and development process, and total quality control (TQC)—an integrated quality control system including statistical quality control, managing supplies, top management support, customer involvement, and other components. To support these approaches, several human resources management practices and organizational characteristics are necessary. The human resources management practices include those designed to encourage a sense of cohesiveness, egalitarian approaches to minimize status differentials, broad training and development, group reward systems, and pay-for-skill systems to encourage the development of broad skills. The organizational characteristics which support WCM include decentralized decision making, formalization of procedures to encourage worker flexibility, integration across functional areas, and control which is based on output rather than behavior.

Q: What is the effect of implementing such practices?

A: Implementing such an integrated system will enable a plant to continuously improve its manufacturing capability and to become better able to produce a product line that is simultaneously innovative, flexible, of high quality, at low cost, and delivered on time. This contradicts traditional wisdom, which says that a plant should focus on only one objective, such as low cost or high quality, and that several objectives can't be accomplished simultaneously. The Japanese, however, are showing us every day that multiple objectives *can* be accomplished simultaneously. This is the ultimate goal of WCM: to meet and exceed global competition on a sustained basis.

Q: How do you do research in such a broad area?

A: I am very lucky to be part of an interdisciplinary team from the University of Minnesota and Iowa State University. It includes researchers with backgrounds in operations management, strategy, sociology, organizational behavior, and Japanese studies. In addition to integrating the theoretical literature in support of WCM from several fields, we are collecting data on WCM in the United States. We are administering a battery of questionnaires to world class, Japanese, and traditional plants in the United States in three industries. These questionnaires collect data on almost 100 characteristics of world class manufacturers. Our findings should be helpful in documenting the "best" management practices, in striving to attain a global competitive advantage.

Barbara B. Flynn (D.B.A., Indiana University) is Assistant Professor of Operations Management at Iowa State University. Her research focuses on two streams, group technology and world class manufacturing. Her articles on group technology use a computer simulation model to investigate various aspects of group technology, including plant layout, scheduling, inventory, and preventive maintenance. The use of a computer simulation also allows the comparison of group technology shops with traditional job shops. Professor Flynn's recent work focuses on world class manufacturing. Her publications have appeared in Decision Sciences, *the* International Journal of Production

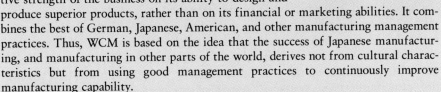

ACADEMIC PROFILE
BARBARA B. FLYNN

Research, *the* Journal of Operations Management, Modeling and Simulation, *and* Industrial Management. *Professor Flynn serves on the editorial board of the* Journal of Operations Management. *In addition, she has held several leadership positions in professional organizations, including the Academy of Management, the Decision Sciences Institute, and The Institute for Management Science.*

Status of the Factory of the Future

While the factory of the future has great promise, some firms are rejecting this approach to go "back to the basics," focusing more on employee motivation and on teaching workers quality-control techniques.[48] Many companies have spent millions of dollars on expensive technology with few tangible results. To a large extent, this disillusionment has been the result of overly optimistic estimates of the impact of robotics and other technology. Also, firms often tried to install new technology on top of the same old structure—paving an old road instead of building a better road.

Now firms are recognizing that if the factory of the future is to realize its potential, reorganization must take place from the ground up. The goal is to work smarter rather than just faster. To accomplish this, artificial intelligence (AI), discussed in the previous chapter, is being built into a new generation of manufacturing systems.[49] Artificial intelligence is often coupled with object-oriented programming. With **object-oriented programming systems (OOPS)**, computers are able to process knowledge—things and concepts— rather than just numbers. With OOPS, software is composed of independent modules, called objects, that describe various attributes of a particular thing, such as a round hole. This has particular benefits for computer-assisted design (CAD) applications.[50] Figure 20–12 shows the steps to automation which may lead to successful implementation of the factory of the future.

Using these approaches, many U.S. firms are recording remarkable successes. At General Dynamics Corp.'s Fort Worth, Texas, plant, the expertise of a master machinist has been installed in a system that oversees a cluster of machine tools and robots. The operation has never scored less than 100 percent quality. At Digital Equipment Corporation, savings from new technology are $135 million annually—on an investment of $30 million annually. These savings are the result of reduced inventories, higher productivity, and faster cycle times for billing and distributing products. The company has launched a five-year project to lift yearly savings to more than $400 million. The B-2 Stealth bomber is one of the most complex products ever made. Using a computer model, Northrup Corp. was able to build the bomber without a mock-up. All but 3 percent of the B-2's parts fit perfectly the first time; the best Northrup had ever done in the past was 50 percent.[51] These and other remarkable successes show the potential of the factory of the future. Nevertheless, new technology carries high start-up costs and risks. Further, recent experience has shown that implementation of the factory of the future must take place as part of an integrated effort. Altered technology may require corresponding changes in structure and management practices.

IMPLICATIONS FOR MANAGEMENT

Some people view operations management as a dull matter, something to do with keeping the boilers running. As we've seen in this chapter, however, operations managers are largely responsible for some of the most important issues facing American business, such as quality, on-time delivery, and productivity. Further, operations management is just as applicable to the rapidly growing service sector as it is to production operations.

THE CRUCIAL STEPS TO AUTOMATION

Many U.S. companies tried to hopscotch their way to computer-integrated manufacturing. Most stumbled, but that hasn't deterred some from trying again. Two new technologies, artificial intelligence and object-oriented programming, could lift U.S. competitiveness. But Japanese noses are catching the scent, too.

1 Simplify and reorganize the shop floor for optimum efficiency—with no automation, or at least no new automation. Only then will further steps yield maximum benefits.

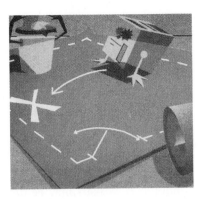

STATUS *Often poorly implemented in the U.S. Done widely and rigorously in Japan. Western Europe lags behind both.*

2 Create "islands of automation" with robots, flexible manufacturing cells, computer controls, and other advanced shop-floor systems.

STATUS *Widely implemented in both the U.S. and Japan, but much more effectively in Japan. Just beginning in Europe.*

3 Link the islands of automation to each other and to computer-aided design (CAD) through a shared data base, either hierarchical or object-oriented.

STATUS *Adopted by many major U.S. manufacturers and being implemented at a growing number of smaller companies. Japan is slightly ahead. Europe is far behind.*

4 Use artificial intelligence (AI) and object-oriented software to integrate some operations with CAD and to automate such complex steps as production scheduling and diagnostics.

STATUS *Now the cutting edge among progressive U.S. companies. Rare in Japan, but done more effectively. Almost nonexistent in Europe.*

5 Extend AI and object-oriented techniques to all decision-making steps, from product planning to customer service. This is the "computer-integrated enterprise."

STATUS *Under way at only a couple of U.S. companies. So far not implemented in Japan, but many Japanese companies could do so rapidly. Nonexistent in Europe.*

Source: Reprinted from May 8, 1989, issue of *Business Week* by special permission, copyright © 1989 by McGraw-Hill, Inc. (Data: Carnegie-Mellon University, Carnegie Group Inc., BW)

FIGURE 20–12
Steps to Successful Implementation of the Factory of the Future

The strategic role of operations management is evident in many of its facets. Capacity planning, for instance, forces the operations manager to anticipate future market and technological trends and developments. Capacity planning decisions, in turn, have an enduring impact on all functions of the firm. Decisions about the ways in which inventory will be maintained and quality assured also have remarkably strong impact, sometimes literally dictating the survival of the firm.

Operations managers are confronted with many of the most exciting new developments in management. The just-in-time inventory system, for instance, not only has major cost consequences for the firm, but also mandates patterns of buyer-supplier relationships, perhaps transforming entire industries. Quality circles provide a forum for worker participation in a crucial area. The emerging factory of the future holds both promise and threat. Its technological innovations offer firms flexibility, information richness, integration, and control. With heavy reliance on robotics, costs can be drastically reduced. Nevertheless, the initial investment required for such technology is great, and individual workers may be displaced.

On the surface, operations management is different from many of the other management topics we have examined. It seems to deal, after all, more with facilities than with people. A bit of reflection, though, will show that such a distinction is inappropriate. This chapter has shown that decisions on plant capacity, materials purchasing, inventory systems, and technological innovation are integral to organizational structure and strategic planning. And we have seen that decisions on facility layout, quality-control methods, and robotics may have consequences for the motivation, performance, and job security of individual workers. The firm, as we have repeatedly stressed, is a system. The strengths of its internal and external linkages are becoming increasingly evident.

It would be wrong to suggest that operations management bears the blame for disappointing productivity growth rates and poor quality, or that it holds the sole promise for their improvement. Motivation, leadership, communications, task design, and even simple respect for the individual may ultimately be just as important. Nevertheless, many of the conspicuous differences between American firms and, for example, their Japanese counterparts fall into the domain of operations management. This is an exciting area which will almost certainly take on greater strategic significance in coming decades. Managers, whatever their specialized interests may be, would do well to explore it.

KEY TERMS AND CONCEPTS

bill of material	critical path
computer-integrated manufacturing (CIM)	dispatching
	economic order quantity (EOQ)
control chart	economies of scope
corrective maintenance	factory of the future

fixed-position layout
follow-up
group technology layout
holding or carrying costs
inspection
inventory record file
just-in-time (JIT) or kanban
lead time
loading
master production schedule
material requirements planning (MRP)
object-oriented programming systems
   (OOPS)
operations
operations management
ordering costs
periodic inventory
perpetual inventory
predictive maintenance

preventive maintenance
process layout
product layout
program evaluation and review
   technique (PERT) chart
quality circles (QC)
quality control
reorder point
reorder quantity
replanning
robot
routing
schedule chart
scheduling
slack time
statistical quality control
stockout costs
transformation process

QUESTIONS FOR REVIEW AND DISCUSSION

1. Which three operations management topics discussed in this chapter do you think are most important for service sector organizations? Least important? Why?

2. Give two examples of companies using each of the following: (a) synthetic transformation processes; (b) analytic transformation processes; (c) temporal transformation processes; and (d) spatial transformation processes.

3. Which of the factors in the facility location decision do you think will become more important in the future? Less important? Why?

4. Describe four key tradeoffs in operations management. Discuss those tradeoffs in the context of a particular firm.

5. What are the three costs in inventory control? How does each vary with quantity ordered? What would it tell you if a company *never* had shortages of inventory?

6. What are the characteristics of a just-in-time inventory system? In view of the apparent benefits of such systems, why do you think they haven't been more widely used in the past?

7. What is material requirements planning? What might be some costs associated with material requirements planning?

8. Choose a project that you have to complete sometime in the future. Discuss how a PERT chart could be applied to that project.

9. Name two countries for which you feel quality of products is higher than in the United States and two for which you feel product quality is lower. Given your knowledge of each of those countries, to what factors can you attribute the quality differences?

10. Consider Deming's 14 Points. Based on material discussed elsewhere in the text and your own views, with which of those points do you agree? Disagree? Why?

11. How does a quality circle work? Do you feel that quality circles are primarily a fad? Why or why not?

12. Give four characteristics of the factory of the future. Relative to traditional factories, how much emphasis does the factory of the future place on flexibility? Efficiency? Coordination and control?

13. In general, do you feel the growth of robotics is desirable or undesirable? Why?

20–1 FLEXIBLE MANUFACTURING SYSTEMS (FMS)

Flexible manufacturing systems—the high-technology solution to factory production—are finally gaining acceptance on the plant floor. The sophisticated units, known as FMS installations, are production systems that contain two or more machine tools served by automated materials-handling equipment and supervised by a computer. They are capable of producing hundreds of different parts in random order as dictated by the computer. Typically, they require little, if any, direct labor.

Fifteen years ago, these systems promised to spark a revolution in domestic manufacturing. U.S. manufacturers thought that FMS, combined with computer-directed systems for assembling the parts produced by FMS, would help counter foreign competitors' lower labor costs. They were expected to be a boon to the domestic machine-tool industry, which is better able to provide the close cooperation with customers required in planning, installing, and debugging the systems.

But FMS have evolved slowly. With each system usually costing between $5 million and $20 million, they frequently aren't the least expensive way to make parts. However, considering their other benefits, from inventory reduction to quality improvement, FMS can still be a good investment.

U.S. manufacturers ordered 14 flexible manufacturing systems during 1984 and 1985, compared to four systems during the two previous years. There are between 20 and 50 systems in the United States today, industry analysts say, with the disparity reflecting an argument over how sophisticated a system has to be before it is considered an FMS.

A main reason for the increased orders is manufacturers' interest in "just-in-time" inventory management, which emphasizes having parts available only as they are needed. An FMS is ideal in such a situation because it permits the economical production of just one part of each type. It can inspect the parts and keep track of what is produced. These parts can be assembled into a product as they come out of the FMS. Once manufacturers have completed the initial round of cost cutting, such as closing excess plant capacity and pushing down materials costs, the largest remaining savings opportunities are to reduce indirect labor, such as fork-lift operators and warehouse workers, and to cut inventories.

Source: Reprinted by permission of *The Wall Street Journal*, © Dow Jones & Company, Inc. (February 28, 1986). All Rights Reserved Worldwide.

1. For what sorts of products and situations would FMS seem to be most useful? Least useful?
2. What do you see as factors inhibiting growth in adoption of FMS? Who might you expect to be opposed to their installation?
3. In what ways is the impact of FMS likely to be similar to that of other automation such as the assembly line? In what ways is it likely to be different?

20–2 PROJECT SATURN

General Motors decided on "Project Saturn" as the name for its multibillion dollar attempt to build a competitive small car. If Saturn fails, GM is likely to give up U.S. small-car production and sharply increase its purchases of small cars from affiliates in Japan, South Korea, and elsewhere.

As initially proposed, GM's Saturn effort was extremely ambitious. The company wasn't just talking about building a new car; it was aiming to come up with a whole new production system. The company hoped to abandon the assembly line that has been standard in the industry since the first Henry Ford, to decrease dramatically the number of parts and the amount of labor needed to build the car, and to leapfrog competitors in the use of highly sophisticated robots. If Saturn is successful, GM could establish itself as one of the world's lowest-cost auto producers and force its domestic competitors to revamp their operations at huge cost.

The overriding idea was to compensate for the Japanese $8-to-$10-an-hour advantage in labor costs by cutting drastically the number of person-hours required to build a car. GM may have to slash person-hours to 30 per car from its current 175 (compared with about 100 for Japanese manufacturers).

The biggest single change slated for Saturn is so-called modular construction. The modular method was first used in 1974 by Volvo AB at Kalmar, Sweden. Under modular construction, the parts are first subassembled into a few fairly large components called "modules." The final assembly isn't done on an assembly line at all. Workers or teams of workers posted at stationary workstations put the modules together, and instead of having one or only a few tasks to do, they perform a whole cluster of tasks, such as building a whole fender or front end. Trolleys carrying the partly completed cars move at command from station to station.

In building the subassemblies, GM initially planned to rely heavily on so-called intelligent robots. Currently, robots are used only in the final assembly process for spot welding and materials handling or for such relatively simple tasks as attaching a tire to a wheel. That is because current robots have sharply limited abilities. Intelligent robots would be able, in contrast, to "see" that a part is out of position, calculate how far out of position it is, and adjust its own operations on the part accordingly. Thus, such robots could perform complex assembly steps such as installing interior trim. As robots get even more intelligent, they could do quick quality-control checks on the dimensions and tolerances of parts as well.

To make Saturn work, GM knew it needed cooperation from the United Auto Workers—possibly a big hurdle. Industry experts predicted that GM would have to drop most of its 140 or so job classifications to permit a single worker to do various assembly, inspection, and equipment-maintenance tasks required under modular construction.

Another projected hurdle was to get GM's thousands of suppliers to make the necessary sacrifices. To cut inventory costs and improve quality, suppliers would have to invest in new equipment and locate plants close to GM's Saturn facilities. But many were wary; they feared they would be stuck with losses if Saturn failed.

Five years later, prototypes of the Saturn car, disguised as Chevrolet Spectrums, were undergoing road tests in the Southwest. GM board chairman Roger Smith's pledge to drive a Saturn car off the assembly line before his retirement in August 1990 seemed safe. But lots had changed. GM's market share had tumbled from 44 percent to 37 percent, and its profits had been badly squeezed. So Saturn's $5 billion budget for its early years was cut to $4 billion, and the emphasis changed from exploring leading-edge technology to building a high-volume car that would capture lost customers. Instead of costing $6,000 as originally planned, the Saturn car will be priced at $10,000 to $12,000. So despite Smith's wishes, there will be no workerless "lights out" factories nor a 50-mile-per-gallon engine.

Nevertheless, freed of the encumbrances of the GM bureaucracy, workers and management already appear to have taken giant steps toward defining a new way of building and marketing cars. Japan wrote the book on high quality, low cost, and relentless productivity gains in auto manufacturing, but Saturn is busily developing its own translation. The silver-gray and maroon offices in the Detroit suburb of Troy are open-style cubicles, and executives eat off paper plates in a spartan cafeteria. Consensus and teamwork are the management bywords. Policy is set by an 11-man Saturn Action Council that includes a United Auto Workers union representative.

The most dramatic evidence of Saturn's Japanization can be seen at the factory complex in Spring Hill, Tennessee. The largest single construction project in GM history, the mile-long installation will combine all the essential operations on one site, much as the Japanese have done. In addition to the usual sheet-metal stamping and body assembly, Spring Hill will include a foundry for casting engine blocks, a power-train assembly line, a plastics-molding unit, and an interior trim shop. Surrounding each operation will be dozens of loading docks so that materials and parts can be delivered close to the assembly lines kanban-style.

Spring Hill represents a big change from recent GM efforts to boost factory productivity and quality. The ranks of robots and armies of car-carrying automatic guided vehicles that populate GM's newest plants will be thinned. Instead, Saturn is pouring its money into people management. It plans to hire exceptionally motivated workers, put them through intensive training, give them more and more say in how their jobs get done, and pay them a salary plus a performance bonus—just like Saturn executives.

Relations with Saturn suppliers are, in the Japanese style, symbiotic. Saturn will have fewer primary suppliers and buy fewer parts from other GM operations. Its suppliers will have to work in lock step with the plant. Some will figure out what to ship by reading production schedules for the coming week. A single miscue could foul the assembly process. "This assumes everybody is going to do jobs right the first time," says Joseph A. Chrzanowski, a Saturn finance manager. "If there is a problem, we inflict pain on the source until it gets fixed."

Sources: Reprinted by permission of *The Wall Street Journal*, © Dow Jones & Company, Inc. (May 14, 1984), All Rights Reserved Worldwide; and adapted from A. Taylor III, "Back to the Future at Saturn," *Fortune* (August 1, 1988): 63-64, 68, 72.

1. Judging from this case, what are some apparent benefits of GM's just-in-time (kanban) emphasis to suppliers? To GM? What are some of the costs or dangers to suppliers and GM?
2. Which of the characteristics of the Saturn approach do you think would enhance employee motivation? Which might dampen it?
3. The case suggests that GM has substantially cut back on its emphasis on new technology at Saturn. What do you think may have led to this cutback?

ENDNOTES

1. B. Wysocki, Jr., "Meeting Mr. Big Face," *Wall Street Journal* (November 14, 1988): B10.
2. T. D. Schellhardt and C. Hymowitz, "U.S. Manufacturers Gird for Competition," *Wall Street Journal* (May 2, 1989): A2, A8. These rather depressing figures notwithstanding, American firms still are world leaders in many areas, from aircraft to flutes to biotechnological drugs to crystal. For instance, see C. Knowlton, "What America Makes Best," *Fortune* (March 28, 1988): 40-53.
3. *Statistical Abstract of the United States*, 109th ed., 1989 (Washington, DC: U.S. Department of Commerce, Bureau of the Census), 831, and "Productivity: Why It's the No. 1 Underachiever," *Business Week* (April 20, 1987): 54-69.
4. W. Skinner, "The Productivity Paradox," *Harvard Business Review* (July-August 1986): 55-59, and "How the New Math of Productivity Adds Up," *Business Week* (June 6, 1988): 103-122.
5. J. O. McClain and L. J. Thomas, *Operations Management: Production of Goods and Services*, 2d ed. (Englewood Cliffs, NJ: Prentice-Hall, 1985), 5.
6. S. E. Barndt and D. W. Carvey, *Essentials of Operations Management* (Englewood Cliffs, NJ: Prentice-Hall, 1982), 1.

7. This section, including the listing of process steps, is drawn primarily from E. S. Buffa, *Essentials of Production/Operations Management* (New York: John Wiley & Sons, 1981), 49-64.

8. Barndt and Carvey, *Operations Management*, 45-46.

9. This description is drawn from R. B. Chase and N. J. Aquilano, *Production and Operations Management: A Life Cycle Approach*, 5th ed. (Homewood, IL: Irwin, 1989), 359. Group technology also refers to the parts classification and coding system that is used to specify machine types that go into a group technology cell. Despite its apparent advantages, group technology implementations have not always been successful. Unfortunately, research on the effectiveness of group technology has often been anecdotal or of questionable quality. For discussions, see C. L. Ang and P. C. Willey, "A Comparative Study of the Performance of Pure and Hybrid Group Technology Manufacturing Systems Using Computer Simulation Techniques," *International Journal of Production Research*, 22 (1984): 193-233; J. L. Burbridge, *The Introduction of Group Technology* (New York, John Wiley & Sons, 1975); and B. B. Flynn and F. R. Jacobs, "An Experimental Comparison of Cellular (Group Technology) Layout with Process Layout," *Decision Sciences* 18, no. 4 (Fall 1987): 568-581.

10. R. A. Johnson, W. T. Newell, and R. C. Vergin, *Production and Operations Management: A Systems Concept* (Boston: Houghton Mifflin, 1974), 339. The reason the amount spent on supplies and raw materials can exceed the gross national product is that purchasing occurs at various points on the way to final delivery of a product or service. Thus, the same material may be purchased, repurchased in an altered form, and so on.

11. *Business Conditions Digest* 29, no. 9 (September 1989): 68.

12. McClain and Thomas, *Operations Management*, 528.

13. M. G. Guiles, "GM, Struggling with High Inventories, Offers Broad New Consumer Incentives," *Wall Street Journal* (March 8, 1989): A6.

14. For an excellent discussion, including a section on JIT for services, see Chase and Aquilano, *Production and Operations Management*.

15. McClain and Thomas, *Operations Management*, 388, 390.

16. R. J. Schonberger and A. Ansari, " 'Just-in-Time' Purchasing Can Improve Quality," *Journal of Purchasing and Materials Management* (1984): 3.

17. S. P. Galante, "Small Manufacturers Shifting to 'Just-in-Time' Techniques," *Wall Street Journal* (December 21, 1987): 21.

18. McClain and Thomas, *Operations Management*, 391, and Chase and Aquilano, *Production and Operations Management*, 802. For more on just-in-time, see B. S. Moskal, "Just in Time: Putting the Squeeze on Suppliers," *Industry Week* (July 9, 1984): 59-63; R. J. Schonberger, "The Transfer of Japanese Manufacturing Management Approaches to U.S. Industry," *Academy of Management Review* 7 (1982): 479-487; R. J. Schonberger and J. P. Gilbert, "Just-in-Time Purchasing: A Challenge for U.S. Industry," *California Management Review* 26, no. 1 (1983): 54-68; and A. Sohal and K. Howard, "Trends in Materials Management," *International Journal of Production Distribution and Materials Management* 17, no. 5 (1987): 3-41.

19. A. C. Laufer, *Production and Operations Management*, 3d ed. (Cincinnati, OH: South-Western Publishing Co., 1984). For more on MRP, see Chase and Aquilano, *Production and Operations Management*, 622-671.

20. The following discussion is based on Laufer, *Production and Operations Management*, 1984.

21. These figures are drawn from Laufer, *Production and Operations Management*, 562.

22. D. A. Garvin, "Quality on the Line," *Harvard Business Review* 61 (September-October 1983): 64-75.

23. M. R. Smith, *Qualitysense: Organizational Approaches to Improving Product Quality and Service* (New York: AMACOM, 1979).

24. For a discussion of dimensions of product quality, see D. A. Garvin, "Product Quality: An Important Strategic Weapon," *Business Horizons* 27, no. 3 (May-June 1984): 40-43.

25. For instance, see A. S. Baillie, "The Deming Approach: Being Better Than the Best," *SAM Advanced Management Journal* (August 1986): 15-23; J. Main, "Under the Spell of the Quality Gurus," *Fortune* (August 18, 1986): 30-32, 34; and W. W. Scherkenback, *The Deming Route to Quality and Assurance* (Washington, DC: Ceepress Books, 1986).

26. This description is based on E. E. Lawler III and S. A. Mohrman, "Quality Circles After the Fad," *Harvard Business Review* (January-February, 1985): 66.

27. E. E. Lawler, *High-Involvement Management* (San Francisco: Jossey-Bass, 1986).

28. Lawler and Mohrman, "Quality Circles," 66.

29. R. Wood, F. Hull, and K. Azumi, "Evaluating Quality Circles: The American Application," *California Management Review* 26, no. 1 (1983): 38. See also M. O'Donnell and R. J. O'Donnell, "Quality Circles—The Latest Fad or a Real Winner?" *Business Horizons* 27, no. 3 (May-June 1984): 48-52.

30. See H. H. Greenbaum, I. T. Kaplan, and W. Metlay, "Evaluation of Problem Solving Groups," *Group and Organization Studies* 13, no. 2 (June 1988): 133-147; M. L. Marks, P. H. Mirvis, E. J. Hackett, and J. F. Grady, Jr., "Employee Involvement in a Quality Circle Program: Impact on Quality of Work Life, Productivity, and Absenteeism," *Journal of Applied Psychology* 71 (1986): 61-69; and A. Rafaeli, "Quality Circles and Employee Attitudes," *Personnel Psychology* 38 (1985): 603-615.

31. P. S. Goodman, "Quality of Work Projects in the 1980s," *Labor Law Journal* (1980): 487-494. For a longitudinal assessment of quality circles showing initial improvements in attitudes, behaviors, and effectiveness but subsequent declines to previous levels, see R. W. Griffin, "Consequences of Quality Circles in an Industrial Setting: A Longitudinal Assessment," *Academy of Management Journal* 31 (1988): 338-358.

32. See T. L.-P. Tang, P. S. Tollison, and H. D. Whiteside, "Quality Circle Productivity As Related to Upper-Management Attendance, Circle Initiation, and Collar Color," *Journal of Management* 15 (1989): 101-113, and M. B. Barrick and R. A. Alexander, "A Review of Quality Circle Efficacy and the Existence of Positive-Findings Bias," *Personnel Psychology* 40 (1988): 579-592.

33. J. D. Blair and K. D. Ramsing, "Quality Circles and Production/Operations Management: Concerns and Caveats," *Journal of Operations Management* 4 (1983): 1.

34. These suggestions are drawn primarily from Blair and Ramsing, "Quality Circles and Production/Operations Management," 8-9.

35. H. T. Amrine, J. A. Ritchey, and O. S. Hulley, *Manufacturing Organization and Management*, 4th ed. (Englewood Cliffs, NJ: Prentice-Hall, 1982), 315.

36. T. G. Gunn, "Factory of the Future—How to Get Started," paper presented at the American Production and Inventory Control Society Operations Management Workshop (East Lansing, MI, July 1982), 1.

37. J. C. Panzer and R. D. Willig, "Economies of Scale and Economies of Scope in Multi-Output Production" (Holmdel, NJ: Bell Laboratories Discussion Paper No. 33, Bell Laboratories, August 1977).

38. M. Jelinek and J. D. Goldhar, "The Strategic Implications of the Factory of the Future," *Sloan Management Review* (Summer 1984): 29-37.

39. For a discussion, see R. B. Blackey, "Will Robots Carry Union Cards?" *Business and Society Review* (Spring 1985): 33. For more on robotics, see E. M. Knod, Jr., et al., "Robotics: Challenges for the Human Resource Manager," *Business Horizons* 27, no. 2 (March-April 1984): 38-46, and F. K. Foulkes and J. L. Hirsch, "People Make Robots Work," *Harvard Business Review* 67 (January-February 1984): 94-102.

40. O. L. Crocker and R. Guelker, "The Effects of Robotics on the Workplace," *Personnel* (September 1988): 26-31, 34, 36.

41. Ibid., 28-29.

42. *New York Times* (October 14, 1981).

43. Jelinek and Goldhar, "Strategic Implications," 30.

44. L. Silk, "Strange New Robotic World," *New York Times* (May 4, 1983): D2.

45. R. Ayres and S. Miller, "Robotics, CAM, and Industrial Productivity," *National Productivity Review* 1, no. 1 (1982).

46. Also, J. A. Mark, "Technological Change and Employment: Some Results from BLS Research," *Monthly Labor Review* (April 1987): 26-29, argues that relatively few employees have been laid off because of technological change. For instance, Mark notes that clerical employment has continued to increase—rather than decrease as had been predicted—despite the introduction of computers for office data-processing applications; the computer created

many new job opportunities for clerical workers. L.-A. Lefebvre and E. Lefebvre, "The Impact of Information Technology on Employment and Productivity: A Survey," *National Productivity Review* (Summer 1988): 219-228, also conclude that, in the majority of firms surveyed, the number of employees remained the same following the introduction of technology.

47. See McClain and Thomas, *Operations Management*, 137-139, for more on this issue. See also S. Deutsch, "Successful Worker Training Programs Help Ease Impact of Technology," *Monthly Labor Review* (November 1987): 14-20.

48. "Business Bulletin" column, *Wall Street Journal* (September 1, 1988): A1.

49. "Smart Factories: America's Turn?" *Business Week* (May 8, 1989): 142-145, 148, 150. See also G. A. Patterson, "Auto Assembly Lines Enter a New Era," *Wall Street Journal* (December 28, 1988): A2.

50. "Smart Factories: America's Turn?" *Business Week* (May 8, 1989): 148.

51. Ibid., 142-144.

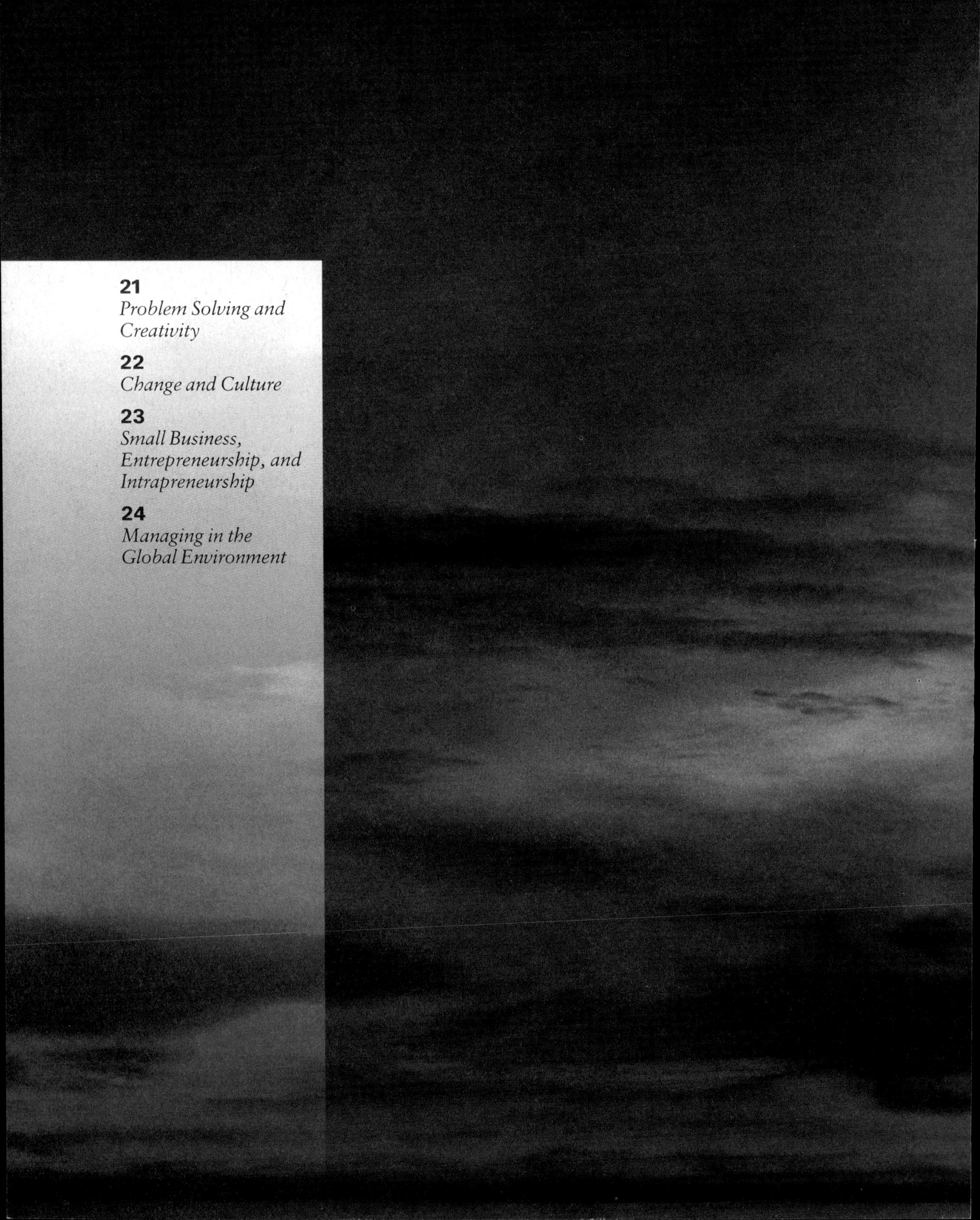

Organizational Vision and Vitality

PART SIX

Problem Solving and Creativity

CHAPTER 21

After studying this chapter, you should be able to:
- *Discuss the five stages of the problem-solving process.*
- *Identify a variety of barriers to effective problem solving.*
- *Discuss consequences of difficulties in problem solving, including usage of heuristics.*
- *Cite advantages and disadvantages of use of groups for problem-solving purposes.*
- *Describe seven group problem-solving processes which are alternatives to the use of traditional interacting groups.*
- *Identify the stages of the creative process.*
- *Discuss seven sets of creativity enhancement techniques.*
- *Describe the creative organization.*

672

Consider these organizational decision situations of the last few years:

- Margarine manufacturers pondered what to do in the face of rumors that Procter & Gamble was going to market sucrose polyester, a fat substitute that looks and tastes like fat but is not absorbed by the body. Sucrose polyester has no calories, can be used like margarine or butter, and actually lowers cholesterol levels.
- Drexel Burnham Lambert Inc. debated whether to plead guilty to six felony charges relating to insider trading and pay $650 million in fines and restitution or to face a lengthy public trial on the charges.
- Manville Corporation was saddled with over 16,500 asbestos-related lawsuits and expected tens of thousands more, totaling $2 billion.
- A growing number of firms encountered threats of greenmail—hostile takeover bids that could be avoided by expensive settlements with the bidder.
- Bioengineering firms wondered whether to continue expensive development of gene-spliced products in view of possible governmental restriction of their use for environmental reasons.
- Energy firms pondered the consequences of an announcement that nuclear fusion had been generated in an inexpensive apparatus, possibly promising limitless cheap energy.
- Margaret Schwartz debated whether to get up and go to work.

In fact, decisions are constantly being made at all levels of organizations. Corporate strategists plot mergers, financial and market gambits, and plant locations. Middle managers consider motivational tools, planning and control techniques, and ways to reduce subordinates' resistance to change. Workers decide whether to go to work, to produce at a certain level, to join informal groups, and to obey orders. Decisions are the fabric of organizations.

There are many reasons why managers care about problem solving. These include the following:[1]

- The decision is the main responsibility of the manager. Traditionally, the key distinction between managers and workers was that managers made decisions. Recall from Chapter 1 that Henry Mintzberg discussed such decision roles of the manager as resource allocator, negotiator, disturbance handler, and entrepreneur.[2] Since managers are increasingly being

evaluated on their problem-solving ability, decisions may affect the careers, rewards, and satisfaction of managers.

- The quality and acceptability of decisions affect organizational performance and the satisfaction of organization members.
- Problem solving takes considerable time and effort in organizations and is often uncomfortable. It makes sense to try to do well something on which we spend so much time and psychic energy.
- Activities in organizations are generally the results of decisions. By examining how decisions are made, we may be able to better understand how organizations work.

In this chapter we will examine problem solving and creativity. We will first consider stages of the problem-solving process. Then, we will discuss barriers to effective problem solving and the consequences of those barriers. We will then present some suggestions for improving problem solving, followed by consideration of group problem-solving processes. The chapter will conclude with examinations of the nature of creativity, creativity enhancement techniques, and characteristics of the creative organization.

Much of our focus in this chapter will be on difficulties encountered in problem solving. These comments are not intended to suggest that managers are poor problem solvers. On the contrary, in view of the tremendous amounts of information managers must deal with, the time constraints and pressures they face, and the often ambiguous nature of the problems they encounter, their decisions are remarkably good. Nevertheless, as suggested by Management in Action 1, the sobering reports of business failures in the daily press suggest that management decisions can often be improved. For this reason, this chapter should be viewed as providing a set of suggestions for improving management decisions, rather than as simply a critique of current practice.

PROBLEM-SOLVING STAGES[3]

Successful problem solvers recognize there is more to a good decision than just choosing one option over another. Instead, they follow the five steps in the problem-solving process shown in Figure 21–1.

Problem Definition

Careful problem definition is crucial. Unless proper time and care are taken at this stage, we may solve the wrong problem. A problem occurs when there

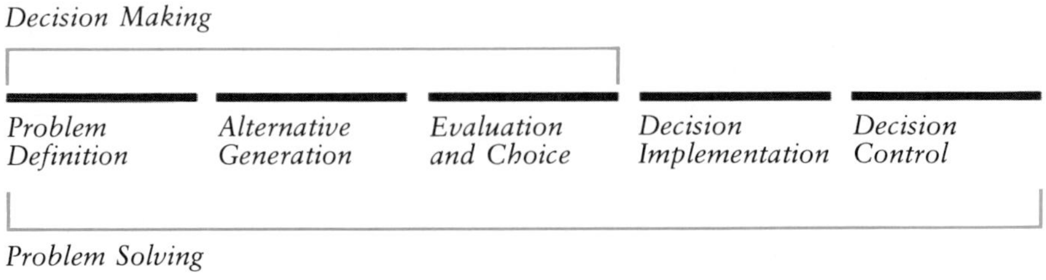

FIGURE 21–1
The Problem-Solving Process

Decision Making

| Problem Definition | Alternative Generation | Evaluation and Choice | Decision Implementation | Decision Control |

Problem Solving

In one of the biggest and most expensive new-product flops in decades, RJR Nabisco in March 1989 began pulling Premier, its revolutionary "smokeless" cigarette, from the shelves of stores in test markets and announced that it had no immediate plans to reintroduce Premier or anything like it. Premier was dead.

The cigarette, which had taken nearly a decade to research and develop, was designed to address many of the concerns that consumers had about smoking. RJR had already spent more than $300 million on Premier and planned to spend a total of more than $1 billion on development and marketing.

In retrospect, Premier seemed doomed from the start. For one thing, RJR couldn't market Premier as a safer cigarette without refuting the industry's age-old claim that smoking hasn't been proved unhealthy. Any chance that consumers might think it safer was doused by an intense and unexpected lobbying effort by health groups and anti-smokers who called the cigarette a "drug-delivery device" and urged that it be regulated by the Food and Drug Administration.

Further, researchers developing and testing the product seemed blind to some fatal flaws, such as the fact that Premier didn't taste right when lighted with a match. It didn't even taste right when lighted by most lighters. The impurities created by anything but a high-quality butane lighter settled in black specks on the cigarette's filter and on smokers' taste buds. Another problem, called the "hernia effect" by some RJR insiders, became apparent in test markets:

smokers often had to inhale furiously to get much smoke.

Even at the time of RJR's 1987 announcement of

MANAGEMENT IN ACTION 1
THE DEATH OF PREMIER

Premier—eight years after the idea of the "smokeless" cigarette was hatched—the company didn't know how to make the product in a factory. Premier required simultaneous assembly of four parts instead of the customary two in normal cigarettes.

Although the company's board of directors was behind Premier, directors raised questions at management presentations. But the people in charge of the project never lacked for confidence or answers, according to one board member. "Management would always say, 'We can fix this; we can fix that,'" he recalls. Another director remembers that the project managers insisted they could make Premier taste however they wanted it to taste.

The tobacco industry was rife with wishful thinking. Everybody knew the product wasn't perfect, insiders say. But within RJR, many had convinced themselves that, like decaffeinated coffee or the early diet sodas, it was a "deprivation product" with benefits for which consumers would make big trade-offs. One tobacco employee says she hated Premier the first time around but stuck with it until she finally began to like it. Adds a former senior RJR scientist who helped mastermind Premier, "What happens is you get into a euphoria where you con yourself."

Source: Reprinted by permission of *The Wall Street Journal*, © Dow Jones & Company, Inc. (March 1, 1989, and March 10, 1989). All Rights Reserved Worldwide.

is a gap between the desired and the actual situation. Declining profits, high scrap rates, or inability to increase market share are all possible problems. Too often, the problem is defined in terms of symptoms. For instance, management may define the problem as employee apathy instead of seeing that apathy as a symptom of a deeper problem, such as low wages. Or the problem may be defined in terms of a preferred solution. A problem statement such as "Gloria is a poor manager" focuses on proposed solutions relating to Gloria rather than directly addressing the criterion of interest, such as declining performance in Gloria's department.

Generation of Alternatives

Alternatives are the various approaches that may be taken to solving the problem. Good solutions require good alternatives. Unfortunately, in their rush to judgment, problem solvers often slight the alternative generation stage. At this stage **divergent thinking** is needed. That is, problem solvers must stretch their minds, seeking new possibilities. Creativity—which we will discuss shortly—is especially important at the alternative generation stage.

Evaluation and Choice

Once alternatives are thoroughly generated, they can be evaluated and a choice can be made. This stage requires **convergent thinking**, a narrowing in on a solution. There are two general approaches to evaluation and choice. With screening approaches, each alternative is identified as satisfactory or unsatisfactory. Unsatisfactory alternatives are screened out, leaving only those that can clear all hurdles. With scoring approaches, a total score is assigned to each alternative. Then the alternative with the best score can be chosen. Together, the first three stages of the problem-solving process are called decision making.

Decision Implementation

Some managers make the mistake of assuming the problem-solving process is over once they have made a choice. Unfortunately, decisions do not implement

THE FAR SIDE   By GARY LARSON

"C'mon, c'mon—it's either one or the other."

THE FAR SIDE. COPYRIGHT 1985 UNIVERSAL PRESS SYNDICATE.

themselves. It is necessary to ensure that resources are available for implementation. It is also important that those who will be involved in implementation understand and accept the solution. For that reason, implementers are often encouraged to participate in the earlier stages of the process.

Decision Control

The final step in the problem-solving process involves monitoring decision outcomes and taking necessary corrective action. If decision control is to be effective, steps must be taken to ensure that necessary information is gathered. Contingency plans must be developed to permit changes if the decision does not turn out well.

As shown in Figure 21–1, problem solving consists of decision making, decision implementation, and decision control.

INFLUENCES ON PROBLEM SOLVING

Figure 21–2 provides a rough outline of the steps information goes through as it is used for problem solving. That is, the manager must perceive and cognitively process available information. A decision is then made and implemented. Finally, the consequences of the decision are evaluated and stored for use in future problem solving.

The Ideal Decision Situation

Ideally, the decision maker would have all the information needed—and no more—when it was needed and in the desired form. The perceptual processes would select and process the information in an unbiased way. The cognitive processes would quickly, accurately, and objectively evaluate the information and arrive at an optimal choice. Subsequent evaluation of consequences would be unbiased and storage would be efficient.

"Real-World" Barriers to Effective Problem Solving

The "real-world" situation is far from this idyllic scenario. Difficulties may occur at each step in the sequence depicted in Figure 21–2.

FIGURE 21–2
Factors Affecting Individual Problem Solving

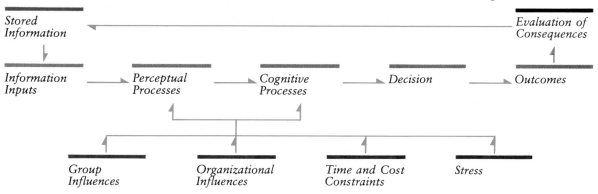

Like a distorting lens, our perceptual processes may give us an inaccurate picture of the information we receive.

INFORMATION INPUTS

Managers must often act on the basis of less than perfect information. It may be incomplete, late, or in the wrong form. There may be too much of it, or it may simply be wrong.

There are many reasons why information may be imperfect. For one, there simply may be too little time to carry out a full information search. In situations that are rapidly changing and complex it is especially difficult to get good information. Some sorts of problem solvers—including those who are younger, who are risk-takers, or who are dogmatic—act on the basis of relatively little information. Their opposites feel especially uncomfortable if information is not abundant.

PERCEPTUAL PROCESSES

As we saw in Chapter 12, our perceptual processes can lead to distortions. Recall, for instance, that we tend to perceive what we're expecting to perceive. Our perceptual selection is influenced by our needs, by personality factors, and by many elements other than the nature of the object being perceived. When we interpret information, we run the risk of stereotyping, halo error, projection, perceptual defense, and a host of other troublesome influences.

COGNITIVE PROCESSES[4]

Human problem solvers face a variety of cognitive constraints. These include the following:

- We have very limited short-term memories, with a capacity for storing only a few pieces of information.
- We are basically serial information processors. That is, we find it difficult to deal with multiple problems simultaneously. As a result, we process information relatively slowly.
- We have limited computational ability. The sorts of calculations implied by theories of maximization, such as the Rational Economic Man so popular in microeconomics, cannot be handled without assistance.
- Unlike computers, we care about the outcomes of our decisions. This causes us to have doubts about whether the decisions we make are correct.
- We evaluate information differently depending on how it is presented to us. Amos Tversky and Daniel Kahneman present the following example to illustrate these **framing effects**:

One group of people was asked the following question:

"Imagine that you have decided to see a play and paid the admission price of $10 per ticket. As you enter the theater you discover that you have lost the ticket. The seat was not marked and the ticket cannot be recovered. Would you pay $10 for another ticket?"

Another group was asked this question:

"Imagine that you have decided to see a play where admission is $10 per ticket. As you enter the theater you discover that you have lost a $10 bill. Would you still pay $10 for a ticket to see the play?"[5]

The outcomes of each of these situations are identical: a $10 cost with no ticket or a $20 cost with a ticket. But of those faced with the first question, most (54 percent) said they would not buy another ticket. Of those asked the second question, only 12 percent indicated they wouldn't buy the ticket.

To explain this apparent paradox, Tversky and Kahneman suggest that people have a psychological account in which they keep track of transactions. The loss registers in the "ticket account" in the first case but not in the second.

GROUP INFLUENCES

Groups influence problem solvers in several ways, as discussed in Chapter 17. For one thing, they exert pressure for conformity to group norms. For another, as we will discuss later in this chapter, they influence the individual's risk preferences, generally in the direction of greater risk-taking for most business-related decisions.

ORGANIZATIONAL INFLUENCES

Problem solvers act within the context of the organization and are continually influenced by it. For instance, the organizational reward system influences the way decisions are made. If it rewards cautious decisions, the manager will learn to play it safe. If it rewards chance-taking, managers will learn to take risks. Rewards for creativity will reinforce creative decision making.

TIME AND COST CONSTRAINTS

Obviously, time and cost constraints restrict our ability to get good, thorough information. Less obviously, time constraints also may cause us to change the nature of our decision processes. When pressed to make a quick decision, for instance, we may seek negative information about alternatives to screen them out quickly instead of carefully balancing positive and negative aspects.[6]

Executives who regularly face hot decision situations may suffer burnout.

STRESS

Decision makers often act under great psychological stress. Especially when the stakes are high, they may find it difficult to react with cool rationality. Notable examples are the chemical disaster in Bhopal, India, the Three Mile Island nuclear incident, and the Tylenol poisonings, but executives face less visible **hot decision situations**—the name given to conditions of extreme psychological stress—regularly. We will see that such situations may lead to inadequate decision making.[7]

PROBLEM SOLVING IN THE FACE OF CONSTRAINTS

The many barriers faced by decision makers have a variety of consequences, some obvious and others not. In view of all the difficulties people face in problem solving, we do remarkably well. For instance, studies show that humans do a very good job of making statistical inferences.[8] Further, we may do even better in the "real world" than lab experiments suggest.[9] Nevertheless, the various barriers we have discussed do hinder problem solving in some important ways.

Use of Heuristics[10]

In his fascinating volume *Hen's Teeth and Horse's Toes*, paleontologist Stephen Jay Gould writes:

When I first went to sea as a petrified urbanite who had never ridden anything larger than a rowboat, an old sailor (and Navy man) told me that I could chart my way through this aqua incognita if I remembered but one simple rule for life and work aboard a ship: if it moves, salute it; if it doesn't move, paint it.[11]

Gould sees the humor of this statement as residing in

the incongruity of placing such a "mindless" model for making decisions inside a human skull. After all, the essence of human intelligence is creative flexibility, our skill in grasping new and complex statements—in short, our ability to make (as we call them) judgments, rather than to act by the dictates of rigid, preset rules. . . . Our enlightened sailor, no matter how successful at combating rust or avoiding the brig, is not following a human style of intelligence.[12]

Actually, there is quite a bit of evidence that humans, no matter how potentially creative or capable of judgment, nevertheless do often behave according to simple guidelines much like those of Gould's "enlightened sailor." The human decision maker, especially when faced with complex decisions such as those faced by managers, shows a combination of creativity and reflex, of judgment and mindlessness.

Heuristics (from the Greek word *heuriskein*, meaning to find or discover) are devices we use—often without knowing it—to simplify decision making. They are simplifying rules of thumb. While they typically do make things easier for the decision maker, they generally lead to less than optimal solutions. Here are some that seem quite important:

- **Satisficing** means choosing the first acceptable alternative rather than looking for the best. Instead of trying to find the sharpest needle in a haystack, we may stop searching once we have located the first needle.[13] Satisficing is certainly a timesaver, since we don't have to gather information about all alternatives, only those we consider before making a choice. The problem with satisficing, of course, is that a far better candidate may be one or two or three alternatives down the list. That alternative will never even be considered.

- Often when we face a great amount of information, such as the full résumés of many job candidates, we may simply ignore most of the information and focus only on one or two attributes, such as previous experience and academic background.

- **Representativeness** is the tendency to place something in a class if it seems representative of the class. If someone looks like an astronaut to us, we may classify that person as an astronaut, even though there are very few astronauts. Making a judgment on the basis of representativeness is closely related to stereotyping and can have serious consequences. For instance, if we think that men "look like" executives and women "look like" secretaries, we may judge them accordingly. This could result in hiring or promotion biases against women.

- **Availability** is the tendency to estimate the probability of an event on the basis of how easy it is to recall examples of the event. Amos Tversky and Daniel Kahneman used the following example to illustrate this tendency: Is it more likely that a word in the English language starts with the letter *r* or has *r* as the third letter?[14] Most people incorrectly guess that *r* is more common as the first letter. The reason for this is that we store information by the first rather than the third letter (witness the phone directory) and can thus retrieve it more easily on that basis. As another example, because certain causes of death are more likely than others to receive publicity in the newspapers and elsewhere, they are more available in our memories than are others. As a result, we tend to overestimate their probabilities.[15]
- When we face a sequence of information, it is often difficult to combine it all properly to come up with a solution. For instance, in one study two groups of high school students had five seconds to estimate the product of a numerical expression on the blackboard. One group was told to estimate the product of the following:

$$8 \times 7 \times 6 \times 5 \times 4 \times 3 \times 2 \times 1$$

The other group was told to estimate the product of the same expression in reverse order:

$$1 \times 2 \times 3 \times 4 \times 5 \times 6 \times 7 \times 8$$

The median estimate for the first group, with the descending sequence, was 2,250. For the second group, with the ascending sequence, it was 512. The correct answer is 40,320.[16]

The inaccuracy of these estimates can be explained as the result of **anchoring and adjustment**, our tendency to use an early bit of information as an anchor and then use new information to adjust that initial anchor. If we weighted all that new information properly this would be fine. However, we tend to give too little weight to new information. The first group started with a higher initial anchor and thus came up with a higher estimate, but both estimates were too low because of insufficient revision.

The use of heuristics, while potentially harmful, may not be all bad. For one thing, the sorts of problems that heuristics cause in laboratory experiments may be less severe in actual job settings. As an example, we often receive continuous feedback concerning our performance; as we trim a hedge, we can see what remains to be trimmed, whether we need to trim a section further, and so on. So, if a heuristic "points us in the right direction," we can often then use feedback later to make adjustments. For this and other reasons, heuristics may actually be helpful in some cases. A danger is that, while managers often use heuristics, they may not know they are using them. For instance, Enzo Valenzi and J. R. Andrews found that job interviewers were unaware that they used simplifying procedures in making their judgments.[17] This inadvertent use of heuristics, especially in one-time decision situations, may be dangerous.

Procrastination

Because we often find decision making uncomfortable, we may put off announcing a decision as long as possible. By the time we commit ourselves to the decision, it is difficult for us to reverse it. Though we may justify our delay on the grounds that we are using the time to gather additional information, we may be secretly wishing that the problem would simply go away.

Incrementalizing

Suppose you wanted to design a perfect mousetrap. How would you begin? Most people would start with the best currently available mousetrap, perhaps the Ronco Rat-O-Matic, and then begin to revise it bit by bit, adding a better spring or disposal mechanism. This process of making a small change in one attribute and then in another is called **incrementalizing**.[18] While incrementalizing may be appropriate if only a "somewhat better" product is needed, it can seriously stifle truly creative alternatives.

Conservatism in Information Processing

Consider the following "experiment":

Let us try an experiment with you as subject. This bookbag contains 1,000 poker chips. I started out with two such bags, one containing 700 red and 300 blue chips, the other containing 300 red and 700 blue. I flipped a fair coin to determine which one to use. Thus, if your opinions are like mine, your probability at the moment that this is the predominantly red bookbag is 0.5. Now, you sample, randomly, with replacement after each chip. In 12 samples, you get 8 reds and 4 blues. Now, on the basis of everything you know, what is the probability that this is the predominantly red bag? Clearly it is higher than 0.5. Please don't continue reading until you have written down your estimate.[19]

The typical subject gives an estimate for this problem ranging between 0.7 and 0.8. The correct answer, 0.97, is much higher. This demonstrates that in general, we tend to show **conservatism in information processing**, characterized by underrevision of our estimates when presented with new information. Conservatism can have serious consequences for decision making.[20]

Attempts at Dissonance Reduction

As discussed in Chapter 12, cognitive dissonance creates tension. To reduce dissonance, individuals take a variety of actions to justify their decisions. These actions include searching for confirming information and avoiding disconfirming information. In the process, decision makers are likely to overestimate the quality of their past decisions.

Decision Confirmation

Dissonance reduction which occurs before a decision is announced has been called **decision confirmation**. Peer Soelberg showed, for instance, that by studying students' decision processes, he could identify their job choices weeks before they announced them. According to Soelberg, the students actually made a decision fairly early in the process and spent the rest of the time building a case for the preferred alternative. Then, when they finally announced a decision, they could present a strong argument in its favor.[21]

Defensive Avoidance

Irving Janis and Leon Mann have argued that the psychological stress caused by hot decision situations can lead to errors in scanning of alternatives.[22] When a hot situation—such as the need for a major decision, the danger of an impending attack, or the prospect of major surgery—occurs and it looks as though important goals cannot be met, stress increases. This stress is especially great if someone—for example, a confirmed smoker hearing the Surgeon General's warnings—is committed to a course of action which is challenged by new information. As stress grows, there is a tendency to lose hope of finding a better solution to the decision conflict, and **defensive avoidance** occurs. This is a condition in which the individual tunes out information about the risks of the chosen alternative or the opportunities associated with an unchosen alternative.

According to Janis and Mann, a state of defensive avoidance is characterized by:

- Lack of vigilant search;
- Distortion of the meanings of warning messages;
- Selective inattention and forgetting; and
- Rationalizing.

Defensive avoidance is at the heart of a phenomenon called groupthink, discussed later in this chapter. It is painfully evident in the Premier example at the beginning of this chapter. Because of defensive avoidance and other undesirable reactions to hot decision situations, many large industrial companies have formal crisis planning and management teams. These teams are trained to ask hard questions before they occur. George Greer, vice-president and coordinator of the crisis management team at H. J. Heinz Co., says, "We try to say, 'What would we do if the president of the company were kidnapped, if a plant burned down, if somebody allegedly tampered with a product?' "[23] The apparently chaotic response of Exxon to the huge Alaskan oil spill in 1989 demonstrates the dangers of failure to carefully consider questions of this magnitude.

IMPROVING PROBLEM SOLVING

The preceding discussion has highlighted the difficulties faced by an unassisted problem solver. Fortunately, there are steps that individuals can take to improve their problem solving in organizations. They can, for instance:

1. Try to be aware of the various barriers to effective problem solving. Simple awareness may help overcome some biases and other problems.
2. Practice self-assessment concerning such dimensions as dogmatism, tolerance for ambiguity, and risk-taking propensity, discussed in Chapter 12.
3. Be careful to move systematically through the problem-solving process. As we have suggested, there is more to problem solving than choice. Fail-

ure to give all stages the attention they deserve can lead to poor decisions.

4. Take steps to ensure that the information used for problem solving is complete and accurate. (On this point, review the suggestions provided in Chapter 15.)

5. Use processes and techniques to generate many unique alternatives. These creativity enhancement techniques will be discussed later in this chapter.

6. Consider use of computers to complement the human problem solver, as discussed in Chapter 19.

7. Apply systematic tools to assist with evaluation and choice, including those discussed in Chapter 8.

8. Review basic statistics to help with probability estimation and revision and other activities relevant to problem solving.

9. Consider using a group problem-solving process. We will address this issue in the next section.

GROUP PROBLEM SOLVING

Difficulties encountered by individual problem solvers have been covered in the previous sections. In this section we will consider problem solving by individuals working in a group. We will first consider the potential benefits and drawbacks of group versus individual problem solving, as well as some other differences between groups and individuals which may be either benefits or drawbacks in the problem-solving process, depending on the situation.

Benefits of Group Problem Solving

Potential benefits of the use of groups for problem-solving purposes include the following:[24]

- Groups bring a variety of perspectives and expertise to the problem. This may result in generation of more alternatives and of more information to evaluate those alternatives.

- Participation in problem solving generally results in greater member acceptance and understanding of decisions. In many instances, such acceptance may be as important to ultimate decision success as the quality of the decision itself.

One of the advantages of group problem solving is that a variety of perspectives and expertise are represented by the individual members.

- When working in the presence of others, individuals experience **social presence effect**. This is a heightened arousal level which, except when individuals are learning a new task, generally translates into improved performance.

- With many inputs to the decision, individual biases, day-to-day mood swings, and other sources of unreliability are dampened. Since a decision cannot be valid if it is not reliable, this should result in improved decision quality.[25]

Drawbacks of Group Problem Solving

While groups have many potential benefits, we all know that they can also be frustrating. We have all sat in group meetings that made us feel we should be getting back to work.

In fact, traditional interacting groups—of which the ubiquitous and much maligned committee is a prime example—are prone to a variety of difficulties. They include the following:[26]

- Dominant or stubborn personalities may control the group process, making it difficult for others to make their views known.
- For a variety of reasons, some members may sit back and make few inputs. Such reluctance to participate may arise from a fear of looking foolish, from threats of sanction, or from a desire to defer to members with higher status. It may also take the form of **social loafing**, in which members don't exert full effort because they expect others to carry the load.[27]
- The group may rush through the problem-solving process. For instance, there is a tendency, called **focus effect**, for groups to focus on just two or three alternatives, begin evaluating them, and never fully generate other alternatives.
- Group members may be less concerned with the group's goals than with their own personal goals. They may, for example, become so sidetracked in trying to win an argument that concerns about group performance and cohesion may be slighted.
- Especially when they are dealing with important and controversial issues, interacting groups may be prone to a phenomenon which Irving Janis has termed groupthink.[28] **Groupthink** is a condition in which members of cohesive groups overemphasize concurrence at the expense of realistic appraisal. Victims of groupthink share an illusion of invulnerability, rationalize to discount warnings and other negative feedback, and believe unquestioningly that what they are doing is morally right. In addition, victims of groupthink hold stereotyped views of members of opposing groups. They take many steps to prevent doubts from surfacing, including applying pressure to anyone who questions the majority's views, practicing self-censorship, and shielding the group from adverse information from outside the group. This leads to an illusion of unanimity within the group concerning judgments expressed by members who speak in favor of the majority view. The result is faulty decision making: members ignore warning signals, make little use of experts, and fail to develop contingency plans in case things go wrong.[29]

These tendencies serve to diminish or neutralize the potential benefits of groups. Benefits of participation, of dampening of unreliability, and of many inputs are effectively lost.

Other Differences Between Groups and Individuals

There are at least three other differences between groups and individuals for problem-solving purposes which, depending on the situation, may be benefits or disadvantages. First, groups take substantially more time than individuals to make a decision. While this will often be a disadvantage, there may be instances where a quick decision is not needed, or even where a manager would like to consciously slow down the problem-solving process.

Second, groups exert pressure on members to conform to group norms. Whether or not this is desirable from the point of view of the organization depends on the nature of those norms. Conformity to norms of creativity, a "fair day's work," and concern for quality would probably be desirable. Generally, organizations would not want norms of rate restriction, defiance of rules, or minimally acceptable behavior to be reinforced.

Finally, group processes tend to make group members' initial risk preferences more extreme; this is called **group polarization**.[30] Group members' initial risk preferences tend to be in the socially desirable direction. For most business-relevant decisions, such as those dealing with money, greater risk-taking is socially desirable. Thus, groups make riskier decisions than individuals. However, when society sees caution as appropriate, such as in cases where the health or welfare of children is at stake, caution is socially acceptable, and as a result groups make more risk-averse decisions than individuals do. For most business decisions, then, group processes may be preferable if individuals seem overly risk averse. On the other hand, use of groups may be dangerous if it is felt that individuals are already too willing to take risks.

Improving Group Problem Solving

This discussion of group benefits and disadvantages, and of other differences between groups and individuals, suggests the following strategies for improving group problem solving. First, it is important to ask whether or not this is a problem-solving situation that calls for a group process. The Vroom and Yetton model, discussed in Chapter 16, was designed to answer this question.

Second, if traditional interacting groups are to be used for problem solving, they should be carefully managed. In this regard, the material on managing committees presented in Chapter 17 should prove useful. If it is felt that groups are showing signs of groupthink or are otherwise overly complacent or failing to show vigilance, additional steps may be necessary. Irving Janis has provided several suggestions for preventing groupthink.[31] He reasons that group leaders should encourage all group members to air doubts and objections and should adopt an impartial stance rather than initially state their preferences. Also, the group should invite outside experts to meetings and encourage them to challenge members' views, and group members should discuss the group's deliberations with trusted associates and then report their reactions back to the group. When the group is considering alternatives, it should from time to time split into subgroups to meet separately, under different chairpersons, and then get together to resolve differences. Also, after a preliminary consensus concerning the preferred alternative, the group should hold a "second-chance" meeting at which members express remaining doubts and rethink the entire issue before making a final choice. Finally, when the issue being dealt with involves a competitor, time should be devoted to assessment of warning signals from the competitor and of alternative scenarios of the competitor's intentions. These are good guidelines to keep in mind any time a group is used to solve important problems.

A third approach to improving group problem solving is to consider alternatives to traditional interacting groups. In this section, we will discuss seven such alternatives, each with its own specific purposes.

THE NOMINAL GROUP TECHNIQUE

The **nominal group technique (NGT)** uses both interacting and noninteracting group processes. Noninteracting groups are called **coacting groups**—because

Q: What led to the development of the nominal group technique?

A: NGT was developed to respond to efforts in the late sixties and early seventies to involve a variety of points of view in public dialogue. This was the period of "maximum feasible participation." Community representatives were asked to officially participate in forming strategy for social programs. This era also saw the evolution of regulatory agencies for the coordination of urban and social services: regional planning bodies, environmental coordinating agencies, health planning councils, et cetera. In all of these efforts, there was a need for a process which would allow diverse constituencies to contribute to and arrive at decisions regarding the identification of needs, the development of solutions, and the specification of priorities despite the widely varied backgrounds, conceptual orientations, and language structures among the participants. For these applications, a structured process was critical.

Q: How widespread is current use of NGT?

A: The technique is virtually a universal tool in developmental planning efforts in the public and service sectors. NGT has also been utilized for peer group quality control in medical and professional settings. Professor David Brown of Boston University indicated that during a World Health Conference in a small village in Botswana, Africa, when the technique was introduced, one of the local participants looked up and cheerfully said, "Ah yes, NGT!"

In the private sector NGT is also a much utilized protocol, particularly where diverse technological perspectives have to be integrated in the establishment of strategic plans. Companies also use NGT in quality control and employee participation efforts. Finally, in recent years there has been substantial adaptation of the technique for computer conferencing, allowing a merger between NGT processes and computer networks.

Q: How would you characterize the evidence concerning the effectiveness of NGT?

ACADEMIC PROFILE
ANDRÉ L. DELBECQ

A: If one utilizes market acceptance as a criterion, there can be no question that NGT is perceived as one of the most effective idea-generating techniques available. Scientifically, evidence concerning structured versus less structured techniques has yielded varied results. My own interpretation is that structured processes are particularly important in circumstances where one is trying to meld heterogeneous groups who do not share common cognitive orientations and communication skills. Given the absence of control regarding both the purposes for using a structured process as well as group composition, it is not surprising the empirical evidence is mixed.

Q: Do you have any suggestions for people who are thinking of using NGT for the first time?

A: Essentially, I would suggest the novice follow the rules as set forth in the handbook *Group Techniques for Program Planning*. In the beginning, following the specific protocol seems to "always work." However, once one gains experience, there emerge many intriguing modifications and adaptations of NGT. As with everyone's favorite four-wheel-drive vehicle, people adjust, modify, add, and subtract.

André L. Delbecq (D.B.A., Indiana University) is Professor of Management at Santa Clara University, where he served as Dean from 1979 to 1989. His research focuses on managerial decision-making techniques, developmental planning, and organizational design for facilitating innovation. He is the developer of the nominal group technique and the program planning model. Professor Delbecq has authored books on organizational decision making and on the nominal group technique and the Delphi process as well as a management readings book. His articles have appeared in the American Sociological Review, Administrative Science Quarterly, Academy of Management Journal, Academy of Management Review, *and elsewhere. He has served on the board of governors and as chair of the Public Sector Division of the Academy of Management and on the editorial boards of the* Academy of Management Journal, Academy of Management Review, *and* Health Services Research. *He is a fellow of the Academy of Management. Professor Delbecq has served as an international consultant, lecturer, and trainer.*

the members are jointly acting toward some goal—or **nominal groups**—because they are groups "in name only." Developed by Andrew Van de Ven and Andre Delbecq, the NGT tries to capture the benefits of groups without falling prey to their problems.[32] It does this by avoiding interaction at early and late stages in the process. Interaction occurs only at the evaluation stage, when multiple views are needed to weight factors and synthesize material. Figure 21–3 presents the stages in the nominal group technique.

Use of nominal groups at early stages of the process may have several benefits, including the following:[33]

- Evaluation is avoided while alternative solutions are being generated. This prevents focus effect and reduces the danger that the search for alternatives will end too soon.
- Each individual has time to search for solutions and must record her or his ideas. Thus, minority opinions are expressed and everyone makes an input.
- The search process is proactive rather than reactive. That is, group members must come up with their own original ideas rather than just responding to or building upon the ideas of others.
- Strong personality types cannot dominate the process.
- Since ideas are expressed in writing, there is a greater feeling of commitment and a greater sense of permanence than spoken expression produces.

The nominal group technique is designed to reduce problems associated with interacting groups while still capturing the benefits of many inputs, feelings of participation, and social presence effect.

FIGURE 21–3
Stages in the Nominal Group Technique

1. Members of the group (called the target group) are selected and brought together.
2. If the group is very large, it is broken down into subgroups of eight or fewer members. This is necessary to prevent the process from being extremely time-consuming.
3. The group leader presents a specific question. For instance, the question might be: "What are some ways to improve creativity in our new product development department?" or "What are the causes of the high absenteeism in this division?"
4. Individual members silently and independently write down their ideas. This is a nominal (noninteracting) stage.
5. Each group member (one at a time, in turn, around the table in round-robin fashion) presents one of his or her ideas to the group without discussion. The ideas are summarized and written on a blackboard or sheet of paper on the wall.
6. After all individuals have presented their ideas, there is a discussion of the recorded ideas for the purposes of clarification and evaluation. This is the interacting stage.
7. The meeting ends with a silent independent voting on priorities by individuals through a rank ordering or rating procedure. The "group decision" is the pooled outcome of the individual votes.

Source: Based on A. L. Delbecq, A. H. Van de Ven, and D. H. Gustafson, *Group Techniques for Program Planning* (Glenview, IL: Scott, Foresman & Company, 1975), 66-69. Reprinted with permission.

The NGT has been widely adopted. Research concerning its effectiveness for generating many unique alternatives, minimizing errors, and satisfying group members has generally been quite positive.[34]

THE DELPHI PROCESS

Many situations require inputs from many individuals who, for one reason or another, can't feasibly be brought together. It may be the case, for instance, that:[35]

- The individuals may be widely scattered geographically.
- They may have time constraints that prevent them from getting together.
- They may want to remain anonymous.
- They may not get along well with one another.
- The problem may be so broad as to require many diverse inputs.

The **Delphi process**, developed by Norman Dalkey and his associates at the Rand Corporation, was designed for such situations. Because its early applications were for forecasting, the process takes its name from the oracle at Delphi. More recently, the Delphi process has been used for many other purposes. These include delineating the pros and cons of policy options, gathering data, examining significance of historical events, putting together the structure of a model, and clarifying human interactions through role-playing concepts.[36]

Delphi has taken on many shapes, but it basically relies on a process in which individuals respond to a series of mailed questionnaires. Figure 21–4 presents the steps of the Delphi process.

The hope of the Delphi process is that after a series of iterations some consensus among participants will emerge and that such consensus will be on a correct solution. By preserving anonymity, Delphi may encourage members to voice unique opinions. Further, Delphi shares with the nominal group technique such benefits as a block of time devoted to alternative generation, proactive search, written expression of ideas, and a structured process.

The Delphi process takes its name from the famous oracle of Apollo at Delphi, a town in ancient Greece.

FIGURE 21–4
Steps in the Delphi Process

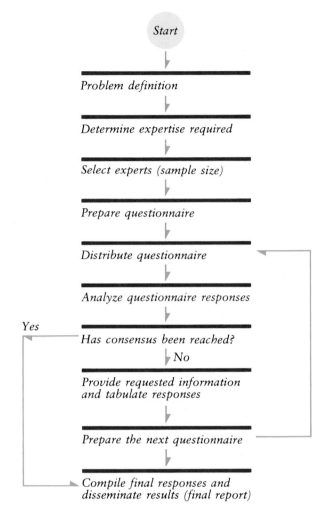

Source: Reprinted from *Business Horizons*, (April, 1976). Copyright 1976 by the Foundation for the School of Business at Indiana University. Used with permission.

Delphi is, however, very time-consuming, requiring weeks or months to complete. Also, unless participants are highly motivated they won't return questionnaires on time, if at all. Finally, Delphi participants miss the opportunities for verbal clarification of questions and for face-to-face problem solving.[37] However, electronic mail and other newer communications technologies may alleviate some of these drawbacks. An "electronic Delphi" can be done very quickly, not only saving time but also reducing demands on participants and giving them a greater sense of immediacy and accomplishment.

SOCIAL JUDGMENT ANALYSIS

Often, people disagree without knowing why they disagree. For instance, in the experiment by Valenzi and Andrews mentioned earlier in the chapter, interviewers rated secretarial job applicants on the basis of information about typing speed, experience, and education. They found that, even though em-

ployment interviewers agreed fairly well on the relative importance of the attributes, they made substantially different choices. Often, in fact, they were
unaware of how they were actually using information to make their choices.

Social judgment analysis is based on the idea that disagreements could be
reduced if members, instead of voicing their choices, could explain how they
arrived at those choices.[38] To accomplish this, social judgment analysis presents a series of tasks to participants. On the basis of their choices, statistical
procedures are used to determine the underlying models participants used in
reaching those choices. Then, pictorial representations of those models are
developed and given to the participants. The participants then compare and
contrast their policies with those of others. Finally, they interact and try to
agree on a final policy.

AUTOMATED DECISION CONFERENCING[39]

When important, complex decisions must be made in a very short time, **automated decision conferencing (ADC)** is becoming popular. An automated decision conference usually lasts 2 or 3 days and may involve 6 to 15 executive
team members and 3 staff members. With the aid of staff members trained in
computer skills, quantitative techniques, and organizational development,
the executive team works on a major organizational problem.

Once a problem is clearly identified, the group leader describes it in detail
and a staff member enters it on a decision support system. As the process continues, additional information is entered on the computer and quantitative
aids are used. The completed computer output is subsequently presented to
the group and is carefully reviewed. The group then refines it until a mutually acceptable solution is achieved. Because of computer support, complex
decisions requiring large amounts of information can be attacked in an open
group process.

SYNTHETIC GROUPS

It may be possible to capture many of the benefits of groups, especially heightened reliability of decisions, without actually using a group process. That is,
a **synthetic group** opinion can be achieved by simply aggregating individual
decisions mathematically. Such aggregation has been shown to markedly improve probability estimates and forecasts.[40]

DEVIL'S ADVOCATE

A **devil's advocate** is a group member who acts as a critic of the plan.[41] The
devil's advocate tries to ferret out problems with the plan and to propose reasons why it should not be adopted. The advocate's role is to create dissonance,
ensuring that the group takes a hard second look at its preferred alternative.
As such, the devil's advocate approach should help prevent groupthink.

Having an individual designated as the devil's advocate makes it clear
that an adversarial stance is legitimate. It brings out criticisms that might not
otherwise emerge, and it highlights underlying assumptions.

Nevertheless, there are problems with the devil's advocate approach. For
one thing, some people become demoralized if their views are constantly criticized. As a result, they may come up with safe solutions, not especially creative or risky but able to stand up to criticism. Also, if the devil's advocate is

successful in finding problems with the plan, there is no new plan to take its place. The devil's advocate approach focuses on what is wrong without pointing out what is right.

DIALECTICAL INQUIRY

Dialectical inquiry tries to accomplish the goals of the devil's advocate approach in a more constructive way. **Dialectical inquiry** is a procedure in which a situation is approached from two opposite points of view. It is hoped that out of this clash of a thesis and an antithesis, a creative synthesis will emerge. The steps of dialectical inquiry include the following:[42]

1. A plan and the data used to derive it are identified.
2. An attempt is made to identify the assumptions underlying the plan.
3. A counterplan is identified which is feasible, politically viable, and generally credible but rests on assumptions which are "opposite" those supporting the plan. These "opposite" assumptions should represent the most serious competition for the assumptions of the plan. Thus, the "opposite" of the assumptions of capitalism might be those of communism.
4. A structured debate is conducted in which those responsible for formulating strategy hear arguments in support of the plan and the counterplan.
5. A "creative synthesis" is arrived at by plan formulators including the best elements of both alternatives.

While dialectical inquiry represents a potentially constructive approach, it is time-consuming and requires considerable training. Also, it may lead to a series of compromises between the original plan and the counterplan. If the original plan was correct, this will be unfortunate.

Evidence on the relative merits of the devil's advocate approach and dialectical inquiry is conflicting. It does seem that if the devil's advocate approach is used, the devil's advocate should adopt an impersonal, lawyer-like demeanor rather than act as a vindictive, carping critic. Many users of dialectical inquiry have found it to be very useful. Nevertheless, experimental evidence comparing dialectical inquiry with the devil's advocate approach has tended to favor the latter.

Use of these processes may involve tradeoffs. For instance, since both the devil's advocate approach and dialectical inquiry are intended to induce conflict, they may make the group process less satisfying for some members. One study showed that both dialectical inquiry and devil's advocacy lead to higher-quality recommendations and assumptions than an approach fostering group consensus. However, the consensus approach proved superior in terms of group members' satisfaction, desire to continue to work with their groups, and acceptance of their groups' decisions. These conditions are critical for the success of ongoing groups. For this reason, the costs and benefits of conflict-generating group techniques must be carefully weighed.[43]

CREATIVITY IN ORGANIZATIONS

Polaroid, once called by its founder Edwin Land "a noble prototype of industry," was by the mid-1980s facing a letdown. Land had resigned in 1982. Many key personnel were leaving and there was a feeling that the company was losing its spark, spending less on research for new technology and more on improvement of current offerings. An employee who resigned said, "The last few years it was control costs, manage this, manage that. The glamour, the excitement, the flair wasn't there." One former director bemoaned the loss of creative risk-taking, saying, "Land grasped at high-risk opportunities. If you aim toward taking advantage of existing products, you can go into a vicious spiral. You search for small differences. Eventually, changing a package becomes a new product."[44]

Such unraveling of the creative fabric is not unique to Polaroid. Many firms, especially those that face growing bureaucratic entanglements, find that innovation is being stifled. And, as previous chapters have suggested, organizational environments are becoming more complex, dynamic, and uncertain. Such conditions demand flexibility and creativity. Thus, firms may find themselves becoming increasingly unresponsive to environmental demands. Further, creativity is important at all levels of the organization, not just in research labs and the CEO's office. In the following sections we will consider the nature of creativity, some specific creativity enhancement techniques, and the characteristics of the creative organization.

THE NATURE OF CREATIVITY

Creative behavior is defined as the production of ideas that are both new and useful. **Creative ability** is the ability to produce ideas that are both new and useful. Since the usefulness of some truly creative ideas may not be immediately evident, these definitions may seem constraining. Sarnoff Mednick has addressed this dilemma by differentiating between originality and creativity. According to Mednick, "7,363,474 is quite an original answer to the problem 'How much is 12 + 12?' However, it is only when conditions are such that the answer is useful that we can also call it creative."[45] Mednick, then, sees the answer "7,363,474" as being original but not creative.

As we have discussed in Chapter 12 and elsewhere, ability may not translate into behavior. Both motivation and a proper setting may be necessary if innate creative ability is to blossom into creative output.[46]

The Creative Process

Creativity involves more than the sudden moment of inspiration in which a cartoon light bulb flashes in the brain. Instead, as shown in Figure 21-5, there are a number of stages to the **creative process**. According to Graham Wallas, the process includes preparation, incubation, insight, and verification.[47]

The preparation stage involves gathering, sorting, and integrating information and other materials to provide a solid base for a later breakthrough. While the discoveries of penicillin, the benzene ring, and gravity each involved a moment of insight, they would have been impossible without a firm grasp of related information. During the incubation stage, the mind is not consciously focused on the problem. The individual may be relaxed, asleep, reflective, or otherwise involved. A. E. Housman wrote that "As I went along, thinking nothing in particular . . . there would flow into my mind, with sudden and unaccountable emotion, sometimes a line or two of verse, sometimes

FIGURE 21–5
The Creative Process

Preparation → Incubation → Insight → Verification

a whole stanza at once."[48] The insight or "Eureka!" stage is the familiar, sudden moment of inspiration. Finally, verification is necessary. Here, the individual carries out the chores involved in carefully checking facts to support the insight, conducting research to determine that the DNA molecule is in fact a double helix or that a meteorite did really create a dust cloud that led to extinction of the dinosaurs.

This process, the elements of which have received research backing, further supports the contention that creativity does not just happen. It is a thorough and often painstaking activity.

Views on Creativity[49]

There are many views on creativity. To 19th-century psychiatrist Cesare Lombroso, creativity was a sign of mental illness associated with "signs of degeneration" such as lesions of the head, stammering, and left-handedness.[50] Abraham Maslow took the opposite stand, seeing creativity as a characteristic of the self-actualized, healthy individual.[51] To B. F. Skinner, creativity is learned like any other behavior.[52]

One influential view of creativity has been developed by J. P. Guilford.[53] According to Guilford's **structure of intellect theory**, humans have 120 different and independent intellectual abilities. As shown in Figure 21–6, those abilities are each the result of application of one of five mental operations to one of four contents to get one of six products. Operations are the things we do with information, such as memorizing or evaluating. Contents are the types of information we may have available, such as figures and symbols and words. Products are the forms taken by the processed information, such as finding relationships and drawing implications.

Guilford's model can be used to draw a distinction between creative ability and intellectual ability. Manipulation of figural and symbolic content is important to creative ability. Divergent production—the ability of the mind to expand and find new approaches—is the most important creative operation. Transformations are valuable products of the creative process. Conversely, intelligence tests focus heavily on semantic content, on the operations of evaluation and convergent production (narrowing in on a solution), and on the products of systems and relations.

Characteristics of Creative Individuals

Creative persons seem to be sensitive and to prefer complexity.[54] They typically value independence, enjoy aesthetic expressions, have high aspiration levels, are nonauthoritarian and nondogmatic, and have a wide range of interests.[55] They were generally given the opportunity to act responsibly early in life.[56]

Studies across a wide range of occupations show that creative behavior peaks in the thirties or early forties,[57] perhaps because of declining motivation to be creative later in life. Consistent with the arguments of the struc-

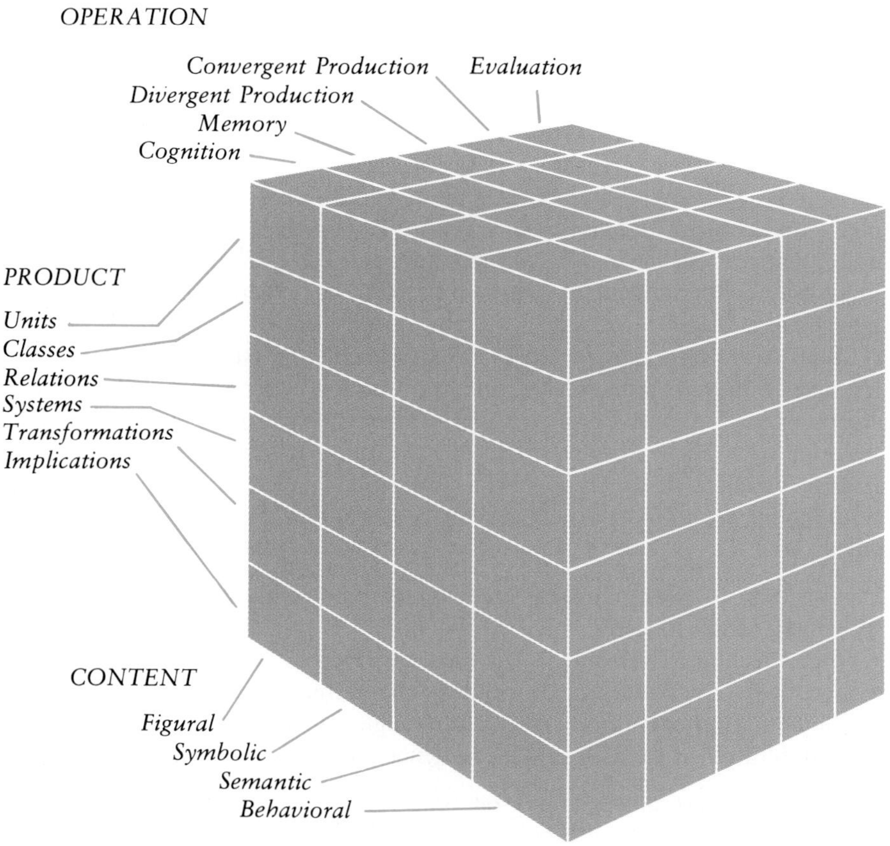

OPERATION

Convergent Production   Evaluation
Divergent Production
Memory
Cognition

FIGURE 21–6
*Guilford's Structure of
Intellect Model*

PRODUCT

Units
Classes
Relations
Systems
Transformations
Implications

CONTENT

Figural
Symbolic
Semantic
Behavioral

Source: From *The Nature of Human Intelligence* by J. P. Guilford. Copyright © 1967 by McGraw-Hill Book
Company. Reproduced with permission.

ture of intellect theory, creativity has only a weak relationship to IQ. Females
outperform males on some figural and all verbal creativity tests after about
age ten in our society, though different patterns appear in other societies.[58]
This suggests that these sex differences may be due to socialization processes.

Creative individuals resist conformity pressures if they see those pressures
as interfering with their creative accomplishments, but otherwise are willing
to conform.[59] They tend to have high turnover rates, leaving schools and jobs
more frequently than those who are less creative.[60]

CREATIVITY ENHANCEMENT TECHNIQUES

Earlier in this chapter we discussed group processes, such as the nominal
group technique and the Delphi process, which may be useful in ensuring
that many unique alternatives are generated. Here are some other creativity
enhancement techniques. What they have in common is the recognition that
good problem solving requires good alternatives.

Brainstorming

There is a small mite, *Acarophenax tribolii*, with an unusual and rather bleak life cycle. Fifteen eggs, including just one male, develop within the mother's body. The male emerges within his mother's shell, mates with all of his sisters, and dies before birth. It somehow seems sad that death should come before birth, even for a mite. Perhaps even sadder, some of our best ideas may meet similar fates. Because we are unsure of ourselves and fearful of evaluation, many of our most creative thoughts never leave our minds. Brainstorming is one technique which tries to ensure that our creative ideas will see the light of day.

Brainstorming was invented by Alex Osborn, a cofounder of the advertising agency Batten, Barton, Durstine and Osborn.[61] Osborn described brainstorming as "using the brain to storm a creative problem . . . commando fashion, with each stormer attacking the same objective." Brainstorming tries to create a situation in which group members feel they can come up with any ideas, no matter how strange, without fear of criticism. It has four rules:

Employees get together for a brainstorming session at Hewlett-Packard, a company that puts strong emphasis on the teamwork approach to problem solving.

- Criticism is ruled out. This creates a climate of psychological safety, reducing inhibitions.
- Freewheeling is welcomed. Any idea, no matter how wild, is sought.
- Quantity is desired. The more ideas, the better.
- Combination and improvement are sought. Members are encouraged to "hitchhike" on each other's ideas, generating a chain of inspiration.

There are several variations on brainstorming.[62] In stop-and-go brainstorming, short periods of brainstorming (ten minutes or so) are interspersed with short periods of evaluation. With large groups, the Phillips 66 technique can be used. Once the problem is clearly understood, small groups of six brainstorm for six minutes. Then a member of each group reports either the best ideas or all ideas to the larger group. Reverse brainstorming brings fresh approaches by turning the problem around. How could we lower productivity? How could we decrease morale? What could be done to stifle creativity?

Group brainstorming had great popularity in the 1950s. Enthusiasm for the technique faded in the 1960s, however, after a series of experiments showed that individuals working alone could produce a greater number of unique ideas than a brainstorming group.[63] More recently, though, it has been argued that a focus just on the number of ideas generated may be misleading. As we suggested earlier, ideas generated by a group may be more acceptable to the members. Further, by using the round-robin technique rather than permitting free interaction, the number of new ideas generated by group brainstorming is similar to that of pooled individuals.[64] With the round-robin technique, group members take turns giving their first idea, then their second idea, and so on.

The Gordon Technique[65]

William J. J. Gordon worked with creative thinking groups and had a variety of other creative pursuits, among them salvage diver, horse handler, ambulance driver, college lecturer, and pig breeder.[66] He observed that when people were asked to come up with a creative new idea, they would instead incrementalize—that is, they would take an available alternative and improve it bit by bit. While this might lead to marginally better alternatives, they probably would not be real breakthroughs.

Gordon decided that one way to avoid this problem would be simply not to tell people what they were inventing. The **Gordon technique** uses an initial focus on function. Rather than being told to build a better mousetrap, the group might first be told that the focus was capturing. Instead of instructing the group to design an improved knife, the function could be given as severing.

Synectics

Gordon also developed a technique called synectics. **Synectics** means the joining of apparently unrelated elements. It means this in two senses. First, very different sorts of people are put together in synectics groups in order to get a great diversity of perspectives. Second, synectics relies heavily on the use of analogies. Synectics techniques have been widely adopted by both businesses and educational institutions.[67] Three of the synectics tools that Gordon identified are direct analogy, personal analogy, and fantasy analogy:

- *Direct analogy.* This involves looking for parallel facts, knowledge, or technology in a different domain from the one being worked on. For instance, can we think of anything similar which occurs in nature? Alexander Graham Bell's words, recalled by Gordon, illustrate this approach:

  It struck me that the bones of the human ear were very massive, indeed, as compared with the delicate thin membrane that operated them, and the thought occurred that if a membrane so delicate could move bones relatively so massive, why should not a thicker and stouter piece of membrane move my piece of steel. And the telephone was conceived.[68]

- *Personal analogy.* With this approach, synectics group members try to identify psychologically with key parts of the problem. In one case, for example, the group was asked to design a mechanism that would run a shaft turning at 400 to 4000 rpm so that the power take-off end of the shaft would turn at a constant 400 rpm. To address this question, members of the group metaphorically entered the box and tried to use their bodies to attain the required speed without undue friction.

- *Fantasy analogy.* Sigmund Freud saw creativity as the fulfillment of a wish or fantasy. Fantasy analogy asks, How in my wildest dreams can I make this happen? Gordon gives the example of a synectics group with the task of inventing a vapor-proof closure for space suits. Their solution was a spring mechanism based on the fantasy analogy of rows of trained insects clasping claws to hold shut the closure.

There is more to synectics than just the use of analogy. The technique follows a structured problem-solving sequence in which a client and other participants interact to develop a workable solution to the client's problem. For instance, after the problem has been introduced and discussed, there is a "springboards" stage in which the problem is opened up by asking the client to convert concerns, opinions, and desires into statements such as "I wish . . ." or "How to . . ." Later, after an initial idea has been developed and refined, an "itemized response" stage requires the client to think of three useful aspects or advantages of the idea and to generate key concerns. Still later, after the group works to modify the suggestion to overcome these concerns, the "possible solution" is checked for elements of newness and feasibility, and whether there is sufficient commitment to the solution to take additional steps. Finally, the client lists actions to be taken to implement the solution, including timing and the personnel to be used.

Idea Checklists

Several **idea checklists** have been developed to enhance creativity.[69] The best known of these is the "73 idea-spurring questions" devised by Osborn. This checklist can be applied to any alternative. Here are some of the questions:

- Put to other uses? New ways to use as is? Other uses if modified?
- Adapt? What else is like it? What other ideas does this suggest? Does past offer parallel? What could I copy? Whom could I emulate?
- Minify? What to subtract? Smaller? Condensed? Miniature? Lower? Shorter? Lighter? Omit? Streamline? Split up? Understate?
- Substitute? Who else instead? What else instead? Other ingredient? Other material? Other process? Other power? Other place? Other approach? Other tone of voice?
- Rearrange? Interchange components? Other pattern? Other layout? Other sequence? Transpose cause and effect? Change pace? Change schedule?
- Combine? How about a blend, an alloy, an assortment, an ensemble? Combine units? Combine purposes? Combine appeals? Combine ideas?

Osborn notes that use of these techniques during World War II improved thinking in war production installations, resulting in estimated savings of 6,000,000 person-hours per year. George Washington Carver asked the question, "How can peanuts be put to other uses?" and came up with over 300 applications. Fiberglass, tapered roller bearings, and freeze-dried foods are all cited by Osborn as outcomes of listing techniques.

Attribute Listing

According to the developer of **attribute listing**, Robert Crawford, "Each time we take a step we do it by changing an attribute or a quality of something, or else by applying that same quality or attribute to some other thing."[70] There are two forms of attribute listing, attribute modifying and attribute transferring.[71]

With attribute modifying, the main attributes of the problem object are listed. Then ways to improve each attribute are listed. For instance, the technique might be used to concentrate on ways to improve the running shoe attributes of weight, stability, cushioning, and durability. Attribute transferring is similar to direct analogy in synectics. Attributes from one thing are transferred to another.

Morphological Analysis

Morphological analysis, sometimes called the checkerboard method, is an extension of attribute modifying. Specific ideas for one attribute or problem dimension are listed along one axis of a matrix. Ideas for a second attribute are listed along the other axis. If desired, a third axis (and attribute) can be added. The cells of the matrix then provide idea combinations. For instance, the axes for a vehicle might be type of energy source (e.g., steam, magnetic fields, compressed air, nuclear); medium of travel (e.g., rollers, air, water, rails); and type of vehicle (e.g., cart, chair, sling, bed).[72]

The benefit of morphological analysis is that it makes us aware of all possible combinations of the attributes. Many, of course, will prove to be of little value, but others may be worthwhile. Like other creativity enhancement techniques, morphological analysis makes us view the world from a different perspective. It has been shown to have promise in stimulating creativity for simple problems, though applications in management have not been systematically examined.[73]

Retroduction

We are the slaves of our assumptions; they dictate the way we behave. **Retroduction** involves changing an assumption. This may serve two purposes. First, our assumptions may be wrong. Second, even if our assumptions are correct, we may gain valuable new perspectives from looking at things from a different angle. Einstein, for instance, revised Newton's assumption that space is flat to the assumption that space is curved and developed a new perspective on time and space. "Images of Organization" shows how an altered perspective can influence the way we think about organizations.

One retroduction technique says "Suppose X were Y." For instance, "Suppose secretaries were chief executives." Another technique pairs apparently distinct concepts, such as power and satisfaction or perception and structure,

IMAGES OF ORGANIZATION

Gareth Morgan has written a very innovative and exciting book. Titled *Images of Organization*, it uses metaphors to encourage new ways of seeing and thinking about organizations. Morgan writes, "Many of our taken-for-granted ideas about organizations are metaphorical, even though we may not recognize them as such. For example, we frequently talk about organizations *as if* they were machines designed to achieve predetermined goals and objectives, and which should operate smoothly and efficiently. And as a result of this kind of thinking we often attempt to organize and manage them in a mechanistic way, forcing their human qualities into a background role" (p. 13). Morgan then examines eight metaphors for organizations: organizations as machines, organisms, brains, cultures, political systems, psychic prisons, flux and transformation, and instruments of domination.

Clearly, the perspective on organizations which we accept will influence our subsequent attitudes and actions. If we see organizations as machines we will tend to manage and design them as if they were made up of interlocking parts, each with a specialized function, and we will try to "fine tune" the organization's performance. If we view organizations as brains, we will attend to information processing, learning, and intelligence. With a perspective on organizations as instruments of domination, we will ask how organizations exploit certain groups, and what can be done to prevent such exploitation.

This metaphorical view of organizations does not see any single perspective as better or worse than the others. Instead, it encourages us to see the power of the metaphors we accept, and to consider the potential benefits of adopting alternative metaphorical perspectives.

Source: Based on Gareth Morgan, *Images of Organization* (Beverly Hills: Sage Publications, 1986).

and sees what new alternatives might be suggested. Yet another asks "What if?" (for example, What if employees could design their own jobs?).[74] One individual who applied these retroduction techniques generated such questions as "What are the structural irregularities of semiconductors?" and "Can arteries have rashes?" Each of these questions is now the subject of study and debate, the first among physicists and the second among researchers on disease processes.[75]

THE CREATIVE ORGANIZATION

Along with the use of specific creativity enhancement techniques, an organization may try to choose appropriate structure and processes to foster creative behavior. There is little hard empirical evidence to provide guidelines here. Instead, some writers have studied creative individuals and their desires and have drawn a picture of an organization that would seem to best suit them. One such picture, presented by George Steiner, is shown in Figure 21–7. The loose, free-flowing, adaptive nature of this organization is quite similar to the organic organization structure discussed in earlier chapters. Recall that such a structure seems appropriate in dynamic, complex, uncertain situations—exactly those most requiring creativity.

The importance of these dimensions is perhaps best seen in their absence. For instance, Japan has in recent years been losing its best and brightest young pure scientists to the United States and other countries. The reason: the scientists are unwilling to accept a system which relies on bureaucratic constraints and seniority and which stifles individualism, job mobility, and open debate. In the Japanese system, young scientists are expected to plug away patiently under the close supervision of older scientists. If they are unhappy, they can't easily move because the notion of lifelong employment is powerful in Japan and job-hoppers are seen as pariahs. Open debate is so rare that when one speaker was challenged at a conference, he froze, unable to an-

FIGURE 21–7
The Creative Organization

Open channels of communication
Encouragement of contact with outside sources
Idea units absolved of other responsibilities
Heterogeneous personnel policy
Investment in basic research
Decentralized; diversified
Risk-taking ethos
Not run as a "tight ship"
Separation of creative from productive functions
Stable, secure internal environment

Source: Excerpted from G. A. Steiner, ed., *The Creative Organization*. Copyright © 1965 by The University of Chicago Press. Reprinted with permission.

We surveyed research and development executives from a variety of industries to learn what techniques or actions their firms use to encourage creativity and innovation. Of the formal techniques described in this chapter, brainstorming was reported to be used most extensively, followed by idea checklists and synectics. Lack of financial resources and resistance to change were most often cited as barriers to innovation.

We also asked the executives, "To what extent do you think each of the following hinders or enhances creativity in organizations?" Executives rated each technique or practice on a scale of 1 to 5, with possible responses including 1 (substantially hinders), 3 (neither enhances nor hinders), and 5 (substantially enhances). Here are the results, ranked from most enhancing to most hindering:

Rank	Description	Average Rating
1	Participative leadership	4.3
2	Goals for creativity	4.0
3	Separate units for creativity	3.8
4	Rewards for creativity	3.8
5	Loosely structured organization	3.3
6	Regular committee meetings	2.8
7	Many deadlines	2.0
8	Many rules and regulations	1.8

These results suggest that managers see many of the topics discussed in this text—including leadership, goal setting, rewards, and organizational design—as possible tools for enhancing creativity. High levels of bureaucratic practices are seen as dampening creativity.

swer. In another case a young scientist held back from questioning the data of an elderly, influential author because the elder "would have lost face and . . . I would have been indirectly punished some day when I filed an application" for a grant. Bureaucratic rules regularly crimp freedom: scientists must apply months ahead for government consent to leave the country. Rather than taking risks and exploring new areas, scholars search Western journals to find research topics. One consequence of this lack of a creative environment is that only five Japanese scientists have ever won the Nobel Prize, compared to more than a score of French scientists and well over 140 Americans.[76]

If it is not possible to change the organization markedly to make it more conducive to creativity, another option is to free some units from bureaucratic entanglements by setting up relatively autonomous units. We will examine such units in the next two chapters. In addition, consider the case of Convergent Technologies discussed in Management in Action 2.

Similarly, when General Motors launched its Saturn project, the first new nameplate in the GM line since 1918, it wanted a clean-slate approach without unnecessary ties to past ways of designing, engineering, manufacturing, or selling the product. As a result, it set up a new organization in order to free Saturn from the inefficiencies and overstaffing of the current GM bureaucracy.[77]

About a year ago, Matt Sanders got kicked out of his office. His belongings were packed in boxes, and two new workers moved into the space at Conver-

MANAGEMENT IN ACTION 2
LARGE COMPUTER FIRMS SPROUT LITTLE DIVISIONS FOR GOOD, FAST WORK

gent Technologies Inc., a Silicon Valley computer maker. Mr. Sanders hung around the building for a few days, borrowing desks, without a phone to call his own.

"If you get into trouble, call me," said his boss, Allen Michels, "and if you get some good news, call me too. But I ain't calling you." Mr. Michels adds:

"Let me tell you, he was scared."

Mr. Sanders wasn't being fired, and he wasn't in trouble with his boss. On the contrary, he had been named leader of what Mr. Michels calls a "strike force" to build a new computer that would enable Convergent, which makes high-priced business computers, to enter the market for lower-priced personal computers in just one year. The idea was to tap into the entrepreneurial forces that energize so many Silicon Valley startups by cutting Mr. Sanders loose and letting him form his own "company within a company." It's an approach that several large or maturing technology companies are turning to.

Source: Reprinted by permission of *The Wall Street Journal*, © Dow Jones & Company, Inc. (August 19, 1983). All Rights Reserved Worldwide.

IMPLICATIONS FOR MANAGEMENT

Problem solving is pervasive at all levels of organizations. As a manager, you will face decisions of varying magnitudes on a daily basis. Remember that problem solving is a process, not simply a choice. To be effective, it also requires proper problem definition, good alternatives, and thoughtful implementation and control.

Many personal and situational factors conspire against effective problem solving. Some of these are largely outside the control of the individual manager, but the effects of others can at least be minimized. Self-awareness, training in statistics, and knowledge of the nature of biases may all serve to offset such difficulties. Attention to information needs and use of systematic procedures for alternative generation, evaluation, and choice may also be helpful.

When called on to make a decision, think about involving others in the process. This may improve both decision quality and acceptability and serve as a developmental experience for others. However, don't automatically select the committee format. Other, more structured group problem-solving processes may prove superior. The nominal group technique seems especially useful. And, with the proliferation of microcomputers and modems, the Delphi process can be applied more quickly and easily. If for some reason a formal process can't be used, even simple averaging of individual inputs can be helpful.

As organizations face increasingly complex, dynamic, and uncertain environments, they must shift their attention from efficiency to creativity. There are at least three approaches to increasing creativity in organizations: selection of individuals who are likely to be creative, use of creativity enhancement techniques, and design of organizations to foster creativity.

However, while creatively behaving individuals do differ in some characteristics from others, attempts to select creative types may be self-defeating.

That is, creativity thrives on diversity. Selection processes which screen out many perspectives and backgrounds stifle that diversity.

All of the creativity enhancement techniques discussed in this chapter have promise for application in organizations. Use them! Finally, remember that creativity, like any other behavior, depends on motivation and the setting as well as on ability. Try to nurture a climate conducive to creativity. Find ways to reward creative accomplishment. Set goals for creativity. And, above all, be a role model for creative behavior.

KEY TERMS AND CONCEPTS

anchoring and adjustment
attribute listing
automated decision conferencing (ADC)
availability
brainstorming
coacting groups
conservatism in information processing
convergent thinking
creative ability
creative behavior
creative process
decision confirmation
defensive avoidance
Delphi process
devil's advocate
dialectical inquiry
divergent thinking
focus effect
framing effects

Gordon technique
group polarization
groupthink
heuristics
hot decision situations
idea checklists
incrementalizing
morphological analysis
nominal groups
nominal group technique (NGT)
representativeness
retroduction
satisficing
social judgment analysis
social loafing
social presence effect
structure of intellect theory
synectics
synthetic group

QUESTIONS FOR REVIEW AND DISCUSSION

1. Consider a major decision you have made. Discuss your problem-solving process in terms of the stages discussed in this chapter. Did you pay attention to all stages? Did you use a screening approach or a scoring approach to make the choice?
2. Do you agree with the concept of a psychological account? Why or why not?
3. What is a heuristic? Choose three heuristics discussed in this chapter and construct organizational scenarios to illustrate how each can lead to inadequate decisions.
4. What is defensive avoidance? Have you ever experienced a stressful situation in which you exhibited characteristics of defensive avoidance? Describe the situation and your behavior.
5. For what sorts of problems would each of the following techniques seem to be most appropriate and least appropriate? (a) The nominal group technique; (b) the Delphi process; (c) social judgment analysis; (d) dialectical inquiry.
6. What might be some of the costs to an organization of a creative climate and creative employees?
7. Think of three individuals whom you consider to be creative. Compare and contrast their characteristics. Do you see any common threads?

8. Choose a common household object. Apply the idea checklist items presented in this chapter to that object.
9. Use morphological analysis to generate new types of mousetraps.
10. You have been approached by the CEO of a company that produces small appliances. The CEO is concerned about the creativity of the firm's managers. What concise and specific recommendations would you make to the CEO concerning easily implementable ways to improve managerial creativity? Justify each of your recommendations.

CASES

21–1 A FATAL ERROR IN JUDGMENT

At 11:38 A.M. on January 28, 1986, the space shuttle *Challenger*, with a crew of seven, rose from its launch pad, briefly ascended to the cheers of onlookers, and exploded in a ball of flames. The immediate result was widespread shock and disbelief. The cover of *Newsweek* shouted the nation's collective question, "What went wrong?" What went wrong, apparently, was the decision-making process.

"My God, Thiokol, when do you want me to launch? April?"

As Allen McDonald told it, that exasperated protest from NASA was the key moment. Under the gun, the managers of Morton Thiokol, Inc., overruled their engineers and signed approval for the space shuttle *Challenger* to blast off, sending six astronauts and a teacher to their immolation. After McDonald's testimony to the Presidential commission investigating the disaster was leaked to the press, the nature of the inquiry and the nation's view of the space program inexorably changed. Whatever technical problem caused the *Challenger* to blow up, it was clear that serious warning flags had been raised. Further, they went unheeded by middle-level officials and evidently were never communicated to the top, "It's not a design defect. There was an error in judgment," said Hank Shuey, a rocket safety expert who has reviewed NASA data. In that case, the implication was as clear as it was disturbing: The astronauts and Christa McAuliffe didn't have to die.

Perhaps most damaging to the fabric of the public trust was the indelible image of the telephone conference call the night before the fatal launch, reconstructed by reporters. A caucus of Morton Thiokol engineers in Brigham City, Utah, concerned about the effect of abnormally low temperatures on the booster-rocket seals, produced an official recommendation: No go. "We all knew if the seals failed, the shuttle would blow up," one engineer later told National Public Radio. But NASA's solid rocket project manager, Lawrence Mulloy, argued that there wasn't enough proof that cold weather stiffens the seals; the agency's George Hardy said he was "appalled" at their insistence that the launch wait for warmer weather. From Cape Canaveral, engineer McDonald protested, "It's so damn cold and none of us are really sure of anything." But as *The Washington Post* reconstructed it, NASA issued a blunt order: "We want a formal written recommendation" to launch. Thiokol, builder of the booster, gave in. The next morning, one Thiokol engineer shakily watched the lift-off. "I thought, Gee, it's going to be all right. It's a piece of cake. A friend turned to me and said, 'Oh, God, we made it. We made it.' Then . . . the shuttle blew up. And we all knew exactly what happened."

1. Would you characterize this as a "hot" or "cool" decision situation? Why?
2. What characteristics of defensive avoidance are seen in this case?
3. What sorts of policies or practices might have served to prevent the breakdowns in decision making that were evidenced?

21–2 GERMAN BOSSES STRESS CONSENSUS DECISIONS

West Germany's postwar "economic miracle" put halos around the heads of its managers. The executives who rebuilt German industry from the ashes of World War II emerged in the 1960s and 1970s as Europe's corporate elite. Their cautious, technical approach made them the ideal captains of the heavy manufacturing industries that formed the powerful base of Germany's postwar economy. As recently as 1980, U.S. management specialists were saying that American executives had much to learn from their German counterparts.

But Germany's economy has sputtered recently, and the old management virtues have come under fire. In the world's fast-changing, high-technology industries of the 1980s, the spoils go to the innovators and improvisers. Markets change too rapidly for plodding, multiyear growth plans. As German executives and management consultants take stock, they discern a worrisome aloofness and rigidity at the top of many German companies—a lack of flexibility that some see imperiling Germany's ability to remain a lasting rival to U.S. and Japanese industry.

"One of the biggest challenges is to fend off bureaucracy and paralysis," says Karl-Heinz Kaske, chief executive of Siemens AG, the giant German electrical company.

For decades, German chief executives have been renowned as technical experts. Whereas top executives in the United States more commonly move up from the financial or legal ranks, nearly 60 percent of Germany's big manufacturing companies are run by engineers with Ph.D.s. This means that subordinates asking bosses technical questions are likely to get direct, useful answers instead of blank stares. But it also means that management is learned on the job; until 1982, no German university offered a formal management degree.

German executives, along with their banks and shareholders, also have a strong tendency to focus on the long term. By looking a few years down the road instead of at problems that must be solved by next week, managers can take time to iron out any disagreements. This more leisurely timetable thus fosters consensus decisions within the managing board, or *Vorstand*. Chief executives provide guidance but rarely charismatic leadership.

The commitment to collective decision making contrasts sharply with the commandments-from-the-top system of most U.S. companies. It runs so deep that one German chemical company, Shering AG, doesn't even have a chief executive officer.

Source: Reprinted by permission of *The Wall Street Journal*, © Dow Jones & Company, Inc. (September 25, 1984). All Rights Reserved Worldwide.

1. What are some specific difficulties which are likely to result from the German decision-making approach described in this case?
2. In what situations and for what sorts of problems would the German decision-making approach be most beneficial? Most harmful?
3. Suggest group problem-solving techniques that German executives might employ to overcome some of the dysfunctional tendencies associated with their current decision-making approach.

ENDNOTES

1. This listing is based primarily on G. P. Huber, *Managerial Decision Making* (Glenview, IL: Scott, Foresman, 1980).
2. H. Mintzberg, "The Manager's Job: Folklore and Fact," *Harvard Business Review* 53 (July-August 1975): 49-61.
3. For a fuller discussion of these stages, see A. Elbing, *Behavioral Decisions in Organizations*, 2d ed. (Glenview, IL: Scott, Foresman, 1978); Huber, *Managerial Decision Making*; and B. M. Bass, *Organizational Decision Making* (Homewood, IL: Richard D. Irwin,

1983). Consideration of these stages will reveal that, while problem solving and creativity are treated separately in this chapter, creativity is an integral part of the problem-solving process.

4. See, for instance, H. A. Simon, "A Behavioral Model of Rational Choice," in *Organizational Decision Making*, ed. M. Alexis and C. Wilson (Englewood Cliffs, NJ: Prentice-Hall, 1967); P. Slovic, "Psychological Study of Human Judgment: Implications for Investment Decision Making," *Journal of Finance* 27 (1972): 779-800; H. A. Simon and A. Newell, "Human Problem Solving: The State of the Theory in 1970," *American Psychologist* 26 (1971): 145-159; and R. N. Taylor, "Psychological Determinants of Bounded Rationality," *Decision Sciences* 6 (1975): 409-429.

5. A. Tversky and D. Kahneman, "The Framing of Decisions and the Psychology of Choice," *Science* 211 (January 30, 1981): 453-458. Copyright 1981 by the AAAS.

6. P. Wright, "The Harassed Decision Maker: Time Pressures, Distractions, and the Use of Evidence," *Journal of Applied Psychology* 59 (1974): 555-561.

7. I. L. Janis and L. Mann, *Decision Making: A Psychological Analysis of Conflict, Choice, and Commitment* (New York: Free Press, 1977), provide a thorough discussion of these situations.

8. C. M. Peterson and L. R. Beach, "Man as an Intuitive Statistician," *Psychological Bulletin* 68 (1967): 29-46, provide one good review of "man as an intuitive statistician."

9. For instance, see R. M. Hogarth, "Beyond Discrete Biases: Functional and Dysfunctional Aspects of Judgmental Heuristics," *Psychological Bulletin* 90 (1981): 197-217.

10. See A. Tversky and D. Kahneman, "Judgment Under Uncertainty: Heuristics and Biases," *Science* 185 (1974): 1124-1131, for a good discussion.

11. S. J. Gould, *Hen's Teeth and Horse's Toes* (New York: W. W. Norton, 1983), 46. Reprinted with permission.

12. Ibid.

13. J. G. March and H. A. Simon, *Organizations* (New York: John Wiley & Sons, 1958).

14. Tversky and Kahneman, "Judgment Under Uncertainty."

15. On this specific point, see S. Lichtenstein et al., "Judged Frequency of Lethal Events," *Journal of Experimental Psychology: Human Learning and Memory* 4 (1978): 551-578. For a detailed discussion of the availability heuristic, see A. Tversky and D. Kahneman, "Availability: A Heuristic for Judging Frequency and Probability," *Cognitive Psychology* 5 (1973): 207-232.

16. This example is from Tversky and Kahneman, "Judgment Under Uncertainty."

17. E. Valenzi and I. R. Andrews, "Individual Differences in the Decision Process of Employment Interviewers," *Journal of Applied Psychology* 58 (1973): 49-53.

18. This choice mode was first proposed by C. E. Lindblom, "The Science of Muddling Through," *Public Administration Review* 19 (1959): 79-88.

19. W. Edwards, "Conservatism in Human Information Processing," in *Formal Representation of Clinical Judgment*, ed. B. Kleinmuntz. Copyright © 1968 by John Wiley & Sons, Inc. Reprinted by permission of John Wiley & Sons, Inc.

20. See Edwards, "Human Information Processing," and H. J. Einhorn, "Overconfidence in Judgment," *New Directions for Methodology of Social and Behavioral Science* 4 (1980): 1-16, for discussions of explanations for this tendency.

21. For a discussion of decision confirmation, see D. J. Power and R. J. Aldag, "Soelberg's Job Search and Choice Model: A Clarification, Review, and Critique," *Academy of Management Review* 10 (1985): 48-58.

22. Janis and Mann, *Decision Making: A Psychological Analysis of Conflict, Choice, and Commitment*.

23. For other examples of crisis planning and management teams, see Nancy Jeffrey, "Preparing for the Worst: Firms Set Up Plans to Help Deal with Corporate Crises," *Wall Street Journal* (December 7, 1987): 25. For a study in crisis management, see Clare Ansberry, "Oil Spill in the Midwest Provides Case Study in Crisis Management," *Wall Street Journal* (January 8, 1988): 17.

24. This listing is based primarily on N. R. F. Maier, "Assets and Liabilities in Group Problem Solving: The Need for an Integrative Function," *Psychological Review* 74 (1967): 239-249. For one empirical comparison of individual and group decision-making performance, see F. C. Miner, Jr., "Group Versus Individual Decision Making: An Investigation of Performance Measures, Decision Strategies, and Process Losses/Gains," *Organizational Behavior and Human Performance* 33 (1984): 112-124.

25. Reliability is important even in the case of a one-time decision. For instance, if a bathroom scale gives a different weight each time we stand on it, it is unreliable. Even though we might wish to use the scale only once, the unreliability of the scale would cause us to be concerned about the validity of its reading.

26. See, for instance, A. L. Delbecq, A. H. Van de Ven, and D. H. Gustafson, *Group Techniques for Program Planning* (Glenview, IL: Scott, Foresman, 1975).

27. For discussions and examinations of social loafing, see E. Weldon and G. M. Gargano, "Cognitive Effort in Additive Task Groups: The Effects of Shared Responsibility on the Quality of Multiattribute Judgments," *Organizational Behavior and Human Decision Processes* 36 (1985): 348-361, and S. G. Harkins, "Social Loafing and Social Facilitation," *Journal of Experimental Social Psychology* 23 (1987): 1-18.

28. I. L. Janis, "Groupthink," *Psychology Today* 5 (1971): 43-46 and 74-76, and *Groupthink*, 2d ed. (Boston: Houghton Mifflin, 1982). For more recent research on groupthink, see M. R. Callaway, R. G. Marriott, and J. K. Esser, "Effects of Dominance on Group Decision Making: Toward a Stress-Reduction Explanation of Groupthink," *Journal of Personality and Social Psychology* 49 (1985): 949-952, and G. Moorhead and J. R. Montanari, "An Empirical Investigation of the Groupthink Phenomenon," *Human Relations* 39 (1986): 399-410. For a recent discussion of groupthink, see G. Whyte, "Groupthink Reconsidered," *Academy of Management Review* 14 (1989): 40-56.

29. Janis saw groupthink as a major contributor to such faulty decisions as the failure to prepare for the attack on Pearl Harbor, the Bay of Pigs invasion, and the escalation of the Vietnam conflict, and he argues that these same processes may occur in business organizations as well. However, no published experimental studies of groupthink have used managerial or other non-student samples.

30. For a good review of group polarization, see D. J. Isenberg, "Group Polarization: A Critical Review and Meta-Analysis," *Journal of Personality and Social Psychology* 50 (1986): 1141-1151.

31. Janis, *Groupthink*, 2d ed.

32. A. H. Van de Ven and A. L. Delbecq, "Nominal Versus Interacting Groups for Committee Decision-Making Effectiveness," *Academy of Management Journal* 14 (1971): 203-212.

33. Ibid.

34. See T. B. Green, "An Empirical Analysis of Nominal and Interacting Groups," *Academy of Management Journal* 18 (1975): 63-73; W. R. Street, "Brainstorming by Individuals, Coacting and Interacting Groups," *Journal of Applied Psychology* 59 (1974): 433-436; and A. H. Van de Ven and A. L. Delbecq, "The Effectiveness of Nominal, Delphi, and Interacting Group Processes," *Academy of Management Journal* 17 (1974): 605-621. For a discussion of a revision of this technique, see S. Frankel, "NGT + MDS: An Adaptation of the Nominal Group Technique for Ill-Structured Problems," *Journal of Applied Behavioral Science* 23 (1987): 543-551.

35. This listing is based on M. Turoff, "Delphi and Its Potential Impact on Information Systems," *AFIPS Conference Proceedings* 39 (1971): 317-326.

36. Ibid.

37. See Delbecq, Van de Ven, and Gustafson, *Group Techniques*, for a thorough discussion of the Delphi process. See also J. Rohrbaugh, "Improving the Quality of Group Judgment: Social Judgment Analysis and the Delphi Technique," *Organizational Behavior and Human Performance* 24 (1979): 73-92.

38. Rohrbaugh, "Improving the Quality of Group Judgment."

39. This section is based on R. E. Quinn and J. Rohrbaugh, "How to Improve Organizational Decision Making: A Report on Automated Decision Conferencing," working paper (Institute for Government and Policy Studies, Rockefeller College of Public Affairs and Policy, State University of New York at Albany, 1983). For another computerized approach to group problem solving, see M. L. G. Shaw, "An Interactive Knowledge-Based System for Group Problem Solving," *IEEE Transactions on Systems, Man, and Cybernetics* 18 (1988): 610-617.

40. For instance, see G. P. Huber, "Methods for Quantifying Subjective Probabilities and Multi-Attribute Utilities," *Decision Sciences* 5 (1974): 430-458.

41. For discussions of the devil's advocate, see R. O. Mason, "A Dialectical Approach to Strategic Planning," *Management Science* 15 (1969): B403-B414, and T. T. Herbert and R. W. Estes, "Improving Executive Decisions by Formalizing Dissent: The Corporate Devil's Advocate," *Academy of Management Review* 2 (1977): 662-667.

42. Dialectical inquiry is based on the writings of G. W. F. Hegel, *The Phenomenology of the Mind* (London: George Allen and Unwin, 1964). These steps are based on Mason, *Dialectical Approach*.

43. D. M. Schweiger, W. R. Sandberg, and J. W. Ragan, "Group Approaches for Improving Strategic Decision Making: A Comparative Analysis of Dialectical Inquiry, Devil's Advocacy, and Consensus," *Academy of Management Journal* 29 (1986): 51-71.

44. These quotes are drawn from *The Wall Street Journal* (May 10, 1983): 20. For a more recent discussion of Polaroid's creativity woes, see Lawrence Ingrassia, "How Polaroid Fights To Regain Creativity After Its Long Slide," *Wall Street Journal* (August 12, 1988): 1. For a variety of perspectives on creativity in organizations, see P. Colemont, P. Groholt, T. Rickards, and H. Smeekes, eds., *Creativity and Innovation: Towards a European Network* (Dordrecht, The Netherlands: Kluwer Academic Publishers, 1988).

45. S. A. Mednick, "The Associative Basis of the Creative Process," *Psychological Review* 69 (1962):221. For a discussion of creative products, see S. P. Besemer and D. J. Treffinger, "Analysis of Creative Products: Review and Synthesis," *Journal of Creative Behavior* 15 (1981): 158-178.

46. G. Halpin and G. Halpin, "The Effect of Motivation on Creative Thinking Abilities," *Journal of Creative Behavior* 7 (1973): 51-53, provide one demonstration of the impact of motivation on creativity.

47. G. Wallas, *The Art of Thought* (New York: Harcourt, Brace, 1926).

48. Quoted in G. A. Davis, *Creativity Is Forever* (Dubuque, IA: Kendall/Hunt, 1983), 9.

49. For discussions of theories of creativity, see T. V. Busse and R. S. Mansfield, "Theories of the Creative Process: A Review and a Perspective," *Journal of Creative Behavior* 14 (1980): 91-103, and M. D. Mumford and S. B. Gustafson, "Creativity Syndrome: Integration, Application, and Innovation," *Psychological Bulletin* 103 (1988): 27-43.

50. C. Lombroso, *The Man of Genius* (London: Charles Scribner's Sons, 1895).

51. A. H. Maslow, ed., *New Knowledge in Human Values* (Chicago: Henry Regnery, 1959).

52. B. F. Skinner, "A Lecture on 'Having' a Poem," in *B. F. Skinner, Cumulative Record: A Selection of Papers*, 3d ed. (Englewood Cliffs, NJ: Prentice-Hall, 1972).

53. J. P. Guilford, *The Nature of Human Intelligence* (New York: McGraw-Hill, 1967).

54. T. R. Amabile, *The Social Psychology of Creativity* (New York: Springer-Verlag, 1983).

55. F. Barron, "The Dream of Art and Poetry," *Psychology Today* 2, no. 12 (1968): 18-23; W. E. Scott, Jr., "The Creative Individual," *Academy of Management Journal* 8 (1965): 211-219; and G. A. Steiner, ed., *The Creative Organization* (Chicago: University of Chicago Press, 1965).

56. T. Christie, "Environmental Factors in Creativity," *Journal of Creative Behavior* 4 (1970): 13-31.

57. H. C. Lehman, *Age and Achievement* (Princeton, NJ: Princeton University Press, 1953). This peaking of creative output in young adulthood is seen primarily for major creative contributions. For minor contributions, creative output peaks in middle age. In general, the peak of the creative output curve occurs earlier in fields highly dependent on native ability and later for fields requiring substantial training and life experience. These observations appear to be stable across cultural groups and historical periods.

58. E. P. Torrance and N. C. Aliotti, "Sex Differences in Levels of Performance and Test-Retest Reliability on the Torrance Tests of Creative Thinking Ability," *Journal of Creative Behavior* 3 (1969): 52-57.

59. J. R. Raia and S. H Osipow, "Creative Thinking Ability and Susceptibility to Persuasion," *Journal of Social Psychology* 28 (1970): 181-186.

60. P. O. Heist, "Creative Students: College Transients," in *The Creative College Student: An Unmet Challenge* (San Francisco: Jossey-Bass, 1968), and E. P. Torrance, "Is Bias Against Job Changing Bias Against Giftedness?" *Gifted Child Quarterly* 15 (1971): 244-248.

61. A. F. Osborn, *Applied Imagination*, 3d ed. (New York: Scribner's, 1963).

62. These are drawn from Davis, *Creativity*.

63. D. W. Taylor, P. C. Berry, and C. H. Block, "Does Group Participation When Using Brainstorming Facilitate or Inhibit Creative Thinking?" *Administrative Science Quarterly* 3 (1958): 23-47, and M. D. Dunnette, J. Campbell, and K. Jostad, "Effect of Group Participation on Brainstorming Effectiveness for Two Industrial Samples," *Journal of Applied Psychology* 47 (1963): 30-37.

64. See R. N. Taylor, *Behavioral Decision Making* (Glenview, IL: Scott, Foresman, 1984), 43-47.

65. W. J. J. Gordon, *Synectics* (New York: Harper & Row, 1961).

66. Davis, *Creativity*, 67.

67. For instance, W. J. J. Gordon, "On Being Explicit About Creative Process," *Journal of Creative Behavior* 6 (1972): 295-300, wrote that more than 200 businesses had spent over $1 million on synectics techniques as early as 1971, and that materials developed by synectics education systems had influenced over 10,000 classrooms. A 1988 Synectics brochure indicated that Synectics Corporation had worked with over 50,000 individuals and with approximately 25 percent of the Fortune 500 companies. For a discussion of the application of Synectics and other creativity enhancement techniques in organizations, see D. Thorn, "Problem Solving for Innovation in Industry," *Journal of Creative Behavior* 21 (1987): 93-107.

68. Gordon, *Synectics*, 42.

69. See Davis, *Creativity*, for a fuller discussion.

70. R. P. Crawford, "The Techniques of Creative Thinking," in *Training Creative Thinking*, ed. G. A. Davis and J. A. Scott (Huntington, NY: Krieger, 1978).

71. Davis, *Creativity*.

72. This example is from J. E. Arnold, "Useful Creative Techniques," in *A Sourcebook of Creative Thinking*, ed. S. Parnes (New York: Scribner's, 1962), 251-268.

73. For studies on morphological analysis, see E. P. Stratton and R. Brown, "Improving Creative Training by Training in the Production and/or Judgment of Solutions," *Journal of Educational Psychology* 61 (1970): 16-23; T. F. Warren and G. A. Davis, "Techniques for Creative Thinking: An Empirical Comparison of Three Methods," *Psychological Reports* 25 (1969): 207-214; F. Zwicky, *Morphological Astronomy* (New York: Springer-Verlag, 1957), and *Discovery, Invention, Research Through the Morphological Approach* (New York: Macmillan, 1969).

74. See B. Olmo, "Retroduction: The Key to Creativity," *Journal of Creative Behavior* 11 (1977): 216, 221.

75. David Stipp, "Patrick Gunkel Is an Idea Man Who Thinks in Lists," *Wall Street Journal* (June 1, 1987): 1, 11.

76. This example is drawn from Stephen Yoder, "Japan's Scientists Find Pure Research Suffers Under Rigid Life Style," *Wall Street Journal* (November 31, 1988): A1.

77. *Wall Street Journal* (January 9, 1985): 3.

Change and Culture

CHAPTER 22

After studying this chapter, you should be able to:
- *Identify the forces that influence organizational change.*
- *Discuss the differences between planned and reactive responses to change.*
- *Identify reasons why change may be resisted and techniques to overcome resistance to change.*
- *Describe three domains of the organization that can be targets for change.*
- *Describe the steps, techniques, and conditions for the success of an organizational development program.*
- *Identify the importance of organization culture for successful management.*
- *Discuss eight attributes that may characterize the culture of a successful company.*

When James L. Dutt ascended to the chairmanship of Beatrice Companies Inc. in 1979, he brought with him a vision of what the company should be. Beatrice was a giant Chicago-based company producing more than 9,000 food and consumer products. Dutt had joined the company in 1947 as a part-time accountant at a local dairy plant in Kansas. As chairman of Beatrice Companies he aggressively sold off divisions, set up a large advertising budget, and imposed tighter controls over employees. This was done to push the company's return on equity higher and to accelerate growth in earnings per share. By 1985, however, Dutt was forced out of the chairmanship of Beatrice. His efforts to change the company had been unsuccessful, leading to a high number of executive resignations and low employee morale. In addition, there were persistent problems in the reorganization of the company and a drop in earnings per share. Former employees claimed that Dutt was prone to deliver tirades that demoralized rather than inspired and that he could not tolerate dissent or debate.[1]

The purposes of this chapter are to suggest how managers can most effectively bring about change in an organization and to explore methods for creating an effective culture within the organization. Organizations can be difficult to change, as James Dutt found out with Beatrice. In spite of his 32 years with the company before being made chairman, Dutt was unable to carry out successfully his vision for Beatrice. However, not all organizations are difficult to change. Some organization managers try to make change a continual process. Other managers may try to resist change, believing that change leads to disruptions and thus to lower performance. As we will see, the need for change is dependent on several external and internal forces that influence the activities of the organization.

This chapter presents ideas and guidelines for managing change. In addition to identifying the external and internal forces that promote change, we will discuss the change process, the targets for change, the techniques associated with organization development, the elements of organization culture, and how organization culture can be managed effectively.

FORCES FOR ORGANIZATIONAL CHANGE

Organizational change is any alteration of activities in an organization. The alteration of activities can be the result of many things: changes in the structure of the organization, transfer of work tasks, introduction of a new product, or changes in attitudes among members. Managers must learn to recognize not only when change is occurring in an organization but also when change is needed. The need for change results from forces that are external and internal to the organization.

External Forces

As we saw in Chapter 3, the environmental domains in which an organization operates can have a significant effect on organization activities. The widely discussed books *Future Shock* and *Megatrends* both underscore that environmental change is occurring at an increasingly rapid rate.[2] Understand-

Growing concern about air pollution has led to government controls affecting the operations of many firms.

ing how that change may affect an organization, for better or worse, is an important task for today's managers.

In the economic domain, inflation, gross national product indicators, and the money supply can affect the ability of organization managers to get needed resources. New laws and regulations, trade tariffs, and court decisions emanating from the political domain can affect the way an organization conducts its business. Changing values, norms, attitudes, customs, and demographic patterns in the social domain often require changes in products and training procedures. In the technological domain, transfer of innovations can either enhance or threaten the organization, depending on how effectively managers can respond. Activities in the competitive domain such as mergers, pricing, and changes in strategies are all critical forces that can lead to organizational change. And finally, most organizations are affected to some degree by the physical domain of the environment.

Changes in the environmental domains of an organization can generate either opportunities or threats. In the 1980s, for example, many savings and loans lent money to governments of countries that were large oil producers. At the time the loans were made, oil prices were rapidly climbing and generating large revenues for producers. This situation changed dramatically, however, when an oil glut drastically reduced the incomes of countries that had borrowed from the banks. Managers who had considered this possibility made changes in their lending and investment practices; many managers who did not foresee the problem were forced into bankruptcy.

Internal Forces

Several areas within an organization can also be a force for change. Broadly speaking, these include (1) structure, where change can result from organizational growth, decline, or a shift in goals; (2) products, as in the case where new products are introduced which may require different production, marketing, and accounting methods; (3) tasks, as when the transfer of existing task technology requires retraining or changes in personnel; and (4) people, as when changes in organization members' attitudes, values, or levels of motivation occur.

Managers must recognize that external and internal forces can be highly interrelated. Attitudes that employees have toward work may change because of a general shift in attitudes among the populace. Efforts to change or install new technologies may be the result of competitive pressures or exposure to new technologies in other industries. Because organizations operate as open systems, a relationship between external and internal forces will always exist. However, managers must be able to identify not only the cause of change, but also the external and internal domains in which the change is taking place. Only then will management be able to respond correctly to the change and adopt activities that will enable the organization to be effective. Figure 22–1 summarizes the external and internal forces for organizational change.

Ideas for change can come from many different sources. For decades, the company suggestion box has been a fixture in many corporate headquarters and on plant floors. It is designed to ask for needs, ideas, and proposals informally from employees. Management in Action 1 shows how one individual

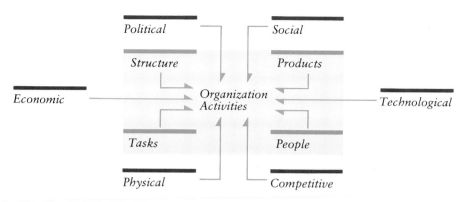

FIGURE 22-1
*External and Internal
Forces for
Organizational Change*

and a suggestion box have become a powerful force for change at General Motors.

THE CHANGE PROCESS

Organization managers must learn to respond to both external and internal forces for change. Pressures for change come from so many factors that many managers spend much of their time planning or reacting to change. To avoid unwanted results, managers need to understand the steps in the change process, reasons why change may be resisted, and techniques that can be applied for overcoming resistance to change.

Planned Versus Reactive Change

Managers can respond to pressures for change by either planning or reacting. **Planned change** occurs when managers develop and install a program that serves to alter organization activities in a timely and orderly way. In many instances, planned change is instigated because managers expect the development of a force for change and thus seek to prepare the organization to adjust activities with minimal disruption. **Reactive change** occurs when managers simply respond to the pressure for change when that pressure comes to their attention. Usually this is a piecemeal approach because managers are facing problems that need immediate resolution.

Planned change is regarded as the superior approach to change. It is often used when change in the organization is to be extensive and lengthy. As such, it requires a greater commitment of time and resources and requires additional expertise in formulating and implementing the change. However, planned change can also be very effective when only modest change in organization activities is required. The key to planned change is that managers must be able to anticipate the types of change that will be necessary.

Reactive change is usually hurried and less expensive to carry out than planned change. It is most effective when applied to small or day-to-day problems in the organization. Examples would include postponing production activities in response to shipping delays, altering a dress code policy to enable office workers to help move belongings to new headquarters, or deciding to hire computer consultants upon learning that the recently bought com-

Michael G. McKay, a 40-year-old machinist for General Motors Corporation, is proof of the power of suggestion. McKay, who carries a picture of inventor

MANAGEMENT IN ACTION 1
HE'S THE KING OF SUGGESTION MAKERS

Thomas Edison, has stuffed his company's suggestion box about 250 times in the past 21 years with ideas he felt would save GM money. The company estimates that about 200 have been implemented at a savings of $3 million. Many of the rest are still being evaluated.

Enlisting employees in the drive for greater efficiency has never been more popular in the United States as managers, economists, politicians, and consultants decry what they see as slipping U.S. productivity and increasing competition from other nations, especially Japan. The modern form of the suggestion box is growing more important in the effort.

Employee suggestion programs have been around a long time; Eastman Kodak Company established the first in 1898. And the National Association of Suggestion Systems began in 1942, when 35 suggestion administrators from different organizations met in Chicago and decided to establish a clearing house

through which affiliated organizations could benefit from the experience of others.

But the key to making the concept work is still the person on the job who sees a better way of doing something. And that describes McKay. For his history of money-saving ideas, he was honored by the association as "Suggester of the Year." For some, the honor would pale beside the $20,000 check one of McKay's latest innovations brought from the company, but he claims his biggest reward is just "having an idea and making it work. It makes me feel good to see the company pick up on my ideas. The reward is minor. Seeing your idea implemented just makes you feel good."

Persistence also pays. "I got $15,000 once on a suggestion that was turned down four times before it was accepted," he said. His suggestions have ranged from his first—in 1964, when he suggested setting up a canteen arrangement for workers to eat their lunches instead of sitting on the floor or on boxes, for which he received $25—to a redesign of a pump the company says will save $3.5 million in the next five years. His most successful year was 1984, when he received about $80,000 from the company for his suggestions.

puter operates in a language unfamiliar to division programmers. These changes usually require minimal planning and are best handled by managers at the time a problem occurs. Other instances in which reactive change may be more appropriate than planned change occur when external and internal forces are themselves changing so rapidly that planning is virtually impossible.

Steps in the Change Process

Whether managers are engaged in planned or reactive change, understanding and implementing the steps in the change process will increase the chances that the change will be successful. One of the first efforts to identify appropriate steps in a change process was made by Kurt Lewin.[3] Lewin, and later Edgar H. Schein,[4] who elaborated on what is known as the **Lewin-Schein model**, identify three general steps in the change process: unfreezing, changing, and refreezing.

THE LEWIN-SCHEIN MODEL

Lewin and Schein noticed that most individuals find it difficult to alter attitudes and behaviors that they have practiced for a long while. When told that their attitude or behavior is inappropriate, they are likely to deny or reject the information. This resistance, according to Lewin, can be countered by

unfreezing the attitude or behavior pattern—that is, by making the need for change so obvious that the individual will be willing to accept the change. This is the first step in the model.

The second general step in the Lewin-Schein model is changing. **Changing** occurs when the individual accepts and internalizes the changes in behavior and attitude that are necessary. The third and final step, **refreezing**, occurs when the changed attitude and behavior are supported and reinforced in a way that is rewarded by the organization. As a result, the new attitude and behavior become the accepted way of doing things in the organization.

SUCCESSFUL CHANGE

Although the Lewin-Schein model is valuable in understanding why efforts to create change in an organization sometimes succeed and sometimes fail, it does not fully identify all the elements necessary for change to be successful. Richard Daft suggests that in order for a new idea or behavior to be successfully adopted, the following elements must be present:[5]

1. *Need*. Recognition of the need for change occurs when organization members become dissatisfied with current activities. Perhaps goals are not being met, product quality may be low, or market share may be shrinking. Dissatisfaction serves to unfreeze acceptance of current activities by organization members.
2. *Idea*. An idea is a new way of doing things. An idea may be a new product, a new technique, or a new machine. However, ideas must be matched with a need. Members of the organization must perceive that the idea, if carried out, will reduce the dissatisfaction caused by current activities.
3. *Proposal*. A proposal is a request by someone in the organization to adopt the new idea. Proposals may take the form of a memo, a formal written document, a suggestion made during a conversation, or a recommendation of an official committee in the organization. A proposal shows how an idea will solve a problem such as unmet goals. A proposal also begins the process of consideration by members concerning whether or not to adopt an idea.
4. *Decision to adopt*. A decision occurs when a choice is made to adopt the proposed idea. This decision may be made by the board of directors if the change is rather large, or by a first-line supervisor if the change is small.
5. *Implementation*. Implementation occurs when organization members actually use the new idea. This may involve a change in attitudes, behaviors, equipment, or products. Without implementation, change cannot take place.
6. *Resources*. Adopting a new idea requires financial, material, human, and information resources. Without resources, change will not take place, and members will return to their previous ways of doing things in the organization.

Often the smallest amount of dissatisfaction or need can lead to a prosperous outcome for an organization. Management in Action 2 describes how the need of one individual resulted in a product that now sits on the desk of virtually every secretary in the country.

Suddenly, they are everywhere! Those tiny yellow sheets of notepaper with sticky backs. You find them clinging to your office door in the mornings. They

MANAGEMENT IN ACTION 2
STICK 'EM UP

are affixed on letters from associates in the mail. You return from lunch to find them hugging the receiver of your phone. A brief trip to the water fountain engenders one on the side of your coffee cup left back at your desk.

Midway through the 1980s, a humble invention called repositional notepaper has quietly but quickly stuck itself into the lives of millions of Americans. Many people cannot recall when they wrote or received their first note on these yellow pages with the quick-gripping adhesive backs. One thing they say they do know for sure: They can never return to a life without them.

The Post-it note pad has been compared to inventions as utilitarian as the paper clip and as imaginative as the shmoo (an imaginary comic-strip character that existed solely to help people). They are simple to use and benign; they leave no trace when you remove them. Like so many great inventions, this one was born of need. It was a sleepy Sunday in 1974, in St. Paul, Minnesota, when Art Fry conceived the idea that has grown into one of the

most successful consumer products of the 1980s.

A scientist at the 3M Company, Fry was singing in his church choir when he was confronted with the problem of finding himself hopelessly lost when the tiny slips of paper he used as bookmarks fell from his hymnal. "I thought, what I need is a bookmark with some adhesive so it would stay put but wouldn't damage the pages if I pulled it off," he said. The next morning at his office at 3M headquarters, he began fiddling with a quick-grip adhesive that a colleague named Spencer Silver had recently discovered. Most people at the giant consumer products company had dismissed this new adhesive as useless, because it wasn't strong enough, wasn't sticky enough. But, Fry realized, that might be its beauty. "It was technology in need of an application," said Fry, who today is a senior scientist at 3M.

It took six years to perfect the product and convince skeptical corporate marketers that the time was right for this idea. But finally, in 1980, the product was released nationally. The rest is consumer product history. Post-it notes quickly claimed a spot in the pantheon of the five top-selling office products, among basics such as paper clips, scotch tape, file folders, and typewriter correction fluid. Although 3M will not release sales figures, industry observers have estimated annual sales reach somewhere between $80 million and $200 million.

Source: Christopher Bogan, *Dallas Times Herald*, as printed in *The Milwaukee Journal* (November 24, 1985): Life/Style section, p. 2 (story distributed by the *Los Angeles Times–Washington Post* News Service).

Resistance to Change

Not all change is greeted warmly by members of an organization. The implementation of a new idea or technique is quite often met with resistance by those who will be affected most. Managers must understand and overcome resistance to change. First, we will identify and discuss the major reasons for resistance to change and then explain strategies managers can apply to overcome it.[6]

SELF-INTEREST

It is natural for organization members to have interests in benefiting themselves directly. Resistance is likely to occur if a proposed change in the organization threatens those interests. Being assigned to manage a new product may increase one's prestige while lessening the prestige of those who did not receive the assignment. Opportunities for promotion may diminish if authority over hiring is shifted from the corporate personnel department to the divisional level in the organization. Installation of new equipment may make a work unit's skills less valuable to the organization. When change is likely to endanger organization members' self-interests, resistance to the change will result.

UNCERTAINTY

With change comes uncertainty. Organization members may resist a change because they cannot be sure how the change will affect their work and lives. Often they expect the worst. This can lead to a dogged resistance and a preference for the existing condition.

LACK OF UNDERSTANDING AND TRUST

Many proposed changes are not adequately explained to those who will be affected by the change. Failure to understand the change increases the chances that members or departments will resist the change. A lack of trust can also support resistance to change. Prior experiences with those supporting or initiating change may have involved misrepresentations or deceit. In this case, resistance may be based simply on who supports the proposed change in the organization.

DIFFERENT PERCEPTIONS

Differences of opinion about the need for change and what the change will accomplish can be a cause of resistance. People tend to see situations and events differently because of prior experiences and training. An engineer is likely to view a change in the production process differently from the way an accountant views it. The engineer may perceive the change in terms of increasing task efficiency in the production of a good. The accountant may perceive the change in terms of the cost increase that will be reflected in the price of the product. Thus, resistance will result from legitimate disagreements over the outcome of the change based on the differing perceptions.

LACK OF TOLERANCE FOR CHANGE

Some organization members feel comfortable with change, while others feel uncomfortable. Even when members are shown that the change will not threaten their self-interest, the results are certain, full understanding and trust exist, and perceptions agree, they may resist change. For example, some people prefer to drive the same route to work even when they agree that a different route is quicker, safer, and less crowded. They are unwilling to make the change because they like the comfortable familiarity of the old route.

Overcoming Resistance to Change

Resistance to change by members in an organization should not necessarily alarm managers. Resistance in some form should be expected. Understanding the cause of the resistance will enable managers to employ techniques to overcome it effectively. Several strategies for overcoming resistance to change can be applied.[7] The advantages and disadvantages of these strategies, and the situations in which the strategies are appropriate, are summarized in Figure 22–2.

Approach	Commonly used where...	Advantages	Disadvantages
Education + Communication	There is a lack of information or inaccurate information and analysis.	Once persuaded, people will often help with the implementation of the change.	Can be very time-consuming if lots of people are involved.
Participation + Involvement	The initiators do not have all the information they need to design the change and where others have considerable power to resist.	People who participate will be committed to implementing change, and any relevant information they have will be integrated into the change plan.	Can be very time-consuming if participators design an inappropriate change.
Facilitation + Support	People are resisting because of adjustment problems.	No other approach works as well with adjustment problems.	Can be time-consuming, expensive, and still fail.
Negotiation + Agreement	Someone or some group will clearly lose out in a change and where that group has considerable power to resist.	Sometimes it is a relatively easy way to avoid major resistance.	Can be too expensive in many cases if it alerts others to negotiate for compliance.
Manipulation + Co-optation	Other tactics will not work or are too expensive.	It can be a relatively quick and inexpensive solution to resistance problems.	Can lead to future problems if people feel manipulated.
Explicit + Implicit Coercion	Speed is essential, and the change initiators possess considerable power.	It is speedy and can overcome any kind of resistance.	Can be risky if it leaves people mad at the initiators.

Source: Reprinted by permission of *Harvard Business Review*. An exhibit from "Choosing Strategies for Change" by John P. Kotter and Leonard A. Schlesinger (March/April 1979). Copyright © 1979 by the President and Fellows of Harvard College; all rights reserved.

FIGURE 22–2
Methods for Dealing with Resistance to Change

EDUCATION AND COMMUNICATION

Explaining the need for and logic of the change is an effective strategy for reducing resistance. Often members lack the information to gauge the change properly or have inaccurate perceptions of how the change will affect them. Education helps members to better understand the need for change.

PARTICIPATION AND INVOLVEMENT

Managers can overcome resistance to change by having members participate in the planning and implementation of the change. This helps reduce uncertainty and misunderstandings about the purpose of the change. Participation also allows members to express their own ideas and listen to the ideas of others, in the process gaining a better picture of why some approaches to change were selected while other approaches were rejected.

FACILITATION AND SUPPORT

Gradual introduction of the change process and provision of support to people affected by the change are effective for overcoming resistance. Support can be provided to those members directly affected by the change by providing training programs, time off during the transition period, and emotional support when the change process is at a difficult stage.

Providing group support to those affected by a change can help to overcome resistance and ease stress.

NEGOTIATION AND AGREEMENT

Often managers must negotiate or bargain to win acceptance or reduce resistance to change. Powerful individuals or departments in an organization may demand more resources to support the change, believing correctly or incorrectly that the change will reduce their power. Managers may want to seek agreements through negotiation before the implementation of change to avoid disrupting the change process.

MANIPULATION AND CO-OPTATION

Managers may select a strategy of covertly steering individuals or groups away from resistance to change through selective use of information. They may also assign potential resisters to a desired position in the change process.

EXPLICIT AND IMPLICIT COERCION

If managers seeking to carry out change hold an advantage of power over resisters, they may demand that members support the change or be threatened with the loss of rewards and resources. Since this strategy has the potential for increasing resistance among members in the future, it is most appropriately used when change must occur quickly and without the opportunity to muster support through other strategies.

TARGETS FOR CHANGE

Change can be targeted to three important areas of an organization: technological, administrative, and human.[8] Change in an organization's technology involves the alteration of equipment, engineering processes, research tech-

FIGURE 22–3
*Areas for Targeting
Organizational Change*

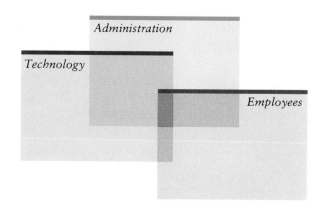

niques, or production methods. Change in the administration of an organization involves approaches that alter the organization's structures, lines of communication, managerial hierarchy, goals, strategies, and reward systems. Change in humans, or employees of the organization, is focused on altering attitudes, values, technical skills, and behaviors. Managers must identify a target or several targets for change that will lead to greater overall effectiveness. As suggested in Figure 22–3, these three areas of an organization overlap, and thus change in one area often requires change in another area. We will examine each of these target areas.

Technological Change

With ever-increasing pressure on American management to increase innovation and improve production efficiency, technological change has received considerable attention. Recall from Chapter 9 that technology is the conversion process that transforms organizational inputs into outputs. As such, an organization's technology consists of machinery, knowledge, tools, techniques, and actions that are necessary to complete the transformation process. Thus, **technological change** involves alterations in the organization's conversion process.

A problem that often faces managers wishing to make technological changes is how to achieve the right balance between creativity and routinization. Creativity, as discussed in Chapter 21, leads to innovation; routiniza-

*Magnetic resonance
imaging is one of many
technological advances
that are changing the
ways medical personnel
diagnose patients'
problems.*

tion often increases efficiencies in production. However, in many situations, promoting creativity can decrease efficiency and promoting efficiency can decrease creativity in the production of goods and services. Moreover, emphasis on creativity is useful for starting change, but the implementation of change is easiest through a routinized technology. How can managers resolve this dilemma?

One answer is to develop organizations with structures set up that are appropriate to both creativity and efficiency.[9] Recall from Chapter 9 that Tom Burns and G. M. Stalker identified two types of organizational designs: organic and mechanistic.[10] Organic organizational designs are those that emphasize decentralized structures and thus promote creativity. Mechanistic designs emphasize centralized structures and are appropriate for tasks that need to be routinized. When managers want to promote creativity to begin technological change, it is best to have an organic design. However, a centralized, mechanistic design would be more appropriate for implementing change to increase production efficiencies. An organization that has separate designs, an organic design for creativity and the initiation of change and a mechanistic design for the implementation of technological change, is called an **ambidextrous organization**. There are four ways organizations can use the ambidextrous approach to achieve technological change: through switching structures, innovation departments, venture teams, and idea champions.[11]

SWITCHING STRUCTURES

Switching structures means that managers change the design of their department or organization between organic and mechanistic depending on whether innovation or implementation is needed. For instance, managers may decide to halt production for a day to conduct informal meetings in which employees can identify problems and generate ideas for solving those problems. Once an agreed-upon solution has been achieved, managers can then change the department back to a mechanistic design to carry out the change. Generally this method works best in smaller organizations such as restaurants or manufacturers of parts.

INNOVATION DEPARTMENTS

In larger organizations, separate departments can be created to deal specifically with creativity and initiation of change. These **innovation departments** are organically designed to aid the development of new ideas and techniques. Ideas that are thought to be worthy are then passed on to a mechanistically designed department for implementation. Research and development departments are often designed organically for generating innovations. The innovation is then communicated to the production department, which carries out the innovation through a mechanistic design. Figure 22–4 identifies the relationship between separate departments where the initiator has an organic design and the implementer a mechanistic design.

Innovating Department (Organic Design)	Initiation	Implementing Department (Mechanistic Design)

FIGURE 22–4
Innovating Versus Implementing

VENTURE TEAMS

An increasingly popular technique for technological change is the use of venture teams. A **venture team** is a temporary grouping of organization members for generating new ideas. So that creative thinking is not stifled, they are freed of the organization's bureaucracy and in many cases have a separate location and facilities. Major corporations such as IBM, 3M Company, Dow Chemical, and Texas Instruments have used venture teams to solve technical problems and promote change.

IDEA CHAMPIONS

An **idea champion** is a member of the organization who is assigned responsibility for the successful implementation of a change. The idea champion may be a senior manager or a non-manager, such as the inventor of the idea that has prompted the change. An idea champion is devoted to the change and is willing to spend time and energy to see that the change takes place. Idea champions will fight resistance to change and will actively pursue resources necessary to carry out the change. Senior managers often make excellent idea champions because they have personal power and prestige that can push the idea through bureaucratic red tape and make sure that the idea comes to the attention of key decision makers. Idea champions may be critical to the success or failure of change. For example, Texas Instruments reviewed 50 successful and unsuccessful technical projects. One consistent finding was that every failure also lacked an idea champion. As a result, Texas Instruments set up as its number one criterion for project approval the presence of an idea champion.[12]

Administrative Change

Administrative change refers to alterations in the organization's structures, lines of communication, managerial hierarchy, goals, strategies, or reward systems. Change is usually carried out in the administrative area of the organization to improve the coordination and control of manager and member activities. Management may, for instance, alter the strategy of the organization, which in turn will require the implementation of new structures to coordinate and control activities that are designed to support the new strategy. Administrative change is important when the organization must adopt new managerial methods to improve performance or to avoid failures.

One way for managers to understand the process of administrative change is represented by the dual-core model.[13] The **dual-core model** suggests that application of organic versus mechanistic designs is partly dependent on the frequency of change that is required. As depicted in Figure 22–5, the dual-core model identifies two cores of an organization: administrative and technical. The administrative core rests above the technical core in the hierarchy. When the administrative core must undergo frequent change, usually due to an uncertain environment, then the proper design would be mechanistic. A mechanistic structure in the administrative core facilitates top-down implementation of changes in goals, strategies, policies, plans, or procedures. If the administrative core has an organic structure, then middle and lower-level managers would have more freedom and thus could easily resist or ignore changes requested from top managers.

FIGURE 22–5
*Dual-Core Model for
Administrative Change*

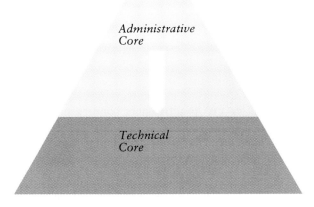

*Administrative
Core*

*Technical
Core*

Human Change

A third area of organizational change, human change, concerns employees of the organization. As a target for change, the emphasis of **human change** is on altering values, attitudes, skills, performance, perceptions, and behavioral patterns of members. Efforts to initiate human change may come from within the organization through training programs or from outside the organization through the use of experts in organization development. The change process directed at humans may involve an individual, a group, or the entire membership of an organization. Since many techniques for human change are discussed in Chapter 10, Chapter 13, and elsewhere in the text, we will focus in this chapter on organization development, a framework of change directed toward the improvement of human relationships.

ORGANIZATION DEVELOPMENT

Organization development (OD) has been defined as "an effort (1) planned, (2) organization wide, and (3) managed from the top, to (4) increase organizational effectiveness and health through (5) planned interventions in the organization's 'process,' using behavioral science knowledge."[14] In this definition, we find the key ideas to the organization development approach to change. First, the OD approach is planned. Change is based not on spontaneity but on careful consideration of the goal of the change and the methods that will lead to the achievement of that goal. Second, OD is an approach to human change that considers and includes all members of the organization, not just certain individuals or groups. Third, OD is a change approach supported by top management. Generally this requires a firm commitment of resources to the change process. Fourth, the change is designed to increase organizational effectiveness as well as to improve the working conditions of its members. Increased effectiveness at the cost of deteriorated working conditions is to be avoided. And finally, OD uses behavioral science approaches to create a more open and honest atmosphere in organizations. Emphasis is on the use of techniques that facilitate communication and problem solving among members.

OD ASSUMPTIONS AND VALUES

The practice of OD is based on several assumptions about people as individuals, as group members, and as members of the organization. These assumptions guide an OD practitioner in her or his efforts to bring about change in the organization.

People as Individuals

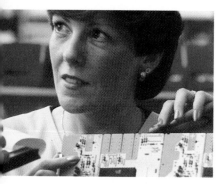

OD recognizes the capacity of the individual to satisfy needs for personal growth through contributions to the work of the organization.

Three basic assumptions are made by OD practitioners concerning people as individuals. First, people in the organization seek to satisfy higher needs such as personal development and growth in their jobs. Second, people desire to make a contribution to the organization. And third, people not only desire to make a contribution to the organization, but they also have the potential to do so. The OD approach seeks to overcome organizational barriers that discourage members from satisfying higher needs and making a contribution to the organization through their work.

People as Group Members

Practitioners of OD assume that the nature of group relationships will determine the satisfaction and contribution of the individual members of the group. It is important to the OD approach that group members feel that acceptance in a work group is important and that the group is capable of generating trust, support, and cooperation among the members. Finally, the nature of the group should be such that members are capable of acting both as leaders and as followers in the group when necessary.

People as Members of the Organization

OD practitioners assume that organizational structures have an impact on member attitudes and behaviors. For instance, if a new policy on dress were communicated to organizational members, there would be an effort to abide by the policy. A second assumption is that win-lose conflict strategies — where conflict is based on one member's winning at the expense of another — are not healthy in the organization. A third assumption is that upper management must have a long-term commitment to change within the organization.

These assumptions of the OD approach are critical to the success of the OD practitioner. If a practitioner of OD were to try to improve the effectiveness and health of an organization in which members did not desire to participate in the change and upper management was unsupportive of the change, the chances of success would be slim.

THE OD PROCESS

Several important steps can be identified in the OD process. Organization development is usually started by what is referred to as a **change agent**, usually an individual outside the organization who intervenes to start the change process. The steps involved in the intervention are to identify a need for change, to select a technique for change, to gather top management support, to plan the change process, to overcome resistance to change, and to evaluate the change process.

Identify a Need for Change

The first step in an OD intervention occurs when the change agent identifies a need for change. This may be the result of work with managers or employees in trying to understand why productivity or satisfaction is low. The change agent must determine whether the situation is temporary or may have long-lasting effects on organization and member effectiveness. If the situation appears to be long-lasting, the change agent will want to identify a change process which will solve the problem.

Select a Technique for Change

Wendell L. French and Cecil H. Bell, Jr., have identified 11 intervention techniques that change agents can use in the organization development approach:[15]

- *Diagnostic techniques.* Once the change agent has identified a need for change, an effort to get more information about the situation is necessary. This can be accomplished through diagnostic techniques which may include such methods as administering questionnaires and surveys, conducting interviews, attending meetings, or reviewing reports and minutes of the organization. Diagnostic techniques are designed to get as much information about the situation as possible.
- *Team building.* Team building consists of a series of activities designed to help individuals who work in groups to develop a sense of teamwork. Teams may consist of members who work alongside one another daily or are together on a project for a short time. The change agent introduces exercises that help communication among members of the team and teaches techniques that apply to solving problems.
- *Survey feedback.* The survey feedback technique of organization development starts with the administering of a questionnaire designed to gauge attitudes and perceptions of members. The information is then collected by the change agent and fed back to members. The feedback may present the results of the survey with time set aside for the group to discuss their meaning and explore possible interpretations. Members may be actively involved in the solution to problems through use of the survey feedback technique.
- *Education.* Educational techniques usually consist of classroom training. The classroom can be used for both the development of skills in relating to others and the exploration of material on specific topics. Emphasis is on the development of human skills rather than technical skills.
- *Intergroup activities.* The change agent may want to focus on techniques designed to improve relationships between groups. The change agent may want to apply techniques that increase communication between groups, develop understanding of one another's goals and problems, and promote cooperation.
- *Third-party peacemaking.* The change agent may want to resort to an approach of mediation or negotiation between two parties engaged in conflict. The parties in conflict may be groups, individuals, organizations, or a mix of the three.
- *Sociotechnical activities.* The term *sociotechnical* refers to the way members relate to the organization technology. The change agent may examine the technology of the organization to see if it is compatible with existing structures. If not, a structural change, such as a move toward decentral-

ization, may be necessary. Or the change agent may want to change the number and composition of tasks for which an employee has responsibility.

- *Process consultation.* Process consultation is a popular technique in which the change agent observes individuals or groups in the organization to develop an understanding of their attitudes and behaviors. The change agent provides immediate feedback to members so they can readily understand how certain processes shape their relationships.
- *Life and career planning.* Another technique that a change agent may want to apply concerns life and career planning of members. This is particularly useful where the goals of members and the goals of the organization are incompatible. The change agent may help individuals in formulating personal goals that coincide with those of the organization or identify specific career maps and training opportunities.
- *Coaching.* Coaching is an effective technique when individuals need feedback to understand how others are responding to them. The information provided is usually nonevaluative and constructive.
- *Planning and goal setting.* Time management, goal setting, and activity planning are important managerial tasks. The change agent can help managers improve their performance in these areas. Increasingly, packaged computer software is being made available to managers for these purposes.

Gather Top Management Support

The successful implementation of any OD technique directed at human change requires the support of top management. Top management should communicate support of the OD change technique to those organizational members who will be involved in the change process. Communication from top management should identify the goals of the change effort, the purpose of the change, and the expected results of the change effort. In this way, members will fully understand why the change effort is taking place and know that top management supports its implementation. Indeed, without the support of top management or in situations when top management has not announced its support, members are likely to treat the change effort as frivolous or inconsequential. If this occurs, the change effort is sure to fail in achieving its goal.

Plan the Change Process

The change process should be well conceived from start to finish. The change agent should break down the change process into subparts, and then each subpart should be carried out sequentially. This will enable the change agent to check and evaluate progress. If some techniques do not work, the change agent can substitute a more effective technique without a large loss of organizational resources invested in the change process.

Overcome Resistance to Change

Resistance to the change process may come from a number of directions. Top management may get cold feet halfway through the change process and begin to withdraw support. Managers of divisions or departments directly affected by the change may feel that their competence or power is under attack. Equally true, managers of divisions or departments left out of the change process may, because of uncertainty, feel that the change will weaken their position. Employees may feel that the change process is an effort to increase

Q: What do you believe are the fundamental differences between organizational change made by consultants hired temporarily and organizational change made through an organization development program?

A: Effective organizational change requires maximum information, participation by the workers, trust in the initiator, and a good experience with a previous change program. Many temporary consultants do not implement lasting change, because they either ignore the above factors or do their faddish thing and run. On the flip side of the coin, some internal OD departments are ineffective because they are part of the problem, are seen as spies of the boss, or can't see the forest for the trees. Unfortunately, effective change is implemented in a large program at about the pace of a turtle with gout. For change to be effective, there must be a proper diagnosis and effective implementation of the change program, and the new behavior must become a habit.

Q: Many management scholars believe the increased use of robots in the workplace will have a profound effect on management processes. Do you believe this to be the case? What, if any, changes will result from this new technology?

A: America is lagging behind international competition such as Japan and Sweden when it comes to introducing robots in the workplace. Between 1974 and 1981, *Business Week* reported that robots increased from 0.8 to 4.0 robots per 10,000 workers in the United States while they increased from 1.9 to 13.0 in Japan and from 1.3 to 29.9 in Sweden. Thus, the use of robots to replace workers in America will be slower than many "experts" predicted in the 1970s. However, because of declining productivity and increased international competition, the 1990s will see robots replacing workers in the United States, and employed workers will need more computer skills. Management will need to develop human and conceptual skills that motivate technical workers to increase productivity.

Q: Many managers are uncomfortable with conflict and try to avoid it. Are there techniques or ideas that managers can use to assist them in learning to manage conflict?

A: As we compete for scarce jobs and resources in the 1990s, managers will have to learn to manage conflict. Managers who keep brushing problems under the rug will be ineffective in the long run. Managers of the future will continue to be promoted based upon superior performance in their technical skills. During college, a course in small-group dynamics should be required for students majoring in engineering, computer science, accounting, physics, and so on. Then, when organizations select managers, they should put greater emphasis on human skills and make greater use of assessment centers to evaluate managerial candidates. Finally, organizations should offer a practical management course with cases and skill development to give candidates an opportunity to experiment with management skills. If the candidate does not show an aptitude for management, there should be a dual-career path to allow the employee to pursue a technical career without moving into management.

Robert A. Zawacki (Ph. D., University of Washington) is Professor and Chairman of Management and Organization at the University of Colorado, Colorado Springs. He was previously Associate Dean of the College of Business and Administration at the University of Colorado and was on the faculty of the United States Air Force Academy. Professor Zawacki is the co-author of Managing and Motivating Computer Personnel; Organization Development: Theory, Practice and Research; People and Organizations; *and* Supervisory Management. *His research on motivation, feedback, and performance appraisal has been published in* Datamation, The Personnel Administrator, *and* Journal of Systems Management. *Professor Zawacki is an international consultant working with such corporations as IBM, Hartford Insurance Group, Prudential, Volvo, Hewlett-Packard, and the European Economic Community. In addition, he has served as a consultant to the United States Navy, the Air Force Academy, and the New York Department of Labor.*

ACADEMIC PROFILE
ROBERT A. ZAWACKI

their work performance without a commensurate increase in pay. Or they may feel that the change process is simply an effort to check their work and that the information will be used by management to decide about firings or lay-offs. Whatever the source or nature of the resistance, the change agent should have a well-thought-out plan to counter the resistance and apply the techniques for overcoming resistance to change discussed in the previous section.

Evaluate the Change Process

Evaluation of the change process is the final step in an organization development program. Measures of the effectiveness of the program can be established through observations of activities, discussions with both participants and nonparticipants, and collection of performance data to determine whether the change process achieved its intended goal.

Evaluation of the change process can be difficult. Contextual factors, such as the environment, size, and linkages, may alter the intended outcome of the change process. Since these factors are generally uncontrollable by the change agent, failure may result in spite of a well-planned and well-executed change program. The change agent should look beyond her or his own efforts in evaluating the causes of success or failure of the change process.

CONDITIONS FOR SUCCESSFUL OD PROGRAMS

While many factors may contribute to the success or failure of an OD program, there are several important conditions thought to be necessary for an OD program to succeed. French and Bell have identified 11 such conditions:[16]

- *Recognition by managers and members that the organization has problems.* Without such recognition, it is unlikely that a change process will receive the required resources to make the effort successful.
- *Use of an external change agent to start the process.* The change agent should not be a member of the organization. Internal change agents often lack the objectivity and autonomy to carry out necessary changes, and their efforts may be seriously hampered by political infighting.
- *Support from top management for the change process.* As previously noted, the lack of top management support can seriously jeopardize the successful implementation of a change program.
- *Involvement of work group leaders.* Where change is directed at work groups or teams, it is important that the work group leaders have an active role in the change process. Without their involvement, implementation of the change process is unlikely to occur.
- *Early success with the OD effort.* Success breeds success. Generally change agents should strive initially to carry out a change process that has a high chance of success. Success motivates members to continue with the process and gives members confidence that more ambitious efforts can also be successful.
- *Understanding of the change process and its goals.* Generally people will respond positively to a change process if they understand why the change is being made. Articulation of the purpose and goals of the change process should be made frequently.
- *Support of managerial strengths.* Change agents often become so focused on the process that they ignore the positives that exist in the organization. Effective managers should be acknowledged and reinforced. The change agent should be wary of overplaying the "expert" role in an organization.

- *Inclusion of personnel managers in the OD program.* The change agent should include managers from the personnel or human resources department in the planning and implementation of the change process. Human resources managers can provide valuable information and insight into members' performance, development, and rewards.
- *Development of internal OD resources.* One goal of an OD program is to make change an ongoing and comfortable process in the organization. The change agent should involve and train organization managers at all levels in OD skills and techniques so that managers of the organization can plan and carry out change long after the change agent has left.
- *Effective management of the OD program.* The change agent should watch and respond to situations to optimize the chances of success. This often requires careful coordination and control of activities to make sure that the change process is correctly carried out and that members support the program.
- *Measurement and evaluation of results.* Measurement and evaluation of results provide the change agent and members of the organization with important information about the effectiveness of the change program. This information can be the basis for planning and implementing change programs in the future.

MANAGING ORGANIZATION CULTURE

Is Hewlett-Packard best known for its success as a manufacturer in the electronics industry or as a company with excellent working conditions? Hewlett-Packard is noteworthy in both areas, and many managers look to the company as a model of how a company can grow, prosper, and still keep a personal feeling in its operations.[17] Hewlett-Packard's sound financial condition as well as its reputation as an excellent place to work is often credited to a credo called "The H-P Way." Developed at a management meeting in 1975, the H-P Way is a list of concepts central to the way the company operates. The H-P Way follows from cofounder Bill Hewlett's dictum: "Men and women want to do a good job, a creative job, and if they are provided the proper environment, they will do so."[18] The H-P Way rests on the following concepts:

- Belief in people; freedom
- Respect and dignity; individual self-esteem
- Recognition; sense of achievement; participation
- Security; permanence; development of people
- Insurance; personal worry protection
- Share benefits and responsibility; help each other
- Management by objectives (rather than directives); decentralization
- Informality; first names; open communication
- A chance to learn by making mistakes
- Training and education; counseling
- Performance and enthusiasm

Management at Hewlett-Packard has successfully formed an organization culture that has many benefits: successful financial performance, high employee satisfaction, and a reputation for quality products. Hewlett-Packard does not stand alone in the esteem in which its organization culture is held. IBM, Northwestern Mutual Life, McDonald's, Wal-Mart, and countless others have achieved this reputation. However, many more companies are unable or unwilling to commit the time and resources necessary to create and manage a culture that provides these benefits.

In this section we explore the basic ingredients of organization culture and discuss the techniques for effective management of culture. We will pay particular attention to how managers can read and influence the culture of their organization.

Ingredients of Organization Culture

According to Terrence Deal and Allan Kennedy, a company's "real existence" lies "in the hearts and minds of its employees." **Organization culture** can be defined as a blend of values, stories, heroes, and rituals and ceremonies that have come to mean a great deal to the people who work for the organization.[19]

VALUES

Values are the things that are most important to us. They are the deep-seated, pervasive standards that influence almost every aspect of our lives: our moral judgments, our responses to others, our commitments to personal and organizational goals. Values are considered the bedrock of corporate culture.[20] Strong organization values let employees know how they are expected to behave and which actions are considered acceptable. In general, organization values have three properties: (1) they stand for something important within the organization; (2) management shapes and communicates them to the members of the organization; and (3) all members of the organization know and share in them.[21] Within an organization context, values can be viewed as either functional or elitist. Functional values focus on how organization members should carry out their work, what service level should be performed, or the quality of the product expected. Elitist values actually serve to give the organization and its members a feeling of superiority.[22] Emphasizing what the firm excels at, recruiting top managerial talent, and promoting the firm to the public all serve to develop elitist values. Sharing of values, whether functional or elitist, is a key element in the development of a successful organization culture. According to Thomas Peters and Robert Waterman, if there is one piece of advice to take to heart from their research on excellent companies it would be: "Figure out your value system. Decide what your company stands for."[23]

The H-P Way is based on a clear listing of values that all employees can understand—belief in people, freedom, respect and dignity, recognition, security, helping each other, and so forth. But more than a simple statement is needed if values are to have a positive impact on the culture of the organization; they must be institutionalized into the daily working lives of employees. At Hewlett-Packard, for instance, units are kept small. There are no time clocks. Employees have a choice of which eight-hour shift to work. Offices are separated by open partitions to increase accessibility and foster teamwork. Management practices MBWA, which stands for "management by wandering around." In addition, Hewlett-Packard has an unwritten policy never to lay people off.[24] Managers should not only inform employees about the values of the organization, but should actively practice behaviors and develop policies that support those values.

STORIES

Stories are another important ingredient of organization culture. Stories, or myths, "are powerful in passing on a culture because they are like maps that help people know how things are done in a particular group."[25] **Stories** are narratives that are repeated among employees and usually based in fact. At 3M, for example, the eleventh commandment is "Never kill a new product idea." The importance of innovation as a 3M value is supported by a story often repeated throughout the organization. According to the story, an employee accidentally developed cellophane tape but was unable to get his superiors to buy the idea. Persistent in his belief in the new product, the employee found a way to sneak into the corporate boardroom and tape down the minutes of board members with his transparent tape. The board was impressed enough with the novelty to give it a try and the product experienced incredible success.[26] This story not only reinforces the importance of innovation but also encourages 3M employees who strongly believe in their ideas not to take "no" from superiors as a final answer.

Another organization story reinforces the value of treating employees with respect and as equals. As the story is told by employees of a large electronics firm, the president had a strong commitment to research and development and would occasionally don a white lab coat to spend time in the labs. A secretary who was closing up the laboratory one evening saw him and asked accusingly, "Were you the one who left the lights and the copying machine on last night?" "Uh, well, I guess I did," was the reply. "Don't you know that we have an energy-saving program in the company and that the president has asked us to be particularly careful about turning off lights and equipment?" she inquired. "I'm very sorry, it won't happen again," returned the president. Several days later the secretary happened to pass the president now dressed in a suit with a name tag. "Oh no," she thought, "I chewed out the company president!"[27] With many repetitions, this story communicates to employees that the company is committed to the value of respect for all employees, whatever their rank.

HEROES

Heroes are company role models in the performance of deeds, embodiment of character, and support of the existing organization culture. They also highlight the values a company wishes to reinforce. "The hero is the great motivator, the magician, the person everyone will count on when things get tough."[28] One often finds heroes as the main characters of stories relayed through an organization. Thomas Watson at IBM, Steven Jobs at Apple Computer, William Paley at CBS, and Lee Iacocca at Chrysler Corporation are all real figures who have taken on heroic qualities in stories that are told in their respective companies, in some cases even after their departure.

RITUALS AND CEREMONIES

A final ingredient of an organization's culture includes rituals and ceremonies, which are outward signs of what the organization values. As symbols, **rituals** are a guide to behavior in daily organizational life. Rituals may include evaluation and reward procedures, regular staff meetings, farewell parties, parking allocations, and work-scheduling procedures.[29] **Ceremonies** are similar to rituals but are more elaborate productions that occur less frequently. Award banquets, gatherings for speeches, and presentation of promotions are all examples of ceremonies.

Through rituals and ceremonies, participants can cement understandings and beliefs that are important to the organization culture by celebrating together.[30] Mary Kay Cosmetics' annual meeting is a good example of a ceremony. With lavish pomp and intense drama, top employees are recognized and rewarded for high sales. The ceremony, however, goes beyond the fancy setting and the presentation of pink Cadillacs to star salespeople. As members accept their rewards, they praise the opportunities provided to them by Mary Kay, the hero of the company. The process gives all Mary Kay employees a sense of purpose in their work—not merely to sell cosmetics but to reach their full potential as women.[31]

Effective Management of Organization Culture

Much of the current interest in the development of a suitable organization culture is based on the emergence of Japanese companies as major players in both the United States and global markets. Comparative studies of Japanese and American management techniques as presented by William Ouchi in his book *Theory Z* (see Chapter 2 for a discussion of this topic) has supported this interest. As Ouchi reported, many successful Japanese companies have strong cultures that emphasize such values as employee participation, open communication, security, and equality.[32]

The most popular writing on the relationship between organization culture and effectiveness is presented by Peters and Waterman in *In Search of Excellence*.[33] Based on their observation of 62 successful firms, including Hewlett-Packard, Delta Air Lines, McDonald's, Disney Productions, Levi Strauss, and Johnson & Johnson, the authors concluded that the following eight attributes of the organization culture contributed to their success:

1. *A bias for action.* While the companies may be analytical in their approach to decision making, they prefer to "do it, fix it, try it." That is, problems are not talked to death nor is time wasted in developing elaborate models for solving problems.
2. *Closeness to the customer.* Learning from customers is important for success. Customer satisfaction becomes a dominant value and can be achieved through excellent customer service and high product quality and reliability.
3. *Autonomy and entrepreneurship.* Excellent companies encourage innovativeness through the development of structures that foster innovation and change. Work units are kept small so that employees have a sense of belonging and feel comfortable about making suggestions.
4. *Productivity through people.* Rank-and-file employees are viewed as valued resources of the organization, the main source of quality and productivity. "We versus them" labor attitudes are avoided.
5. *Hands-on, value driven.* Managers of excellent companies have clearly defined the value system of the firm. Both managers and employees understand what values guide the activities of the firm. For example, McDonald's incorporates quality, service, cleanliness, and value in all aspects of the company's activities.

Company ceremonies are an important part of an organization's culture.

6. *Stick to the knitting.* Successful companies will stay close to the business they know. This may mean a focus on a single product line or a related group of product lines rather than a diverse mix of products.

7. *Simple form, lean staff.* Keeping the company simple in its structure with few staff positions was found to be important to company success. In general, no more than five layers of management are encouraged. When the company increases in size, divisions are broken down into subdivisions to avoid additional layers of management.

8. *Simultaneous loose-tight properties.* Excellent companies are both centralized and decentralized. This may sound paradoxical, but centralization/decentralization can be split. Centralized or tight controls can be applied to the company's core values. In other areas, such as innovation and creativity, controls on employees are loose or decentralized.

Not every company studied by Peters and Waterman scored high on all eight attributes. However, success in promoting some of these attributes and a desire to score well on others were part of the organization culture. While the findings of Peters and Waterman have received widespread attention, there has been some questioning of the results.[34] For instance, the authors' primary focus was successful companies. Could these same attributes be characteristic of companies that are poor performers? Measures of excellence were limited to the financial performance of the company.[35] Are they successful in terms of customer satisfaction? Are they socially responsible? Several years after the publication of *In Search of Excellence,* several of the "excellent" companies suffered financially, such as Dana, Johnson & Johnson, and 3M.[36] A final question about the Peters and Waterman research concerns the extent to which the eight attributes should be applied. Recall that contingency theory is a response to the fact that organizations operate in different environments, under different strategic conditions, with different structures and technologies. Contingency theory would discourage the idea that there is "one best way" to manage a culture. Rather, different environments, strategic conditions, and structures and technology should call for different types of cultures.

An emphasis on culture as an effective means for making change in the performance of an organization will be a relevant topic for some time. Many corporations have turned to Japanese techniques as a means to change their culture. However, managers should be cautious in assuming that Japanese techniques can be directly applied to American corporate settings. Management in Action 3 describes the problems with direct application of Japanese techniques to American managers.

IMPLICATIONS FOR MANAGEMENT

As a manager you will want to devote considerable attention to the processes and results of change. Both the methods of change and the existing organization culture can have strong effects on the performance and overall effectiveness of an organization. Learn to identify the sources of problems so that an effective change technique can be applied. Too often, managers attack the

For many Japanese executives, the road to the top leads through Hell Camp, Japan's famous quasi-military management training school. Every month

the school puts 500 or so of that nation's best and brightest middle managers through an ordeal so tough that it leaves some broken and sobbing.

Now, Hell Camp's operator, Kanrisha Yosi Gakko Corporation, has opened a U.S. version on a ranch near Malibu, California. But the school is off to a hellish start. Having failed to attract real American executives, Kanrisha staged its first U.S. course using mostly shills—its own employees and their friends and relatives—as students. The 13-day charade succeeded in bringing out the media, ever in search of some secret formula to explain Japan's economic success. But in the end, Hell Camp, Malibu-style, seemed little more than an elaborate cross-cultural misunderstanding.

The course foundered on a basic point, all too familiar to most Americans who have spent time in Japan: Japanese and Americans don't think alike. Ethics and beliefs that hark back hundreds of years in Japanese culture and still permeate Japanese attitudes today aren't easily transferred to a cowboy setting like the Calamigos Ranch conference center, Kanrisha's U.S. campus.

But don't blame the students. For a dozen cold mornings they rose at 5 A.M. for a flag ceremony; they bowed deeply and frequently on command;

they braved humiliation singing solos at a shopping mall; they even memorized pages of nonsensical speeches written by the school's reclusive founder, Ichiro Takurabe. None of them questioned the purpose of Walking Training, a daily, stopwatched stroll through the ranch in perfect single file, or wondered aloud why the Japanese were teaching Americans Quick Writing, Correct Reading, and Telephone Training.

Founded nine years ago in the foothills of Mount Fuji, Hell Camp claims to have subjected some 100,000 Japanese "salary-men" to 13 days each of speed drills, speechifying, and hazing rituals. Its main message—"100 liters of sweat; 100 liters of tears"—was designed to counteract a growing fear among Japan's corporate and government elite that the nation's workers are becoming too "Americanized," too soft.

The school's solution, for nearly $3,000 a pop: to crush the individual ego with mindless and humiliating exercises and then rebuild it with a modern version of the Samurai code of selfless servitude called *bushido*.

But the real question is how long the school will go on ignoring the vast cultural differences between Japan and its new market. "The school needs to understand how Americans feel about being ordered around," says Kyoko Maemura, the ad agency employee who attended the first course. "They're assuming everybody knows the importance of obedience and discipline."

Source: Reprinted by permission of *The Wall Street Journal*, © Dow Jones & Company, Inc. (March 1, 1988). All Rights Reserved Worldwide.

symptoms of a problem rather than the underlying cause. When only the symptom is treated, managers will be forced to deal with the problem's recurrence.

Many managers find it useful to identify steps they want to take to carry out change before they proceed. Identifying these steps requires a keen understanding of how both external and internal forces affect activities in the organization. As a manager, you should develop a list of each external and internal force you believe affects the activities of your organization. You may want to keep such a list handy at all times. It can serve as a reminder of what factors must be considered before change is to take place in the organization. If possible, try to avoid reactive responses to change. While many times throughout your career you will have to react to (as opposed to plan for) change, the change process has greater potential for success when it is planned. Remember that managers are paid to anticipate problems.

Regardless of how well thought out and beautifully conceived your plan for change is, expect resistance. Resistance to change can arise from many unexpected sources. However, if you anticipate the kinds of resistance your plan may encounter, you may be able to make an effective response.

If you have determined that the source of a problem rests with the administrative area of the organization, you will want to aid the change process by altering policies, goals, structure, or evaluation systems. Create an organic system in the administrative unit for formulating the change. This can be accomplished by developing workshops or sessions that allow employees to offer suggestions. Or create a separate organizational department whose goal is to formulate solutions to problems. When it is time to carry out the change, develop a mechanistic system. This will enable you to check the change process and identify trouble spots.

If you believe the problem to be solved rests with the technological area of the organization, you will want to change the tasks or technology in the organization. Again, you may halt the production line and develop workshops or sessions in which employees are encouraged to contribute to the solution of the problem. Once a solution has been identified, a mechanistic system can be used to carry out the solution to the problem. More common is the creation of an organic department, such as research and development, whose goal is to create new ideas to be carried out by a mechanistic production department.

When a change in the human area is necessary, consider an organization development program. While more costly than hiring an outside consultant, it has many long-term benefits. Make a commitment to greet change as a natural process in the organization and develop your own ideas as to how the workplace of members can be improved. Remember that any successful change through an OD program is going to require support from management. If you display lack of enthusiasm for the program, others will catch that attitude and the program's chances for success will be greatly reduced.

As a manager you must be aware of the values that are at the core of the organization's culture. An organization's culture will have a direct impact on employee morale, effort expended in work, and commitment to product quality. Managers of low-performing organizations should audit the values of their company. You can do so by examining the values and then identifying how those values are being reinforced through storytelling, identification of heroes, and meetings and other company events. Do people tell stories about workers who contributed little to the firm but commanded a big paycheck? If so, this may reflect an undesirable value. Are the company heroes those who outsmarted senior managers? If so, the behaviors of management may need to be evaluated. Are ceremonies sparsely attended with little enthusiasm? Perhaps the wrong values are being displayed. The creation of a desired culture in a firm may take time and effort, but for many companies the investment is well worth it.

KEY TERMS AND CONCEPTS

administrative change	changing
ambidextrous organization	dual-core model
ceremonies	heroes
change agent	human change

idea champion   refreezing
innovation departments   rituals
Lewin-Schein model   stories
organizational change   switching structures
organization culture   technological change
organization development (OD)   values
planned change   venture team
reactive change   unfreezing

QUESTIONS FOR REVIEW AND DISCUSSION

1. What are the key external and internal forces that influence change in an organization?
2. How does planned change differ from reactive change? Which is considered to be the most effective approach to change?
3. Do you believe business schools should offer a degree in "organization change" as they do in finance or marketing? Why or why not?
4. Why does the Lewin-Schein model use the terms "unfreeze" and "freeze" in its conceptualization of the change process? What exactly is being unfrozen and frozen?
5. What is the ambidextrous method of technological change? On what basis is one design chosen rather than the other?
6. Where do you consider yourself in regard to a tolerance for change: high, low, or somewhere in the middle? What aspects of your personality or upbringing do you believe have resulted in this level of tolerance for change?
7. What is organization development? How does OD differ from hiring a consultant to institute change?
8. Which of the six approaches for overcoming resistance to change do you believe is most effective? Explain why.
9. Identify stories, heroes, rituals, and ceremonies that exist on your college campus. How do these ingredients of the culture reinforce values within your college?
10. Identify and discuss those organization values that the eight attributes from the book *In Search of Excellence* would support the most. Which values would they support the least?

CASES

22–1 BOOT CAMP THE GE WAY

As a boss, do you have this problem? "Your budget has been cut, but the work load increases. You've been told to reduce staff while maintaining the current level of productivity, but receive no advice on how people are to keep up."

Or how about this one: "She complains about everything—vacation policy, someone else's promotion, fringe benefits, the work assignments that you give others (too light) or to her (too heavy), the position of her desk or the location of her office. . . . Her work is good enough to justify retaining her. . . . How do you live with her—and perhaps cut down on some of the complaining?"

If you were a new manager at General Electric Company, you would find answers to these and 80 other problems in the "Trouble-Shooting Guide" of your New Manager Starter Kit. The kit as well as mandatory attendance at a one-week course at GE's Crotonville Management Development Institute in Ossining, N.Y., are among the tools GE is using these days to develop its future leaders—and help assimilate the diverse operations it recently has acquired.

As GE has increased its pace of acquisitions and divestitures to focus on services and technology under Chairman John F. Welch, Jr., it has stepped up the importance of the 31-year-old Crotonville program. The campuslike facility, spread over 50 rolling acres near the Hudson River, has become much more than an in-house school for accounting, finance, and marketing. It also spreads Chairman Welch's vision of the company and molds a common GE culture.

Other companies have management development programs, but Crotonville is one of the most intense and systematic. As a result, it is closely studied by other companies establishing their own schools. Hitachi Ltd., for instance, built a virtual replica of Crotonville in Japan. In recent months, executives from Ford Motor Company, Eastman Kodak Company, and Prudential Life Insurance Company of America have come to study the Crotonville program.

Although Crotonville is given much credit for helping instill GE's often-praised management style, some say such programs can be too insular. Jean Hauser, associate director of Duke University's Fuqua School of Business, says in-house training can foster a "foxhole mentality," with managers believing that "nobody understands our world but us."

GE is aware of that risk, says James Baughman, manager of corporate organization, management development, and executive compensation. But because of the acquisition of RCA Corporation, Kidder, Peabody & Company, and other concerns in recent years, as well as major changes within the parent company, he says, GE needs a program such as Crotonville to rally managers around common goals.

That program ranges from 2½-day mandatory sessions for the 2,500 new college graduates GE hires each year, to month-long programs for mid-level and upper-level managers. Lecturers include GE executives, a retired officer from the U.S. Military Academy at West Point, and visiting professors from top business schools including Harvard, Emory, and Yale. The program includes lectures on GE's goals and philosophy, but such sessions are only part of the course work. A marketing class last year, for instance, studied the advertising techniques of MCI Communications Corporation to see how an upstart service concern uses advertising to compete against a much larger company.

Along with the standard management courses and lectures, more unusual problem-solving workshops are taught. At the start of a recent month-long program, for example, a class of 40 middle managers divide into groups to solve a hurricane-survival exercise developed by a Yale professor. In the exercises, the group's chartered yacht, *Snowflake*, has been wrecked just off the eastern shore of Tobago, leaving the crew to swim ashore and wait out the hurricane. Each team has to develop a survival strategy, which includes ranking a list of 15 items that would be most necessary to survive. Earlier, individual class members rank the list on their own.

In each group but one, the team list turns out to be more correct than the individual rankings. The team that didn't do as well, says George Roy, a financial manager in major appliances, relied too much on the advice of two members who had been Eagle Scouts—and who seemed to be experts on such outdoor predicaments—instead of reaching a consensus. Besides breaking the ice and teaching consensus management, the workshop "taught us that sometimes the expert isn't an expert," says David J. Illingworth, a sales manager for medical systems.

And what does GE recommend in the cases cited at the top of this story? In the first example, the "Trouble-Shooting Guide" advises, hold brainstorming sessions with staff, don't discourage negative comments, look for more efficient methods, and focus on top-priority tasks. In the second, give recognition to the employee, reassure her of her abilities, accept her feelings, and check to see whether the complaints are more widely held.

Source: Reprinted by permission of *The Wall Street Journal*, © Dow Jones & Company, Inc. (August 10, 1987). All Rights Reserved Worldwide.

1. How would you apply the Lewin-Schein model of change to the practices followed at GE's Management Development Institute?
2. What OD techniques are being applied to students in the classroom?
3. What values does the Management Development Institute try to reinforce in its managers? Is the Institute an effective way to change the culture of GE? Explain.

22–2 WHICH CORPORATE CULTURE FITS YOU?

"Academy" or "fortress"? "Baseball team" or "club"? According to one management scholar, those four descriptions of corporate culture are more than mere fodder for gossip around the water cooler. Understanding the culture you work in—and knowing whether it matches your career personality—can affect how far or how easily you scurry up the management ranks.

"We've taught managers how to assess their own abilities but not how to match those with the right company," says Jeffrey Sonnenfeld, director of Emory University's Center for Leadership and Career Change, who is researching career paths in different corporate cultures. A risk-taker, for instance, will thrive at a baseball-team company but fall flat on his face at an academy. But take note, a team player who craves security won't last at a baseball team, says Mr. Sonnenfeld, who is also a professor at Emory.

Analyzing a company's corporate culture doesn't guarantee landing a job or a promotion, career experts and managers agree. But it can illuminate why achievements and a sense of belonging come easier in some settings than in others.

Academies

For the steady climber who wants to thoroughly master each new job and make one company his or her career home, Mr. Sonnenfeld recommends the academy. There, new recruits are invariably young college graduates who are steered through a myriad of specialized jobs. A classic academy is International Business Machines Corporation, where every manager spends at least 40 hours each year in management-training school, with 32 hours devoted to people management.

IBM identifies fast-trackers early on and "carefully grooms them to become expert in a particular function," Mr. Sonnenfeld says. "They'll tell you they're IBMers first and foremost but then add they're an IBMer who cares about data-entry systems or applications technology."

Clubs

While managers in academies must stand out to move ahead, "those in clubs must strive to fit in," says Mr. Sonnenfeld, describing his second grouping. "What counts isn't individual achievement but seniority, commitment, and doing things for the good of the group," he says. "If you like quick upward mobility and notoriety, clubs aren't for you."

And unlike academies, clubs groom managers as generalists, with initiation beginning at an entry-level job. At United Parcel Service of America Inc., chief executive John W. Rogers and his management committee began their careers as clerks, drivers, and management trainees. Instead of becoming narrow specialists, they learned a little of everything from distribution to marketing as they crisscrossed their way up the corporate ladder. The chief executive, a 32-year UPS veteran, still does his own photocopying, eats lunch in the cafeteria alongside packagers and junior managers, and shares a secretary. "When decisions have to be made, we get everyone's opinion, and the company feels like a family to a lot of us," says John Tranfo, a staff vice-president who will soon be celebrating his 40th year at UPS. "In management, we have hardly any turnover," he adds.

Baseball Teams

Baseball-team companies, which include accounting and law firms, consulting, advertising, and software development, are a different breed entirely. Entrepreneurial in style, baseball teams seek out talent of all ages and experience and reward them by what they produce. "They don't care how committed you'll be tomorrow," says Mr. Sonnenfeld. "They want cutting-edge results today. And they don't train their employees; either you come in with skills or develop them quickly on the job."

Managers at baseball-team companies perceive themselves as free agents, much like professional athletes. If one company doesn't give them the freedom or rewards they think they deserve, they'll leave for a company that does—or form their own. Such was the case with Bruce Wasserstein and Joseph Perella, two young investment banking wizards who made mergers and acquisitions Wall Street's most lucrative business. First Boston Corporation paid them more than the firm's top executives. Yet last year they quit to form their own company, Wasserstein Perella & Co., because they felt the profits they were producing shouldn't be used to subsidize money-losing operations, like securities trading.

After working as a consultant at Booz, Allen & Hamilton Inc. and as an executive at Time Inc., Sandra Kresch concludes that "Booz Allen's baseball-team meritocracy works better for me. At Time (where the culture is clubby), who you knew seemed more important than anything you did, and that didn't fit my style." Ms. Kresch is now an independent consultant.

Fortresses

Whereas baseball-team companies value inventiveness, fortresses are concerned with survival. Many fortresses are academies, clubs, or baseball teams that have failed in the marketplace and are struggling to reverse their fortunes. Others, including retailing and natural-resources companies, are in a perpetual boom-and-bust cycle. Fortresses can't promise job security or reward people simply on the basis of how well they perform. The most competent fortress managers may find themselves suddenly out of a job when the businesses they oversee are sold or restructured.

Yet for those who relish the challenge of a turnaround, fortresses can be exciting. "I like the fact that there's adrenaline flowing, because you're doing an overhaul, not just a refining, and you have the chance to really create something," says Bruce McKinnon, senior vice-president of Microband Wireless Cable of New York. In the past six years, he's worked at three other cable-television companies, recruited to each as a "portable warlord to help them back on track," he says. Managers who crave security and conviviality may not be able to tolerate fortresses. "No one likes to be told they're overweight, but when you're doing a turnaround you're usually putting everyone on a diet," says Mr. McKinnon. "I elicit strong emotions from subordinates."

1. What values seem to be dominant in each of the four corporate cultures?
2. Suppose you were able to interview employees of companies that differ by culture. What types of people might they identify as heroes within the firm?
3. Review the eight attributes of corporate culture that Peters and Waterman say lead to success. Which attributes are most important for which culture? Which attributes are least important?

ENDNOTES

1. A. M. Louis, "The Controversial Boss of Beatrice," *Fortune* (July 22, 1985): 110-116.
2. A. Toffler, *Future Shock* (New York: Random House, 1970), and J. Naisbett, *Megatrends* (New York: Warner Books, 1982).
3. K. Lewin, "Frontiers in Group Dynamics: Concept, Method, and Reality in Social Science," *Human Relations* (June 1947): 5-41.
4. E. H. Schein, *Organizational Psychology*, 3d ed. (Englewood Cliffs, NJ: Prentice-Hall, 1980), 243-247.
5. R. L. Daft, "Bureaucratic Versus Nonbureaucratic Structure in the Process of Innovation and Change," in *Perspectives in Organizational Sociology: Theory and Research*, ed. Samuel B. Bacharach (Greenwich, CT: JAI Press, 1982), 129-166.
6. P. R. Lawrence, "How to Deal with Resistance to Change," in *Organizational Change and Development*, ed. G. W. Dalton, P. R. Lawrence, and L. E. Greiner (Homewood, IL: Irwin and Dorsey, 1970), 181-197, and J. P. Kotter and L. A. Schlesinger, "Choosing Strategies for Change," *Harvard Business Review* 57 (March-April 1979): 106-114.
7. Kotter and Schlesinger, "Choosing Strategies for Change."
8. H. J. Leavitt, "Applied Organization Change in Industry: Structural, Technical, and Human Approaches," in *New Perspectives in Organization Research*, ed. W. W. Cooper, H. J. Leavitt, and M. W. Shelly II (New York: John Wiley & Sons, 1964), 55-71.
9. R. B. Duncan, "The Ambidextrous Organization: Designing Dual Structures for Innovation," in *The Management of Organization,* vol. 1, ed. R. H. Killman, L. R. Pondy, and D. Slevin (New York: North-Holland, 1976), 167-188.
10. T. Burns and G. M. Stalker, *The Management of Innovation* (London: Tavistock, 1961).
11. R. L. Daft, *Organization Theory and Design*, 2d ed. (St. Paul, MN: West Publishing Co., 1986), 273-275.
12. T. J. Peters and R. H. Waterman, Jr., *In Search of Excellence: Lessons from America's Best-Run Companies* (New York: Harper & Row, 1982), 203-204.
13. R. L. Daft, "A Dual-Core Model of Organizational Innovation," *Academy of Management Journal* 21 (1978): 193-210.
14. R. Beckhard, *Organization Development: Strategies and Models* (Reading, MA: Addison-Wesley, 1969), 9.
15. W. L. French and C. H. Bell, Jr., *Organization Development: Behavioral Science interventions for Organization Improvement*, 2d ed. (Englewood Cliffs, NJ: Prentice-Hall, 1978).
16. Ibid., 215-228.
17. R. Levering, M. Moskowitz, and M. Katz, *The 100 Best Companies to Work For in America* (Reading, MA: Addison-Wesley, 1984), 142.
18. Ibid., 143.
19. T. E. Deal and A. A. Kennedy, *Corporate Cultures: The Rites and Rituals of Corporate Life* (Reading, MA: Addison-Wesley, 1982), 4.
20. B. Z. Posner, J. M. Kouzes, and W. H. Schmidt, "Shared Values Make a Difference: An Empirical Test of Corporate Culture," *Human Resource Management* 24 (1985): 293-294.
21. Deal and Kennedy, *Corporate Cultures*, 4.
22. Y. Wiener, "Forms of Value Systems: A Focus on Organizational Effectiveness and Cultural Change and Maintenance," *Academy of Management Review* 13 (1988): 537.
23. Peters and Waterman, *In Search of Excellence*.
24. Levering, Moskowitz, and Katz, *100 Best Companies*, 143-144.
25. S. L. Solberg, "Changing Culture Through Ceremony: An Example from GM," *Human Resource Management* 24 (1985): 338.
26. A. L. Wilkins, "The Creation of Company Cultures: The Role of Stories and Human Resource Systems," *Human Resource Management* 23 (1984): 43.
27. Ibid., 54.
28. Deal and Kennedy, *Corporate Cultures*, 37.
29. W. L. Ulrich, "HRM and Culture: History, Ritual, and Myth," *Human Resource Management* 23 (1984): 121.
30. Deal and Kennedy, *Corporate Cultures*.
31. Solberg, "Changing Culture Through Ceremony," 330.

32. W. Ouchi, *Theory Z: How American Business Can Meet the Japanese Challenge* (Reading, MA: Addison-Wesley, 1979).
33. Peters and Waterman, *In Search of Excellence.*
34. D. Carroll, "A Disappointing Search for Excellence," *Harvard Business Review* 61 (November-December 1983): 78-88.
35. B. Johnson, A. Natarajan, and A. Rappaport, "Shareholder Returns and Corporate Excellence," *Journal of Business Strategy* (Fall 1985).
36. "Who's Excellent Now?" *Business Week* 5 (November 1984): 76-88.

Small Business, Entrepreneurship, and Intrapreneurship

CHAPTER 23

After studying this chapter, you should be able to:
- *Understand the contributions of entrepreneurship and small business to the national economy.*
- *Discuss entrepreneurship, including entrepreneurial characteristics and strategies.*
- *Identify guidelines for starting a business.*
- *Explain why entrepreneurs may encounter difficulties as the firm grows.*
- *Describe the small business environment.*
- *Summarize the factors which make the small business effective.*
- *Describe intrapreneurship and discuss ways it may be encouraged.*

Steven Jobs, Ray Kroc, and Mary Kay Ash are people who have successfully started their own businesses—entrepreneurs who have added value to society. Jobs is credited with starting the personal computer revolution; Kroc, at the age of 52, founded the hamburger chain McDonald's; and Ash has influenced the lives of millions through her cosmetics and personal care products.

Many college students wonder what it would be like to start their own business. Even more think about being their own boss. Others are faced with decisions about working in the family business. Some of these enterprises do well, but almost 60 percent of new businesses started today are likely to fail within the next five years.[1] New businesses and small businesses typically face serious management challenges.

One purpose of this chapter is to present some of the distinctive issues that one might face while starting and managing a small business. Many college graduates will work in small businesses at some time during their working careers, because small businesses are common in the United States. Ninety-eight percent of firms in this country have fewer than 100 employees,[2] and firms with fewer than 100 workers employ almost 60 percent of the work force.[3] Approximately 1.2 million small firms opened their doors between 1983 and 1989, and in 1989 an additional 200,000 entrepreneurs struck out on their own.[4] Entrepreneurship is often equated with small business ownership and management because of the common, and generally accurate, perception that much of the nation's innovation and growth comes from this sector. This chapter explores small business and entrepreneurship and also discusses how entrepreneurship may be fostered within large organizations.

THE ROLE OF SMALL BUSINESS IN THE ECONOMY

When people use the term small business, they are usually thinking of so-called mom and pop stores like the neighborhood grocery, reserving the term big business for "giant" corporations like IBM and General Motors. A more general definition of **small business** suggests that businesses financed by the owners and their personal funding resources should be considered small. Further, the same person or small group owns and manages the business; resources are secured locally; and products or services are distributed locally. Also, most businesses are considered small if they are small relative to others in the same industry. In the U.S. Chamber of Commerce classification, a business that employs fewer than 500 individuals is considered small.[5]

Not only are there substantially more small businesses than big businesses, but a great many more new jobs are created by small businesses than by big businesses. During the past ten years, a total of 20 million new jobs have been created by small businesses, compared with a net loss in jobs in the Fortune 500 companies.[6] In addition, small businesses outperform big businesses in critical areas such as return on owners' equity.[7] There are at least two reasons for this success. First, small businesses are able to respond more quickly and at less cost than big businesses to the fast pace of change in products, services,

---

This chapter is based in part on material prepared by Dr. Gary Roberts and Dr. Janet Adams for the first edition of this text.

processes, and markets. Second, small business has become more attractive to talented, individualistic men and women.

ENTREPRENEURSHIP

Entrepreneurship means the creation of wealth-adding value. This wealth is created by individuals who assume the major risks in terms of equity, time, and/or career commitment of providing value for some product or service. The product or service may or may not be new or unique, but value must somehow be imparted by the entrepreneur.[8] When this activity takes place within the confines of a large organization, it is often referred to as **intrapreneurship**.

Though the preceding discussion makes it clear that there is considerable overlap between small business and entrepreneurship, the concepts are not the same. Small businesses are not all entrepreneurial in nature. Entrepreneurial firms are not all small—they may begin at any size level but key in on growth over time. Some new small firms may grow, but many will remain small businesses.

Entrepreneurial Characteristics

Several characteristics of entrepreneurs have been found to be associated with their success. Here are some of the most important:[9]

- *Commitment, determination, and perseverance.* Successful entrepreneurs almost always give their all in order to succeed. Case studies of successful entrepreneurs indicate that they make many sacrifices in their family life, their standards of living, and often their health.
- *Strong achievement motivation.* Successful entrepreneurs are self-starters who are driven by a need to succeed and to accomplish something. They are constantly keeping score.
- *Goal directedness.* Successful entrepreneurs typically challenge themselves by setting difficult, yet obtainable, goals. Both goal-directed behavior and achievement motivation were discussed in detail in Chapter 13.
- *Acceptance of personal responsibility.* Successful entrepreneurs do not avoid situations where they are personally responsible for the success or

Kroger's growth from one modest store to a large supermarket chain with its own food manufacturing and processing facilities is an example of entrepreneurial success.

failure of any given activity or event. They have a strong inclination toward doing and are self-reliant.

- *Peripheral awareness.* Successful entrepreneurs are characterized by an extremely sharp peripheral vision. They are often aware of things that most people miss.
- *Internal locus of control.* Successful entrepreneurs generally hold the belief that one's accomplishments and failures lie within one's personal control and influence. They downplay the importance of luck.
- *Tolerance for ambiguity.* The successful entrepreneur is able to live with a substantial amount of uncertainty regarding job and career security, work-related events, and other aspects of independence. Self-confidence is related to this perspective.
- *Calculated risk-taking.* The successful entrepreneur is not risk averse; in other words, he or she will take risks. In a calculated risk, the chances of winning are neither so small as to be a gamble nor so large as to be a sure thing. The entrepreneur's managerial efforts are heavily directed toward reducing the level of risk by lowering the odds against his or her enterprise.
- *Low needs for status and power.* Achievement—not status and power—is the driving force in the lives of successful entrepreneurs.
- *Creative expression.* Successful entrepreneurs tend to need and value creative expression. They also place high values on aesthetics and variety.
- *Ability to deal with failure.* Successful entrepreneurs often fail, only to recover and keep on going. Failures are seen as temporary setbacks and are valued as learning experiences. Colonel Sanders, of Kentucky Fried Chicken fame, failed at many businesses until he opened a chicken stand at the age of 47.

These characteristics don't necessarily distinguish successful entrepreneurs from successful managers; successful managers also have high levels of achievement motivation, perseverance, and tolerance for ambiguity. And, of course, there are many successful entrepreneurs who don't exhibit certain of these characteristics. Nevertheless, an individual with this pattern of characteristics would be a good candidate for entrepreneurial success.

These characteristics provide some clues to the sorts of things that are necessary for entrepreneurial success. Nevertheless, a focus on characteristics of entrepreneurs may obscure the fact that entrepreneurship involves a set of behaviors, and that those behaviors may be learned. We will next discuss entrepreneurial strategies and then will examine the entrepreneurial firm in transition. Later in the chapter we will consider specific guidelines for successfully starting a business.

Entrepreneurial Strategies

Peter Drucker has discussed three distinct strategies available to entrepreneurs.[10] He calls these "fustest with the mostest," "creative imitation," and "entrepreneurial judo." Each of these approaches aims at obtaining a leadership position and eventual dominance. Each has benefits and risks.

"FUSTEST WITH THE MOSTEST"

Being **"fustest with the mostest"** was how a Confederate cavalry general explained his consistent success in battles. When applying this strategy, the entrepreneur aims at leadership, if not dominance, in a new market or industry. This doesn't necessarily imply creating a big business right from the start, though this is often a goal. However, it does from the start aim at achieving a permanent leadership position.

While this is often viewed as the primary entrepreneurial strategy, Drucker argues that it is not the dominant entrepreneurial strategy, let alone the one with the lowest risk or highest success ratio. Of all entrepreneurial strategies, it is the greatest gamble, and it is unforgiving, making no allowance for mistakes. If successful, though, it is highly rewarding. This strategy has spawned notable successes, such as when An Wang developed the word processor, or when two young entrepreneurs started Apple Computer in a garage. The fustest with the mostest strategy aims at creating a new industry, a new market or, at the very least, a new process. This strategy requires thought and careful analysis of the opportunities for innovation. Even then, it requires great concentration of effort. When this effort begins to produce results, the innovator has to be ready to mobilize resources massively. Then, after the innovation has become a successful business, substantial and continuing efforts are required to retain the leadership position.

"CREATIVE IMITATION"

"Creative imitation" is one of two "Hit them where they ain't" strategies discussed by Drucker. While creative imitation sounds like a contradiction in terms, Drucker argues that the term is appropriate since the entrepreneur who applies this strategy understands what the innovation represents better than the people who made the innovation. Creative imitation goes to work after somebody else has introduced the new, but only in a limited way. Then it sets out to truly satisfy the customer. It does not invent a product or service; it perfects and positions it. It is market focused and market driven. If well done, creative imitation then sets the standard and takes over the market.

This is the strategy practiced by IBM with the personal computer. Although Apple was the initial market leader, IBM set to work to develop a personal computer that would dominate the field; within two years, the IBM PC had wrested the leadership position from Apple to become the fastest-selling brand and the standard in the field. Johnson & Johnson also used creative imitation with Tylenol. Acetaminophen, the substance in Tylenol, had long been used as a painkiller, and the first brand on the market was promoted as a drug for those who suffered side effects from aspirin. Johnson & Johnson recognized that there was a market for a drug that would *replace* aspirin as the painkiller of choice. Tylenol was promoted as the safe, *universal* painkiller and quickly took over the market.

Creative imitation is less risky than fustest with the mostest. By the time the creative imitator moves, the market has been established and the new has been accepted. Indeed, there is often more demand than the original innovator can easily supply. Most of the uncertainties that abound when the first innovator appears have been dispelled or at least analyzed and studied. On the other hand, creative imitation does require a growing market, and there is always the danger that the wrong thing will be imitated. What creative imitation lacks in risk it makes up for in the need for alertness, flexibility, and willingness to accept the verdict of the market.

"ENTREPRENEURIAL JUDO"

Another "Hit them where they ain't" strategy, **"entrepreneurial judo"** takes advantage of the weaknesses of the firm holding the leadership position. Drucker writes that entrepreneurial judo first aims at securing a beachhead, one that the leaders either do not defend at all or defend only halfheartedly. Once that beachhead is secured, the newcomers have adequate market and revenue and move in on the rest of the territory. They then repeat the strategy, designing a product or service which is specific to a given market segment and optimal for it. The Japanese have had notable success in implementing this strategy. Drucker identifies five common "bad habits" which enable newcomers to use entrepreneurial judo:

- *"NIH" ("not invented here").* This is the arrogance that leads a company or industry to believe that something new cannot be any good unless they themselves thought of it. Thus, the new invention is spurned. This occurred when the transistor was developed at Bell Laboratories. American manufacturers moved slowly to convert to transistors, partly because the innovation hadn't been developed internally. Sony jumped in and quickly dominated the world radio market.
- *The tendency to "cream" the market.* "Creaming" the market means getting the high-profit portion of it. Xerox used this strategy with its copying machines, focusing its strategy on the buyers of large numbers of machines or of expensive high-performance machines. This made it an easy target for Japanese imitators who provided service to small customers.
- *The belief in "quality."* Drucker points out that "quality" is what the consumer gets from a product or service and is willing to pay for. American electronics manufacturers in the 1950s believed that their radios—big, filled with vacuum tubes, and requiring considerable skill to make—were "quality." But from the consumer's point of view, the transistor radio—lightweight, reliable, and inexpensive—was clearly of far superior "quality."
- *The delusion of the "premium" price.* Drucker argues that attempting to achieve a higher profit margin through a higher price is always self-defeating. What looks like higher profit for the established leader is in effect a subsidy to the newcomer who will soon unseat the leader and claim the throne. Charging premium prices puts the leader in a highly vulnerable position.
- *Maximizing rather than optimizing.* As a market grows and develops, some firms try to satisfy every user through the same product or service; they try to maximize what the product or service can do. This raises price, and nobody is really satisfied. The newcomer can then enter with a lower-priced product that is optimal for one market segment. Sony used this approach to enter the copier field. Xerox had developed expensive, full-featured machines. Sony provided simple machines at low cost for small offices. It quickly established itself in that market and then moved on to others, with products designed to optimally serve a specific market segment.

Entrepreneurial judo is market focused and market driven. It requires analysis of the industry: the producers and their suppliers, their habits (especially their bad habits), and their policies. Then one looks at the markets and seeks the place where an alternative strategy would meet with the greatest success and the least resistance. Drucker views entrepreneurial judo as the least risky and most likely to succeed of the three entrepreneurial strategies he discusses.

THE ENTREPRENEURIAL FIRM IN TRANSITION

In an interesting discussion of the archetypal life of the hero in mythology, FitzRoy Raglan has presented 22 features or incidents that are common to many accounts of heroes' lives.[11] Often, for instance, the hero's father is a king, an attempt is made to kill the hero at birth, the hero is spirited away to a far country but returns upon reaching manhood, has a great victory, becomes king, and so on. Barbara Bird suggests that the entrepreneur may be considered a type of mythological hero, in search of adventure and treasure; a kind of heroic charisma attaches itself to the notion of entrepreneurship. Bird says the following elements are common in the adult years of many entrepreneurs:[12]

1. The entrepreneur, reaching a plateau or experiencing a displacement, finds a need to prove himself or herself.
2. In starting a new venture, he or she finds that competition, bankers, suppliers, and customers present serious, venture-threatening problems, which he or she solves.
3. The entrepreneur establishes a business, which is often experienced as "mistress," "child," or "family."
4. The entrepreneur becomes CEO.
5. For a time the entrepreneur runs the business smoothly.
6. The entrepreneur designs the organization, establishes procedures, hires and trains managers and other employees, and builds organizational momentum.
7. The entrepreneur loses the favor of outside investors who want return on their investments or of employees who want more pay, respect, or control.
8. The entrepreneur is forced to change the organization (e.g., through public offering, acquisition, or unionizing) or leave.

This scenario suggests that the entrepreneurial form may be unstable. That is, the skills needed to successfully start and nurture a firm may be very different from those required to successfully maintain a larger organization. Lucien Rhodes has written:

In the fullness of your accomplishment, you find it strangely hollow. The company is too big, too complex. What is that person's name? Where did the family feeling go, and where's the magic? You find yourself stranded in the breach where impulse and improvisation must give way to systems and planning, and the fires of creation are cooling on the routines of disciplined technique. You sense . . . that your own talents, so productive at the start, are no longer of the kind and quality to carry the enterprise further. Others around you see it as well. But it's your enterprise, isn't it? You birthed it. You are its loving parent. How can you let it go? What can you do?[13]

Alan Filley and his colleagues have classified organizations into three types, called craft, promotion, and administrative types.[14] The **craft type or-**

ganization is strongly influenced by a chief executive who seeks comfort and company survival objectives and who engages in duties which are primarily technical rather than administrative. There are low levels of risk-taking, innovation, and growth, and the organization exists at the mercy of a benevolent environment. The **promotion type organization** is strongly influenced by a chief executive who is charismatic and the promoter of the firm's innovative advantage. The organization exists as an extension of the chief executive's personality. Morale is high as long as organization members share high expectations about future outcomes. The organization is innovative and is readily redirected by the chief executive. It exists and succeeds primarily to exploit some product or market advantage, and the advantage ends when competitors or imitators enter the market. The **administrative type organization** is characterized by professional management and by an institutional character which exists independent of organization members. Its management seeks to adapt to its competitive situation through planning and the use of formal organization. Of most relevance here, the promotion type of organization is similar to the entrepreneurial firm. Filley has shown that this type of firm is short-lived. According to Filley and Aldag:

Steven Jobs, whose outstanding entrepreneurial skills led to the success of Apple Computer, relinquished leadership during the company's transition period.

The promotion type of organization is also vulnerable, containing within itself the seeds of its own destruction. The organization is inefficient, making it vulnerable to competitors who are efficient. The newness of its innovation is subject to imitation. The leader's charisma may well end, either through personal failure or through failure to achieve idealistic goals. Finally, the personal influence of the leader may cease when contact with organization members is no longer practical.[15]

Filley's research suggests that these organizations typically must either evolve into administrative types or die. Entrepreneurs must deal with the fact that the skills needed to start a business may be very different from those needed to keep it running effectively. As their firms grow, entrepreneurs must be willing to seek guidance in dealing with management problems and to give up some measure of control. For many entrepreneurs, this is difficult advice to accept. If it is not heeded, however, failure of the enterprise may result, as reflected in Management in Action 1.

THE SMALL BUSINESS ENVIRONMENT

Small businesses are affected by the same environmental domains and dimensions as those affecting larger businesses. However, because they have fewer means of buffering themselves from the environment and responding to changes, small businesses are especially susceptible to environmental forces. As a result, managers of small businesses must pay especially careful attention to the domains of their environment.

Economic Domain

Because they have fewer resources to fall back on during lean times, small businesses are particularly vulnerable to downturns in the business cycle. Borrowing is likely to be more expensive for small businesses since they lack

When Marc Hyman started a delivery service in New York four years ago, he was obsessed with being "on top of everything."

MANAGEMENT IN ACTION 1
ENTREPRENEURS OFTEN FAIL AS MANAGERS

"I wasn't willing to listen to other people," he recalls. "I thought, 'I am the daddy of this. I put in thousands of hours. I know better than anyone else.'" Now Mr. Hyman is trying to sell his business, and he frankly admits that he was wrong to have relied only on himself. "I didn't have what it took to make [the business] a success." Mr. Hyman believes he has learned from his mistakes, and that a new business he has begun will be much more successful.

The very traits that lead people to start their own businesses—ambition, self-confidence, creativity, even obsessiveness—often lead to both financial and personal grief as the enterprises grow. The starting entrepreneur commonly relishes the hands-on involvement in perfecting every detail as he builds his enterprise. This helps make the business fly.

But after the start-up, growth requires a radical shift in management style. Some find it easy, but many can't accept it. In a growing business, an inability to delegate authority can spell disaster. Making the problem all the tougher, the proprietor often finds it hard to cede control when all the money that flows out of the company ultimately flows out of his pocket.

Growth pushes entrepreneurs "into areas where most entrepreneurs aren't good," says William C. Dunkelberg, chief economist of the National Federation of Independent Business in Washington, D.C. For the small-business executive, delegating authority "can be like getting a baby sitter for the first time. You don't trust anybody," he says.

Some entrepreneurs recognize their limitations but find it hard to change roles. "I think I'm a pretty poor manager," concedes Nolan Bushnell, a perpetual entrepreneur who also admits being "really bad" at hiring. Of the eight companies he has started, some grew fast, some failed—and some did both. Mr. Bushnell now heads Axlon Inc., a Sunnyvale, Calif., toy company that even he describes as "kind of a basket case." Still, he won't bring in a turnaround specialist to help his struggling company. His resistance, he says, boils down to one word: "Ego."

The problems facing a growing company aren't new to Mr. Bushnell. When his restaurant chain, Pizza Time Theater Inc., was growing rapidly in the early 1980s, he felt he was on a roll and turned his attention to other ventures—instead of monitoring the chain's growth. "I got off track, and got too many businesses going," he says. Within a five-month period, the company went through two reorganizations, and Mr. Bushnell resigned as chairman in 1984. The company filed for protection under Chapter 11 of the federal Bankruptcy Code the following month.

the economic power to qualify for the prime rate from lenders. The small business frequently lacks surplus resources in the forms of inventories of raw materials and finished goods as well as operating capital; thus, the business may be unable to survive the difficult economic times that a larger firm can weather by living off the surpluses built up during more prosperous times.

The economic affluence of the small business's customers obviously affects their demand for the products and services offered. Factors in the general economic environment that impact on small business customers include such things as the general availability of credit, amount of disposable income, interest rates, rate of inflation, and growth trends in the overall economy and in sectors targeted by the business. Slower growth in the GNP means that any growth for one business must come at the expense of another company's market share rather than from the expansion of the total market. One implication of this is that marketing practices must be adjusted for no-growth segments.

Political Domain

The political environment establishes the legal aspects of engaging in business. It produces both opportunities and restrictions. Some government regulations protect small businesses: antitrust laws, patent protection, fair-trade decisions, subsidies, product research grants, and import restrictions may all aid small businesses.

Government support for particular businesses spawns development, as in the space program under Kennedy and synthetic fuels (less successfully) under Carter. Government social policies affect hiring, safety, and environmental policies of all businesses; however, the effect may be particularly strong on small businesses that are overwhelmed by the red tape and paperwork required to document compliance and the expense of safety and environmental protection features that may require large-scale production to be economically feasible. The expenditures required to meet environmental and other standards and to handle the paperwork necessary to document compliance have a greater impact on small businesses than on large ones. With simply less output, the cost of compliance per unit is greater for the small firm. Small firms also typically do not have access to long-term debt available to larger firms to finance regulatory compliance. Because small businesses usually find themselves in such competitive environments, they are less able to recoup the costs by raising their prices. In the late 1960s and early 1970s, many small foundries in the United States failed at least in part because they could not meet new Environmental Protection Agency requirements. Small companies that do manage to survive are still at a disadvantage in dealing with the proportionately larger share of regulatory costs. One small trucking company's president figured that his truck drivers had to maintain about 60 different forms to comply with various regulations. And small companies cannot hire additional staff to handle the accompanying paperwork.[16]

Small businesses spend billions of dollars filling out hundreds of millions of pages of government reports. The owner of a small seed and grain business claimed such government reports increased clerical costs by 42 percent. Another small business owner estimated that IRS regulations on biweekly payrolls increased monthly record-keeping requirements by $200.[17] The 1986 Tax Reform Act added to these problems, creating both uncertainty and paperwork for small businesses. One paragraph of this act reads:

(a) Except as provided in paragraph (b) of this section and hereafter in this subdivision (i), if at the close of any calendar month the aggregate of undeposited taxes (as defined in paragraph (a) (a) (iii) of this section) is $500 or more, the employer shall deposit the undeposited taxes in a Federal Reserve Bank or authorized financial institution (see subparagraph (3) (iii) of this paragraph) within 125 calendar days after the close of such calendar month.

Complaints about the regulatory load on small businesses have led to some relief. Firms employing fewer than 250 workers are no longer required to file EEOC written affirmative-action plans for hiring and promoting minorities; OSHA has dropped regular inspections on all except high-hazard manufacturing operations; and reporting requirements have been relaxed for small carriers. In addition, about 10 percent of small businesses making stock offerings have been exempted from SEC disclosure requirements. Finally, pressure has been building to exempt small businesses from one particularly vexing section of the 1986 Tax Reform Act.[18]

Small businesses have also been given help in meeting the legal costs of protesting regulatory loads. The **Equal Access to Justice Act** enables businesses to recover costs of litigation from the government when they challenge what they believe to be unreasonable government regulation—provided they win. No compensation is available, however, if the small business is not successful in its challenge, and the law does not cover disputed IRS tax rulings.

Another attempt to offer some protection to small businesses is the **Regulatory Flexibility Act**, which requires the government to take into account the size of the business and its ability to comply with regulations. Public notice must be given of proposed rules which can be expected to have a large economic impact on small businesses, and record-keeping requirements must be estimated. According to a government official, the Regulatory Flexibility Act "goes after crazy regulations and Equal Access aims at crazy enforcement."[19] On the other hand, small businesses may benefit from government requirements dictating that a certain percentage of contracts be set aside for minority contractors.

The most overt political help for small businesses comes through the **Small Business Administration (SBA)**, which was formed in 1953 to promote free competitive enterprise by making credit, contracts, and management advice available to small businesses.

The role of the federal government in determining the political environment of business has at times overshadowed that of state and local governments. Nevertheless, it is necessary for all businesses to comply with state and local ordinances. States, for example, set requirements for worker's compensation coverage and have varying other insurance requirements. The effect of local political factors is felt in the zoning ordinances that limit location decisions for businesses.

Technological Domain

A major technological change can revolutionize an industry. Less major changes can lead to product improvement, changes in production techniques, need for different marketing approaches, or new product development. Businesses are increasingly affected by technological changes in other industries that can create new and unexpected competitors. Small businesses may be particularly vulnerable to changes in technology that can create substitutes for their products from unexpected sources.

However, small businesses may actually enjoy an advantage where technological innovation is concerned. Because they are less constrained by large investments in plants and equipment for producing large amounts of current products using existing technologies, small businesses lead the way in innovations. Small businesses produce two and a half times as many innovations as large firms relative to the number of employees.[20] Small businesses have brought the world instant cameras, heart pacemakers, the vacuum tube, and the zipper. IBM may be the giant in the computer industry, but it is not known for technological innovation. It was another company (Univac) that produced the first full-scale commercial electronic computer; and Apple Computer, starting out as a small business in the owner's garage, developed the concept, product, and market for the personal computer.

Social Domain

The importance and pervasiveness of economic, political, and technological factors are undeniable, but social factors are also necessary considerations for small businesses. People—who they are, where they are, and what they think—must be taken into account in managing the small business. All businesses have to be concerned with changes in society as a whole. Day-care centers, many of which are small businesses, are one example of opportunities for businesses that result from changes in society.

Values and cultural patterns in society at large affect businesses, as discussed in Chapter 4. Public concern with environmental issues, the safety of nuclear power plants, and demands for more-fuel-efficient cars have all affected what is produced and how it is produced in the American economy.

Day-care centers are an example of opportunities for businesses that result from changes in society.

Competitive Domain

Small businesses usually operate in oligopolistic and monopolistic competition markets. The degree of competition in these markets is influenced by at least five factors: rivalry among competitors, potential entrants, substitute products or services, the bargaining power of customers, and the bargaining power of suppliers.[21]

Rivalry among competitors is likely to be the most important environmental force faced by the small business in day-to-day operations. Awareness of what competitors are doing, anticipating what they are likely to do, and planning responses to their changes in tactics and strategies are key activities in managing the small business. In addition, any contemplated change in the operation of the business must be assessed in light of the probable response of competitors. Price cuts by one firm are likely to produce price cuts by competitors, for example. Such price competition may leave all firms in the industry with lower profits or even losses, but the firm that fails to meet its competitors' prices in a highly competitive market will suffer most.

Since small businesses usually operate in markets with relatively low barriers to entry, the threat of new entrants is a constant concern. Barriers to entry, such as inability to achieve economies of scale and high capital requirements, are usually prohibitive to small business, of course. But product differentiation, in which a small business achieves a unique niche in terms of quality, design, customer service, or brand image, may be achieved by a small business and act as a barrier to entry into its market segment. Because of resource limitations, however, most small businesses enter markets having low entry barriers; once established, they must constantly be concerned with the threat of new competitors.

There is also the threat that competitors will produce substitute products or services that will give customers new ways to meet the needs that are currently being met by the small business. The specter of new substitutes for existing products is increased by the accelerating rate of change in technology.

The bargaining power of customers and suppliers also affects the competitive domain of the firm. Small businesses that sell most of their output to one or a few customers are put in a very dependent position. Likewise, if the small business is one of many customers of its key suppliers, it will have little power in relation to those suppliers. Small businesses rarely have great amounts of bargaining power in dealing with their customers or suppliers.

Their larger competitors may be able to negotiate more favorable terms with suppliers because their larger purchases give them more clout in the bargaining process.

Physical Domain

Small businesses must attempt to protect themselves from elements in their physical environment such as damaging weather conditions. The 1980s crisis in the insurance industry hit small businesses especially hard and made the physical domain more threatening to the business than in times when insurance against physical damage was cheaper and easier to obtain. Increasing expenses in this area may affect a company's pricing policies and hence its ability to compete against larger companies that can spread the expense across a larger number of products or incidents of service provision.

GUIDELINES FOR STARTING A BUSINESS

The Chinese philosopher Confucius once said, "Choose a job you love, and you will never have to work a day in your life." For many students reading this text, that job will involve starting their own business.

Starting one's own business involves answering three central questions in detail: (1) What business should be started? (2) Is this business feasible? (3) What steps must be taken to start the business?

What Business Should Be Started?

Choosing what business to start depends upon one's marketing skills, technological skills, and personal finances, and often entails doing a self-assessment before making a commitment. If one has several thousand dollars to spend, a professional consultant can be hired to do a study. Normally, a person will need to have a well-defined idea of what it is that he or she wants to do. Most people conduct their own initial study, focusing on what interests them and where they feel they might make money.

It is usually a mistake to compete head to head with an ongoing operation. While it may be true that one can take away a lot of the competition's business by competing on a price basis, remember that competitors can always choose to "bite the bullet" and match the lower prices. The resulting price competition can play real havoc with profit margins. A person who is considering starting a business should have a number of good reasons, other than price, which will cause customers to switch over. These could include a distinctly better product, better service, a more convenient location, or some other competitive advantage.

Is This Business Feasible?

Once your idea for a business has been evaluated, you must still analyze the market for your product or service. A **market feasibility study** will allow you to satisfy yourself that a good market exists for whatever you are planning to sell. Figure 23–1 shows a worksheet for a market feasibility study. The answers should be written in as much detail as possible.

FIGURE 23–1
*Format for a Market
Feasibility Study*

Your Product or Service

1. Describe the nature of the product or service you will offer.
2. Which stage of the product life cycle is your product or service in: introduction, growth, maturity, or decline?
3. What edge do you believe your product or service will have over similar products that are already offered or that may be introduced by new competitors?
4. How do you intend to take market share away from competitors?

Your Customers

5. Describe your customers in terms of their geographic area; age and/or sex group; income level; and social, cultural, and ethnic factors.

Your Competition

6. The main competitors in my market area are as follows:
7. Three reasons why customers would buy from me rather than from my competitors:
8. Three weaknesses my business will have as compared with those of my competitors:
9. I will overcome these weaknesses by:

What Steps Are Needed to Start the Business?

Eight major steps are needed to get a business going. Individual situations will vary, of course, and these steps will probably need to be adjusted to suit the particular situation:

1. Prepare a written business plan for your venture. Developing and implementing a sound business plan are discussed in detail in the next section.
2. Consult the professionals needed to get the business off to a good start. An accountant can offer sound advice on a variety of business-related topics and make an important contribution to the successful start-up and operation of the firm. An attorney has information on the licenses and permits needed, the forms that must be completed, and the decisions that must be made before the doors are opened. He or she will save you from unintentionally breaking laws. A banker will probably be one of your most frequent professional contacts, whether the business is just starting up or has been in operation for some time. If you borrow money from a bank, the banker will be keenly interested in the success of the venture, because the bank wants to see that the loan is made good. Insurance agents will help with decisions about how much and what types of coverage are essential in the start-up situation. Talk to several agents in order to compare rates.
3. Make a decision about the legal form of organization your business will follow. Sole proprietorships, partnerships, and corporations each have advantages and disadvantages.
4. Determine the type of financing that best fits the situation. Start-ups generally find that there are many sources of money available. These sources are listed in order of accessibility:

   - Personal savings, family, and friends
   - Life insurance policies

Deciding on the best location is an important step in starting a business.

- Mortgaging real estate
- Commercial bank financing
- Savings and loan associations
- The U.S. Small Business Administration (SBA)
- Farmer's Home Administration
- External financing by selling ownership of the business
- Private venture capital

5. Decide on the best location for the firm. Choosing a location is crucial to the success of most small businesses. A detailed analysis of the type of business that you are in, coupled with an analysis of the type of customers that you are dealing with, is the first step in choosing a good location.

6. Obtain the required licenses and permits for the particular business location chosen. Businesses are subject to regulation by three different governmental jurisdictions—local, state, and federal. Men and women managing small businesses must check with each of these levels of government to make certain they are complying with all regulations which pertain to their business. An attorney should help with this stage of the start-up.

7. Register with the appropriate authorities for tax collection, employee withholding, and safety, health, and pollution control inspections if applicable to the business. At this stage, an accountant and an attorney can offer appropriate advice.

8. Become involved with professional and community organizations in the area, and participate in the educational programs they offer. The local chamber of commerce is a key organization in most communities. The chamber will help business owners in a variety of ways, including sponsorship of seminars on business topics. It also offers individual counseling.

MAKING THE SMALL BUSINESS EFFECTIVE

The early years of a business are treacherous. There are many liabilities of newness that conspire against young firms.[22] There are new roles to be learned and no "old hands" to teach them; people are uncertain about who is, or isn't, doing what; members haven't yet had a chance to develop relationships of trust; there are as yet no stable ties to suppliers or customers. During this start-up period, many things can, and will, go wrong.

A survey by the National Federation of Independent Businesses (NFIB), summarized in Figure 23–2, asked small business owners about the single most important problem they faced. Taxes, poor sales, and interest rates for financing were mentioned most frequently.[23]

Another survey asked the owners of a large number of small businesses what they regarded as major pitfalls in managing a small business. The replies identified nine roadblocks:[24]

1. Lack of experience with the business
2. Lack of enough money for start-up and continuation
3. Choosing the wrong location
4. Inventory mismanagement
5. Tying up too much money in fixed assets
6. Poor credit-granting policies

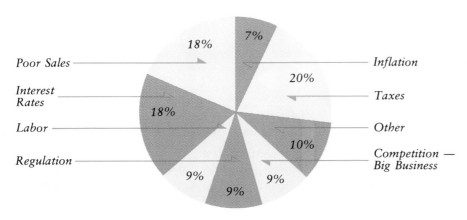

FIGURE 23–2
Single Most Important Problem of Small Business

Source: From "Quarterly Economic Report for Small Business," The NFIB Foundation. Reprinted by permission of the National Federation of Independent Business, Research and Education Division.

7. Taking too much out for yourself
8. Unplanned expansion
9. Having the wrong mental attitude

These surveys highlight the myriad of factors—some associated with the environment but many within the control of the manager—which may jeopardize small business success.

The ideas and the skills identified during the discussion of the functional areas of management presented earlier in this book are as applicable to managing in a small business as they are in a large business. Further, careful attention to the development and implementation of a sound business plan may help ensure success of the small business. A **business plan** helps the owner determine what resources are needed and provides a standard against which to evaluate results. The Small Business Administration publishes a series called *Management Aids* that is designed to help small business owners make successful business plans. The discussion that follows is based on SBA aids for developing business plans in small retail, service, and manufacturing firms.[25]

A business plan offers at least four benefits:

• A plan sets out a path to follow. Without a path, it is impossible to determine whether the business is going in the right direction.
• Having a plan makes it easier to communicate with bankers and others who can aid the business. It indicates to others that the entrepreneur has thought out what he or she wants to do and what he or she needs in order to do it. The plan shows details that will be requested by anyone who considers lending money.
• A plan helps to communicate to salespeople, suppliers, and others the business's goals and how they will be reached.
• Working through the process of considering factors that are likely to have an impact on the business can help one develop as a manager.

The SBA approach to developing a business plan for any kind of business starts by requesting answers to basic questions. Why are you in business?

Rocky Aoki is the founder and chairman of the board of Benihana of Tokyo, a nationwide chain of Japanese-style steakhouses. A former Olympic wrestler, Aoki opened his first restaurant in New York in 1964 with $10,000 of his own money and a $20,000 loan. The restaurant was based on the age-old idea of teppanyaki (steel grill) cooking. Aoki developed a formula combining a meal and theatrics, with chefs dicing, slicing, and cooking food on a hibachi table in front of the patrons.

Today, Benihana companies employ approximately 2,500 people from New York to Honolulu serving more than three million guests a year at their 78 restaurants. Included in that success is the publicly traded Benihana National Corporation, created in the early 1980s to tackle debt, perpetuate restaurant growth, and provide seed money for the development of a line of premium oriental frozen entrees marketed through supermarkets across the United States. Among Aoki's other endeavors are an urbanized dining concept called Benihana Cafe, where only one chef performs for an entire restaurant. Aoki also associates his name with a line of wines, videotapes on cooking, and several best-selling Japanese business books.

Aoki is also involved in promoting cultural exchanges between Japan and the United States. These include sponsorship of sporting and cultural events, such as the first professional heavyweight fight to be held in the Far East, the Muhammad Ali–Mac Foster fight in 1972; becoming Broadway's first "Japanese angel"; and being a patron to young Japanese artists in the United States and producing films about them for release in Japan. Aoki's love of sports has led him to become a premier competitor on the offshore powerboat racing circuit and a crew member on the first balloon to successfully cross the Pacific Ocean.

Q: You are often cited as an extraordinary entrepreneurial success story. Do you have any suggestions for prospective entrepreneurs?

A: You have to want to succeed. In your search for success you'll have to surround yourself with the right people and brains. Work smarter and harder and keep focused. Look for opportunities in everything you do. Be daring and different.

Q: How do you maintain an entrepreneurial spirit in a large organization such as Benihana of Tokyo?

A: Sometimes keeping an entrepreneurial spirit in a large company can be more challenging than finding new opportunities on the outside. Many people fall into place and simply want to follow. You have to keep people excited. I'm not afraid to say that I've failed in the past, so what I do when hiring is really ensure that the brains I am buying are ripe for success, mine and theirs. At the senior management level in our company, the newest executive has been with us six years already.

Q: You seem to be a risk-taker, both in business and in personal pursuits such as powerboat racing and ballooning. Have you found risk-taking to be helpful or a detriment in business?

A: Everyone should know that to succeed in something a risk must be taken. To cross the street involves taking a risk. Who knows, you could be waysided by a

MANAGERIAL PROFILE
ROCKY AOKI

speeding car. The point is to take calculated risks. Study all that is available about a subject before jumping in head first. Before I flew across the Pacific Ocean in a balloon my crew and I spent a year preparing: studying weather patterns, getting in good physical shape, practicing rescue procedures, learning radio equipment, etc. If I hadn't taken the risks I took, my company wouldn't be as well known as it is. I believe risks have led to my success. One of the first risks taken for Benihana was a full-page—that's right, *full*-page—ad in the *New York Times* during the late 1960s when it was unheard of for restaurants to even advertise. Even then the expense was astronomical, but the ad paid for itself within days.

What are your personal goals—making a profit, being your own boss, or producing a quality product? What business are you really in? Although this last question may sound silly, not knowing the answer almost cost one owner his business. He thought he was in the marina business maintaining a dock and renting boats. However, he was really in several businesses because he served meals to boating parties (the restaurant business); he bought and sold lots (the real estate business); and he bought parts and hired mechanics to repair boats (the boat repair business). He was, in fact, in so many businesses that he was unsure of where to put his limited resources. He had no idea what kind of return he should expect. He finally decided he was really in the marina business and should concentrate on buying, selling, and servicing boats.

We will first discuss the business plan for service and retail businesses and will then point out how the plan might differ for small manufacturing firms. For service and retail businesses, the next steps in developing a business plan are the same. They involve developing a marketing plan. The marketing plan can be broken down into three sections: determining sales potential, attracting customers, and selling to customers.

Determining Sales Potential

Sales potential depends on the location of the service or retail business. In what part of town should the business be located? What is the population and growth potential of the area? What are the ages, incomes, and occupations of the population? Is adequate space available for the business? Are there zoning restrictions that will affect the business? If leasing property, what services does the landlord supply? Are the leasing terms favorable? Is parking or public transportation available to customers? Is there a strong economic base in the area? Does competition exist in this location? What do competitors in the area charge for their products or services? If you locate in a particular area, what is your sales potential? What other businesses have failed in this location and why?

Attracting Customers

Small retail and service businesses often find that they have or can develop some competitive advantage in attracting customers. Image—the view of the business you want to project—can be crucial in retail and service businesses. Cleanliness, treatment of customers, and employee conduct all contribute to the image of the business. It is important for the owner to know what image she or he wants to project and to make it concrete enough to use in advertising. For example, a small restaurant might project an image of home-cooked meals in a home-like atmosphere.

Pricing also plays an important role in attracting customers. Pricing decisions are based on costs of materials and supplies, expenses of labor and other operating costs, planned profit, and what the competition charges for similar products or services. If your prices are higher than your competitors', what are you offering to justify the higher prices you charge? If you offer credit, the cost of this service will have to be covered in your price.

Store layout and lighting are part of the image of a business.

Selling to Customers

What services do your competitors offer? What do these services cost? Are there other services you could offer that might attract customers away from your competitors? Can you offer the services you want to offer without pricing yourself out of the market?

Before customers can buy, they must know what you have to offer. Advertising informs them. Advertising is the last consideration in the marketing plan. Know what you have to offer before you consider how to advertise it. Image, price range, and services are the kinds of things you will want to tell prospective customers about when advertising. Decide what you want advertising to do for your business. What facts do you want to get across, and to whom? Your customer profile becomes very important, because it clearly identifies the target of your advertising efforts. Determine what it will cost to advertise for the next 12 months. Is this above or below what the competition spends? Keep in mind that no single area in your budget plan can be too far out of line if you expect to be able to make a profit.

The next steps in developing the business plan differ by type of business. In the retail business, the buying function must be considered at this point. The retailer must identify sources of goods to sell—whether they can be bought directly from the manufacturer or through wholesalers and distributors, the buying terms, whether credit is available for the business, how quickly sources deliver goods, if fill-in orders are available (do you have to buy a dozen or a gross, or will the supplier ship only one or two items?), freight costs and whose responsibility they are, and delivery time.

In a service business, concerns are different at this point in developing the business plan. The emphasis is on selling—repeat selling—to customers who come to you for services. Identify the types of fixtures and equipment needed to provide your services. From whom are they available? Do these suppliers offer a discount? How many days or weeks does it take the supplier to deliver the parts and materials needed in your business? What are the freight costs, and who has to pay them? What is the supplier's fill-in policy? What kind of stock-control system is needed to help you keep track of what is on hand, what is on order, and what has been used? What overhead items will be needed to provide the services (rent, utilities, postage, telephone, accountant, licenses, local taxes, payroll taxes, etc.)? If you have employees, their salaries will be part of your overhead.

In the retail business, you also will be concerned with stock control and with stock turnover. What is the average stock turnover of other similar retailing businesses? How many times do you expect your stock to turn over in the next 12 months? How will the behind-the-scenes work of retailing be handled? That is, who will receive merchandise, prepare and maintain displays, and keep the store clean? What equipment will be needed? How much time will be allotted for these activities?

Getting the Work Done

How will your service or retail business be organized? How will you find and train employees and delegate work, responsibility, and authority as the business grows? A helpful tool for answering these questions is an organization chart showing who is responsible for what and who answers to whom in the organization. It may also be helpful to list all the activities that are necessary in carrying out your business. Determine who will do each activity.

Converting the Plan into Dollars

This is the next step in the planning process for both retail and service businesses. It is necessary to estimate the start-up costs for fixtures and equipment, starting inventory, decorating and remodeling, installation of equipment, deposits for utilities, legal and professional fees, licenses and permits, advertising for the opening, an allowance for accounts receivable, and the operating cash needed. Whether the start-up costs come from your personal savings or from a lender, the business has to make enough to pay back the start-up costs.

The next step is to estimate expenses for each of the next 12 months. Will your estimated sales cover your cash needs on a month-by-month basis? If not, where will you get the money you need that is not generated by your sales? If you intend to borrow from a bank to tide you over the lean months, prepare a balance sheet to show your firm's financial condition.

Control and Feedback

The record-keeping system should be set up before the business opens. If this is neglected, the business may never have the time to establish the system properly. Controls should be included to give current information on stock control, sales, and disbursements. It is also important to know the break-even point before starting.

Because the stock-control system keeps the business up-to-date on the status of inventory, the business is better able to offer efficient service to customers while tying up as little money as possible in inventory. Inventory costs include not only the cost of the stock but also the costs of purchasing, keeping inventory-control records, and receiving and storing parts and materials.

Control and feedback are most important in the areas of sales and disbursements. Once a firm is operating, it must have systems that can provide answers to the following questions: How much did we sell today? How many separate sales were made and on what credit terms? In the very small business, this feedback can come from sales slips and cash register tapes. Are bills being paid on time to get suppliers' discounts? How are funds being used? Are payroll taxes being deposited at the proper times?

Putting Your Plan into Action

At this point in the planning process, it is time to take a look at whether or not the plan is workable. If break-even analysis shows that the business has to have a level of sales considered unreachable, or if any cost items look too high or too low, a revision in the plan is needed. It is also a good idea to have someone who has not been involved in developing the plan take a look at it. A banker, an SBA representative, or some other knowledgeable advisor may be able to identify weaknesses. It is far easier to revise or to make a no-go decision before you invest your money than it is after the business is already under way.

Planning is for action, and unless the plan is put into action, it is merely a dream. Make a list of the steps that must be taken to put the plan into action, and include the dates by which each action is to be taken. Then do it.

Finally, it is necessary to keep the plan current by staying on top of the conditions that affect the business and by adjusting the plan to meet the new conditions. A regular review of the plan is a good idea, perhaps monthly or bimonthly. After you have been in business for a while, there will be more accurate information to work with. The plan should be revised to reflect this new information. "A good business plan must evolve from experience and the best current information."[26]

Differences in the Business Plan for Small Manufacturing Firms

The planning steps outlined in the previous sections are for small retail and service firms. How does a business plan for a small manufacturing business differ? The SBA guide for small manufacturers suggests that after deciding why one is in business and what business one is in, it is a good idea to identify the standard industrial classification (SIC) of the product and industry. The **standard industrial classification**, a method of categorizing the products of a company by type and industry, gives information that may be helpful in planning the marketing effort.

Next, identify market area and competitors. Careful analysis is needed to determine what advantage(s) the business has over its competitors. Is it price? performance? durability? versatility? speed? accuracy? ease of operation, maintenance, repair, or installation? size or weight? style or appearance? What unique features does the product have? As a manufacturer, one also must determine how and where the product will be distributed and what the distribution costs will be.

For the manufacturer, trade associations may be good sources of information in identifying market trends for the past few years and in making predictions about future trends. An estimate of the share of the market you expect to serve once your enterprise is in full operation is an important part of a manufacturing business plan.

In a manufacturing plan, attention must be given to planning production. Determining what production facilities are needed requires that the production process be analyzed. What basic manufacturing operations are necessary? What raw materials are required and where will you get them? How much raw materials inventory will have to be maintained? Are there special storage requirements for any of your raw materials, such as flammable materials or materials with limited shelf lives? What manufacturing equipment is required? How will you comply with the Occupational Safety and Health Administration (OSHA) requirements for your operation? What labor skills are necessary to run the equipment, handle materials, and otherwise keep the plant operating? Where will you find people with the needed skills? How much space is required for manufacturing and supporting facilities? What local ordinances apply? Estimate your overhead (indirect labor, tools, supplies, utilities, office help, salaries for key people, etc.).

At this point, the manufacturing business plan proceeds as do plans for other small businesses by estimating the money needed for start-up and the first year's cash flow, developing an organization chart, setting up control systems, and systematically revising the plan and keeping it up-to-date.

INTRAPRENEURSHIP

To this point we have focused primarily on small firms. In this section, we will ask how the flexibility, creativity, risk-taking, and energy which are often associated with small firms and entrepreneurship may be instilled in larger organizations. As noted earlier, intrapreneurship is a name given to entrepreneurial activities within a larger organization. Management in Action 2 shows how some large firms are trying to foster intrapreneurship.

Intrapreneurial Characteristics

Intrapreneurs and entrepreneurs have many things in common.[27] For instance, they value creativity and autonomy and have high achievement motivation. On the other hand, there are important differences between intrapreneurs and entrepreneurs. Most important, since intrapreneurs work within a corporate system, they face the benefits and constraints of that system. Unlike entrepreneurs, they operate under a corporate accounting system and must report to hierarchical superiors. They do not personally face the financial risks that entrepreneurs do, nor do they enjoy the same rewards. They can draw on the rich financial resources of the corporation.

These differences in actual and perceived autonomy, risk, and resource availability may influence decision making, relationships, commitment, and

Go beyond the traditional strongholds of Du Pont Co.—beyond the mainstay chemicals, the oil rigs, the coal mines—and you run into little surprises.

MANAGEMENT IN ACTION 2
MONEY FROM THE BOSS

Here someone is selling a chemically improved fish bait. There somebody else is trying new ways to catch and kill flies. Another fellow thinks carpet underlay will serve as cushion in running shoes.

Du Pont (1988 sales: $32.92 billion) is first a colossus, marshaling huge resources to huge tasks. Yet it is something else, too—a breeding ground for small businesses.

The employees who run these businesses harbor an idea, find a sugar daddy, and then go to work on the margins of the corporation. They still tap into their employer for help. But they may also line up their own production capacity on the outside, or do their own market research or hire their own staffs.

If the corporate bureaucracy in Wilmington, Del., all but loses track of them for a while, that may be just as well with them. Like so many small-business people, they prize their leeway.

"I worked within the company, I worked outside the company, I worked around the company," says Charles Atkinson, a Du Pont employee who has come up with an animal-repelling garbage bag.

Du Pont is hardly alone in backing new ventures, though the methods among big companies vary. Minnesota Mining & Manufacturing Co. runs a grant program that any employee with a business idea may apply to. Xerox Corp. forms small companies around the technologies it pioneers and then keeps a stake in them. SmithKline Beckman Corp. has its own venture-capital fund; it is supporting, among others, a former scientist who has started his own biotechnology concern.

At Du Pont, top executives have preached for five years now that more ideas should bubble up from the ranks. The result is what might be called internal venture capital. Perhaps 100 projects inside Du Pont have advanced beyond bare concepts but have yet to be sluiced into mainstream businesses.

other behavior. Further, intrapreneurs may need different competencies to succeed than do entrepreneurs. For instance, intrapreneurs must be somewhat skilled at organizational politics, something that entrepreneurs may find reprehensible and that may, in fact, motivate them to work for themselves. Further, while entrepreneurs must practice self-management, providing their own goals and rewards, intrapreneurs are within the reward system of the formal organization.

The Intrapreneurial Process

Gifford Pinchot III, who coined the term intrapreneur, suggests that the intrapreneurial process has four key phases:[28]

THE SOLO PHASE

In the beginning, the intrapreneur generally works alone to develop an intrapreneurial idea. When the idea is complete enough to face scrutiny, it is ready to be presented to others. If the idea is presented too soon, it may be coopted by others, causing the intrapreneur to lose interest. Those others, with less commitment and understanding, may fail to adequately implement the idea.

THE NETWORK PHASE

Once the idea is clear, most intrapreneurs share it with a few close friends in the company and a few trusted customers. Their reactions provide informa-

Dr. Spencer Silver (left) and Art Fry are the 3M intrapreneurs who developed the enormously popular Post-it Notes.

tion about strengths and weaknesses of the concept. At this stage, the intrapreneur is not yet leading others into action, but is simply getting feedback and casual help.

THE BOOTLEG PHASE

As the network phase proceeds, some people begin doing more than just providing encouragement and facts. Even though no one has been officially assigned to the project, these people begin working to develop a product or explore the market. This informal team gives the intrapreneur support as well as the responsibilities of leadership. The team may meet together away from work, such as at a home or restaurant. In this phase, the team nurtures the idea to the point at which it can be presented in a well-developed form to the rest of the organization.

THE FORMAL TEAM PHASE

Here, the intraprise becomes a formal organizational entity and must deal with regular organizational practices and policies. The team now works together, from development through commercialization and beyond.

Nurturing Intrapreneurs

Pinchot has identified a number of "freedom factors" that he says serve as scissors to cut away excessive paperwork controls and to create a nurturing environment for intrapreneurship. These "freedom factors" include the following:[29]

1. *Self-selection.* Intrapreneurs appoint themselves to their role and receive the corporation's blessing for their self-appointed task. Management cannot appoint someone an intrapreneur, tell him or her to become passionately committed to an idea, and then expect success. The self-selection process often begins with bootlegging; the intrapreneur works nights or weekends or on time borrowed from approved projects to build the case for official sanction of self-appointed tasks.
2. *No handoffs.* Innovation is not a relay race in which an idea can be handed off from runner to runner. When a developing business or product is "handed off" from a committed intrapreneur to whoever is next in line, commitment to the project may suffer.
3. *The doer decides.* The intrapreneur's job is to create a vision of a new business reality and then make it happen. The primary problem in big organizations is not blocking the vision, but blocking the action. The solution lies in letting the doer decide; the intrapreneur must be allowed to act.
4. *Corporate "slack."* When all corporate resources are committed to what is planned, nothing is left for trying the unplannable. Yet innovation is inherently unplannable. Intrapreneurs need discretionary resources to explore and develop new ideas. Employees should be given the freedom to use a percentage of their time on projects of their own choosing and to set aside funds to explore new ideas when they occur.

5. *Ending the home-run philosophy.* Today's corporate culture favors a few well-studied, well-planned attempts to hit a home run. But nobody bats a thousand, and it is better to try more times with less careful and expensive preparation for each. Companies that demand projection of the huge payoff before entering a market rarely get in on the ground floor of new industries, and even if they do they rarely find the high-profit segments.

6. *Tolerance of risk, failure, and mistakes.* Innovation cannot be achieved without risk and mistakes. Even successful innovation generally begins with blunders and false starts.

7. *Patient money.* Innovation takes time, even decades, but the rhythm of corporations is annual planning. Sophisticated investors in innovation have the courage and patience to let their investments prove themselves or go bust.

8. *Freedom from "turfiness."* Executives' emphasis on beating their peers in the race to the top leads to an obsession with turf. Because new ideas almost always cross the boundaries of existing patterns of organizations, a jealous tendency to turfiness blocks innovation. An effective organization must focus competition on performance and contribution, not politics.

9. *Cross-functional teams.* Small teams with full responsibility for developing an intraprise solve many of the basic problems of bigness in innovation. Since whenever a new idea begins, it encounters resistance from other functional areas, each idea needs the support of all functions before it can be a success. But some companies resist the formation of cross-functional teams.

10. *Multiple options.* Entrepreneurs live in a multioption universe. If one venture capitalist or supplier can't or won't meet their needs, there are many more to choose from. Intrapreneurs, however, often face single-option situations that may be called internal monopolies. They must have their product made by a certain factory or sold by a certain sales force. Too often these groups lack motivation or are simply wrong for the job, and a good idea dies an unnecessary death. Intrapreneurs should have the freedom to select from all possible ways to get the job done—internal or external.

In addition to these "freedom factors," Pinchot provides additional suggestions for intrapreneurial success. For one, sponsorship of intrapreneurs is important. Sponsors ensure that the intraprise gets the required resources, and they can help temper the grievances of those who feel threatened by the innovation. Many intrapreneurs have several sponsors: lower-level sponsors to take care of day-to-day support needs, and higher-level sponsors to fend off threatening strategic attacks. For another, there must be suitable rewards for intrapreneurship. Traditional rewards for success don't match the risks of innovating or intrapreneuring, and the basic reward in most companies is promotion, which doesn't work well for most intrapreneurs; they seek freedom to use their intuition, take risks, and invest the company's money in building new businesses and launching new products and services. For this reason, Pinchot argues that a key reward for intrapreneurs is intracapital. **Intracapital** is a discretionary budget earned by the intrapreneur and used to fund the creation of new intraprises and innovation for the corporation. This is a powerful motivator since it gives intrapreneurs what they crave—the freedom to make their ideas happen. It is also cost-effective, since it may be spent more carefully and wisely than money that is just a small part of a senior manager's budget.

IMPLICATIONS FOR MANAGEMENT

As an entrepreneur or small business owner, an individual is placed in the position of having to handle all aspects of the business. Planning, organizing and staffing, directing, and controlling functions are the owner's responsibility, whether she or he assumes these responsibilities or assigns them to someone else. Few managers in a larger business are in a position to be entrusted with that level of responsibility, but for the small business owner, such responsibility goes with the territory.

For the small business owner, all the preceding sections of the text are important. If the owner does not know and practice the principles and functions discussed, who will do so in the small business? As the top manager in the organization, the small business owner must divide the work to structure the organization; set objectives; create communication systems; see to it that staff members are selected, trained, and compensated; apply motivation theory and practice leadership; gather information and make decisions; select a strategy for competing in the industry; make sure the appropriate legal and regulatory requirements are met; set standards and measure results; and manage planned change as necessary.

The chances are quite high that a good number of those of you who read this text will at some point in your working lives start your own small businesses. This chapter has attempted to acquaint you with the values and characteristics of small business owners and entrepreneurs, the opportunities for creating your own business, and the contributions that small businesses make to the economy as a whole. It has shown that small businesses create many new jobs and foster innovation, but that they are also risky and prone to failure. It has demonstrated that several entrepreneurial characteristics, such as perseverance, achievement motivation, and tolerance for ambiguity, are associated with success, but that the development and execution of an entrepreneurial strategy and careful planning are also needed.

If you do decide to start a business, consider the entrepreneurial strategies discussed by Drucker. Weigh their merits in view of your goals, resources, and risk preferences. Also, think carefully about the sort of business you would like to start and whether it is feasible, and then pay attention to the steps suggested in this chapter for starting a business. Remember, too, that starting a business is only one hurdle; you must then manage it as it grows and matures. This may require different skills from those needed to start a business, and it is very difficult for many entrepreneurs. And, if the business is to be successful, it is important to pay careful attention to the domains of the environment and to develop and follow a sound business plan.

Finally, enlightened larger firms are increasingly recognizing entrepreneurs as models for the development of internal programs and practices to encourage innovation. These intrapreneurial ventures promise substantial rewards for organizations as well as exciting opportunities for employees.

KEY TERMS AND CONCEPTS

administrative type organization

business plan

craft type organization

creative imitation

entrepreneurial judo

entrepreneurship

Equal Access to Justice Act

fustest with the mostest

intracapital

intrapreneurship

market feasibility study

promotion type organization

Regulatory Flexibility Act

small business

Small Business Administration (SBA)

standard industrial classification (SIC)

QUESTIONS FOR REVIEW AND DISCUSSION

1. Discuss the causes and consequences of the very high failure rates of new firms. What are some of the costs of these high failure rates? Some of the benefits?
2. Discuss reasons why small firms may be especially innovative.
3. Which of the characteristics of successful entrepreneurs do you think would be shared by successful managers of large established firms? On which characteristics do you think successful entrepreneurs and successful managers of large established firms would differ?
4. Which of Drucker's entrepreneurial strategies do you find most appealing? Why?
5. Cite the eight major steps needed to start a business.
6. Which factors in the environment do you think have *more* of an impact on small businesses than on large businesses? Which might have *less*?
7. Small businesses complain about government regulatory requirements. Describe some of these requirements and how they may harm small businesses.
8. Why is planning important to the small business?
9. What aids are available from the Small Business Administration for individuals who want to start their own businesses?
10. Do you think a person with strong entrepreneurial tendencies could ever be really happy as an intrapreneur? Why or why not?
11. Consider Pinchot's "freedom factors." Can you think of dangers associated with any of these factors?

CASES

23–1 HOW THE COOKIE CRUMBLED AT MRS. FIELDS

The saga of Mrs. Fields has never been just another entrepreneurial success story. Rather, it's one of those classic business legends that seem almost too perfect: how Debra "Debbi" Fields, a housewife without a college degree, became chief executive of a multimillion-dollar cookie-store chain; how that chain grew from a single store in 1977 to nearly 600 cookie outlets, despite its steadfast refusal to franchise; and how the company was so obsessed with quality that it wouldn't sell any cookie that was more than two hours old.

Now, it turns out that perhaps the story *was* too good to be true.

Mrs. Fields, based in Park City, Utah, last year closed or made plans to close a large number of its cookie stores. Because of the costs involved, the move plunged the company into red ink and sent the price of its shares, which are traded on the London Stock Exchange's unlisted-securities market, plummeting. Mrs. Fields also recently yielded control of its European operations to a French company.

Of course, the end of the story isn't written yet. But just as the company's fairy-tale rise inspired other fast-growing companies, so its troubles now offer lessons on the dangers of being a single-product company and on the difficulty of sustaining—and controlling—rapid growth. A look at Mrs. Fields provides a "live" case study as it struggles to recover from its missteps and transform itself into a diversified "specialty-foods retailer."

For now, Mrs. Fields plans to redirect nearly all of its future growth into "combination stores" that will eventually merge Mrs. Fields stores with those of La Petite Boulangerie, the chain of about 105 bakery stores it acquired from PepsiCo Inc. in 1987. Mrs. Fields has already opened 32 combination outlets and plans to open as many as 30 more this year.

This strategy is a risky one, for Mrs. Fields is basically moving away from its area of expertise into a more complex market. Its combination stores are three times the size of its cookie outlets, and besides cookies they sell such items as soup, bagels, and sandwiches. Even if the stores succeed, Mrs. Fields, by dividing its attention, could lose its leadership position in the market niche it helped to create.

Mrs. Fields's efforts could also muddle its identity with consumers. Indeed, the company seems confused about the proper identity for the combination stores. In some areas it is calling them Mrs. Fields Cafe, while in others they will operate under both the Mrs. Fields and La Petite Boulangerie names.

Still, the company clearly has to do something. It lost $15.1 million in the first half of 1988—contrasted with a $6.3 million profit in the year-earlier period—despite a 26 percent increase in sales, to $52.8 million. And it is expected to report a sizable loss for 1988 overall, contrasted with 1987 net income of $17.7 million. Mrs. Fields also closed or made provisions to close some 95—or about 16 percent—of its cookie stores in 1988, which will number about 498 after the closings. And its share price has fallen 85 percent, to 41 pence (about 73 cents) from a high of 272 pence (about $4.83) in 1987.

Debra Fields and her husband blame the company's current troubles solely on expenses related to the combination-store concept. But analysts—and competitors—say Mrs. Fields's problems run deeper. Even excluding write-downs related to the store closings, the company's pretax income in the first half of 1988 fell 96 percent.

One reason for the problems, analysts say, was a management structure that didn't keep pace with the company's growth. They note that Mrs. Fields's policy of running all of its stores itself to maintain quality backfired when the company moved to such far-flung places as London and Hong Kong.

Analysts generally applaud the company's recent efforts to address its problems, and its move to diversify. But some critics say Mrs. Fields is acting belatedly—and is rushing headlong into a strategy that is still largely unproved.

Source: Reprinted by permission of *The Wall Street Journal*, © Dow Jones & Company, Inc. (January 26, 1989). All Rights Reserved Worldwide.

1. What are the benefits of the sort of niche specialization historically shown by Mrs. Fields? The dangers?
2. Discuss the problems at Mrs. Fields in terms of the chapter's discussion of the entrepreneurial firm in transition.
3. What do you see as the benefits of Mrs. Fields's plans to direct future growth into "combination stores"? The costs?

23–2 BRAL-STAT

Bral-Stat, a polyester substitute for paper in Braille publications, recently became one of Du Pont's thousands of products. It started in a one-man shop.

Steven Morganti has traveled the United States trying to find markets among agencies and schools for the blind, which produce many of their own Braille materials. He keeps tabs on the orders phoned to the part-time secretary at his office in Rochester, N.Y. And he occasionally drops in on a Du Pont plant in Rochester to check on new-sized cuts of Bral-Stat.

It adds up to a different job for Mr. Morganti, 37, who once worked on the production line of that plant. Visiting an agency for the blind during a United Way campaign, he saw the frustration of a secretary operating a braille machine, which repeatedly jammed as the paper tore. He returned with a sheet of polyester. It took the embossing. It didn't tear.

Soon Mr. Morganti was in libraries researching such matters as state laws requiring books in Braille. He asked the plant, which mostly makes photographic films, to turn out batches of polyester with coatings of varying tactile qualities. Then he had blind people tell him which ones were easiest to read. "They definitely had a touch that they wanted," he says, "and it was very consistent."

Throughout, he has shown a knack for connecting with people in Du Pont who will sponsor him. The first group at company headquarters that freed up some money fell apart last year when most of its members took early retirement. Mr. Morganti ended up back on the production line. But soon he found more patrons in a group that has a tradition of innovation in recovering silver and other materials.

"He just got on the phone and started finding out who was who," says Steven Enes, a buyer at the Rochester plant who served as a sounding board for Mr. Morganti. Says Howard Koch, a marketing manager in the materials-recovery group, "We decided to take a flier on him."

No one can say whether Bral-Stat will really take off as a Du Pont product. It is more durable than paper—Brailled paper wears down with use—but twice as expensive.

But now that Bral-Stat is commercial, Du Pont is about to assign more people to its marketing and production. Where Mr. Morganti will land next? "I have no idea," he says.

Source: Reprinted by permission of *The Wall Street Journal*, © Dow Jones & Company, Inc. (February 24, 1989). All Rights Reserved Worldwide.

1. Discuss Bral-Stat in terms of the intrapreneurial process.
2. Which of Pinchot's "freedom factors" are evident in the case of Bral-Stat? Which are apparently missing?
3. Do you think an entrepreneurial individual would be happy working as an intrapreneur in Du Pont? Why or why not?

ENDNOTES

1. "The 1990 Guide to Small Business," *U.S. News & World Report* (October 23, 1989): 72.
2. *Handbook of Small Business Data, 1988* (November), 111, U.S. Small Business Administration, Office of Advocacy. Published by the Small Business Data Base.
3. "1990 Guide to Small Business," 72.
4. Ibid.
5. The U.S. Small Business Administration has a very detailed set of criteria, including limits on sales revenues and employment, that can be used to define exactly what a small business is. The government's intent is to require that the business be independent and not dominant in its field in order to be considered a small business. The government also recognizes that different sectors of the economy are characterized by different levels of employment and sales revenues.
6. Small firms are often credited with creating about 80 percent of the new jobs in the United States, though this figure is debatable. See W. Wessel and B. Brown, "The Hyping of Small-Firm Job Growth," *Wall Street Journal* (November 8, 1988): B1.

7. T. Peters and N. Austin, *A Passion for Excellence* (New York: Random House, 1985).

8. R. Ronstadt, *Entrepreneurship* (Dover, MA: Lord Publishing, 1984), 3. For good discussions of entrepreneurship, see B. Bird, *Entrepreneurial Behavior* (Glenview, IL: Scott, Foresman, 1989), and P. F. Drucker, *Innovation and Entrepreneurship: Practices and Principles* (New York: Harper & Row, 1985). For suggestions about future research on entrepreneurship, see M. B. Low and I. C. MacMillan, "Entrepreneurship: Past Research and Future Challenges," *Journal of Management* (June 1988): 139-161.

9. For additional information on the subject of entrepreneurial characteristics, see Bird, *Entrepreneurial Behavior*, Chapter 4; W. B. Gartner, " 'Who Is an Entrepreneur?' Is the Wrong Question," *American Journal of Small Business* (Spring 1988): 11-32; M. B. Low and I. C. MacMillan, "Entrepreneurship: Past Research and Future Challenges," *Journal of Management* (June 1988): 139-161; and J. A. Timmons, *New Venture Creation* (Homewood, IL: Richard D. Irwin, 1985), 311-386.

10. P. F. Drucker, "Entrepreneurial Strategies," *California Management Review* (Winter 1985): 9-25. This section draws heavily from this article.

11. F. Raglan, *The Hero: A Study in Tradition, Myth, and Drama* (Westport, CT: Greenwood Press, 1956).

12. Bird, *Entrepreneurial Behavior*, 130.

13. L. Rhodes, "Kuolt's Complex." Reprinted with permission, *Inc.* magazine (April, 1986). Copyright © 1986 by Goldhirsh Group, Inc., 38 Commercial Wharf, Boston, MA 02110.

14. For instance, see A. C. Filley and R. J. Aldag, "Organizational Growth and Types: Lessons from Small Institutions," in *Research in Organizational Behavior*, vol. 2, ed. B. M. Staw and L. L. Cummings (Greenwich, CT: JAI Press, 1980), 279-320.

15. Filley and Aldag, "Organizational Growth and Types," 287. Reprinted with permission of JAI Press Inc.

16. N. M. Scarborough and T. W. Zimmerer, *Effective Small Business Management* (Columbus, OH: Merrill, 1984).

17. "End a Federal Rule and a New One Replaces It," *U.S. News and World Report* 88, no. 8 (March 3, 1980): 61-62.

18. See S. Griffin del Villar, "Small Businesses Find It Tough to Keep Abreast of Complex Tax Laws," *Washington Post* (May 15, 1989): 16, and "Small Business Shows Its Clout with Big Victories on Capitol Hill," *Washington Post* (October 2, 1989).

19. M. Thoryn, "A Fairer Shake for Small Business," *Nation's Business* 70, no. 2 (February 1982): 39-40.

20. *The State of Small Business: A Report to the President* (Washington, DC: U.S. Government Printing Office, 1983), 122.

21. M. E. Porter, *Competitive Strategy: Techniques for Analyzing Industries and Competitors* (New York: Free Press, 1980).

22. See A. L. Stinchcombe, "Social Structure and Organizations," in *Handbook of Organizations*, ed. J. G. March (Chicago: Rand McNally, 1965), 142-193.

23. *The Small Business Economy—1984* (Washington, DC: Research and Education Foundation, National Federation of Independent Business), 2.

24. *The Pitfalls in Managing a Small Business* (Dun and Bradstreet, 1977), 1-20.

25. For additional information on planning, see the following U.S. Small Business Administration publications: *Business Plan for Small Service Firms, Management Aids, no. 2.002; Business Plan for Small Manufacturers, Management Aids, no. 2.007*; and *Business Plan for Retailers, Management Aids, no. 2.020*.

26. *Business Plan for Retailers*, 10.

27. This section is based on Bird, *Entrepreneurial Behavior*, 28.

28. This discussion is drawn from G. F. Pinchot III, *Intrapreneuring* (New York: Harper & Row, 1985), 181-184. For more on intrapreneurship, see R. A. Burgelman, "Designs for Corporate Entrepreneurship in Established Firms," *California Management Review* (Spring 1984): 154-166, and R. S. Schuler, "Fostering and Facilitating Entrepreneurship in Organizations: Implications for Organization Structure and Human Resource Management Practices," *Human Resource Management* (Winter 1986): 607-629. Also, *SAM Advanced Management Journal* (Summer 1987) is an entire issue devoted to intrapreneurship.

29. This material is adapted from Pinchot, *Intrapreneuring*, 198-256.

Managing in the Global Environment

After studying this chapter, you should be able to:

- *Give reasons why international management is important.*
- *Explain why international business exists.*
- *Identify basic features of the economic, legal/political, and sociocultural environment of international management.*
- *Define the basic modes of entry used by firms when going international.*
- *Understand some of the adaptations that need to be made in the management process because of cultural differences among countries.*
- *Describe the frameworks that can be applied to the study of comparative management.*

In the spring of 1989, the People's Republic of China was paralyzed by a student strike. Students and workers were demanding greater freedom of speech, more individual control over career paths, and an end to corruption in the government and businesses. After many weeks, the government stepped in with a show of military force and violently cleared the student throngs gathered in Tiananmen Square in the heart of Beijing. While the student uprising and the resulting response from the government captured headlines around the world for months, less noticeable dramas were being played out in corporate boardrooms as managers with plant and office facilities in the People's Republic of China gathered to decide what to do. Should they evacuate their personnel? Was the PRC on the verge of a bloody civil war? Would their entire investment in the country be lost? Should they begin rethinking their strategy in light of these events and perhaps seek a course that carries less risk? Do operations in other countries face the same threats?

Ever since the "opening" of China began in the 1970s, American companies have sought ways to invest in the country having the world's largest population. Companies such as General Electric, Eastman Kodak, Procter & Gamble, Corning, Dow Chemical, IBM, General Motors, Bechtel Group, Boeing, and Chrysler each have had a large and long investment in China. Each company decided after the military suppression of the student uprising to pull their people out of the country temporarily until more information could be gathered.

The events in China dramatize the complexity of expanding operations into foreign countries. Though not all foreign countries are as politically unstable as China in 1989, differences in culture, economic systems, technology, and physical conditions can all pose unique problems to managers of American companies entering international markets.

The purpose of this chapter is to outline the concepts that make managing a global organization different from managing a domestic organization. We will suggest ways in which managers can gain understanding of diverse cultures. We will examine various strategies that managers may choose for gaining access to foreign markets. Some strategies carry less risk than others and were certainly the topic of boardroom discussions during the crisis in China. Finally, we will discuss how the functional tasks of planning, organizing and staffing, directing, and controlling can be adapted for effective international management.

THE MULTINATIONAL CORPORATION

A rapid expansion into international markets began in the decades of the 1950s and 1960s. This expansion was in large part a response to two political events—the lowering of tariff levels from their peak during the Depression of the 1930s and the creation of a large tariff-free Common Market in Western Europe. It was also during this period that public awareness of large corporations labeled multinationals came about. A **multinational corporation (MNC)** is a company whose goods and services have significant market shares in several countries and whose senior managers plan for a global rather than a purely domestic market.

This chapter is based in part on material prepared by Dr. James D. Goodnow for the first edition of this text.

With a world map as a backdrop, First Interstate Bancorp Vice-President and Chief Economist Jerry L. Jordan lectures on aspects of international business.

Some MNCs have been criticized by governments because of the perceived economic power of these corporations. As Figure 24–1 shows, the annual sales of some multinationals in the petroleum and automotive businesses are larger than the gross national products of many countries. The assets of many of these companies, however, are largely illiquid (i.e., in the form of plants and equipment). Thus their economic power is less than that shown by a direct comparison between total sales and GNP. Nevertheless, many foreign governments have chosen to restrict activities of MNCs in their coun

FIGURE 24–1

Total Sales vs. GNP

Firm	Total Sales for 1986 ($ billions)	GNP ($ billions)	Nation
GM	102.8	91.0	Belgium
Exxon	69.9	64.4	Norway
Ford	62.7	60.0	Finland
		57.1	Turkey
IBM	51.3		
Mobil	44.9	36.7	Greece

Sources: From "The 500," *Fortune* 117, no. 9 (1986), and *Statistical Abstract of the United States* (U.S. Department of Commerce, Bureau of the Census, 1986).

Since World War II, the typical corporate chief executive officer has looked something like this:

He started out as a finance man with an undergraduate degree in accounting. He methodically worked his way up through the company from the controller's office in a division, to running that division to the top job. His military background shows: He is used to giving orders—and to having them obeyed. As the head of the United Way drive, he is a big man in his community. However, the first time he traveled overseas on business was as chief executive. Computers make him nervous.

But peer into the executive suite of the year 2000 and see a completely different person.

His undergraduate degree is in French literature,

but he also has a joint MBA/engineering degree. He started in research and was quickly picked out as a potential CEO. He zigzagged from research to mar-

MANAGEMENT IN ACTION 1
THE GLOBAL EXECUTIVE

keting to finance. He proved himself in Brazil by turning around a failing joint venture. He speaks Portuguese and French and is on a first-name basis with commerce ministers in half a dozen countries. Unlike his predecessor's predecessor, he isn't a drill sergeant. He's first among equals in a five-person Office of the Chief Executive.

And he may very well be a she.

Source: Reprinted by permission of *The Wall Street Journal*, © Dow Jones & Company, Inc. (February 27, 1989). All Rights Reserved Worldwide.

tries. For this reason among others, some companies have divested assets, linked up with joint-venture partners, or transferred technology without making capital investments in some foreign countries.

Other problems have plagued international companies of all sizes in recent years. Worldwide inflation, growing competition from newly industrialized nations in Asia and Latin America, and changes in the international financial system have threatened operations of international companies. Underlying many of these problems is the difficulty that many managers have in understanding the cultural climate of foreign nations. No doubt, more and more American firms in the future will seek to expand their operations internationally. The manager of the future, as Management in Action 1 suggests, will have to be markedly different from the manager of bygone years.

UNDERSTANDING INTERNATIONAL BUSINESS

An understanding of international management begins with an understanding of international business. International management is the management of business operations in more than one country. International business is the method by which goods and services are produced and transferred between countries. We can begin our understanding of international business by examining the concepts of absolute advantage, comparative advantage, the international product life cycle, and direct investment.

One of the oldest explanations of international business appears in the writings of David Ricardo, an English stockbroker who lived in the early 1800s. Ricardo was trying to convince the British government to permit the unregulated import of certain wines and foodstuffs from the Mediterranean countries. As a basis for his argument, Ricardo used the concept of the **labor theory of value**. In brief, the theory stated that the price of any product could be approximated by the number of hours it took a worker to produce one unit. Trade would take place if a worker could make item A faster than item B as long as another worker could make item B faster than this second worker could make item A. We recognize this principle in our previous discussions of the division of labor. Ricardo, however, sought to apply this concept to trade between nations. Ricardo's application leads us to a distinction between absolute advantage and comparative advantage.

Absolute Advantage

Suppose British workers could produce either 100 shirts or 25 kegs of wine per day and that Spanish workers could produce 100 kegs of wine or 25 shirts per day. If the British specialized in shirts and the Spanish specialized in wine and if the two countries traded their excess production with one another, the citizens of both countries would be better off. The theory of specializing in what we can do fastest and most inexpensively is called **absolute advantage**.

Comparative Advantage

Next, suppose there is an executive who is also a speedy typist. The executive could make a lot more money managing people and arranging business deals than he or she could make typing letters. Suppose this executive were to hire a secretary to do the necessary typing. Further, assume the secretary could type only half as fast as the executive and had no prior business experience. Should the executive hire the secretary? No question about it, since the executive could make a lot more money managing and negotiating than devoting time to typing. This is an example of the theory of **comparative advantage**. Under comparative advantage, the executive has an absolute advantage over the secretary in both typing and managing but has a larger comparative advantage in managerial tasks. The secretary has a lesser absolute disadvantage in typing than the larger disadvantage he or she has in managerial tasks.

Let's take this example one step further. Suppose the secretary stays with the company several years and learns a lot about managing and negotiating by handling correspondence and intercepting phone calls for the executive. Meanwhile, the executive has decided to spend less time making deals and more time on the golf course. In time, the secretary might become better at managing than the executive. Upon the executive's retirement, it is conceivable that the secretary could replace the executive.

Likewise in international trade, one nation might have an absolute advantage in the production of two commodities. But it may choose to import the item in which it has the lesser absolute advantage and to export the item in which it has the greater absolute advantage. Following the analogy above, the country might find that over time, its absolute advantage declines as other nations learn to produce its original specialty item more efficiently. The nation may then import both items and may need to find something else to export if it wants to continue to pay its international debts. This, of course, is what occurred in the trade relationship between the United States and Japan over several decades. Initially, we maintained an absolute advantage in many areas. Over time, however, as the Japanese learned how to make these products more efficiently, the United States found itself with a trade deficit.

Japan's success in world markets has made Tokyo a center of international business activity.

Q: *How important is the concept of comparative advantage when thinking about competing in foreign markets?*

A: The concept of comparative advantage is very important in any competitive situation. Unless a product or process has an advantage in quality or cost, survival—much less success—is not assured in today's global environment. At Kimberly-Clark de Mexico we always ask ourselves whether we will benefit from quality, productivity, and comparative advantage in any investment we consider. If the answer is yes, then we will go ahead with the investment.

Q: *1992 will bring significant changes to Europe in terms of trade, commerce, and investment. How will corporations in Mexico be influenced by these changes?*

A: Corporations in Mexico will have to become even more competitive and more focused on our comparative advantage in order to compete in Europe. One important disadvantage that Mexican corporations have is in cost of shipping. However, we are very well positioned to participate in the United States market, in the Pacific Rim countries, and in Europe. We will use our comparative advantage of physical location when we compete in these three rapidly growing and changing marketplaces.

Q: *If I were a young executive about to be transferred to Mexico from the United States, what would you tell me about managers in Mexico that would help me to be effective in my new job?*

A: I would tell you that you are about to compete in a rapidly changing and dynamic marketplace in an open economy. Mexico's managers are rapidly learning the skills necessary to be more competitive.

Q: *By the year 2000, where do you think the best opportunities for economic growth will be in the world?*

A: Undoubtedly the United States, Canada, Europe, and the Pacific Rim will be areas of high opportunity for firms with products that enjoy an advantage. I think, however, that Mexico will also offer a strong growth opportunity because of its large population, its unmet needs, and its forward-looking, market-oriented economic policies.

Claudio X. Gonzalez is Chairman of the Board and Managing Director of Kimberly-Clark de Mexico, S. A. de C.V. He also serves as Special Advisor to the President of Mexico on foreign investment. Mr. Gonzalez received a bachelor's degree in chemical engineering from Stanford University and has engaged in postgraduate studies at the Mexican Institute of Business Administration. Currently he serves on the board of directors of Kimberly-Clark Corporation, IBM World Trade Latin America, Kellogg Company, Banco Nacional de Mexico, Corporacion Industrial San Luis, Impulsora del Fondo Mexico, and the Stanford University Graduate School of Business Advisory Council.

MANAGERIAL PROFILE

CLAUDIO X. GONZALEZ

International Product Life Cycle

During the 1960s, many companies began making more money from their investments in plants and equipment in other countries than they did from international merchandise trade. One reason for this, advanced by Raymond Vernon and his associates, was the operation of the **international product life cycle**.[1] The concept of product life cycle is well developed in marketing. Business firms see sales of their new products go through four stages: slow growth, fast growth, a plateau of steady revenue, and decline. Vernon observed that these cycles occurred at different points in time in different countries. Therefore, he hypothesized that firms could extend the growth periods of their products by exporting to foreign markets when the domestic market was nearing saturation. But he also observed that as more competitors entered the foreign market, there would be pressures to reduce the costs resulting from tariffs, labor, and transportation to the foreign market. Managers seeking to reduce costs would consider the option of manufacturing locally in the foreign country. Meanwhile, since the domestic market is saturated or on the decline, operations in the domestic market would most likely be ended. The remaining demand in the domestic market can, after all, be satisfied by importing from the foreign market.

The international product life cycle theory helps to explain shifts of production from one country to another over time. The textile and consumer electronics businesses are examples. The heaviest concentration of textile manufacturing has moved from the United Kingdom to the United States to East Asia (Japan, Hong Kong, Korea, and Taiwan) and is now moving toward Southeast and South Asia (the Philippines, Singapore, Malaysia, Thailand, India, and Pakistan). Consumer electronics has shifted from the United States to Japan and now to other East Asian countries.

Other Direct Investment Theories

Scholars have suggested a wide number of other reasons why managers may opt for direct investment in a foreign country as opposed to simply exporting their goods. The theory of oligopoly (see Chapter 3) suggests that firms are motivated to follow their major competitors into various foreign markets to protect their worldwide market shares.[2] Honda, and then Nissan, followed Toyota into the U.S. market. The theory of internalization suggests that firms prefer to own their marketing and production facilities in other countries because this allows them to withhold their patents, trademarks, copyrights, and other corporate secrets from business partners.[3] IBM operates facilities throughout the world, though these facilities are largely staffed by nationals. The behavioral theory of international business states that managers of companies decide about direct investment for noneconomic reasons such as prestige, proximity to a vacation spot, or support/rejection of a political or ethnic cause.[4] The behavioral theory, for instance, would explain why some companies choose to build plants in Israel and why others choose to terminate investment in South Africa. The theory of environmental determinants suggests that firms are willing to make large direct financial commitments in those countries believed to be rich and politically stable.[5] Hence, the theory would predict that one should find greater direct investments in European countries than in South American countries.

All of these theories help to explain why managers of international companies seek direct investment in foreign countries. Different industry conditions may be a factor in the decision. For instance, a company in an oligopolistic industry may directly invest in a competing foreign firm to keep abreast with its major competitors. Managers of a company that operates in a technological industry may directly invest in a foreign company to protect their patents. Understanding the context of the industry can be important for understanding the motives for direct foreign investment.

THE ENVIRONMENT OF INTERNATIONAL MANAGEMENT

In this section, we will focus on the economic, legal/political, and sociocultural domains to which managers of international companies must adapt. Managers who are successful at operating in the international arena often relate their successes to an understanding of the various environmental domains that directly affect operations in foreign markets.

International Economic Domain

Countries around the world have widely diverging per capita income levels, economic growth rates, and levels of development. Scholars have devised several ways of classifying countries by levels of economic growth. One useful classification was suggested by Walt W. Rostow.[6] Rostow likened the five stages of economic growth to an airplane flight. The first stage is traditional, consisting of countries who have yet to get off the ground. These countries rely almost exclusively on the primary sector (agriculture and raw materials) of their economy for their existence. The second stage of economic growth starts with industrialization, which Rostow suggests is when the nation has the necessary preconditions for takeoff. During this stage, investment from foreign countries is needed to support economic growth. Third is the takeoff stage, where nations have adequate internal financial resources to sustain continued growth without dependence on outside funding. The fourth stage is the industrialized society, which is likened to an airplane climbing to cruising altitude. Here the industrial sector makes the greatest overall contribution to the country's gross national product. Finally, countries reach the mass consumption stage (similar to maintaining a cruising altitude) when the service sector contributes heavily to the national output.

Other scholars have suggested that several economic, political, and cultural statistics could be examined simultaneously to put countries having common characteristics into groups or clusters.[7] Most attempts to classify countries by this method have shown that there are two distinct groups. One is a group of wealthy "developed" countries. The other consists of several types of "developing" countries—those that are newly industrialized, those that are rich in certain needed resources such as petroleum, and those that are largely poor with nonexistent, untapped, or undiscovered resources. "Developing" countries are also commonly referred to as "less-developed countries" (LDCs). Limited access to statistical data and the gathering of data in noncomparable ways prevent the inclusion of the Soviet Union and its Eastern European allies in most analyses. Most scholars agree, however, that these socialist countries

In the first stage of economic growth a country relies almost exclusively on agriculture and raw materials for its existence.

have reached levels of development about equal to or slightly surpassing those of the less-developed countries. Based on this judgment, a third group of primarily socialist countries can be identified as well. Figure 24–2 divides the world's economies into these three groupings.

Recognition of the diversity of economic conditions in countries around the globe is necessary for effective international management. Although most international firms are located in developed countries because of their greater wealth, developing countries offer large and promising markets for future growth. And, near the end of the last decade, many socialist countries expressed a strong desire to import products from many developed countries such as West Germany, the United States, and Great Britain. As plant facilities are set up in these countries, managers will have to be trained to work effectively under these different economic conditions.

In the international economic domain managers must also consider exchange rates. Exchange rates are the rate at which one country's currency is exchanged for another country's. Since the world is no longer on a gold or silver standard, imbalances in trade and investment transactions among nations have to be covered by purchases and sales of many national currencies by various banks and governments. Before 1971, this foreign exchange market was fairly predictable, since governments related the value of their currencies to the price of an ounce of gold. The system permitted **fixed exchange rates**. Nations could settle their payment imbalances with key currencies such as the U.S. dollar and the British pound, whose values in relation to gold did not fluctuate. The system was coordinated by an agency known as the International Monetary Fund (IMF). The IMF also served member nations by offering short-term loans to cover temporary fluctuations in their overall international credit or debt positions.

Today there is a system of **freely floating exchange rates** in which market supply and demand can affect the relationship between the day-to-day values of one country's currency and another country's. Yet governments often intervene in the market to stabilize the values of currencies through a process called a **managed float**. For instance, a closely watched floating exchange rate is that between the U.S. dollar and the Japanese yen. A "strong" dollar implies that the dollar is increasing in value in relation to the yen. When the dollar gets strong, the price of American goods in Japan goes up, as more yen are required to buy the good. This can reduce the demand for American goods on Japanese soil and also decrease the price of Japanese goods on American soil. If either the U.S. or the Japanese government believes this to be undesirable, it may intervene by buying or selling dollars at prices that will increase or decrease the exchange rate.

The international manager must be prepared to cope with the uncertainties of currency values, which can have a direct effect on costs and prices of international transactions. In the early 1980s, many industries in the United States such as consumer electronics and automobiles were hit hard by a strong dollar. With the dollar strong, many Japanese companies were able to provide products at prices lower than or comparable to those of similar products manufactured in the United States. By the late 1980s, the dollar had weakened, reducing the price advantage of Japanese products and opening up opportunities for U.S. firms to enter the Japanese market.

Legal/Political Domain

Some of the major economic factors facing international managers are closely related to laws restraining or encouraging international transactions. These include the following:

- **Tariffs.** Taxes imposed on imported products.
- **Quotas.** Legal limitations on the quantities of particular products that can enter a country during a particular time period.
- **Administrative measures.** Measures such as health and safety laws, time-consuming customs inspection procedures, and regulations impacting minimum pricing of foreign-made goods.
- **Exchange controls.** Limitations or prohibitions on exchanging the home-country currency for foreign currencies.
- **Local content laws.** Requirements that certain percentages of finished goods be made of parts produced in the importing country.
- **Subsidies.** Special tax incentives that encourage the production of goods for export rather than domestic consumption.
- **Trade promotion assistance.** Government underwriting of certain expenses associated with the marketing of goods in other countries.
- **Commodity agreements** and **producers' cartels.** International arrangements to stabilize the prices of food or raw materials rather than to allow free-market price competition to take place.

Governments have also devised regulations to discriminate against foreign investors in plants and equipment. These laws may require that a certain percentage of local nationals be employed in the managerial and labor work force in the plant. Or they may require all or a portion of the foreign firm's assets in the host country to be owned by local governmental agencies or local private investors. As a firm begins operating in a multiplicity of political jurisdictions, it finds a need for local legal representation to handle variations in laws. These laws can affect taxation, commercial ventures, intangible property (patents, trademarks, copyrights), contractual relationships with local partners, and labor relations.

Fortunately, ways have been devised to improve international cooperation to reduce trade barriers among nations. One example is the **General Agreement on Trade and Tariffs (GATT).** This is an association of most of the nations in the free world which oversees and provides a forum for the multilateral reduction of tariff and nontariff barriers. Member nations meet periodically to negotiate reciprocal reductions in such barriers.

A second way of progressing toward the international reduction of trade barriers is through economic integration. This method takes many forms:

- **Free trade areas.** Groups of nations that agree to reduce all barriers to international trade among themselves.
- **Customs unions.** Groups of nations that set up free trade areas and also agree to have one common set of regulations for trade relationships with nonmember countries. This replaces having each member country set its own unique rules regulating trade with nonmember countries.
- **Common markets.** Groups of nations that agree not only to set up customs unions but also to find ways to further harmonize their economic

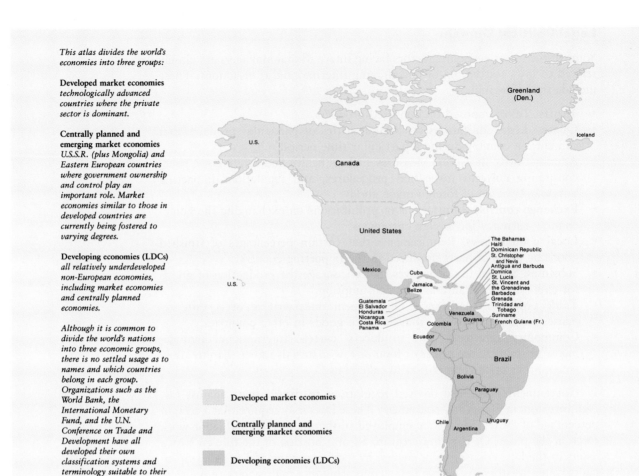

This atlas divides the world's economies into three groups:

Developed market economies *technologically advanced countries where the private sector is dominant.*

Centrally planned and emerging market economies *U.S.S.R. (plus Mongolia) and Eastern European countries where government ownership and control play an important role. Market economies similar to those in developed countries are currently being fostered to varying degrees.*

Developing economies (LDCs) *all relatively underdeveloped non-European economies, including market economies and centrally planned economies.*

Although it is common to divide the world's nations into three economic groups, there is no settled usage as to names and which countries belong in each group. Organizations such as the World Bank, the International Monetary Fund, and the U.N. Conference on Trade and Development have all developed their own classification systems and terminology suitable to their needs.

☐ Developed market economies

☐ Centrally planned and emerging market economies

☐ Developing economies (LDCs)

FIGURE 24–2
World Economic Classifications

Source: Adapted from United States Department of State, Bureau of Public Affairs, *Atlas of United States Foreign Relations*, 2d ed. (Washington, D.C.: U.S. Government Printing Office, December 1985), 39.

policies in such areas as agricultural price supports, work permits, antitrust regulations, transportation, and communication.

• **Economic unions.** Common market member countries that agree to issue an international common currency and to set up a central tax agency to collect revenues directly from private individuals rather than from their respective governments. When countries form an economic union, they are very close to becoming a political union or a nation-state. The only additional requirement is a common foreign policy, including a common defense policy.

Another major concern of managers engaged in international business is political risk. Political risk refers to a company's risk of loss of assets, managerial control of plants and facilities, and access to markets due to actions taken by the host government. Many American firms, for instance, lost major assets and access to the Iranian market when the Shah of Iran was overthrown in 1979.

To assess the future political/legal climate in various countries, some companies have developed an assortment of political risk-assessment techniques.

The United States has not recognized the incorporation of Estonia, Latvia, and Lithuania into the U.S.S.R. Boundary representation is not necessarily authoritative.

These include monitoring the world press and appropriate statistical indicators, on-site visits to various countries, discussions with experts on various countries, and a variety of conceptual frameworks such as multiple-factor indices and mathematical probability models.[8] They also use a variety of methods such as those shown in Figure 24–3 to lessen conflicts with host governments.

Sociocultural Domain

Economic and political differences among countries are usually the result of basic social and cultural differences among the ethnic groups who populate the nations of the earth. Such differences will have a direct effect on the selection of a managerial style, the adaptation of products and promotional messages, communication with employees, and the relative levels of productive efficiency among the operating facilities in various countries. The study of comparative culture is very broad in scope. We will focus on only a few important conceptual areas for our brief overview.[9]

FIGURE 24–3

Methods Companies Use to Lessen Conflicts with Host Governments

1. Get materials and parts from host-country sources.
2. Set up joint ventures with host-government partners.
3. Employ local nationals as workers and managers.
4. Develop a profit-sharing program in the host country.
5. Set up a research and development facility in the host country.
6. Reinvest earnings in the host country.
7. Train foreign managers to better interact with the local culture.
8. Support public welfare projects.
9. Avoid bribing top government officials.
10. Sell stock to host-country shareholders.
11. Borrow from host-country banks and lending agencies.
12. Plan to divest assets by selling equity shares to local nationals.
13. Purchase political-risk insurance from home-government agencies.
14. Learn effective bargaining.
    a. Keep control over critical elements such as international transportation, international marketing channels, patents, trademarks, copyrights, and manufacturing processes. This can be accomplished by signing management contracts or licensing agreements.
    b. Threaten to cut off future inflows of capital.
15. Keep local equity low. Use more debt financing.
16. Develop an international image by having international headquarters in a neutral country and/or by having worldwide ownership of corporate equity shares.
17. Develop an effective lobbying presence with the host government.
18. Have legal representation in the host country.

The first critical area is communication—spoken, written, and visual (body language). Many nations are populated by people who speak several different languages or dialects. In the United States, there is a growing proportion of the population whose primary language is Spanish. India is composed of 14 major language groupings and many local dialects. In both countries, English serves as an official language for international business and for government activities. A spoken or written language is only a part of the cross-cultural communication concept. Visual or body language such as gestures may be equally critical for international managerial success. Different cultures have norms about the distances between people engaged in conversation, the exactness of meeting times, the giving of gifts and bribes, and the establishing of personal trust and friendship versus the use of formal written contracts. There are also different norms for aesthetic values such as colors, designs, symbols, and the appreciation of food flavorings. Management in Action 2 provides examples of many of these unique differences.

Differences in religion and values can have far-reaching implications for managerial style and effectiveness. Policies affecting holidays, work breaks, sex discrimination, job advancement, retirement, charitable contributions, the role of interest and profits, selection of employees, and the introduction of new technology can all be influenced by religious factors. For example, followers of Islam observe Fridays as religious holidays, observe prayer breaks five times a day, refrain from eating or drinking during daylight hours one month each year, give a percentage of their incomes to the poor, and abhor the taking of interest on loans. They also have the fatalistic belief that many misfortunes are the will of God rather than the result of human error. Fol-

Want to avoid making a fool of yourself in different languages or in other cultures? Here are some tips:

- In Chinese, the surname comes first and given name last. Remember this to avoid calling the chairman of the board Mr. Ed. Don't be afraid to ask the person what he or she prefers to be called.
- In Togo, what looks like a necklace probably is used to hold up a loin cloth, and wearing beads around the neck looks to every Togoese like part of a pair of underpants.
- Travel with a cast-iron stomach and eat everything, everywhere. Delicacies might include such items as bear's paw soup in China, sheep's eyes in Saudi Arabia, or roast gorilla in some parts of Africa. Refusing them would be similar to a Frenchman refusing a bite of homemade apple pie or sizzling sirloin in the United States.
- In dress, the rule is button up: conservative suit and tie for men, dress or skirt-suit for women. Avoid jeans, jogging shoes, T-shirts, shorts, funny hats, tight sweaters for women, and open-to-the-navel shirts for men.
- Try your hand at speaking another language. But be warned that the wrong pronunciation in Chinese, for example, can have you saying, "The girth of my donkey's saddle is loose," when you

meant to say, "Thank you very much for the dinner. I am so full I must loosen my belt."

- In Saudi Arabia, to cross your legs in such a way

MANAGEMENT IN ACTION 2

IN BRAZIL, OK IS NOT OK

that you display the sole of your foot to your host is a grievous affront. In Spain, it is grossly insulting to offer to split the bill in a restaurant. And in Japan, don't sneeze in public even if you have to.

- Nodding your head means "Yes" in most countries, but it means "No" in Bulgaria and Greece.
- Outside the United States and Western Europe, it's not a good idea for women to eat or drink alone in restaurants. Locals and business travelers use some, including many European-style restaurants and even hotel dining rooms, as places to pick up women.
- Be careful with hand gestures. The classic American OK sign of thumb and forefinger forming a circle is considered an obscene gesture in Brazil. This same obscenity can be delivered in Mexico if you lift your left forearm vertically and hit the bottom of the elbow with the palm of the other hand—precisely the action you might take to swat a mosquito.

Source: Adapted from Roger E. Axtell, *Do's and Taboo's Around the World.* Copyright © 1986 by John Wiley & Sons. Reprinted by permission of John Wiley & Sons, Inc.

---

lowers of Hinduism have traditionally denied advancement to certain workers because they belong to the wrong castes. Believing that the cause of all human suffering is a desire for material goods, fundamentalist Buddhists shun the acquisition of wealth. Those who come from a Confucian ethic accord high status to the elderly and therefore relate job advancement more to seniority than to proven skill. Followers of Calvinist Protestantism traditionally believed that hard work brought one closer to admission to heaven. Followers of Japan's national religion, Shintoism, believe that hard work is in accord with the spirits of nature.

Cultural value systems also have an impact on the nature of the decision-making system (scientific and rational versus impulsive and inspirational), the influence of the family on the individual, the degree of politeness in negotiation (face-saving versus frankness), and the role of authority versus participation in decisions. We will return to some of these issues later in this chapter in the section on comparative management.

Another area to be compared across cultures is the nature and extent of education. Although basic literacy levels are rising in the less-developed nations, there is a minimum of vocational and managerial education available. Many developing countries were formerly colonies of Western European countries that imposed traditional content in advanced education, stressing the humanities and preparation for certain professions such as law and medicine. Until recently, there was relatively little advanced education outside the United States for developing business leaders and skilled laborers. Therefore, foreign investors had to do much personnel training in-house. Today, however, many countries are setting up business schools and vocational training centers. Many are set up with the cooperation of business schools in the United States.

A manager should understand that cultural change can come about as the result either of armed conflict or of the peaceful introduction of new ideas, products, and technologies. Some of the conflicts in today's world have their roots in interreligious strife—for example, Islam versus Judaism in the Middle East, Hinduism versus Sikhism in India, Catholicism versus Protestantism in Northern Ireland, and Sunni versus Shiite Moslems in Iraq and Iran. Yet we see evidence that international businesses can bring about cultural change in peaceful ways, as exemplified by the worldwide consumption of cola drinks or the nearly universal acceptance of Levi's jeans and British-originated rock music.

A knowledge of the environment facing the international manager is essential in deciding on proper strategies and human relations approaches when exporting and marketing in other countries. International management becomes particularly difficult when firms operate in several countries that vary in their economic, legal/political, and sociocultural domains. Strategies must be carefully developed to account for global diversity.

STRATEGIC ASPECTS OF INTERNATIONAL MANAGEMENT

Managers of international business can select from among three basic strategies for access to markets in foreign countries: trade, technology transfer, and direct equity investment in overseas operations.

International Trade

International trade can be conducted indirectly through intermediaries in the exporting, or sourcing, country or directly through intermediaries in the importing, or target market, country. If sales to specific end-users are large enough, intermediaries between the domestic exporter and the foreign end-user can be bypassed. The variety of export intermediaries ranges from foreign companies with buying agents in the exporter's country to specialized intermediaries who take on a number of responsibilities. Export merchants and trading companies as well as foreign distributors and dealers buy goods outright and take inventory-carrying risk off the exporter's shoulders. Certain types of agent middlemen, such as export management companies in the exporter's home country or manufacturer's representatives in the importing country, often do not take title to goods but act as part-time additions to the exporting firm's sales force. Still others, such as switch traders, specialize in barter and other types of countertrade (goods exchanged for goods) transactions.

Technology Transfer

Sometimes transportation costs, tariffs, favorable cost factors for host-country competitors, and wholesale/retail margins result in export prices which are neither competitive nor profitable. In such cases, it becomes necessary to seek ways of making products in host-country locations. If firms are unable to afford the outright purchase of additional facilities in the host country or if host governments discourage foreign investment in certain industries, they may resort to some type of **technology transfer**. This transfer might take the form of a manufacturing contract that establishes a host-country manufacturing firm as the sole supplier of a product made to the home-country firm's specifications. The home-country firm still oversees the marketing of the product in the host country. Another approach is for the home-country firm to look for a host-country licensee to manufacture and market the product using the home-country firm's specifications and brand identification. Although licensing requires little or no capital investment on the part of the home-country firm, it runs the risk of creating a competitor upon the expiration of the contract. Moreover, most licensing agreements give the licensor a fixed percentage of licensee sales. In the long term, these cumulative returns may be less than the cumulative amounts that could be earned on a direct equity investment.

Direct Investment

Direct equity investment may take the form of a joint venture in service, distribution, or manufacturing facilities. Or it may be a wholly owned venture either built from scratch or resulting from merger with or acquisition of a going concern in the host country. Manufacturing facilities can act as centers for assembling imported parts or can involve the production of parts as well. Multinational corporations often manufacture parts in a variety of countries. These parts are then shipped to the various countries where final assembly takes place. Joint ventures involve the sharing of expenses and risks, with the home-country firm taking either a minority, equal, or majority equity position in the venture. Misunderstandings can result if the parent firms fail to assess one another carefully before forming the new company. Wholly owned operations, on the other hand, involve large investment and risk. Such operations also limit the financial flexibility of firms with modest cash resources. Yet, if they are successful, wholly owned branches or subsidiaries can generate large long-term returns.

The selection of a proper strategy for entry into a foreign country is part of the international strategic planning process undertaken by firms. This process is the topic of the next section.

INTERNATIONAL STRATEGIC PLANNING

International managers need to make the same kinds of decisions that managers make domestically. They must identify appropriate products or services to introduce to various market segments; select ways of reaching these market segments; select and manage sources of supply; select sources of funds; oversee the development of proper technologies; structure organizations for the formal flow of intracorporate communications; and devise schemes for the selection, training, and development of labor and managerial resources. The complexity of the international environment makes these tasks more difficult and challenging. Not only do managers face different economic, legal/ political, and sociocultural conditions, but they also need to coordinate decisions affecting strategic business units in far-flung geographic locations. A framework for developing an international strategic plan is critical.

One such framework follows a chronological sequence of decisions that must be made when planning for international business activity. This framework answers the following questions:

1. Does international activity fit into the overall mission of the corporation?
2. Which products or services should the firm introduce to foreign markets?
3. Which countries should the company enter and when?
4. Which modes of entry should the firm use to enter each of the selected countries?
5. With which specific business partners should the firm deal within each market?
6. Which provisions should be included in the contracts the firm negotiates with each of its foreign partners?
7. How should the firm adapt its marketing mix (prices, products, distribution systems, and communications with potential buyers) in light of differing external environmental conditions (including competition) in each national market or submarket segment?
8. How should the firm select methods of supporting its marketing or revenue-generating program? The answer includes decisions on financing, personnel, research and development, and sourcing (including production).
9. How should the firm develop ways to ensure the attainment of desired results? The answer includes decisions about the structuring of intrafirm communications, selecting a proper degree of delegation of authority, and selecting proper leadership styles.
10. How should the firm devise a system to monitor operations and their results to provide feedback for future decisions? The answer includes developing an international accounting system and a system for monitoring internal and external environmental conditions that could have a positive or negative impact on operating results.

Providing in-depth answers to these questions is beyond the scope of an introductory management text. However, the remaining sections of this chapter give brief overviews of the managerial functions of planning, organizing and staffing, directing, and controlling in the international context.

Planning

The process of planning in an international corporation is very similar to that followed in a domestic context. It involves periodic assessment of the company's progress in achieving financial objectives, analysis of likely strategies of competitors, and forecasts of changes in the economic, political/legal, and social domain during the planning time-horizon. Based on this analysis, the firm develops a strategic plan covering its whole range of functional activities (marketing, finance, production, personnel, research and development, and administration). In an international context, this process becomes more complex because of the greater number of country settings in which the company hopes to conduct business.

Larger multinational corporations develop subplans for each product grouping (or strategic business unit) and for each country or region. These subplans are interrelated through a process known as **global planning**. Global planning is most successful when the concept of rationalization is incorporated. **Rationalization** in an international context is buying parts or finished goods from sources whose prices are the lowest anywhere in the world and selling finished products where they will command the highest prices.

Ideally, managers of a multinational firm will include rationalization in their global plans. However, some conditions can affect its success. Changes in government regulations may make transfer of goods difficult. Variations in market demand, competition, and operating costs may lead to losses when goods are transferred. Although these constraints also exist in domestic business, they are magnified in an international setting.

Often firms new to the international market fail to use a global planning approach. Instead, they take advantage of opportunities as they come along, following a reactive rather than proactive planning strategy. The result may be mistakes such as selecting the wrong foreign partner or signing a licensing or distributorship agreement that gives too many benefits to the foreign partner. Such problems can often be averted by more careful planning before entry into the foreign market.

Organizing and Staffing

Most manufacturing companies first enter the international market through occasional exporting. Since this activity is often supervised by a sales manager who has little or no international experience, the person responsible for exporting is often frustrated in his or her attempts to develop markets outside the home country. Time and money for travel and other promotional activities are often very limited during this start-up phase.

Over time, some smaller firms find that their export sales grow to a level where they can no longer be handled by a single salesperson on a part-time basis. The salesperson may need help with correspondence, documentation, and scheduling. Therefore, an inside specialist is added to the sales group to handle these functions. Eventually, international trade becomes important enough to require the formation of an export department separate from the domestic sales department. With the addition of more levels of managerial supervision and the possible opening of foreign production facilities, the export department may become an international division. In some very large corporations, such as IBM, the international division may become equal in importance to the domestic division.

At this point, some corporate leaders feel that lines of communication between domestic and international operations need to be blended. In some companies, functional vice-presidents for marketing, finance, production, and human resources will take on global responsibilities. In others, heads of product divisions will assume global responsibilities. In still others, the com-

A joint venture between IBM and Japan's Nippon Telegraph & Telephone Company provides telecommunication services and products.

pany is divided into world regions. Domestic operations in the home country make up just one of these regions. The functional organizational structure is used when the company is selling related goods or services that do not require a great deal of adaptation from country to country. The product-division structure is used by firms that sell a variety of product lines, each of which reaches a very different set of customers through a very different set of distribution channels. The geographic structure is used for companies that offer a few product lines but need to make major marketing adjustments as they go from region to region. Some companies have developed a matrix (hybrid or umbrella) structure to interrelate functional, product, and country specialists and to reduce costs of duplicating expertise. Formal reporting normally follows functional, product, or geographic lines, but informal relationships and project groups interrelate all three methods for structuring organizations.

When multinational corporations entered their greatest period of international expansion during the 1950s and early 1960s, many of them sent executives and their families to foreign locations for extended stays. Staffing international offices through extended foreign assignments is less common today because of problems with culture shock and the high cost of international relocation of the executive work force. Long-term foreign assignments are still common for bankers and engineers but less so for managers in other industries. However, there is a growing amount of international market development, contract negotiation, and trouble-shooting going on today. This calls for a new breed of international manager.

During the rest of this century, there will be a need for managers with ability to adapt very rapidly to a variety of cultural and political environments. The executive who is bilingual or multilingual, well versed in techniques for negotiating in a variety of national or regional settings, and familiar with ways for evaluating future strategies under changing environmental conditions will be better able to adapt to short-term assignments in many countries.

Directing

Directing the performance of employees in an international setting depends on a knowledge of cultural similarities and differences. This knowledge will help the manager select a proper leadership style and a proper degree of delegation of responsibility. Frameworks for analyzing the directing function in international management will be discussed in a later section on comparative management.

Controlling

As in a domestic firm, a good control system in an international firm should be based on a regularly scheduled comprehensive overview of the firm's activities and operating results. This review should be conducted in a systematic fashion with the help of independent outside auditors. Major accounting firms maintain offices on a worldwide basis to help in financial auditing. However, one must also audit other areas of the firm's activities such as marketing and production.

Many successful international firms develop their annual plans from such operations audits. They apply company-wide approaches similar to the management by objectives (MBO) approach used for setting goals and evaluating the performance of individual employees. Geographic distances, multiple languages, changes in the values of foreign currencies, and political/cultural factors complicate the control function for an international firm, but jet travel and worldwide electronic information networks are making it easier to hold regular meetings and obtain needed data.

Control questions, including the optimal number of persons reporting to one manager and the decentralization of decision-making responsibility, are closely related to cross-cultural communication and mutual understanding. These skills can be enhanced by an understanding of comparative management.

COMPARATIVE MANAGEMENT

Comparative management is the study of culturally defined management practices. The management styles associated with a variety of cultural environments are compared to discover their similarities and differences. Some observers seek universal management principles; others feel that management practices need to be individualized from culture to culture. At least two conceptual frameworks for such comparisons have been advanced.

The first framework involves descriptive comparisons of management in two countries, such as Japan and the United States. Recent successes of Japanese businesses in major world markets have sparked an interest in a managerial style which can be seen as almost the polar opposite of the style commonly called "Western management." Can Japan's success be attributed to a managerial approach reflecting its cultural values? And more important, is this managerial style transferable to other countries? What are the differences between Japanese and American approaches to leadership, control, and delegation of authority that appear to have given Japan a competitive advantage in world markets?

The American perception of Japanese management style generally regards the custom of lifetime commitments (*shushin koyo*) between employers and employees as its most salient characteristic.[10] Because of this custom, Japanese workers feel greater loyalty to their companies than do their American counterparts, and their off-hours socializing typically involves company-planned activities with work associates. In the United States, on the other hand, workers often feel greater loyalty to their professions than to their current employers, and their off-hours social activities are more likely to be centered on the broader community.

Other elements associated with Japanese management are seniority rule (*nenko seido*) and a participatory or consensus decision-making process (*shuden ishi kettei*). These elements, which reflect the culture and value orientation of Japanese society, are incorporated in managerial approaches to work assignments, methods of operation, work habits, and mobility. For example, in making work assignments, the Japanese practice fits broadly defined jobs to workers who are assigned to groups. The American practice fits workers to more narrowly defined jobs. Thus, the American worker might be unwilling to perform a task not specifically contained in his or her job description. The Japanese worker would be willing to perform a broader range of tasks. In addition, the function of a Japanese manager is to serve as a liaison between workers, their tasks, and their tools. In a Western business, managers serve in more of a supervisory role. The Japanese approach is based on a cooperative group consciousness rather than the competitive (and often conflicting) individual consciousness that characterizes the American approach.

There can be much more fluidity of job movement between labor and management in Japan than in the United States. For example, the senior manager of Procter & Gamble's manufacturing operations in Japan joined the company as a factory worker. He later served as chief spokesperson for the company workers' union before being promoted to a management position. One would not normally expect a shop steward in a traditional American company to be promoted to a senior management post.

The essential differences between these two styles of management have cultural origins. A manager's choice of style is not based on the deliberate adoption of a formula because it is uniquely Japanese or uniquely American. Rather, the Japanese culture, which emphasizes obligations and relationships within a collectivistic entity, gives rise naturally to a management system that reflects these cultural values. The emphasis on individuality inherent in American culture is characteristic of the American management system. For this reason, it is probably difficult to transfer management styles across cultural boundaries.

Are managerial philosophies and processes becoming more similar or dissimilar on an international basis? Ross Webber suggested in a 1969 article that forces of convergence, or uniformity, in machine technology, improved educational standards, and pragmatic laissez-faire free-enterprise philosophies were on the rise. He saw these trends replacing forces of divergence, or diversity, such as cultural inertia (resistance to change), scarcities of natural resources, and demographic trends such as high population growth rates in developing countries.[11]

In more recent years some observers have suggested that forces leading toward convergence in management philosophies and practices are weaker than those leading toward more divergence.[12] Deeply embedded cultural value systems do not change rapidly. Moreover, certain worldwide concerns such as scarcities of resources, overpopulation, and pollution may require somewhat greater government regulation and central planning than might be considered proper by those who subscribe to a laissez-faire philosophy.

How is it possible to determine which management concepts can be transferred universally, which need adaptation, and which are unique to specific cultures? By comparing management practices in two different countries, comparative management serves to highlight specific contextual differences in cultures. However, such a framework does not identify factors basic to all cultures which permit a broader understanding of how management practices can be selected and adapted among nations.

Geert Hofstede suggests a framework that may be more useful than the purely descriptive type illustrated here.[13] Although Hofstede acknowledges national roots of cultural differences, he defines four dimensions which are applicable to all cultures. These are power distance, uncertainty avoidance, individualism, and sex roles.[14] These dimensions serve as guides to effective leadership styles, control practices, and ways of delegating authority. Hofstede suggests that each dimension is measurable by its presence or absence. Thus his framework makes it easier to compare many different cultures and their associated management practices with one another.

Power Distance

Power distance addresses the basic issue of inequalities in prestige, wealth, and power. Different cultures place varying emphases on the importance associated with certain levels of power. Hofstede suggests that power distance can be seen in superior-subordinate relationships where the former prefers to widen the distance and the latter strives to close it. The typical distance between superiors and subordinates in each culture is socially determined. Power distance can be measured by getting subordinates' opinions of their superiors' styles of decision making, the degree to which they fear disagreeing with their superiors, and the types of decision making by superiors they think their peers prefer.

Uncertainty Avoidance

Hofstede suggests that varying degrees of **uncertainty avoidance** are basic to all cultures. To make the future more predictable, societies have developed certain "innovations" in technology as well as in law and religion. In business organizations, these innovations emerge as rules (corporate policy), ceremonies, and technological advancements. Data from Hofstede's study show that tolerance for uncertainty about the future, such as changing company policies, varies considerably among countries. This may help to explain why long-term planning is more readily accepted in some countries than in others.

Individualism

Individualism describes typical relationships between individual persons and the collective society within various national cultures. The degree of individualism in a particular culture is reflected in its basic societal units. As primary units of a specific culture, nuclear families (spouses and their immediate offspring) represent a high degree of individualism. In contrast, societies whose primary units are extended families and tribal groupings represent a lesser degree of individualism. Societies with a high degree of individualism consider individuality to be a source of well-being. A group-oriented society may regard emphasis on the individual as alienating and undesirable.

Employees in group-oriented societies depend emotionally on the organizations for which they work. The organization should in turn assume a broad responsibility for the welfare of its employees in areas such as housing, education, health, and recreation. The failure of a company to do so may result in worker disharmony, with possible negative implications for the broader host-country society.

Sex Roles

Societies differ in the ways they cope with issues of gender. Cultures put differing weights on the importance of biological differences as they relate to attainable social roles. Some cultures put greater emphasis than others on sex roles, such as the male's provider role and the female's maternal function. Likewise, there can be a relationship between organizational goals and career chances for men and women. In some cultures, for example, a merchandising concern would prefer to have males handle aggressive personal selling. In the same cultures, hospitals may prefer female nurses because of their presumed biological fit with nurturing and healing goals.

Hofstede's framework provides a more practical approach to comparative management than does the purely descriptive approach. The four dimensions described above allow us to compare how cultural factors affect group motivation, advancement criteria, and the delegation of responsibility—all critical concerns for the international manager.

IMPLICATIONS FOR MANAGEMENT

We have seen the critical importance of examining the management process in light of similarities and differences in economic, legal/political, and sociocultural domains of global nations. An understanding of these external environmental considerations will become more critical in the future as global interdependence and global information systems become more common. Yet international managers are faced with several unresolved issues, such as the inability of countries to pay their international debts, competition from foreign countries, and disputes among political and cultural groups. Although the world's economic and literacy standards are improving universally, these standards do not grow at a constant rate everywhere and for every participant in the world economy. When people's wishes and expectations exceed their current level of progress, envy and suspicion can grow. The international manager of the future needs to discover ways to lessen the differences among nations by improving communication and cross-cultural understanding. The future will see more joint ventures between businesses and governments, more trade in the socialist sector, and more foreign activity in the U.S. economy.

The foregoing issues suggest the need for the globalization of management. This chapter has provided only a quick survey of the issues involved. We strongly encourage you to pursue these topics further through formal courses (or even advanced degree work) in international business as well as through lifelong self-education. Overseas travel, the study of modern languages, and area studies are certainly helpful. If a challenging international opportunity is offered to you during your business career, remember that success comes with careful preparation.

KEY TERMS AND CONCEPTS

absolute advantage
administrative measures
commodity agreements
common markets
comparative advantage
comparative management
customs unions
direct equity investment
economic unions
exchange controls
fixed exchange rates
free trade areas
freely floating exchange rates
General Agreement on Trade and
    Tariffs (GATT)
global planning

individualism
international product life cycle
labor theory of value
local content laws
managed float
multinational corporation (MNC)
power distance
producers' cartels
quotas
rationalization
subsidies
tariffs
technology transfer
trade promotion assistance
uncertainty avoidance

QUESTIONS FOR REVIEW AND DISCUSSION

1. What are multinational corporations?
2. What is the theory of comparative advantage?
3. Apply Rostow's five stages of economic growth to the United States.
4. Give examples of three ways that governments restrain international business activities.
5. What are some of the major pros and cons of entering overseas markets by licensing? Why do firms set up joint ventures? How can companies know whether joint ventures will be successes or failures?
6. Why do some companies enter foreign markets by direct investment rather than by exporting finished products from their home countries?
7. Select any two countries and compare them on the basis of Hofstede's four dimensions. How would your answers relate to the use of participative versus autocratic management styles?

8. Describe six major ways of formally organizing international corporations.
9. Discuss two major differences between the Japanese and Western management styles.
10. Identify a country or group of countries that you believe are on the verge of becoming developed. What special managerial techniques would be proper for these countries? How would you suggest that a toy manufacturer (or other type of firm) enter this country's market?

24-1 A SLICE OF THINGS TO COME?

By opening its doors to Western businesses, the Soviet Union hopes to acquire advanced technology and management techniques to help revitalize its flagging economy.

That may be so someday. For now, the Soviets have acquired American pizza.

Chilled by an icy wind and snow flurries, Shelley M. Zeiger, a businessman from Trenton, N.J., yesterday officially launched a U.S.-Soviet joint venture to bring the citizens of Moscow a cornucopia of capitalism: pizza neapolitan, pizza primavera, manicotti, lasagna, and stuffed shells. The portions, at the equivalent of $2 each, are made from imported ingredients, cooked on imported equipment, and served from an imported mobile van.

"It's pizza perestroika," Mr. Zeiger says, using Soviet leader Mikhail Gorbachev's term for his program of economic reform. With Sergei A. Goryachev, the mayor of Moscow's Lenin district, the American cut the blue and red ribbons in front of the Astropizza van, parked on a hill outside Moscow University.

Mr. Zeiger and his American partner, Louis Piancone, hope the venture will be just the antipasto before a bigger attempt to win the palates and wallets of Muscovites and hungry foreigners. "Nationwide franchises available," read a hopeful slogan emblazoned on the van in English and Russian. The two men invested about $350,000 in the venture and reckon that, at best, it could be profitable in a year or so.

"I see that fast food is the future in the Soviet Union," Mr. Zeiger says. "It's just like the U.S. Men and women both work, so there's no time for cooking."

Ludmilla isn't so sure. A thin mother in a beige overcoat and head scarf, she clearly relishes the free slice given out at the grand opening. "It is very good," she says. "You can't compare it with Soviet pizza, which tastes different." Would she pay $2 a slice for it, or the equivalent of about two hours' pay? "It isn't worth the money," comes the swift retort.

As for Nadezhda, a stout matron with a smart gray woolen coat and a broad grin, her first encounter with American pizza brought back memories. "Nice," she says, swallowing quickly. "In Bulgaria I have eaten something similar."

While the pizza venture is small, its details reveal the typical obstacles that bigger companies with more significant plans must overcome. The two Americans showed a flexibility and willingness to take risks that seem to scare off many others. Even now, they don't let euphoria entirely cloud their business judgment. "We aren't that clear about it ourselves. We're testing the waters," Mr. Zeiger says.

The Soviets implemented a law last year authorizing joint ventures with foreign companies, and about 50 agreements have so far been signed. But, under the law, the foreign companies can't take profits out of the Soviet Union in dollars unless the venture itself earns hard currency. This is a major obstacle for Western businesses, which want to gain access to the Soviet market and not worry about exporting the products of any venture to earn dollars, marks, or pounds.

Thus, few of the completed joint ventures are in manufacturing, as the Soviets would like, while several are in services such as hotels for foreign tourists that won't do much to modernize creaky Soviet industry.

Mr. Zeiger and Mr. Piancone hope to leap the currency hurdle by selling both to Muscovites and to foreign tourists. They plan to open pizza outlets soon in two Moscow hotels exclusively for foreigners. The hard currency they earn will pay for the imported pizza ingredients and equipment, they hope, while the rubles earned from Russians will finance new outlets.

And they don't seem to mind not getting profits in cash. Mr. Zeiger, who already imports Russian dolls and Ukrainian carvings into the U.S., has a barter agreement with the Ministry of Foreign Economic Relations under which he will be paid in anything from cement to souvenirs. Eventually, the Americans may use some Soviet ingredients in the pizzas, if they can persuade the Ministry of Agriculture to provide tomatoes with less acid and cheese with less fat.

"I don't want to sound cocky," Mr. Zeiger says sounding just that, "but we may wind up being a model for other industries."

The venture may soon have tough competition, however, as PepsiCo.'s Pizza Hut unit is discussing opening up in Moscow. Until that happens, the two men from New Jersey will only have the local alternative to worry about.

It isn't much of a threat. Down the road at the Pizza Krostiny on Kutuzovsky Prospekt, a grumpy maitre d' in a white sweater refuses to give two visitors a seat. "There are no spare places," she says, pointing behind her to the almost-empty restaurant. Grudgingly she shows the menu instead. "We have pizza with chicken," she points to the first and most expensive item on the menu. What about the second item? "That is pizza with fish," she frowns. "No, no, we don't have it."

Source: Reprinted by permission of *The Wall Street Journal*, © Dow Jones & Company, Inc. (April 18, 1988). All Rights Reserved Worldwide.

1. Discuss how each environmental domain affects the operations of Astropizza in Moscow. Which environmental domain do you believe has the greatest effect on the success of Astropizza in Moscow? Which has the least effect? Explain.
2. What method of access to the Soviet market are the owners of Astropizza using? Do you believe this is the best approach?
3. If you were to buy and manage an Astropizza franchise, what dimension of Hofstede's framework would be most important in considering your management style?

24–2 ONE BIG MARKET?

One television commercial that isn't preserved in Procter & Gamble Company's archives is a spot for Camay soap that ran on Japanese TV in 1983. In the advertisement, a Japanese woman is bathing when her husband walks into the bathroom. She begins telling him about her new beauty soap, but the husband, stroking her shoulder, hints that suds aren't what's on his mind.

Although popular in Europe, the ad flopped in Japan. "It was considered bad manners" for the man to intrude on his wife, says Edwin L. Artzt, P&G vice-chairman and its international chief. "And the Japanese didn't think it was very funny."

Procter & Gamble has had its share of marketing and other missteps in entering foreign markets, but clearly the consumer-products giant has been learning from its mistakes. Last month, the company reported that second-quarter profit rose 25 percent largely because of strength in its foreign operations. In fiscal 1988, overseas sales accounted for $7 billion, or 36 percent, of the company's $19.3 billion in sales, up from 28.5 percent a decade earlier. And P&G predicts that foreign sales will generate half of its revenue by some time in the 1990s.

Some of that rise reflects the foreign sales of P&G acquisitions, such as Richardson-Vicks, Inc., a pharmaceutical company it bought in 1985 that has extensive overseas operations. But much of the growth represents the payoff from years of struggling to overcome trade barriers and cultural differences in selling P&G's staples, such as diapers and detergents, overseas. The company now sells its products in 140 countries, with two-thirds of its sales coming from 24 brands, including Crest toothpaste, Head & Shoulders shampoo, and Pampers diapers.

"The huge surprise [at P&G] is this turnaround and how fast its international business is growing," says Jay Freedman, consumer-products analyst with Kidder, Peabody & Co.; "they're knocking the cover off the ball." Many of P&G's early stumbles came in Japan, which Mr. Artzt considers its biggest challenge so far. P&G entered Japan in 1972, trying to snare a share of the potentially lucrative diaper and detergent business there. Ten years later, the company had piled up $200 million in losses.

One crucial mistake was failing to understand cultural differences, as in the Camay ad. P&G now tries to address this, in Japan and elsewhere, by hiring natives to work in marketing and other areas. But perhaps P&G's biggest problem in Japan was simply failing to understand what consumers wanted. Initially, the diapers P&G sold there were the bulky and shapeless U.S. version of Pampers. Japanese mothers considered cloth diapers and sleek Japanese-made disposable diapers superior in comfort and absorbency. "It was clear we were out of the ball game," recalls Mr. Artzt.

P&G soon launched in Japan its own superabsorbent, sleek diaper. But sales lagged because the brand bore the stigma of the earlier version. So in 1985 the company rolled out an ad campaign with a talking diaper describing the improved product to babies. Those ads have helped Pampers grab a 28 percent share in parts of Japan, though company officials won't give a figure for the nation as a whole.

P&G's other disaster in Japan was Cheer laundry detergent, which it first promoted as being effective in all water temperatures. The problem, as P&G soon learned, was that many Japanese wash clothes in cold water—either tap water or leftover bath water—so they don't care about all-temperature washing. Also, if a lot of fabric softener was added to the water, Cheer didn't produce much suds, and at the time "the fabric-softener market was exploding in Japan," Mr. Artzt says.

Procter & Gamble reformulated the detergent so it wouldn't be affected by fabric softeners, and in ads it pledged "superior" cleaning in cold water, not all temperatures. P&G officials say Cheer has become one of their best-selling products in Japan though they won't be more specific. Sometimes the company has to adapt not so much to different consumers as to different circumstances. In Europe, P&G's biggest headache involved its liquid laundry detergents. The liquids didn't work in European washing machines, which had dispensers only for powdered detergents. P&G engineers set out to make dispensers for liquids that would fit on the washers, but soon discovered that each brand of machine required a different design. "At that point, we were sure the devil was working against us," Mr. Artzt says.

The solution: a plastic "dosing ball" supplied with each bottle that gets filled with detergent and placed in each load of clothes. P&G now has 50 percent of the liquid-detergent market in Europe, with brands such as Vizir and Ariel.

In the next decade, company officials say, much of the company's growth overseas is likely to come from an expansion of Richardson-Vicks' operations. But this effort faces obstacles: Some countries require that many more products be registered as drugs than does the U.S. For instance, Vicks cough drops are considered a drug in Japan and elsewhere. Other local laws and demands have limited P&G's growth. In Mexico, the government won't allow P&G to build a second detergent plant unless the company agrees to sell a majority stake in it to a Mexican company. For now, P&G has retooled its existing plant to increase efficiency.

Joint ventures have helped crack some trade barriers. In recent months P&G announced a joint venture with the South Korean government to sell a variety of its products. It also recently began producing Head & Shoulders shampoo in China. Similar ventures probably will be vital to what company officials hope will be P&G's next move: into the Soviet Union. The company is optimistic that current talks with the

Soviet government will give it access to the nation's vast market. Mr. Artzt cites reforms of the farm program and proposals for reduced military spending as signs that Soviet buyers will have more cash for consumer goods. And that, Mr. Artzt believes, will translate into a "happier Russian public."

Source: Reprinted by permission of *The Wall Street Journal*, © Dow Jones & Company, Inc. (February 6, 1989). All Rights Reserved Worldwide.

1. Identify those factors in each environmental domain that present obstacles to P&G in terms of marketing its products successfully.
2. Procter & Gamble is now considering going into the Soviet Union with its products. Based on the information in Case 24–1, what tactic would you recommend to Mr. Artzt so that P&G's venture in the Soviet market would be successful?
3. Do you believe Mr. Artzt should oversee all international operations at P&G, or should each country be assigned its own international vice-president? Explain.

ENDNOTES

1. See R. Vernon, "International Investment and International Trade in the Product Life Cycle," *Quarterly Journal of Economics* (May 1966): 190-207, for a full explanation of the international product life cycle concept.
2. The application of oligopoly theory to international business was explained in a doctoral dissertation by F. T. Knickerbocker, "Oligopolistic Reaction and the Multinational Enterprise" (Boston: Harvard Graduate School of Business Administration, 1973).
3. The internalization theory has been advanced by J. H. Dunning, "Towards an Eclectic Theory of International Production," *Journal of International Business Studies* (Spring-Summer 1980): 9-31, and A. M. Rugman, "A New Theory of Multinational Enterprise: Internationalization Versus Internalization," *Columbia Journal of World Business* (Spring 1980).
4. The behavioral theory of the international firm was first explained by Y. Aharoni, "The Foreign Investment Decision Process" (Boston: Harvard Graduate School of Business Administration, Division of Research, 1966). Later, Scandinavian researchers such as J. E. Wahlne and F. Weidersheim-Paul, "Psychic Distance—An Inhibiting Factor in International Trade," unpublished working paper (Uppsala, Sweden: Center for International Business Studies, Department of Business Administration, University of Uppsala, 1977), and R. Luostarinen, "Lateral Rigidity in International Business Decision Making," *Working Papers in International Business*, no. 3 (Helsinki, Finland: The Helsinki School of Economics, 1978), elaborated on the importance of "noneconomic" behavior in the international entry mode decision process, especially the notion of psychic (cultural) distance as opposed to geographic distance.
5. The environmental determinants theory was advanced by I. A. Litvak and P. M. Banting, "A Conceptual Framework for International Business Arrangements," *Marketing and the New Science of Planning* (Chicago: American Marketing Association Fall Conference Proceedings, 1968). The first empirical test of the theory appeared in an article by J. D. Goodnow and J. E. Hansz, "Environmental Determinants of Overseas Market Entry Strategies," *Journal of International Business Studies* (Spring 1972): 33-50.
6. See W. W. Rostow, *The Stages of Economic Growth*, 2d ed. (New York: Cambridge University Press, 1960), for a full explanation of the stages of growth concept.
7. The use of cluster analysis for the classification of countries was discussed by S. Prakash Sethi, "Comparative Cluster Analysis for World Markets," *Journal of Marketing Research* 8 (August 1971): 348-354, and Goodnow and Hansz, "Environmental Determinants," 33-50.
8. A method for evaluating political uncertainties as they impact international business was suggested by R. Stobaugh, "How to Analyze Foreign Investment Climates," *Harvard Business Review* (September-October 1969): 100-108. Several private consulting firms such as Business International, Frost and Sullivan, and BERI (Business Environmental Risk Incorporated) publish reports on the political outlooks in various countries as they might affect international business activities.

   9. For the most comprehensive discussion of the cultural impact on international business, see V. Terpstra and K. David, *The Cultural Environment of International Business*, 2d ed. (Cincinnati: South-Western Publishing Co., 1985).

  10. For example, see A. R. Neghandi, *Functioning of the Multinational Corporation: A Global Comparative Study* (New York: Pergamon Press, 1980).

  11. See R. A. Webber, "Convergence or Divergence?" *Columbia Journal of World Business* (May-June 1969): 75-83, for his views on convergence and divergence.

  12. See G. S. Vozikis and T. S. Mescon, "Convergence or Divergence? A Vital Managerial Quest Revisited," *Columbia Journal of World Business* (Summer 1981): 79-87, for a critique of Webber's earlier views.

  13. See G. Hofstede, *Culture's Consequences: International Differences in Work-Related Values* (Beverly Hills, CA: Sage Publications, 1980), for a full explanation of the many variables that underlie each of his dimensions.

  14. Hofstede originally used the term masculinity for the fourth dimension. We have adopted the term sex roles to be more consistent with current terminology.

A

ability the capacity to perform; along with effort, it is a key determinant of performance.

ability test a test which measures whether an applicant is able to perform the tasks required on the job.

absolute advantage the advantage a firm has over its competitors in its ability to produce something faster and more inexpensively than they can.

acceptance theory Chester Barnard's view that authority resides in subordinates, because they can choose to either accept or reject the directives of their superiors.

achievement-oriented leadership leadership in which the leader sets challenging goals, expects subordinates to perform at their highest level, and shows confidence that subordinates will meet such expectations.

action plans plans that identify day-to-day activities in support of the goals of the organization; include single-use plans and standing plans.

action points points in a plan at which conditions may be moving in a direction that requires the modification or abandonment of the original plan.

ad hoc committees committees created for a short-term purpose.

adaptation model a model contending that a major thrust of strategic management should be the alignment of organization activities with key dimensions of the organization's environment.

adaptive subsystems organization units or departments that oversee organizational planning and change.

adhocracy an organizational design in which coordination is achieved through mutual adjustment, avoiding specialization, formality, and centralized authority.

administrative change alterations in an organization's structures, lines of communication, managerial hierarchy, goals, strategies, or reward systems.

administrative measures measures such as health and safety laws, customs inspection procedures, and regulations that have an impact on minimum pricing of foreign-made goods.

administrative problem the need to develop an appropriate administrative system within the organization to support a strategy.

administrative theory a branch of classical management theory that focuses on the total organization, attempting to develop guidelines for managers that will improve the efficiency of the organization.

administrative type organization an organization characterized by professional management and by an institutional character which exists independent of organization members.

affirmative action a legal requirement that employers must actively recruit, hire, and promote members of minority groups if such groups are underrepresented in the firm.

allocation models models that permit the decision maker to make optimal use of scarce resources by allocating them where they will do the most good.

ambidextrous organization an organization that has two designs: an organic design for creativity and the initiation of change and a mechanistic design for the implementation of technological change.

analyzer strategy a strategy which identifies two areas of activity for the organization, a stable market and an unstable market, to solve the engineering, administrative, and entrepreneurial problems.

anchoring and adjustment the tendency, in an often unconscious attempt to simplify decision making, to use an early bit of information as an anchor and then use new information to adjust that initial anchor.

application blank a form that provides the hiring firm with information about the educational background, work experience, and outside interests of an applicant.

artificial intelligence (AI) the capacity of a computer to reason as people do, learn from experience, and communicate in human language.

assessment center a place where many different employee-selection procedures can be performed in order to make the hiring process more systematic.

attendance the degree of regularity in reporting for work on a given day.

attitudes the beliefs, feelings, and behavioral tendencies held by a person about an object, event, or person.

attribute listing the compilation of a list of attributes of something in order to create ways of improving those attributes.

audit an independent and unbiased evaluation of the data reported and the procedures used in a control system.

authoritarian an individual who believes that power and status should be clearly defined and that there should be a hierarchy of authority.

authority in the context of leadership, the right to exert force on another.

autocratic leaders leaders who make decisions without inputs from subordinates.

automated decision conferencing (ADC) a method for making complex decisions quickly which uses computers and quantitative aids to reach a decision that is then reviewed carefully by staff members.

availability the tendency, in an often unconscious attempt to simplify decision making, to estimate the probability of an event on the basis of how easy it is to recall examples of the event.

avoidance conditioning in the application of learning theory, conditioning achieved by giving an individual the power to prevent the onset of an unpleasant consequence.

B

bargaining a method of formulating goals to match agreements for the exchange of goods or services with other organizations.

basic corrective action action taken to prevent the future occurrence of deviations from expected standards.

BCG matrix a portfolio strategy model which emphasizes the nature of the internal mix, or the diversification, of business units that are under the control of management.

behavior modeling training which gives supervisory trainees an opportunity to deal with actual employee problems and provides managers with immediate feedback on the trainees' performance. Trainees observe the behavior of a model supervisor and then attempt to emulate that behavior.

behavioral accounting the study of the financial impact of attitudes and behaviors such as turnover and absenteeism on organizations.

behavioral controls controls that monitor, measure, and evaluate behavior as it occurs.

behavioral management theory a body of theory based on the assumption that increased worker satisfaction leads to better performance.

behavioral shaping in organizational behavior modification (OB Mod), the learning of a complex behavior through successive approximations of the desired behavior, where responses are "shaped" until the desired complex behavior is achieved.

behaviorally anchored rating scale (BARS) a performance measure which involves rating employees against a list of possible employee actions, ranging from very desirable to very undesirable.

bill of material a listing of the components of an end item.

bottom-up approach an approach to control in which subordinates influence the goals and standards of top management.

boundary or boundary-spanning subsystems organization units or departments that handle transactions involving the procurement and disposal of necessary resources.

boundary spanners employees at the boundary between the organization and its environment.

boundary spanning creating roles to open exchanges and coordinate activities with factors in the environment.

brainstorming a group problem-solving technique which promotes creativity by encouraging members to come up with any ideas, no matter how strange, without fear of criticism.

break-even analysis a method for analyzing at what point a project will cover its costs.

break-even point the point at which there is neither a profit nor a loss to an organization.

budget as a means of financial control, a formal statement of the expenditures needed for a future time period; in the planning process, a single-use plan that specifies allocations of financial resources to support specific activities within a given period.

budgeting the process by which a firm divides its resources and allocates them to various business units.

buffering setting up buffers for both the input and output sides of organizational activities in order to absorb and cope with environmental uncertainty.

buffers programs or practices instituted to prevent environmental factors from upsetting the smooth functioning of the production process.

bureaucracy Weber's term for an ideal type of organization structured around rational guidelines to promote maximum efficiency.

bureaucratic control strategy a strategy which depends on tight controls based on rules that ensure standardization and on data management that reports the current level of activity to management.

bureaupathology pathological reliance on control mechanisms in order to overcome personal anxiety.

business ethics rules about how businesses and their employees ought to behave.

business plan a plan that helps the owner of a small business determine what resources are needed and provides a standard against which to evaluate results.

C

cafeteria-style benefit plans benefit plans in which employees can choose from a wide range of alternative benefits, tailoring them to their particular situations.

capacity controls controls that link long-range forecasts to the amount of product or service being produced in order to generate alternative capacity plans, to schedule operations, and to decide on a plan for implementation.

career anchors "master motives," or things such as values and self-perceptions that guide and constrain a person's entire career and will not be relinquished under any circumstances.

career concept types Driver's categories of career behavior and patterns.

career plateau the point in a career where the likelihood of additional hierarchical promotion is very low.

cash cow a business-unit product line which is a good performer in a low-growth market.

causal attribution the process of forming perceptions of the causes underlying others' behaviors.

centralization a measure of the variability in member relative centralities in a communication network.

centralized authority the concentration of decision-making authority in the hands of higher-level managers.

ceremonies elaborate organizational events that occur less frequently than rituals and include award banquets and the presentation of promotions.

certainty a decision situation in which the problem solver knows which event will occur.

chain of command a management principle that establishes clear, unbroken lines of authority and responsibility from the highest to the lowest level in the organization.

change agent an individual, usually from outside the organization, who intervenes to start the change process.

changing accepting and internalizing necessary changes in behavior and attitude; the second step in the Lewin-Schein model of the change process.

charismatic leadership leadership characterized by the leader's ability to arouse enthusiasm, faith, loyalty, and pride and trust in the leader and his or her aims.

choice-making models models used when a decision maker is faced with an array of alternatives and can choose only a subset of those alternatives.

citizenship behaviors actions taken by an employee which help the organization but are not necessarily reflected in the quantity or quality of that employee's output, such as helping co-workers, following orders, and protecting and conserving organizational resources.

clan control strategy a control strategy that capitalizes on people's need to belong to a group and develops control through rituals and myths.

classical management theory a body of theory that evolved to develop management techniques to solve problems of organizational efficiency in the production of goods and services.

classical or Pavlovian conditioning conditioning that uses pairing of stimuli so that a new stimulus is responded to in the same way as the original stimulus.

classical view the view propounded by the English economist Adam Smith that when businesses attempt to maximize their profits in a competitive market environment, they also unintentionally promote the public or social interest.

closed system a system that does not rely on inputs from or outputs to the environment in order to survive.

closure organizing stimuli to "close up" or "fill in" missing parts to create a meaningful whole.

co-optation absorbing new elements into the goal-formulation process to avert threats to the organization's stability or survival.

coacting groups noninteracting groups whose members are jointly acting toward some goal.

coalition a combination of two or more organizations joined to achieve a common purpose.

code noise the difference between the meaning of a message to the sender and its meaning to the recipient.

code of ethics a formal statement setting forth an organization's principles of appropriate behavior.

coercive power power based on one person's ability to affect punishment that another receives.

cognitive dissonance a situation in which an individual has conflicting thoughts.

command groups or functional groups groups consisting of managers and their subordinates.

commodity agreements international arrangements to stabilize the prices of food or raw materials rather than allow free-market price competition to take place.

common markets groups of nations that agree not only to set up customs unions but also to find ways to further harmonize their economic policies in such areas as agricultural price supports, work permits, antitrust regulations, transportation, and communication.

communication the transfer of information from one person to another.

communication networks communication channels that are linked together to structure the information flows among network members.

comparable worth the view that if the work of different employee positions is of equal worth, individuals in those positions should be paid the same amount.

comparative advantage the greater of the absolute advantages a firm or a nation has in the production of two different items.

comparative management the study of management practices in different cultures to discover and compare their similarities and differences.

competition rivalry between two or more organizations.

competitive model a model contending that the nature and degree of competition in an industry determine what strategy is appropriate.

complexity the degree of similarity or diversity between the factors in an organization's environment.

computer-assisted design (CAD) the use of computers to improve and speed up design projects and reduce the number of drafters needed.

computer-integrated manufacturing (CIM) a manufacturing method which links computer-aided engineering, computer-assisted design, and computer-aided manufacturing, multiplying their individual benefits.

concentration the degree to which factors are distributed in the environment.

conceptual skills the ability to understand the degree of complexity in a given situation and to reduce that complexity to a level at which specific courses of action can be derived.

conflict a decision situation in which the events are actions of a competitor, and their probabilities are unknown.

consensus the degree to which an organization's claim to a specific activity is recognized or disputed by other organizations.

conservatism in information processing the underrevision of estimates when one is presented with new information.

consideration leader behavior which demonstrates friendship, mutual trust, respect, and warmth toward subordinates.

constrainers critics of the classical view of economics who believe that businesses are indifferent to the social consequences of their actions and tend to act irresponsibly unless constrained by legal and political means.

content theories theories of motivation that focus on the underlying needs which motivate a person.

context the combination of characteristics that identify the organizational system and its relationship to the environment.

contextual condition a characteristic that is either external or internal to the boundaries of an organization.

contingency model of leadership a model contending that leadership effectiveness depends upon whether situational characteristics fit the manager.

contingency planning identifying alternative courses of action before implementation of a plan in order to meet possible future conditions.

contingency theory a body of theory stating that the solution to any one managerial problem is contingent on the other factors that impinge on the situation.

continuous reinforcement in the application of learning theory, reinforcing behavior every time it occurs.

continuous-process technology a transformation process in which machines handle the production process almost entirely.

contributions rule in equity theory, the rule that distributive fairness is determined by equating contributions (inputs) with outcomes.

control in the context of leadership, the exertion of enough force on another to alter behavior; as a function of management, the process that tries to ensure that activities performed match the desired activities, or goals, that have been set.

control chart a chart used in conjunction with statistical control that shows, for example, an average dimension for a particular product component, an upper control limit, and a lower control limit.

control process a process of setting standards, measuring actual performance, comparing actual performance to the standards, and taking corrective action when necessary.

control technique a mechanism designed to help achieve desired performance.

controlling the managerial function of collecting, evaluating, and comparing information in order to correct for tasks that are improperly performed as well as to identify where activities by members in the organization can be improved.

convergent thinking narrowing in on a solution to a problem after many alternatives have been generated and evaluated.

cooperation a goal-formulation strategy used when other organizations in the environment have a strong influence over an organization; includes bargaining, co-optation, and coalition.

coordination the linking of activities in the organization that serve to achieve a common goal or objective.

coping strategies mechanisms set up to "seal off" the technical core from environmental factors that might disrupt the internal operations of the organization; these include buffering, smoothing, forecasting, rationing, boundary spanning, structural complexity, and executive succession.

core task dimensions in the job characteristics model of job design, the five characteristics of a job that are believed to be key influences on employee motivation.

corrective maintenance the repair of something that is not working properly.

craft type organization an organization which is strongly influenced by a chief executive who seeks comfort and company survival objectives and who engages in duties which are primarily technical rather than administrative.

creative ability the ability to produce ideas that are both new and useful.

creative behavior the production of ideas that are both new and useful.

creative imitation a strategy involving the perfecting and positioning of a product by one firm after the product has been introduced by another firm.

creative process the stages of creativity, including preparation, incubation, insight, and verification.

crisis management the scramble for answers to problems within a very short time frame.

criterion of optimism the assumption that things will work out as well as they possibly could.

criterion of pessimism the assumption that for any alternative the decision maker chooses, the worst possible event will take place.

critical incidents method a performance measure in which the appraiser keeps a list of all the things the employee did that were especially good or bad.

critical path the sequence of in-series activities in

an operation requiring the longest time for completion.

critical psychological states in the job characteristics model of job design, an employee's experienced meaningfulness of work, experienced responsibility for work outcomes, and knowledge of the actual results of work activities.

crucial subordinate a subordinate that the boss needs as much as that person needs the boss.

customer division a divisional design used when the organization produces and sells products to a diverse group of customers.

customs unions agreements between nations to set up free trade areas and to have one common set of regulations for trade relationships with non-member countries.

cybernetic control the use of self-operating, self-regulating systems which have built-in devices to correct automatically any deviations that occur.

D

decentralized authority the delegation of decision-making authority to middle- and lower-level positions in an organization.

decision confirmation dissonance reduction which occurs before a decision is announced.

decision insight system a computer program that leads the manager through the problem-solving process.

decision matrix a method of displaying the sorts of information a decision maker needs to make an optimal choice; alternatives are arrayed on the vertical axis and events on the horizontal axis.

decision structure table an arrangement of information used to screen out unsatisfactory alternatives.

decision support system (DSS) a class of computer systems which support the process of making decisions by allowing managers to ask "what if" questions about the problems they face.

decision tree a way to display the information needed to make a decision under risk; alternatives are arrayed as act forks and events as event forks in a tree structure.

decisional roles ways in which managers make decisions that affect organizational outcomes; one of Mintzberg's three general groupings of managerial roles.

decoder the element of the communication process that translates the message from the sender into a form that will have meaning to the recipient.

defender strategy a strategy that seeks or creates an environment that is stable in order to protect market share.

defense mechanisms ways in which an employee may try to reduce the tensions caused by frustration.

defensive avoidance a condition in which an individual tunes out information about the risks of a chosen alternative or the opportunities associated with an unchosen alternative in an effort to avoid stress.

delegation of authority granting decision-making authority to those in middle- and low-level positions.

Delphi process a decision process in which group members respond to a series of mailed questionnaires, in the hope that after a series of iterations a consensus among participants will emerge.

demanders critics of the classical view of economics who believe that businesses must be willing to exhibit a level of social involvement in proportion to their resources and power.

democratic leaders leaders who let subordinates participate in decision making.

demotion a movement downward in title, responsibility, or benefits.

departmentation the grouping of jobs based on criteria that managers believe help in the coordination and control of activities.

devil's advocate a group member who acts as a critic of a plan in order to ferret out problems with the plan and to propose reasons why it should not be adopted.

dialectical inquiry a procedure in which a situation is approached from two opposite points of view in hopes that out of this clash a creative synthesis will emerge.

differentiation the extent to which the organization is broken down into departments that differ by managers' orientations and structures.

differentiation strategy a strategy which emphasizes that a firm's product is unique in relation to other products in the industry.

direct equity investment a joint venture in service, distribution, or manufacturing facilities or a wholly owned venture, either built from scratch or resulting from a merger with or an acquisition of a going concern in the host country.

directing the managerial function of motivating, leading, and influencing the activities of subordinates.

directive leadership leadership in which a leader tells subordinates what is expected of them and how to do it.

dispatching preparing and issuing work orders.

dissatisfiers or hygiene factors in Herzberg's theory,

factors in organizations that cause dissatisfaction when deficient.

disseminator role informational role that involves evaluating and transmitting information to subordinates, peers, or superiors in the organization.

distributive fairness in equity theory, the perception that people are getting what they deserve.

disturbance handler role decisional role that requires quick action in a crisis situation to restore the organization's stability.

divergent thinking a technique used when problem solvers are not generating alternatives to an idea and must stretch their minds and seek new possibilities.

division of labor breaking a job down into specialized tasks to increase productivity.

divisional design an organizational form in which all activities needed to produce a good or service are grouped together into an independent unit.

divisionalized form a form of organizational design that achieves coordination through standardization of output.

dog a business unit which is a poor performer because of little growth in the market and small market share.

dogmatic closed-minded; descriptive of individuals who refuse to revise their opinions even in the face of conflicting evidence.

domain of power the number of individuals over whom someone can exert influence with respect to a specified range.

downward communication messages that travel from senders relatively high in the organizational structure to receivers in lower-level positions.

dual-core model an approach to the process of administrative change which suggests that application of organic versus mechanistic designs is partly dependent on the frequency of change that is required.

dynamism the degree of turnover in environmental factors.

E

economic order quantity (EOQ) an amount determined by balancing holding costs against ordering and stockout costs to find the least-cost reorder quantity.

economic unions agreements between common market member countries to issue an international common currency and to set up a central tax agency to collect revenues directly from private individuals rather than from their respective governments.

economies of scope concept from the factory of the future in which computerized controls allow automated machinery to produce a variety of products cheaply.

effort behavior directed toward some goal.

electronic bulletin boards "bulletin boards" which, when called with a modem, allow microcomputer users to read or leave messages.

electronic cottage the name given to work done on computers by employees who stay at home and transfer their output electronically to the office.

electronic mail or E-mail the long-distance electronic transmission of written information.

elimination-by-aspects rule a rule that screens out unacceptable alternatives on an attribute-by-attribute basis, usually working from the most important to the least important.

employee assistance programs (EAPs) training programs offered by companies to build skills, promote career development, provide counseling, or focus on other issues important to the company.

encoder the element of the communication process that puts the meaning of the message in an appropriate form, such as words, symbols, or body gestures.

engineering problem the need to determine which methods are appropriate for the production and distribution of goods and services to support a strategy.

entrepreneur role decisional role which involves efforts to improve the work unit by adapting new techniques or modifying old techniques.

entrepreneurial judo a strategy that takes advantage of the weaknesses of the firm holding the leadership position by securing a part of the market that the leader does not adequately defend and from there moving in on the rest of the leader's territory.

entrepreneurial problem the need to determine the market of the organization to support a strategy.

entrepreneurship the creation of wealth-adding value.

environment all factors outside an organization's boundaries that can affect activities of the organization.

environmental factors information, capital, material, people, and other organizations that reside outside an organization's boundaries that can affect the internal activities of the organization.

Equal Access to Justice Act an act which enables businesses to recover costs of litigation from the government when they challenge what they believe to be unreasonable government regulation—provided they win.

Equal Employment Opportunity Commission (EEOC) the government body responsible for enforcing federal law relating to job discrimination.

equality rule a rule that argues that it is fair for everyone to receive the same amount of outcomes.

equity theory a theory which argues that people want to maintain a balance between their inputs and the outcomes they receive.

escape conditioning in the application of learning theory, conditioning that rewards desired behavior by removing some unpleasant consequence.

exception principle the principle that only exceptions to the norm should be reported to supervisors in order to reduce the supervisors' communication overload.

exchange controls limitations or prohibitions on exchanging the home-country currency for foreign currencies.

executive succession the replacement of a top manager by another manager.

existence needs in Alderfer's ERG theory, all forms of material and physical desires.

existence-relatedness-growth (ERG) theory Alderfer's revision of Maslow's hierarchy theory which holds that individuals have only three sets of needs and that growth needs become increasingly important as they are satisfied.

expectancy in expectancy theory, the perceived linkage between effort and the first-order outcome.

expectancy theory an approach to motivation theory which examines the links in the process from effort to ultimate rewards.

expected utilities the products of the utilities of outcomes and their probabilities of occurrence.

expert power power based on one person's perception that another has needed relevant knowledge in a given area.

expert system a computer application that guides the performance of ill-structured tasks, which usually require experience and specialized knowledge.

exponential smoothing a forecasting technique that provides an estimate which weights all previous observations, but those weights diminish with the age of the observation.

exposure how often subordinates are seen by those above them in the organization.

extinction the elimination of an undesired behavior or failure to continue a desired behavior.

extrinsic factors in Herzberg's theory, factors in a job which are under the control of the supervisor or someone else other than the employee.

F

4/40 a work schedule in which employees work ten hours a day four days a week.

factory of the future the computer-based integration of design, process, and control functions in the manufacturing environment.

fantasy stage the stage of career choice that occurs between the ages of 6 and 11; expectations at this stage are typically unrealistic.

faxing the use of facsimile machines to send and reproduce copies of a document over telephone lines.

feasible region in linear programming, the area that satisfies all constraints.

feedback information received about activities in the organization.

figurehead role interpersonal role that involves conducting ceremonial activities as a representative of the organization.

financial analysis an analysis that identifies the major financial strengths and weaknesses of a firm by determining whether funds are used efficiently and the firm is financially viable.

financial budget a budget that estimates the amount of cash needed to support the expected level of activities during a specified time period.

financial ratio a relationship that indicates something about a firm's activities, such as the ratio between the firm's assets and liabilities.

first-line managers managers at the lowest level in the managerial hierarchy who lead employees in day-to-day tasks.

first-order outcome in expectancy theory, the direct result of effort.

fixed exchange rates rates of currency exchange that do not fluctuate because the value of all currencies is related to the price of an ounce of gold.

fixed-interval schedule in the application of learning theory, a schedule that provides a reinforcer at fixed time intervals, such as once a week.

fixed-position layout a facility design in which the workers, rather than the material or part, move from one work center or machine to another.

fixed-ratio schedule in the application of learning theory, a schedule that provides a reinforcer after a given number of acceptable behaviors.

flat organization an organization with wide spans of control and thus fewer levels of management.

flextime a work schedule that requires employees to work during a core work period in the middle of the day, but leaves them free to decide when they want to come to work and when they want to leave.

focus effect the tendency for groups to focus on just two or three alternatives, begin evaluating them, and never fully generate other alternatives.

focus strategy a strategy that pursues either an overall cost leadership strategy or a differentiation strategy by focusing on a narrow customer group, product line, or geographic market.

follow-up keeping track of work completed and any time lags or delays that may have occurred.

force to perform, or effort in expectancy theory, the degree of effort that an employee exerts, which depends on both the expectancy that effort will lead to an increase in the first-order outcome and the valence of the first-order outcome.

foreboders critics of the classical view of economics who believe that unless businesses contribute to social improvement, social problems will worsen and government will be forced to step in.

forecasting the collection of past and current information to make predictions about the future.

forecasting models models that allow the decision maker to obtain estimates of future levels of variables, such as sales, employment levels, or prices.

formal behavioral controls controls tied to the rules and regulations of the firm which serve to formalize hiring practices, the assignment of work, and evaluation procedures.

formal groups groups created by an organization to help accomplish some organizational objective.

framing effects the tendency to evaluate information differently depending on how the information is presented.

free trade areas regions where groups of nations have agreed to reduce all barriers to international trade among themselves.

freely floating exchange rates rates of currency exchange subject to market supply and demand, which can affect the relationship between the day-to-day values of one country's currency and another country's.

friendship groups groups formed because of some attraction such as similar values, backgrounds, or ages.

frustration regression in Alderfer's ERG theory, a movement down the hierarchy of needs which occurs when an inability to satisfy needs at a particular level in the hierarchy causes an individual to regress and focus on more concrete needs.

functional design an organizational form in which employees are grouped together in separate departments on the basis of common tasks, skills, or activities.

fustest with the mostest a strategy which from the start aims at achieving a permanent leadership position in a new market or industry (its name comes from the way a Confederate cavalry general explained his consistent success in battles).

futurists analysts who attempt to identify social or political trends and determine their relevance to a firm's future.

G

game theory a method of finding the optimal strategy or mix of strategies of each competitor, or player, in a zero-sum conflict situation.

Gantt chart a graph that shows the scheduling of work to be done and itemizes the work that has been completed.

gatekeepers members of an organization who decide who should receive information; they open and close the gates of information.

GE matrix a portfolio strategy model for evaluating business units in which the business units are plotted in a matrix on two dimensions: industry attractiveness and business strength.

General Agreement on Trade and Tariffs (GATT) an association of most of the nations in the free world which oversees and provides a forum for the multilateral reduction of tariff and nontariff barriers.

geographic division a divisional design used when the organization produces and sells products in diverse regions of the country or the world.

global planning interrelating a multinational corporation's subplans for each product grouping (or strategic business unit) and for each country or region.

goal a desired end state.

Gordon technique a creative technique which uses an initial focus on function.

grand strategy a broad plan to guide an organization toward completion of its official goals.

grapevine an informal information network among employees.

group a collection of individuals who have a common goal, are interdependent, and perceive themselves as a unit.

group cohesiveness the degree to which members are attracted to one another, reflected in their desires to retain membership and to resist leaving the group.

group polarization the tendency of group processes to make group members' initial risk preferences more extreme.

group technology layout a facility design that groups dissimilar machines into work centers (or cells) to work on products having similar shapes and processing requirements.

group territory a fixed area over which a group takes a proprietary interest.

groupthink a condition in which members of cohesive groups overemphasize concurrence-seeking at the expense of realistic appraisal.

growth needs in Alderfer's ERG theory, all needs involving creative efforts.

growth strategy a strategy in which companies grow through internal development or external acquisition of additional business units.

H

hackers computer buffs who illegally gain access to, and sometimes tamper with, computer files.

halo effect the tendency to judge specific traits on the basis of a general impression.

Hawthorne effect the tendency for participants in a field study to behave differently simply because they know they are being studied.

heroes company role models in the performance of deeds, embodiment of character, and support of the existing organization culture.

heuristics devices used, often unconsciously, to simplify decision making.

hierarchy of goals the linkage of official, operative, and operational goals within the organization.

hierarchy of plans the integration of the plans of all four levels of management.

higher order need strength (HONS) the degree to which an individual wants such things as challenge and responsibility.

holding or carrying costs the expense of storing inventory in the firm's warehouse or on its stock shelves.

horizontal communication communication among individuals or groups at the same organizational level.

hot decision situations situations in which decision makers must act under great psychological stress, such as when stakes are high.

human change the area of organizational change that emphasizes altering values, attitudes, skills, performance, perceptions, and behavioral patterns of members.

human resource planning the process of analyzing an organization's human resource needs under changing conditions and developing the activities necessary to satisfy those needs.

human skills the ability to work with, motivate, and direct individuals or groups.

humanistic-existential theories theories that focus on the total personality of the individual instead of on the separate behaviors that make up the personality, stressing individual choice and personal responsibility.

hybrid design a divisional design which includes divisional units as well as functional departments centralized at corporate headquarters.

I

idea champion a member of the organization who is assigned responsibility for the successful implementation of a change.

idea checklists lists of questions to stimulate creativity.

ill structure a decision situation in which the problem solver does not have enough information to construct the decision matrix.

ill-structured, or wicked, decision situation a situation which is nonroutine and unprogrammed, with delayed feedback and incomplete information.

immediate corrective action action taken to influence present performance.

implicit theories preconceptions that influence perceptions at the selection, organization, and translation stages.

impression management an effort by workers to beat controls by appearing to be busy or to otherwise be meeting job requirements.

income statement a financial statement that shows revenues, expenses, taxes, and profits.

incrementalizing the process of making a small change in one product attribute and then in another instead of seeking creative ways to develop something entirely new.

individual territory a fixed area over which an individual takes a proprietary interest.

individualism the relationship between individual persons and the collective society within various national cultures.

influence in the context of leadership, the actual exertion of force on another.

informal behavioral controls controls that try to influence employees through unobtrusive methods such as culture and socialization.

informal groups groups within an organization which are created by the members themselves.

information knowledge communicated or received concerning a particular fact or circumstance.

information resource management a field that has developed in recognition of the fact that information is a valuable resource in need of systematic management.

informational roles ways in which managers gather, receive, and transmit information that concerns members of the organization; one of Mintzberg's three general groupings of managerial roles.

initiating structure leader behavior characterized by the leader's tendency to organize and define the relationship between himself or herself and subordinates.

innovation the creation or modification of a process, product, or service.

innovation departments departments of organizations that deal specifically with creativity and initiation of change.

inspection the process of comparing products with the standards, approving those that meet them, and rejecting those that do not.

instrumentality in expectancy theory, the perceived linkage between a first-order outcome and a second-order outcome.

integration the degree of collaboration that exists among departments.

interest groups groups formed when individuals unite to achieve some common purpose.

interest test a measure of a person's likes and dislikes.

interlocking directorates boards of directors with members who also serve on the board of directors of other organizations.

intermediate planning identifying activities to be carried out over a period of one to five years at the middle or divisional levels of the organization.

international product life cycle the stages through which sales of a product introduced into a foreign market go; since these cycles occur at different times in different countries, firms can extend the growth periods of their products' life cycles by exporting to foreign markets when the domestic market nears saturation.

interpersonal dimensions in the job characteristics model of job design, the two characteristics that influence the degree to which employees engage in relationships with others on the job.

interpersonal roles ways in which managers relate to members of the organization; one of Mintzberg's three general groupings of managerial roles.

interviews asking job candidates a series of questions to determine their qualifications for a position.

intimate zone a zone of personal space which extends, for Americans, to about 18 inches from the skin; reserved for such things as lovemaking and comforting.

intracapital a discretionary budget earned by the intrapreneur and used to fund the creation of new intraprises and innovation for the corporation.

intrapreneurship the creation of wealth-adding value which takes place within the confines of a large organization.

intrinsic factors in Herzberg's theory, factors which are part of the job itself or are otherwise under the control of the employee.

inventory control management of the costs of ordering, storing, and handling inventory.

inventory record file a file containing information about the status of each item held in inventory.

"invisible hand" Adam Smith's term for the influence responsible for ensuring that decisions made by buyers and sellers in a freely operating market to promote their own self-interests will promote the general good of society as well.

iron law of responsibility the belief that responsibility must equal power.

issues managers analysts who identify social issues and make specific recommendations for company response.

J

just-in-time (JIT) or kanban a method of inventory control in which the firm maintains very small inventories.

job analysis the systematic study of a job to determine its characteristics.

job characteristics model a model of job design that describes jobs as having five core task dimensions and two interpersonal dimensions which influence employees' responses to job design efforts.

job depth the degree to which employees can influence their work environments and carry out planning and control functions.

job description a short summary of the basic tasks that make up a job.

job enlargement an increase in job scope.

job enrichment an increase in job depth.

job evaluation determining the relative worth of a job in the firm.

job involvement the degree to which employees are involved with their jobs, often reflected in the job's importance to the employee's life or to the employee's self-concept.

job pathing a carefully planned sequence of job assignments aimed at developing certain job-related skills.

job satisfaction the overall affective reactions of an employee to a job.

job scope the number of different activities the worker performs, regardless of their content.

job sharing or worksharing a work schedule in which two or more people share a single job.

job specification a summary of the qualifications needed for a specific job.

joint venture a legal arrangement between two competing companies to work together on the production of a particular product or service.

L

labor theory of value the theory that the price of any product can be approximated by the number of hours it takes a worker to produce one unit.

Laplace criterion (criterion of insufficient reason) criterion arguing that if the probabilities of events are unknown, it is reasonable to assume that the probabilities are equal.

large-batch, or mass-production, technology a transformation process using an assembly-line approach characterized by long production runs with standardized parts.

law of effect a law stating that behavior which is rewarded will tend to be repeated; behavior which is not rewarded will tend not to be repeated.

lead time the time from order placement to delivery.

leader role interpersonal role that involves the coordination and control of the work of subordinates.

leadership the behavior and characteristics of individuals who use influence to coordinate and direct the activities of others toward group objectives.

learning any relatively permanent change in behavior produced by experience.

legitimacy the acceptance of the organization's activities by non-members of the organization.

legitimate power power attained because one individual feels it is legitimate, or right, for another to give orders or otherwise exercise force.

Lewin-Schein model a model of change which proposes three general steps in the change process: unfreezing, changing, and refreezing.

liaison role interpersonal role enacted when managers obtain from others the information or resources needed to complete the work performed by their departments or work units.

linear programming a technique that seeks to optimize something subject to various constraints.

linear regression a technique that predicts future levels of a variable by identifying and extrapolating the line that best fits through past levels of the variable.

linking pin the leader of a task group who is also a member of a higher-level group and helps to coordinate activities and communications between levels.

loading the process of determining how long it takes to perform a particular operation at a machine or workstation and then adding that amount of time to the time needed for work already scheduled there.

lobbying trying to influence decisions made by governmental agencies or legislators.

local content laws requirements that certain percentages of finished goods be made of parts produced in the importing country.

locus of control the degree to which people feel that what happens to them is the result of their own actions (internal locus of control) or is controlled by fate or circumstance (external locus of control).

long-range planning identifying activities to be performed over an extended period of time.

LPC scale a measure of whether a leader is relationship-oriented or task-oriented based on asking the leader to describe on several dimensions the individual he or she least liked to work with in the past (the least-preferred co-worker).

M

Machiavellian a person who feels that any behavior is acceptable if it achieves his or her goals.

machine bureaucracy a design configuration in which the organization is large and old, and tasks are divided according to an assembly-line technology.

maintenance subsystem organization unit or department concerned with the stable operation of activities in the organization.

managed float the intervention of a government in the international market to stabilize the values of currencies.

management a process of planning, organizing and staffing, directing, and controlling activities in an organization in a systematic way in order to achieve a common goal.

management by exception taking corrective actions only when there is an unusual deviation from the norm.

management by objectives (MBO) a management technique in which an employee and his or her supervisor regularly set goals for the employee, whose performance is evaluated against these goals.

management games training methods in which trainees are faced with a simulated situation and are required to make an ongoing series of decisions about that situation.

management information system (MIS) an integrated system of information flows designed to enhance decision-making effectiveness.

managerial control the allocation of resources so that businesses, units, and departments have what they need to accomplish their goals, to schedule activities, and to monitor progress.

managerial Grid® a tool for evaluating the attitudes of managers in which the axes of the Grid are concern for people and concern for production.

managerial subsystem organization unit or department that oversees the activities of the other subsystems, placing its emphasis on coordinating them, resolving conflicts, establishing strategies, and directing them toward system-level goals.

managers individuals responsible for completing tasks that require the supervision of other members or organizational resources.

market control strategy a strategy based on the assumption that the price of certain exchanges or transactions can be set most efficiently through market mechanisms such as competition.

market feasibility study an analysis of the market for a product or service.

master production schedule the overall production plan for end items, expressed in terms of timing and quantity requirements.

material requirements planning (MRP) a method of planning and controlling inventories in which projected inventory levels are computed from present inventories and from planned transactions affecting inventory levels.

matrix design a design which implements functional and divisional structures simultaneously in each department.

mechanistic design a design in which the structures emphasize rules, specialized jobs, and centralized authority.

mechanistic organization an organization type appropriate for a task that is routine and unchanging; *see* mechanistic design.

mentor an older adult who contributes to the career development of a younger adult.

merger the combining of two or more firms to create one company.

message channel the medium of information exchange.

middle managers managers who supervise first-line managers and some non-management personnel and are responsible for the coordination of tasks performed to achieve organizational goals.

minimum resource theory the theory that members would like to form a coalition that controls the minimum amount of resources necessary to gain the upper hand.

mission the path managers choose to achieve the stated purpose of the organization.

mobicentric man someone who values mobility as an end rather than as a means.

models simplifications of reality that can be manipulated more easily and inexpensively than the real situation they depict.

modem a device that permits computers to communicate over telephone lines (short for *modulator-demodulator*).

monitor role informational role that involves scanning the environment for information and events that represent opportunities or threats to the functioning of the work unit.

monopolistic competition a competitive market structure that exists when many firms offer a similar good or service with only minor price differentials.

monopoly a market structure in which one organization has sole access to the market for its goods and services.

morphological analysis creativity enhancement technique in which specific ideas for one attribute or problem dimension are listed along one axis of a matrix and ideas for a second attribute or problem dimension are listed along the other axis; the cells of the matrix then provide idea combinations.

motivating potential score in the job characteristics model of job design, an evaluation of how perceptions of the core task dimensions fit together to determine the job's intrinsic motivating potential.

motivation a set of forces, originating both within and outside the individual, that initiate behavior and determine its form, direction, intensity, and duration.

moving average a technique used to forecast the next period on the basis of the average of actual levels over a particular number of past periods.

multi-attribute utility (MAU) model a tool used to determine the overall satisfactoriness of something that has a number of relevant characteristics by considering the utility of each alternative;

attribute levels and attribute weights are used to compute the overall utility of each alternative.

multinational corporation (MNC) a company whose goods and services have significant market shares in several countries and whose senior managers plan for a global rather than a purely domestic market.

munificence the level of resources in the environment available to an organization.

N

need for achievement the need to accomplish a difficult task or develop a particular talent in an attempt to increase self-esteem.

need for affiliation the desire to establish and maintain friendly and warm relations with other persons.

need for power the desire to control other persons, to influence their behavior, and to be responsible for them.

needs rule in equity theory, a rule of distributive fairness which argues that it is fair to give people what they need rather than what they deserve according to their contributions.

negotiator role a decisional role resting on the manager's authority to commit organizational resources.

networking linking computers together to permit them to communicate without modems and to access tremendous amounts of information.

new careerism the set of changes in career expectations that include the increasingly personal dimensions of career success, a focus on career development, and more women in the work force than ever before.

noise anything that distorts an intended message.

nominal group technique (NGT) a technique which uses both interacting and noninteracting group processes in order to capture the benefits of groups without falling prey to their problems.

nominal groups groups whose members are jointly acting toward some goal but who never interact; groups "in name only."

noncybernetic controls controls in which managers use their own discretion in deciding how best to complete an activity and meet performance goals.

nonreinforcement in the application of learning theory, removal of the reinforcing consequence that previously followed an undesired behavior in order to cause extinction of that behavior.

nonverbal communication communication that either does not use words at all or uses words in a way that conveys meaning beyond their strict definition.

norms expectations about how group members ought to behave.

numerical control a computer system that relies on punched tape or some other automatic control mechanism to direct machine operations.

O

object-oriented programming systems (OOPS) systems that allow computers to process knowledge—things and concepts—rather than just numbers.

objective function the element of a linear programming problem that one attempts to maximize or minimize.

Occupational Safety and Health Administration (OSHA) the government body which attempts to reduce the number of safety and health hazards in the workplace.

official goals formally stated organizational goals formulated by top management.

oligopoly a market structure in which only a few firms are in competition to provide goods and services to a market.

on-the-job training training conducted while employees perform job-related tasks.

one-way communication communication that gives a message without opportunity for immediate feedback.

open system a system that must continually seek resources from the environment in order to survive.

operant or Skinnerian conditioning conditioning which relies on the law of effect.

operating budget a budget that summarizes the raw materials, goods, and services a unit expects to consume during a specified time period.

operational control control that involves overseeing individual tasks and performance and is concerned with the integration of work groups.

operational goals goals formulated by first-line supervisors and employees that include standards of behavior, performance criteria, and completion time.

operations any process that accepts inputs and uses resources to change those inputs in useful ways.

operations control the management of the transformation of inputs into outputs.

operations management the process of planning, organizing, and controlling operations to reach objectives efficiently and effectively.

operative goals goals formulated by middle management that identify the ends sought through the actual operating policies of the organization.

ordering costs the expenses involved in placing an order.

organic design an organizational design in which rules and regulations are minimal, tasks are more often done in groups than individually, and authority is decentralized.

organic organization an organization type appropriate for a task that is nonroutine and changing; *see* organic design.

organization a collectivity of people engaged in a systematic effort to produce a good or an activity.

organization context dimensions of activities and events that exist outside an organization's boundaries as well as dimensions that are unique to the organization.

organization culture a blend of values, stories, heroes, and rituals and ceremonies that have come to mean a great deal to the people who work for an organization.

organization development (OD) a planned, organization-wide effort that is supported by top management and directed toward increasing organizational effectiveness and encouraging honest communication between organization members.

organization set all of the organizations with which a firm has an exchange in order to get necessary resources and achieve goals.

organizational adaptation the transformation of part or all of an organization to make its activities more compatible with existing environmental conditions.

organizational audit group a group which tries to ferret out the points at which omissions or distortions in the communication process are taking place.

organizational behavior modification (OB Mod) the use of the principles of learning theory to manage behavior in organizations.

organizational change any alteration of activities in an organization.

organizational commitment the degree to which the employee is committed to the organization's values and goals.

organizational effectiveness the extent to which an organization realizes its goals.

organizational efficiency the ratio of an organization's outputs to its inputs, used to determine the degree to which the organization achieves its goals.

organizational goal a desired state of affairs which the organization tries to realize.

organizational slack the difference between the total resources available to the organization and the total side payments made to induce goal support among organizational groups.

organizational structure a structure characterized by mechanisms that serve to coordinate and control activities of organizational members.

organizing and staffing the assignment and coordination of tasks to be performed by organization members and the assignment and distribution of resources necessary to perform each task.

orientation introducing new employees to their jobs and to the company.

output control measurement and evaluation of the results of an activity after it is completed; also called post-action control.

overall cost leadership strategy a strategy that focuses on maintaining an efficient and low-cost organization.

P

partial reinforcement schedule in the application of learning theory, a schedule that is time-based or behavior-based rather than continuous, administered on a fixed, unchanging basis, or varied around some mean.

participation being at work to do one's job.

participative leadership leadership in which the leader consults with subordinates and asks for their suggestions, which he or she seriously considers before making a decision.

path-goal theory of leader effectiveness the theory that leaders are effective because they can influence subordinates' perceptions of their work goals, personal goals, and paths to goal attainment.

perception the complex process by which we select, organize, and interpret sensory stimuli into a meaningful and coherent picture of the world.

perceptual readiness the fact that people are more likely to see things they are expecting to see.

perfect competition a market structure that exists when many organizations offer essentially the same good or service, and price becomes the primary discriminator for the customer.

performance the accomplishment of an organizational goal.

performance appraisal measuring employee performance.

performance standards standards used to define the goals to be achieved by a worker over a specified period of time.

periodic inventory a system in which the firm takes a physical count of inventory at the end of each accounting period.

perpetual inventory a running count of inventory levels.

personal space the self-established area of privacy and control which surrounds a person.

personal zone the zone of personal space ranging from about one and a half to four feet from a person; used for confortable interaction with others and connotes friendship and closeness.

personality the organized and distinctive pattern of behavior that characterizes an individual's adaptation to a situation and endures over time.

personality test a test to measure personality characteristics that might be important on the job.

personalized power seekers people who try to dominate others for the sake of dominating, deriving satisfaction from conquering others.

Peter Principle the theory that employees are ultimately promoted to positions for which they are not qualified.

piece-rate system a financial incentive system that bases pay on what workers produce rather than on the number of hours they work.

placement fitting people and jobs together.

plan a framework that details the methods and tasks involved in achieving a defined goal.

planned change an effort by management to develop and install a program that serves to alter organization activities in a timely and orderly way.

planning the selection and sequential ordering of tasks required to achieve an organizational goal.

planning, programming, budgeting system (PPBS) a system used for analyzing and deciding among program or activity proposals in an effort to tie together strategic and long-range planning with conventional budgeting.

planning horizon the length of time a plan specifies for activities to be carried out; can be long-range, intermediate, or short-range.

planning staff a group of individuals whose sole responsibility is the formulation of plans.

policy a standing plan that provides managers with a general guideline for decision making.

pooled interdependence a situation of minimal direct contact between individuals or groups performing an activity.

portfolio strategy a strategy that considers the types of business units and product lines the company controls.

positive reinforcement in the application of learning theory, rewarding desired behavior in order to increase the likelihood that the behavior will be repeated.

post-action control measurement and evaluation of the results of an activity after it is completed; also called output control.

power in the context of leadership, the ability to exert force on another.

power distance the issue of inequalities in prestige, wealth, and power.

predictive maintenance the use of monitoring instruments to estimate when machine failure is most likely to occur.

preference ordering ranking goals according to priorities.

preliminary or feedforward control a control system that anticipates results and guides activities before an operation begins; also called steering control.

preventive maintenance designing, inspecting, and servicing machinery so that breakdowns are less likely to occur.

primacy effect the strong influence that the first information received has on final impressions.

primary data sources sources of data gathered specifically for the current purpose.

prior commitments guarantees or promises made to others on actions to be taken in the future.

Prisoner's Dilemma a classic example of a non-zero-sum game in which each of two accused criminals is given the one-time choice of confessing or not confessing. Each is much better off if neither confesses than if both confess, but one will be badly hurt if the other is the only one to confess.

pro-con comparison a comparison of the advantages and disadvantages of alternatives.

procedural fairness in equity theory, the perception that the process used to allocate rewards is fair.

process controls long-term controls that address the method of transformation and facility planning.

process layout a facility layout that groups work of a similar function in a single department or work center.

process theories motivation theories that consider the processes which lead a person to behave in a certain way.

producers' cartels international arrangements to stabilize the prices of food or raw materials rather than to allow free-market price competition to take place.

product division a divisional design in which each unit is responsible for a single product or a group of related products.

product layout a facility layout in which the organization of the work is dictated by the sequence of production or service steps common to all jobs.

production subsystem unit or department of the organization that produces a good or service to be exported to customers in the environment.

productivity a measure of the output of goods or services per unit of input such as human resources, land, and capital.

professional bureaucracy an organizational design characterized by an operating core primarily composed of professionals.

profit-sharing plans compensation plans in which employees are given a bonus in the form of either a cash payment or company stock when company profits are high.

program a single-use plan designed to coordinate a large set of activities.

program evaluation and review technique (PERT) chart a diagram depicting each activity involved in the completion of a project, the sequencing of these activities, and the time allotted for each activity.

programmed instruction a training method in which subject matter is broken down into organized, logical sequences; only when the trainee gives a correct response is he or she presented with the next segment of material.

project a single-use plan that is usually more limited in scope than a program and is sometimes formed to support a program.

projection an unconscious tendency to see one's own characteristics in others.

promotion advancement within a company, generally involving a new title, more responsibility, and greater financial rewards.

promotion type organization an organization that is strongly influenced by a chief executive who is charismatic and the promoter of the firm's innovative advantage.

prospector strategy a strategy which seeks or creates an unstable environment in the form of rapid change and high growth in the market.

protean career a career viewed as an ongoing sequence of events as a person seeks self-fulfillment through a variety of educational experiences, training, and changes in job orientation.

Protestant work ethic the belief that work is valuable, important, and a central life interest.

psychoanalytic theory Sigmund Freud's theory that people are motivated by drives or instincts that are largely out of their control.

psychological noise a communication breakdown in which a recipient does not understand the sender's message because he or she is thinking about something else.

public zone the zone of personal space that begins 12 feet away from a person; beyond the range for comfortable interaction.

punishment in the application of learning theory, the presentation of an unpleasant consequence, or the removal of a desired consequence, whenever an undesired behavior occurs.

purpose the reason for an organization's existence; compare **mission**.

Pygmalion effect the influence of perceptual readiness on how stimuli are interpreted; also called the self-fulfilling prophecy. An individual's interpretation of stimuli causes him or her to behave in ways that cause the interpretation to be valid.

Q

quality circles (QC) committees of workers who analyze and solve quality problems.

quality control a control that monitors the transformation process and corrects deviations in order to make a product that meets certain specifications.

quality of work life a term used to mean many different things, ranging from fair compensation to the full use and development of human capacities to the social relevance and social responsibility of the company.

quantitative management theory the application of mathematical models to production problems.

question mark a business unit that exists in a rapidly growing market but has a small market share.

queuing models models used to determine the sorts of waiting lines which are likely to develop at machines, service stations, or other facilities.

quotas legal limitations on the quantities of particular products that can enter a country during a particular time period.

R

range of power the number of different areas in which one person can influence another.

rationalization in the context of international business, the purchase of parts or finished goods from sources whose prices are the lowest any-where in the world and selling finished products where they will command the highest prices.

rationing a coping strategy that takes place when organizations ignore some operations and empha-size others in order to preserve the most critical functions of the technical core.

reactive change a response by management to pres-sure for change.

reactor strategy a strategy forced on managers by strategic failure.

realistic job preview (RJP) an unbiased, accurate pic-ture of what a company and a job are like, pro-vided to a new recruit.

realistic stage the stage of career choice in which peo-ple seriously explore career options, firm up their preferences, and make an occupational choice.

receiver the element of the communication process that picks up the message.

recency effect the strong influence that information received most recently has on final impressions.

reciprocal interdependence a situation in which units provide each other with activity inputs.

recruiting assembling a group of job applicants from which to choose.

references written evaluations of an applicant pro-vided by the applicant's previous employers, co-workers, teachers, or other acquaintances.

referent power power that comes from the feeling of identity, or oneness, that one person has with an-other or the desire for such identity.

refreezing the third step in the Lewin-Schein model of the change process, in which the changed atti-tude and behavior are supported and reinforced in a way that is rewarded by the organization.

Regulatory Flexibility Act an act requiring the gov-ernment to take into account the size of a busi-ness and its ability to comply with regulations.

reinforcement theories theories of motivation that focus on the environmental events which influ-ence behavior.

relatedness needs in Alderfer's ERG theory, all needs that involve relationships with other people.

relative centrality the degree of centrality of an indi-vidual in a communication network.

reorder point the inventory level at which an order for new supplies is placed.

reorder quantity the size of an order for new supplies.

replanning the development of new routing, loading, and scheduling.

representativeness the tendency, in an often uncon-scious attempt to simplify decision making, to place something in a class if it seems representa-tive of the class.

resource allocator role decisional role that involves deciding to whom and in what quantity resources will be dispensed.

resource flows the pattern of resource exchanges with other organizations in the environment.

responsibility center a unit responsible for achieving certain goals.

retained earnings statement a financial statement that provides a summary of the changes in the earnings retained in a business for a specific pe-riod of time.

retention remaining with the organization.

retrenchment strategy a strategy of attempting to im-prove operational efficiency in order to counter-act declining performance.

retroduction the changing of an assumption.

reward power power based on the ability to reward, either by providing desired outcomes or by decreasing or removing outcomes that are not desired.

risk a decision situation in which the event which will occur is not known, but the probabilities of events are known.

rituals company procedures, regular meetings, parties, etc., that serve as a guide to behavior in daily organizational life.

robot a machine that can be programmed to do a variety of tasks automatically.

role a set of shared expectations concerning appro-priate behavior.

role ambiguity lack of clarity about role expectations.

role conflict conflict that occurs in a business setting when employees are expected to engage in activi-ties that clash with their own expectations or are somehow inconsistent.

routing the process of determining the movement of a mechanical part or other piece of work from one operation to the next.

rules and regulations statements that either require or forbid a certain action; the most explicit form of standing plan.

S

saddle point the point in a decision matrix where the maximin value of the player on the vertical axis is equal to the minimax value of the player on the horizontal axis.

satisfaction progression movement up Maslow's hier-archy of needs.

satisficing choosing the first acceptable alternative rather than looking for the best; in goal selec-tion, identifying satisfactory or suboptimal rather than optimal levels of performance to be attained.

satisficing rule a rule used to screen out unacceptable alternatives in which alternatives are considered sequentially and the first alternative which satisfies all constraints is chosen.

satisfiers or motivators in Herzberg's theory, factors in an organization which, when adequate, result in satisfaction.

Savage criterion (criterion of minimax regret) the view that people should act in ways to minimize their maximum possible regret.

schedule chart a chart showing when each of a series of job orders is to be performed at each machine, workstation, or department.

scheduling the process of determining when an operation is to be performed at a machine or workstation.

schemas cognitive frameworks that an individual uses to give structure and meaning to social information.

scientific management a branch of classical management theory that advocates the application of scientific principles to improve task efficiency.

scoring approach an approach to choosing between alternatives when an optimal alternative is needed; a score is computed for each alternative and the alternative with the best score is chosen.

screening approach an approach to choosing between alternatives that identifies each alternative as satisfactory or unsatisfactory and screens out those that are unsatisfactory.

scripts schemas in one's memory that describe events or behaviors appropriate for a given context.

second-order outcome in expectancy theory, any outcome, good or bad, that results from attainment of the first-order outcome.

secondary data sources sources of data initially collected for other purposes but which fit the current needs.

selection and hiring the process of evaluating each candidate and picking the best one for the position available.

self-managing work groups work groups having the authority to deal with their own internal management without consulting others in order to produce a group product, service, or decision.

self-monitoring the extent to which people emulate the behavior of others.

self-serving bias the tendency to take credit for successes and deny personal responsibility for failures.

seniority the number of years an employee has spent with the company.

sensitivity training training which attempts to develop participants' sensitivity, self-insight, and awareness of group processes while focusing on job- and organization-related issues.

sequential attention shifting attention from one goal to another as required by market demands or special problems.

sequential interdependence a situation in which the output of one activity becomes the input of another activity.

shadow price the price associated with a constraint which shows how much the objective function would improve if the constraint were loosened by one unit.

short-range planning developing plans for implementation within a planning horizon of less than one year.

side payments the price a group pays others to join it in support of an organization goal.

simple structure an organizational structure in which coordination of activities is maintained by a top manager who directly supervises employees in the operating core.

simulation models models developed to deal specifically with problems of such complexity that analysis by other techniques is not feasible.

single-use plans action plans used to direct activities in the achievement of a specific goal which will not be repeated in the future.

slack the amount left over on each constraint in linear programming when the objective function is optimized.

slack time the length of time a project activity could be delayed without slowing project completion.

small business a business financed by the owners and their personal funding resources.

Small Business Administration (SBA) a federal agency which promotes free competitive enterprise by making credit, contracts, and management advice available to small businesses.

smoothing adjusting the operations of an organization to expected changes in demand.

social audit a step-by-step examination of all of the activities comprising a firm's social programs.

social forecasting a process of identifying and analyzing social trends to anticipate those issues that will be important to an organization in the future.

social information-processing approach the view that socially provided information, such as comments from peers or supervisors, plays a major role in determining how people perceive jobs and respond to them.

social judgment analysis approach based on the idea

that disagreements could be reduced if group members, instead of voicing their choices, could explain how they arrived at those choices.

social learning learning that occurs through any of a variety of social channels—newspapers, books, television, conversations with family members, friends, and co-workers, and so on.

social loafing the failure of group members to exert full effort because they expect others in the group to carry the load.

social presence effect a heightened arousal level experienced by individuals when they are working in the presence of others.

social responsibility business's concern for the social as well as the economic effects of its decisions.

social zone the zone of personal space extending from 4 to 12 feet from the individual; used for most impersonal business.

socialization the process of gaining an understanding of the norms, values, and behavior patterns of a group to which one is a newcomer.

socialized power seekers people who satisfy their power needs through means that help the organization.

span of control the number of subordinates reporting to a single supervisor.

spokesperson role informational role that involves speaking on behalf of the work unit to people inside or outside the organization.

stability strategy a strategy that allows corporate managers to concentrate on increasing the internal strengths of the firm.

staff those who serve as advisers to managers faced with critical decisions.

staffing bringing new people into the organization and making sure they serve as valuable additions to the work force.

standard industrial classification (SIC) a method of categorizing the products of a company by type and industry.

standard operating procedure (SOP) a form of standing plan which governs specific actions that members of the organization are required to perform under certain circumstances.

standing committees relatively permanent task groups that deal with issues on an ongoing basis.

standing plans action plans developed to guide activities toward achievement of recurring goals.

star a business unit that has both high market growth rate and a relatively large share of the market.

statistical quality control a control system based on the assumption that most quality problems are

the result of flaws in manufacturing systems, not of errors by production workers.

status social ranking within a group.

status symbols concrete signs of status.

steering control a control that tries to control an activity before it occurs; also called preliminary, or feedforward, control.

stereotyping forming an opinion of a person based not on individual characteristics but on the group to which the person belongs.

stockout costs the costs to a firm when it runs out of inventory.

stories narratives that are repeated among employees and usually based in fact.

strategic alternatives different methods of competition for attaining organizational goals.

strategic constituency any group internal or external to the organization that has a stake in the organization's performance.

strategic control a long-term control concerned with the direction of the firm, the evaluation of strategy, the interrelationships of the business units, external reporting, and the maintenance of cash flows across business units.

strategic management the set of managerial decisions and actions that determines the long-run competitive performance of the organization.

strategic plan the answers of an organization's management to three questions: What will we do and for whom will we do it? What goals do we want to achieve? and How are we going to manage the organization's activities so as to achieve the chosen goal?

strategy a method of competition.

stress a physiological state in which adrenaline courses into the bloodstream and then to muscles and organs.

stress reactions mental and physical responses to stress.

stressors environmental factors that influence stress levels.

structural complexity adapting to the environment by setting up organization departments (or subsystems) that will respond to specific groupings of environmental factors.

structure of intellect theory the idea that humans have 120 different and independent intellectual abilities.

subjective probabilities the decision maker's estimates of the probabilities of events when the true probabilities are unknown.

subsidies special tax incentives that encourage the production of goods for export rather than domestic consumption.

substitutes for leadership various characteristics of situations or of subordinates that tend to neutralize or make ineffective certain leadership behaviors.

success chess Eugene Jennings' rules for maximizing career mobility.

supportive leadership leadership characterized by friendliness and concern for the status, well-being, and needs of subordinates.

switching structures changing the design of a department or organization between organic and mechanistic depending on whether innovation or implementation is needed.

SWOT an acronym for Strengths and Weaknesses of an organization's capabilities and Opportunities and Threats in the organization's environment; SWOT analysis produces a strategic profile of the organization.

synectics a creative enhancement technique whereby people attempt to join together apparently unrelated elements.

synthetic group a "group" of individuals whose decisions have been aggregated mathematically, although the group may never have met.

system an interrelated set of elements functioning as a whole.

systems theory the theory that the survival or failure of the system, or organization, is dependent on the interrelation of subsystems and their contribution to the overall purpose of the system.

T

tall organization an organization with narrow spans of control and thus increased levels of management.

tariffs taxes imposed on imported products.

task groups or committees groups formed for a specific purpose, such as exchange of information, coordination of activities, generation of recommendations, development of new procedures, or solution of specific problems.

task knowledge the degree to which the transformation process is well understood.

task variety the frequency of unexpected and novel events that occur as inputs are transformed into outputs.

task-and-bonus wage system a modification of the piece-rate system whereby production goals are established for the worker and, if the goals are achieved, both the worker and the supervisor receive a bonus.

team interdependence a situation in which work is interactive or acted on jointly by members of different groups or units rather than simply being transferred back and forth.

technical core internal operations of an organization that must be conducted in a predictable and orderly manner to work efficiently.

technical skills skills necessary to carry out a specific task.

technological change alterations in an organization's conversion process.

technology a conversion process that transforms organizational inputs into outputs.

technology transfer a tactic used by firms that are unable to afford facilities in a host country or are prevented by the host government from investing in certain industries, whereby they either continue to oversee the operations of their facility or license their brand name to a domestic company that will manufacture the product.

teleconferencing two-way communication by both video and audio equipment between persons at different locations.

tentative stage the stage of career choice that usually occurs between the ages of 11 and 16, when people realize they have an important decision to make about their future and begin to consider how various careers might fit their abilities, interests, and values.

termination at will the view that management has the right to fire employees for any reason.

testing a relatively objective means of determining how well a person may do on the job.

Theory X the assumption that workers dislike work, prefer to be directed by supervisors, and are more interested in monetary gains than in performing their jobs well.

Theory Y the assumption that workers can enjoy their work under favorable conditions and can provide valued input to the decision-making process.

Theory Z a theory developed by William Ouchi that attempts to combine the best of Japanese and American management practices to solve human resource management problems.

time studies observation and measurement of all task movements made by a worker in an attempt to eliminate those that do not lead to increased productivity.

timeliness a measure of the degree to which employees come to work on time.

tolerance for ambiguity the degree to which individuals welcome uncertainty and change.

top-down approach a control approach in which management sets the direction and gives directives to subordinates.

tournament model of mobility a model in which careers are seen as a series of competitions, each of which has implications for an individual's chances of mobility.

trade associations associations made up of organizations that share a common interest.

trade promotion assistance government underwriting of certain expenses associated with the marketing of goods in other countries.

training and development the training of employees and the development of their skills and careers.

transaction costs costs incurred by an organization in such activities as the purchase of goods, employment of labor, or distribution of services because of the incomplete information, mistakes, or irrational behavior of managers.

transactional leaders leaders who recognize what actions subordinates must take to achieve outcomes, clarify these roles and task requirements, and recognize subordinates' needs and clarify how they will be satisfied if necessary efforts are made.

transformation process the process that alters inputs (labor, capital, or materials) in some useful way to produce outputs (goods or services).

transformational leaders leaders who motivate followers to do more than they expected to do.

transmitter the element of the communication process that places the message into the message channel.

turbulence the extent to which environments are being disturbed by an increasing rate of exchanges between factors.

two-factor theory or motivation-hygiene theory Herzberg's theory that there are two relatively distinct sets of factors in organizations, one that results in satisfaction when adequate and one that causes dissatisfaction when deficient.

two-way communication communication that allows the message recipient to ask questions and provide feedback.

Type A behavior pattern behavior characterized by feelings of great time pressure and impatience.

Type B behavior pattern behavior typical of people who are relaxed, steady-paced, and easygoing.

U

uncertainty a decision situation in which the event which will occur is not known, and the probabilities of events are not known.

uncertainty absorbers individuals who summarize information or change its form in other ways to make it more understandable or concise.

uncertainty avoidance reducing uncertainty through innovations in technology, law, religion, and, in an organization, rules and ceremonies.

unfreezing making the need for change so obvious that an individual will be willing to accept the change; the first step in the Lewin-Schein model of the change process.

unit, or small-batch, technology a transformation process in which the production process is primarily in the hands of individuals who must provide knowledge and skill to the transformation process.

unity of command the principle that no individual should have more than one supervisor.

upper managers typically the smallest grouping of managers in an organization; responsible for the overall performance of the organization.

upward communication communication from senders in lower-level positions to receivers in relatively higher positions.

utility the relative satisfactoriness of something to an individual.

utility curve a plot of the utiles (units of utility) corresponding to the various levels of an attribute.

V

valence in expectancy theory, the value an individual attaches to an outcome.

value of the game in game theory, the expected return to the player on the vertical axis.

values broad, general beliefs about some way of behaving or some desired end state; often expressed as standards, moral judgments, and commitments that people have in an organization.

variable-interval schedule in the application of learning theory, a time-based schedule in which a reinforcer is administered randomly around some average interval.

variable-ratio schedule in the application of learning theory, a schedule that reinforces a behavior on average every *n* responses.

venture team a temporary grouping of organization members for generating new ideas.

vestibule training a training method in which trainees are given instruction in the operation of equipment like that found in their departments.

visibility how often subordinates see their superiors.

Vroom and Yetton normative model of leadership a model that prescribes the proper leadership style(s) for various situations; the model focuses on the appropriate degree of delegation of decision-making authority.

W

whistleblowers employees who tell people outside the organization that their company engages in bribery or some other illegal activity.

work involvement the degree to which an employee is involved with work in general, rather than with a specific job.

work sample test a measure of how well applicants perform selected job tasks.

work specialization the degree to which tasks are divided in the organization.

Y

yes-no control a control that assesses an activity while it is in progress so that at specified checkpoints progress is approved, progress is halted, or corrective action is taken.

Z

zero-based budgeting (ZBB) a budgeting system in which managers begin from scratch each budgeting period and justify the entire budget.

A

PART 1 Photo Courtesy of Apple Computer, Inc., 5; © Mark E. Gibson 1989/THE STOCK MARKET, 10; USDA Photo, 11; Photo Courtesy of Hewlett-Packard Company, 15; © TRW, Inc., 1983, 17; Courtesy of IBM Corporation, 22; The Bettmann Archive, 33; The Bettmann Archive, 37 (top); Charles Babbage Institute, University of Minnesota, 37 (bottom); Courtesy of Ronald Greenwood, 38; The Bettmann Archive, 40; Historical Pictures Service, Inc., 41 (top); The Bettmann Archive, 41 (bottom); Courtesy of Peter B. Peterson, 43; Courtesy of Ronald Greenwood, 44 (top and bottom); Baker Library/Harvard Business School, 46; The MIT Museum, 48 (bottom); Yale University, 49 (top); The Bettmann Archive, 49 (bottom); Zenith Data Systems, 54; UPI/Bettmann Newsphotos, 59; Harvard Business School, 61; Photo Courtesy of Bethesda Oak Hospital, 75; © Larry Lee/WEST LIGHT, 79; Marathon Oil Company, 84; First Interstate Bancorp, 90; Bethlehem Steel, 95; Photo Courtesy of Cincinnati Gas & Electric Company, 112; Metropolitan Detroit Convention & Visitors Bureau, 116; Dean Foods Company, 117; Larry Bellante for The Statue of Liberty–Ellis Island Foundation, Inc., 121.

PART 2 TRW, Inc., 142; Cincinnati Milacron, 151; © Martha Swope/PepsiCo, Inc./Purchase, N.Y., 154; Florida Division of Tourism, 166 (left); American Petroleum Institute, 166 (right); © Miro Vintoniv/STOCK, BOSTON, 169; Courtesy of IBM Corporation, 174; Courtesy of Honeywell, Inc., 180; Salt Lake City Convention & Visitors Bureau, 197; Photo Courtesy of Hewlett-Packard Company, 201;

Walgreen Company, 203; Photo Courtesy of Goodyear Tire & Rubber Co., 215; Ron Forth Photography, 228; United Airlines, 230; Delta Air Lines, 246.

PART 3 Photo Courtesy of Hewlett-Packard Company, 264; ITT Corporation, 267; Courtesy of IBM Corporation, 270; © 1989 Chris Springmann Esprit/San Francisco/THE STOCK MARKET, 275; Dow Corning Corporation, 282; Texaco Inc. © Todd T. Weinstein, 303; Cincinnati Milacron, Industrial Robot Division, 317; © David Woods 1988/THE STOCK MARKET, 321; Indiana University–Purdue University at Indianapolis, 337; © Chuck O'Rear/WEST LIGHT, 340; Eastman Kodak Company, 345; Florida Department of Commerce, Division of Tourism, 347; Good Samaritan Hospital, 356.

PART 4 Photo Courtesy of Hewlett-Packard Company, 377; AMERICAN RECREATION COALITION, American Petroleum Institute, 388; Westinghouse Furniture Systems, 395; WIDE WORLD PHOTOS, INC., 413 and 415; © Palmer/Kane, Inc. 1982/THE STOCK MARKET, 426; Courtesy United Technologies Corporation, 454; Courtesy of IBM Corporation, 455 and 461; Ron Watts/WEST LIGHT, 464; Arthur Grace/STOCK, BOSTON, 473; Courtesy of IBM Corporation, 478; SUPERSTOCK, 480; Photo Courtesy of Xerox Corporation, 493; Courtesy of Chrysler Motor Corporation, 501; General Electric Credit Corporation, 513; Courtesy of The Coca-Cola Company, 522; Courtesy of Unisys Corporation, 549; Photo Courtesy of Delta Air Lines, Inc., 551; Virginia State Travel Service, 556.

PART 5 The Coca-Cola Company, 568; Ford Motor Company, 577; The Lincoln Electric Company, 583; FPG International, 604; THE STOCK MARKET, 606; © Michael A. Keller 1987/THE STOCK MARKET, 611; Hayes Microcomputer Products, Inc., 614; Courtesy of IBM Corporation, 616; Digital Equipment Corporation, 617; American Petroleum Institute, 635; © Bill Ross/WEST LIGHT, 639; © George Disario 1989/THE STOCK MARKET, 643; Courtesy of Ford Motor Company, 650; FPG International, 657.

PART 6 © Al Francekevich/THE STOCK MARKET, 679; Courtesy of The Rowland Company, 689; Photo Courtesy of Hewlett-Packard Company, 696; © David Pollack 1987/THE STOCK MARKET, 712; Photo Courtesy of Hewlett-Packard Company, 719; © Pete Saloutos 1987/THE STOCK MARKET, 720; Honeywell, Inc., 724; Courtesy of Quality International, 732; Courtesy of The Kroger Company, 744 (left); © Rick Browne/STOCK, BOSTON, INC., 749; Courtesy of 3M, 764; First Interstate Bancorp, 774; © Ken Straiton, 1988/THE STOCK MARKET, 776; World Bank Photo, 779; Courtesy of IBM Corporation, 790.